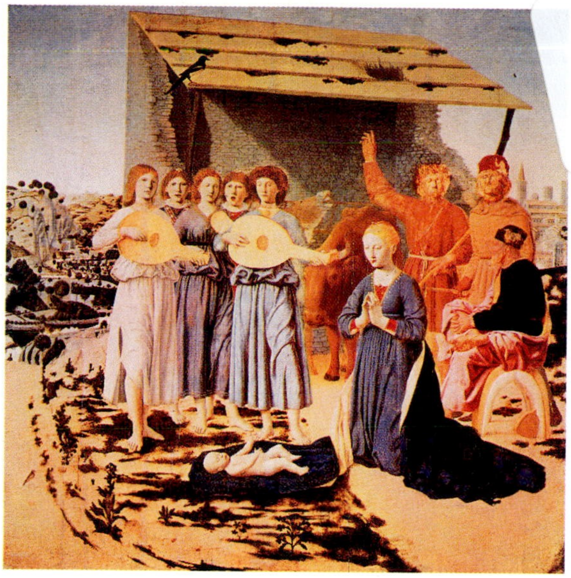

A World of Art

SECOND EDITION

HENRY M. SAYRE

Oregon State University

PRENTICE HALL

Upper Saddle River, New Jersey 07458

Library of Congress Cataloging-in-Publication Data

Sayre, Henry M. (date)
A world of art / Henry M. Sayre. — 2nd ed.
p. cm.
Includes index.
ISBN 0-13-476011-5 (pbk.)
1. Arts I. Title
NX620.S28 1997
700'.1–dc20 96-26340
CIP

Editor-in-Chief: Charlyce Jones Owen
Acquisitions Editor: Bud Therien
Editorial Assistant: Lee Mamunes
Development Editor: Elaine Silverstein
Director of Production and Manufacturing: Barbara Kittle
Production Editor: Barbara DeVries
Manufacturing Manager: Nick Sklitsis
Prepress and Manufacturing Buyer: Robert Anderson
Marketing Manager: Alison Pendergast
Copyeditor: Sylvia Moore
Proofreader: Carolyn Gauntt
Creative Design Director: Leslie Osher
Interior Design: Anne DeMarinis, Function Thru Form
Photo Director: Lorinda Morris-Nantz
Photo Editor: Melinda Reo
Photo Research: Joelle Burrows
Cover Design: Anne DeMarinis, Function Thru Form
Cover Image: Piero della Francesca, *Navity.* National Gallery, London, Great Britain. (Bridgeman/Art Resource, N.Y.)

This book was set in 11/13 Sabon by Function Thru Form, and was printed by RR Donnelley & Sons Company. Color separation and film was supplied by Lehigh Press Colortronics. The cover was printed by The Lehigh Press, Inc.

Printed in the United States of America
10 9 8 7 6 5 4 3 2

ISBN 0-13-476011-5

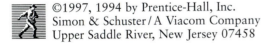

Prentice-Hall International (UK) Limited, *London*
Prentice-Hall of Australia Pty. Limited, *Sydney*
Prentice-Hall Canada Inc., *Toronto*
Prentice-Hall Hispanoamericana, S.A., *Mexico*
Prentice-Hall of India Private Limited, *New Delhi*
Prentice-Hall of Japan, Inc., *Tokyo*
Simon & Schuster Asia Pte. Ltd., *Singapore*
Editora Prentice-Hall do Brasil, Ltda., *Rio de Janeiro*

For my boys, Rob and John, and for Sandy

CONTENTS

PART III

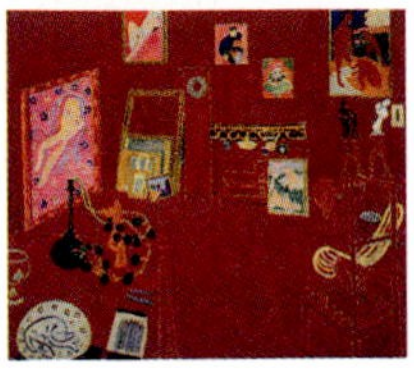

THE FINE ARTS MEDIA

LEARNING HOW ART IS MADE

PART IV

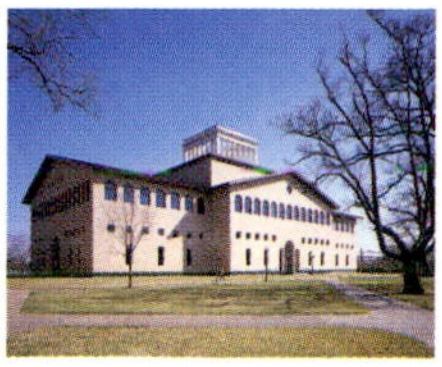

THE VISUAL ARTS IN EVERYDAY LIFE

RECOGNIZING THE ART OF DESIGN

PART V

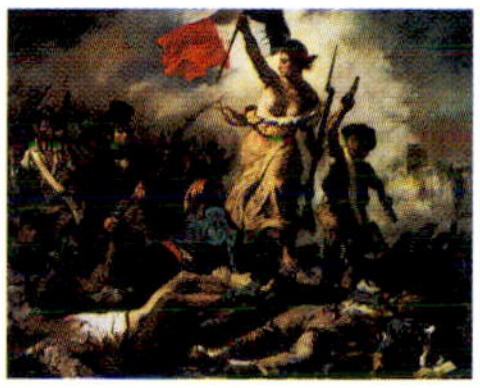

THE VISUAL RECORD

PLACING THE ARTS IN HISTORICAL CONTEXT

PREFACE

I began the preface to the first edition of *A World of Art* by saying that it was written out of a felt need. What I said then remains true today. Art appreciation is a course I enjoy teaching because in the darkness of a large lecture hall, illuminated only by the slide on the screen, I can sense my students' excitement. Sometimes, when I'm teaching color theory, or explaining a purposeful violation of perspective, or when I analyze a favorite painting like Monet's *The Railroad Bridge at Argenteuil,* I feel like a magician. I can hear their oohs and ahhs, and I know that I've brought them something of the joy I feel before great art.

But it seemed to me when I first conceived of this book, as it seems to me now, that as we approach the twenty-first century, our mission as educators is changing, and our courses and our texts must change as well. This book is designed around the cornerstones of the Western tradition. I have not forsaken them, nor do I believe that we should or must. They are, after all, what most of us teaching today are best equipped to explain and discuss. But I am convinced, as I was when I wrote the first edition, that if we do not compare our tradition to others, we are unable to see how special, how unique are its many assumptions. In comparing works of art from our own tradition to works from other traditions, we gain a better sense of who we are and what we are about. As a result, we are better equipped to recognize not only our achievements but also our shortcomings.

Over the course of the last two decades, we have become increasingly sensitized as teachers to the ways in which traditional art history has systematically excluded certain works and traditions from the "master" narrative. We have witnessed the "admission" of works by women and black Americans into the canon, and their representation in the basic art texts and histories has dramatically increased. The second edition, like the first, builds on this and strives to introduce "a world of art" into the art appreciation curriculum. We have consistently tried to juxtapose works from the "master" tradition to works not so well known. For instance, the book opens with a consideration of landscape works by a nineteenth-century American artist, a fourteenth-century Chinese master, a self-taught contemporary aboriginal Australian, and a contemporary American sculptor. Thus, without sacrificing traditional coverage, we are able to introduce new work into the art appreciation curriculum. The result is a much more varied and lively approach.

The second edition of *A World of Art* looks very different from the first, and a number of new elements have been introduced:

- A series of two-page spreads entitled *Works in Progress* focuses on the *process* of artistic creation. Discussion of the artists' materials, techniques and strategies to achieve intended, and sometimes unintended, results is presented in a dynamic way (see page x).

- The original five-part, nine-chapter text followed by the timeline has been revised into a five-part, twenty-chapter text. The new structure has allowed us to add subheadings and thus to make the relationship between different themes, techniques, and periods clearer to students. In addition, a brief, convenient outline of these subheadings occurs at the beginning of each chapter.

- The timeline, a popular feature of the first edition, has been made an integral part of the text. We have provided a selection of world historical events to put the art history material in context for students.

- Seven maps have been added in order to help students conceptualize the geographic and historical world in which the art under discussion has been created.

- In response to readers who felt that architecture was not dealt with in sufficient depth in the first edition, a new, full discussion of architecture now precedes the design chapter.

- New sections on the crafts have been incorporated, primarily into Chapter 12.

Many of these changes came as a result of being awarded a grant from the Annenberg Project at the Corporation for Public Broadcasting. We reconceived the book so that in addition to being used in a traditional classroom setting it could function in a distance learning environment as part of a complete video telecourse based on our new PBS series entitled, "A World of Art: Works in Progress." We think the second edition of the book sets a new standard for art appreciation texts in its own right, but together with the materials designed for the distance education package, it is unsurpassed.

WORKS IN PROGRESS

The major new feature in the second of edition of *A World of Art* is the series of over 30 two-page spreads called *Works in Progress.* These are intended to give students insight into the *process* of artistic creation. My greatest frustration as an instructor teaching art appreciation is that students almost inevitably believe that art is the result of some quasi-mystical, mysterious act of genius. But art, like most things, is the result of hard work and, especially, of a *critical thinking* process of questioning, exploration, trial and error, and discovery that I long to convey effectively and in a manner that students can generalize to their own experience. Many of the spreads focus on accepted masterpieces, ranging from Pablo Picasso's *Les Demoiselles d'Avignon* and Henri Matisse's *Dance II* to Albrecht Dürer's *Adam and Eve* and Raphael's *Alba Madonna.* In addition, eleven of the artists treated in these spreads are also the subjects of an eleven-part video series *A World of Art: Works in Progress* produced for public television as part of the Annenberg/CPB grant. These half-hour videos develop the materials in the text to an even greater degree. We hope that in these videos, as we follow each individual artist through the process of making a single work of art from start to finish, the creative process will literally come alive.

In the order of their appearance in *A World of Art,* the artists treated in the video series are Lorna Simpson, Guillermo Gómez-Peña, Bill Viola, Hung Liu, Beverly Buchanan, June Wayne, Milton Resnick, Judy Baca, Goat Island, Fred Wilson, and Mierle Ukeles. We asked each of them to describe their working process in their own words, and each of them is extraordinarily articulate. As a group, they are also extraordinarily diverse in terms of their cultural and ethnic backgrounds and equally diverse in terms of the media in which they work. While it would have been easy to concentrate discussion of them in Part III, the media section, we have attempted to spread them throughout the book in order to allow instructors and students the opportunity to view a program on a more or less weekly basis.

A WORLD OF ART – THE CD-ROM

To further the student's sense of the process of making art, we have also prepared an interactive CD-ROM to accompany the text. The CD-ROM consists of two rooms. In the first, there is a wide variety of interactive exercises designed to give the student practical, hands-on experience manipulating the elements of art—exercises demonstrating and applying the principles of color theory, perspective, value, balance, and so on. The second room consists of a series of QuickTime video demonstrations. As an author, I have never been satisfied with the diagrams in art appreciation books that illustrate the printmaking processes, for instance, or lost-wax bronze pours (an especially difficult process both to illustrate and to discuss). Here, we have live demonstrations of those processes—and many others, such as making and mixing oil paint—which can be run in either real time or slow motion, together with text that sequentially outlines what the student is watching.

THE ANNENBERG/CORPORATION FOR PUBLIC BROADCASTING PROJECT

The video series *A World of Art: Works in Progress* and the CD-ROM were conceived in response to the demands of creating a distance education curriculum for the Annenberg/CPB Project, but both cannot help but improve teaching and learning in the standard classroom environment as well. The television series itself is a production of Oregon Public Broadcasting, in cooperation with Oregon State University. Our directors are of national stature, and the quality of the production is of the highest level. John Lindsay, of Oregon Public Broadcasting, and I have served as co-executive producers of the series. I closely supervised the writing, editing, and shooting of each segment, and I exercised complete control over the content of each episode. But I am not a filmmaker—though I have learned a lot about it in recent months—and without the extraordinarily talented people at OPB, the resulting programs would have been considerably less distinguished.

The artists for the series were chosen in consultation with an advisory board, whose members have overseen the project at every level: David Antin, of the University of California, San Diego; Bruce Jenkins, of the Walker Art Center in Minneapolis; Lynn Hershman, of the

University of California, Davis; Suzanne Lacy, of the California College of Arts and Crafts; George Roeder, of the School of the Art Institute of Chicago; and John Weber, of the San Francisco Musuem of Modern Art. In addition, two members of the Annenberg/CPB staff have made major contributions, Hilda Moskowitz and Pete Neal. While I must accept responsibility for any of the weaknesses of what we have done, most of the strengths of the project are the result of these people's expert advice. I owe them more thanks than I can even begin to measure.

The video series is available from the Annenberg/CPB Project. For further details call 1-800-LEARNER (532-7637), or ask your Prentice Hall representative for more information.

OTHER ANCILLARY MATERIALS

Taken together, the text, the CD-ROM, and the *Works in Progress* television series offer the teacher and student what we believe is the strongest teaching package available anywhere. But there are other important elements in our package as well.

Teacher's Guide. My colleague at Oregon State University, John Maul, has authored a *Teacher's Guide* for the second edition that helps the instructor integrate the different aspects of the teaching package into a coherent whole by providing many ideas about ways to extend lectures beyond the scope of the text itself. Of note is background information about artists and artwork present in the *Works in Progress* text and video segments. The *Guide* also includes test banks.

Student Guide. With John's help, I have authored a *Student Guide*. This is directed particularly at distance learners, whose study plans are often self-directed and self-sustaining, but every student should find it useful. It includes, for each chapter, a set of Learning Objectives, a list of Key Concepts, an Overview of the chapter, and a Viewing Guide to each video, including an overview of the episode, an outline of what students should pay particular attention to, questions they should ask themselves about the video, and answers to frequently asked questions about the materials presented. In addition, each study lesson includes a CD-ROM Study Guide, Supplemental Exercises, two kinds of Writing Assignments—one on the subject of the chapter itself, and another entitled Writing to Explore New Ideas—and Suggested Further Reading.

Slides. Finally, a set of slides is available from Prentice Hall. In addition to providing the standard set of masterpieces, we have included a wide variety of hard-to-find images and images pertaining to each of the videotapes. The slide set should, as a result, be a significant addition to every slide library. Ask your Prentice Hall representative for details.

Henry Sayre
Oregon State University
April 1996

The New York Times and **Prentice Hall** are sponsoring **Themes of the Times:** a program designed to enhance access to current information of relevance in the classroom.

Through this program, the core subject matter provided in the text is supplemented by a collection of time-sensitive articles from one of the world's most distinguished newspapers, **The New York Times.** These articles demonstrate the vital, ongoing connection between what is learned in the classroom and what is happening in the world around us.

To enjoy the wealth of information of **The New York Times** daily, a reduced subscription rate is available. For information, call toll-free: 1-800-631-1222.

Prentice Hall and **The New York Times** are proud to co-sponsor **Themes of the Times.** We hope it will make the reading of both textbooks and newspapers a more dynamic, involving process.

PART I

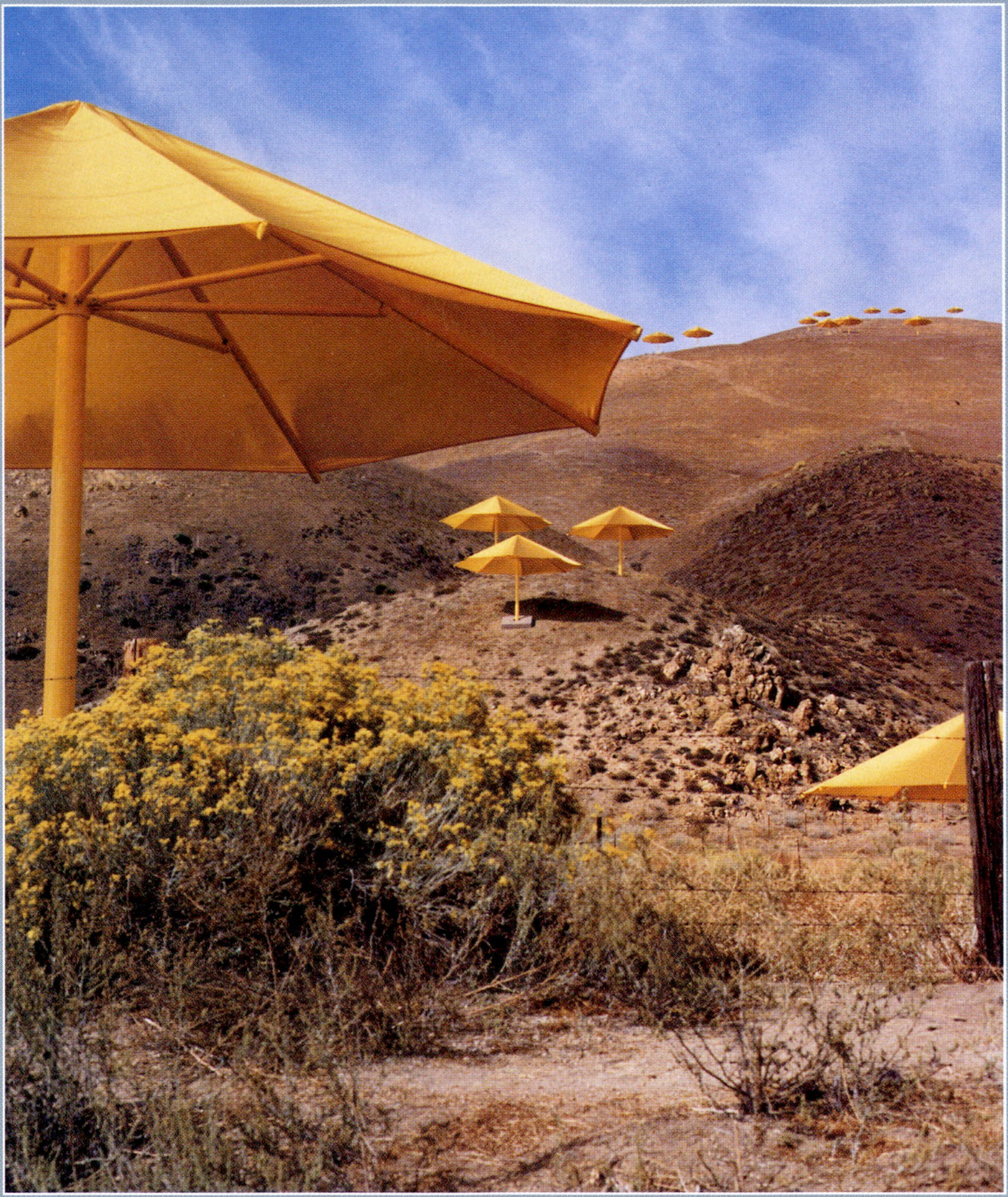

Fig. 1 Christo and Jeanne-Claude, *The Umbrellas, Japan–U.S.A.,* 1984–1991.
©Christo, 1991. Photograph by the author.

THE VISUAL WORLD

UNDERSTANDING THE ART YOU SEE

CHAPTER 1

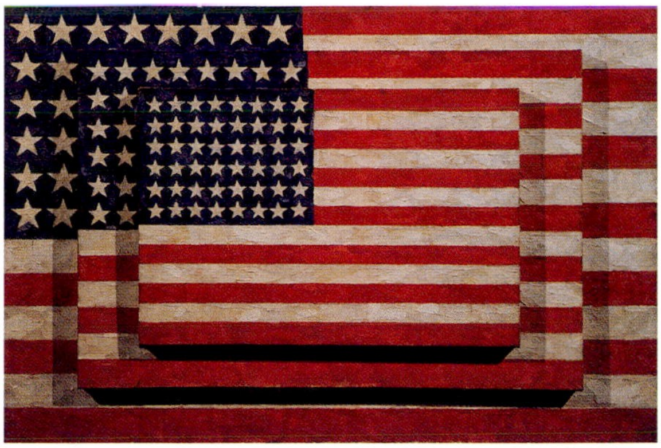

A World of Art

Throughout the morning of October 9, 1991, along a stretch of interstate highway at Tejon Pass, north of downtown Los Angeles, 1,760 yellow umbrellas, each 19 feet 8 inches in height, 28 feet 5 inches in diameter, and weighing 448 pounds, slowly opened across the parched gold hills and valleys of the Tehachapi Mountains (Fig. 1). Sixteen hours earlier—but that same morning, given the time change—1,340 blue umbrellas opened in the prefecture of Ibaraki, Japan, north of Tokyo, 90 of them in the valley's river (Fig. 2).

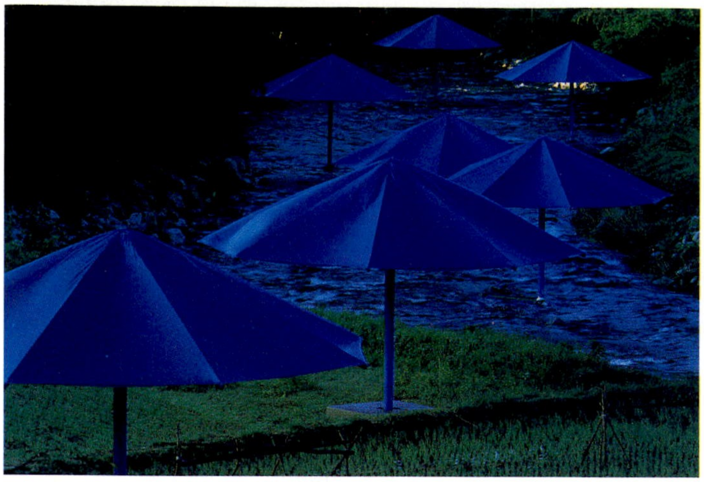

Fig. 2 Christo and Jeanne-Claude, *The Umbrellas, Japan–U.S.A.*, 1984–1991.
Photo: Wolfgang Ibaraki, Japan Site ©Christo, 1991.

Built at a cost of $26 million, which the artists Christo, and Jeanne-Claude raised entirely through the sale of his work, *The Umbrellas* symbolized for him how vast and various the world of art has become. *The Umbrellas* changes with each shift in our point of view, with each change of light and weather. Their aspects—yellow or blue, seen from near or far, from above or below, surrounded by many others or isolated on a ridge—are virtually infinite. No single photograph of *The Umbrellas* can capture the many different experiences of it. To experience the work in California was to experience only half of it. In California *The Umbrellas* seemed to stretch to the horizon and beyond. Their yellow color echoed the dry grass on the hills and the aridity of the parched California landscape, which in 1991 was deep in drought. In Japan, the blue umbrellas, identical but for their color to the yellow ones in California, had a completely different feel. In the fertile, green Japanese valley, with its small villages, farms, gardens, and fields, they appeared to grow out of the landscape itself, as if they were mushrooms or flowers. Placed closely together, they seemed almost intimate by comparison to those in California. They seemed to embody the precious and limited space of Japan itself. Blue on one side of the world and yellow on the other, the umbrellas symbolized crucial differences between the two cultures.

And yet, for all their differences, they had a common meaning. In both cultures, the umbrella is an image of shelter and protection, and therefore a symbol of community life. The extraordinary amount of collaborative activity required to mount the project—the vast numbers of workers, the complex logistics of bringing everything together—itself underscored the communal meaning of the piece. The event became a sort of cultural umbrella, stretching across the Pacific Ocean to bring Japan and the United States together.

The Umbrellas project teaches us that while art is something we all share, something all cultures appreciate and value, it does not carry the same meaning from culture to culture. In every culture it serves different ends, it is motivated by different needs, and it is shared, circulated, and appreciated in different ways. The experience of art depends on many things—not only who makes it and why, but also who sees it and where. We in the West are used to approaching objects made in African, Oceanic, Native American, or Asian cultures in museums as "works of art." But in their cultures of origin, such objects might be sacred tools that provide divine insight and inspiration. Or they might serve to define family and community relationships, establishing social order and structure. Or they might document momentous events in the history of a people. Or they might serve a simple utilitarian function, such as a pot to carry water in or a spoon to eat with. They might also be thought of as **aesthetic** objects—that is, as works that stimulate a sense of beauty in the viewer—but this aesthetic function, often considered the main purpose of art in our own culture, might be secondary, or even peripheral in cultures other than our own. As we will see, the aesthetic function has traditionally been primary to Western art, but today many artists question this purpose. Instead, they want art to define and underscore important political, social, and moral dilemmas. They want art actively to engage the world.

THE WORLD AS ARTISTS SEE IT

The Umbrellas project demonstrates how the landscape is not only different in its appearance in two different parts of the world, but is appreciated and valued in different ways. Let us consider four different approaches to the

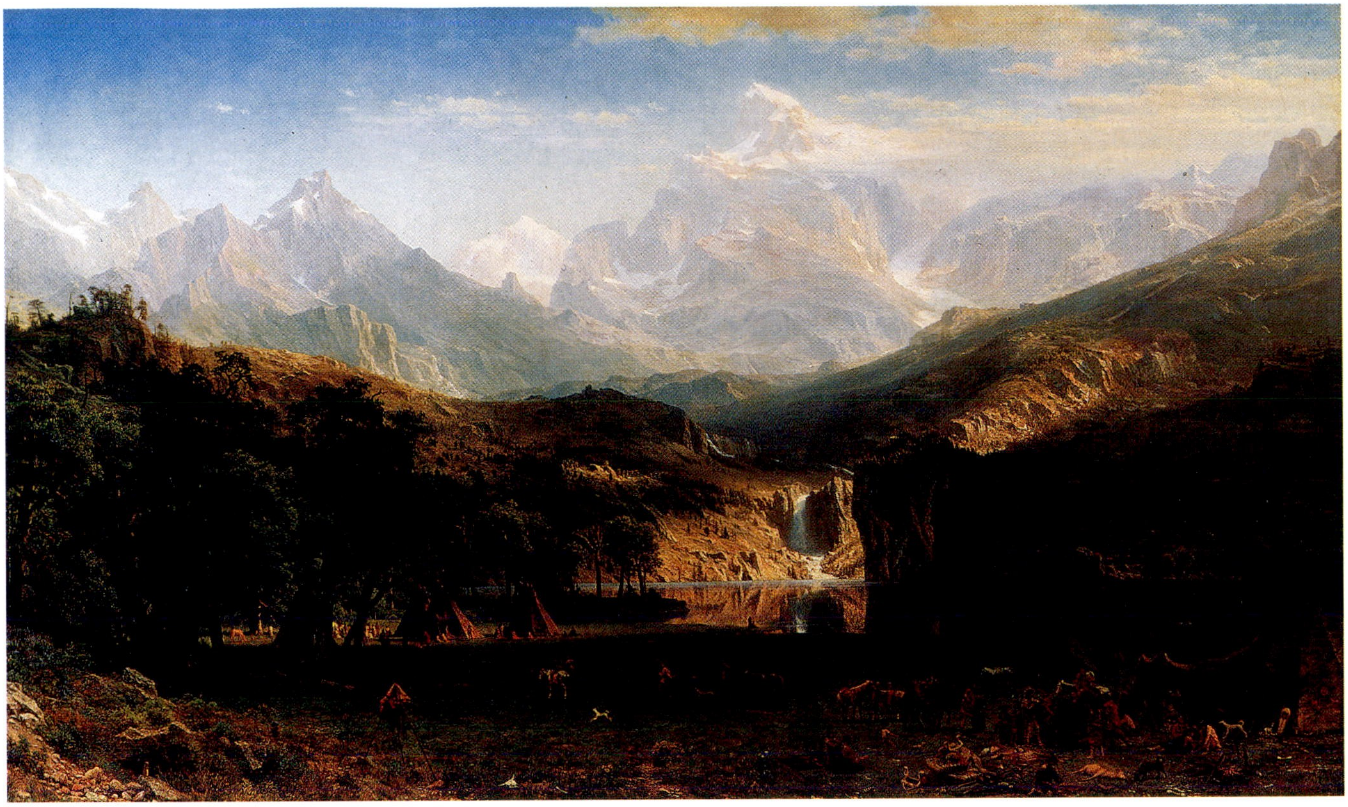

Fig. 3 Albert Bierstadt (1830–1902), *The Rocky Mountains, Lander's Peak,* 1863.
Oil on canvas. 73½ in. × 120¾ in. © 1979 by The Metropolitan Museum of Art, Rogers Fund, 1907. Photograph by Schecter Lee.

landscape—works by a nineteenth-century American, a Chinese, an aboriginal Australian, and a twentieth-century American—in order to see how four different artists, from four very different times and places, respond to the same fundamental phenomenon, the world that surrounds them. But rather than emphasizing their differences, let's ask if they have anything in common.

An American Vista

Albert Bierstadt's *The Rocky Mountains* (Fig. 3), painted in 1863, was one of the most popular paintings of its time. An enormous work, over 6 feet high and 10 feet long, it captured, in the American imagination, the vastness and majesty of the then still largely unexplored West. Writing about the painting in his 1867 *Book of the Artists*, the critic H. T. Tuckerman described the painting in glowing terms: "Representing the sublime range which guards the remote West, its subject is eminently national; and the spirit in which it is executed is at once patient and comprehensive—patient in the careful reproduction of the tints and traits which make up and identify its local character, and comprehensive in the breadth, elevation, and grandeur of the composition." In its breadth and grandeur, the painting seemed to Tuckerman an image of the nation itself. If it was **sublime**—that is, if it captured an immensity so large that it could hardly be comprehended by the imagination—the same was true of the United States as a whole. *The Rocky Mountains* was a truly democratic painting, vast enough to accommodate the aspirations of the nation.

But if it was truly democratic, it was not true to life. Despite Tuckerman's assertion that Beirstadt has captured the "tints and traits" of the scene, no landscape quite like this exists in the American West. Rather, Bierstadt has painted the Alps, and the painting's central peak is a barely disguised version of the Matterhorn. Trained as a painter in Europe, Bierstadt sees the landscape through European eyes. He is not interested in representing the Rockies accurately. Rather, it is as if he secretly longs for America to be Europe, and so paints it that way.

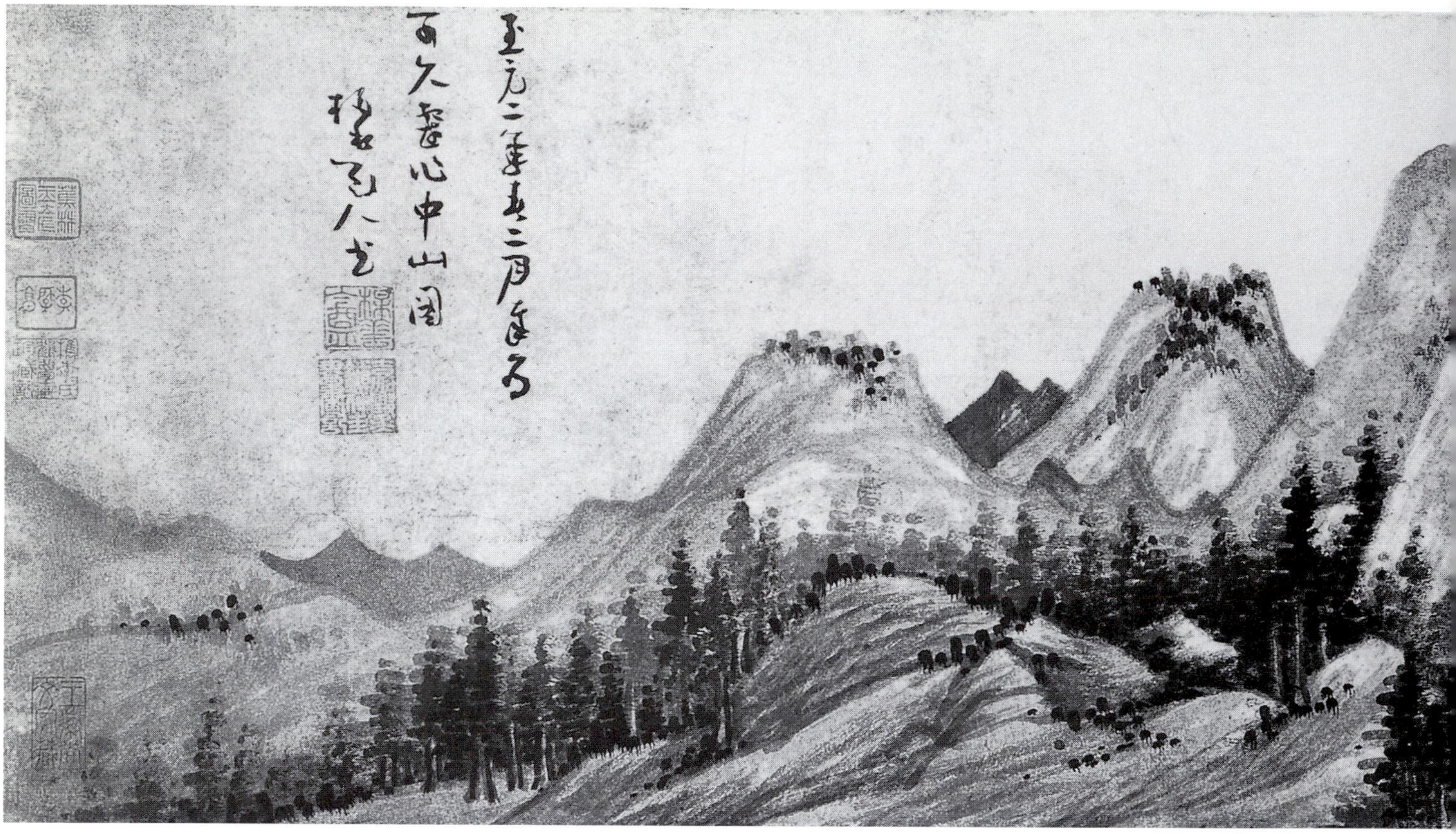

Fig. 4 Wu Chen, *The Central Mountain,* 1336.
Handscroll, ink on paper, $10\frac{1}{6} \times 35\frac{1}{3}$ in. Collection of the National Palace Museum, Taipei, Taiwan, Republic of China.

Tuckerman assumed that Bierstadt's aim in painting this scene was to record it accurately. And, in fact, one of the traditional roles of the artist is *to record the world,* to make a visual record of the places, people, and events that surround them. To a certain degree—in his accurate representation of Western flora and fauna, and in his equally accurate depiction of native dress and costume—Bierstadt accepts this role. But he also clearly wishes to accomplish something more. If the painting does not accurately reflect the American scene, it almost certainly reflects Bierstadt's own *feelings* about it. The Rockies, for him, are at least as sublime as the Alps. He wants us to share in his feeling.

A Chinese Landscape

A second traditional role of the artist, it follows, is *to give visible or tangible form to feelings.* Wu Chen's classic handscroll, *The Central Mountain* (Fig. 4), is a masterpiece of Chinese art. Composed according to strict artistic principles of unity and simplicity, it elevates the most bland, plain, and uninteresting view—the kind of scene the Chinese call *p'ing-tan*—to the highest levels of beauty, and reveals, in the process, profound truths about nature. In fact, if Wu Chen's deep feelings and reverence for nature are evident in his handscroll, it is clear that he wants to reveal something more as well. He assumes a third traditional role for the artist: He seeks to reveal hidden or universal truths.

Wu Chen was one of the Four Great Masters of the Yuan Dynasty, the period of history dominated by Mongol rulers and lasting from 1279 until 1368, when Zhu Yuanzhang drove the Mongols back to the northern deserts and restored China to the Han people. Wu Chen worked in an intensely creative cultural atmosphere, dominated by gatherings of intellectuals organized for the appreciation and criticism of poetry, calligraphy, and painting, and for the appreciation of good wine. In addition, the

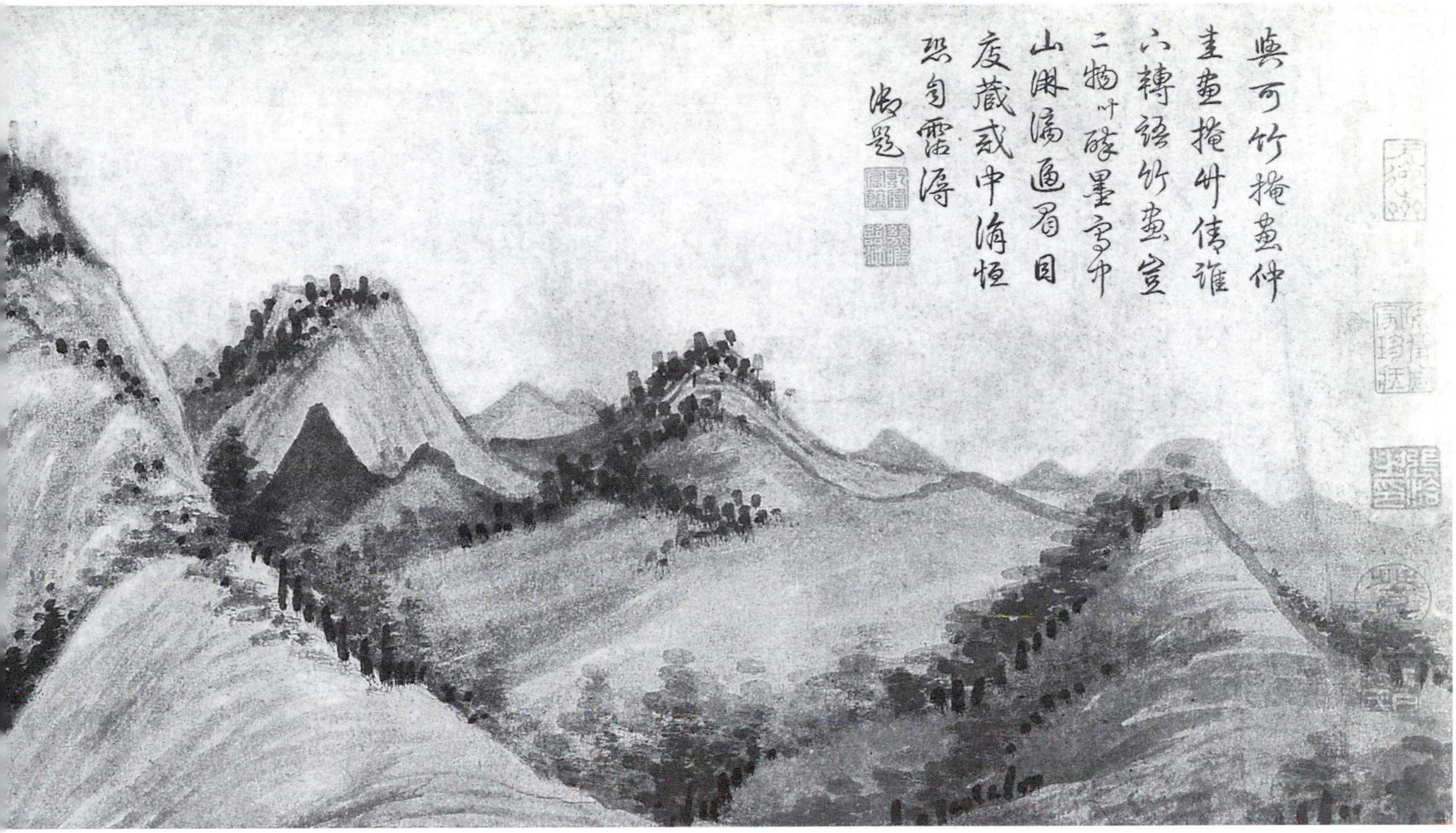

culture was dominated by deep interest in both Buddhist and Taoist thought. Of the Four Masters, Wu Chen's tastes were perhaps the simplest and most devout. *The Central Mountain* embodies the teachings of the Tao.

In Chinese thought, the Tao is the source of life. It gives form to all things, and yet it is beyond description. It manifests itself in our world through the principle of complementarity known as *yin* and *yang*. Representing unity within diversity, opposites organized in perfect harmony, the ancient symbol for this principle is the famous *yin* and *yang:*

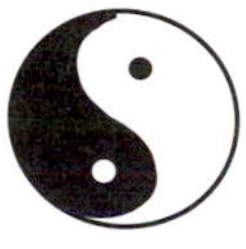

Yin is nurturing and passive, and is represented by the earth in general and by the cool, moist valleys of the landscape in particular. *Yang* is generative and active. It is represented by the sun and the mountain.

In the natural world, the variety of visual experience obscures these principles, making it difficult to recognize them. The goal of the artist, therefore, must be to reveal the Tao's presence. In Wu Chen's handscroll only trees and mountains are depicted. The trees are simple dots of ink; the grassy slopes of the mountainsides are painted in a uniform flat, gray wash. There are no roads, houses, or people to distract us. The scene is without action, devoid of any movement or sense of change. The mountains roll across the scroll with a regular rhythm, as if measuring the serene breath of the spectator. The entire composition, both the mountains and the sky, is symmetrically balanced around the central mountain. Heaven and earth, solid and void, fold into one, as if to reveal the absolute essence and universal presence of *yin* and *yang* lying at the heart of all our visual experience.

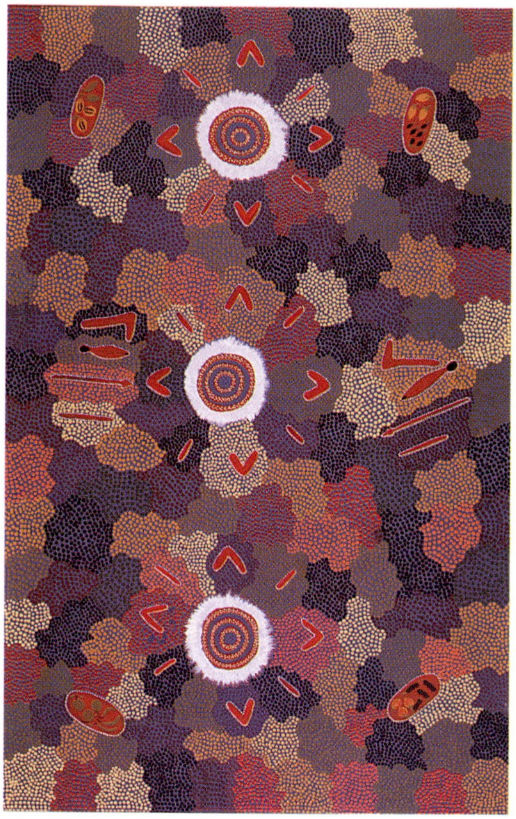

Fig. 5 **Erna Motna, *Bushfire and Corroboree Dreaming,* 1988.** Acrylic on canvas, 48 × 32 in. Australia Gallery, New York.

An Aboriginal "Dreaming"

Like Wu Chen, the Australian aboriginal artist Erna Motna wishes to reveal something larger than himself in his *Bushfire and Corroboree Dreaming* (Fig. 5). The organizing logic of most Aboriginal art is the so-called Dreaming, a system of belief unlike that of most other religions in the world. The Dreaming is not literally dreaming as we think of it. For the Aborigine, the Dreaming is the presence, or mark, of an Ancestral Being in the world. Images of these Beings—representations of the myths about them, maps of their travels, depictions of the places and landscapes they inhabited—make up the great bulk of Aboriginal art. To the Aboriginal people, the entire landscape is thought of as a series of marks made upon the earth by the Dreaming. Thus the landscape itself is a record of the Ancestral Being's passing. Geography is thus full of meaning and history. And painting is understood as a concise vocabulary of abstract marks conceived to reveal the ancestor's being, both present and past, in the Australian landscape.

Ceremonial paintings on rocks, on the ground, and on people's bodies were made for centuries by the Aboriginal peoples of Central Australia's Western Desert region. Acrylic paintings, similar in form and content to these traditional works, began to be produced in the region in 1971. In that year a young white art teacher named Geoff Bardon arrived in Papunya, a settlement on the edge of the Western Desert organized by the government to provide health care, education, and housing for the Aboriginal peoples. Several of the older Aboriginal men became interested in Bardon's classes, and he encouraged them to paint in acrylic, using traditional motifs. By 1987, prices for works executed by well-known painters ranged from $2,000 to $15,000, though Western buyers clearly valued the works for their aesthetic appeal and not for their traditional meanings.

Each design still carries with it, however, its traditional ceremonial power and is actual proof of the identity of those involved in making it. The artist who paints a Dreaming is called *kirda*. Artists are *kirda* if they have inherited the "rights" to the Dreaming from their father. Every Dreaming is also inherited through the mother's line, and a person who is related to a Dreaming in this way is said to be *kurdungurlu*. Thus a woman who is *kirda* for a particular Dreaming will have children who are *kurdungurlu* for that same myth and the landscape associated with it. *Kurdungurlu* must ensure that the *kirda* fulfill their proper social and ritual obligations to the Dreaming. As a result, several people usually work on a given painting. The *kirda* who is most knowledgeable about the Dreaming might direct it, overseen by *kurdungurlu* who make sure everything is properly depicted. Another *kirda* skillful with the brush might paint it. Because the process of composing with so many small dots of paint is so arduous, still other *kirda,* and sometimes *kurdungurlu,* help with the painting as well. The person that Westerners designate as the "artist"—a distinction not employed in Aboriginal culture before the advent of acrylic painting—is generally the person who has chosen the specific Dreaming to be depicted.

Erna Motna's *Bushfire and Corroboree Dreaming* depicts the preparations for a *corroboree,* or celebration ceremony. The circular features at the top and bottom of the painting represent small bush fires that have been started by women. As small animals run from the fire (symbolized by the small red dots at the edge of each circle), they are caught by the women and hit with digging sticks, also visible around each fire, and then carried with fruit and vegetables to the central fire, the site of the corroboree itself. Other implements that will be used by the men to kill larger animals driven out of the bush by the fires are depicted as well—boomerangs, spears, clubs, and spear throwers.

Unlike most other forms of Aboriginal art, acrylic paintings are permanent and are not destroyed after serving the ceremonial purposes for which they were produced. In this sense, the paintings have tended to turn dynamic religious practice into static representations, and, even worse, into commodities. Conflicts have arisen over the potential revelation of secret ritual information contained in the paintings, and the star status bestowed upon certain painters, particularly younger ones, has had destructive effects on traditional hierarchies within the community. On the other hand, these paintings have tended to revitalize and strengthen traditions that were, as late as the 1960s, thought doomed to extinction.

A Contemporary Earthwork

The abstract marks that make up Erna Motna's painting are not readily legible to us in the West. In fact, it is difficult for Westerners to view the painting in terms of landscape. Yet Robert Smithson's giant earthwork, *Spiral Jetty* (Fig. 6), is a large-scale mark very similar to Motna's. Stretching into the Great Salt Lake at a point near the Golden Spike monument, which marks the spot where the rails of the first transcontinental railroad were joined, *Spiral Jetty* literally *is* landscape. Made of mud, salt crystals, rocks, and water, it is a record of the geological history of the place. But it is landscape that has been created by man. The spiral form makes this clear. The spiral is one of the most widespread of all ornamental and symbolic designs on earth. In Egyptian culture, the spiral designated the motion of cosmic forms and the relationship between unity and multiplicity, in a manner similar to the Chinese *yin* and *yang*. The spiral is, furthermore, found in three main natural forms: expanding like a nebula, contracting like a whirlpool, or ossified like a snail's shell. Smithson's work suggests the way in which these contradictory forces are simultaneously at work in the universe—to reveal that hidden truth. Thus the *Jetty* gives form to the feelings of contradiction he felt as a contemporary inhabitant of his world. Motion and stasis, expansion and contraction, life and death, all are simultaneously suggested by the 1500-foot coil, the artist's creation extending into the Great Salt Lake, America's Dead Sea.

Smithson's work, furthermore, exemplifies the fourth traditional role of the artist: *to help us see the world in a new or innovative way.* Art can transform our experience of the world. It can jar us out of our complacency. It can create new ways for us to see and think about the world around us. It can literally cause us to open up our eyes.

To a greater or lesser degree, all four of the artists we have discussed assume all four of the traditional roles. What else do they share? However diverse their backgrounds and their

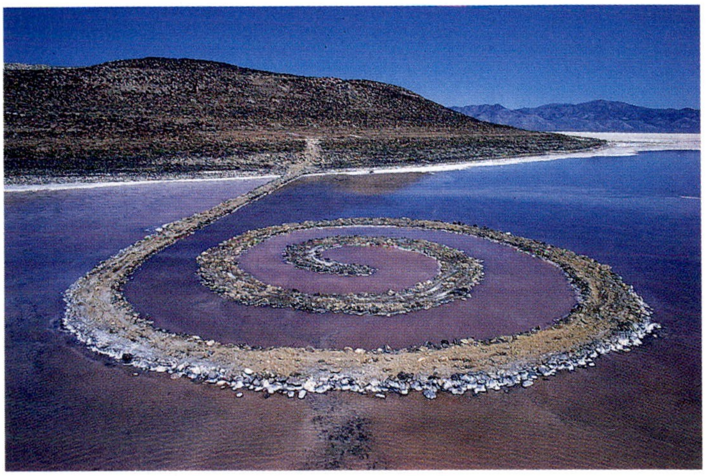

Fig. 6 Robert Smithson, "*Spiral Jetty*," Great Salt Lake, Utah, April 1970.
Photograph by Gianfranco Gorgoni.
Mud, precipitated salt crystals, rock, water, coil 1500 ft. long and 15 ft. wide.
Woodfin Camp & Associates.

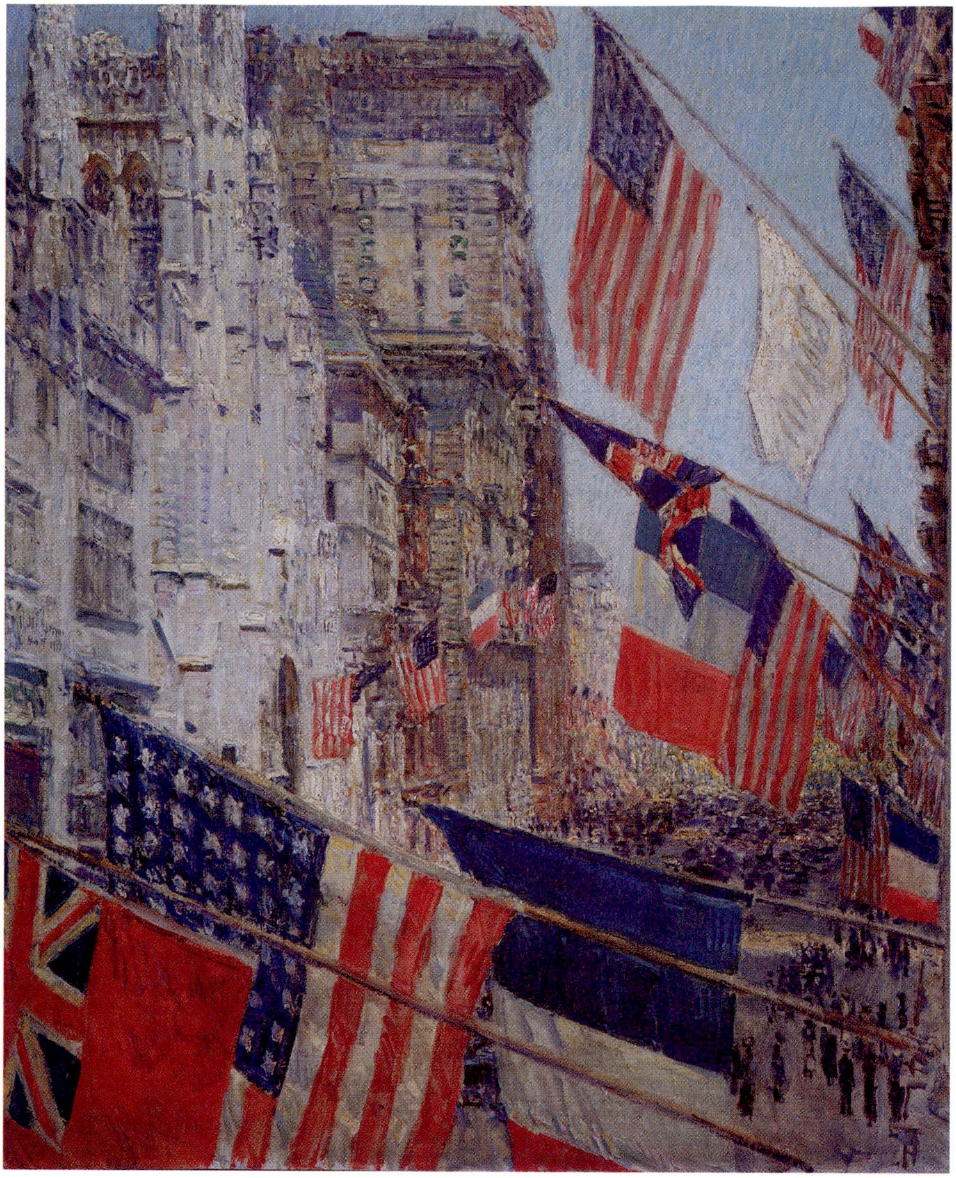

Fig. 7 Childe Hassam, *Allies Day, May 1917*, 1917.
Oil on canvas. 36 3/4 × 30 1/4 in. © 1992 National Gallery of Art, Washington, DC.
Gift of Ethelyn McKinney in memory of her brother, Glenn Ford McKinney.

worlds, all four *create visual images.* All people are creative, but not all people possess the energy, flexibility, and courage of conviction that is required to make art. **Creativity** is the ability to bring to fruition, or produce, whatever is imagined or envisioned. But it is also much more. In order to produce a work of art, the artist must be able to respond to the unexpected, the chance occurences or results that are part of the creative process. In other words, the artist must be something of an explorer and inventor. The artist must always be open to new ways of seeing. And if we are to appreciate art, we must be willing to open ourselves to new ways of seeing as well. In the second half of this chapter we will explore what we are really doing when we look at art.

THE WORLD AS WE PERCEIVE IT

Many of us assume, almost without question, that we can trust in the reality of what we see. Seeing, as we say, is believing. Our word "idea" derives, in fact, from the Greek word *idein,* meaning "to see," and it is no accident that when we say "I see" we really mean "I understand."

Nevertheless, though visual information dominates our perceptions of the world around us, we do not always understand what we see. More to the point, no two people, seeing the same thing, will come to the same understanding of its meaning or significance. Consider the images on the two pages before you. Almost all of us can agree, I think without difficulty, on the subject matter. Both images depict flags. Childe Hassam's *Allies Day, May 1917* (Fig. 7) is patriotic in tone. It celebrates the American entry into World War I, something that the nation had put off until April 6, 1917, after five American ships had been sunk in a span of nine days. The scene is Fifth Avenue in New York City, viewed from 52nd Street, where the flags decorated the route of the parades held on May 9 and 11 to honor the Allied leaders, who had come to New York to consult on strategy.

If Hassam's painting seems straightforward, Jasper Johns's *Three Flags* (Fig. 8) is, at first sight, a perplexing image. It is constructed out of three progressively smaller canvases that have been bolted to one another, and because the flag undeniably shrinks before your eyes, becoming less grand and physically smaller the closer it gets to you, it seems to many viewers to diminish the very idea of America for which it stands. According to Johns, when he created this work the flag was something "seen but not looked at, not examined." *Three Flags* was painted at a time when the nation was obsessed with patriotism, spawned by Senator Joseph McCarthy's anti-Communist hearings in 1954, by President Eisenhower's affirmation of all things American, and by the Soviet Union's challenge of American supremacy, shown clearly by the launching of Sputnik in 1957. Against that background, Johns's work asks us to consider just what our flag means to us. It asks us to examine our assumptions about ourselves.

However we feel about the Johns painting, however easily we all *read* it as the image of a flag, its *meaning* is not clear. In a book called *The Languages of Art,* Nelson Goodman suggests why. "The eye," he says, "functions not as an instrument self-powered and alone, but as a dutiful member of a complex and capricious organism. Not only how but what it sees is regulated by need and prejudice. It selects, rejects, organizes, discriminates, associates, classifies, analyzes, constructs. It does not so much mirror as take and make." In other words, the eye mirrors each individual's complex perceptions of the world. There are at least two sets of eyes at issue when we discuss Johns's work: Johns's (what exact ideas influenced him when he chose to paint the flag?) and ours (what needs and prejudices regulate our vision?). In the next two sections, we will explore the related processes of seeing and perceiving.

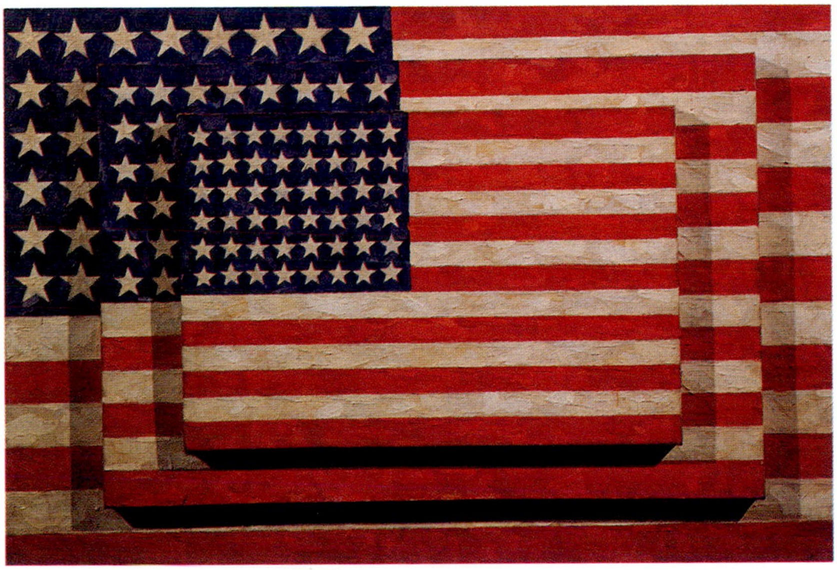

Fig. 8 Jasper Johns, *Three Flags,* 1958.
Encaustic on canvas, 30 7/8 × 45 1/2 in. Collection of Whitney Museum of American Art.
50th Anniversary Gift of the Gilman Foundation, Inc., The Lauder Foundation, A. Alfred Taubman, an anonymous donor, and purchaser 80.32.

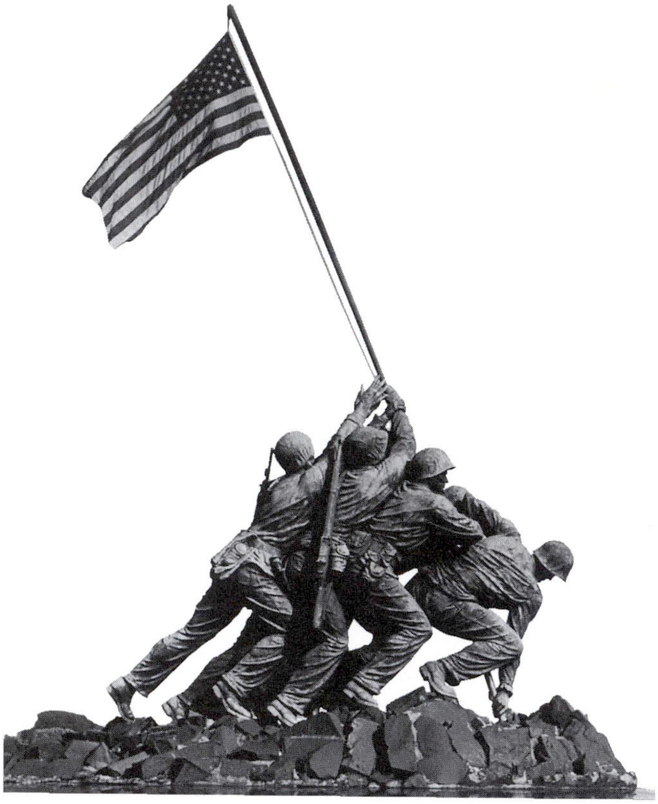

Fig. 9 Felix W. de Weldon, *Marine Corps War Memorial,* Arlington, Virginia, 1954.
Cast bronze, over lifesize. Superstock.

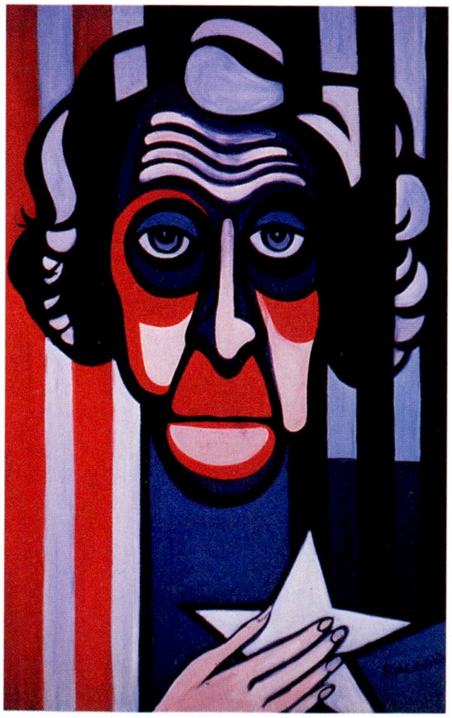

Fig. 10 Faith Ringgold, *God Bless America,* 1964.
Oil on canvas, 31 × 19 in. © Faith Ringgold.

The Physical Process of Seeing

Seeing is both a physical and psychological process. We know that, physically, visual processing can be divided into three steps:

reception → *extraction* → *inference.*

In the first step, *reception,* external stimuli enter the nervous system through our eyes—"we see the light." Next, the retina, which is a collection of nerve cells at the back of the eye, extracts the basic information it needs and sends this information to the visual cortex, the part of the brain that processes visual stimuli. There are approximately 100 million sensors in the retina, but only 5 million channels to the visual cortex. In other words, the retina does a lot of "editing," and so does the visual cortex. There, special mechanisms capable of extracting specific information about features such as color, motion, orientation, and size "create" what is finally seen. What you see is the *inference* your visual cortex extracts from the information your retina sends it.

Seeing, in other words, is an inherently creative process. The visual system makes conclusions about the world. It represents the world for you by selecting out information, deciding what is important and what is not. What sort of information, for example, have you visually assimilated about the U.S. flag? You know its colors—red, white, and blue—and that it has 50 stars and 13 stripes. You know, roughly, its shape—rectangular. But do you know its proportions? Do you even know, without looking, what color stripe is at the flag's top, or what color is at the bottom? How many short stripes are there, and how many long ones? How many horizontal rows of stars are there? How many long rows? How many short ones? Of course, even looking back at Johns's painting will not help you answer the last three questions, since it was finished before the admission of Hawaii and Alaska to the Union. The point is that not only do we each perceive the same things differently, remembering different details, but also we do not usually see things as thoroughly or accurately as we might suppose.

The Psychological Process of Seeing

If seeing is a physically creative process, psychologically it is even more so. If you wanted to draw a flag, for instance, you would concentrate on the

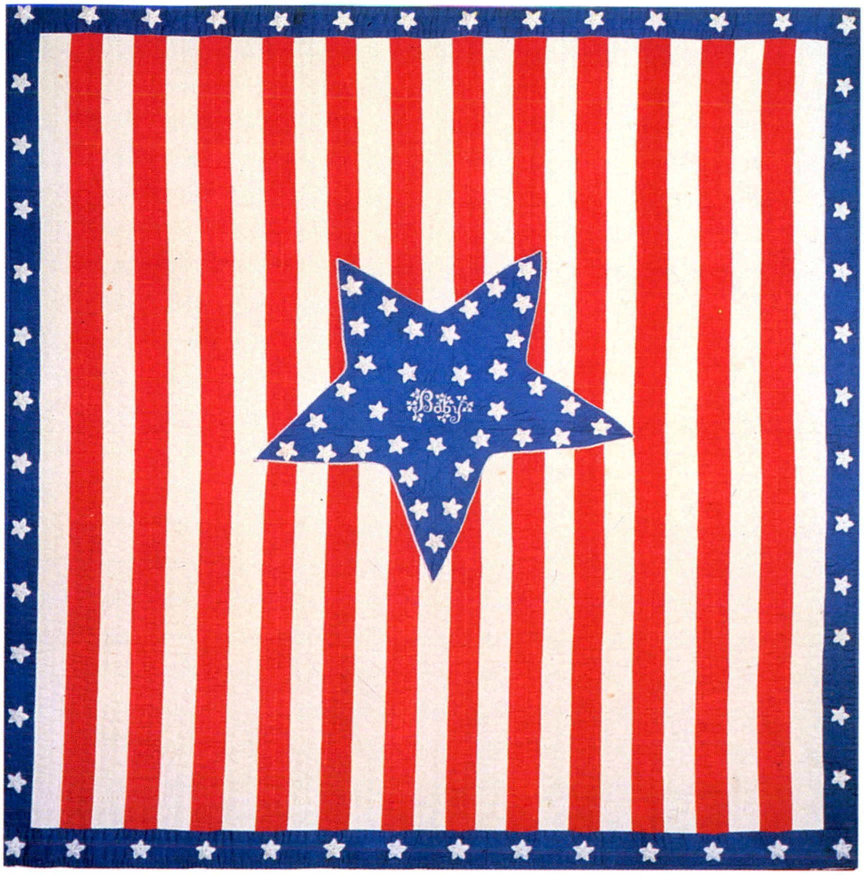

Fig. 11 Artist Unknown, *"Baby" Crib Quilt*, Kansas, c. 1861.
Hand dyed, homespun cotton, 36 7/8 × 36 3/4 in.
Collection of the Museum of American Folk Art, New York.
Gift of Phyllis Haders. 1978.42.1.

kinds of formal details listed in the previous paragraph. But the context in which you see a thing has a lot to do with how you see it. Everything you see is filtered through a long history of fears, prejudices, desires, emotions, customs, and beliefs—both your own and the artist's. Figures 9, 10, and 11 show three widely different interpretations of the U.S. flag. In the *Marine Corps War Memorial* (Fig. 9), the flag becomes the symbol not merely of the nation but of freedom itself. In Faith Ringgold's *God Bless America* (Fig. 10), it has been turned into a prison. Painted during the Civil Rights movement, as Martin Luther King, Jr. was delivering the great speeches that mark that era, the star of the flag becomes a sheriff's badge and its red and white stripes are transformed into the black bars of a jail cell. The white woman portrayed in the painting is the very image of contradiction, at once a patriot, pledging allegiance to the flag, and a racist, denying blacks the right to vote. The artists' intentions in these two works are different, and so, potentially, are our reactions to them.

The crib quilt (Fig. 11) represents still another meaning for the flag. Created in Kansas in about the year 1861, it is a far more complex image than it at first appears. The blue center star contains 34 smaller white stars, and this allows us to date the quilt, because Kansas joined the Union as the 34th state in 1861. The quilt celebrates two "newcomers," Kansas and the baby for whom it was sewn. It might even be said to transform the new state's motto—"To the Stars Through Difficulty"—into a story about childbirth. But it is important to remember that the Kansas of 1861 was a state torn by the Civil War and the issue of slavery. John Brown had attempted to begin a war for the abolition of slavery at Potawatomie in 1856, and five years later the state was forced to choose between joining the Union or the Confederacy. This quilt, then, is a political statement—it could even be called Republican, the party of Lincoln—emphatically asserting the family's position concerning the issue of slavery.

One of the most controversial works of art concerning the flag in recent years is "Dred" Scott Tyler's installation, *What Is the Proper Way to Display the American Flag?* (Fig. 12). The piece was first seen on February 20, 1989, when the School of the Art Institute of Chicago opened an exhibition of works of art by 66 students who were members of minority groups. Tyler's work consisted of a 34 × 57 inch American flag draped on the floor beneath photographs of flag-draped coffins and South Koreans burning the flag. Beneath the photos was a ledger in which viewers were asked to record their opinions. The problem was not only that the flag was on the floor, but that it was difficult to write in the ledger without stepping on the flag. Thus the flag became a barrier to the freedom of expression it was meant to defend. Viewers had to choose which they revered most—the flag itself or freedom of speech.

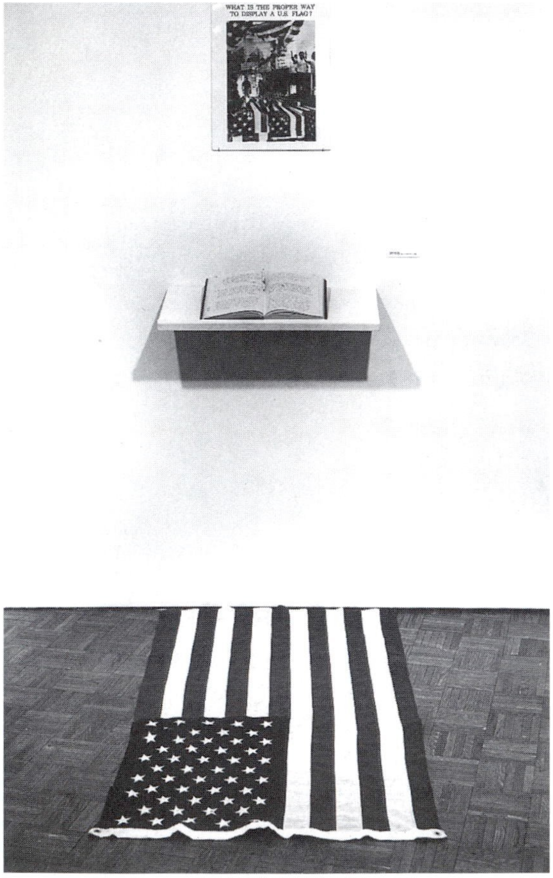

Fig. 12 Scott Tyler, *What Is the Proper Way to Display the American Flag?* 1989.
Installation. Photograph by Michael Tropea.

Angry veterans wearing combat fatigues protested the exhibit soon after it opened, waving American flags, singing the national anthem, and carrying signs saying, "The American flag is not a doormat." Said one: "When I walked in there and saw those muddy footprints on the flag, I was disgusted. It would be different if it was his own rendering of the flag. But it was a real flag. And it belongs to the American people." Tyler responded that he had purchased the flag at a store for $3.95. It had been made in Taiwan.

By February 24, school officials had closed the show. A week later it reopened, and a school teacher from Virginia was arrested when she walked on the flag to write in the ledger. Finally, on March 12, 2,500 veterans and supporters from nine states marched on the Art Institute. Students reacted, brawls broke out, and five more people were arrested.

Because of the exhibition, the United States Senate, the Illinois Legislature, and the Chicago City Council all passed legislation banning display of the flag on the floor. These laws were all subsequently overturned when the United States Supreme Court ruled that even flag burning is protected as free speech by the First Amendment. Freedom of speech is a difficult issue, even for the courts, and in taking freedom of speech as its subject, Tyler's installation was equally problematic.

In this chapter we have discovered that the world of art is as vast and various as it is not only because different artists in different cultures see and respond to the world in different ways, but because each of us sees and responds to a given work of art in different ways as well. The traditional roles of the artist—to record the world, to give visible or tangible form to feelings, to reveal hidden or universal truths, and to help us see the world in new or innovative ways—are all part of a more general creative impulse that leads, ultimately, to the work of art. But once the work of art is made, it remains for us, its audience, to see it and come to understand it. And though we might all agree that the images in the last half of this chapter are all of the U.S. flag, we would not all agree what these images mean. What we see in the world of art and what we understand about it are two very different things.

CHAPTER 2

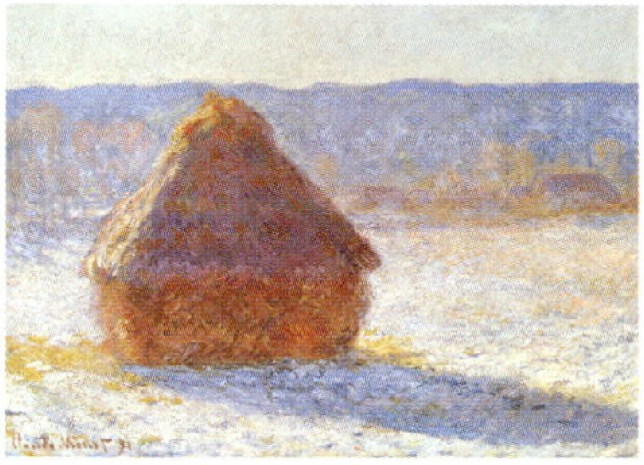

Understanding Visual Art

Visual art can be powerfully persuasive , and one of the purposes of this book is to help you to recognize how this is so. Yet it is important for you to understand from the outset that you can neither recognize nor understand—let alone communicate—how visual art affects you without using language. In other words, one of the primary purposes of any art appreciation text is to provide you with a descriptive vocabulary, a set of terms, phrases, concepts,

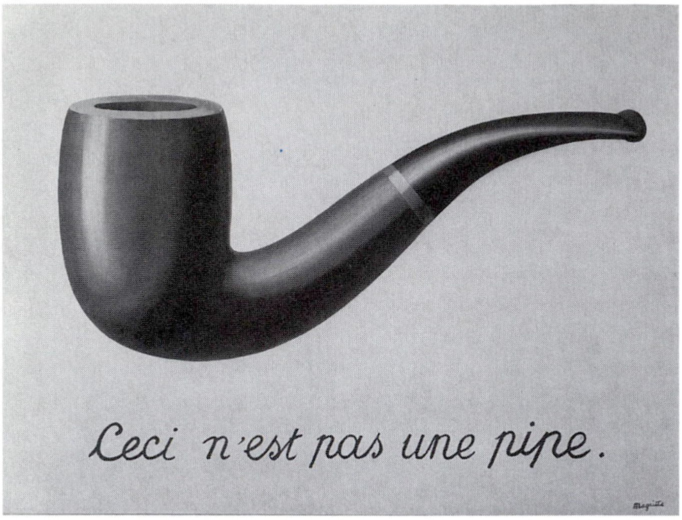

Fig. 13 René Magritte, *The Treason of Images,* 1929.
Oil on canvas, 21 ½ × 28 ½ in. Los Angeles County Museum.

and approaches that will allow you to think critically about visual images. It is not sufficient to say, "I like this or that painting." You need to be able to recognize why you like it, how it communicates to you. This ability is given the name **visual literacy.**

The fact is, most of us take the visual world for granted. We assume that we understand what we see. Those of us born and raised in the television era are often accused of being nonverbal, passive receivers, like TV monitors themselves. If television—and the mass media generally, from *Time* to MTV—has made us virtually dependent on visual information, we have not necessarily become visually *literate* in the process. To introduce you to the idea of visual literacy, this chapter will begin by introducing you to the main tools needed for our discussion—the relationship between words, images, and objects in the real world, the idea of representation, and the distinction between form and content in art. With these in hand, we will then consider some of the major themes of art: representing God, the mind, and the beautiful.

WORDS AND IMAGES

The degrees of distance between things in the world and the words and images with which we refer to them is precisely the point of René Magritte's *The Treason of Images* (Fig. 13). We tend to look at the image of a pipe as if it were really a pipe, but of course it isn't. It is the *representation* of a pipe. *Ceci n'est pas une pipe,* the painting tells us: "This is not a pipe." Nor is the word "pipe" the same as an image of it. The word is an abstract set of marks that "represents," in language, both the thing and its image. Language is even further removed from the real world than visual representation. And within language there are different degrees of distance as well. "This," finally, is not a "pipe." These two words are not the same: "This" is a pronoun that could point to anything, and only in this context does it point to a "pipe."

In the West, we tend to confuse words and the things they represent. This is not true in other cultures. For example, in Muslim culture, the removal of the word from what it refers to is seen as a virtue. Traditionally, those who make pictures with human figures in them are labeled "the worst of men," and to possess such a picture is comparable to owning a dog, an animal held in contempt because it is associated with filth. In creating a human likeness, the artist is thought to be competing with the Creator himself, and such *hubris,* or excessive pride, is, of course, a sin. As a result, **calligraphy**—that is, the fine art of handwriting—is the chief form of Islamic art.

The Muslim calligrapher does not so much express himself—in the way that we, individually, express ourselves through our style of writing—as act as a medium through which Allah can express himself in the most beautiful manner possible. Thus all properly pious writing, especially poetry, is sacred. This is the case with the page from the poet Firdausi's *Shahnamah* at the right (Fig. 14).

Sacred texts are almost always completely abstract designs that have no relation to the world of things. They demand to be considered at least as much for their visual properties as for their literary or spiritual content. Until recent times, in the Muslim world, every book, indeed almost every sustained statement, began with the phrase "In the name of Allah"—the *bismillah,* as it is called—the same phrase that opens the Koran. On this folio page from the *Shahnamah,* the *bismillah* is in the top right-hand corner (Arabic texts read from right to left). To write the *bismillah* in as beautiful a form as possible is believed to bring the scribe forgiveness for his sins.

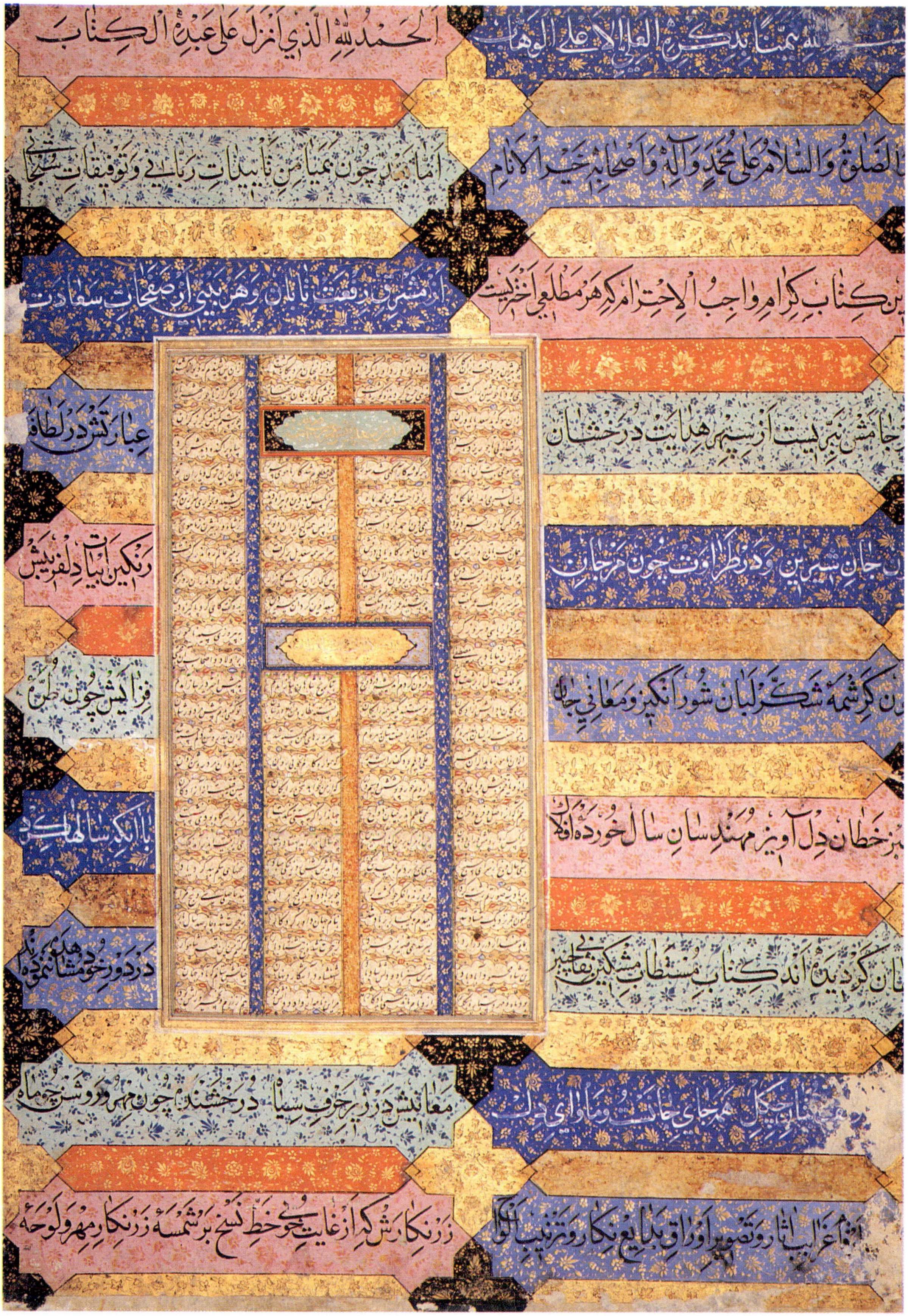

Fig. 14 Page from a manuscript of the *Shahnamah* of Firdausi, Iran and Turkey, 1562–1583.
Watercolor and gold on paper, 18 ½ × 13 in. Museum of Fine Arts, Boston. Francis Bartlett Donation of 1912 and Picture Fund.

Yet words, however beautifully written, have limitations. If you allow yourself to believe for a moment that the photograph of the tree in the diagram below (Fig. 15) represents a "real" tree, and that the drawing in the middle is its "image," the question arises: Should we trust the word "tree" more or less than the image of it? It is no more "real" than the drawing. It is made from a series of pen strokes on paper—not an action radically removed, at least in a physical sense, from the set of gestures used to draw the tree. In fact, the word might seem even more arbitrary and culturally determined than the drawing. Most people would understand what the drawing depicts. Only English speakers understand "tree." In French the word is *arbre,* in German *baum,* in Turkish *agaç,* and in Swahili *mti.*

An excellent case can be made, in other words, for the primacy of images over words. Most of us trust a photograph of an unusual event more than some witness's verbal description of it. "The camera never lies," we tell ourselves, while the reliability of a given witness is always in doubt.

Cameras, of course, can and do lie. Consider Duane Michals's photograph of an embracing couple (Fig. 16). The **subject matter** of the work—what the image depicts—and its **content**—what the image means—are radically opposed. The man in this photograph insists on using it as if it were proof in a court of law, and we are the jury. Evidently the relationship is over, but the man wants us to believe that "once upon a time" he was loved by someone, that this woman was happy in his company. His insistence is embarrassing. We read his protestation as a fairy tale that he has created in order to deceive himself.

Whichever we tend to trust more, the visual or the verbal (and it probably depends on the context of any given situation), it should nevertheless be clear that words and images need to work together. Each is insufficient in itself to tell the whole "truth." It should be equally clear that any distrust of visual imagery we might feel is, at least in part, a result of the visual's power. When, in Exodus, the worship of "graven images," that is, idols, is forbidden, the assumption is that such images are powerfully attractive, even dangerously seductive. As we have noted, the page of Arab poetry reproduced previously (Fig. 14) depends for its power at least as much on its visual presence and beauty as it does on what it actually says.

REPRESENTING THE WORLD

In the last section, we explored the topic of visual literacy by considering the relationship between words and images. Words and images are two different systems of **representation.** In a representation, things in the real world are literally re-presented in different form. Representation, in other words, involves the relation of the word or image to the natural world. This relation is especially important in the visual arts, since traditionally one of the primary goals of the visual arts has been to capture and portray the way the natural world looks. But, as we all know, some works of art look more like the natural world than others, and some artists are more interested than others in representing the world. As a result, a vocabulary has developed that describes how closely, or not, the image resembles visual reality itself. This basic set of terms is where we need to begin in order to talk or write intelligently about works of art.

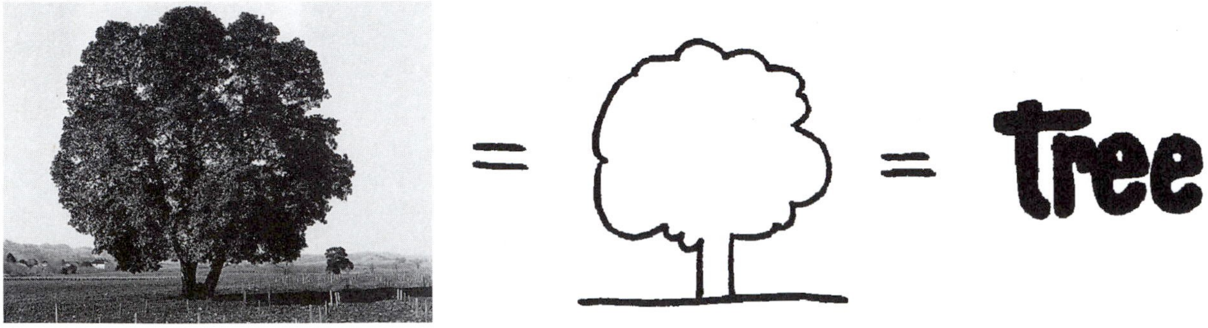

Fig. 15 The visual to the verbal. On the left: C. E. Watkins, *Arbutus Menziesii Pursh,* California, 1861.
Albumen print, 14 × 21 ¼ in. Collection, Museum of Modern Art, New York. Purchase.

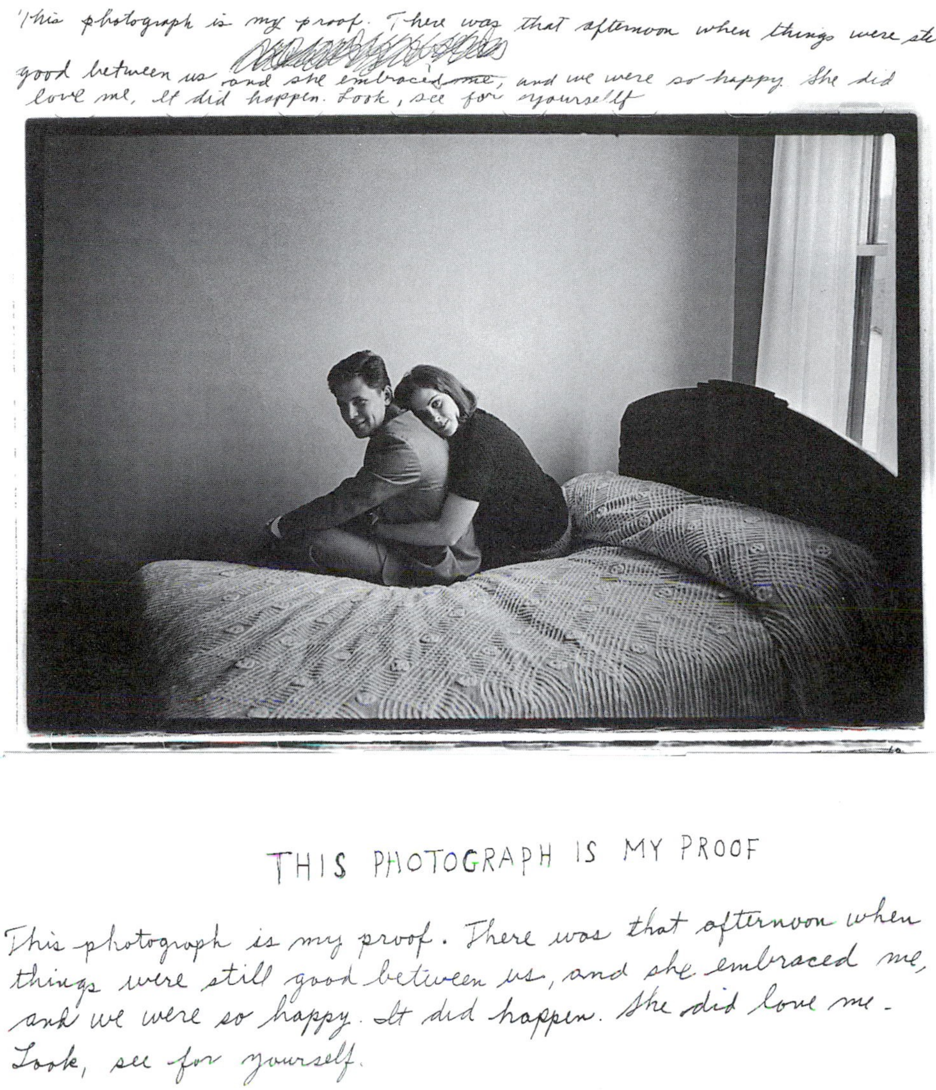
This photograph is my proof. There was that afternoon when things were still
good between us and she embraced me, and we were so happy. She did
love me, it did happen. Look, see for yourself
THIS PHOTOGRAPH IS MY PROOF
This photograph is my proof. There was that afternoon when
things were still good between us, and she embraced me,
and we were so happy. It did happen. She did love me.
Look, see for yourself.

Fig. 16 Duane Michals, *This Photograph Is My Proof,* 1967 and 1974.
Silver print, 8 × 10 in. ©Duane Michals.

Representational, Abstract, and Nonobjective Art

Generally we refer to works of art as either **representational, abstract,** or **nonobjective** (or **nonrepresentational**). The more a work resembles real things in the real world, the more **representational,** or **realistic,** it is said to be. You may also encounter the related terms, **naturalistic,** meaning "like nature," and **illusionistic,** which refers to an image so natural that it creates the illusion of being real. Traditional photography is, in many ways, the most representational medium, because its transcription of what lies before the viewfinder appears to be direct and unmanipulated. The photograph, therefore, seems to capture the immediacy of visual experience. It seems equivalent to what we actually see. It is important to remember, however, that photography captures only what is visible. As in the Duane Michals photograph, the photographic image does not necessarily capture the emotional world that lies beneath the surface. Photography offers up only a replica of the world.

The four images on these pages, all by different artists, proceed in steps from so-called photographic realism to the most abstract art. As a series, they embody a continuum from the most representational through the abstract to the nonobjective.

Lorna Simpson's The Park

As a photographer, Lorna Simpson is preoccupied with the question of representation and its limitations. All of her works, of which the multipanel *Necklines* (Fig. 17) is a good example, deal with the ways in which words and images function together to make meaning.

Simpson presents us with three different photographs of the same woman's neck and the neckline of her dress. Below these images are two panels with four words on each, each word in turn playing on the idea of the neck itself. The sensuality of the photographs is affirmed by words such as "necking" and "neck-ed" (that is, "naked"), while the phrases "neck & neck" and "breakneck"

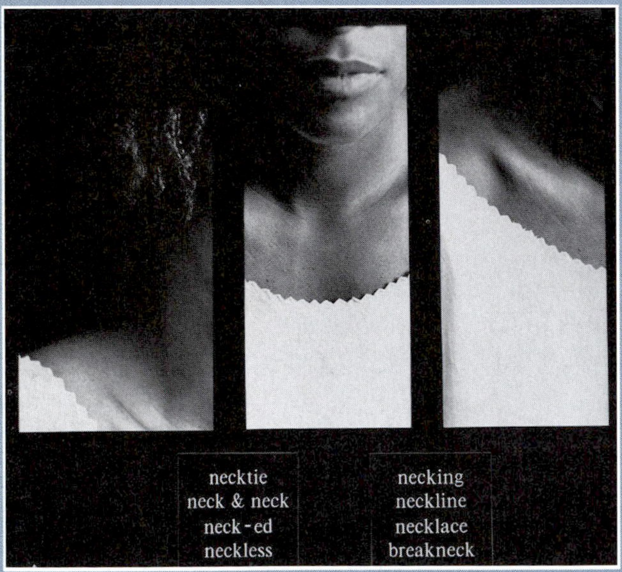

Fig. 17 Lorna Simpson, *Necklines*, 1989.
Three silver prints, two plastic plaques, 68 ½ × 70 in.
Courtesy Josh Baer Gallery, New York.

introduce the idea of speed or running. The question is, what do these two sets of terms have to do with one another? Necklaces and neckties go around the neck. So do nooses at hangings. In fact, "necktie parties" involve hangings, hangings break necks, and a person runs from a "necktie party" precisely because, instead of wearing a necklace, in being hanged one becomes "neckless."

If this set of verbal associations runs contrary to the sensuality and seeming passivity of Simpson's photographs, they do not run contrary to the social reality faced, throughout American history, by black people in general. The anonymity of Simpson's model serves not only to universalize the situation that her words begin to explore, but also to depersonalize the subject in a way that suggests how such situations become possible. Simpson seeks to articulate this tension—the violence that always lies beneath the surface of the black's world—by bringing words and images together.

A group of large-scale black-and-white serigraphs, or silkscreen prints, on felt take up different subject matter but remain committed to investigating the relationship between words and images. Created for the premier opening of the Sean Kelly Gallery in New York City in October 1995, all of the works but one are multipanel photographs of landscapes (the one exception is a view of two almost identical hotel rooms). They employ a unique process. Simpson first photographed the scenes. Then she arranged with Jean Noblet, one of the primier serigraph printers in the world, to print them, blown up into several large panels, on felt, a material never before utilized in the silkscreen printing process. The felt absorbed vast quantities of ink, and each panel had to be printed several times to achieve the correct density of black. Furthermore, each panel had to match the others in the image. In less than two weeks time, the entire suite of seven images, consisting of over fifty panels, was miraculously printed, just in time for the show.

Each of the images is accompanied by a wall text that, when read, transforms the image. On one side of *The Park* (Fig. 18), for instance, the viewer reads:

> *Just unpacked a new shiny silver telescope. And we are up high enough for a really good view of all the buildings and the park. The living room window seems to be the best spot for it. On the sidewalk below a man watches figures from across the path.*

On the other side of the image, a second wall text reads:

> *It is early evening, the lone sociologist walks through the park, to observe private acts in the men's public bathrooms. . . . He decides to adopt the role of voyeur and look out in order to go unnoticed and noticed at the same time. His research takes several years . . . .*

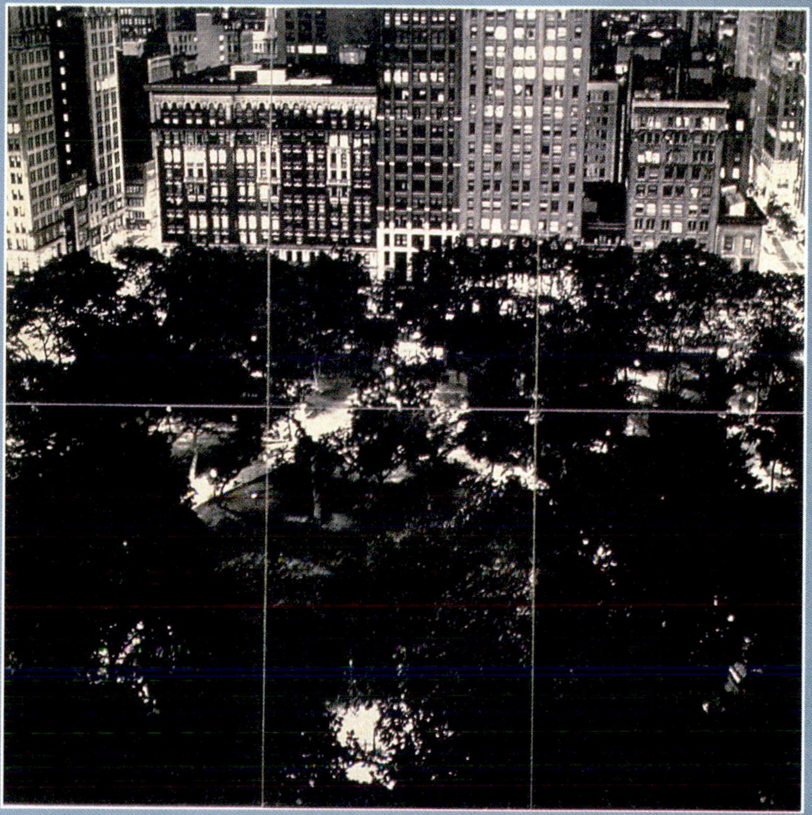

Fig. 18 Lorna Simpson, *The Park*, 1995.
Edition of 3, serigraph on six felt panels with felt text panel, 67 × 67 ½ in. overall.
Courtesy Sean Kelly Gallery, New York.

These texts effectively involve Simpson's audience in a complex network of voyeurism. The photographer's position is the same as the person's who has purchased the telescope, and our viewpoint is the same. Equipped with a telescope (or the telescopic lens of a camera) apparently purchased for viewing the very kind of scene described in the second text, we want to zoom in to see what's going on below.

There is, in fact, a kind of telescopic feel to the work itself. The image itself is over 5½ feet square and can be readily taken in from across the room. But to understand it, we need to come in close to read the texts. Close-up, the image is too large to see as a whole, and the crisp contrasts of the print as seen from across the room are lost in the soft texture of the felt. The felt even seems to absorb light rather than reflect it as most photographic prints do, blurring our vision in the process. As an audience, we zoom in and out, viewing the scene as a whole, and then coming in to read the texts. As we move from the general to the particular, from the panoramic view to the close-up text, the innocuous scene becomes charged with meaning. The reality beneath surface appearances is once again Simpson's theme—the photographer challenging the camera view.

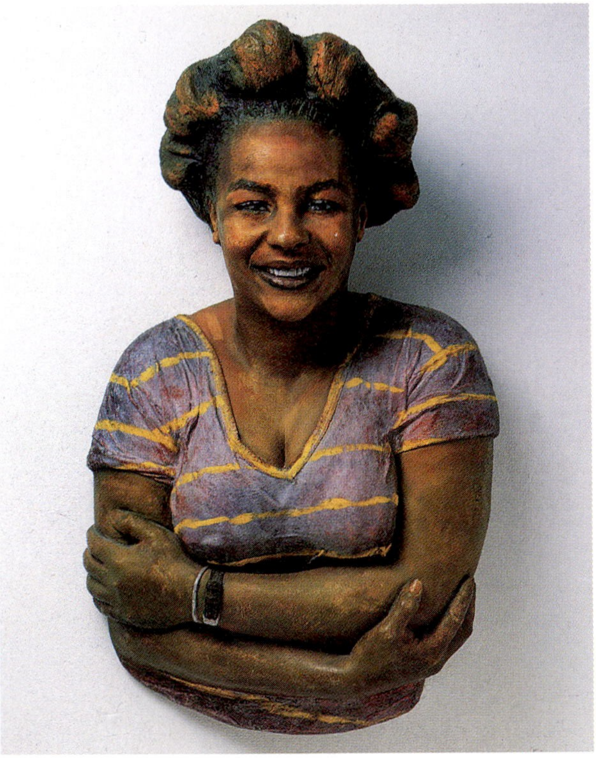

Fig. 19 John Ahearn and Rigoberto Torres, *Pat,* 1982.
Painted cast plaster, 28 ½ × 16 ½ × 11 in. Courtesy Alexander and Bonin, New York. Collection Norma and William Ross, Winterhaven, Florida; photo courtesy of Sotheby's.

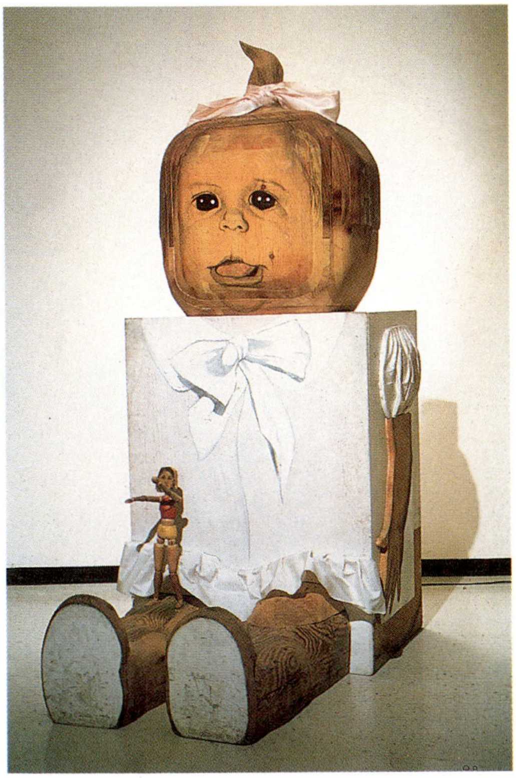

Fig. 20 Marisol Escobar, *"Baby Girl,"* 1963. © 1966 Marisol Escobar/ Licensed by VAGA, New York, NY
Wood, paint, pencil, H. 74 in. Albright-Knox Museum, Buffalo, New York.

The sculpture of *Pat,* on the left (Fig. 19), is so representational that it almost looks real. Sculpture this true to life is called **super realist** (a related term, **photorealist**—i.e., as real as a photograph—is generally reserved for two-dimensional, or flat, images). In fact, *Pat* is one of many plaster casts made from life by John Ahearn and Rigoberto Torres, residents of the South Bronx in New York City. In 1980, Ahearn moved to the South Bronx and began to work in collaboration with local resident Torres. Torres had learned the art of plaster casting from his uncle, who had cast plaster statues for churches and cemeteries. Together Ahearn and Torres set out to capture the spirit of a community that was financially impoverished, but that possessed real, if unrecognized dignity. "The key to my work is life—lifecasting," says Ahearn. "The people I've casted have given me more life experiences than any art education of college could ever hope to. . . . The people I cast know that they are as responsible for my work as I am, even more so. The people make my sculptures."

The next image in our continuum, Marisol's *Baby Girl* (Fig. 20), is still recognizable as a representation of a little girl, but it is much less realistic than *Pat.* Instead of rendering the human form exactly, Marisol simply draws the human form on the large, barely rounded blocks of wood. As a result, the work seems half sculpture, half drawing.

The less a work resembles real things in the real world, the more **abstract** it is said to be. Abstract art does not try to duplicate the world exactly, but instead reduces the world to its essential qualities. It is concerned with the formal qualities of an image (such as line and form and color), or in the emotions that may be expressed through it. For example, Marisol's *Baby Girl* is over six feet tall, sitting down. Her exaggerated size lends her the emotional presence of a monster, an all-consuming, all-demanding force far larger than her actual size.

Joel Shapiro's *Untitled* (Fig. 21) is a barely representational, highly abstract version of a human figure lying on its side. Shapiro believes that we all inevitably see representational forms in any configuration (just as we see representational shapes in cloud formations), so he lets us see these nine wooden blocks as a figure. Nevertheless, their abstraction, their formal quality as wooden retangular volumes, is asserted even more completely than in Marisol's work.

Shapiro's work is very close to becoming as **nonobjective**—that is, without reference to the objective world—as Carl Andre's *Redan* (Fig. 22). Composed of 27 wooden blocks piled in a zig-zag formation, Andre's work seems to have no reference to the world of things at all. If we look up its title in a dictionary, however, we discover that it refers to an architectural feature of fortifications in which two walls are set at an angle facing the enemy. Nevertheless, Andre is more interested in the form of his piece, its angles and its presence in the room, than its actual reference.

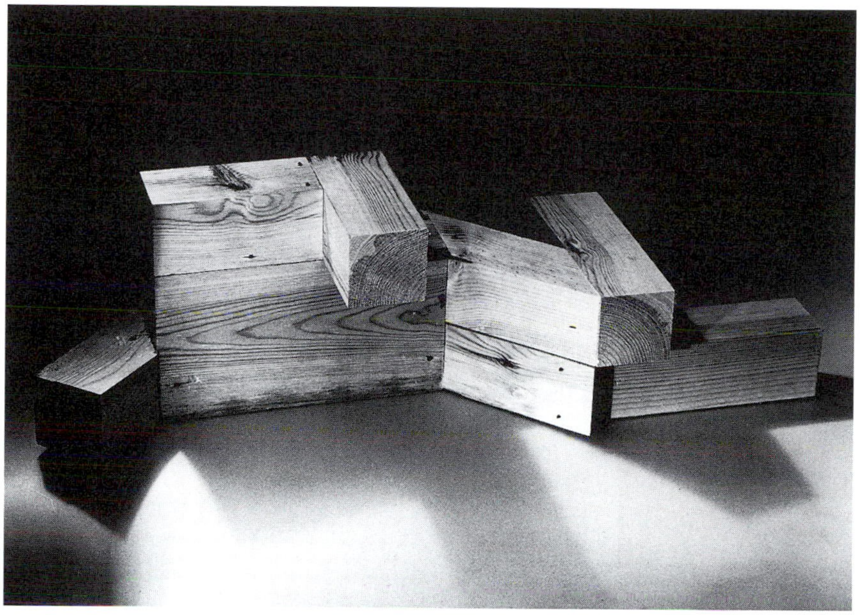

Fig. 21 Joel Shapiro, *Untitled,* 1981.
Wood, approx. 8 3/4 × 31 1/4 × 8 1/2 in. (21.8 × 78 × 21 cm.).
Photograph courtesy of PaceWilderstein.

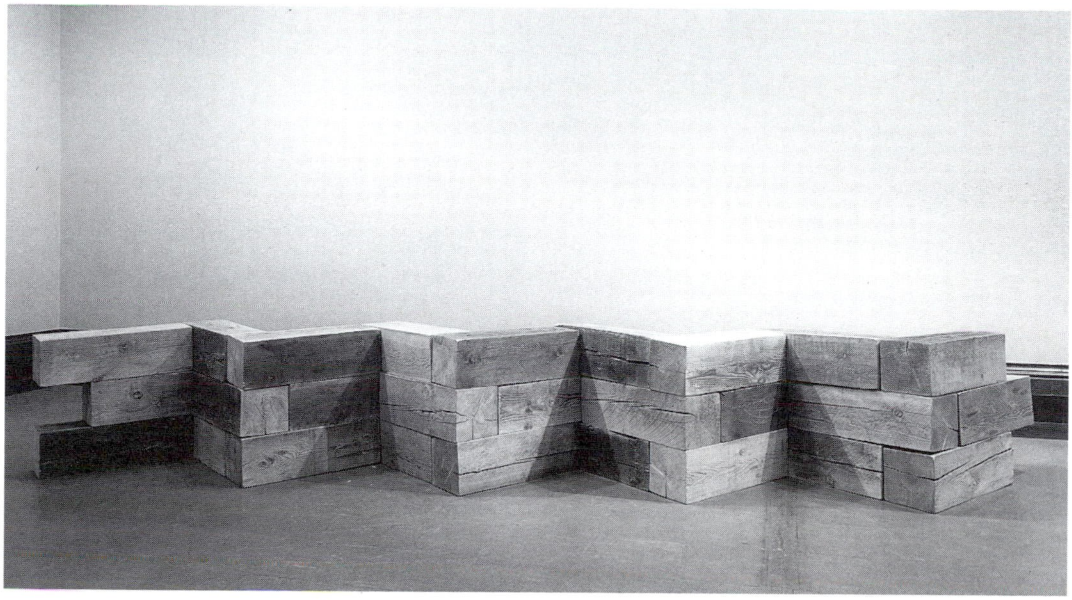

Fig. 22 Carl Andre, *Redan,* 1964 (destroyed; reconstructed 1970).
Wood, 27 units, 12 × 12 × 36 in. each; 36 × 42 × 245 in. overall. Art Gallery of Ontario, Toronto.
Purchased with assistance from the Women's Committee Fund, 1971.

It is not always easy, or even necessary, to make absolute distinctions between the representational, the abstract, and the nonobjective. Joel Shapiro's work, Fig. 21, is a good example. A given work of art may be more or less representational, more or less abstract. Very often certain elements of a representational painting will be more abstract, or generalized, than other elements. Likewise, a work may appear totally nonobjective until you read the title, and see that, in fact, it does refer to things in the actual world, however loosely. Purely nonobjective art, such as Kasimir Malevich's *Suprematist Painting* (Fig. 23), is concerned only with questions of form, and we turn now to those considerations.

Form and Content

When we speak of a work's **form,** we mean everything from the materials used to make it, to the way it employs the various formal elements (discussed in Part II), to the ways in which those elements are organized into a **composition.** Form, somewhat misleadingly, is generally opposed to **content,** which is what the work of art expresses or means. Obviously, the

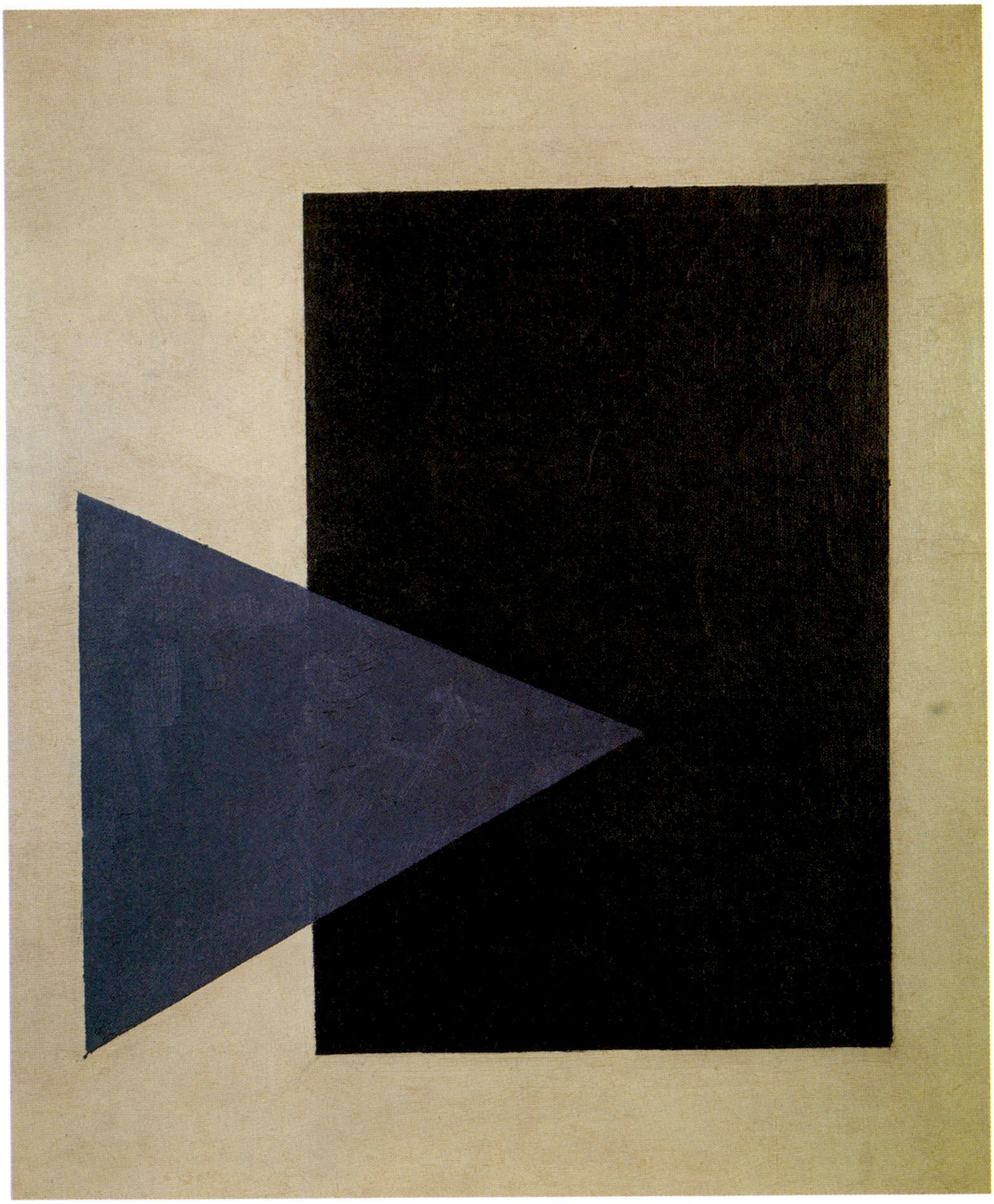

Fig. 23 Kasimir Malevich, *Suprematist Painting, Black Rectangle, Blue Triangle,* 1915.
Oil on canvas, 26 ⅛ × 22 ½ in. Stedelijk Museum, Amsterdam.

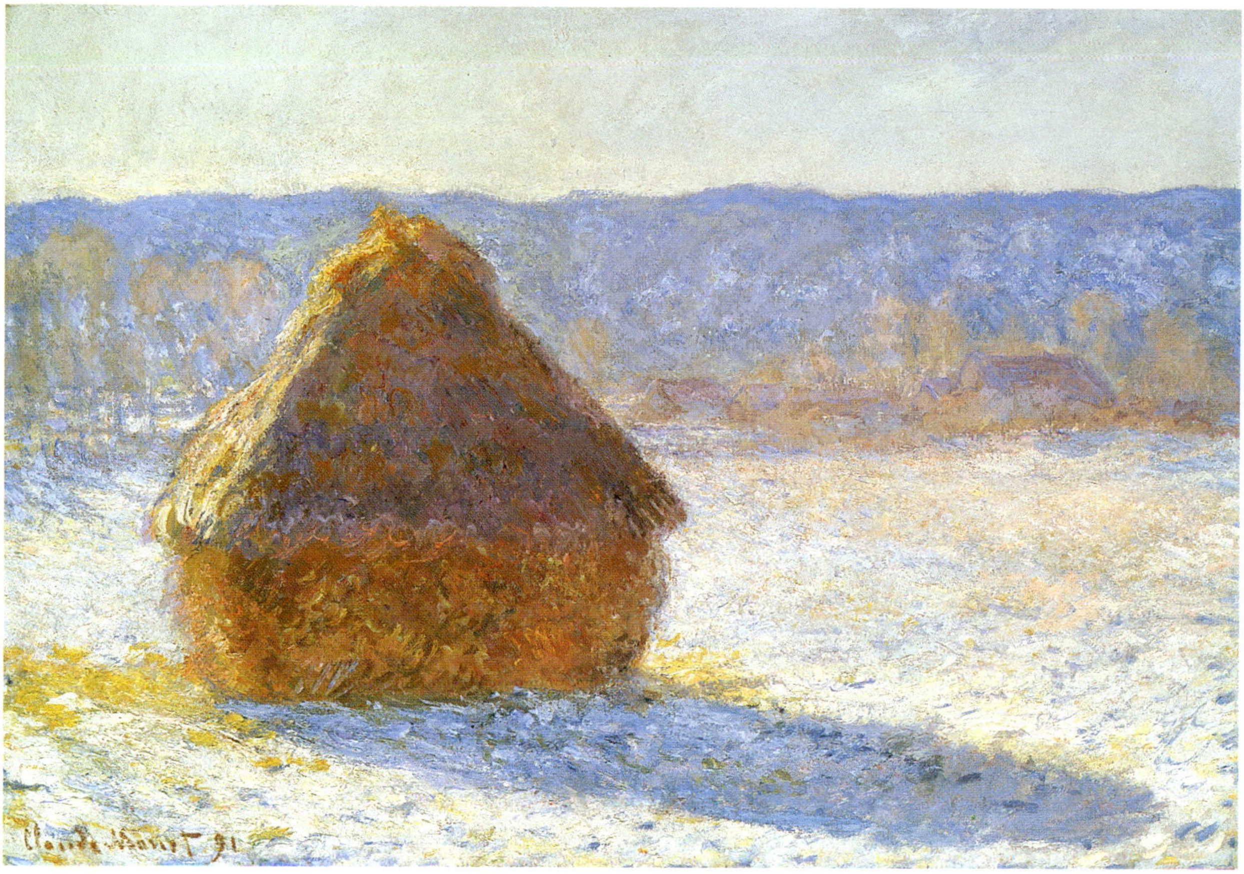

Fig. 24 Claude Monet, *Grainstack (Snow Effect)*, 1891.
Oil on canvas, 25 3/4 × 36 3/8 in. Museum of Fine Arts, Boston.
Gift of Misses Aimee and Rosamond Lamb in memory of Mr. and Mrs. Horatio A. Lamb.

content of nonobjective art *is* its form. Malevich's painting is really *about* the relation between the black rectangle, the blue triangle, and the white ground behind them. Though it is a uniform blue, notice that the blue triangle's color seems to be lighter where it is backed by the black triangle and darker when seen against the white ground. This phenomenon occurs because our perception of the relative lightness or darkness of a color depends on the context in which we see it, even though the color never actually changes. If you stare for a moment at the line where the triangle crosses from white to black, you will begin to see a vibration. The two parts of the triangle will seem, in fact, to be at different visual depths. Malevich's painting demonstrates how purely formal relationships can transform otherwise static forms into a visually dynamic composition.

Claude Monet uses the same forms in his *Grainstack* (Fig. 24). In fact, compositionally, this work is almost as simple as Malevich's. That is, the haystack is a triangle set on a rectangle, both set on a rectangular ground. Only the cast shadow adds compositional complexity. Yet Monet's painting has clear content. For nearly three years, from 1888 to 1891, Monet painted the haystacks near his home in Giverny, France, over and over again, in all kinds of weather and in all kinds of light. When these paintings were exhibited in May 1891, the critic Gustave Geffroy summed up their meaning: "These stacks, in this deserted field, are transient objects whose surfaces, like mirrors, catch the mood of the environment. . . . Light and shade radiate from them, sun and shadow revolve around them in relentless pursuit; they reflect the dying heat, its last rays; they are shrouded in mist, soaked with rain, frozen with snow, in harmony with the distant horizon, the earth, the sky." This series of paintings, in other words, attempts to reveal the dynamism of the natural world, the variety of its cyclic change.

In a successful work of art, form and content are inseparable. Consider another two examples of the relation between form and content. To our eyes, the two heads on this page (Figs. 25 and 26) possess radically different formal characteristics, and, as a result, differ radically in content. Kenneth Clark compares the two on the second page of his famous book *Civilisation:* "I don't think there is any doubt that the Apollo embodies a higher state of civilisation than the mask. They both represent spirits, messengers from another world—that is to say, from a world of our own imagining. To the Negro imagination it is a world of fear and darkness, ready to inflict horrible punishment for the smallest infringement of a taboo. To the Hellenistic imagination it is a world of light and confidence, in which the gods are like ourselves, only more beautiful, and descend to earth in order to teach men reason and the laws of harmony."

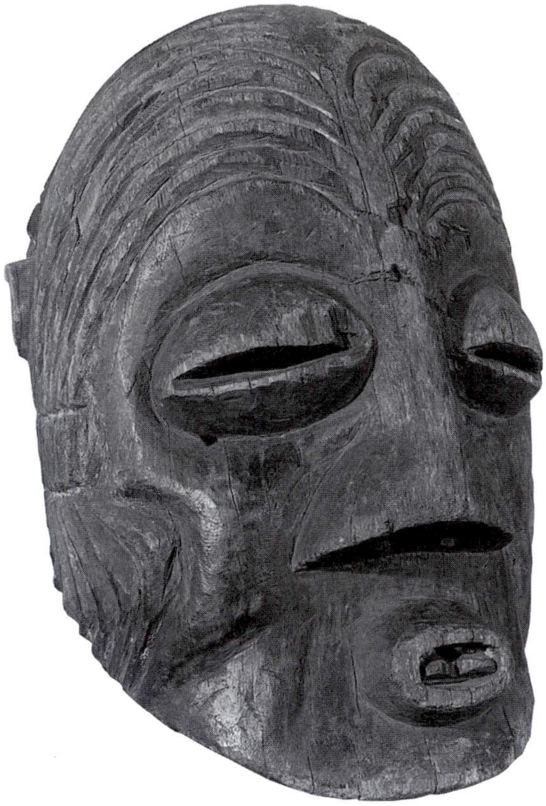

Fig. 26 African mask, Sang tribe, Gabon, West Africa.
Courtauld Institute Galleries, London.

Conventions in Art

Clark is wrong about the African mask. Its features are exaggerated, at least in part, to separate it from the "real" and to underscore its ceremonial function. Clark is reading it through the eyes of Western civilization, which has referred to the African continent as "darkest" Africa ever since the Europeans first arrived there in the sixteenth century. It is important to recognize that what we think is expressed by the particular formal treatment of a subject sometimes results from our own prejudice, and often results from our conventional expectations. The best light in which Clark's reading of the African mask can be seen is to think of it as the manifestation of a **convention**—that is, a habitual or generally accepted way of thinking in a given culture. This particular convention can be traced back at least as far as Leonardo da Vinci's studies of grotesque heads (Fig. 27). Each of these visages, we would generally agree, is *expressive* of the inner, psychological state of the being that lies behind the mask of its physical appearance. The face is the outer expression, we believe, of the reality within, and distortions in the human face indicate or imply distortions or aberrations in the human psyche beneath.

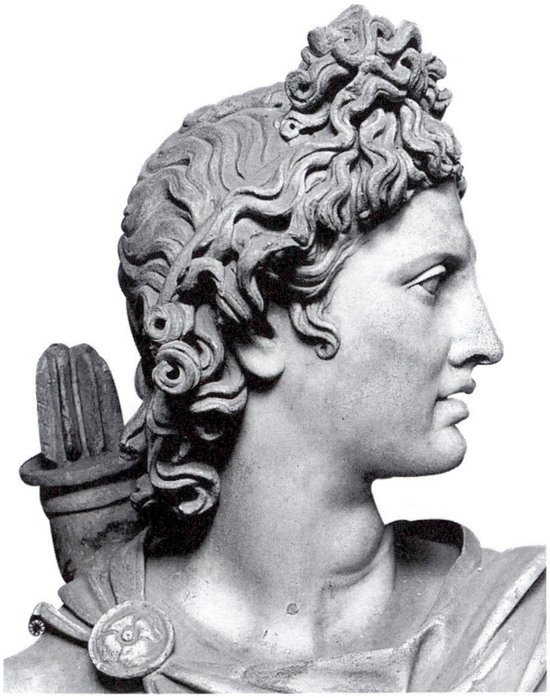

Fig. 25 Apollo Belvedere (detail), Roman copy after a 4th Century BCE Greek original.
Vatican Museums, Rome. Alinari/Art Resource.

Thus when Clark sees an African mask, he reads into its features his own preconceptions of the psychic realities—violence, horror, or fright—that might create it.

The properties for which many in the Western world value African masks—the abstractness of their forms and their often horrifying emotional expressiveness—are not necessarily those most valued by their makers. For the Baule carvers of the Yamoussoukio area of the Ivory Coast, the Helmet Mask (Fig. 28) is a pleasing and beautiful object. But it has other conventional meanings as well.

This is the Dye sacred mask, according to one carver cited in Susan Vogel's *Perspectives: Angles on African Art.* "The god is a dance of rejoicing for me. So when I see the mask, my heart is filled with joy. I like it because of the horns and the eyes. The horns curve nicely, and I like the placement of the eyes and ears. In addition, it executes very interesting and graceful dance steps. . . . This is a sacred mask danced in our village. It makes us happy when we see it. There are days when we want to look at it. At that time, we take it out and contemplate it."

The Baule carvers pay attention to formal elements, but the mask is seen as much as part of a process—the dance—as an object. To the Baule eye, the mask projects its performance. It is a vehicle through which the spirit world is made available to humankind. In performance, the wearer of the mask takes on the spirit of the place, and the carver quoted above apparently imagines this as he contemplates it.

If we do not immediately share with the Baule carvers the feelings evoked by the mask, we can be educated to see it in their terms. When we see the mask only through the conventions of our own culture, then we not only radically alter its meaning and function but implicitly denigrate the African viewpoint or refuse to acknowledge it at all.

Such a reading is **ethnocentric.** That is, it imposes upon the art of another culture the meanings and prejudices of our own. Individual cultures always develop a traditional or *conventional* repertoire of visual images that they tend to understand in a particular way. Another culture, however, might read the same image in an entirely different way. Even within a culture, the meaning of an image may change

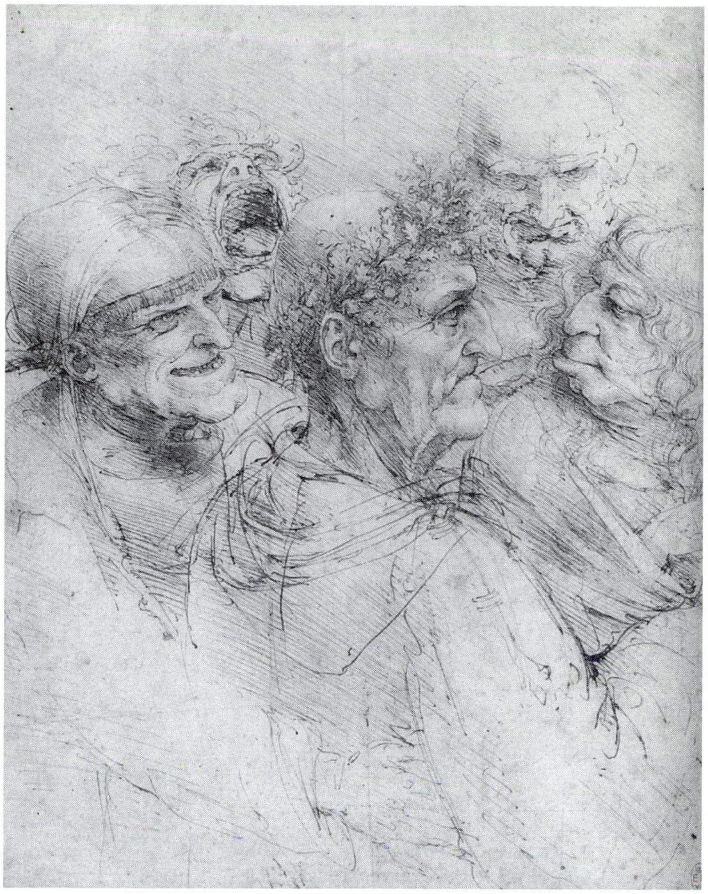

Fig. 27 Leonardo da Vinci, *Five Characters in a Comic Scene,* c. 1490.
Pen and ink, $10\frac{3}{16} \times 8\frac{3}{8}$ in.

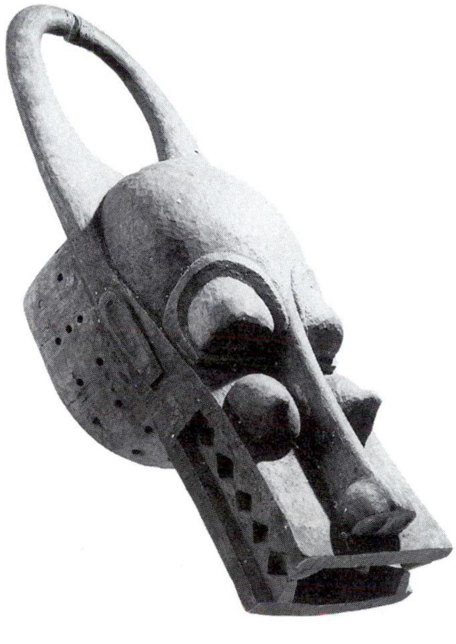

Fig. 28 Helmet mask, Baule, Ivory Coast, 19th–20th century.
Woodwork sculpture. Metropolitan Museum of Art. Michael C. Rockefeller Memorial Collection, Gift of Adrian Pascal. LaGamma, 1973. (1978.412.664).

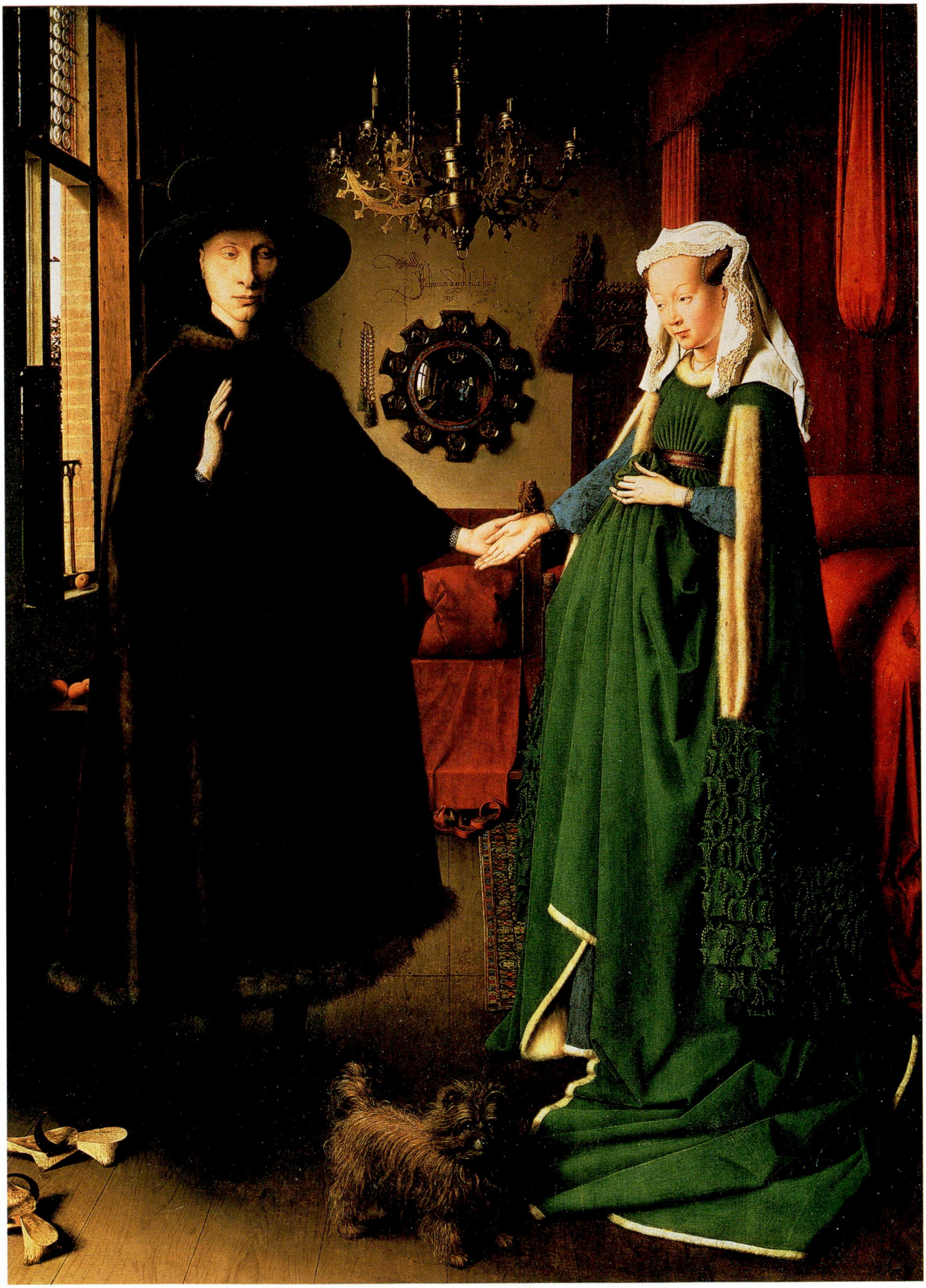

Fig. 29 Jan van Eyck, *The Marriage of Giovanni Amolfini and Giovanna Cenami,* 1434.
Oil on oak panel, 32 1/2 × 23 1/2 in. The National Gallery, London, Great Britain. Bridgeman/Art Resource, New York.

or be lost over time. When Jan van Eyck painted *The Marriage of Giovanni Arnolfini and Giovanna Cenami* in 1434 (Fig. 29), its repertoire of visual images was well understood, but today much of its meaning is lost to the average viewer. For example, the bride's green dress, a traditional color for weddings, was meant to suggest her natural fertility. She is not pregnant—her swelling stomach was a convention of female beauty at the time, and she stands in a way to accentuate it. The groom's removal of his shoes is a reference to God's commandment to Moses to take off his shoes when standing on holy ground. A single candle burns in the chandelier above the couple, symbolizing the presence of Christ at the scene. And the dog, as most of us recognize even today, is symbolic of marital fidelity.

Iconography

The study or description of such visual images or symbolic systems is called **iconography.** Every culture has its specific iconographic practices, its own system of images that are understood by the culture at large to mean specific things. But what would Arab culture make of the dog in the van Eyck painting, since in the Muslim world dogs are traditionally viewed as filthy and degraded? From the Muslim point of view, the painting verges on nonsense.

Similarly, most of us in the West probably recognize a Buddha when we see one, but most of us do not know that the position of the Buddha's hands carries iconographic significance. Buddhism, which originated in India in the fourth century BCE, is traditionally associated with the worldly existence of Sakyamuni, or Gautama, the Sage of the Sakya clan, who lived and taught around 500 BCE In his thirty-fifth year, Sakyamuni experienced enlightenment under a tree at Gaya (near modern Patna), and became Buddha or the Enlightened One.

The religion spread to China in the third century BCE, and from there into Southeast Asia during the first century CE. Long before it reached Japan, by way of Korea in the middle of the fifth century CE, it had developed a more or less consistent iconography, especially related to the representation of Buddha himself. The symbolic hand gestures, or *mudra,* refer both to general states of mind and to specific events in the life of Buddha. The *mudra* best known to Westerners, the hands folded in the seated Buddha's lap, symbolizes meditation (Fig. 30). The snake motif, seen here, illustrates a specific episode from the life of the Buddha in which the serpent-king Mucilinda made a seat out of its coiled body and spread a canopy of seven heads over Buddha to protect him, as he meditated, from a violent storm.

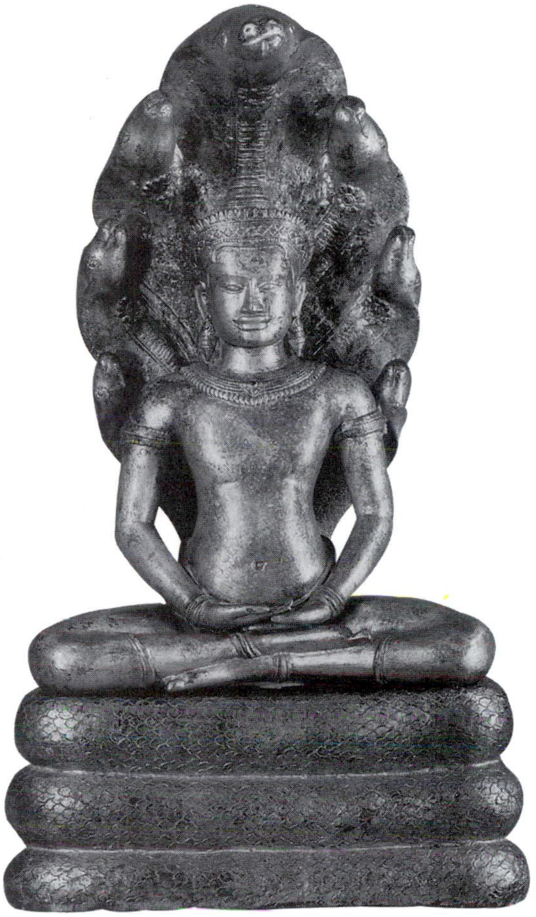

Fig. 30 Buddha, adomed, seated in meditation on the serpent Mucilinda, c. 1100–1150.
Photograph by Superstock.

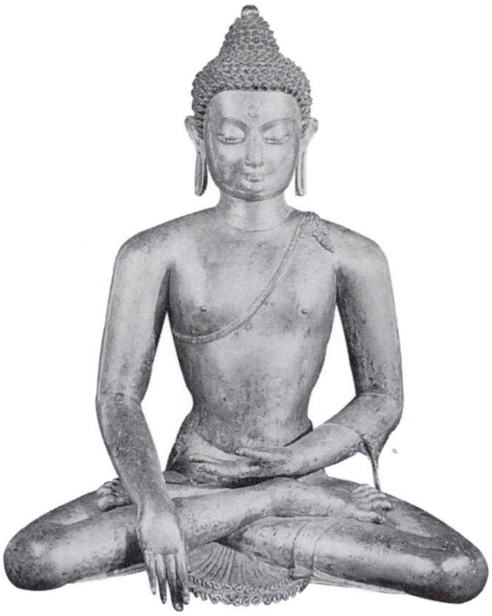

Fig. 31 Buddha subduing Mara, Nepal, late 14th century.
Gilted copper. Photograph by Superstock.

One of the most popular of the *mudra*, especially in East India, Nepal, and Thailand, is the gesture of touching the earth, right hand down over the leg, the left lying in the lap (Fig. 31). Biographically, it represents the moment when Sakyamuni achieved Enlightenment and became Buddha. Challenged by the Evil One, Mara, as he sat meditating at Gaya, Sakyamuni proved his readiness to reach Nirvana, the highest spiritual state, by calling the earth goddess to witness his worthiness with a simple touch of his hand. The gesture symbolizes, then, not only Buddha's absolute serenity, but the state of Enlightment itself.

A Buddhist audience can read these gestures as readily as we, in the predominantly Christian West, can read incidents from the story of Christ. Figure 32 shows the lower nine panels of the center window in the west front of Chartres Cathedral in France. This window

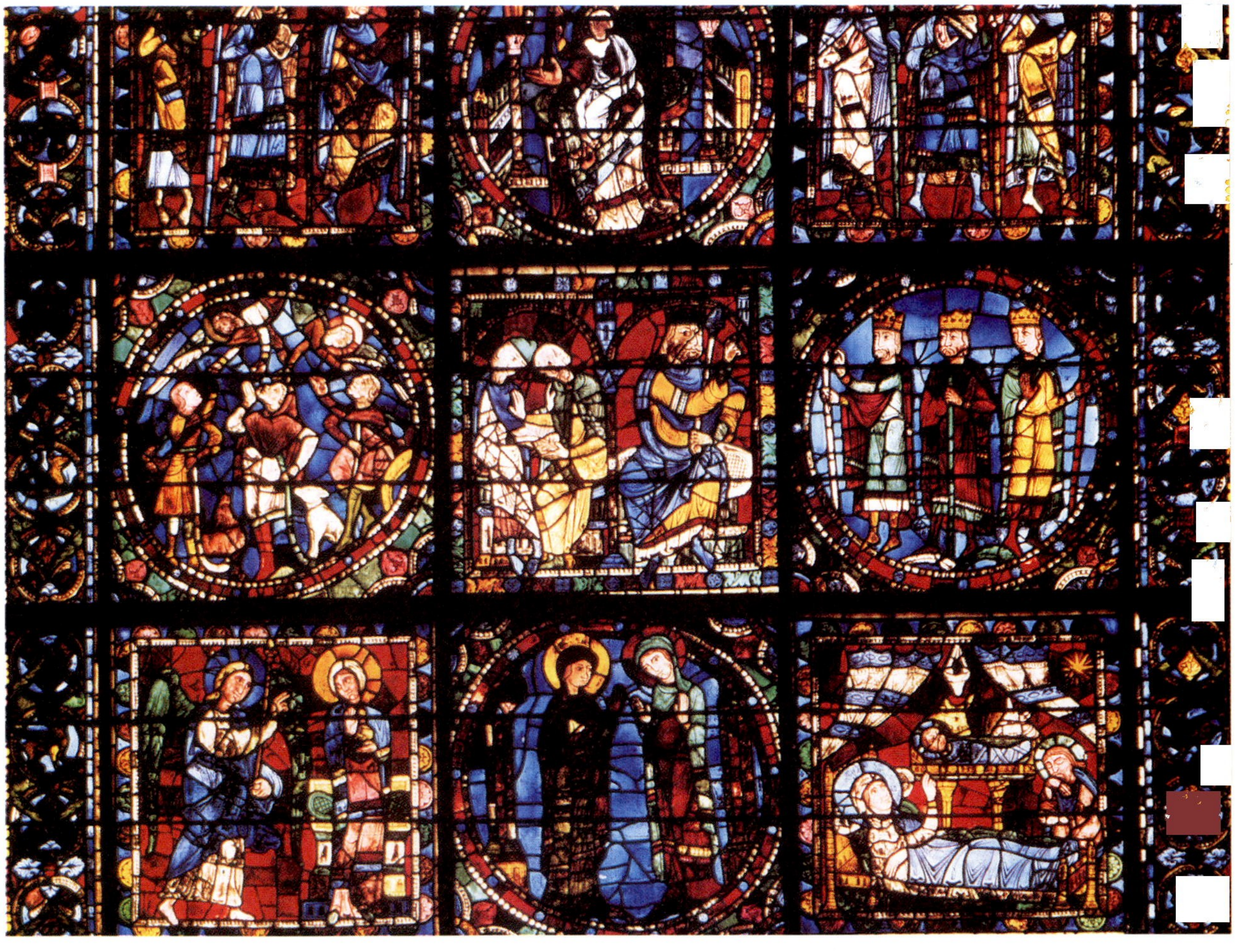

Fig. 32 Lower nine panels of the center lancet window in the west front of Chartres Cathedral, showing the Nativity, Annunciation of the Shepherds, and the Adoration of the Magi, c. 1150.
Chartres Cathedral, France. Giraudon/Art Resource.

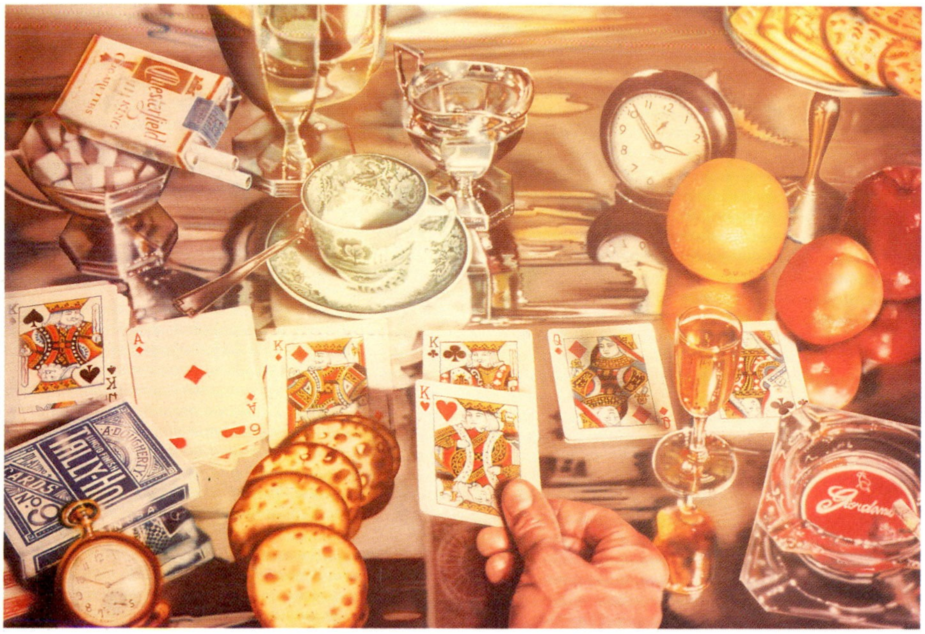

Fig. 33 Audrey Flack, *Solitaire,* 1974.
Acrylic on canvas, 60 × 84 in. Courtesy Louis K. Meisel Gallery, New York.

was made about 1150, and it is one of the oldest and finest surviving stained-glass windows in the world. The story can be read like a cartoon-strip, beginning at the bottom left and moving right and up, from the Immaculate Conception through the Nativity, the Annunciation of the Shepherds, and the Adoration of the Magi. The window is usually considered the work of the same artist who was commissioned by the Abbot Suger to make the windows of the relic chapels at Saint-Denis, which portray many of the same incidents. "The pictures in the windows are there," the Abbot explains in his writings, "for the sole purpose of showing simple people, who cannot read the Holy Scriptures, what they must believe." But he understood as well the expressive power of this beautiful glass. It transforms, he said, "that which is material into that which is immaterial." Suger understood that whatever story the pictures in the window tell, whatever iconographic significance they contain, and whatever words they generate, above all it is their art that lends them power.

REPRESENTING OTHER REALITIES

Audrey Flack's *Solitaire* (Fig. 33) is an example of a kind of painting called **photorealism,** or sometimes **super realism,** because it looks like a photograph. Yet for all its representational realism, it alludes to other realities, not the least of which is the obsessive card playing of the artist's family. The clock and the pocket watch tell us the time, but it is unclear whether it is day or night. We know from the empty coffee cup and the untouched sherry glass that the game has gone on for a while and will continue for a while more. In making her paintings, Flack first arranges a group of objects into a sort of still life, which she photographs. Then she paints from the photograph. In spite of the real subject matter, and however fascinated we might be with the image and Flack's scrupulous rendering of it, what interests the artist herself is not so much the reality of the scene as its color. This is not "real" color. It is the highly intensified color of a slide transparency projected onto a white screen.

Flack's subject matter could be said, in fact, to be the reality of representation, the way in which, in contemporary life, reality is more often "image" than not. We know about the real world *through* film, *through* television, *through* photographs, as much as or more than we know it through actual experience. But assuming that much of what we see in film, television, and photography is at least potentially manipulated, how "real" is our knowledge? What do we *really* know? And how can we represent what we cannot see?

Representing God

The idea of daring to represent God has, throughout the history of the Western world, aroused controversy. In seventeenth-century Holland, images of God were banned from Protestant churches, as Peter Saenredam's stark architectural rendering of the interior of the Church of Assendelft attests (Fig. 34). As one contemporary Protestant theologian put it, "The image of God is His Word"—that is, the Bible—and "statues in human form, being an earthen image of visible, earthborn man [are] far away from the truth." One of the reasons that Jesus, the son of God, is so often represented in Western art is that representing the son, a real person, is far easier than representing the father, a spiritual unknown.

In this context it is easy to see why, in the early nineteenth century, William Blake's *The Ancient of Days* (Fig. 35) was considered by some to be an outrageous violation of propriety. Not only had Blake chosen to name his God "Urizen," creating his own personal mythology in the place of Christianity, but his God was *nude*. This image was a little *too* human. Moreover, Blake attributes to God a quandary that is really his own. God is depicted here as the powerful but aged father of us all, a father, in Blake's view of things, less merciful than cruel. The scene is the second day of Creation, and God holds a pair of compasses as he measures out and delineates the firmament, imposing order upon chaos. For Blake, the creation of the world was not a particularly happy moment. Creation represents a double bind: On the one hand, to create or make something—for example, a world, or an image—is limiting, because it sets boundaries upon the imagination. On the other hand, the imagination is defined by its ability to create. Blake's God is distinctly ambiguous.

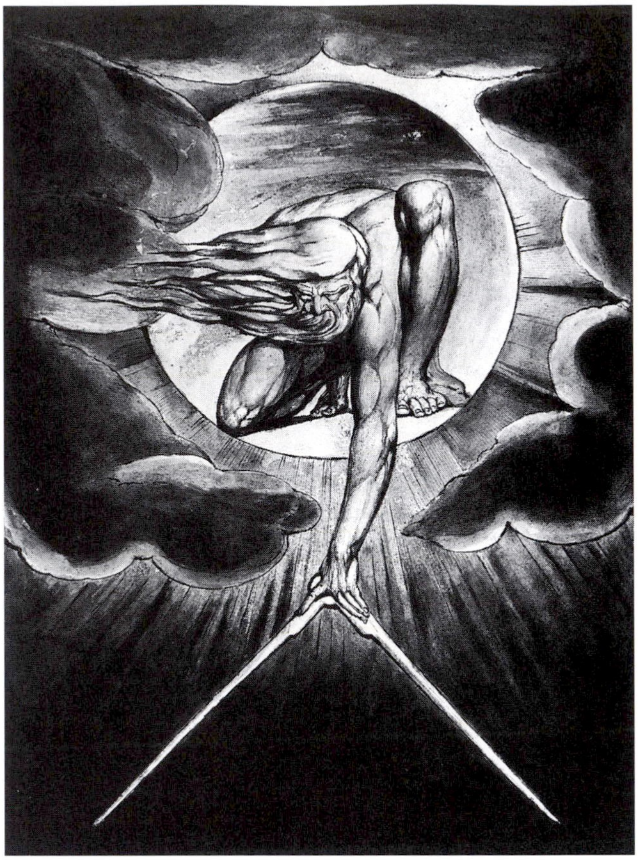

Fig. 35 William Blake, *The Ancient of Days*, from *Europe, a Prophecy*, frontispiece, 1794–1827.
Watercolor, black ink, and gold paint on etched matrix, 9 × 6¾ in. Fitzwilliam Museum, University of Cambridge, England.

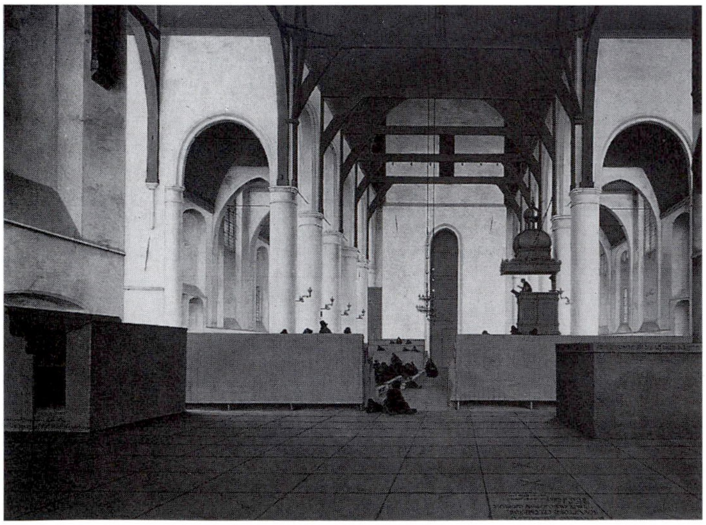

Fig. 34 Peter Saenredam, *Interior of the Church of Assendelft*, 1649.
Oil on panel, 19⅝ × 28⅞ in. Rijksmuseum, Amsterdam.

And Blake's perplexing God is very different from Jan van Eyck's (Fig. 36). Van Eyck's God, painted 400 years earlier than Blake's, is much frailer, younger, apparently more merciful and kind, and certainly more richly adorned. Indeed, judging from the richness of his vestments, van Eyck's God values worldly things more than Blake's. Where Blake despised the material world—the world in which things get made—van Eyck admired and

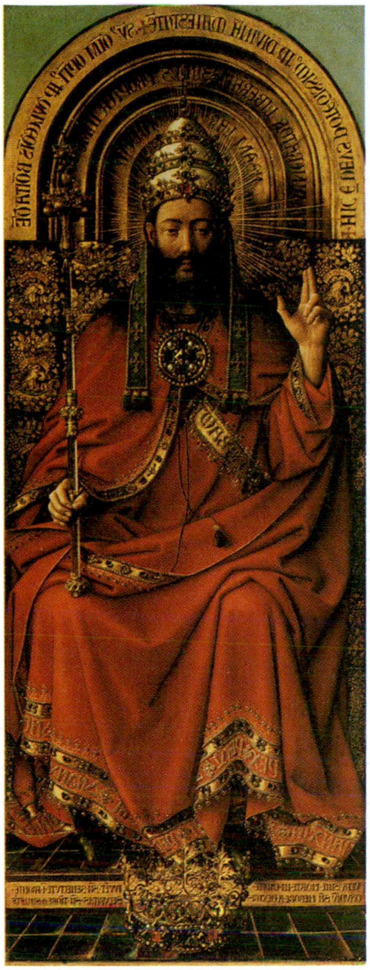

Fig. 36 Jan van Eyck, *God,* panel from the Ghent Altarpiece, c. 1432.
St. Bavo's, Ghent. Scala/Art Resource.

trusted it. He celebrates a materialism that is the proper right of benevolent kings. Behind God's head, across the top of the throne, are Latin words that, translated into English, read: "This is God, all powerful in his divine majesty; of all the best, by the gentleness of his goodness; the most liberal giver, because of his infinite generosity." God's mercy and love are indicated by the pelicans embroidered on the tapestry behind him, which in Christian tradition symbolize self-sacrificing love, since pelicans were believed to wound themselves in order to feed their young with their own blood if other food was unavailable.

In the nineteenth century, the van Eyck portrait of God was one model for Ingres's portrait of Napoleon (Fig. 37), the French general and emperor. Significantly, the pelicans have disappeared, and an eagle, symbol of imperial power, has taken their place on the carpet at Napoleon's feet. The grandness of Napoleon's pose—his wide shoulders, his raised right hand—suggests that he is not only a good deal closer to God than he is to us mortals but grander even than the Christian God. This idea was possible only in France and only for a short time after the Revolution in which the government had banned the Church altogether. While the opulence of Ingres's figure refers back to van Eyck's work, the pose here is in fact based on an engraved Roman gem representing Jupiter, the chief Roman god and god of the Roman state. Ingres consciously substitutes the Roman imperial ideal for the Christian one.

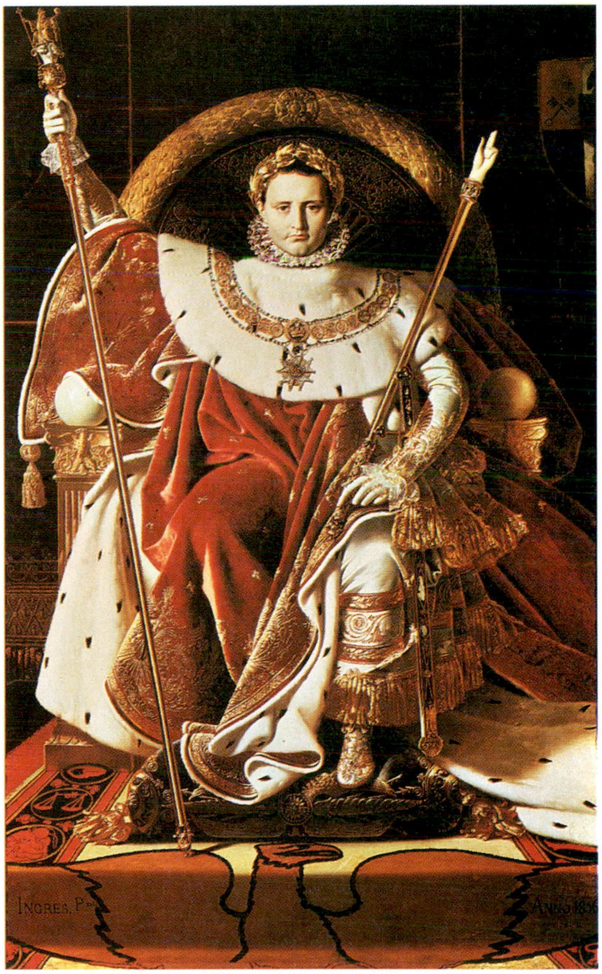

Fig. 37 Jean-Auguste-Dominique Ingres, *Napoleon on His Imperial Throne,* 1806.
Oil on canvas, $104 \times 65\frac{1}{2}$ in.
Musée de l'Armée, Paris. Giraudon/Art Resource.

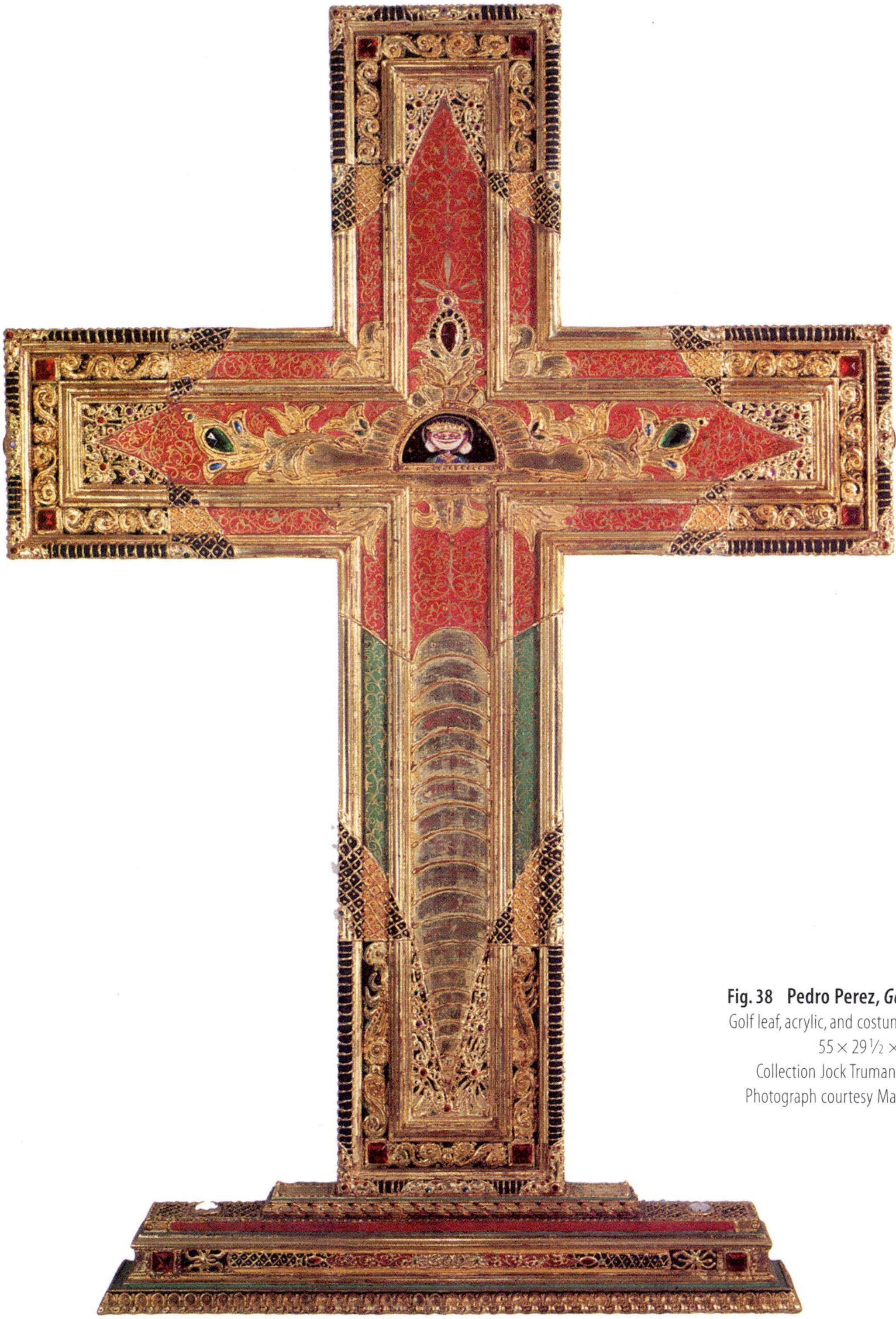

Fig. 38 Pedro Perez, *God* (detail), 1981.
Golf leaf, acrylic, and costume jewelry on wood, 55 × 29½ × 2 in.
Collection Jock Truman and Eric Green.
Photograph courtesy Marilyn Pearl Gallery.

For Pedro Perez, an artist born in Cuba in 1952 who emigrated to the United States at the age of 14, God is caught up in the collision of two cultures (Fig. 38). Here the rich imagery of traditional Spanish Catholicism, embodied in the actual gold leaf that Perez has used to decorate the cross, is countered not only by his use of gaudy costume jewelry but also by the deeply satiric depiction of God at the work's center. Perez's God is not a conventional, dignified, white-bearded patriarch but a mellow, aging hippie, a gurulike and undeniably "cool" Santa Claus.

Representing the Mind

If most people were told that they had to hang in their own home one of the two paintings on this page, either Helen Frankenthaler's *For E. M.* (Fig. 39) or Edouard Manet's *Still Life with Carp* (Fig. 40), most would choose the Manet. The Manet would seem more "real" to them than the Frankenthaler, the subject matter of which is not at all obvious. That is, just as an actual table is more objectively "real" than a painting of one, so the Manet is a more **objective** rendering of reality than the Frankenthaler. Frankenthaler's painting seems, by comparison, wholly **subjective,** manifesting her personal interest in purely formal matters of painting. In fact, her painting is a rendering of the Manet in abstract terms, hence its title, *For E(douard) M(anet)*. Although most people are generous enough to grant Frankenthaler her intentions, they do not readily share in her sensibility. They begin to appreciate what she is up to only when her intentions are made plain.

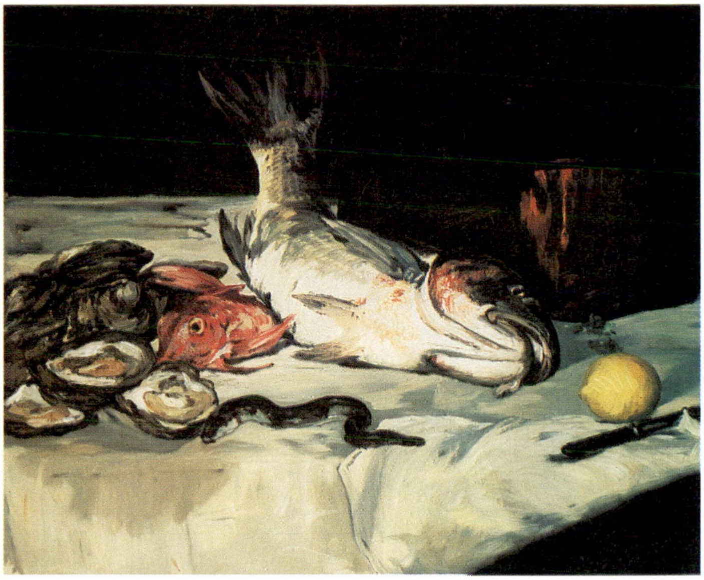

Fig. 40 Edouard Manet, *Still Life with Carp,* 1864.
Oil on canvas, 28 7/8 × 36 1/4 in. Mr. and Mrs. Lewis Larned Coburn Memorial Collection. © The Art Institute of Chicago, all rights reserved.

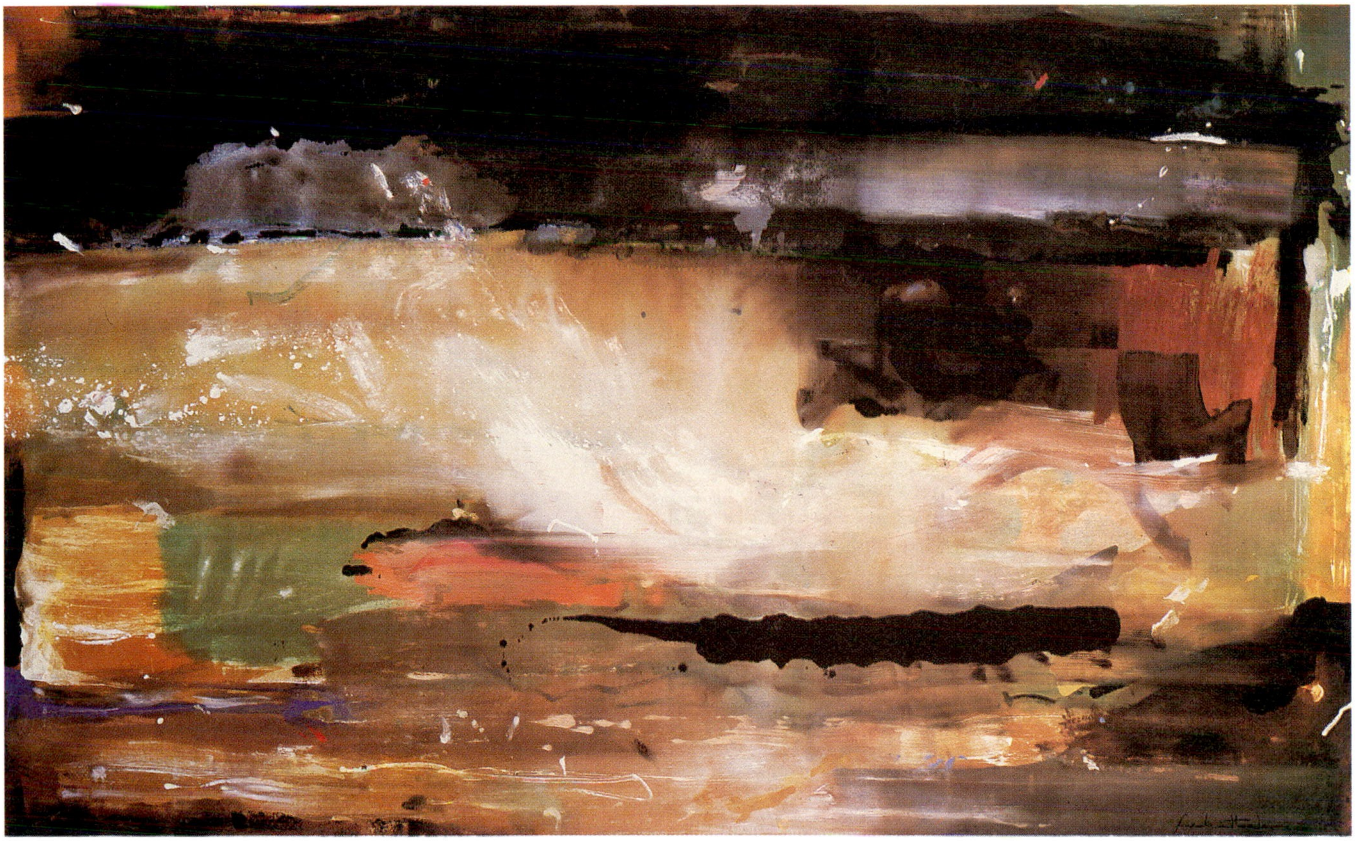

Fig. 39 Helen Frankenthaler, *For E. M.,* 1981.
Acrylic on canvas, 71 × 115 in. Collection of the artist. © Helen Frankenthaler 1993.

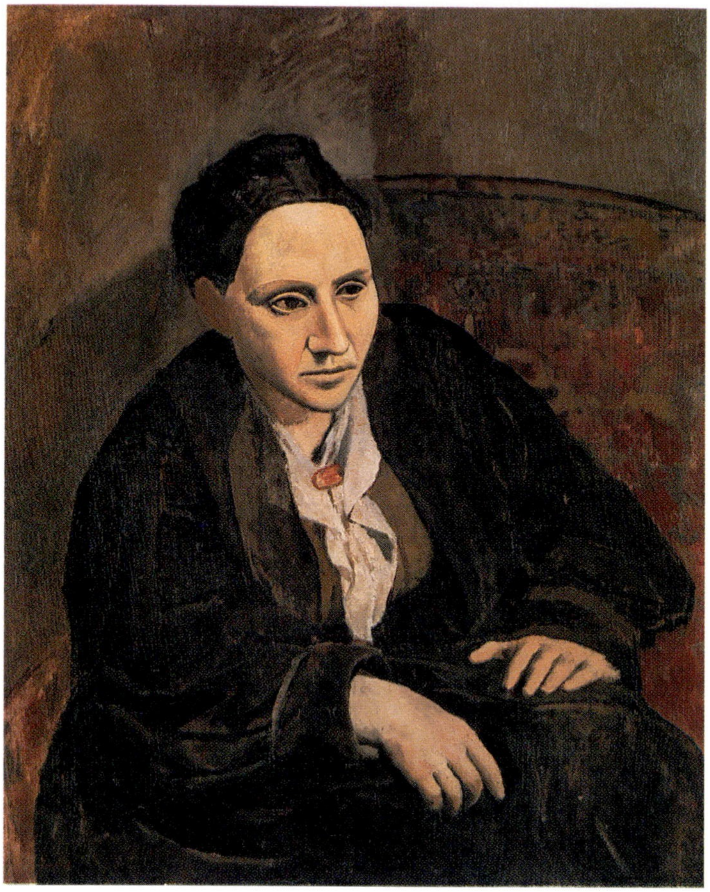

Fig. 41 Pablo Picasso, *Gertrude Stein,* 1906.
Oil on canvas, 39 1/4 × 32 in.
The Metropolitan Museum of Art, New York.
Bequest of Gertrude Stein, 1946. 47.106.

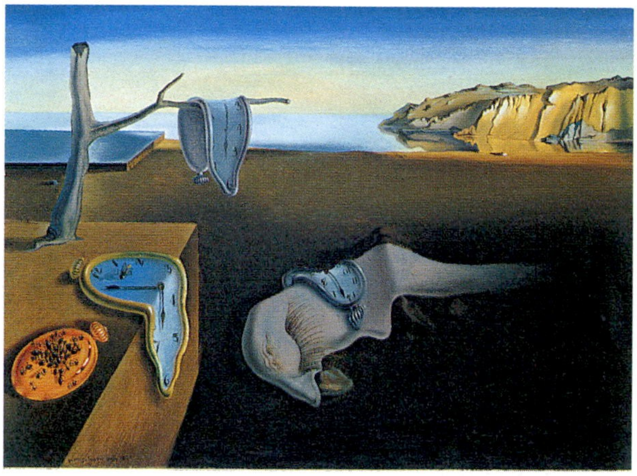

Fig. 42 Salvador Dali, *The Persistence of Memory,* 1931.
Oil on canvas, 9 1/2 × 13 in.
Collection, The Museum of Modern Art, New York. Given anonymously.

Abstract and nonobjective art have always been open to the charge of being so subjective that they are virtually inaccessible to the average person. This subjectivity is, nevertheless, fundamental to the history of modern art. Picasso's portrait of *Gertrude Stein* (Fig. 41) is a case in point. The painting was begun in the winter of 1905–1906. Stein would visit Picasso's studio nearly every day to pose for the portrait. But he had a terrible time with the face. Finally, after over 80 sittings, Picasso, in complete frustration, painted out Stein's head and departed for Spain, leaving a great blank in the middle of the canvas. In the late summer he returned, stood before the canvas, and painted the face from memory. When, some months later, Stein's friend Alice B. Toklas told Picasso how much she admired the painting, he thanked her. "Everyone says that she does not look like it," Picasso said, smiling, "but that does not make any difference—she will."

The story could be said to mark the moment when painters no longer felt compelled to represent the world as it is and instead became free to paint what they felt or imagined it to be. In other words, for Picasso, his own subjective knowledge of Stein was more "real" than what she objectively looked like. This belief in the reality of the interior world dominates the history of modern art. In his 1928 book *Surrealism and Painting,* André Breton, the leader of the French Surrealists, asserted that the mistake of painters "has been to believe that a model could be derived only from the exterior world. . . . [Painters must] either seek a *purely interior model* or cease to exist." **Surrealism** is a style of art in which the reality of the dream, or the subconscious mind, is seen as more "real" than the surface reality of everyday life. Its reality is a higher reality. The Surrealist Salvador Dali called paintings such as *The Persistence of Memory* (Fig. 42) "hand-painted dream photographs." The limbless figure lying on the ground like a giant slug is actually a self-portrait of the artist, who seems to have moved into a landscape removed from time and mind.

Similarly, because he believed that he was directly presenting the reality of his own feelings and emotions on canvas, the abstract expressionist painter Robert Motherwell

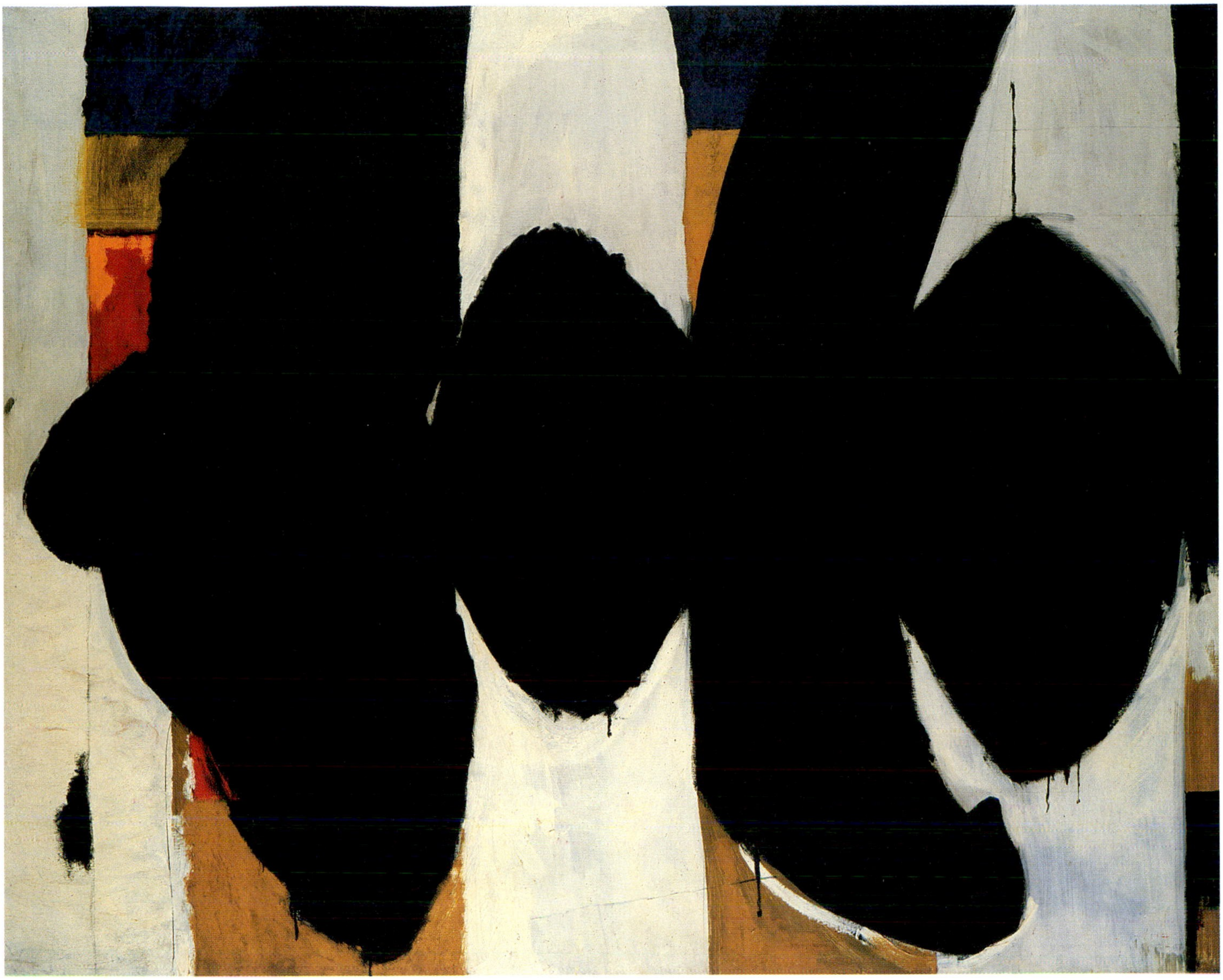

Fig. 43 Robert Motherwell, *Elegy to the Spanish Republic XXXIV,* 1953–1954.
Oil on canvas, 80 × 100 in. Albright-Knox Art Gallery, Buffalo, New York.
Gift of Seymour H. Knox, 1957.

refused to admit that his paintings were abstract. Speaking of works such as *Elegy to the Spanish Republic XXXIV* (Fig. 43), he would write in 1955: "I never think of my pictures as 'abstract'. . . . Nothing can be more concrete to a man than his own felt thought, his own thought feeling. I feel most real to myself in the studio, and resent any description of what transpires there as 'abstract'—which nowadays . . . signifies something remote from reality. From whose reality? And on what level?" The painting's title refers to the Fascist defeat of the democratic Spanish Republican forces by General Franco's forces just before World War II. It marks for Motherwell the terrible death of liberty itself, a reality he was unwilling to think of as being "abstract" in any sense of the word. He thought of the black forms and their lighter background as elemental "protagonists in the struggle between life and death." Nothing, for him, could be more real than that struggle.

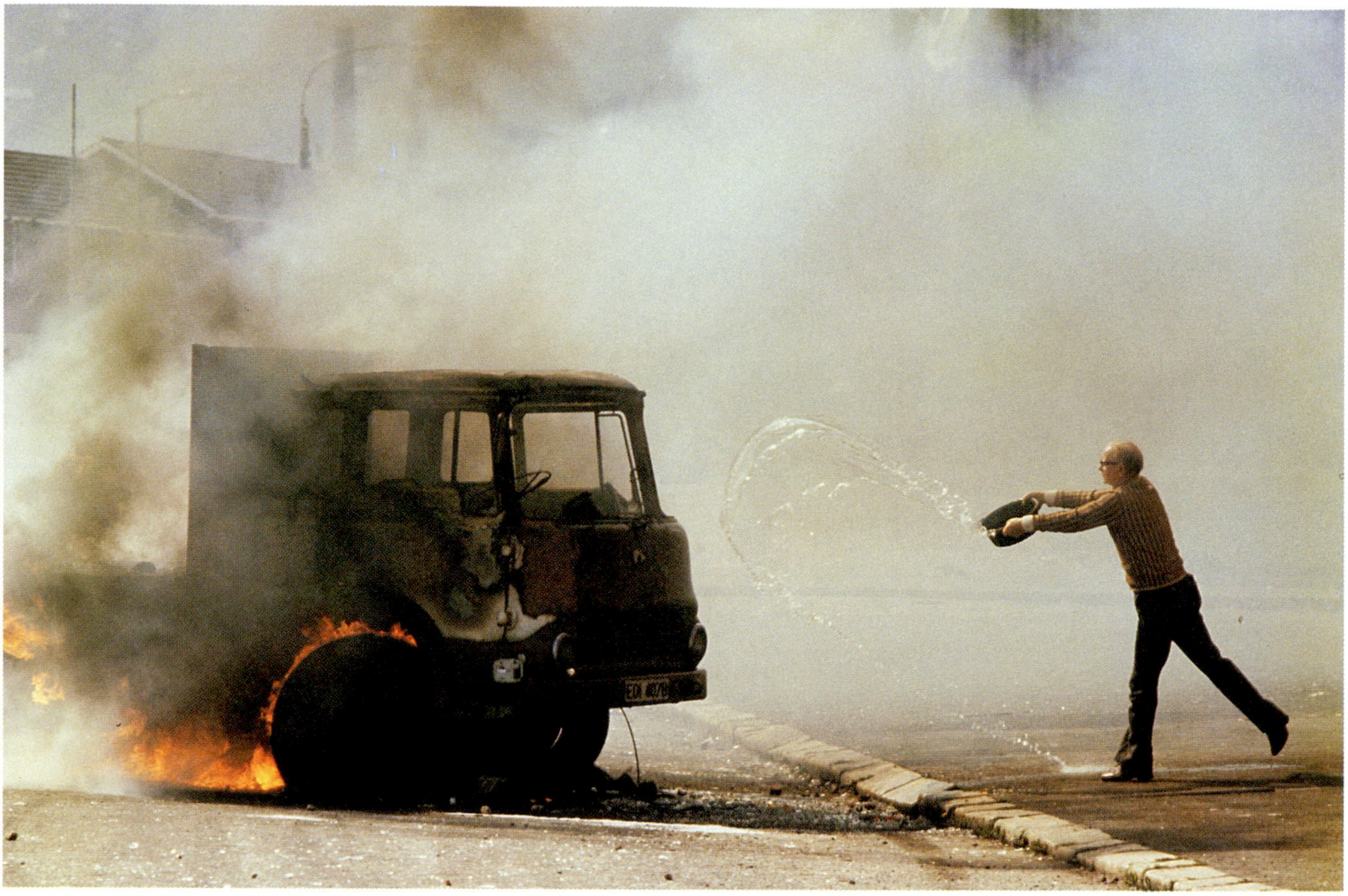

Fig. 44 James Nachtwey, *Belfast, Northern Ireland,* 1981.
Magnum Photos.

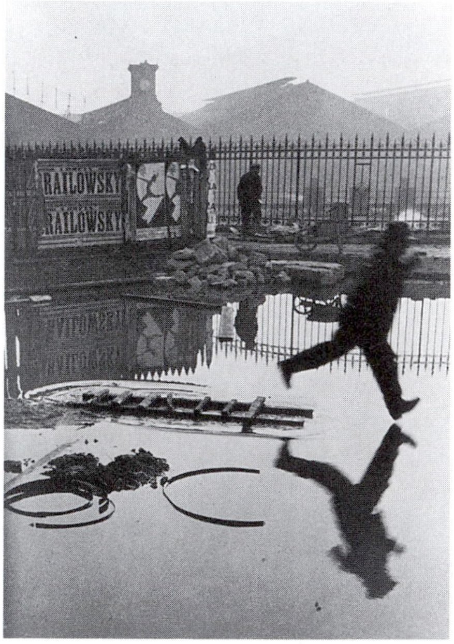

Fig. 45 Henri Cartier-Bresson, *Place de l'Europe, Paris,* 1932.
Magnum Photos.

Representing the Beautiful

For many people, the main purpose of art is to satisfy our **aesthetic** sense, our desire to see and experience the beautiful. But as both Robert Motherwell's representation of "the struggle between life and death" in his *Elegy to the Spanish Republic* and Picasso's *Les Demoiselles* demonstrate, art often represents other truths, other realities that seem to have little to do with a purely aesthetic response to the world.

James Nachtwey's photograph, *Belfast, Northern Ireland* (Fig. 44) offers a precise example of the difficulties inherent in considering questions of beauty. In many ways, the picture is reminiscent of Henri Cartier-Bresson's famous 1932 photograph of a man jumping a puddle in Paris (Fig. 45). Each involves an intricate choreography of leaps and arcs, a sense of the futility (and comedy) of human activity, and a dramatic sense of contrast between light and dark, stasis and motion, and in Nachtwey's photograph, fire and water. To

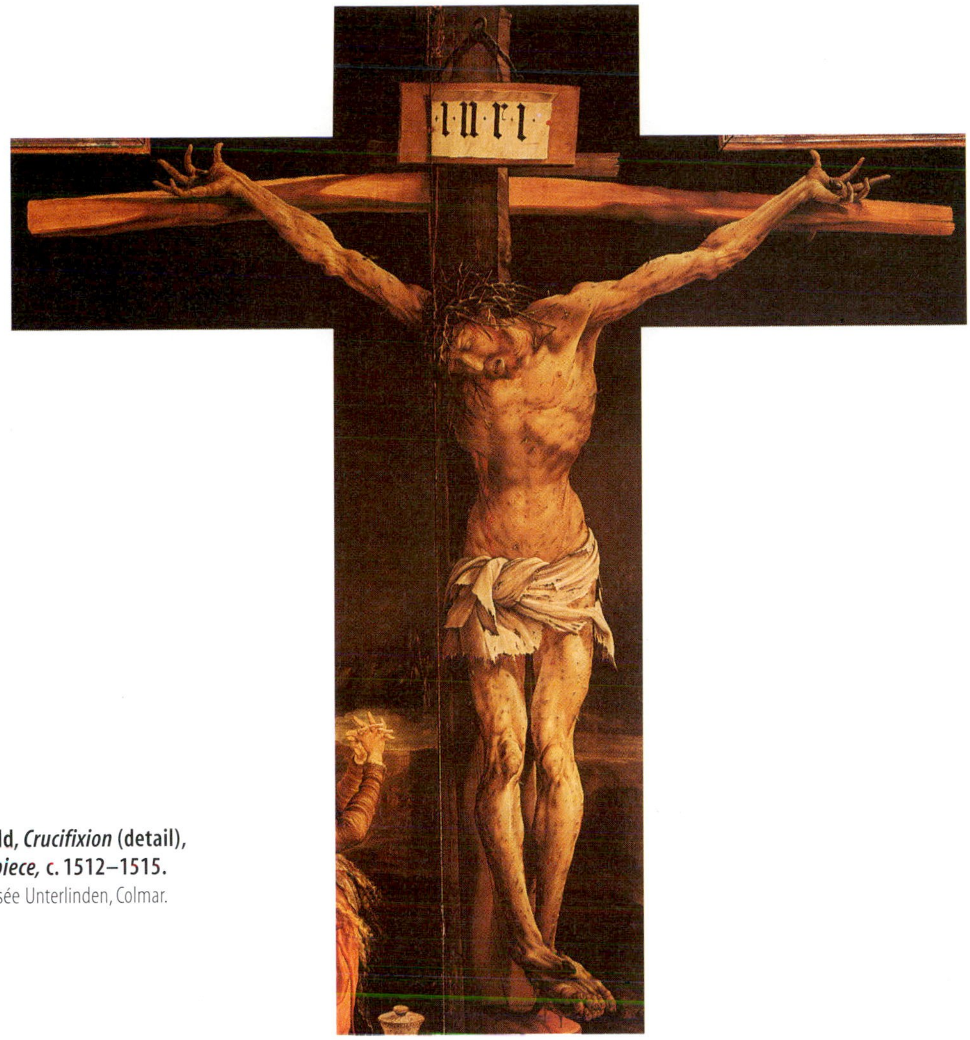

Fig. 46 Matthias Grünewald, *Crucifixion* (detail), from the *Isenheim Altarpiece,* c. 1512–1515.
Oil on panel, H. 117 ½ in. Musée Unterlinden, Colmar.

the eye of the art historian, this analogy itself lends a certain beauty to Nachtwey's piece. That is, we often judge a work's beauty by comparing it to other work that is generally acknowledged to be aesthetically pleasing. Yet, judged in the context of the civil war in Northern Ireland, Nachtwey's photograph becomes far less "beautiful." It is as if the innocence of Cartier-Bresson's photo has been stripped away, and the full brutality of modern life revealed in its stead.

Nachtwey's photograph causes us to ask some difficult questions. Can the ugly itself ever be art? Can the ugly be made, by the artist, to appear beautiful, and if so, does that cause us to ignore the reality of the situation? The central *Crucifixion* in Matthias Grünewald's *Isenheim Altarpiece* (Fig. 46) is one of the most tragic and horrifying depictions of Christ on the cross ever painted. Many people cannot bear to look at it. Rigor mortis has set in, Christ's body is torn with wounds and scars, his flesh is a greenish gray, his feet are mangled, and his hands are stiffly contorted in the agony of death. The painting portrays suffering, pure and simple. However, Grünewald painted this altarpiece for a hospital chapel, and it was assumed that patients would find solace in knowing that Christ had suffered at least as much as they. In this painting, the ugly and horrible are transformed into art, not least of all because, as Christians believe, resurrection and salvation await the Christ after his suffering. The line that runs down Christ's right side is, in fact, the edge of a double door that opens to reveal the Annunciation and the Resurrection behind. In the latter, Christ's body has been transformed into a pure, unblemished white, his hair and beard are gold, and his wounds are rubies.

Pablo Picasso's *Les Demoiselles d'Avignon*

Not long after finishing his portrait of Gertrude Stein (Fig. 41), Picasso began working on a large canvas, nearly eight feet square, that would come to be considered one of the first major paintings of the modern era, *Les Demoiselles d'Avignon* (Fig. 49). The title, chosen not by Picasso but by a close friend, literally means "the young ladies of Avignon," but its somewhat tongue-in-cheek reference is specifically to the prostitutes of Avignon Street, the red-light district of Barcelona, Spain, Picasso's hometown. We know a great deal about Picasso's process as he worked on the canvas from late 1906 into the early summer months of 1907, not only because many of his working sketches survive but also because the canvas itself has been submitted to extensive examination, including X-ray analysis. This reveals early versions of certain passages, particularly the figure at the left and the two figures on the right, which lie under the final layers of paint.

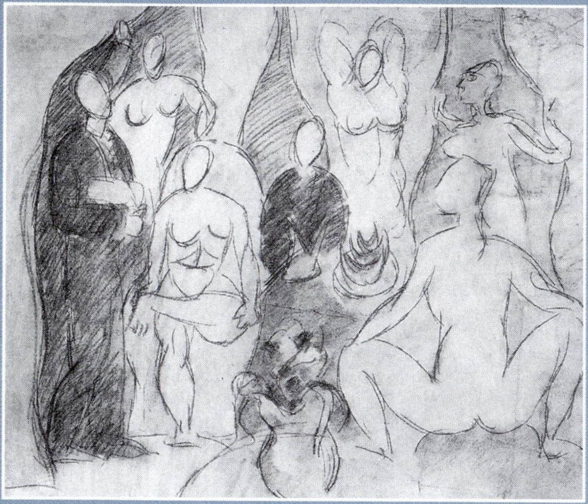

Fig. 47 Pablo Picasso, *Medical Student, Sailor, and Five Nudes in a Bordello (Study for Les Demoiselles d'Avignon)*, 1907.
Charcoal and pastel. 18 1/2 × 25 in.
Oeffentliche Kunstsammlung Basel Hausaufnahme.

An early sketch (Fig. 47) reveals that it was originally conceived to include seven figures—five prostitutes, a sailor seated in their midst, and, entering from the left, a medical student carrying a book. Picasso probably had in mind some anecdotal or narrative idea contrasting the dangers and joys of both work and pleasure, but he soon abandoned the male figures. By doing so, he involved the viewer much more fully in the scene. No longer does the curtain open up at the left to allow the medical student to enter. Now the curtain is opened by one of the prostitutes as if she is admitting us, the audience, into the bordello. We are implicated in the scene.

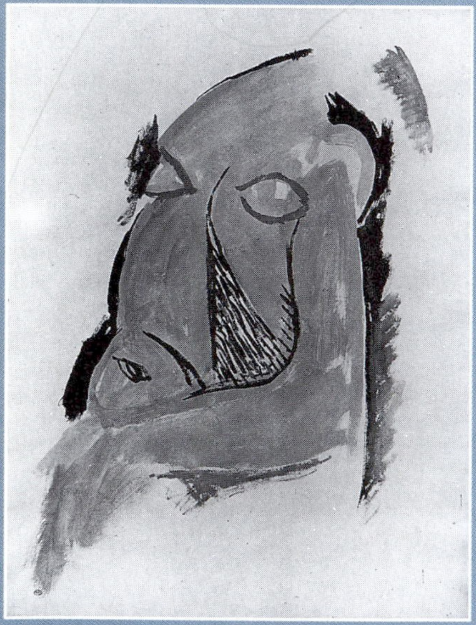

Fig. 48 Pablo Picasso, *Study for the Crouching Demoiselle*, 1907.
Gouache on paper, 24 3/4 × 18 7/8 in.
Musée Picasso, Paris.
Reunion des Musees Nationaux.

And an extraordinary scene it is. Picasso seems to have willingly abdicated any traditional aesthetic sense of beauty. There is nothing enticing or alluring here. Of all the nudes, the two central ones are the most traditional, and their facial features, particularly their brows and oval eyes, are closely related to Gertrude Stein's in his portrait of her. But their bodies are composed of a series of long lozenge shapes, hard angles, and only a few traditional curves. It is unclear whether the second nude from the left is standing or sitting, or possibly even lying down. (In the early drawing, she is clearly seated.) Picasso seems to have made her position in space intentionally ambiguous.

We know, through X-rays, that all five nudes originally looked like the central two. We also know that sometime after he began painting *Les Demoiselles,* Picasso visited the Trocadero, now the Museum of Man, in Paris and saw in its collection of African sculpture, particularly African masks, an approach to the representation of the human face that was extraordinarily powerful. As in his portrait of Gertrude Stein, the masks freed him from representing exactly what his subjects looked like and allowed him to represent his *idea* of them instead.

That idea is clearly ambivalent. Picasso probably saw in these masks something of the same "fear and darkness" that Kenneth Clark would find in them 60 years later in his book *Civilisation* (see the discussion of the African masks on pages 26-27). But it is also clear that he found something liberating in them. They freed him from a slavish concern for accurate representation, and they allowed him to create a much more emotionally charged scene than he would have otherwise been able to accomplish. Rather than offering us a single point of view, he offers us many, both literally and figuratively. The painting is about the ambiguity of experience.

Nowhere is this more clear than in the squatting figure in the lower right hand corner of the painting. She seems twisted around on herself in the final version, her back to us, but her head impossibly turned to face us, her chin resting on her grotesque, clawlike hand. We see her, in other words, from both front and back. (Notice, incidentally, that even the nudes in the sketch possess something of this "double" point of view: their noses are in profile though they face the viewer.) But this crouching figure is even more complex. An early drawing of her (Fig. 48) reveals that her face was originally conceived as a headless torso. What would become her hand is originally her arm. What would become her eyes were her breasts. And her mouth would begin as her belly button. Here we are witness to the extraordinary freedom of invention that defines all of Picasso's art.

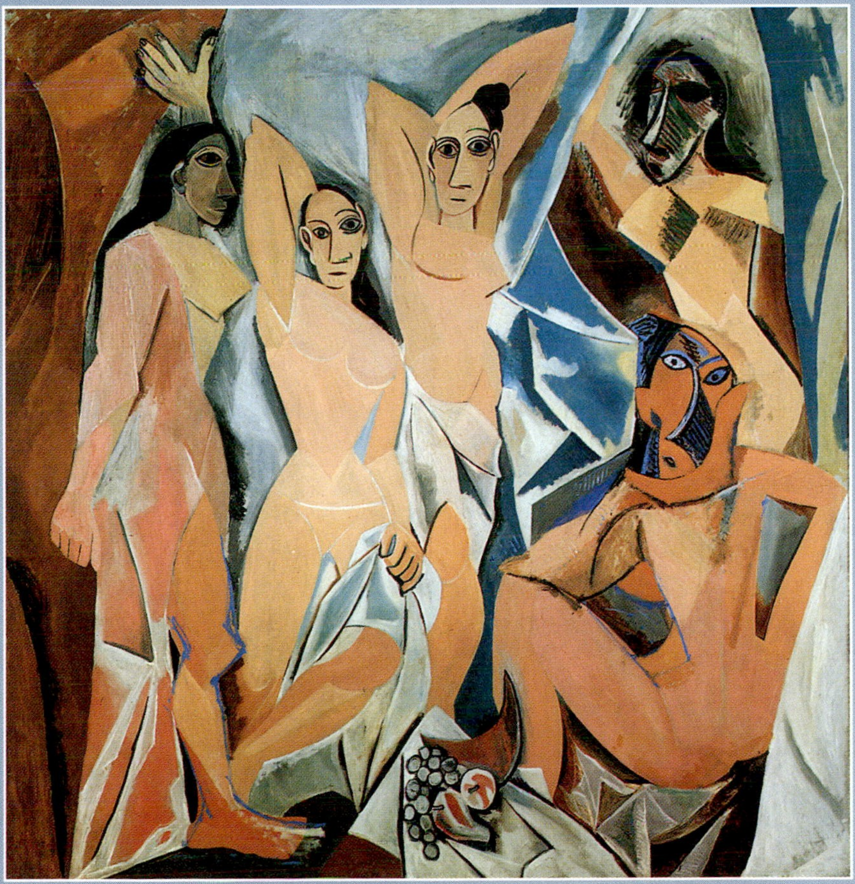

Fig. 49 Pablo Picasso, *Les Demoiselles d'Avignon,* 1907. Oil on canvas, 8 ft. × 7 ft. 8 in. Collection, The Museum of Modern Art, New York. Acquired through the Lillie P. Bliss Bequest.

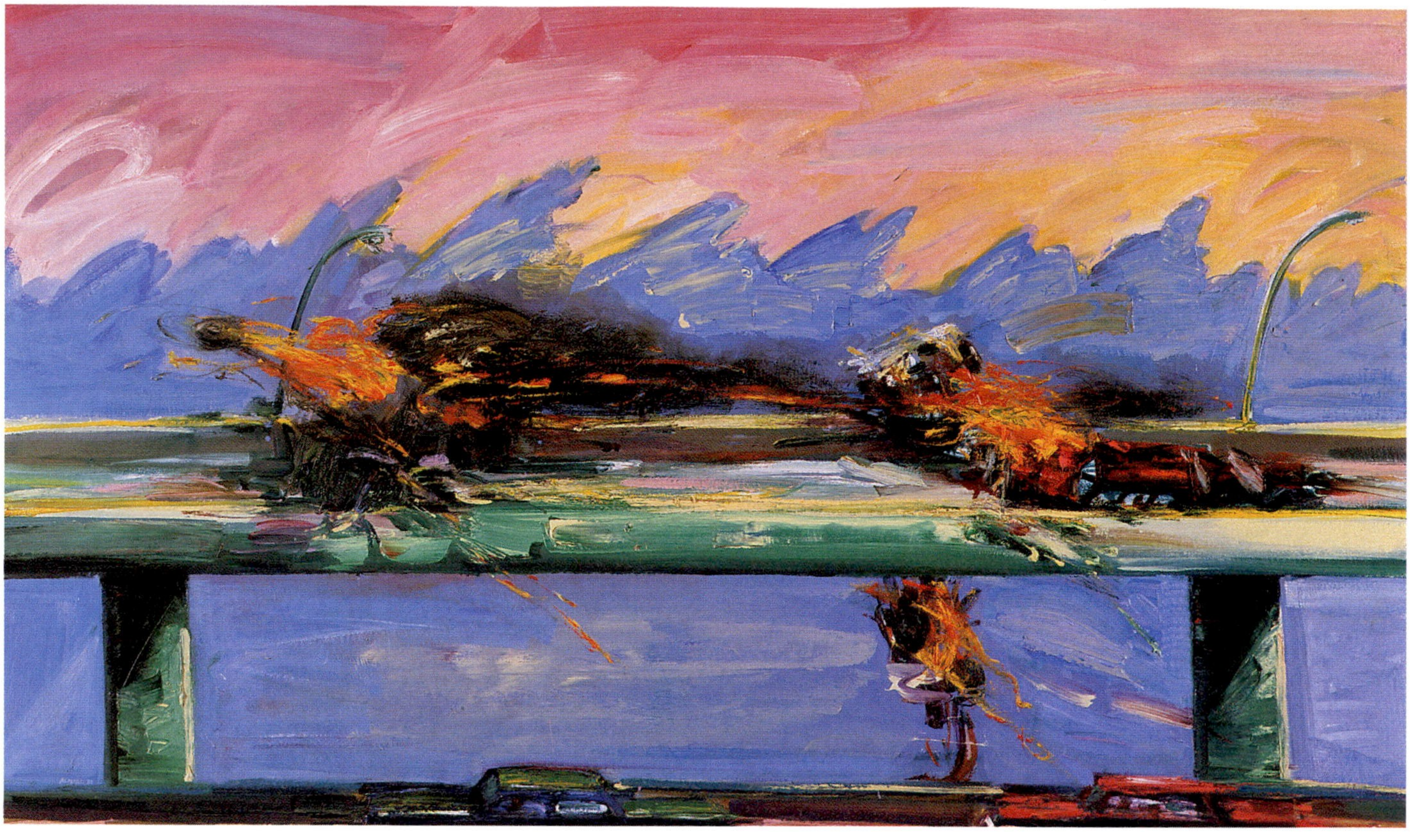

Fig. 50 Carlos Almaraz, *Crash in Pthalo Green,* 1984.
Oil on canvas, 42 × 72 in. Los Angeles County Museum of Art.
Gift of 1992 Collectors Committee.

Grünewald's *Crucifixion* shows how beauty can arise out of horror. Similarly, *Crash in Pthalo Green* by Carlos Almaraz (Fig. 50), is the representation of a two-tier freeway with a violent, fiery automobile accident occurring on the top level. The horror of the scene is countered by the richness of the painting's color, its sensual and expressive brushwork, and, above all, by the work's very abstraction. It is as if Almaraz wants us to consider everything *but* the work's subject matter. The ancient Greek philosopher Socrates, in fact, argued that painters should be exiled from his ideal Republic on just these grounds. To him, the painter's ability to attend to and delight in the sensory pleasures of seeing, to create an emotionally charged (and hence, he believed, illogical and irrational) sense of the beautiful, was destructive to a society that should strive, instead, to attain truth, wisdom, and order. But for an artist like Almaraz, it is precisely the disjunction between the horror of what he depicts and the beauty of how he depicts it that makes a work interesting. By making our relation to the painting so problematic, he creates a sense of tension that makes the work *dynamic*. Our feelings about it are not easily resolved. The painting demands our active response.

From a certain point of view, the experience of such dynamic tension is itself pleasing, and it is the ability of works of art to create and sustain such moments that many people value most about them. That is, many people find such moments **aesthetically** pleasing. The work of art may not itself be beautiful, but it triggers a higher level of thought and awareness in the viewer, and the viewer experiences this intellectual and imaginative stimulus—this higher order of thought—as a form of beauty in its own right.

The ***vanitas*** tradition of still life painting is specifically designed to induce in the spectator a higher order of thought. *Vanitas* is the Latin term for "vanity," and vanitas paintings, especially popular in Northern Europe in the seventeenth century, remind us of the vanity, or frivolous quality, of human existence. One ordinarily associates the contemplation of the normal subjects of still life paintings—flowers, food, books, and so on, set on a tabletop—with the enjoyment of the pleasurable things in life. The key element in a *vanitas* painting, however, is the presence of a human skull among these objects. The skull reminds the viewer that the material world—the world of still life—is fleeting, and that death is the end of all things. In Philippe de Champaigne's *Vanitas* (Fig. 51), the skull reminds us that the other elements in the painting are themselves short-lived. The hourglass embodies the quick passage of time. The cut flower will quickly fade, its petals dropping to the tabletop, its beauty temporary and conditional. Even the light in the room will soon disappear as darkness falls. Nevertheless, the *vanitas* is not about death, it is about the right way to live. It reminds the viewer that the material world is not as longlasting as the spiritual, and that spiritual well-being is of greater importance than material wealth.

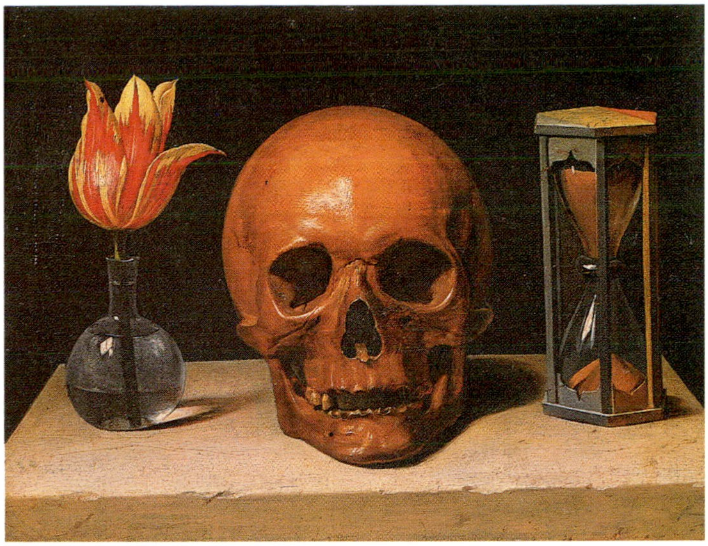

Fig. 51 Philippe de Champaigne (1602–1674), *Still Life* or *Vanitas* (tulip, skull, and hour glass).
Oil on panel, 11 1/4 × 14 3/4 in. Musée des Tesse, Le Mans, France.
Photo Giraudon/Art Resource, New York.

Robert Mapplethorpe's *Self-Portrait* of 1988 (Fig. 52) purposefully invokes these same themes, but with a certain irony. Mapplethorpe means to draw an analogy between his own face and the skull that tops the cane he holds. We are invited to see death in his face. When this self-portrait was taken, Mapplethorpe was HIV-positive. Soon after, in the spring of 1989, he died of AIDS. Mapplethorpe frankly acknowledges the vanity of his lifestyle in the *Self-Portrait*. He accepts death as the price of his pleasure, turning the *vanitas* tradition on its head. But he also means the *Self-Portrait* to be read as a mirror—as all photography is in some sense a mirror—a mirror that he holds up to us. He means us to see ourselves in its light.

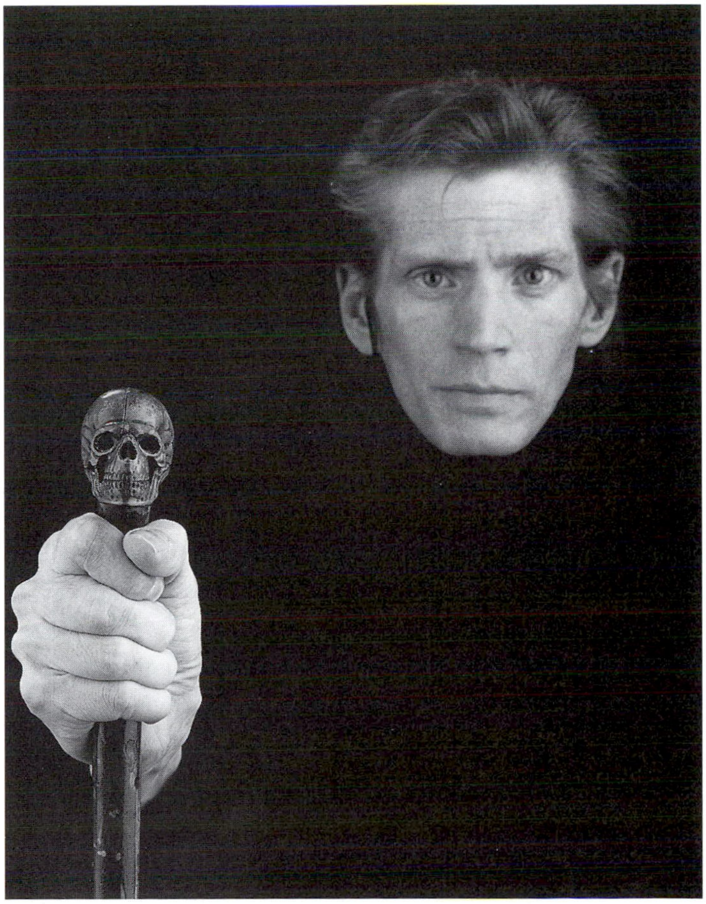

Fig. 52 Robert Mapplethorpe, *Self-Portrait*, 1988.
© 1988 The Estate of Robert Mapplethorpe.

At the time of his death and for long afterward, Mapplethorpe was probably the world's most notorious photographer, known to the general public chiefly for his photographs of sadomasochistic and homoerotic acts. Known as the "X Portfolio," these photographs were the focus of a continuing Congressional debate, headed by Senator Jesse Helms of North Carolina, over funding of the National Endowment for the Arts, which partially funded their scheduled exhibition at the Corcoran Gallery in Washington, D.C. the summer after

Mapplethorpe's death. Many of these same photographs were seized, a year after his death, when they were exhibited at the Cincinnati Arts Center, as police arrested the Center's director, Dennis Barrie, for pandering and the use of a minor in pornography. In the midst of these controversies, the remainder of Mapplethorpe's work was ignored. The "X Portfolio" was meant to be seen, for instance, in conjunction with a "Y Portfolio," a series of still lifes of flowers. Mapplethorpe's many stunningly beautiful flower photographs, such as *Parrot Tulip* (Fig. 53), take on a special poignancy in relation to his other work. They are not merely still lifes. Drooping over the edge of its vase, the tulip not only acknowledges the *vanitas* tradition, the photograph capturing the flower's imminent demise as surely as Mapplethorpe captures his own in his *Self-Portrait*. It also becomes subtly eroticized as well, the flower announcing itself as the sexual organ—stamen and pistil—that it is.

In this chapter we have begun to examine the complex ways in which images such as Mapplethorpe's represent our world. Because our world is composed of more than just physical things, because there are orders of mind, intellect, and sensibility that surpass the world of things, images do more than just represent objects. They capture, in some sense, what objects mean to the artist and to us, its audience, and they often require us to find words to express that meaning. If the image is nonobjective, it may capture our emotional feelings, or our sense of order, or our understanding of higher realities. The meaning of a work of art is always more than what we actually see. It remains to be seen, however, how we come to value works of art, how we judge if they are good or bad. And why does it matter? How does art affect our world?

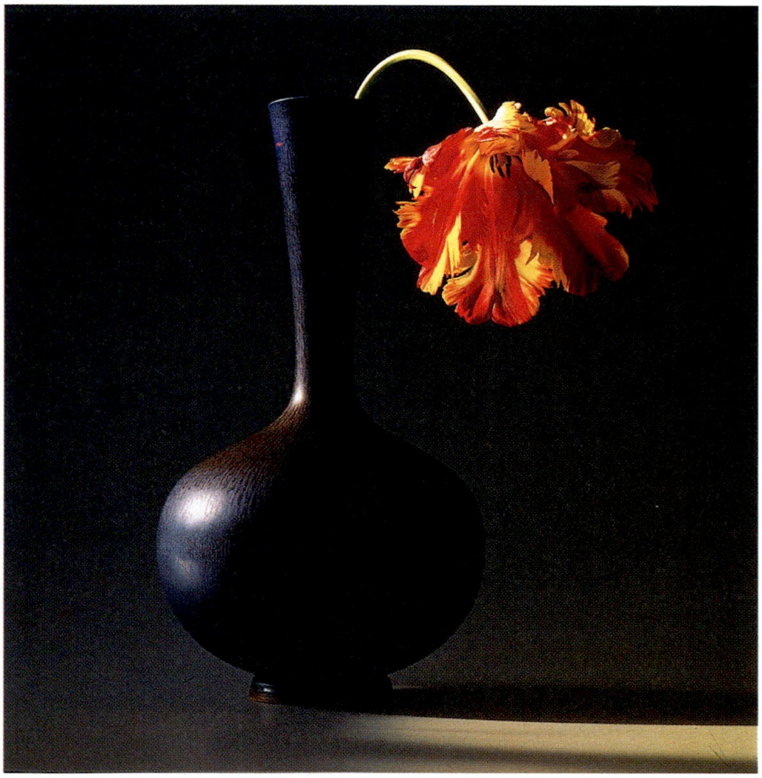

Fig. 53 Robert Mapplethorpe, *Parrot Tulip*, 1985.

CHAPTER 3

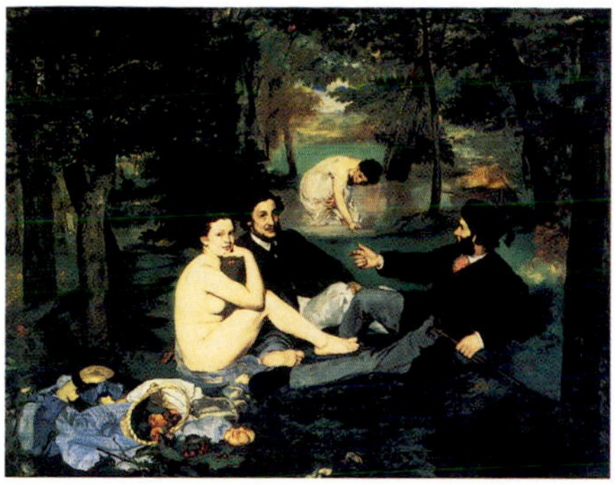

Seeing the Value in Art

At the end of Chapter 2, we used Robert Mapplethorpe's *Parrot Tulip* to suggest the many complex meanings that works of art can have. Mapplethorpe's photography raises key questions about the **value** of art—not its monetary worth, but its intrinsic value to the individual and to society as a whole. When the Corcoran Gallery decided not to exhibit Mapplethorpe's work in the summer of 1989, fearing that to do so would be to jeopardize Congress's continued funding of the National Endowment for the Arts, the show quickly moved to a smaller Washington gallery, Project for the Arts, where nearly 50,000 people visited it in 25 days. After leaving Washington, the exhibition ran without incident in both Hartford, Connecticut, and Berkeley, California. And as mentioned in Chapter 2, the show drew record crowds in Cincinnati, at least in part because people wanted to decide for themselves whether the work was "criminally obscene" as the county sheriff alleged. The Cincinnati Arts Center, the Robert Mapplethorpe Foundation, and the Mapplethorpe estate together countered the sheriff's action by filing suit to determine if the photographs were obscene under Ohio state law. "We want a decision on whether the work as a whole has serious artistic value," they stated.

And it is, of course, the question of *artistic* value that confronts us. The monetary value of the works was, at least, confirmed. *The New York Times* reported that the national publicity surrounding the exhibition had notably increased the prices of Mapplethorpe's work. And its popularity with the public seemed established—the Mapplethorpe Foundation was realizing significant new dollars from the sale of books, T-shirts, and posters. But do monetary value and popularity determine the artistic value of the works?

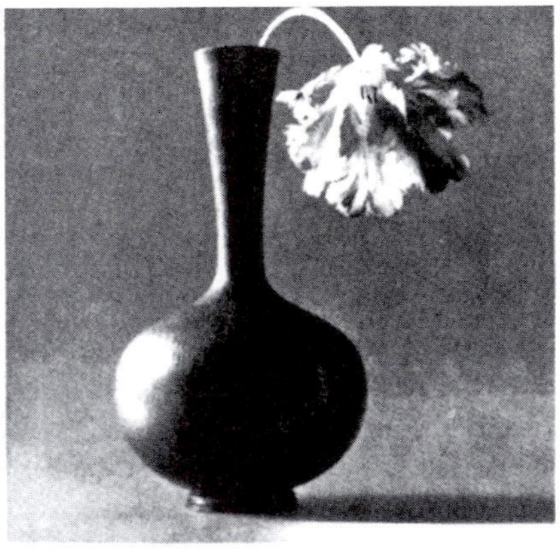

Are you going to let politics kill Art?

Art should be supported by government and protected from politics.

Until now that has been the enlightened principle that has guided all legislation affecting the Arts in America.

Art must live free to survive.

That is why it is crucial that every friend of the Arts send a message to Washington right now.

There is still time for cool heads and common sense to prevail over the Helms amendment to the appropriations bill for the National Endowment for the Arts.

But the Arts desperately need your help now. Today.

It is with a sense of the greatest urgency that we ask you to write to the people in Congress who will be meeting in the next few days in a crucial conference between the Appropriations Subcommittees of both Houses to resolve differences in the National Endowment for the Arts legislation.

The names and addresses of the Congressional people to contact are listed below.

You are probably aware of the controversy that inspired the devastating amendment by Senator Jesse Helms. In a July 28 editorial, entitled "The Helms Process," the New York Times wisely urged Congress to protect the legislation that insulates art from politics. It observed:

"The Helms process would drain art of creativity, controversy – of life... and would plunge one esthetic question after another into the boiling bath of politics. That's unlikely to be good for politics; it would surely be fatal to Art."

Don't let moral panic and political pressure kill the Arts.

Don't assume that "someone else" will fight this battle for you.

Write, call, fax, or telegram the Congressional leaders listed below *now* and urge them to delete the Helms provisions from the conference report on H.R. 2788.

Trustees of the Whitney Museum of American Art

Fig. 54 Whitney Museum of American Art Advertisement,
The New York Times, Sept. 7, 1989. "Are You Going to Let Politics Kill Art?"
Courtesy of the Trustees of the Whitney Museum of American Art.

Senator Jesse Helms certainly didn't think that Mapplethorpe's works possessed artistic value. He introduced an amendment to an Interior Department appropriations bill prohibiting the use of National Endowment funds for the "dissemination, promotion, or production of obscene or indecent materials or materials denigrating a particular religion." The amendment passed by voice vote in a nearly empty Senate chamber. Within five weeks, the Whitney Museum of American Art responded by running a highly critical ad in both *The New York Times* and *The Washington Post* (Fig. 54).

The judge in the Cincinnati trial of Dennis Barrie and the Cincinnati Art Center sided with Helms. Judge David J. Albanese ruled that the jury should not consider whether Mapplethorpe's "work as a whole has serious artistic value," as the defendents had hoped. Rather, he said, "the Court finds that each photograph has a separate identity; each photograph has a visual and unique image permanently recorded." Nevertheless, the jury acquitted Dennis Barrie and the Cincinnati Art Center.

Even though the jury was barred from drawing comparisons between Mapplethorpe's sadomasochistic and homoerotic photographs and his flowers, as we did in Chapter 2, they found that each of the images possessed serious artistic value. A good deal of testimony focused on the formal qualities of Mapplethorpe's work, for example, the way that in his portrait of *Ajitto* (Fig. 55) the human body assumes the geometrical precision of a pentagon. (We will study art's formal qualities in detail in Part II.) But one of the most compelling witnesses was Robert Sobieszek, senior curator of the International Museum of Photography in Rochester, New York. Mapplethorpe, said Sobieszek, "wanted to document what was beautiful and what was torturous—in his personal experience. If something is truly obscene or pornographic, then it's not art." But Mapplethorpe's coping with his problems in his work, he said, is "not unlike van Gogh painting himself with his ear cut off."

Thus the jury found that considered in the context of art as a whole, in the context of art's concerns with form, and in the context of the history of art and its tradition of confronting those parts of our lives that give us pain as well as those that give us pleasure, Mapplethorpe's work seemed to them to possess "serious artistic value." What the Mapplethorpe story makes clear is that "value," like beauty, as discussed in the last chapter, is a relative term. What some people value, others do not and cannot.

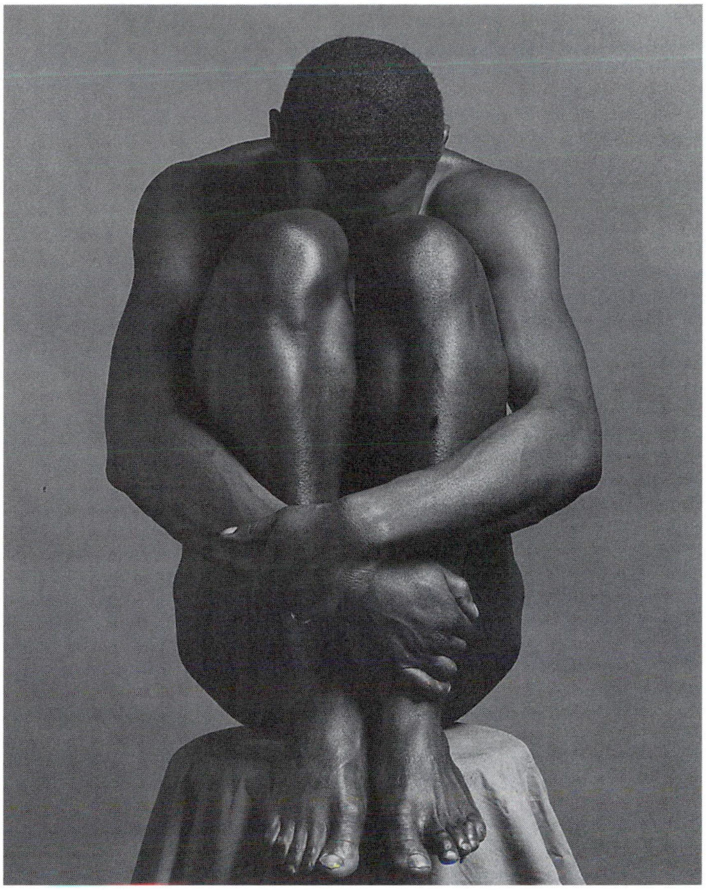

Fig. 55 Robert Mapplethorpe, *Ajitto,* 1981.

Mapplethorpe's work has been discussed at some length to show the many complex factors that go into a judgment of art's value. In the rest of this chapter, we will explore the public nature of art in order to reach some conclusions about how our culture comes to value it. We have already discussed the question of aesthetic value in Chapter 2. Now we will consider the social value of art. But the two must be considered together if we are to understand the value of art in its fullest sense.

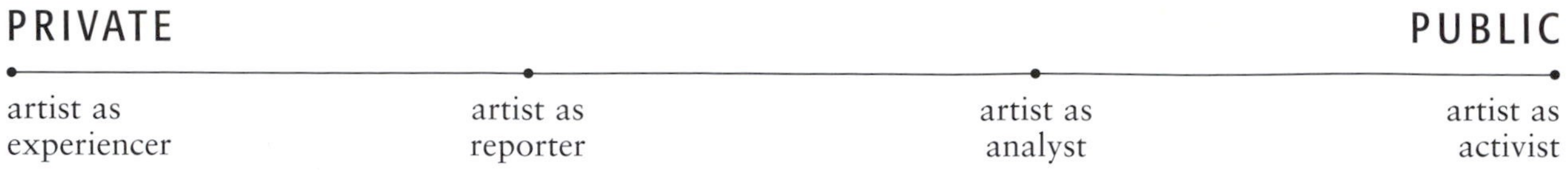

Fig. 56 Suzanne Lacy, Spectrum of Artists' Roles, from *Mapping the Terrain: New Genre Public Art,* 1995.

ART AND ITS RECEPTION

In a recent book on public art, artist and activist Suzanne Lacy, whose own art we will consider at the end of this chapter, provided a chart representing a spectrum of possible roles for the artist, from private to public (Fig. 56). These roles correspond closely to those outlined in Chapter 1. Artists as reporters *represent* their world. Artists as experiencers *give tangible form to their feelings* about their world. Artists as analysts look beyond the immediate *to reveal hidden or universal truths.* And artists as activists *help us see the world in new ways.* They even expect their work to have an impact on the world. Questions of the *aesthetic*—that is, questions about knowing and appreciating the beautiful—are supplanted by questions of *transformation*—how artists can affect and change the world to make it a better, more beautiful place.

Lacy's chart is useful because it helps us to see that from the extremely private moment when the artist first experiences the world, each of these possible roles is increasingly public in nature. The experiencer has no necessary audience—the experiencer is a like a television receiver, taking information in. But the reporter assumes an audience, a public, and so does the analyst. They are like transmitters, putting information out which they hope will be understood. The activist, finally, puts information out not only to be understood but to make things happen.

The artist's relation to the public, it should be clear, depends on the public's understanding what the artist is trying to say. But the history of the public's reception of art abounds in instances of the public's misunderstanding. In 1863, for example, Edouard Manet submitted his painting *Luncheon on the Grass,* more commonly known by its French name, *Déjeuner sur l'herbe* (Fig. 57), to the conservative jury that picked paintings for the annual Salon exhibition in Paris. It was rejected along with many other paintings considered "modern," and the resulting outcry forced Napoleon III to create a Salon des Refusés, an exhibition of works refused by the Salon proper, in order to let the public judge for themselves the individual merits of the rejected works. Even at the Salon des Refusés, however, Manet's painting created a scandal. Some years later, in his novel *The Masterpiece,* Manet's friend Emile Zola wrote a barely fictionalized account of the painting's reception:

> *It was one long-drawn-out explosion of laughter, rising in intensity to hysteria . . . . A group of young men on the opposite side of the room were writhing as if their ribs were being tickled. One woman had collapsed on to a bench, her knees pressed tightly together, gasping, struggling to regain her breath . . . . The ones who did not laugh lost their tempers . . . . It was an outrage and should be stopped, according to elderly gentlemen who brandished their walking sticks in indignation. One very serious individual, as he stalked away in anger, was heard announcing to his wife that he had no use for bad jokes . . . . It was beginning to look like a riot . . . and as the heat grew more intense faces grew more and more purple.*

Though it was not widely recognized at the time, Manet had, in this painting, by no means abandoned tradition completely to depict everyday life in all its sordid detail. *Déjeuner sur l'herbe* was based on a composition by Raphael that Manet knew through an engraving, *The Judgment of Paris,* copied from the original by one of Raphael's students, Marcantonio Raimondi (Fig. 58). The pose of the three main figures in Manet's painting directly copies

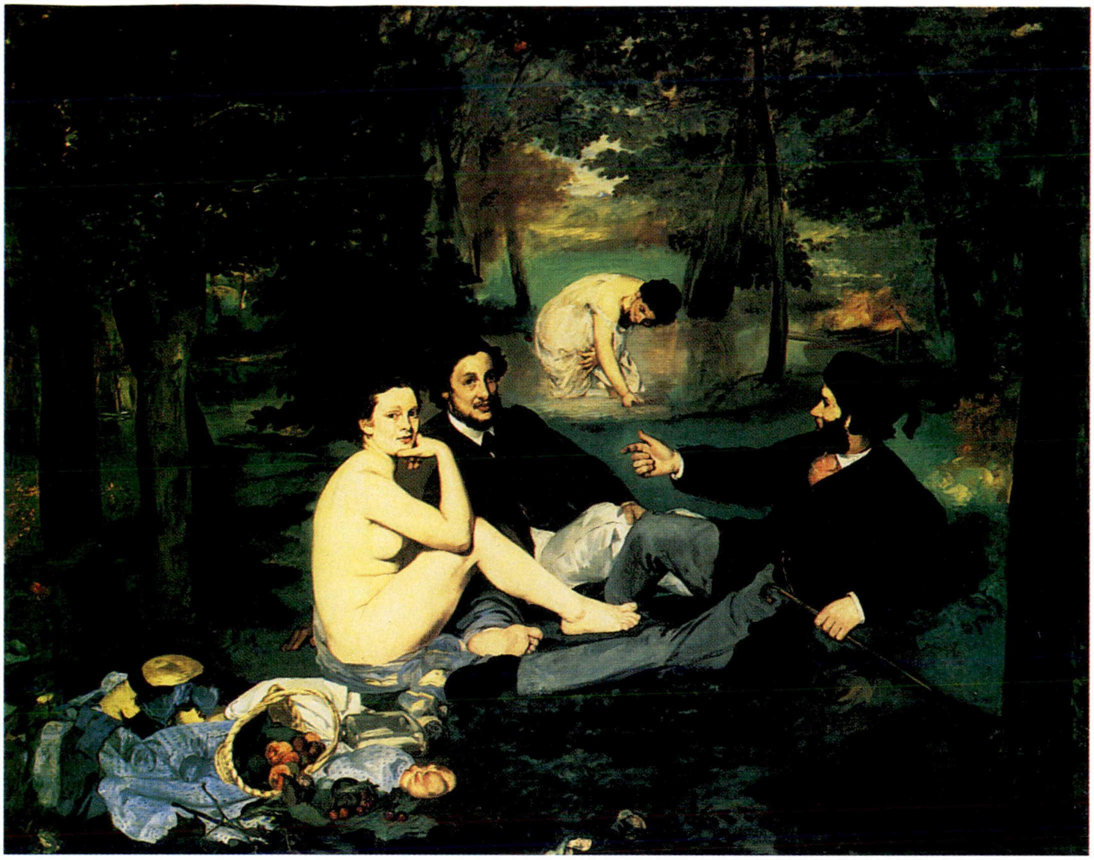

Fig 57 Edouard Manet, *"Luncheon on the Grass" (Déjeuner sur l'herbe)*, 1863.
Oil on canvas, 7 ft. × 8 ft. 10 in. Musée d'Orsay, Paris. Cliche des Musées Nationaux – Paris. © Photo R.M.N. – SPADEM.

the pose of the three wood nymphs in the lower right corner of the engraving. However, if Manet's sources were classical, his treatment was anything but. In fact, what most irritated both critics and public was the apparently "slipshod" nature of his painting technique. The body of the seated nude in *Le Déjeuner* seems flat. The painting's sense of space seems distorted, and the bather in the background and the stream she stands in both seem about to spill forward into the picnic.

Manet's rejection of traditional painting techniques was intentional. He was drawing attention to his very modernity, to the fact that he was breaking with the past. His manipulation of his traditional sources supported the same intentions. In the words of his contemporary, Karl Marx, Manet was looking "with open eyes upon his conditions of life and true social relations." Raphael had depicted the classical judgment of Paris, the mythological contest in which Paris chose Venus as the most beautiful of the goddesses, a choice that led to

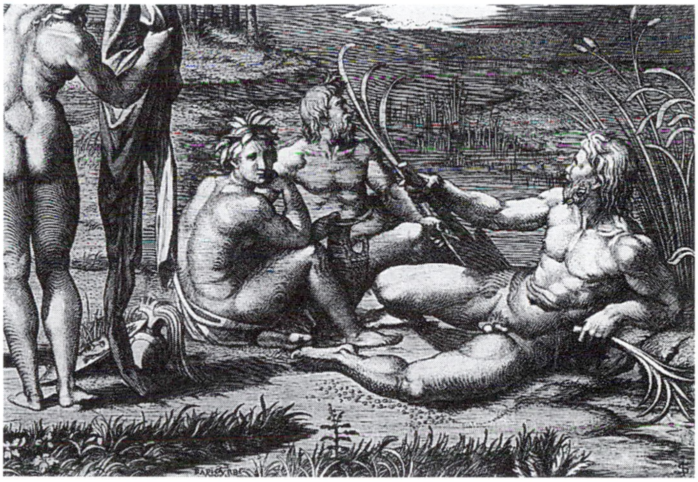

Fig. 58 Marcantonio Raimondi, after Raphael, *"The Judgment of Paris"* (detail), c. 1488 – 1530.
Italian Prints. Engraving. The Metropolitan Museum of Art, Rogers Fund, 1919. (19.74.1).

the Trojan War. In his depiction of a decadent picnic in the Bois de Bologne, Manet passed judgment upon a different Paris, the modern city in which he lived. His world had changed. It was less heroic, its ideals less grand.

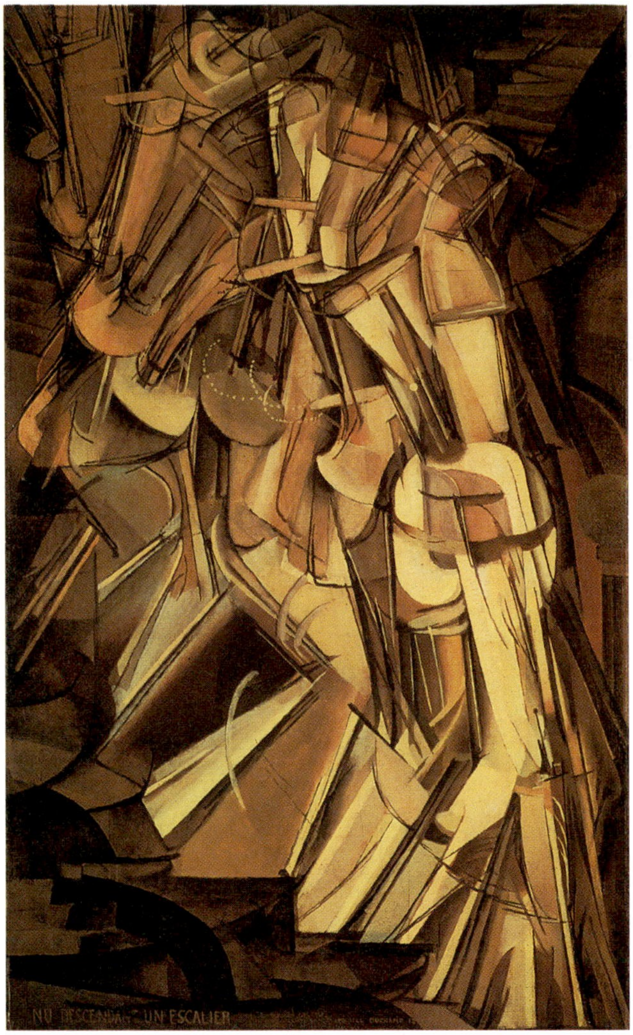

Fig. 59 Marcel Duchamp, *Nude Descending a Staircase, No. 2,* 1912.
Oil on canvas, 58 × 35 in. Philadelphia Museum of Art.
Louise and Walter Arensberg Collection.

The public tends to receive innovative art work with reservation because it usually has little context, historical or otherwise, in which to view the work. It is not easy to appreciate, let alone value, what they do not understand. When Marcel Duchamp exhibited his *Nude Descending a Staircase* (Fig. 59) at the Armory Show in New York City in 1913, it was a scandalous success, parodied and ridiculed in the newspapers. Former President Teddy Roosevelt told the papers, to their delight, that the painting reminded him of a Navajo blanket. Others called it "an explosion in a shingle factory," or "a staircase descending a nude." *The American Art News* held a contest to find the "nude" in the painting. The winning entry declared, "It isn't a lady but only a man."

The Armory Show was most Americans' first exposure to modern art, and over 70,000 people saw it in New York. By the time it closed, after also traveling to Boston and Chicago, nearly 300,000 people had seen the exhibition. If not many understood the *Nude* then, today it is easier for us to see what Duchamp was representing. He had read, we know, a book called *Movement,* published in Paris in 1894, a treatise on human and animal locomotion. It was written by Etienne-Jules Marey, a French physiologist who had long been fascinated with the possibility of breaking down the flow of movement into isolated data that could be analyzed. Marey himself had seen the photographs of a horse trotting, published by Eadweard Muybridge in *La Nature* in 1878

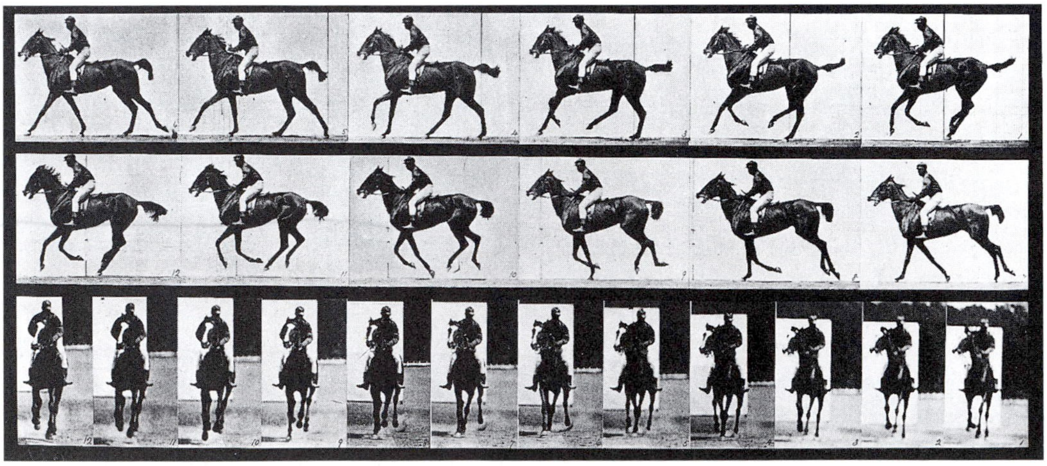

Fig. 60 Eadweard Muybridge (English 1830–1904), *Annie G, Cantering, Saddled,* 1887.
Size: sheet: 19 × 24 in., image: 7 1/2 × 16 1/4 in., collotype print. Philadelphia Museum of Art:
City of Philadelphia, Trade & Convention Center, Dept. of Commerce (Commercial Museum).

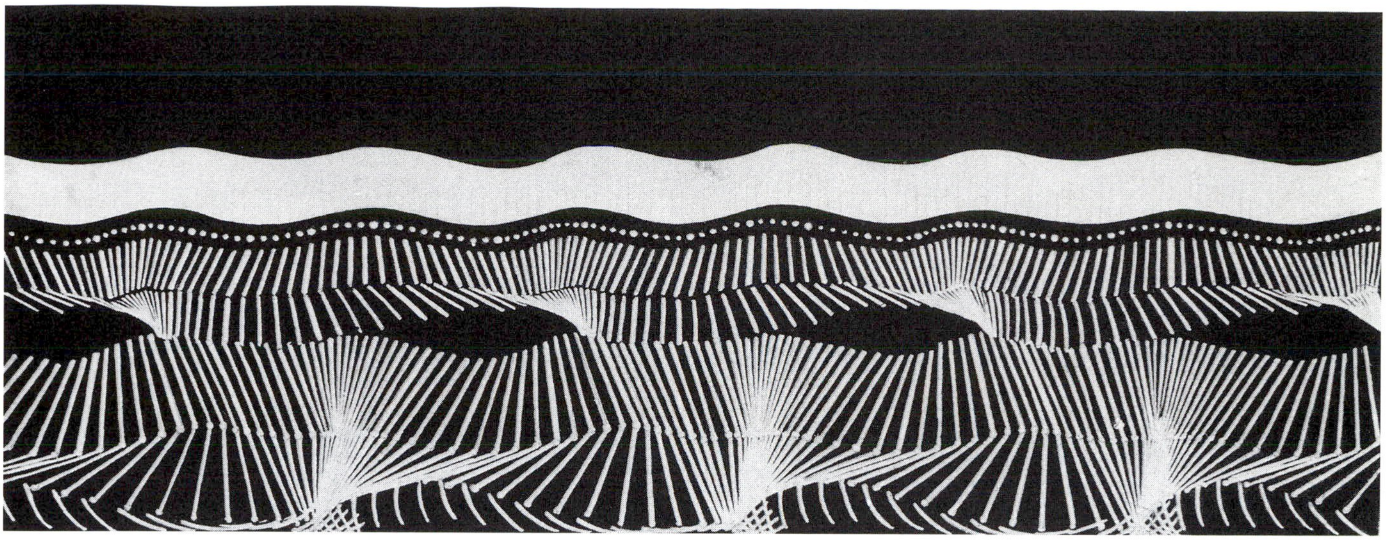

Fig. 61 **Etienne-Jules Marey, *Man Walking in Black Suit with White Stripe Down Sides,* 1886.**
Collection Musée Marey, Beaune, France. Photograph by Jean-Claude Couval.

(Fig. 60). Muybridge had used a trip-wire device in an experiment commissioned by California governor Leland Stanford to settle a bet about whether there were moments in the stride of a trotting or galloping horse when it was entirely free of the ground. As a result of Muybridge's photographs, Marey began to use the camera himself, using models dressed in black suits with white points and stripes (Fig. 62) that allowed him to study, in images created out of a rapid succession of photographs, the flow of their motion. These images, called "chrono-photographs," literally "photographs of time," (Fig. 61) are startlingly like Duchamp's painting. "In one of Marey's books," Duchamp later explained, "I saw an illustration of how he indicated [movement] . . . with a system of dots delimiting the different movements. . . . That's what gave me the idea for the execution of [the] *Nude.*"

Marey, Muybridge, and Duchamp had all embarked, we can now see, on the same path, a path that led to the invention of the motion picture. On December 28, 1895, at the Grand Café on the Boulevard des Capucines in Paris, the Lumière brothers, who knew Marey and his work well, projected motion pictures of a baby being fed its dinner, a gardener being doused by a hose, and a train racing directly at the viewers, causing them to jump from their seats. Duchamp's vision had already been confirmed, but the public had not yet learned to see it.

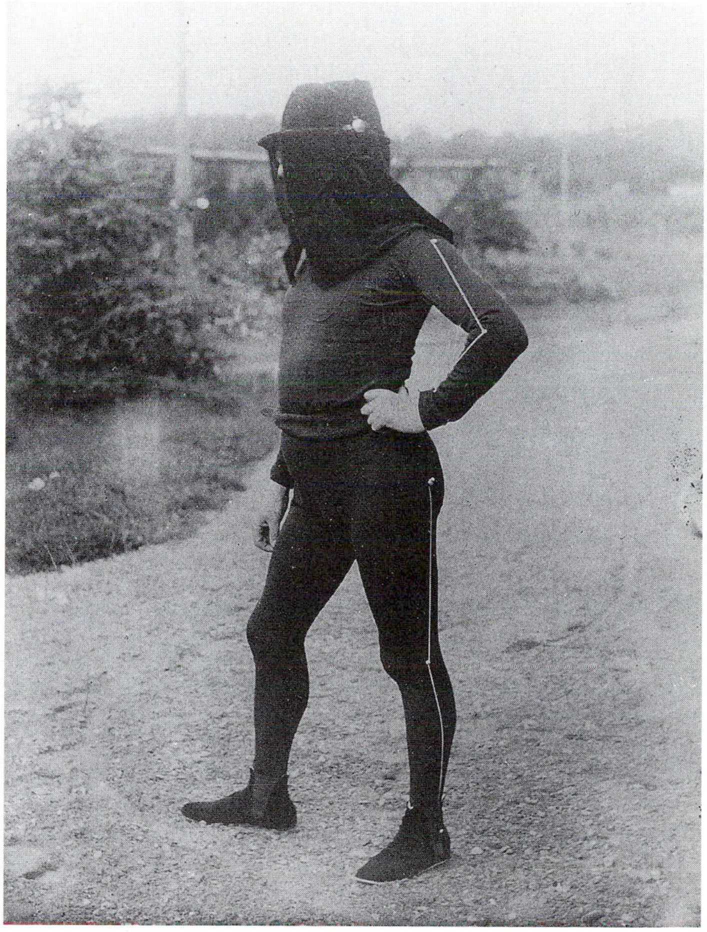

Fig. 62 **Etienne-Jules Marey, *Man in Black Suit with White Stripe Down Side of Chronophotograph Motion Experiment,* 1883.**
Collection Musée Marey, Beaune, France. Photograph by Jean-Claude Couval.

A more recent example of the same phenomenon, of a public first rejecting and then coming to understand and accept a work of art, is Maya Lin's *Vietnam Memorial* in Washington, D.C. Lin's work was selected from a group of over 1,400 entries in a national competition. At the time her proposal was selected, Lin was 22 years old, a recent graduate of Yale University where she had majored in architecture.

Many people at first viewed the monument as an insult to the memory of the very soldiers to whom it was supposed to pay honor. Rather than rise in majesty and dignity above the Washington Mall, like the Washington Monument or the Jefferson Memorial, it descends below earth level in a giant V, over two hundred feet long on each side. It represents nothing in particular, unlike the monument to the planting of the flag on the hill at Iwo Jima, which stands in Arlington National Cemetery, directly across the river. If Lin's memorial commemorates the war dead, it does so only abstractly.

And yet, this anti-monumental monument has become the most visited site in Washington. In part, people recognize that it symbolizes the history of the Vietnam War itself, which began barely perceptibly, like the gentle slope that leads down into the V, then deepened and deepened in crisis, and then ended almost as slowly and imperceptibly as it began. It also symbolizes, for many, the process of grief, a process experienced by many visitors as they descend into the site and then rise out of it again. Cut into the flat expanse of the Mall, it also represents a sort of wound in the American psyche, and for many, to visit it is to begin to heal. The names of the 58,000 men and women who died in Vietnam are chiseled into the wall in the order in which they were killed. One finds the name of a loved one or a friend by looking it up in a register. As you descend into the space to find that name, or simply to stare in humility at all the names, the polished black granite reflects your own image back at you, as if to say that your life is what these names fought for.

Like Manet's *Luncheon* and Duchamp's *Nude,* Lin's piece was misunderstood by the public. But unlike either, it was designed for

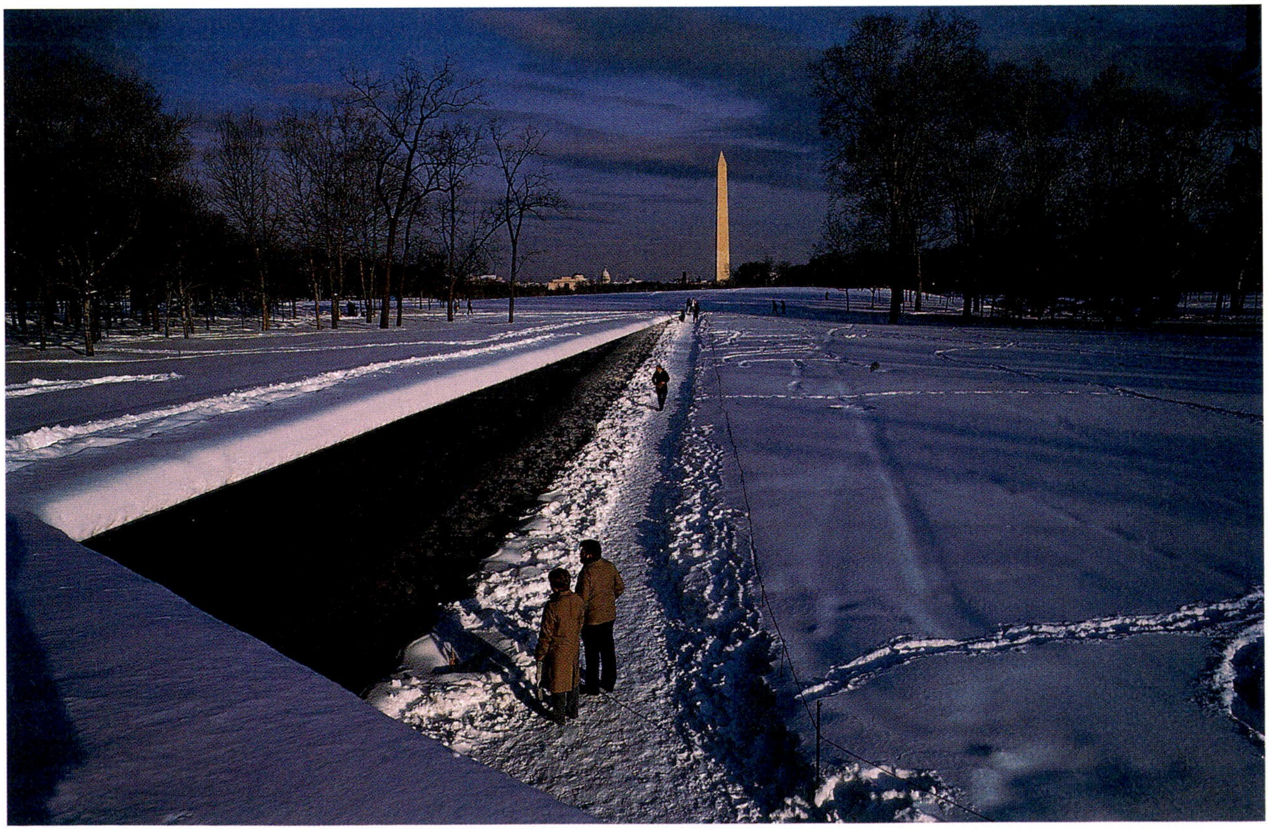

Fig. 63 Maya Ying Lin, Vietnam Memorial, Washington, DC, 1982.
Polished black granite, length 492 ft. Woodfin Camp & Associates.

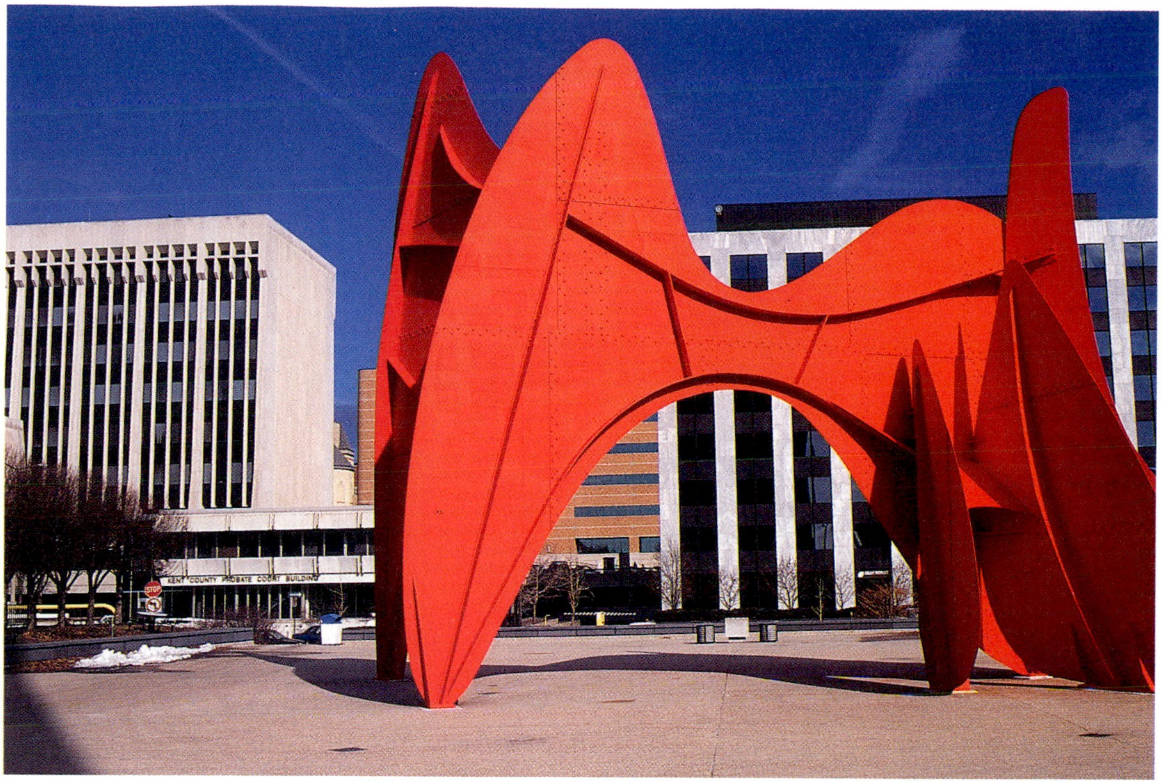

Fig. 64 Alexander Calder, *La Grande Vitesse,* 1969.
Painted steel plate, 43 ft. × 55 ft. Calder Plaza, Vandenberg Center, Grand Rapids, Michigan. © John Corriveau.

public space. As we have seen, as a whole the public is a fickle audience, and the fate of art in public places can teach us much about how and why we value art as a culture.

ART, POLITICS, AND PUBLIC SPACE

A certain segment of the public has always sought out art, in galleries and museums. But as a general rule, except for statues commemorating local heroes, often mounted on horseback in the middle of a square and attracting the interest mostly of pigeons, if the general public wished to ignore art, they could. In 1967, when the Congress first funded the National Endowment for the Arts, that changed. An Arts in Public Places Program was initiated, which was quickly followed by state and local programs nationwide, usually requiring that 1 percent of the cost of new public buildings be dedicated to purchasing art to enhance their public spaces. Where artists previously had assumed an interested, self-selected audience, now everyone was potentially their audience. And like it or not, artists were thrust into an activist role—their job, as the NEA defined it, to educate the general public about the value of art.

The Endowment's plan was to expose the nation's communities to "advanced" art, and the Arts in Public Places Program was conceived as a mass-audience art appreciation course. Time and again, throughout its history, it commissioned pieces that the public initially resisted but learned to love. Alexander Calder's *La Grande Vitesse* (Fig. 64) in Grand Rapids, Michigan, was the first piece commissioned by the Program. The selection committee was a group of four well-known outsiders, including New York painter Adolph Gottlieb and Gordon Smith, director of the Albright-Knox Art Gallery in Buffalo, along with three local representatives, giving the edge to the outside experts, who were, it was assumed, more knowledgable about art matters than their local counterparts. In the case of *La Grande Vitesse,* the public reacted negatively to the long organic curves of Calder's praying mantis-like forms, but soon adopted the sculpture as a civic symbol and a source of civic pride. The NEA and its artists were succeeding in teaching the public to value art for art's sake.

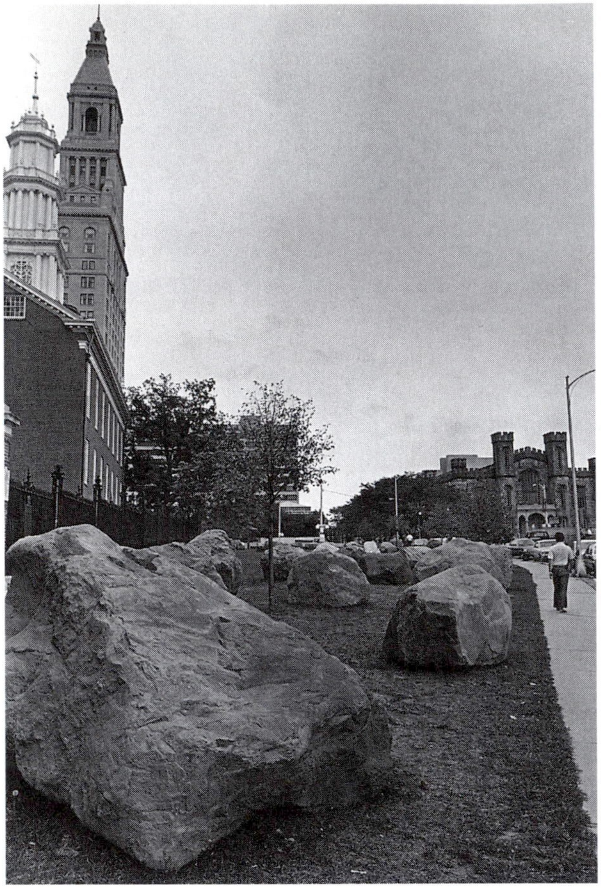

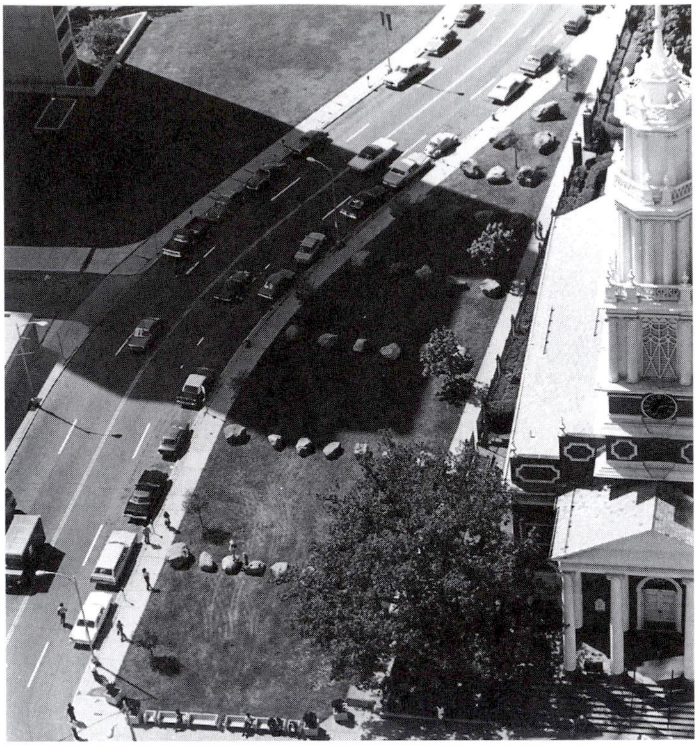

Figs. 65 and 66 Carl Andre, *Stone Field Sculpture,* Hartford, Connecticut 1977. 36 glacial boulders, overall 53′ × 290′, Collection: City of Hartford, Connecticut. Courtesy, Paula Cooper Gallery, New York.

Three Public Sculptures

To value art for art's sake is to value it as an aesthetic object, to value the beauty of its forms rather than its functional practicality or its impact on social life. The NEA assumed, however, that by teaching people to appreciate art, the social life of the nation would be enhanced. Public art, the Endowment believed, would make everyone's life better by making the places we live more beautiful, or at least more interesting. The three public sculptures considered in this section have all tested this hypothesis.

Carl Andre's *Stone Field Sculpture* (Figs. 65 and 66), was commissioned in 1977 by the Arts in Public Places Program. Designed for a triangular public green at the corner of Gold and Main Streets in downtown Hartford, Connecticut, it offers a particularly clear example of how the community came to appreciate a work of art that it at first regarded as a frivolous waste of tax dollars. The work consists of 36 boulders, ranging in weight from 1,000 pounds to 11 tons, placed in eight rows, beginning with one boulder in the first row and increasing by one boulder in each subsequent row. The largest boulder is situated at the narrowest end of the green, and the row containing the eight smallest boulders is at the other end. The stones themselves are uncut, natural boulders from a sand and gravel pit in nearby Bristol, Connecticut. About a third of them are Connecticut sandstone, the same material used in many Hartford buildings, and the rest are granite, basalt, schist, gneiss, and serpentine.

Many people in Hartford felt that the work hardly qualified as art at all. They were doubly incensed that money had been spent on it at a time when the jobless rate was very high. For example, the Republican candidate for mayor at the time called it "another slap in the face for the poor and elderly." Residents in the apartment tower across the street called meetings to discuss having the boulders removed. "There was a lot of real hostility during the installation," Andre told *The New Yorker* magazine. "People would come up and start screaming at me—really screaming. People from all social and economic classes. I was quite startled by the vehemence." But as people came more and more to understand Andre's intentions—the issue was constantly before them in the press—they began to change their minds.

In the first place, Andre wanted to create a tranquil space that would parallel, both emotionally and physically, the 300-year-old graveyard of Center Church alongside it. He also wanted to juxtapose human time—Center Church's first minister, appointed in 1633, was the great Puritan preacher Thomas Hooker—with the far vaster scale of geological time embodied in the rocks. He saw the site as facilitating a sort of dialogue between gravestones and quarry stones, as the meeting place of human history and natural history. Finally, he wanted to create a different, and to his way of thinking better, kind of public sculpture. "What I really hate," he said, "is to see a piece of abstract art in a public space that's nothing more than a disguised man-on-horseback. That just doesn't interest me at all." He thinks of his work, instead, in terms of movement in and around the work. "My idea of a piece of sculpture is a road," he has said. "We don't have a single point of view for a road at all, except a moving one, moving along it. Most of my works—certainly the successful ones—have been ones that are in a way causeways—they cause you to make your way along them or around them . . . . There should be no one place, nor even group of places . . . where you should be."

Richard Serra's controversial *Tilted Arc* (Figs. 67 and 68) received an entirely different reception. When it was originally installed in 1981 in Federal Plaza in lower Manhattan, there was only a minor flurry of negative reaction. However, beginning in March 1985, William Diamond, newly appointed Regional Administrator of the General Services Administration, which had originally commissioned the piece, began an active campaign to have it removed. At the time, nearly everyone believed that the vast majority of people working in the Federal Plaza complex despised the work. In fact, of the approximately 12,000 employees in the complex, only 3,791 signed the petition to have it removed, while nearly as many—3,763—signed a petition to save it. Yet the public perception

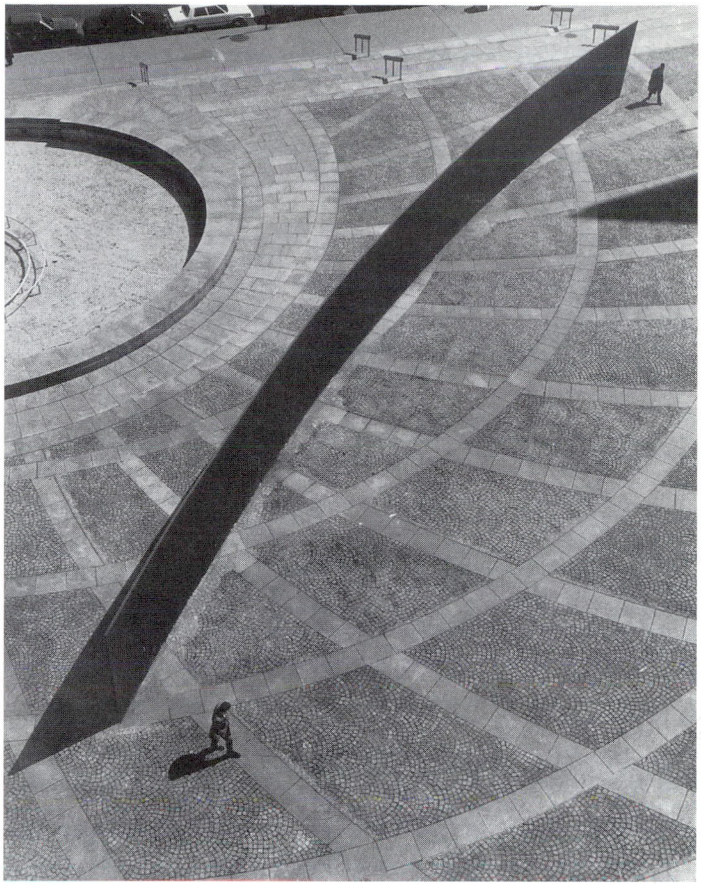

Fig. 67 Richard Serra, *Tilted Arc,* 1981.
Cor-Ten steel, 12 ft. × 120 ft. × 2½ in. Federal Plaza, New York City. Destroyed by the U.S. Government, 3/15/89. ARS.

was that the piece was "a scar on the plaza" and "an arrogant, nose-thumbing gesture," in the words of one observer. During the night of March 15, 1989, against the artist's vehement protests and after he had filed a lawsuit to block its removal, the sculpture was dismantled and its parts stored in a Brooklyn warehouse. It has subsequently been destroyed.

From Serra's point of view, *Tilted Arc* was destroyed when it was removed from Federal Plaza. He had created it specifically for the site, and once removed, it lost its reason for being. In Serra's words: "Site-specific works primarily engender a dialogue with their surroundings . . . . It is necessary to work in opposition to the constraints of the context, so that the work cannot be read as an affirmation of questionable ideologies and political power." Serra *intended* his work to be confrontational. It was political. He had assumed the role of the artist as *analyst*. That is, he felt that Americans were divided from their government, and the Arc divided the plaza in the same way. Its tilt was ominous—it seemed ready to topple over at any instant. Serra succeeded in questioning political power probably more dramatically than he ever intended, but he lost the resulting battle. He made his intentions known and understood, and the work was judged as fulfilling those intentions. But those in power judged his intentions negatively, which is hardly surprising, considering that Serra was challenging their very position and authority.

One of the reasons that the public has had difficulty, at least initially, accepting so many of the public art projects that have been funded by both the NEA and "1%-for-art" programs is that they have not found them to be aesthetically pleasing. The negative reactions to Andre's boulders and Serra's arc are typical. If art must be beautiful, then neither is evidently art. Yet as the public learned what each piece meant, many came to value the works not for their beauty but for their insight, for what they revealed about the places they were in. Serra's work teaches us a further lesson about the value of art. Once public art becomes activist, promoting a specific political or social agenda, there are bound to be segments of the public that disagree with its point of view.

A classic example is Michelangelo's *David* (Fig. 69). Today it is one of the world's most famous sculptures, considered a masterpiece of Renaissance art. But it did not meet with

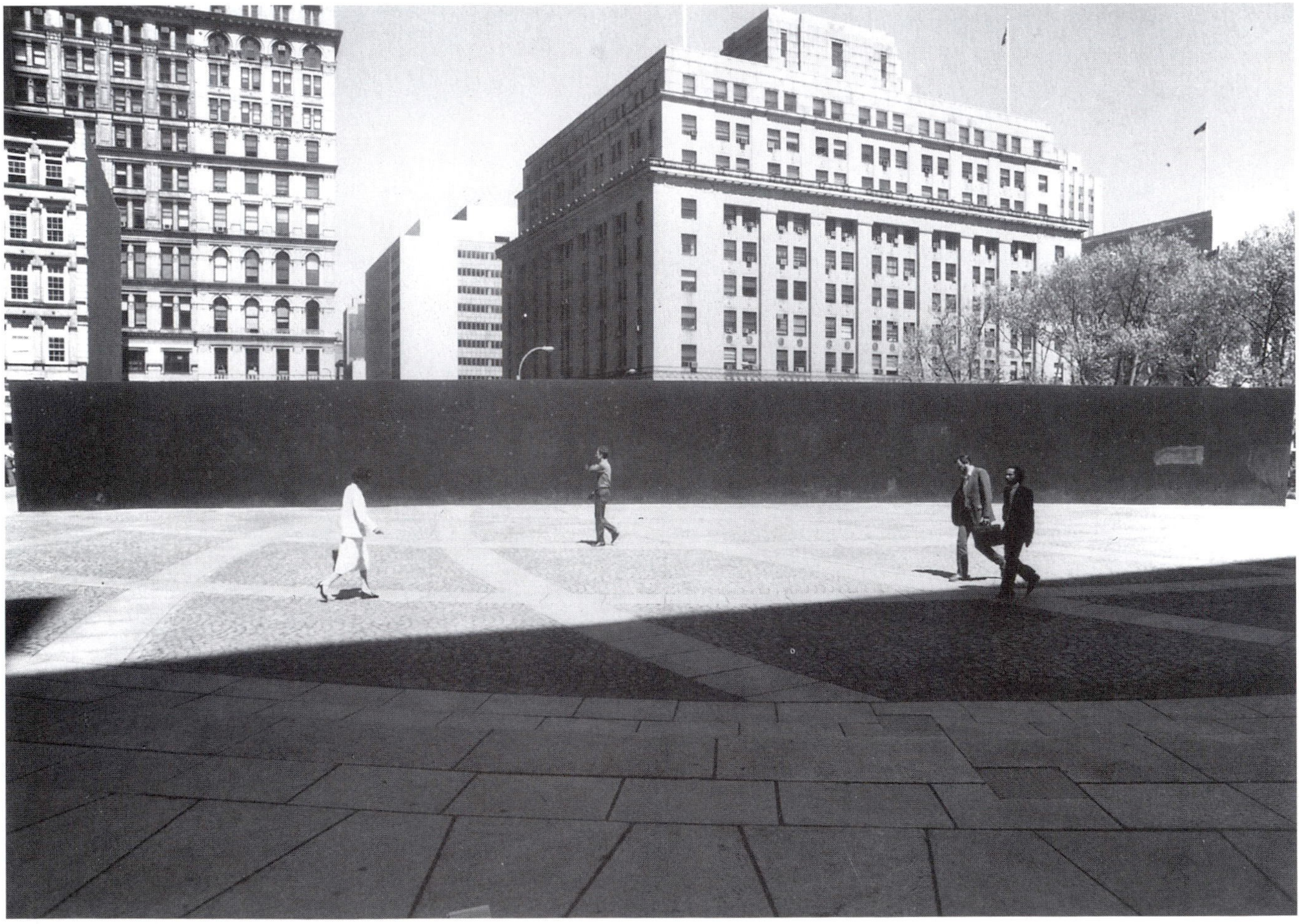

Fig. 68 Richard Serra, *Tilted Arc,* 1981.
Cor-Ten steel, 12 ft. × 120 ft. × 2½ in. Federal Plaza, New York City.
Destroyed by the U.S. Government, 3/15/89. ARS.

universal approval when it was first displayed in Florence, Italy, in 1504. The sculpture was originally commissioned three years earlier, when Michelangelo was 26 years old, by the Opera del Duomo ("Works of the Cathedral"), a group founded in the thirteenth century to look after the Florence cathedral and to maintain works of art. It was to be a public piece, designed for outdoor display in the Piazza della Signoria, the plaza where public political meetings took place on a raised platform called the *arringhiera* (from which the English word "harangue" derives). Its political context, in other words, was clear. It represented David's triumph over the tyrant Goliath and was meant to symbolize Republican Florence, and the city's freedom from foreign and papal domination and from the rule of the Medici family as well.

The *David* was itself, as everyone in the city knew, a sculptural triumph in its own right. It was carved from a giant 16-foot-high block of marble that had been quarried 40 years earlier. Not only was the block riddled with cracks, forcing Michelangelo to bring all his skills to bear, but earlier sculptors, including Leonardo da Vinci, had been offered the problem stone and refused.

When the *David* was finished in 1504, it was moved out of the Opera del Duomo at eight in the evening. It took 40 men four days to move it the 600 yards to the Piazza della Signoria. It required another 20 days to raise it onto the *arringhiera*. The entire time its politics hounded it. Each night, stones were hurled at it by supporters of the Medici, and guards had to be hired to keep watch over it. Inevitably, a second group of citizens objected to its nudity, and before its installation a skirt of copper leaves was prepared to spare the general public any possible offense. The skirt is today long gone. By the time the Medici returned to power in 1512, the *David* was a revered public shrine. It remained in place until 1873, when the sculpture was replaced by a copy and moved to the Opera del Duomo to protect it from a far greater enemy than the Medici, the natural elements. Michelangelo's *David* suggests another lesson about the value of art. Today, we no longer value the sculpture for its politics but rather for its sheer aesthetic beauty and accomplishment. It teaches us how important aesthetic issues remain, even in the public arena.

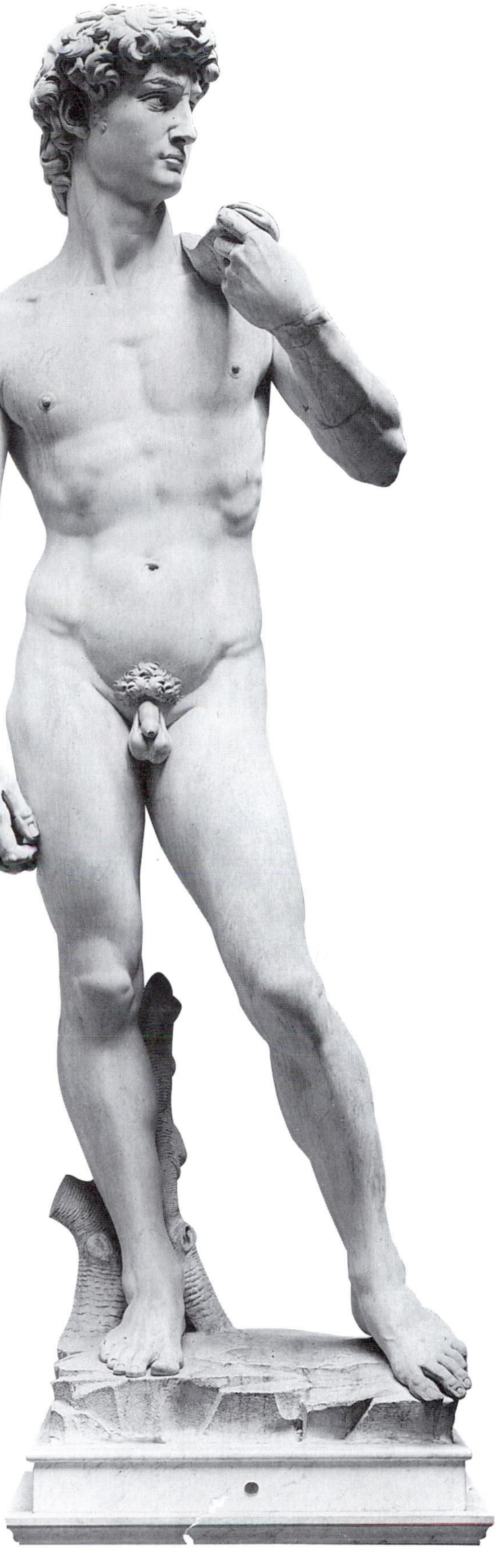

Fig. 69 Michelangelo, *David*, 1501–1504.
Marble, H. 13 ft. Galleria dell'Accademia, Florence. Alinari/Art Resource.

Guillermo Gómez-Peña's Temple of Confessions

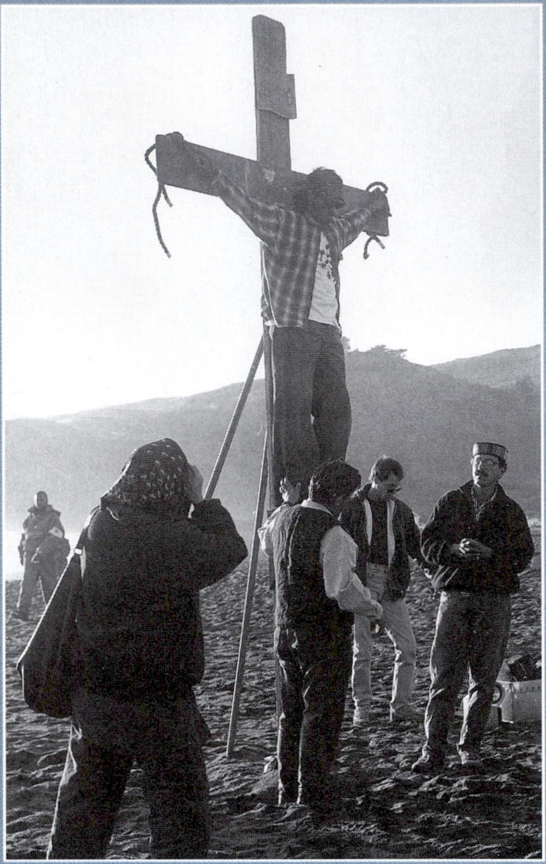

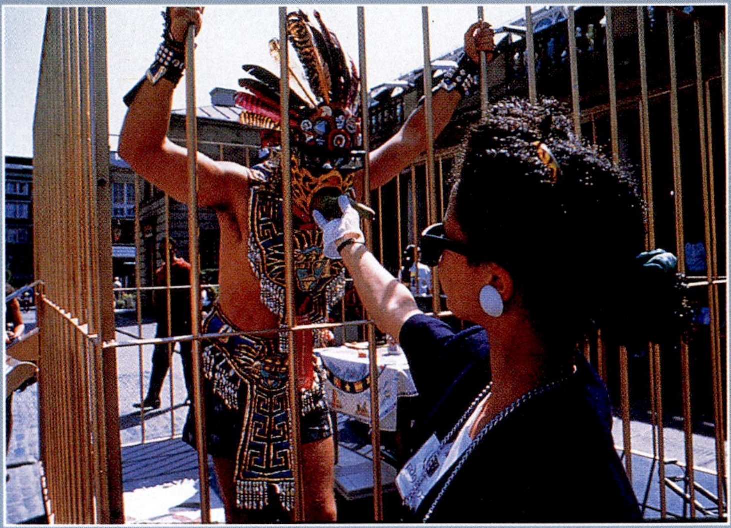

Fig. 70 (above) Guillermo Gómez-Peña and Coco Fusco, *Two Undiscovered Amerindians Visit London,* May, 1992.
Site-specific performance, London, England. Photograph by Peter Barker.

Fig. 71 (left) Guillermo Gómez-Peña and Roberto Sifuentes, *The Cruci-fiction Project,* 1994.
Site-specific performance, Marin headlands, California. Photograph by Neph Navas.

In his work, Mexican artist and activist Guillermo Gómez-Peña has chosen to address what he considers to be the major political question facing North America—relations between the United States and Mexico.

For him, the entire problem is embodied in the idea of the "border." His work dramatizes how the geographical pseudo-"reality" of the border allows us, in the United States, to keep out what we do not want to see. The "border" is a metaphor for the division between ourselves and our neighbors, just as the difference in our national languages, English and Spanish, bars us from understanding one another. Gómez-Peña's work is an ongoing series of what he calls "border crossings," purposeful transgressions of this barrier.

Gómez-Peña asks his audience in the United States to examine their own sense of their cultural superiority. He laces all his performances with Spanish in order to underscore to his largely English-speaking audience that he, the Mexican, is bilingual, and that they are not. In one of his most famous pieces, *Two Undiscovered Amerindians* (Fig. 70), a collaboration with Coco Fusco, he and Fusco dressed as recently discovered, wholly uncivilized "natives" of the fictitious island of Guatinaui in the middle of the Gulf of Mexico. To the artists' astonishment, many audience members didn't find the idea of supposed natives locked in a cage as part of an "art" or "anthropological" exhibit

WORKS IN PROGRESS

objectionable or even unusual. The project pointed out just how barbaric the assumptions of Western culture sometimes are.

Since 1994, Gómez-Peña has been collaborating with Roberto Sifuentes. In *The Cruci-fiction Project* (Fig. 71), the two, dressed as Mexican stereotypes as a migrant worker and a lowrider, tied themselves to two 12 × 8 foot wooden crosses to protest immigration policy. In an artists' statement they identified themselves as modern-day versions of Dimas and Gestas, the two small-time thieves who were crucified along with Jesus Christ. Over 300 audience members watched them suffer for nearly three hours until, finally, someone took it upon themselves to set them free.

Another ongoing performance and installation work is entitled *The Temple of Confessions* (Fig. 72). Gómez-Peña and Sifuentes exhibit themselves, for five to seven hours a day, inside Plexiglass booths. Sifuentes' arms and face are painted with tattoos, his bloody T-shirt is riddled with bullet holes. He shares his booth with 50 cockroaches, a four-foot iguana, and an assortment of weapons and drug paraphernalia. In his own booth, Gómez-Peña sits on a toilet (or wheelchair), dressed as what he calls a "curio shop shaman." Hundreds of souvenirs hang from his chest and waist. He shares his box with live crickets, stuffed animals, tribal musical instruments, and a giant ghetto blaster. A violet neon light frames the entire altar and a highly "techno" soundtrack plays constantly.

In front of each booth, there is a church kneeler with a microphone to allow audience members to confess their "intercultural fears and desires." At least a third of all visitors eventually do so. Gómez-Peña describes the effect: "Emotions begin to pour forth from both sides. Some people cry, and in doing so, they make me cry. Some express their sexual desire for me. Others spell their hatred, their contempt, and their fear. . . . The range goes from confessions of extreme violence and racism toward Mexicans and other people of color, to expressions of incommensurable tenderness and solidarity with us. Some confessions are filled with guilt, or with fear of invasion, violence, rape and disease. Others are fantasies about wanting to be Mexican or Indian, or vice versa: Mexicans and Latinos suffused in self-hatred wanting to be Anglo, Spanish, or 'blond.'" At night, after each performance, Sifuentes and Gómez-Peña listen to tapes of all the confessions of the day. The most revealing ones are edited and incorporated into the installation soundtrack.

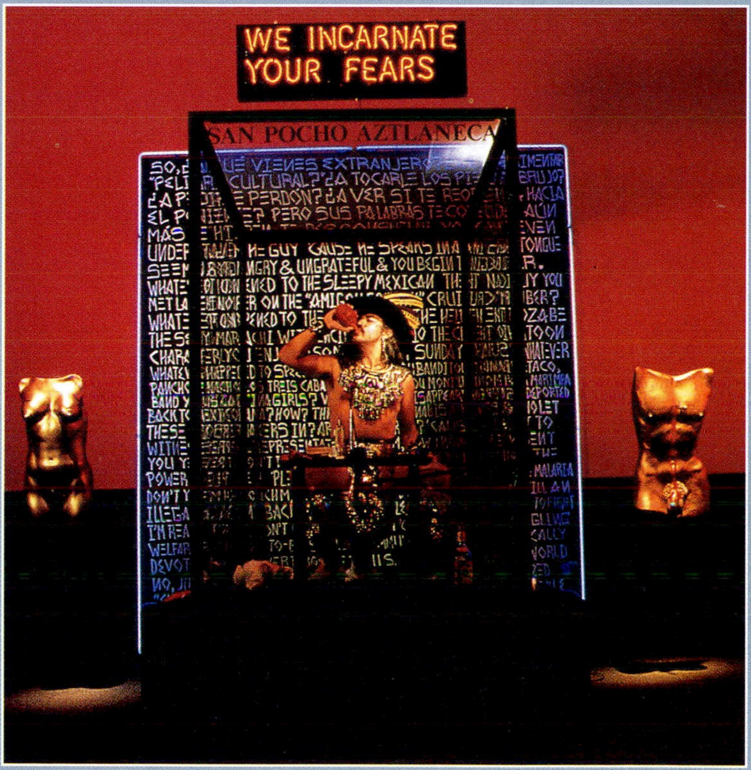

Fig. 72 Guillermo Gómez-Peña and Roberto Sifuentes, *The Temple of Confessions,* 1994. Site-specific performance, Detroit Institute of the Arts, 1994. Photograph by Dirk Bakker.

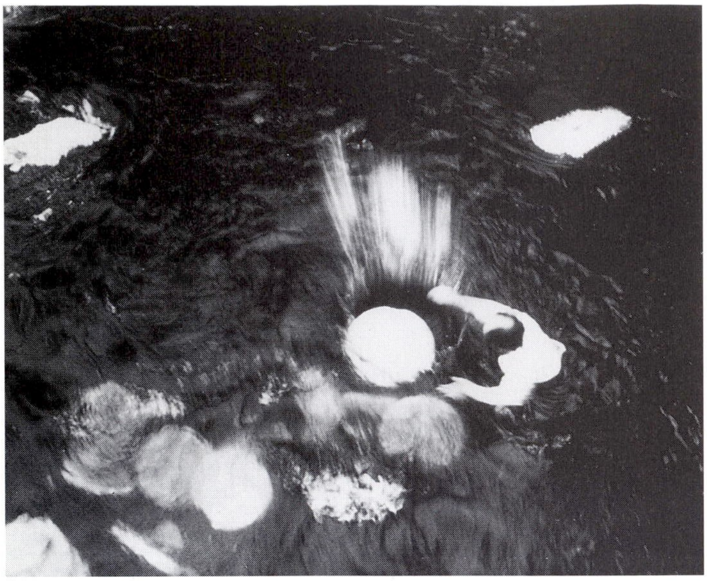

Fig. 73 Buster Simpson, *Anti-Acid Placement in Headwaters of Hudson River, South of Lake Placid, New York,* 1991.
Limestone disk, 3 × 24 in. Courtesy of the artist.

The "Other" Public Art

Public art, as these last three examples make clear, has been associated particularly with sculptural works. Whatever social issues or civic pride they may symbolize, they are not active agents of change.

But there are other fully activist kinds of public art that aim to have direct impact on our lives. For example, Seattle-based artist Buster Simpson is less interested in making beautiful objects to grace public spaces than works that have environmental consequences. His series of *River Rolaids* (Fig. 73), located in several watersheds around Seattle and around the nation, are a direct response to acid rain, a problem compounded by the urban environment. The disks are literal "anti-acid" pills that slowly break down to sweeten and neutralize the acidity of the river water, bringing it back to health.

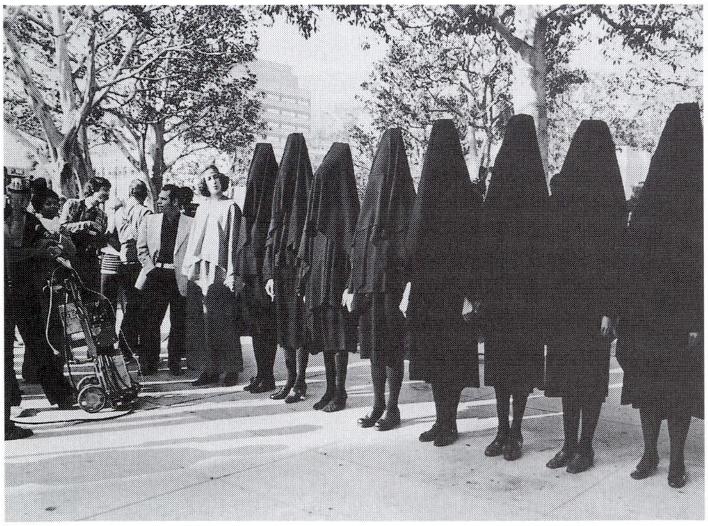

Fig. 74 Performance by Suzanne Lacy and Leslie Labowitz.
Photograph by Susan R. Mogul.

Another example of this activist direction in art is the collaborative performance piece created by Suzanne Lacy and Leslie Labowitz, *In Mourning and in Rage* (Fig. 74), which was performed in December 1977 outside the Los Angeles City Hall to protest violence against women in America's cities. It was timed to coincide with a Los Angeles city council meeting. Lacy and Labowitz wanted to ensure media coverage of the performance, an elaborately staged event conceived to be both visually powerful and politically telling. Ten women stepped from a hearse wearing veils draped over structures that, headdress-like, made each figure seven feet tall. Representing the ten victims of the Hillside Strangler, a serial killer then on the loose in Los Angeles, each of the figures, in turn, addressed the media. They linked the so-called Strangler's crimes to a national climate of violence against women and the sensationalized media coverage that supports it. As Lacy and Labowitz have explained: "The *art* is in making it compelling; the *politics* is in making it clear . . . . *In Mourning and in Rage* took this culture's trivialized images of mourners as old, powerless women and transformed them into commanding seven-foot-tall figures angrily demanding an end to violence against women." To maximize the educational and emotional impact of the event, the performance itself was followed up by a number of talk show appearances and activities organized in conjunction with a local rape hot line program.

This model for political art represents the end of Lacy's spectrum of possible roles for the artist that opened this chapter. On the day of *In Mourning and in Rage*'s performance in 1977, the artists assumed an activist role, engaging the public and the press in a confrontational way. It is worth remembering, however, that to get to this point, Lacy and Labowitz had probably functioned in the other roles as well—first experiencing, on a private level, the sense of mourning and rage that gives the work its title, then determining how to report or visualize that mourning and rage (the image of headless, seven-foot women), then analyzing what aspects of American social behavior had led to it in the first place.

For Group Material, a collaborative team made up of John Ault, Doug Ashford, Felix Gonzalez-Torres, and Karen Ramspacher, the AIDS crisis is the central problem that we all must face. For an 1989 exhibition at the University Art Museum, Berkeley, California, they created a ten-year timeline (Fig. 75) in an attempt to make visible the course of an epidemic from which we too easily, and at our peril, avert our eyes. The work has since been installed in many museums, including the Whitney Museum in New York. A related Group Material project occupies an entire wall near the top floor elevators of the San Francisco Museum of Modern Art. Its reception is not unlike that afforded most new art that the public confronts without any sense of its context. People scoff at it—"That's art!?" Or, because it is barely visible—and as a result, not reproducible here—people often ignore it. It simply consists of four letters:

AI
DS

stenciled in block form in white on white paper in the middle of the wall, and then surrounding it, on the wall itself, the same letters, white on white, only smaller. It takes effort to see it. It is a plea for us to open our eyes. It is a lesson in both art and life.

Whatever role artists assume—experiencer, reporter, analyst, or activist—it is finally us, their audience, that must judge the value of their work. Works of art can possess aesthetic value—they can make our world a more beautiful place. Or they can have social value—they can enter the public arena to make our world a better place in which to live. Many works of art do both. What each of us values in art is different, but when we say we value a given work, we should be able to explain what we mean, whether we find it aesthetically pleasing, socially effective, or both.

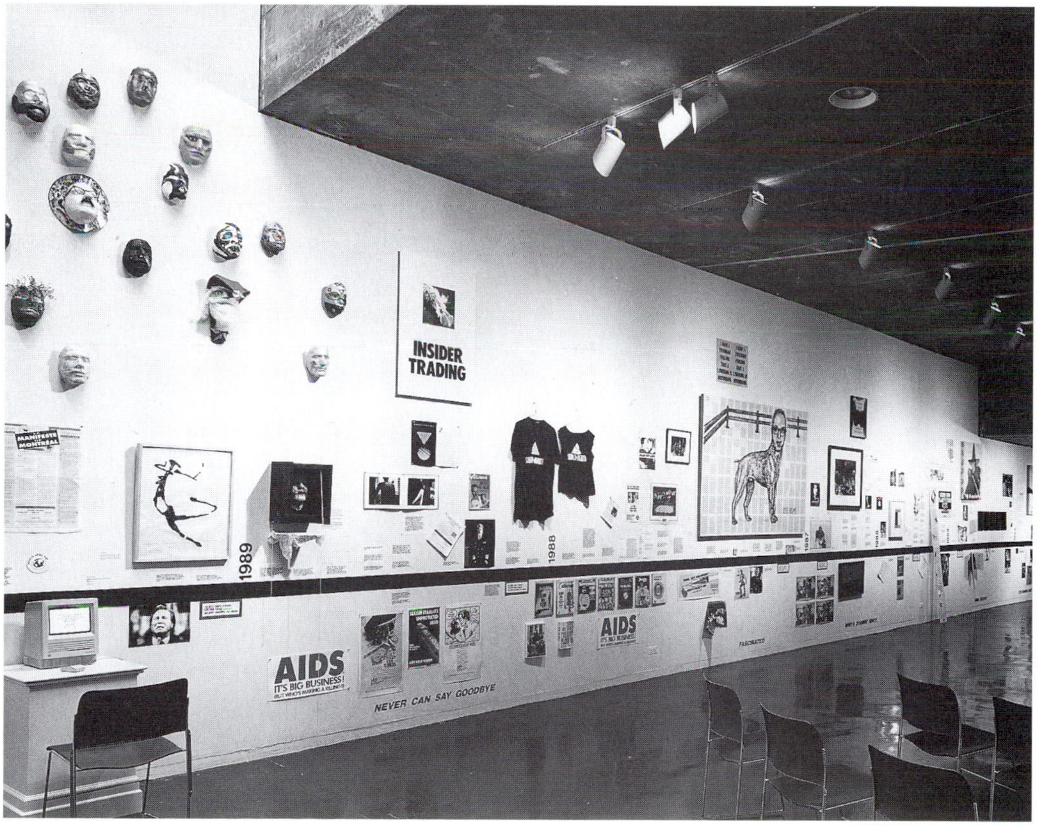

Fig. 75 Group Material, *Group Material Installation View (AIDS Timeline)*, 1989.
Courtesy University Art Museum, University of California at Berkeley.

PART II

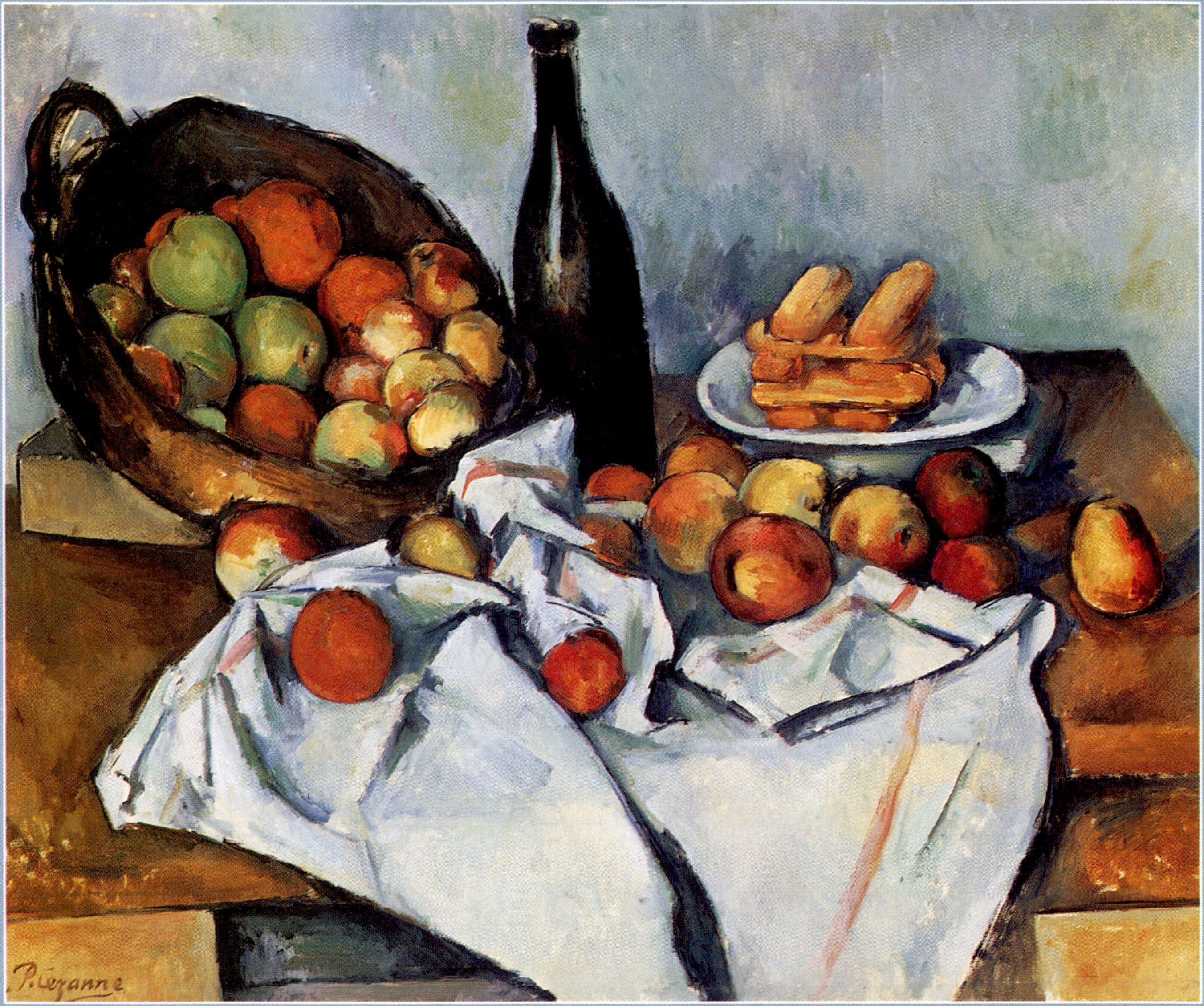

Fig. 76 Paul Cézanne, *The Basket of Apples*, c. 1895.
Oil on canvas, 21 3/8 × 31 in.

THE FORMAL ELEMENTS AND THEIR DESIGN

DESCRIBING THE ART YOU SEE

CHAPTER 4

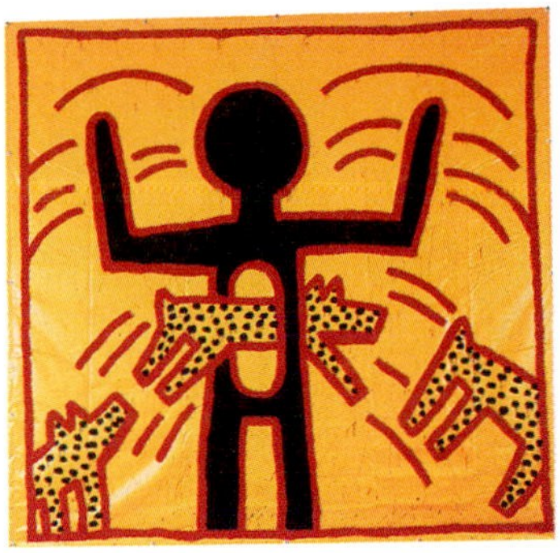

Line

Varieties of Line
Outline and Contour Line
Implied Line

Qualities of Line
Expressive Line

WORKS IN PROGRESS
Vincent van Gogh's *The Sower*

Analytic or Classical Line
Line and Cultural Convention

The painting at the left, Paul Cézanne's *The Basket of Apples* (Fig. 76), is a still life, but it is also a complex arrangement of visual elements: lines and shapes, light and color, space, and, despite the fact that it is a "still" life, time. Upon first encountering the painting, most people sense immediately that it is full of what appear to be visual "mistakes." The edges of the table, both front and back, do not line up. The wine bottle is tilted sideways, and the apples appear to be spilling forward, out of the basket, onto the white napkin, which in turn seems to project forward, out of the picture plane.

Fig. 77 (below) Jean Tinguely, Plate from *La Vittoria,* 1972.
Plate (folio 9). Milan, Sergio Tosi Stampatore, 1972.
Photolithograph and rubber stamp, printed in color, with collage and pencil additions, composition: 17 15/16 × 13 1/8 in. (irregular).
The Museum of Modern Art, New York. Purchase.
Photograph © 1996 The Museum of Modern, Art, New York.

Fig. 78 (right) Pablo Picasso, *Pitcher, Candle, and Casserole,* 1945.
Oil on canvas, 32 1/4 × 41 3/4 in. Musée National d'Art Moderne, Centre National d'Art et de Culture Georges Pompidou, Paris.

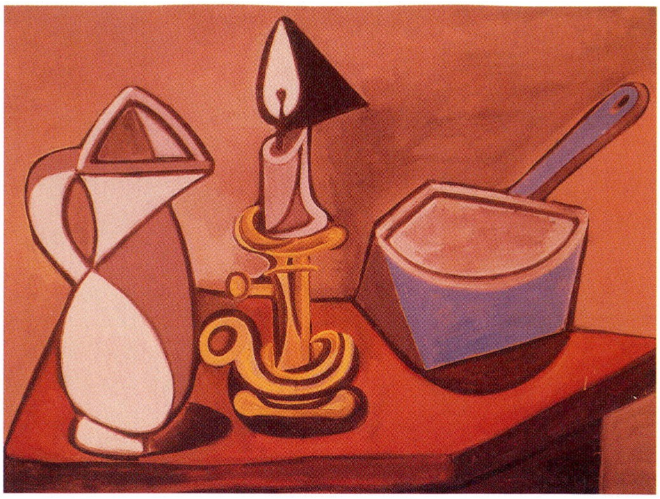

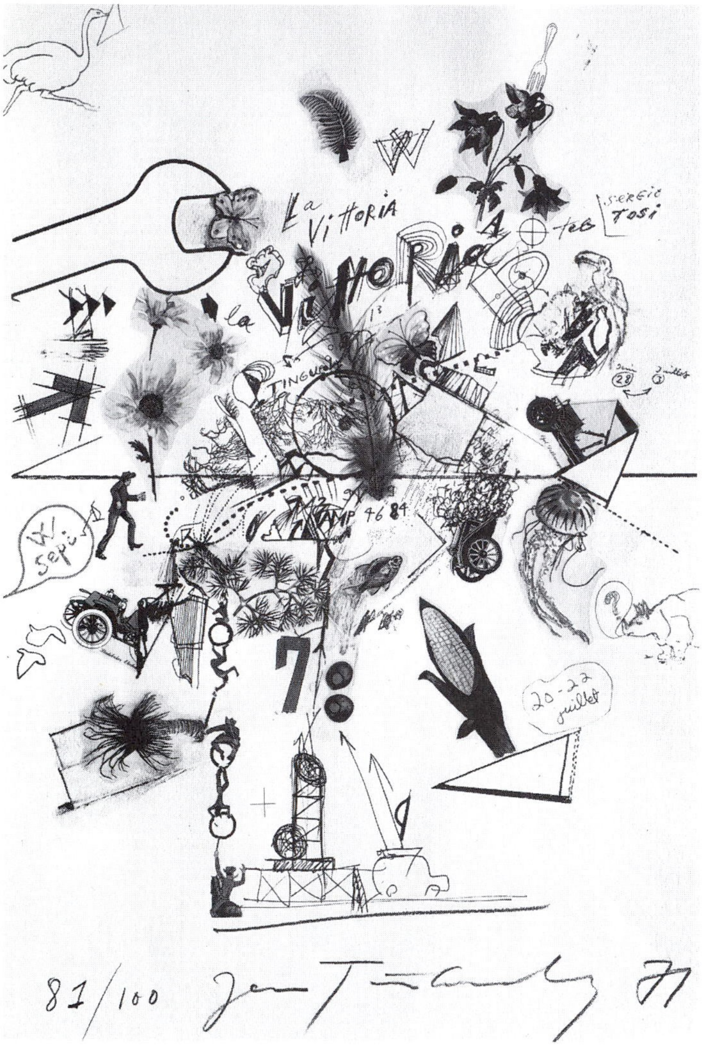

Indeed, looking at this work, one feels compelled to reach out and catch that first apple as it rolls down the napkin's central fold and falls into our space.

However, Cézanne has not made any mistakes at all. Each decision is part of a strategy designed to give back life to the "still life"—which in French is called *nature morte*—"dead nature." He wants to animate the picture plane, to make its space *dynamic* rather than *static,* to engage the imagination of the viewer. He has taken the visual elements of line, space, and texture and deliberately manipulated them as part of his *composition,* the way he has chosen to organize the canvas. As we begin to appreciate how the visual elements routinely function—the topic of this and the next four chapters—we will better appreciate how Cézanne manipulates them to achieve the wide variety of effects in this still life.

VARIETIES OF LINE

One of the most fundamental elements of art is **line.** If you take pencil to paper, you can draw a straight line or a curved one. Straight lines can be vertical, horizontal, or diagonal. Curved lines can be circular, or oval (or segments of circles and ovals), or they can be free-form. Lines can abuptly change direction, in an angle or a curve. They seem to possess direction—they can rise or fall, head off to the left or to the right, disappear in the distance. Lines can divide one thing from another, or they can connect things together. They can be thick or thin, long or short, smooth or agitated. Almost all types of line are apparent in Jean Tinguely's work from his portfolio of prints, *La Vittoria* (Fig. 77). Tinguely's frenzied image is an explosion of lines, each playing off the others in a manner as odd, and as full of imaginative possibility, as the wrench, in the print's upper left, which turns a butterfly.

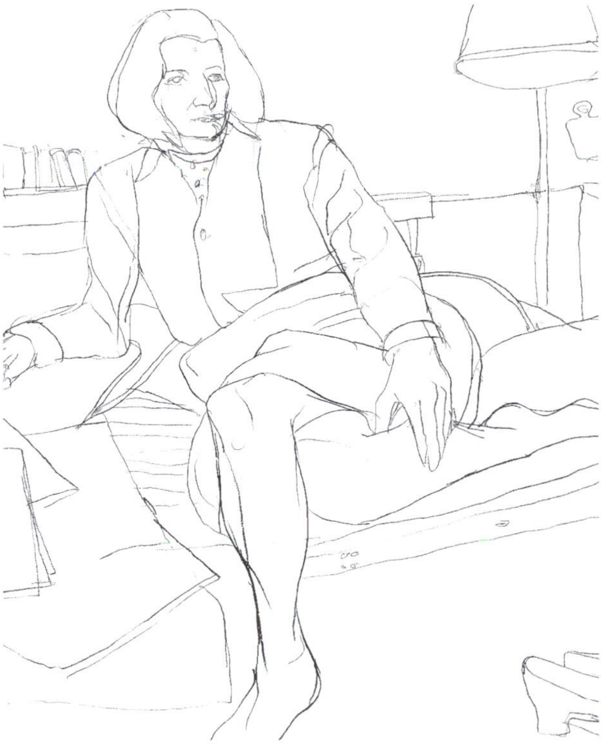

Fig. 79 Richard Diebenkorn, *Untitled,* c. 1961.
Pencil on paper, 17 × 14 in. Acquavella Contemporary Art, Inc.

Outline and Contour Line

Another important feature of line is that it indicates the edge of two- or three-dimensional shapes or forms. This edge can be indicated either directly, by means of an actual **outline,** as in Picasso's *Pitcher, Candle, and Casserole* (Fig. 78), or indirectly, as in Richard Diebenkorn's untitled drawing (Fig. 79). In Picasso's painting, each of the objects on the table, and the table itself, is established by *actual* black outlines drawn at their edge. Picasso has then filled in each of the outlined areas with large fields of color. Unlike Picasso, Diebenkorn has not drawn lines in order to indicate the edges of his figure, such as her arm, or the crossed leg under her dress. Rather, it is as if each line surrounds and establishes a volume. This is perhaps clearest in the line that establishes the model's left leg and hip, which does not define a flat shape but rather the fullness and recession of her anatomy. From the point of view of the artist, there are no actual lines in this work, even though, perceptually, they are quite apparent. There are only volumes that make lines *appear* to us as they curve away. We call these **contour lines.**

Implied Line

Another variety of line that depends on perception is *implied.* We perceive **implied lines** even though they neither exist in or mark the edge of our visual field. We visually "follow," for instance, the line indicated by a pointing finger. If someone nods toward us, we recognize the direction of that nod, the line of communication thus established between us. Movement also creates implied lines, as we saw in Chapter 3 in the photographs of Eadweard Muybridge and Etienne-Jules Marey (Figs. 60–62). In his untitled drawing (Fig. 80), Keith Haring draws actual lines to indicate the motion of waving hands and jumping dogs. Haring began his career as a graffiti artist in the New York City subways and made his work available to a large audience through a retail outlet called the Pop Shop. Though Haring died of AIDS in 1990, the Pop Shop still sells Haring-designed posters, T-shirts, refrigerator magnets, radios, buttons, Swatch watches, and other items. The piece reproduced here is typical of Haring's work. Deceptively simple in its outlines, it is not just a "fun" line drawing. It is meant to represent the fatal shooting of John Lennon. Lennon's asssasin is only one in an endless line of hyenas, a hideous, all-consuming public that believes it has the right to enter into any star's heart and soul.

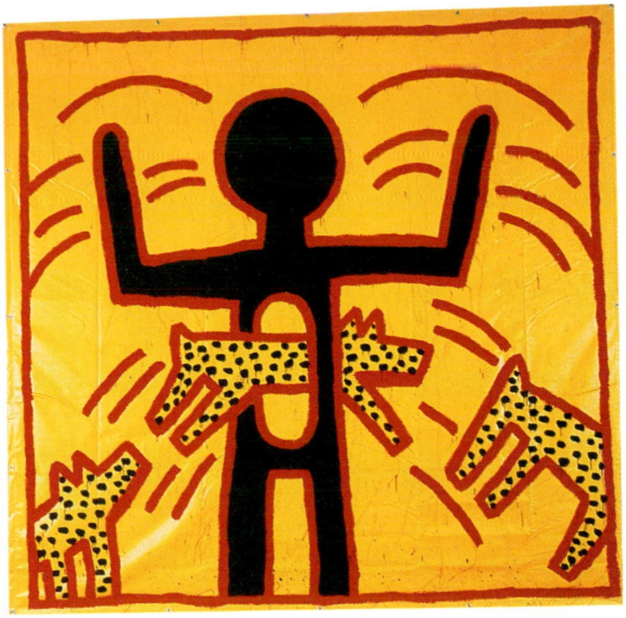

Fig. 80 Keith Haring, *Untitled,* March 24th, 1982.
Vinyl ink on vinyl tarp, 12 × 12 ft.
Courtesy Tony Shafrazi Gallery, New York.

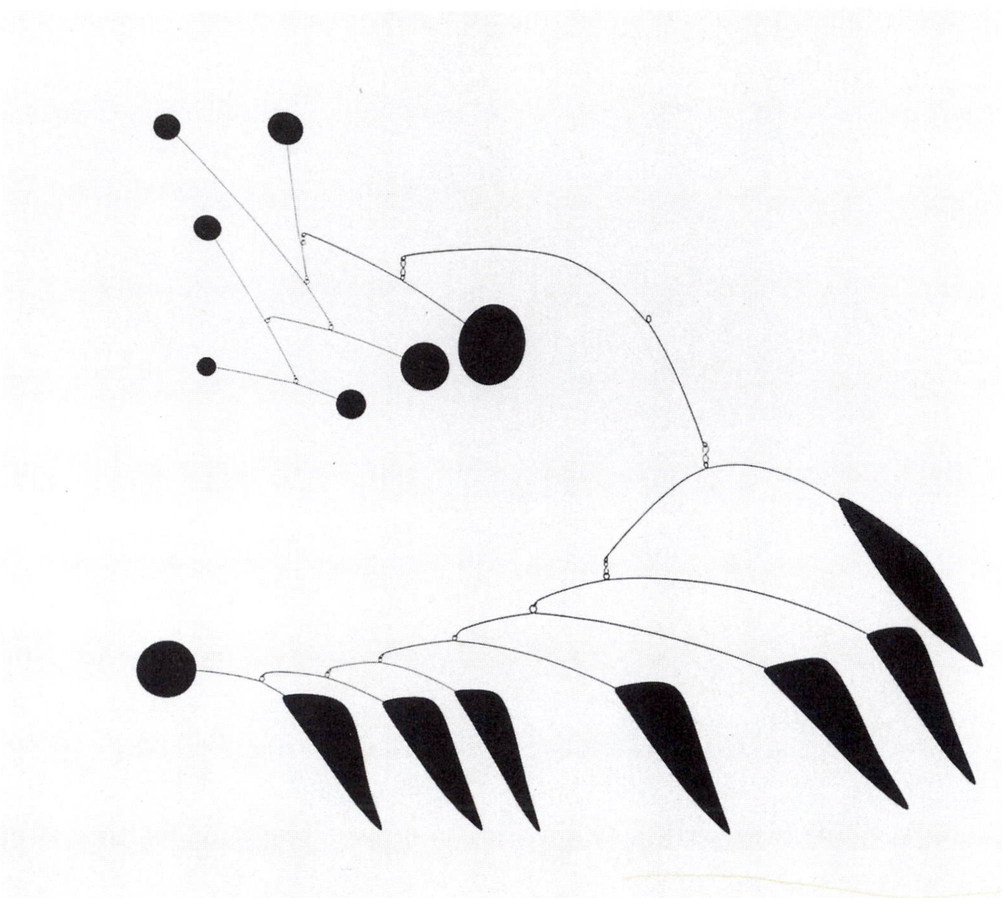

Fig. 81 Alexander Calder, *Dots and Dashes,* 1959.
Painted sheet metal, wire, W. 60 in. Collection of Peter and Beverly Lipman.

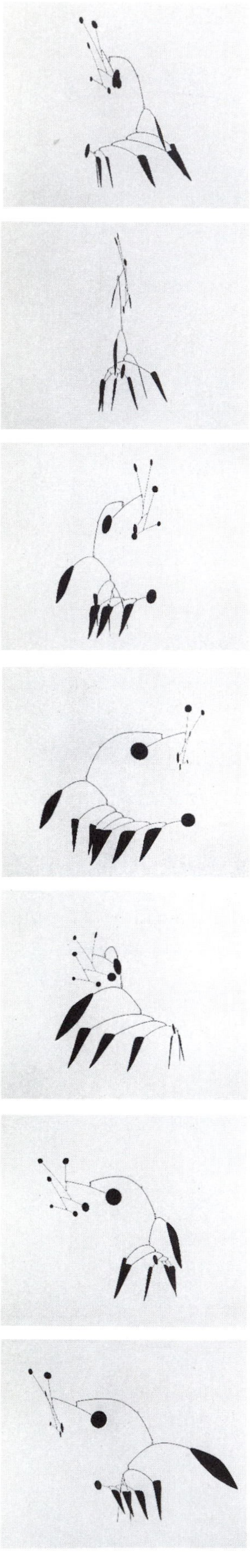

Fig. 82 Sequential sequence of *Dots and Dashes* in motion.
Reproduced from *Alexander Calder and His Magical Mobiles,* by Jean Lipman, Hudson Hills Press in Association with the Whitney Museum of American Art. Photographs by Jerry Thompson.

Many **kinetic** works—works that *move*—rely on our ability to remember the path that particular elements in the work have followed. Alexander Calder's mobiles (Fig. 81), composed of circular disks and wing-shaped discs that spin around their points of balance on arched cantilevers, are designed to create a sense of virtual volume as space is filled out by implied line. The sequence of photographs of *Dots and Dashes* (Fig. 82) clearly reveals how Calder's sculpture changes as it moves. The lines generated here are equivalent, in Calder's mind, to the lines created by a dancer moving through space.

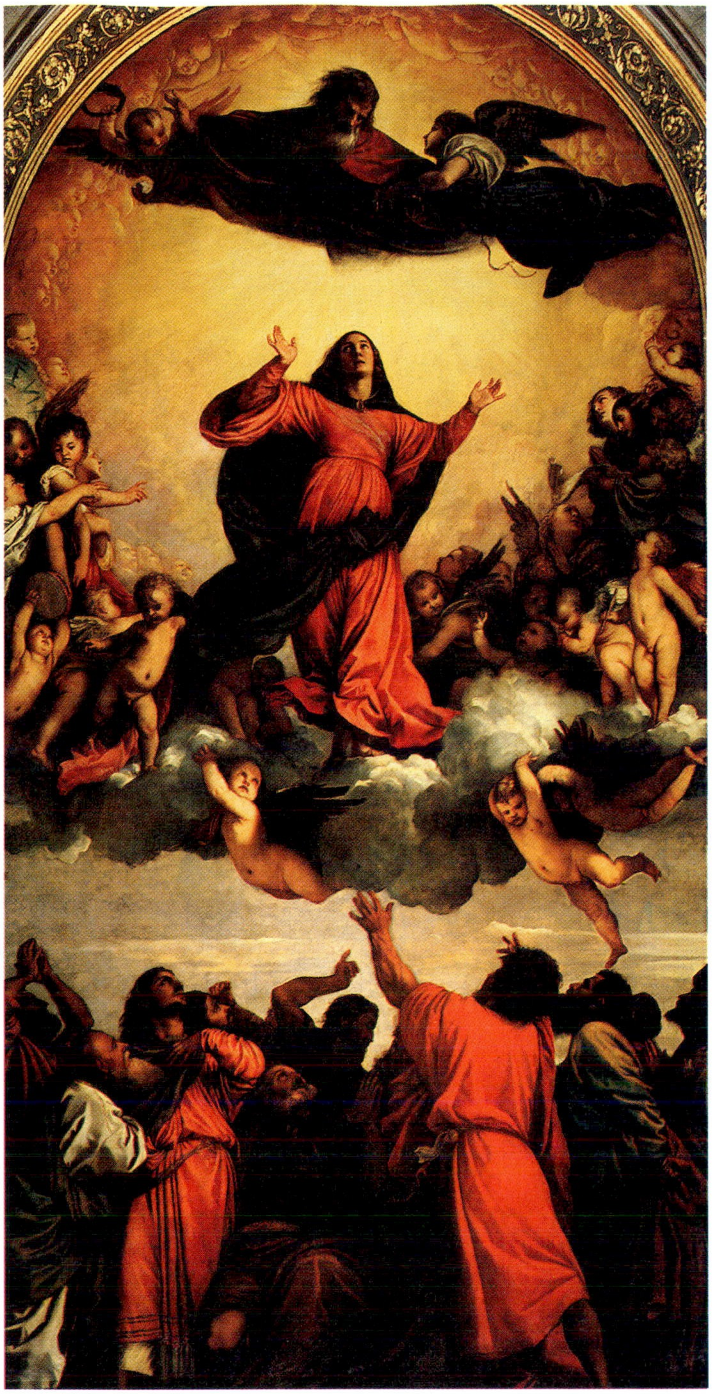

Fig. 83 Titian, *Assumption and Consecration of the Virgin,* c. 1516–1518.
Oil on wood, 22 1/2 × 11 4/5 ft.
Santa Maria Gloriosa dei Frari, Venice. Scala/Art Resource.

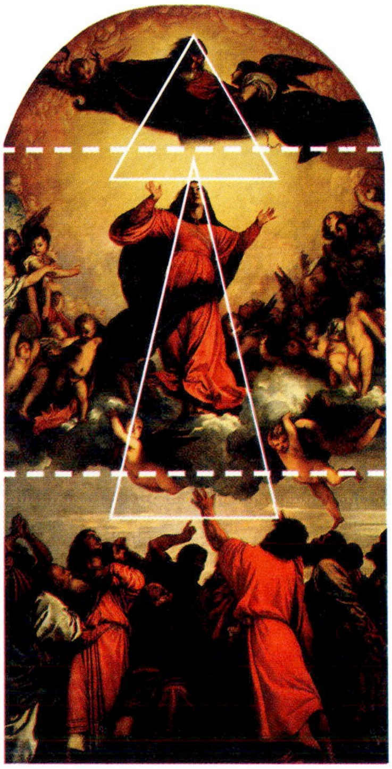

Fig. 84 Line analysis of Titian's *Assumption and Consecration of the Virgin.*

One of the most powerful kinds of implied line is a function of *line of sight,* the direction the figures in a given composition are looking. In his *Assumption and Consecration of the Virgin* (Fig. 83), Titian ties together the three separate horizontal areas of the piece—God the Father above, the Virgin Mary in the middle, and the Apostles below—by implied lines that create simple, interlocking symmetrical triangles (Fig. 84) that serve to unify the worlds of the divine and the mortal.

QUALITIES OF LINE

Line delineates form and shape, by means of outline and contour line. Implied lines also create a sense of movement and direction. But line also possesses certain intellectual, emotional, and expressive qualities.

In a series of six works entitled *Drawing Lesson, Part I, Line,* Pat Steir has created what she calls "a dictionary of marks," derived from the ways in which artists whom she admires employ line. Each pair of works represents a particular intellectual, emotional, or expressive quality of line. One pair, of which Figure 85 at the left is an example, refers to the work of Rembrandt, particularly to the kinds of effects Rembrandt achieved in works like *The Three Crosses* (Fig. 86). The center square of Steir's piece is a sort of "blow-up" of Rembrandt's basic line; the outside frame shows the wide variety of effects achieved by Rembrandt as he draws this line with greater or lesser density. Rembrandt's lines seem to envelop the scene, shrouding it in a darkness that moves in upon the crucified Christ like a curtain closing upon a play or a storm descending upon a landscape. Rembrandt's line—and Steir's too—becomes more charged emotionally as it becomes denser and darker.

A second pair of Steir's "drawing lessons" is even more emotionally charged. In the center of Figure 87 is a dripping line, one of the basic "signatures" of contemporary abstract painting. It indicates the presence of the artist's brush in front of the canvas. Surrounding it is a series of gestures evocative of Vincent van Gogh. Of the swirling turmoil of line that makes up *The Starry Night* (Fig. 88), van Gogh would write to his brother Theo, "Is it not

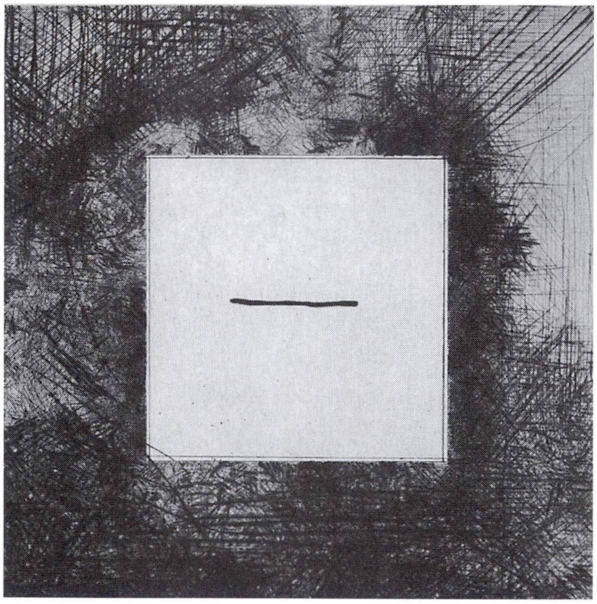

Fig. 85 (above) Pat Steir, *Drawing Lesson, Part I, Line #1,* 1978.
Drypoint with aquatint, from a portfolio of 7 etchings, each 16 × 16 in., edition of 25. Courtesy of Crown Point Press, San Francisco.

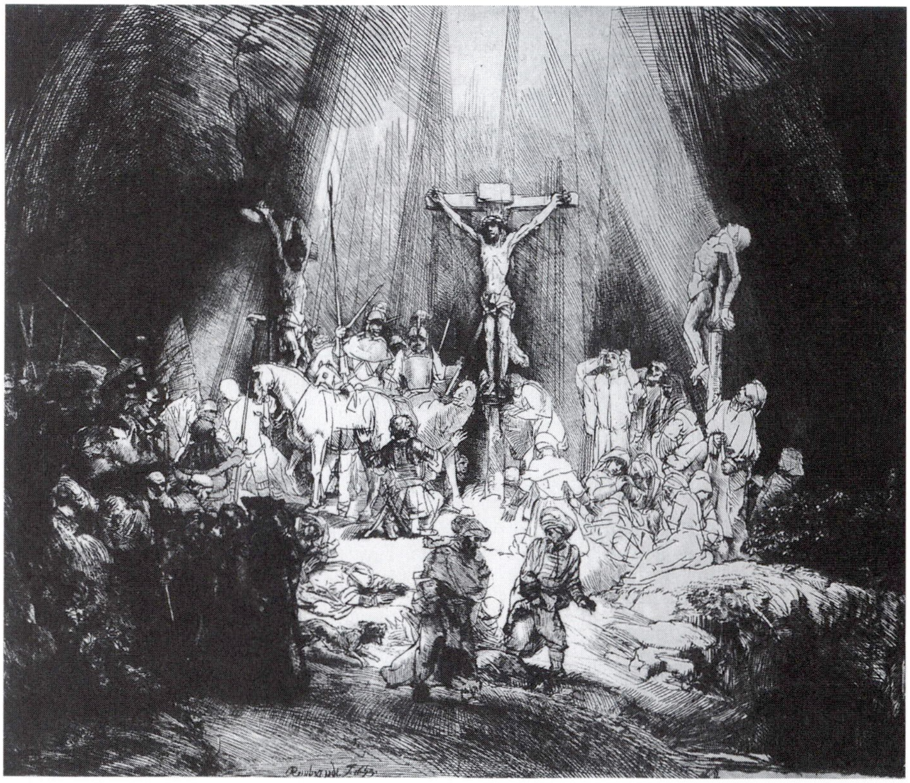

Fig. 86 (right) Rembrandt van Rijn, *The Three Crosses,* 1653.
Etching, 15 ¼ × 17 ¾ in. Reproduced by courtesy of the Trustees of the British Museum.

emotion, the sincerity of one's feeling for nature, that draws us?" Steir has willingly submitted herself to van Gogh's emotion and style. "Getting into his mark," she says, "is like getting onto a merry-go-round, you can't stop. . . . . It's like endless movement."

Expressive Line

Van Gogh's paintings are, for many, some of the most personally expressive in the history of art. When we speak of the **expressive** use of a formal element, such as line, we mean that it expresses powerful emotions. The expressive line of van Gogh is loose and free, so much so that it seems almost out of control. It remains, nevertheless, consistent enough that it is recognizably van Gogh's. It has become, in this sense, **autographic.** Like a signature, it identifies the artist himself, his deeply anguished and creative genius.

During the 15 months just before *The Starry Night* was painted, while he was living in the southern French town of Arles, van Gogh produced a truly amazing quantity of work: 200 paintings, over 100 drawings and watercolors, and roughly 200 letters, mostly written to his brother Theo. Many of these letters help us understand the expressive energies released in this creative outburst. In *Starry Night,* life and death—the town and the heavens—collide, and they are connected by both the church spire and the swaying cypress, a tree traditionally used to mark graves in southern France and Italy. "My paintings are almost a cry of anguish," van Gogh wrote. On July 27, 1890, a little over a year after *The Starry Night* was painted, the artist shot himself in the chest. He died two days later at the age of 37.

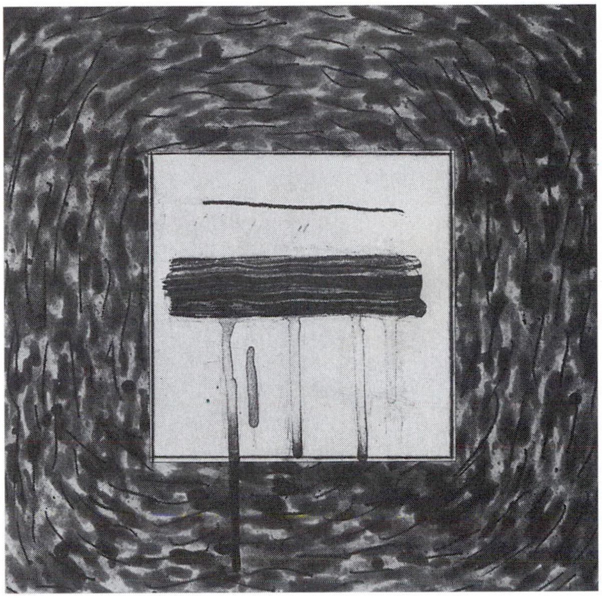

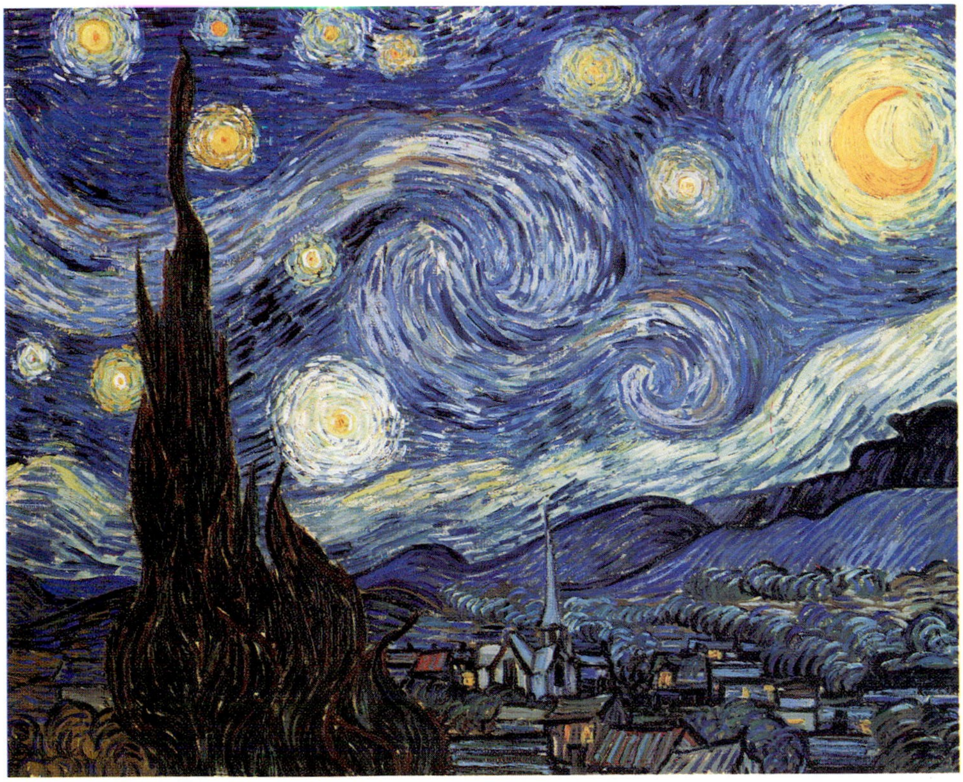

Fig. 87 (above) Pat Steir, *Drawing Lesson, Part I, Line #5,* 1978. Sugar lift aquatint with soft ground etchings, from portfolio of 7 etchings, each 16 × 16 in., edition of 25. Courtesy of Crown Point Press, San Francisco.

Fig. 88 (left) Vincent van Gogh, *The Starry Night,* 1889. Oil on canvas, 29 × 36 1/4 in. The Museum of Modern Art, New York. Acquired through the Lillie P. Bliss Bequest.

Vincent van Gogh's The Sower

We know more about the genesis and development of *The Sower* than almost all of Vincent van Gogh's other paintings, and we can follow the work's progress in some detail.

There are four different descriptions of it in his letters, the first on June 17, 1888, in a letter to Austrian painter John Russell (Fig. 89) that includes a preliminary sketch of his idea. "Am working at a Sower," van Gogh writes in the letter, "the great field all violet the sky & sun very yellow. It is a hard subject to treat."

The difficulties he was facing in the painting were numerous, having particularly to do with a color problem. At sunset, he wrote in a letter to the painter Emile Bernard on the very next day, June 18, the artist was faced with a moment when the "excessive" contrast between the yellow sun and the violet shadows on the field would necessarily "irritate" the beholder's eye. He had to be true to that contrast, and yet find a way to soften it. For approximately eight days he worked on the painting. First he tried making the sower's trousers white in an effort to create a place in the painting that would "allow the eye to rest and distract it." That strategy apparently failing, he tried modifying the yellow and violet areas of the painting. On June 26, he wrote to his brother Theo: "Yesterday and today

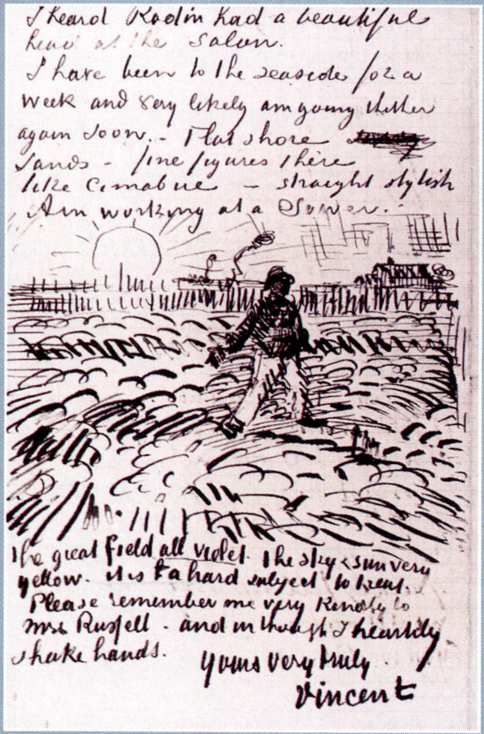
I heard Rodin had a beautiful head at the Salon.
I have been to the seaside for a week and very likely am going thither again soon. - Flat shore sands - fine figures there like Cimabue - straight stylish.
Am working at a Sower.
the great field all violet the sky & sun very yellow. It is a hard subject to treat.
Please remember me very kindly to Mrs Russell - and in thought I heartily shake hands.
Yours very truly
Vincent

Fig. 89 Vincent van Gogh, *"Letter to John Russell"* (with drawing of Sower), April 1888.
Ink on wove paper. Thannhauser Collection: Courtesy of the Thannhauser Foundation. Photograph by Robert E. Mates.

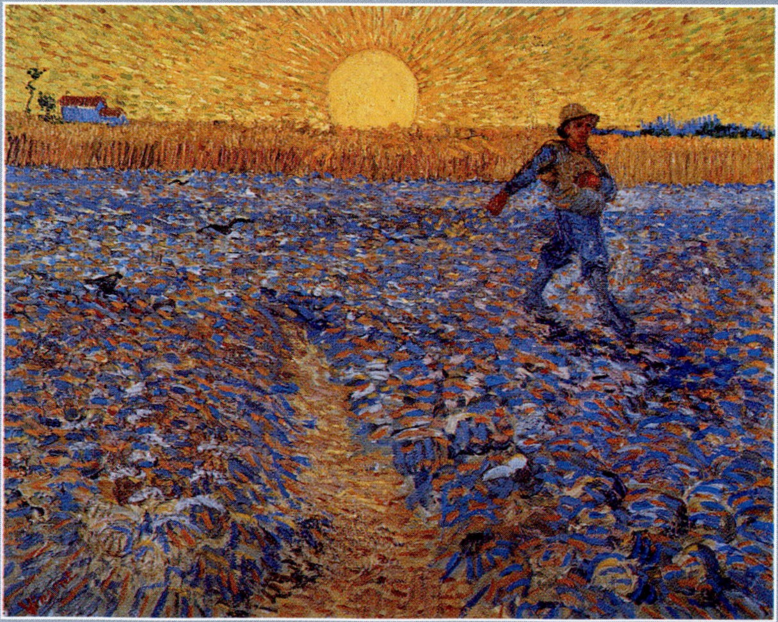

...h. *The Sower,* 1888.
...d, lower left: Vincent.
...tterlo, The Netherlands.

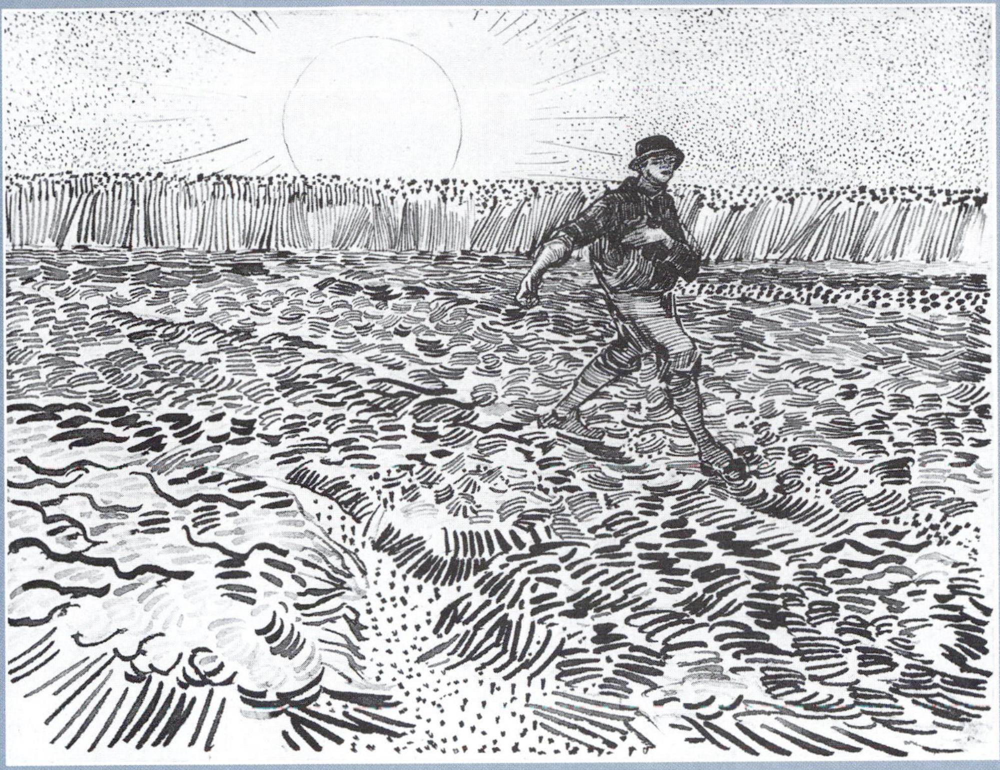

Fig. 91 Vincent van Gogh, *The Sower*, 1888.
Pencil, reed pen, brown and black ink on wove paper, 9 5/8 × 12 1/2 in.
Rijksmuseum Vincent van Gogh, Amsterdam. Vincent van Gogh Foundation.

I worked on the sower, which is completely recast. The sky is yellow and green, the ground violet and orange." This plan succeeded (Fig. 90). Each area of the painting now contained color that connected it to the opposite area, green to violet and orange to yellow.

The sower was, for van Gogh, the symbol of his own "longing for the infinite," as he wrote to Bernard, and having finished the painting, he remained, in August, still obsessed with the image. "The idea of the Sower continues to haunt me all the time," he would write to Theo. In fact, he had begun to think of the finished painting as a study that was itself a preliminary work leading to drawing (Fig. 91). "Now the harvest, the Garden, the Sower . . . are sketches after painted studies. I think all these ideas are good," he wrote to Theo on August 8, "but the painted studies lack clearness of touch. That is [the] reason why I felt it necessary to draw them."

In the drawing, sun, wheat, and the sower himself are enlarged, made more monumental. The house and tree on the left have been eliminated, causing us to focus more on the sower himself, whose stride is now wider and who seems more intent on his task. But it is the clarity of van Gogh's line that is especially astonishing. Here we have a sort of anthology of line types: short and long, curved and straight, wide and narrow. Lines of each type seem to group themselves into bundles of five or ten, and each bundle seems to possess its own direction and flow, creating a sense of the tilled field's uneven but regular furrows. It is as if, wanting to represent his longing for the infinite, as it is contained at the moment of the genesis of life, sowing the field, van Gogh himself returns to the most fundamental element in art—line itself.

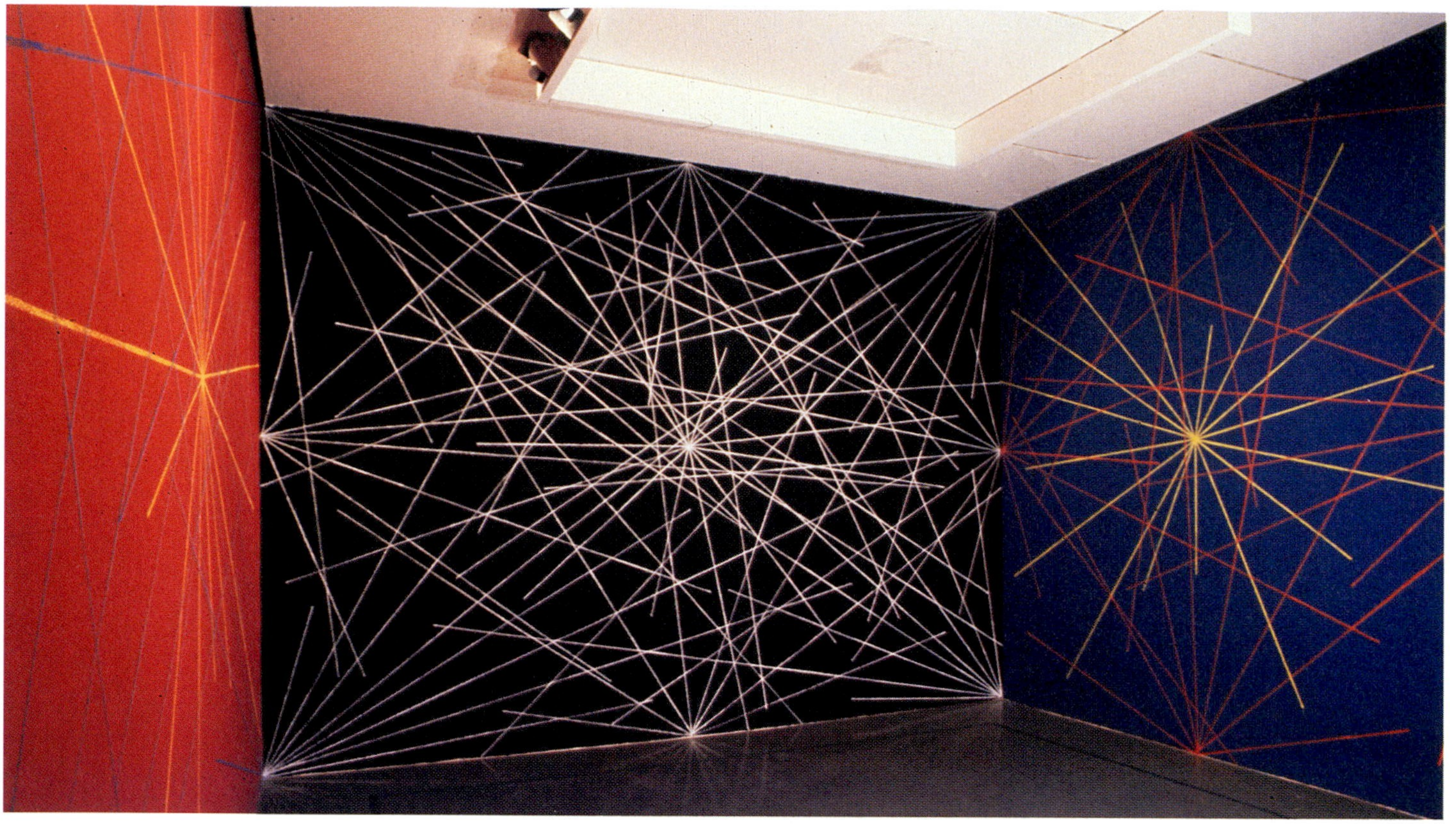

Fig 92 Sol LeWitt, *Lines from Four Corners to Points on a Grid,* 1976.
Chalk on four painted walls. Installation, Museum of Modern Art, New York, 1978.
Collection The Whitney Museum of American Art, New York.
Photograph: John Weber Gallery, New York.

Analytic or Classical Line

Sol LeWitt, whose work is the source, incidentally, of another pair of Steir's *Drawing Lessons,* employs a line that is equally autographic, recognizably his own, but one that reveals to us a personality very different from van Gogh's (Figs. 89, 90, and 91). LeWitt's line is *analytical* where van Gogh's is expressive. LeWitt's **analytic line** is precise, controlled, mathematically rigorous, logical, and rationally organized, where van Gogh's **expressive line** is imprecise, emotionally charged, and almost chaotic. One seems a product of the mind, the other of the heart.

A measure of the removal of LeWitt's art from personal expression is that very often LeWitt does not even draw his own lines. The works are usually generated by museum staff according to LeWitt's instructions. If a museum "owns" a LeWitt, it does not own the actual wall drawing but only the instructions on how to make it. As a result, LeWitt's works are temporary, but they are always resurrectable. *Lines from Four Corners to Points on a Grid* (Fig. 92) is, in fact, in the collection of the Whitney Museum—that is to say, the instructions for making it are in the Whitney's collection—but it was "borrowed" by the Museum of Modern Art for the installation illustrated here. Since LeWitt often writes his instructions so that the staff executing the drawing must make their own decisions about the placement and arrangement of the lines, the work changes from appearance to appearance.

In LeWitt's drawing, the geometry of the room's architecture, with its strong sense of the vertical, the horizontal, and the right angle, helps lend the work a sense of mathematical precision and regularity. But it is probably the **grid,** the pattern of vertical and horizontal lines crossing each other to make squares, that most characteristically dominates compositions of this variety. So strong is the grid's sense of orderliness and regularity that it can easily lend a sense of rational organization and logical operations to even the most expressive compositions. Jasper Johns's *Numbers in Colors* (Fig. 93) is a case in point. Johns's brushwork—what we call his *gesture*—is fluid and loose, almost as expressive as van Gogh's, yet the grid here seems to contain and control it, to exercise some sort of rational authority over it. The numbers themselves repeat regularly, and like the alphabet, which arbitrarily organizes random elements into a coherent system, they impose a sense of logic where none necessarily exists.

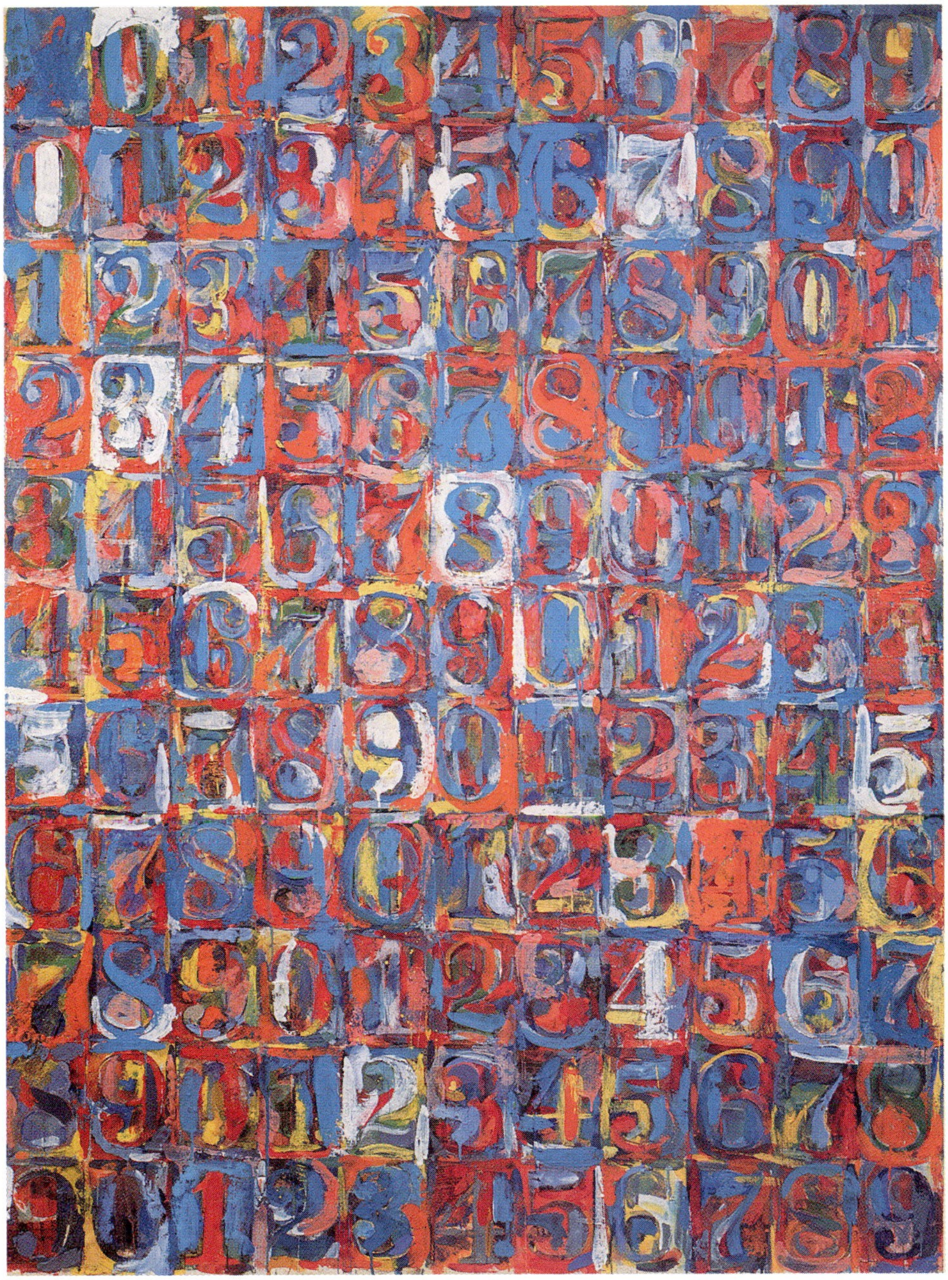

Fig. 93 Jasper Johns, "*Numbers in Color*," 1958–1959.
Encaustic and collage on canvas, 67 × 49 1/2 in. Albright-Knox Art Gallery, Buffalo, New York. Gift of Seymour H. Knox. Leo Castelli Gallery. © Jasper Johns/Licensed by VAGA, New York.

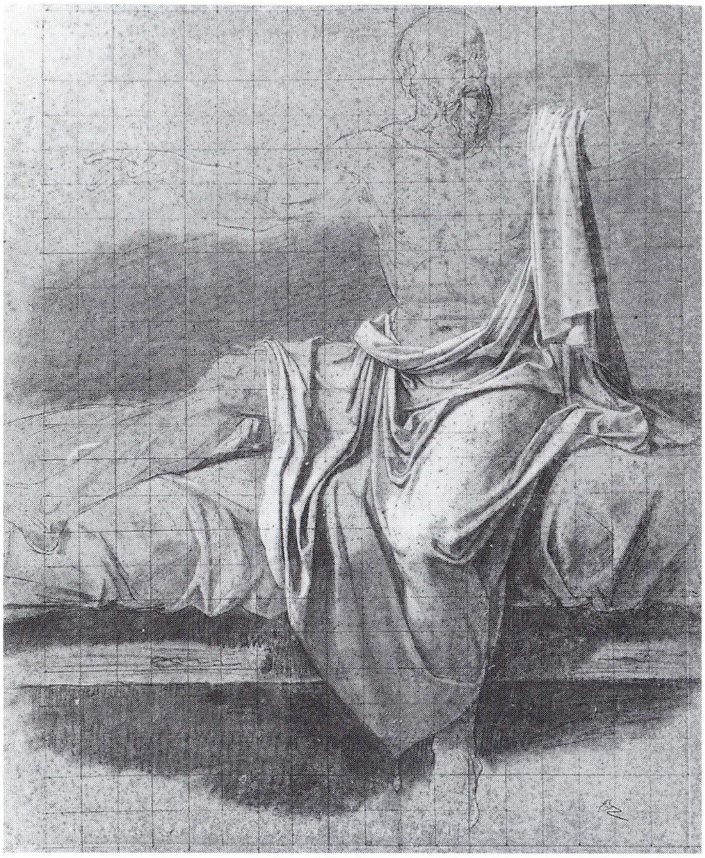

Fig. 94 Jacques Louis David,
***Study for the Death of Socrates,* 1787.**
Charcoal heightened in white on gray-brown paper, 20 1/2 × 17 in. Musée Bonnat, Bayonne.

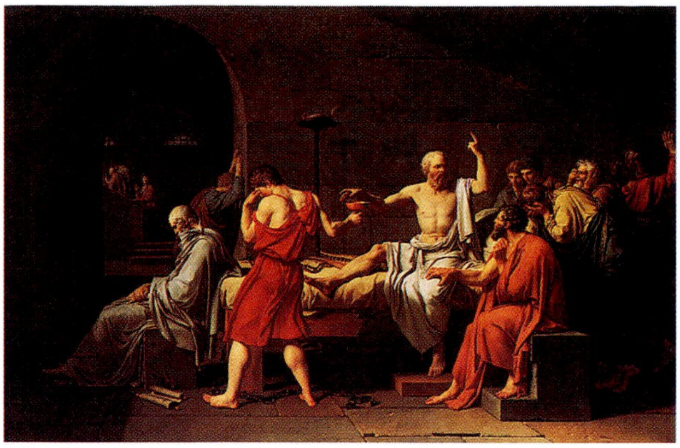

Fig. 95 Jacques Louis David,
***The Death of Socrates,* 1787.**
Oil on canvas, 51 × 77 1/4 in. Metropolitan Museum of Art, New York. Wolfe Fund, 1931. Catherine Lorillard Collection. 31.45.

Analytic line is closely related to what is widely referred to as **classical line.** The word "classical" refers to the Greek art of the fifth century BCE, but by association it has come to refer to any art that is based on logical, rational principles, and that is executed in a deliberate, precise manner. In his *Study for the Death of Socrates* (Fig. 94), Jacques Louis David portrays Socrates, the father of philosophy, about to drink deadly hemlock after the Greek state convicted him of corrupting his students, the youth of Athens, by his teaching. In this preliminary drawing, David has submitted the figure of Socrates to a mathematical grid that survives into the final painting (Fig. 95). Notice especially the gridwork of stone blocks that form the wall behind the figures. The human body is not constructed of parallels and perpendiculars, of course, but David has rendered it almost as if it is.

The structure and control evident in David's classical line is underscored by comparing it to Eugène Delacroix's much more expressive and romantic *Study for The Death of Sardanapalus* (Fig. 96). (The term **romantic,** often used to describe nineteenth-century art such as Delacroix's, does not refer just to the expression of love, but to the expression of all feelings and passions.) The finished painting (Fig. 97) shows Sardanapalus, the last king of the second Assyrian dynasty at the end of the ninth century BCE, who was besieged in his city by an enemy army. He ordered all his horses, dogs, servants, and wives slain before him, and all his belongings destroyed, so that none of his pleasures would survive him when his kingdom was overthrown. The drawing is a study for the lower corner of the bed, with its elephant-head bedpost, and, below it, on the floor, a pile of jewelry and musical instruments. The figure of the nude leaning back against the bed in the finished work, perhaps already dead, can be seen at the right edge of the study. Delacroix's line is quick, imprecise, and fluid. Compared to David's, his final painting seems a flurry of curves, knots, and linear webs. It is emotional, almost violent, while David's painting is calm, in exactly the spirit of Socrates.

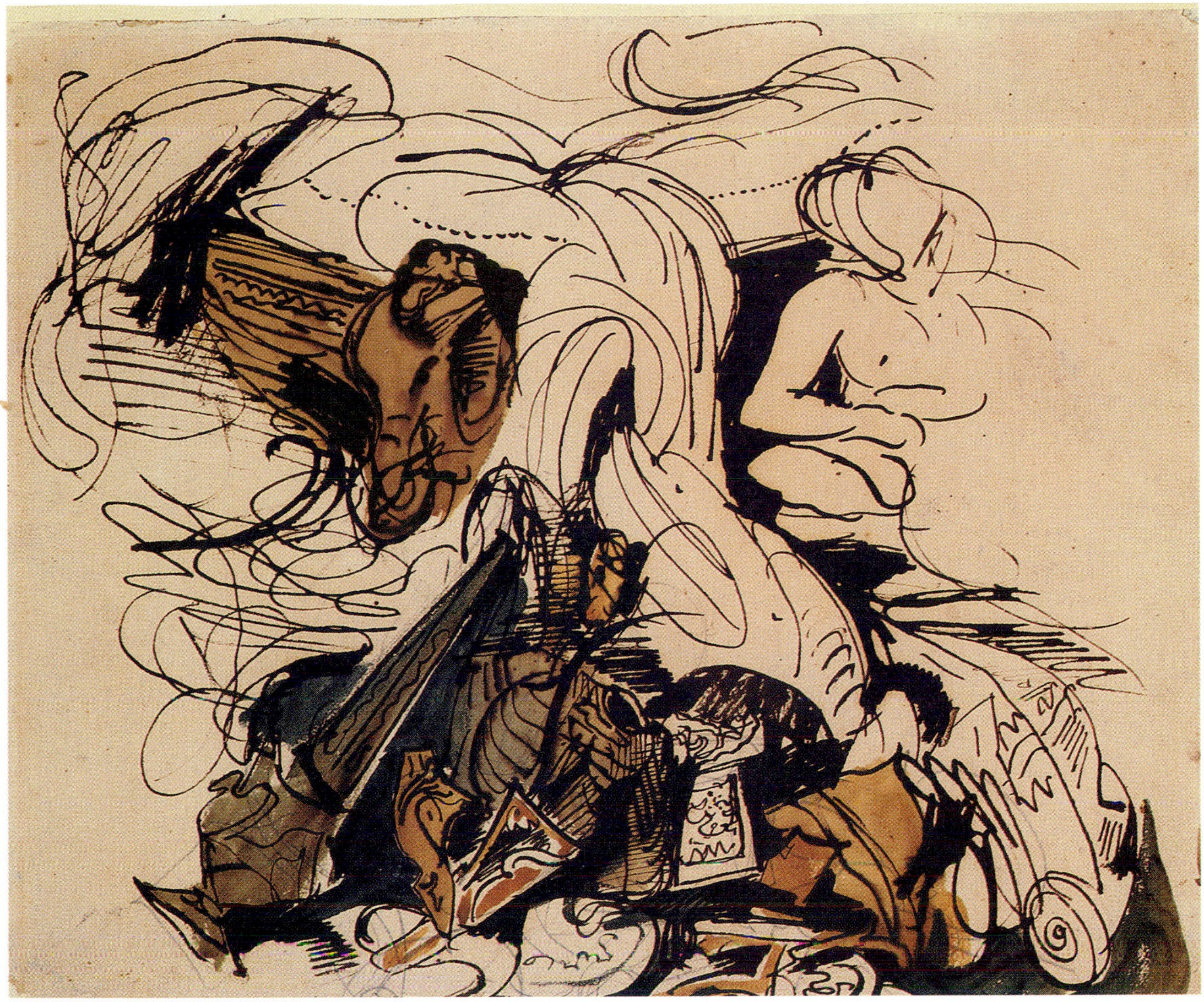

Fig. 96 Eugène Delacroix, "*Study for The Death of Sardanapalus*," 1827–1828.
Pen, watercolor, and pencil, 10 ¼ × 12 ½ in. Cabinet des Dessins, Musée du Louvre, Paris. Cliche des Musées Nationaux – Paris © Photo R.M.N. – SPADEM.

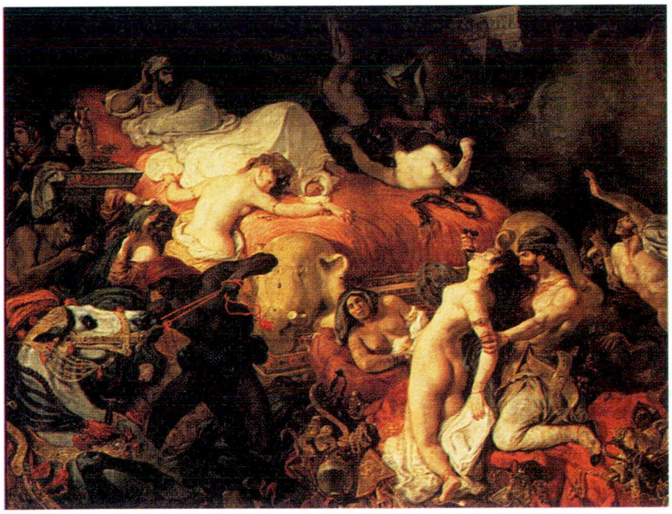

Fig. 97 Eugène Delacroix, *The Death of Sardanapalus,* 1828.
Oil on canvas, 153 ½ × 195 in. Musée du Louvre, Paris.

LINE AND CULTURAL CONVENTION

Especially in the depiction of human anatomy, certain cultural assumptions have come to be associated with the use of line. Conventionally, classical line is "logical," "rational," and closely identified with the male form. Expressive line is less clear, less "logical," more emotional and intuitive, and characteristically identified with the female form. The implications of this convention are worth exploring in some detail.

Compare, for example, the sculptures of the male and female figures above. The Greek bronze (Fig. 98), identified by some as Zeus, king of the Greek gods, and by others as Poseidon, Greek god of the sea, has been submitted to very nearly the same mathematical grid as David's Socrates. This is especially evident in the definition of the god's chest and stomach muscles, which have been sculpted with great attention to detail, and in the extraordinary horizontality of the outstretched left arm. The severe intensity and powerful muscularity of the male god is far removed from Praxiteles's more spontaneous and casual treatment of the female figure (Fig. 99). Completed more than 100 years after the Zeus, it renders Aphrodite, the Greek goddess of beauty and love, in very different terms. Every angle of her figure is softened and rounded, so that her body seems to echo the gentle folds of the drapery that she drops over the vase to her left. Her weight is shifted entirely over her right foot, and her hip is thus thrust out to the right, to emphasize the essential curvilinear structure of her anatomy. Though in fact she is composed using essentially the same mathematical grid as the Zeus, the logic of that grid has been suppressed by the curve.

Consider also Ingres's giant *Jupiter and Thetis* of 1811 (Fig. 100). Not only is the adoring Thetis composed of an array of curves as soft as the folds of the drapery covering her lower body, but she is much smaller than the giant god at whose feet she kneels. The grand and indifferent Jupiter, like the vertical and horizontal lines that define him, is the personification of reason and power—the male—while Thetis is the embodiment of the sensual and the submissive—the female.

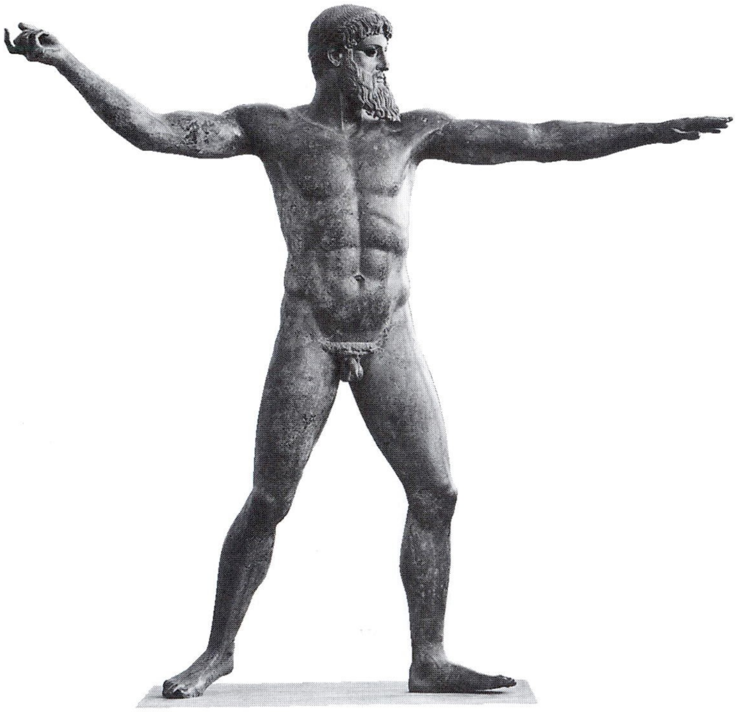

Fig. 98 ***Zeus,* or *Poseidon,* c. 460 BCE.**
Bronze, H. 82 in.
National Archeological Museum, Athens.

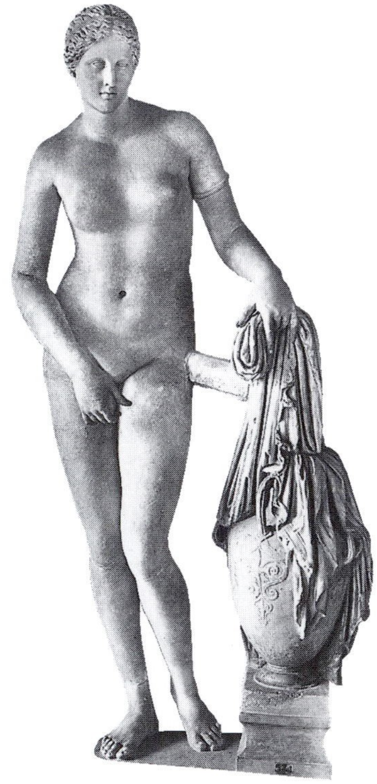

Fig. 99 Roman copy after Praxiteles, *Aphrodite of Knidos,* 4th century BCE original.
Marble, H. 80 in. Vatican Museums, Rome. Alinari/Art Resource.

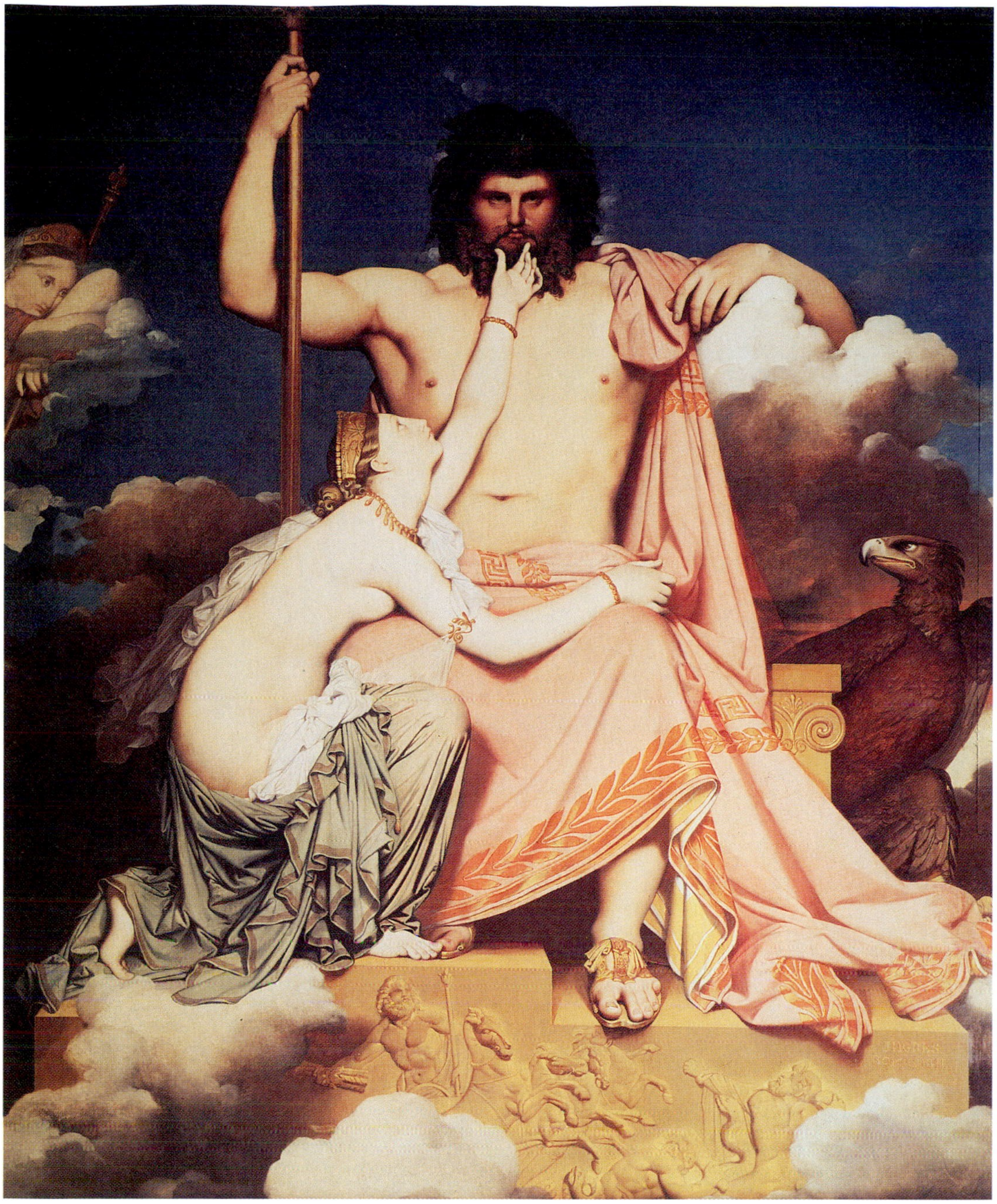

Fig. 100 Jean-Auguste-Dominique Ingres, *Jupiter and Thetis,* 1811.
Oil on canvas, 130 5/8 × 101 1/4 in. Musée Granet, Aix-en-Provence.

While conventional representations of the male and female nude carry with them recognizably sexist implications—man as strong and rational, woman as weak and given to emotional outbursts—these same conventions are nonetheless important to our understanding of much of Western art. It should come as no surprise that the biases of our culture are reflected in its art, even in the most fundamental of art's formal elements—line.

Line is, in summation, an extremely versatile element. Thick or thin, short or long, straight or curved, line can outline shapes and forms, indicate the contour of a volume, and imply direction and movement. Lines of sight can connect widely separated parts of a composition. Depending on how it is employed, line can seem extremely intellectual and rational or highly expressive and emotional. It is, above all, the artist's most basic tool.

CHAPTER 5

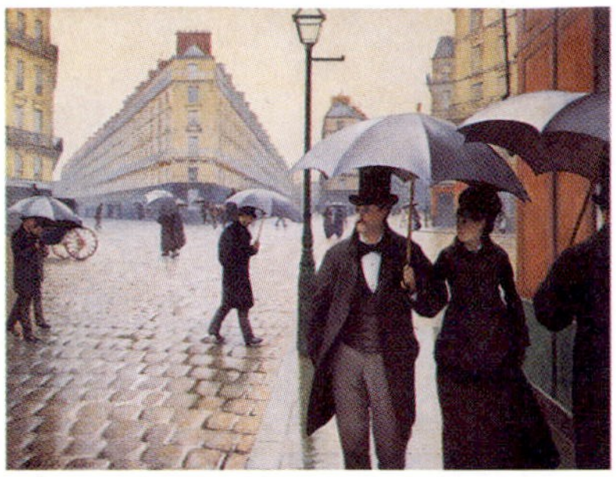

Space

Shape and Mass

Three-Dimensional Space

Two-Dimensional Space

Linear Perspective

WORKS IN PROGRESS
Bill Viola's *The Greeting*

Some Other Means of Representing Space

Distortions of Space and Foreshortening

Modern Experiments and New Dimensions

We live in a physical world whose properties are familiar, and, together with line, space is one of the most familiar. It is all around us, all the time. We talk about outer space—the space outside our world—and "inner" space—the space inside our own minds. We cherish our own "space." We give "space" to people or things that scare us. But in the twentieth century, space has become a more and more contested issue. Since Einstein, we have come to recognize that the space in which we live is fluid.

It takes place in time. We have developed new kinds of space as well—the space of mass media, the Internet, the computer screen, "virtual reality," and cyberspace. All these new kinds of space result, as we shall see, in new media for artists to work in. But first, we need to define some elementary concepts of shape and mass.

SHAPE AND MASS

A **shape** is flat. In mathematical terms, a shape is a two-dimensional *area,* that is, its boundaries can be measured in terms of height and width. A **mass,** on the other hand, is a solid that occupies a three-dimensional *volume.* It must be measured in terms of height, width, and depth. Though mass also implies density and weight, in the simplest terms, the difference between shape and mass is the difference between a square and a cube, a circle and a sphere.

Donald Sultan's *Lemons, May 16, 1984* (Fig. 101) is an image of three lemons, but it consists of a single yellow shape on a black ground nearly eight feet square. To create the image, Sultan covered vinyl composite tile with tar. Then he drew the outline of the lemons, scraped out the area inside the outline, filled it with plaster, and painted the plaster area yellow. The shape of the three lemons is created not only by the outline Sultan drew but also by the contrasting colors and textures, black and yellow, tar and plaster.

Martin Puryear's *Self* (Fig. 102) is a sculptural mass standing nearly six feet high. Made of wood, it looms out of the floor like a giant basalt outcropping, and it seems to satisfy the other implied meanings of mass—that is, it seems to possess weight and density as well as volume. "It looks as though it might have been created by erosion," Puryear has said, "like a rock worn by sand and weather until the angles are all gone. . . . It's meant to be a visual notion of the self, rather than any particular self—the self as a secret entity, as a secret, hidden place." And in fact, it does not possess the mass it visually announces. It is actually very lightweight, built of thin layers of wood over a hollow core. This hidden, almost secret fragility is the "self" of Puryear's title.

One of the most interesting things about Sultan's *Lemons* is that, though it is completely flat, it implies three-dimensional space. We

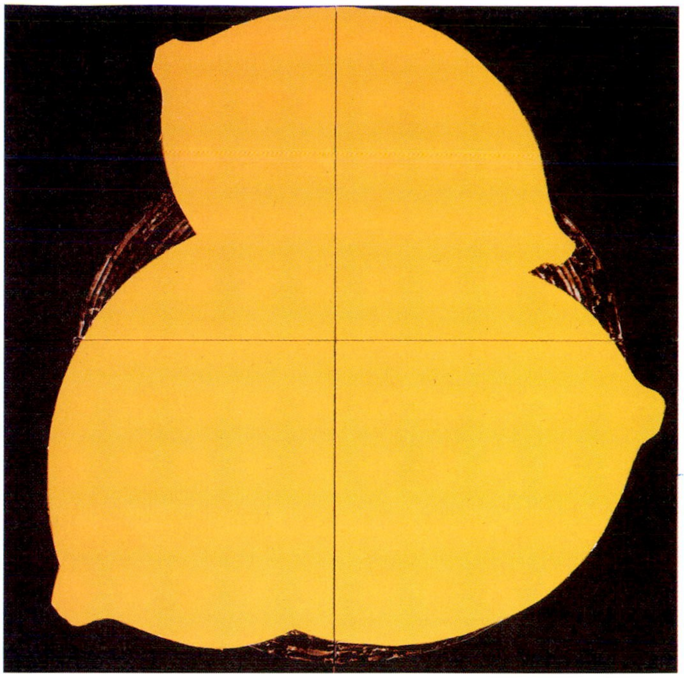

Fig. 101 Donald Sultan, *Lemons, May 16, 1984,* 1984.
Latex, tar on vinyl tile over wood, 97 × 97 ½ in.
Virginia Museum of Fine Arts, Richmond, Virginia. Gift of The Sydney and Frances Lewis Foundation. Photograph: Katherine Wetzel, © 1996 Virginia Museum of Fine Arts.

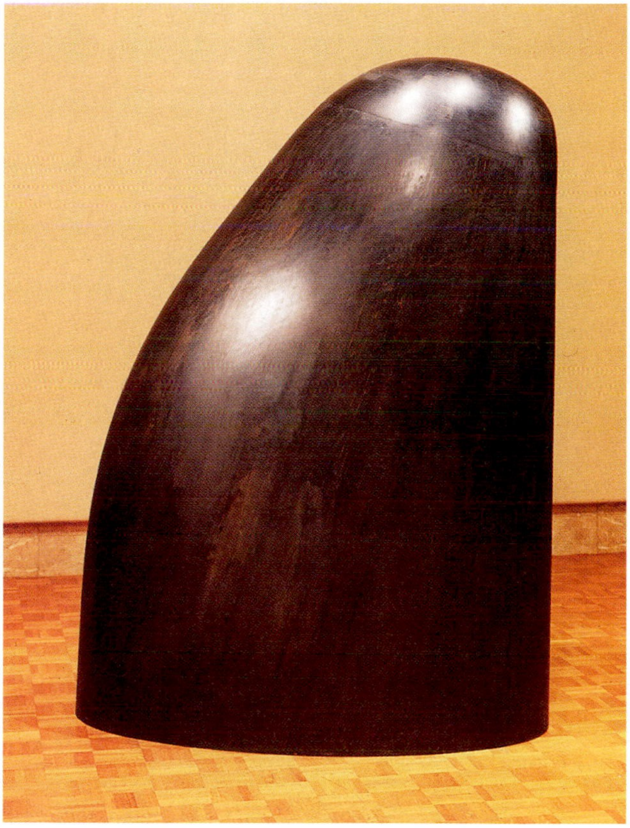

Fig. 102 Martin Puryear (b. 1941), *Self,* 1978.
Polychromed red cedar and mahogany, 69 × 48 × 25 in.
Joslyn Art Museum, Omaha, Nebraska.

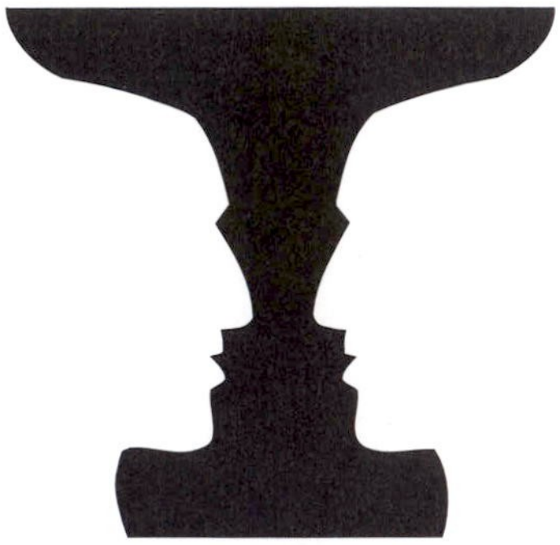

Fig. 103 Rubin vase.

tend to read the painting from the bottom to the top—the left-hand lemon as closest to us and the top lemon as furthest away—although it is simple enough to imagine any one of the lemons as lying on top of the other two. But the point is that the instant we place any shape on a ground, a sense of space is activated. In Figure 103, the black vase seems to sit on a white ground. When, conversely, we look at the white as shape and the black as ground, our perceptual experience of the same space is radically altered. What was the foreground vase becomes the background space, and we see two faces peering at one another. Such **figure-ground reversals** help us recognize how our perceptual experience fundamentally depends on our recognition of the spatial relationships between an object and what lies beside and behind it.

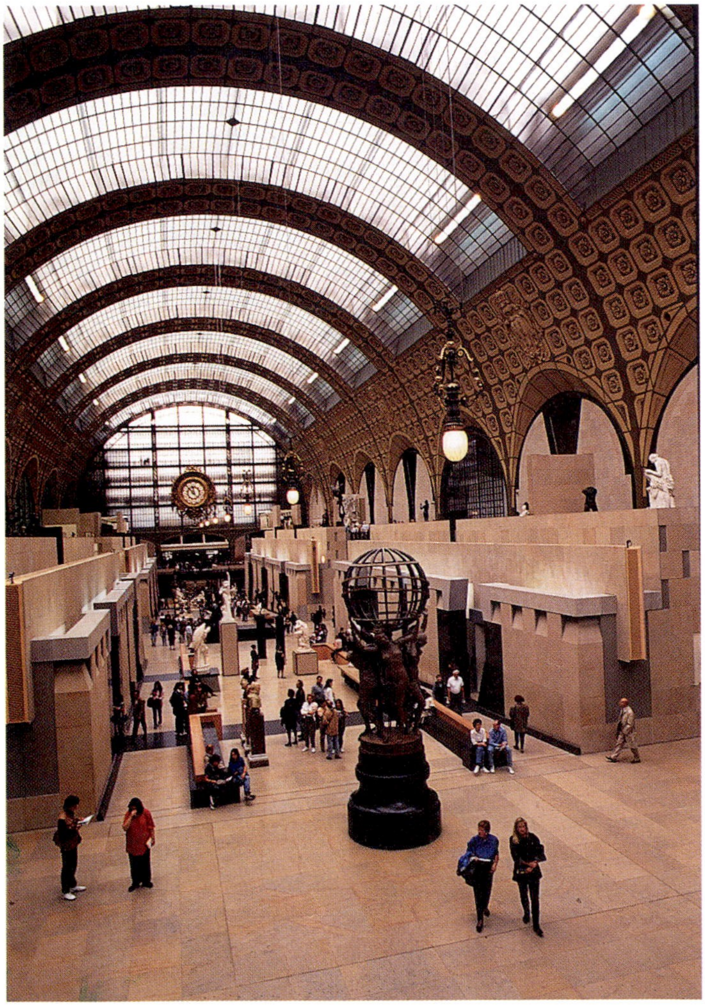

Fig. 104 Musée d'Orsay, Paris, Gae Aluenti architect, 1986.
John Brooks/Gamma–Liaison, Inc.

THREE-DIMENSIONAL SPACE

The world that we live in (our homes, our streets, our cities), has been carved out of **three-dimensional space.** A building surrounds empty space in such a way as to frame it or outline it. Walls shape the space they contain, and rooms acquire a sense of volume and form. In 1986, architect Gae Aluenti transformed a nineteenth-century Parisian railroad station into the new home for late-nineteenth- and early-twentieth-century art, the now famous Musée d'Orsay (Fig. 104). Aluenti maintained the space defined by the architecture of the original station, with its arched 100-hundred foot ceiling stretching to a length of 150 yards, but across the bottom of this space he carved new cubical and rectilinear gallery rooms. The sculptural quality of these rooms is underscored by the way in which their lines are echoed in the benches and actual sculptures that fill the central walkway through the space. The massive presence of all these new forms stands in marked contrast to the airiness of the original building, but these new spaces also lend the building a sense of monumentality and solidity, a dignity befitting the works of art they contain.

Barbara Hepworth's *Two Figures* (Fig. 105) consists of two standing vertical masses that occupy three-dimensional space in a manner similar to standing human forms. Into each of these figures she has carved out **negative shapes**

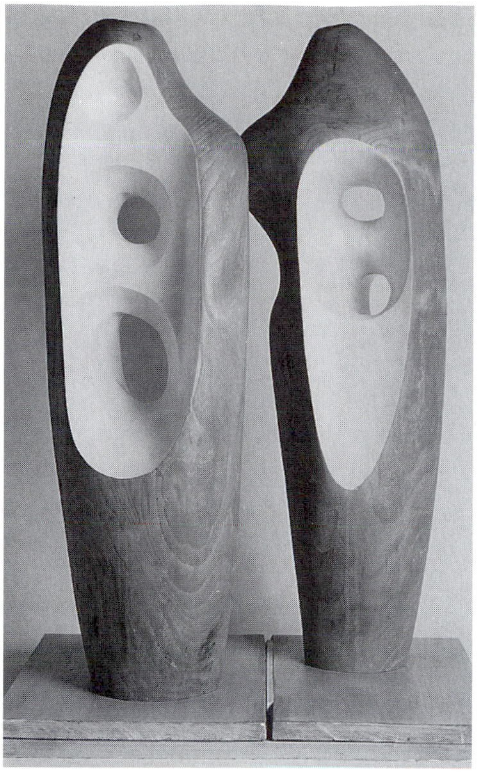

Fig. 105 Barbara Hepworth, *Two Figures,* 1947–1948.
Elmwood and white paint, 38 × 17 in. Frederick R. Weisman Art Museum, University of Minnesota, Minneapolis.

or **negative spaces,** so called because they are empty spaces that acquire a sense of volume and form by means of the outline or frame that surrounds them, like the rooms in the Musée d'Orsay. Hepworth has painted these negative spaces white. Especially in the left-hand figure, the negative shapes suggest anatomical features: the top round indentation suggests a head, the middle hollow a breast, and the bottom hole a belly, with the elmwood wrapping around the figure like a cloak.

The negative space formed by the bowl of the ceremonial spoon of the Dan people native to Liberia and the Ivory Coast (Fig. 106) likewise suggests anatomy. Nearly a foot in length and called the "belly pregnant with rice," the bowl represents the generosity of the most hospitable woman of the clan, who is known as the *wunkirle.* The *wunkirle* carries this spoon at festivals, where she dances and sings. As *wunkirles* from other clans arrive, the festivals become competitions, each woman striving to give away more than the others. Finally the most generous *wunkirle* of all is proclaimed, and the men sing in her honor.

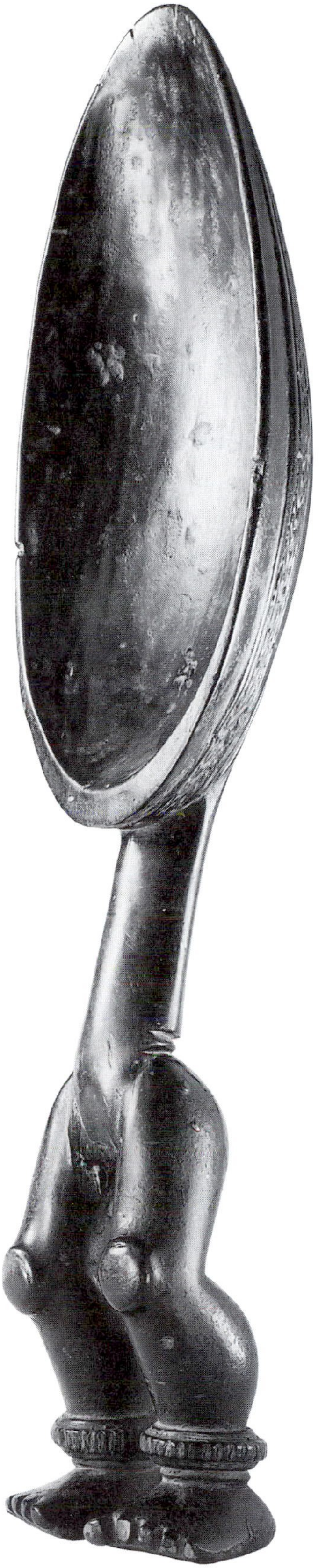

Fig. 106 Feast-making spoon, Liberia/Ivory Coast, Dan, 20th century.
Wood and iron, H. 24 1/4 in. The Seattle Art Museum, Gift of Katherine C. White and the Boeing Company. 81.17.204.

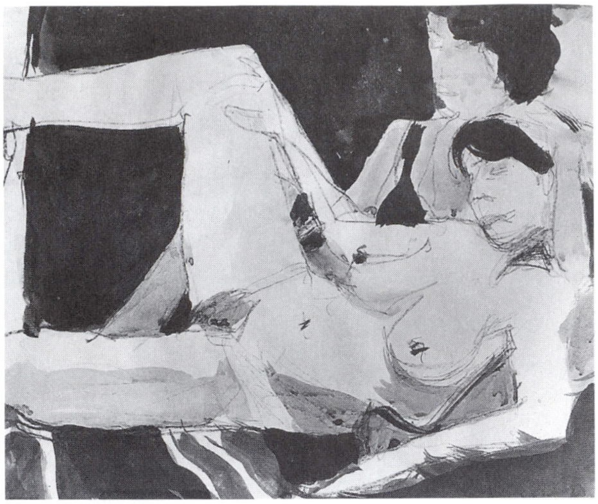

Fig. 107 Richard Diebenkorn, *Two Nudes*, 1962.
Graphite and gouache on paper, 13 15/16 × 16 7/8 in. Glenn C. Janss Collection.

TWO-DIMENSIONAL SPACE

While sculptors and architects define forms out of empty three-dimensional space, painters begin with an empty canvas, a two-dimensional space. **Two-dimensional space** is flat, possessing height and width, but no depth. A sense of depth, of three dimensions, can only be achieved by means of *illusion*.

In Richard Diebenkorn's *Two Nudes* (Fig. 107), the untouched white ground of the paper—also called the **reserve**—is surrounded by drawing in ink so that it seems to stand forward from the paper itself to become the nude's body. As in the figure-ground reversal discussed at the beginning of this section, we no longer read the drawing's white space as background, but rather as illuminated flesh. The figure-ground reversal creates an illusion. Our eyes read the whiteness as representing the model's body, but it is literally the whiteness of the paper that we see.

There are many ways to create the illusion of deep space on the flat surface of the paper or canvas, and most are used simultaneously. For example, we recognize that objects close to us appear larger than objects farther away, creating a change in **scale.** Objects closer to the viewer **overlap** and cover other objects behind them. Both a change in scale and overlapping inform the creation of the space in Caspar David Friedrich's *Woman in Morning Light* (Fig. 108). The woman looking out at the rising sun is *literally* larger than the mountains in the "distance," and she blocks out our view of the sun, overlapping it. But we do not think of her as a giant. We simply recognize that she is closer than the mountain to the surface of the painting, which is called the **picture plane.** Her position is, in fact, similar to our own as viewers, and together, we look out on the new day with all its possibility and promise.

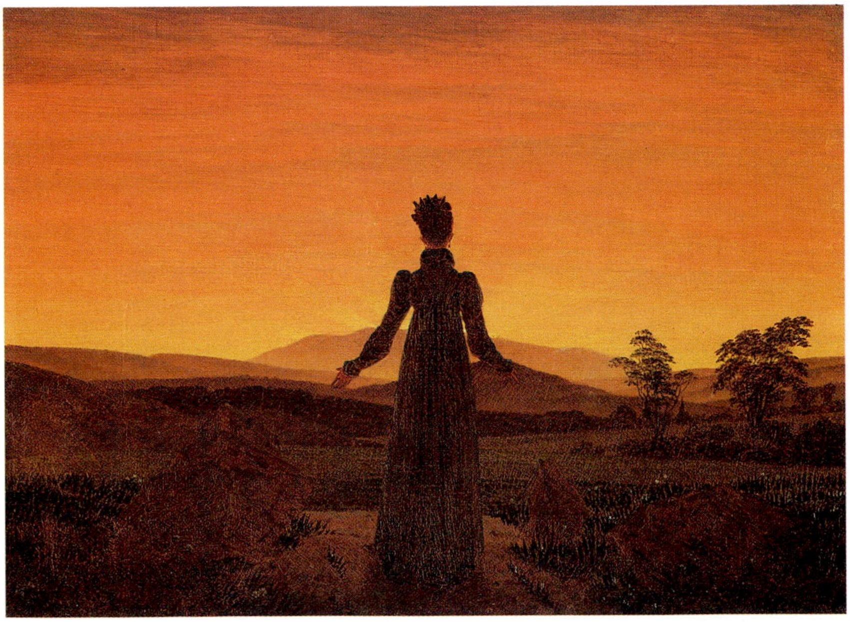

Fig. 108 Caspar David Friedrich, *Woman in Morning Light*, 1818.
Oil on canvas, 8 3/4 × 11 3/4 in. Museum Folkwang, Essen, Germany.

LINEAR PERSPECTIVE

The lines emanating from Friedrich's sun evoke certain principles of perspective, one of the most convincing means of representing three-dimensional space on a two-dimensional surface. **Perspective** is a system, known to the Greeks and Romans but not mathematically codified until the Renaissance, that, in simplest terms, allows the picture plane to function as a window through which a specific scene is presented to the viewer. In **one-point linear perspective** (Fig. 109), lines are drawn on the picture plane in such a way to represent parallel lines receding to a single point on the viewer's horizon called the **vanishing point.** When the vanishing point is directly across from the viewer's **vantage point,** the recession is said to be **frontal,** as in the drawing at the left. If the vanishing point is to one side or the other, the recession is said to be **diagonal,** as in the drawing on the right in Figure 109.

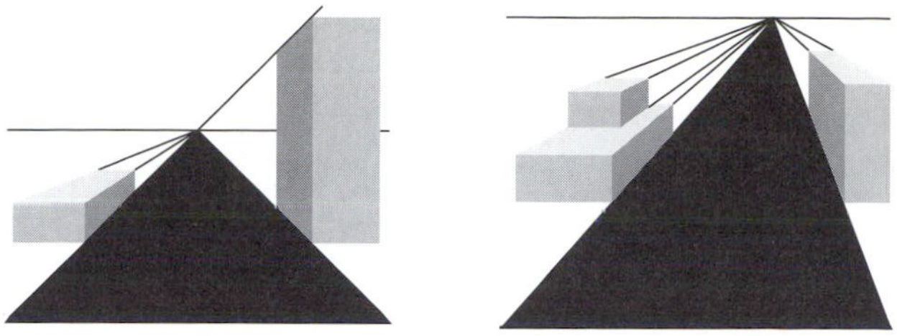

Fig. 109 One-point linear perspective.
Left: frontal recession, street level. Right: diagonal recession, elevated position.

To judge the effectiveness of linear perspective as a system capable of creating the illusion of real space on a two-dimensional surface, we need only look at an example of a work painted before linear perspective was fully understood and then compare it to works in which the system is successfully employed. In 1228, just two years after the death of St. Francis, a basilica was built in his honor in Assisi, Italy. The greatest painters of the day were sought to decorate it. The laws of perspective would not be worked out for nearly 200 years, but in a series of 28 frescoes depicting the life of St. Francis, often thought to be the work of Giotto, we can witness an artist attempting to grasp the principles intuitively. Notice how, in the scene *St. Francis Renouncing His Earthly Possessions* (Fig. 110), the feet of St. Francis, standing on the right (with the halo) seem unnaturally close to the building behind him and how the column supporting the building on the far right seems to descend into the head of his follower. In fact, if we draw perspective lines along the major elements of this building (Fig. 111), we can see that they fly off in any number of directions and never come together at a common vanishing point. Thus, the space of this painting seems unrealistic and artificial.

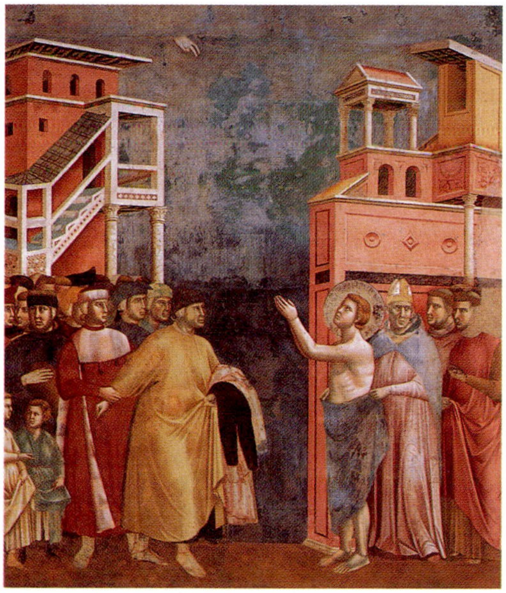

Fig. 110 Assisi, Upper Church of S. Francesco. Giotto and pupils, *St. Francis Renouncing His Earthly Possessions,* Fresco c. 1295–1330.

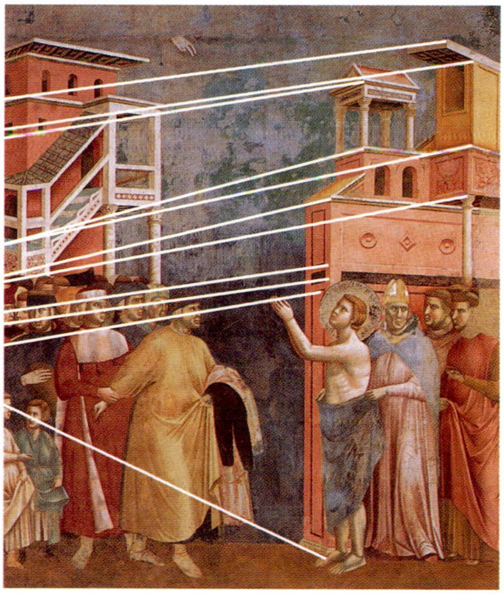

Fig. 111 Perspective analysis of *St. Francis Renouncing His Earthly Possessions.*

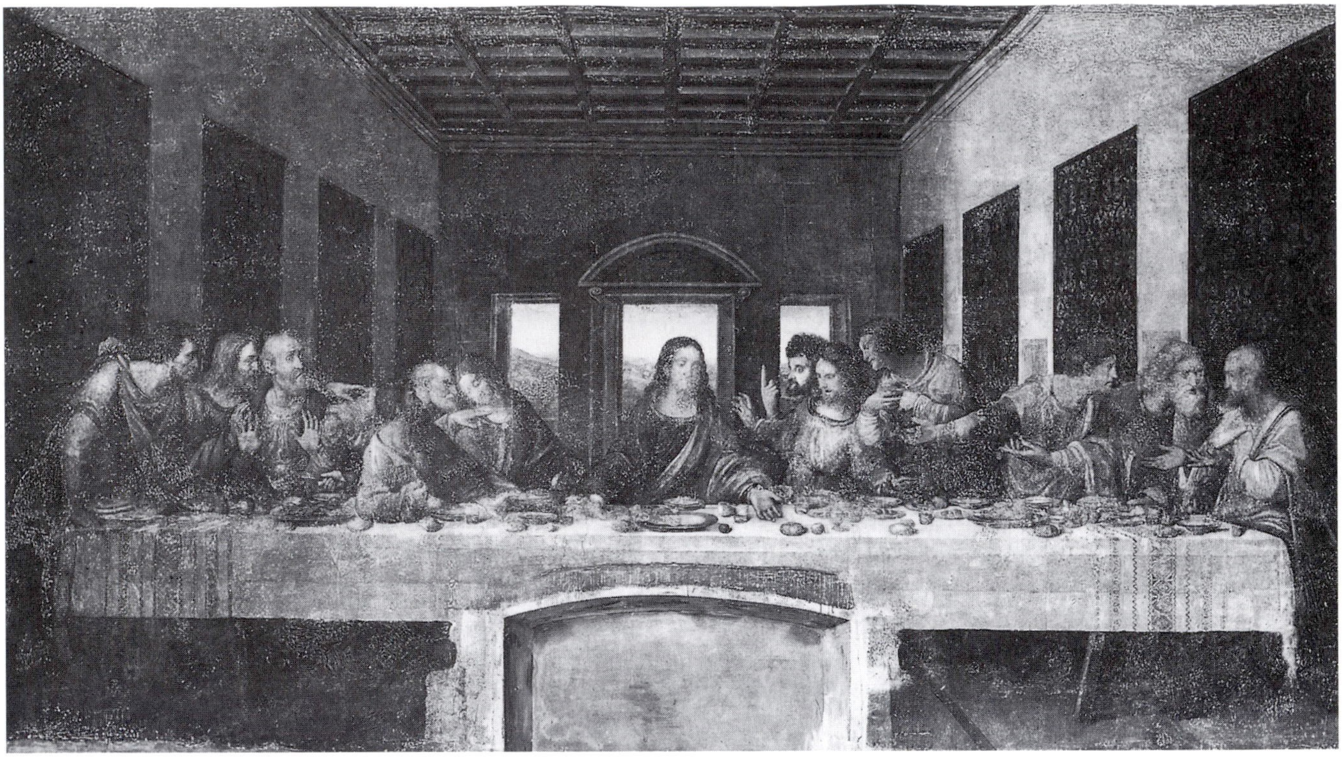

Fig. 112 Leonardo da Vinci, *The Last Supper*, c. 1495–1498.
Mural (oil and tempera on plaster), 15 ft. 1 ⅛ in. × 28 ft. 10 ½ in.
Refectory, Monastery of Santa Maria delle Grazie, Milan, Italy.

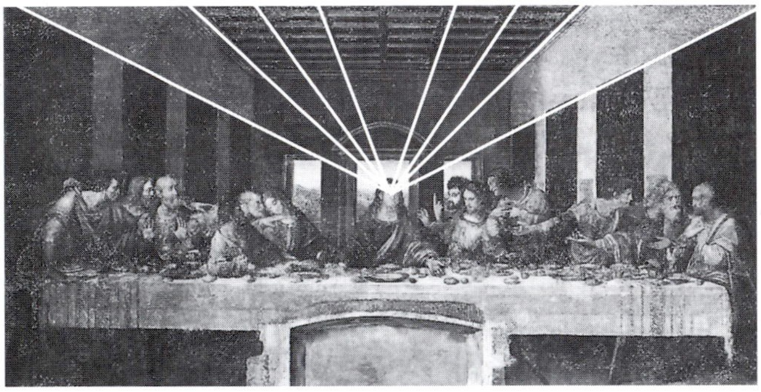

Fig. 113 Perspective analysis of *The Last Supper*.

By way of contrast, the space of Leonardo da Vinci's famous depiction of *The Last Supper* (Fig. 112) is completely convincing. Leonardo employs a fully frontal one-point perspective system, as the perspective analysis shows (Fig. 113). This system focuses our attention on Christ, since the perspective lines appear almost as rays of light radiating from Christ's head. *The Last Supper* itself is a wall painting created in the refectory—dining hall—of the Monastery of Santa Maria delle Grazie in Milan, Italy. Because the painting's architecture appears to be continuous with the actual architecture of the refectory, it seems as if the world outside the space of the painting is organized around Christ as well. Everything in the architecture of the painting and the refectory draws our attention to Him. His gaze controls the world.

The complex illusion of real space that perspective makes possible is evident in Gustave Caillebotte's *Place de l'Europe on a Rainy Day* (Fig. 114). Two (and even more) vanishing points organize a complex array of parallel lines emanating from the intersection of the five Paris streets depicted (Fig. 115). More than one vanishing point—that is, **two-point linear perspective** (Fig. 116)—help to create a more lively composition, in part because the perspective recedes in several diagonal directions from the viewer, rather than frontally as in Leonardo's *Last Supper*. Caillebotte nevertheless imposes order on this scene by dividing the canvas into four equal rectangles formed by the vertical lamp post and the horizon line.

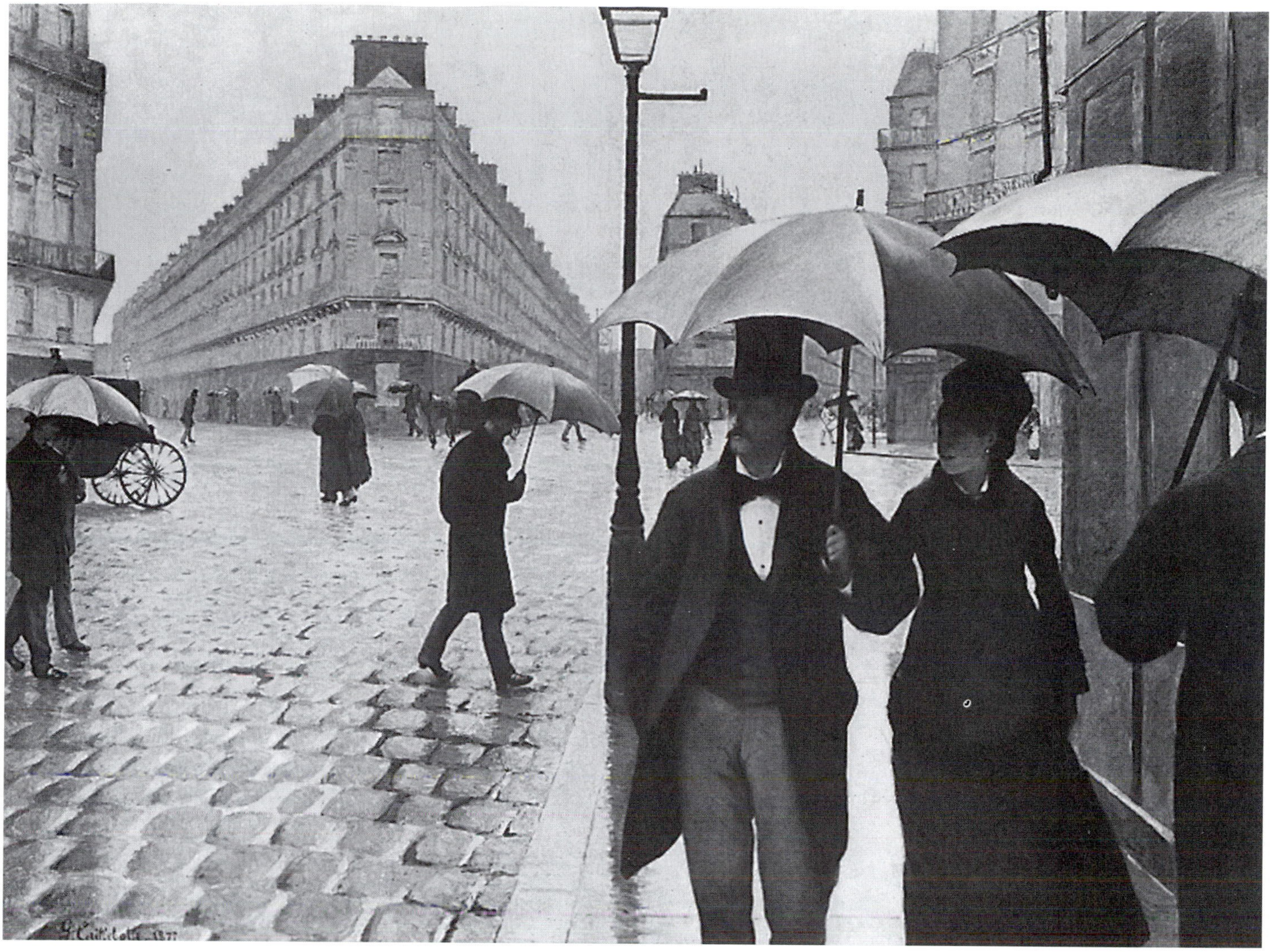

Fig. 114 Gustave Caillebotte (1848–1894), Paris Street, *Place de l'Europe on a Rainy Day,* 1876–1877.
Oil on canvas, 83 1/2 × 108 3/4 in. Photograph © 1995, The Art Institute of Chicago, all rights reserved. Charles H. and Mary F. S. Worcester Collection.

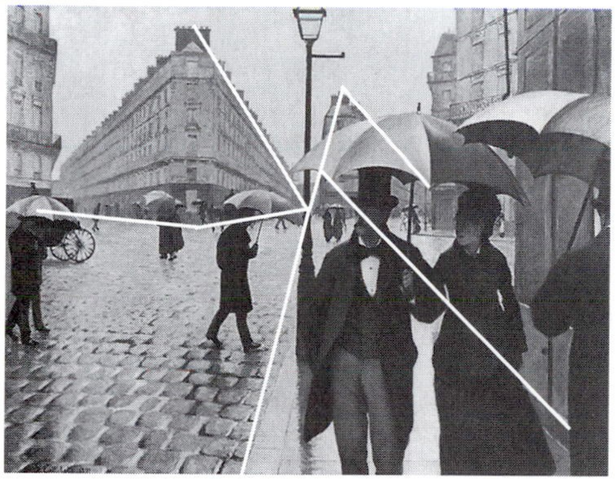

Fig. 115 Perspective analysis of *Place de l'Europe on a Rainy Day.*

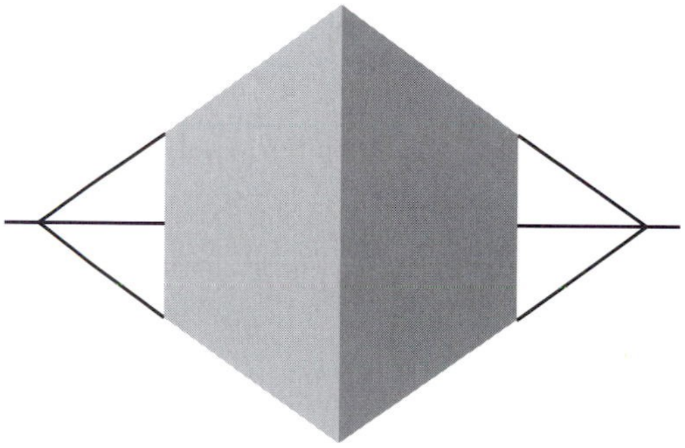

Fig. 116 Two-point linear perspective.

Bill Viola's The Greeting

When video artist Bill Viola first saw a reproduction of Jacopo Pontormo's 1528 painting *The Visitation* (Fig. 118), he knew that he had to do something with it. Asked to be the American representative at the 1995 Venice Biennale, perhaps the oldest and most prestigious international arts festival, he decided to see if he could create a piece based on Pontormo's painting for the exhibition. He intended to convert the entire United States Pavilion into a series of five independent video installations, which he called, as a whole, "Buried Secrets." By "buried secrets" he meant to refer to our emotions, which have for too long lain hidden within us. "Emotions," he says, "are precisely the missing key that has thrown things out of balance, and the restoration to their right place as one of the higher orders of the mind of a human being cannot happen fast enough."

What fascinated Viola about Pontormo's painting was, first of all, the scene itself. Two women meet each other in the street. They embrace as two other women look on. An instantaneous knowledge and understanding seems to pass between their eyes. The visit, as told in the Bible by Luke (I:36–56), is of the Virgin Mary to Elizabeth. Mary has just been told by the angel Gabriel: "You shall conceive and bear a son, and you shall give him the name Jesus," the moment of the Annunciation. In Pontormo's painting, the two women, one just pregnant with Jesus, the other six months pregnant, after a lifetime of barrenness, with the child who would grow to be John the Baptist, share each other's joy. For Viola, looking at this work, it is their shared intimacy—that moment of contact in which the nature of their relationship is permanently changed—that most fascinated him. Here was the instant when we leave the isolation of ourselves and enter into social relations with others. Viola decided that he wanted to recreate this encounter, to try and capture in a medium such as film or video—mediums that can depict the passing of time—the emotions buried in the moment of greeting itself.

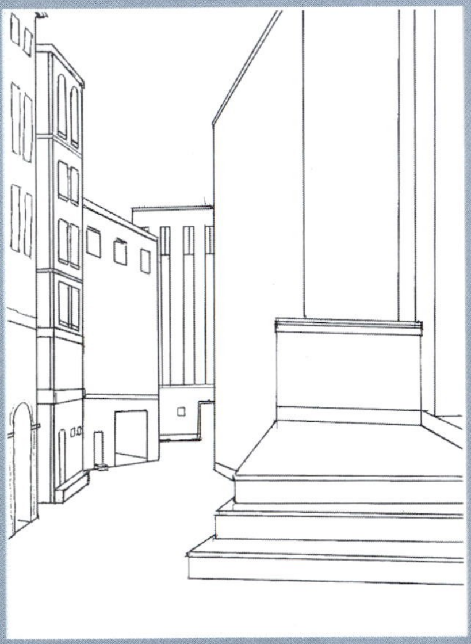

Fig. 117 Bill Viola, sketch for *The Greeting*, 1995.
Courtesy Bill Viola Studio.

In order to recreate the work, Viola turned his attention to other aspects of the composition. He was particularly interested in how the piece depicted space. There seemed to him to be a clear tension between the deep space of the street behind the women and the space occupied by the women themselves. It is as if a giant gulf lies between the foot of the woman on the left and the two tiny men sitting in the doorway to the left of her knee. To recreate the painting he had to recreate that space.

He made a series of sketches of the hypothetical street behind the women (Fig. 117); then, working with a set designer, recreated it. The

WORKS IN PROGRESS

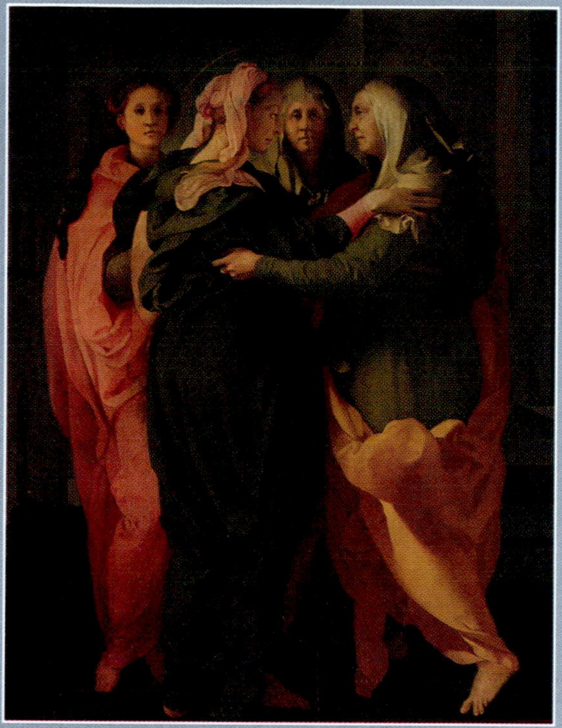

Fig. 118 Jacopo Pontormo, *The Visitation,* 1528.
Oil on canvas, 79 ½ × 61 ⅜ in. Pieve di S. Michele, Carmignano, Italy.
© Canali Photobank, Capriolo, Italy.

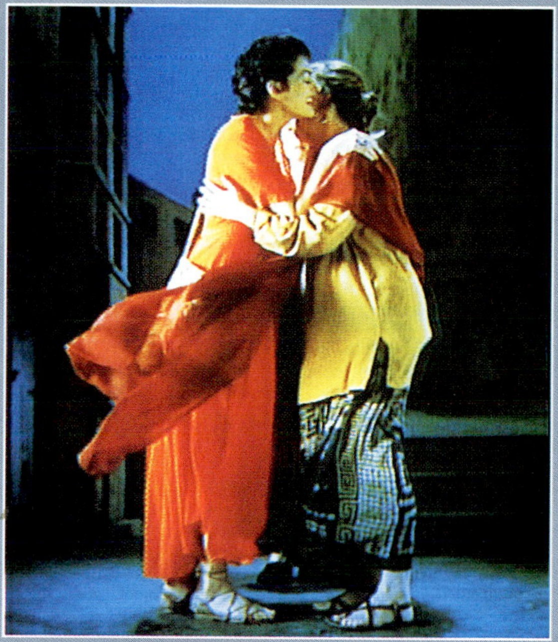

Fig. 119 Bill Viola, *The Greeting,* 1995.
Video/sound installation exhibition, *Buried Secrets.*
United States Pavilion, Venice Biennale 1995
commissioner, Marilyn Zeitlin.
Arizona State University Art Museum, Tempe, Arizona.
© Bill Viola Studio. Photograph: Roman Mensing.

steep, odd perspective of the buildings had to fit into a 20-foot-deep sound stage. Obviously, the two figures in the doorway would seem incredibly large if they were, as they would have to be on the stage, only ten feet behind the women. In order to make them as small as the the two figures in the painting—who must be nearly one hundred yards behind the women—Viola constructed an elaborate and ingenious system of mirrors. In the doorway of the stage set he placed a mirror that reflected the image from another mirror across the street, hidden by the women. This second mirror, in turn, reflected two actors leaning against a wall some 75 feet to the left of the set. Since their size diminished by half in each reflection, they appeared, reflected in the doorway, the size of the men in Pontormo's painting.

A costume designer was hired; actors auditioned and then rehearsed. On Monday, April 3, 1995, on a sound stage in Culver City, California, Viola shot *The Greeting*. He had earlier decided to shoot the piece on film, not video, because he wanted to capture every nuance of the moment. On an earlier project he had utilized a special high-speed 35-millimeter camera that was capable of shooting an entire role of film in about 45 seconds at a rate of 300 frames per second. The camera was exactly what he needed for this project. The finished film would run for over 10 minutes. The action it would record would last for 45 seconds.

"I never felt more like a painter," Viola says of the piece. "It was like I was moving color around, but on film." For ten slow-motion minutes, the camera never shifts its point of view. Two women stand talking on a street, and a third enters from the left to greet them. There is the sound of wind, and then the third woman leans across and whispers, "Can you help me? I need to talk with you right away." Joy rises to their faces (Fig. 119). Their emotions surface. The wind lifts their dresses, and they are transformed.

SOME OTHER MEANS OF REPRESENTING SPACE

Linear perspective creates the illusion of three-dimensional space on a two-dimensional surface. Other systems of projecting space, however, are available. These so-called **axonometric projections** (Fig. 120), employed by architects and engineers, have the advantage of translating space in such a way that the distortions of scale common in linear perspective are eliminated. In axonometric projections all lines remain parallel, rather than receding to a common vanishing point, and all sides of the object are at an angle to the picture plane. There are three types of axonometric projection, **isometric, dimetric,** and **trimetric.** In isometric projection, all the measurements—height, width, and depth—are to the same scale: for instance, each inch might represent one foot. In dimetric projection, two of the measurements maintain the same scale, while the third is reduced, often by half. Figure 120 is an example of dimetric projection, its height employing a smaller scale than its width and depth. In trimetric projection all three measurements use different scales.

Another related type of projection commonly found in Japanese art is **oblique projection.** As in axonometric projection, the sides of the object are parallel, but in this system, one face is parallel to the picture plane as well. The same scale is utilized for height and width, while depth is reduced. This hanging scroll (Fig. 121) depicts the three sacred Shinto-Buddhist shrines of Kumano, south of Osaka, Japan, in oblique perspective. The shrines are actually about 80 miles apart, the one at the bottom of the scroll high in the mountains of the Kii Peninsula in a cypress forest, the middle one on the eastern coast of the peninsula, and the top one near a famous waterfall that can be seen to its right. In addition to oblique projection, the artist employs two other devices to give a sense of spatial depth as well. As is common in traditional perspective, each shrine appears smaller the further away it is. But spatial depth is also indicated here by **position**—the further away the shrine, the *higher* it is in the composition.

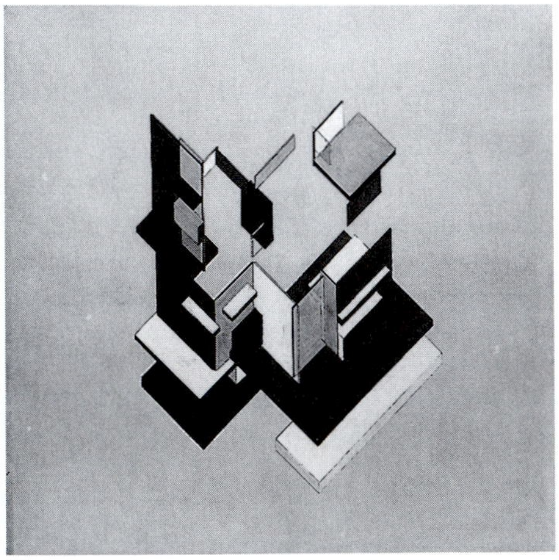

Fig. 120 Theo van Doesburg and Cornelius van Eesteren, *Color Construction,* Project for a private house, 1922.
Gouache, 22 1/2 × 22 1/2 in. Collection, The Museum of Modern Art, New York. Edgar J. Kaufmann, Jr. Fund.

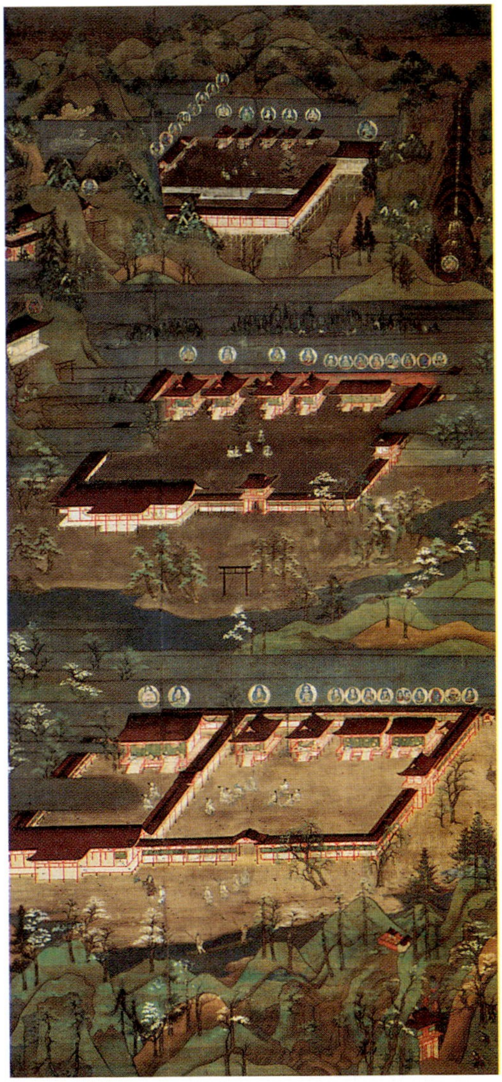

Fig. 121 Kumano Mandala: *The Three Sacred Shrines,* Kamakura period, c. 1300.
Hanging scroll, ink and color on silk, 52 1/4 × 24 1/4 in. Cleveland Museum of Art. Purchase, John L. Severance Fund.

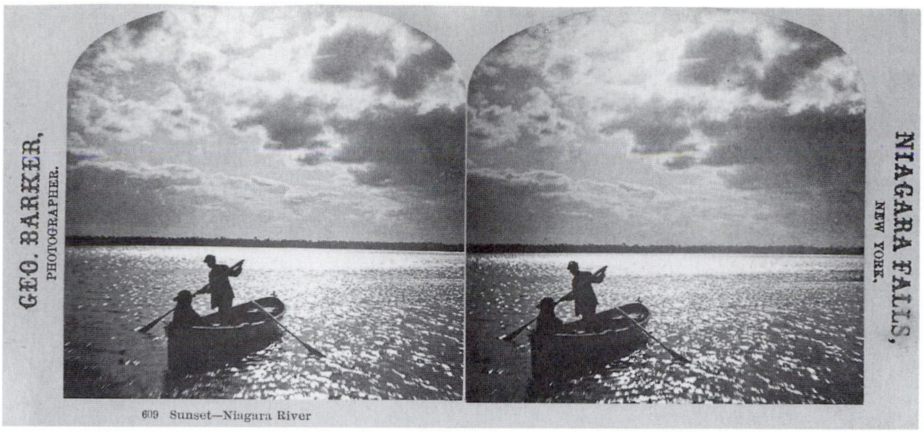

Fig. 122 George Barker, *Sunset—Niagara River (no. 609)*, c. 1870–1875.
Stereograph. International Museum of Photography at George Eastman House, Rochester, NY.

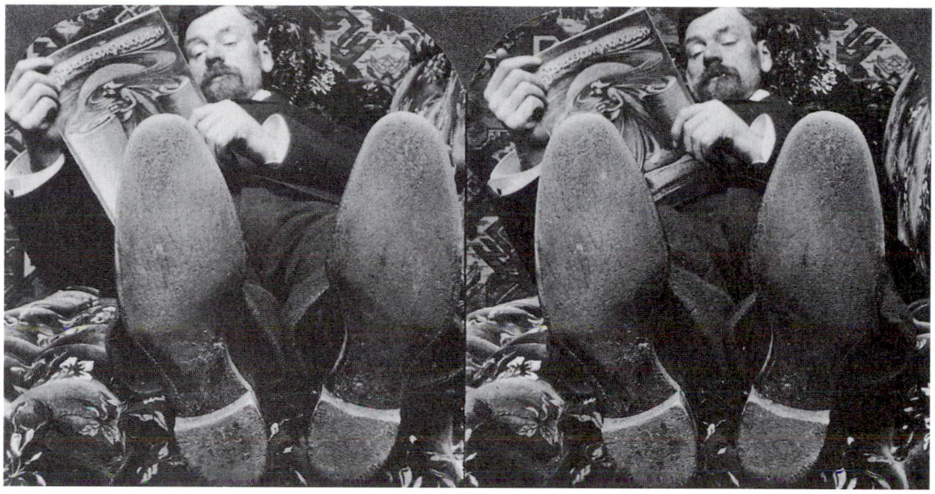

Fig. 123 Photographer unknown, *Man with Big Shoes*, c. 1890.
Stereograph.

DISTORTIONS OF SPACE AND FORESHORTENING

The space created by means of linear perspective is closely related to the space created by photography, the medium we accept as representing "real" space with the highest degree of accuracy. The picture drawn in perspective and the photograph both employ a *monocular,* that is, one-eyed, point of view that defines the picture plane as the base of a pyramid, the apex of which is the single lens or eye. Our actual vision, however, is *binocular.* We see with both eyes. If you hold your finger up before your eyes and look at it first with one eye closed and then with the other, you will readily see that the point of view of each eye is different. Under most conditions, the human organism has the capacity to synthesize these differing points of view into a unitary image.

In the nineteenth century, the stereoscope was invented precisely to imitate binocular vision. Two pictures of the same subject, taken from slightly different points of view, were viewed through the stereoscope, one by each eye. The effect of a single picture was produced, with the appearance of depth or relief, a result of the divergence of the point of view. As George Barker's stereoscope of *Sunset—Niagara River* (Fig. 122) makes clear, the difference between the two points of view is barely discernible if we are looking at relatively distant objects. But if we look at objects that are nearby, as in the stereoscopic view of the *Man with Big Shoes* (Fig. 123), then the difference is readily apparent.

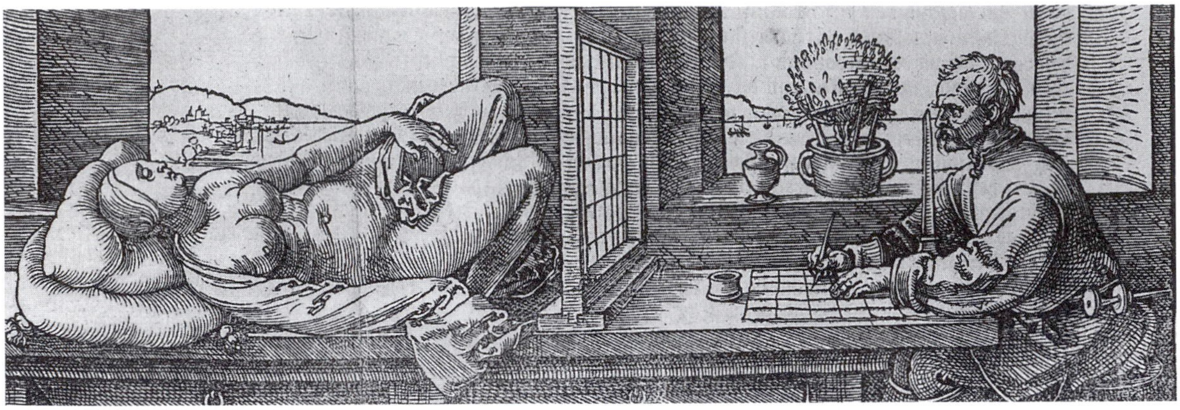

Fig. 124 Albrect Dürer, *Draftsman Drawing a Reclining Nude,* from *The Art of Measurement,* c. 1527.
Woodcut 3 × 8 ½ in. Museum of Fine Arts, Boston, Horatio Greenough Curtis Fund.

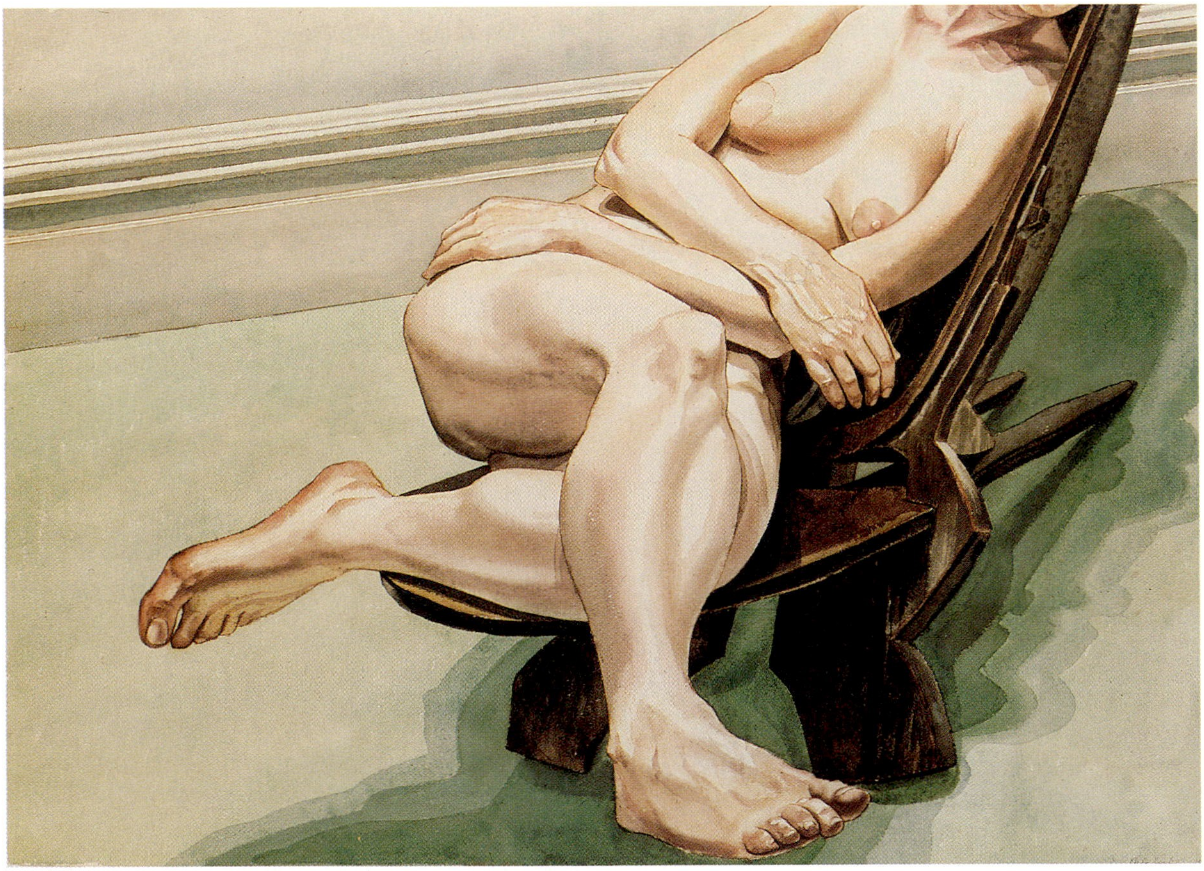

Fig. 125 Phillip Pearlstein, *Model on Dogon Chair, Legs Crossed,* 1979.
Watercolor, 29 ½ × 49 ¼ in. Hirschl & Adler Modern, New York.

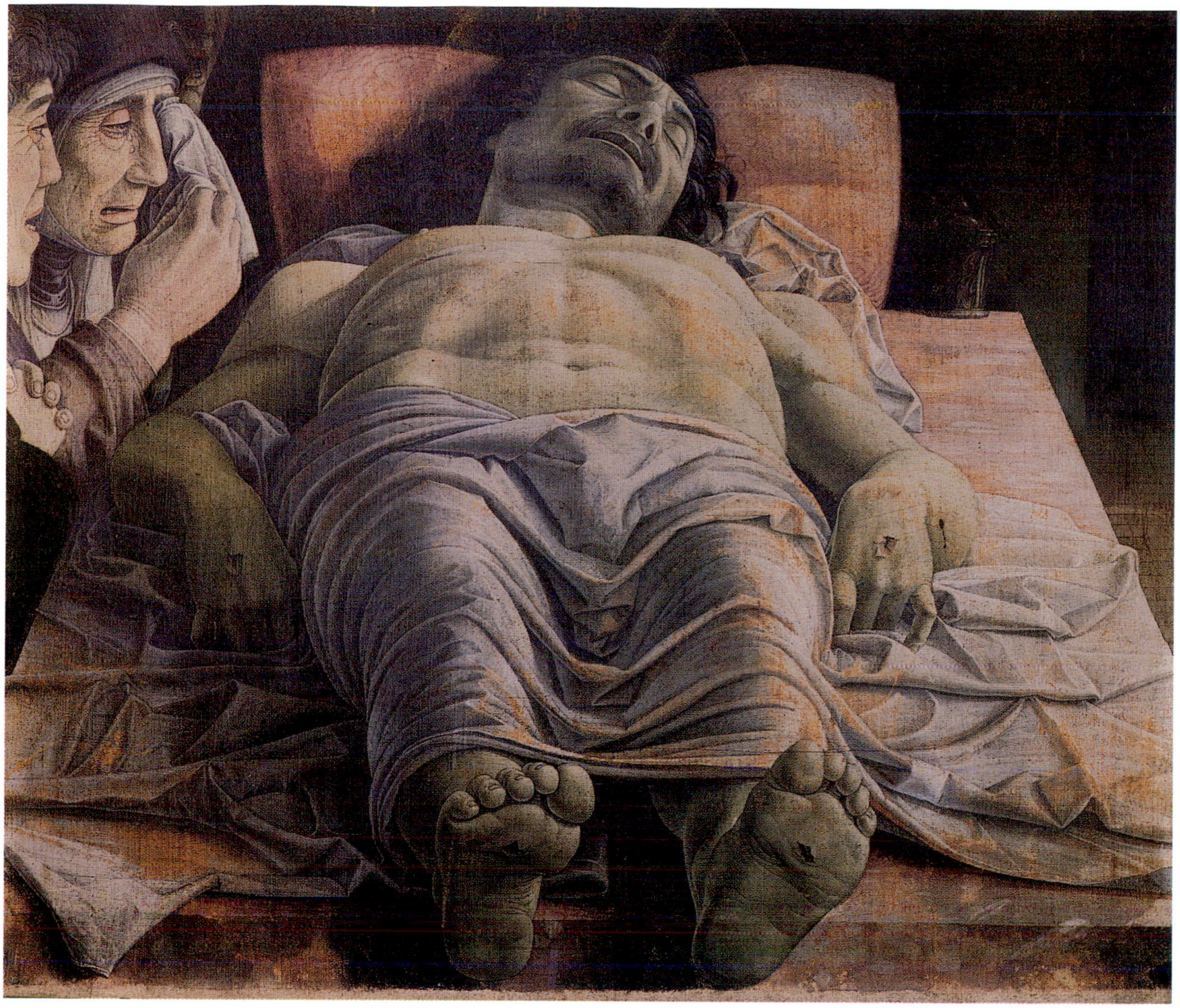

Fig. 126 Andrea Mantegna, *The Dead Christ,* c. 1501.
Tempera on canvas, 26 × 30 in. Brera Gallery, Milan.

Painters can make up for such distortions in ways that photographers cannot. If the artist portrayed in Dürer's woodcut (Fig. 124) were to draw exactly what he sees before his eyes, he would end up with a composition not unlike that achieved by Phillip Pearlstein in his watercolor (Fig. 125), a nude whose feet and calves are much larger than the rest of her body. Pearlstein is deliberately painting exactly what he sees, in order to draw our attention to certain formal repetitions and patterns in the figure. Note, for instance, the way that the shape of the nearest foot repeats the shape of the shadowed area beneath the model's buttocks and thigh. But Andrea Mantegna was not interested at all in depicting *The Dead Christ* (Fig. 126) with disproportionately large feet. Such a representation would make comic or ridiculous a scene of high seriousness and consequence. It would be *indecorous.* Thus Mantegna has employed **foreshortening** in order to represent Christ's body. In foreshortening, the dimensions of the closer extremities are adjusted in order to make up for the distortion created by the point of view.

MODERN EXPERIMENTS AND NEW DIMENSIONS

As we saw in the Pearlstein watercolor, modern artists often intentionally violate the rules of perspective to draw the attention of the viewer to elements of the composition other than its **verisimilitude,** or the apparent "truth" of its representation of reality. In his large painting *Harmony in Red* (Fig. 127), Henri Matisse has almost completely eliminated any sense of three-dimensionality by uniting the different spaces of the painting in one large field of uniform color and design. The wallpaper and the tablecloth are made of the same fabric. The chair at the left seems abnormally large, as if very close to our point of view, yet its back stands at the same height as the chair between the table and the wall. Shapes are repeated throughout: the spindles of the chairs and the tops of the decanters echo one another, as do the maid's hair and the white foliage of the large tree outside the window. The tree's trunk repeats the arabesque design on the tablecloth directly below it. Even the window can be read in two ways: it could, in fact, be a window opening to the world outside, or it could be the corner of a painting, a framed canvas lying flat against the wall. In traditional perspective, the picture frame functions as a window. Here the window has been transformed into a frame.

What one notices most of all in Cézanne's *Mme. Cézanne in a Red Chair* (Fig. 128) is its very lack of spatial depth. Although the arm of the chair seems to project forward on the right, on the left the painting is almost totally flat. The blue flower pattern on the wallpaper seems to float above the spiraled end of the arm, as does the tassel that hangs below it, drawing the wall far forward into the composition. The line that establishes the bottom of the baseboard on the left seems to ripple on through Mme. Cézanne's dress. But most of all, the assertive vertical stripes of that dress, which appear to rise straight up from her feet parallel to the picture plane, deny Mme. Cézanne her lap. It is almost as if a second, striped vertical plane lies between her and the viewer. By this means Cézanne announces that it is not so much the accurate representation of the figure that interests him as it is the *design* of the canvas and the activity of painting itself, the play of pattern and color.

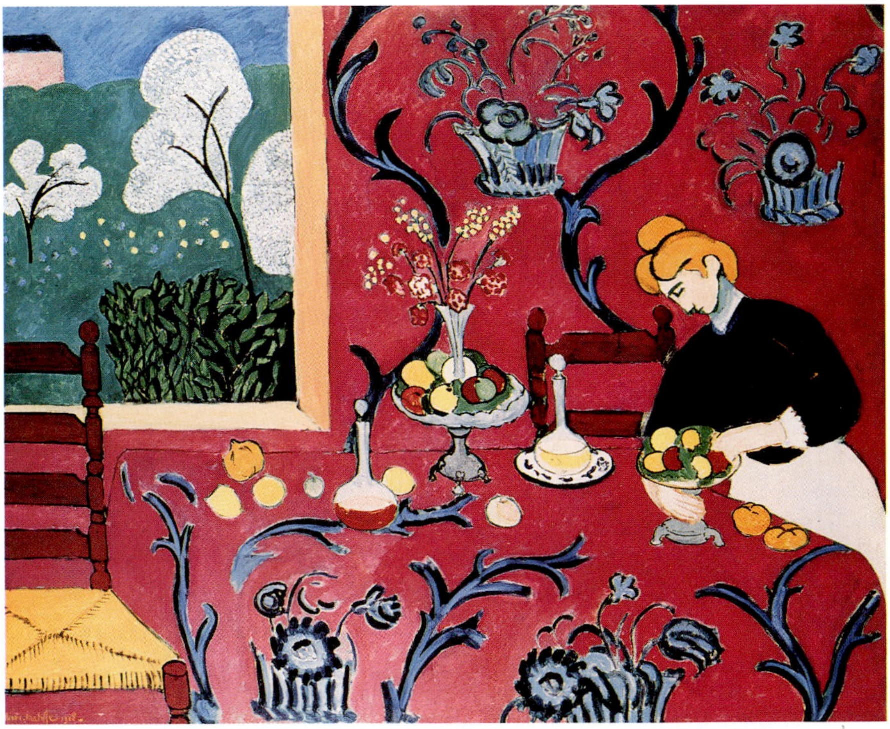

Fig. 127 Henri Matisse, *Harmony in Red (The Red Room)*, 1908–1909.
Oil on canvas, 70⅞ × 86⅝ in. Leningrad, Hermitage. George Roos/Art Resource, New York.

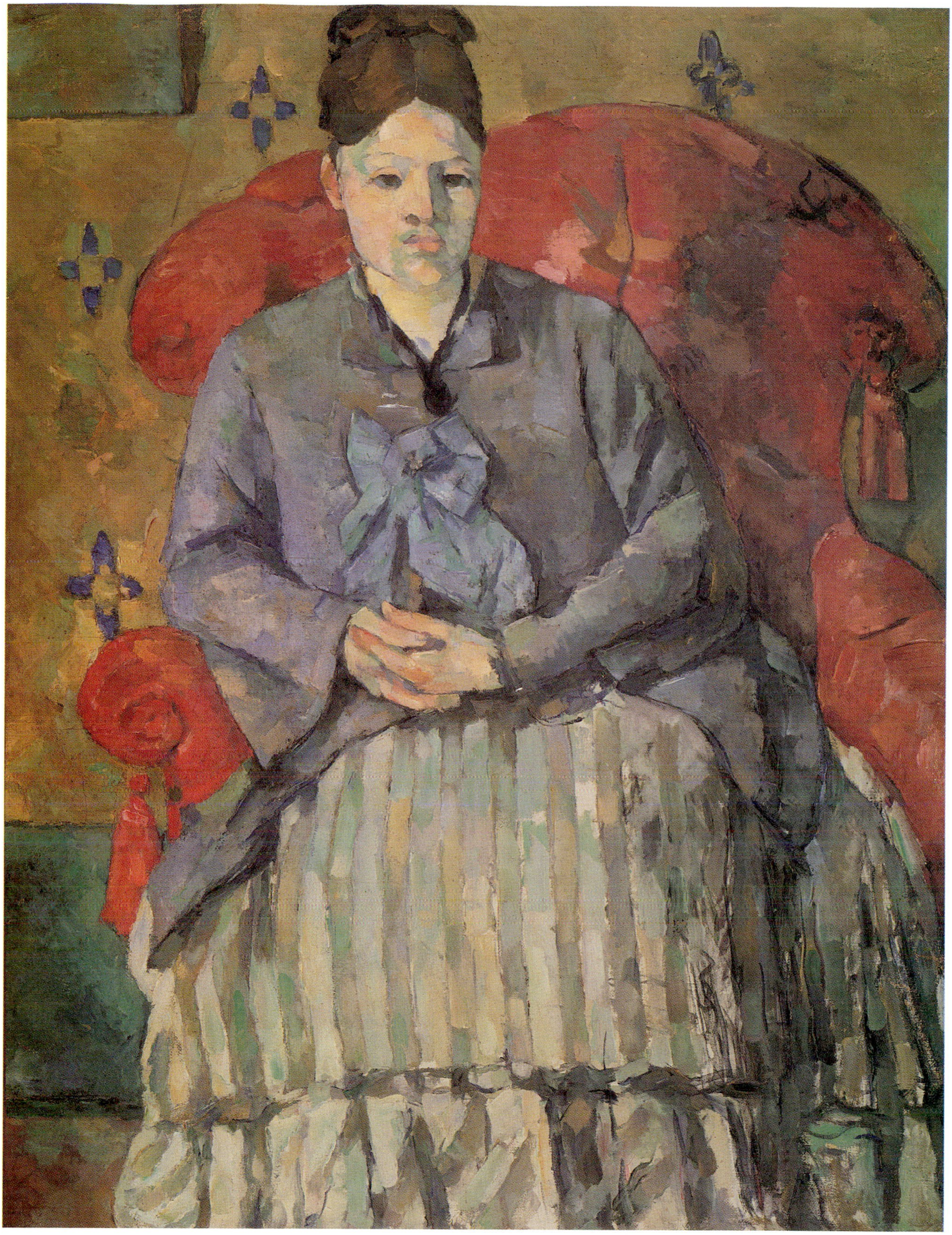

Fig. 128 Paul Cézanne, *Mme. Cézanne in a Red Chair,* 1877.
Oil on canvas, 28 ½ × 22 in.
Museum of Fine Arts, Boston. Bequest of Robert Treat Paine II.

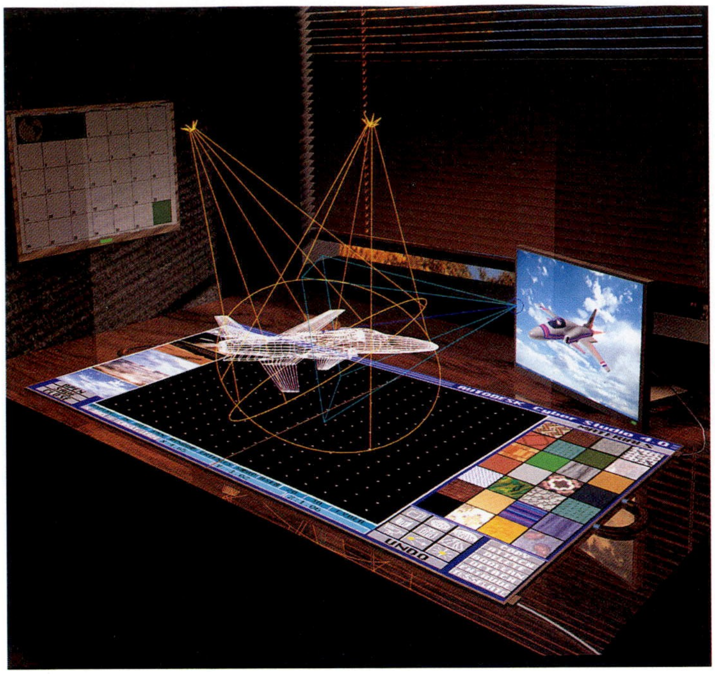

Fig. 129 Jamie Clay, *Dream System,* 1992.
Computer-generated image, using 3-D Studio.
Courtesy Autodesk, Inc.

The history of modern art has often been summarized as the growing refusal of painters to represent three-dimensional space and the resulting emphasis placed on the two-dimensional space of the picture plane. It is perhaps better to think in terms of the modern artist's growing interest in bringing the three-dimensional into dialogue with the two-dimensional. While modern art diminished the importance of representing "real" space in order to draw attention to other types of reality, recent developments in video and computer technologies have begun to make it possible to create artificial environments that the viewer experiences as real space. Variously known as **cyberspace, hyperspace,** or **virtual reality,** these spaces are becoming increasingly realistic. The viewer "enters" one such space by donning a set of goggles containing two small video monitors, one in front of each eye, and a glove covered with optic fibers for tracking purposes. Point a finger, which means "fly," and you dart into the space depicted on the monitors. Relax your hand, and you slow to a stop. You feel as if you inhabit and move in the space before your eyes, though you are actually in the completely controlled environment of the lab. "It's all about illusion," says Randal Walser of the Cyberspace Project at Autodesk, Inc., in Sausalito, California. "We're building imaginary worlds, and we're putting people in them. . . . Instead of being like TVs, which are windows you look through, cyberspace is a door. You walk through the door and you're *there.*"

Our sense of space helps us to define not only where we are, but who we are, because we define ourselves personally through our relations to the things around us. In this technology, traditional distinctions about the nature of space begin to collapse. The far becomes near, and the small becomes large. The world, which was once so vast, is today as close as the Internet, that "worldwide web" of computer interactivity and exchange. As a result, our sense of space is today open to redefinition, a redefinition perhaps as fundamental as that which occurred in the fifteenth century when the laws of linear perspective were finally codified.

We have seen, in this chapter, that space is no simple construction. But construction it is, an organization of shapes and masses. We grasp space through illusion—through, that is, the way we *represent* it, whatever perspective or projection system we choose, as simple as overlapping shapes, or as complex as a computer generated image (Fig. 129). Space remains important even for those who, like the moderns, deny illusion—flat space becomes their subject rather than deep space, shapes in and for themselves rather than illusions of mass. Space, finally, is the arena in which art takes place. And in that arena, almost anything is possible.

CHAPTER 6

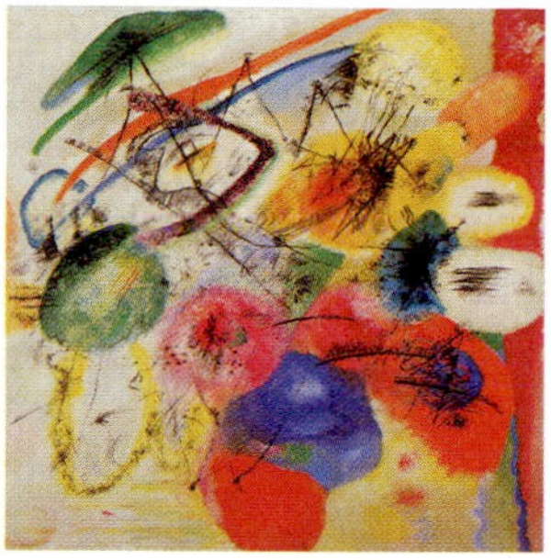

Light and Color

Light
Atmospheric Perspective
Chiaroscuro
Hatching and Cross-hatching
Key

Color
Basic Color Vocabulary
Color Schemes

WORKS IN PROGRESS
Chuck Close's *Stanley*

Color in Representational Art

WORKS IN PROGRESS
Henri Matisse's *Dance II*

Symbolic Use of Color

The manipulation of perspective systems is by no means the only way that space is created in art. Light is at least as important to the rendering of space. For instance, light creates shadow, and thus helps to define the contour of a figure or mass. Our experience of color is itself a direct function of light. In 1666, Sir Isaac Newton demonstrated that objects appear to be a certain color because they absorb and reflect different parts of the visible spectrum.

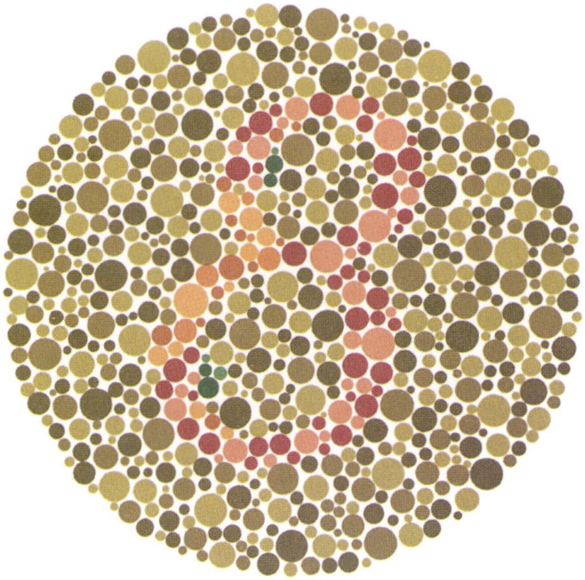

Fig. 130 **Ishihara, *Test for Color Deficiency.***
Courtesy Kanehara Shuppan Co., Ltd.
Offered exclusively in the USA by Graham-Field Inc., Hauppauge, New York.

In the simplest terms, when light strikes an object that appears blue, the object has absorbed all the colors of the spectrum but wavelengths of blue. If it appears yellow-green—or chartreuse—it has screened out all but yellow and green wavelengths. Color is essential in defining shape and mass. It allows us, for instance, to see a red object against a green one, and thus establish their relation in space. So-called "color-blind" people (who actually can see colors, just not those that most of us see) cannot detect, for reasons that are not entirely understood, one or both of the numerals in Figure 130. Interestingly, if you were to photocopy this pattern of dots, the numerals would not be visible. The machine, like the eye of the color-blind person, reads the light brown and light red dots as if they were the same, and the dark brown and red dots as if they were the same. Because they are unable to see some shapes overlapping others, color-blind people experience spatial relationships differently than the rest of us, but their difficulty helps demonstrate how important color—and, by extension, light—is to our experience of space.

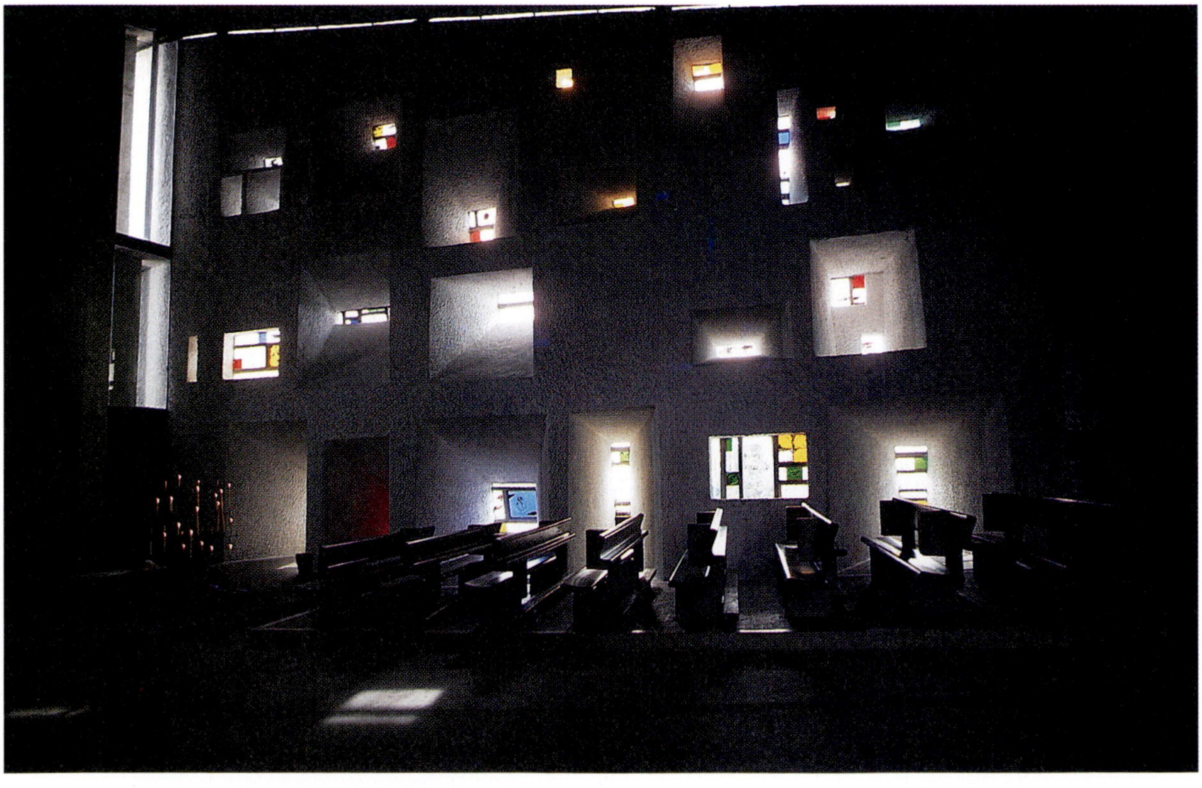

Fig. 131 **Le Corbusier, *Interior, Chapelle de Ronchamp, Notre-Dame-du-Haut,* Ronchamp, France, 1950–1955.**
Explorer/Photo Researchers, Inc.

LIGHT

Since natural light helps us to define spatial relationships, it stands to reason that artists are interested in manipulating it. By doing so, they can control our experience of their work. Architects, particularly, must concern themselves with light. Interior spaces demand lighting, either natural or artificial, and our experience of a given space can be deeply affected by the quality of its light.

One of the most dramatically lit spaces in all modern architecture is Le Corbusier's church of Notre-Dame-du-Haut at Ronchamp in eastern France (Fig. 131). The light is admitted through narrow stained-glass windows on the exterior southern wall, but as the window boxes expand through the thick wall, the light broadens into wide shafts that possess an unmistakable spiritual quality. The effect is one of extraordinary beauty.

Obviously, not all artists are able to utilize light as fully as architects. But, especially if they are interested in representing the world, they must learn to imitate the effects of light in their work. Before turning to a discussion of color—the most complex effect of light—we need to consider some of the more general ways in which the properties of light are utilized in art.

Atmospheric Perspective

For Leonardo da Vinci, representing the effects of light was at least as important in creating believable space as perspective. The effect of the atmosphere on the appearance of elements in a landscape is one of the chief preoccupations of his *Notebooks,* and it is fair to say that Leonardo is responsible for formulating the "rules" of what we call **atmospheric** or **aerial perspective.** Briefly, these rules state that the quality of the atmosphere (the haze and relative humidity) between us and large objects, such as mountains, changes their appearance. Objects further away from us appear less distinct, often cooler or bluer in color, and the contrast between light and dark is reduced.

Clarity, precision, and contrast between light and dark dominate the foreground elements in Leonardo's *Madonna of the Rocks* (Fig. 132). The Madonna's hand extends over the head of the infant Jesus in an instance of almost perfect perspectival foreshortening. Yet perspective has little to do with the way in which we perceive the distant mountains over the Madonna's right shoulder. We assume that the rocks in the far distance are the same brown as those nearer us, yet the atmosphere has changed them, making them appear blue. We know that of these three distant rock formations, the one nearest us is on the right, and the one farthest away is on the left. Since they are approximately the same size, if they were painted with the same clarity and the same amount of contrast between light and dark, we would be unable to place them spatially. We would see them as a horizontal wall of rock, parallel to the picture plane, rather than as a series of mountains, receding diagonally into space.

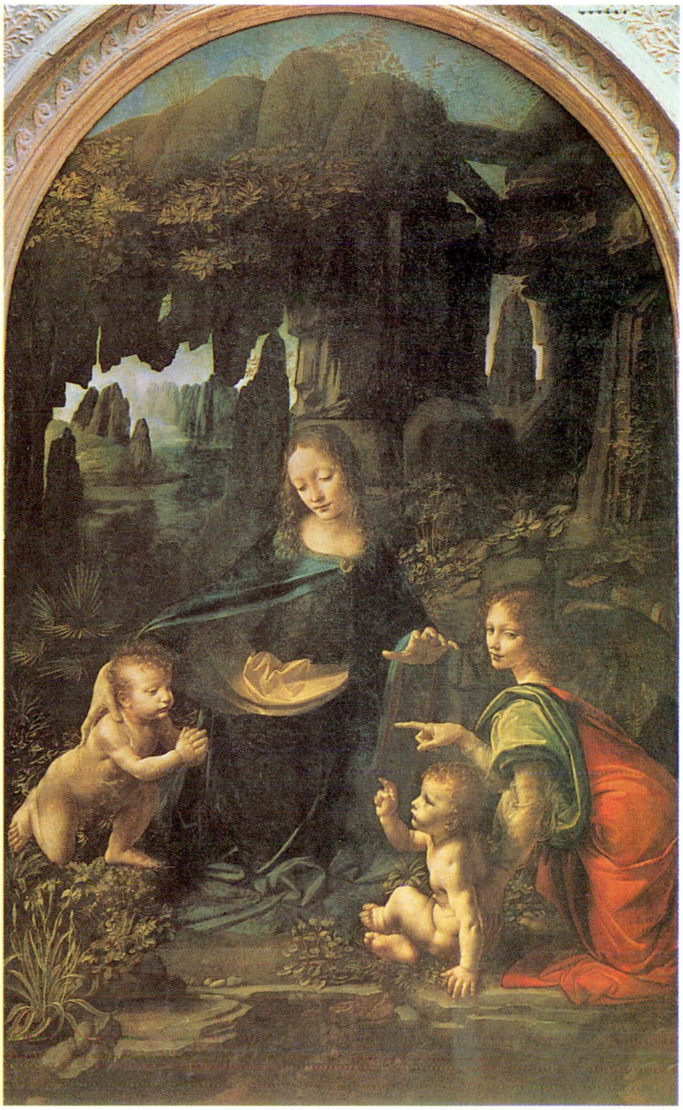

Fig. 132 Leonardo da Vinci, *Madonna of the Rocks,* c. 1495–1508.
Oil on panel, 75 × 47 in. National Gallery, London.

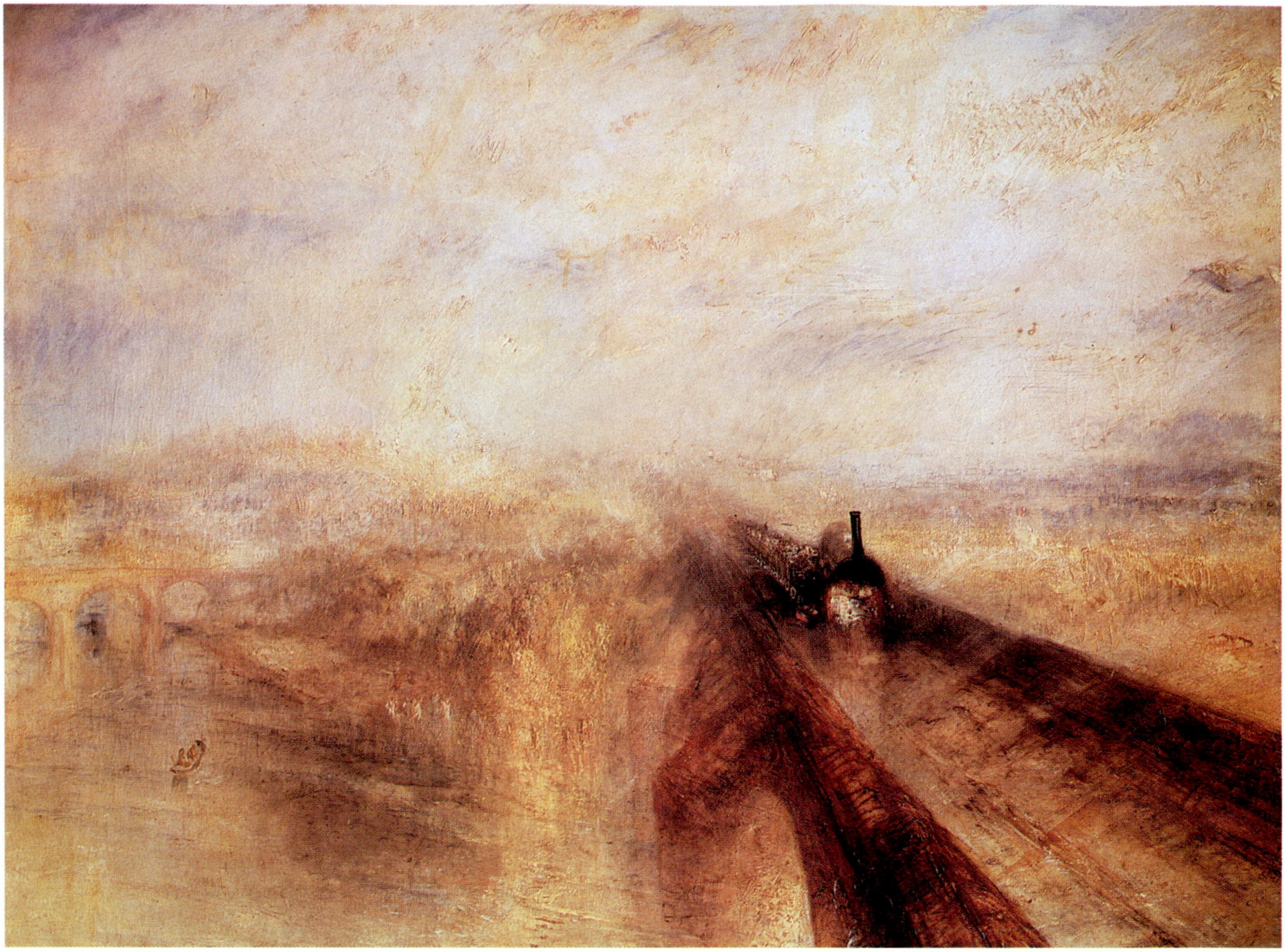

Fig. 133 J. M. W. Turner, *Rain, Steam, and Speed—The Great Western Railway,* 1844.
Oil on canvas, 33 3/4 × 48 in. Clore Collection, Tate Gallery, London.

By the nineteenth century, aerial perspective had come to dominate the thinking of landscape painters. A painting like *Rain, Steam, and Speed—The Great Western Railway* (Fig. 133) certainly employs linear perspective: we stare over the River Thames across the Maidenhead Bridge, which was completed for the railway's new Bristol and Exeter line in 1844, the year Turner painted the scene. But the space of this painting does not depend on linear perspective. Rather, it is light and atmosphere that dominate it, creating a sense of space that in fact overwhelms the painting's linear elements in luminous and intense light. Turner's light is at once so opaque that it conceals everything behind it and so deep that it seems to stretch beyond the limits of vision. Describing the power of Rembrandt's *The Mill* (Fig. 134) in a lecture delivered in 1811, Turner would praise such ambiguity: "Over [the Mill] he has thrown that veil of matchless color, that lucid interval of Morning dawn and dewy light on which the Eye dwells . . . [and he] thinks it a sacrilege to pierce the mystic shell of color in search of form." With linear perspective one might adequately describe physical reality—a building, for instance—but through light one could reveal a greater spiritual reality.

The dominance of light over line, fully developed in Turner's work, had begun to assert itself in painting as early as the late Renaissance. When compared to Leonardo's classical rendering of the scene (Fig. 112), painted almost exactly 100 years earlier, Tintoretto's version of *The Last Supper* (Fig. 135) seems much more expressive. It is, in large part, the dramatic play of light and dark in the painting that contributes to this expressivity. As in Leonardo's mural, Tintoretto's *Last Supper* places Christ in the center of the composition. But where the perspective system employed by Leonardo is used to focus our attention on Christ, it is light that draws our attention to His actions in the Tintoretto.

The heavenly light surrounding Christ contrasts dramatically with the darkness of the rest of the composition. Christ, in fact, is offering bread to the disciples, and in so doing performs the Eucharist of the Mass, symbolically offering them His body as nourishment. This purely spiritual act contrasts with the gluttonous worldly activity going on in the foreground, where a dog knaws at a bone and a cat searches for leftovers. Light here symbolizes the spiritual world, and darkness our earthly home.

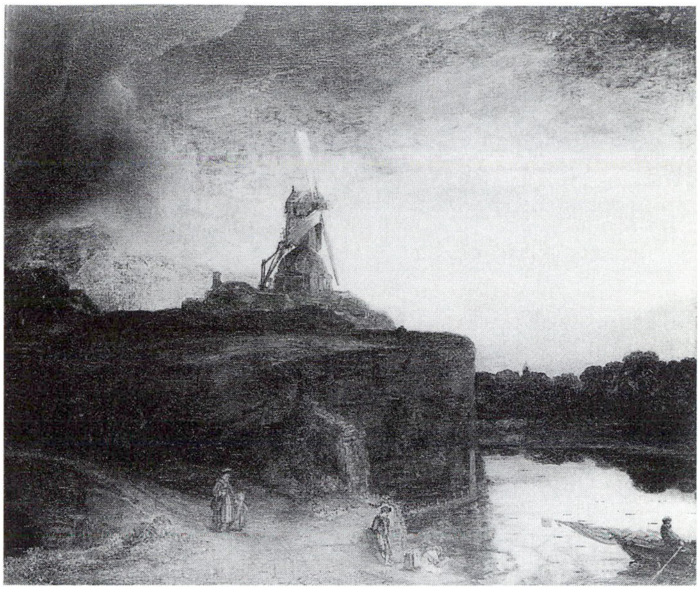

Fig. 134 Formerly attributed to Rembrandt van Rijn, *The Mill,* c. 1650.
Oil on canvas, 34 3/8 × 41 1/2 in. National Gallery of Art, Washington, DC.

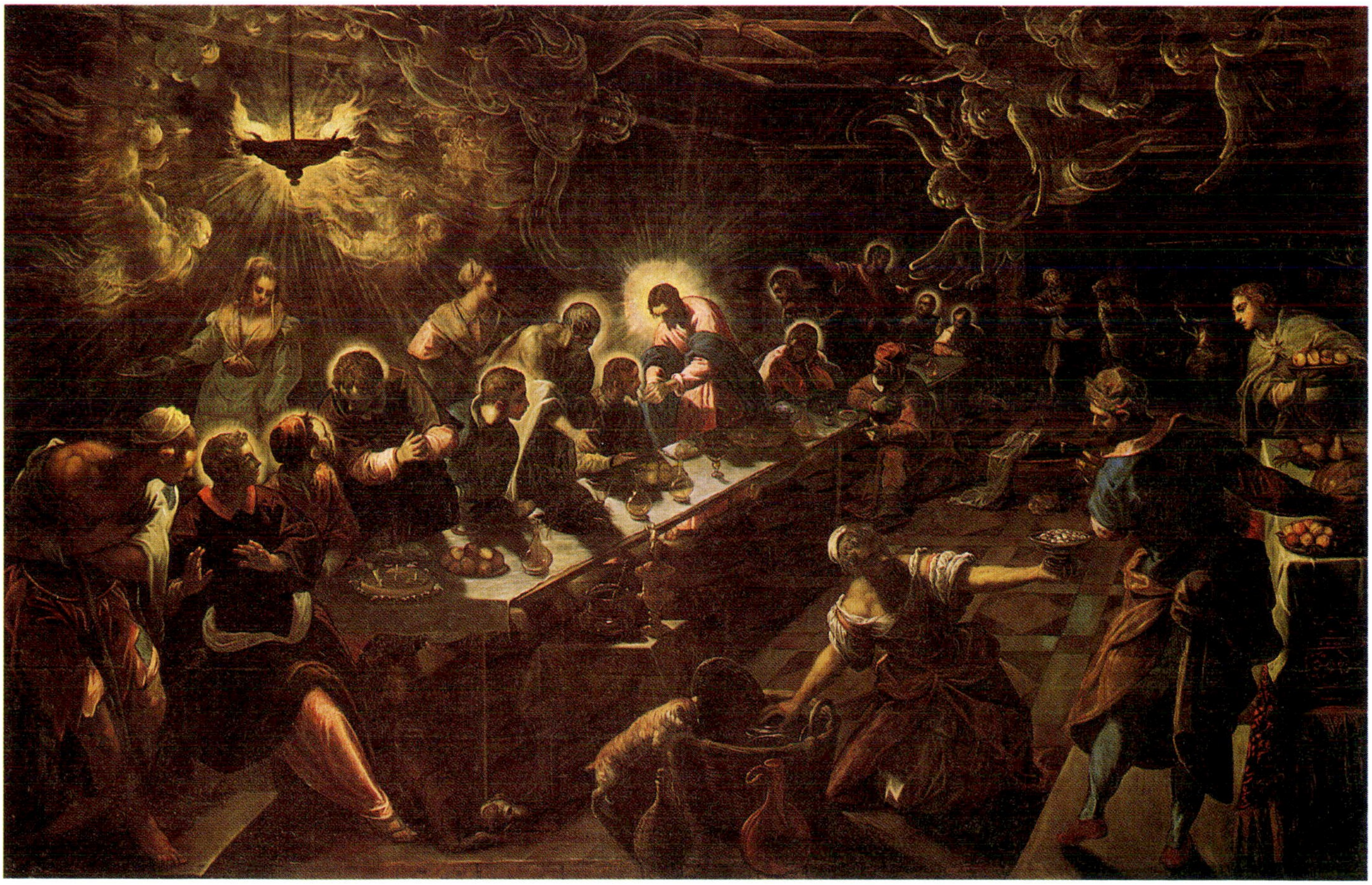

Fig. 135 Tintoretto, *The Last Supper,* 1592–1594.
Oil on canvas, 12 × 18 2/3 ft. San Giorgio Maggiore, Venice.

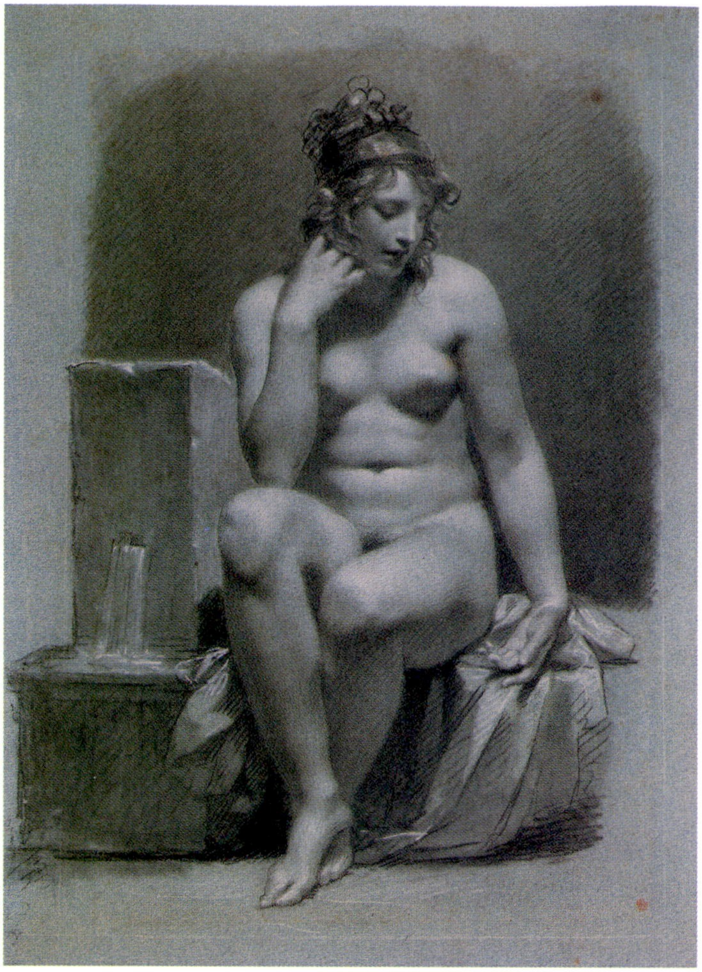

Fig. 136 Pierre Paul Prud'hon, *Study for La Source*, c. 1801.
Black and white chalk, 21 ¾ × 15 ¼ in.
Sterling and Francine Clark Art Institute, Williamstown, MA.

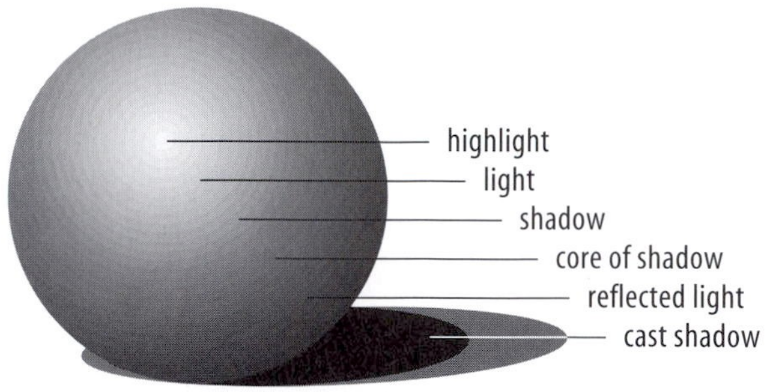

Fig. 137 A sphere represented by means of modeling.

Chiaroscuro

One of the chief tools employed by artists of the Renaissance to render the effects of light is ***chiaroscuro.*** In Italian, the word *chiaro* means "light" and the word *oscuro* means "dark." Thus, the word *chiaroscuro* refers to the balance of light and shade in a picture, especially its skillful use by the artist in representing the gradual transition around a curved surface from light to dark. The use of chiaroscuro to represent light falling across a curved or rounded surface is called **modeling.**

In his *Study for La Source* (Fig. 136), Pierre Paul Prud'hon has employed the techniques of chiaroscuro to model his figure. Drawing on blue tinted paper, he has indicated shadow by means of charcoal and created the impression of light with white chalk. The *reserve*—or the tinted paper upon which the drawing is made—functions as the light area. Thus, Prud'hon leaves all of the normally lit areas of the model's body, as it were, "blank"—they are not drawn upon.

The basic types of shading and light employed in chiaroscuro can be observed in Figure 137. **Highlights,** which directly reflect the light source, are indicated by white, and the various degrees of shadow are noted by darker and darker areas of black. There are three basic areas of shadow: the **penumbra,** which provides the transition to the **umbra,** the core of the shadow, and the **cast shadow,** the darkest area of all. Finally, areas of reflected light, cast indirectly on the table on which the sphere rests lighten the underside of shadowed surfaces. The effect can be seen on the underside of the model's left thigh in the Prud'hon drawing.

In her *Judith and Maidservant with the Head of Holofernes* (Fig. 138), Artemisia Gentileschi heightens the drama inherent in the conflict between light and dark, taking the technique of chiaroscuro to a new level. One of the most important painters of her day, Gentileschi utilizes a technique that came to be known as **tenebrism,** from the Italian *tenebroso,* meaning murky. Competing against the very deep shadows of the painting are dramatic spots of light. Based on the tale in the book of Judith in the Bible in which the noble Judith seduces the invading general Holofernes and then kills him, thereby saving her people from destruction, the painting is larger than lifesize. Its figures are heroic, illuminated in a strong artificial spotlight, and modeled in both their physical features and the folds of their clothing with a skill that lends them astonishing spatial reality and dimension. Not only does Judith's outstretched hand cast a shadow across her face, suggesting a more powerful, revealing source of light off canvas to the left, it invokes our silence. Like the light itself, danger lurks just offstage. If Judith is to escape, even we must remain still. Gentileschi represents a woman of heroic stature in a painting of heroic scale, a painting that dominates, even controls the viewer.

Hatching and Cross-hatching

Other techniques used to model figures include hatching and cross-hatching. Employed especially in drawing in ink and printmaking, where the artist's tools do not readily lend themselves to creating shaded areas, hatching and cross-hatching are linear methods of modeling. **Hatching** is an area of closely spaced parallel lines, or hatches. The closer the spacing between the lines, the darker the area. If you look closely you will see that Prud'hon has employed black hatches to deepen the shadows of his *Study for La Source*. They are especially evident along her left thigh and upper left arm. Hatching can also be seen in Michelangelo's *Head of a Satyr* (Fig. 139) at the top and back of the satyr's head, and at the base of his neck. But in Michelangelo's drawing, it is through cross-hatching that the greatest sense of volume and form in space is achieved. In **cross-hatching** one set of hatches is crossed at an angle by a second, and sometimes a third, set. The denser the lines, the darker the area. The hollows of the satyr's face are tightly cross-hatched. In contrast, the most prominent aspects of the satyr's face, its highlights at the top of his nose and on his cheekbone, are almost completely free of line. Michelangelo employs line to create a sense of volume not unlike that achieved in the sphere modeled in Figure 137.

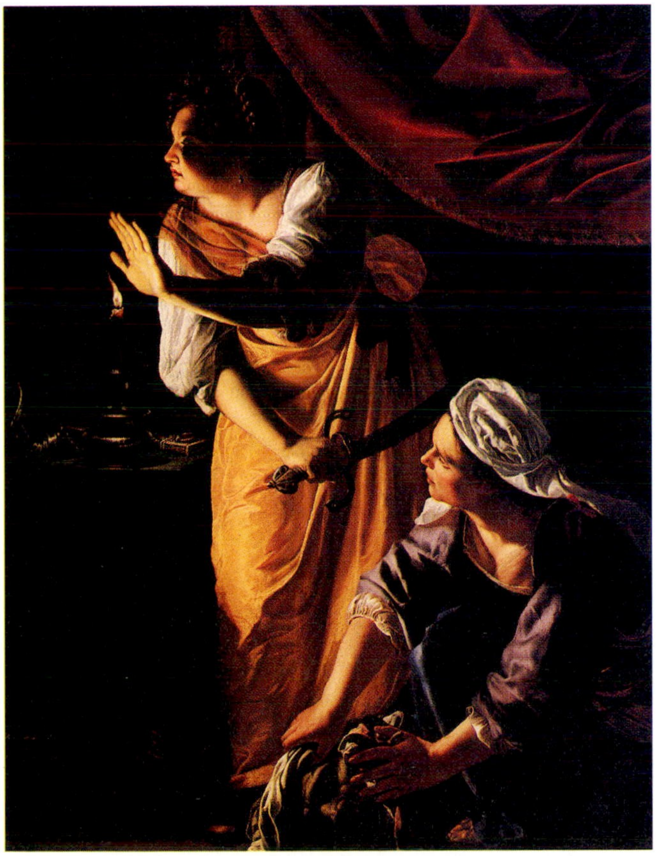

Fig. 138 Artemisia Gentileschi, *Judith and Maidservant with the Head of Holofernes,* c. 1625.
Oil on canvas, 72 1/2 × 55 3/4 in. © The Detroit Institute of the Arts, Gift of Mr. Leslie H. Green.

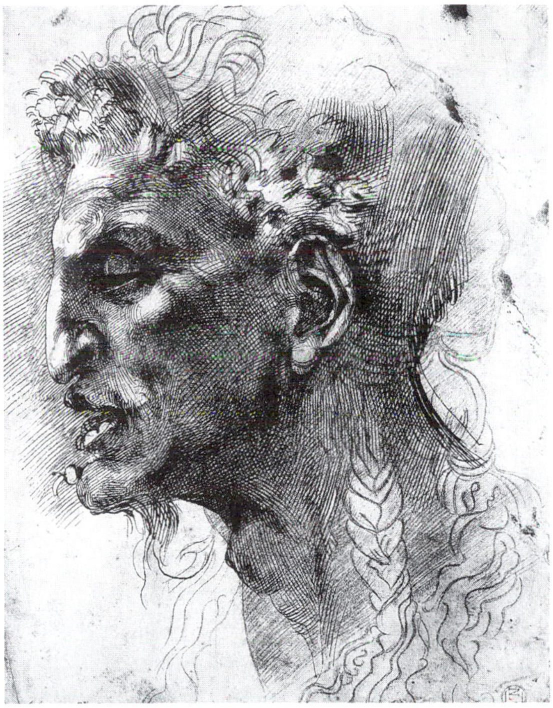

Fig. 139 Michelangelo, *Head of a Satyr,* c. 1620–1630.
Pen and ink over chalk, 10 5/8 × 7 7/8 in.
Musée du Louvre, Paris. Giraudon/Art Resource.

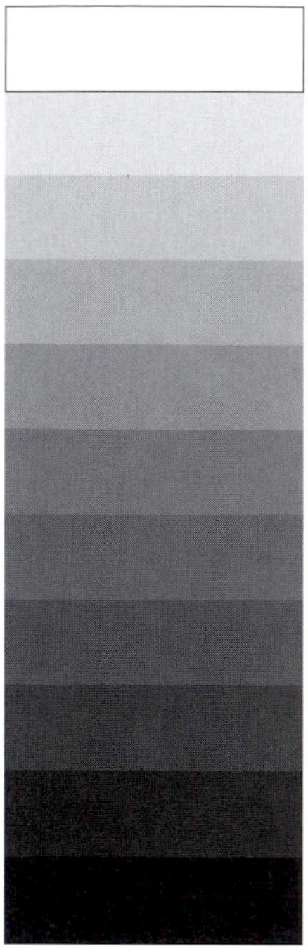

Fig. 140 Gray scale.

Key

The gradual shift from light to dark that characterizes both chiaroscuro and atmospheric perspective is illustrated by the gray scale at the left (Fig. 140). The lighter or whiter an area or object, the more filled it is with light, the *higher* it is in **key** (also called **value**). The darker or blacker an area, the more it is shrouded in shadow, the *lower* it is in key or value. Colors, too, change key or value in similar gradients. Imagine, for example, substituting the lightest blue near the top of this scale, and the darkest cobalt near its bottom. The mountains in the back of Leonardo's *Madonna of the Rocks* (Fig. 132) are depicted in a blue of higher and higher key or value the farther they are away from us.

Likewise, light pink is high in key and dark maroon low in key. In terms of color, whenever white is added to the basic **hue** or color, we are dealing with a **tint** of that color. Whenever black is added to the hue, we are dealing with a **shade** of that color. Thus pink is a tint and maroon a shade of red. Pat Steir's two large paintings, *Pink Chrysanthemum (*Fig. 141) and

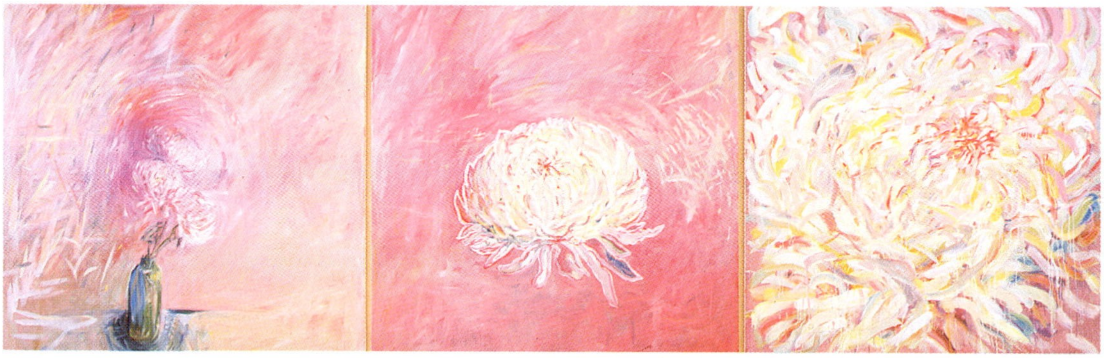

Fig. 141 Pat Steir, *Pink Chrysanthemum,* 1984.
Oil on canvas, 5 × 15 ft. Robert Miller Gallery, New York.

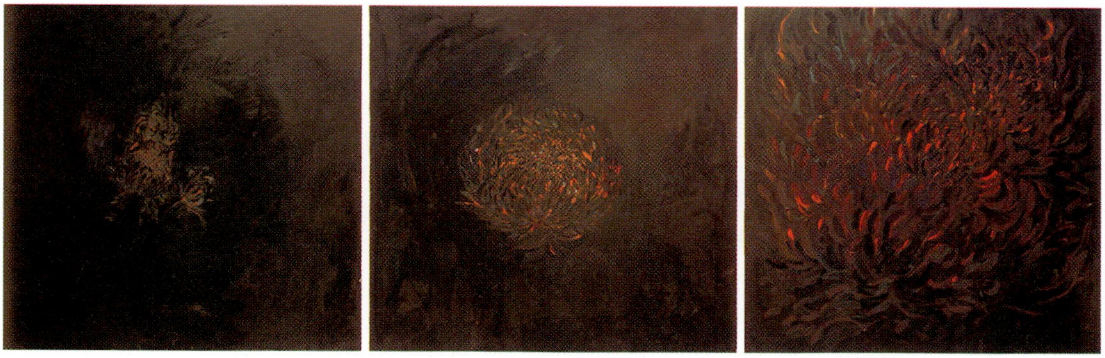

Fig. 142 Pat Steir, *Night Chrysanthemum,* 1984.
Oil on canvas, 5 × 15 ft. Robert Miller Gallery, New York.

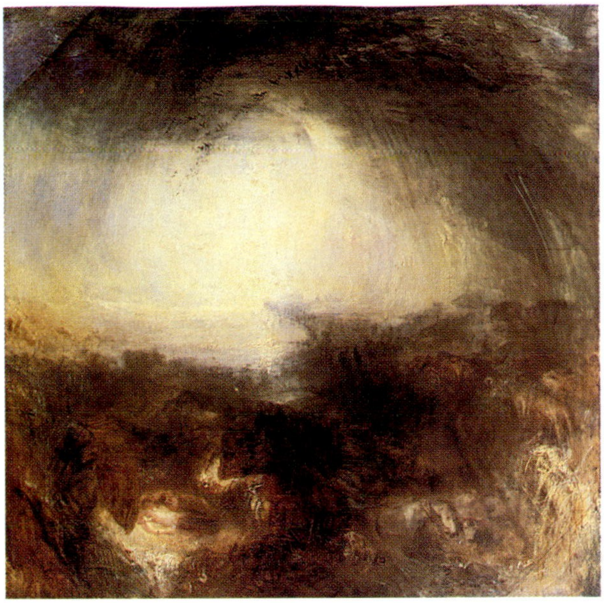

Fig. 143 J. M. W. Turner, *Shade and Darkness—The Evening of the Deluge,* 1843.
Oil on canvas, 30 1/2 × 30 1/2 in. Clore Collection, Tate Gallery, London.

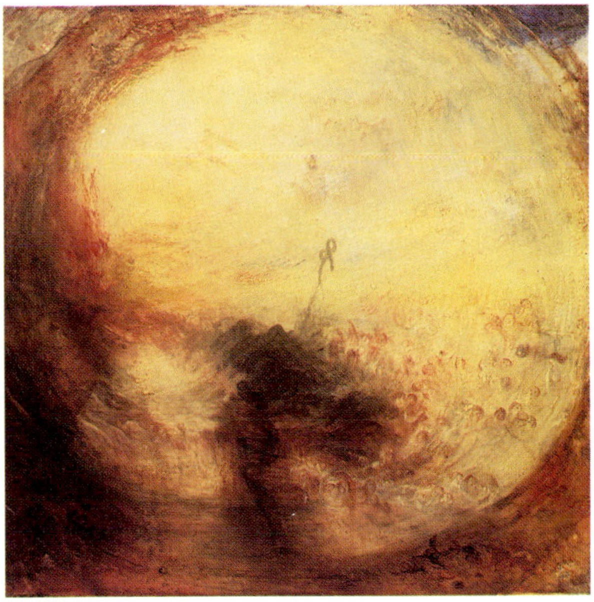

Fig. 144 J. M. W. Turner, *Light and Colour (Goethe's Theory)—The Morning after the Deluge—Moses Writing the Book of Genesis,* 1843.
Oil on canvas, 30 1/2 × 30 1/2. Clore Collection, Tate Gallery, London.

Night Chrysanthemum (Fig. 142), are each composed of three panels, each of which depicts the same flower in the same light viewed increasingly closeup, left to right. Not only does each panel become more and more abstract as our point of view focuses in on the flower, so that in the last panel we are looking at almost pure gestural line and brushwork, but also the feeling of each panel shifts, depending on its relative key. The light painting becomes increasingly energetic and alive, while the dark one becomes increasingly somber and threatening.

Light and dark have traditionally had strong symbolic meaning in Western culture. We have only to think of the Bible, and the first lines of the Book of Genesis, which very openly associates the dark with the bad and the light with the good:

> *In the beginning God created the heaven and the earth. And the earth was without form, and void; and darkness was upon the face of the deep. And the Spirit of God moved upon the face of the waters. And God said, Let there be light: and there was light. And God saw the light, that it was good: and God divided the light from the darkness.*

In the history of art, this association of light or white with good and darkness or black with evil was first fully developed in the late eighteenth- and early nineteenth-century color theory of the German poet and dramatist Johann Wolfgang von Goethe. For Goethe, colors were not just phenomena to be explained by scientific laws. They also had moral and religious significance, existing halfway between the goodness of pure light and the damnation of pure blackness. In heaven there is only pure light, but the fact that we can experience color—which, according to the laws of optics, depends upon light mixing with darkness—promises us at least the hope of salvation.

J. M. W. Turner was deeply impressed with Goethe's color theory and illustrated it in a pair of paintings executed late in life, though he is certainly accepting darkness here in a way that Goethe did not, recognizing that his painting depends on an equal give-and-take between light and darkness. *Shade and Darkness* (Fig. 143) is dominated by blues, grays, and browns, while *Light and Colour* (Fig. 144) is alive with reds and yellows. In the first, the figures are all passive, sleeping, or dead. In the second, bathed in an almost pure white light and barely recognizable at the top center of the painting, Moses writes the words we have quoted from Genesis. Figures swirl around him as if life itself is being born out of the vortex.

Although this opposition between dark and light is taken for granted in our culture, many people of color, with reason, find such thinking offensive. They are especially offended by the use of the term *value* to describe gradations of light and dark, so that black is "low" and white is "high" in value. Like Goethe's theory, the term *value* entered art discourse in the late eighteenth century, the first instance of its use in English being in the lectures of Sir Joshua Reynolds, with whom Turner probably studied at the Royal Academy between 1789 and 1792. Since then, artists and art historians alike use the term as part of a specialized descriptive vocabulary that, in itself, would seem to be at the furthest remove from issues of race and the relative "worth" of human beings. Nevertheless, it is clear that since Biblical times Western culture has tended to associate blackness with negative qualities and whiteness with positive ones, and it is understandable why people might take offense at this usage. For this reason, this book uses the word **key** instead of **value**, substituting the musical metaphor for the moral and economic one.

If for Goethe blackness is not merely the absence of color but the absence of good, for African Americans blackness is just the opposite. In poet Ted Wilson's words:

> *Mighty drums echoing the voices*
> *of Spirits. . . .*
> *these sounds are rhythmatic*
> *The rhythm of vitality,*
> *The rhythm of exuberance*
> *and the rhythms of Life*
> *These are the sounds of blackness*
> *Blackness—the presence of all color.*

The example of a Nigerian funeral cloth (Fig. 145), commissioned by a collector in the late 1970s, similarly illustrates the limits of white Western assumptions about the meaning of light and dark, black and white. The cloth is the featured element of a shrine, called a *nwomo*, constructed of bamboo poles to commemorate the death of a member of Ebie-owo, a Nigerian warriors' association. A deceased elder, wearing a woolen hat, is depicted in the center of this cloth. His eldest daughter, at the left, pours liquor into his glass. The woman on the right wears the hairdo of a mourning widow. She is cooking two dried fish for the funeral feast.

But the dominant colors of the cloth—red, black, and white—are what is most interesting.

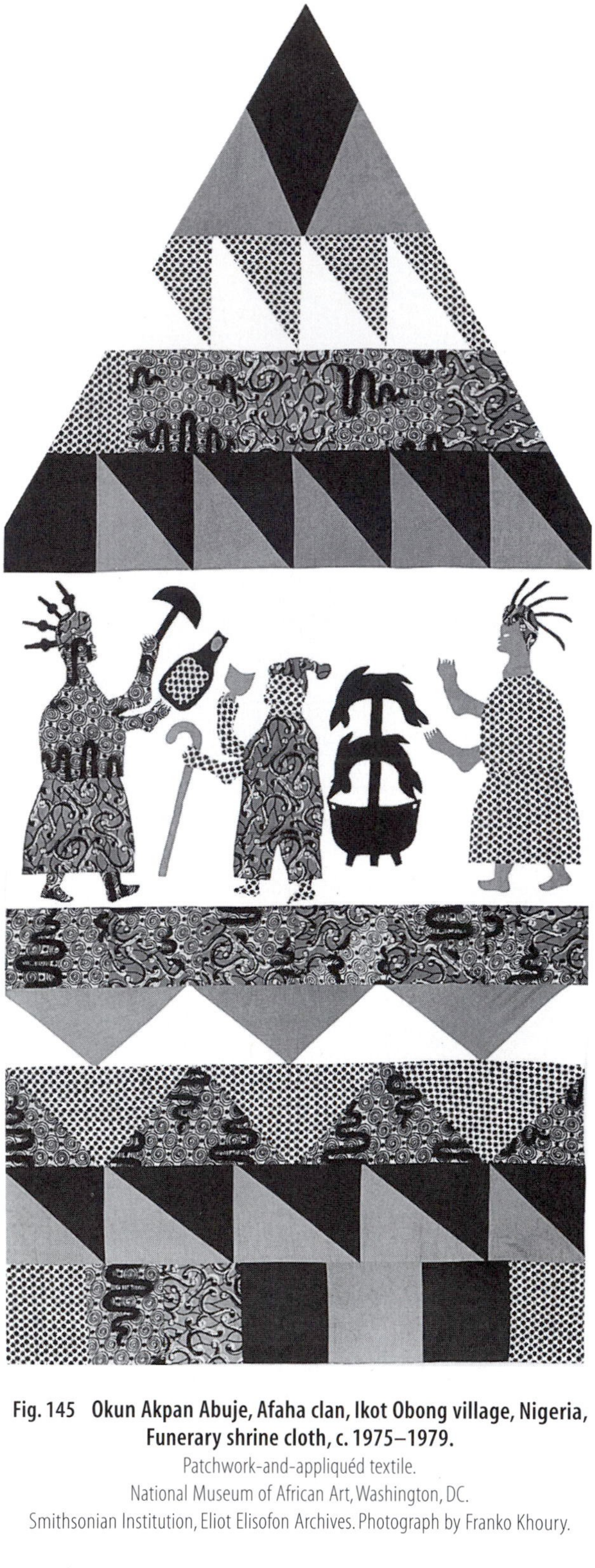

Fig. 145 Okun Akpan Abuje, Afaha clan, Ikot Obong village, Nigeria, Funerary shrine cloth, c. 1975–1979.
Patchwork-and-appliquéd textile.
National Museum of African Art, Washington, DC.
Smithsonian Institution, Eliot Elisofon Archives. Photograph by Franko Khoury.

While in the West we associate black with funerals and mourning, here it signifies life and the ancestral spirits. White, on the other hand, signifies death. Though red is the color of blood, it is meant to inspire the warrior's valorous deeds.

COLOR

Both the ambiguity of Goethe's color theory and the example of the Nigerian funeral cloth make clear that, of all the formal elements, color is perhaps the most complex. Not only do different colors mean different things to different people and cultures, but our individual perception of a given color can change as its relationship to other colors changes. The human eye may be able to distinguish as many as 10 million different colors, but we have nowhere near that many words to differentiate among them. Different cultures, furthermore, tend to emphasize different ranges of color. Although apparently able to distinguish visually between green and blue, many cultures do not possess different words for them. The Maoris of New Zealand regularly employ over 100 words for what most of us would simply call "red." Color is so complex that no one—neither scientists, nor artists, nor theoreticians such as Goethe—has ever fully explained it to everyone's satisfaction.

Basic Color Vocabulary

As we have said, color is a direct function of light. Sunlight passed through a prism breaks into bands of different colors, in what is known as the **spectrum** (Fig. 146). By reorganizing the visible spectrum into a circle, we have what is recognized as the conventional **color wheel** (Fig. 147). The three **primary colors**—red, yellow, and blue (designated by the number 1 on the color wheel)—are those that, in theory at least, cannot be made by any mixture of the other colors. Each of the **secondary colors**—orange, green, and violet (designated by the number 2)—are mixtures of the two primaries that each lies between. Thus, as we all learn in elementary school, green is made by mixing yellow and blue. The **intermediate colors** (designated by the number 3) are mixtures of a primary and a neighboring secondary. If we mix the primary yellow with the secondary orange, for instance, the result is yellow-orange.

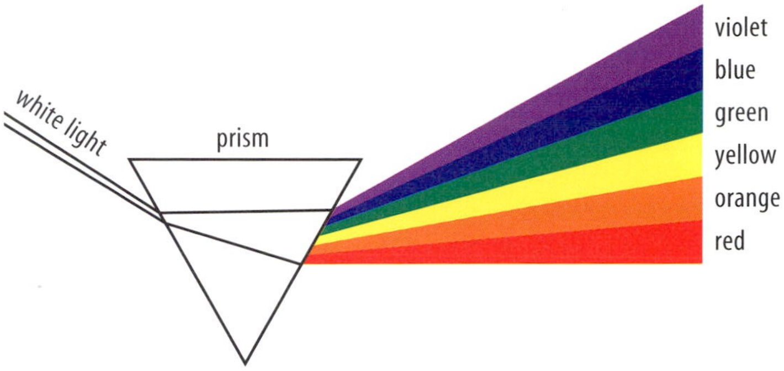

Fig. 146 Colors separated by a prism.

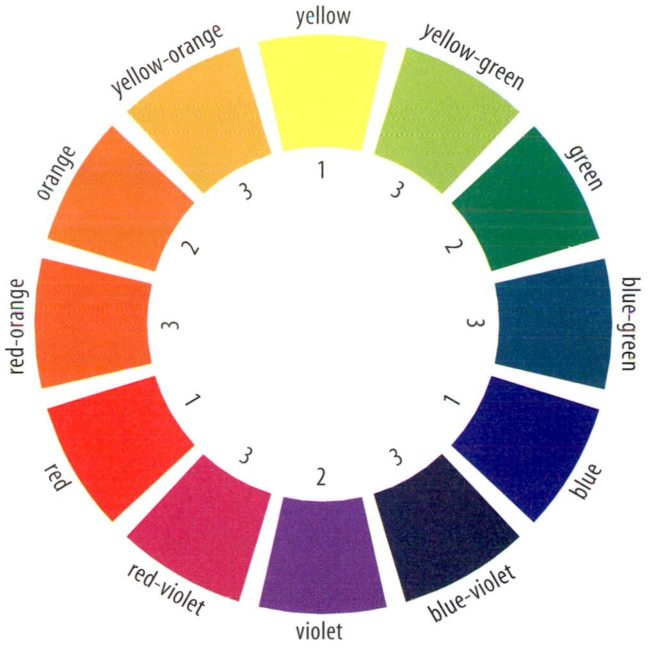

Fig. 147 Conventional color wheel.

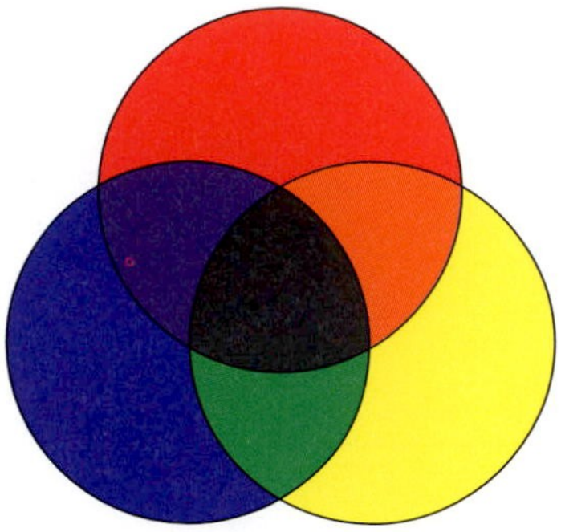

Fig. 148 Color mixtures of reflected pigment—subtractive process.

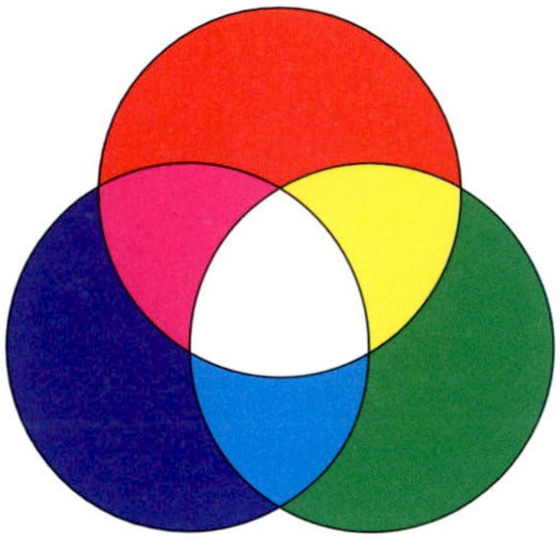

Fig. 149 Color mixtures of refracted light—additive process.

As we have already noted in our discussion of tint and shade, each primary and secondary color of the visible spectrum is called a hue. Thus all shades and tints of red—from pink to deep maroon—are said to be of the same red hue, though they are different keys of that hue. One of the more complex problems presented to us by color is that the primary and secondary hues change depending on whether we are dealing with *refracted* light or *reflected* pigment. The conventional color wheel illustrated on the previous page demonstrates the relationship among the various hues as reflected pigment. When we mix pigments, we are involved in a **subtractive** process (Fig. 148). That is, in mixing two primaries, the secondary that results is of a lower key and seems duller than either of the original two primaries because each given primary absorbs a different range of white light. Thus when we combine red and yellow, the resulting orange absorbs twice the light of either of its source primaries taken alone. Theoretically, if we combine all the pigments, we would absorb all light and end up with black, the absence of color altogether.

Refracted light, on the other hand, works in a very different manner. With refracted light, the primary colors are red-orange, green, and blue-violet. The secondaries are yellow, magenta, and cyan. When we mix light, we are involved in an **additive** process (Fig. 149). That is, if we mix two primaries of colored light, the resulting secondary is higher in key and seems brighter than either primary. Our most usual exposure to this process occurs when we watch television. This is especially apparent on a large screen monitor, where yellow, if viewed close up, can be seen to result from the overlapping of many red and green dots. In the additive color process, as more and more colors are combined, more and more light is added to the mixture, and the colors that result are brighter than either source taken alone. As Newton discovered, when the total spectrum of refracted light is recombined, white light results.

Color is described first by reference to its hue (red), then to its relative key or value (pink or maroon), and then also by its **intensity** or **saturation** (bright pink). Intensity is a function of a color's relative brightness or dullness. One lowers the intensity of a hue by adding to it either gray or the hue opposite it on the color wheel (in the case of red, we would add green). Intensity may also be reduced by adding **medium**—a liquid that makes paint easier to manipulate—to the hue.

There is perhaps no better evidence of the psychological impact a change in intensity can make than to look at the newly restored frescoes of the Sistine Chapel ceiling at the Vatican in Rome, painted by Michelangelo between 1508 and 1512 (Figs. 150 and 151). Restoration was begun in 1980 and was completed in 1995. The process was relatively simple. A solvent called AB 57, mixed with a fungicide and antibacterial agent and a cellulose gel so that it would not drip from the ceiling, was painted on to a small section of the fresco with a bristle brush. The AB 57 mixture was allowed to sit for three minutes, and then it was removed with a sponge and water that also removed the grime. The process was repeated in the dirtiest areas. The entire operation was documented in great detail by the Nippon Television Network of Japan, which funded the entire restoration project.

Restorers have discovered that the dull, somber hues always associated with Michelangelo were not the result of his **palette,** that is, the range of colors he preferred to use, but of centuries of accumulated dust, smoke, grease, and varnishes made of animal glue painted over the ceiling by earlier restorers. The colors are in fact much more saturated and intense than anyone had previously supposed. Some experts in fact find them so intense that they seem, beside the golden tones of the unrestored surface, almost garish. As a result, there has been some debate about the merits of the cleaning. But, in the words of one observer: "It's not a controversy. It's culture shock."

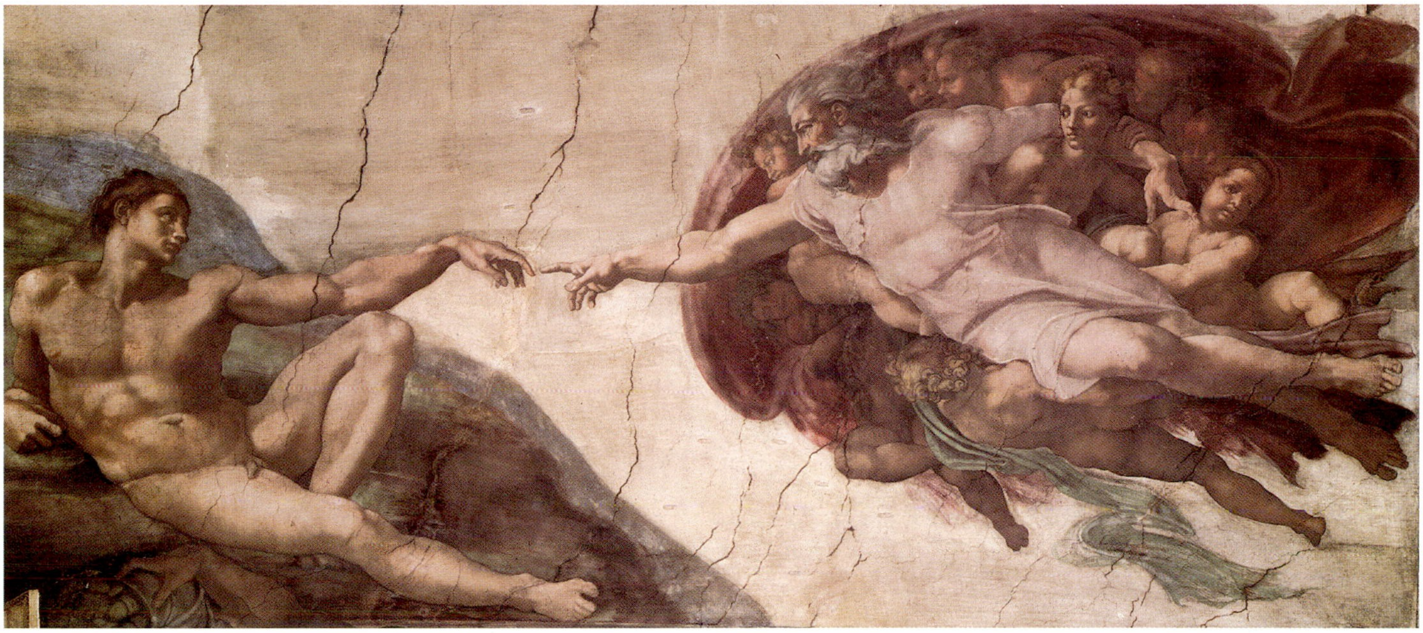

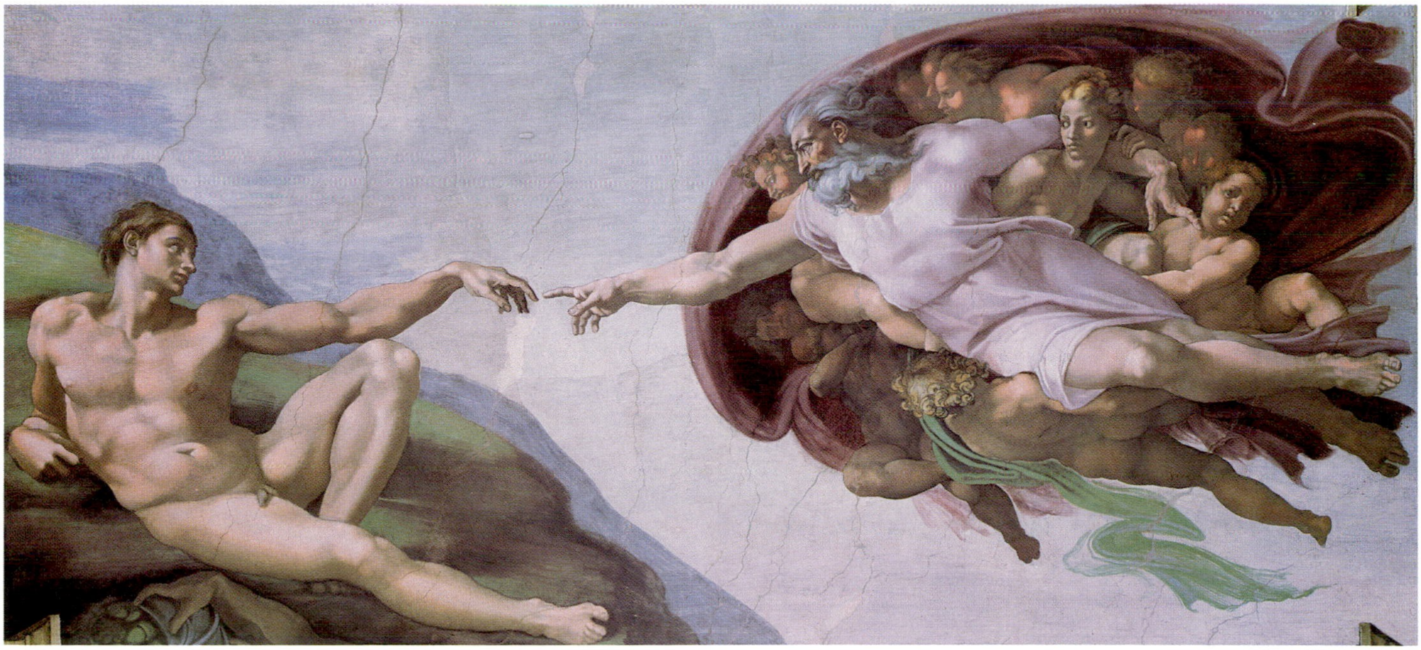

Figs. 150 and 151 Michelangelo, *The Creation of Adam* (top: unrestored; bottom: restored), ceiling of the Sistine Chapel, 1508–1512.
Fresco. The Vatican, Rome. Restored image ©Nippon TV, Tokyo.

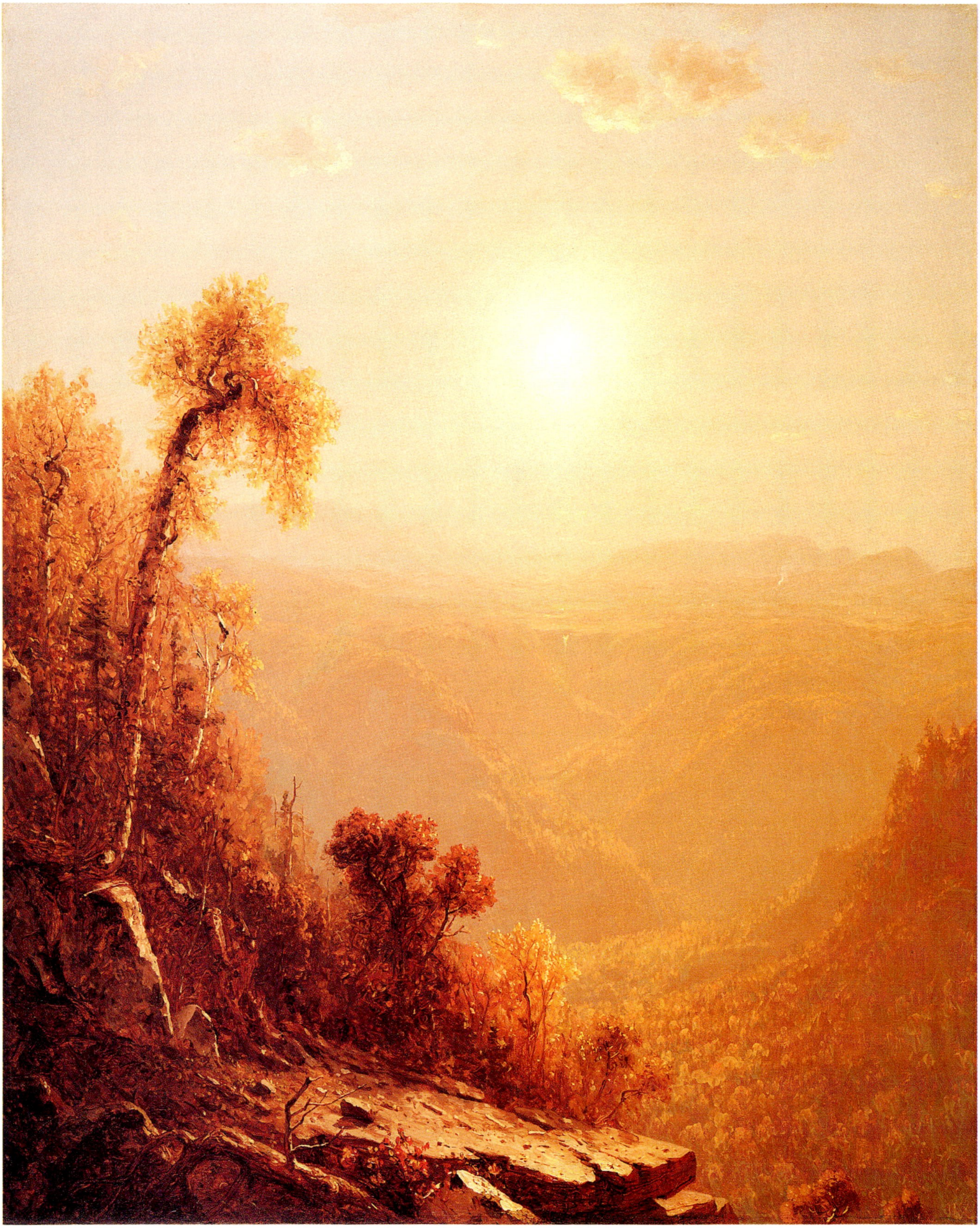

Fig. 152 Sanford R. Gifford, *October in the Catskills,* 1880.
Oil on canvas, 36 3/8 × 29 3/8 in. Los Angeles County Museum of Art.
Gift of Mr. and Mrs. Charles C. Shoemaker, Mr. and Mrs. J. Douglas Pardee, and Mr. and Mrs. John McGreevey.

Color schemes

Colors can be employed by painters in different ways to achieve a wide variety of effects. **Analogous** color schemes are those composed of hues that neighbor each other on the color wheel. Such color schemes are often organized on the basis of color **temperature.** Most of us respond to the range from yellow through orange and red as *warm,* and to the opposite side of the color wheel, from green through blue to violet, as *cool.* Sanford Gifford's *October in the Catskills* (Fig. 152) is a decidedly warm painting—just like a sunny fall day. The color scheme consists of yellows, oranges, and reds in varying degrees of intensity and key. Even what appears to be brown in this composition is a the result of mixing this spectrum of warm colors. Its warmth is so powerful that even the blue of the sky is barely perceptible through the all-consuming yellow atmosphere. The painting is a study in atmospheric perspective, though it modifies Leonardo's formula somewhat, since the distant hills do not appear "bluer," only softer in hue. Representing the effects of atmosphere was Gifford's chief goal in painting. "The really important matter," he would say, "is not the natural object itself, but the veil or medium through which we see it."

Just as warm and cool temperatures literally create contrasting physical sensations, when both warm and cool hues occur together in the same work of art they tend to evoke a sense of contrast and tension. Romare Bearden's *She-ba* (Fig. 153) is dominated by cool blues and greens, but surrounding and accenting these great blocks of color are contrasting areas of red, yellow, and orange. "Sometimes, in order to heighten the character of a painting," Bearden wrote in 1969, just a year before this painting was completed, "I introduce what appears to be a dissonant color where the red, browns, and yellows disrupt the placidity of the blues and greens." Queen of the Arab culture that brought the Muslim religion to Ethiopia, Sheba here imparts a regal serenity to all that surrounds her. It is as if, in her every gesture, she cools the atmosphere, like rain in a time of drought, or shade at an oasis in the desert.

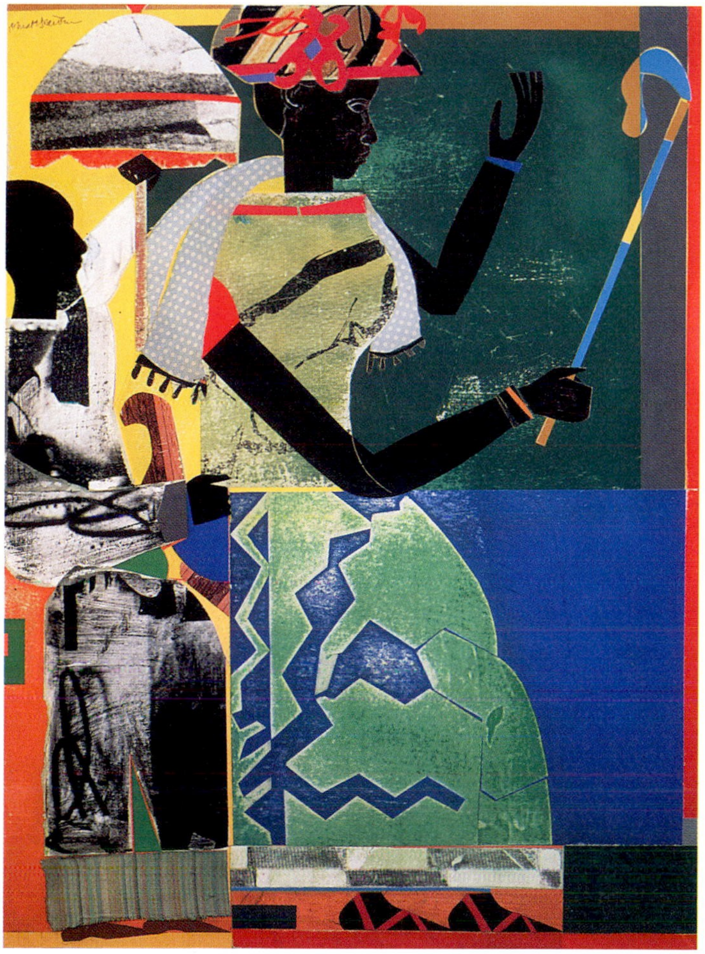

Fig. 153 Romare Bearden, *She-ba,* 1970.
Collage on composition board, 48 × 35 7/8 in.
Wadsworth Atheneum, Hartford, Connecticut.
Ella Gallup Sumner and Mary Catlin Sumner Collection.

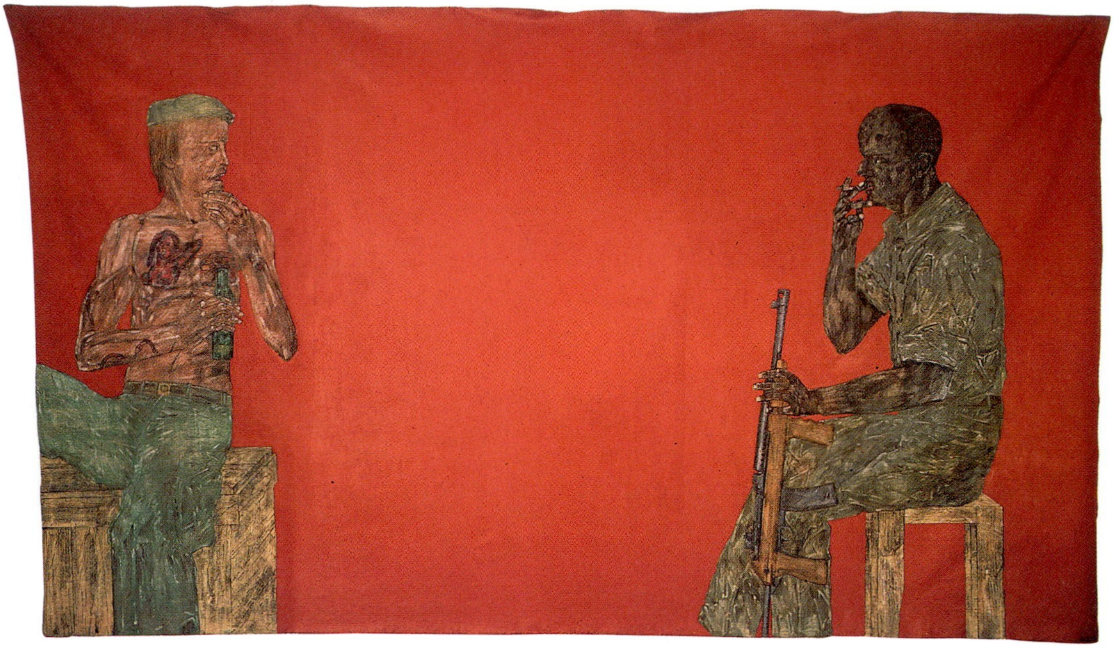

Fig. 154 Leon Golub, *Mercenaries III*, 1980.
Acrylic on canvas, 120 in. × 198 in. Collection Eli Broad Family Foundation, Los Angeles.

Color schemes composed of hues that lie opposite each other on the color wheel, as opposed to next to one another, are called **complementary.** Thus, on the traditional color wheel, there are three basic sets of complementary relations: orange/blue, yellow/violet, and red/green. Each intermediate color has its complement as well. When two complements appear in the same composition, especially if they are pure hues, each will appear more intense. If placed next to each other, without mixing, complements seem brighter than if

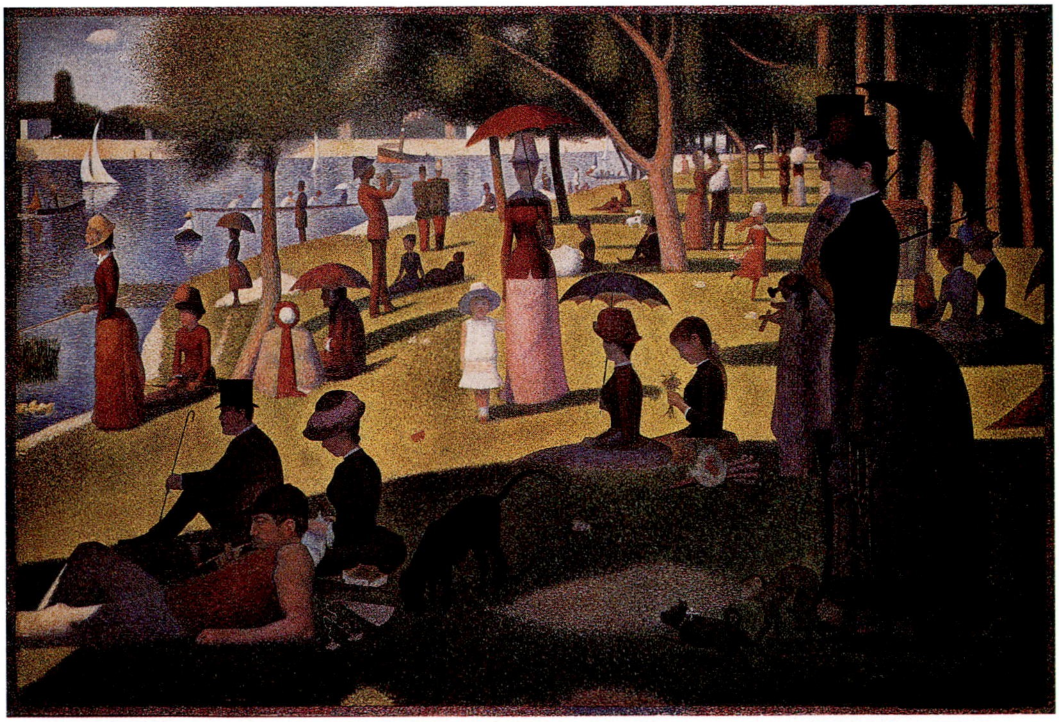

Fig. 155 Georges Seurat (1859–1891), *A Sunday on La Grande Jatte*, 1884–1886.
Oil on canvas, 71¾ in. × 10 ft. 1¼ in. The Art Institute of Chicago. Helen Birch Bartlett Memorial Collection. Photograph © 1995, The Art Institute of Chicago. All rights reserved.

they appear alone. This effect, known as **simultaneous contrast,** is due to the physiology of the eye. If, for example, you stare intensely at the color red for about 30 seconds, and then shift your vision to a field of pure white, you will see not red but a variety of green. Physiologically, the eye supplies an **afterimage** of a given hue in the color of its complement. This effect can be experienced in Leon Golub's *Mercenaries III* (Fig. 154). Based on news photos, Golub's painting attempts, in his words, to "have a sense of the contemporaneity of events. They are poised to be almost physically palpable, a tactile tension of events." The almost neon, electric red and green of the canvas clash dramatically. The color seems as explosive as the situation Golub depicts.

In his *A Sunday on La Grande Jatte* (Fig. 155), Georges Seurat has tried to *harmonize* his complementary colors rather than create a sense of tension with them. With what almost amounts to fanaticism, Seurat painted this giant canvas with thousands of tiny dots, or points, of pure color in a process that came to be known as *pointillism.* Instead of mixing color on the palette or canvas, he believed that the eye of the perceiver would be able to mix colors optically. He strongly believed that if he placed complements side by side—particularly orange and blue in the shadowed areas of the painting—that the intensity of the color would be dramatically enhanced. But to Seurat's dismay, most viewers found the painting "lusterless" and "murky." This is because there is a rather limited zone in which the viewer does in fact optically mix the pointillist dots. For most viewers, Seurat's painting works from about six feet away—closer, and the painting breaks down into abstract dots, further away, and the colors muddy, turning almost brown.

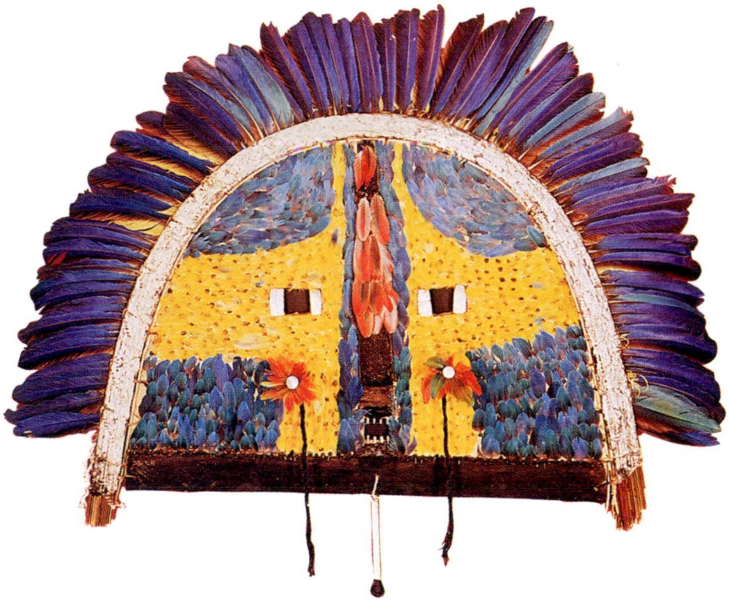

Fig. 156 Cara Grande feather mask, *Tapirapé,* Rio Tapirapé, Brazil, c. 1960.
H. 31 in. National Museum of the American Indian, New York.

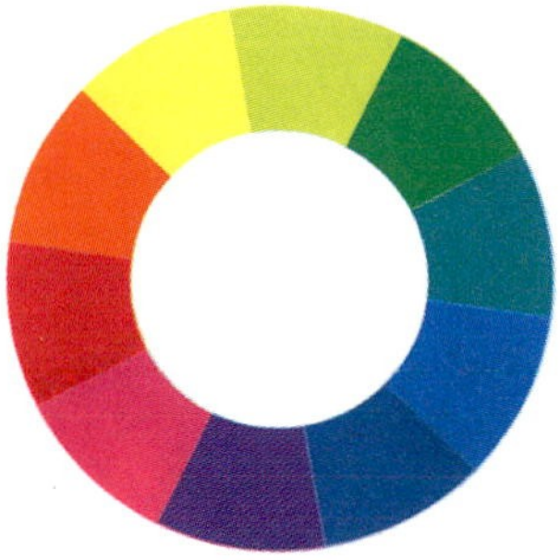

Fig. 157 Munsell color wheel.

One of the more vexing issues that the study of color presents is that the traditional color wheel really does not adequately describe true complementary color relations. For instance, the afterimage of red is not really green, but blue-green. In 1905, Albert Munsell created a color wheel based on five, rather than three, primary hues: yellow, green, blue, violet, and red (Fig. 157). The complement of each of these five is a secondary. Munsell's color wheel accounts for what is, to many eyes, one of the most powerful complementary color schemes, the relation between yellow and blue-violet. The Brazilian feather mask, known as a *Cara Grande* in Fig. 156, illustrates this contrast. The mask is worn during the annual Banana Fiesta in the Amazon basin; it is almost three feet tall. It is made of wood and covered with pitch to which feathers are attached. The brilliantly colored feathers are not dyed, but are the natural plumage of tropical birds, and the intensity of their color is heightened by the simultaneous contrast between yellow and blue-violet, which is especially apparent at the outer edge of the mask.

Chuck Close's Stanley

Chuck Close's 1981 oil painting *Stanley* (Fig. 159) might best be described as "layered" pointillism (refer to Fig. 155). Like all of his paintings, the piece is based on a photograph.

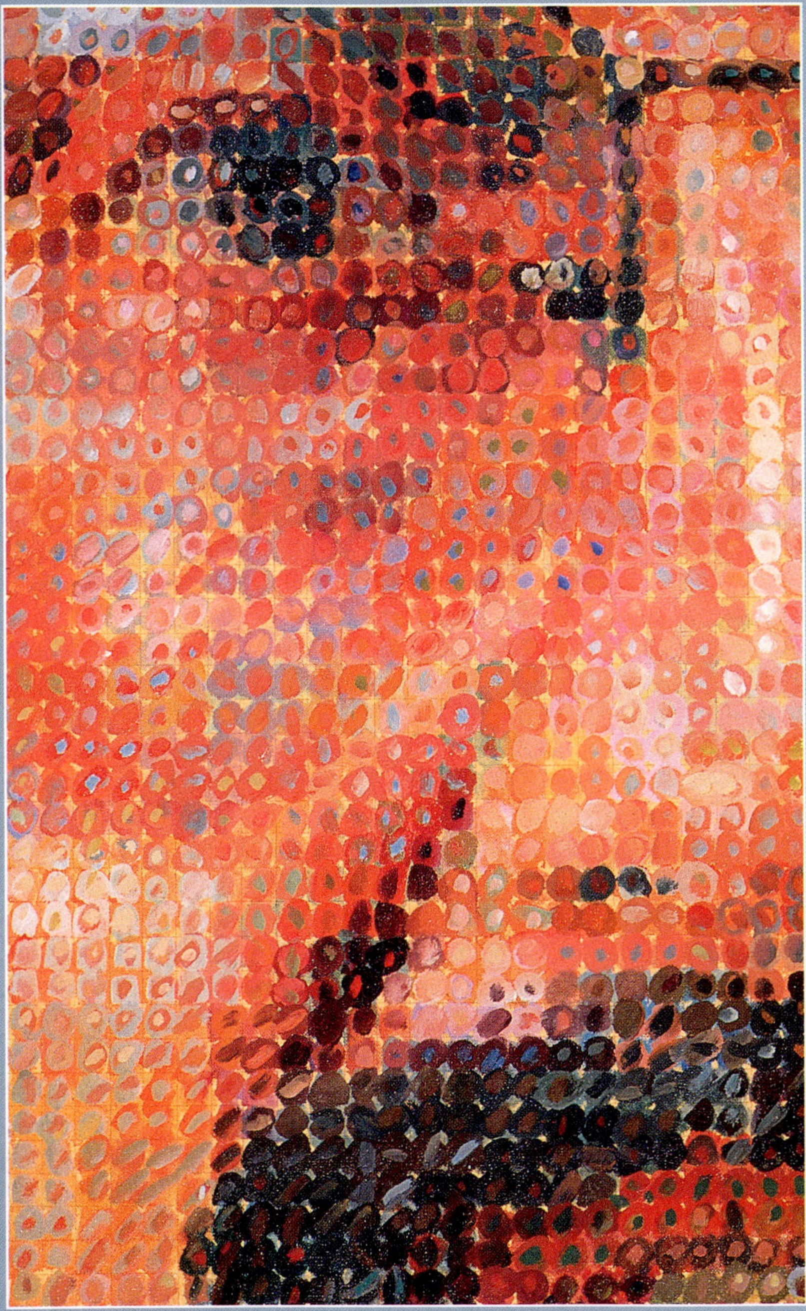

Fig. 158 Chuck Close, *Stanley* (large version), 1980–1981, and detail. Oil on canvas 101 × 84 in. The Solomon R. Guggenheim Museum, New York. Photograph by David Heald. © The Solomon R. Guggenheim Foundation, New York.

Close's working method is to overlay the original photograph with a grid. Then he draws a grid with the same number of squares on a canvas. Close is not so much interested in representing the person whose portrait he is painting, as reproducing, as accurately as possible, the completely abstract design that occurs in each square of the photo's grid. In essence, Close's large paintings—Stanley is nearly eight feet high and six feet wide—are made up of thousands of little square paintings, as the detail (Fig. 158) makes clear. Each of these "micro"-paintings is composed as a small target, an arrangement of between two, three, or four concentric circles. Viewed up close, it is hard to see anything but the design of each square of the grid. But as the viewer moves further away, the design of the individual squares of the composition dissolves, and the sitter's features emerge with greater and greater clarity.

In an interview conducted by art critic Lisa Lyons for an essay that appears in the book *Chuck Close*, published by Rizzoli International in 1987, Close describes his working method in *Stanley* at some length, comparing his technique to, of all things, the game of golf:

WORKS IN PROGRESS

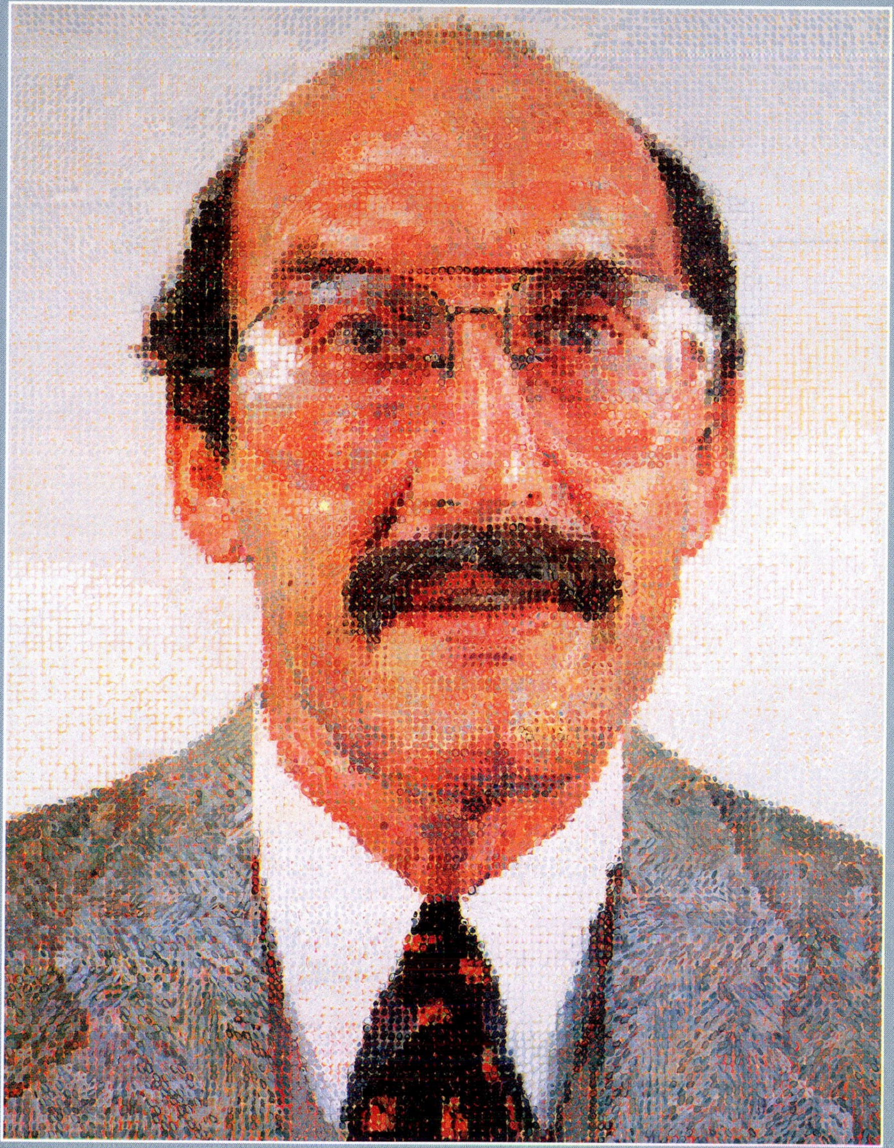

Fig. 159 Chuck Close, *Stanley* (large version), 1980–1981. Oil on canvas, 101 × 84 in. The Solomon R. Guggenheim Museum, New York. Photograph by David Heald. © The Solomon R. Guggenheim Foundation, New York.

Golf is the only sport in which you move from the general to the specific. In the beginning when you take your first shot, you can't even see the pin. And in a matter of three or four strokes, you're supposed to be in the cup, a very small, specific place a very long ways away. I thought of the gridded canvas as a golf course, and each square of the grid as a par-four hole. Then just to complicate things and make the game more interesting, I teed off in the opposite direction of the pin. For example, I knew that the color of the skin was going to be in the orange family, so I started out by putting down a thin wash of blue, green, or purple—something very different from what the final color would be. The second color then had to go miles to alter the first one. So for this big correcting stroke, I chose a hue that moved me into the generic color family I should have been aiming for. Now I had moved into orange, but it was too yellow, so in the middle of that stroke, I put down a gob of red to move into a reddish orange. Then I was at the equivalent of being "on the green" and hopefully quite close to the cup. But the color was still much too bright. So the final stroke was a little dot of blue, the complementary color, which optically mixed with the orange and lowered its intensity, dropping it down to an orangish brown. I was in the cup.

[It was possible] to have a birdie—to come in a stroke early. It was even possible to have an eagle—to come in two [strokes] under par. Of course, it was also equally possible to have a bogie or a double bogie [one or two strokes over par], and even get mired in some aesthetic sandtrap, just making strokes and getting nowhere at all.

Close's "game" with color is exacting and demanding, requiring a knowlege of the optical effects of color mixing that is virtually unparalleled in the history of art. He is able to achieve, in his work, two seemingly contradictory goals at once. On the one hand, his work is fully representational. On the other, it is fully abstract, even nonobjective in its purely formal interest in color. Close has it both ways.

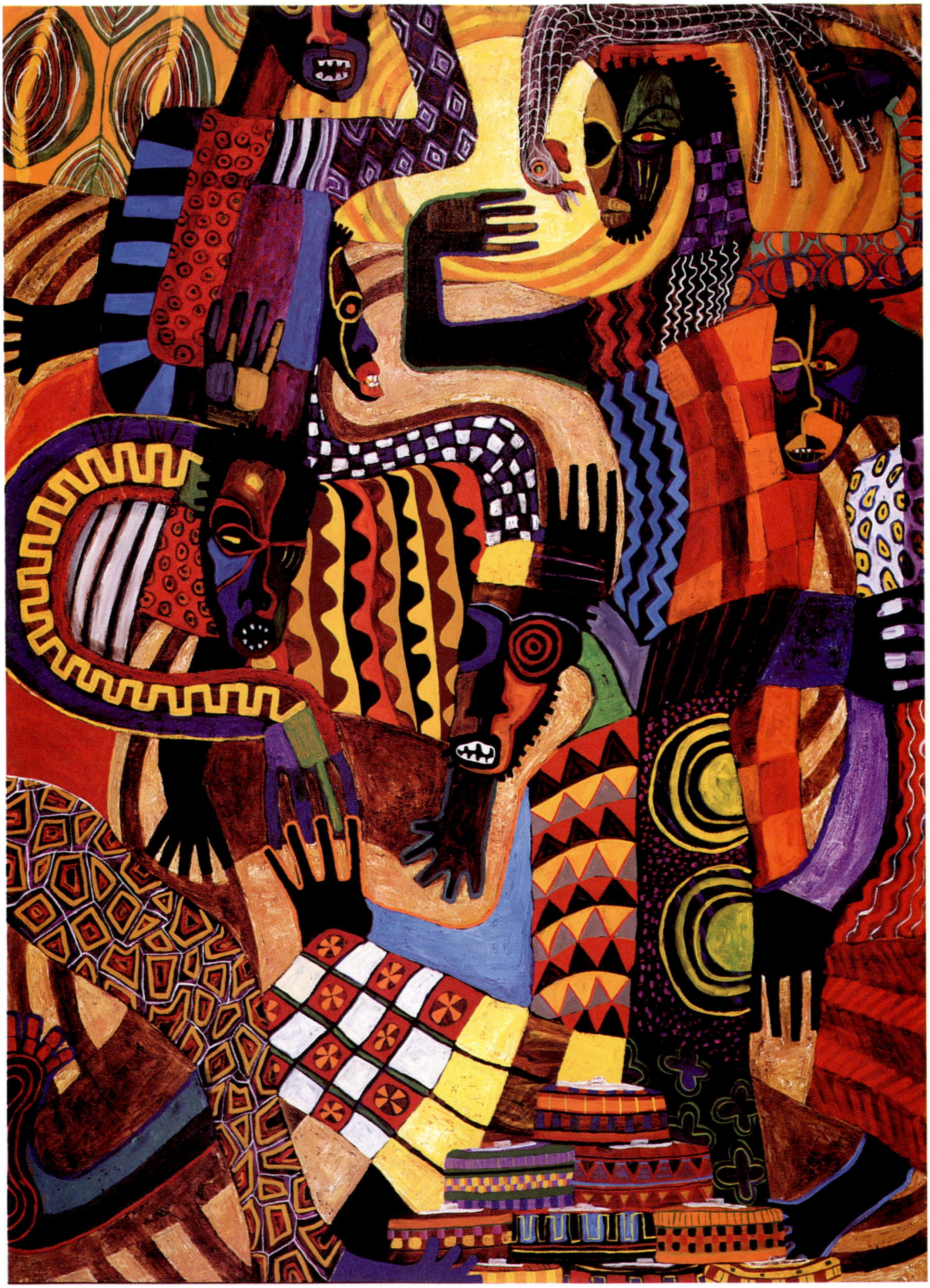

Fig. 160 Charles Searles, *Filàs for Sale* (from the *Nigerian Impressions* series), 1972.
Acrylic on canvas, 72 × 50 in. National Center of Afro-American Artists, Roxbury, Massachusetts.

Artists working with either analogous or complementary color schemes chose to limit the range of their color selection. In his painting *Filàs for Sale* (Fig. 160), Charles Searles has rejected such a *closed* or *restricted palette* in favor of an *open palette,* in which he employs the entire range of hues in a wide variety of values and intensities. Such a painting is **polychromatic.** The painting depicts a Nigerian marketplace and was inspired by a trip Searles took to Nigeria, Ghana, and Morocco in 1972. "What really hit me," Searles says, "is that the art is in the people. The way the people carried themselves, dressed, decorated their houses became the art to me, like a living art." A pile of *filàs,* or brightly patterned skullcaps, occupies the right foreground of this painting. The confusion and turmoil of the crowded marketplace is mirrored in the swirl of the variously colored textile patterns. Each pattern has its own color scheme—yellow arcs against a set of violet dots, for instance, in the swatch of cloth just above the pile of hats—but all combine to create an almost disorienting sense of movement and activity.

Color in Representational Art

There are four different ways of using color in representational art. The artist can employ local color, represent perceptual color, create an optical mix like Seurat, or simply use color arbitrarily. The green tree and the red brick building in Stuart Davis's *Summer Landscape* (Fig. 161) are examples of **local color,** or the color of objects viewed close-up in even lighting conditions. Local color is the color we

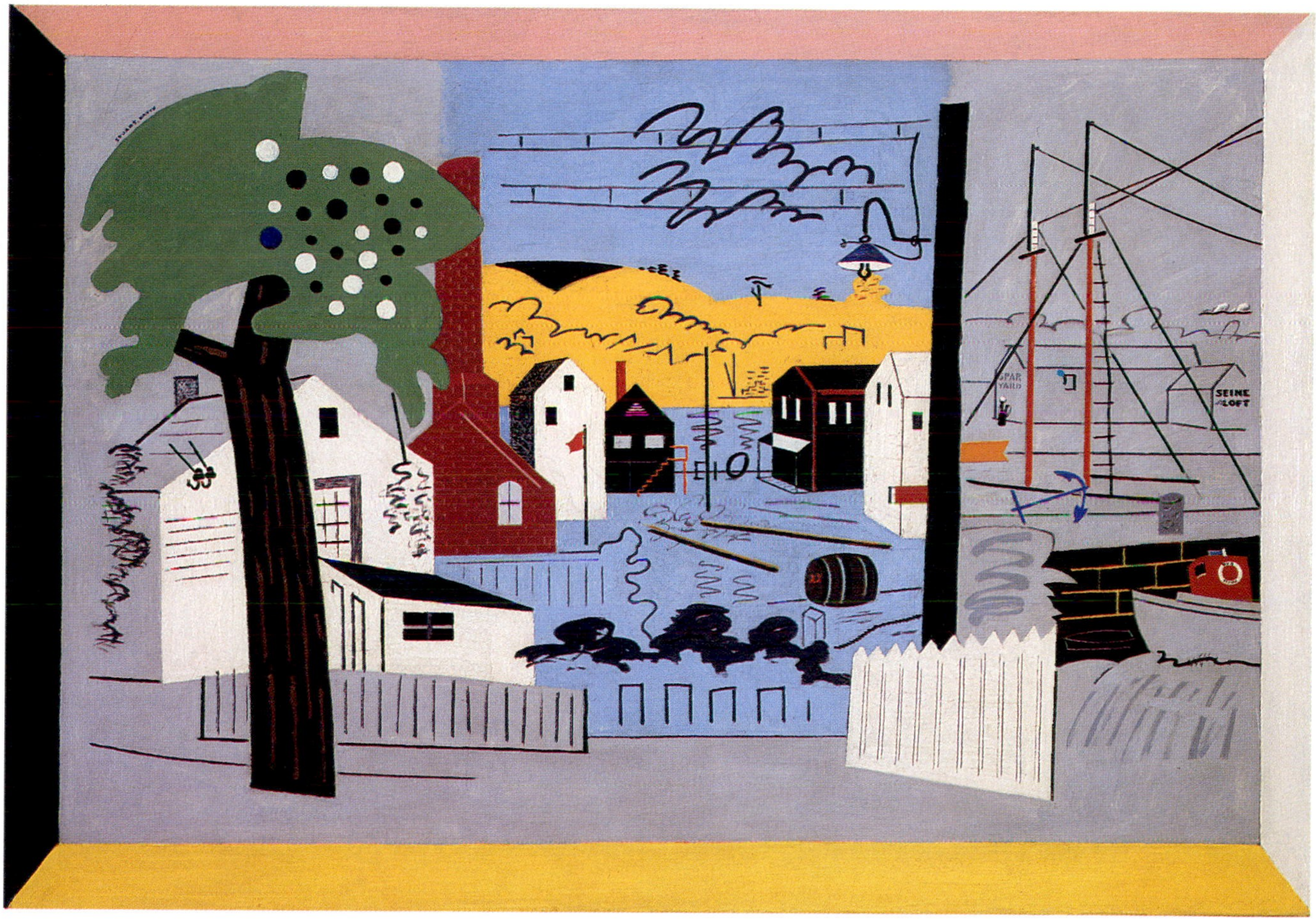

Fig. 161 Stuart Davis, *Summer Landscape,* 1930.
Oil on canvas, 29 × 42 in. Collection, The Museum of Modern Art, New York. Purchase.

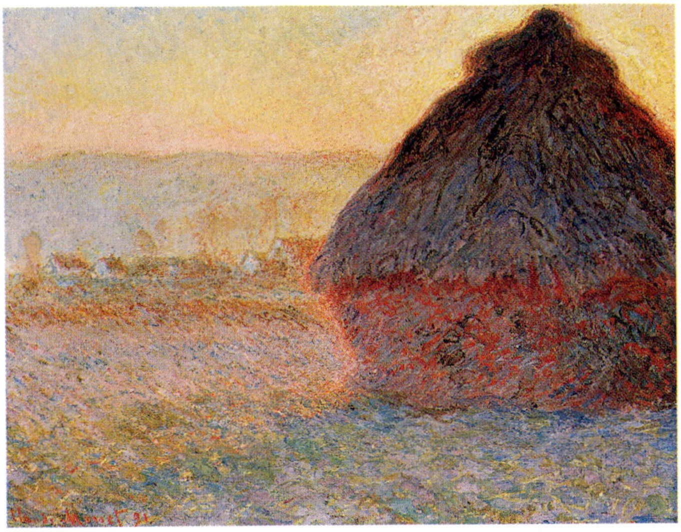

Fig. 162 Claude Monet, *Grainstack (Sunset)*, 1891.
Oil on canvas, 28 7/8 × 36 1/2 in. Museum of Fine Arts, Boston. Juliana Cheney Edwards Collection.

"know" an object to be, in the way that we know a banana is yellow or a fire truck is red. But we are also aware that as the effects of light and atmosphere on an object change, we will perceive its color as different. As we know from the example of atmospheric perspective, we actually see a distant pine-covered hill as blue, not green. The Impressionist painters were especially concerned with rendering such **perceptual colors.** Monet painted his landscapes outdoors, in front of his subject—**plein air painting** is the technical term, the French word for "open air"—so as to be true to the optical colors of the scene before him. He did not paint a haystack yellow simply because he knew hay to be yellow. He painted it in the colors that natural light rendered it to his eyes. Thus this *Grainstack (Sunset)* (Fig. 162) is dominated by reds, with after-images of green flashing throughout.

The Impressionists' attempt to render the effects of light by representing *perceptual reality* is different than Seurat's attempt to reproduce light's effects by means of **optical color** mixing. Monet mixes color on the canvas. Seurat expects color to mix in your own eye. He put two hues next to each other, and a third, new hue results in the beholder's eye. Seurat's experiments were carried further by his student Paul Signac. Signac recognized that Seurat's dots had been too small to be read legibly from very far away. So, abandoning the dot, Signac began to utilize a much larger square, mozaic pattern of brushstrokes, visible in his 1905 canvas *The Windmills at Owerschie* (Fig. 163). To distinguish his method from *pointillism,* he insisted that his style be known as *divisionism*—the

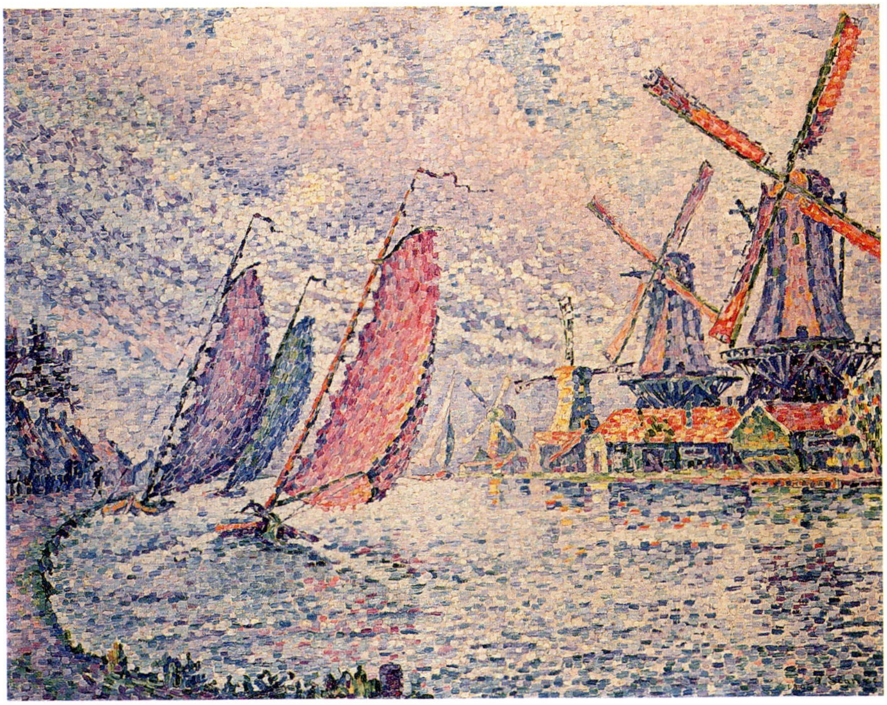

Fig. 163 Paul Signac, *The Mills at Owerschie*, 1905.
Oil on canvas, 25 × 31 1/2 in. Museum of Fine Arts, Springfield, Massachusetts. Robert J. Freedman Memorial Collection.

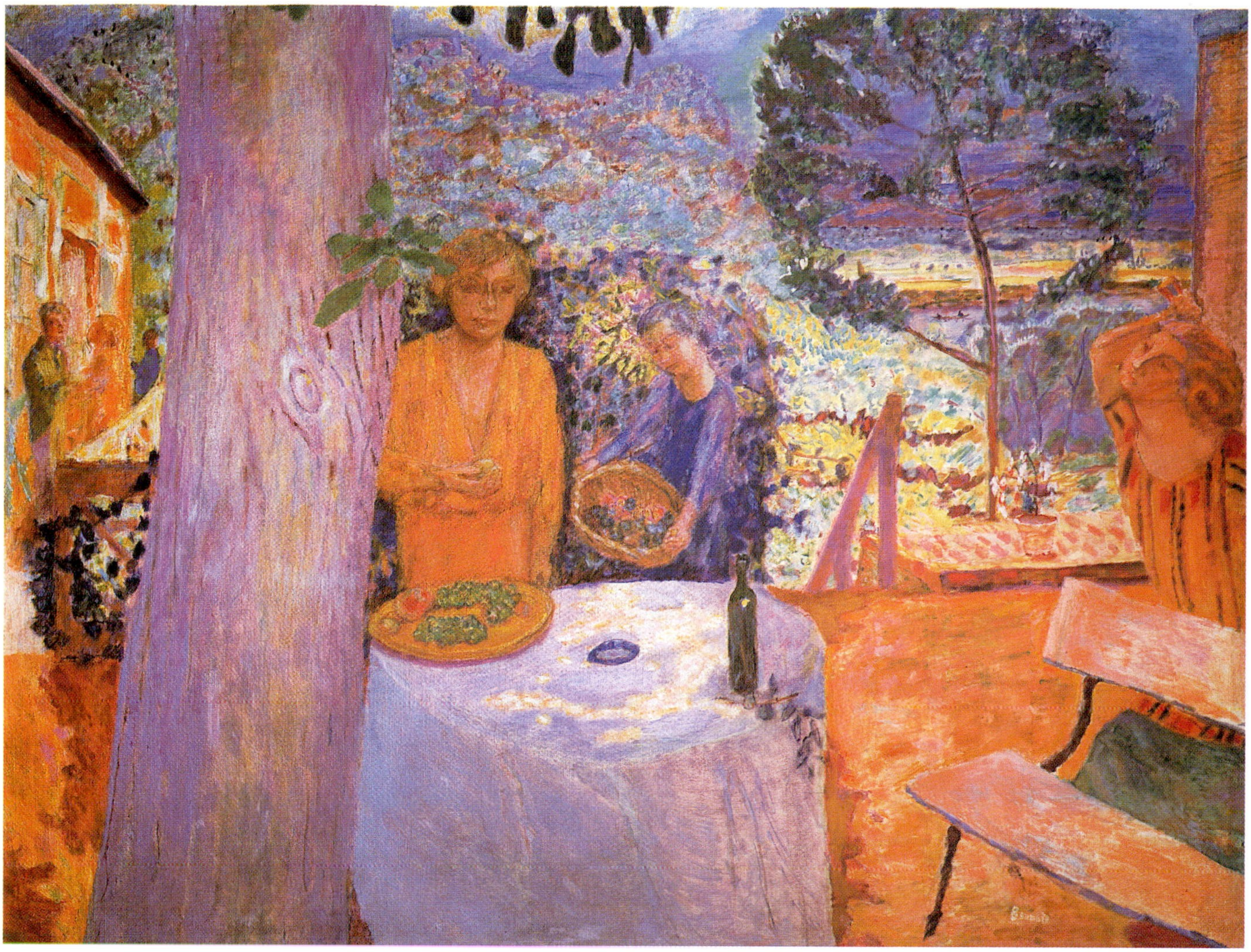

Fig. 164 Pierre Bonnard, *The Terrace at Vernon*, c. 1920–1939.
Oil on canvas, 57 11/16 × 76 1/2 in. The Metropolitan Museum of Art, New York. Gift of Mrs. Frank Jay Gould, 1968. 68.1.

painter, he wrote, "does not paint with *dots,* he *divides.*" That is, the optical mix is created by the practice of dividing the paint on the canvas by means of separate, unmixed strokes of different pigments. Depending on the nature of each stroke—depending, that is, on such variables as its hue, intensity, and size—a whole range of effects could be achieved. The painting might shimmer, vibrate, glow, or even turn muddy and pale.

Artists sometimes choose to paint things in colors that are not "true" to either their optical or local colors. Bonnard's painting *The Terrace at Vernon* (Fig. 164) is an example of the expressive use of **arbitrary color.** No tree is "really" violet, and yet this large foreground tree is. The woman at the left holds an apple, but the apple is as orange as her dress. Next to her a young woman carrying a basket seems almost to disappear into the background, painted, as she is, in almost the same hues as the landscape (or is it a hedge?) behind her. At the right, another young woman in orange reaches above her head, melding into the ground around her. Everything in the composition is sacrificed to Bonnard's interest in the play between warm and cool colors, chiefly orange and violet or blue-violet, which he uses to flatten the composition, so that fore-, middle-, and backgrounds all seem to coexist in the same space. "The main subject," Bonnard would explain, "is the surface which has its color, its laws, over and above those of the objects." He sacrifices both the local and optical color of things to the arbitrary color scheme of the composition.

Henri Matisse's Dance II

Matisse's giant painting *Dance II* (Fig. 167) is one of two paintings commissioned in 1909 by the Russian collector Sergei Shchukin for the stairway of his home in Moscow, each designed to decorate a different landing. The circle of dancing young women or nymphs, revelling in their freedom, first appears in Matisse's work in the center background of his famous *Le Bonheur de vivre*, or *Joy of Life*, which was painted in 1905–1906 (Fig. 165). The scene of the earlier painting is Bacchanalian—that is, it takes place under the sign of Bacchus, god of wine—and *Dance II* was conceived in the same spirit. It represents an orgiastic indulgence in sensual pleasure, a peaceful, pastoral world in which lovers embrace, wine flows, and the sun eternally warms both flesh and spirit.

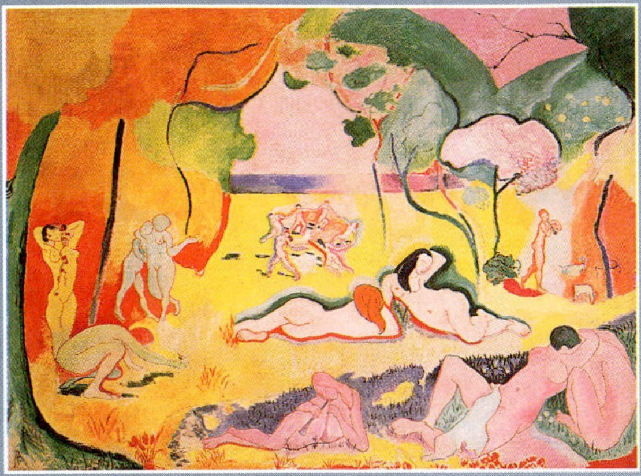

Fig. 165 Henri Matisse (1869–1954), *Le Bonheur de vivre*, 1905–1906.
Oil on canvas, 69 1/8 × 94 7/8 in.
Photograph ©1997 by The Barnes Foundation, all rights reserved.

Probably no other modern painter was as determined as Matisse to celebrate the good life in his work. His first major success had been the sale, in 1905, of a large divisionist canvas entitled *Luxe, calme et volupté, Luxury, calm and voluptuousness* (Fig. 166), to the divisionist master Paul Signac, who hung the painting in his dining room. Signac saw Matisse as a disciple and invited him to spend the summer in the south of France near his own home on the Mediterranean coast. But no sooner did Matisse arrive in the South than he began to question the divisionist approach to painting. He wrote to Signac complaining that the color and drawing in *Luxe, calme, et volupté* were not in accord. Divisionism's "breaking up of color led," he felt, "to the breaking up of form, of contour." Matisse, in other words, fully appreciated the sensuousness of Signac's color, but he missed, in the application of short strokes of color all over the canvas, the sensuous curves of line. The *Bonheur de vivre,* with its broad sweeps of color and its sensually outlined figures, represents Matisse's break with divisionism and the beginnings of his own mature style. He has begun to enlarge the divisionist stroke into the large, strongly outlined fields of color that are evident in *Dance II*.

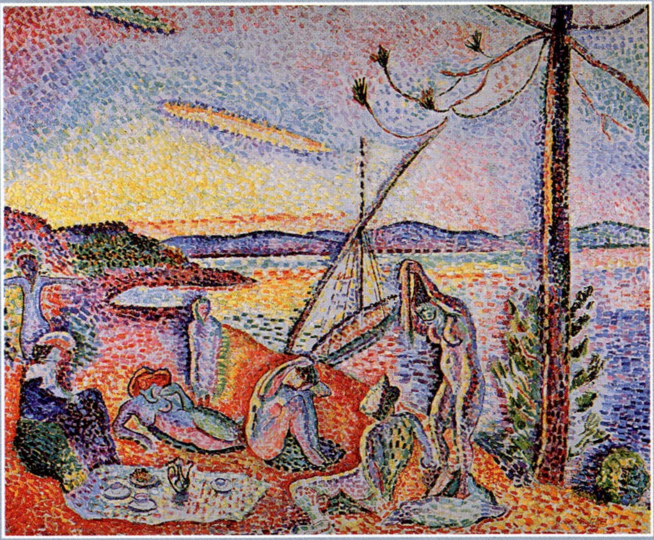

Fig. 166 Henri Matisse, *Luxe, calme et volupté*, 1904.
Oil on canvas, 38 1/2 × 46 1/2 in. Musée d'Orsay, Paris, France.
Photograph by Erich Lessing/ARS/Art Resource, New York.

WORKS IN PROGRESS

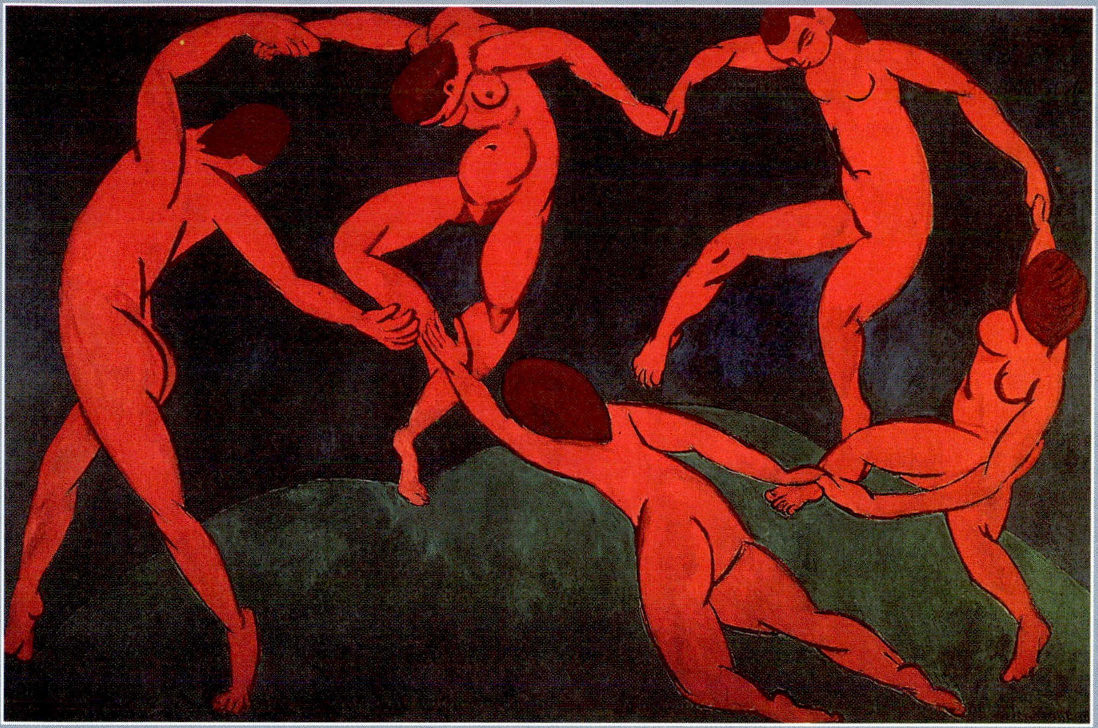

Fig. 167 Henri Matisse, *Dance II (La Danse II)*, 1910.
Oil on canvas, 8 ft. 5⅝ in. × 12 ft. 9½ in. The Hermitage Museum, St. Petersburg. Formerly Collection Sergei Shchukin. Scala/ARS/Art Resource, New York.

Dance II not only represents a simplification of the *Bonheur de vivre's* themes but a simplification of its presentation. Matisse's palette has been reduced to three colors. In his first full-scale sketch for the painting—known as *Dance* (first version) (Fig. 168)—the figures are flesh-toned and local in nature. The sky is blue, the grass is green, and flesh is pink. But in the final work the figures become vermillion. The green of the hillside seems more intense—in part because the extraordinarily intense vermillion contrasts with it so—and blue-violet sky is equally brilliant.

What moved Matisse to abandon local color for this arbitrary color scheme? When *Dance II* and *Music*, its companion painting, were exhibited in the autumn of 1910, they were widely attacked. Shchukin himself decided not to accept them (though he would later change his mind). The colors are, in fact, the primary colors of light—red-orange (vermillion), green, and blue-violet (see Fig. 149). Where Seurat and Signac had attempted to create light in the eye, Matisse, he would admit, tried to "generate" it. It is as if the painting is a turbine, generating the electricity we feel standing before it.

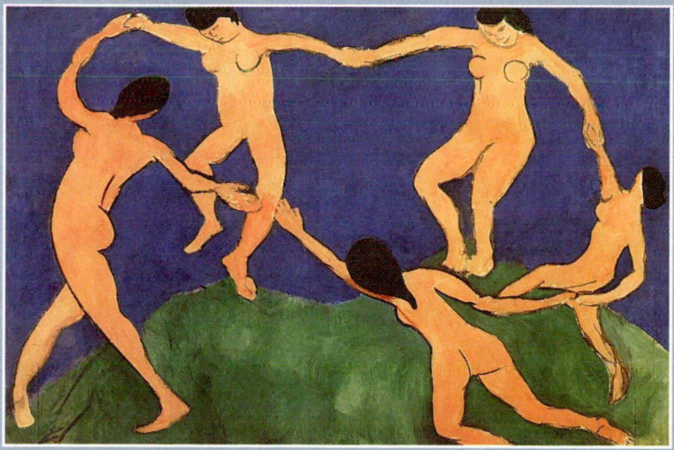

Fig. 168 Henri Matisse, *Dance* (first version), Paris, March 1909.
Oil on canvas, 8 ft. 6½ in. × 12 ft. 9½ in. The Museum of Modern Art, New York. Gift of Nelson A. Rockefeller in honor of Alfred H. Barr, Jr. Photograph © 1996 The Museum of Modern Art, New York.

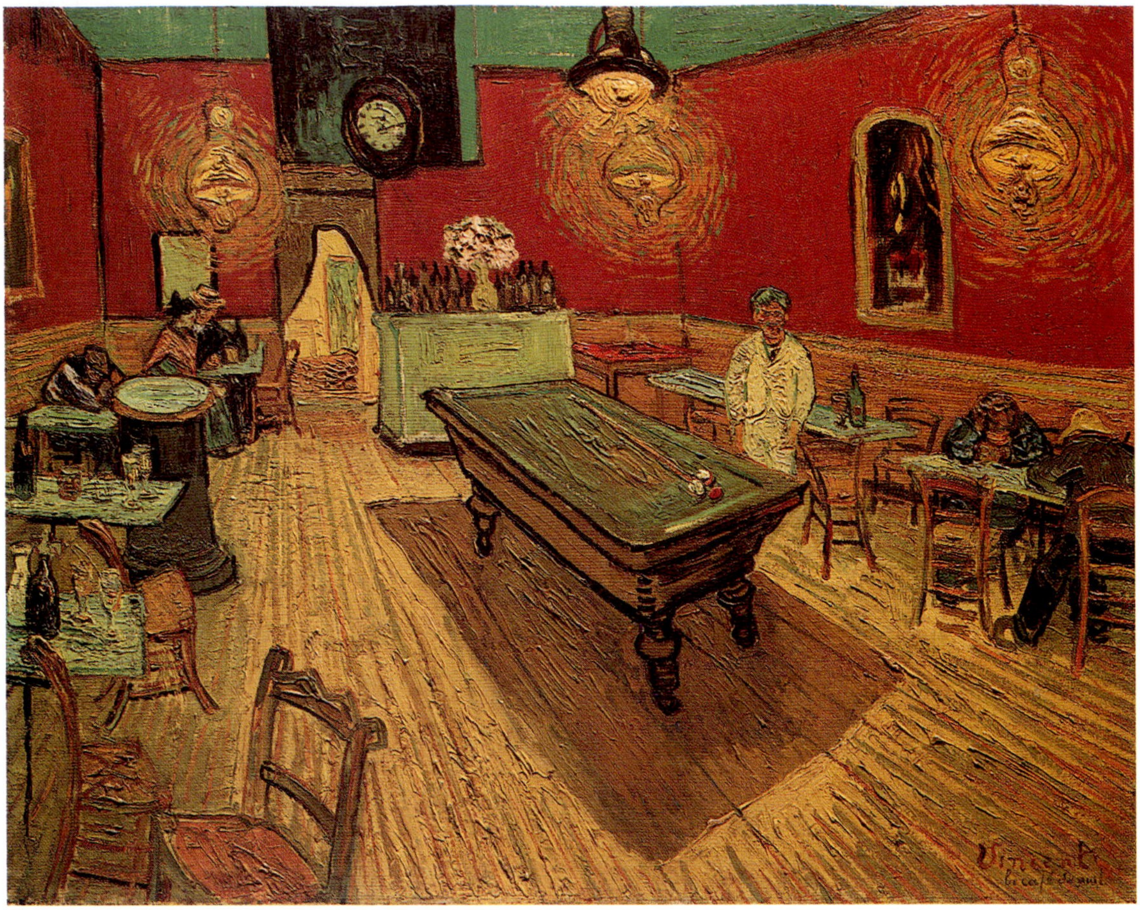

Fig. 169 Vincent van Gogh, *The Night Café,* 1888.
Oil on canvas, 28 1/2 × 36 1/4 in. Yale University Art Gallery, New Haven, Connecticut. Bequest of Stephen Carlton Clark.

Symbolic Use of Color

As we have seen in the example of Leon Golub's *Mercenaries* painting (Fig. 154), the complementary opposition between red and green *symbolizes* larger thematic oppositions of the work. To different people in different situations and in different contexts, color symbolizes different things. There is no one meaning for any given color, though in a particular cultural environment, there may be a shared understanding of it. So, for instance, when we see a stop light, we assume that everyone understands that red means "stop," and green means "go." In China, however, this distinction does not exist. In the context of war, red might mean "death" or "blood," or "anger." In the context of Valentine's Day, it means "love." Most Americans, when confronted by the complementary pair of red and green, think first of all of Christmas.

In his painting *The Night Café* (Fig. 169), van Gogh employs red and green to his own expressive ends. In a letter to his brother Theo, written September 8, 1888, he described how the complements work to create a sense of visual tension and emotional imbalance:

> *In my picture of the* Night Café *I have tried to express the idea that the café is a place where one can ruin oneself, run mad, or commit a crime. I have tried to express the terrible passions of humanity by means of red and green. . . . Everywhere there is a clash and contrast of the most alien reds and greens. . . . So I have tried to express, as it were, the powers of darkness in a low wine-shop, and all this in an atmosphere like a devil's furnace of pale sulphur. . . . It is color not locally true from the point of view of the stereoscopic realist, but color to suggest the emotion of an ardent temperament.*

While there is a sense of opposition in Wassily Kandinsky's *Black Lines* (Fig. 170) as well, the atmosphere of the painting is nowhere near so ominous. The work is virtually nonobjective, though a hint of landscape can be seen in the upper left where three mountainlike forms rise in front of and above what appears to be a horizon line defined by a lake or an ocean at sunset. The round shapes that dominate the painting seem to burst into flowers. Emerging like pods from the red-orange border at the painting's right, they suffuse the atmosphere with color, as if to overwhelm and dominate the nervous black lines that give the painting its title.

Color had specific symbolic meaning for Kandinsky. "Blue," he says, "is the heavenly color." Its opposite is yellow, "the color of the earth." Green is a mixture of the two; as a result, it is "passive and static, and can be compared to the so-called 'bourgeoisie'—self-satisfied, fat, and healthy." Red, on the other hand, "stimulates and excites the heart." The complementary pair of red and green juxtaposes the passive and the active. "In the open air," he writes, "the harmony of red and green is very charming," recalling for him not the "powers of darkness" that van Gogh witnessed in the pair, but the simplicity and pastoral harmony of an idealized peasant life.

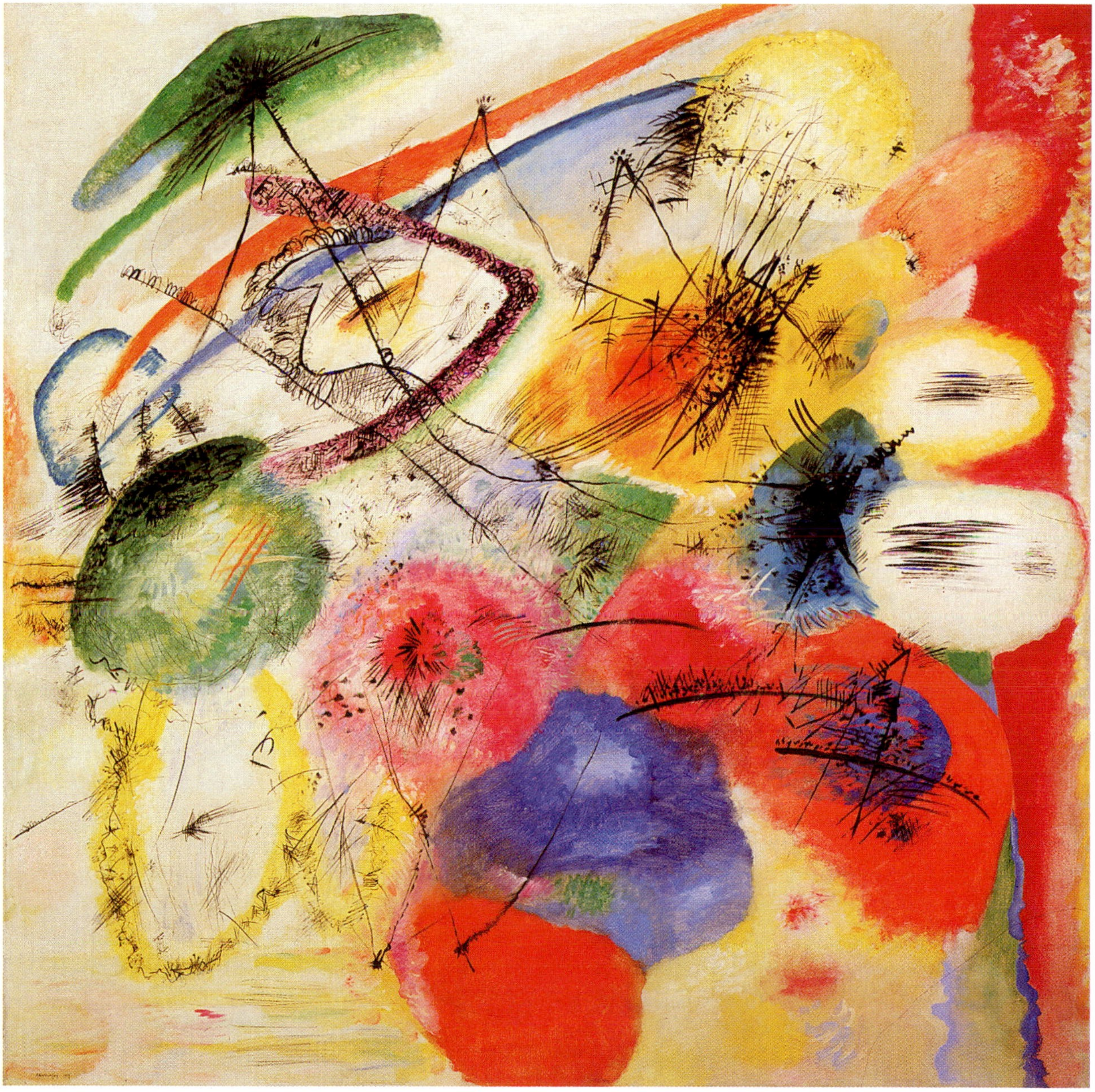

Fig. 170 Wassily Kandinsky, *Black Lines,* 1913.
Oil on canvas, 51 × 51⅝ in. Solomon R. Guggenheim Museum, New York.
Gift, Solomon R. Guggenheim, 1937. Photograph: David Heald © The Solomon R. Guggenheim Foundation, New York. FN 37.241.

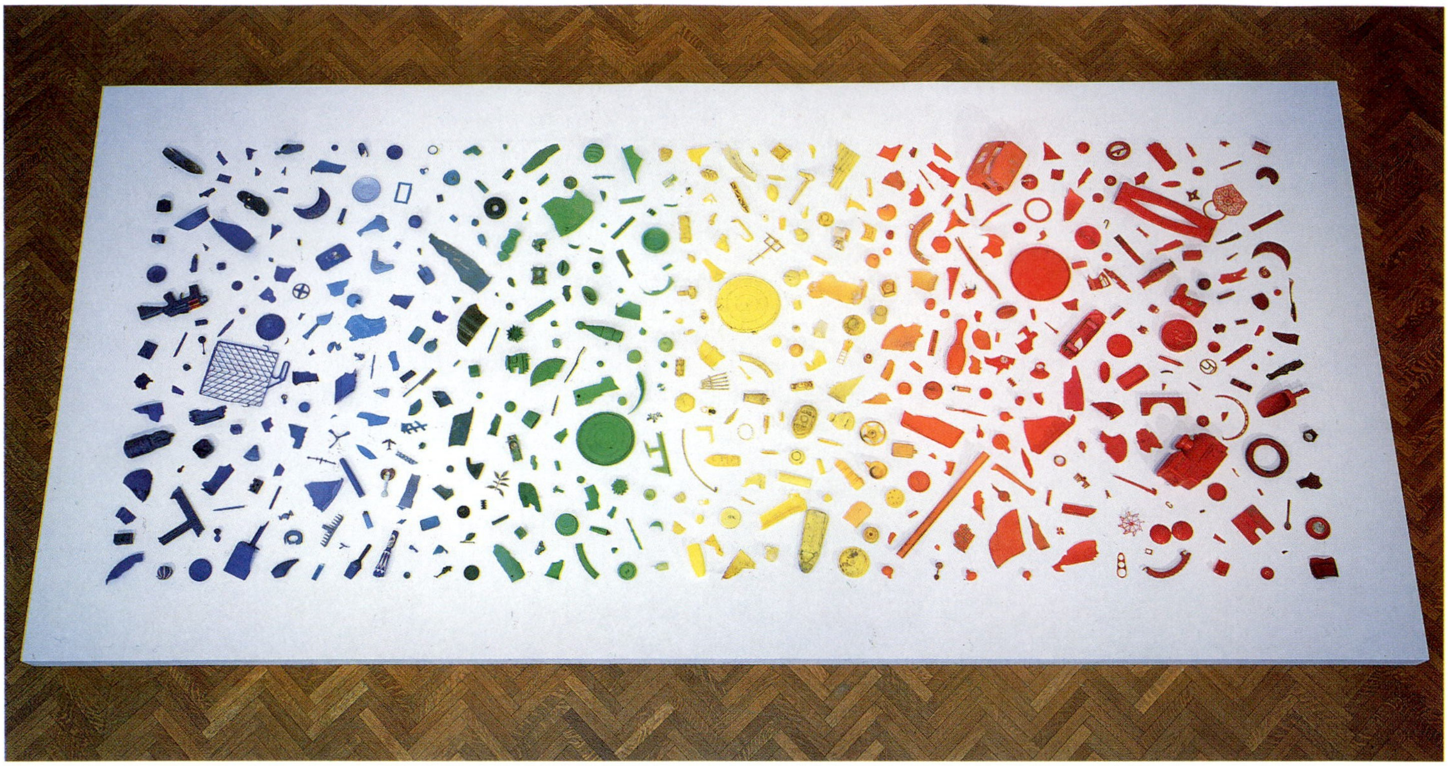

Fig. 171 Tony Cragg, ***Newton's Tones/New Stones,*** **1982.**
Plastic floor construction, 197 × 72 in. (16 ft. 5 in. × 6 ft.). Courtesy Marian Goodman Gallery, New York.

British artist Tony Cragg's *Newton's Tones/New Stones* (Fig. 171) reminds us, finally, that color is a function of light. Trained as a scientist, Cragg turned to art in order to create works that demonstrate the complexities of the modern world in straightforward, even simple terms that the average person on the street can understand. In this piece, Cragg reinvents Sir Isaac Newton's spectrum, but it is not merely white light that has passed through Cragg's prism, exploding into a rainbow of colors. The material world has passed through it as well. Colorfast plastic toys, tools, and kitchen utensils, all debris gathered on a Sussex, England beach, have fallen into their "proper" place on the spectrum. This is light transformed into waste, the "new stones" of postindustrial society. The sheer beauty of the "natural" color spectrum is undercut by the unnatural matter of which it is composed.

In this chapter, we have witnessed how artists use the properties of light to help us define spatial relationships in atmospheric perspective, to define volume by means of chiaroscuro and other modeling techniques such as cross-hatching, and to manipulate key or value in order to create a range of moods. We have seen how the contrast between light and dark can be an effective expressive tool, and how in different cultures light and dark mean different things. And we have paid detailed attention to the properties of light that result in color. Color is an extraordinarily versatile tool for the artist, allowing for an almost limitless range of color schemes. In representing the world, artists can utilize color's local effects, its perceptual qualities, the way in which it mixes optically in the viewer's eye. Or, forsaking fidelity to the world, they can use it arbitrarily, seeking other effects. Finally, color can be employed, like the contrast between light and dark, to symbolize many different things, depending on the artist's sensibility and intentions.

CHAPTER 7

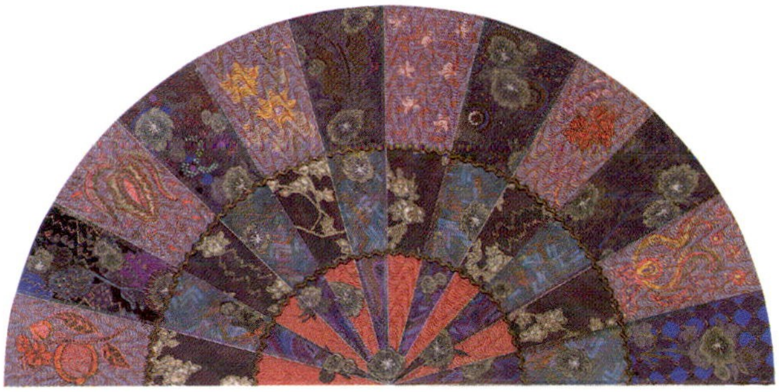

Other Formal Elements

Texture
Actual Texture
Visual Texture

Pattern

Time and Motion

WORKS IN PROGRESS
Jackson Pollock's *Autumn Rhythm*

To this point, we have discussed some of the most important of the formal elements—line, space, light, and color—but several other elements employed by artists can contribute significantly to an effective work of art. **Texture** refers to the surface quality of a work. **Pattern** is a repetitive motif or design. And **time and motion** can be introduced into a work of art in a variety of ways. A work can *suggest* the passing of time by telling, for instance, a story in a sequence of panels or actions. It can create the *illusion* of movement, optically, before the eye. Or the work can *actually* move, as Alexander Calder's mobiles (see Figures 83 and 84) or video and film do.

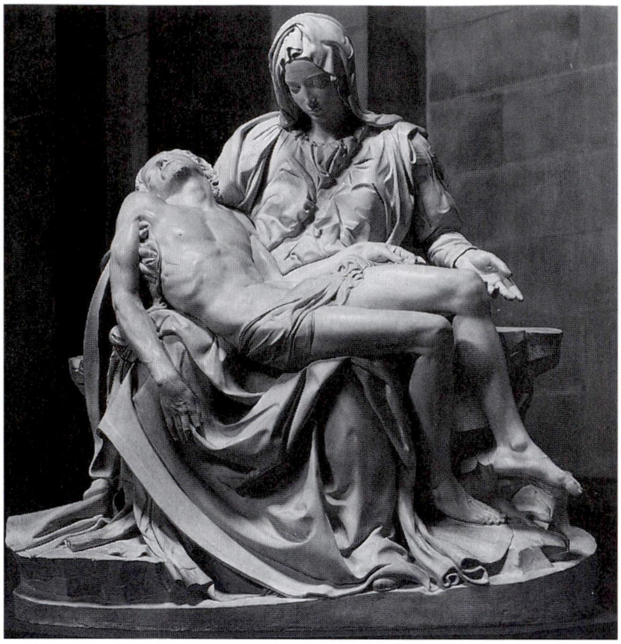

Fig. 172 Michelangelo, *Pietà,* 1501.
Marble, H. 6 ft. 8 ½ in. Vatican, Rome.

TEXTURE

Texture is the word we use to describe the work of art's ability to call forth certain *tactile* sensations and feelings. It may seem rough or smooth, as coarse as sandpaper or as fine as powder. If it seems slimy, like a slug, it may repel us. If it seems as soft as fur, it may make us want to touch it. In fact, most of us are compelled to touch what we see. It is one of the ways we come to understand our world. That's why signs in museums and galleries saying "Please Do Not Touch" are so necessary: if, for example, every visitor to the Vatican in Rome had touched the marble body of Christ in Michelangelo's *Pietà* (Fig. 172), the rounded, sculptural forms would have been reduced to utter flatness long ago.

Actual Texture

Marble is one of the most tactile of all artistic mediums. Confronted with Michelangelo's almost uncanny ability to transform marble into lifelike form, we are virtually compelled to reach out and confirm that Christ's dead body is made of hard, cold stone and not the real, yielding flesh that the grieving Mary seems to hold in her arms. Even the wound on his side, which Mary almost touches with her own hand, seems real. The drapery seems soft, falling in gentle folds. The visual experience of this work defies what we know is materially true. Beyond its emotional content, part of the power of this work derives from the stone's extraordinary texture, from Michelangelo's ability to make stone come to life.

Another actual texture that we often encounter in art is paint applied in a thick, heavy manner. Each brushstroke is not only evident but seems to have a "body" of its own. This textural effect is called **impasto.** Joan Snyder is known for the expressive impasto of her

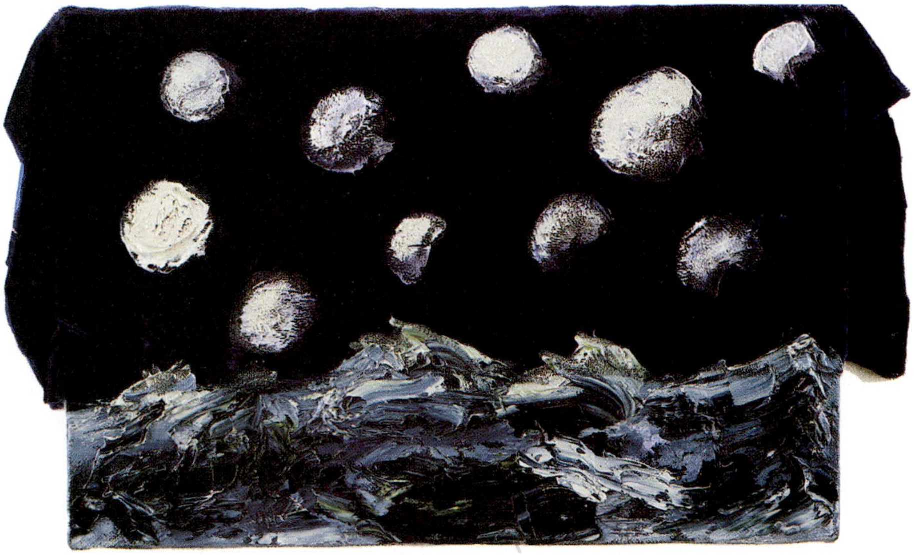

Fig. 173 Joan Snyder, *Sea Moons,* 1989.
Oil and velvet on linen, 11 ¼ × 19 ½ in. Courtesy of Hirschl & Adler Modern, New York.

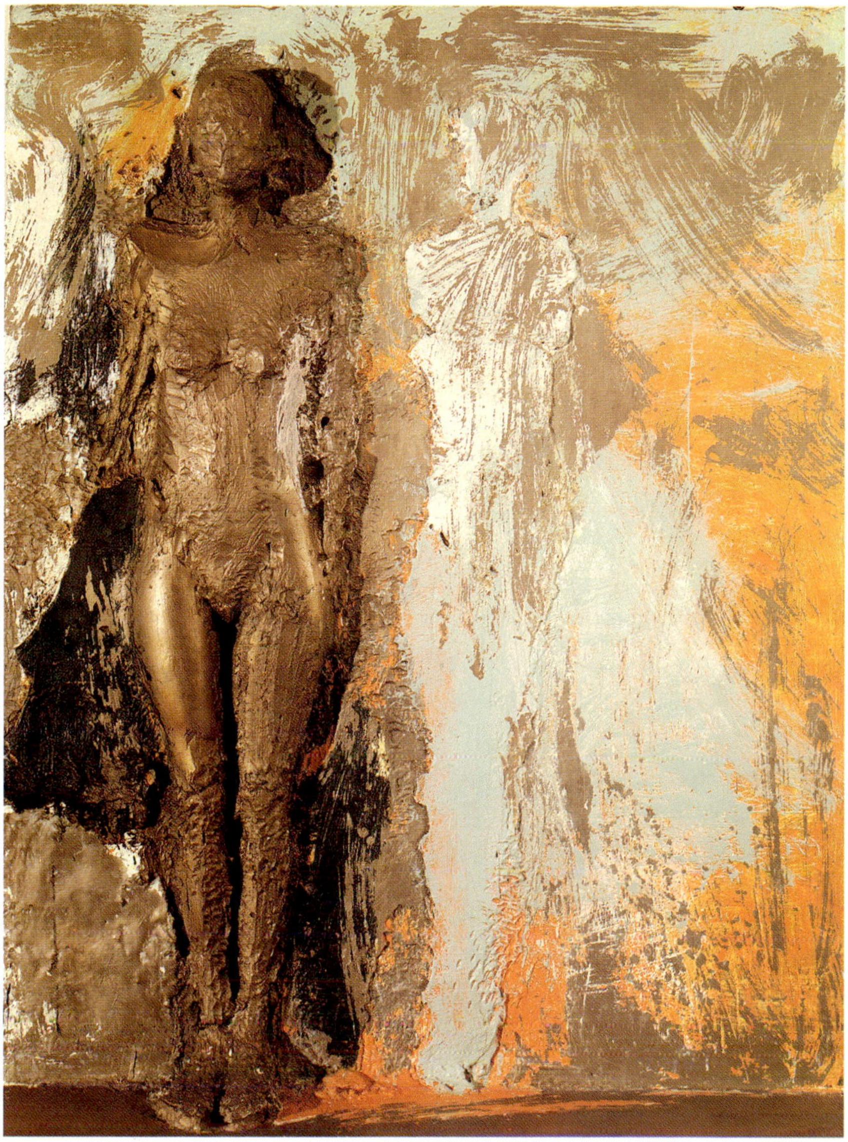

Fig. 174 Manuel Neri, *Mujer Pegada Series No. 2,* 1985–1986.
Bronze with oil-based enamel, 70 × 56 × 11 in. Courtesy Anne Kohs & Associates, San Francisco. Photograph by M. Lee Fatheree.

abstract "stroke" paintings of the late 1960s. Recently, Snyder has begun to use this brushstroke in landscape paintings done on a ground of red or black velvet. *Sea Moons* (Fig. 173), for example, consists of a canvas draped with a swath of black velvet. The thick impasto of the sea sweeps up from the canvas across the bottom of the hanging fabric; a night sky, dotted with van Gogh-like moons and stars, descends across the painting like a shroud. The shift in texture, from paint to velvet, differentiates space. The line between sea and sky, heaven and earth, is underscored by this shift in texture.

In Manuel Neri's bronze sculpture from the *Mujer Pegada Series* (Fig. 174), the actual texture of the bronze is both smooth, where it implies the texture of skin on the figure's thigh, for instance, and rough, where it indicates the "unfinished" quality of the work. It is as if Neri can only begin to capture the whole woman who is his subject, as she emerges half-realized from the sheet of bronze. Our sense of the transitory nature of the image, its fleeting quality, is underscored by the enamel paint that Neri has applied in broad, loosely gestural strokes to the bronze. This paint adds yet another texture to the piece, the texture of the brushstroke. This brushstroke helps, in turn, to emphasize the work's two-dimensional quality. It is as if Neri's three-dimensional sculpture is attempting to escape the two-dimensional space of the wall, to escape, that is, the space of painting.

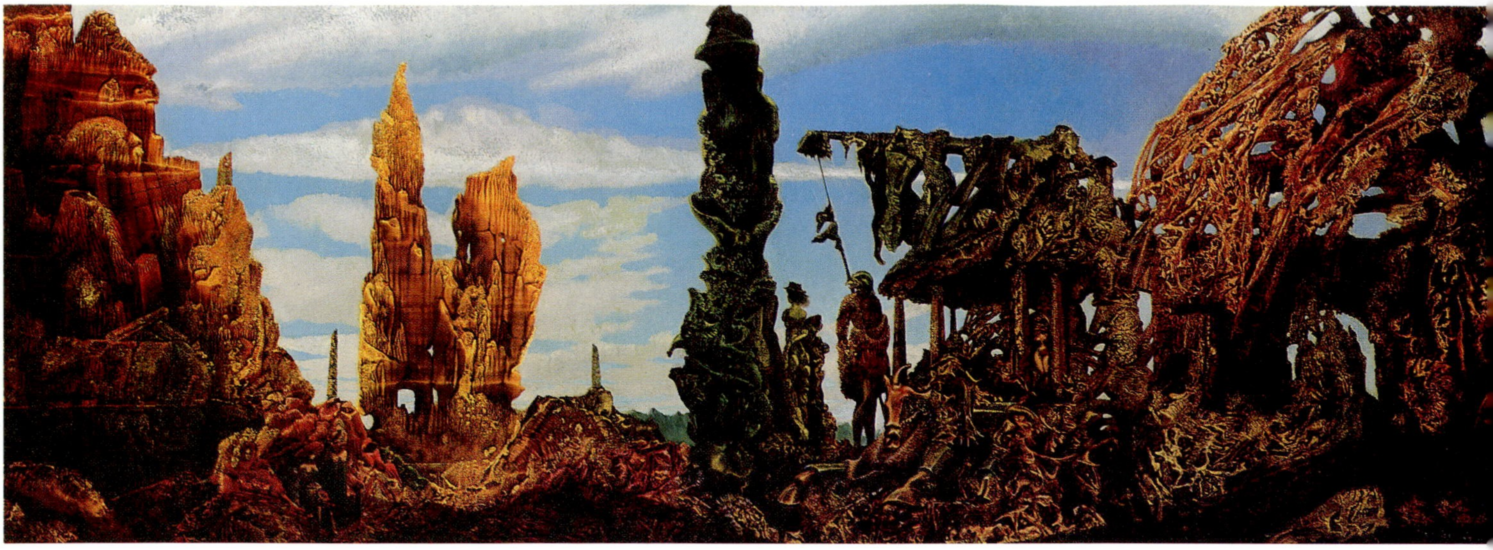

Fig. 175 Max Ernst, *Europe after the Rain,* 1940–1942.
Oil on canvas, 21 9/16 × 58 3/16 in. Wadsworth Atheneum, Hartford, Connecticut. The Ella Gallup Sumner and Mary Catlin Sumner Collection Fund.

Visual Texture

Visual texture appears to be actual but is not. Like the representation of three-dimensional space on a two-dimensional surface, a visual texture is an illusion. If we were to touch the painting above, *Europe after the Rain* (Fig. 175), it would feel primarily smooth, despite the fact that it seems to possess all sorts of actual surface texture, bumps and hollows of fungus-like growth.

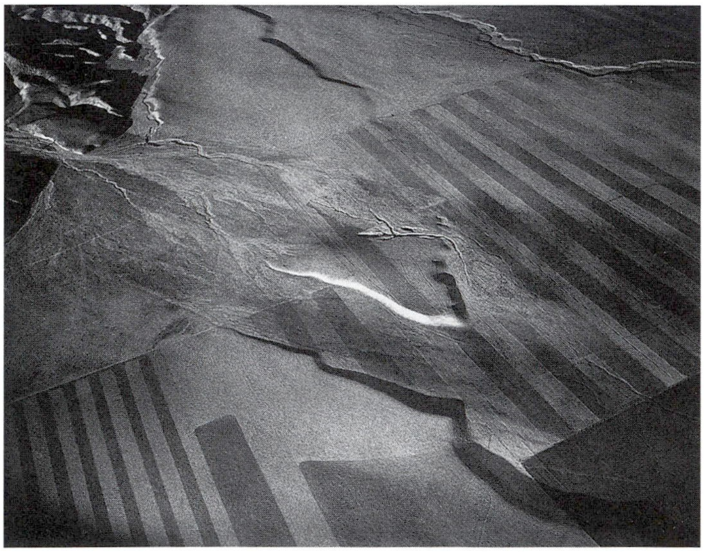

Fig. 176 William A. Garnett, *Erosion and Strip Farms,* 1951.
Gelatin–silver print, 15 9/16 × 19 1/2 in. The Museum of Modern Art, New York, Purchase. Copy Print © 1996 The Museum of Modern Art, New York.

The painting is by Max Ernst, the inventor of a technique called ***frottage,*** from the French word *frotter,* "to rub." By putting a sheet of paper over textured surfaces, especially floorboards and other wooden surfaces, and then rubbing a soft pencil across the paper, he was able to create a wide variety of textural effects. He would then arrange these textures into visions of surrealistic "forests" and fantastic landscapes.

William Garnett's stunning aerial view of strip farms stretching across an eroding landscape (Fig. 176) is a study in visual texture. The plowed strips of earth contrast dramatically with the strips that have been left fallow. And the predictable, geometric textures of the farmed landscape also contrast with the irregular veins and valleys of the unfarmed and eroded landscape in the photograph's upper left.

The evocation of visual textures is, in fact, one of the primary tools of the photographer. When light falls across actual textures, especially *raking* light, or light that illuminates the surface from an oblique angle, the resulting patterns of light and shadow emphasize the texture of the surface. In this way, the Garrett photograph reveals the most subtle details of the land surface. But remember, the photograph itself is smooth and flat, and its textures are therefore visual. The textures of its subject, revealed by the light, are actual ones.

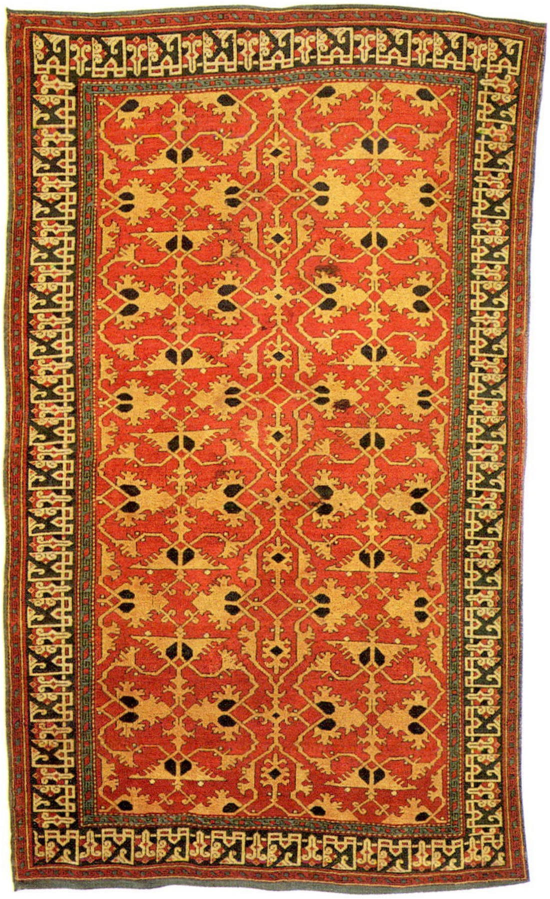

Fig. 177 "Lotto" rug, Konya (?), Anatolia, 16th century. Wool, 6 ft. 9 in. × 4 ft. 1 in. Philadelphia Museum of Art, The Joseph Lees Williams Memorial Collection.

PATTERN

The textures of the landscape in Garnett's photograph reveal themselves as a pattern of light and dark stripes. Any formal element that repeats itself in a composition—line, shape, mass, color, or texture—creates a recognizable **pattern.**

The carpet illustrated here (Fig. 177) was probably made in Anatolian Turkey in the sixteenth century, and its design may have originated among Asian nomads. The pattern, a repetitive interlace of lines and shapes, was apparently based on a widely available master plan, and it rarely changed. It developed as a court design in central Turkey and subsequently spread through exportation to Europe, where it was copied by local manufacturers in Spain, Flanders, England, and Italy, as well as in North Africa and India.

In its systematic and repetitive use of the same motif or design, pattern is an especially important *decorative* tool. Throughout history decorative patterns have been applied to utilitarian objects, such this rug, in order to make them more pleasing to the eye. Early manuscripts, for instance, such as the page reproduced here from the eighth-century *Lindisfarne Gospels* (Fig. 178), were *illuminated,* or elaborately decorated with drawings, paintings, and large capital letters, to beautify the sacred text. This page represents the ways in which Christian imagery—the cross—and earlier pre-Christian pagan motifs came together in the early Christian era in the British Isles. The simple design of the traditional Celtic cross, found across Ireland, is almost lost in the checkerboard pattern and the interlace of fighting beasts with spiraling tails, extended necks, and clawing legs that borders the page. These beasts are examples of the pagan *animal style,* which consists of intricate, ribbonlike traceries of line that suggest wild and fantastic beasts. The animal style was used not only in England but also in Scandinavia, Germany, and France.

Because decorative pattern is associated with the beautifying of utilitarian objects in the crafts, with folk art, and with "women's work" such as quilt-making, it has not been held in the highest esteem among artists. But since the early 1980s, as the value of "women's work"

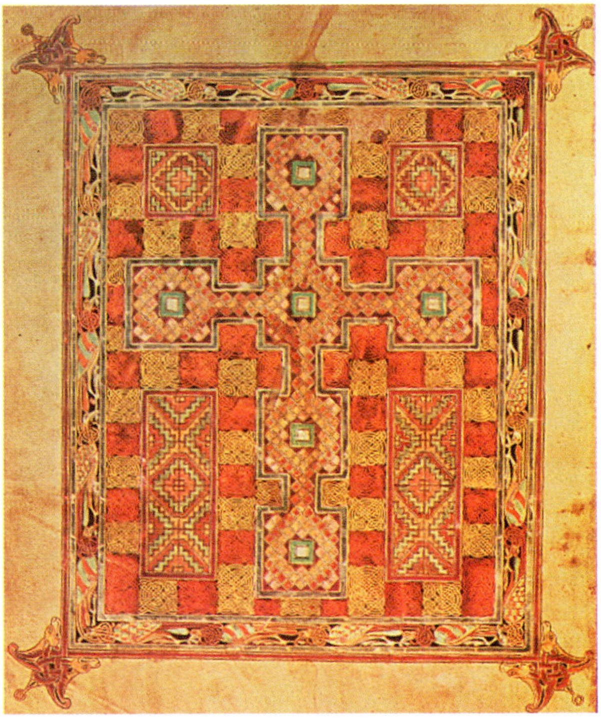

Fig. 178 Cross page from the *Lindisfarne Gospels,* c. 700. $13\frac{1}{2} \times 9\frac{1}{4}$ in. British Library.

has been rethought, and as the traditional "folk" arts of other cultures have come to be appreciated by the Western art world, its importance in art has been reassessed by many.

Of all the artists working with pattern and decoration, Miriam Schapiro has perhaps done the most to legitimate pattern's important place in the arts. Schapiro creates what she calls "femmages," a bilingual pun, contracting the French words *femme* and *hommage*, "homage to woman," and the English words "female" and "image." "I wanted to explore and express," Schapiro explains, "a part of my life which I had always dismissed—my homemaking, my

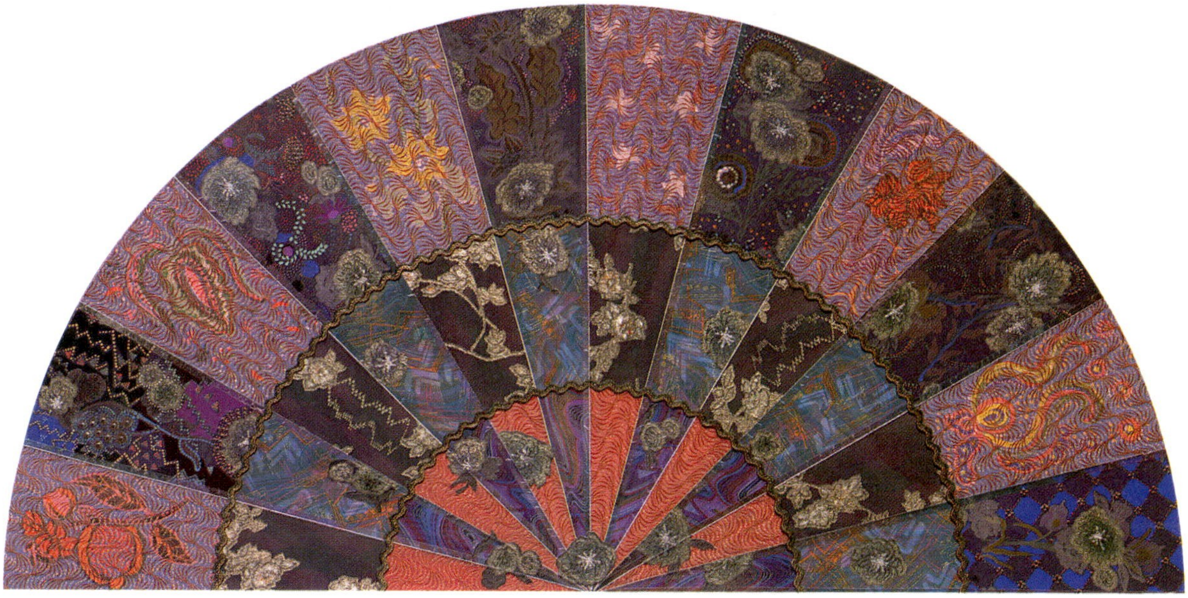

Fig. 179 Miriam Schapiro, *Night Shade,* 1986.
Acrylic and fabric collage on canvas, 48 × 96 in. Private collection.

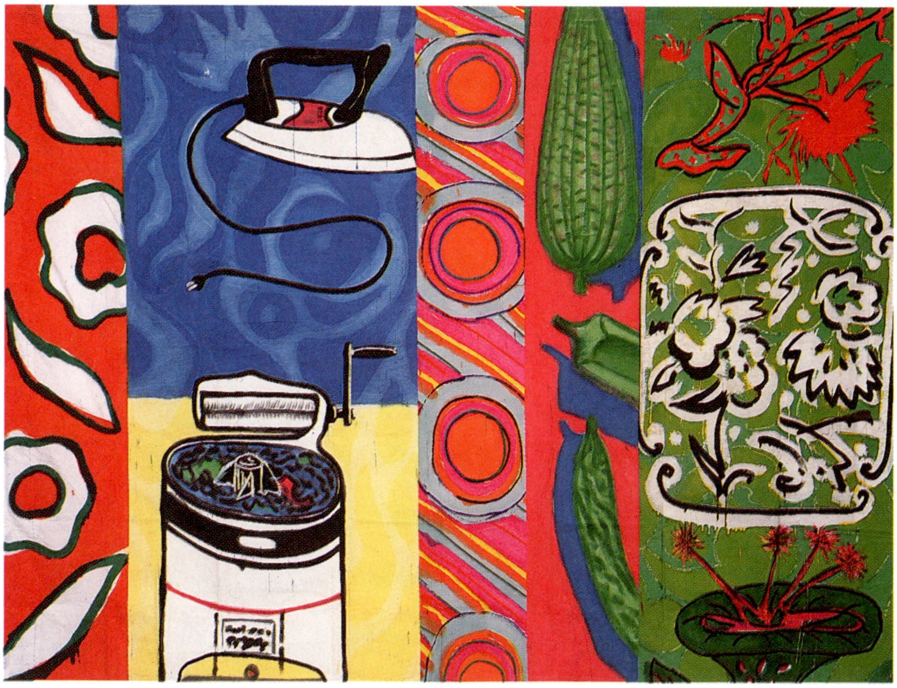

Fig. 180 Kim McConnel, *Miracle,* 1980.
Acrylic on cotton with metallic paint, 93 × 123 in. Courtesy Holly Solomon Gallery, New York. Photograph by D. James Dee.

nesting." In her monumental multimedia work *Night Shade* (Fig. 179), Schapiro has chosen an explicitly feminine image, the fan which fashionable women, in earlier days, used to cool themselves. Partially painted and partially sewn out of fabric, it intentionally brings to mind the kinds of domestic handiwork traditionally assigned to women as well as the life of leisure of the aristocratic lady.

Because of its associations with home decoration—with wallpaper, upholstery, linen, and so on—pattern symbolizes for many the home itself. For Kim McConnel, born soon after World War II and raised in the 1950s, the prints and patterns of his childhood combine to create a half-nostalgic, half-ironic tribute to American family life. *Miracle* (Fig. 180) combines images of an early wringer washing machine, a home iron, a hot pad, and the kind of vegetables one might see on a kitchen handcloth, with two designs for wallpaper, or perhaps shower curtains, that reproduce what verges on the worst taste of the decade. The "miracle" of the painting's title may be the sheer wonder of all these patterns co-existing in the same space, or it may be more than that: the miraculous sense of well-being that characterized American life in the 1950s.

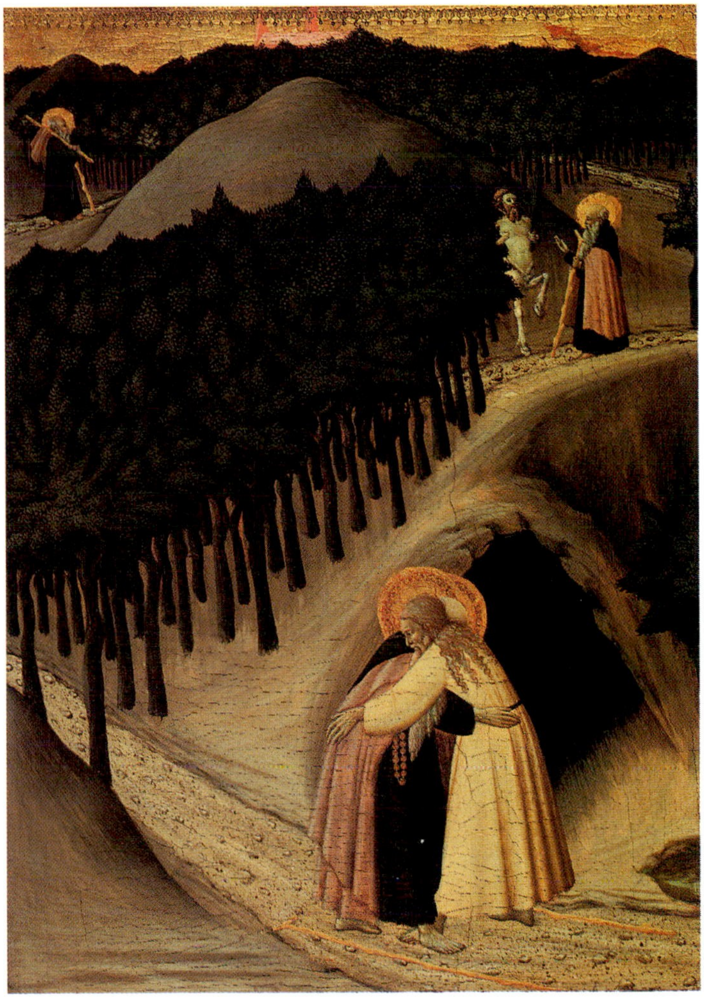

Fig. 181 Sassetta, and workshop of Sassetta, *The Meeting of Saint Anthony and Saint Paul*, c. 1440.
Tempera on wood, 18 3/4 × 13 5/8 in.

TIME AND MOTION

Pattern's repetitive quality creates a sense of linear and directional movement. Anyone who has ever stared at a wallpaper pattern, trying to determine where and how it begins to repeat itself, knows how the eye will follow a pattern. Nevertheless, one of the most traditional distinctions made between the *plastic arts*—painting and sculpture—and the written arts, such as music and literature, is that the former are *spatial* and the latter **temporal** media. That is, we experience a painting or sculpture all at once; the work of art is before us in its totality at all times. But we experience music and literature over time, in a linear way; a temporal work possesses a clear beginning, middle, and end.

While there is a certain truth to this distinction, time plays a greater role in the plastic arts than such a formulation might suggest. Even in the case where the depiction of a given event implies that we are witness to a photographic "frozen moment," an instant of time taken from a larger sequence of events, the single image may be understood as part of a larger **narrative** sequence: a story.

A work of art can also, in and of itself, invite us to experience it in a linear or temporal way. *The Meeting of Saint Anthony and Saint Paul* (Fig. 181), for example, depicts Saint Anthony at three different points as he travels down a winding road, away from the city in the distant background and toward his meeting with the hermit, Saint Paul. First, he enters a wood, then he confronts a centaur, and finally he meets Saint Paul. The road here represents Saint Anthony's movement through space and time.

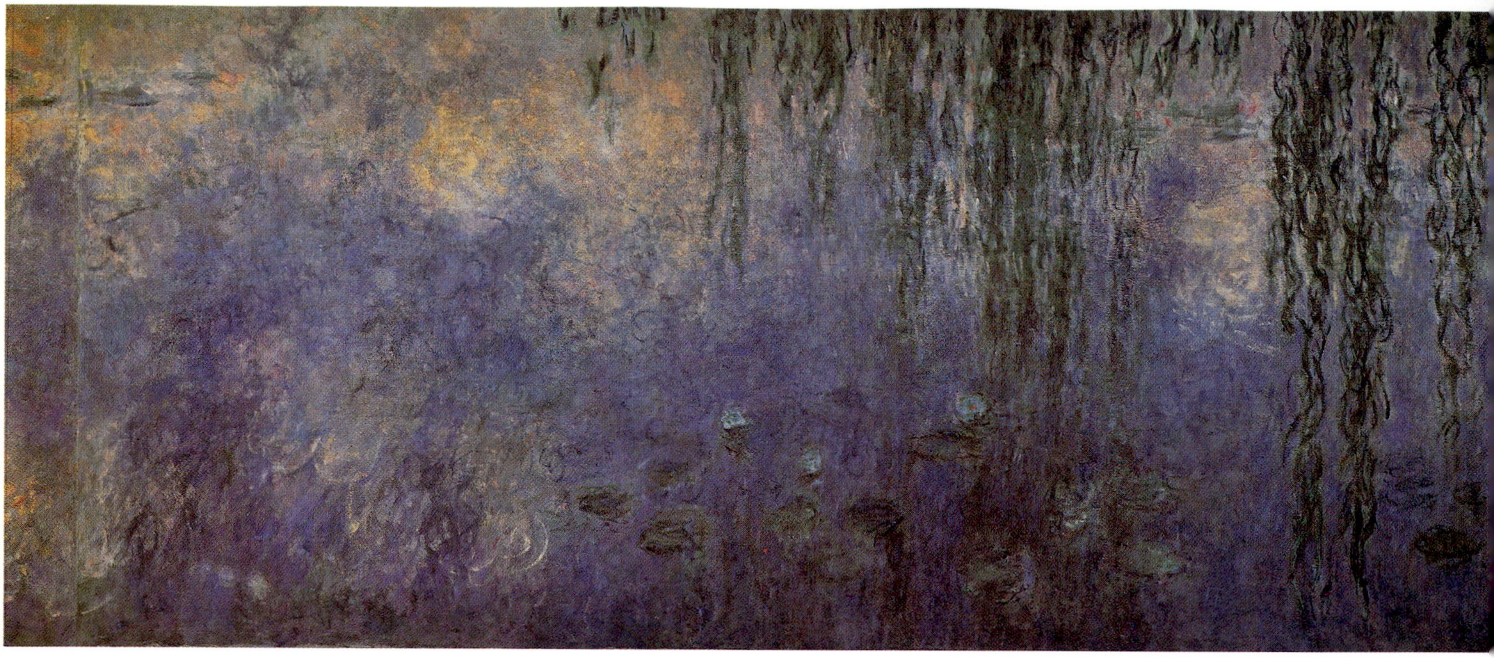

Fig. 182a Claude Monet, *Waterlilies, Morning: Willows* (central section), 1916–1926.
Triptych, each panel 80 × 170 in. Musée de l'Orangerie, Paris, France. Giraudon/Art Resource, New York.

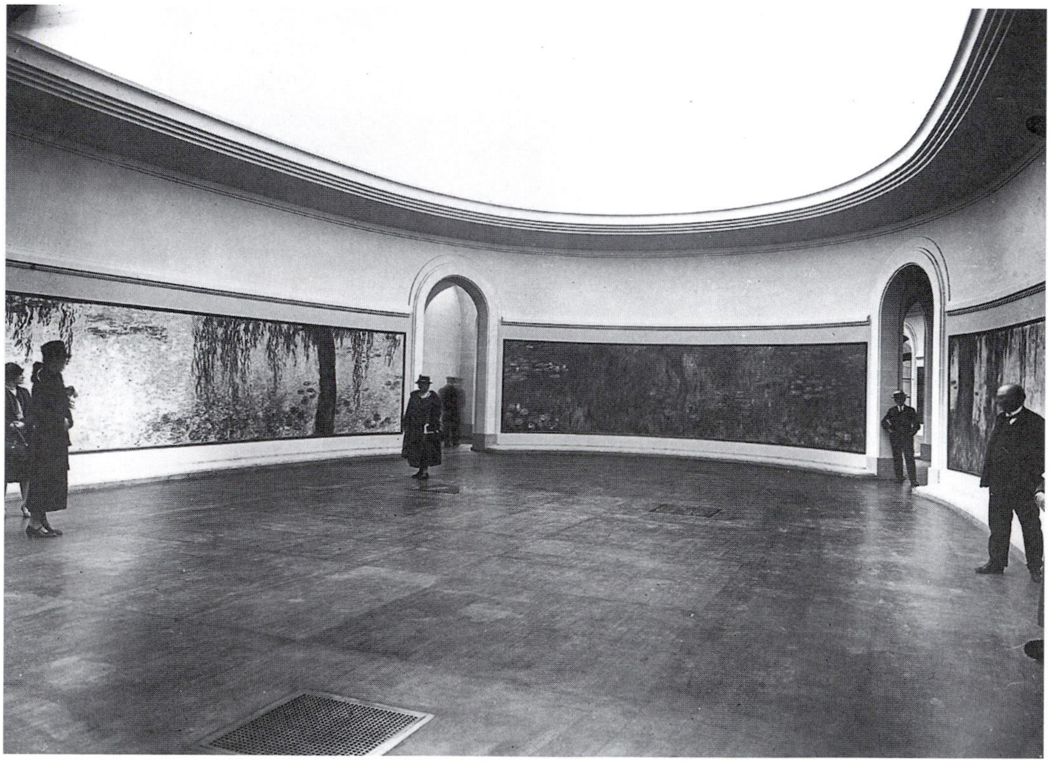

Fig. 183 Claude Monet, *Reflections of Trees* on the far wall, *Waterlilies, Morning: Willows* on each side.
Room II, Musée de l'Orangerie, Paris, France.

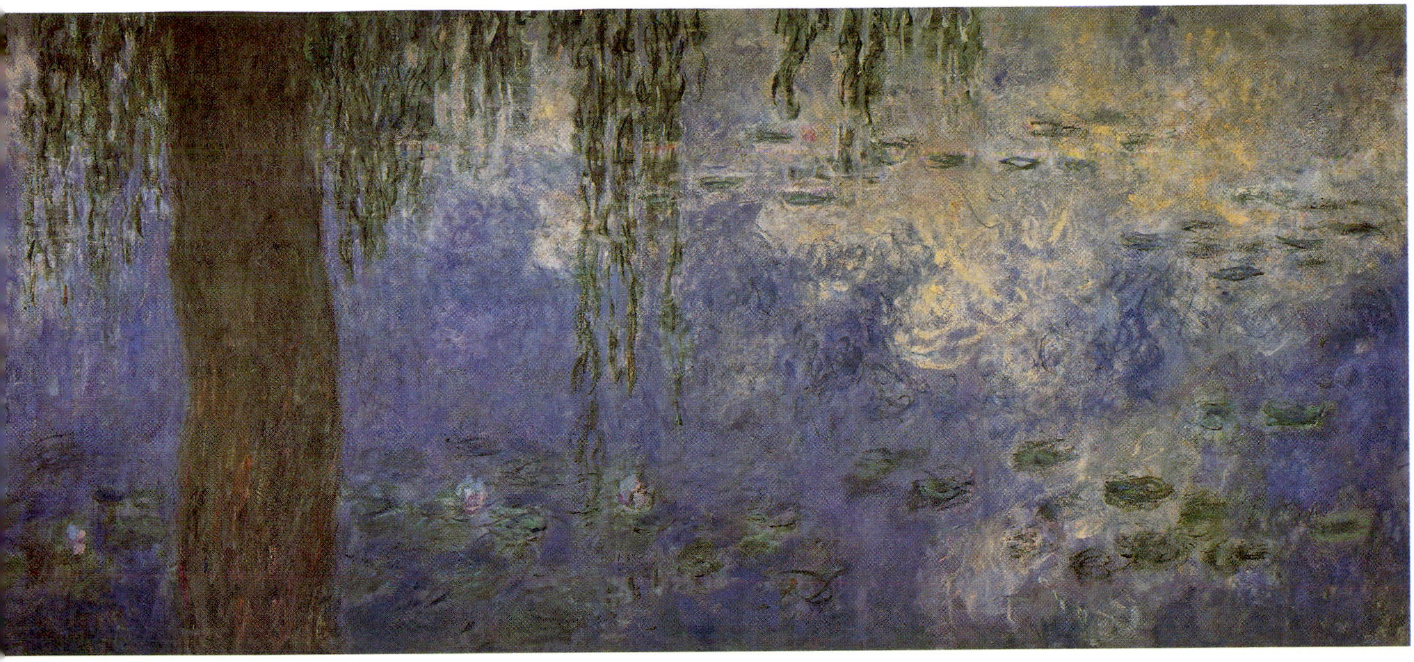

Fig. 182b Claude Monet, *Waterlilies, Morning: Willows* (right side), 1916–1926.
Triptych, each panel 80 × 170 in. Musée de l'Orangerie, Paris, France. Giraudon/Art Resource, New York.

Likewise, we naturally "read" Pat Steir's Chrysanthemum paintings (Figs. 141 and 142) from left to right, in linear progression. While each of Monet's Grainstack paintings (Figs. 24 and 162) can be appreciated as a wholly unified totality, each can also be seen as part of a larger whole, a time sequence. Viewed in series, they are not so much "frozen moments" removed from time as they are *about* time itself, the ways in which our sense of place changes over time.

To appreciate large-scale works of art, it may be necessary to move around and view them from all sides, or to see them from a number of vantage points—to view them over time. Monet's famous paintings of his lily pond at Giverny, which were installed in the Orangerie in Paris in 1927, are also designed to compel the viewer to move (Fig. 182). They encircle the room (Fig. 183), and to be in the midst of this work is to find oneself suddenly in the middle of a world that has been curiously turned inside out: the work is painted from the shoreline, but the viewer seems to be surrounded by water, as if the room were an island in the middle of the pond itself. The paintings cannot be seen all at once. There is always a part of the work behind you. There is no focal point, no sense of unified perspective. In fact, the series of paintings seems to organize itself around and through the viewer's own acts of perception and movement.

According to Georges Clemenceau, the French statesman who was Monet's close friend and who arranged for the giant paintings to hang in the Orangerie, the paintings could be understood as "a representation of Brownian motion." First described by the Scottish scientist Robert Brown in 1827, Brownian motion is a result of the physical movement of minute particles of solid matter suspended in fluid. Any sufficiently small particle of matter suspended in water will be buffeted by the molecules of the liquid and driven at random throughout it. Standing in the midst of Monet's panorama, the viewer's eye is likewise driven randomly through the space of the paintings. The viewer is encircled by them, and there is no place for the eye to rest.

Jackson Pollock's Autumn Rhythm

While not as large as Monet's paintings at the Orangerie, Pollock's works are still large enough to engulf the viewer. The eye travels in what one critic has accurately called "galactic" space, following first one line, then another, unable quite ever to locate itself or complete its visual circuit through the web of paint. Work such as this has been labeled "Action Painting" not only because it prompts the viewer to become actively engaged with it, but also because the lines that trace themselves out across the sweep of the canvas seem to chart the path of Pollock's own motions as he stood over the canvas. The drips and sweeps of paint record his action as a painter and document it, a fact captured by Hans Namuth in October of 1950 in a famous series of photographs (Figs. 184 and 185) of Pollock at work on the canvas *Autumn Rhythm* (Fig. 186).

Namuth's photographs teach us much about Pollock's working method. Pollock longed to be completely involved in the process of painting. He wanted to become wholly absorbed in the work. As he had written in a short article called "My Painting," published in 1947, "When I am *in* my painting, I'm not aware of what I'm doing . . . the painting has a life

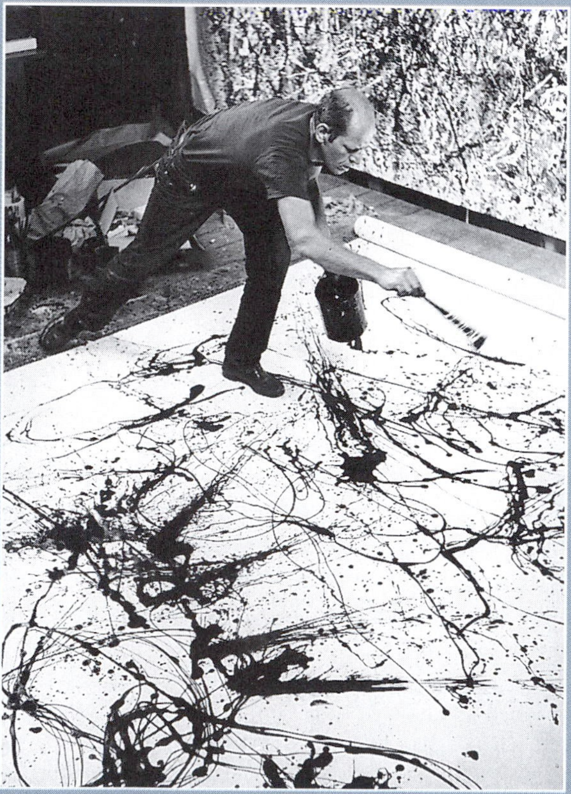

Fig. 184 Hans Namuth, Jackson Pollock Painting *Autumn Rhythm,* 1950.
Center for Creative Photography, Tucson. Photograph by Hans Namuth.

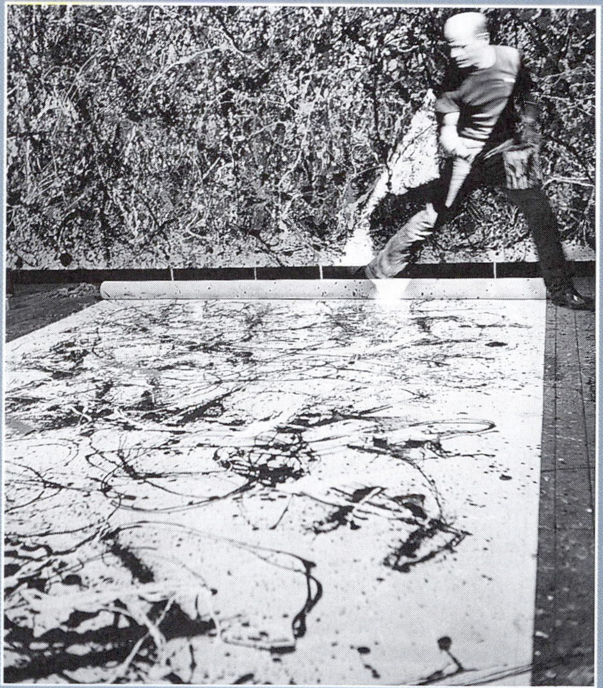

Fig. 185 Hans Namuth, Jackson Pollock Painting *Autumn Rhythm,* 1950.
Courtesy, Center for Creative Photography, Tucson. Photographs, The University of Arizona. © 1991 Hans Namuth Estate. Photograph by Hans Namuth.

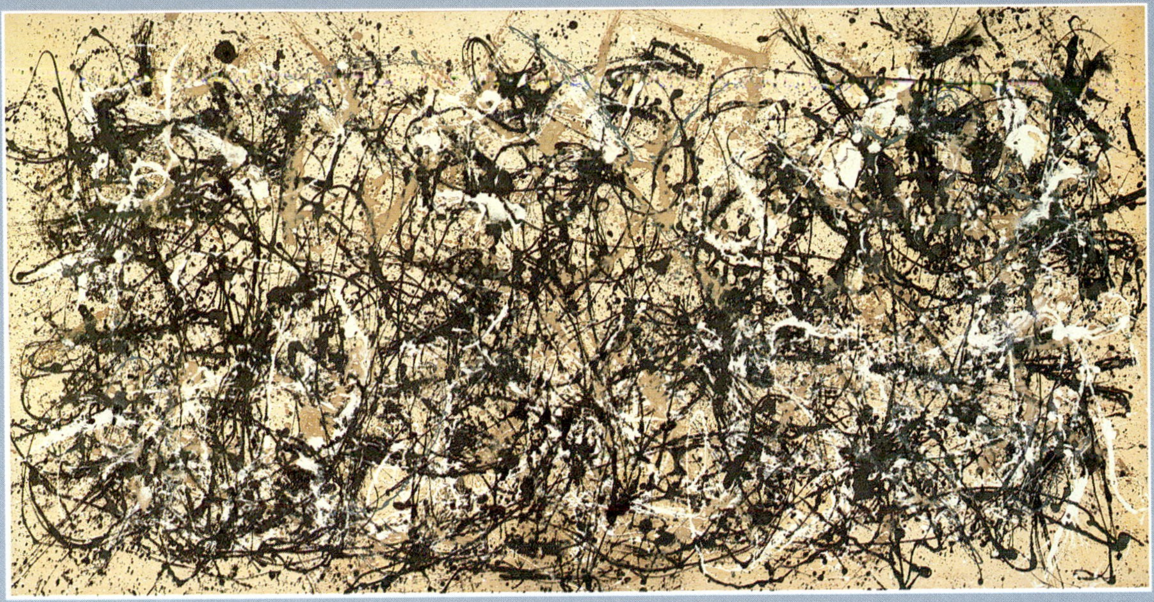

Fig. 186 Jackson Pollock, *Autumn Rhythm,* 1950.
Oil on canvas, 105 × 207 in. The Metropolitan Museum of Art, George A. Hearn Fund, 1957. 57.92.

of its own. I try to let it come through. It is only when I lose contact with the painting that the result is a mess. Otherwise there is pure harmony, an easy give and take, and the painting comes out well."

In Namuth's photographs we are witness to Pollock's absorption in the canvas. We see the immediacy of his gesture as he flings paint, moving around the work, the paint tracing his path. He worked on the floor, in fact, in order to heighten his sense of being in the work. "On the floor I am more at ease," he wrote in "My Painting." "I feel nearer, more a part of the painting, since this way I can walk round it, work from the four sides and literally be *in* the painting." We also see, in the photographs, something of the speed with which Pollock worked. Many of Namuth's photographs have blurred body and hand movements, the result of his having to shoot inside with relatively low light and slow shutter speeds, as Pollock moved swiftly around the canvas. Namuth was disturbed by the lack of sharpness in some of these photographs, and he did not show them to Pollock. "It was not until years later," Namuth admitted, "that I understood how exciting these photographs really were." In them, the motions of Pollock's body seem to blur together into the canvases on the floor and on the wall behind him.

According to Namuth, when Pollock was painting, "his movements, slow at first, gradually became faster and more dancelike as he flung black, white, and rust-colored paint onto the canvas." In fact, the traceries of line on the canvas are like choreographies, complex charts of a dancer's movement. In Pollock's words, the paintings are

> *energy and motion*
> *made visible—*
> *memories arrested in space.*

Pollock's process soon would move Namuth to other media. "To make a film was the next logical step," he knew. "Pollock's method of painting suggested a moving picture—the dance around the canvas, the continuous movement, the drama." Namuth, finally, would make two films, one in black-and-white and one in color, the second shot from below up through a sheet of glass on which Pollock is painting, vividly capturing the motion embodied in Pollock's work.

Some art works are created precisely to give us the *illusion* of movement. In **Optical Painting,** or "Op Art" as it is more popularly known, the physical characteristics of certain formal elements—line and color particularly—are subtly manipulated to stimulate the nervous system into thinking it perceives movement. Bridget Riley's *Drift 2* (Fig. 187) is a large canvas that seems to wave and roll before our eyes even though it is stretched taut across its support. One of Riley's earliest paintings was an attempt to find a visual equivalent to heat. She had been crossing a wide plain in Italy: "The heat off the plain was quite incredible—it shattered the topographical structure of it and set up violent color vibrations. . . . The important thing was to bring about an equivalent shimmering sensation on the canvas." In *Drift 2,* we encounter not heat, but wave action, as though we were, visually, out at sea.

Other works of art, of course, do *actually* move. Often driven by motors, such works are examples of **kinetic art.** Alexander Calder's mobiles, such as *Dots and Dashes* (see Figs. 80 and 81) are an example. One of the most fascinating of kinetic sculptors was Jean Tinguely, who dedicated his career to making large machines out of the refuse of industrial culture. On the rainy evening of March 7, 1960, he set in motion a machine in the sculpture garden of the Museum of Modern Art in New York (Fig. 188). The piece sputtered, stalled, started up again. A big balloon inflated over the mass of pulleys and gears. A player piano began to play. Fire erupted, the piano burned, stink bombs exploded, and a small wheeled machine was released and, all aflame, careened toward the audience, chasing a TV cameraman up a ladder. A fireman, in attendance as a safety precaution, was eventually summoned, and to the robust boos of the audience, finally doused the flames with a fire extinguisher. The piece—or the event, actually—was entitled *Homage to New York*. Asked what he thought of it, one critic replied, with tongue in cheek, "It's the end of civilization as we know it," which is something of what Tinguely himself must have felt. In modern-day New York, he seems to say, creative energy is mechanical, self-destructive—and entirely amusing.

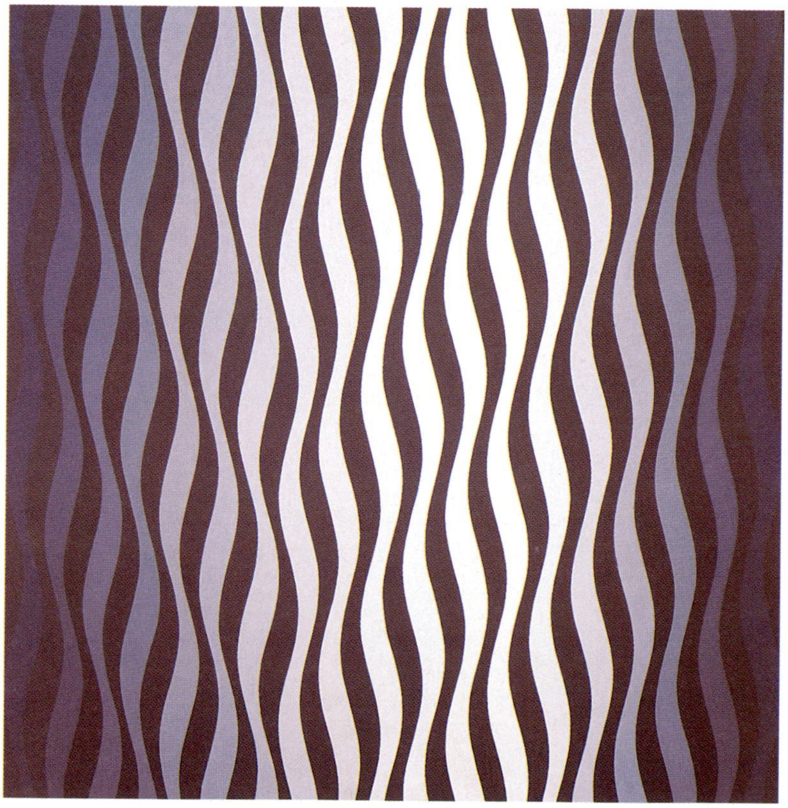

Fig. 187 Bridget Riley, *Drift 2,* 1966.
Emulsion on canvas, 91½ × 89½ in. The Albright-Knox Art Gallery, Buffalo, NY. Gift of Seymour H. Knox, 1967.

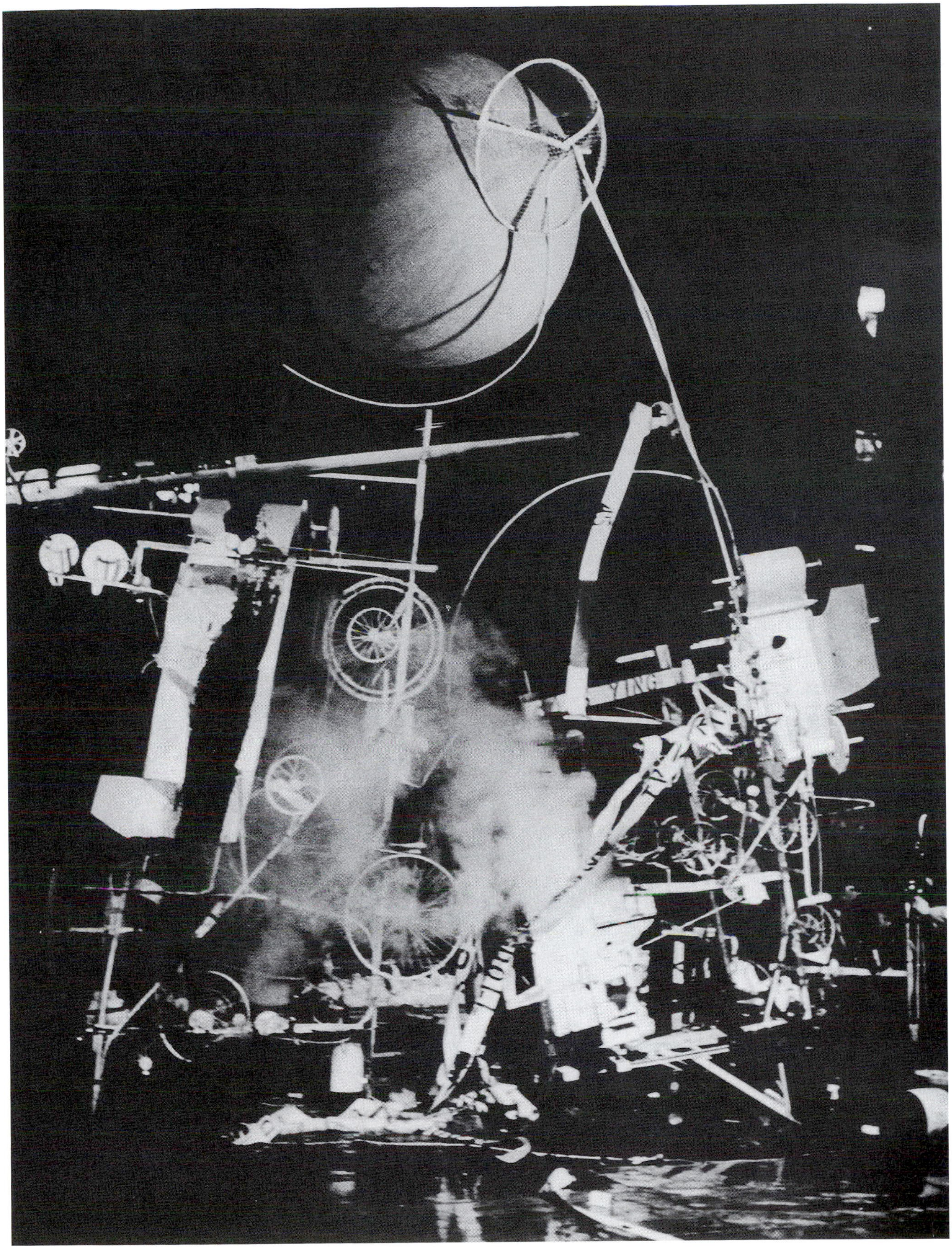

Fig. 188 Jean Tinguely, *Homage to New York,* March 7, 1960.
Museum of Modern Art, New York. Photograph by David Gahr.

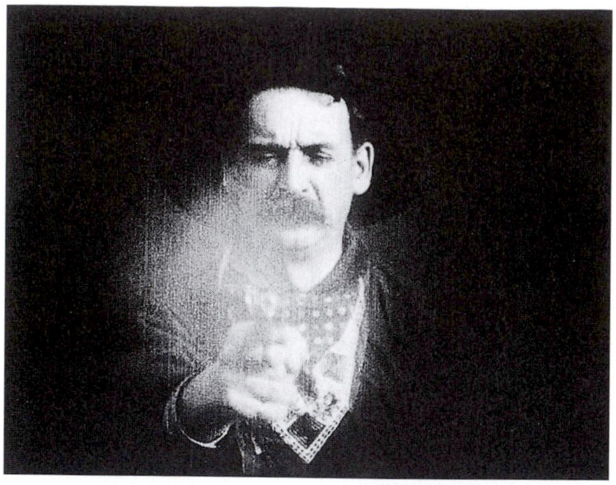

Fig. 189 Edwin S. Porter, *The Great Train Robbery,* 1903.

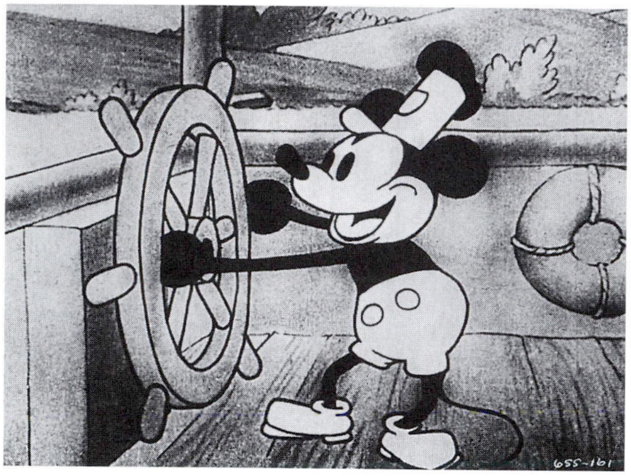

Fig. 190 Walt Disney, *Steamboat Willie,* 1928.

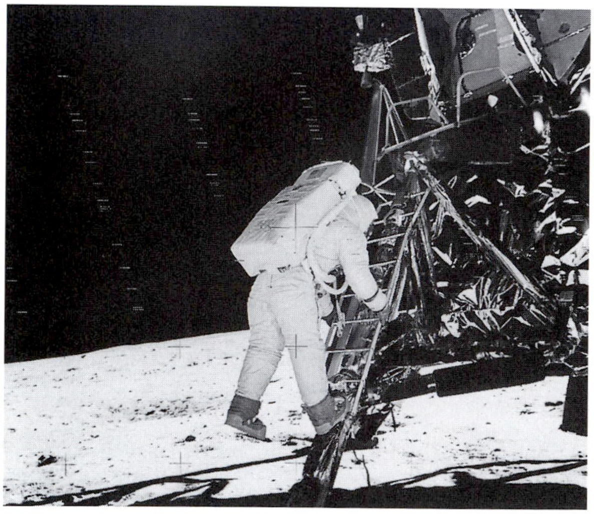

Fig. 191 Apollo XI Astronaut Neil Armstrong Stepping onto the Moon, July 20, 1969.
Courtesy of NASA.

The spatial and the temporal have been most successfully combined in the twentieth century in the arts of film and video. In 1903, Edwin S. Porter released the groundbreaking film *The Great Train Robbery,* the first narrative action chase scene in the history of the cinema, which ended with the shockingly direct act of the bandit turning to fire his gun into the audience (Fig. 189). Fifteen minutes in length, the film opened in 1905 at John P. Harris's Nickelodeon in Pittsburgh, the first theater in the United States devoted to the showing of movies, where it played to packed houses. Within months, thousands of "nickelodeons" were springing up across the continent as millions of people rushed to experience "moving pictures." By the late 1920s Walt Disney had perfected the animated cartoon, and Mickey Mouse had become an American institution (Fig. 190). Hollywood was making over 450 movies a year by 1936, and the average American saw two films a week.

After World War II, this thirst for the moving image was satisfied as much by television, the first medium in history to bring the primary image directly into the viewer's home. Many early television shows were actually "live"—that is, the show was broadcast live, before a live studio audience, without any taping or even tape delay. The directness, immediacy, and realism of the television image (further heightened by the rise of the color monitor, which began to have a real impact in the late 1950s) have made it, at least seemingly, the most *realistic* of media. Though its images are constantly manipulated, and its stage space almost totally artificial (notice how many television "families" sit on the same side of the kitchen table, facing the camera), we accept it as "real." When 400 million people watched Neil Armstrong step onto the moon in July 1969 (Fig. 191), only the most die-hard skeptics distrusted what they saw. It is fair to say, in fact, that television has shrunk the world. In 1985, one-third of the world's population—approximately 1.6 billion people—watched the Live Aid Telethon together.

Time and motion in television are very different from time and motion in video art, as Bill Viola's *Room for St. John of the Cross* (Fig. 192) demonstrates. Like film, television is made of sequences of "shots"—close-ups (showing head and shoulders), medium shots (from the waist up), full shots (showing actors or television personalities from head to toe), and long shots (seen from a distance). The camera might "pan" the scene, that is, move from side to side, or it might "travel," move forward or backward on a track. All of these shots usually last between five and ten seconds each. In contemporary television—MTV, for instance—the pace is even faster, and as a culture we have grown very accustomed to these rapidly changing sequences. By way of contrast, in the interior of the black cubicle in Viola's *Room for St. John of the Cross* is a small television monitor that shows a color image of a snow-covered mountain (Fig. 193). Barely audible is a voice reading St. John's poetry. The videotape consists of a single "shot." The camera never moves. The only visible movement is wind blowing through the trees and bushes.

This cubicle is like the cell of the Spanish mystic and poet St. John of the Cross, who was imprisoned in 1577 for nine months in a windowless cell too small to allow him to stand upright. In this cell he wrote most of the poems for which he is known, poems in which he often flies out of captivity, over the city walls and across the mountains. The image on the small monitor is the landscape that St. John remembers. On the large screen, behind the cubicle, Viola has projected a black-and-white video image of snow-covered mountains, shot with an unstable hand-held camera. These mountains move in wild, breathless flights, image after image filing by in an uneven, rapid rhythm, like the imagination escaping imprisonment on the loud roaring wind that fills the room, making the voice reading in the cubicle even harder to hear.

Neither of these two video images would normally be seen on television. The small one is too monotonous to be entertaining, the large one too amateurish to be acceptable "broadcast quality." But as we ourselves move in this installation—and we must move in order to view the piece—we experience many of the formal elements of art all at once. The quiet analytic geometry of the cell contrasts with the loud expressive swirl on the large screen. The space is both constricted and immense, both interior and exterior. We move between light and dark, black-and-white and color imagery. The actual textures of the pitcher, glass, and table contrast with the implied textures of the images on the videotapes. These are the raw materials of art, the formal elements, playing upon one another in real time. Viola has set them in motion together, in a single composition. We will now turn our attention to the principles of design that Viola and other artists employ in bringing the formal elements together in their work.

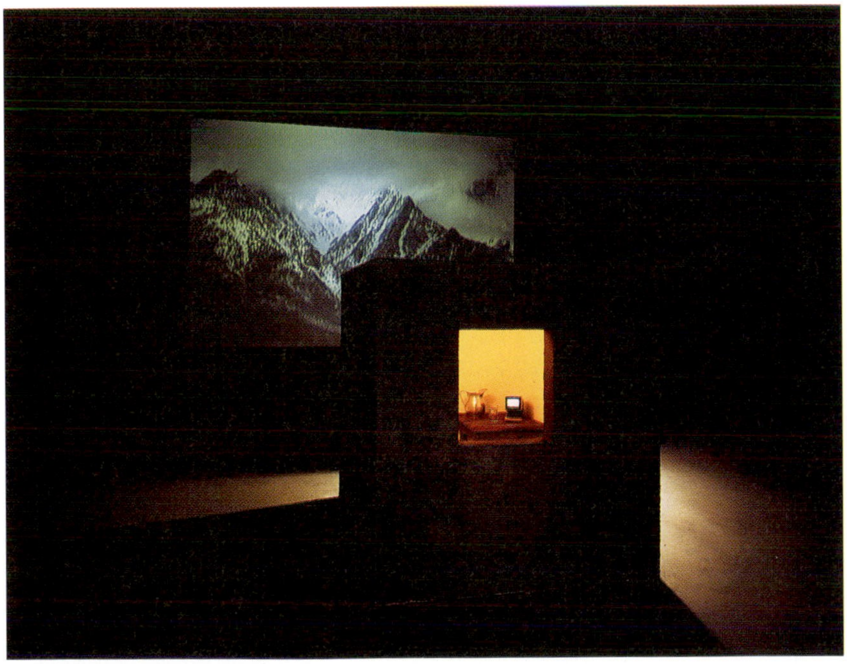

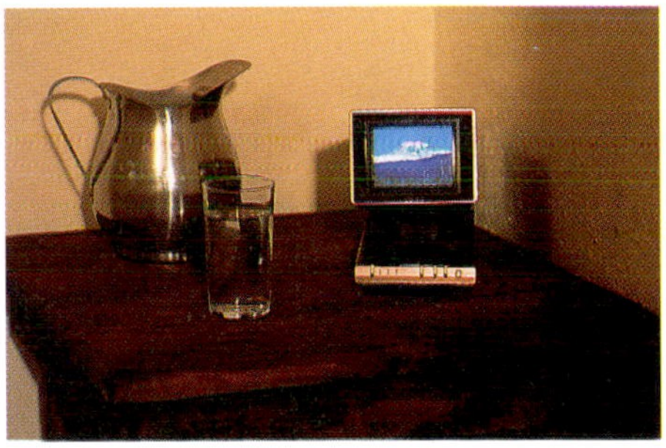

Fig. 192 (left) Bill Viola, *Room for St. John of the Cross*, 1983. Video/sound installation. © Bill Viola Studio. Collection: Museum of Contemporary Art, Los Angeles. Photograph by Kira Perov/Squidds and Nunns.

Fig. 193 (above) Bill Viola, *Room for St. John of the Cross*, 1983. Video/sound installation. © Bill Viola Studio. Photograph by Kira Perov.

CHAPTER 8

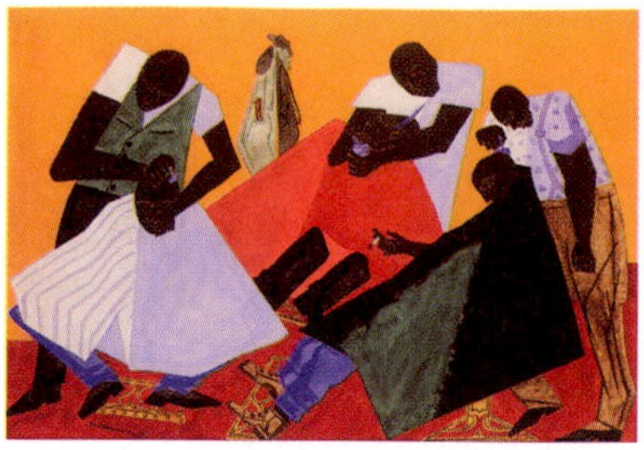

The Principles of Design

The word *design* is both a verb and a noun. Thus design is both a process and a product. To design something, the process, is to organize the various various aspects of a work of art—line, space, light and color, texture, pattern, time and motion, the formal elements that we have studied in the last four chapters—into a totality, a unified whole. We are able to see in that totality something

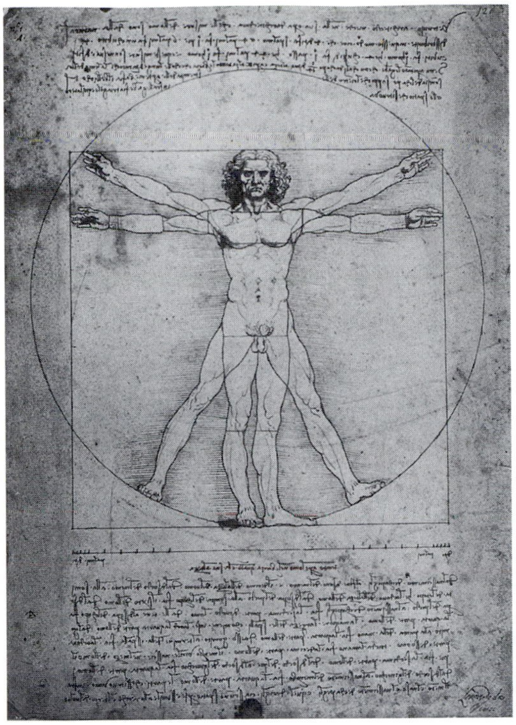

Fig. 194 Leonardo da Vinci, *Illustration of Proportions of the Human Figure,* c. 1485–1490.
Pen and ink, $13\frac{1}{2} \times 9\frac{3}{4}$ in. Galleria dell' Accademia, Venice.

we call its "design"—that is, the product. And we can recognize in the finished product the process of its organization and composition.

The principles of design are usually discussed in terms of the qualities of balance, emphasis, proportion and scale, rhythm and repetition, and unity and variety. For the sake of clarity, we must discuss these qualities one by one, but artists unite them. For example, Leonardo's famous *Illustration of Proportions of the Human Figure* (Fig. 194) embodies them all. The figure is perfectly balanced and is symmetrical. The very center of the composition is the figure's belly button, a focal point that represents the source of life itself, the fetus's connection by the umbilical cord to its mother's womb. Each of the figure's limbs appears twice, once to fit in the square, symbol of the finite, earthly world, and once to fit in the circle, symbol of the heavenly world, the infinite and the universal. Thus, all the various aspects of existence—mind and matter, the material and the transcendental—are unified by the design into a coherent whole.

By way of contrast, architect Frank Gehry's 1976 redesign of his house in Santa Monica, California (Figs. 195 and 196), seems anything but unified. He surrounded the original structure with an outer shell constructed of plywood, concrete blocks, corrugated metal, and chain-link fence. The result shocked and bewildered his neighbors. They could not understand what principles of design had guided the architect in both his choice of materials and their construction. To many it seemed that he had destroyed a perfectly good house, and in the process destroyed the neighborhood.

Certain principles of design did, of course, guide Gehry, and looking closely at the house we can begin to guess what they are. He apparently values common, everyday materials. It was important to him to establish a sense of discontinuity between the original house and its addition; they were not meant to blend into a harmonious, unified whole. Most of all, the house is different from its neighbors. It does not fit in—willfully, almost gleefully so.

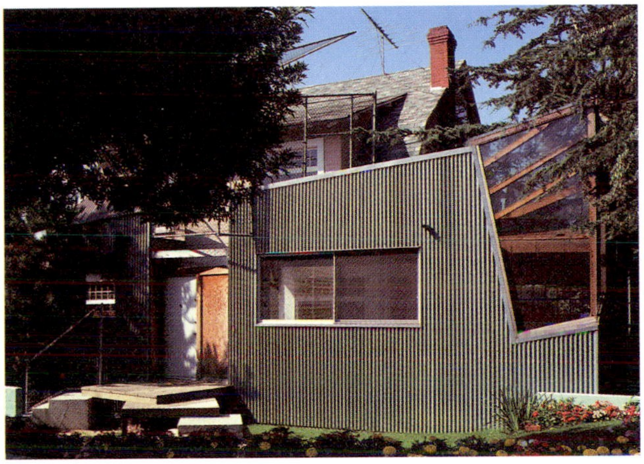

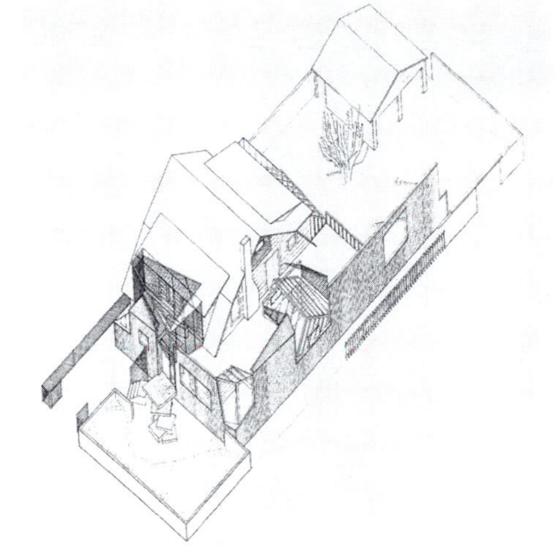

Figs. 195 and 196 Frank Gehry, Gehry house, Santa Monica, California 1977–1978, and axonometric drawing.
Photograph by Tim Street-Porter.

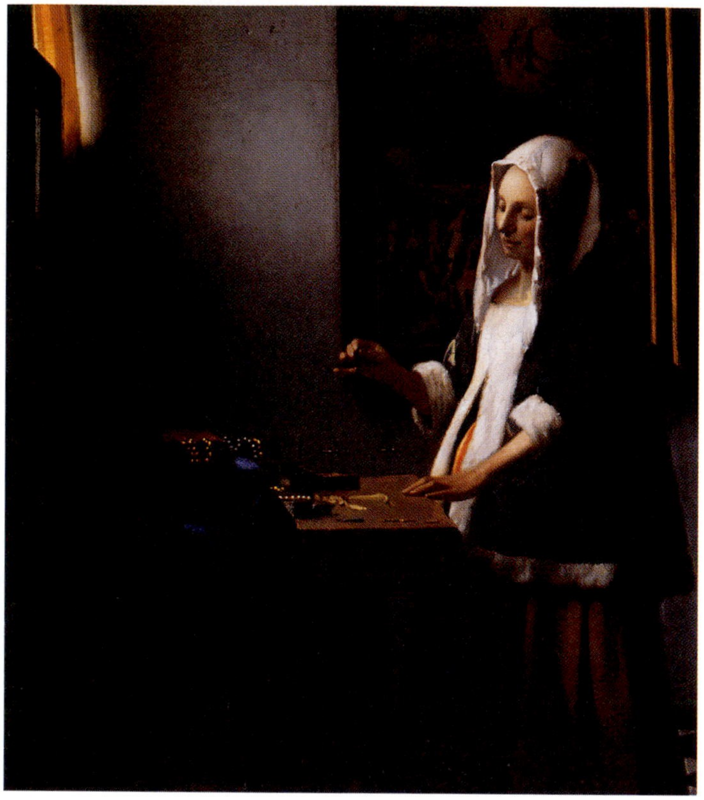

Fig. 197 Johannes Vermeer (1632–1675), *Woman Holding a Balance*, c. 1664. Oil on canvas, 16 3/4 × 15 in.; framed: 24 3/4 × 23 × 3 in. Widener Collection, © 1996 Board of Trustees, National Gallery of Art, Washington, DC Photograph by Bob Grove.

Leonardo's illustration is a remarkable example of the "rules" of proportion, yet the inventiveness and originality of Gehry's work teaches us, from the outset, that the "rules" guiding the creative process are, perhaps, made to be broken. In fact, the very idea of creativity implies a certain willingness on the part of the artist to go beyond the norm, to extend the rules, and to discover new principles around which artistic expression can organize itself. As we have seen, artists can easily create visual interest by purposefully breaking with conventions such as the traditional rules of perspective; likewise, any artist can stimulate our interest by purposefully manipulating the principles of design.

In the remainder of this chapter, we discuss the way artists combine the formal elements with classical design principles to create inventive, original work. Once we have seen how the formal elements and their design come together, we will be ready to survey the various materials, or media, that artists employ to make their art.

BALANCE

If you have ever skied in a heavy fog, unable to distinguish between the white of the atmosphere and the white of the snow, the mountain dropping away beneath your feet, you will know that you quickly lose your balance. Your sense of balance is something you maintain by means of your powers of sight, and this is perhaps why most of us value balance when we look at works of art. Instability is threatening. It makes us uncomfortable.

We need to see the space around us in order to distribute our **actual weight** evenly over our feet. If our weight is evenly distributed, we are able to stay balanced. In sculpture and architecture, actual weight, or the physical weight of materials in pounds, comes into play, but all art deals with **visual weight,** the *apparent* "heaviness" or "lightness" of the shapes and forms arranged in the composition. When both sides of a composition have the same visual weight they are balanced. Artists achieve visual balance in compositions by one of three means—symmetrical balance, asymmetrical balance, or radial balance.

Symmetrical Balance

If you were to draw a line down the middle of your body, each side of it would be, more or less, a mirror reflection of the other. When children make "angels" in the snow, they are creating, almost instinctively, **symmetrical** representations of themselves that recall Leonardo's *Illustration of Proportions.* When each side is exactly the same, we have **absolute symmetry.** But even when they are not, as is true of most human bodies, when there are minor discrepancies side to side, the overall effect is still one of symmetry, what we call **bilateral symmetry.** The two sides seem to line up.

A clear example of bilateral symmetry can be seen in Johannes Vermeer's *Woman Holding a Balance* (Fig. 197). If you look closely at the scales you will see they are not symmetrical—the left is larger than the right—but they are perfectly balanced. The woman is evidently in the process of weighing her jewelry, which is scattered on the table before her, but she seems to be distracted, as if the scales themselves have evoked other thoughts. It appears, in fact, that the scales are empty. Since scales are the traditional symbol of justice, and since behind her on the wall is a painting of *The Last Judgment,* when Christ judges the worth of all souls for entry into heaven, perhaps she is weighing nothing less than the worth of her own life. Her peaceful gaze suggests, at least, her contentment.

One of the dominant images of symmetry in Western art is the crucifix, which is, in itself, a construction of absolute symmetry. In Enguerrand Quarton's remarkable *Coronation of the Virgin* (Fig. 198), the crucifix at the lower center of the composition is a comparatively small detail in the overall composition. Nevertheless, its *cruciform* shape dominates the whole, and all the formal elements in the work are organized around it. Thus God, the Father, and Jesus, the Son, flank Mary in almost perfect symmetry, identical in their major features (though the robes of each fall a little differently). On earth below, the two centers of the Christian faith flank the cross, Rome on the left and Jerusalem on the right. And at the very bottom of the painting, below ground level, Purgatory, on the left, out of which an angel assists a newly redeemed soul, balances Hell on the right. Each element balances out another, picturing a unified theological universe.

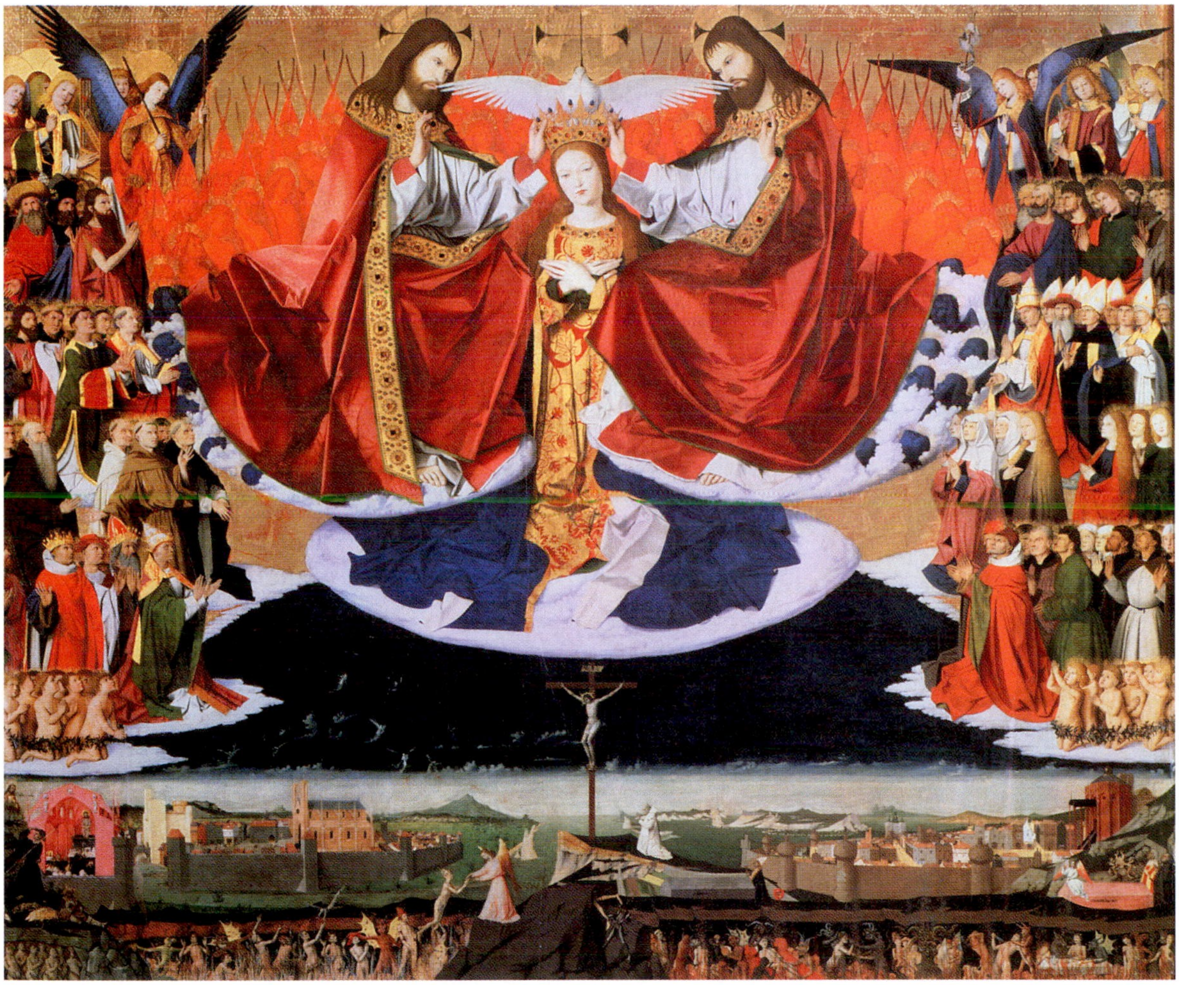

Fig. 198 Enguerrand Quarton, *Coronation of the Virgin,* 1453–1454.
Panel painting, 72 × 86 5/8 in. Musée de l'Hospice, Villeneuve-lès-Avignon.

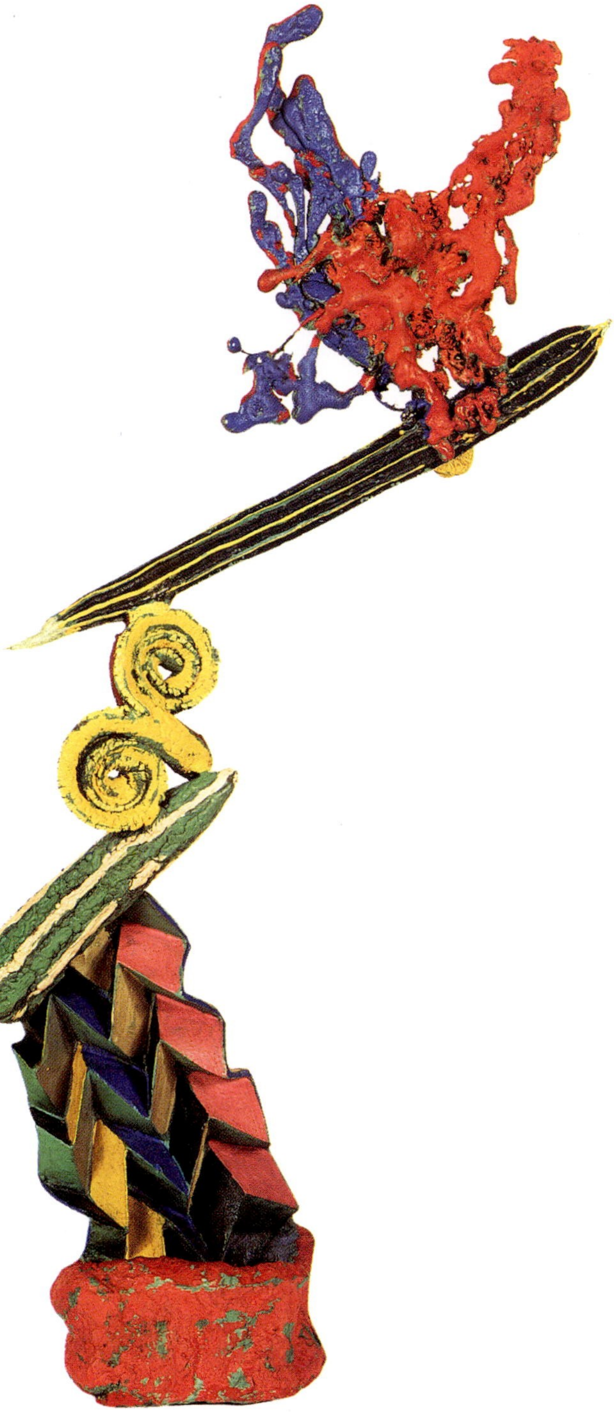

Fig. 199 **Nancy Graves, *Zeeg,* 1983.**
Bronze with polychrome patina, 28 ½ × 14 × 11 in. © VAGA. Private collection.

Asymmetrical Balance

The *Coronation of the Virgin* is symmetrically balanced. Compositions that have two apparently balanced halves that are not mirror images of one another are said to be **asymmetrically balanced.** That is, though the two sides of the composition do not match, they seem to possess the same visual weight. Visual weight refers to the apparent lightness or heaviness of the visual elements on each side of the composition. In Vermeer's painting (Fig. 197), the scales themselves are symmetrically balanced but the composition as a whole is asymmetrically balanced. This is because the light falling on the woman, which is massed near the center right of the composition, visually balances the great dark mass of the left side of the painting.

We intuitively know that Nancy Graves's *Zeeg* (Fig. 199) is balanced—otherwise it would topple over—but this bronze sculpture consisting, from the bottom up, of billows, a squash, what appears to be a sweetroll, an English cucumber, and finally two large abstract expressionist drips is completely asymmetrical. Compare it, for instance, to the symmetrical balance of a cruciform construction, or to the asymmetrical balance of Michelangelo's *Pietà* (Fig. 172). Neither side of Michelangelo's sculpture is a mirror image of the other, but the entire compostion is achieved in a perfectly balanced equilateral triangle. Graves does not fit her composition into any such geometrical scheme. Rather, she relies on your seeing the large abstract expressionist drips at the top of the sculpture as rising, not falling. They appear to defy gravity, and thus put no downward pressure on the cucumber. In fact, they appear to be holding the end of the cucumber up. But despite the sculpture's apparent balance, Graves has depended on actual weight to balance it. She has heavily weighted the bottom left of the sculpture so that the lighter upper thrust of the zucchini and its attendant drips do not fall to the right.

The change in actual weight that allows three-dimensional sculpture to achieve equilibrium has a number of visual equivalents in two-dimensional terms. You probably remember from childhood what happened when an older and larger child got on the other end of the seesaw. Up you shot, like a catapult. In

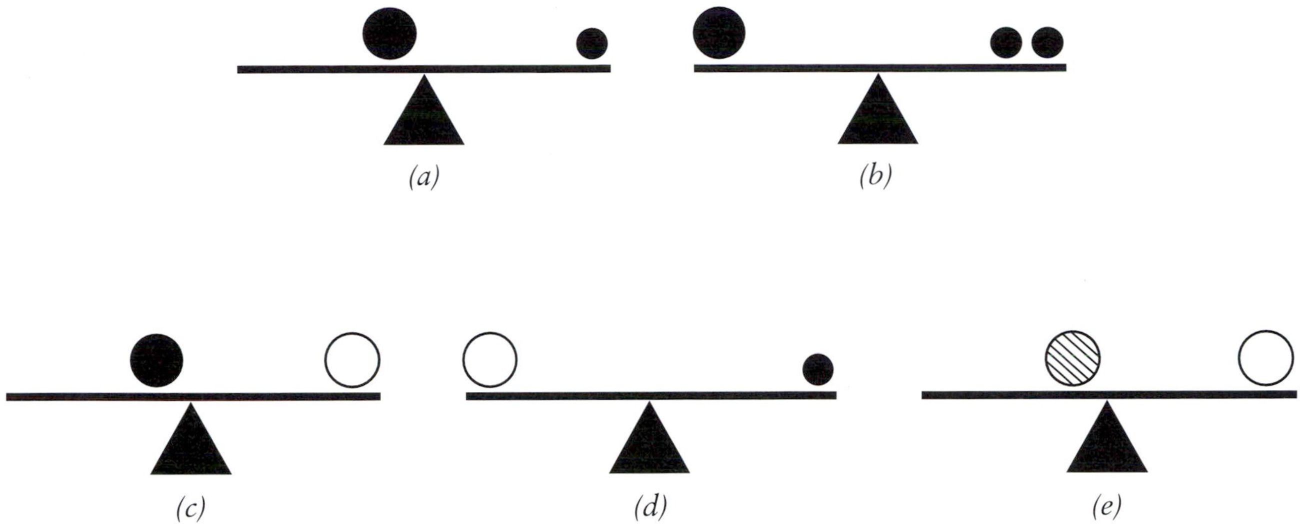

Fig. 200 Some different varieties of asymmetrical balance.

order to right the balance, the larger child had to move toward the fulcrum of the seesaw, giving your smaller self more leverage and allowing the plank to balance. The illustrations (Fig. 200) show, in visual terms, some of the ways this balance can be attained (in a work of art, the center axis of the work is equivalent to the fulcrum):

(a) *A large area closer to the fulcrum is balanced by a smaller area further away.* We instinctively see something large as heavier than something small.

(b) *Two small areas balance one large area.* We see the combined weight of the two small areas as equivalent to the larger mass.

(c) *A dark area closer to the fulcrum is balanced by a light area of the same size further away.* We instinctively see light-colored areas as light in weight, and dark-colored areas as dense and heavy.

(d) *A large light area is balanced by a small dark one.* Because it appears to weigh less, the light area can be far larger than the dark one that balances it.

(e) *A textured area closer to the fulcrum is balanced by a smooth, even area further away.* Visually, textured surfaces appear heavier than smooth ones because texture lends the shape an appearance of added density—it seems "thicker" or more substantial.

These are only a few of the possible ways in which works might appear balanced. There are, however, no "laws" or "rules" about how to go about visually balancing a work of art. Artists generally trust their own eyes. When a work looks balanced, it is balanced.

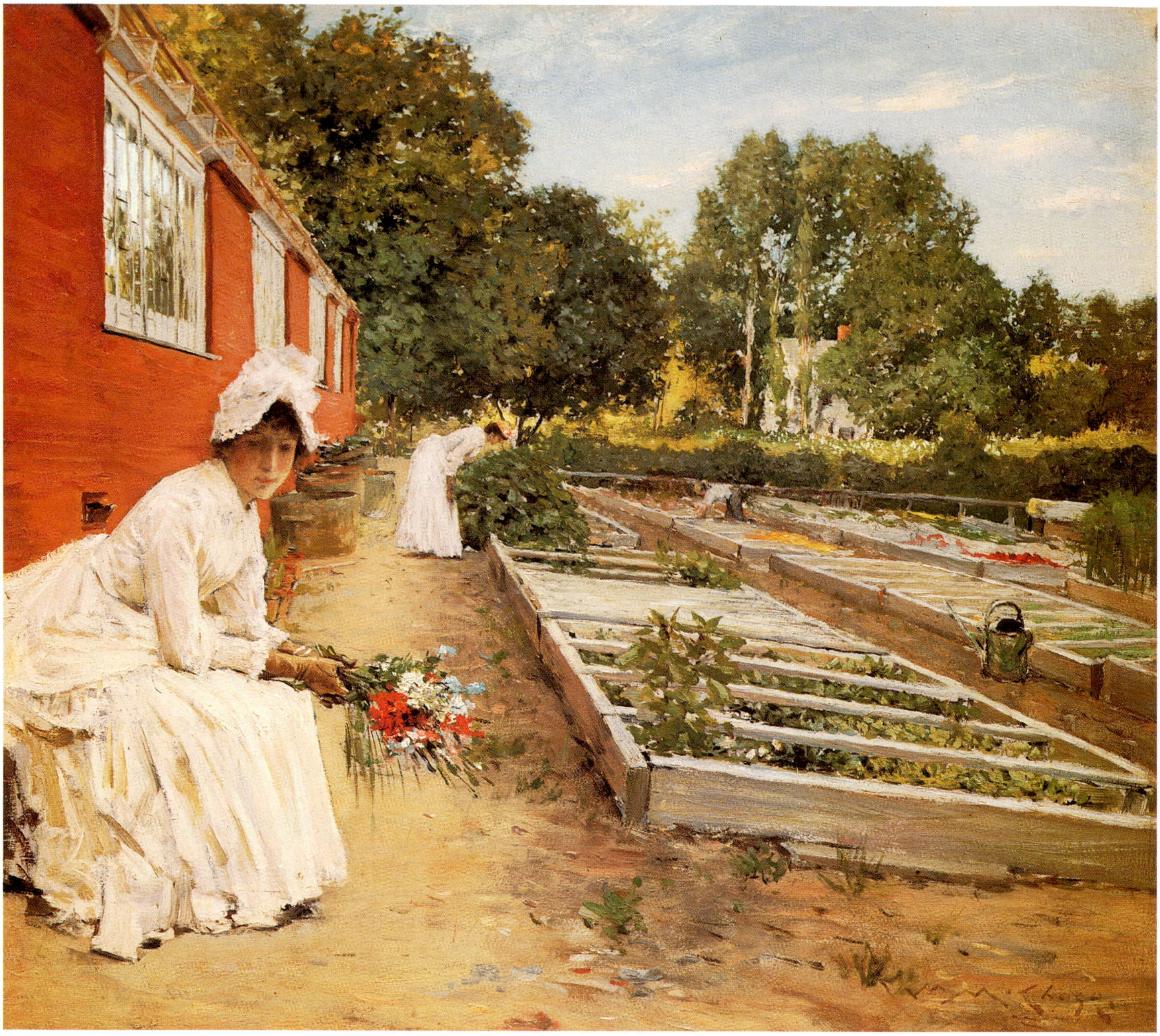

Fig. 201 William Merritt Chase, *The Nursery,* 1890.
Oil on panel, $14\frac{1}{8} \times 16$ in. Manoogian Collection, Detroit.

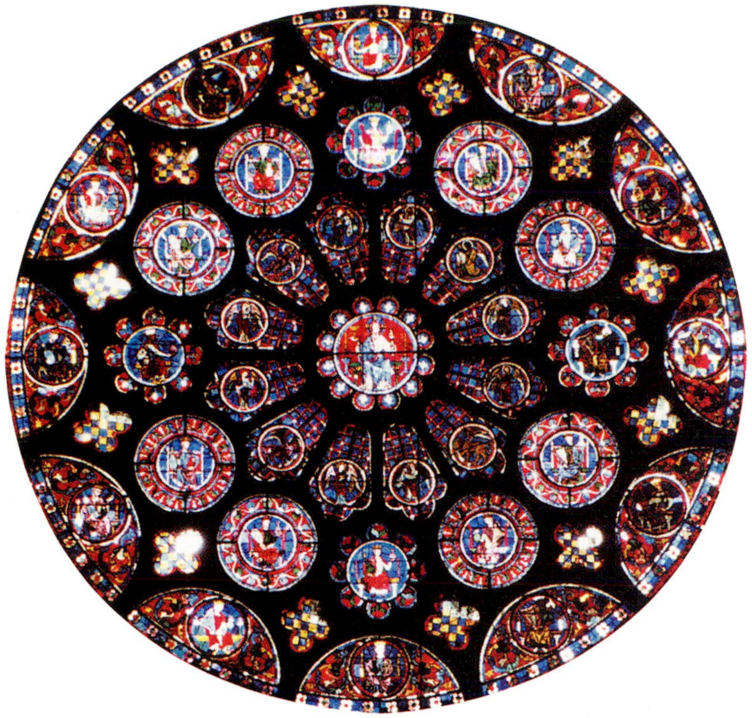

Fig. 202 Rose window, west façade, Chartres Cathedral, c. 1215.
Chartres, France. Art Resource.

William Merritt Chase's *The Nursery* (Fig. 201) is a good example of asymmetrical balance functioning in yet another way. The central axis around which this painting is balanced is not in the middle, but to the left. The setting is the nursery in New York's Central Park, where seedlings are started each year and then transplanted to the flowerbeds thoughout the park. It is evidently early summer, and many of the plants have already been moved. The left side of this painting is much heavier than the right. The bright white dress of the seated young woman, together with the red building behind her, are the largest shapes in the composition. The complementary color scheme enforces our sense of asymmetrical balance. The larger right side is predominantly green, with only two hints of red. But the smaller left-hand side of the painting is dominated by a red that tints even the young woman's cheeks. Except for the leaves above the building, there is very little green on the left side, and the leaves themselves are more a warm yellow than green. If we were to imagine a fulcrum beneath the painting that would balance the composition, it would in effect divide the red from the green, exactly, as it turns out, below the vanishing point established by the building and the lines of planting frames. Instinctively, we place ourselves at this fulcrum.

Radial Balance

A final type of balance is **radial balance,** in which everything *radiates* outward from a central point. The large, dominating, and round stained-glass window above the front portal of Chartres Cathedral in France (Fig. 202) is a perfect example. Called a rose window because of its dominant color and its flowerlike structure, it represents the Last Judgment. At its center is Jesus, surrounded by the symbols of Matthew, Mark, Luke, and John, the writers of the Gospels, and of angels and seraphim. The Apostles, depicted in pairs, surround these, and on the outer ring are scenes from the Book of Revelations. In other words, the entire New Testament of the Bible emanates from Jesus in the center.

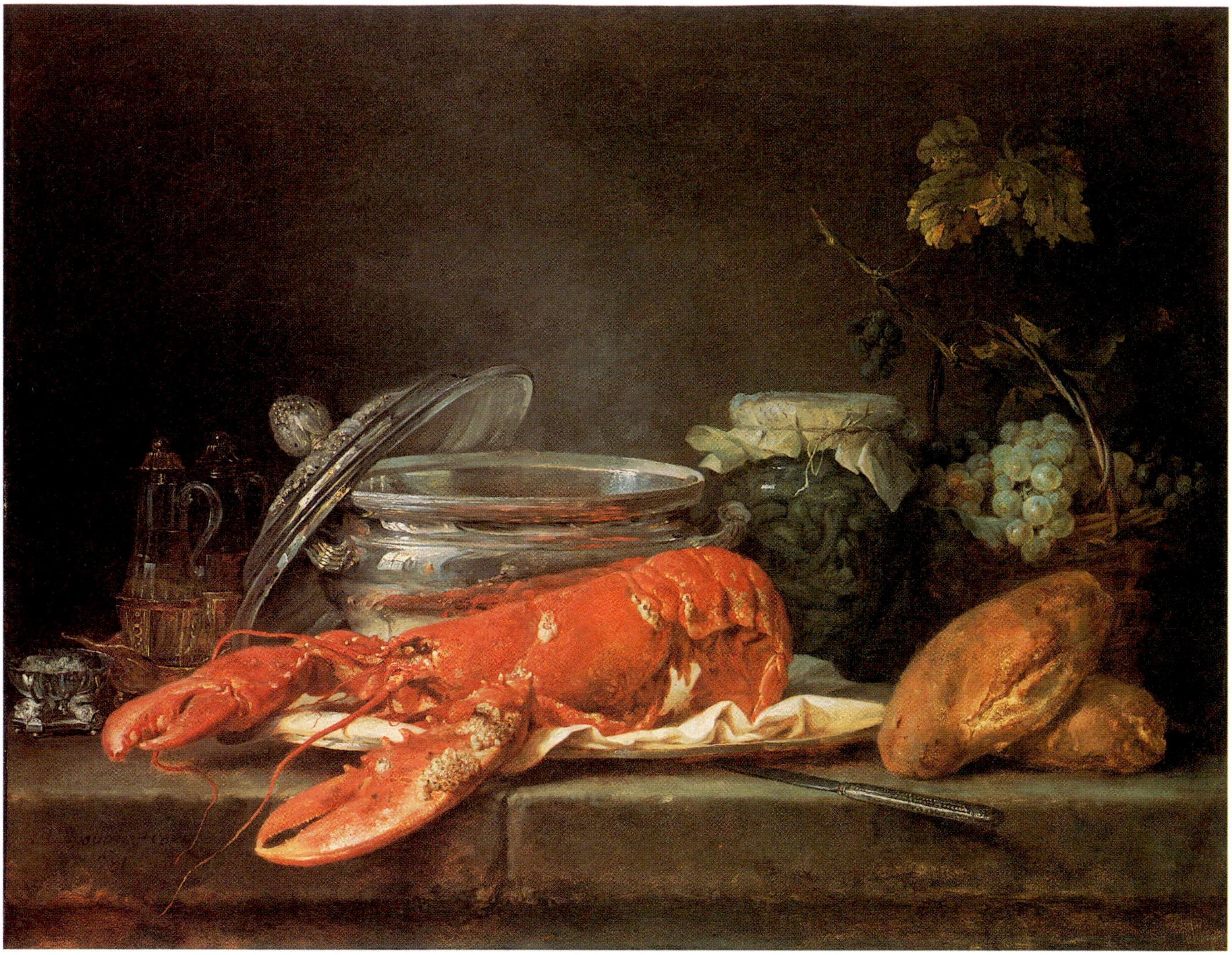

Fig. 203 **Anna Vallayer-Coster, *Still Life,* 1767.**
Oil on canvas, 27 3/4 × 35 1/4 in. The Toledo Art Museum, Toledo, Ohio. Gift of Edward Drummond Libbey.

EMPHASIS AND FOCAL POINT

Artists employ *emphasis* in order to draw the viewer's attention to one area of the work. We refer to this area as the **focal point** of the composition. The focal point of a radially balanced composition is obvious. The center of the rose window in the west façade of Chartres Cathedral (Fig. 202) is its focal point, and fittingly the crucified Christ occupies that spot. The focal point of Quarton's *Coronation of the Virgin* (Fig. 198) is Mary, who is also, not coincidentally, the object of everyone's attention. The focal point of Chase's *The Nursery* (Fig. 201) is the vanishing point—though the eye, in that painting, is quickly drawn to the seated woman in the foreground, herself a second, important focus of the composition.

One important way that emphasis can be established is through the manipulation of light and color. The two paintings illustrated here employ the same complementary color scheme to widely different ends. Both are by women who painted in the court of the French king Louis XVI. Both were members of the Académie Royale, the official organization of French painters, though it is important to note that after Anna Vallayer-Coster was elected to the Académie in 1770, membership by women was limited to four, perhaps because the male-dominated Académie felt threatened by women's success.

By painting everything else in the composition a shade of green, Anna Vallayer-Coster focuses our attention in her *Still Life* (Fig. 203) on the delicious red lobster in the foreground. Lush in its brushwork, and with a sense of luminosity that we can almost feel, the painting celebrates Vallayer-Coster's skill as a painter, her ability to control both color and light. In essence—and the double meaning is intentional—the painting is an exercise in "good taste."

Marie-Louise-Elisabeth Vigée-Lebrun's portrait of Marie Antoinette (Fig. 204) emphasizes its subject by means of the same color contrast, the Queen's red dress contrasting with the predominantly green shades of her surroundings. Vigée-Lebrun, Marie Antoinette's favorite painter, was entrusted with the difficult task of portraying the unpopular Queen in a favorable light. Commissioned by the Court to restore the Queen's reputation among the people, the painting idealizes the unattractive Marie, not only by portraying her as a loving mother surrounded by her children but that role as well—her yo empty cradle that is mea the recent death of This is an example of emphasis by means of of sight. The little boy no eyes but draws them to the emp

We have already seen, in Tinto *Supper* (Fig. 135), how light, functioning stage spotlight, can draw the eye away fro the perspectival lines of the scene and cause us to focus our attention elsewhere. The light in Georges de La Tour's *Joseph the Carpenter* (Fig. 205) draws our attention away from the painting's apparent subject, Joseph, the father of Jesus, and to the brightly lit visage of Christ himself. The candlelight here is comparable to the Divine Light, casting an ethereal glow across the young boy's face.

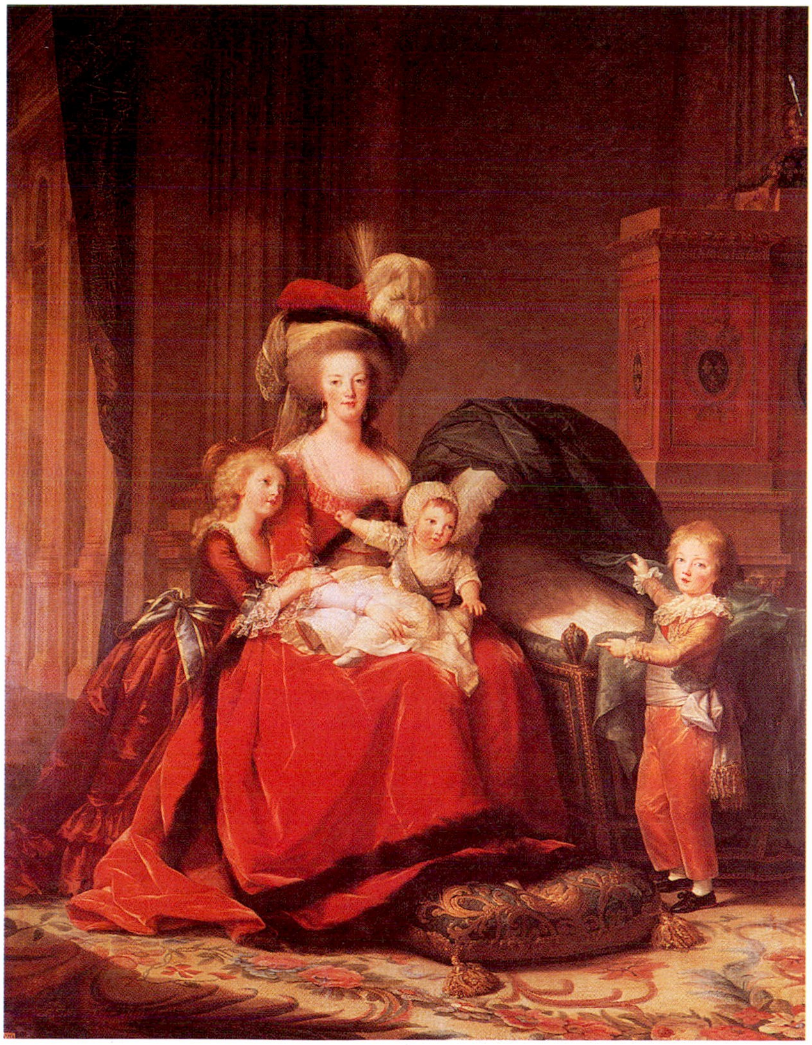

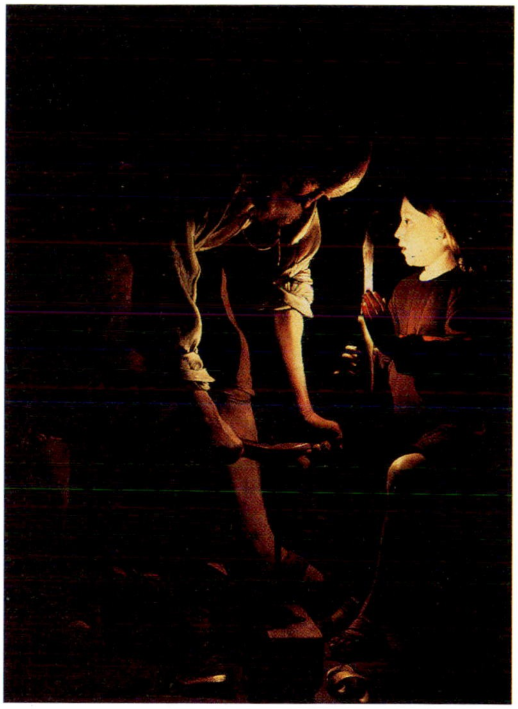

Fig. 204 (left) Marie-Louise-Elisabeth Vigée-Lebrun, *Portrait of Marie Antoinette with Her Children,* 1787.
Oil on canvas, 108 1/4 × 84 5/8 in.
Musée de Versailles, France. Giraudon/Art Resource.

Fig. 205 (above) Georges de La Tour, *Joseph the Carpenter,* c. 1645.
Oil on canvas, 18 1/2 × 25 1/2 in.
Musée du Louvre, Paris. Scala/Art Resource.

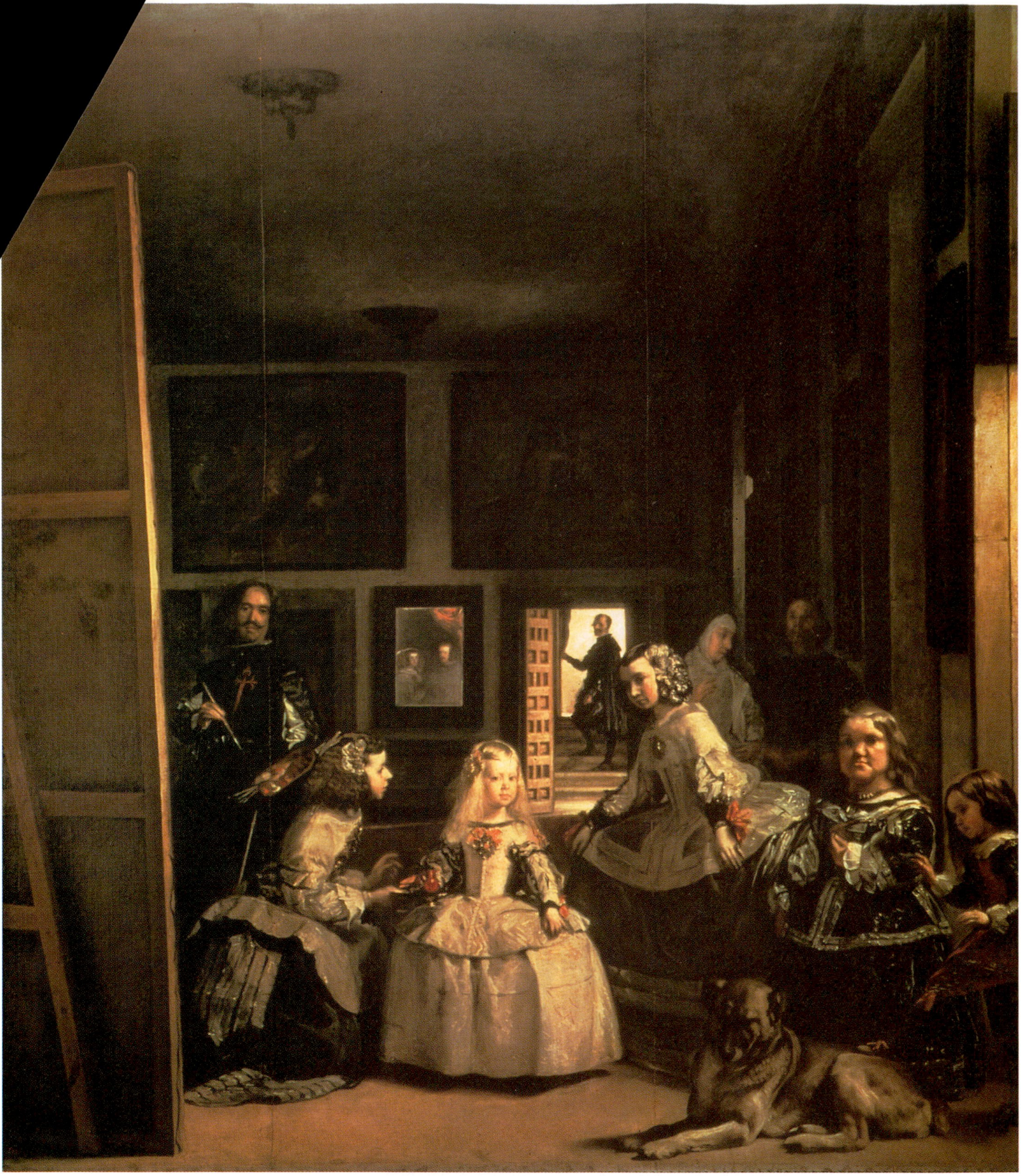

Fig. 206 Diego Velázquez, *Las Meninas (The Maids of Honor)*, 1656.
Oil on canvas, 10 ft. ¾ in. × 9 ft. ¾ in. Prado, Madrid. Giraudon/Art Resource.

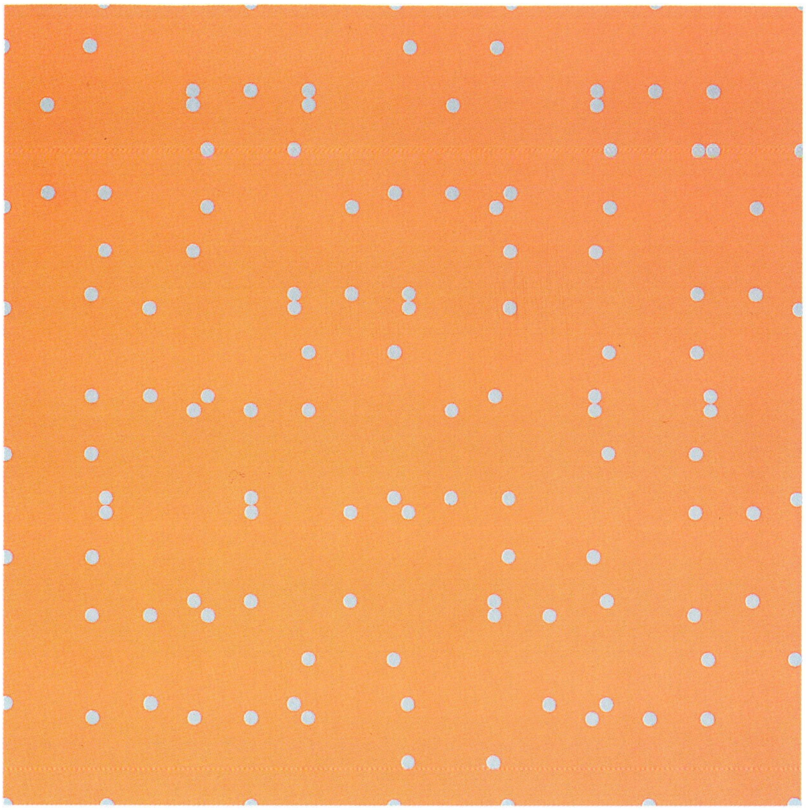

Fig. 207 Larry Poons, *Orange Crush,* 1963.
Acrylic on canvas, 80 × 80 in. Albright-Knox Art Gallery, Buffalo, New York. Gift of Seymour H. Knox, 1964.

In his masterpiece *Las Meninas (The Maids of Honor)* (Fig. 206), Diego Velázquez creates competing points of emphasis. The scene is the Spanish court of King Philip IV. The most obvious focal point of the composition is the young princess, the *infanta* Margarita, who is emphasized by her position in the center of the painting, by the light that shines brilliantly on her alone, and by the implied lines created by the gazes of the two maids of honor who bracket her. But the figures outside this central group, that of the dwarf on the right, who is also a maid of honor, and the painter on the left (a self-portrait of Velázquez) gaze away from the *infanta*. In fact, they seem to be looking at us, and so too is the *infanta* herself. The focal point of their attention, in other words, lies outside the picture plane. In fact, they are looking at a spot that appears to be occupied by the couple reflected in the mirror at the opposite end of the room, over the *infanta's* shoulder—a couple that turns out to be the king and queen themselves. It seems likely that they are the subject of the painting that Velázquez depicts himself as painting, since they are in the position that would be occupied normally by persons sitting for a portrait. The *infanta* Margarita and her maids of honor have come, it would seem, to watch the royal couple have their portrait painted by the great Velázquez. And Velázquez has turned the table on everyone—the focal point of *Las Meninas* is not the focal point of what he is painting.

Finally, it is possible, as the earlier example of Pollock's *Autumn Rhythm* (Fig. 186) indicates, to make a work of art that is **afocal**—that is, not merely a work in which no single point of the composition demands our attention any more or less than any other, but also one in which the eye can find no place to rest. In fact, if you stare for a while at the dots in at Larry Poons's painting *Orange Crush* (Fig. 207), and then transfer your attention quickly to the more solid orange area that surrounds them, dots of an even more intense orange will appear. Your vision seems to want to float aimlessly through the space of this painting, focusing on nothing at all.

Jacques Louis David's Oath of the Horatii

Jacques Louis David's *Oath of the Horatii* (Fig. 210) was painted in 1784, five years before the French Revolution. Its focal point, upon which all the male figures are focused, is a compositional "X" just to the left of center. This "X" is created by the central figure's outstretched right arm and the three swords he holds in his left hand. This focal point is, in fact, the subject of the painting, the oath being taken by the three figures on the left.

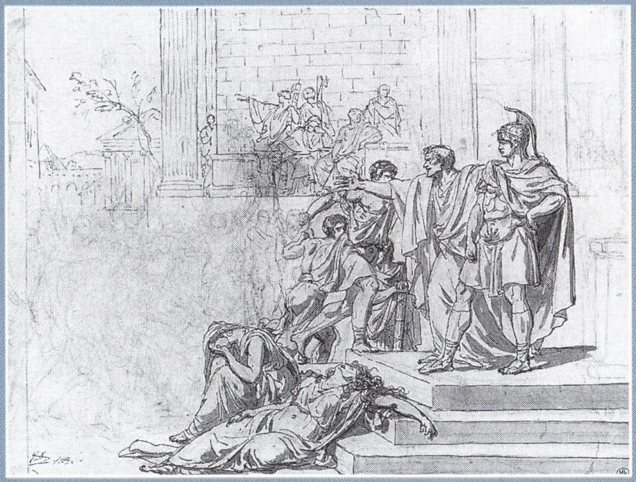

Fig. 208 Jacques-Louis David (1748–1825), *Old Horatius Defending His Son*, c. 1781.
Drawing in black crayon and ink with Indian white wash, $8^4/_5 \times 11^3/_5$ in.
Cabinet des Dessins (RF 1917), Musee du Louvre/Photo Reunion des Musees Nationaux.

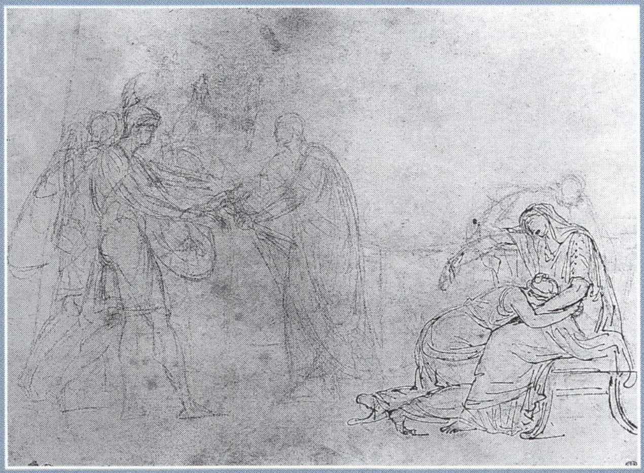

Fig. 209 Jacques-Louis David, *Etude pour Le Serment des Horaces (Oath, Study)*, c. 1782.
Ecole Nat. Superieure Des Beaux-Arts, Paris, France.
Giraudon/Art Resource.

The Horatii, the three sons of Horatius of Rome, are shown swearing before their father to fight to the death the Curatii, the three sons of Curatius, who have been picked to represent Rome's enemy, the Albans. Each set of sons has been chosen for this duty by their respective leaders, who have agreed that rather than sacrificing their entire armies in combat they will accept the outcome of a battle between these representatives. Behind the proud father, the women weep, as much for the Curatii as for the Horatii, since Camilla, a sister of the Horatii, is engaged to be married to one of the Curatii. In fact, the eldest son will murder Camilla for her allegiance to her betrothed. The loss of at least a single loved one is thus inevitable, the loss of more entirely probable. But such sacrifice, the painting suggests, is the necessary price of patriotism. The demands of civic responsibility must eclipse the joys of domestic life. The painting's emphasis on the oath-taking itself supports and clarifies this meaning.

David did not arrive at the focal point for his painting quickly. In the first sketch for the project (Fig. 208), the composition is organized completely differently. The subject is not even the same. The battle is over, not just about to begin. Horatius stands at the top of a set of stairs, holding back a group of men rushing up the stairs to arrest his eldest son for the murder

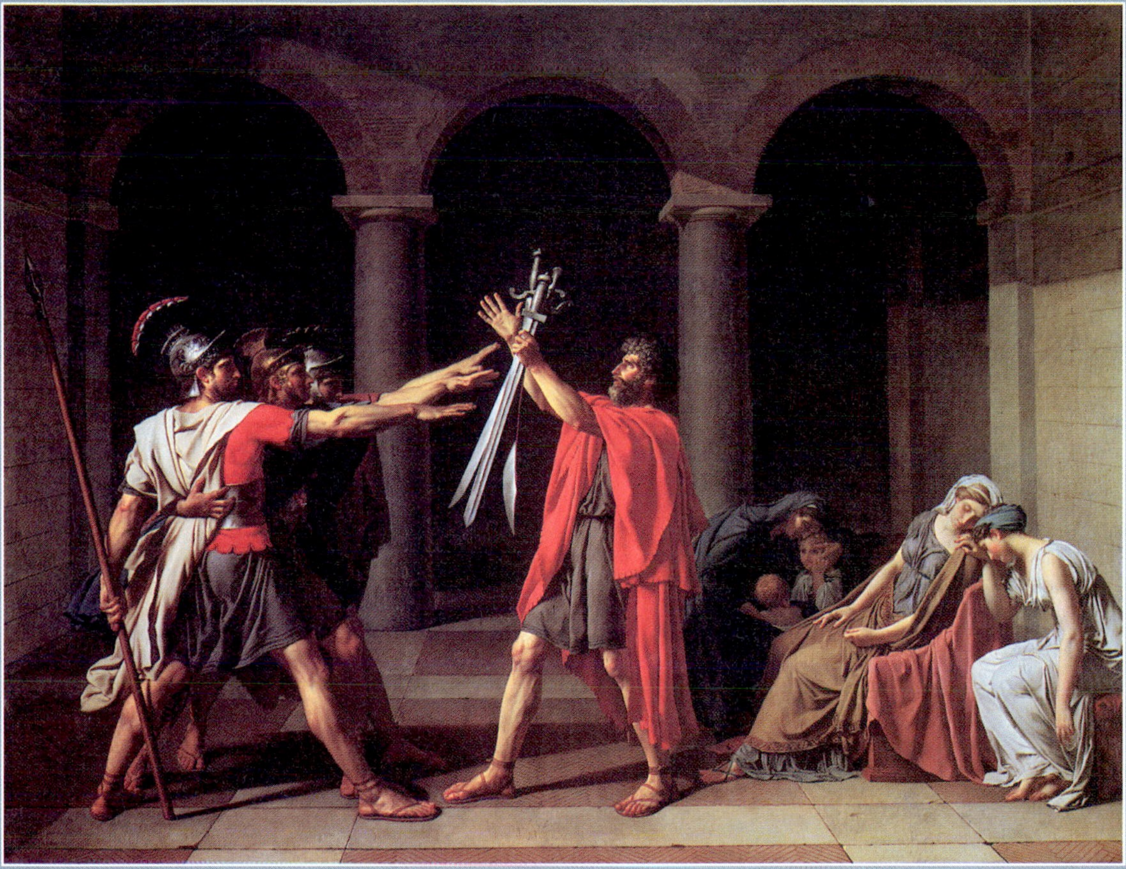

Fig. 210 Jacques-Louis David, *The Oath of the Horatii,* 1784.
Oil on canvas, approx. 11 × 14 ft. Musée du Louvre, Paris.

of Camilla. In a moment, the public, touched by the scene and moved by his sacrifice for his country, will absolve the son. At the bottom of the stairs lies the dead Camilla, a grieving sister beside her. Horatius and his son are the focal point, the apex, as it were, of a mound of bodies. But the drawing lacks both the emotional and compositional clarity of the final painting, and David would turn to a different scheme.

In a later sketch (Fig. 209), we can see that he has chosen the moment before the battle as the subject of the painting and begun to organize the composition much more along the painting's final lines. But here the women are the focus of the composition. In the background, the father is arming the sons, but they are not yet swearing the oath. Rather, the women's grief, the sacrifice of domestic tranquility to the affairs of state, seems to be David's subject.

In the final painting, it is the oath that is the focus. The women form a second, subordinate, point of emphasis. The men are standing, the women sitting. The men look up, the women look down. The men are composed with a geometric rigor, the women with a set of soft, expressive curves. The men occupy two-thirds of the composition, the women only one-third. It is, clearly, the men's action that takes compositional precedence. And it is the nobility of their action that David champions.

Once David arrived at his final compositional scheme, the final work took 11 months to paint. According to contemporary accounts, "the only part of the painting that really gave him any trouble was the left foot of the father. He rubbed it out and redid it at least twenty times."

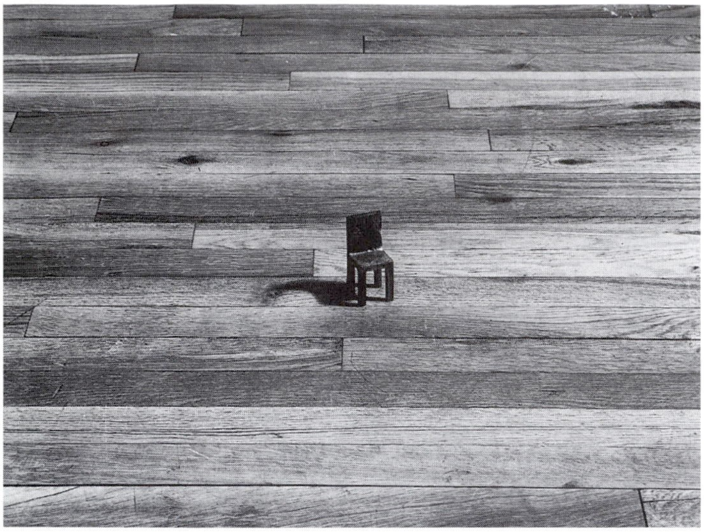

Fig. 211 Joel Shapiro, *Untitled,* 1973–1974.
Cast iron, 3 × 1 ¼ × 1 ¼ in.
Photograph courtesy of PaceWildenstein. Photograph by Geoffrey Clements.

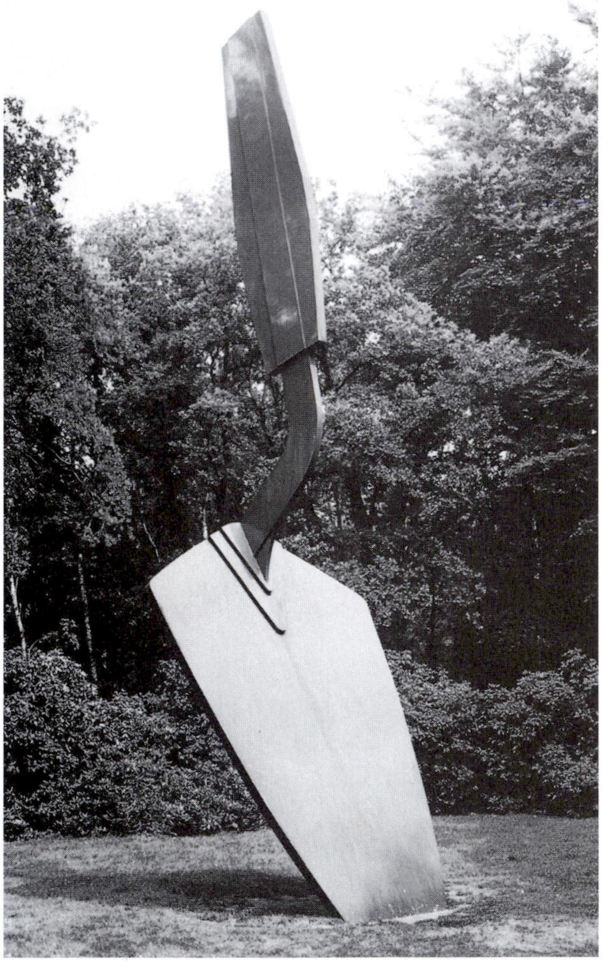

Fig. 212 Claes Oldenburg, *Giant Trowel,* 1971.
Zinc-coated steel, 144 × 46 in. Rijksmuseum Kröller-Müller, Otterlo, The Netherlands.

SCALE AND PROPORTION

Scale is the word we use to describe the dimensions of an art object in relation to the original object that it depicts or in relation to the objects around it. Thus we speak of a miniature as a "small-scale" portrait, or of a big mural as a "large-scale" work. Scale is an issue that is important when you read a textbook such as this. You must always remember that the reproductions you look at do not usually give us much sense of the actual size of the work. The scale is by no means consistent throughout. That is, a relatively small painting might be reproduced on a full page, and a very large painting on a half page. In order to make the artwork fit on the book page we must—however unintentionally—manipulate its scale.

In both Joel Shapiro's *Untitled* (Fig. 211) and Claes Oldenburg's *Giant Trowel* (Fig. 212), the artist is intentionally manipulating the scale of the object depicted. In Shapiro's case, he has diminished the scale of a normal chair. In the context of a dollhouse, it would be appropriately scaled, but set in the middle of a large room, as it is here, it is startlingly small. Twelve feet high, Oldenburg's trowel is gigantic in scale. It is an intentional exaggeration that parodies the idea of garden sculpture.

Proportion refers to the relationship between the parts of an object and the whole, or to the relationship between an object and its surroundings. Thus the internal proportions of each of these objects are accurate. However, each of these objects is "out of proportion" in relationship to its environment. When something is disproportionate to its surroundings, its scale is either too large or too small.

The painting on the right, John Singer Sargent's *The Daughters of Edward Darley Boit* (Fig. 213) has a certain "Alice in Wonderland" feel to it. It is as if the young ladies depicted here had swallowed a piece of cookie and suddenly shrunk to a size smaller than a Chinese vase. The scale of the vases appears to be too large. They are out of proportion with the room. The painting, executed in 1882 in the Boit family's Paris apartment, is not merely a group portrait, but a stunning psychological study, granting us access into the complicated reality of these young girls' lives. Writing about it in *Harper's Magazine,* Sargent's contempo-

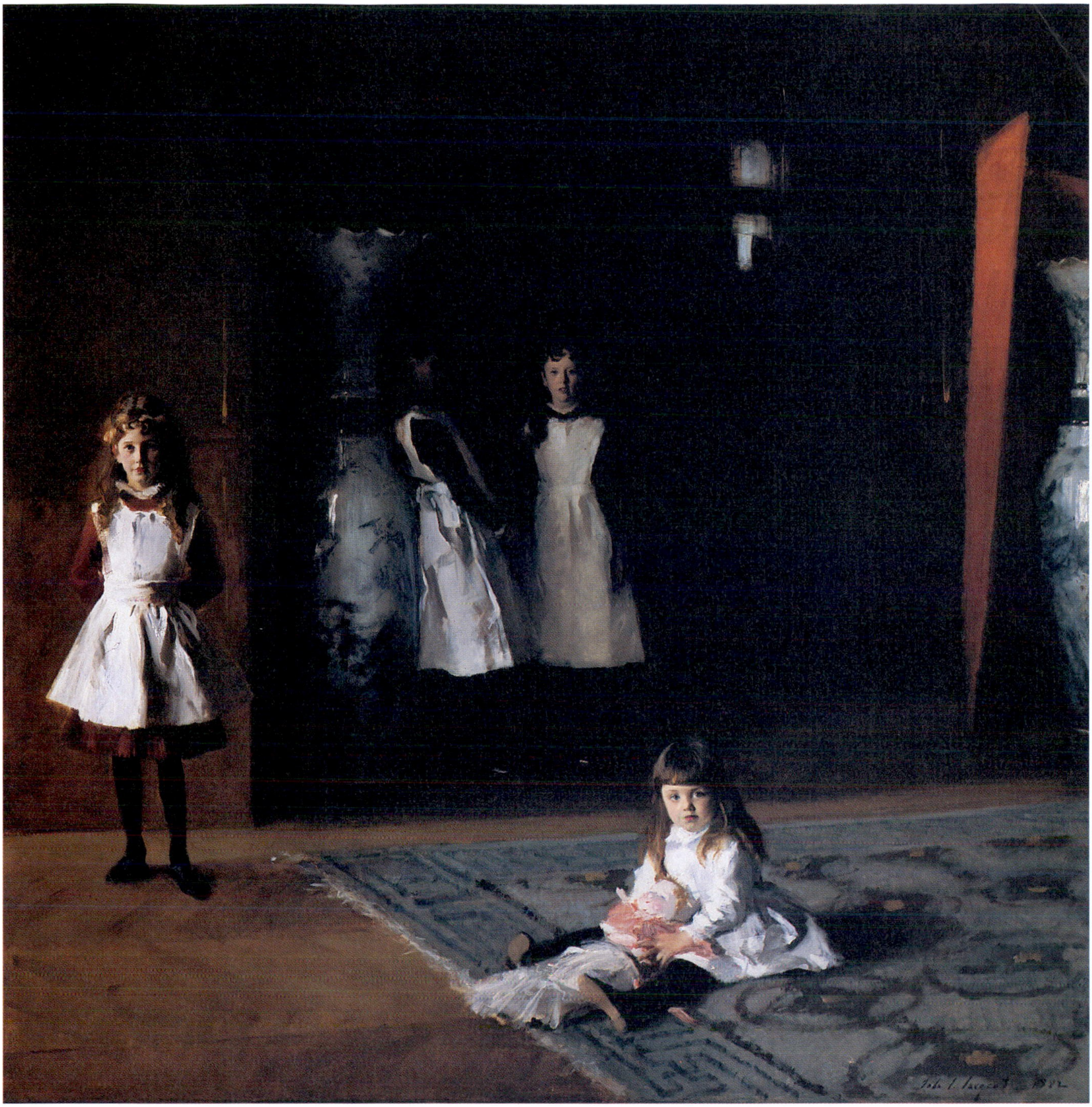

Fig. 213 John Singer Sargent, *The Daughters of Edward Darley Boit,* 1882.
Oil on canvas, $87\,^5/_8 \times 87\,^5/_8$ in. Museum of Fine Arts, Boston. Gift of the daughters of Edward D. Boit in memory of their father.

rary, the novelist Henry James, found in this depiction of privileged children the same mysterious depth that he tried to convey in his own fiction—"the sense," he called it, "of assimilated secrets." The older girls are further back in space than the youngest child, in the darkness rather than the light, as if their psychological world were becoming increasingly private as they become more mature. The giant vases that loom over them, especially in combination with the bright red gash of the screen at the right, function like parental hands, at once threatening and caressing, but dominating their social world at every turn.

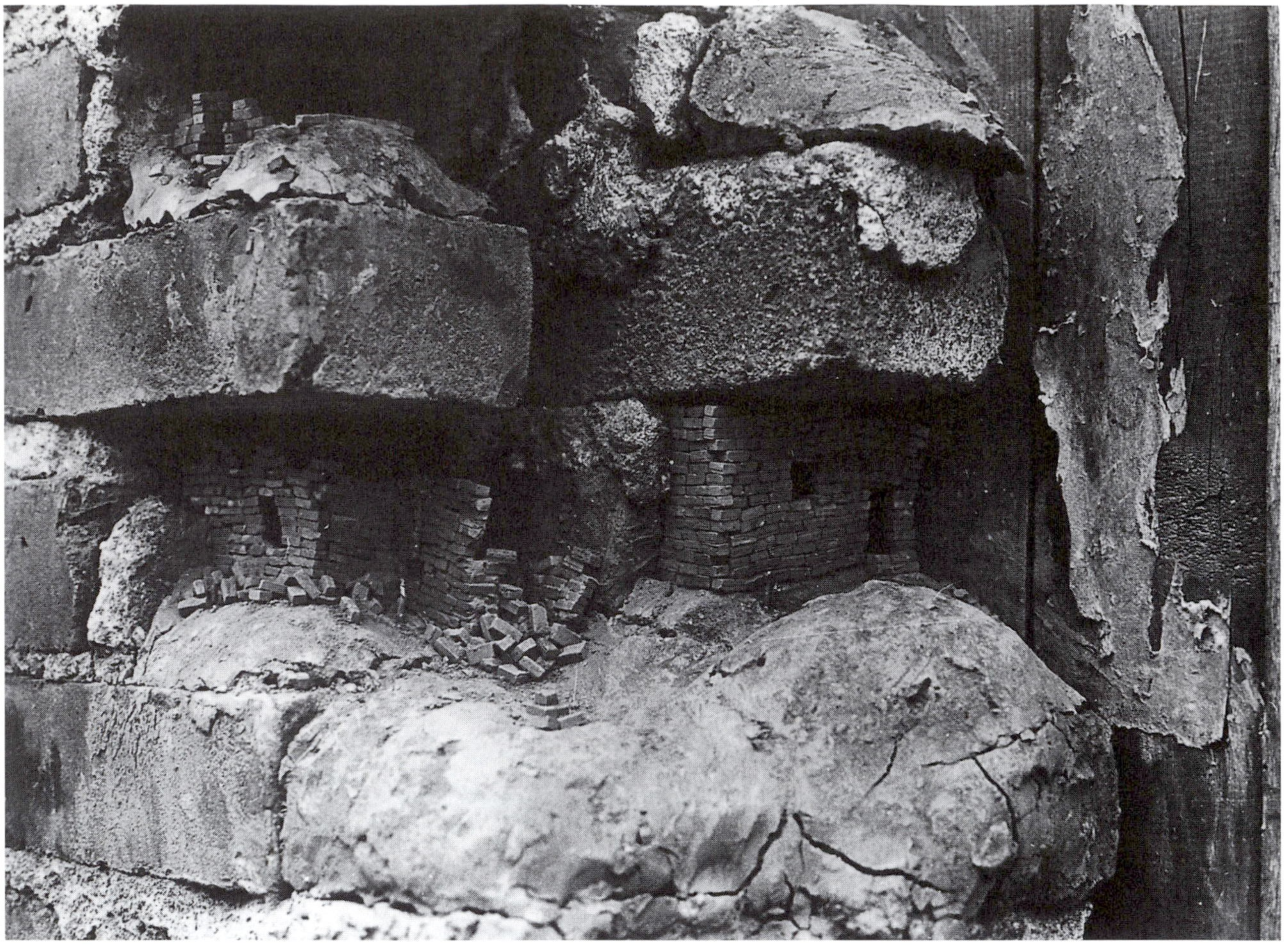

Fig. 214 Charles Simonds, *Dwelling, East Houston Street, New York,* 1972.
Unfired clay brick installation. Photograph by Charles Simonds.

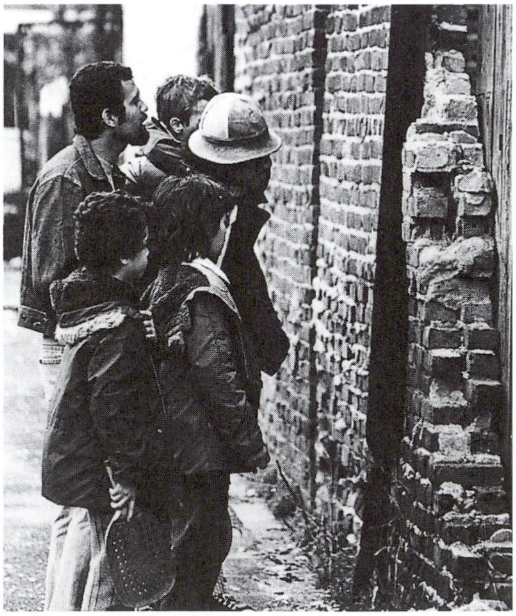

Fig. 215 Passersby with *Dwelling, East Houston Street, New York,* 1972.
Photograph by Charles Simonds.

By manipulating scale and flouting the viewer's expectations, the artist can achieve some startling effects. During the 1970s, Charles Simonds constructed over 300 dwellings and ritual structures—200 of them on the Lower East Side of Manhattan alone, the others all over the world, from Ireland to China. These structures purported to be the traces of an imaginary race of "Little People" who once inhabited them (Figs. 214 and 215) Made of tiny unfired clay bricks deposited in the walls of our decaying urban environment, these cliff dwellings speak to us of a lost tribe of people who have abandoned the sites we now occupy, presumably because they have found them unlivable. Because these works exist literally in the streets, very few have survived. Passersby take souvenir bricks, children play games in the ruins, weather destroys them. It is evident that the Little People are not only smaller than us, but that time is contracted for them as well. They have come and gone in our midst, and we have been blind to them.

Artists also manipulate scale by the way they depict the relative size of objects. As we know from our study of perspective, one of the most important ways to represent recessional space is to depict a thing closer to us as larger than a thing the same size farther away. This change in scale helps us to visually measure the space in the scene before us. When a mountain fills a small percentage of the space of a painting we know that it is lies somewhere in the distance. We judge its actual size relative to other elements in the painting and our sense of the average real mountain's size.

Because everybody in Japan knows just how large Mount Fuji is, many of Hokusai's various views of the mountain take advantage of this knowledge and, by manipulating scale, play with the viewer's expectations. His most famous view of the mountain, (Fig. 216), is a case in point. In the foreground, two boats descend into a trough beneath a great crashing wave that hangs over the scene like a giant, menacing claw. In the distance, Fuji rises above the horizon, framed in a vortex of wave and foam. Hokusai has echoed its shape in the foremost wave of the composition. While the wave is visually larger than the distant mountain, our sense of scale causes us to diminish its importance. The wave will imminently collapse, Fuji will remain. For the Japanese, Fuji symbolizes not only the everlasting, but Japan itself, and the print juxtaposes the perils of the moment with the enduring life of the nation.

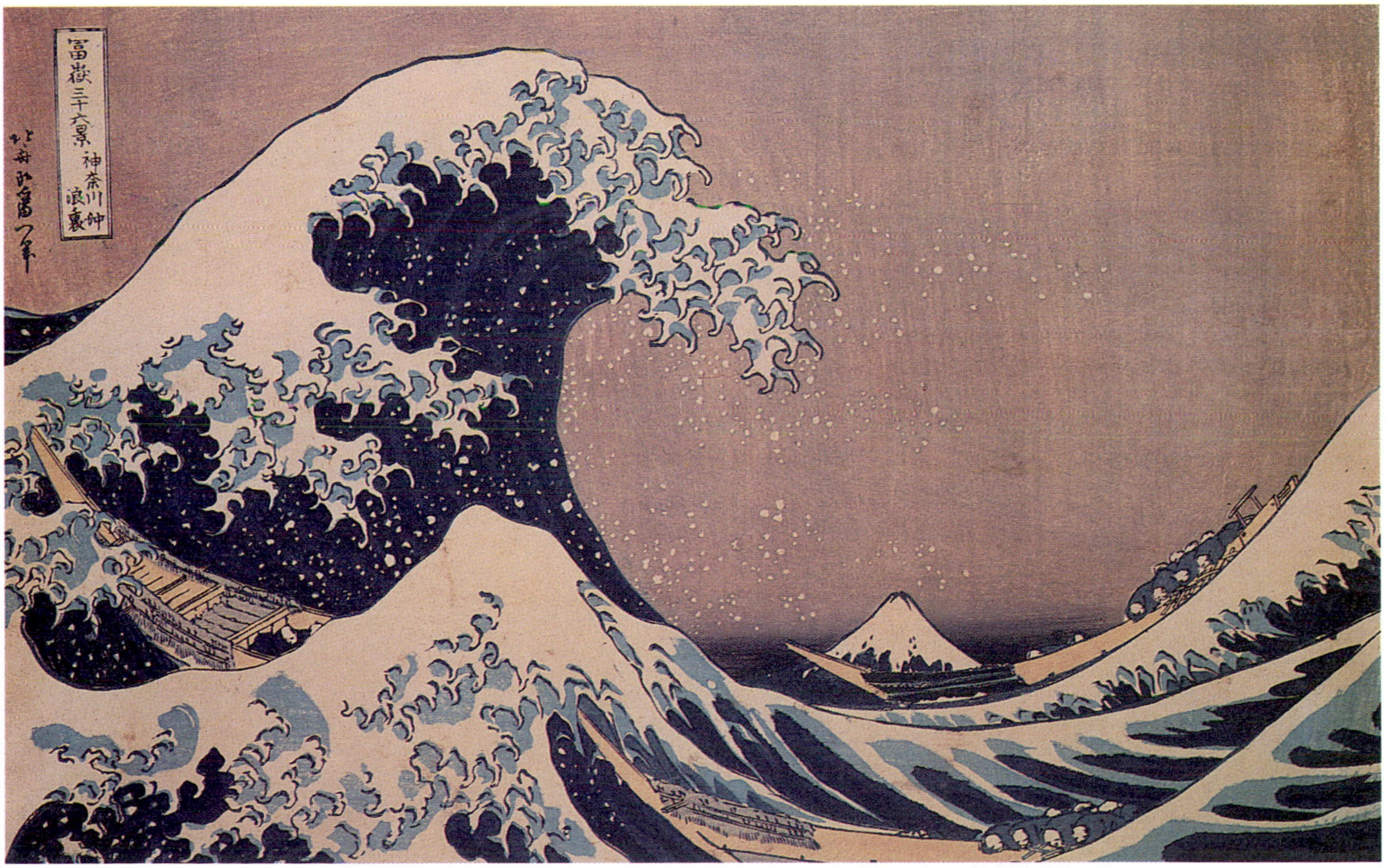

Fig. 216 Hokusai, *The Great Wave off Kanagawa*, from the series *Thirty-Six Views of Mount Fuji*, 1823–1829.
Color woodcut, 10 × 15 in. Giraudon/Art Resource.

Artists can also manipulate proportion to interesting ends. Picasso's *Woman with Stiletto (Death of Marat)* (Fig. 217) depicts one of the most famous moments in French history, when Charlotte Corday assassinated the revolutionary hero Jean-Paul Marat in his bath. Every element in Picasso's painting is grotesquely disproportionate. Marat lies in his tub with a tiny head and tiny left arm in which he holds a pen. His right arm is somewhat larger; in it he holds the letter that Corday wrote in order to gain entrance to his house. His right leg is swollen to gigantic size. Corday stretches out above him like a praying mantis, her giant mouth opened as if to consume the minuscule Marat, her stiletto, the size of a sewing needle, piercing his heart, her lower body hugely distorted. Blood falls in a rush to the floor, and its red becomes, behind Marat's gigantic foot, part and parcel of the tricolor, the flag of the French Revolution. By radically distorting the normal proportions of the human body, Picasso is able convincingly to dramatize the horror of this scene.

When the proportions of a figure seem normal, on the other hand, the representation is more likely to seem harmonious and balanced. The classical Greeks, in fact, believed that beauty itself was a function of proper proportion. In terms of the human body, these perfect proportions were determined by the sculptor Polykleitos, who not only described them in a now lost text called the *Canon* (from the Greek *kanon,* or "rule") but who also executed a sculpture to embody them. This is the *Doryphoros,* or

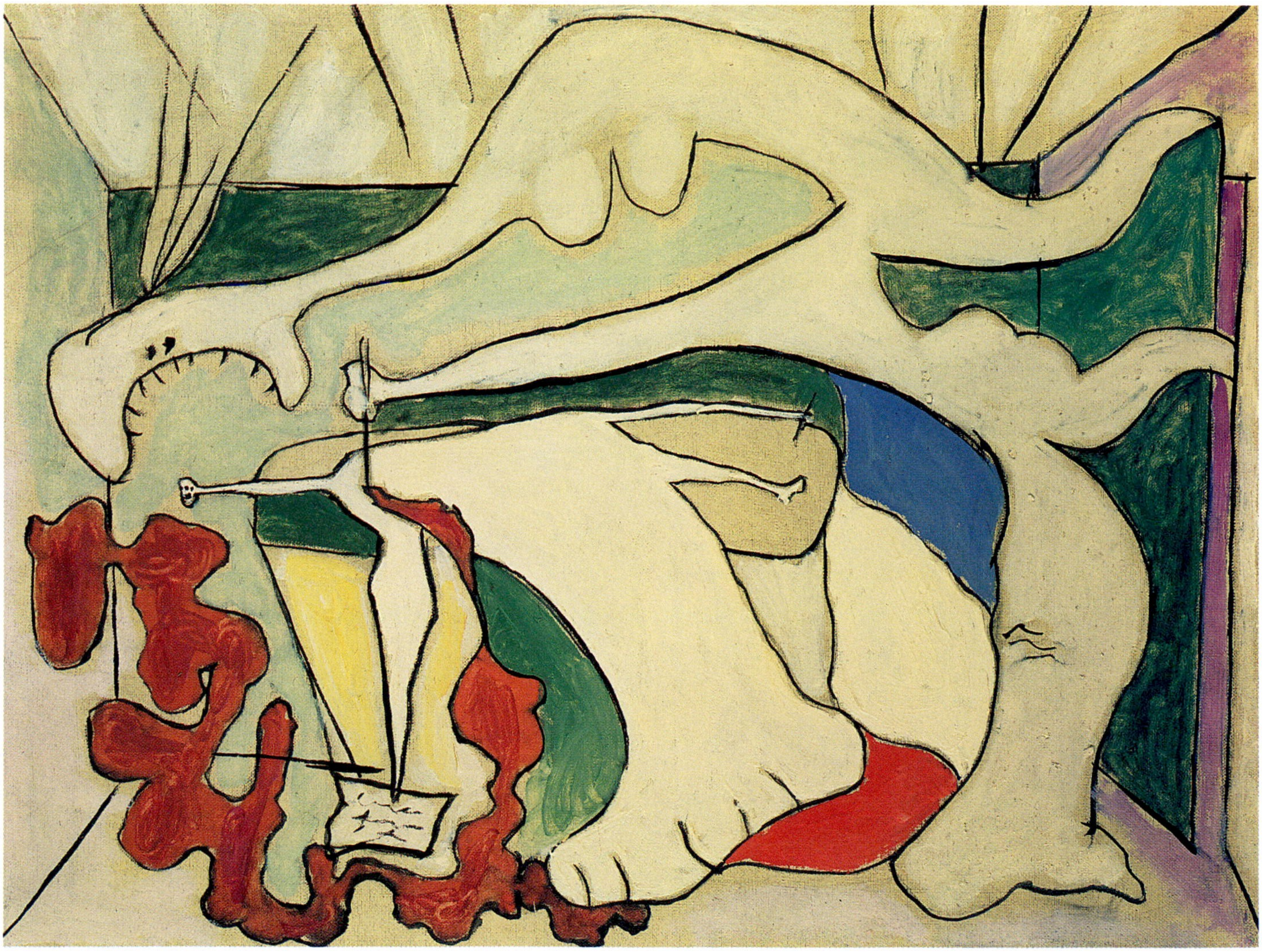

Fig. 217 Pablo Picasso, "*Woman with Stiletto (Death of Marat)*", 1931.
Oil on canvas, 18 1/8 × 24 in. Musée Picasso, Paris. Cliche des Musées Nationaux – Paris. © R.M.N. – SPADEM.

"spear carrier," the original of which is also lost, although numerous copies survive (Fig. 218). The perfection of this figure is based on the fact that each part of the body is a common fraction of the figure's total height. According to the **Canon,** the height of the head ought to be one-eighth and the breadth of the shoulders one-fourth of the total height of the body.

This sense of mathematical harmony was utilized by the Greeks in their architecture as well. The proportions of the facade of the Parthenon, constructed in the fifth century BCE on the top of the Acropolis in Athens (Fig. 219), are based on the so-called **Golden Section:** the width of the building is 1.618 times the height. In terms of proportions, the height is to the width as 1 is to 1.618, or in less precise terms, approximately a ratio of 5:8. Plato regarded this proportion as the key to understanding the cosmos, and many years later, in the thirteenth century CE, the mathematician Leonardo Fibonacci discovered that this ratio is part of an infinite sequence (1, 2, 3, 5, 8, 13, 21, 34, 55, 89, etc.) in which each number is the sum of the two numbers before it, and each pair of numbers is a ratio that, as the numbers increase, more and more closely approximates 1:1.618. That the Parthenon should be constructed according to this proportion is hardly accidental. It is a temple to Athena, not only the protectress of Athens but the goddess of wisdom, and the Golden Section represents to the ancient Greeks not merely beauty, but the ultimate wisdom of the universe.

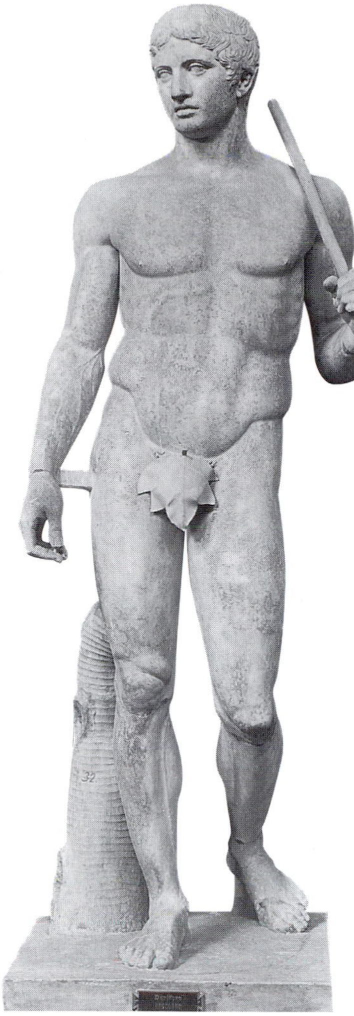

Fig. 218 Polykleitos, *Doryphoros,* 450 BCE.
Marble, Roman copy after lost bronze original, H. 84 in. National Museum, Naples.

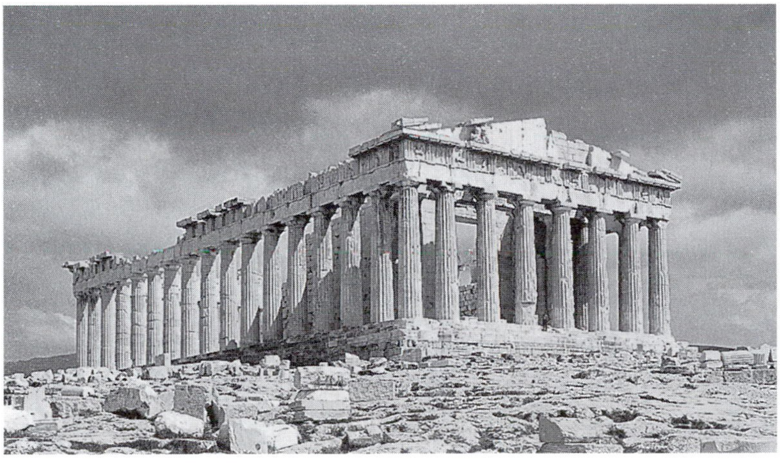

Fig. 219 Parthenon, 447–438 BCE.
Pentelic marble, 111 × 237 ft. at base. Athens, Greece. D.A. Harissiadis, Athens.

REPETITION AND RHYTHM

Repetition often implies monotony. If we see the same thing over and over again, it tends to get boring. The sterile world of suburban life depicted in Frank Gohlke's photograph *Housing Devlopment South of Fort Worth, Texas* (Fig. 220) is, precisely, the image of such monotony, as the eye travels down a street where house after house is the same.

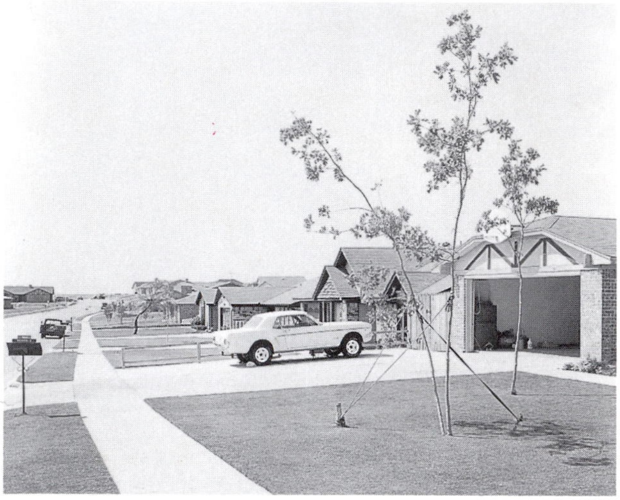

Fig. 220 Frank Gohlke, *Housing Development South of Fort Worth, Texas,* 1978.
Gelatin silver print, 14 1/8 × 17 1/4 in.

Nevertheless, when the same or like elements—shapes, colors, or a regular pattern of any kind—are repeated over and over again in a composition, a certain visual **rhythm** will result. In Jacob Lawrence's *Barber Shop* (Fig. 221), this rhythm is established through the repetition of both shapes and colors. One pattern is based on the diamond-shaped figures sitting in the barber chairs, each of whom is covered with a different-colored apron: one lavendar and white, one red, and one black and green. The color and pattern of the left-hand patron's apron is echoed in the shirts of the two barbers on the right, while the pattern of the right-hand patron's apron is repeated in the vest of the barber on the left. Hands, shoulders, feet—all work into the triangulated format of the design. "The painting," Lawrence explained in 1979, "is one of the many works . . . executed out of my experience . . . my everyday visual encounters." It is meant to capture the rhythm of life in Harlem, where Lawrence grew up in the 1930s. "It was inevitable," he says, "that the barber shop with

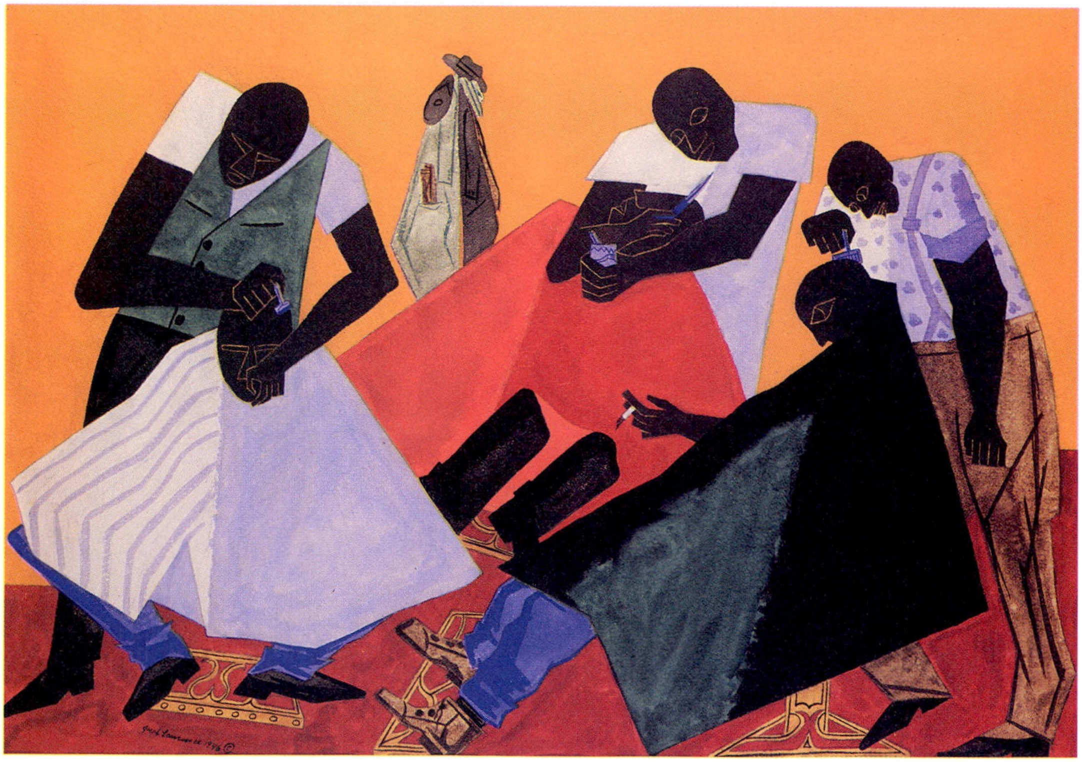

Fig. 221 Jacob Lawrence, *Barber Shop,* 1946.
Gouache on paper, 21 3/8 × 29 1/8 in. The Toledo Museum of Art, Toledo, Ohio. Gift of Edward Drummond Libbey.

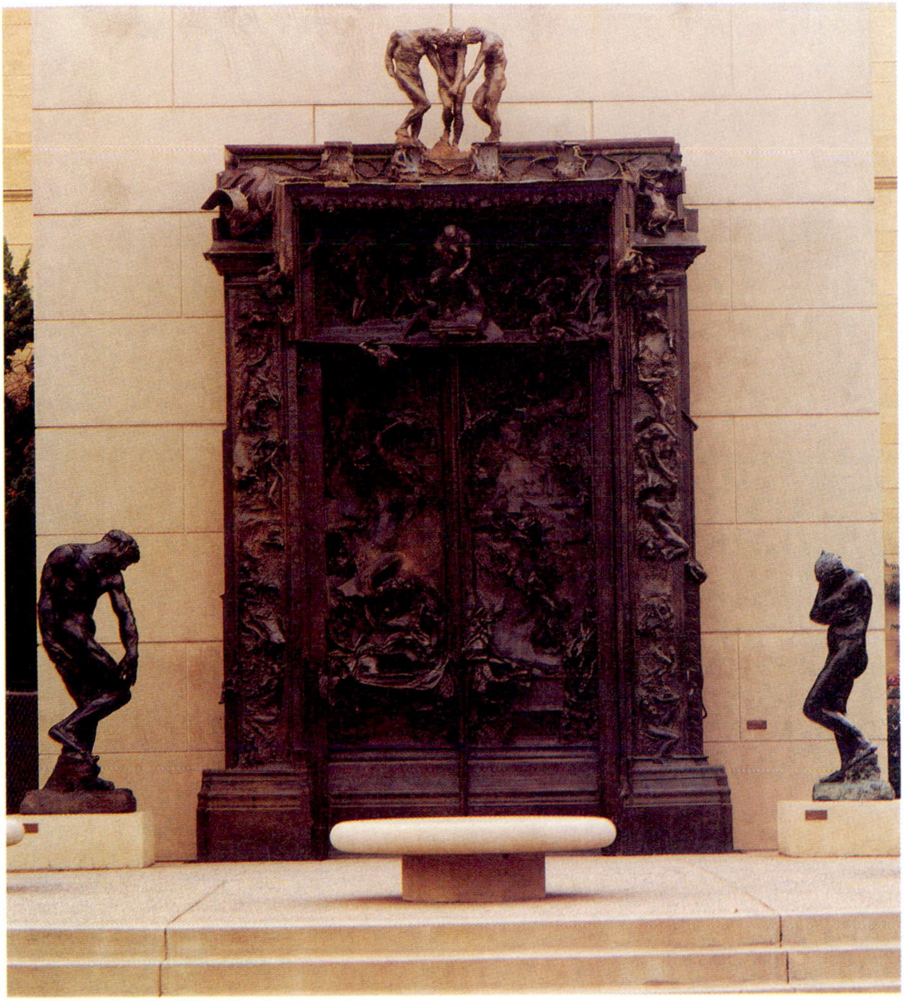

Fig. 222 Auguste Rodin, *Gates of Hell with Adam and Eve*, 1880–1917.
Bronze, 251 × 158 × 33 in. Stanford University Museum of Art. Photograph by Frank Wing.

its daily gathering of Harlemites, its clippers, mirror, razors, the overall pattern and the many conversations that took place there . . . was to become the subject of many of my paintings. Even now, in my imagination, whenever I relive my early years in the Harlem community, the barber shop, in both form and content . . . is one of the scenes that I still see and remember."

As we all know from listening to music, and as Lawrence's painting demonstrates, repetition is not necessarily boring. The *Gates of Hell* (Fig. 222), by Auguste Rodin, were conceived in 1880 as the entry for the Museum of Decorative Arts in Paris, which was never built. The work is based on the *Inferno* section of Dante's *Divine Comedy* and is filled with nearly 200 figures who swirl in hell-fire, reaching out as if continually striving to escape the surface of the door. Rodin's famous *Thinker* sits atop the door panels, looking down as if in contemplation of man's fate, and to each side of the door, in its original conception, stand Adam and Eve. At the very top of the door is a group of three figures, the Three Shades, guardians of the dark inferno beneath.

What is startling is that the Three Shades are not different, but, in fact, all the same. Rodin cast his Shade three times and then arranged the three identical casts in the format of a semicircle. The figure remains the same, but it looks different when seen from different sides. Furthermore, the posture of the figure of Adam, in front and to the left, echoes that of the Shades above. This formal repetition, and the downward pull that unites all four figures, implies that Adam is not merely the father of us all, but, in his sin, the man responsible for hell itself.

Piet Mondrian's Broadway Boogie-Woogie

The Dutch painter Piet Mondrian left Europe and World War II in 1940 and moved to New York City, where he spent the last four years of his life. The pulsing, staccato rhythms of his last masterpiece, *Broadway Boogie-Woogie* (Fig. 226), are intentionally reminiscent of American jazz, the music that reflected, in Mondrian's eyes, America itself—its pace, its vitality, and its energy. The painting, however, is not merely a celebration of American jazz, it is also a summation of Mondrian's painting career, the culmination of a life-long process.

In three paintings of trees executed early in his career, between 1908 and 1912 (Figs. 223. 224, and 225), we can see that his treatment becomes increasingly abstract. The first painting, *Red Tree,* is executed under the influence of his fellow countryman, Vincent van Gogh. But already here, his interest in the pattern of positive and negative spaces created by the branches is evident. Four years later, in *The Gray Tree,* the gridlike pattern that delineates the ground in the earlier painting seems to consume the entire background. A rhythmic pattern of ovals and curves competes with the geometric grid of horizontals and verticals, forms derived from his study, in Paris, of Picasso, whose canvases—*Les Demoiselles d'Avignon* (Fig. 49), for instance—utilized both oval and right-angled shapes concurrently. By the time Mondrian painted *Flowering Apple Trees* in 1912, his reference to the real world has almost disappeared. Given the painting's title, we can discern the tree's trunk and its branches, but the painting is more a pure pattern of ovoid shapes set into a simple grid.

Mondrian considered himself one of the leaders of a group dedicated to discovering a new, purer kind of art, freed from the necessity of depicting recognizable objects or expressing personal feelings. "The new painting," he wrote, "by employing 'neutral,'

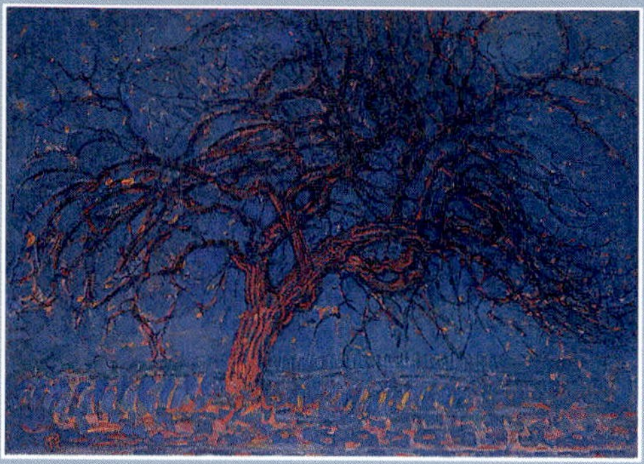

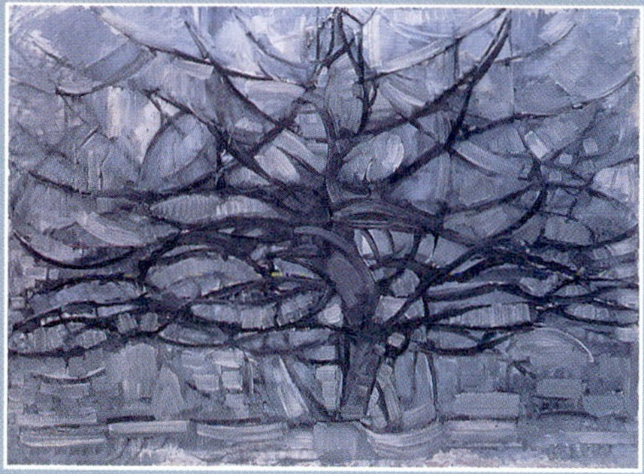

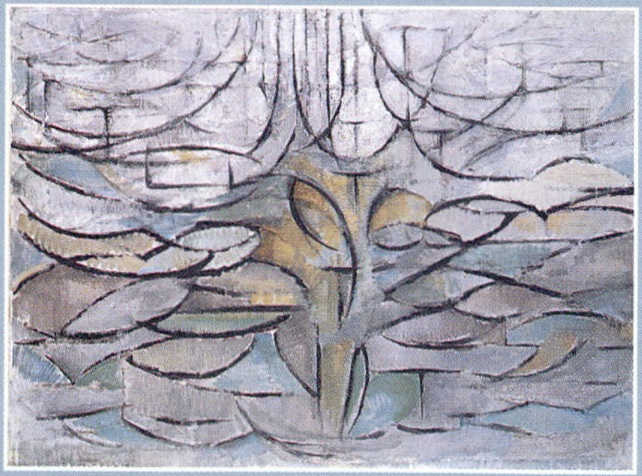

Fig. 223 (top) Piet Mondrian, *Red Tree,* 1908.
Oil on canvas, 27 1/2 × 39 in. Collection Haags Gemeentemuseum

Fig. 224 (middle) Piet Mondrian, *The Gray Tree,* 1912.
31 2/5 × 43 in. Collection Haags Gemeentemuseum, The Hague.

Fig. 225 (bottom) Piet Mondrian, *Flowering Apple Trees,* 1912.
Oil on canvas, 30 3/4 × 41 3/4 in. Collection Haags Gemeentemuseum, The Hague.

or universal forms, expresses itself only through the relationships of line and color." He quickly reduced his palette to the three primary colors plus white, black, and sometimes gray. The straight line became his primary tool, the right angle the focal point of all activity in the work. In works like *Composition with Blue and Yellow* (Fig. 227), for instance, he is particularly interested in the way that when the black lines cross each other, the black seems to lighten and flicker before the viewer's eye. At this point, the most stable of images suddenly destabilizes. A composition that we begin by assuming is static begins to shake and shimmer, to move in a rhythm all its own.

Mondrian placed greater and greater emphasis on the principles of design, particularly asymmetrical balance and repetition and rhythm. He seemed to measure space in his work, and he sought to unify positive and negative space, as well as the horizontal and vertical, in what he called an "equilibrium of opposites."

The balance of *Broadway Boogie-Woogie* is asymmetrical, denser on the right, lighter and wider on the left. Its visual rhythms are improvisational. No set pattern of repetition can be detected in the canvas. And yet the painting has something of the effect of a musical score, or a pattern of dance steps set down on paper, or the grid of New York City's streets, as if we are looking down from the top of a skyscraper at automobiles moving through the maze of streets in time to the rhythm of changing traffic lights.

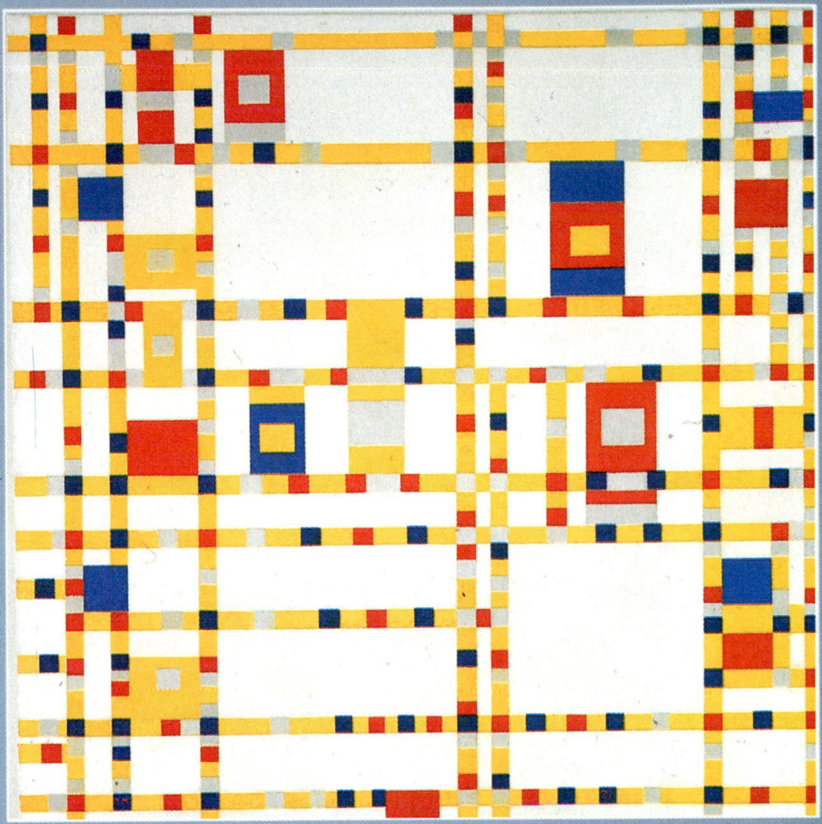

Fig. 226 Piet Mondrian, *Broadway Boogie-Woogie,* 1942–1943.
Oil on canvas, 50 × 50 in.
The Museum of Modern Art, New York. Given anonymously.
Photograph © 1996 The Museum of Modern Art, New York.

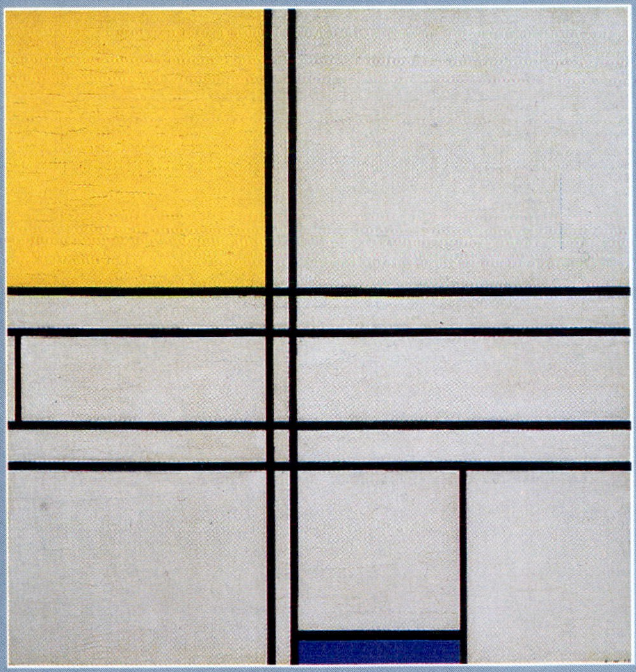

Fig. 227 Piet Mondrian, *Composition with Blue and Yellow,* 1935.
Oil on canvas, 28 3/4 × 27 1/4 in. Photograph by Lee Stalsworth.
Hirshhorn Museum and Sculpture Garden, Smithsonian Institution, Washington, DC.
Gift of Joseph H. Hirshhorn Foundation, 1972.

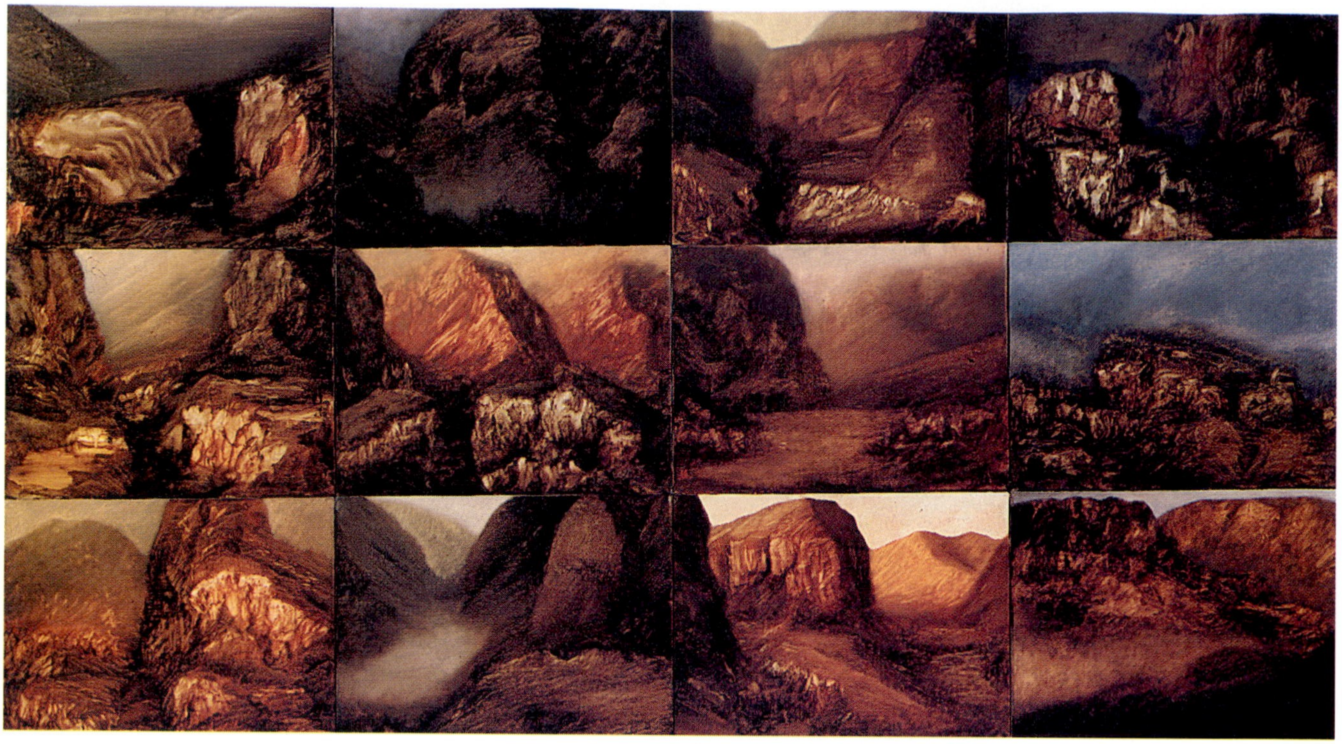

Fig. 228 James Lavadour, *The Seven Valleys and the Five Valleys,* 1988.
Oil on canvas, 54 × 96 in. Collection of Ida Cole. Courtesy of Elezabeth Leach Gallery, Portland, Oregon.

UNITY AND VARIETY

Repetition and rhythm are employed by artists in order to unify the different elements of the work. In *Barber Shop,* (Fig. 221) Jacob Lawrence gives the painting a sense of coherence by repeating shapes and color patterns. Each of the principles of design that we have discussed leads to this idea of organization, the sense that we are looking at a unified whole—balanced, focused, and so on. Even Lawrence's figures, with their strange, clumsy hands, their oversimplified features, and their oddly extended legs and feet, are *uniform* throughout. Such consistency lends the picture its feeling of being complete.

It is as if, in *Barber Shop,* Lawrence is painting the idea of community itself, bringing together the diversity of the Harlem streets through the unifying patterns of his art. In fact, if everything were the same, in art as in life, there would be no need for us to discuss the concept of "unity." But things are not the same. The visual world is made up of different lines, forms, colors, textures—the various visual elements themselves—and they must be made to work together. Still, Rodin's Three Shades atop the *Gates of Hell* (Fig. 222) teaches us an important lesson. Even when each element of a composition is identical, it is variety—in this case, the fact that our point of view changes with each of the Shades—that sustains our interest. In general, unity and variety must coexist in a work of art. The artist must strike a balance between the two.

James Lavadour's *The Seven Valleys and the Five Valleys* (Fig. 228) is a stylistically unified composition of 12 landscape views, but each of the views is quite different from the others. Lavadour's paintings constantly negotiate the boundaries betweeen realism and abstraction. Close up, they seem to dissolve into a scraped, dripped, and brushed abstract surface, but seen from a distance, they become expansive landscape views, capturing the light and weather of the Pacific Northwest plateau country where Lavadour lives. Viewing a painting such as this is like viewing a series of Monet haystacks, all rolled into one.

By way of contrast, this untitled painting by Jean-Michel Basquiat (Fig. 229) seems purposefully to avoid any sense of unity. Basquiat was the middle-class son of a Brooklyn accountant who, at age 20, moved from painting graffiti on walls throughout Manhattan to painting and drawing on large canvases. His loose, expressionist brushwork is painted over a body of scrawled notations the content of which is willfully arbitrary. On the one hand, we sense Basquiat's alienation from his community in the work, in the contorted masks that grin menacingly out of the space of the composition and in the very crudeness of his style, a purposeful affront to traditional notions of artistic "quality." But on the other hand, Basquiat's painting is distinguished by the sheer energy and exuberance of his style, the vitality of his color, and the sense of freedom that his brushwork seems to embody. If Basquiat was himself alienated from an art world that had granted him instant success, he also always seemed to have fun with it, spoofing its high seriousness and mocking, particularly, its preoccupation with money and fame.

It is this sense of disjunction, the sense that the parts can never form a unified whole, that we have come to identify with what is commonly called **postmodernism.** The discontinuity between the old and the new that marks Frank Gehry's house (Figs. 195 and 196), discussed at the beginning of this chapter, is an example of this postmodern sensibility, a sensibility defined particularly well by another architect, Robert Venturi, in his important 1972 book, *Learning from Las Vegas*. For Venturi, the collision of styles, signs, and symbols that marks the American "strip," especially the Las Vegas strip (Fig. 230) could be seen in light of a new sort of unity. "Disorder," Venturi writes, "[is] an order we cannot see. . . . The commercial strip with the urban sprawl . . . [is an order that] includes; it includes at all levels, from the mixture of seemingly incongruous land uses to the mixture of seemingly incongruous advertising media plus a system of neo-organic . . . restaurant motifs in Walnut Formica." The strip declares that anything can be put next to anything else. While traditional art has tended to exclude things that it deemed unartful, postmodern art lets everything in. In this sense, it is democratic. It could even be said to achieve a unity larger than the comparatively elitist art of high culture could ever imagine.

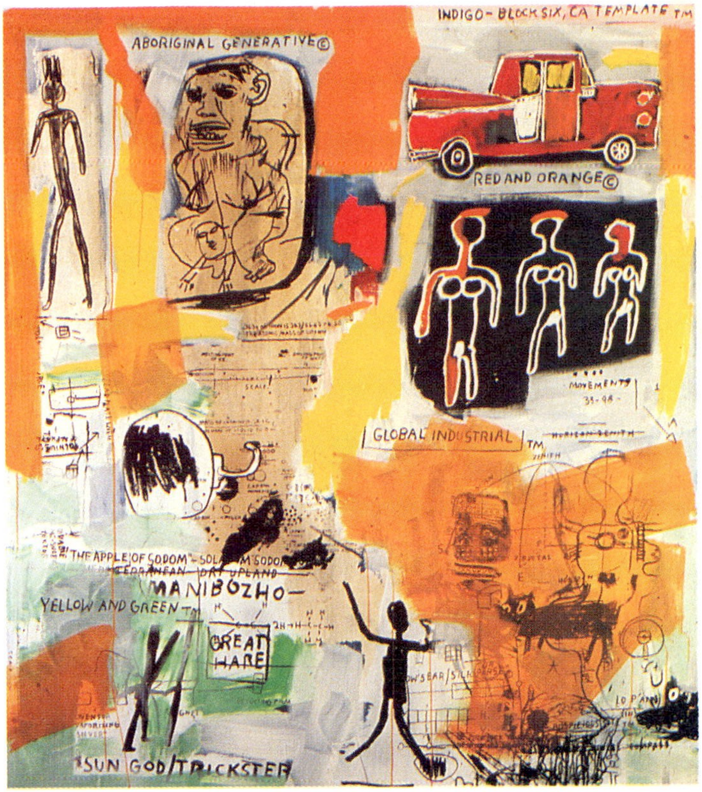

Fig. 229 Jean-Michel Basquiat, *Untitled,* 1984.
Acrylic, silkscreen and oilstick on canvas, 88 × 77 in.

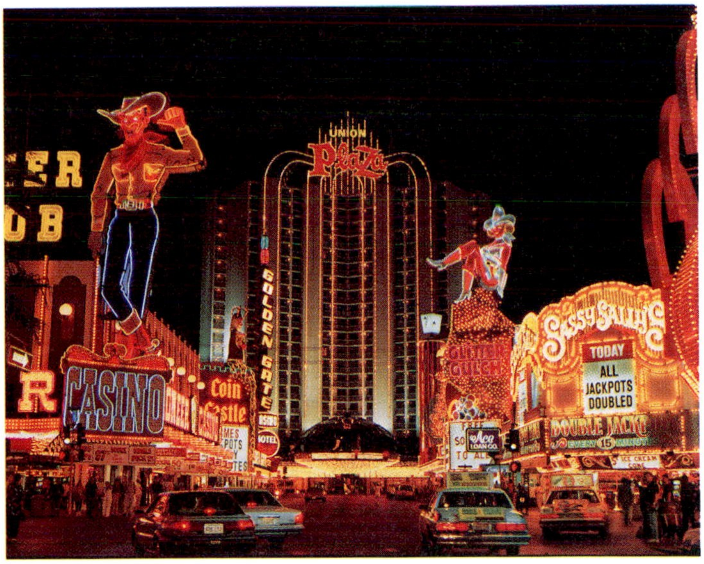

Fig. 230 Las Vegas, Nevada.
Superstock, Inc.

Hung Liu's Three Fujins

Born in Changchun, China, in 1948, the year that Chairman Mao forced the Nationalist Chinese off the mainland to Taiwan, painter Hung Liu lived in China until 1984. Beginning in 1966, during Mao's Cultural Revolution, she worked for four years as a peasant in the fields. Successfully "reeducated" by the working class, she returned to Beijing where she studied, and later taught, painting of a strict Russian Social Realist style—propaganda portraits of Mao's new society. In 1980, she applied for a passport to study painting in the United States, and in 1984 her request was granted. An extraordinarily independent spirit, raised and educated in a society that values social conformity above individual identity, Liu depends as a painter on the interplay between unity and variety, not only as a principle of design but as the very subject of her art.

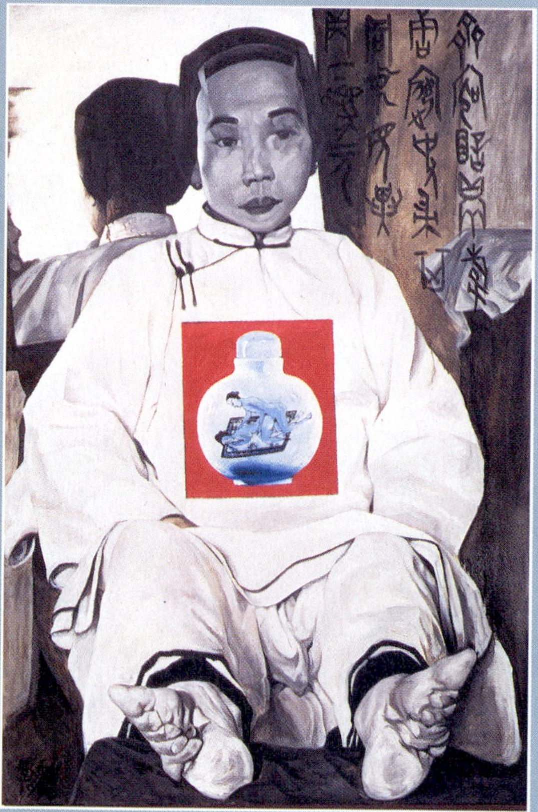

Fig. 231 Hung Liu, *Virgin/Vessel,* 1995.
Oil on canvas, 72 × 48 in. Collection Bernice and Harold Steinbaum.

During the Cultural Revolution, Liu had begun photographing peasant families, not for herself, but as gifts for the villagers. She has painted from photographs ever since, particularly archival photographs that she has discovered on research trips back to China in both 1991 and 1993. "I am not copying photographs," she explains. "I release information from them. There's a tiny bit of information there—the photograph was taken in a very short moment, maybe 1/100 or 1/50 of a second—and I look for clues. The clues give me an excuse to do things." In other words, for Liu, to paint from a photograph is to liberate something locked inside it. For example, the disfigured feet of the "virgin" in the painting on the left (Fig. 231) are the result of traditional Chinese foot-binding. Unable to walk, even upper-class women were forced into prostitution after Mao's Revolution confiscated their material possessions and left them without servants to transport them. In the painting, the woman's body will inevitably become a sexual vessel, like the one in front of her. She is completely isolated and vulnerable.

Three Fujins (Fig. 232) is also a depiction of women bound by the system in which they live. These are the three concubines of the famous "last prince," Yi Huan of the Qing Dynasty, which was overthrown in

1911. Projecting in front of each concubine is an actual birdcage, purchased by Liu in San Francisco's Chinatown, symbolizing the women's spiritual captivity. But even the excessively unified formality of their pose—its perfect balance, its repetitious rhythms—belies their submission to the rule of tyrannical social forces. The unified composition of the photograph upon which this painting is based, the sense that these women have given up themselves—and made themselves up—in order to fit into their proscribed roles, Liu sees as symbolizing "relationships of power, and I want to dissolve them in my paintings."

Speaking specifically about *Three Fujins,* Liu explains how that dissolution takes place: "Contrast is very important. If you don't have contrast, everything just cancels each other thing out. So I draw, very carefully, and then I let the paint drip—two kinds of contrasting line." One is controlled, the line representing power, and the other is free, liberated. It introduces the necessary variety into the composition. "Linseed oil is very thick," Liu goes on, "it drips very slowly, sometimes overnight. You don't know when you leave what's going to be there in the morning. You hope the best. You plant your seed. You work hard. But for the harvest, you have to wait." The drip, she says, gives her "a sense of liberation, of freedom from what I've been painting. I could never have done this work in China. But the real Chinese tradition—landscape painters, calligraphers—are pretty crazy. My drip is closer to the real Chinese tradition than my training. It's part of me, the deeply rooted traditional Chinese ways."

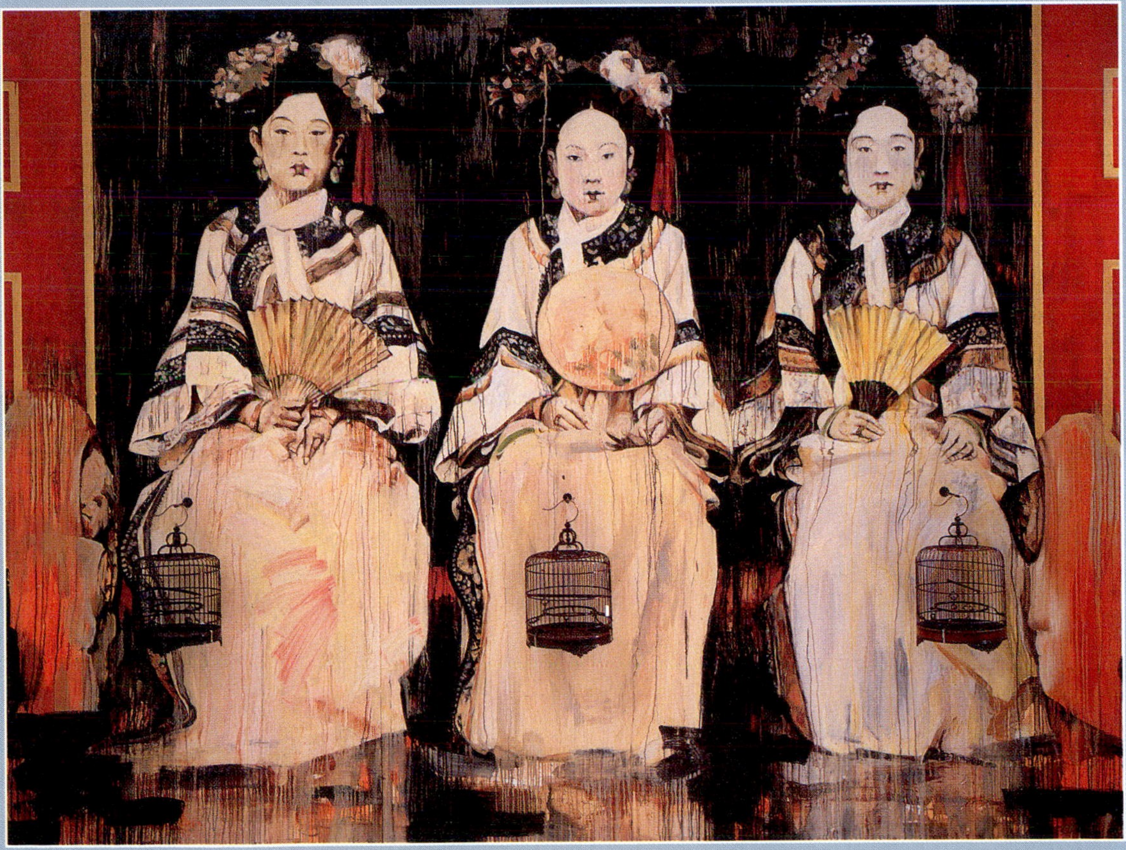

Fig. 232 Hung Liu, *Three Fujins,* 1995.
Oil on canvas, bird cages, 86 × 126 × 12 in. Private collection, Washington, DC. Courtesy Steinbaum Krauss Gallery, New York. Photograph by Ben Blackwell.

Elizabeth Murray's shaped canvas *Just in Time* (Fig. 233) is, at first glance, a two-panel abstract construction of rhythmic curves oddly, and not quite evenly, cut in half. But on second glance, it announces its postmodernity. For the construction is also an ordinary tea cup, with a pink cloud of steam rising above its rim. In a move that calls to mind Claes Oldenburg's *Giant Trowel* (Fig. 212), the scale of this cup—it is nearly nine feet high—monumentalizes the banal, domestic subject matter. Animal forms seem to arise out of the design—a rabbit on the left, an animated, Disney-like, laughing teacup in profile on the right. The title recalls pop lyrics—"Just in time, I found you just in time." Yet it remains an abstract painting, interesting as painting and as design. It is even, for Murray, deeply serious. She has defined the significance of the break down the middle of the painting in a poem:

The desert sighs in the cupboard
The glacier knocks in the bed
And a crack in the tea-cup opens
A lane to the land of the dead.

Who knows what meanings are rising up out of this crack in the cup, this structural gap. Murray's painting is at once an ordinary teacup and an image rich in possible meanings, stylistically coherent and physically fragmented. The endless play of unity and variety is what it's about.

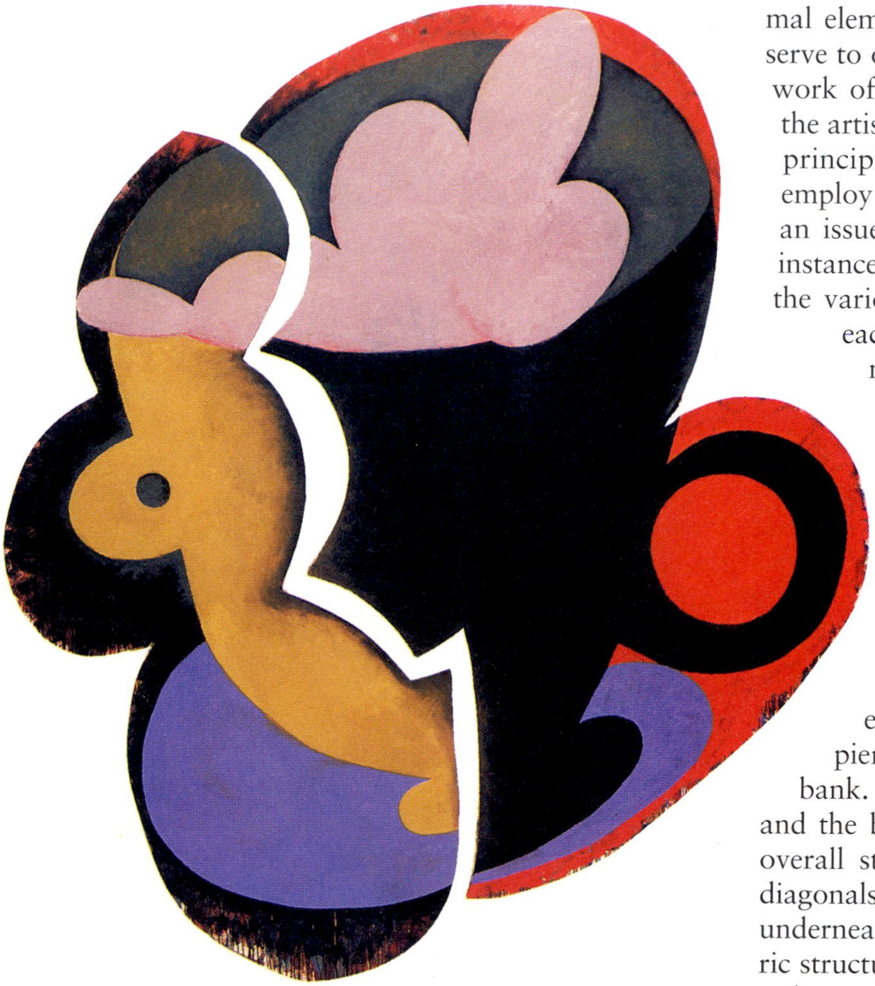

Fig. 233 Elizabeth Murray, *Just in Time*, 1981.
Oil on canvas in two sections, 106 × 97 in.
Philadelphia Museum of Art. Purchased: The Eadward and Althea Budd Fund, the Adele Haas Turner and Beatrice Pastorius Fund and funds contributed by Marion Stroud Swingle and Lorine E. Vogt.

SUMMARY

In the last five chapters we have studied the formal elements and the principles of design that serve to organize them. Whenever you discuss a work of art, you should take care to see how the artist manipulates each of the elements and principles. A given work of art may not employ every element or principle—color isn't an issue in black-and-white photography, for instance—but ask yourself how artists employ the various elements and principles and what each one tells you about the work of art's meaning.

By way of concluding this part of the book, let's consider how the various elements and principles inform a particular work, Monet's *The Railroad Bridge at Argenteuil* (Fig. 234). Line comes into play here in any number of ways. Monet employs one-point linear perspective to create the bridge. A gridlike geometry is established where the bridge's piers cross the horizon and the far riverbank. Two strong diagonals—the near bank and the bridge itself—cross this grid, and this overall structure of verticals, horizontals, and diagonals is echoed in the wooden structure underneath the bridge. Countering this geometric structure is the single expressive curve of the sail, a curve echoed in the implied line that marks the edge of the bushes at the top right. These contrasting types of line underscore two opposing directional lines—the train's and the boat's. In fact, the boat is apparently tacking

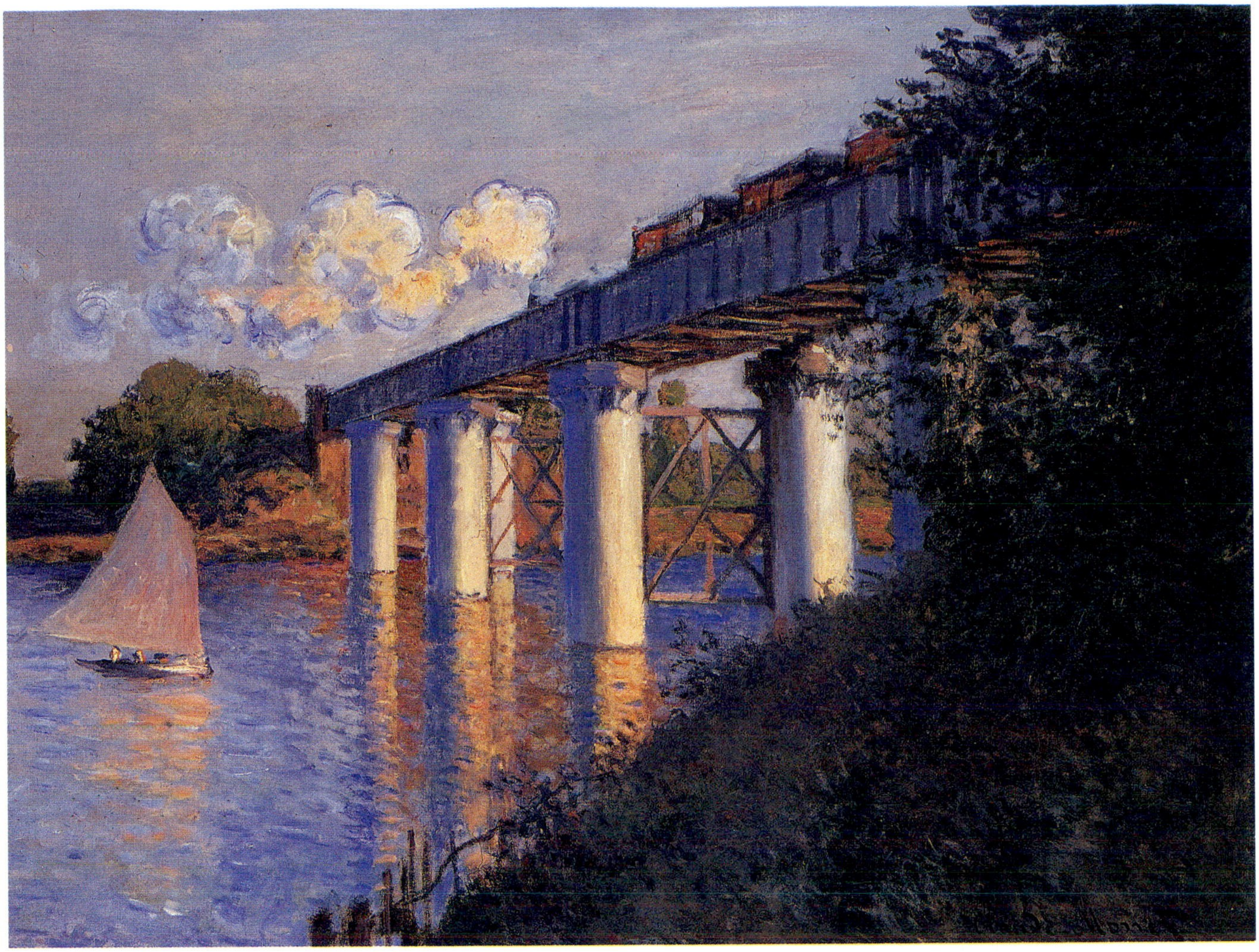

Fig. 234 Claude Monet (1840–1926), *The Railroad Bridge at Argenteuil,* 1874.
Oil on canvas, 21 4/5 × 29 2/5 in. Philadelphia Museum of Art. The John G. Johnson Collection.

left. We recognize the direction of the wind only when we see that what at first appears to be a cloud in the sky is actually, in a remarkable play of proportion and scale, smoke coming from the train's engine.

The contrast Monet develops with line, the sense of opposing forces, is everywhere at work in the composition—in the alternating rhythm of light to dark established by the bridge's pier and in the complementary color scheme of orange and blue that is especially utilized in the reflections and in the smoke above. The almost perfect symmetrical balance of the painting's grid structure is countered by the asymmetrical balance of the composition as a whole. There seem to be two points of emphasis, the bridge and the boat, and they are, we feel, somehow at odds.

What appears at first to be a simple landscape view upon analysis reveals itself to be a much more complicated painting. In the same way, what at first appears to be a cloud becomes, rather disturbingly, a cloud of smoke. Out of the dense growth of the near bank, a train emerges. We are witness here to nature in the process of giving way to the forces of civilization. Finally, time becomes a factor in the composition—eternal nature pitted against the contemporary moment. When Monet painted it, the railroad bridge at Argenteuil was a new bridge, and this painting captures the dawn of a new world, a world of opposition and contradiction. Every formal element and principle of design at work in the painting supports this reading.

PART III

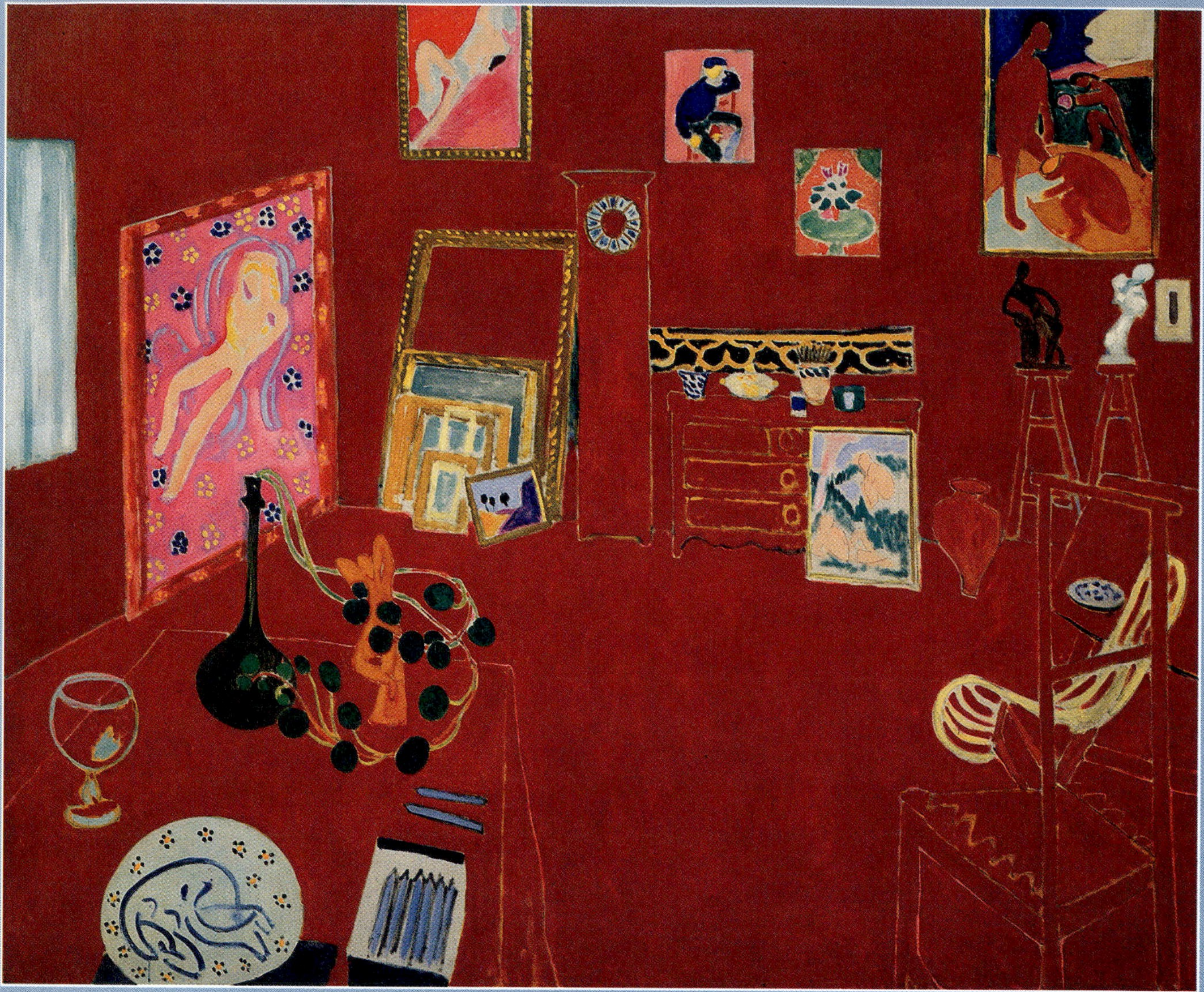

Fig. 235 Henri Matisse, *The Red Studio,* 1911.
Oil on canvas, 71 ¼ in. × 7 ft. 2 ¼ in. Collection, The Museum of Modern Art. Mrs. Simon Guggenheim Fund.

THE FINE ARTS MEDIA

LEARNING HOW ART IS MADE

CHAPTER 9

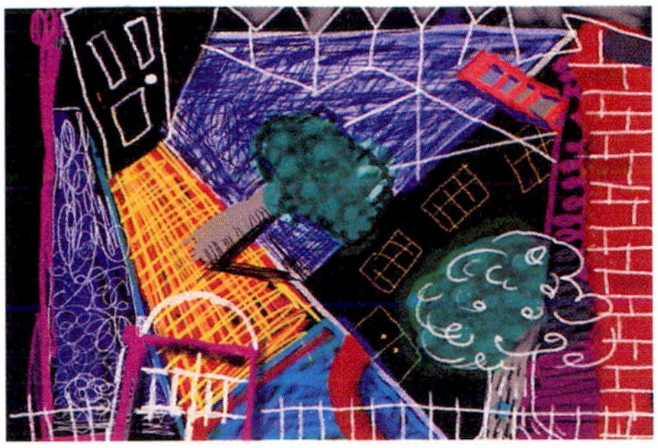

Drawing

Drawing as an Art

Drawing Materials

WORKS IN PROGRESS
Raphael's *Alba Madonna*

Dry Media

WORKS IN PROGRESS
Beverly Buchanan's *Shackworks*

Liquid Media
Innovative Drawing Media

In his 1911 painting *The Red Studio* (Fig. 235), Henri Matisse depicts a stunning variety of media. Stacked around the room and hanging on the wall are a number of his own paintings. On the right, for instance, is *Le Luxe (Luxury)*, painted in 1908, and *The Young Sailor*, which dates from 1906, is next to the clock in the middle. On the table, surrounded by a vine, is a small bronze sculpture of a reclining nude and under *Le Luxe*, the bronze *Decorative Figure* of 1908 and a plaster cast for the 1910 sculpture *Jeannette*. On the table is a painted ceramic dish, charcoal pencils for drawing, glassware, and a vase.

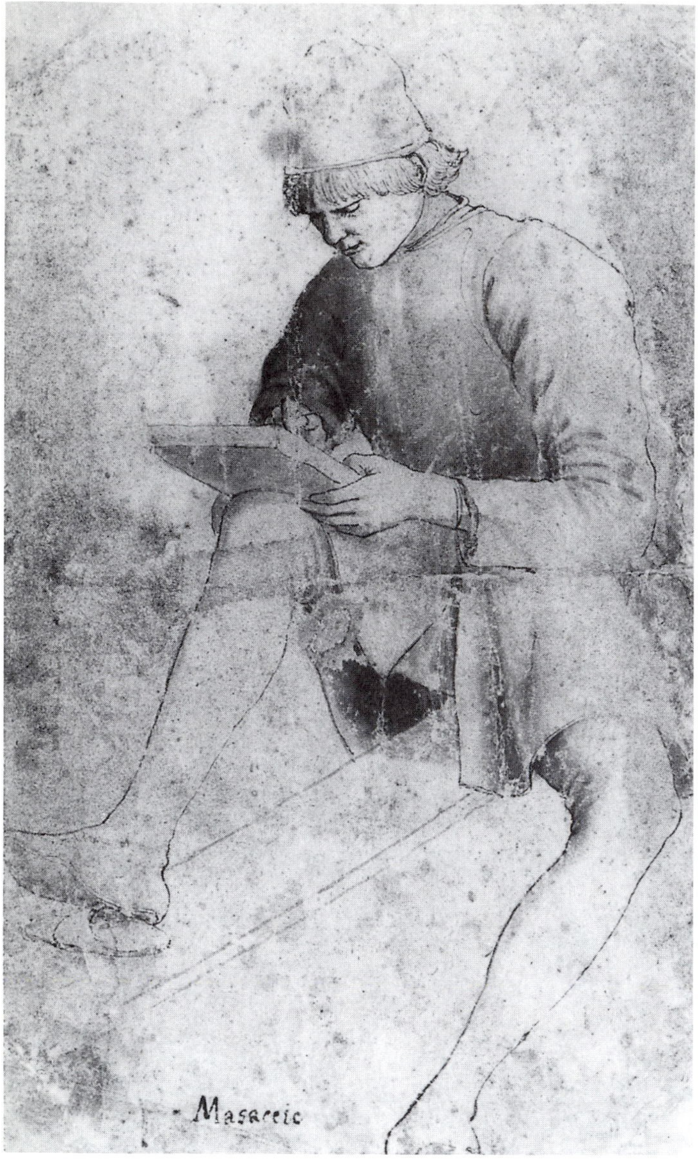

Fig. 236 Workshop of Pollaiuolo (?), *Youth Drawing,* late 15th century.
Pen and ink with wash on paper, $7\frac{5}{8} \times 4\frac{1}{2}$ in.
By permission of the Trustees of the British Museum, London.

Each of the materials in Matisse's work—the paintings, sculptures, ceramics, and glassware—is what we call a **medium.** The history of the various media used to create art is, in essence, the history of the various **technologies** that artists have employed. These technologies have helped artists both to achieve their desired effects more readily and to discover new modes of creation and expression. A technology, literally, is the "word" or "discourse" (from the Greek *logos)* about a "techne" (from the Greek word for art, which in turn comes from the Greek verb *tekein,* "to make, prepare, or fabricate"). A medium is, in this sense, a *techne,* a means for making art.

In Part III we will study all of the various media, but we turn our attention first to drawing, perhaps the most basic of medium of all. Drawing has many purposes, but chief among them is preliminary study. Through drawing, artists can experiment with different approaches to their compositions. They illustrate, for themselves, what they are going to do. And, in fact, illustration is another important purpose of drawing. Before the advent of the camera, illustration was the primary way that we recorded history, and today it provides visual interpretations of written texts, particularly in children's books. Finally, because it is so direct, tracing the path of the artist's hand recorded directly on paper, artists also find drawing to be a ready-made means for self-expression. It is as if, in the act of drawing, the soul or spirit of the artist finds its way to paper.

DRAWING AS AN ART

The young man in this picture (Fig. 236) seems to be doing the most ordinary thing in the world—drawing. We think of drawing as an everyday activity that everyone, artists and ordinary people, does all the time. You doodle on a pad; you throw away the marked-up sheet and start again with a fresh one. Artists often make dozens of sketches before deciding on the composition of a major work. But people have not always been able or willing to casually toss out marked-up paper and begin again fresh. Before the late fifteenth century, paper was costly and expensive.

Look closely at Figure 236. The young man shown here is sketching on a wooden tablet that he would sand clean after each drawing. The artist who drew him at work, however, worked in pen and ink on rare, expensive paper. This work thus repersents a transition point in Western art—the point at which artists began to draw on paper before they committed their idea to canvas or plaster.

Until the late fifteenth century, drawing was generally considered a student medium. Copying a master's work was the means by which a student learned the higher art of painting. Thus, in 1493, the Italian religious zealot

Savonarola outlined the ideal relation between student and master: "What does the pupil look for in the master? I'll tell you. The master draws from his mind an image which his hands trace on paper and it carries the imprint of his idea. The pupil studies the drawing, and tries to imitate it. Little by little, in this way, he appropriates the style of his master. That is how all natural things, and all creatures, have derived from the divine intellect." Savonarola thus describes drawing as both the banal, everyday business of beginners and also as equal in its creativity to God's handiwork in nature. For Savonarola, the master's idea is comparable to "divine intellect." The master is to the student as God is to humanity. Drawing is, furthermore, autographic: it bears the master's imprint, his style.

By the end of the fifteenth century, then, drawing had come into its own. It was seen as embodying, perhaps more clearly than even the finished work, the artist's personality and creative genius. As one watched an artist's ideas develop through a series of preparatory sketches, it became possible to speak knowingly about the creative process itself. By the time Giorgio Vasari wrote his famous *Lives of the Painters* in 1550, the tendency was to see, in drawing, the foundation of Renaissance painting itself. Vasari had one of the largest collections of fifteenth-century—or so-called *quattrocento*—drawings ever assembled, and he wrote as if these drawings were a dictionary of the styles of the artists who had come before him.

In the *Lives* he recalls how, in 1501, crowds rushed to see Leonardo's *Virgin and Child with St. Anne and Infant St. John,* a **cartoon** (from the Italian *cartone,* meaning "paper"), a drawing done to scale for a painting or a fresco. "The work not only won the astonished admiration of all the artists," Vasari reported, "but when finished for two days it attracted to the room where it was exhibited a crowd of men and women, young and old, who flocked there, as if they were attending a great festival, to gaze in amazement at the marvels he had created." Though this cartoon apparently does not survive, we can get some notion of it from the later cartoon illustrated here (Fig. 237). Vasari's account, at any rate, is the earliest recorded example we have of the public actually admiring a drawing.

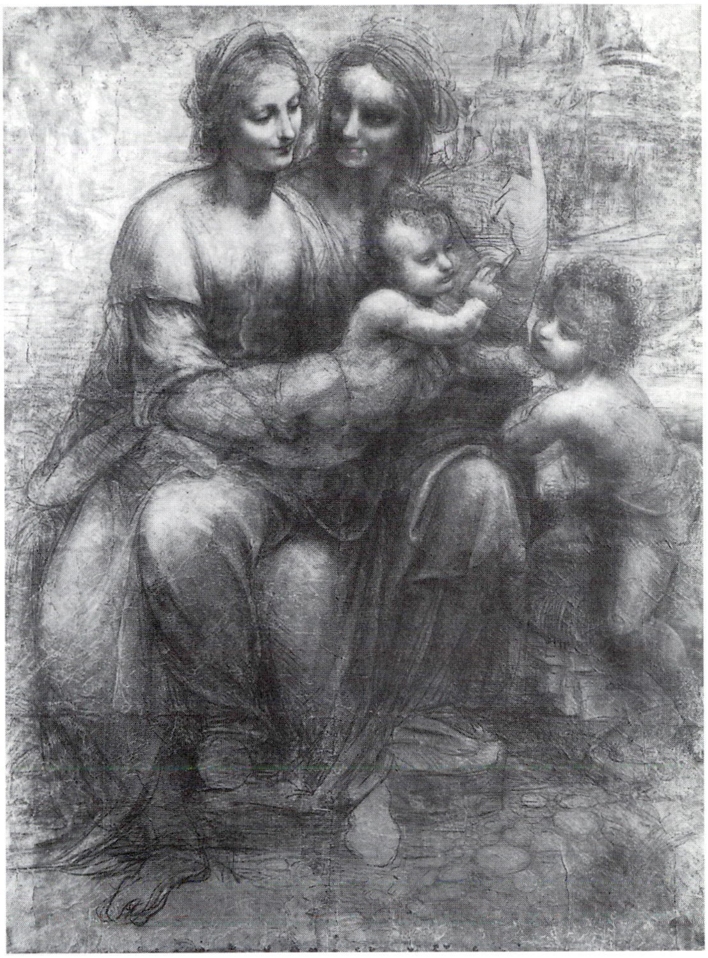

Fig. 237 Leonardo da Vinci,
***Virgin and Child with St. Anne and Infant St. John,* c. 1505–1507.**
Black chalk, 55 3/4 × 41 in. The National Gallery, London.

The two works shown here illustrate why drawing merits serious consideration as an art form in its own right. In Leonardo's *Study for a Sleeve* (Fig. 238), witness the extraordinary fluidity and spontaneity of the master's line. In contrast to the stillness of the resting arm (the hand, which is comparatively crude, was probably added later), the drapery is portrayed as if it were a whirlpool or vortex. The directness of the medium, the ability of the artist's hand to move quickly over paper, allows Leonardo to bring this turbulence out. Through the intensity of his line, Leonardo imparts a degree of emotional complexity to the sitter, who is revealed in the part as well as in the whole. But the drawing also reveals the movements of the artist's own mind. It is as if the still sitter were at odds with the turbulence of the artist's imagination, an imagination that will not hold still whatever its object of contemplation.

Movement, in fact, fascinated Leonardo. And nothing obsessed him more than the movement of water, in particular the swirling forms of the Deluge (Fig. 239), the great flood that would come at the end of the world. It is as if, even in this sleeve, we are witness to the artist's fantastic preoccupation with the destructive forces of nature. We can see it also in his famous notebooks, where he instructs the painter how to represent a storm:

> *O what fearful noises were heard throughout the dark air as it was pounded by the discharged bolts of thunder and lightning that violently shot through it to strike whatever opposed their course. O how many you might have seen covering their ears with their hands in abhorrence at the uproar. . . . O how much weeping and wailing! O how many terrified beings hurled themselves from the rocks! Let there be shown huge branches of great oaks weighed down with men and borne through the air by the impetuous winds. . . . You might see herds of horses, oxen, goats and sheep, already encircled by the waters and left marooned on the high peaks of the*

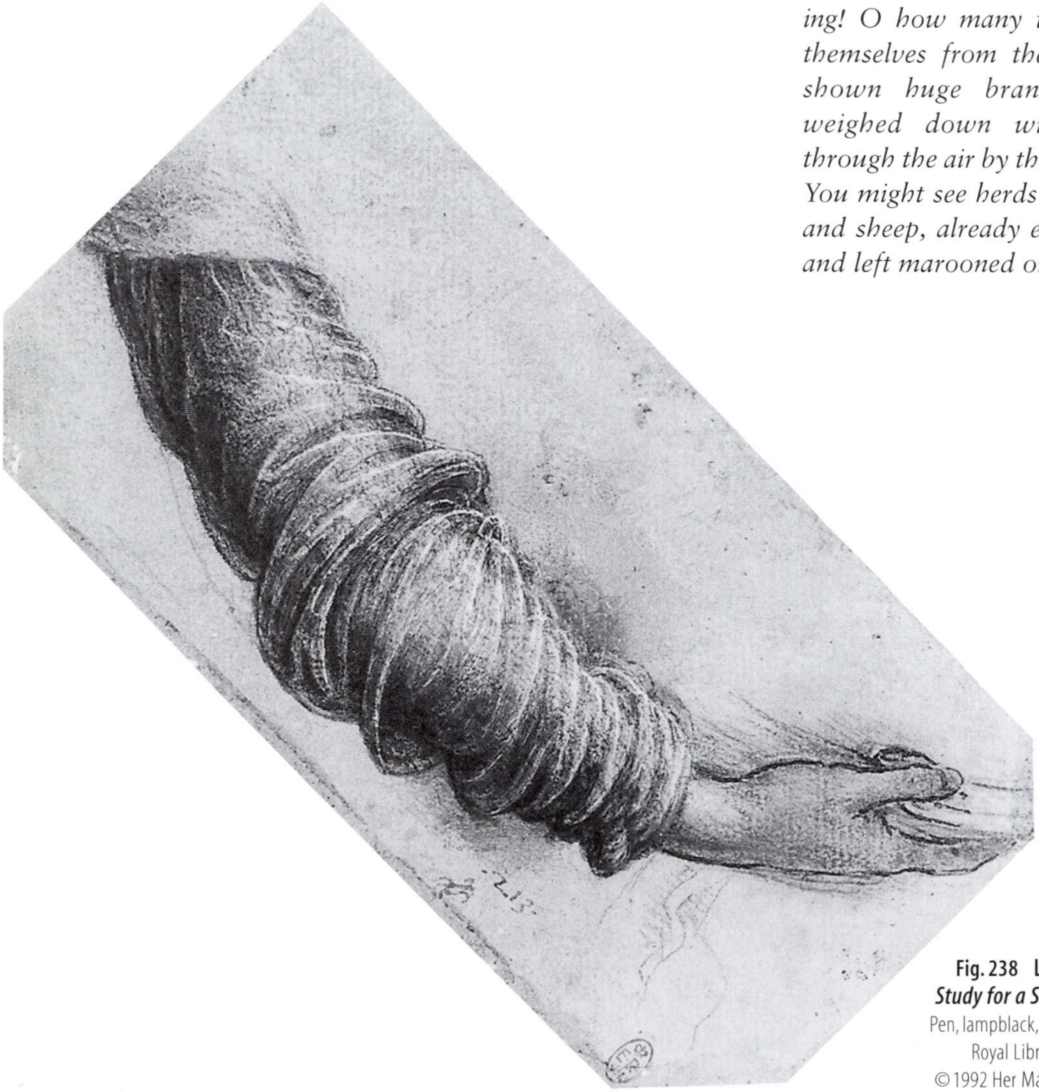

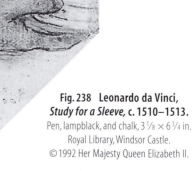

Fig. 238 Leonardo da Vinci, *Study for a Sleeve,* c. 1510–1513.
Pen, lampblack, and chalk, $3\frac{1}{8} \times 6\frac{3}{4}$ in.
Royal Library, Windsor Castle.

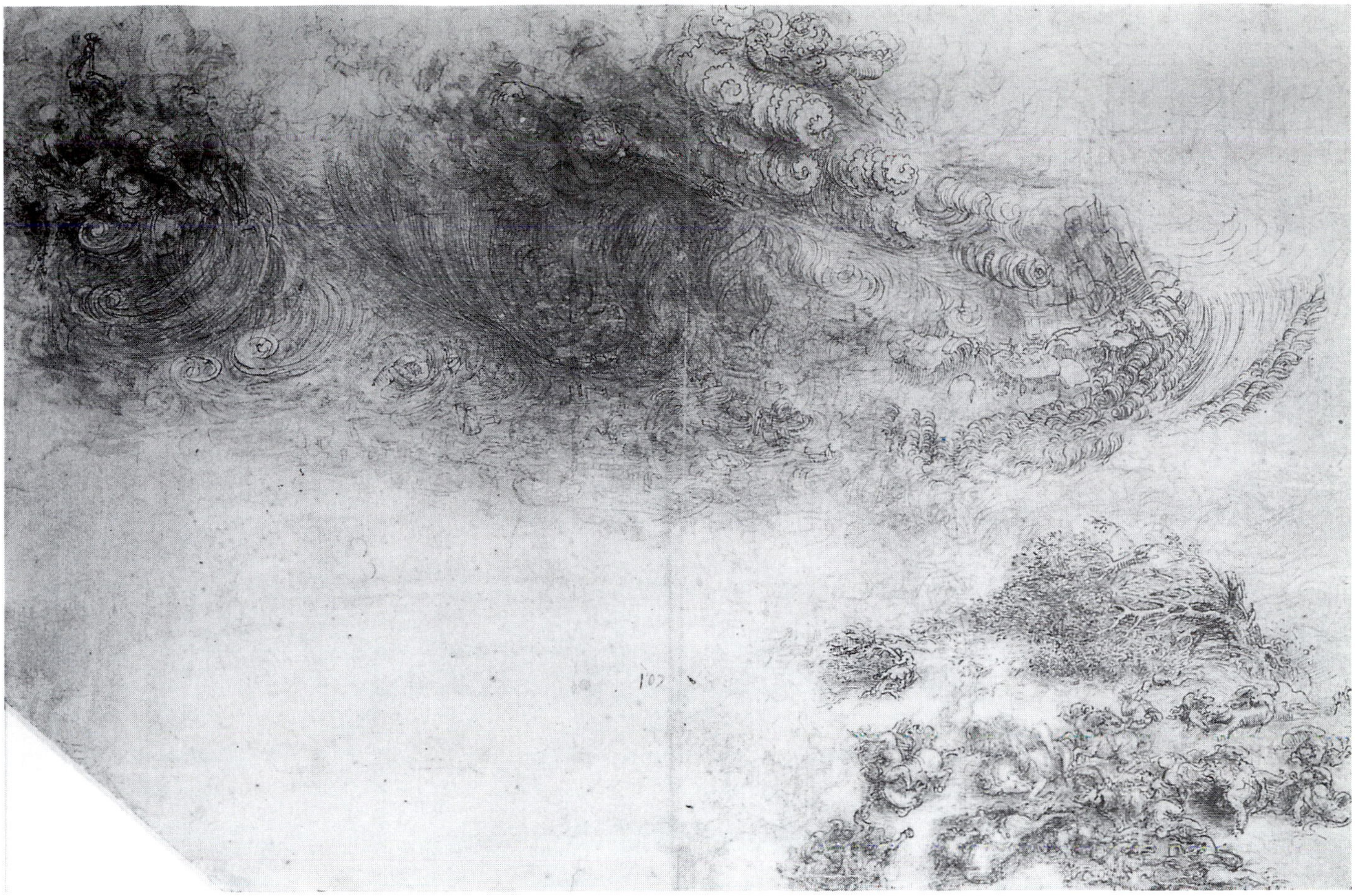

Fig. 239 Leonardo da Vinci, *Hurricane over Horsemen and Trees*, c. 1518.
Pen and ink over black chalk, 10 1/4 × 16 1/8 in. Royal Library, Windsor Castle. © 1992 Her Majesty Queen Elizabeth II.

mountains. Now they . . . huddled together with those in the middle clambering on top of the others, and all scuffling fiercely amongst themselves. . . . The air was darkened by the heavy rain that, driven aslant by the crosswinds and wafted up and down through the air, resembled nothing other than dust, differing only in that this inundation was streaked through by the lines drops of water make as they fall.

Because we can see in the earlier drawing of the sleeve a fascination with swirling line that erupts in the later drawings of the Deluge, we feel we know something important not only about Leonardo's technique but about what drove his imagination. More than any other reason, this was why, in the sixteenth century, drawings began to be preserved by artists and, simultaneously, collected by connoisseurs, experts on and appreciators of fine art.

DRAWING MATERIALS

Just as the different fine arts media produce different kinds of images, different drawing materials produce different effects as well. Drawing materials are generally divided into two categories—dry media and liquid media. The dry media—metalpoint, chalk, charcoal, graphite, and pastel—consist of coloring agents—or **pigments**—that are sometimes ground or mixed with substances that hold the pigment together called **binders.** Binders, however, are not necessary if the natural pigment—for instance, charcoal made from vine wood heated in a hot kiln until only the carbon charcoal remains—can be applied directly to the surface of the work. In liquid media, pigments are suspended in liquid binders, like the ink in Leonardo's drawing of the hurricane. The liquid ink flows much more easily onto Leonardo's surface than the dry chalk below it.

Raphael's Alba Madonna

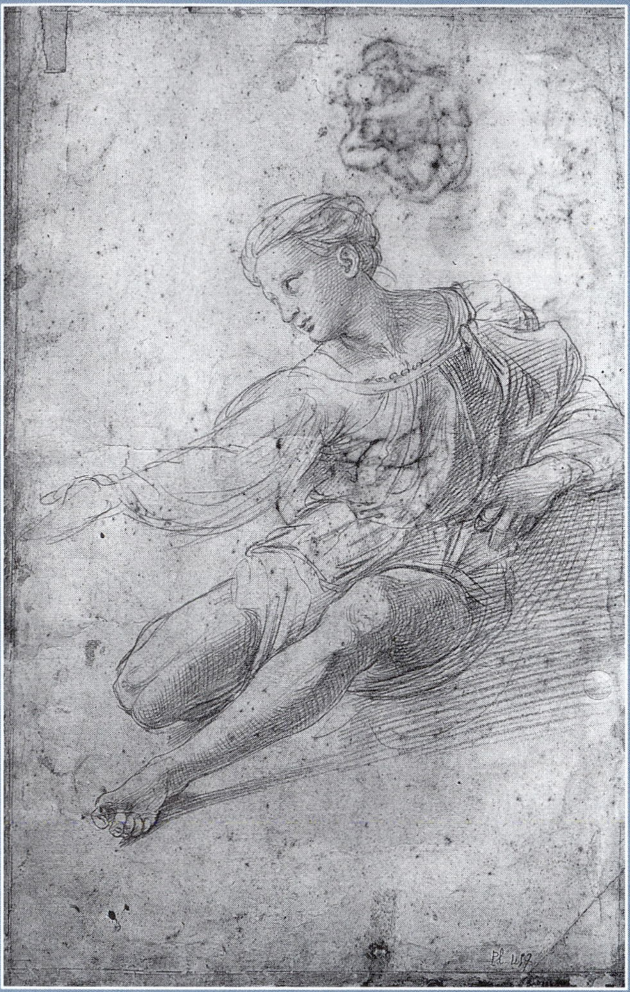

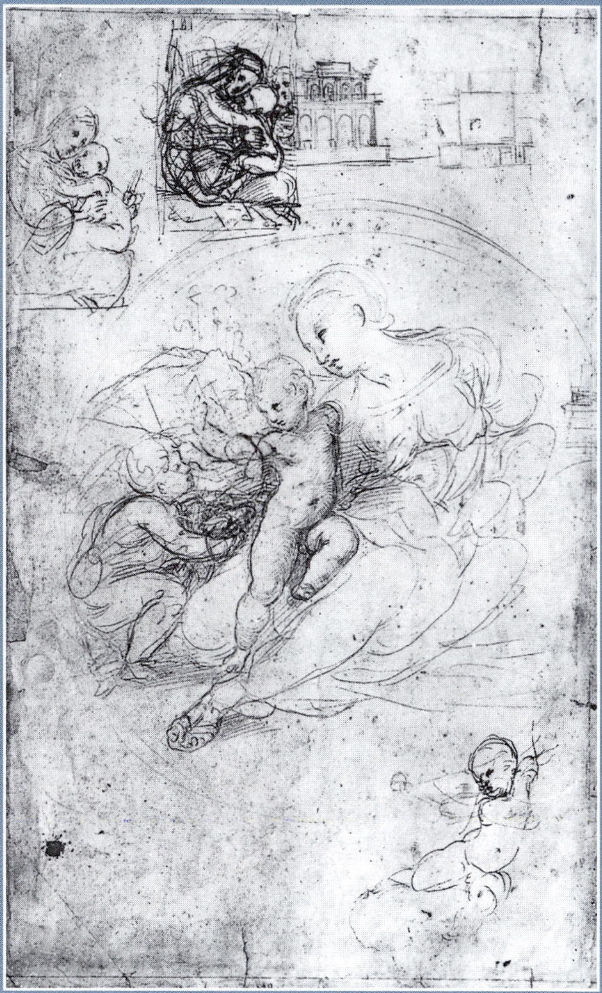

Figs. 240 and 241 Raphael (1483–1520), *Studies for The Alba Madonna* (recto and verso), c. 1511.
Left: red chalk; right: red chalk and pen and ink, both $16\frac{5}{8} \times 10\frac{3}{4}$ in. Lille, Musée des Beaux Arts.

In a series of studies for *The Alba Madonna* (Fig. 242), the great Renaissance draughtsman Raphael demonstrates many of the ways that artists utilize drawings to plan the final work. It is as if Raphael, in these sketches, had been instructed by Leonardo himself. We do know, in fact, that when Raphael arrived in Florence, in 1504, he was stunned by the freedom of movement and invention that he discovered in Leonardo's drawings. "Sketch subjects quickly," Leonardo admonished his students. "Rough out the arrangement of the limbs of your figures and first attend to the movements appropriate to the mental state of the creatures that make up your picture rather than to the beauty and perfection of their parts."

In the studies illustrated here, Raphael worked on both sides of a single sheet of paper (Figs. 240 and 241). On one side he has drawn a male model from life, and posed him as the Madonna. In the sweeping cross-hatching below the figure in the sketch on the right, one can already sense the circular format of the final painting, as these lines rise and turn up the arm and shoulder and around to the model's head. Inside this curve is another, rising from the knee bent under the model up across his chest to his neck and face. Even the folds of the drapery under his extended arm echo this curvilinear structure.

On the other side of the paper, all the figures present in the final composition are included. The major difference between this and the final painting is that infant St. John offers up a bowl of fruit in the drawing and Christ does not yet carry a cross in his hand. But the circular format of the final painting is fully realized in this drawing. A hastily drawn circular frame encircles the group (outside this frame, above it, are first ideas for yet another Madonna and Child, and below it, in the bottom right corner, an early version of the Christ figure for this one). The speed and fluency of this drawing's execution is readily apparent, and if the complex facial expressions of the final painting are not yet indicated here, the emotional tenor of the body language is. The postures are both tense and relaxed. Christ seems to move away from St. John even as he turns toward him. Mary reaches out, possibly to comfort the young saint, but equally possibly to hold him at bay. Raphael has done precisely as Leonardo directed, attending to the precise movements and gestures that will indicate the mental states of his subjects in the final painting.

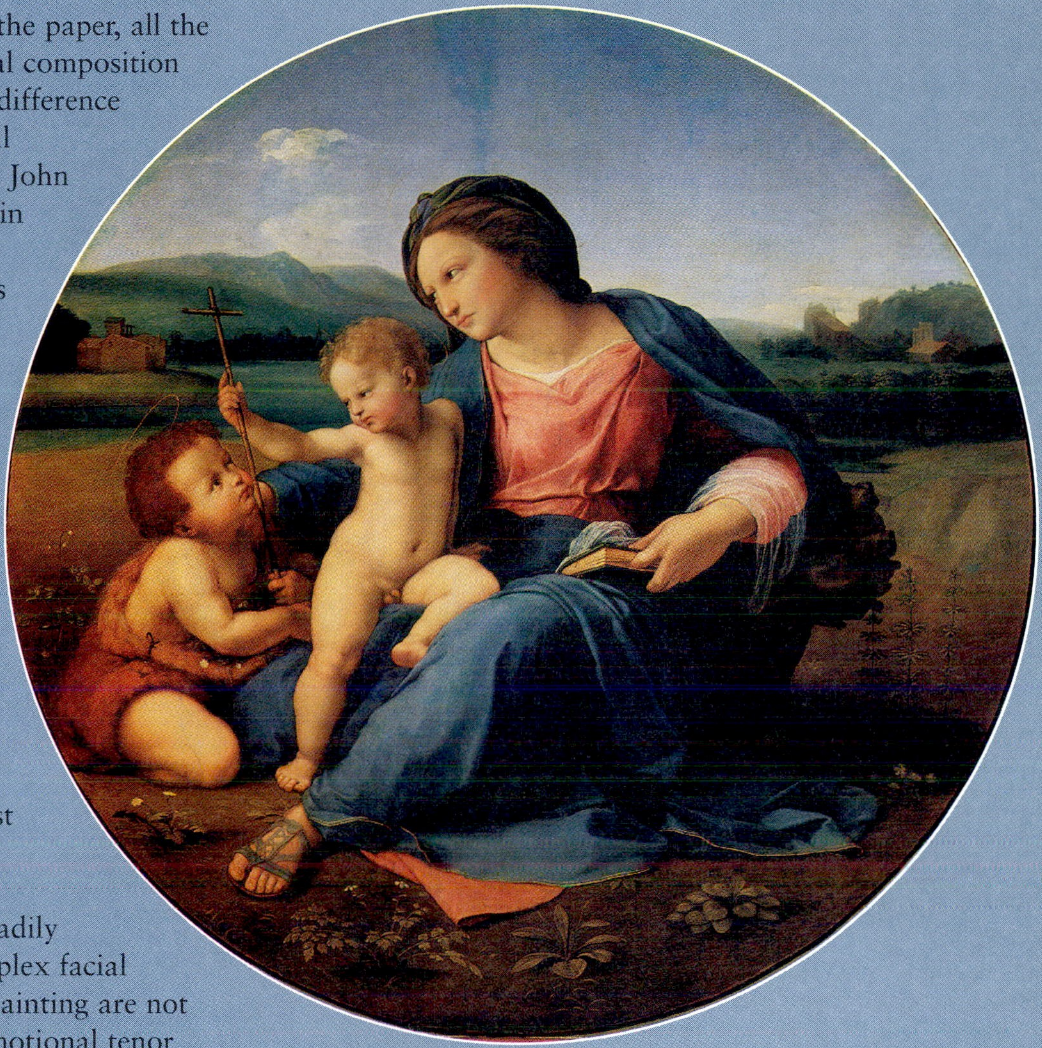

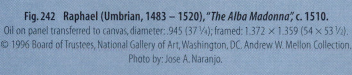

Fig. 242 Raphael (Umbrian, 1483 – 1520), *"The Alba Madonna"*, c. 1510.
Oil on panel transferred to canvas, diameter: .945 (37 ¼); framed: 1.372 × 1.359 (54 × 53 ½).

Photo by: Jose A. Naranjo.

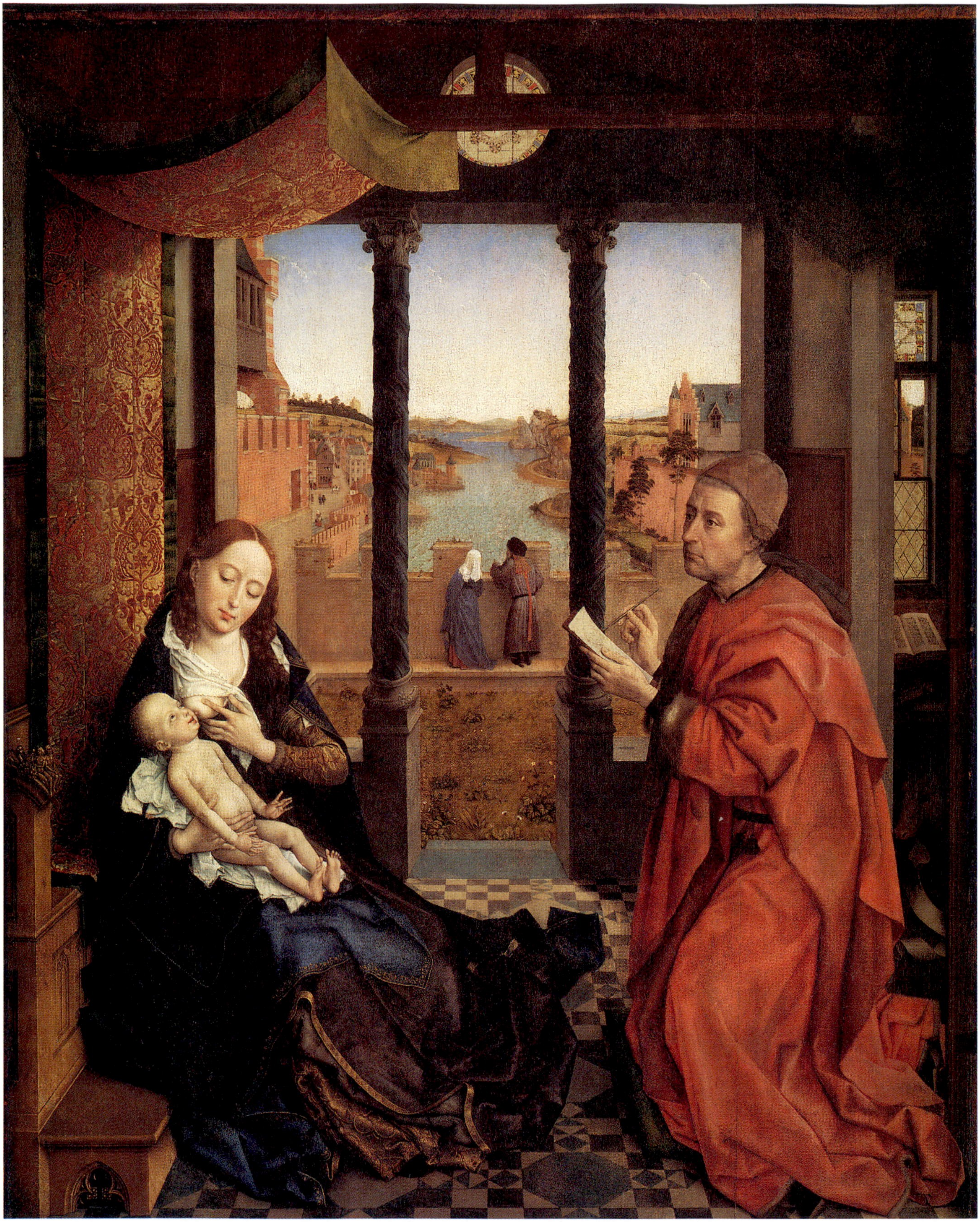

Fig. 243 Rogier van der Weyden, *St. Luke Painting the Virgin and Child,* c. 1440.
Oil and tempera on panel, 54 1/8 × 43 5/8 in. Museum of Fine Arts, Boston. Gift of Mr. and Mrs. Henry Lee Higginson.

Dry Media

Metalpoint One of the most common tools used in drawing in late fifteenth- and early sixteenth-century Italy was **metalpoint.** A *stylus* (point) made of gold, silver, or some other metal is applied to a sheet of paper prepared with a mixture of powdered bones (or lead white) and gumwater (when the stylus was silver, as it often was, the medium was called **silverpoint**). Sometimes pigments other than white were added to this preparation in order to color the paper. When the metalpoint is applied to this ground, a chemical reaction results, and line is produced.

Rogier van der Weyden's *St. Luke Painting the Virgin and Child* (Fig. 243), actually depicts St. Luke drawing with metalpoint on parchment. The figure of St. Luke is believed to be a self-portrait of Rogier himself. Probably executed for the chapel of the Painters Guild in Brussels, of which Rogier was the head, the painting is, then, a compendium of the artist's craft, and represents the entire process of making a painting from drawing to finished product. The painting, incidentally, is indebted to Jan van Eyck's *The Madonna of Chancellor Rolin* (see Fig. 313), which was painted six years earlier. Van der Weyden's painting reverses van Eyck's composition; its format is more vertical than van Eyck's, and it is considerably simpler in its details.

A metalpoint line, which is pale gray, is very delicate, and cannot be widened by increasing pressure upon the point. To make a thicker line, the artist must switch to a thicker point. Often, the same stylus would have a fine point on one end and a blunt one on the other, as does St. Luke's in the van der Weyden. Since a line cannot be erased without resurfacing the paper, drawing with metalpoint required extreme patience and skill. Raphael's metalpoint drawing of *Paul Rending His Garments* (Fig. 244) shows this skill. Shadow is rendered here by means of careful hatching. At the same time, a sense of movement and energy is evoked not only by the directional force of these parallels, but also by the freedom of Raphael's outline, the looseness of the gesture even in this most demanding of formats. The highlights in the drawing are known as **heightening,** and are created by applying an opaque white to the design after the metalpoint lines have been drawn.

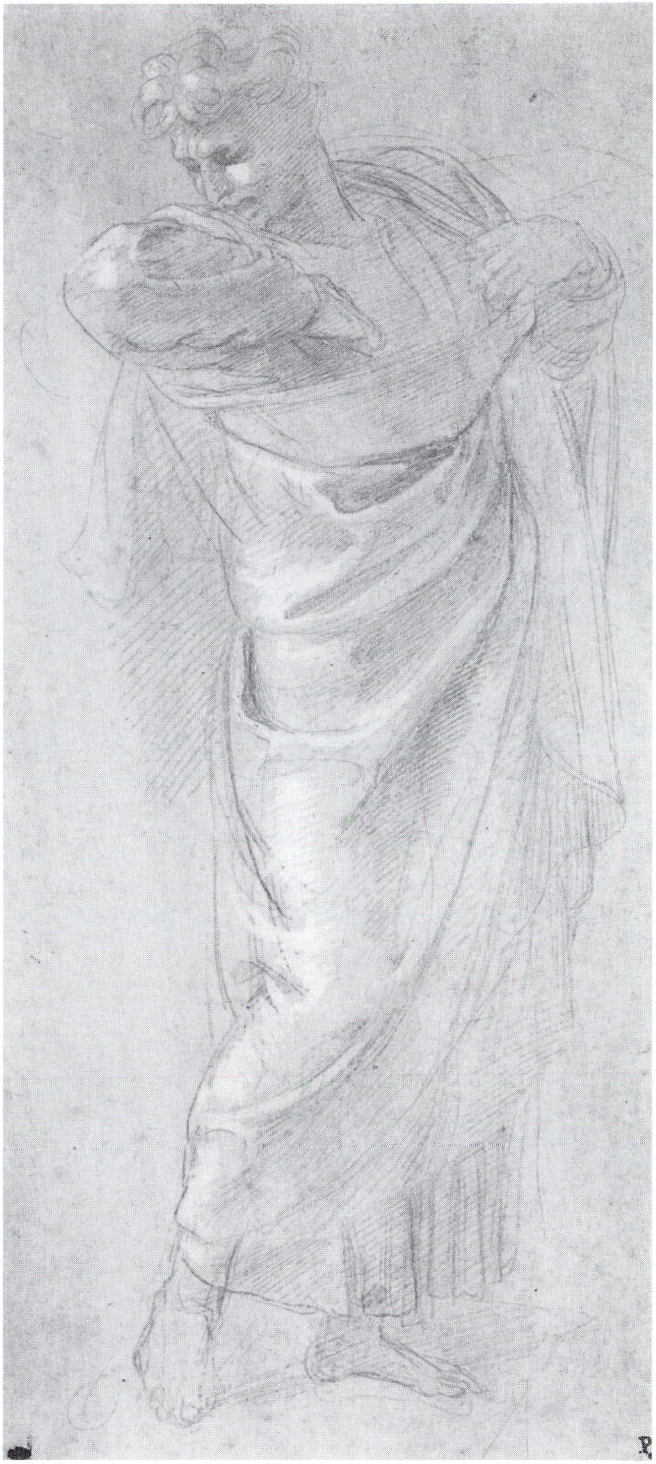

Fig. 244 Raphael, *Paul Rending His Garments*, c. 1514–1515.
Metalpoint heightened with white gouache on lilac-gray prepared paper, 9 1/16 × 4 1/16 in.
Collection of the J. Paul Getty Museum, Malibu, California.

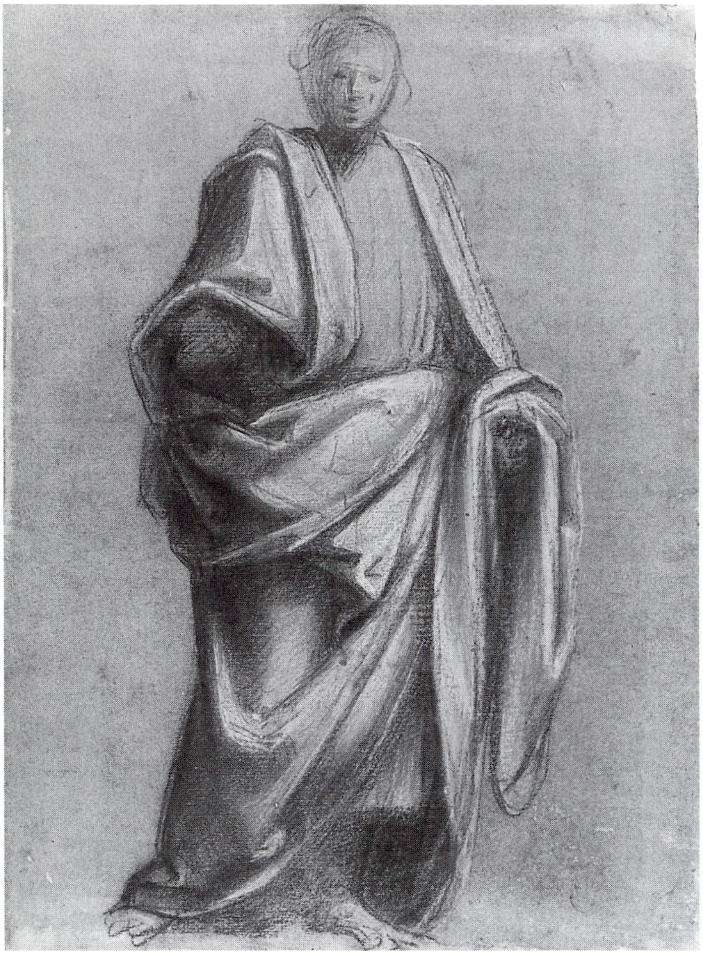

Fig. 245 Fra Bartolommeo, *Study for a Prophet Seen from the Front,* 1499–1500. Black chalk, heightened with white chalk, on brown prepared paper, 11 5/8 × 8 5/8 in. Museum Boymans-Van Beuningen, Rotterdam, The Netherlands.

Chalk and Charcoal Metalpoint is a mode of drawing that is chiefly concerned with **delineation**—that is, with a descriptive representation of the thing seen through an outline or contour drawing. Effects of light and shadow are essentially "added" to the finished drawing by means of hatching or heightening. With the softer media of chalk and charcoal, however, it is much easier to give a sense of the *volumetric*—that is, of three-dimensional form—through modulations of light and dark. While some degree of hatching is visible in Fra Bartolommeo's *Study for a Prophet Seen from the Front* (Fig. 245), the primary impression is not one of linearity or two-dimensionality. Instead, the artist uses *chiaroscuro* to realize the three-dimensional form of the figure in space (see Chapter 6).

By the middle of the sixteenth century, artists used natural chalks, derived from red ocher hematite, white soapstone, and black carbonaceous shale, which were fitted into holders and shaved to a point. With these chalks, it became possible to realize gradual transitions from light to dark, either by adjusting the pressure of one's hand or by merging individual strokes by gently rubbing over a given area with a finger, cloth, or eraser. Charcoal sticks are made from burnt wood, and the best are made from hardwood, especially vines. They can be either hard or soft, sharpened to so precise a point that they draw like a pencil, or held on their sides and dragged in large bold gestures across the surface of the paper.

In her charcoal drawing of a *Banana Flower* (Fig. 246), Georgia O'Keeffe achieves a sense of volume and space comparable to that realized by means of chalk. Though she is noted for her stunning oil paintings of flowers, this is a rare example in her work of a colorless flower composition. O'Keeffe's interest here is in creating three-dimensional space with a minimum of means, and the result is a study in light and dark in many ways comparable to a black-and-white photograph.

Because of its tendency to smudge easily, charcoal was not widely used during the Renaissance except in ***sinopie,*** tracings of the outlines of compositions drawn on the wall before the painting of frescoes. Such *sinopie* have come to light only recently, as the plaster supports for frescoes have been removed for conservation purposes. Drawing with both charcoal and chalk requires a paper with *tooth*—a rough surface to which the media can adhere. Today charcoal drawings can be kept from smudging by spraying synthetic resin **fixatives** over the finished work.

In the hands of modern artists, charcoal has become one of the more popular drawing media, in large part because of its expressive directness and immediacy. In her *Self-Portrait* (Fig. 247), Käthe Kollwitz has revealed the extraordinary expressive capabilities of charcoal as a medium. Much of the figure was realized by dragging the stick up and down in sharp angular gestures along her arm from her chest to her hand. It is as if this line, which mediates between the two much more carefully rendered areas of hand and face, embodies the dynamics of her work. This area of raw drawing literally connects her mind to her hand, her intellectual and spiritual capacity to her technical facility. She seems to hold the very piece of charcoal that has made this mark sideways between her fingers. She has rubbed so hard, and with such fury, that it has almost disappeared.

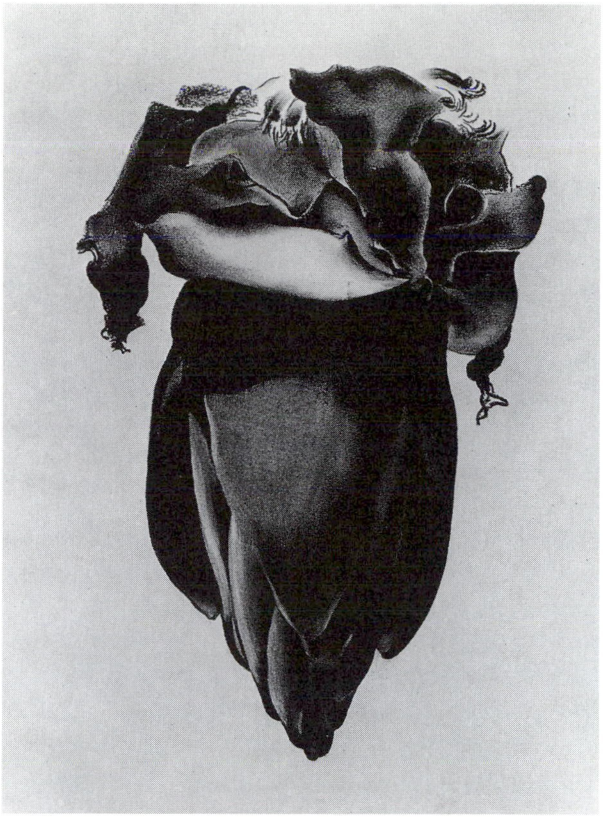

Fig. 246 Georgia O'Keeffe, *Banana Flower,* 1933.
Charcoal, 21 3/4 × 14 3/4 in.
Collection, The Museum of Modern Art, New York. Purchase.

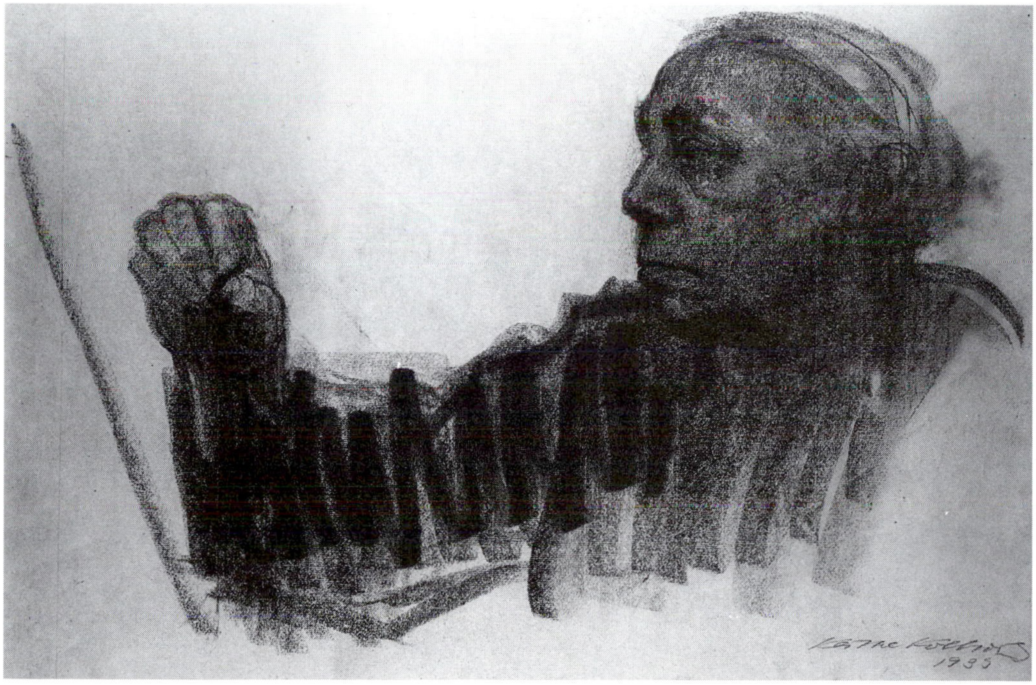

Fig. 247 Käthe Kollwitz, (German 1867 – 1945) "*Self-Portrait*," 1933.
Charcoal on brown laid Ingres paper, (Nagel 1972 1240), .477 × .635 (18 3/4 × 25 in.).
© 1996 Board of Trustees, National Gallery of Art, Washington, DC. Rosenwald Collection.

Graphite Graphite, a soft form of carbon similar to coal, was discovered in 1564 in Borrowdale, England. As good black chalk became more and more difficult to obtain, the lead **pencil**—graphite enclosed in a cylinder of soft wood—increasingly became one of the most common of all drawing tools. It became even more popular during the Napoleonic Wars early in the nineteenth century. Then, because supplies of English graphite were cut off from the continent, the Frenchman Nicholas-Jacques Conté invented, at the request of Napoleon himself, a substitute for imported pencils that became known as the **Conté crayon** (not to be confused with the so-called Conté Crayons marketed today, which are made with chalk). Conté substituted clay for some of the graphite. This technology was quickly adapted to the making of pencils generally. Thus the relative hardness of the pencil could be controlled—the less graphite, the harder the pencil—and a greater range of lights (hard pencils) and darks (soft pencils, employing more graphite) became available.

Georges Seurat's Conté crayon studies (Fig. 248) indicate the powerful range of tonal effects afforded by the new medium. As Seurat presses harder, in the lower areas of the composition depicting the shadows of the orchestra pit, the coarsely textured paper is filled by the crayon. Above, pressing less firmly, Seurat creates a sense of light dancing on the surface of the stage. Where he has not drawn on the surface at all—across the stage and on the singer's dress—the glare of the white paper is almost as intense as light itself.

Don Eddy's drawing for *Glassware I* (Fig. 249) is an example of a highly developed photorealist graphite drawing. About the size of a standard sheet of typing paper, the drawing is an extraordinarily detailed rendering of three glass shelves packed with a variety of glassware. The front of each of the top two shelves is represented by a hard black horizontal line. The drawing is not a sketch but a fully finished representation of reflected light.

Graphite drawings can be erased, and erasure itself can become an important element in the composition. In 1953, a young Robert Rauschenberg, just at the beginning of his career, was thinking about the possibility of making an entire drawing by erasing. He told Willem de Kooning, a generation older than

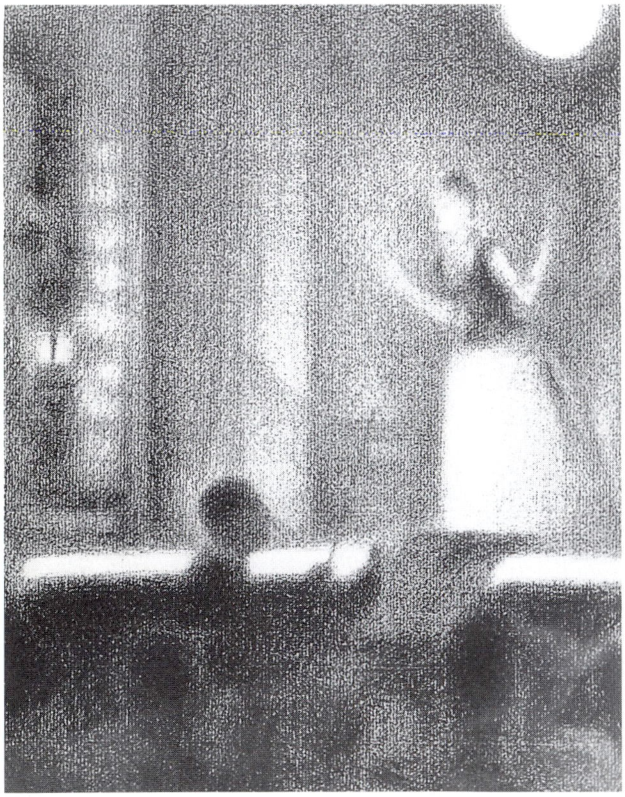

Fig. 248 Georges Seurat, *Café Concert*, c. 1887–1888.
Conté crayon with white heightening on Ingres paper, 12 × 9 1/4 in. Museum of Art, Rhode Island School of Design, Providence. Gift of Mrs. Murray S. Danforth.

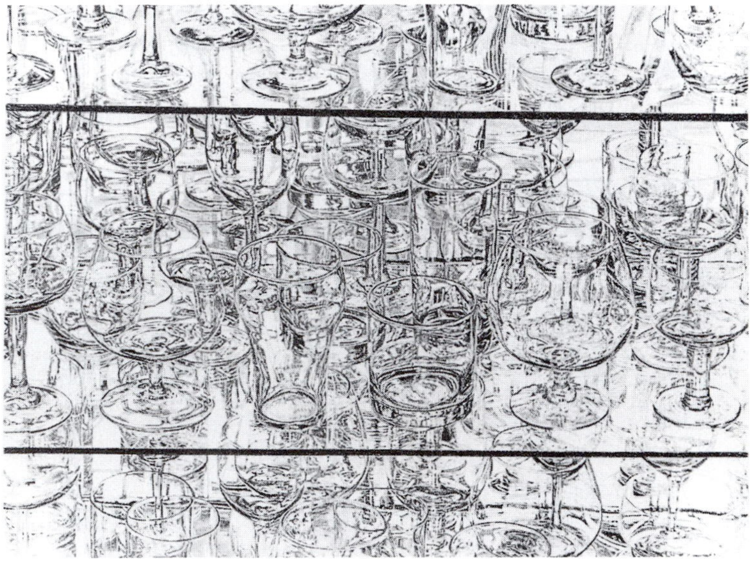

Fig. 249 Don Eddy, drawing for *Glassware I*, 1978.
Graphite on paper, 8 9/16 × 11 3/16 in. Collection of Glenn C. Janss.

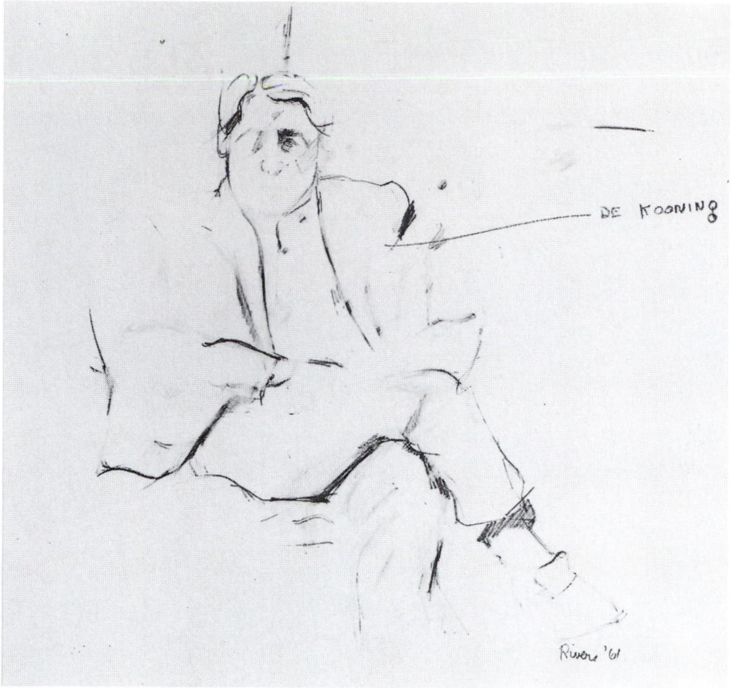

Fig. 250 Larry Rivers, *Willem de Kooning,* 1961.
Pencil on paper, 10 ³⁄₄ × 10 in.
© The Detroit Institute of Arts,
Founders Society Purchase, Director's Discretionary Fund.

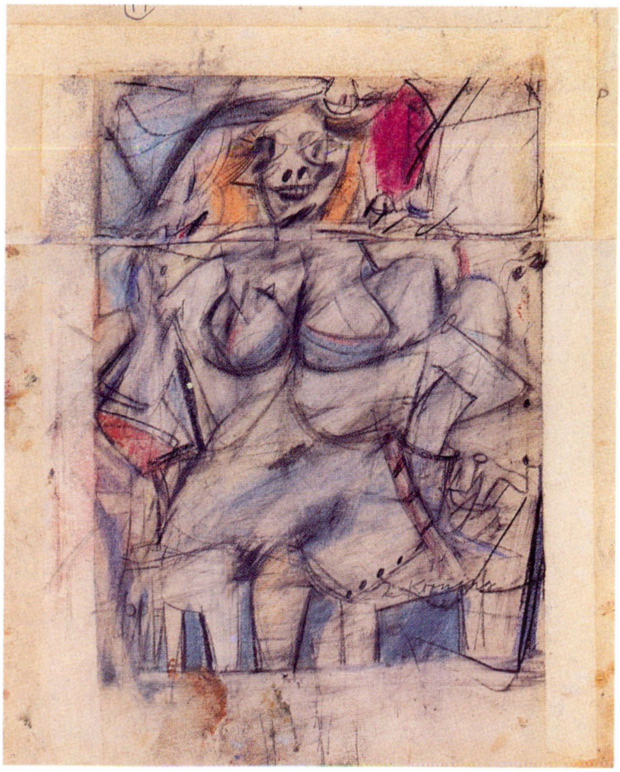

Fig. 251 Willem de Kooning, *Seated Woman,* 1952.
Pastel and pencil on cut and pasted paper, 12 × 9 ¹⁄₂ in.
The Museum of Modern Art, The Lauder Foundation Fund.
Photograph © 1996 The Museum of Modern Art, New York.

himself and an established abstract expressionist painter, about his musings. "I'd been trying with my own drawings, and it didn't work, because that was only 50 percent of what I wanted to get. I had to start with something that was 100 percent art, which mine might not be; but his work was definitely art." De Kooning reluctantly agreed to give Rauschenberg a drawing to erase. "It was a drawing done partly with a hard line, and also with grease pencil, and ink, and heavy crayon. It took me a month, and about forty erasers, to do it." The result is not easy to reproduce. It is a white sheet of paper with a faint shadow of its original gestures barely visible on it.

Larry Rivers's full figure of Willem de Kooning (Fig. 250) is a more traditional homage of a younger artist to his mentor, but it too is concerned with erasure. Rivers has described the process and the rationale behind it:

> *I tend to erase it, erase it, erase it, keep trying, erase, keep trying, erase, and finally . . . well, let the observer make up more than I can represent. . . . This drawing is in the tradition of those kinds of work in which the history of the work became part of the quality of the work. De Kooning's work is full of that. His whole genre is that. His work is all about sweeping away, putting in . . . struggle, struggle, struggle and poof—masterpiece!*

What Rivers says about de Kooning's work is evident if we consider one of the master's own drawings (Fig. 251), itself a study for a famous series of paintings of women executed between 1950 and 1953. One can see that the drawing has been erased, smudged out, and drawn over. Part of the comic effect of the drawing is the result of the fact that the porportions of the woman are odd, her breasts too big, her eyelashes huge, her head too small for the torso. In fact, this work probably began as two separate drawings—de Kooning cut the head off another drawing and pasted it to the top of this one—putting in and sweeping away, as Rivers described his process.

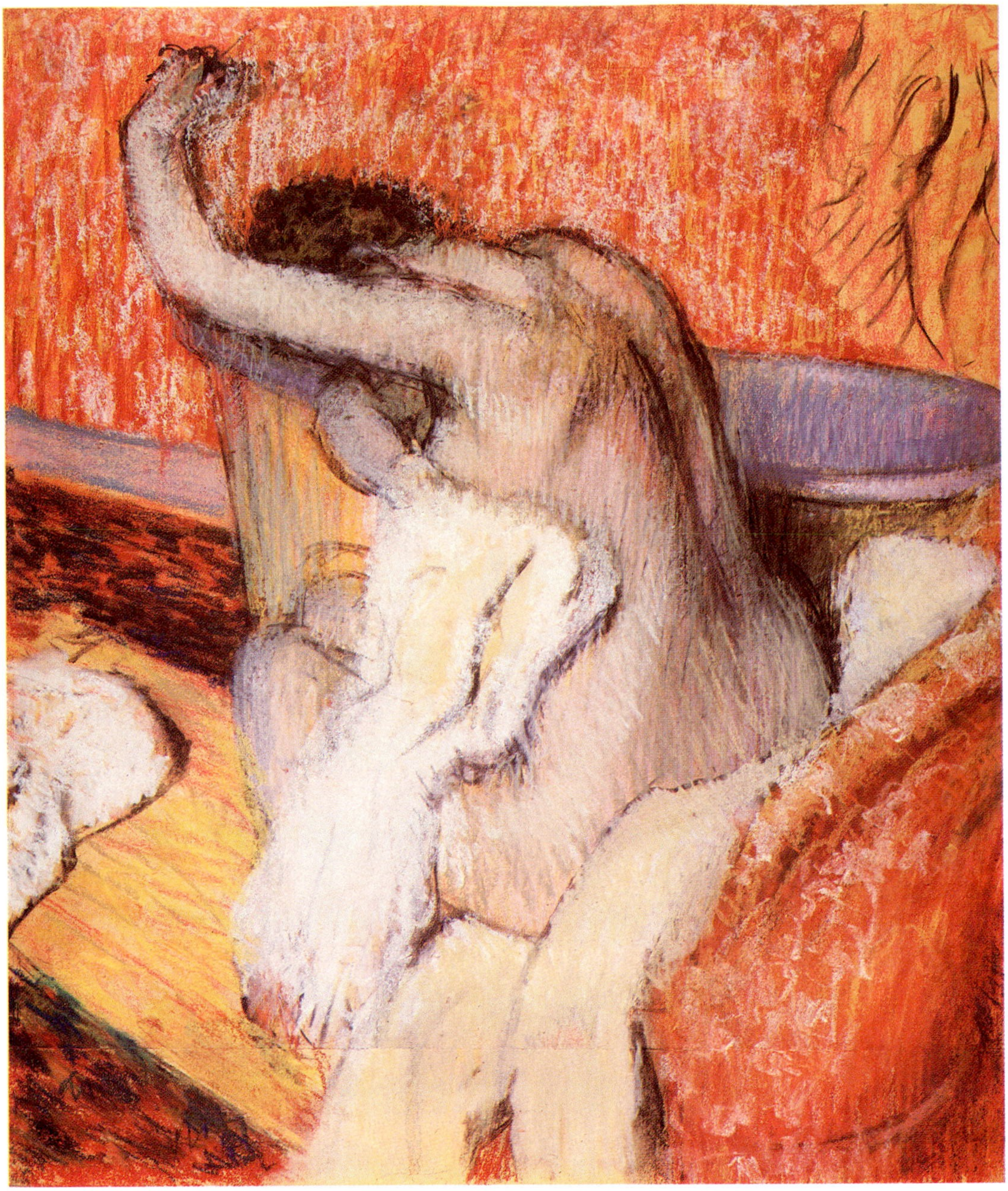

Fig. 252 Edgar Degas, *After the Bath, Woman Drying Herself,* c. 1889–1890.
Pastel on paper, 26 5/8 × 22 3/4 in. Courtauld Institute Galleries, London.

Pastel The color in de Kooning's drawing is the result of **pastel,** which is essentially a chalk medium with colored pigment and a nongreasy binder added to it. Pastels come in sticks the dimension of an index finger, and are labeled soft, medium, and hard, depending on how much binder is incorporated in the medium—the more binder the harder the stick. Since the pigment is, in effect, diluted by increased quantities of binder, the harder the stick, the less intense its color. This is why we tend to associate the word "pastel" with pale, light colors. Although the harder sticks are much easier to use than the softer ones, some of the more interesting effects of the medium can only be achieved with the more intense colors of the softer sticks. The lack of binder in pastels makes them extremely fragile. Before the final drawing is fixed, the marks created by the chalky powder can literally fall off the paper, despite the fact that, since the middle of the eighteenth century, special ribbed and textured papers have been made that help hold the medium to the surface.

Of all artists who have ever used pastel, perhaps Edgar Degas was the most proficient and inventive. He was probably attracted to the medium because it was more direct than painting, and its unfinished quality seemed particularly well suited to his artistic goal of capturing the reality of the contemporary scene. According to George Moore, a friend of Degas's who began his career as a painter in Paris but gave it up to become an essayist and novelist, Degas's intention in works such as *After the Bath, Woman Drying Herself* (Fig. 252) was to show "a human figure preoccupied with herself—a cat who licks herself; hitherto, the nude has always been represented in poses which presuppose an audience, but these women of mine are honest and simple folk, unconcerned by any other interests than those involved in their physical condition. . . . It is as if you looked through a keyhole." It is disturbing that Degas is so comfortable in his position as voyeur, and that he assumes that his model possesses little or no intelligence. His comparison of his model to a cat is demeaning. But he is also to be admired for giving up the academic studio pose.

And his use of his medium is equally unconventional, incorporating into the "finished" work both improvised gesture and a loose, sketchlike drawing. Degas invented a new way to use pastel, building up the pigments in successive layers. Normally, this would not have been possible because the powdery chalks of the medium would not hold to the surface. But Degas worked with a fixative, the formula for which has been lost, that allowed him to build up layers of pastel without affecting the intensity of their color. Laid on the surface in hatches, these successive layers create an optical mixture of color that shimmers before the eyes in a virtually abstract design.

The American painter Mary Cassatt met Degas in Paris in 1877, and he became her artistic mentor. Known for her pictures of mothers and children, Cassatt learned to use the pastel medium with an even greater freedom and looseness than Degas. In this drawing of *Young Mother, Daughter, and Son* (Fig. 253), one of Cassatt's last works, the gestures of her pastel line again and again exceed the boundaries of the forms that contain them, and loosely drawn, arbitrary blue strokes extend across almost every element of the composition.

The owner of this work, Mrs. H. O. Havemeyer, Cassatt's oldest and best friend, saw in works such as this one an almost virtuoso display of "strong line, great freedom of technique and a supreme mastery of color." When Mrs. Havemeyer organized a benefit exhibition of Cassatt's and Degas's works in New York in 1915, its proceeds to be donated to the cause of woman's suffrage, she included works such as this one because Cassatt's freedom of line was, to her, the very symbol of the strength of women and their equality to men. Seen beside the works by Degas, it would be evident that the pupil had equaled, and in many ways surpassed, the achievement of Degas himself.

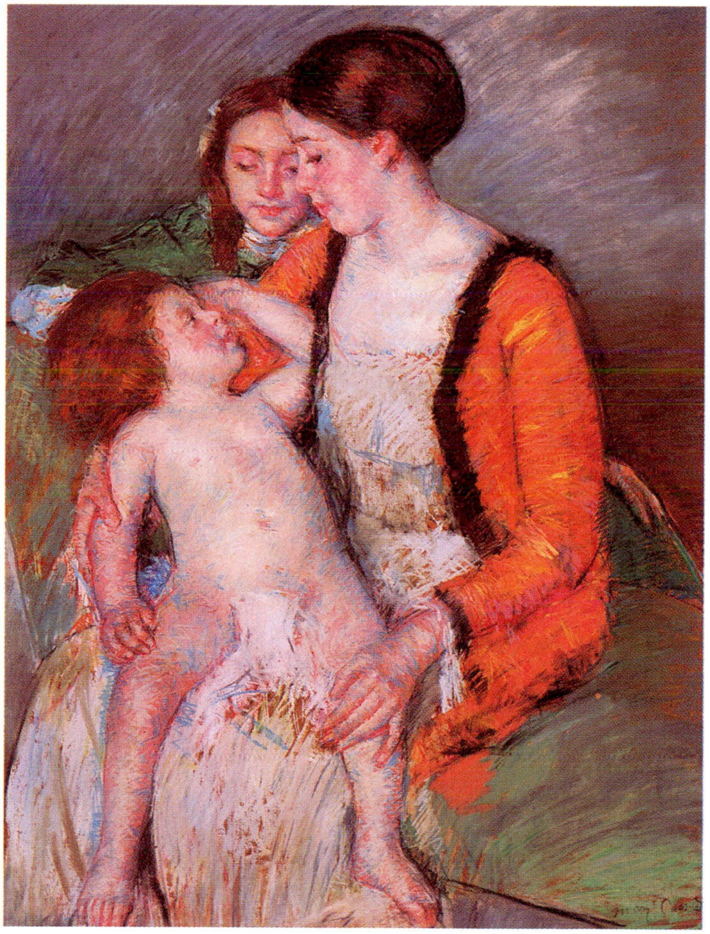

Fig. 253 Mary Cassatt, *Young Mother, Daughter, and Son*, 1913.
Pastel on paper, 43 1/4 × 33 1/4 in.
Memorial Art Gallery of the University of Rochester, Marion Stratten Gould Fund.

Beverly Buchanan's Shackworks

Pastels are an extremely fragile medium, but they can be combined with oil to make pastel oilsticks that not only flow more easily onto the surface of the drawing but adhere to the surface more readily.

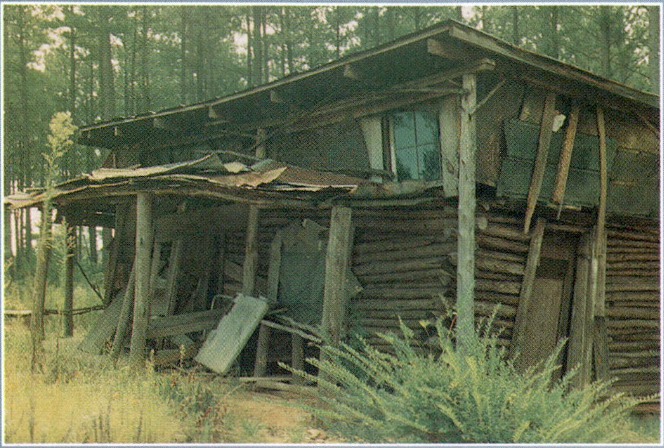

Fig. 254 Beverly Buchanan, *Ms. Mary Lou Furcron's House, deserted,* 1989. Color photograph, 16 × 20 in. Courtesy of the artist and Steinbaum Krauss Gallery, New York.

Pastel oilstick drawings are central to the art of Beverly Buchanan, whose work is about the makeshift shacks that dot the Southern landscape near her home in Athens, Georgia.

Beginning in the early 1980s, Buchanan started photographing these shacks, an enterprise she has carried on ever since (Fig. 254). "At some point," she says, "I had to realize that for me the structure was related to the people who built it. I would look at shacks and the ones that attracted me always had something a little different or odd about them. This evolved into my having to deal with [the fact that] I'm making portraits of a family or person."

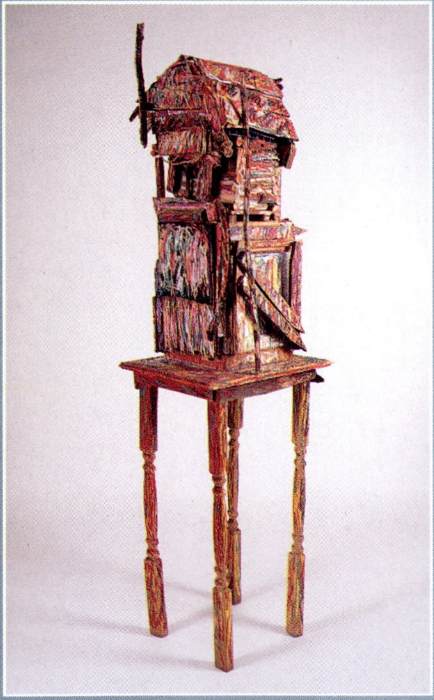

Fig. 255 Beverly Buchanan, *Richard's Home,* 1993. Oil crayon on wood and mixed media, 78 × 16 × 21 in. Photo by Adam Reich. Collection: Barbara and Eric Dobkin. Courtesy of the artist and Steinbaum Krauss Gallery, New York.

Buchanan soon began to make drawings and sculptural models of the shacks. Each of these models tells a story. This legend, for instance, accompanies the sculpture of *Richard's Home* (Fig. 255):

> *Some of Richard's friends had already moved north, to freedom, when he got on the bus to New York. Richard had been "free" for fifteen years and homeless now for seven. . . . After eight years as a foreman, he was "let go." He never imagined it would be so hard and cruel to look for something else. Selling his blood barely fed him. At night, dreams took him back to a childhood of good food, hard work, and his Grandmother's yard of flowers and pinestraw and wood. Late one night, his cardboard house collapsed during a heaving rain. Looking down at a soggy heap, he heard a voice, like thunder, roar this message through his brains, RICHARD GO HOME!*

Buchanan's sculpture does not represent the collapsed cardboard house in the North, but Richard's new home in the South. It is not just a ramshackle symbol of poverty. Rather, in its improvisational design, in its builder's determination to use whatever materials are available, to make something of nothing, as it were, the shack is a

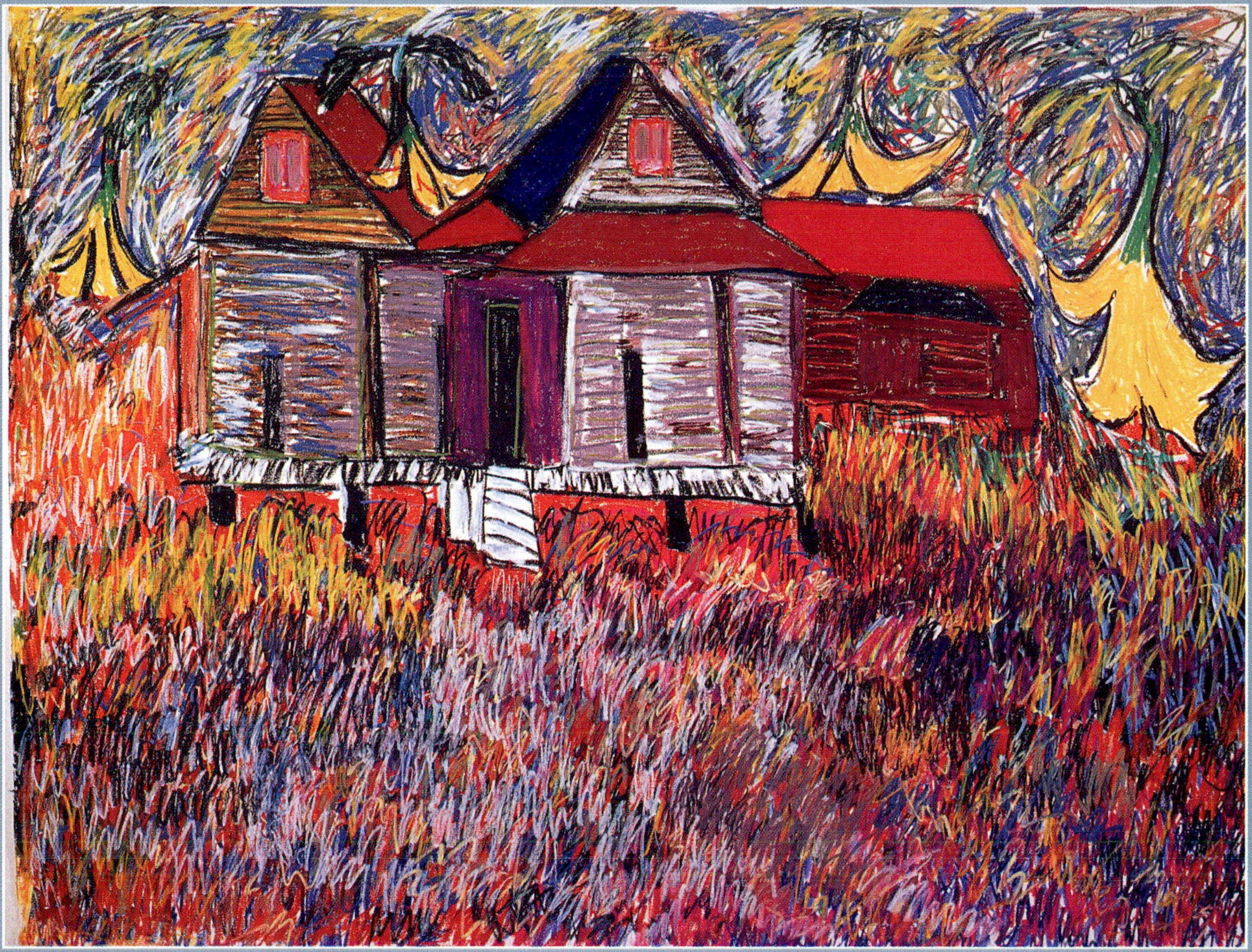

Fig. 256 Beverly Buchanan, *Monroe County House with Yellow Datura,* 1994.
Oil pastel on paper, 60 × 79 in. Photo by Adam Reich. Courtesy Steinbaum Krauss Gallery, New York.

testament to the energy and spirit of its creator. More than just testifying to Richard's will to survive, his shack underscores his creative and aesthetic genius.

Buchanan's oilstick drawings such as *Monroe County House with Yellow Datura* (Fig. 256) are embodiments of this same energy and spirit. In their use of expressive line and color, they are almost abstract, especially in the fields of color that surround the shacks. Their distinctive scribble-like marks are based on the handwriting of Walter Buchanan, Beverly Buchanan's great-uncle and the man who raised her. Late in his life he suffered a series of strokes, and before he died he started writing letters to family members that he considered very important. "Some of the words were legible," Buchanan explains, "and some were in this kind of script that I later tried to imitate. . . . What I thought about in his scribbling was an interior image. It took me a long time to absorb that. . . . And I can also see the relation of his markings to sea grasses, the tall grasses, the marsh grasses that I paint." The pastel oilstick is the perfect tool for this line, the seemingly untutored rawness of its application mirroring the haphazard construction of the shacks. And it results in images of great beauty, as beautiful as the shacks themselves.

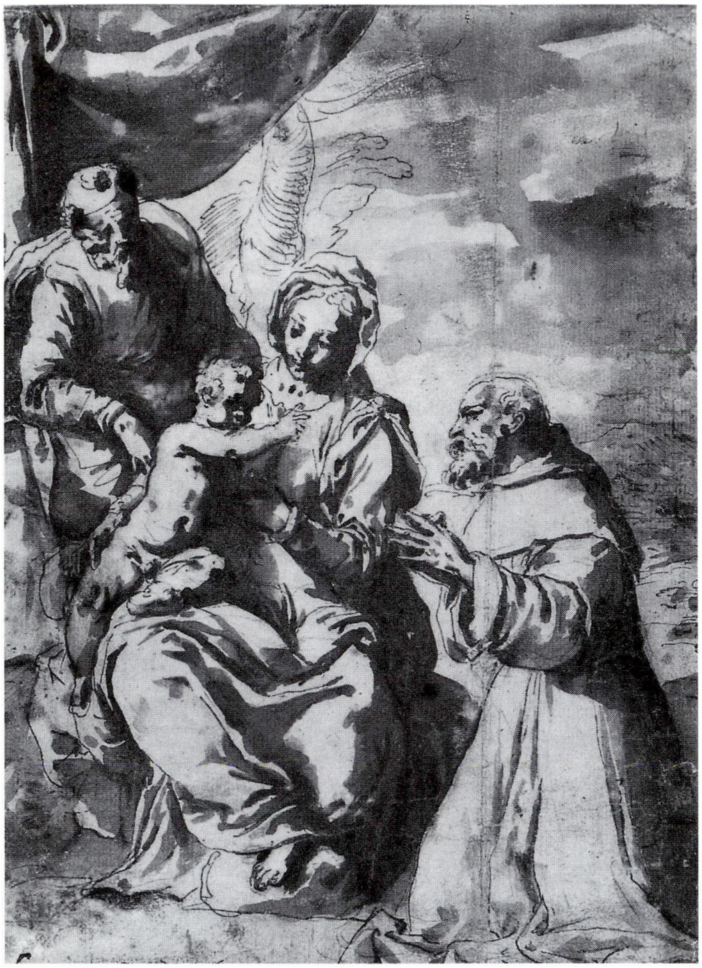

Fig. 257 Elisabetta Sirani,
***The Holy Family with a Kneeling Monastic Saint,* c. 1660.**
Pen and brown ink, black chalk, on paper, 10 3/8 × 7 3/8 in.
Private collection. Photograph courtesy of Christie's, London.

Liquid Media

Pen and Ink During the Renaissance, after the invention of paper, most drawings were made with iron-gall ink, which was made from a mixture of iron salts and an acid obtained from the nutgall, a swelling on an oak tree caused by disease. The characteristic brown color of most Renaissance pen and ink drawings results from the fact that this ink, though black at application, browns with age.

The quill pen used by most Renaissance artists, which was most often made from a goose or swan feather, allows for far greater variation in line and texture than is possible with a metalpoint stylus or even with a pencil. As we can see in this drawing by Elisabetta Sirani (Fig. 257), one of the leading artists in Bologna during the seventeenth century, the line can be thickened or thinned, depending on the artist's manipulation of the flexible quill and the absorbency of the paper (the more absorbent the paper, the more freely the ink will flow through its fibers). Diluted to a greater or lesser degree, ink also provides her with a more fluid and expressive means to render light and shadow than the elaborate and tedious hatching that was necessary when using stylus or chalk. Drawing with pen and ink is fast and expressive. Sirani, in fact, displayed such speed and facility in her compositions that, in a story that most women will find familiar, she was forced to work in public in order to demonstrate that her work was her own and not done by a man.

In this example from Jean Dubuffet's series of drawings *Corps de Dame* (Fig. 258) ("corps" means both a group of women and the bodies of women), the whorl of line, which ranges from the finest hairline to strokes nearly a half-inch thick, defines a female form, her two small arms raised as if to ward off the violent gestures of the artist's pen itself. Though many see Dubuffet's work as misogynistic—the product of someone who hates women—it can also be read as an attack on academic figure drawing, the pursuit of formal perfection and beauty that has been used traditionally to justify drawing from the nude. Dubuffet does not so much render form as flatten it, and in a gesture that insists on the modern artist's liberation from traditional techniques and values, his use of pen and ink threatens to transform drawing into scribbling, conscious draftsmanship into automatism, that is, unconscious and random automatic marking. In this, his work is very close to surrealist experiments designed to make contact with the unconscious mind.

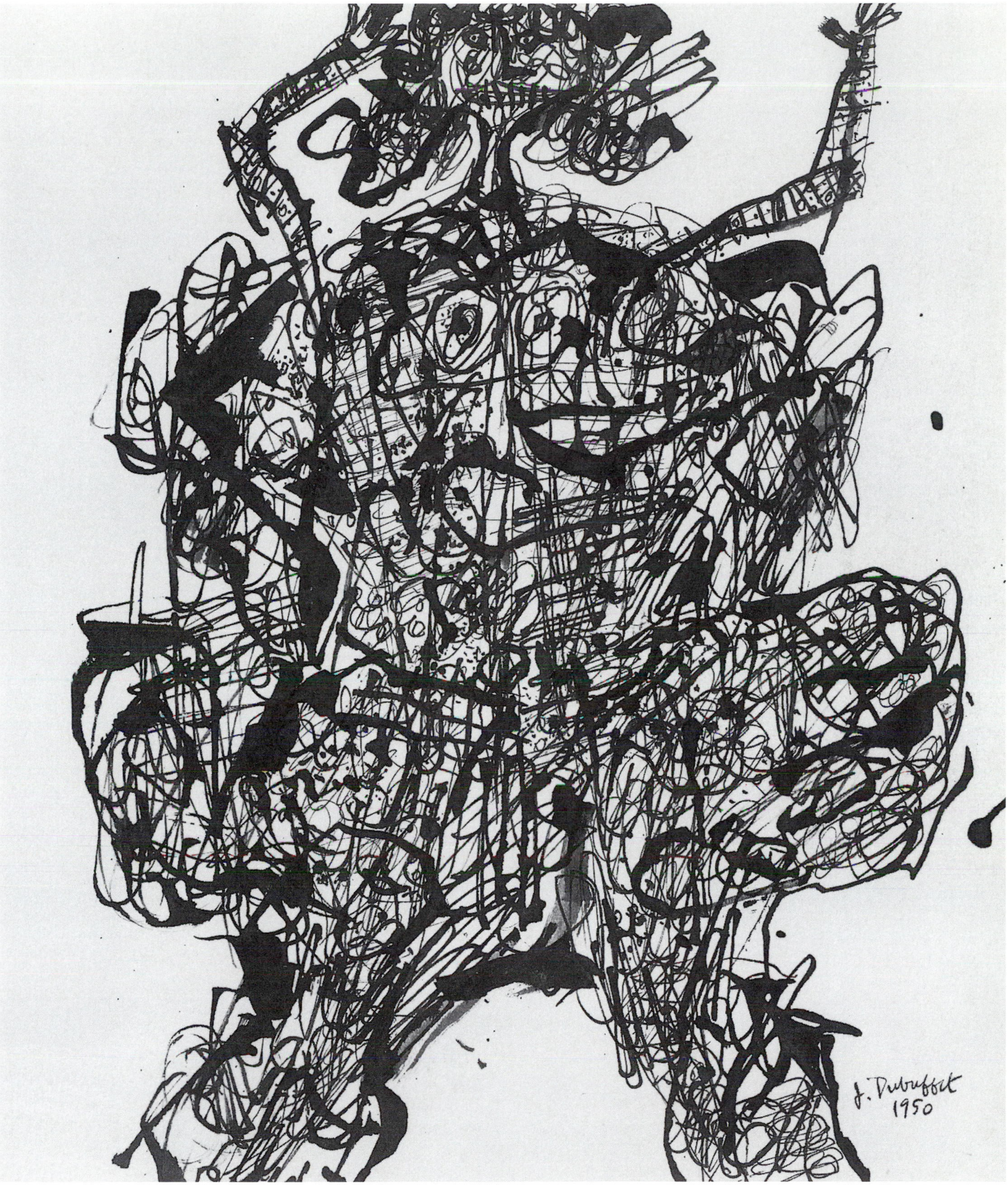

Fig. 258 Jean Dubuffet, *Corps de Dame,* June–December 1950.
Pen, reed pen, and ink, 10 5/8 × 8 3/8 in. Collection, The Museum of Modern Art, New York. The Jean and Lester Avnet Collection.

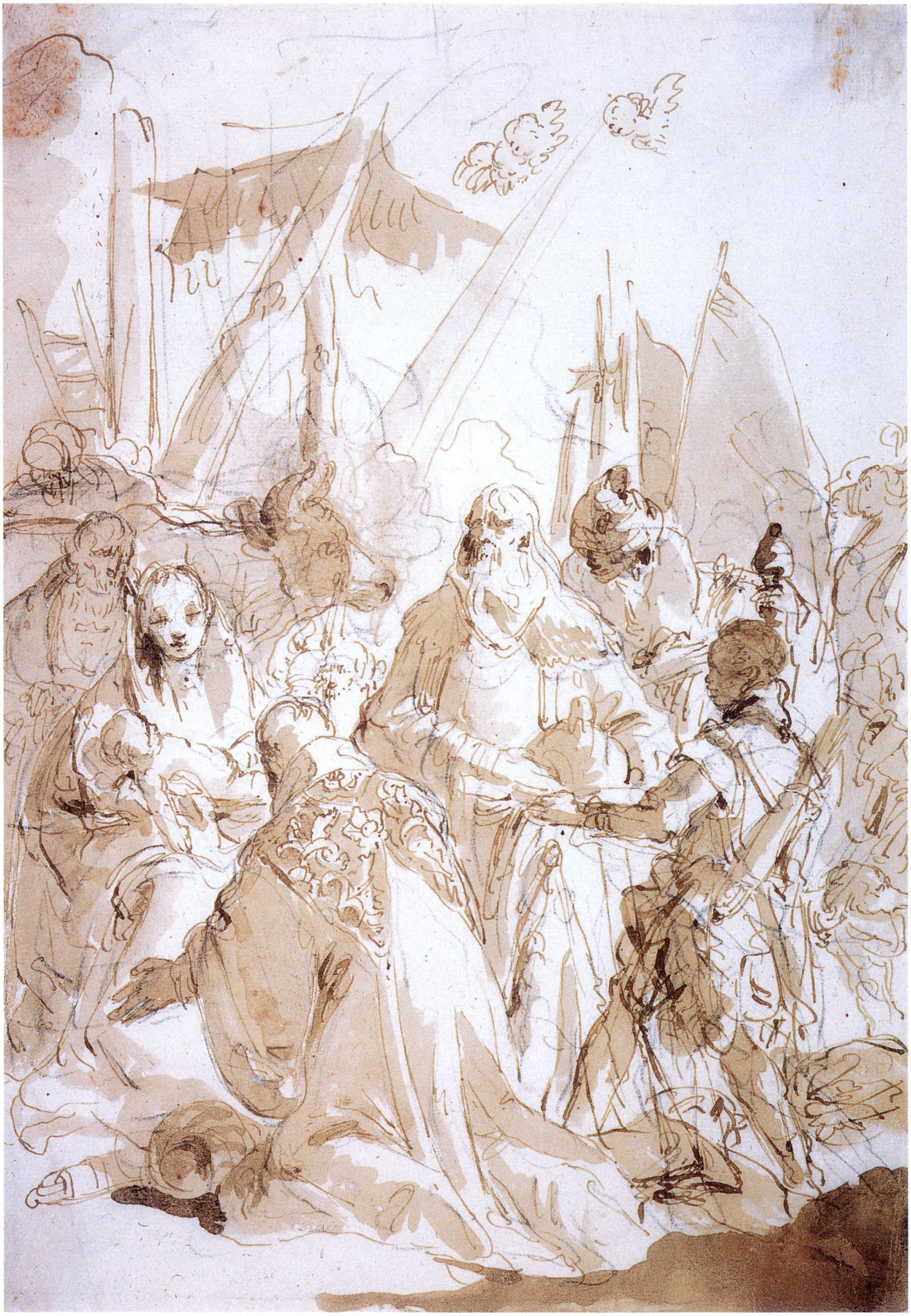

Fig. 259 Giovanni Battista Tiepolo (1696–1770), *The Adoration of the Magi*, c. 1740s.
Pen and brown wash over graphite sketch, $11\frac{3}{5} \times 8\frac{1}{5}$ in.
Stanford University Museum of Art. Gift of Mortimer C. Leventritt.

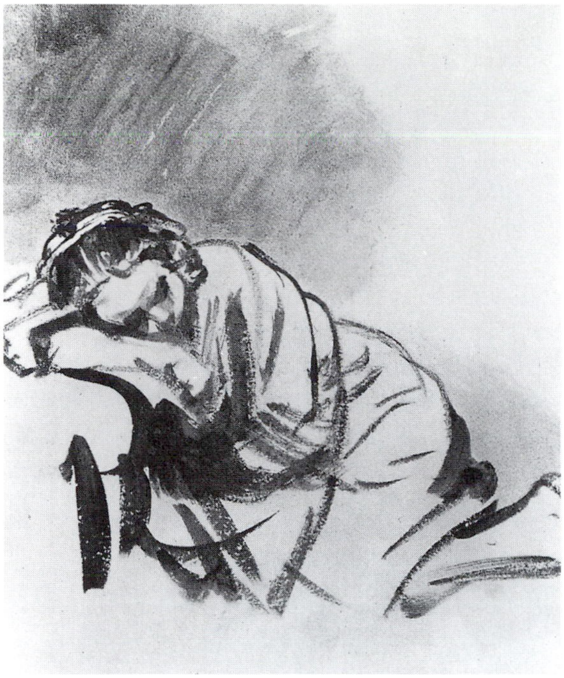

Fig. 260 Rembrandt van Rijn, *A Sleeping Woman*, c. 1660–1669. Brush drawing in brown ink and wash, $9\frac{5}{8} \times 8$ in. The British Museum, London.

Wash and Brush When ink is diluted with water and applied by brush in broad, flat areas, the result is called a **wash.** Tiepolo's *Adoration of the Magi* (Fig. 259) is essentially three layers deep. Over a preliminary graphite sketch is a pen and ink drawing, and over both Tiepolo has laid a brown wash. The wash serves two purposes here. First, it helps to define volume and form by adding shadow. But it also creates a visual pattern of alternating light and dark elements that help to make the drawing much more dynamic than it would otherwise be. As we move from right to left across the scene, deeper and deeper into its space, this alternating pattern leads us to a cental moment of light, which seems to flood from the upper right, falling on the infant Jesus himself.

Many artists prefer to draw with a brush. It affords them a sense of immediacy and spontaneity, as Rembrandt's brush drawing of *A Sleeping Woman* (Fig. 260) makes clear. The work seems so spontaneous, so quick and impetuous, that one can imagine Rembrandt drawing the scene quickly, so as not to wake the woman. And the drawing possesses an equally powerful sense of intimacy. It is as if the ability to draw this fast is the result of knowing very well who it is one draws.

Drawing with a brush is a technique with a long tradition in the East, perhaps because the brush is used there as a writing instrument. Chinese calligraphy requires that each line in a written character begin very thinly, then broaden in the middle and taper again to a point. The soft brushtip allows calligraphers to control the width of their line. Thus, in the same gesture, a line can move from broad and sweeping to fragile and narrow, and back again. Such ribbons of line are extremely expressive. In his depiction of the Tang poet Li Bo (Fig. 261), Liang Kai juxtaposes—contrasts—the quick strokes of diluted ink that form the robe with the fine, detailed brushwork of his face. This opposition contrasts the fleeting materiality of the poet's body—as insubstantial as his chant, which drifts away on the wind—with the enduring permanence of his poetry.

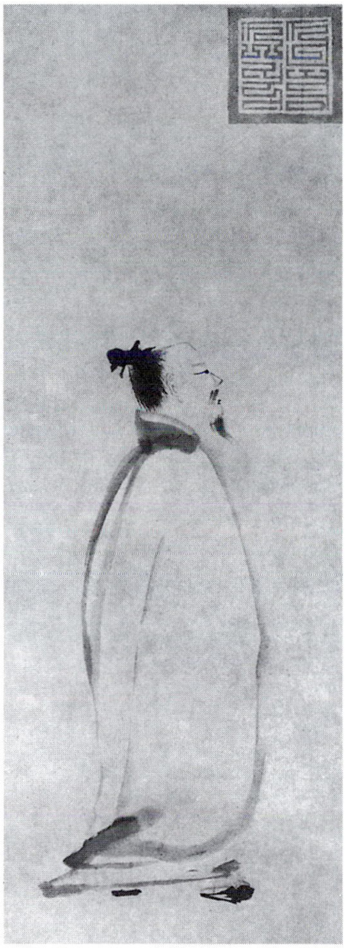

Fig. 261 Liang Kai, *The Poet Li Bo Walking and Chanting a Poem*, Southern Song Dynasty, c. 1200. Hanging scroll, ink on paper, $31\frac{3}{4} \times 11\frac{7}{8}$ in. Tokyo National Museum, Japan.

Innovative Drawing Media

Drawing is by its nature an exploratory medium. It invites experiment. Taking up a sheet of heavy prepainted paper, Henri Matisse was often inspired, beginning in the early 1940s, to cut out a shape in the paper with a pair of wide-open scissors, using them like a knife to carve through the paper. "Scissors," he says, "can acquire more feeling for line than pencil or charcoal." Sketching with the scissors, Matisse discovered what he considered to be the essence of a form. Cut-outs, in fact, dominated Matisse's artistic production from 1951 until his death in 1954. In this *Venus* (Fig. 262), the figure of the goddess is revealed in the negative space of the composition. It is as if the goddess of love—and hence love itself—were immaterial. In the blue positive space to the right we discover the profile of a man, as if love springs, fleetingly, from his very breath.

Walter De Maria's *Las Vegas Piece* (Fig. 263) is a "drawing" made in 1969 in the central Nevada desert with the six-foot blade of a bulldozer. The photograph shows one side of a square that is one-half mile on each side. Two sides of this square extend an additional half-mile at opposite corners. As the photograph

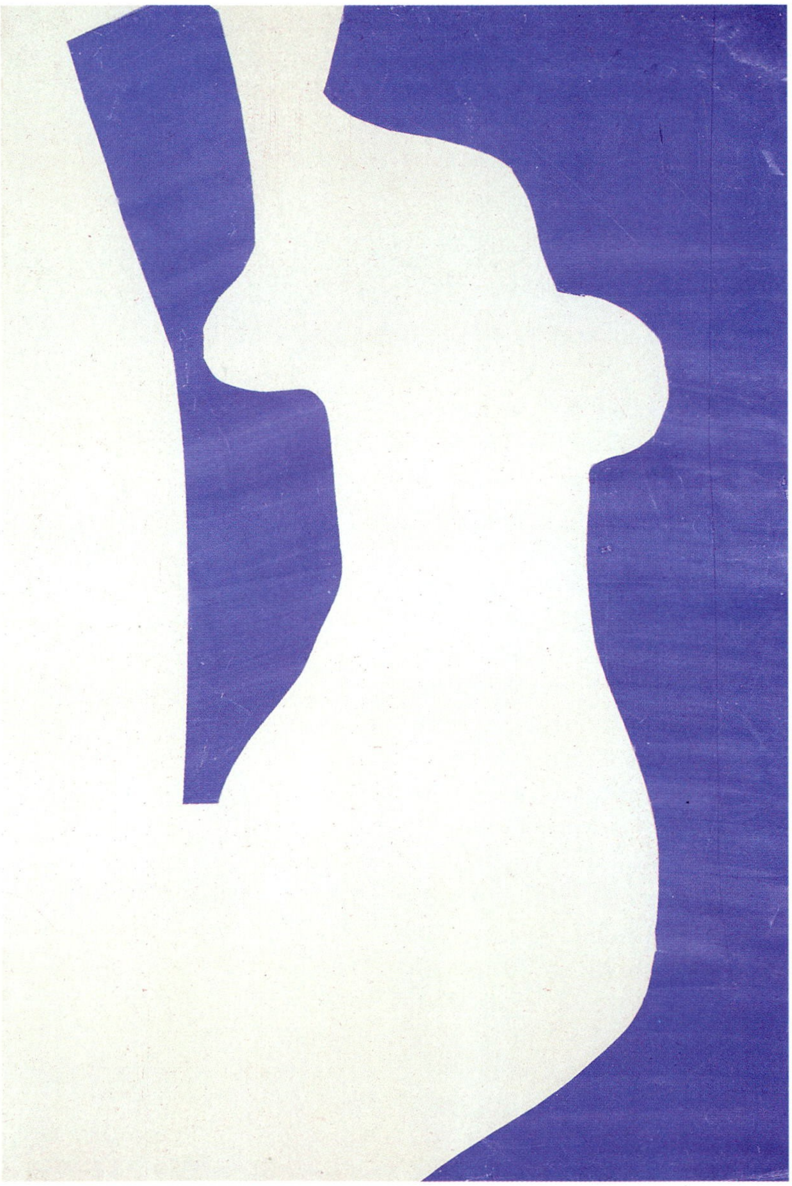

Fig. 262 Henri Matisse, *Venus*, 1952.
Paper cut-out, 39 7/8 × 30 1/8 in. ©1992 National Gallery of Art, Washington, DC. Ailsa Mellon Bruce Fund.

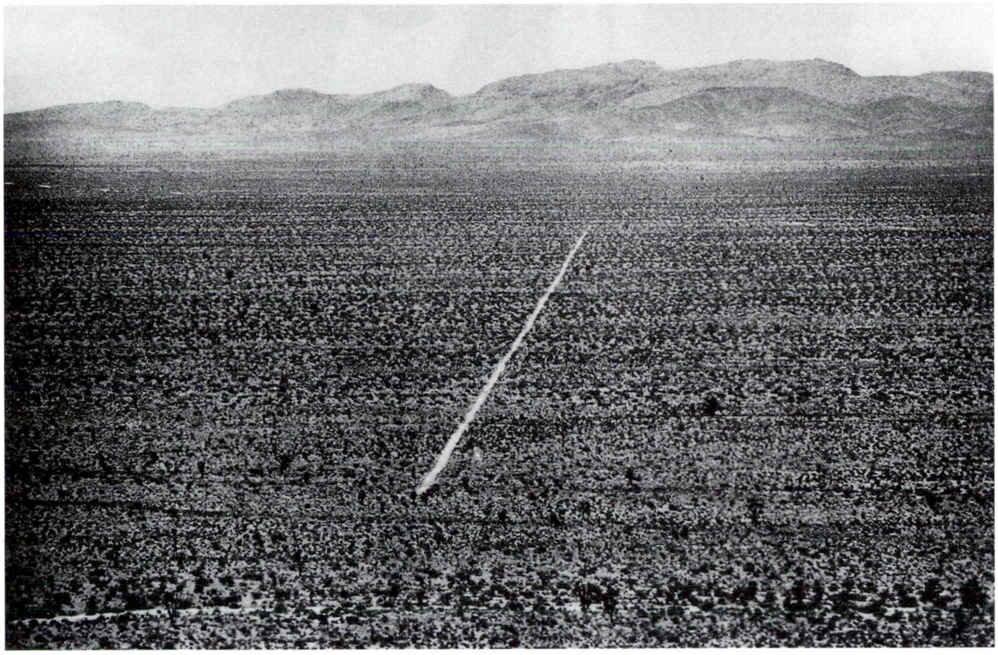

Fig. 263 Walter De Maria, *Las Vegas Piece,* 1969.
Overall length: 3 mi. Desert Valley, Nevada. All reproduction rights reserved: © Walter De Maria.

suggests, the piece is never entirely visible except from the air. Oriented on precise north-south and east-west coordinates, it has something of the mystery of the famous Nazca lines in Peru (Fig. 264). These lines, drawn by sweeping away the top layer of the desert with a broom, have been roughly dated as originating in the first century CE. Their significance is enormously controversial. They have been seen as highways, as part of a calendar system, as representative of kinship lines between clans, as ritual dance grounds, as UFO landing strips, and so on. Writing in *Artforum* in 1975, sculptor Robert Morris described them as marks drawn by a culture obsessed with "space as a palpable emptiness."

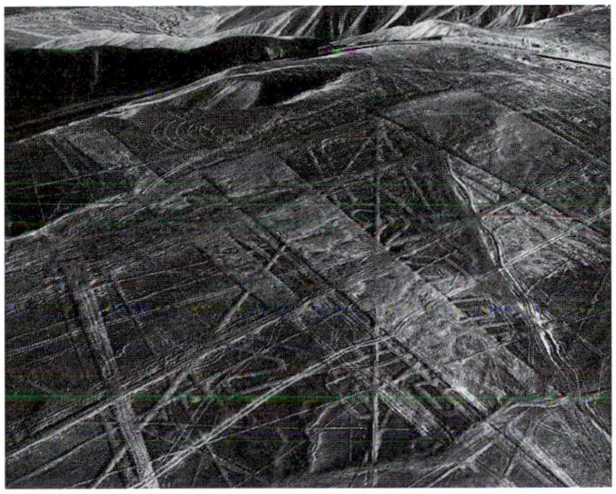

Fig. 264 Marilyn Bridges, *Overview,* Nazca, Peru, 1979.

To fully comprehend such drawings it would seem necessary to view them from an aerial vantage point. Of course, this was impossible for a first-century Peruvian. Even today, viewing De Maria's piece from the air involves chartering a helicopter or plane, an extremely expensive proposition. But the aerial point of view requires, literally for the ancient Peruvian and figuratively for the modern observer, an imaginative flight more than a real one. It is as if both the Nazca lines and De Maria's simultaneously lay claim to two discontinuous spaces. From the air, one imagines they would be experienced as huge tracings across the vastness of the earth's surface. But encountered on the ground, these huge scars seem rather innocent. As Elizabeth Baker, the editor of *Art in America,* put it in 1976 when describing *Las Vegas Piece:* "This piece requires that you walk on it. At ground level . . . knee-high scrub growth hides it unless one is right on it—its track is shallower than all sorts of natural washes and holes." On the ground one's attention quickly moves away from the drawing itself. In Baker's words: "It provides an experience of a specific place, random apprehension of surroundings, and an intensified sense of self which seems to transcend visual apprehension alone."

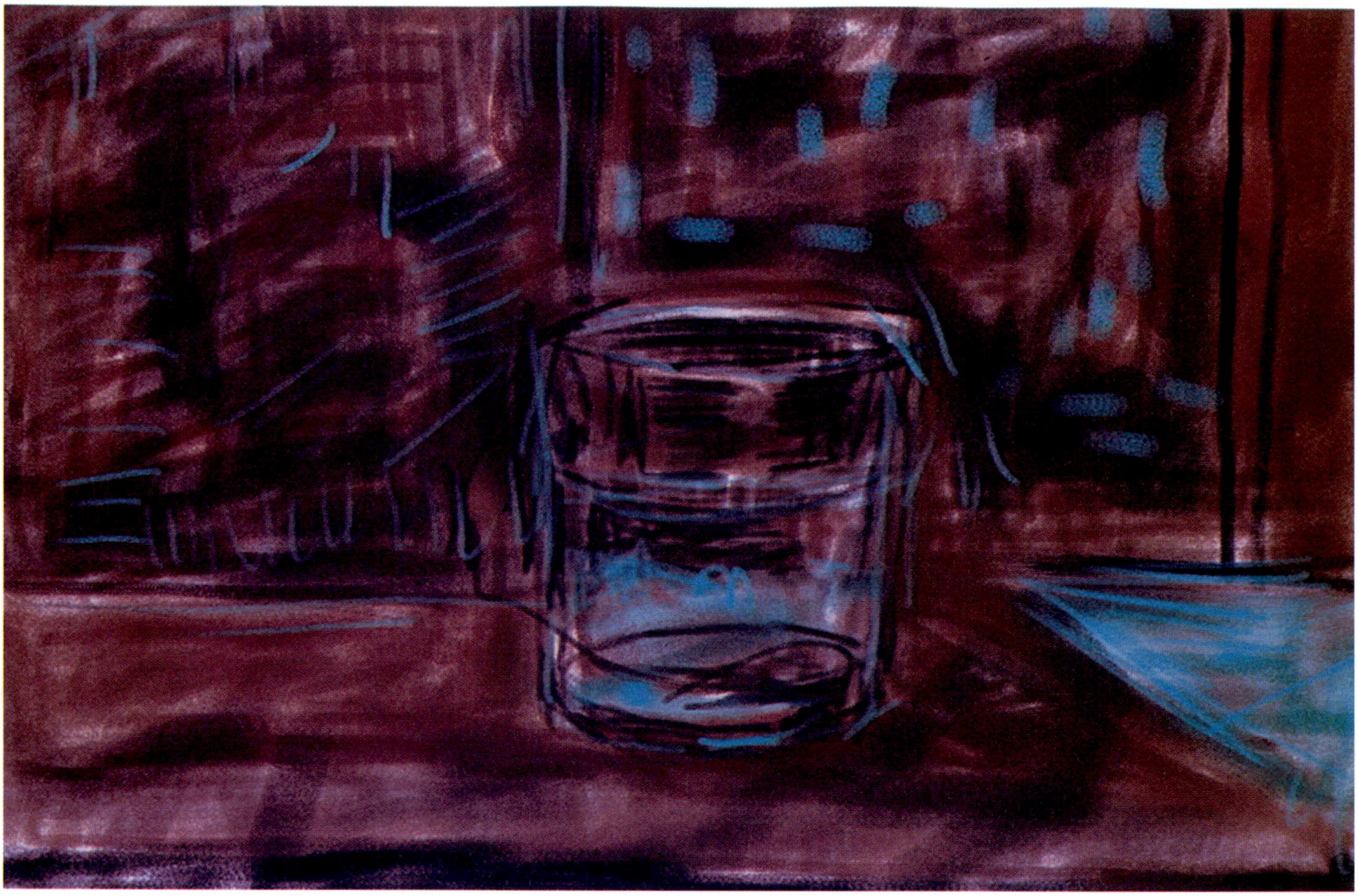

Fig. 265 Jennifer Bartlett, *Untitled,* 1986.
From *Painting with Light,* a BBC television series by Griffin Productions produced on the Quantel Paintbox ®, a registered trademark of Quantel.

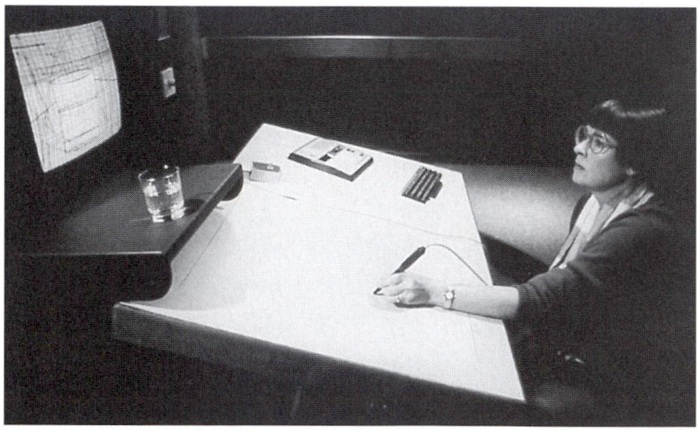

Fig. 266 Jennifer Bartlett, *Untitled,* 1986.
From *Painting with Light,* a BBC television series by Griffin Productions produced on the Quantel Paintbox ®, a registered trademark of Quantel.

Increasingly, drawing is accomplished by electronic means, especially with the aid of computers. The introduction of relatively inexpensive personal computers, electronic palettes, and increasingly sophisticated user-friendly software "paint" programs has made drawing on the computer more and more commonplace. Computers make experimentation easy. It is possible to explore in a matter of minutes what might take years to accomplish at the drawing board.

It is best to think of the computer as an electronic sketchpad. At the left, the painter Jennifer Bartlett is at work on a digitized tablet provided for her use by Quantel, the manufacturer of the computer hardware system Paintbox (Fig. 266). Her subject, a glass of water, sits before her. As she moves her light pen on the pad, each line appears on the screen above. She can choose a variety of colors, line widths, textures, and so on from a software menu, and change them at will. The ability of the program to adopt to a given artist's style is obvious if we compare Bartlett's final computer drawing (Fig. 265) with a landscape by David Hockney (Fig. 267), also done in 1986 at the invitation of Quantel. Once the artist learns to coordinate the hand with the image on the screen, the process is essentially the same as work in traditional media, only faster and more versatile because a vast array of possible effects of line, color, and so on, can be rapidly explored.

As we have seen, drawing is one of the most basic and one of the most direct of all media. Initially, drawing was not considered an art in its own right, but only a tool for teaching and preliminary study. However, by the time of the Renaissance, drawing was seen to possess a vitality and immediacy that revealed significant details about an artist's personality and style. The primary drawing materials, both dry and liquid, are capable of producing a variety of effects, and each medium produces effects uniquely its own. The dry media include metal-point, chalk, charcoal, graphite, and pastel. The liquid media include pen and ink, wash, and drawing with a brush. But it is possible to draw with almost anything that will make a line—from a scissor's edge to a bulldozer to a computer screen.

Drawing plays a fundamental role in almost all the other media that we will explore. Not only is it a tool utilized universally for preliminary study, but it is fundamental to the process of all the other media. Printmakers draw, but with the printmaker's tools. Painters often draw, but with a brush. Photography literally means "drawing with light." Even sculpture could be considered a sort of three-dimensional drawing in space. Drawing informs all of the arts. It is simply something all artists do.

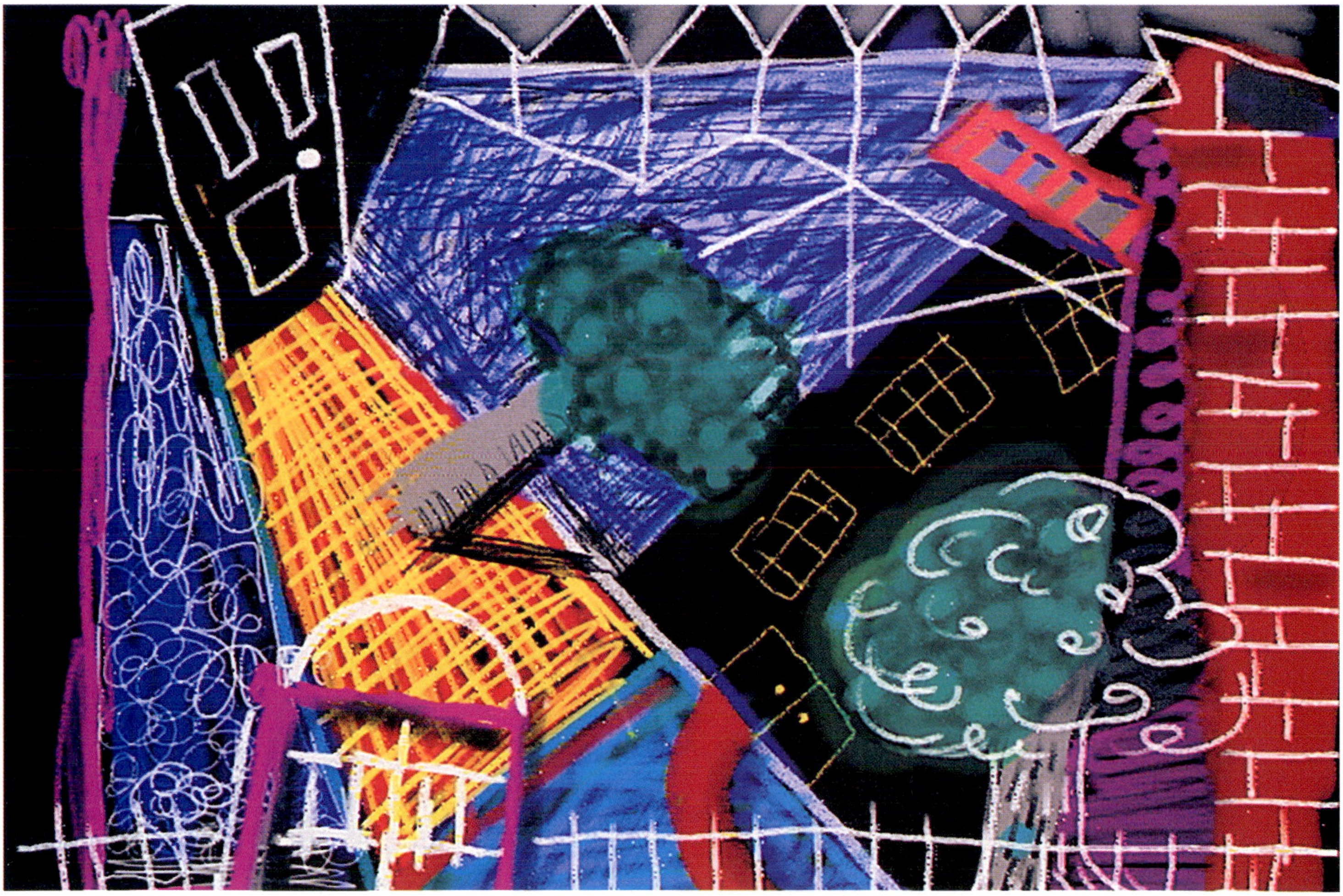

Fig. 267 David Hockney, *Untitled,* 1986.
From *Painting with Light,* a BBC television series by Griffin Productions, produced on the Quantel Paintbox ®, a registered trademark of Quantel.

CHAPTER 10

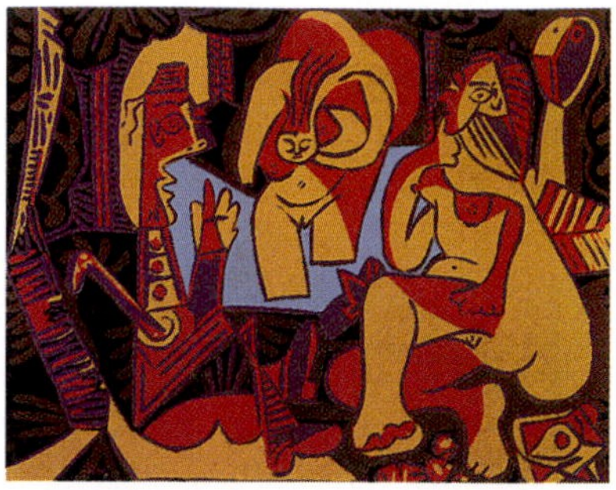

Printmaking

The medium of printmaking originated in the West very soon after the appearance of the first book printed with movable type, the Gutenberg Bible (1450–1456). At first, printmaking was used almost exclusively as a mode of illustration for books. In post-medieval Western culture, prints not only served to codify and regularize scientific knowledge, which depends on the dissemination of exact reproductions, but they were fundamental to the creation of our shared visual culture.

This illustration for *The Nuremberg Chronicle* (Fig. 268) was published in 1493 by one of the first professional book publishers in history, Anton Koberger. Appearing in two editions, one in black-and-white, and another much more costly edition with hand-colored illustrations, *The Nuremberg Chronicle* was intended as a history of the world. A best-seller in its day, it contained over 1,800 pictures, though only 654 different blocks were employed. Forty-four images of men and women were repeated 226 times to represent different famous historical characters, and depictions of many different cities utilized the same woodcut.

For centuries, prints were primarily used in books, but since the nineteenth century, and increasingly since World War II, the art world has witnessed what might well be called an explosion of prints. The reasons for this are many. For one thing, the fact that prints exist in multiple numbers seemed to many artists absolutely in keeping with an era of mass production and distribution. The print allows the contemporary artist, in an age increasingly dominated by the mass media and mechanical modes of reproduction, such as photography, to investigate the meaning of mechanically reproduced imagery itself. An even more important reason is that the unique work of art—a painting or a sculpture—has become, during the twentieth century, too expensive for the average collector, and the size of the purchasing public has as a consequence diminished considerably. Far less expensive than unique paintings, prints are an avenue through which artists can more readily reach a wider audience.

A **print** is defined as a single **impression,** or example, of a multiple **edition** of impressions, made on paper from the same **matrix,** the master image on the working surface. As collectors have come to value prints more and more highly, the somewhat confusing concept of the **original print** has come into being. How, one wonders, can an image that exists in multiple be considered "original"? By and large, an original print consists of an image that the artist alone has created, and that has been printed by the artist or under the artist's supervision. Since the late nineteenth century, artists have signed and numbered each impression—for example, the number 3⁄35 at the bottom of a print means that this is the third impression in an edition of thirty-five. Often the artist reserves a small number of additional **proofs**—trial impressions made before the final edition is run—for personal use. These are usually designated "AP," meaning "artist's proof." After the edition is made, the original plate is destroyed or canceled by incising lines across it. This is done to protect the collector against a misrepresentation about the number of prints in a given edition.

Today, prints provide many people with aesthetic pleasure. There are five basic processes of printmaking—relief, intaglio, lithography, silkscreen, and monotype—and we will consider them all in this chapter.

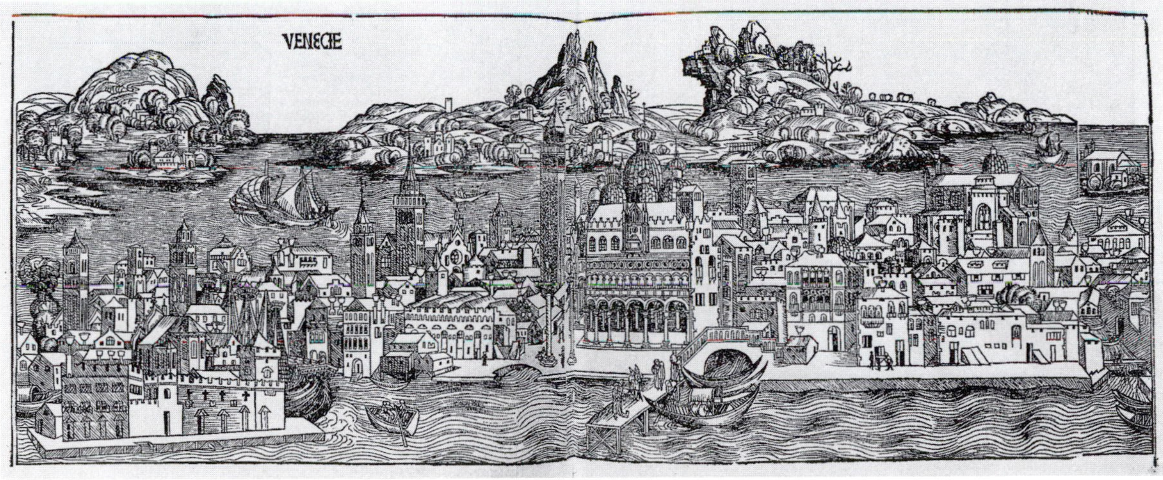

Fig. 268 Hartmann Schedel, *Venice,* illustration for *The Nuremberg Chronicle,* 1493.
Woodcut, illustration size 10 × 20 in. Metropolitan Museum of Art, New York. Rogers Fund, 1921.21.36.145.

RELIEF PROCESSES

The term **relief** refers to any printmaking process in which the image to be printed is raised off the background in reverse. Common rubber stamps utilize the relief process. If you have a stamp with your name on it, you will know that the letters of your name are raised off it in reverse. You press the letters into an ink pad, and then to paper, and your name is printed right side up. All relief processes rely on this basic principle.

Woodcut

The earliest prints, such as the illustrations for *The Nuremberg Chronicle,* were **woodcuts.** A design is drawn on the surface of a wood block, and the parts that are to print white are cut or gouged away, usually with a knife. This process leaves the areas that are to be black elevated. A black line is created, for instance, by cutting away the block on each side of it. This elevated surface is then rolled with a relatively viscous ink, thick and sticky enough that it will not flow into the hollows (Fig. 269). Paper is then rolled through a press directly against this inked and raised surface.

The woodcut print offers the artist a means of achieving great contrast between light and dark, and as a result, dramatic emotional effects. In the twentieth century, the expressive potential of the medium was recognized, particularly by the German Expressionists. In Emile Nolde's *Prophet* (Fig. 270), we do not merely sense the pain and anguish of the prophet's life, the burden that prophecy entails, but we feel the portrait emerging out of the very gouges Nolde's knife made in the block.

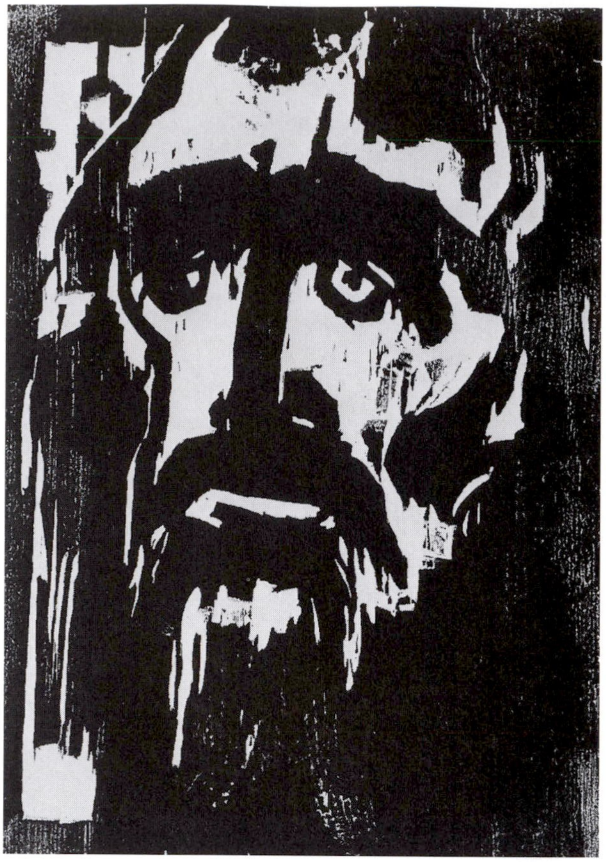

Fig. 270 Emile Nolde, *Prophet,* 1912.
Woodcut, 12 5/8 × 8 7/8 in.
National Gallery of Art, Washington, DC. Rosenwald Collection.

European artists became particularly interested in the woodblock process in the nineteenth century though their introduction to the Japanese woodblock print. Woodblock printing

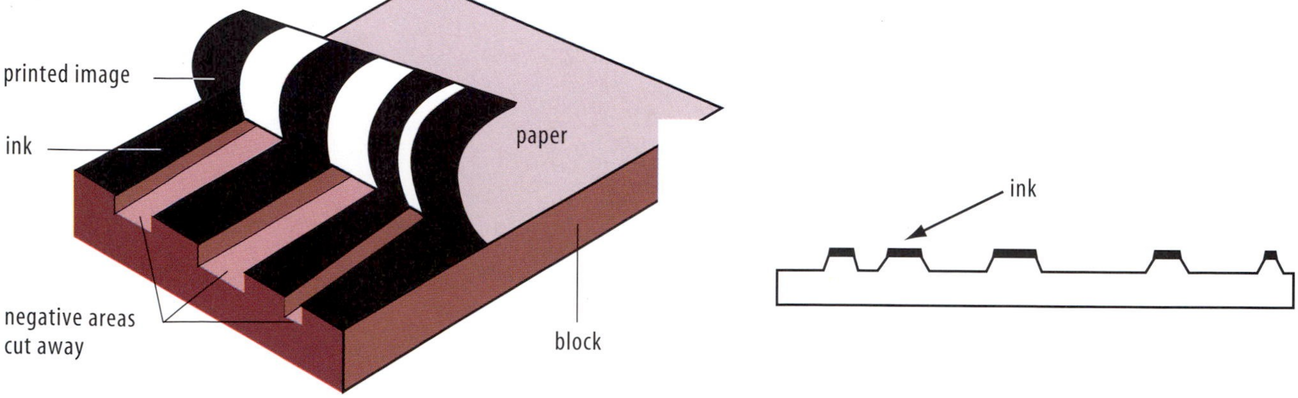

Fig. 269 Relief printing technique.

had essentially died as an art form in Europe as early as the Renaissance, but not long after Commodore Matthew C. Perry's arrival in Japan in July 1853, ending 215 years of isolation from the rest of the world, Japanese prints flooded the European market, and they were received with enthusiasm. Part of their attraction was their exotic subject matter, but artists were also intrigued by the range of color in the prints, their subtle and economical use of line, and their novel use of pictorial space.

Artists such as Edouard Manet, Edgar Degas, and Mary Cassatt were particularly influenced by Japanese prints. But the artist most enthusiastic about Japanese prints was Vincent van Gogh. He owned prints by the hundreds, and on numerous occasions he copied them directly. *Japonaiserie: The Courtesan (after Kesai Eisen)* (Fig. 272) is an example. The central figure in the painting is copied from a print by Kesai Eisen that van Gogh saw on the cover of a special Japanese number of *Paris Illustré* published in May 1886 (Fig. 271). All the other elements of the painting are derived from other Japanese prints, except perhaps the boat at the very top, which appears Western in conception. The frogs were copied from Yoshimaro's *New Book of Insects*, and both the cranes and the bamboo stalks are derived from prints by Hokusai, whose *Great Wave Off Kanagawa* we saw in Chapter 8 (Fig. 216). Van Gogh's intentions in combining all these elements becomes clear when we recognize that the central figure is a courtesan (her tortoiseshell hair ornaments signify her profession), and that the words *grue* (crane) and *grenouille* (frog) were common Parisian words for prostitutes. Van Gogh explained his interest in Japanese prints in a letter of September 1988: "Whatever one says," he wrote, "I admire the most popular Japanese prints, colored in flat areas, and for the same reasons that I admire Rubens and Veronese. I am absolutely certain that this is no primitive art."

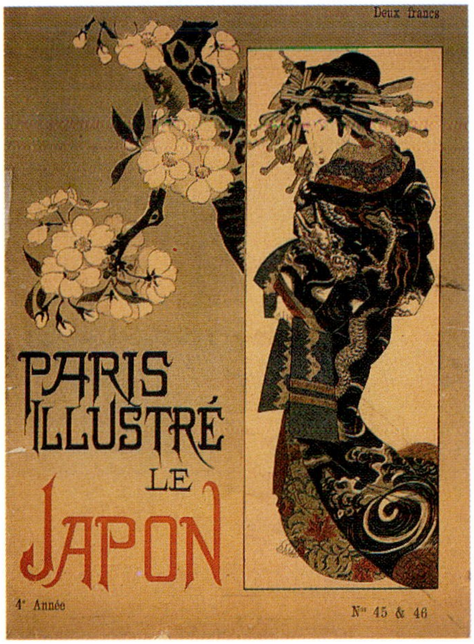

Fig. 271 "Le Japon," cover of *Paris Illustré*, May 1886.
© Amsterdam, van Gogh Museum (Vincent van Gogh Foundation).

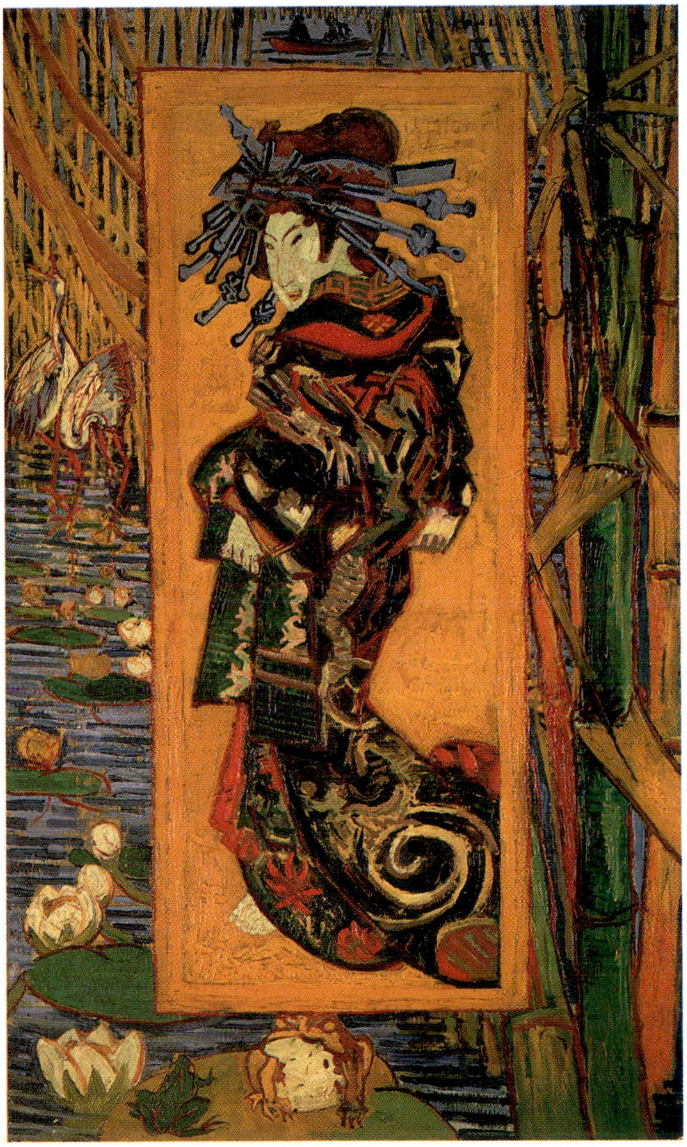

Fig. 272 Vincent van Gogh, *Japonaiserie: The Courtesan (after Kesai Eisen)*, 1887.
Oil on canvas, 41 3/8 × 24 in. Amsterdam, van Gogh Museum (Vincent van Gogh Foundation).

Utamaro's Studio

Most Japanese prints are examples of what is called *ukiyo-e,* or "pictures of the transient world of everyday life." Inspired in the late seventeenth century by a Chinese manual on the art of painting entitled *The Mustard-Seed Garden,* which contained many woodcuts in both color and black-and-white, *ukiyo-e* prints were commonplace in Japan by the middle of the eighteenth century. Between 1743 and 1765, Japanese artists developed their distinctive method for color printing from multiple blocks.

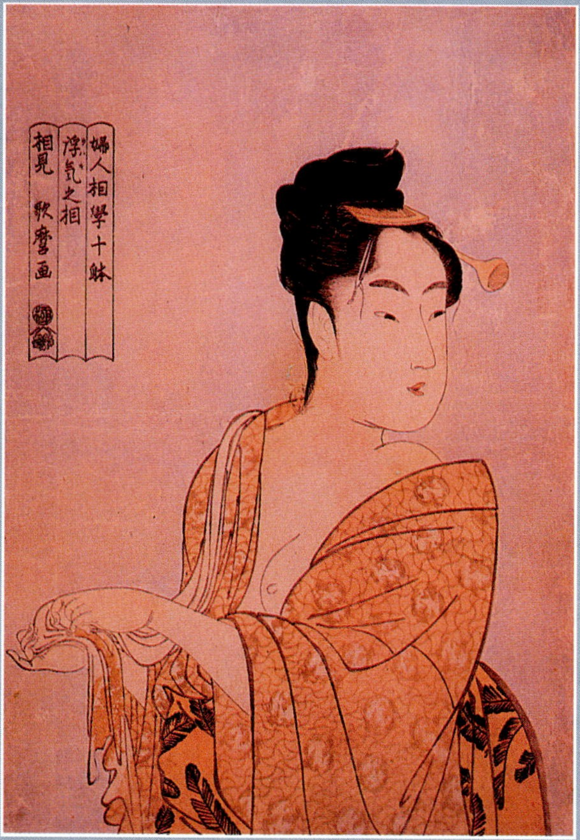

Fig. 273 Kitagawa Utamaro, *The Fickle Type,* from the series *Ten Physiognomies of Women,* c. 1793. Woodcut, 14 × 9⅞ in. Asian Art & Archeology/Art Resource.

The subject matter of these prints is usually concerned with the pleasures of contemporary life—hairdos and wardrobes, daily rituals such as bathing, theatrical entertainments, life in the Tokyo brothels, and so on, in endless combination. Utamaro's depiction of *The Fickle Type,* from his series *Ten Physiognomies of Women* (Fig. 273) embodies the sensuality of the world that the *ukiyo-e* print so often reveals. Hokusai's views of the eternal Mount Fuji (Fig. 216), which we have already studied in connection with their play with questions of scale, were probably conceived as commentaries on the self-indulgence of the genre of *ukiyo-e* as a whole. The mountain—and by extension, the values it stood for, the traditional values of the nation itself—is depicted in these works as transcending the fleeting pleasures of daily life.

Traditionally, the creation of a Japanese print was a team effort, and the publisher, the designer (such as Utamaro), the carver, and the printer were all considered essentially equal in the creative process. The head of the project was the publisher, who often conceived of the ideas for the prints, financing individual works or series of works that the public would, in his estimation, be likely to buy. Utamaro's depiction of his studio in a publisher's establishment (Fig. 274) is a *mitate*, or fanciful picture. Each of the workers in the studio is a pretty girl—hence, the print's status as a *mitate*—and they are engaged, according to the caption on the print in "making the famous Edo [present day Tokyo] color prints." Utamaro depicts himself at the right, dressed in women's

WORKS IN PROGRESS

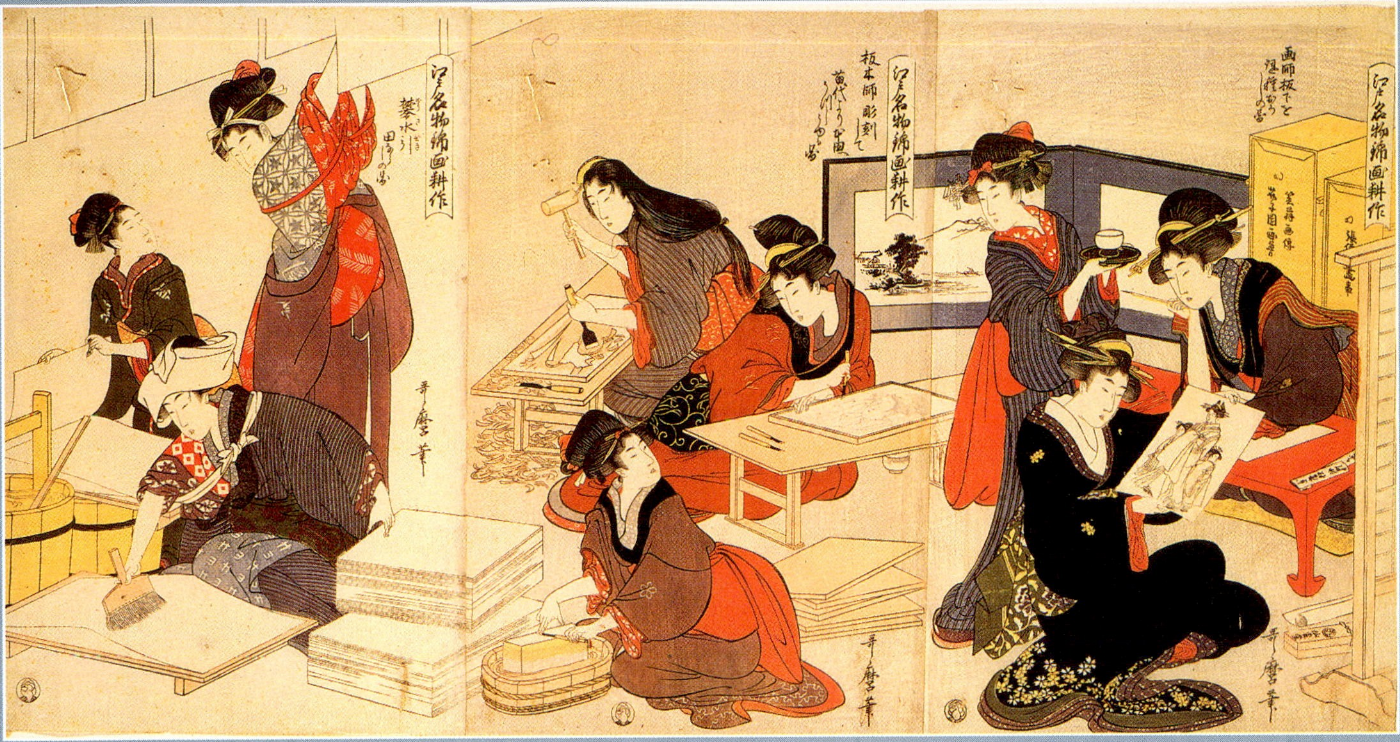

Fig. 274 Utamaro, A fanciful picture of *Utamaro's Studio*, with all the artisans represented as women, c. 1790.
From the series Edo meibutsu-e kosaku, ink and color on paper. Oban triptyph, $24\frac{3}{4} \times 9\frac{5}{8}$ in., published by Tsuruya. The Art Institue of Chicago.

clothing and holding a finished print. His publisher, also dressed as a woman, looks on from behind his desk. On the left of the triptych is a depiction of workers preparing paper. They are **sizing** it—that is, brushing the surface with an astringent crystalline substance called alum that reduces the absorbancy of the paper so that ink will not run along its fibers—then hanging the sized prints to dry. The paper was traditionally made from the inside of the bark of the mulberry tree mixed with bamboo fiber, and, after sizing, it was kept damp for six hours before printing.

In the middle section of the print, the block is actually prepared. In the foreground, a worker sharpens her chisel on a stone. Behind her is a stack of blocks with brush drawings made by Utamaro stuck face down on them with a weak rice-starch dissolved in water. The woman seated at the desk in the middle rubs the back of the drawing to remove several layers of fiber. She then saturates what remains with oil until it becomes transparent. At this point, the original drawing looks as if it were drawn on the block.

Next the workers carve the block, and we can see here large white areas being chiseled out of the block by the woman seated in the back. Black-and-white prints of this design are made and then returned to the artist, who indicates the colors for the prints, one color to a sheet. The cutter then carves each sheet on a separate block. The final print is, in essence, an accumulation of the individually colored blocks, requiring a separate printing for each color.

Wood Engraving

By the late nineteenth century, woodcut illustration had reached a level of extraordinary refinement. Illustrators commonly employed a method known as **wood engraving.** Wood engraving is a "white-line" technique in which the fine, narrow grooves cut into the block do not hold ink. The grainy end of a section of wood—comparable to the rough end of a 4 × 4—is utilized instead of the smooth side of a board as it is in woodcut proper. The end grain can be cut in any direction without splintering, and thus extremely delicate modeling can be achieved by means of careful hatching in any direction.

The wood engraving below (Fig. 275) was copied by a professional wood engraver from an original sketch, executed on the site, by American painter Thomas Moran (his signature mark, in the lower left corner, is an "M" crossed by a "T" with an arrow pointing downward). It was used to illustrate Captain J. W. Powell's 1875 *Exploration of the Colorado River of the West,* a narrative of the first exploration of the Colorado River canyon from Green River, in Wyoming, to the lower end of the Grand Canyon. The wood

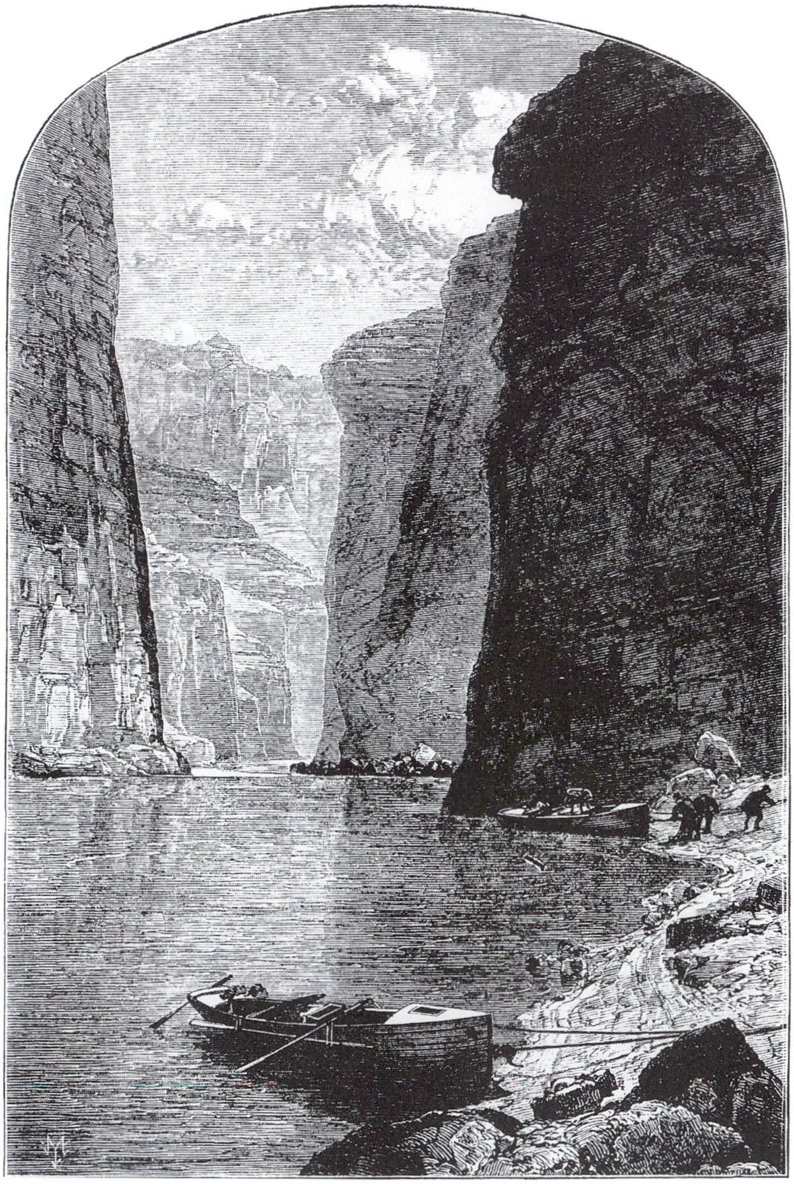

Fig. 275 ***Noon-Day Rest in Marble Canyon,*** **from J. W. Powell's *Exploration of the Colorado River of the West,* 1875.**
Wood engraving after an original sketch by Thomas Moran, 6½ × 4⅜ in.

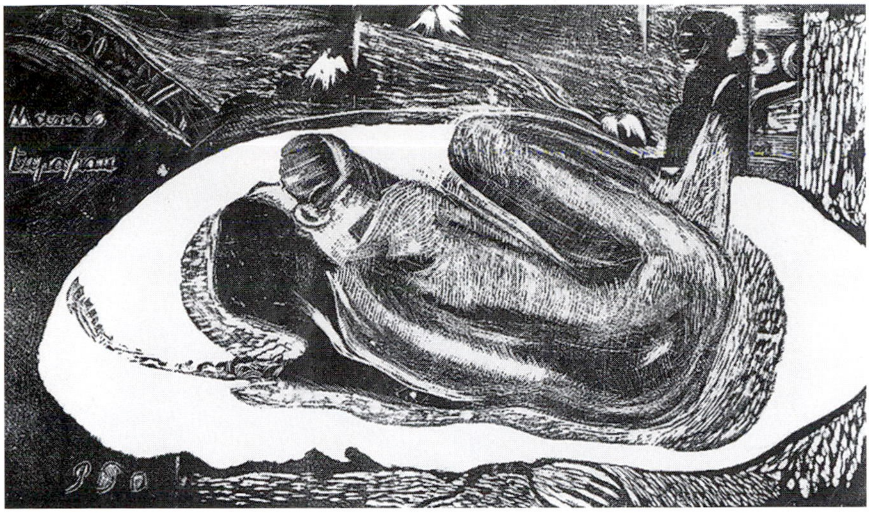

Fig. 276 Paul Gauguin, *Watched by the Spirit of the Dead (Manao Tupapau)*, 1893.
Woodcut, printed in black, block, $8\frac{1}{16} \times 14$ in. Collection, The Museum of Modern Art, New York. Lillie P. Bliss Collection.

engravings of Moran's work—together with a number of paintings executed by him from the same sketches—were America's first views of the great western canyonlands.

The French artist Paul Gauguin detested the detailed effects achievable in wood engraving. He felt they made the print look more like a photograph than a woodcut. He considered his own wood engravings interesting because, he said, they "recall the primitive era."

Gauguin gave up the detailed linear representation achieved by expert cutting, and opted instead to compose with broad, bold, purposely coarse gestures. Whereas in a traditional woodcut the surface of the block would be cut away leaving black line on a predominantly white surface, Gauguin chose to leave large areas of surface uncut so that they would print in black. In a purposefully unrefined example of the wood engravers' method, he would scratch raggedly across this black surface to reveal form by means of white line on black. Every detail of Gauguin's print, *Watched by the Spirit of the Dead* (Fig. 276), reveals the presence of the artist at work—poking, gouging, slicing, scraping, and scratching into the block.

Linocut

Color can also be added to a print by creating a series of different blocks, one for each different color, each of which is aligned with the others in a process known as **registration.** In 1959, Picasso, working with linoleum instead of wood, simplified the process. This **linocut,** as it is called, is made from one linoleum block. After each successive stage of carving is completed, the block is printed. An all-yellow run of the print below (Fig. 277) was first made from an uncarved block. Picasso then cut into the linoleum, hollowing out the areas that now appear yellow on the print, so that they would not print again. Then he printed in blue. The blue area was then hollowed out, the plate reprinted again, in violet, and so on, through red, green, and finally black.

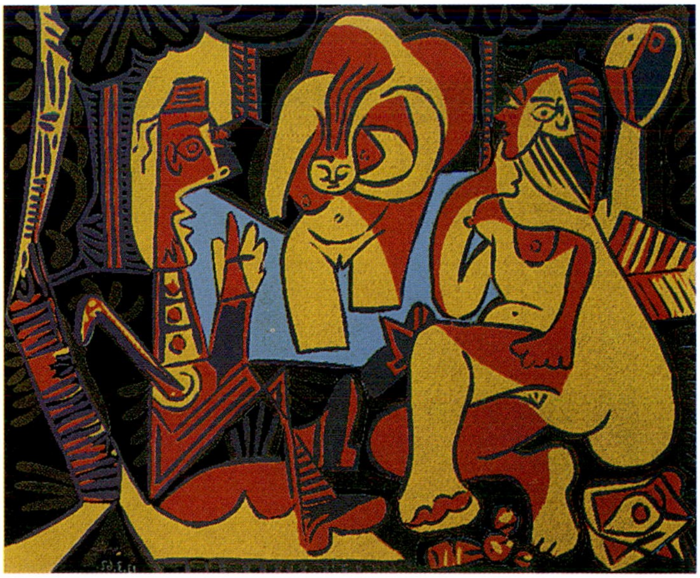

Fig. 277 Pablo Picasso, *Luncheon on the Grass, after Edouard Manet*, 1962.
Linoleum cut on Arches paper, $24\frac{3}{8} \times 29\frac{5}{8}$ in. The Metropolitan Museum of Art, New York. The Mr. and Mrs. Charles Kramer Collection, 1979. 1979.620.50.

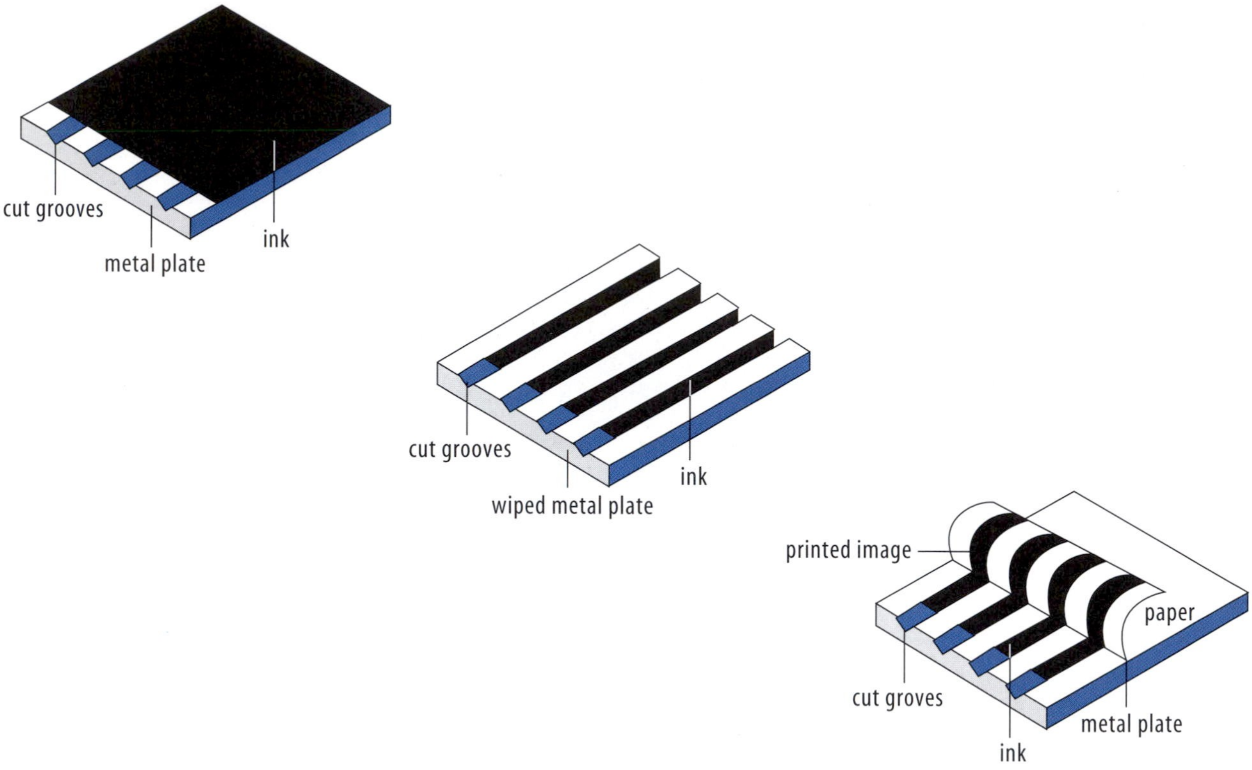

Fig. 278 Intaglio printmaking technique, general view.

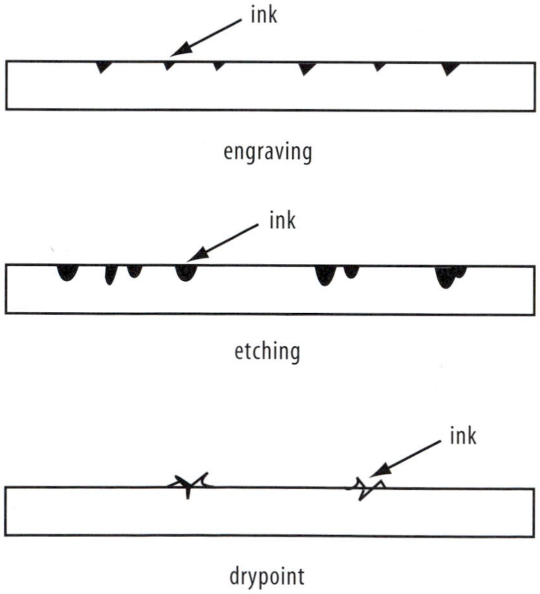

Fig. 279 Intaglio printmaking techniques, side views.

INTAGLIO PROCESSES

Relief processes rely on a *raised* surface for printing. With the **intaglio** process, on the other hand, the areas to be printed are *below* the surface of the plate. *Intaglio* is the Italian word for "engraving," and the method itself was derived from engraving techniques practiced by goldsmiths and armorers in the Middle Ages. In general, intaglio refers to any process in which the cut or incised lines on the plate are filled with ink (Figs. 278 and 279). The surface of the plate is wiped clean, and a sheet of dampened paper is pressed into the plate with a very powerful roller so that the paper picks up the ink in the depressed grooves. Since the paper is essentially pushed into the plate in order to be inked, a subtle but detectable elevation of the lines that result is always evident in the final print. Modeling and shading are achieved in the same way as in drawing, by hatching, cross-hatching, and often **stippling**—where, instead of lines, dots are employed in greater and greater density the deeper and darker the shadow.

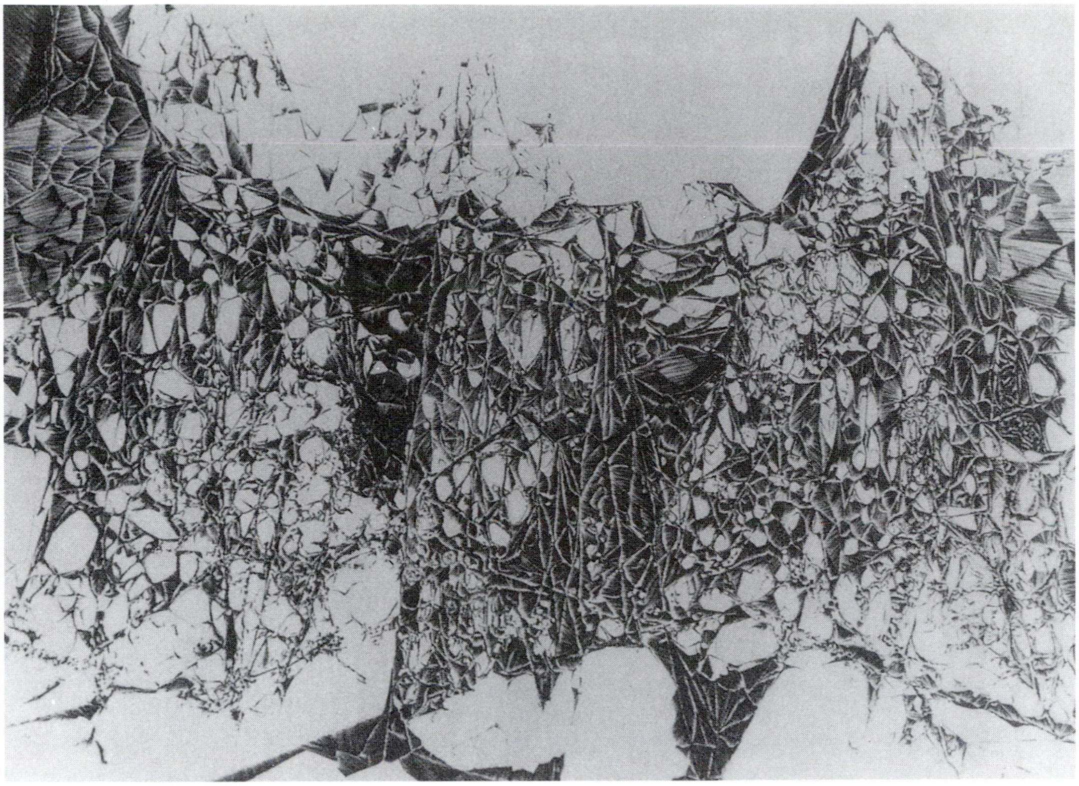

Fig. 280 Wendell H. "Bud" Black, *Mountainscape,* 1956.
Engraving on copper, 19 × 26 in. Private collection.

Engraving

Engraving is accomplished by pushing a small V-shaped metal rod, called a **burin,** across a metal plate, usually of copper or zinc, forcing the metal up in slivers in front of the line. These slivers are then removed from the plate with a hard metal scraper. Depending on the size of the burin used and the force with which it is applied to the plate, the results can range from almost microscopically fine lines to ones so broad and coarse that they can be felt with a finger tip.

The wide variety of lines possible in engraving can be seen in Bud Black's *Mountainscape* (Fig. 280). The finest hatching is visible throughout, creating the many-faceted landscape of the glacial morain. Contrasting with these heavily engraved dark areas are white shapes defined by lightly engraved outlines that take on the appearance of the finest lace.

Black was among the first students of Mauricio Lasansky, an Argentinean who was hired by the University of Iowa in 1945 expressly to make it the leading printmaking school in the United States. Lasansky initiated what was then a new model for arts education in the United States, championing a spirit of individual creativity within a community of artists. This community promised to result in ever more innovative and interesting work, as each teacher inspired the students, and as the students in turn became teachers, inspiring a new generation of students themselves. When Black graduated from Iowa he moved to the University of Colorado, where by 1963 he had created one of the most respected printmaking facilities in the nation.

The first time *Mountainscape* was seen, at the Oakland Print and Sculpture Annual in California, few members of the selection committee believed it was actually an engraving. They did not believe that such long lines could be achieved with a burin. The drawing seemed too fluid and light. But Black had discovered, in England, a Sellers hand-made burin called a model 0000, a "quadruple-ought," which was shaped something like a straightened bobby-pin. The result is a completely unique print.

Albrecht Dürer's Adam and Eve

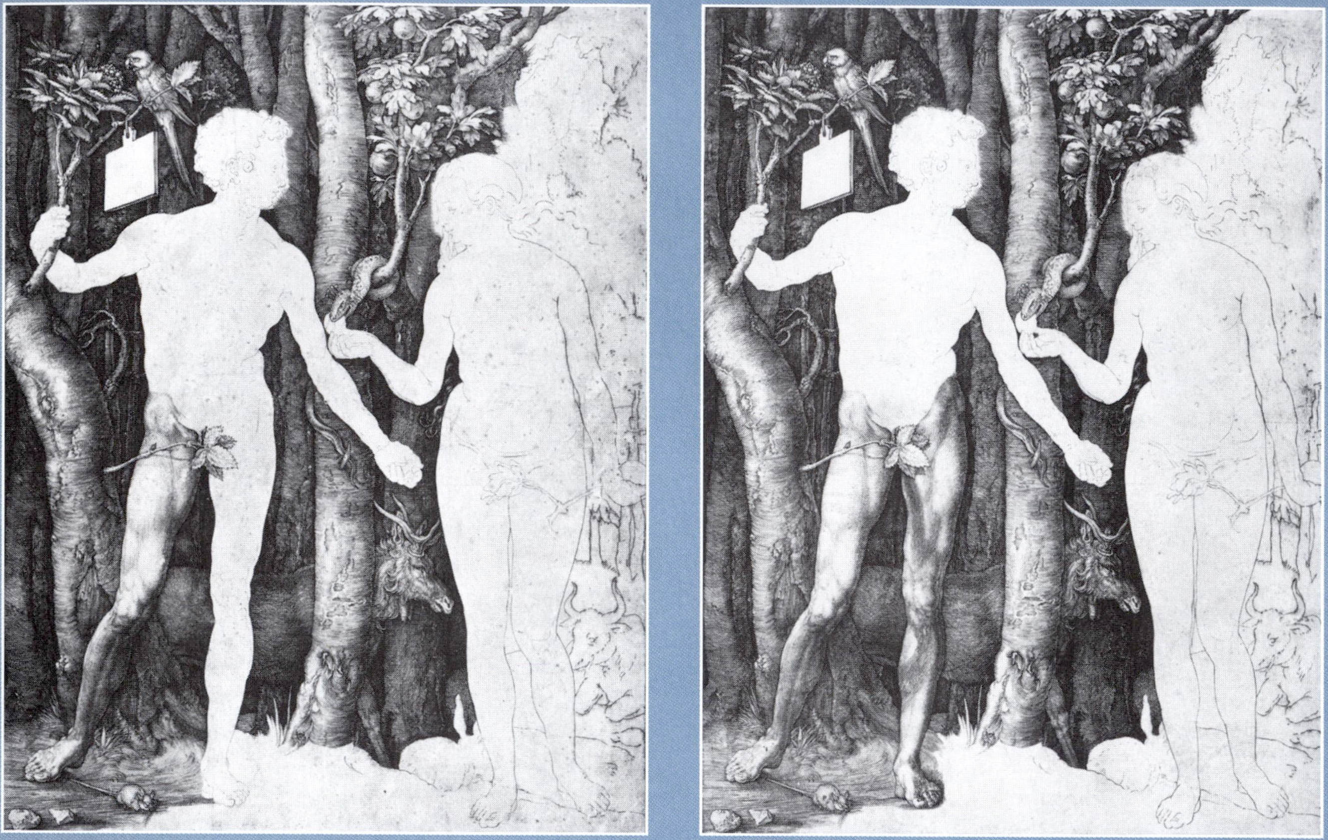

Figs. 281 and 282 Albrecht Dürer, *Adam and Eve,* 1st state and 2nd state, 1504.
Engravings, each $9\frac{7}{8} \times 7\frac{5}{8}$ in. Graphische Sannlung, Albertina, Wien.

One of the greatest of the early masters of the intaglio process was Albrecht Dürer. Trained in Nuremberg from 1486 to 1490, he was the godson of Anton Koberger, publisher of *The Nuremberg Chronicle.*

As an apprentice in the studio of Michael Wolgemut, who was responsible for many of the major designs in the *Chronicle,* Dürer may, in fact, have carved several of the book's woodcuts. By the end of the century, at any rate, Dürer was recognized as the preeminent woodcut artist of the day, and he had mastered the art of engraving as well.

Dürer's engraving of *Adam and Eve* (Fig. 283) is one of his finest. It is also the first of his works to be "signed" with the artist's characteristic tablet, including his Latinized name and the date of composition, here tied to a bough of the tree above Adam's right shoulder. Two of Dürer's trial proofs (Figs. 281 and 282) survive, providing us the opportunity to consider the progress of Dürer's print. The artist pulled each of these **states,** or stages in the process, so that he could consider how well his incised lines would hold ink and transfer it to paper, as well as to see the actual image, since on the plate it is reversed. In the white areas of both states we can see how Dürer outlined his entire composition with lightly incised lines. In the first state all of the background has been incised, except for the area behind Eve's left shoulder. Adam himself is barely realized. Dürer has only just begun to define his leg with hatching and cross-hatching. In the second state, Adam's entire lower body and the ground around his left foot have been realized. Notice how hatching and cross-hatching serve to create a sense of real volume in Adam's figure.

The print is rich in iconographical meaning. The cat at Eve's feet—a symbol of deceit, and perhaps sexuality as well—suggests not only Eve's feline character but, as it prepares to pounce on the mouse at Adam's feet, Adam's susceptibility to the female's wiles. The parrot perched over the sign is the embodiment of both wisdom and language. It contrasts with the evil snake that Eve is feeding. Spatially, then, the parrot and its attributes are associated with Adam, the snake and its characteristics with Eve. An early sixteenth-century audience would have immediately understood that the four animals on the right were intended to represent the four *humors*, the four bodily fluids thought to make up the human constitution. The elk represents melancholy (black bile), the cat anger and cruelty (yellow bile), the rabbit sensuality (blood), and the ox sluggishness or laziness (phlegm). The engraving technique makes it possible for Dürer to realize this wealth of detail.

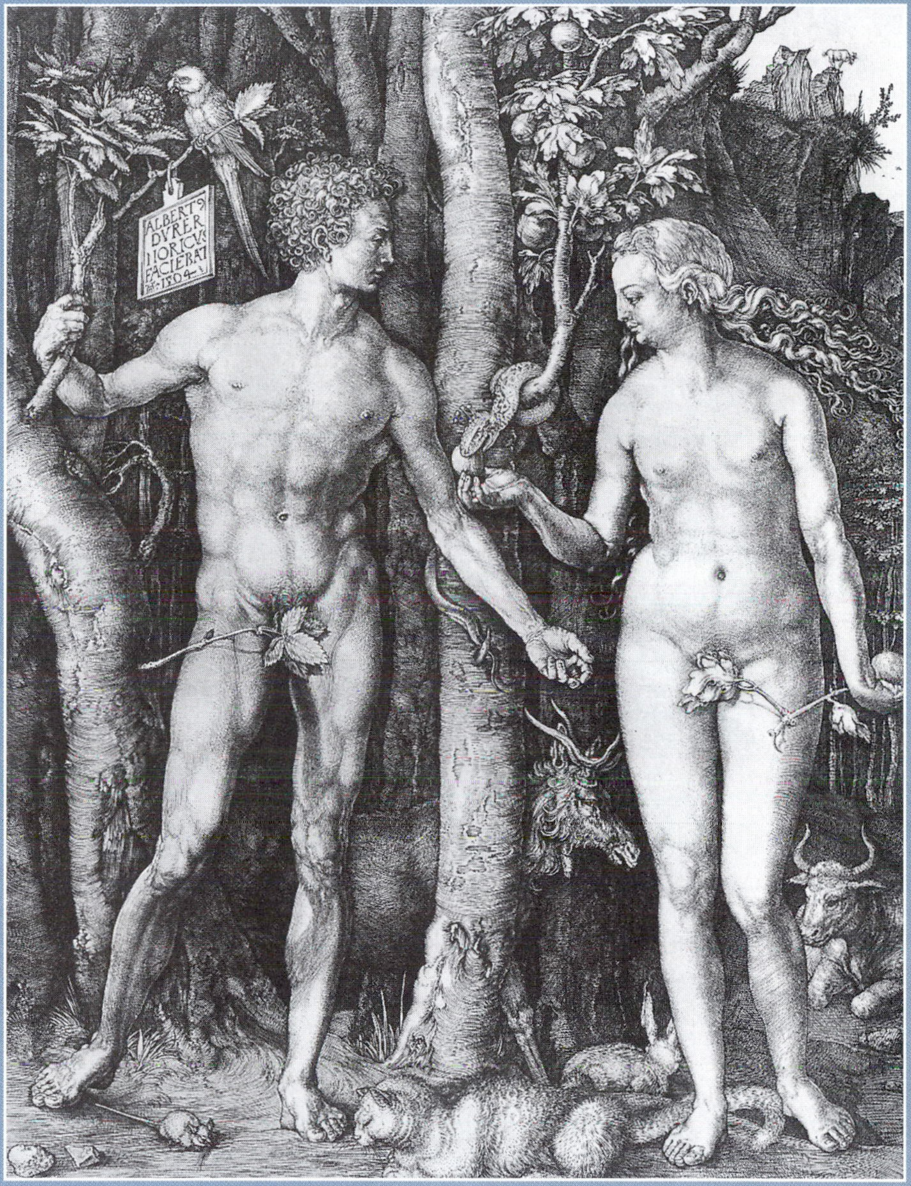

Fig. 283 Albrecht Dürer, *Adam and Eve,* 1504.
Engraving, 9 7/8 × 7 5/8 in. The Metropolitan Museum of Art, New York. Fletcher Fund, 1919. 19.73.1.

Etching

Etching is a much more fluid and free process than engraving and is capable of capturing something of the same sense of immediacy as the sketch. As a result, master draughtsmen, such as Rembrandt, readily took to the medium. It satisfied their love for spontaneity of line. Yet the medium requires, in addition, the utmost calculation and planning, an ability to manipulate chemicals that verges, especially in Rembrandt's greatest etchings, on wizardry, and a certain willingness to risk losing everything in order to achieve the desired effect.

Creating an etching is a twofold process, consisting of a drawing stage and an etching stage. The metal plate is first coated with an acid-resistant substance called a **ground,** and this ground is drawn upon. If a hard ground is chosen, then an etching needle is required to break through the ground and expose the plate. Hard grounds are employed for finely detailed linear work. Soft grounds, made of tallow or petroleum jelly, can also be utilized, and virtually any tool, including the artist's finger, can be used to expose the plate. The traditional soft-ground technique is often called *crayon*

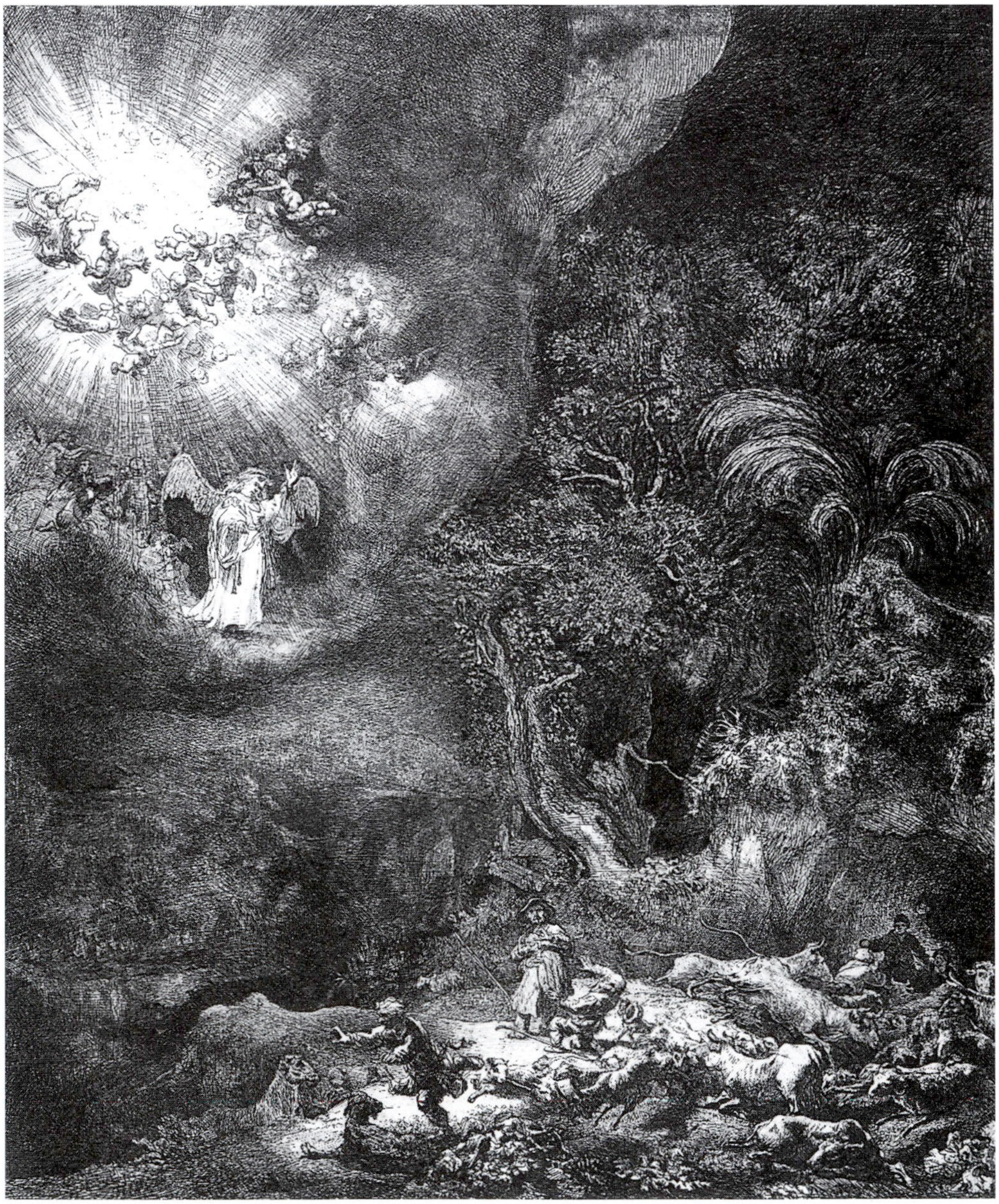

Fig. 284 Rembrandt van Rijn, *The Angel Appearing to the Shepherds,* 1634.
Etching, 10¼ × 8½ in. Rijksmuseum, Amsterdam.

or *pencil manner* because the final product so closely resembles pencil and crayon drawing. In this technique, a thin sheet of paper is placed on top of the ground and is drawn on with a soft pencil or crayon. When the paper is removed, it lifts the ground where the drawing instrument was pressed into the paper.

Whichever kind of ground is employed, the drawn plate is then set in an acid bath, and those areas that have been drawn are eaten into, or *etched,* by the acid. The undrawn areas of the plate are, of course, unaffected by the acid. The longer the exposed plate is left in the bath, and the stronger the solution, the greater the width and depth of the etched line. The strength of individual lines or areas can be controlled by removing the plate from the bath and **stopping out** a section by applying a varnish or another coat of ground over the etched surface. The plate is then resubmerged in the bath. The stopped-out lines will be lighter than those that are again exposed to the acid. When the plate is ready for printing, the ground is removed with solvent, and the print is made in the intaglio method.

Rembrandt's *The Angel Appearing to the Shepherds* (Fig. 284) is one of the most fully realized etchings ever printed, pushing the medium to its very limits. For this print Rembrandt altered the usual etching process. Fascinated by the play of light and dark, he wanted to create the feeling that the angel, and the light associated with her, was emerging *out* of the darkness. Normally, in etching, the background is white, since it is unetched and there are no lines on it to hold ink. Here Rembrandt wanted a black background, and he worked first on the darkest areas of the composition, creating an intricately crosshatched landscape of ever-deepening shadow. Only the white areas bathed in the angel's light remained undrawn. At this point, the plate was placed in acid and bitten as deeply as possible. Finally, the angel and the frightened shepherds in the foreground were worked up in a more traditional manner of etched line on a largely white ground. It is as if, at this crucial moment of the New Testament, when the angel announces the birth of Jesus, Rembrandt reenacts, in his manipulation of light and dark, the opening scenes of the Old Testament—God's pronouncement in Genesis, "Let there be light."

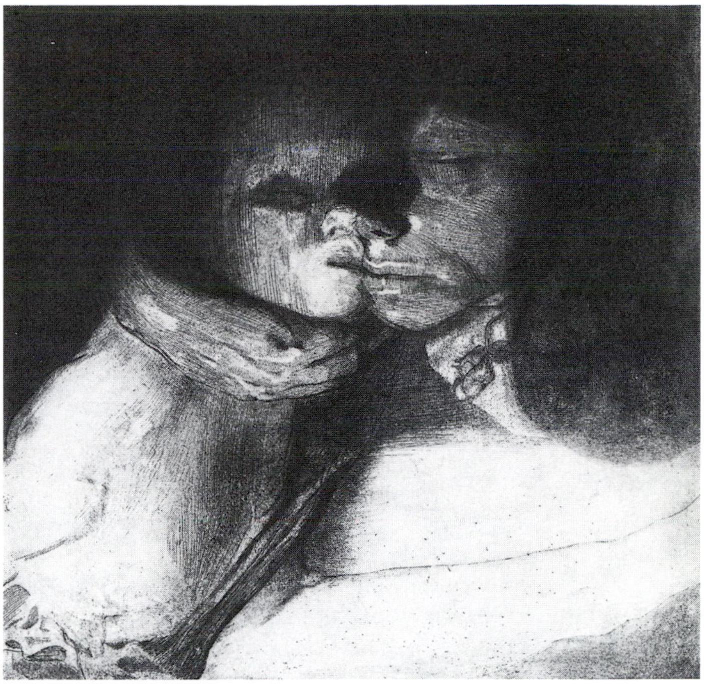

Fig. 285 Käthe Kollwitz, *Death and a Woman Struggling for a Child,* 1911.
Etching, 16 1/8 × 16 3/16 in. Museum of Modern Art, New York. Gift of Mrs. Theodore Boettger.

The dynamic play between dark and light achieved by Rembrandt would be used to great expressive effect in the work of the German Expressionist artist Käthe Kollwitz. Kollwitz, renowned for the quality of her graphic work, chose as her artistic subject matter the poor and downtrodden, especially mothers and children. Deliberately avoiding the use of color in her work, she preferred the sense of emotional conflict and opposition that could be realized in black and white.

In 1914, at the beginning of World War I, Kollwitz's son Peter was killed. The drama of the battle between the life-giving mother and the forces of death that we witness in *Death and a Woman Struggling for a Child* (Fig. 285) painfully foreshadows her own tragedy. It is hard to say just whose hand is reaching around the child's throat—the mother's or death's. What is clear, however, is that in the dark and deeply inked shadow created where the mother presses her child's forehead hard against her own face is expressed a depth of feeling and compassion virtually unsurpassed in the history of art.

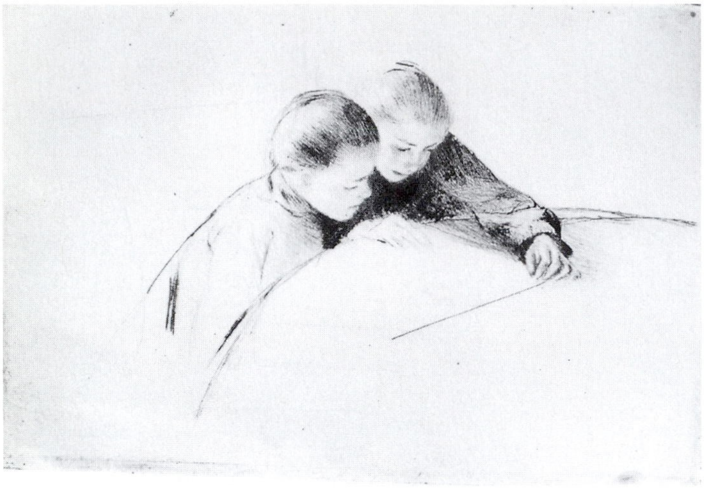

Fig. 286 Mary Cassatt, *The Map (The Lesson)*, 1890.
Drypoint, $6\,^3/_{16} \times 9\,^3/_{16}$ in.
Joseph Brooks Fair Collection,

Drypoint

A third form of intaglio printing is known as **drypoint.** The drypoint line is scratched into the copper plate with a metal point that is pulled across the surface, not pushed as is the case in engraving. A ridge of metal, called a **burr,** is pushed up along each side of the line, giving a rich, velvety, soft texture to the print when inked, as is evident in Mary Cassatt's *The Map* (Fig. 286). The softness of line generated by the drypoint process is especially appealing to Vija Celmins, whose obsessive attention to detail in *Drypoint—Ocean Surface* (Fig. 287) results in an almost photorealist representation of the sea. It is as if a haze sits over these waves, the softness of the drypoint burr imitating the thickness of the atmosphere itself. Because this burr quickly wears off in the printing process, it is rare to find a drypoint edition of more than 25 numbers, and the earliest numbers in the edition are often the finest.

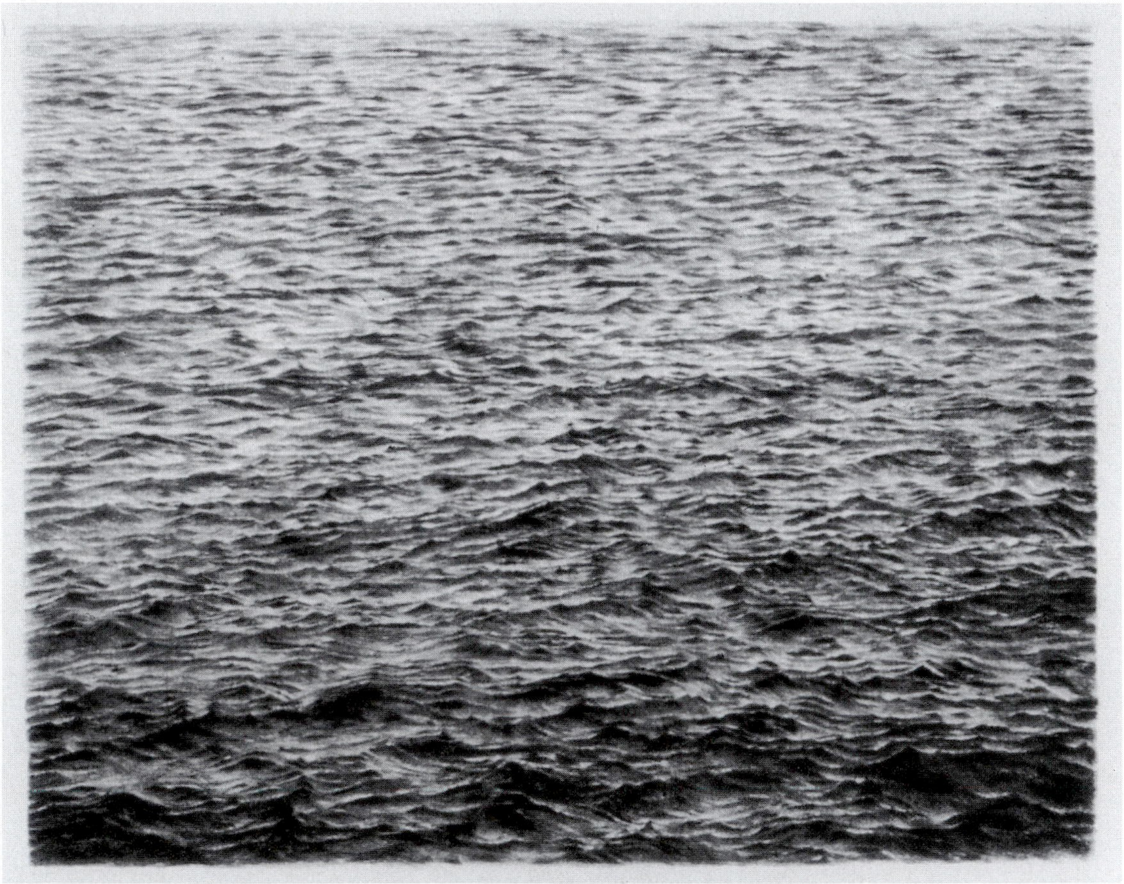

Fig. 287 Vija Celmins, *Drypoint—Ocean Surface*, 1984.
Drypoint, $26 \times 20\,^1/_4$ in. Courtesy of McKee Gallery, New York.

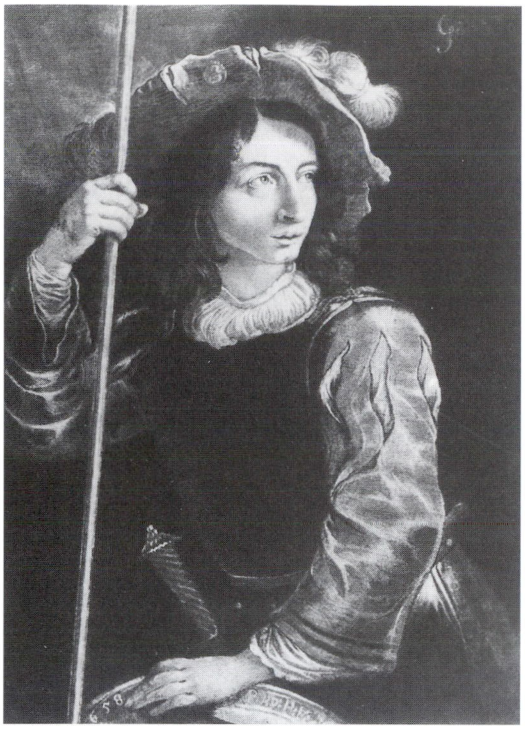

Fig. 288 Prince Rupert, *The Standard Bearer,* 1658.
Mezzotint. The Metropolitan Museum of Art, New York. Harris Brisbane Dick Fund, 1933. 32.52.32.

Mezzotint and Aquatint

Two other intaglio techniques should be mentioned, mezzotint and aquatint. **Mezzotint** is, in effect, a negative process. That is, the plate is first ground all over using a sharp, curved tool called a **rocker,** leaving a burr over the entire surface that, if inked, would result in a solid black print. The surface is then lightened by scraping away the burr to a greater or lesser degree. One of the earliest practitioners of the mezzotint process was Prince Rupert, son of Elizabeth Stuart of the British royal family and Frederick V of Germany, who learned the process from its inventor in 1654. Rupert is credited, in fact, with the invention of the rocking tool used to darken the plate. His *Standard Bearer* (Fig. 288) reveals the deep blacks from which the image has been scraped.

Like mezzotint, **aquatint** relies for its effect not on line but on tonal areas of light and dark. Invented in France in the 1760s, the method involves coating the surface of the plate with a porous ground through which acid can penetrate. Usually consisting of particles of resin or powder, the ground is dusted onto the plate, then set in place by heating it until it melts. The acid bites around each particle into the surface of the plate, creating a sandpaperlike texture. The denser the resin, the lighter the tone of the resulting surface. Line is often added later, usually by means of etching or drypoint.

Jane Dickson's *Stairwell* (Fig. 289) is a pure aquatint, printed in three colors, in which the roughness of the method's surface serves to underscore the emotional turmoil and psychological isolation embodied in her subject matter. "I'm interested," Dickson says, "in the ominous underside of contemporary culture that lurks as an ever present possibility in our lives. . . . I aim to portray psychological states that everyone experiences." In looking at this print, one can almost feel the acid biting into the plate, as if the process itself is a metaphor for the pain and isolation of the figure leaning forlornly over the bannister.

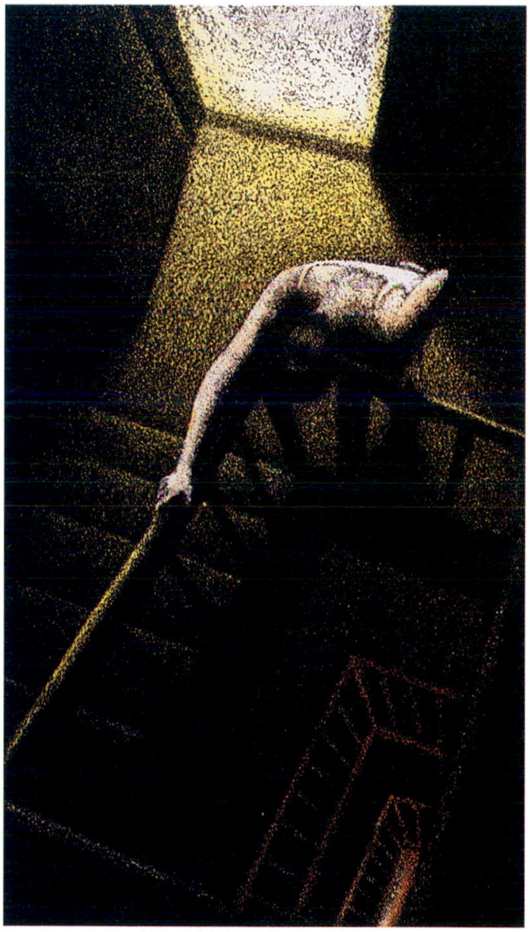

Fig. 289 Jane Dickson, *Stairwell,* 1984.
Aquatint on Rives BFK paper, $35\frac{3}{4} \times 22\frac{3}{4}$ in.
Mount Holyoke College Art Museum. The Henry Rox Memorial Fund for the Acquisition of Works by Contemporary Women Artists.

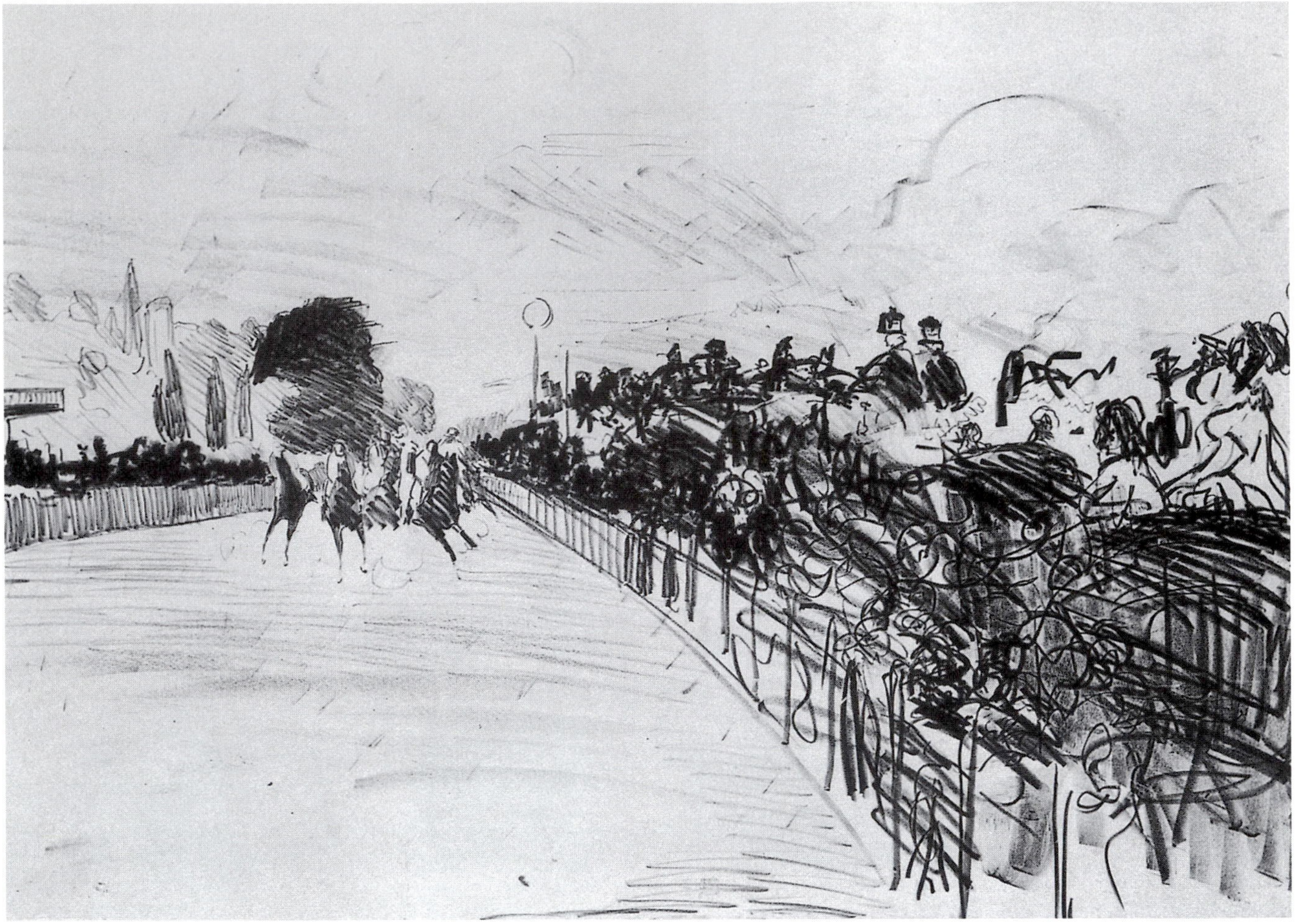

Fig. 290 Edouard Manet, *The Races,* 1865.
Lithograph, $14\frac{5}{8} \times 20\frac{1}{2}$ in. National Gallery of Art, Washington, DC. Rosenwald Collection.

LITHOGRAPHY

Lithography—meaning, literally, "stone writing"—is the chief **planographic print-making process,** meaning that the printing surface is flat. There is no raised or depressed surface on the plate to hold ink. Rather, the method depends on the fact that grease and water don't mix.

The process was discovered accidentally by a young German playwright named Alois Senefelder in the 1790s in Munich. Unsuccessful in his occupation, Senefelder was determined to reduce the cost of publishing his plays by writing them backwards on a copper plate in a wax and soap ground and then etching the text. But with only one good piece of copper to his name, he knew he needed to practice writing backwards on less expensive material, and he chose a smooth piece of Kelheim limestone, the material used to line the Munich streets and abundantly available. As he was practicing one day, his laundry woman arrived to pick up his clothes and, with no paper or ink on the premises, he jotted down what she had taken on the ground of the prepared limestone slab. It dawned on him to bathe the stone with nitric acid and water, and when he did so, he found that the acid had etched the stone and left his writing raised in relief above its surface.

Recognizing the commercial potential of his invention, he abandoned playwrighting to perfect the process. By 1798, he had discovered that if he drew directly on the stone with a greasy crayon, and then treated the entire stone with nitric acid, water, and gum arabic (a very tough substance, obtained from the acacia tree, that attracts and holds water), then ink would stick to the grease drawing but not to the treated and dampened stone. He also discovered that the acid and gum arabic solution did not actually *etch* the limestone. As a result, the same stone could be used again and again. The essential processes of lithography had been invented.

Possibly because it is so direct a process, actually a kind of drawing on stone, lithography has been the favorite printmaking medium of nineteenth- and twentieth-century artists. The gestural freedom it offers the artist, the sense of spontaneity and immediacy that can be captured in its line, is readily apparent in Edouard Manet's *The Races* (Fig. 290). More than a simple sketch of the event, the print is almost abstract, a whirl of motion and line that captures the furious pace of the race itself.

In the hands of Honoré Daumier, who turned to lithography to depict actual current events, the feeling of immediacy that the lithograph could inspire was most fully realized. From the early 1830s until his death in 1872, Daumier was employed by the French press as an illustrator and political caricaturist. Recognized as the greatest lithographer of his day, Daumier did some of his finest work in the 1830s for the monthly publication *L'Association Mensuelle*, each issue of which contained an original lithograph. His famous print *Rue Transnonain* (Fig. 291) is direct reportage of the outrages committed by government troops during an insurrection in the Parisian workers' quarters. He illustrates what happened in a building at 12 rue Transnonain on the night of April 15, 1834, when police, responding to a sniper's bullet that had killed one of their number and had appeared to originate from the building, revenged their colleague's death by slaughtering everyone inside. The father of a family, who had evidently been sleeping, lies dead by his bed, his child crushed beneath him, his dead wife to his right and an elder parent to his left. The foreshortening of the scene draws us into the lithograph's visual space, making the horror of the scene all the more real.

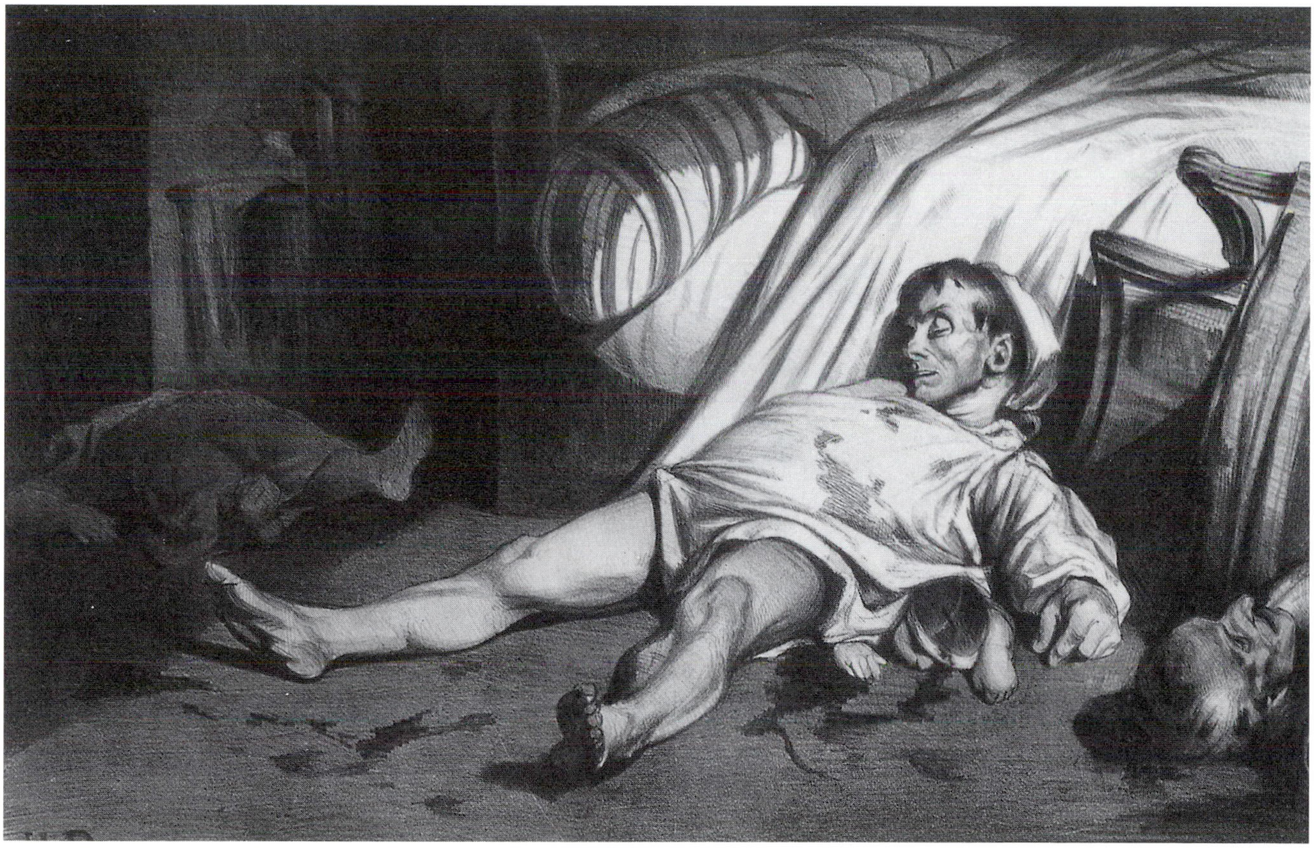

Fig. 291 Honoré Daumier, *Rue Transnonain, April 15, 1834*, 1834.
Lithograph, 11 ½ × 17 ⅝ in.
The Charles Derring Collection,

While lithography flourished as a medium throughout the twentieth century, it has enjoyed a marked increase in popularity since the late 1950s. In 1957 Tatyana Grosman established Universal Limited Art Editions (ULAE) in West Islip, New York. Three years later, June Wayne founded the Tamarind Lithography Workshop in Los Angeles with a grant from the Ford Foundation. While Grosman's primary motivation was to make available to the best artists a quality printmaking environment, one of Wayne's primary purposes was to train the printers themselves. Due to her influence, workshops sprang up across the country, including Gemini G.E.L. in Los Angeles, Tyler Graphics in Mount Kisco, New York, Landfall Press in Chicago, Cirrus Editions in Los Angeles, and Derrière l'Etoile in New York. In 1987, an exhibition of prints by women artists was held at the Mount Holyoke College Art Museum, which was inspired by Nancy Campbell's founding of the Mount Holyoke College Printmaking Workshop in 1984. Elaine de Kooning was the first resident artist at this workshop, and the series of prints she created there, one of which is reproduced here (Fig. 292), was inspired by the prehistoric cave drawings at Lascaux, France (see Chapter 16, "The Ancient World"). The medium of lithography allows de Kooning to use to best advantage the broad painterly gesture that she developed as an abstract expressionist painter in the 1950s and 1960s. In these prints she develops a remarkable tension between what might be called "the present tense" of her gesture, the sense that we can feel the very motion of her hand, and the "past tense" of her chosen image, the timelessness and permanence of the drawings at Lascaux.

Robert Rauschenberg's *Accident* (Fig. 293), printed at Universal Limited Art Editions in 1963, represents the spirit of innovation and experiment found in so much contemporary printmaking. At first, Rauschenberg, a post-abstract expressionist painter who included everyday materials and objects in his canvases, was reluctant to undertake printmaking. "Drawing on rocks," as he put it, seemed to him archaic. But Grosman was insistent that he try his hand at making lithographs at her West Islip studio. "Tatyana called me so often that I figured the only way I could stop her was to go out there," Rauschenberg says. He experimented with pressing all manner of materials down on the stone in order to see if they contained enough natural oil to leave an imprint that would hold ink. He dipped zinc cuts of old

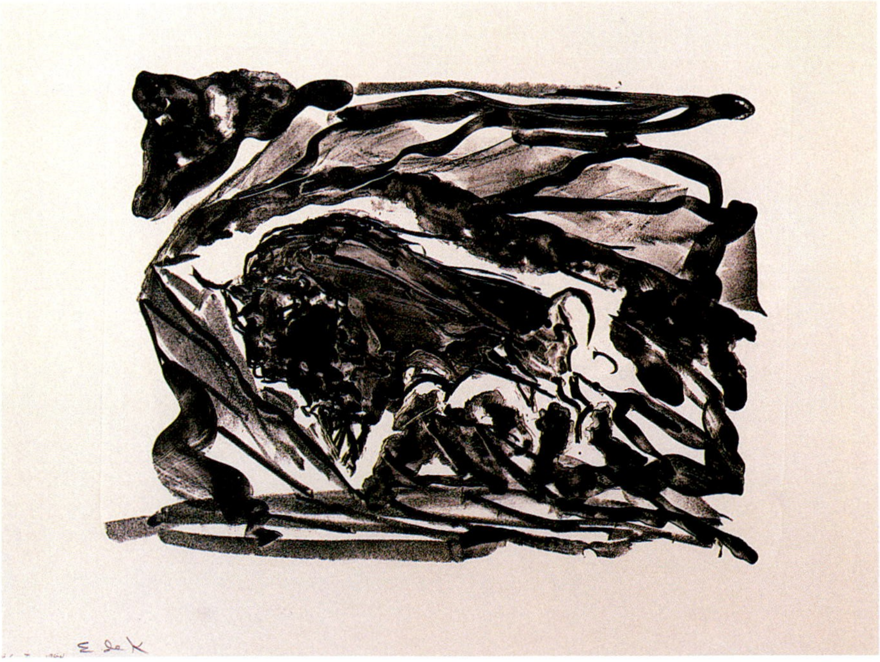

Fig. 292 Elaine de Kooning, *Lascaux #4,* 1984.
Lithograph on Arches paper, 15 × 21 in.
Mount Holyoke College Art Museum. Gift of the Mount Holyoke College Printmaking Workshop.

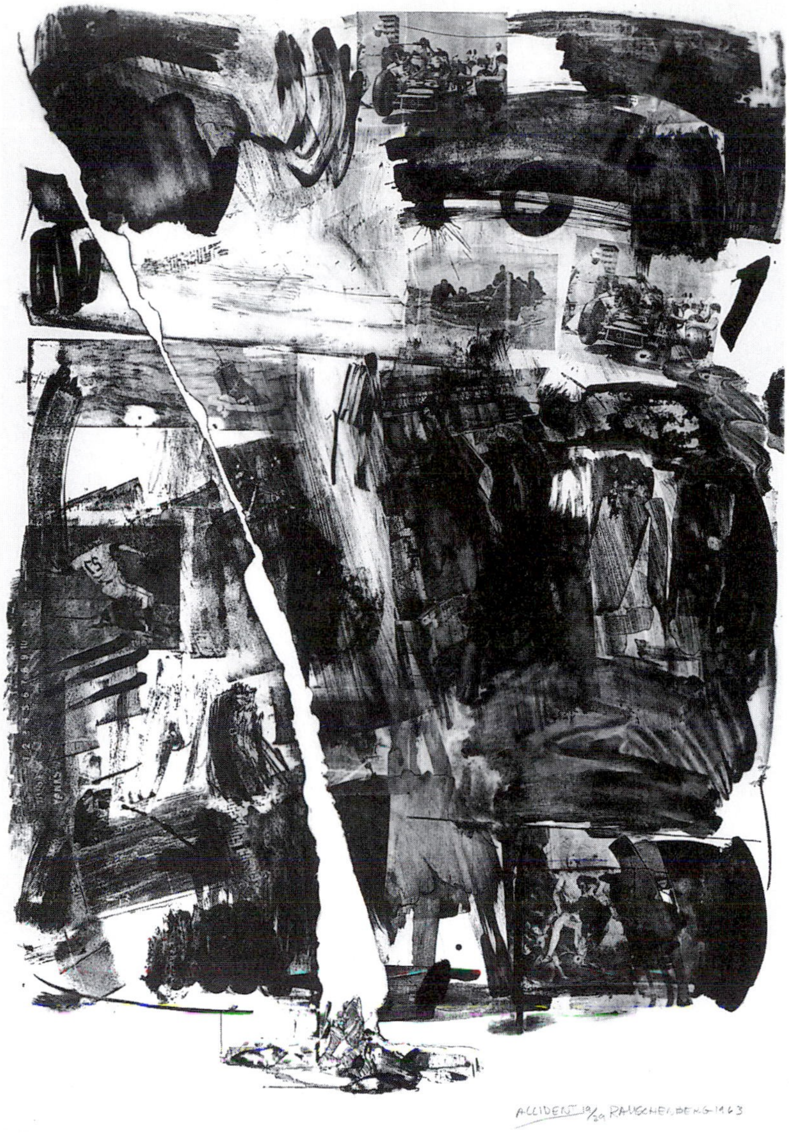

Fig. 293 Robert Rauschenberg, *Accident,* 1963.
Lithograph on paper, 41 × 29 in. In the Collection of The Corcoran Gallery of Art, Gift of the Women's Committee.

newspaper photos in **tusche**—a greasing liquid, which also comes in a hardened, crayon-like form, made of wax, tallow, soap, shellac, and lampblack, and which is the best material for drawing on a lithographic stone. *Accident* was created with these tusche-dipped zinc cuts.

As the first printing began, the stone broke under the press, and Rauschenberg was forced to prepare a new version of the piece on a second stone. Only a few proofs of this second state had been pulled when it too broke, an almost unprecedented series of catastrophes. It turned out that a small piece of cardboard lodged under the press's roller was causing uneven pressure to be applied to the stones. Rauschenberg was undaunted. He dipped the broken chips of the second stone in tusche, set the two large pieces back on the press, and lay the chips beneath them. Then, with great difficulty, his printer, Robert Blackburn, printed the edition of 29 plus artist's proofs. *Accident* was awarded the grand prize at the Fifth International Print Exhibition in Ljubljana, Yugoslavia, in 1963. Says Grosman: "Bob is always bringing something new, some new discovery" to the printmaking process.

June Wayne's Knockout

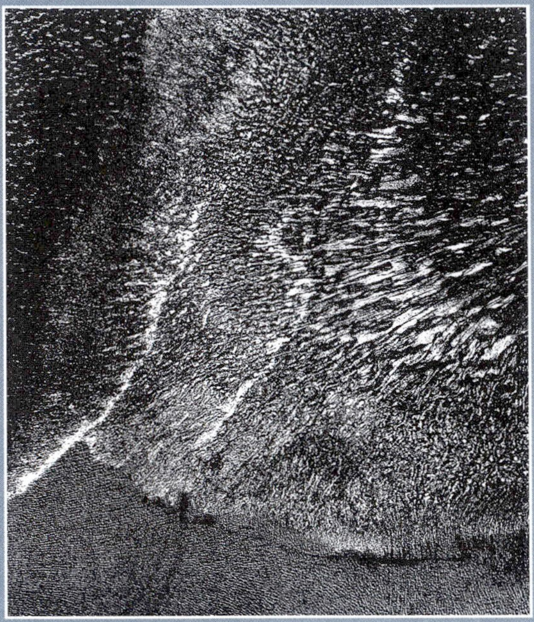

Fig. 294 June Wayne, *Stellar Roil, Stellar Winds 5,* 1978.
Lithograph, 11 × 9¼ in. (image). 18¾ × 14¾ in. (paper).

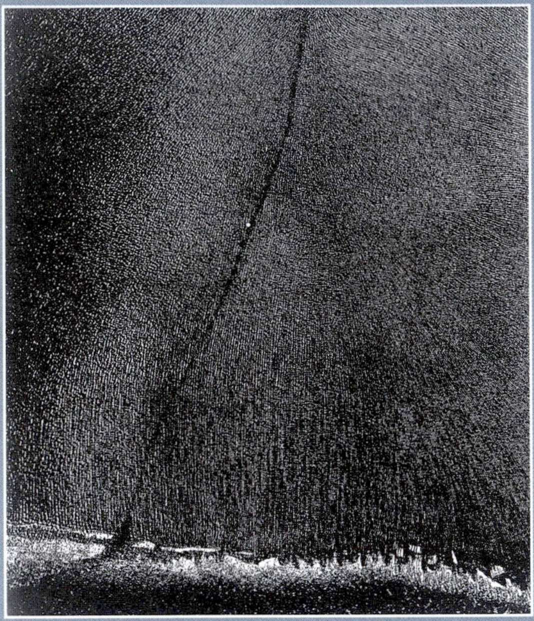

Fig. 295 June Wayne, *Wind Veil, Stellar Winds 3,* 1978.
Lithograph, 11⅛ × 9⅝ in. (image). 18¾ × 14¾ in. (paper).

One of the great innovators of the lithographic process in the last 50 years has been June Wayne, founder of the Tamarind Lithography Workshop. She founded the workshop because lithography was, in 1960, on the verge of extinction, like "the great white whooping crane," she says. "In all the world there were only 36 cranes left, and in the United States there were no master printers able to work with the creative spectrum of our artists. The artist-lithographers, like the cranes, needed a protected environment and a concerned public so that, once rescued from extinction, they could make a go of it on their own." By 1970, Wayne felt that lithography had been saved, and she arranged for Tamarind to move to the University of New Mexico, where it remains, training master printers and bringing artists to Albuquerque to work with them.

Wayne still lives and works in the original Tamarind Avenue studio in Los Angeles. "Every day," she says, "I push lithography and it reveals something new." With Edward Hamilton, who was trained at Tamarind and who was her personal printer for 14 years, beginning in 1974, Wayne has continually discovered new processes. She is inspired by the energy made visible in Leonardo da Vinci's deluge drawings (see Fig. 239), and she is equally inspired by modern science and space exploration—in her own words, by "the ineffably beautiful but hostile wilderness of astrophysical space." She regularly visits the observatory at Mount Palomar above Los Angeles, she is acquainted with leading physicists and astronauts, and she routinely reviews the images returned to earth by unmanned space probes. In 1975, experimenting with zinc plates and liquid tusche, she discovered that the two oxidized when combined and that the resultant textures created patterns reminiscent of skin, clusters of nebulae, magnetic fields, solar flares, or astral winds. In prints such as *Stellar Roil* (Fig. 294) and *Wind Veil* (Fig. 295), she felt that she was harnessing in the lithographic process the same primordial energies that drive the universe.

A long-time feminist, who sponsored the famous "Joan of Art" seminars in the 1970s designed to help women understand their professional possibilities, Wayne has turned her attention, in her 1996 print *Knockout* (Fig. 296), to a scientific discovery with implications about sexual politics. In November 1995, *The New York Times* reported that scientists had discovered that a brain chemical, nitric oxide, which plays a significant role in human strokes, also controls aggressive and sexual behaviour in male mice. Experiments in mice had indicated that by blocking the enzyme responsible for producing nitric oxide, incidence of stroke can be reduced by 70 percent. But in the course of experiments on so-called "knockout" mice, from whom the gene responsible for the enzyme had been genetically eliminated, scientists found that the male mice would fight until the dominant one in any cage would kill the others. Furthermore, paired with females, the male mice were violently ardent. "They would keep trying to mount the female no matter how much she screamed," according to the *Times*. It would appear, then, that nitric oxide curbs aggressive and sexual appetites, and it also appears that this function is sex-specific. Female mice lacking the same gene show no significant change in behavior.

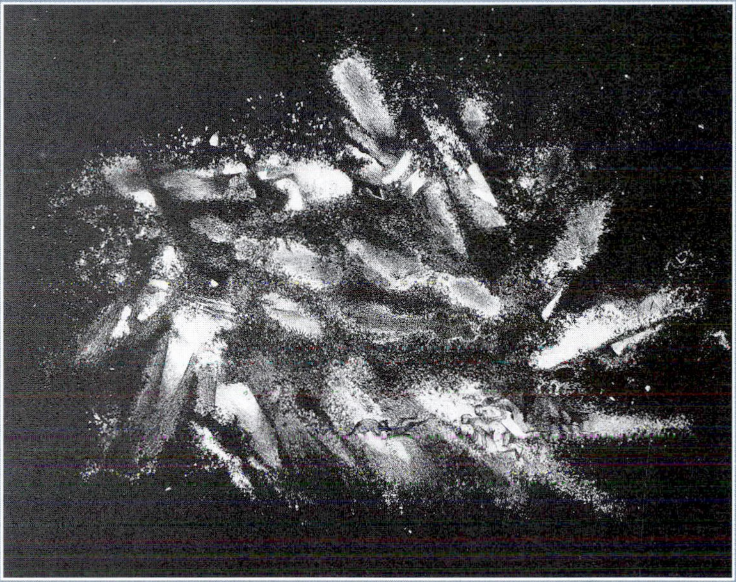

Fig. 296 June Wayne, *Knockout*, 1996.
Lithograph, 28¼ × 35⅞ in. (image). Bleed (paper).
© 1996 June Wayne, all rights reserved. Courtesy of the artist.

It is, of course, dangerous to extrapolate human behavior from the behavior of rodents, but from a feminist point of view, the implications of this discovery are enormous. The study suggests that male violence may in fact be genetically coded. *Knockout* is, in this sense, a feminist print, and Wayne's choice of a printer underscores this—Judith Solodkin of Solo Impression Inc. in New York, the first woman trained at Tamarind to become a master printer.

Knockout is an explosion of light, its deep black inks accentuating the whiteness of the paper, the shattered white bands piercing the darkness like screams of horror. At the bottom, three crouching spectators look on as a giant mouse, perhaps a product of genetic engineering, attacks a human victim.

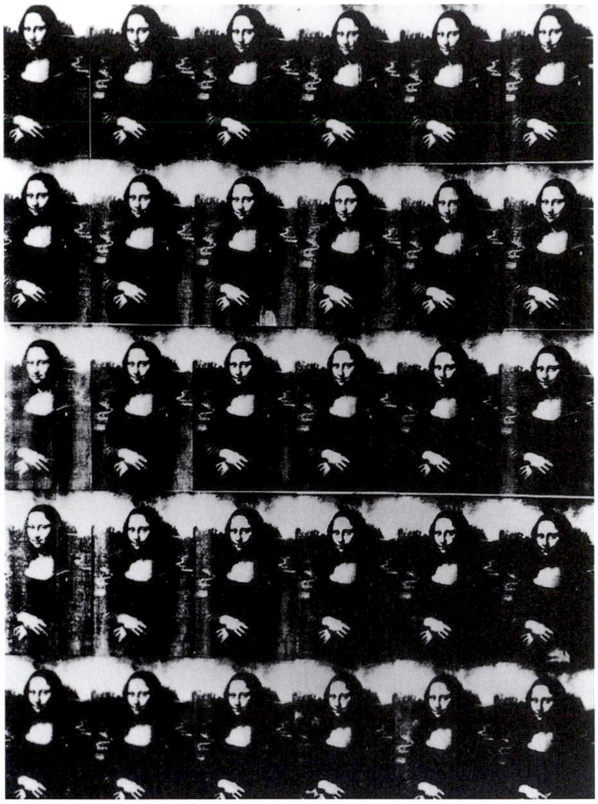

Fig. 297 Andy Warhol,
***30 Are Better than One,* 1963.**
Silkscreen ink and synthetic polymer paint on canvas, 110 × 82 in.

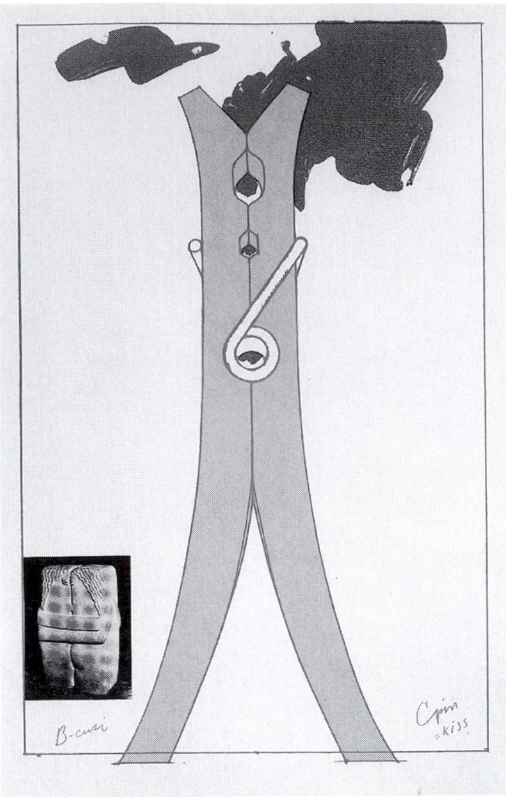

Fig. 298 Claes Oldenburg,
***Design for a Colossal Clothespin Compared to Brancusi's Kiss,* 1972.**
Silkscreen, $21\frac{1}{2} \times 13\frac{7}{8}$ in. Philadelphia Museum of Art: From the Friends of the Philadelphia Museum of Art.

SILKSCREEN PRINTING

Silkscreens are more formally known as **serigraphs,** from the Greek *graphos,* "to write," and the Latin *seri,* "silk." Unlike other printmaking media, no expensive, heavy machinery is needed to make a serigraph. The principles used are essentially the same as those required for stenciling, where a shape is cut out of a piece of material and that shape is reproduced over and over again on other surfaces by spreading ink or paint over the cutout. In serigraphy proper, shapes are not actually cut out. Rather, the fabric—silk, or more commonly today, nylon and polyester—is stretched tightly on a frame, and a stencil is made by painting a substance such as glue across the fabric in the areas where the artist does not want ink to pass through to the paper. Alternately, special films can be cut out and stuck to the fabric, or tusche can be utilized. This last allows the artist a freedom of drawing that is close to the lithographic process. The areas that are left uncovered are those that will print. Silkscreen inks are very thick, so that they will not run beneath the edge of the cutout, and must be pushed through the open areas of the fabric with the blade of a tool called a *squeegee.*

Serigraphy is the newest form of printmaking, though related stencil techniques were employed in textile printing in China and Japan as early as CE 550. Until the 1960s, serigraphy was used primarily in commercial printing, especially by the advertising industry. In fact the word "serigraphy" was coined in 1935 by the curator of the Philadelphia Museum of Fine Arts in order to differentiate the work of artists using the silkscreen in creative ways from that of their commercially oriented counterparts.

In the 1960s, serigraphy became an especially popular medium for Pop artists. Both Andy Warhol's *30 Are Better Than One* (Fig. 297) and

Claes Oldenburg's *Design for a Colossal Clothespin Compared to Brancusi's Kiss* (Fig. 298) take advantage of the fact that photographs can be transferred directly to the screen. Warhol repeats Leonardo's *Mona Lisa* thirty times, emphasizing its status as an artistic cliché and as a commodity comparable, in the American mind, to a can of Campbell's tomato soup. Oldenburg's print compares his own giant clothespin to Brancusi's famous sculpture *The Kiss* not merely to underscore their formal similarity—and it is striking—but, with tongue in cheek, to lend his own design the status of Brancusi's modern masterpiece. The print not only celebrates, with intentional irony, the commonplace and our culture's ability to monumentalize virtually anything, but also makes fun of art criticism's tendency to regard art in formal terms alone, the logic that might lead one to see the Brancusi and the clothespin in the same light.

MONOTYPES

There is one last kind of printmaking for us to consider, one that has much in common with painting and drawing. However, **monotypes** are generally classified as a kind of printmaking because they utilize both a plate and a press in the making of the image. Unlike other prints, however, a monotype is a unique image. Once it is printed, it can never be printed again.

In monotypes, the artist forms an image on a plate with printer's ink or paints, and the image is transferred to paper under pressure, usually by means of an etching press. Part of the difficulty and challenge of the process is that if a top layer of paint is applied over a bottom layer of paint on the plate, when printed, the original bottom layer will be the top layer and vice versa. Thus the foreground elements of a composition must be painted first on the plate, and the background elements over them. The process requires considerable planning.

Native American artist Fritz Scholder is a master of the medium. Scholder often works in series. Whenever he lifts a full impression of an image, a "ghost" of the original remains on the plate. He then reworks that ghost, revising and renewing it to make a new image. Since each print is itself a surprise—the artist never knows until the image is printed just what the work will look like—and since each print leaves a "ghost" that will spur him to new discoveries, the process is one of perpetual discovery and renewal. His *Dream Horse* monotypes, of which Figure 299 is an example, are symbolic of this process. The artist figuratively "rides" the horse, and its image, on his continuing imaginative journey.

Scholder's process is, in another sense, a summation of the possibilities of printmaking as a whole. As new techniques have been invented—from the relief processes to those of intaglio, to ligthography, silkscreen printing, and the monotype—the artist's imagination has been freed to discover new means of representation and expression. The variety of visual effects achievable in printmaking is virtually unlimited.

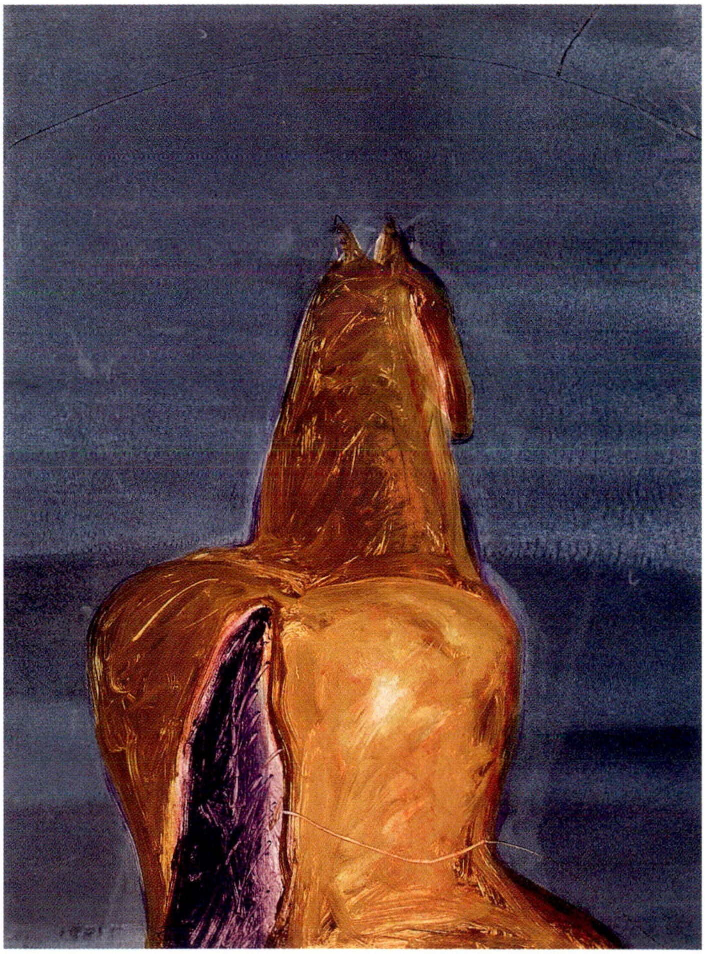

Fig. 299 Fritz Scholder, *Dream Horse G*, 1986.
Monotype, 30 × 22 in. Courtesy of the artist, Fritz Scholder.

CHAPTER 11

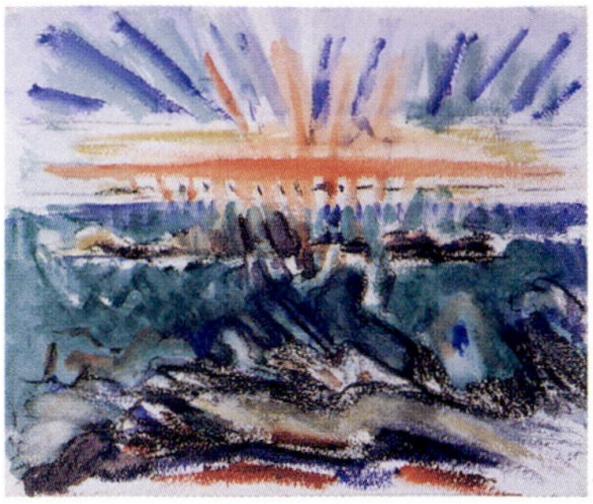

Painting

Early in the fifteenth century, a figure known as *La Pittura*—literally, "the picture"—began to appear in Italian art (Fig. 300). As art historian Mary D. Garrard has noted, the emergence of the figure of *La Pittura,* the personification of painting, could be said to announce the cultural arrival of painting as an art. In the Middle Ages, painting was never included among the liberal arts—those areas of knowledge that were thought to develop general intellectual capacity—which included rhetoric, arithmetic, geometry, astrology, and music.

While the liberal arts were understood to involve inspiration and creative invention, painting was considered merely a mechanical skill, involving, at most, the ability to copy. The emergence of *La Pittura* announced that painting was finally something more than mere copywork, that it was an intellectual pursuit equal to the other liberal arts, all of which had been given similar personification early in the Middle Ages.

In her *Self-Portrait as the Allegory of Painting* (Fig. 301), Artemisia Gentileschi presents herself as both a real person and as the personification of *La Pittura*. Iconographically speaking, Gentileschi may be recognized as *La Pittura* by virtue of the pendant around her neck that symbolizes *imitation*. And Gentileschi can imitate the appearance of things very well. She presents us a portrait of herself as she really looks. Still, in Renaissance terms, imitation means more than simply copying appearances; it is the representation of nature as seen by and through the artist's imagination. On the one hand, Gentileschi's multicolored garment alludes to her craft and skill as a copyist—she can imitate the effects of color—but on the other hand, her unruly hair stands for the imaginative frenzy of the artist's temperament. Thus, in this painting, she portrays herself both as a real woman and as an idealized personification of artistic genius, possessing all the intellectual authority and dignity of a Leonardo or a Michelangelo. Though in her time it was commonplace to think of women as intellectually inferior to men—"women have long dresses and short intellects" was a popular saying—here Gentileschi transforms painting from mere copywork, and transforms her own possibilities as a creative person in the process.

Nevertheless, from the earliest times, one of the major concerns of painting in the Western world has been representing the appearance of things. There is a famous story told by the historian Pliny about a contest between the Greek painters Parrhasius and Zeuxis as to who could make the most realistic image:

> *Zeuxis produced a picture of grapes so dexterously represented that birds began to fly down to eat from the painted vine. Whereupon Parrhasius designed so lifelike*

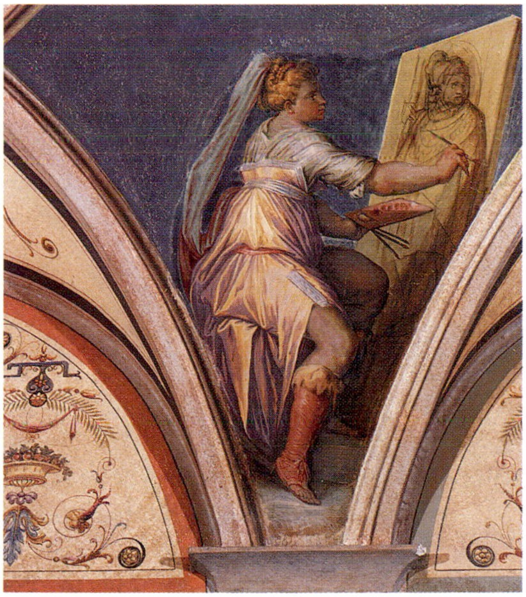

Fig. 300 Giorgio Vasari, *The Art of Painting,* 1542.
Fresco of the vault of the Main Room. Arezzo, Casa Vasari.
Canali Photobank, Capriolo, Italy.

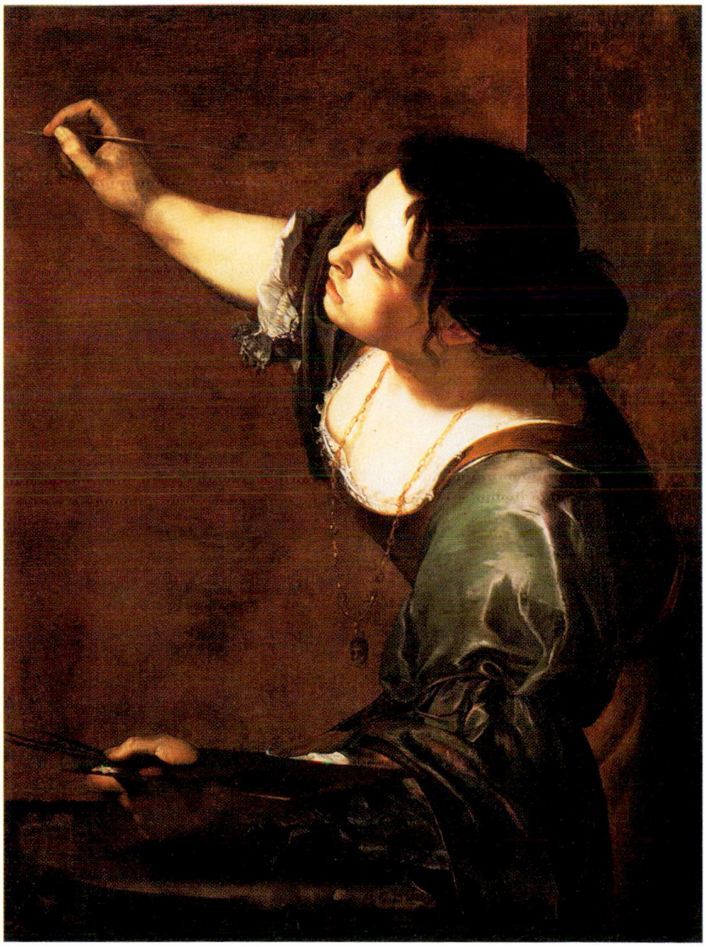

Fig. 301 Artemisia Gentileschi, *Self-Portrait as the Allegory of Painting,* 1630.
Oil on canvas, 35 1/4 × 29 in. London, Kensington Palace.
Collection of Her Majesty the Queen. Copyright reserved to Her Majesty Queen Elizabeth II.

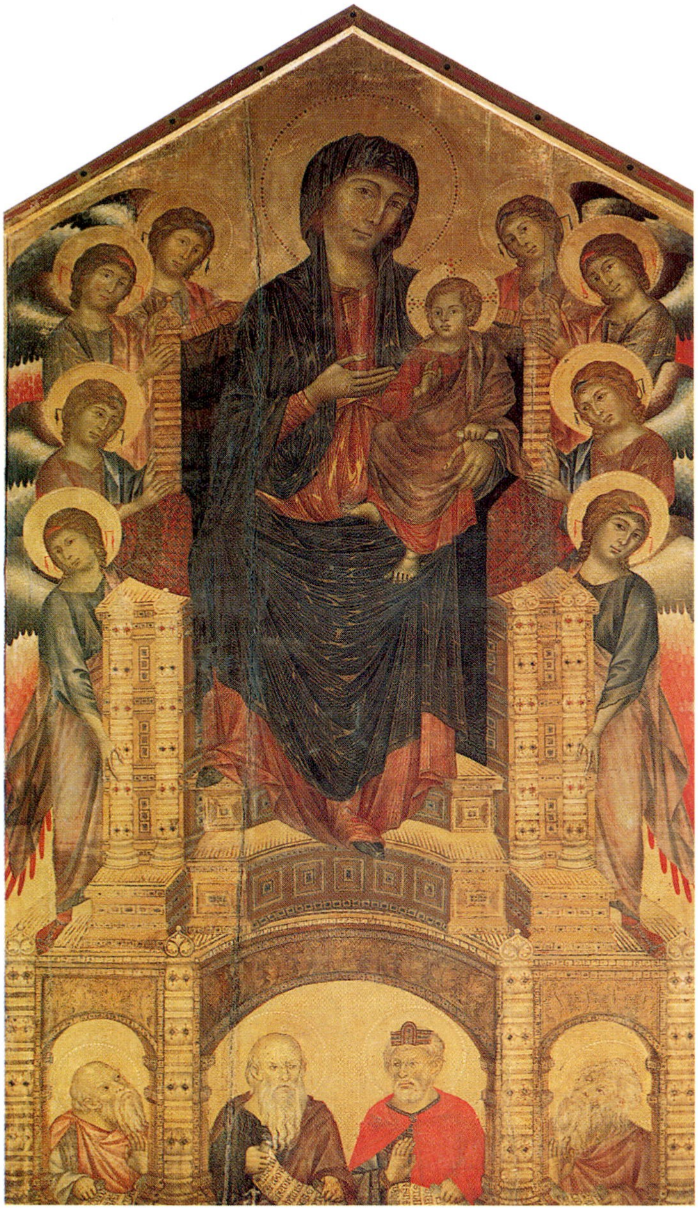

Fig. 302 Cimabue, *Madonna Enthroned,* c. 1280.
Tempera on panel, 12 ft 7 ½ in. × 7 ft. 4 in.
Galleria degli Uffizi, Florence.

a picture of a curtain that Zeuxis, proud of the verdict of the birds, requested that the curtain should now be drawn back and the picture displayed. When he realized his mistake, with a modesty that did him honor, he yielded up the palm, saying that whereas he had managed to deceive only birds, Parrhasius had deceived an artist.

This tradition, which views the painter's task as rivalling the truth of nature, has survived to the present day.

In the late Middle Ages, Dante wrote in the *Purgatory* section of his *Divine Comedy* about the painters Cimabue and Giotto: "Once, Cimabue was thought to hold the field / In painting; now it is Giotto's turn." If we compare altarpieces painted by both artists (Figs. 302 and 303), Giotto's only 30 years after Cimabue's, we can readily see that Giotto's is the more "realistic." However, this is not the realism to which we have since grown accustomed in, for instance, photography. For one thing, Giotto's Madonna and Child are far larger than the angels, raising all sorts of problems of scale. To early Renaissance eyes, however, Giotto's painting was a significant "advance" over the work of Cimabue. It is possible, for instance, to feel the volume of the Madonna's knee in Giotto's altarpiece, to sense actual bodies beneath the draperies that clothe his models. The neck of Cimabue's Madonna is a flat surface, while the neck of Giotto's Madonna is modeled and curves round beneath her cape. Cimabue's Madonna is chinless, her nose almost rendered in profile; the face of Giotto's Virgin is far more sculptural, as if real bones lie beneath her skin.

By this measure, the more faithful to nature a painting is, the more accurately it represents the real world, the greater is its aesthetic value. But if this were all there was to painting, then abstraction would be of little or no value. However, there are many types and styles of painting for which truth to nature is not of paramount importance. Think of modern abstract art. Even during the Renaissance, the concept of imitation, or **mimesis,** involved the creation of representations that transcended mere appearance, that implied the sacred or spiritual essence of things. This is the truth Gentileschi sought to reveal.

Painting, in other words, can outstrip physical reality, leave it behind, even when it is fully representational. It need not simply point at what it represents. It can suggest at least as much, and probably more, than it portrays. Another way to say this is that painting can be **connotative** as well as **denotative.** What a painting denotes is clearly before us: both Cimabue and Giotto have painted a Madonna and Child surrounded by angels. But what these paintings connote is something else again. To a thirteenth- or fourteenth-century Italian audience, both altarpieces would have been understood as depicting the ideal of love that lies between mother and child and, by extension, the greater love of God for mankind. The meaning, then, of these altarpieces exits on many levels. And although the relative realism of Giotto's painting is what secures its place in art history, its *didactic* function—that is, its ability to teach, to elevate the mind, in this case, to the contemplation of salvation—was at least as important to its original audience. Its truth to nature was, in fact, probably inspired by Giotto's desire to make an image with which its audience could readily identify.

In this chapter we will consider the art of painting. We will pay particular attention to how its various media developed in response to artists' desire to imitate reality and express themselves more and more fluently. But before we begin our discussion of these various painting media, we should be familiar with a number of terms that all the media share, and which are crucial to understanding how painting are made.

From prehistoric times to the present day, the painting process has remained basically the same. As in drawing, artists use **pigments,** or powdered colors, suspended in a **medium** or **binder** that holds the particles of pigment together. The binder protects the pigment from changes and serves as an adhesive to anchor the pigment to the **support,** or the surface on which the artist paints—a wall, a panel of wood, a sheet of paper, or a canvas. Different binders have different characteristics. Some dry more quickly than others. Some create an almost transparent paint, while others are *opaque*—that is, they cannot be seen through. The same pigment used in different binders will look different because of the differing degrees of each binder's transparency.

Since most supports are too absorbent to allow the easy application of paint, artists often *prime* (pre-treat) a support with a paint-like material called a **ground.** Grounds also make the support surface smoother or more uniform in texture. Many grounds, especially white grounds, increase the brightness of the final picture.

Finally, artists use **solvent** or **vehicle,** a thinner that enables the paint to flow more readily and that also cleans brushes. All water-based paints use water for a vehicle. Other paints, such as oil-based paints, require a different thinner—turpentine in the case of oil paint.

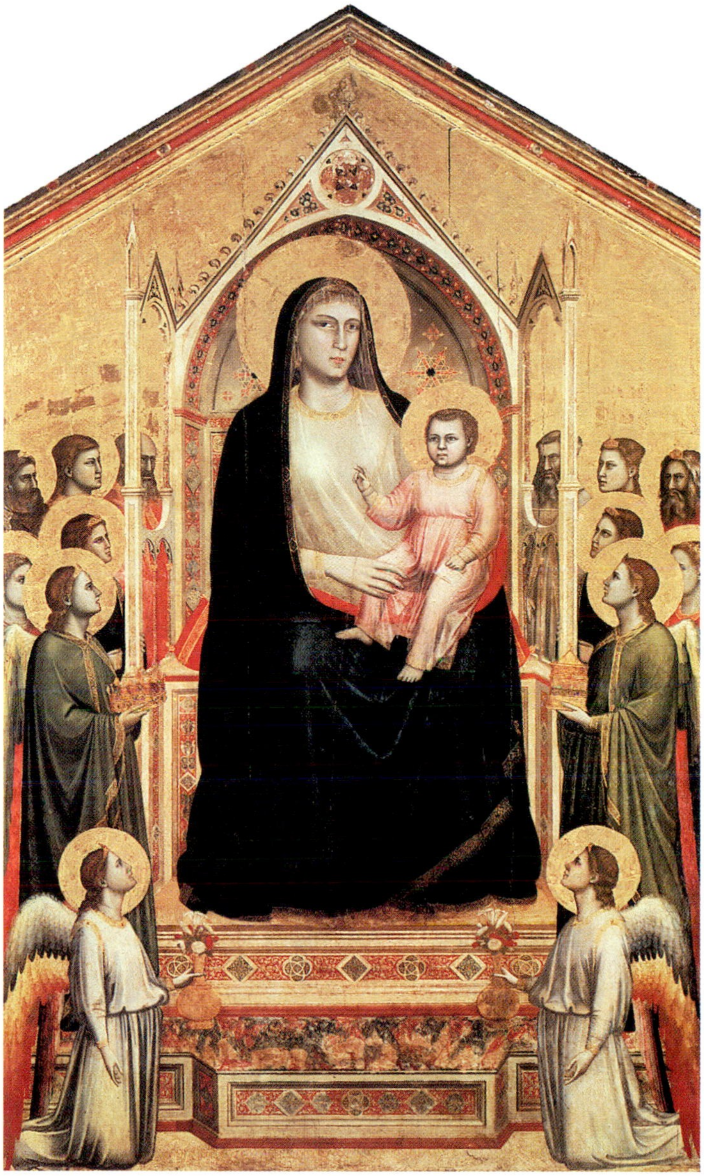

Fig. 303 Giotto, *Madonna and Child Enthroned,* c. 1310. Tempera on panel, 10 ft. 8 in. × 6 ft. 8 1/4 in. Galleria degli Uffizi, Florence.

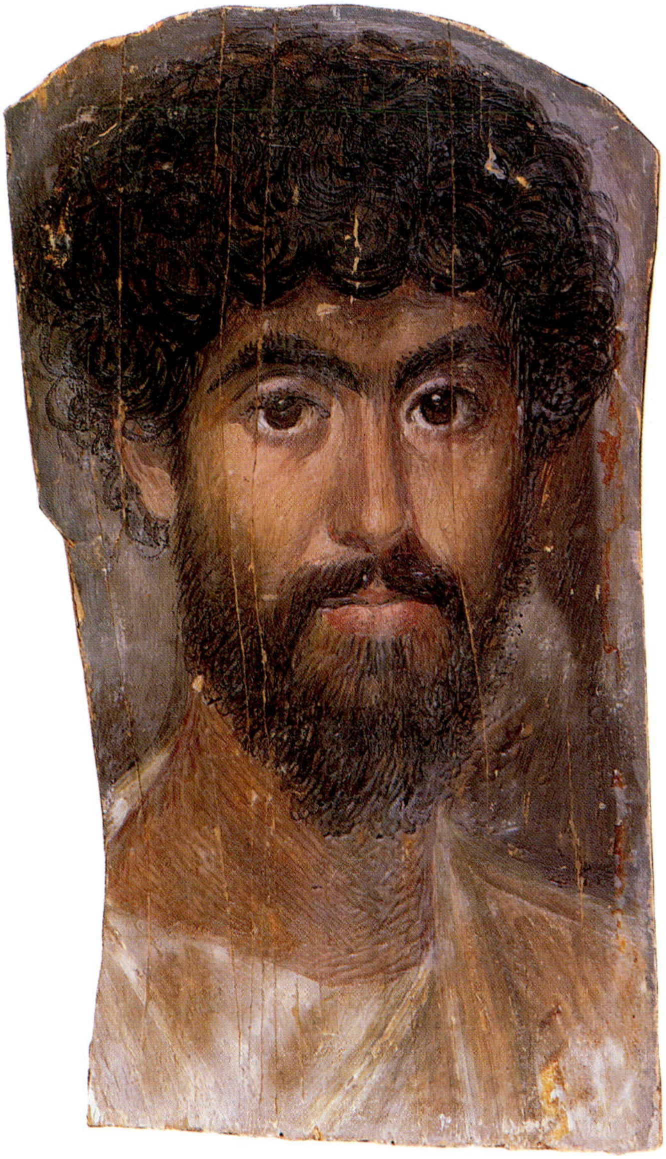

Fig. 304 ***Mummy Portrait of a Man,*** **Faiyum, c. CE 160–170.**
Encaustic on wood, 14 × 18 in.
Albright-Knox Art Gallery, Buffalo, New York. Charles Clifton Fund, 1938.

Each painting medium has unique characteristics and has flourished at particular historical moments. Though many have been largely abandoned as new media have been discovered—media that allow the artist to create a more believable image or that are simply easier to use—almost all continue to be used to some extent, and older media, such as encaustic and fresco, sometimes find fresh uses in the hands of contemporary artists.

ENCAUSTIC

Encaustic, made by combining pigment with a binder of hot wax, is one of the oldest painting media. It was widely used in classical Greece, most famously by Polygnotus, but very few paintings from that period survive. (The contest between Zeuxis and Parrhasius was probably conducted in encaustic.) The Hellenistic Greeks used it as well.

The largest number of surviving encaustic paintings comes from Faiyum in Egypt which, in the second century CE, was a thriving Roman province about 60 miles south of present-day Cairo. The Faiyum paintings are funeral portraits, which were attached to the mummy cases of the deceased, and they are the only indication we have of the painting techniques used by the Greeks. A transplanted Greek artist may, in fact, have been responsible for *Mummy Portrait of a Man* (Fig. 304), though we cannot be sure.

What is clear, though, is the artist's remarkable skill with the brush. The encaustic medium is a demanding one, requiring the painter to work quickly so that the wax will stay liquid. Looking at *Mummy Portrait of a Man*, we notice that while the neck and shoulders have been rendered with simplified forms, which gives them a sense of strength that is almost tangible, the face has been painted in a very naturalistic and sensitive way. The wide, expressive eyes and the delicate modeling of the cheeks make us feel that we are looking at a "real" person, which was clearly the artist's intention.

The extraordinary luminosity of the encaustic medium has led to its revival in recent years. Of all contemporary artists working in the medium, no one has perfected its use more than Jasper Johns, whose encaustic *Three Flags* (Fig. 8) we saw in Chapter 1.

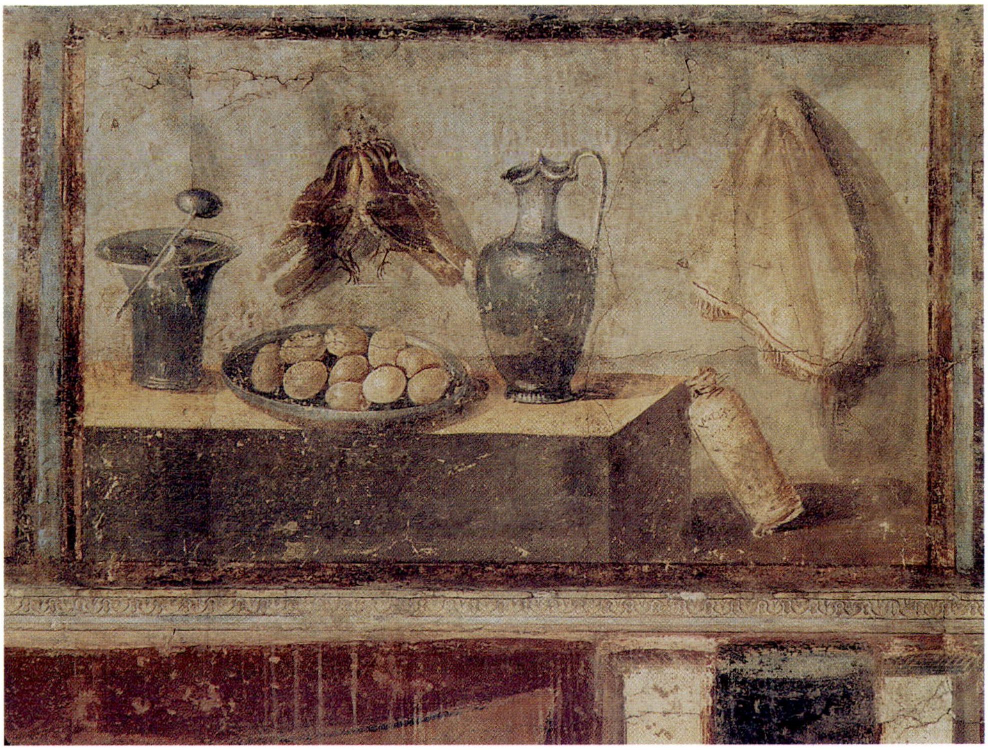

Fig. 305 ***Still Life with Eggs and Thrushes,*** **Villa of Julia Felix, Pompeii, before CE 79.**
Fresco, 35 × 48 in. National Museum, Naples.

FRESCO

Wall painting was practiced by the ancient Egyptians, Greeks, and Romans, as well as by Italian painters of the Renaissance. The preferred medium was **fresco,** in which pigment is mixed generally with limewater (a solution containing calcium hydroxide, or slaked lime), and then applied to a lime plaster wall that is either still wet or hardened and dry. If the paint is applied to a wet wall, the process is called ***buon fresco*** (Italian for "good" or "true fresco"), and if applied to a dry wall, ***fresco secco,*** or "dry fresco." In *buon fresco,* the wet plaster absorbs the wet pigment, and the painting literally becomes part of the wall. The artist must work quickly, plastering only as much wall as can be painted before it dries, but the advantage of the process is that it is extremely durable. In *fresco secco,* on the other hand, the pigment is combined with binders such as egg yolk, oil, or wax, and applied separately, at virtually any pace the artist desires. As a result, the artist can render an object with extraordinary care and meticulousness. The disadvantage of the *fresco secco* technique is that moisture can creep in between the plaster and the paint, causing the paint to flake off the wall. This is what happened to Leonardo da Vinci's *Last Supper* in Milan, which has peeled away to such a tragic degree that the image has almost disappeared, though it is today being carefully restored.

In the eighteenth century, many frescoes were discovered at Pompeii and nearby Herculaneum, where they had been buried under volcanic ash since the eruption of Mt. Vesuvius in CE 79. A series of still life paintings was unearthed in the years 1755–1757 that proved so popular in France that they led to the renewed popularity of the still life genre. This *Still Life with Eggs and Thrushes* (Fig. 305), from the Villa of Julia Felix, is particularly notable, especially the realism of the dish of eggs, which seems to hang over the edge of the painting and push forward into our space. The fact that all the objects in the still life have been painted lifesize adds to the work's sense of realism.

One of the most remarkable frescoes to survive Roman times is a wall-size rendering of a garden, found in the Villa of Livia, wife of the Emperor Augustus, in Prima Porta near Rome

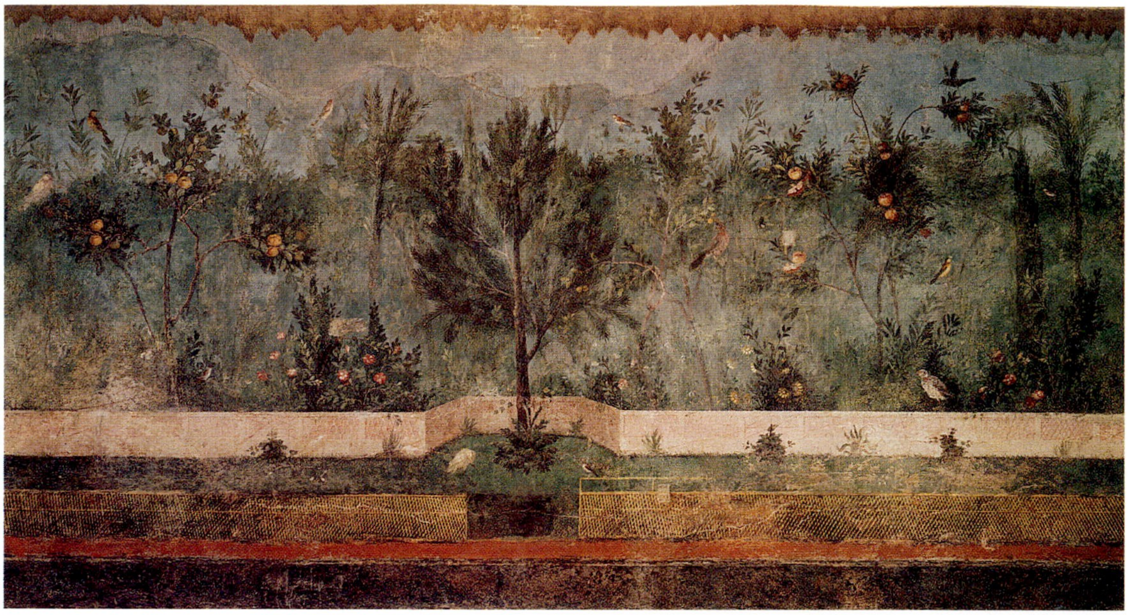

Fig. 306 (above) ***Garden,* Villa of Livia, Prima Porta, near Rome, late 1st century BCE.**
Fresco, H. 10 ft. Museo delle Terme, Rome.

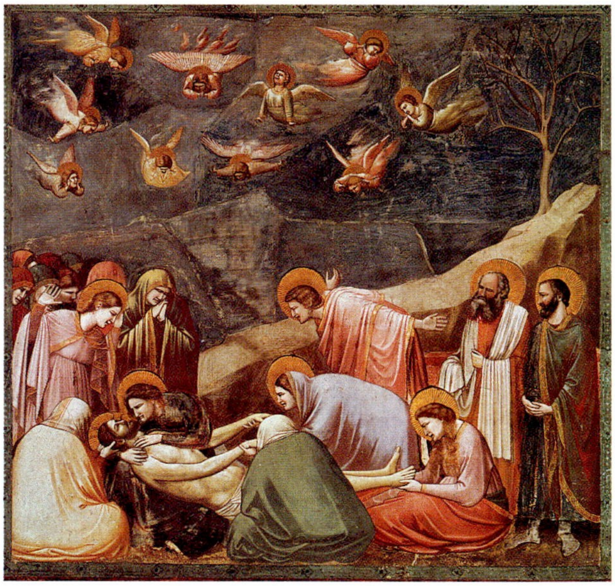

Fig. 307 (right) Giotto, *Lamentation,* c. 1305.
Fresco, approx. 70 × 78 in. Arena Chapel, Padua, Italy.

(Fig. 306). Not unlike certain back-lighted beer advertisements of rushing mountain streams commonly found in taverns today, the painting is designed to "open" the closed room to the out-of-doors, lending it the airiness and light of a cool summer evening. The artist is attempting to render an illusionistic, that is, realistic, space by means of both linear and atmospheric perspective.

This goal of creating the illusion of reality dominates fresco painting from the early Renaissance in the fourteenth century through the Baroque period of the late seventeenth century. It is as if painting at the scale of the wall invites, even demands, the creation of "real" space. In one of the great sets of frescoes of the early Renaissance, painted by Giotto in the Arena Chapel in Padua, Italy, this realist impulse is especially apparent.

The Arena Chapel was designed, possibly by Giotto himself, especially to house frescoes, and it contains 38 individual scenes that tell the stories of the lives of the Virgin and Christ. In the *Lamentation* (Fig. 307), the two crouching figures with their backs to us extend into our space in a manner similar to the bowl of eggs in the Roman fresco. Here, the result is to involve us in the sorrow of the scene. As the hand of the leftmost figure cradles Christ's head, it is almost as if it were our own. One of the more remarkable aspects of this fresco, however, is the placement of its focal point—Christ's face—in the lower left-hand corner of the composition, at the base of the diagonal formed by the stone ledge. Just as the angels in the sky above seem to be plummeting toward the fallen Christ, the tall figure on the right leans forward in a sweeping gesture of grief that mimics their descending flight.

The fresco artist's interest in illusionism culminated in the Baroque ceiling designs of the late seventeenth century. Among the most remarkable of these is *The Glorification of St. Ignatius* (Fig. 308), which Fra Andrea Pozzo painted for the church of Sant' Ignazio in Rome. Standing

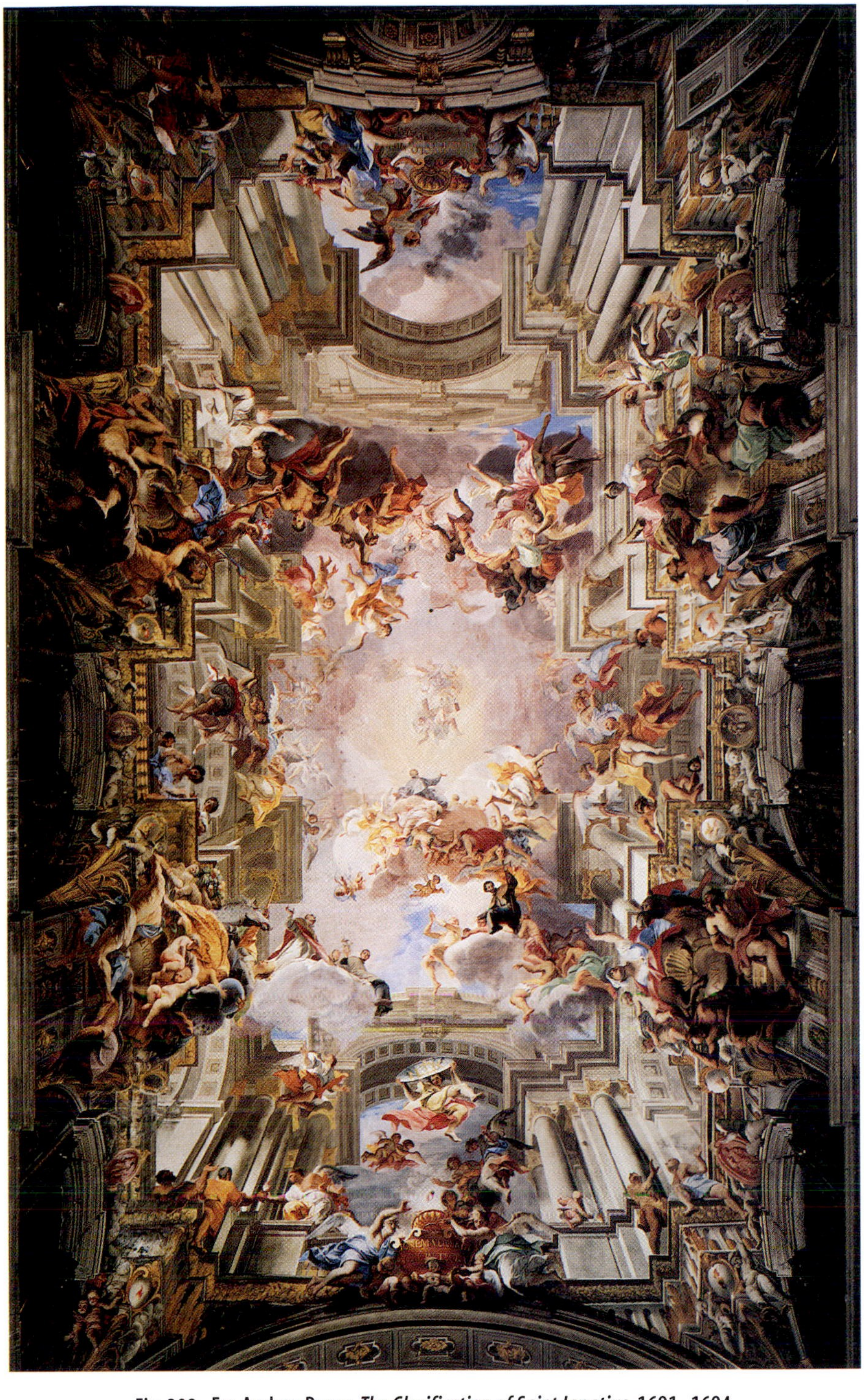

Fig. 308 Fra Andrea Pozzo, *The Glorification of Saint Ignatius,* 1691–1694.
Ceiling fresco. Nave of Sant' Ignazio, Rome.

in the nave, or central portion of the church, and looking upward, the congregation had the illusion that the roof of the church had been removed, revealing the glories of Heaven. A master of perspective, about which he wrote an influential treatise, Pozzo realized his effects by extending the architecture in paint one story above the actual windows in the vault. St. Ignatius, the founder of the Jesuit order, is shown being transported on a cloud toward the waiting Christ. The foreshortening of the many figures, becoming ever smaller in size as they rise toward the center of the ceiling, greatly adds to the realistic, yet awe-inspiring effect.

A revival of fresco painting occurred in Mexico in the 1920s when the new revolutionary Mexican government decided to support a public mural project that would teach and inform the public about revolutionary history. Diego Rivera's *Sugar Cane* (Fig. 309), one of eight portable murals created especially for a 1931 exhibition at the Museum of Modern Art, replicates an actual mural at the Palace of Cortez in Cuernavaca, Mexico. It depicts, on the one hand, the suppression of the working class by landowners, and on the other, the nobility of the suppressed workers.

TEMPERA

Until the end of the Middle Ages, most paintings were done in **tempera,** a medium made by combining water, pigment, and some gummy material, usually egg yolk. The paint was meticulously applied with the point of a fine red sable brush. Colors could not readily be blended, and, as a result, effects of *chiaroscuro* were accomplished by means of careful and gradual hatching. In order to use tempera, the painting surface, often a wood panel, had to be prepared with a very smooth ground not unlike the smooth plaster wall prepared for *buon fresco.* **Gesso,** made from glue and plaster of Paris or chalk, is the most common ground, and like wet plaster, it is fully absorbent, combining with the tempera paint to create an extremely durable and softly glowing surface unmatched by any other medium.

Sandro Botticelli's *Primavera* (Fig. 310), painted for a chamber next to the bedroom of his patron Lorenzo di Pierfrancesco de'Medici, is one of the greatest tempera paintings ever made. As a result of its restoration in 1978, we know a good deal about how it was painted. The support consists of eight poplar panels, arranged vertically and fastened by two horizontal strips of spruce. This support was covered with a gesso ground that hid the seams between the panels. Botticelli next outlined the trees and his human figures on the gesso and then painted the sky, laying blue tempera directly on the ground. The figures and trees

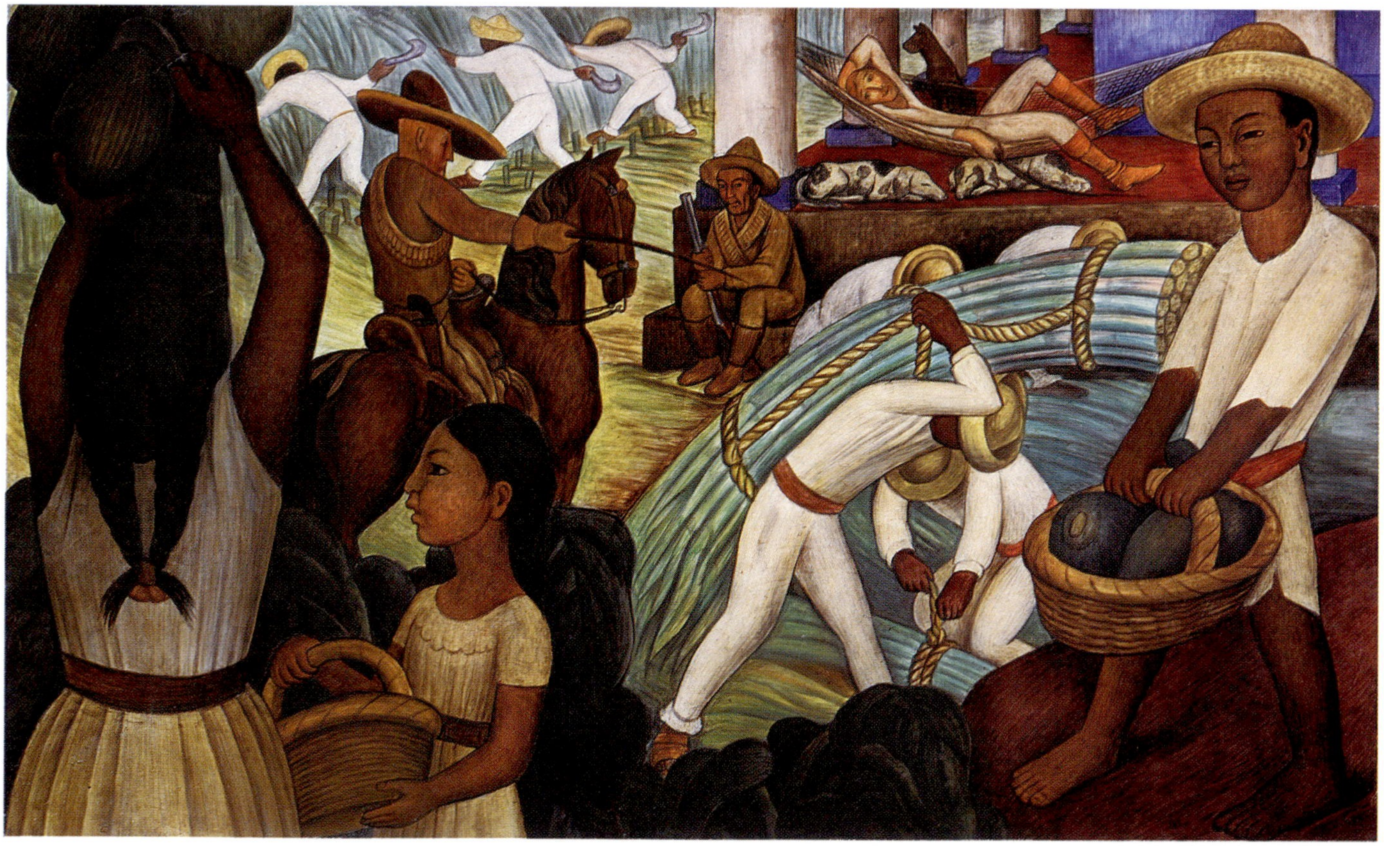

Fig. 309 José Diego Maria Rivera, *Sugar Cane,* 1931.
Fresco, 57 1/8 × 94 1/8 in. Philadelphia Museum of Art. Gift of Mr. and Mrs. Herbert Cameron Morris.

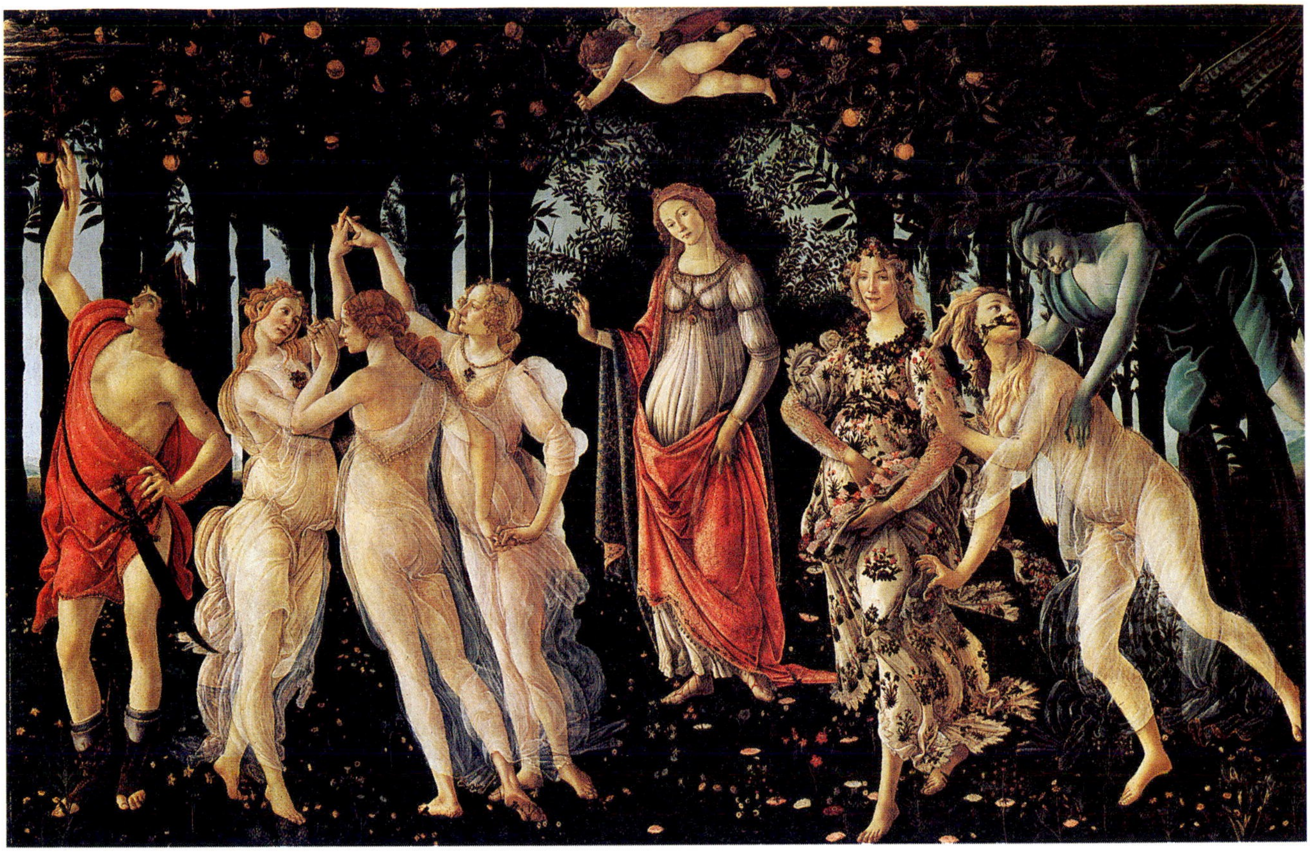

Fig. 310 Sandro Botticelli, *Primavera*, c. 1482.
Tempera on a gesso ground on poplar panel, 80 × 123 ¼ in. Galleria degli Uffizi, Florence.

were painted on an undercoat, white for the figures, black for the trees. The transparency of the drapery was achieved by layering thin yellow washes of transparent medium over the white undercoat. As many as thirty coats of color, transparent or opaque depending on the relative light or shadow of the area being painted, were required to create each figure.

The kind of detail the artist is able to achieve using egg termpera is readily apparent in *Braids* (Fig. 311) by Andrew Wyeth, one of the few contemporary artists to work almost exclusively in the medium. Wyeth's brushwork is so fine that each strand of hair escaping from his model's braids seems caught individually in the light. In fact, the most obvious effect that Wyeth achieves with the medium is that of light. Wyeth's figures often seem posed in the most intense late afternoon sun. The intensity is achieved by Wyeth setting his palette of warm colors against a deep black background. Thus, the inherently glowing surface of the tempera medium seems to glow even more acutely.

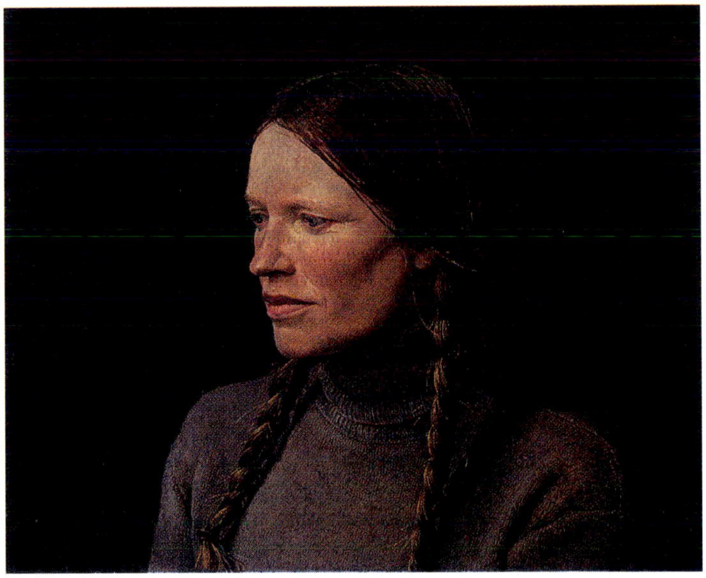

Fig. 311 Andrew Wyeth, *Braids*, 1979.
Egg tempera on canvas, 16 ½ × 20 ½ in.
Copyright © 1986 Leonard E. B. Andrews. Private Collection.
Photograph courtesy of Ann Kendall Richards, Inc., New York.

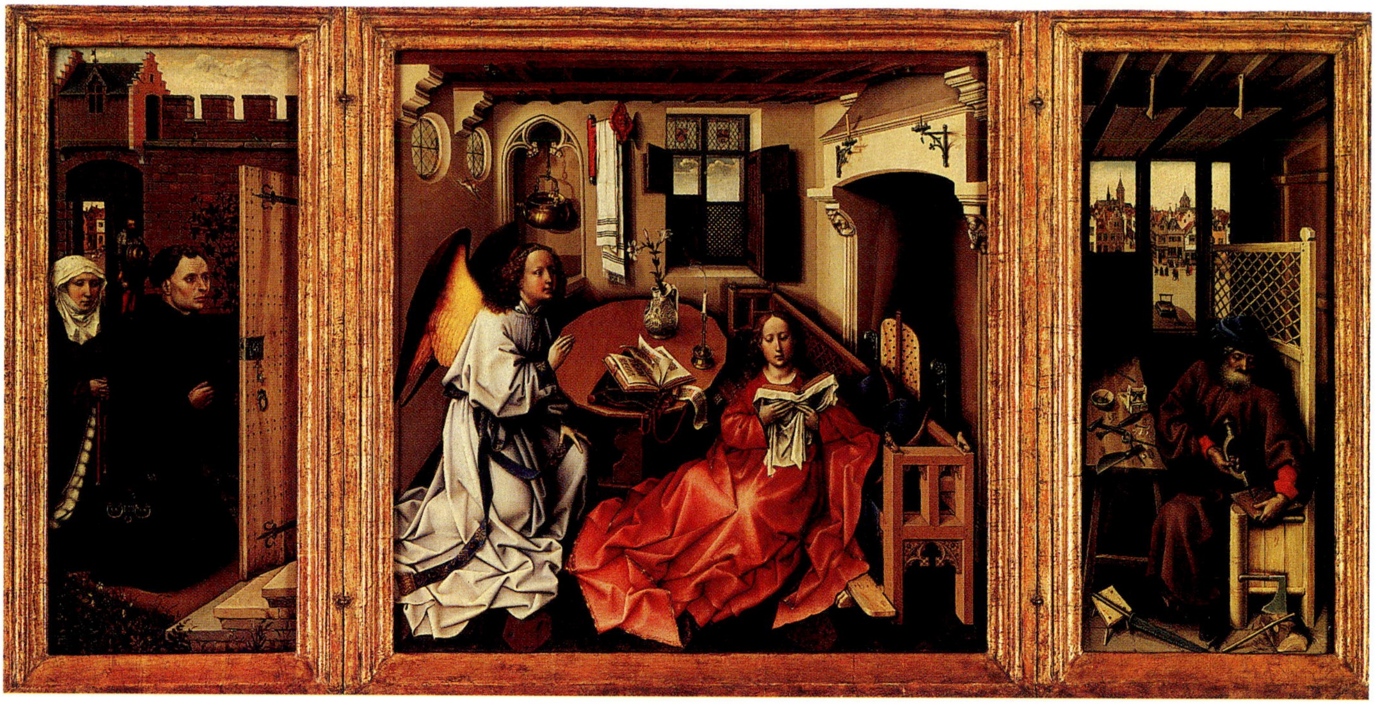

Fig. 312 The Master of Flémalle (Robert Campin?), ***Merode Altarpiece*, c. 1425–1430.**
Oil on wood panels, center 25 ¼ × 24 ⅞ in.; each wing 25 ⅜ × 10 ¾ in.
The Metropolitan Museum of Art, New York. The Cloisters Collection, 1956. 56.70.

OIL PAINTING

Oil paint is a far more versatile medium than tempera. It can be blended on the painting surface to create a continuous scale of tones and hues, many of which, especially darker shades, were not possible before its invention. As a result, the painter who uses oils can render the most subtle changes in light and achieve the most realistic three-dimensional effects, rivaling sculpture in this regard. Thinned with turpentine, it can become almost transparent. Used directly from the tube, with no thinner at all, it can be molded and shaped to create three-dimensional surfaces, a technique referred to as **impasto.** Perhaps most important, because its binder is linseed oil, oil painting is slow to dry. Whereas with other painting media artists had to work quickly, with oil they could rework their images almost endlessly.

It was the so-called Master of Flémalle, probably the artist Robert Campin, who first recognized the realistic effects that could be achieved with the new medium. In the *Merode Altarpiece* (Fig. 312), the Annunciation of the Virgin takes place in a fully realized Flemish domestic interior. The scene is not idealized. In the right-hand panel, Joseph the carpenter works as a real fifteenth-century carpenter might have. Shown kneeling outside the door in the left-hand panel are the donors, the couple who commissioned the altarpiece, dressed in fashionable fifteenth-century clothing.

The Master of Flémalle's contemporary, Jan van Eyck, developed oil painting even further. Van Eyck was particularly skilled both at realizing the effects of atmospheric perspective and at rendering the visible world in the utmost detail. What fascinates the viewer, in fact, about a painting like *The Madonna of Chancellor Rolin* (Fig. 313) is at least as much what can be seen out the window—from the garden to the distant mountains—as what is seen in the figures of the chancellor and the Virgin and Child who occupy the foreground. Our interest, like that of the two figures who lean over the wall beyond the garden, is drawn from the interior scene to the world beyond, almost as if we were being drawn away from the representation of an ideal world in art and into the representation of a real one.

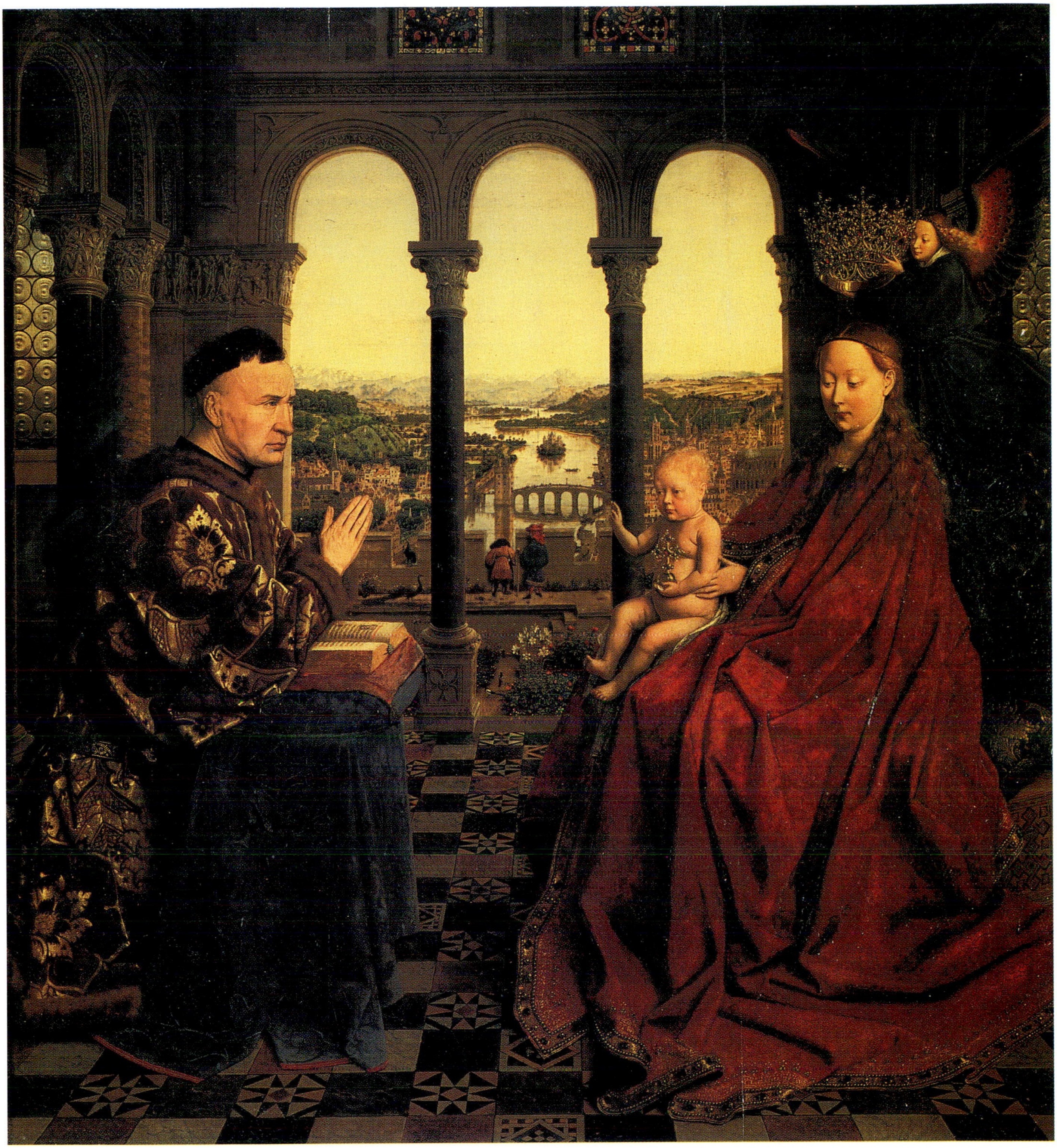

Fig. 313 Jan van Eyck, *The Madonna of Chancellor Rolin*, c. 1433–1434.
Oil on panel, 26 × 24 3/4 in. Musée du Louvre, Paris.

In 1608, the Netherlands freed itself of Spanish rule and became, by virtue of its almost total dominance of world trade, the wealthiest nation in the world. By that time, artists had become extremely skillful at representing these material riches—with the medium of oil paint. One critic has called the Dutch preoccupation with still life "a dialogue between the newly affluent society and its material possessions." In a painting such as Jan de Heem's *Still Life with Lobster* (Fig. 314), we are witness to the remains of a most extravagant meal, most of which has been left uneaten. This luxuriant and conspicuous display of wealth is deliberate. Southern fruit in a cold climate is a luxury, and the peeled lemon, otherwise untouched, is a sign of almost wanton consumption. And though we might want to read into this image our own sense of its decadence, for de Heem the painting was more a celebration, an invitation to share, at least visually and thus imaginatively, in its world. The feast on the table was a feast for the eyes.

The ability to create such a sense of tactile reality is a virtue of oil painting that makes the medium particularly suitable to the celebration of material things. By **glazing** the surface of the painting with thin films of transparent color, the artist creates a sense of luminous materiality. Light penetrates this glaze, bounces off the opaque underpainting beneath, and is reflected back up through the glaze. Painted objects thus seem to reflect light as if they were real, and the play of light through the painted surfaces gives them a sense of tangible presence.

The more real a painting appears to be, the more it is said to be an example of ***trompe l'oeil,*** a French phrase meaning "deceit of the eye." It

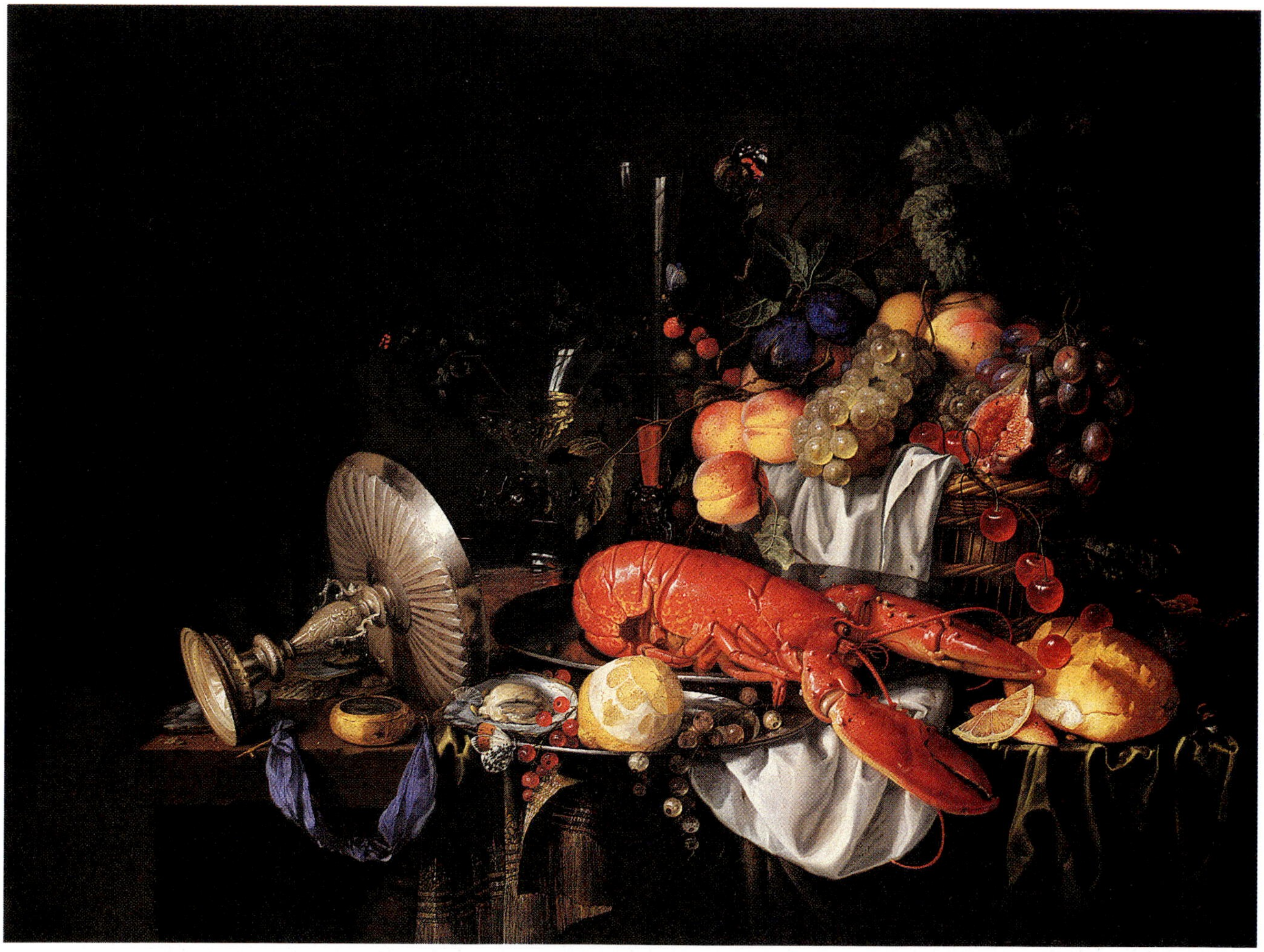

Fig. 314 Jan Davidsz. de Heem, *Still Life with Lobster,* c. 1650.
Oil on canvas, 25 ⅛ × 33 ¼ in. The Toledo Museum of Art, Toledo, Ohio. Gift of Edward Drummond Libbey.

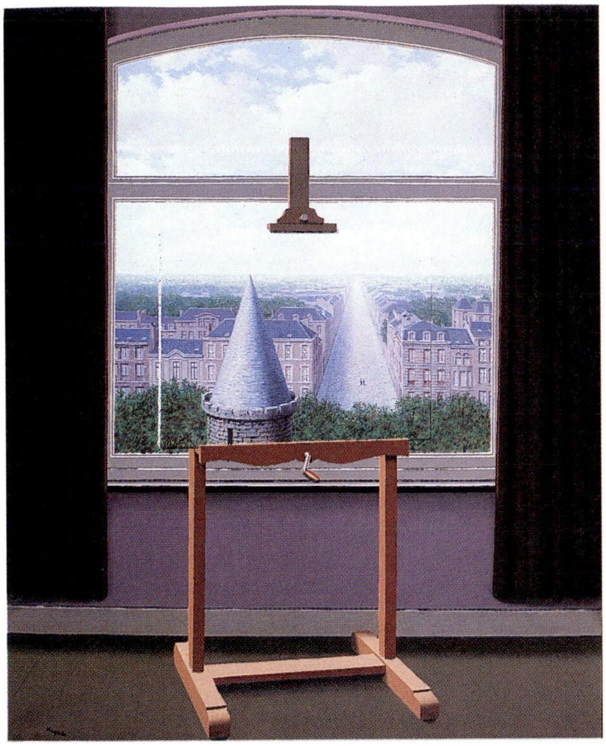

Fig. 315 René Magritte, *Euclidean Walks,* 1955.
Oil on canvas, 64 × 51 1/2 in. The Minneapolis Institute of the Arts.

is precisely painting's ability to deceive the eye, to substitute itself for reality, that is the subject of René Magritte's *Euclidean Walks* (Fig. 315). Here a painting-within-a-painting is set in front of a window so that it hides, but exactly duplicates, the scene outside. The painting confuses the interior of the room with the exterior landscape, and by analogy, the world of the mind with the physical world outside it. In Magritte's words, this is "how we see the world: we see it as being outside ourselves even though it is only a mental representation of it that we experience inside ourselves." The artificial nature of this superficially *trompe-l'oeil* scene is underscored by the way in which the shape of the tower is identical to the shape of the avenue that recedes to a distant vanishing point. A painting is, after all, a mental construction, an artificial reality, not reality itself.

If oil painting exists in the mind, and for the mind, it need not necessarily reflect the world outside it. Since virtually its inception, oil painting's *expressive* potential has also been recognized. Much more than in fresco, where the artist's gesture was lost in the plaster, and much more than in tempera, where the artist was forced to use brushes so small that gestural freedom was absorbed by the scale of the image, oil paint could record and trace the artist's presence before the canvas. In the swirls and dashes of paint that make up Susan Rothenberg's *Biker* (Fig. 316), we can detect a cyclist charging through a puddle or a stream straight at us, water splashing up from the bike's tires. A windswept tree reaches into the painting from the right, like a claw ready to bring the biker down. The biker himself seems disembodied. All we can see of him is head and his right arm which reaches up to his brow as if to shade his eyes. Rothenberg's paint seems to want to capture the image and at the same time reject it. It is as if the artist's hand, caught in the act of painting a figure rejects reality (representation) and insists on abstraction. We feel, in other words, that Rothenberg has been moved by something she has seen, but that she can express it only through the expressive agitation of her brushwork and the glimmering beauty of her color.

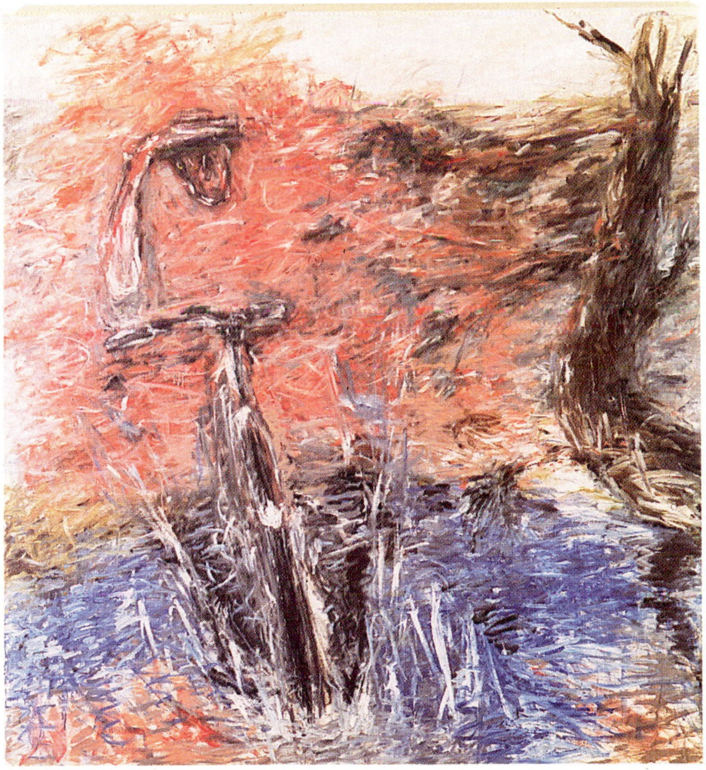

Fig. 316 Susan Rothenberg, *Biker,* 1985.
Oil on canvas, 74 × 69 1/2 in.
Collection, The Museum of Modern Art, New York. Fractional gift of Paine Webber Group, Inc.

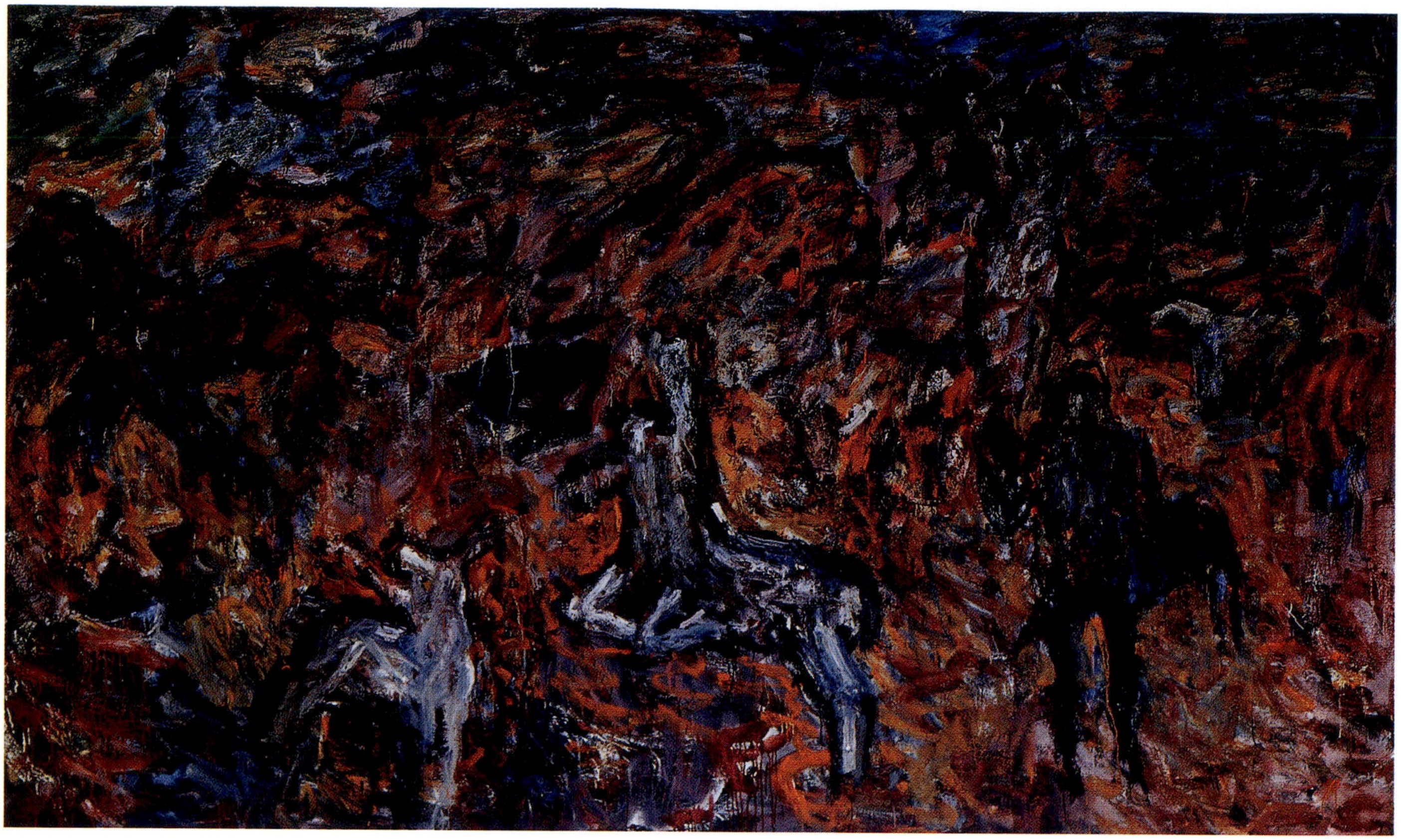

Fig. 317 Pat Passlof, *Centaurs and Caryatid,* 1995.
Oil on canvas, 36 × 42 in. Courtesy of the artist.

Where Rothenberg begins with the thing seen, Pat Passlof begins with abstraction. She begins painting without any plan, without even knowing what it is she is going to paint. Her painting *Centaurs and Caryatid* (Fig. 317) is painted over an older painting that she had overworked (in her words, "killed") a painting of horses in a field. Though painted out, "ghosts" of the original painting began to give rise to new images. Over a period of days and even months, she began to recognize, in the lines and shapes she had painted, hints of real things—or, in this case, semi-real things, the stuff of legend. Centaurs are the imaginary creatures, half man and half horse, that inhabit Greek mythology. A caryatid is a figure of a woman used as a supporting column for a temple—in the painting it rises above the blue centaur on the right. By means of abstraction, then, Passlof returns us to the ideal world of Greek art. Oil paint allows this process to take place. Because the paint stays wet for days, Passlof can continue to push and maneuver the paint in order to fully realize the suggestions that arise as she works.

Many of Passlof's attitudes about painting were developed working with New York painters such as Willem de Kooning, whom she first met when she attended Black Mountain College in North Carolina in the early 1950s. Even more of an influence was Milton Resnick, to whom she is married, and who was himself a close friend of de Kooning's in the 1940s and 1950s. In paintings like de Kooning's *Door to the River* (Fig. 318) there is no reference to visual reality at all. He has described the subject matter of this painting, and others like it, as a mixture of raw sensations: "landscapes and highways and sensations of that, outside the city—with the feeling of going to the city or coming from it." What we feel here, especially, is energy, the energy of the city translated into the energy of painting itself.

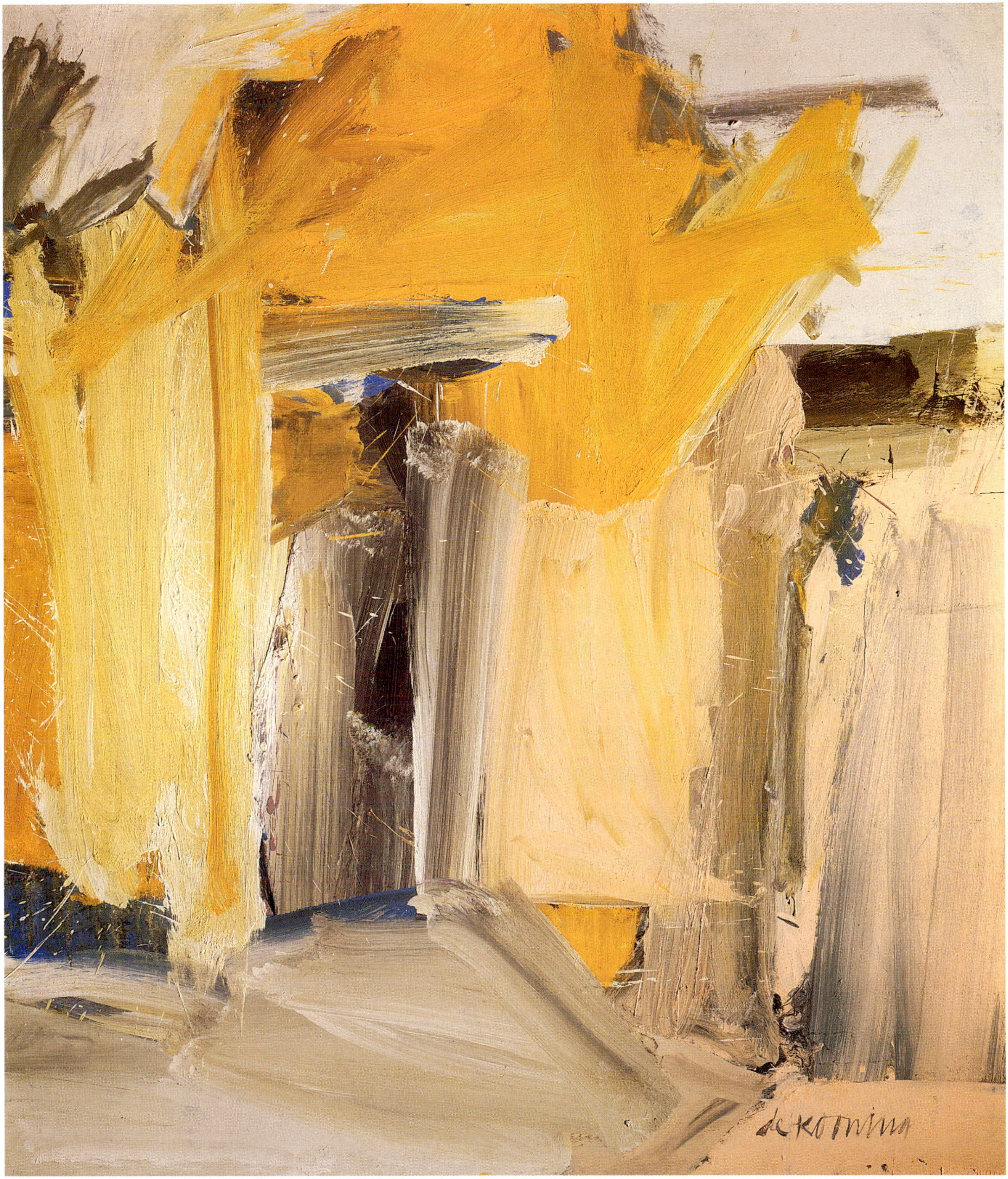

Fig. 318 Willem de Kooning, *Door to the River,* 1960.
Oil on canvas, 80 × 70 in.
Collection of Whitney Museum of American Art.
Purchase, with funds from the Friends of the Whitney Museum of American Art. (60.63).

Milton Resnick's U + Me

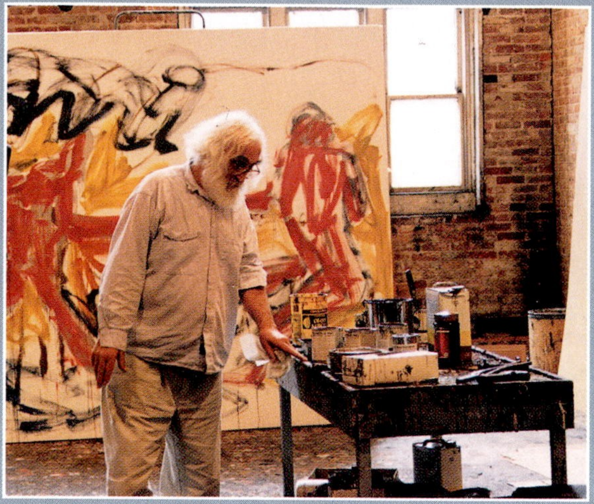

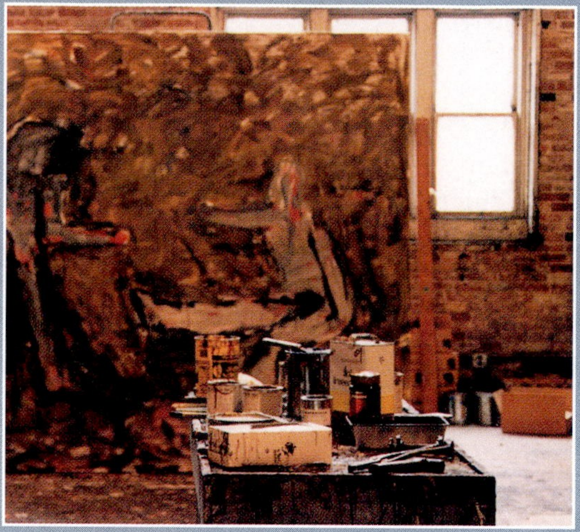

Fig. 319 Milton Resnick's *U + Me* in progress.
Left: June 25, 1995. Right: June 26, 1995.

On July 25, 1995, abstract expressionist painter Milton Resnick began five new large paintings. They would sum up, he hoped, what he had learned over the years as a painter. He had left home in his late teens to become an artist, lived through the heyday of abstract expressionist painting in New York, where, as one of the leaders of what would come to be known as the New York School, he had worked together with Willem de Kooning, Jackson Pollock, and Hans Hofmann, and had continued to work down to the present, longer than any of his contemporaries. These new paintings would take him full circle, back to his beginnings and forward again into the present. And it was, in fact, beginnings that would lend the new paintings their theme—Genesis, the first book of the Bible, Adam and Eve, the Garden of Eden, the Tree of the Knowledge of Good and Evil, and the serpent, Satan. Pat Passlof, Resnick's wife and fellow painter, suggested that the figures in the new work really weren't Adam and Eve at all, but "you and me." And the name stuck, though modified to *U + Me*, because, Resnick says, "it's easier to write."

On July 25, he painted on all five canvases in his Eldridge Street studio in Chinatown, a two-story brick-walled space with large windows that had been, in the first decades of this century, a Jewish synagogue. He begins without a plan, and without preliminary drawing, with nothing but a brushmark and a feeling about where he's going. "This feeling doesn't have to be physical," he says, "but it has to be as if I come at you and you're frightened. That's the feeling. It's like if you have a glass and there's something in it and it's a kind of funny color. And someone says, 'Drink it.' And you say, 'What's in it?' And they say, 'Drink it or else!' And so you have to drink it. So that's the feeling. I'm going to drink something, and I don't know what's going to happen to me."

Pictured on these pages is one of the *U + Me* paintings at three different stages in its development—two studio photographs taken on each of the first two days, July 25 and

July 26 (Fig. 319), and the finished painting as it appeared in February 1996 in an exhibition of the new *U + Me* paintings at the Robert Miller Gallery in New York (Fig. 320).

In the first stages of the painting there are two figures, the one on the right kicking forward to meet the other who seems to be striding forward in greeting. The major difference in the work from day one to day two is color. The exuberant red and yellow of the first brushstrokes is suppressed in an overall brownish-green **scumbling**—the working of an opaque layer of oil-paint over another layer of a different tone or color so that the lower layer is not entirely obliterated. The final painting, in fact, is a culmination of layer upon layer of paint being added to the work, each revealing itself at different points across the canvas. For instance, the second day's brownish-green layer can be seen in the final work above the top of the tree, and rich dapples of differently colored layers appear throughout the dark layer of paint of the ground behind the figures and tree.

The final work, in fact, seems dramatically different from its beginnings. For one thing, Resnick has added a tree. "I put it in the middle," he says, "because that's the most difficult spot"—difficult because the tree makes the painting so symmetrical and balanced that it loses any sense of tension or energy. But Resnick's tree also has symbolic resonance, prefiguring the cross. By looking forward to the crucifixion from the Garden of Eden, Resnick charges the image. The figures have changed as well, giving up their sense of physical motion. "The figures have to have a vitality but not be in motion," Resnick says. "They have to be animated with some force . . . with some energy. That's what the paint is doing. Paint has the energy."

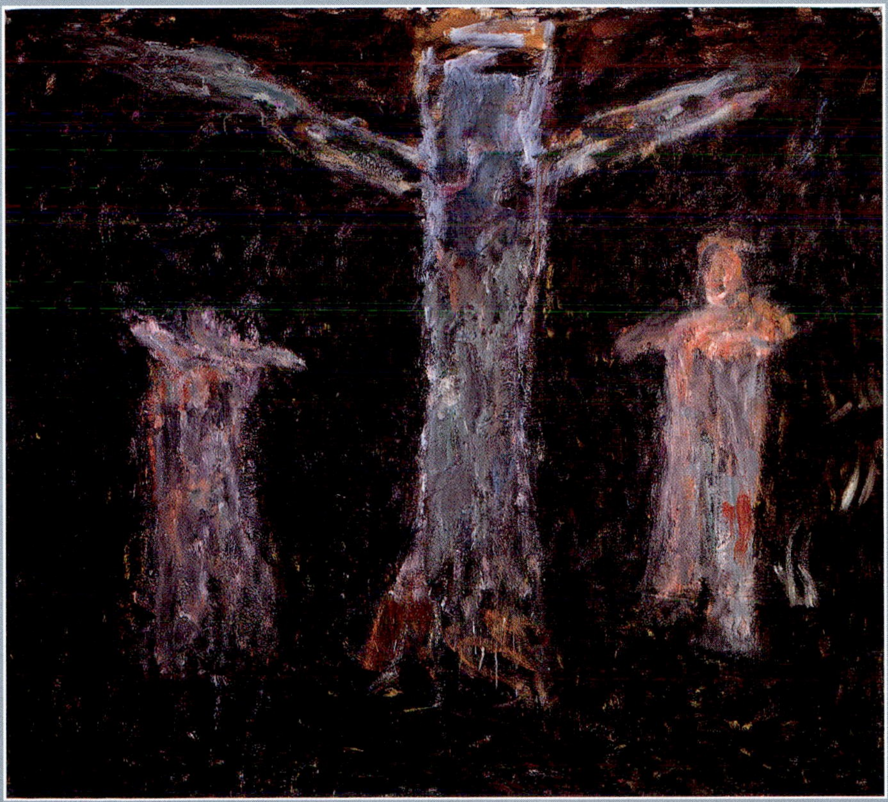

Fig. 320 Milton Resnick, *U + Me,* 1995.
Oil on canvas, 93 1/4 × 104 1/2 in. © Robert Miller Gallery, New York.

WATERCOLOR

Of all the painting media, **watercolor** is at least potentially one of the most expressive. The ancient Egyptians used it to illustrate papyrus scrolls, and it was employed intermittently by other artists down through the centuries, notably by Albrecht Dürer and Peter Paul Rubens. But it was not until artists began to exploit the expressive potential of painting, rather than pursuing purely representational ends, that the characteristics of the medium were fully explored.

Watercolor paintings are made by applying pigments suspended in a solution of water and gum arabic to dampened paper. Working quickly, it is possible to achieve gestural effects that are very close to those possible with brush and ink, and many people think of watercolor as a form of drawing. Historically, it has often been utilized as a sketching tool. Certainly, as a medium, it can possess all of the spontaneity of a high-quality sketch.

Depending on the absorbency of the paper and the amount of watercolor on the brush, the paint spreads along the fibers of the paper when it is applied. Thin solutions of pigment and binder have the appearance of soft, transparent washes, while dense solutions can become almost opaque. The play between the transparent and the opaque qualities of the medium is central to Winslow Homer's *A Wall, Nassau* (Fig. 321). Both the wall and the sky behind it are transparent washes, and the textural ribbons and spots of white on the coral limestone wall are actually unpainted paper. Between these two light bands of color lies the densely painted foliage of the garden and, to the right, the sea, which becomes a deeper and deeper

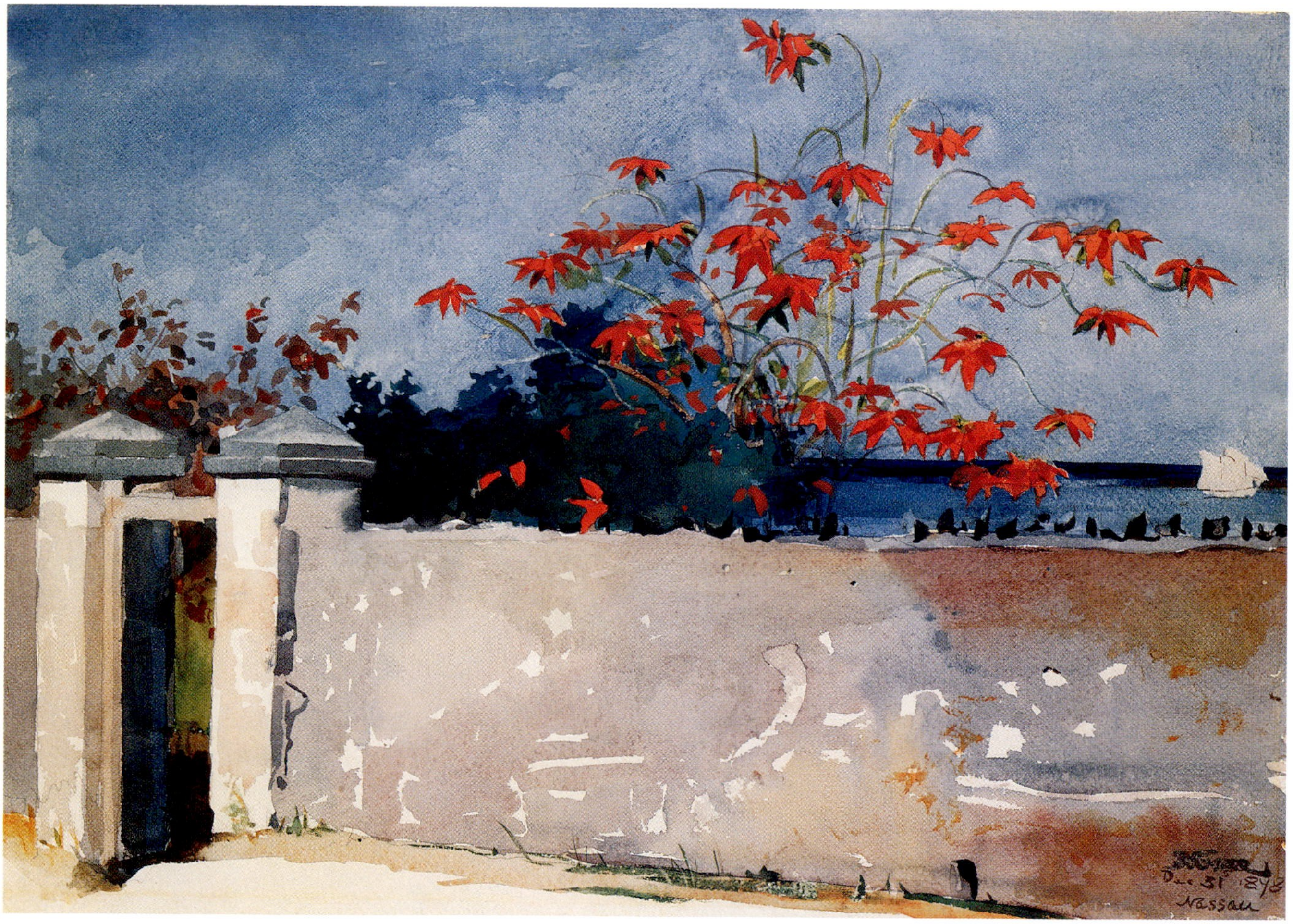

Fig. 321 Winslow Homer, *A Wall, Nassau,* 1898.
Watercolor and pencil on paper, 14 3/4 × 21 1/2 in. © The Metropolitan Museum of Art, Amelia B. Lazarus Fund, 1910.

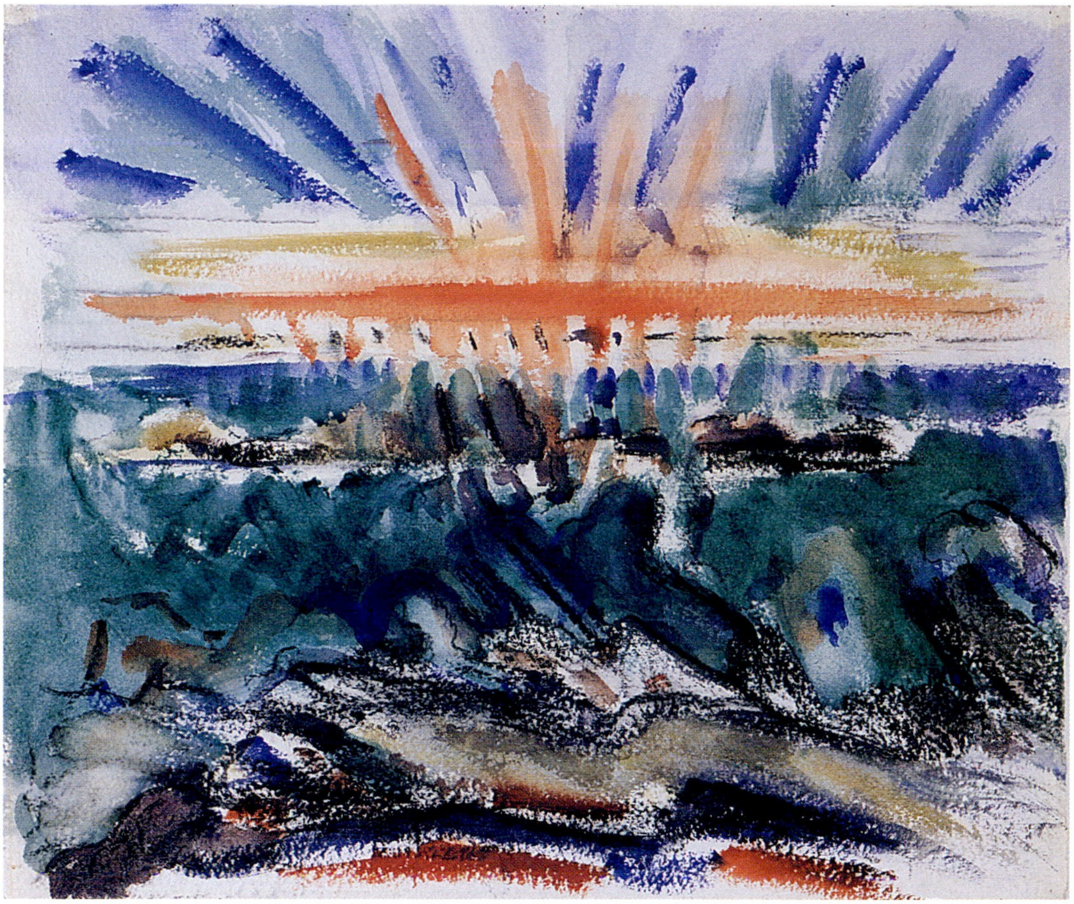

Fig. 322 John Marin, *Sunset, Maine Coast,* 1919.
Watercolor, 16 1/4 × 19 1/4 in. Columbus Museum of Art, Ohio. Gift of Ferdinand Howald.

blue as it stretches toward the horizon. A white sailboat heads out to sea on the right. Almost everything of visual interest in this painting takes place between the sky above and the wall below. Even the red leaves of the giant poinsettia plant that is the painting's focal point turn down toward this middle ground. Pointing up from the top of the wall, framing this middle area from below, is something far more ominous—dark, almost black shards of broken glass. Suddenly, the painting is transformed. No longer just a pretty view of a garden, it begins to speak of privacy and intrusion, and of the divided social world of the Bahamas at the turn of the century, the islands given over to tourism and its associated wealth at the expense of the local black population. The wall holds back those outside it from the beauty and luxury within, separating them from the freedom offered, for instance, by the boat as it sails away.

It is worth comparing Homer's watercolor style with that of another American master of the medium, John Marin. Homer's career was ending at the turn of the century—he would paint for only one more decade—just as Marin's was beginning. Marin's style is much more expressive than Homer's, as his watercolor *Sunset, Maine Coast* (Fig. 322) makes evident. The delicate lines of Homer's painting, which could only be achieved with a fine pointed brush, are transformed by Marin into bold, broad strokes of color. Where Homer uses the paper reserve to create the elegant speckled texture of the wall, Marin uses it to create bands of light. And gone in Marin's painting are Homer's soft washes. Marin is a fully modern painter, whose energetic use of the watercolor medium, even in the depiction of a landscape, is comparable to the speed and energy of the modern age.

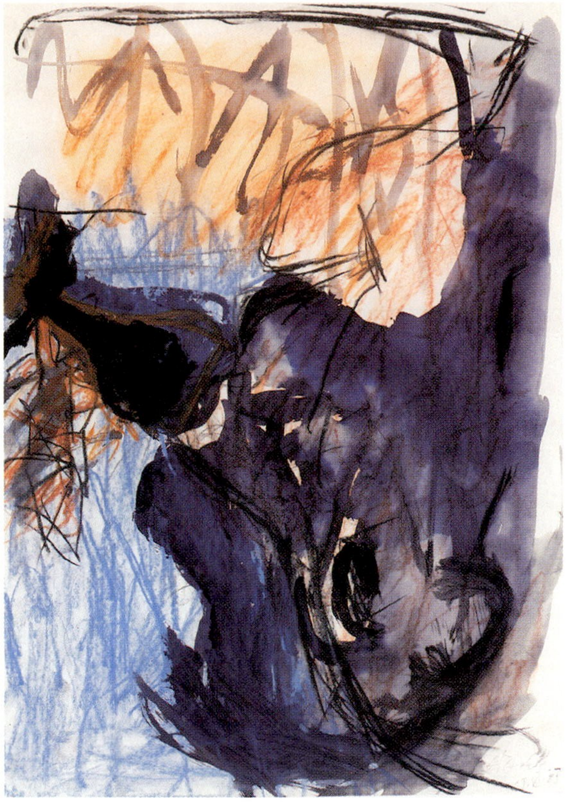

Fig. 323 Georg Baselitz, *Untitled,* 1981.
Watercolor and chalk pastel on white paper, 23 3/4 × 16 3/4 in.
Harvard University Art Museums (Fogg Art Museum).
Acquired through the Deknatel Purchase Fund.

The expressive potential of watercolor is fully realized in Georg Baselitz's *Untitled* (Fig. 323). At first glance, the painting seems to be an almost totally abstract sunset landscape, close in mood to Marin's, representing perhaps a lake, at the left, emptying into a distant sea. Baselitz's title, however, indicates that our temptation to read this image figuratively is probably mistaken. When we realize that, viewed upside down, this is not a landscape, but the image of a man eating a drumstick or singing into a microphone, we begin to understand that Baselitz wishes us to value his painting *as* painting, subject matter aside. For Baselitz, painting reveals the mind, not the world, an idea realized in his transformation of the representational into the abstract.

GOUACHE

Derived from the Italian word *guazzo,* meaning "puddle," **gouache** is essentially watercolor mixed with Chinese white chalk. The medium is opaque, and, while gouache colors display a light-reflecting brilliance, it is difficult to blend brushstrokes of gouache together. Thus the medium lends itself to the creation of large flat, colored forms. It is this abstract quality that attracted Jacob Lawrence to it. Everything in

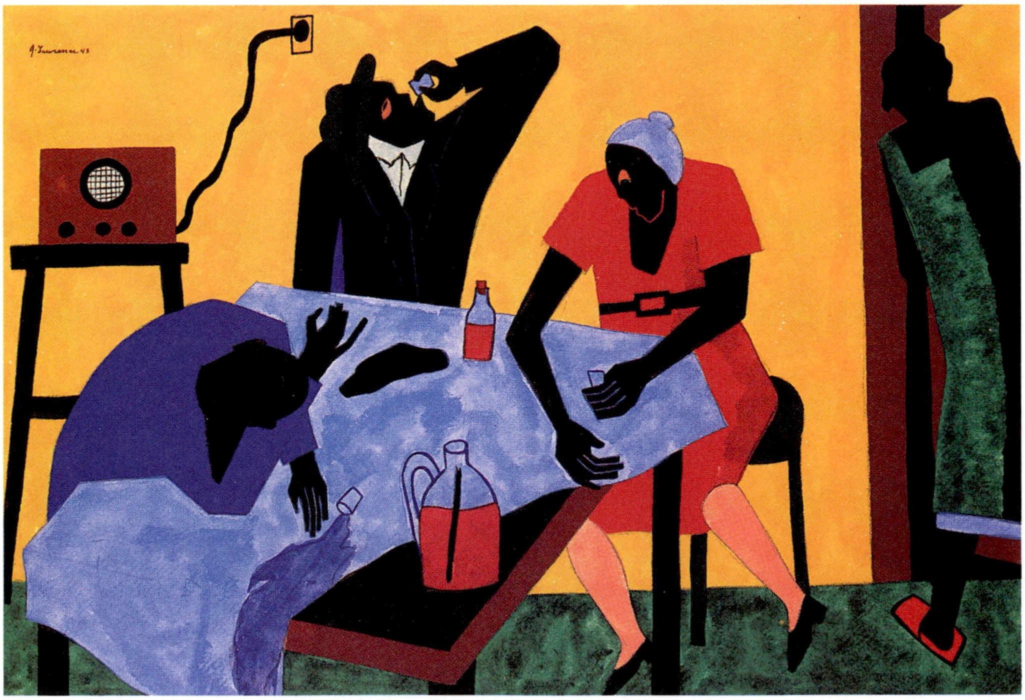

Fig. 324 Jacob Lawrence, *No. 15: You can buy bootleg whiskey for twenty-five cents a quart,* from the *Harlem Series,* 1942–1943.
Gouache on paper, 15 1/2 × 22 1/2 in. Collection of the Portland, Oregon Art Museum; Helen Thurston Ayer Fund.

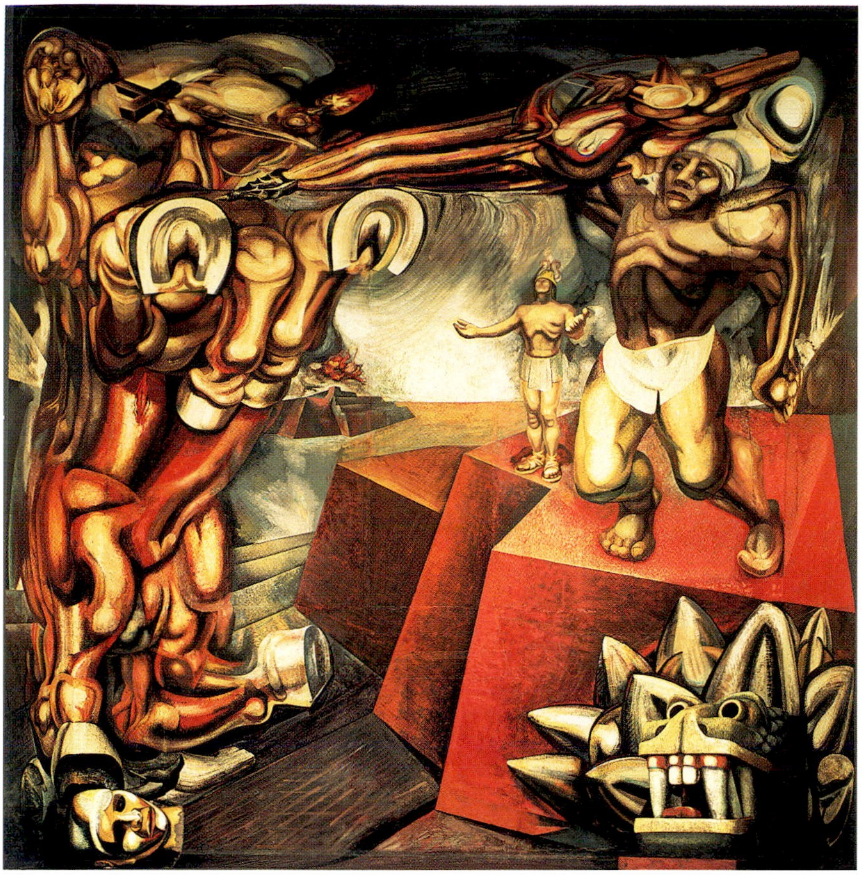

Fig. 325 David Alfaro Siqueiros, *Cuauhtémoc against the Myth,* 1944.
Mural, pyroxylin on celotex and plywood, 1000 sq. ft. Teepan Union Housing Project, Tlatelco, Mexico. INAH/CNCA.

the painting *You can buy bootleg whiskey for twenty-five cents a quart* (Fig. 324) tips forward. This not only creates a sense of disorienting and drunken imbalance, but emphasizes the flat two-dimensional quality of the painting's space. Lawrence's dramatically intense complementary colors blare like the jazz we can almost hear coming from the radio.

SYNTHETIC MEDIA

Because of its slow-drying characteristics and the preparation necessary to ready the painting surface, oil painting lacks the sense of immediacy so readily apparent in more direct media like drawing or watercolor. For the same reasons, the medium is not particularly suitable for painting out-of-doors, where one is continually exposed to the elements.

The first artists to experiment with synthetic media were a group of Mexican painters, led by David Alfaro Siqueiros, whose goal was to create a large-scale revolutionary mural art. Painting outdoors, where their celebrations of the struggles of the working class could easily be seen, Siqueiros, Diego Rivera, and José Clemente Orozco—*Los Tres Grandes,* as they are known—worked first in fresco, then in oil paint, but the sun, rain, and humidity of Mexico quickly ruined their efforts. In 1937 Siqueiros organized a workshop in New York, closer to the chemical industry, expressly to develop and experiment with new synthetic paints. One of the first media used at the workshop was pyroxylin, commonly known as Duco, a lacquer developed as an automobile paint. Housed in the Union Housing Project at Tlatelco since 1964, *Cuauhtémoc against the Myth* (Fig. 325) depicts the story of the Aztec hero who shattered the myth of the conquering Spanish army's invulnerability to attack. Meant as a commentary on the vulnerability of the Nazi army as well, the mural was painted on a 1,000-square-foot panel instead of a wall in order to withstand damage from earthquakes.

Judy Baca's Great Wall of Los Angeles

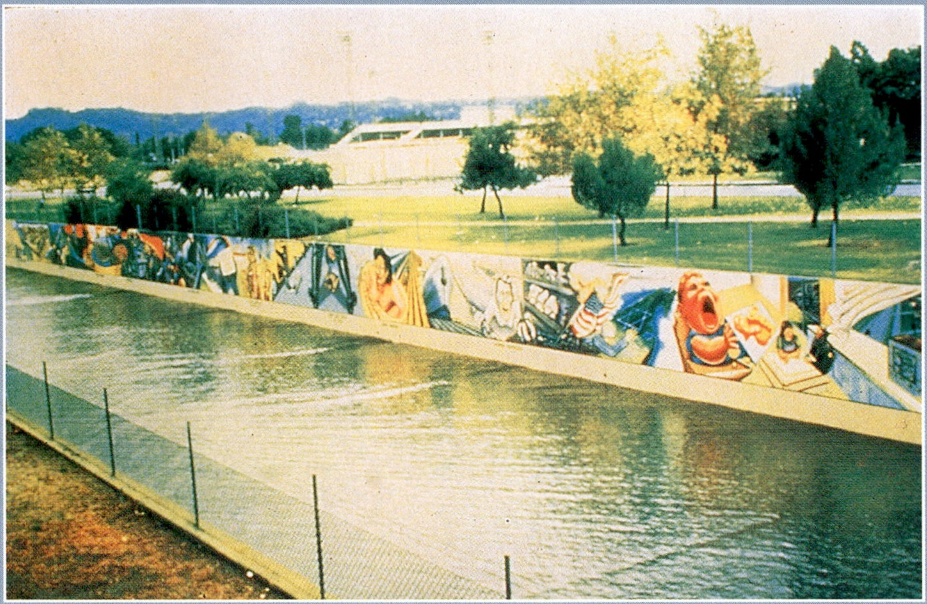

Fig. 326 **Judy F. Baca, *Great Wall of Los Angeles*, 1983.**
Acrylic on cast concrete, 13 × 2400 ft.

In 1933, David Alfaro Siqueiros painted a mural, *America Tropical*, on Olvera Street, the historic center of Chicano and Mexican culture in Los Angeles. It was quickly painted over by city fathers, who objected to its portrayal of the plight of Mexicans and Chicanos in California. Currently under restoration with funds provided by the Getty Foundation, the mural depicts a mestizo shooting at an American eagle and a crucified Chicano, one of the inspirations for Guillermo Gómez-Peña's *Cruci-fiction Project* (see Fig. 71). The mural—and the work of *Los Tres Grandes* as a whole—has also inspired activist artist Judy Baca, who has dedicated her career to "giving voice" to the marginalized communities of California, empowering people through art.

"Murals," Baca says, "have been the only interventions in public spaces that articulate the presence of ethnicity. . . . A rich legacy of murals has been produced since *America Tropical* was painted on Olvera Street by the maestro. Thousands of public murals in places where people live and work have become tangible public monuments to the shared experience of communities of color." In 1974, Baca inaugurated the Citywide Mural Project in Los Angeles, which completed 250 murals, 150 of which she directed herself. Since then, she has continued to sponsor and direct murals through SPARC, the Social and Public Art Resource Center, which she founded.

The *Great Wall of Los Angeles* (Fig. 326), begun in 1976 and still in progress, is her most ambitious project. It is located in the Tujunga Wash of the Los Angeles River, which was entirely concreted by developers as Los Angeles grew. This concrete conduit is, says Baca, "a giant scar across the land which served to further divide an already divided city. . . . Just as young Chicanos tattoo battle scars on their bodies, *Great Wall of Los*

Angeles is a tattoo on a scar where the river once ran." The wall narrates the history of California, and Los Angeles in particular, but not the history told in textbooks. It tells the history of indigenous peoples, immigrant minorities—Portuguese, Chinese, Japanese, Korean, and Basque, as well as Chicano—and of women from prehistory to the present. The detail below (Fig. 327) represents the kind of history Baca tells. It depicts how four major freeways intersected in the middle of East Los Angeles's Chicano communities, dividing them, weakening them, and turning them against each other. To the right a Mexican woman protests the building of Dodger Stadium, which displaced a historic Mexican community in Chavez Ravine.

Baca has worked on the *Great Wall* project more as a director and facilitator than painter. Nearly 400 inner-city youths, many of them recruited through the juvenile justice system, have done the actual painting and design. Rival gang members, of different races, and from different neighborhoods in the city, find themselves working on the project. They represent, in real terms, the divided city itself, and Baca's goal is to help them understand how to communicate with one another and how to work together. "The thing about muralism," she says, "is that collaboration is a requirement. . . . [The *Great Wall*'s] focus is cooperation in the process underlying its creation." For Baca, the collaborative process heals wounds, brings people together, and helps to recreate communities that have been destroyed.

"For me," Baca explains, "the process of making art is the transforming of pain. First there's rage, below that rage is indignation, below that indignation is shame, below that hope, and at its corniest base, love. After I got through all of that I could love myself, my art, my people, who I really was. That's how the *Great Wall* got done. The art process takes pain to its furthest transformation." Baca's own progress through this series of transformations is the progress that each person who comes to work on the *Wall* must go through themselves. To work on the *Great Wall* is to be transformed.

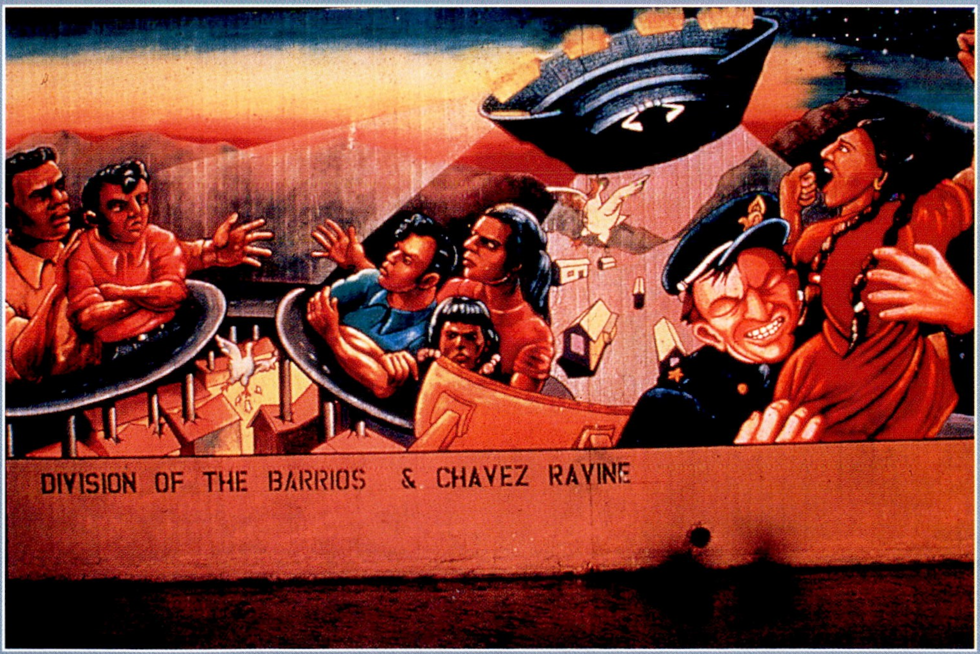

Fig. 327 Judy Baca, *The Great Wall of Los Angeles* (detail: *Division of the Barrios and Chavez Ravine*), 1976–continuing. Mural, H. 13 ft. (whole mural over 1 mile long), Tujunga Wash, Los Angeles, CA. Photo © SPARC, Venice, CA.

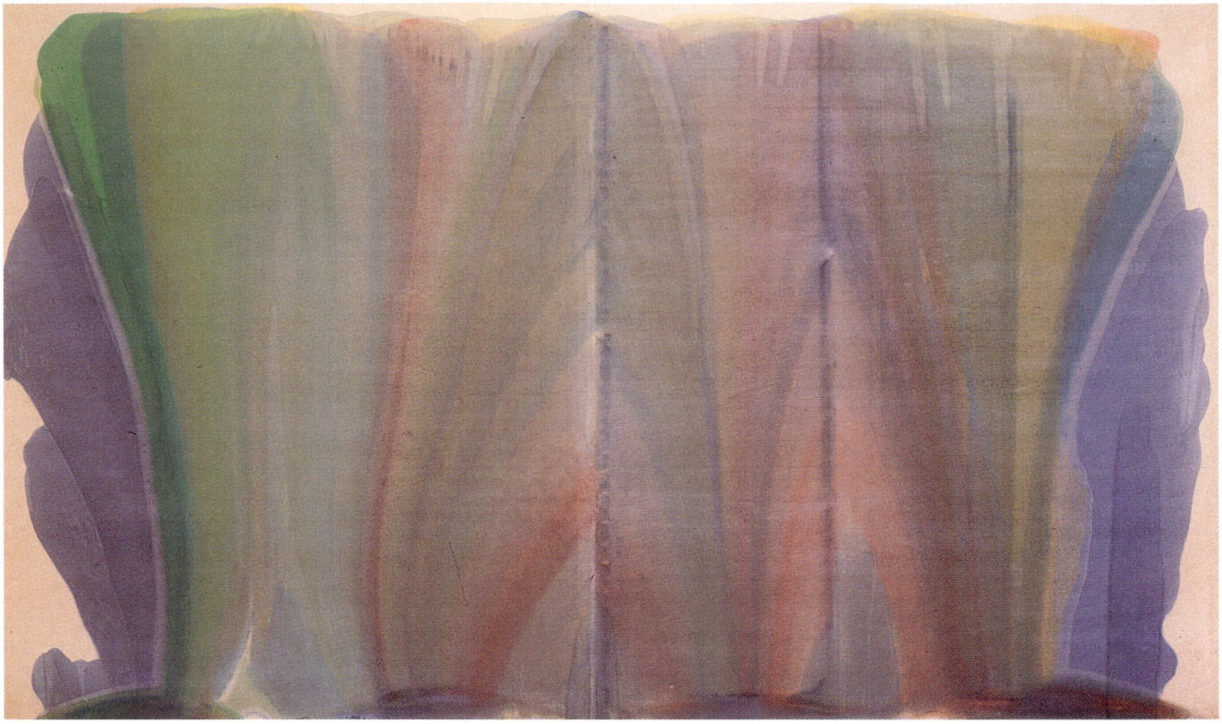

Fig. 328 Morris Louis, *Blue Veil,* 1958–1959.
Acrylic resin paint on canvas, 100 1/2 × 149 in.
Courtesy of the Fogg Art Museum, Harvard University; Gift of Lois Orswell and Gifts for Special Uses Fund.

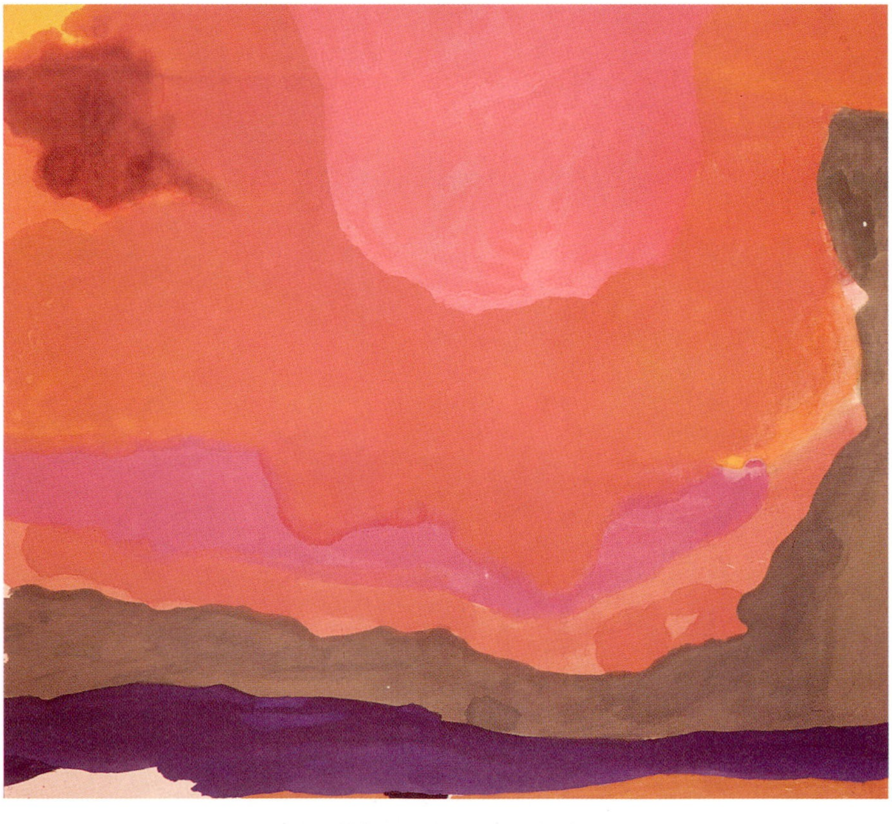

Fig. 329 Helen Frankenthaler, *Flood,* 1967.
Synthetic polymer on canvas, 10 ft. 4 in. × 11 ft. 8 in.
Collection of Whitney Museum of American Art. Purchase, with funds from the Friends of the Whitney Museum of American Art. (68.12).

In the early 1950s, Helen Frankenthaler gave up the gestural qualities of the brush loaded with oil paint and began to stain raw, unprimed canvas with greatly thinned oil pigments, soaking color into the surface in what has been called an art of "stain-gesture." Her technique soon attracted a number of painters, Morris Louis among them, who were themselves experimenting with Magna, a paint made from **acrylic** resins—materials used to make plastic—mixed with turpentine. Staining canvas with oil created a messy, brownish "halo" around each stain or puddle of paint, but Louis quickly realized that the "halo" disappeared when he stained canvas with Magna, the paint and canvas really becoming one.

At almost exactly this time, researchers in both Mexico and the United States discovered a way to mix acrylic resins with water, and by 1956 water-based acrylic paints were on the market. These media were inorganic and, as a result, much better suited to staining raw canvas than turpentine or oil-based media, since no chemical interaction could take place that might threaten the life of the painting.

Louis's *Blue Veil* (Fig. 328) consists of multicolored translucent washes of acrylic paint thinned to the consistency of watercolor. Inevitably, Frankenthaler gave up staining her canvases with oil and moved to acrylic in 1963. With this medium she was able to create such intensely atmospheric paintings as *Flood* (Fig. 329). Working on the floor and pouring paint directly on canvas, the artist was able to make the painting seem spontaneous, even though it is quite large. "A really good picture," Frankenthaler says, "looks as if it's happened at once. . . . It looks as if it were born in a minute." This sense of spontaneity manifests itself as a sort of aggressive good humor in the giant poured pieces of Lynda Benglis (Fig. 330). Her liquid rubber materials find their own form as they spill, not onto canvas, but directly onto the floor, creating what might be called "soft" painting.

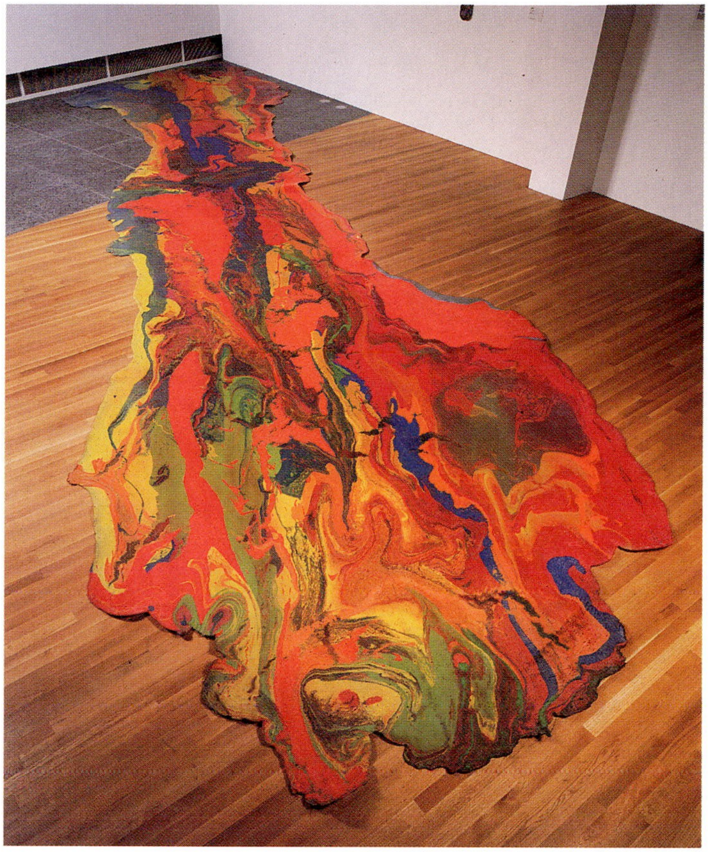

Fig. 330 Lynda Benglis, *Contraband,* 1969. Poured pigmented latex, 33 ft. 9 in. × 9 ft. × 1 in. Courtesy Paula Cooper Gallery, New York.

In this chapter, we have considered all of the painting media—encaustic, fresco, tempera, oil paint, watercolor, gouache, and acrylic paints—and we have discussed not only how these media are used but why artists have favored them. One of the most important factors in the development of new painting media has always been the desire of artists to represent the world more and more faithfully. But representation is not the only goal of painting. If we recall Artemesia Gentileschi's *Self-Portrait* at the beginning of this chapter, she is not simply representing the way she looks but also the way she feels. In her hands, paint becomes an *expressive* tool. Some painting media—oil paint, watercolor, and acrylics—are better suited to expressive ends than others because they are more fluid or can be manipulated more easily. But the possibilities of painting are as vast as the human imagination itself. In painting, anything is possible.

CHAPTER 12

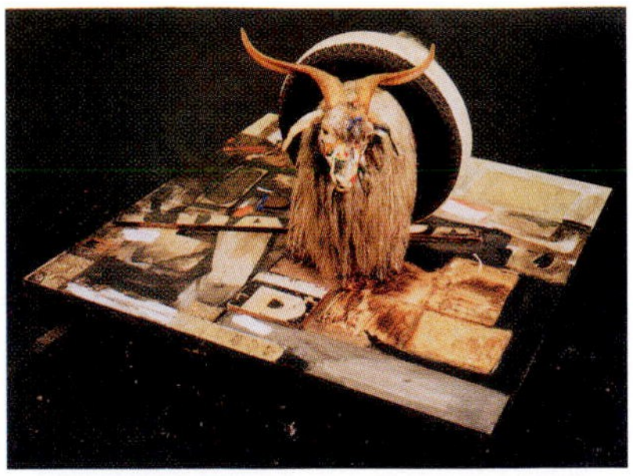

Three-Dimensional Media

All of the media we have considered thus far—drawing, printmaking, and painting—are generally considered two-dimensional media. However, we ended the last chapter with *Contraband* (Fig. 330), a painting that spills out and escapes across the floor. We begin this chapter with Marcia Gygli King's *Springs Upstate* (Fig. 331), which travels even farther into three-dimensional space. *Springs Upstate* is half painting, half sculpture. The stream and boulders on the floor, and the frame of the painting itself, are created with carved styrofoam that is covered with epoxy and fiberglass. King's painting leaves two-dimensional space behind and embraces three dimensions. It moves off the wall and into our space. As we will see in this chapter, this movement of art into the room, and then out of the room and into our lives, is one of the defining characteristics of many contemporary art forms, from earthworks to performance art.

Thus, in this chapter we turn to a discussion of the three-dimensional media and its relation to the space we ourselves occupy. Sculpture, one of the oldest and most enduring of all the arts, is our primary focus. But we will also consider the many so-called "craft" media—ceramics, glass, and fiber in particular—which have traditionally been distinguished from the fine arts because they are employed to make functional objects, from the utensils we eat with to the clothes we wear. In the hands of a skilled artist, however, these media can be employed to make objects that are not only of great beauty but that must be appreciated as sculptures in their own right. Finally, we will consider a number of so-called "mixed" media forms—works of art that combine two- and three-dimensional media in innovative and exciting ways.

SCULPTURE

All the types of sculpture we will study in this chapter—carving, modeling, casting, construction and assemblage, and earthworks—employ two basic processes: they are either subtractive or additive in nature. In **subtractive** processes, the sculptor begins with a mass of material larger than the finished work and removes material, or subtracts from that mass until the work achieves its finished form. Carving is a subtractive process. In **additive** processes, the sculptor builds the work, adding material as the work proceeds. Modeling, construction, and assemblage are additive processes. Casting, in which material in a liquid state is poured into a mold and allowed to harden, has additive aspects, but as we shall see, it is in many ways a process of its own. Earthworks often utilize both additive and subtractive processes.

In addition to these basic processes, there are three basic ways in which we experience sculpture in three-dimensional space—as relief, in-the-round, and as an environment. If you recall the process for making woodblock prints, which are described in Chapter 10, you will quickly understand that the raised portion of a woodblock plate stands out in relief against the background. The woodblock plate is, in essence, a carved relief sculpture, a sculpture that has three-dimensional depth but is meant to be seen from only one side.

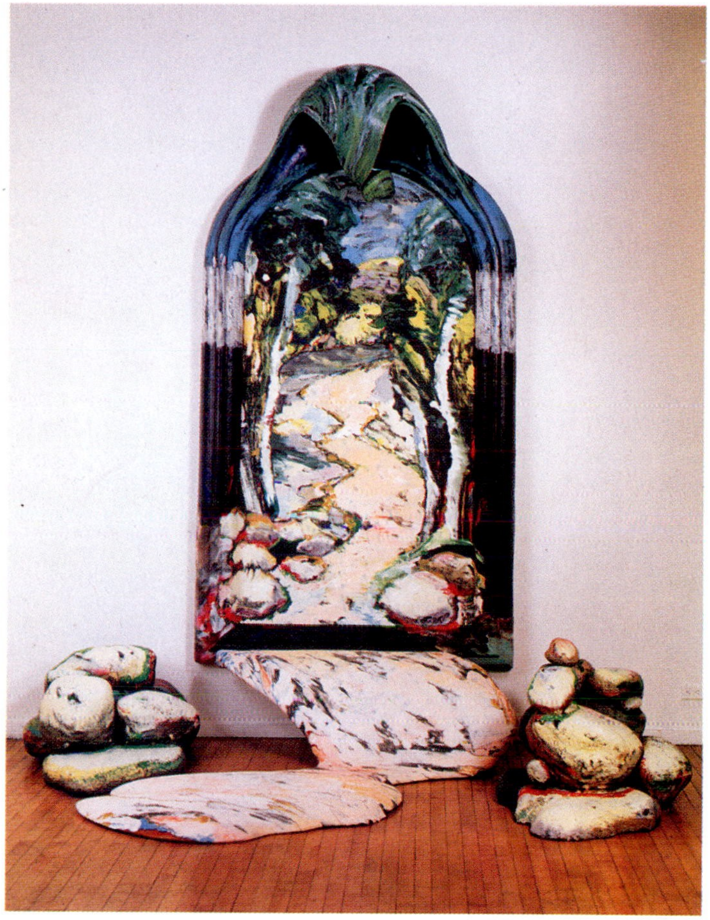

Fig. 331 Marcia Gygli King, *Springs Upstate*, 1990–1992.
Oil on canvas, mixed media frame, 6 ft. × 9 ft. × 10 ft. 6 in. painting, 9 ft. × 5 ft. × 7 in. sceptural projection. Photograph by Allan Finkelman.

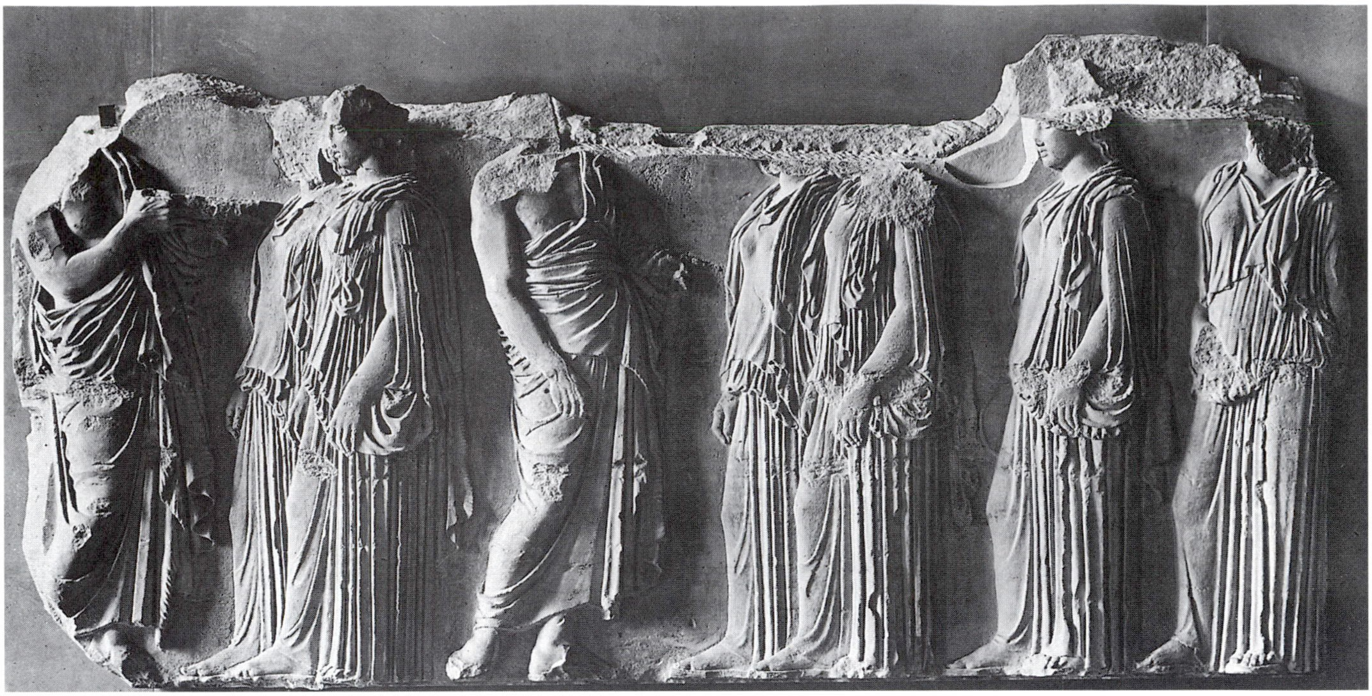

Fig. 332 ***Maidens and Stewards,*** **fragment of the** ***Panathenaic Procession,*** **from the east frieze of the Parthenon, Acropolis, Athens, 438–432 BCE.**
Marble, H. approx. 43 in. Musée du Louvre, Paris.

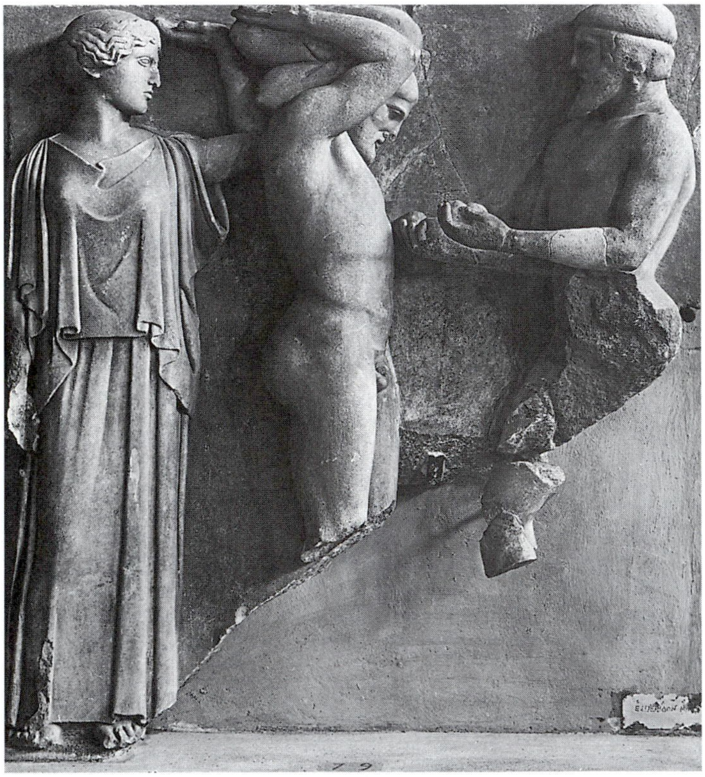

Fig. 333 ***Atlas Bringing Herakles the Golden Apples,*** **The Temple of Zeus, Olympia, c. 470–456 BCE.**
Marble, H. 63 in. Archaeological Museum, Olympia.

The Greeks perfected the sculptural art of relief as a means to decorate and embellish the beauty of their great architectural achievements. Forms and figures carved in relief are spoken of as done in either **low relief** or **high relief.** (Some people prefer the French terms, *bas-relief* and *haut-relief*.) Low relief sculptures project only a short distance from their base. High relief sculptures project forward from their base by at least half their depth, and often several elements will be fully in the round. The *Maidens and Stewards*, for example, a fragment in low relief from the **frieze,** or sculptural band, on the Parthenon (Fig. 332), projects only a little distance from the background, and no sculptural element is detached entirely from it. By contrast, *Atlas Bringing Herakles the Golden Apples* (Fig. 333), from the Temple of Zeus at Olympia, is an example of high relief. Here the figures project from the background at least half their circumference, and other elements, like the left arm of Herakles, the central figure, float free.

Of the two, the relief from the Temple of Zeus is the more simple and direct in carving style. It depicts the moment in the story of Herakles when the giant Atlas returns from the Hesperides with the Golden Apples of immortality. In Atlas's absence, Herakles had assumed the giant's normal task of holding up the heavens on his back, assisted by a pillow that rests upon his shoulders. In the relief, his protectress, Athena, the goddess of wisdom, helps Herakles to support the weight of the sky so that he can exchange places with Atlas. The frontality of Athena's body is countered by the pure profile of her face, a profile repeated in the positioning of both Herakles and Atlas. The composition of this relief is dominated by right angles, and as a result, it is stiff and rigid, as if the urge to naturalism, realized, for instance, in the figure of Herakles, is as burdened by tradition as Herakles is himself weighed down.

The naturalism of the Parthenon frieze is much more fully developed. Figures overlap one another and are shown in three-quarter view, making the space seem far more natural and even deeper than that at Olympia, though it is, in fact, much shallower. The figures themselves seem almost to move in slow procession, and the garments they wear reveal real flesh and limbs beneath them. The carving of this drapery invites a play of light and shadow that further activates the surface, increasing the sense of movement.

Perhaps because the human figure has traditionally been one of the chief subjects of sculpture, movement is one of the defining characteristics of the medium. Even in relief sculptures it is as if the figures want to escape the confines of their base. Sculpture **in-the-round** literally demands movement. It is meant to be seen from all sides, and the viewer must move around it. Giovanni da Bologna's *The Rape of the Sabine Women* (Fig. 334) is impossible to represent in a single photograph. As its figures rise in a spiral, the sculpture changes dramatically as the viewer walks around it and experiences it from each side. It is in part the horror of the scene that lends the sculpture its power, for as it draws us around it, in order to see more of what is happening, it involves us both physically and emotionally in the scene it depicts.

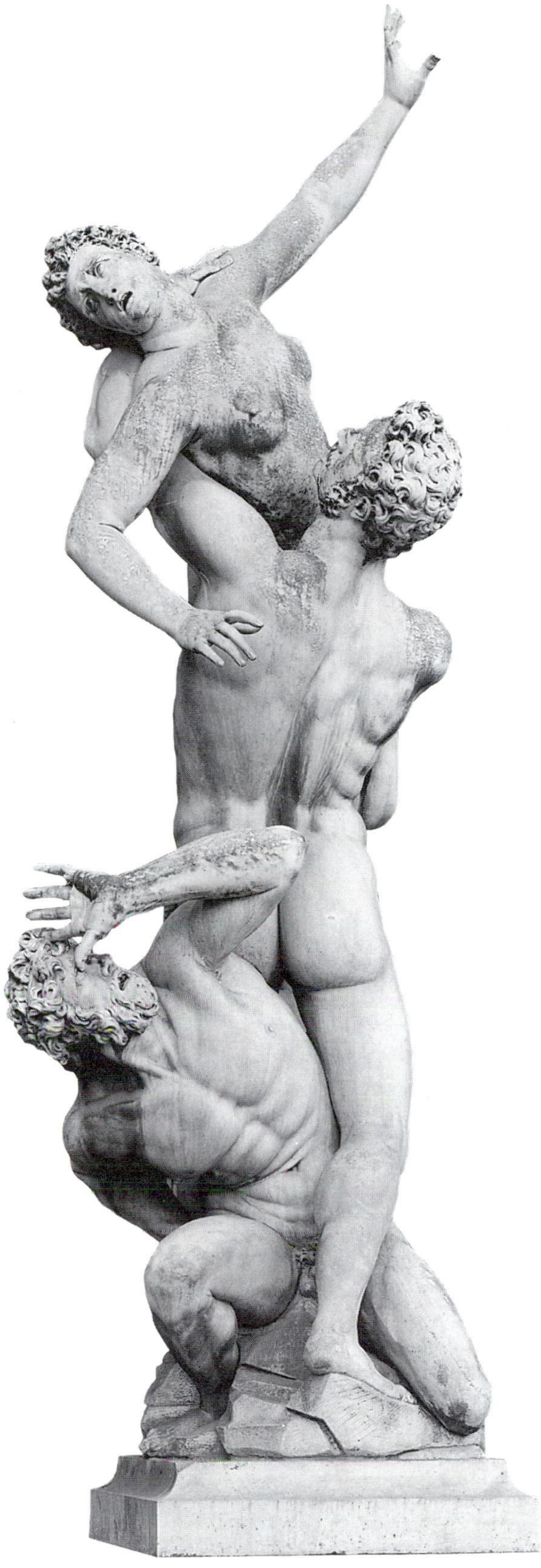

Fig. 334 Giovanni da Bologna, *The Rape of the Sabine Women,* completed 1583.
Marble, H. 13 ft. 6 in.
Loggia dei Lanzi, Florence.

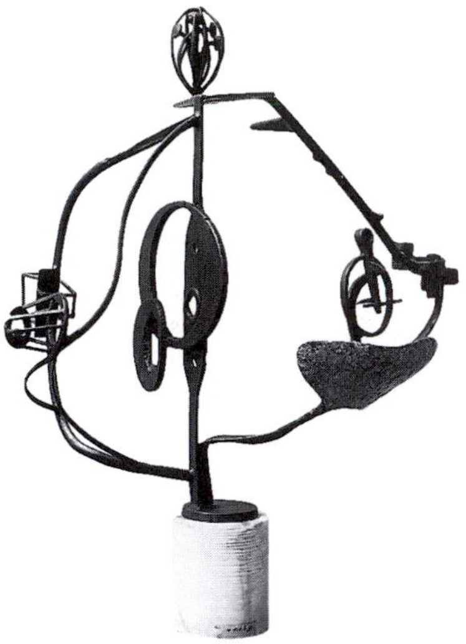

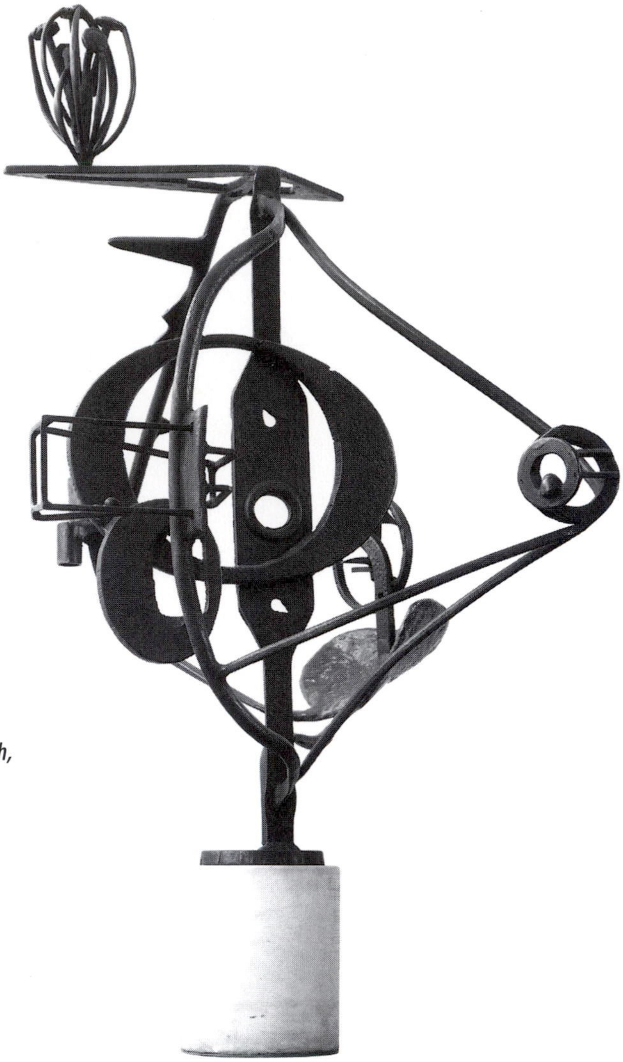

Figs. 335 and 336 David Smith, *Blackburn: Song of an Irish Blacksmith*, frontal view above; profile view at right, 1949–1950.
Steel and bronze, 46 1/4 × 49 3/4 × 24 in.
Wilhelm Lehmbruck Museum, Duisburg, Germany.

Looked at from different points of view, David Smith's *Blackburn: Song of an Irish Blacksmith* (Figs. 335 and 336) appears to be two entirely different works of art. The frontal view is airy and open, the work seeming to float in space like a series of notes and chords, while the profile view reveals the sculpture as densely compacted, a confusing jumble of forms from which two seem to want to escape, one at the top left, the other on the extreme right. The frontal view is almost symmetrical, the profile view radically asymmetrical.

The viewer is even more engaged in the other sculptural media we will discuss in this chapter—environments. An **environment** is a sculptural space into which you can physically enter either indoors, where it is generally referred to as an **installation,** or out-of-doors, where its most common form is that of the **earthwork.** With these terms in mind—relief sculpture, sculpture in-the-round, and environments—we can turn now to the specific methods of making sculpture.

Carving

Carving is a subtractive process in which the material being carved is chipped, gouged, or hammered away from an inert, raw block of material. Wood and stone are the two most common carving materials. Both materials present problems for the artist to solve. Sculptors who work in wood must pay attention to the wood's grain, since wood will only split in the direction it grew. To work "against the grain" is to risk destroying the block. Sculptors who work in stone must take into account the different characteristics of each type of stone. Sandstone is gritty and coarse, marble soft and crystalline, granite dense and hard. Each must be dealt with differently. For Michelangelo, each stone held within it the secret of what it might become as a sculpture. "The best artist," he wrote, "has no concept which some single marble does not enclose within its mass. . . . Taking away . . . brings out a living figure in alpine and hard stone, which . . . grows the more as the stone is chipped away." But carving is so difficult that even Michelangelo often failed to realize his concept. In his *"Atlas" Slave* (Fig. 337), he has given up. The block of stone resists Michelangelo's desire to transform it, as if refusing to release the figure it holds enslaved within. Atlas, condemned to bearing the weight of the world on his shoulders forever as punishment for challenging the Greek gods, is literally held captive in the stone.

Nativity (Fig. 338), by the Taos, New Mexico-born Hispanic sculptor Patrocinio Barela, is carved out of the aromatic juniper tree that grows across the arid landscape of the Southwest. Barela's forms are clearly dependent upon the original shape of the juniper itself. The lines of his figures, verging on abstraction, follow the natural contours of the wood and its grain. The group of animals at the far left, for instance, are supported by a natural fork in the branch that is incorporated into the sculpture. The human figures in Barela's work are closely related to *santos,* images of the saints. Those who carve *santos* are known as *santeros*. Both have been an important part of Southwestern Hispanic culture since the seventeenth century, serving to give concrete identity to the abstractions of Catholic religious doctrine. By choosing to work in local wood, Barela ties the local world of the everyday to the universal realm of religion, uniting material reality and the spiritual.

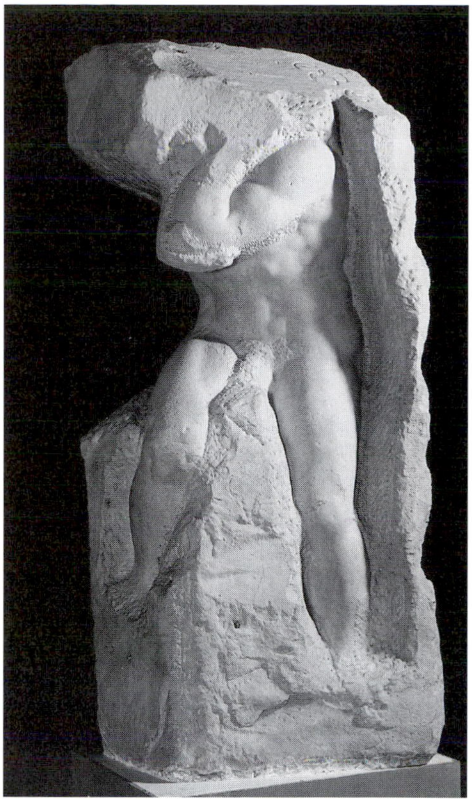

Fig. 337 Michelangelo, *"Atlas" Slave,* c. 1513–1520.
Marble, 9 ft. 2 in. Accademia, Florence.

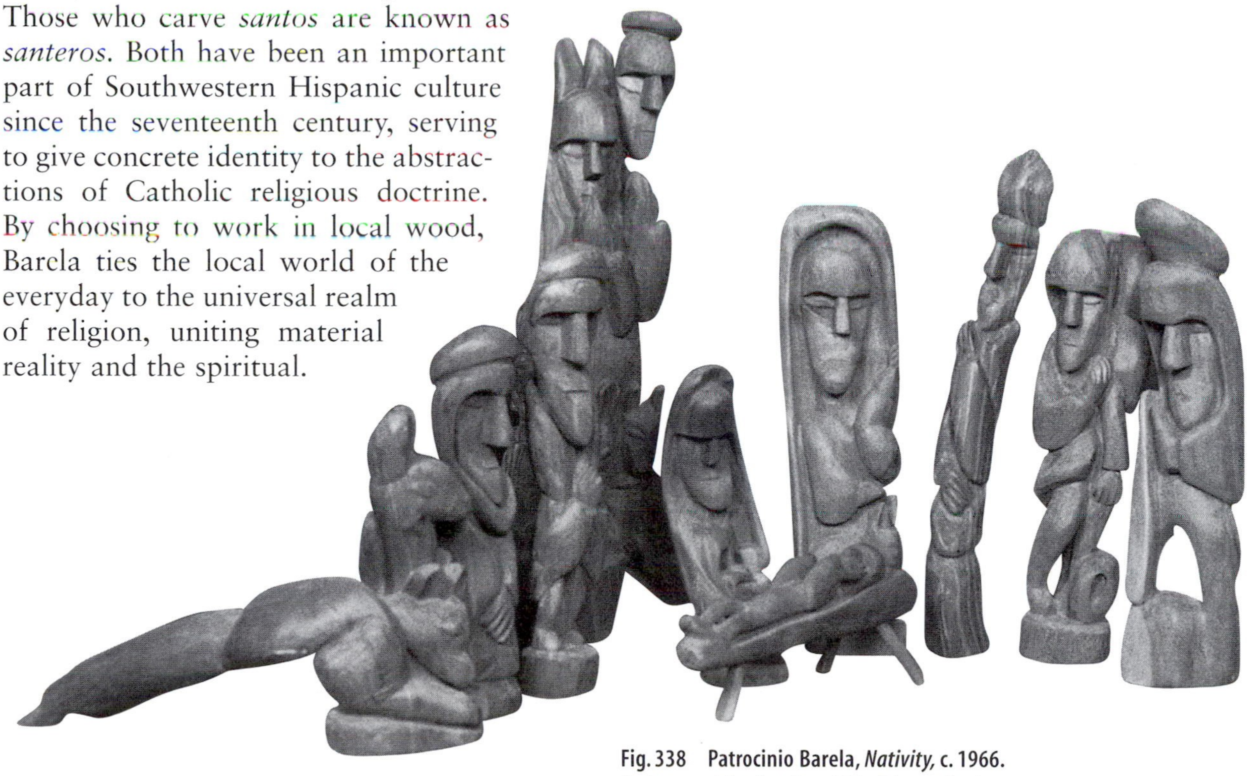

Fig. 338 Patrocinio Barela, *Nativity,* c. 1966.
Juniper wood, H. tallest figure 33 in. Private collection.

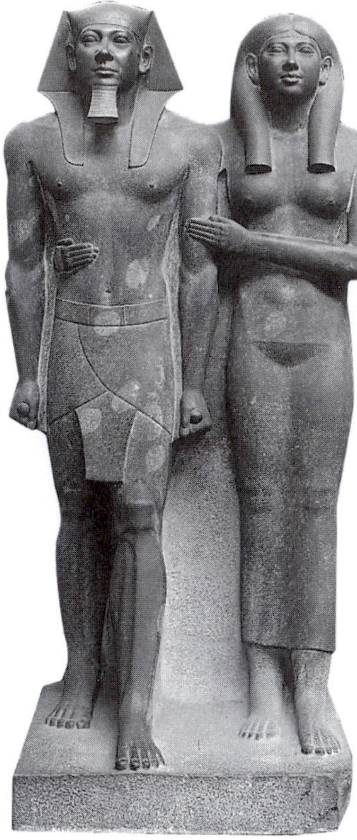

Fig. 339 ***Mycerinus and His Queen, Kha-Merer-Nebty II,* Giza, c. 2599–2571 BCE.**
Slate schist, H. 54 ½ in. Museum of Fine Arts, Boston.

This desire to unify the material and the spiritual worlds has been a goal of sculpture from the earliest times. In Egypt, for example, larger-than-lifesize stone funerary figures (Fig. 339) were carved to bear the ***ka,*** or individual spirit, of the deceased into the eternity of the afterlife. The permanence of the stone was felt to guarantee the *ka*'s immortality. For the ancient Greeks, only the gods were immortal. What tied the world of the gods to the world of humanity was beauty itself, and the most beautiful thing of all was the perfectly proportioned, usually athletic male form.

Egyptian sculpture was known to the Greeks as early as the seventh century BCE, and Greek sculpture is indebted to it, but the Greeks quickly evolved a much more *naturalistic* style. In other words, compared with the rigidity of the Egyptian figures, this *Kouros,* or youth (Fig. 340), is both more at ease and more lifelike. Despite the fact that his feet have been lost, we can see that the weight of his body is on his left leg, allowing his right leg to relax completely. This youth, then, begins to move—we see him shift his weight to his left foot to take a step in one of the earliest examples of the principle of **ponderation,** or weight shift. The sculpture begins to be animated, to portray not just the figure but its movement. It is as if the stone has begun to come to life. Furthermore, the *Kouros* is much more anatomically correct than his Egyptian forebear. In fact, by the fifth century BCE, the practice of medicine had established itself as a respected field of study in Greece, and anatomical investigations were commonplace. At the time that the *Kouros* was sculpted, the body was an object of empirical study, and its parts were understood to be unified in a single, flowing harmony.

Such naturalism is perhaps nowhere more fully realized in Greek sculpture than in the grouping *Three Goddesses* (Fig. 341) on the east pediment, or triangular roof gable, of the Parthenon. Though actually freestanding

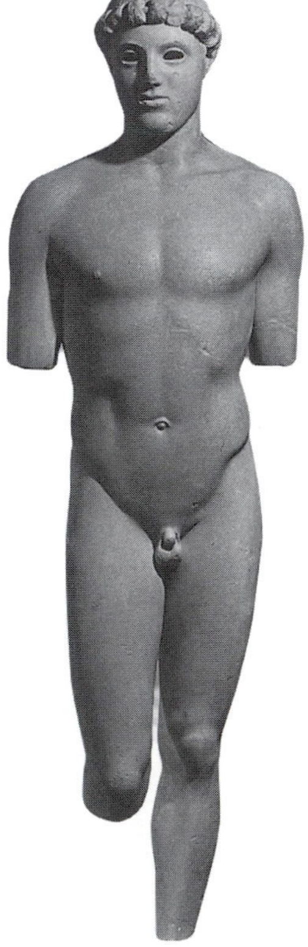

Fig. 340 ***Kouros*** **(also known as the *Kritios Boy*), c. 480 BCE.**
Marble fragment, H. 36 in. Acropolis Museum, Athens.

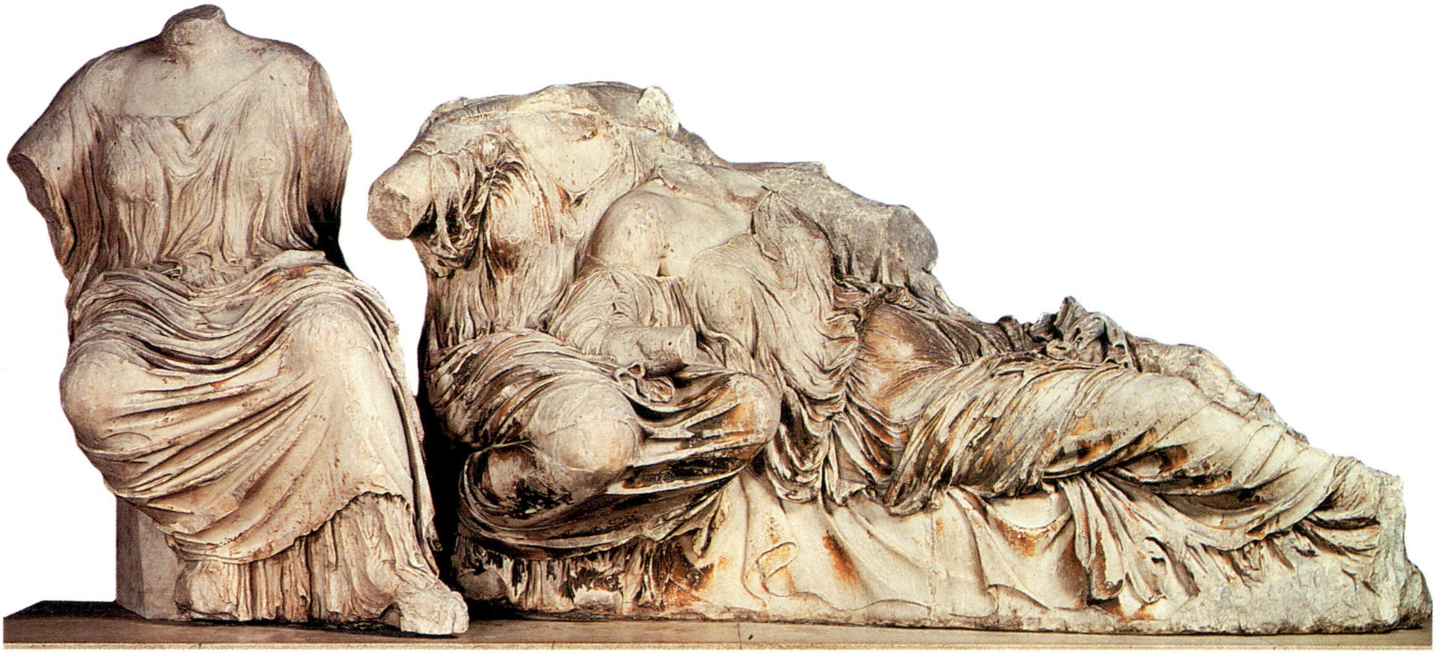

Fig. 341 ***Three Goddesses,*** **from the east pediment of the Parthenon, Acropolis, Athens, c. 438–432 BCE.**
Marble, over lifesize. British Museum, London.

when seen from the ground, as it is displayed today in the British Museum, with the wall of the pediment behind them, Aphrodite, the goddess of beauty, her mother Dione, and Hestia, the goddess of the hearth, would have looked as if they had been carved in high relief. As daylight shifted across the surface of their bodies, it is easy to imagine the goddesses seeming to move beneath the swirling, clinging, almost transparent folds of cloth, as if brought to life by light itself.

The life inherent in stone is the very subject of Auguste Rodin's *The Kiss* (Fig. 342). Rodin leaves the mark of the chisel, like a painter's brushstroke, readily visible in the stone in order to reveal the *process* of sculpture, wherein formal beauty slowly emerges out of raw stone. Marble, as we have seen in Chapter 7, is one of the most tactile of all artistic media. It invites touch. Here the sensuality and passion of the lovers' embrace is heightened in the contrast between the smooth surface of their bodies and the rough-hewn stone on which they sit and out of which they have emerged. Our desire to touch the stone, to feel it beneath our fingers, animates the sculpture. *The Kiss* breathes life into the stone itself.

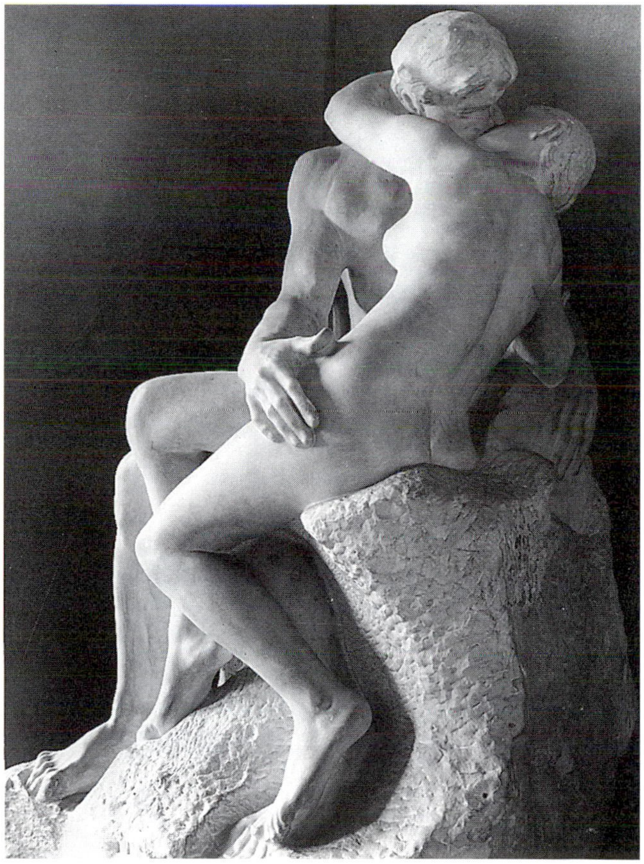

Fig. 342 Auguste Rodin, *The Kiss,* 1886–1898.
Marble, over lifesize. Rodin Museum, Paris.

Modeling

When you pick up a handful of clay, you almost instinctively know what to do with it. You smack it with your hand, pull it, squeeze it, bend it, pinch it between your fingers, roll it, slice it with a knife, and shape it. Then you grab another handful, repeat the process, and add it to the first, building a form piece by piece These are the basic gestures of the additive process of **modeling,** in which a pliant substance, usually clay, is molded.

Clay, a natural material found worldwide, has been used by artists to make everything from pots to sculptures since the earliest times. Its appeal is largely due to its capacity to be molded into forms that retain their shape. Once formed, the durability of the material can be ensured by firing it—that is, baking it—at

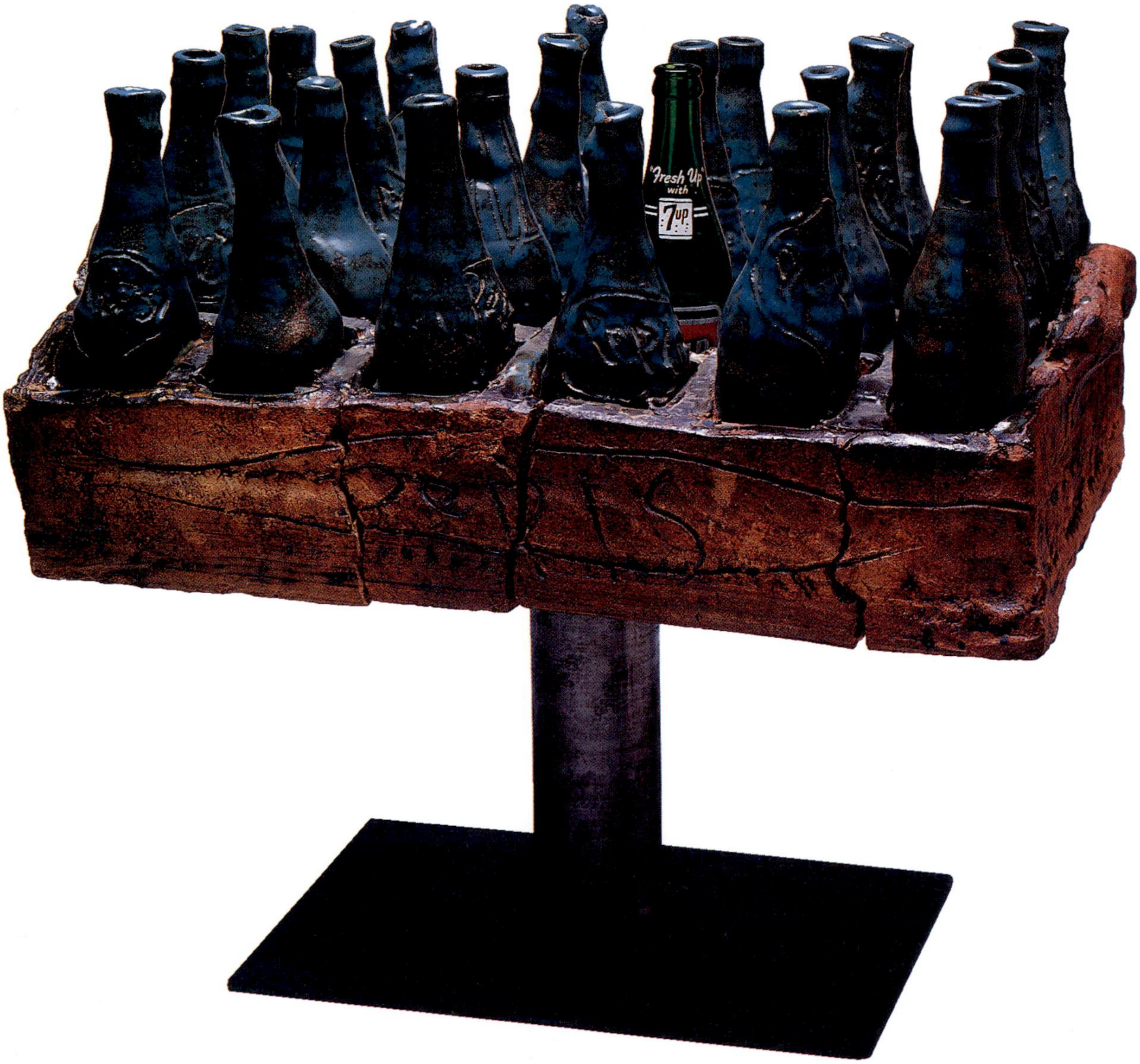

Fig. 343 Robert Arneson, *Case of Bottles,* 1963.
Glazed ceramic (stoneware) and glass, 10 1/2 × 22 × 15 in.
The Santa Barbara Museum of Art. Gift of Mr. and Mrs. Stanley Sheinbaum.

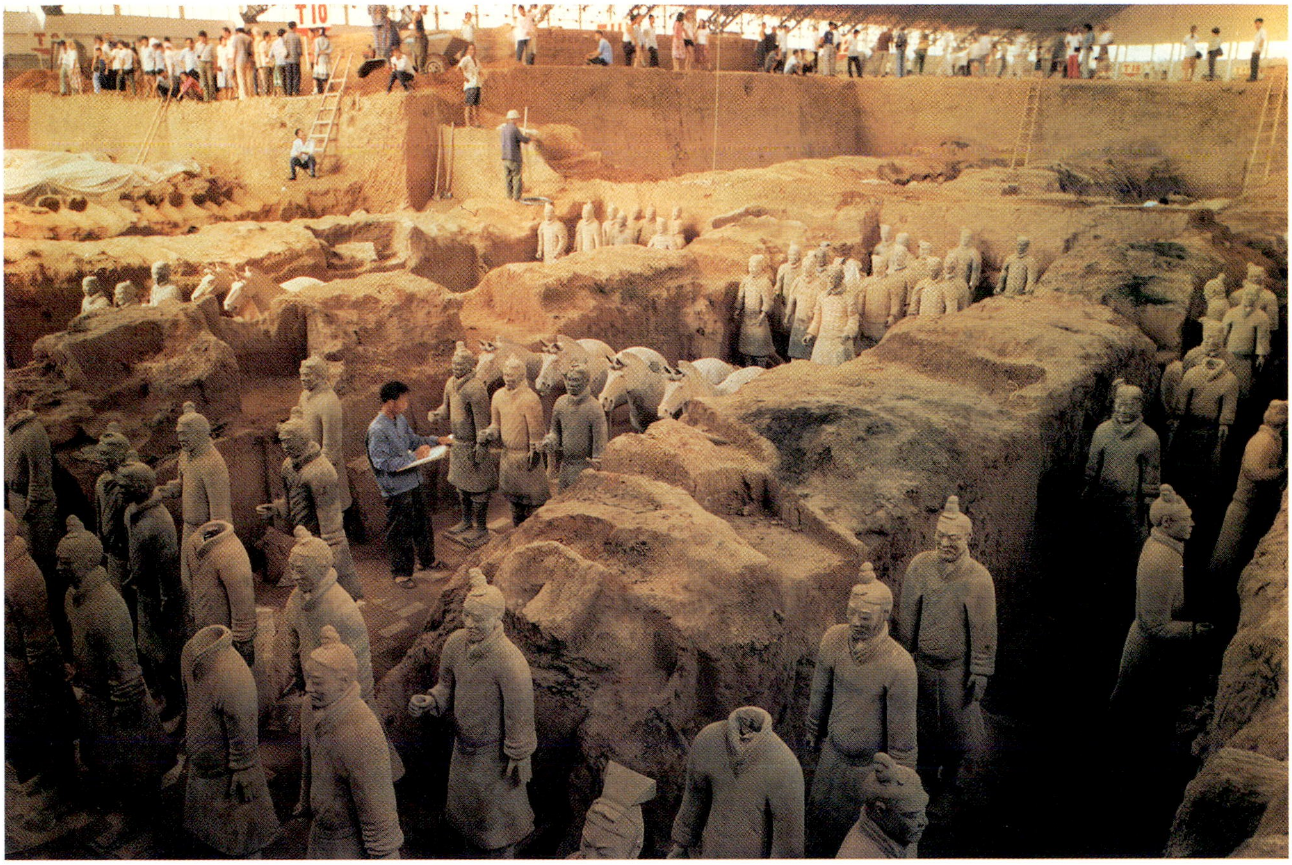

Fig. 344 Tomb of Emperor Shih Huang Ti, 221–206 BCE.
Painted ceramic figures, lifesize.

temperatures normally ranging between 1200 and 2700 degrees Fahrenheit in a **kiln**, or oven, designed especially for the process. This causes it to become hard and waterproof. We call all works made of clay **ceramics.**

Robert Arneson's *Case of Bottles* (Fig. 343) is a ceramic sculpture. The rough handmade quality of Arneson's work, a quality that clay lends itself to especially well, contrasts dramatically with his subject matter, mass-produced consumer products. He underscores this contrast by including in the case of Pepsi a single real 7-Up bottle. He has even allowed the work to crack by firing it too quickly. The piece stands in stark defiance to the assembly line.

Throughout history, the Chinese have made extraordinary ceramic works, including the finest porcelains of fine, pure white clay. We tacitly acknowledge their expertise when we refer to our own "best" dinner plates as "china." But the most massive display of the Chinese mastery of ceramic art was discovered in 1974 by well diggers who accidentally drilled into the tomb of Shih Huang Ti, the first emperor of China (Fig. 344). In 221 BCE, Shih Huang Ti united the country under one rule and imposed order, establishing a single code of law and requiring the use of a single language. Under his rule the Great Wall was built, and construction of his tomb required a force of over 700,000 men. Shih was buried near the central Chinese city of Xian, or Ch-in (the origin of the name China), and his tomb contained more than 6,000 lifesize, and extraordinarily life-like, ceramic figures of soldiers and horses, immortal bodyguards for the emperor. More recently, clerks, scribes, and other court figures have been discovered, as well as a set of magnificent bronze horses and chariots. Compared to Arneson's rough work, the figures created by the ancient Chinese masters are incredibly refined, but between the two of them we can see how versatile clay is as a material.

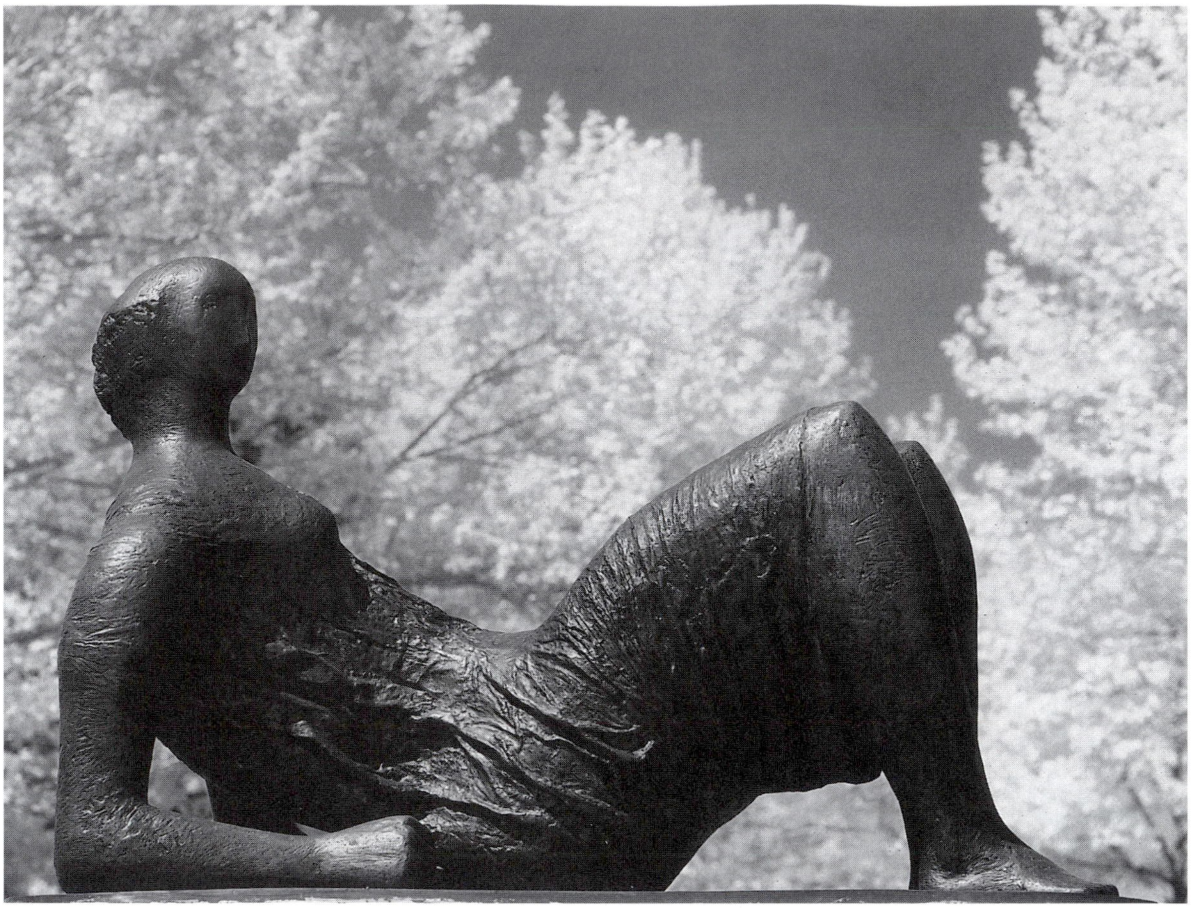

Fig. 345 Henry Moore, *Draped Reclining Figure,* 1952–1953.
Bronze, $40\frac{7}{8} \times 66\frac{5}{8} \times 34\frac{1}{8}$ in.
Hirshhorn Museum and Sculpture Garden, Smithsonian Institution; Gift of Joseph H. Hirshhorn, 1966.

Casting

When the sculptor Henry Moore visited Greece in 1951, he was immediately enthralled by the use of drapery in classical sculpture. "Drapery can emphasize the tension in a figure," he wrote, "For where the form pushes outwards such as on the shoulders, the thighs, the breasts, etc., it can be pulled tight across the form (almost like a bandage)." Moore's *Draped Reclining Figure* (Fig. 345) was inspired by what he saw in Greece. "Although static," he said, "this figure is not meant to be in slack repose, but, as it were, alerted."

Moore's work is cast in bronze, a metal made by mixing copper and tin. **Casting** is an invention of the Bronze Age (beginning approximately 2500 BCE), when it was first utilized to make various utensils by simply pouring liquid bronze into open-faced molds. The technology is not much more complicated than that of a Jello mold. You pour Jello into the mold and let

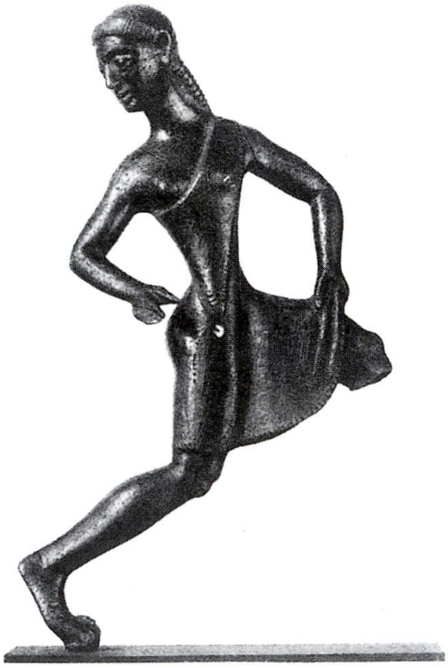

Fig. 346 *Girl Running,* Greece, probably Sparta, c. 500 BCE.
H. $4\frac{1}{2}$ in. British Museum, London.

it harden. When you remove the Jello, it is shaped like the inside of the mold. Small figures made of bronze are similarly produced by making a simple mold of an original modeled form, filling the mold with bronze, and then breaking the mold away. The early Greek *Girl Running* (Fig. 346) is a small, solid cast-bronze figure almost certainly made by this most straightforward of bronze casting methods.

As the example of Jello demonstrates, bronze is not the only material that can be cast. In the kingdom of Benin, located in southern Nigeria, on the coastal plain west of the Niger River, brass casting reached a level of extraordinary accomplishment as early as the late fourteenth century. Brass, which is a compound composed of copper and zinc, is similar to bronze but contains less copper and is yellower in color. When, after 1475, the people of Benin began to trade with the Portuguese for copper and brass, an explosion of brass casting occurred. Shown below is a brass head of an Oba dating from the eighteenth century (Fig. 347). The Oba is the king of a dynasty. When an Oba dies, one of the first duties of the new Oba is to establish an altar commemorating his father and to decorate it with newly cast brass heads. The heads are not portraits. Rather, they are generalized images that emphasize the king's coral-bead crown and high bead collar, the symbols of his authority. The head has a special significance in Benin ritual. According to British anthropologist R. E. Bradbury, the head "symbolizes life and behavior in this world, the capacity to organize one's actions in such a way as to survive and prosper. It is one's Head that 'leads one through life.'. . . On a man's Head depends not only his own wellbeing but that of his wives and children. . . . At the state level, the welfare of the people as a whole depends on the Oba's Head which is the object of worship at the main event of the state ritual year."

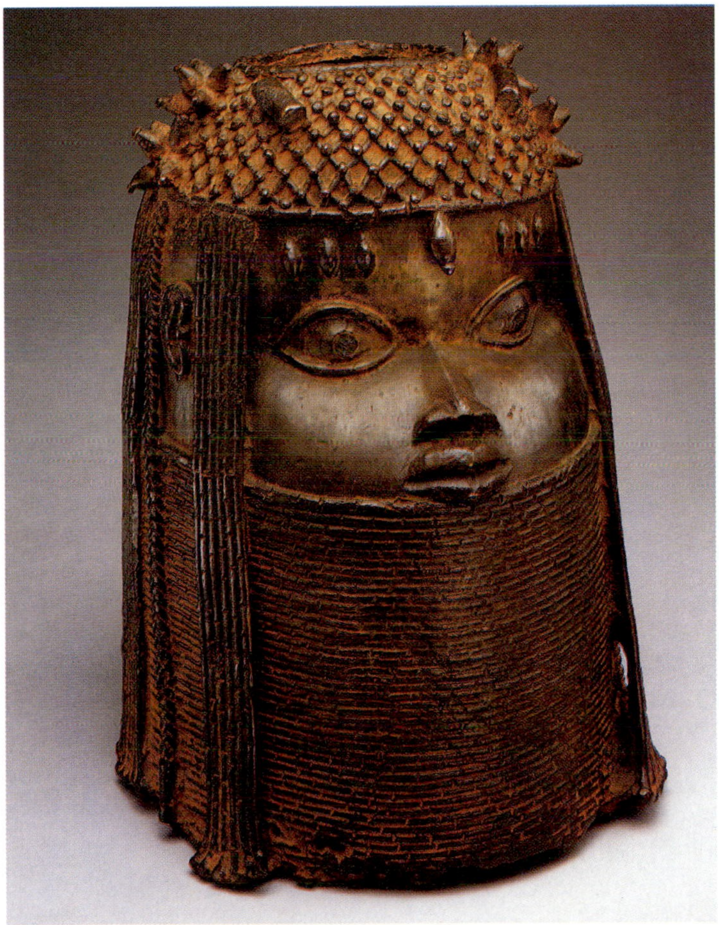

Fig. 347 Nigeria, Edo; Court of Benin, *Head of an Oba,* 18th century.
Brass, iron, H. 13 1/8 in. The Metropolitan Museum of Art, Gift of Mr. and Mrs. Klaus G. Perls, 1991.

The Oba head is an example of one of the most enduring, and one of the most complicated processes for casting metal. The **lost-wax** method, also known as ***cire-perdue,*** was perfected by the Greeks if not actually invented by them. Because metal is both expensive and heavy, a technique had to be developed to create hollow images rather than solid ones. The illustrations of the method on these two pages (Figs. 348–350) give some indication of its complexity. These images are from the *Encyclopedia of Trades and Industry,* compiled in the eighteenth century by the French encyclopedist, art critic, dramatist, and writer Denis Diderot. They depict the casting process of a mounted figure of Louis XIV, which was erected in Paris in 1699.

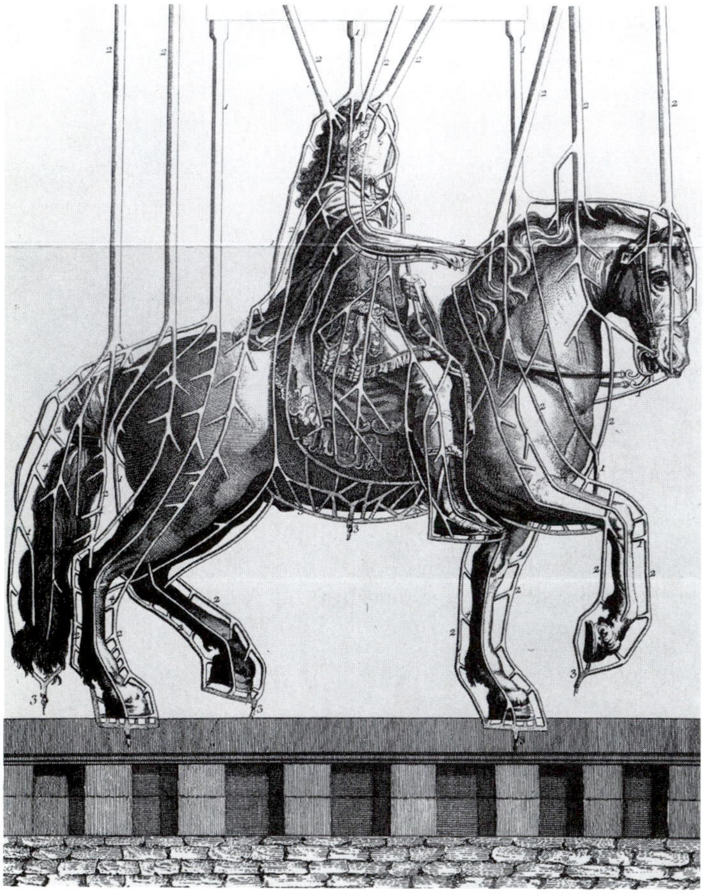

Fig. 348 ***Casting a Large Equestrian Statue I,***
from Diderot's *Encyclopaedia of Trades and Industries,* Vol. VIII, 1771.
Sculpture, Fonte des Statues Equestres, Pl. IV. Courtesy of the New York Public Library.

In the lost-wax method, the sculpture is first modeled in some soft, pliable material, such as clay, wax, or plaster in a putty state. This model looks just like the finished sculpture, but, of course, the material of which it is composed is nowhere near as durable as metal.

A mold is then made of the model (today, synthetic rubber is most commonly used to make this mold), and when it is removed, we are left with a *negative* impression of the original—in other words, something like a Jello mold of the object. Molten wax is then poured or brushed into this impression to the same thickness desired for the final sculpture—about an eighth of an inch. The space inside this wax lining is filled with an **investment**—a mixture of water, plaster, and powder made from ground-up pottery. The mold is then removed, and we are left with a wax casting, identical to the original model, that is filled with the investment material. Rods of wax are then applied to the wax casting. They stick out from it like giant hairs. They will carry off melted wax during baking and will eventually provide channels through which the molten bronze will be poured. Figure 348 depicts the wax model of the stature of Louis XIV surrounded by a latticework of wax channels. Note how the channels descend from the top, where the bronze will eventually be poured. The statue's surface is a thin layer of wax supported by the investment. Bronze pins have been driven through the wax into the investment in order to hold investment, casting, and channels in place.

This wax cast, with its wax channels, is ready to be covered with another outer mold, of investment. In the left panel of Figure 349, we see a cutaway of the wax cast surrounded by the investment. When this outer mold cures, it is then baked in a kiln at a temperature of 1500° F., with the wax replica inside it. The wax rods melt, providing channels for the rest of the wax to run out as well—hence the term *lost-wax*. A thin space where the wax once was

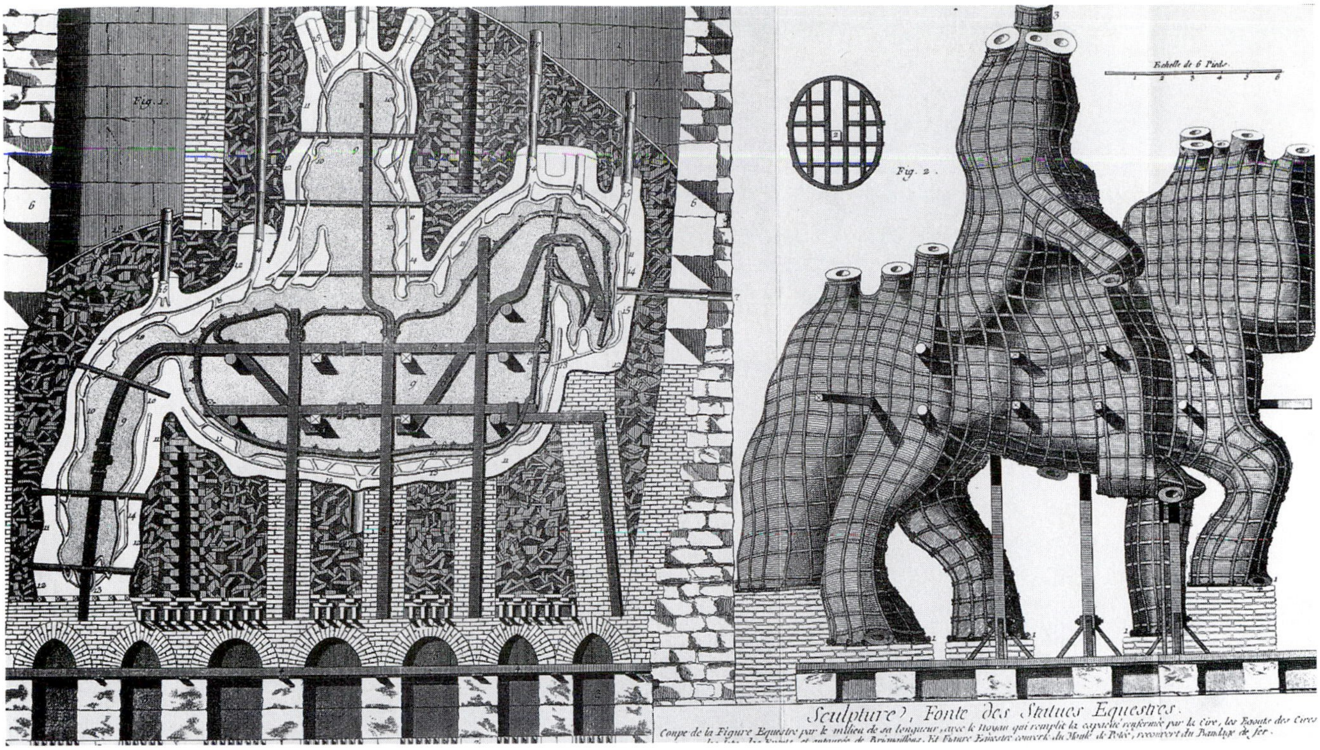

Fig. 349 (above) ***Casting a Large Equestrian Statue II,***
from Diderot's *Encyclopaedia of Trades and Industries,* Vol. VIII, 1771.
Sculpture, Fonte des Statues Equestres, Pl. V. Courtesy of the New York Public Library.

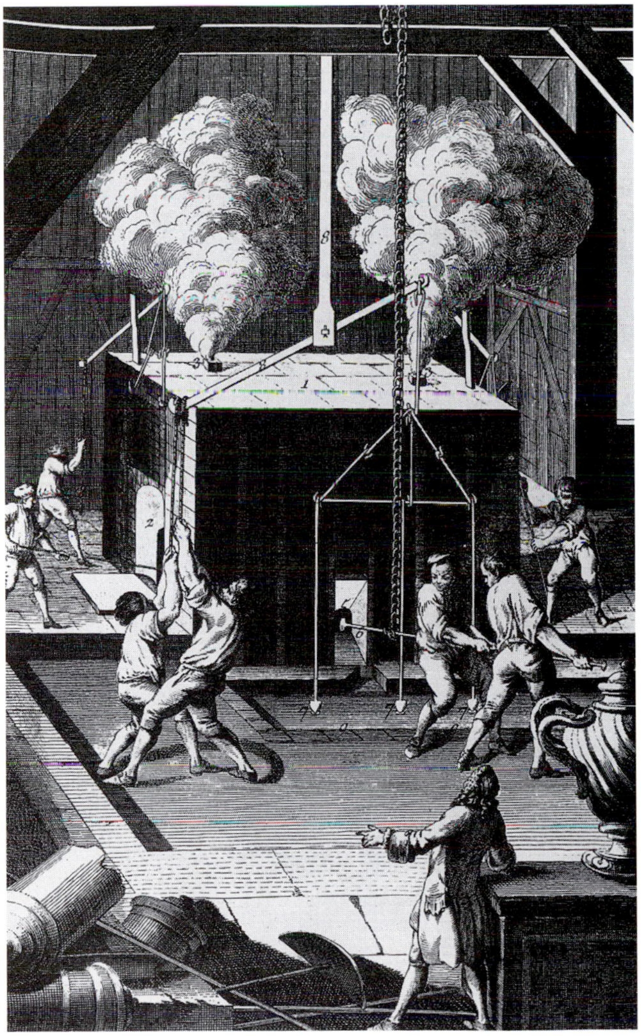

Fig. 350 (right) ***Casting a Large Equestrian Statue III,***
from Diderot's *Encyclopaedia of Trades and Industries,* Vol. VIII, 1771.
Sculpture, Fonte des Statues Equestres, Pl. I. Courtesy of the New York Public Library.

now lies empty between the inner core and the outer mold, the separation maintained by the bronze pins. The right hand side of Figure 349 shows the burned-out mold ready to be lowered into the casting pit, its exterior reinforced by iron bands.

In Figure 350, the bronze pour is about to take place. The casting pit is located beneath the foundry floor, where the mold is encased in sand. The large box in the background is the furnace, where the bronze is melted. Molten bronze is poured into the *casting gate,* the large opening in the top of the mold directly in front of the furnace, filling the cavity where the wax once was. Hence, many people refer to casting as a **replacement** method—bronze replaces wax. When the bronze has cooled, the mold and the investment are removed, and we are left with a bronze replica of the wax form complete with the latticework of rods. The rods are cut from the bronze cast and the surface smoothed and finished.

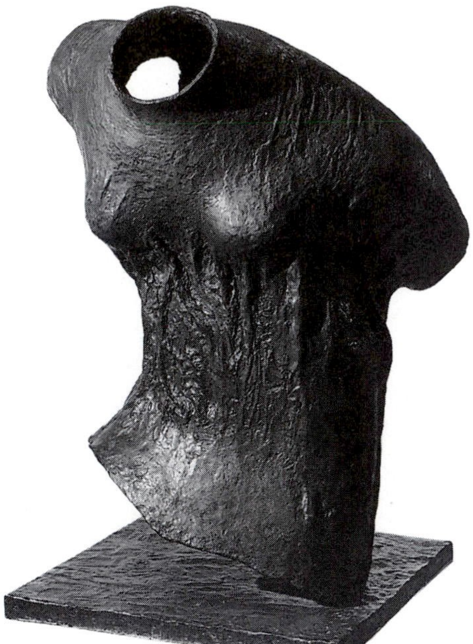

Fig. 351 Henry Moore, *Draped Torso,* 1953.
Bronze, H. 35 in. Ferens Art Gallery: Hull City Museums, Art Galleries and Archives. Hull, England.

Large pieces such as Moore's *Draped Reclining Figure* (Fig. 345) must be cast in several pieces and then welded together. Bronze is so soft and malleable that the individual pieces can easily be joined in either of two ways: pounded together with a hammer, the procedure used in Greek times, or welded, the more usual procedure today. Finally, the shell is reassembled to form a perfect hollow replica of the original model. In fact, when Moore saw the torso part of his *Draped Reclining Figure,* cast separately from the rest, he was struck by what he called "its completeness and impressiveness just as a thing in its own right." Thus, after the *Draped Reclining Figure* was completed, he had a wax version of the figure's torso made, and he reworked it, alternately modeling and carving it until it looked appropriately poised in an upright position. *Draped Torso* (Fig. 351) is the result.

It is possible that the process of making body armor might have suggested to the Greeks that the living human body could be used to create molds for cast bronze sculptures, such as the magnificent Zeus we described in Chapter 4

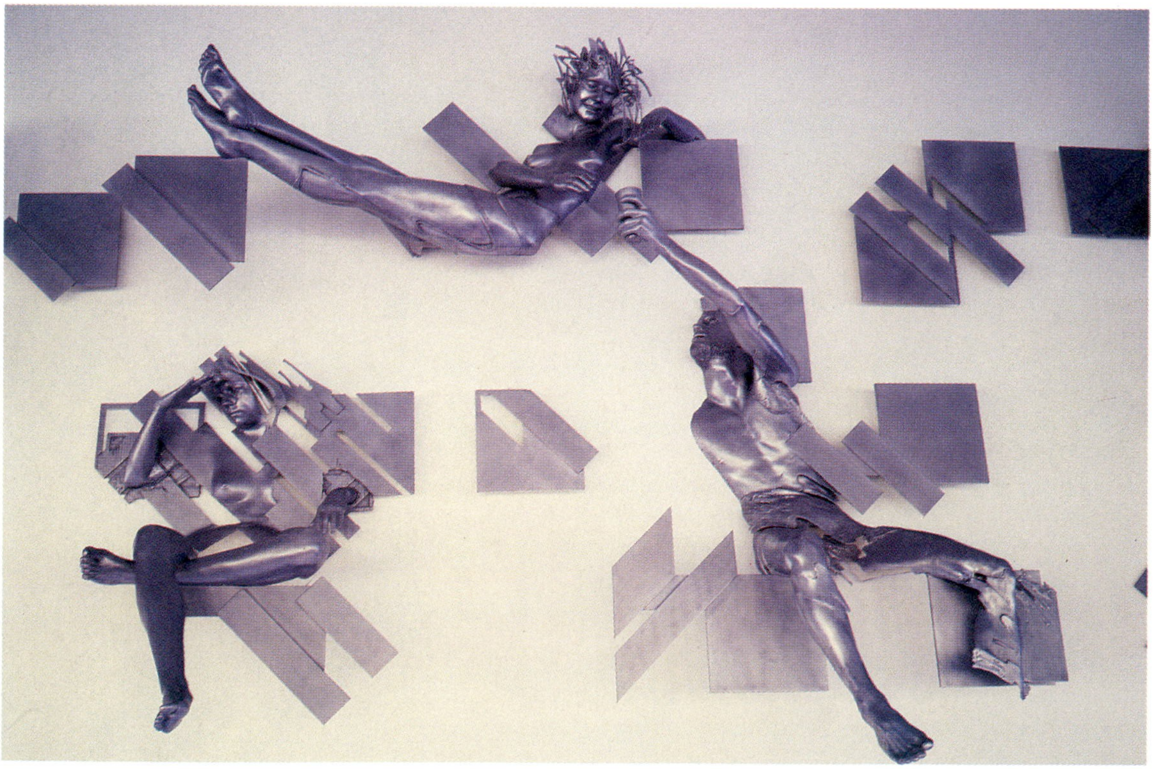

Fig. 352 Tom Morandi, detail from *The Audience,* 1991.
Aluminum, 3 of 10 lifesize figures. Fine and Performing Arts Building, Eastern Oregon State College, La Grande, Oregon.

(Fig. 98). In his huge aluminum relief *The Audience* (Fig. 352), contemporary sculptor Tom Morandi has, in fact, cast his figures from real people by wrapping small sections of their bodies in cheesecloth that has been impregnated with plaster. Small "hinges" were left in the material so that after drying, it could be easily opened and removed. These plaster casts were then used as molds in a lost-wax casting process.

The Audience is composed of ten figures in all, stretched above the main lobby doors of a theater. They variously stare down upon the arriving theatergoers or ignore them, as the figures illustrated here seem to. The piece is a compendium of styles and references, ranging from the Greek pediment to the Pop icon, from realism to idealism (the outstretched arms of the two figures at the right parody the Creation scene in Michelangelo's Sistine Chapel), from the minimalist geometric pattern of the backdrop to the expressive gesture and abstraction of areas such as the bottom right-hand figure's left calf and foot.

Assemblage

Many of the same thematic concerns that we saw in Michelangelo's *"Atlas" Slave* (Fig. 337) are at work in David Hammons's *Spade with Chains* (Fig. 353). Both address, particularly, the issue of enslavement. By means of **assemblage**—creating a sculpture by compiling objects taken from the environment—Hammons has combined "found" materials, a common spade and a set of chains, into a face that recalls an African mask. The piece represents a wealth of transformations. Just as Michelangelo could see in the raw block of stone the figure within, Hammons can see, in the most common materials of everyday life, the figures of his world. This transformation of common materials into art is a defining characteristic of assemblage. As a process, assemblage evokes the myth of the phoenix, the bird that, consumed by fire, is reborn out of its own ashes. That rebirth, or rejuvenation, is also expressed at a cultural level in Hammons's work. The transformation of the materials of slave labor—the spade and the chain—into a mask is an affirmation of the American slave's African heritage. The richness of this transformation is embodied in the double-meaning of the word "spade"—at once a racist epithet and the appropriate name of the object in question. But faced with this image, it is no longer possible, in the words of a common cliché, to "call a spade a spade." The piece literally liberates us from that simple and reductive possibility.

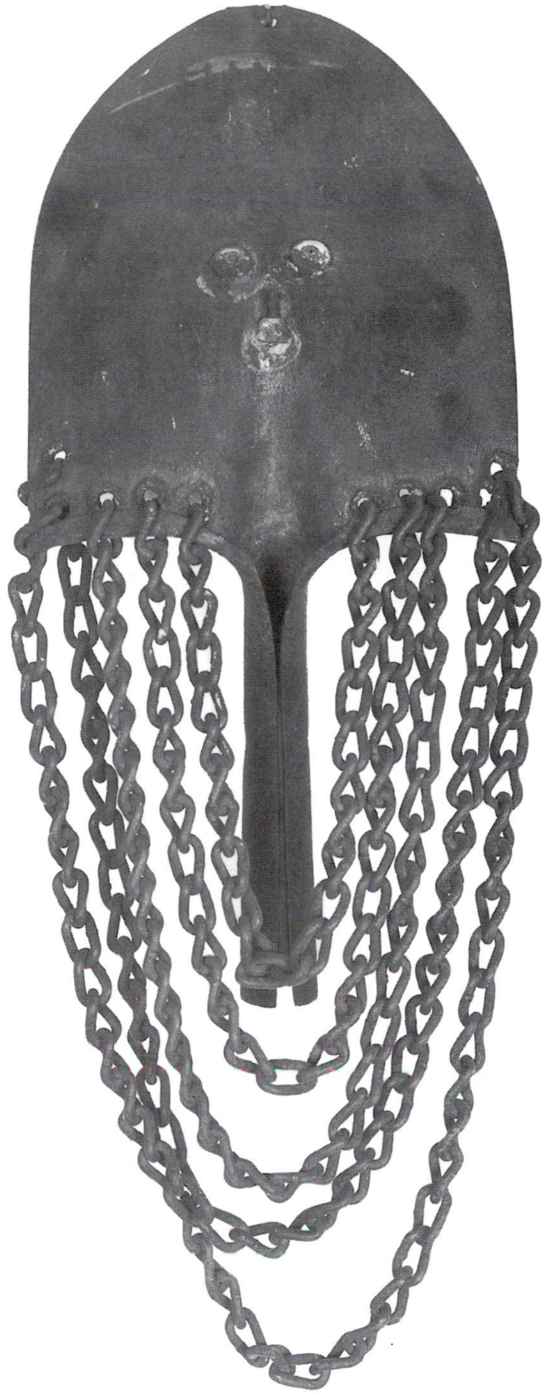

Fig. 353 David Hammons, *Spade with Chains*, 1973.
Spade, chains, 24 × 10 × 5 in.
Courtesy Jack Tilton Gallery, New York. Photograph by Dawoud Bey

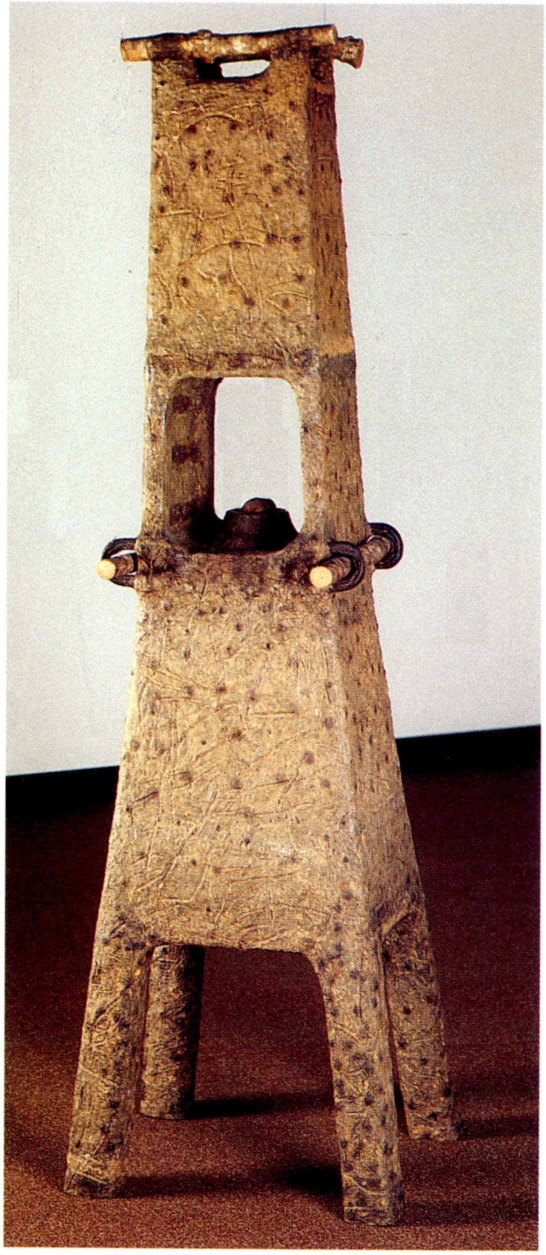

Fig. 354 Clyde Connell, *Swamp Ritual,* 1972.
Mixed media, 81 × 24 × 22 in.
Collection Tyler Museum of Art, Tyler, Texas.
A gift from Alantic Richfield Company.

To the degree that they are composed of separately cast pieces later welded together, works like Moore's *Draped Reclining Figure* (Fig. 345) and Morandi's *The Audience* (Fig. 352) might themselves seem to be assemblages. But it is better to think of them as *constructions*—works in which the artist forms all of the parts that are put together rather than finding the parts in the world. Clyde Connell's assemblage, *Swamp Ritual* (Fig. 354), on the other hand, is fabricated of parts from rusted-out tractors and machines, discarded building materials and logs, and papier-mâché made from the classified sections of the *Shreveport Journal and Times.* The use of papier-mâché developed out of Connell's desire to find a material capable of binding the wooden and iron elements of her work. By soaking the newsprint in hot water until its ink began to turn it a uniform gray, and then mixing it with Elmer's Glue, she was able to create a claylike material possessing, when dry, the texture of wasps' nests or rough gray stone.

Connell developed her method of working very slowly, over the course of about a decade, beginning in 1959 when, at age 58, she moved to a small cabin on Lake Bistineau, 17 miles southeast of Shreveport, Louisiana. She was totally isolated. "Nobody is going to look at these sculptures," she thought. "Nobody was coming here. It was just for me because I wanted to do it. . . . I said to myself, 'I'm just going to start to make sculpture because I think it would be great if there were sculptures here under the trees.'"

In the late 1960s, Connell, by then in her late sixties, discovered the work of another assembler of nontraditional materials, the much younger artist Eva Hesse, who died at age 34 in 1970. Hesse's work is marked by its use of the most outlandish materials—rope, latex, rubberized cheesecloth, fiberglass, and cheap synthetic fabrics—which she used in strangely appealing, even elegant assemblages. Connell particularly admired Hesse's desire to make art in the face of all odds. She sensed in Hesse's work an almost obstinate insistence on *being:* "No matter what it was," she said about Hesse's work, "it looked like it had life in it." Connell wanted to capture this sense of life in her own sculpture—what she calls Hesse's "deep quality." In *Swamp Ritual,* the middle of Connell's figure is hollowed out, creating a cavity filled with stones. Rather than thinking of this space in sexual terms—as a womb, for instance—it is, in Connell's words, a "ritual space" in which she might deposit small objects from nature. "I began to think about putting things in there, of having a gathering place not for mementos but for things you wanted to save. The ritual place is an inner sanctuary. . . . Everybody has this interior space."

While Connell's piece is assembled from many parts, the result is a unified, even organic whole. Anthony Caro's *Early One Morning* (Fig. 355), made of sheet metal, I-beams, pipe, and bolts, lacks this sense of unity. Indeed, it seems to insist on the fact that it is man-made, even artificial. Through the materials of which it is made, the materials of contemporary industrial construction, it boldly declares itself separate from the natural world. Like David Smith's *Blackburn: Song of the Irish Blacksmith* (Figs. 335 and 336), the sculpture changes dramatically depending on the side from which it is seen. Seen directly on—that is, slightly to the right of the view here—both the large vertical sheet at the back and the two central I-beams below it visually combine into an almost solid backdrop, and all of the other elements seem to project off the "flat" rear surface in relief. Seen from the side, however—and the reader must imagine this—the work appears as a series of separate architectural units dispersed along a low horizontal beam over 20 feet long. Like Smith's *Blackburn,* from one side it is airy, almost light, and from the other, it is densely packed, almost two-dimensional. Not only is the work itself an assemblage of disparate elements, but our visual experience of it is itself an assemblage, a construction of multiple points of view.

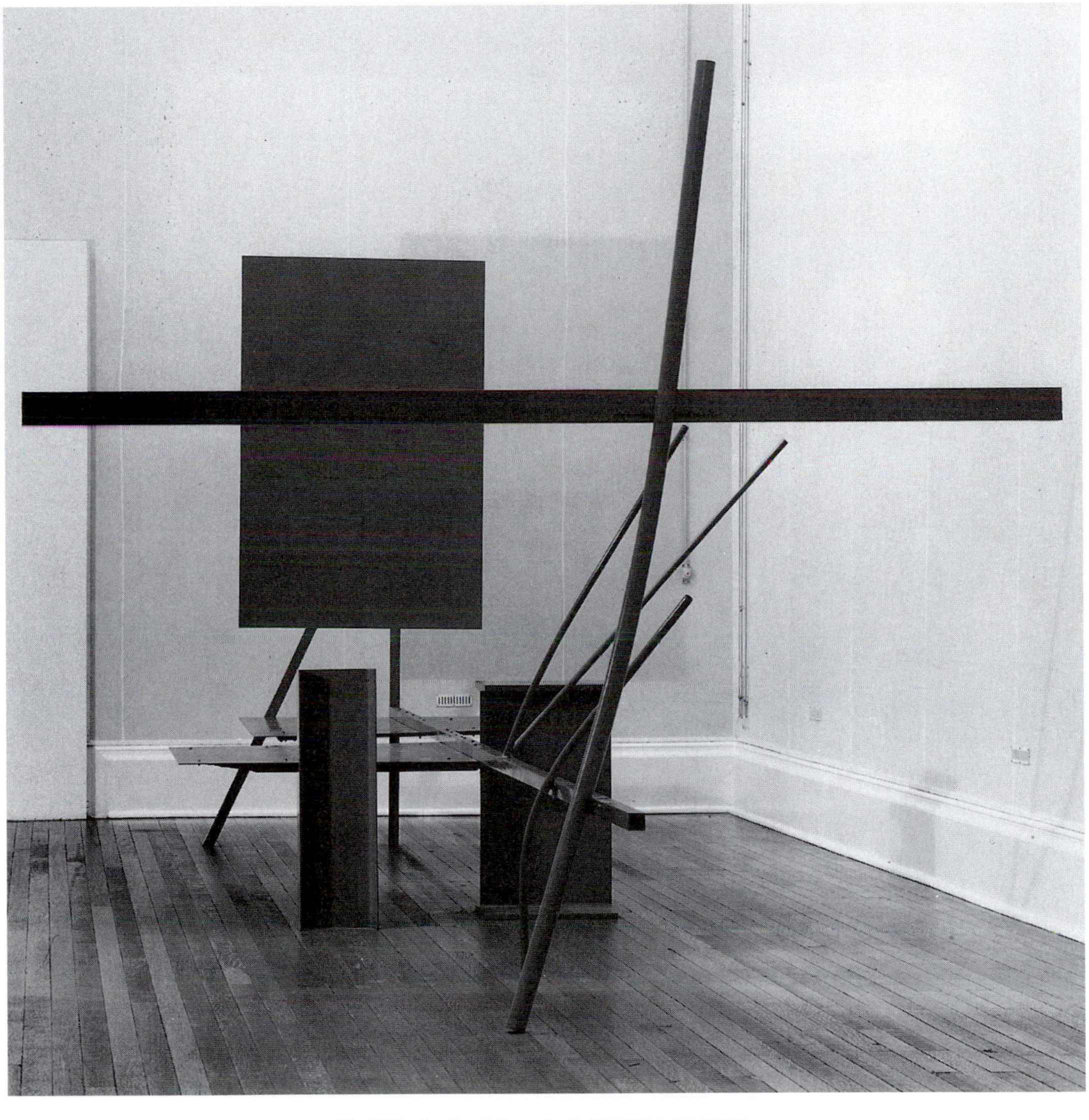

Fig. 355 Anthony Caro, *Early One Morning,* 1962.
Painted metal, 114 × 244 × 132 in.
Tate Gallery, London.

Eva Hesse's Contingent

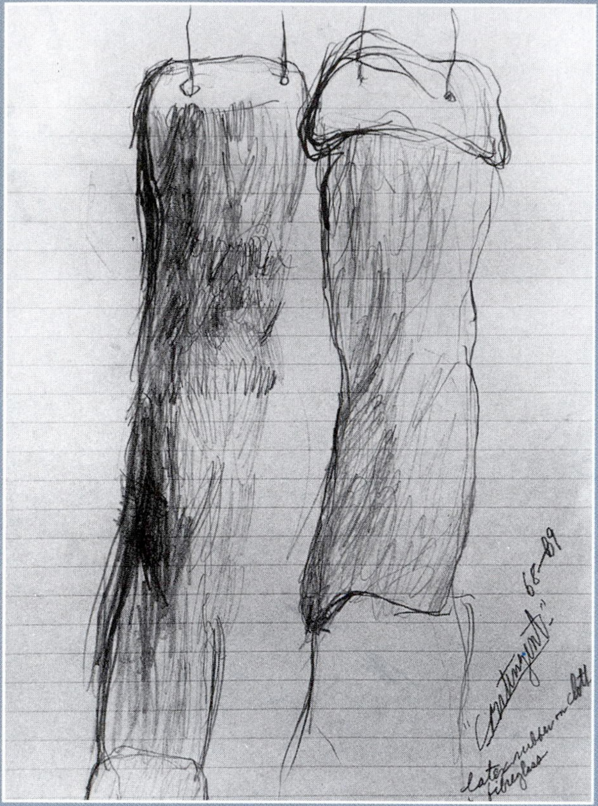

Fig. 356 Eva Hesse, drawing for *Contingent,* 1968–1969.
Pencil on paper, 8 ¼ × 11 in.

Courtesy of The Robert Miller Gallery, New York. Private Collection.

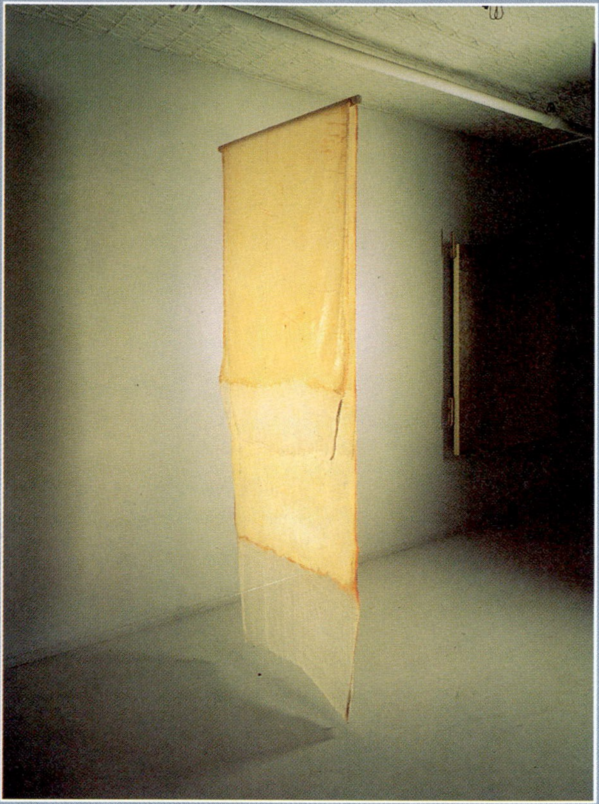

Fig. 357 Eva Hesse, test piece for *Contingent,* 1969.
Latex over cheesecloth, 144 × 44 in.
Collection of Naomi Spector and Stephen Antonakos Private Collection.
 Courtesy of The Robert Miller Gallery, New York.

Between September 1965 and her death in May 1970, Eva Hesse completed over 70 sculptural works. *Contingent* (Fig. 358) is one of the last four pieces she made. For most of the last two years of her life she was ill, suffering from the effects of a brain tumor that was not diagnosed until April 1969. Clyde Connell's admiration for her work is partly a response to Hesse's heroic insistence on making art in the face of her illness and, to use Connell's word, infusing it with "life." But it is also a result of Hesse's feminist sensibilities, for Hesse was a feminist long before the Women's Movement of the early 1970s. "A woman is side-tracked by all her feminine roles," she wrote in 1965. "She's at a disadvantage from the beginning. . . . She also lacks the conviction that she has the 'right' to achievement. . . . [But] we want to achieve something meaningful and to feel our involvements make of us valuable thinking persons." *Contingent* embodies Hesse's personal strength.

Hesse's first ideas for the piece took the form of drawing (Fig. 356). "I always did drawings," Hesse said, "but they were always separate from the sculpture. . . . They were just sketches. . . . [A drawing] is just a quickie to develop it in the process rather than working out a whole model in small and following it—that doesn't interest me." In the drawing, it appears as if Hesse initially conceived of the piece as hanging against the wall, but by the time she was fabricating it, she had turned it sideways, as her "test piece" (Fig. 357) shows.

The final work consists of eight cheesecloth and fiberglass sheets that catch light in different ways producing different colors, an effect almost impossible to capture in a photograph. The sheets seem at once to hang ponderously and to float effortlessly away. Hesse's catalogue statement for the first exhibition of the piece at Finch College in the fall of 1969 speaks eloquently of her thinking about the work:

Began somewhere in November-December, 1968.
Worked.
Collapsed April 6, 1969. I have been very ill.
Statement.
Resuming work on piece,
have one complete from back then. . . .
Piece is in many parts.
Each in itself is a complete statement. . . .
textures, coarse, rough, changing.
see through, not see through, consistent, inconsistent.
they are tight and formal but very ethereal. sensitive. fragile. . . .
not painting, not sculpture. it's there though. . . .
non, nothing,
everything, but of another kind, vision, sort. . . .
I have learned anything is possible. I know that.
that vision or concept will come through total risk,
freedom, discipline.
I will do it.

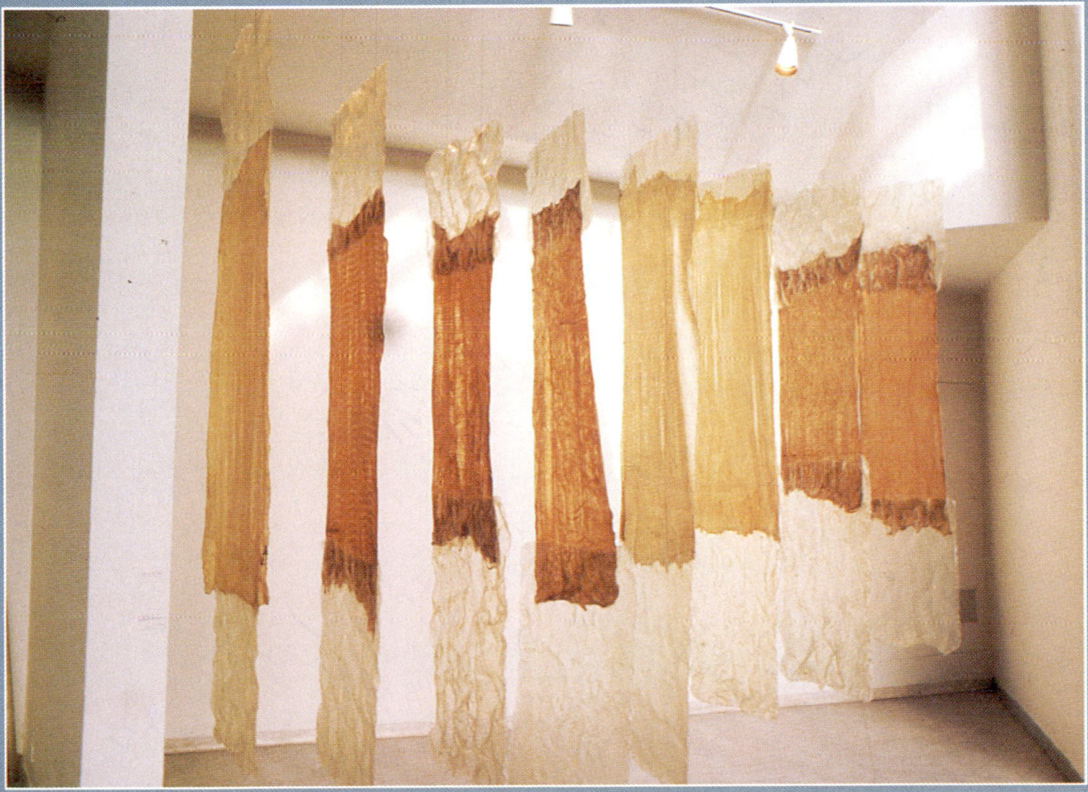

Fig. 358 Eva Hesse, *Contingent*, 1969.
Reinforced fiberglass and latex over cheesecloth, H. each of 8 units, 114–118 in.; W. each of 8 units, 36–48 in.
Collection of the National Gallery of Australia, Canberra. © The Estate of Eva Hesse. Courtesy of The Robert Miller Gallery, New York.

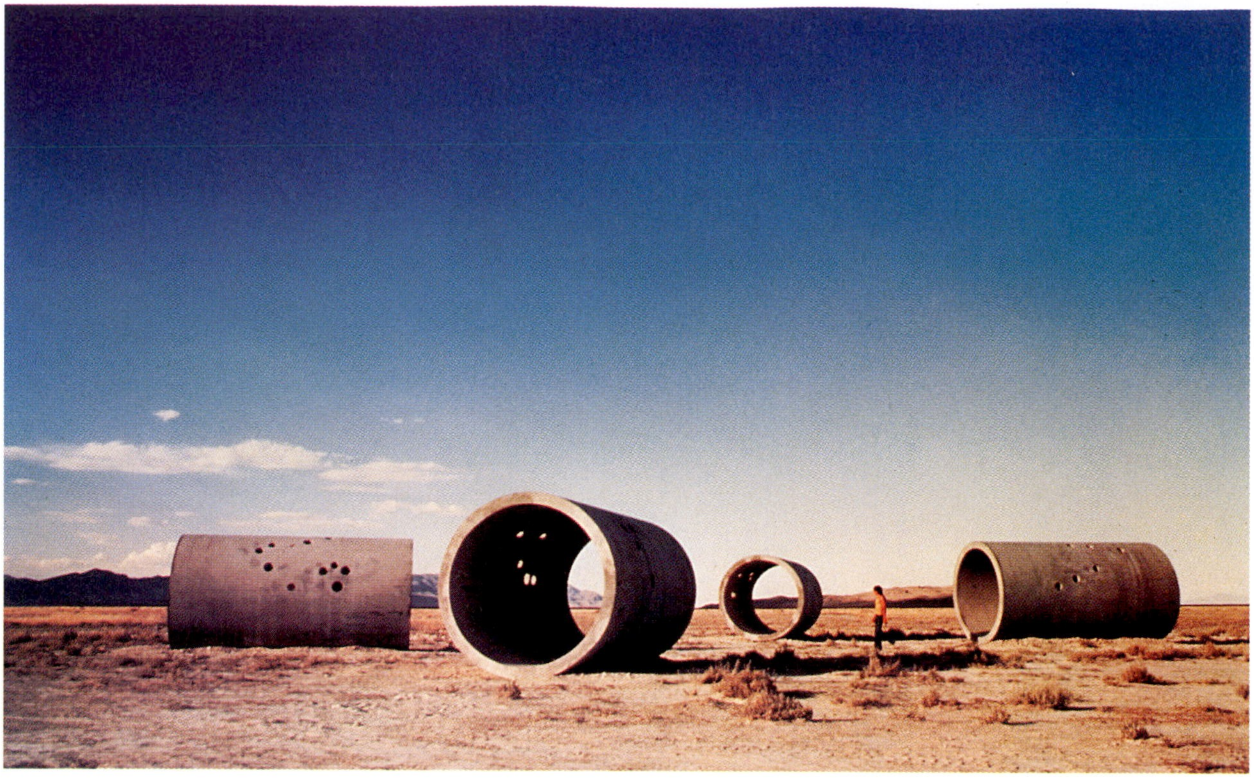

Fig. 359 **Nancy Holt, *Sun Tunnels,* Great Basin Desert, Utah, 1973–1976.**
Four tunnels, each 18 ft. long × 9 ft. 4 in. diameter; each axis 86 ft. long. Courtesy John Weber Gallery, New York.

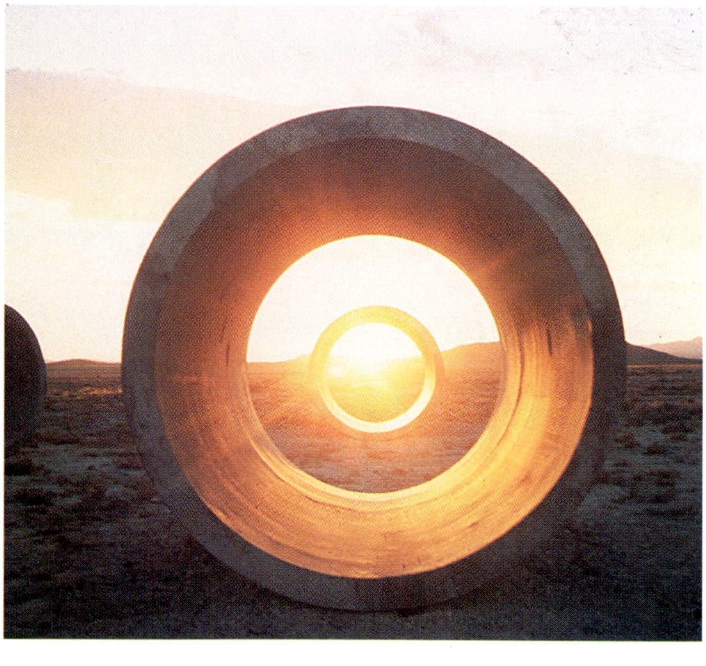

Fig. 360 **Nancy Holt, *Sun Tunnels,* Great Basin Desert, Utah, 1973–1976.**
Four tunnels, each 18 ft. long × 9 ft. 4 in. diameter; each axis 86 ft. long.
Courtesy John Weber Gallery, New York.

Earthworks

The larger a work, the more our visual experience depends on multiple points of view, in the same way that both David Smith's and Anthony Caro's sculptures (Figs. 335–36 and 355) depend on multiple points of view. Since the late 1960s, one of the focuses of modern sculpture has been the creation of large-scale out-of-doors environments, generally referred to as **earthworks.** We have already seen several examples. Both Christo and Jeanne-Claude's *Umbrellas* (Figs. 1 and 2) and Robert Smithson's *Spiral Jetty* (Fig. 6) are classic examples of the medium, as is Walter de Maria's *Las Vegas Piece* (Fig. 263). As the lines (Fig. 264) drawn on the landscape in Nazca, Peru indicate, humans have set out to sculpt the landscape, and to impose sculpture into the landscape, since the earliest times.

Nancy Holt's *Sun Tunnels* (Figs. 359 and 360) consists of four 22-ton concrete tunnels aligned with the rising and setting of the sun during the summer and winter solstices. The

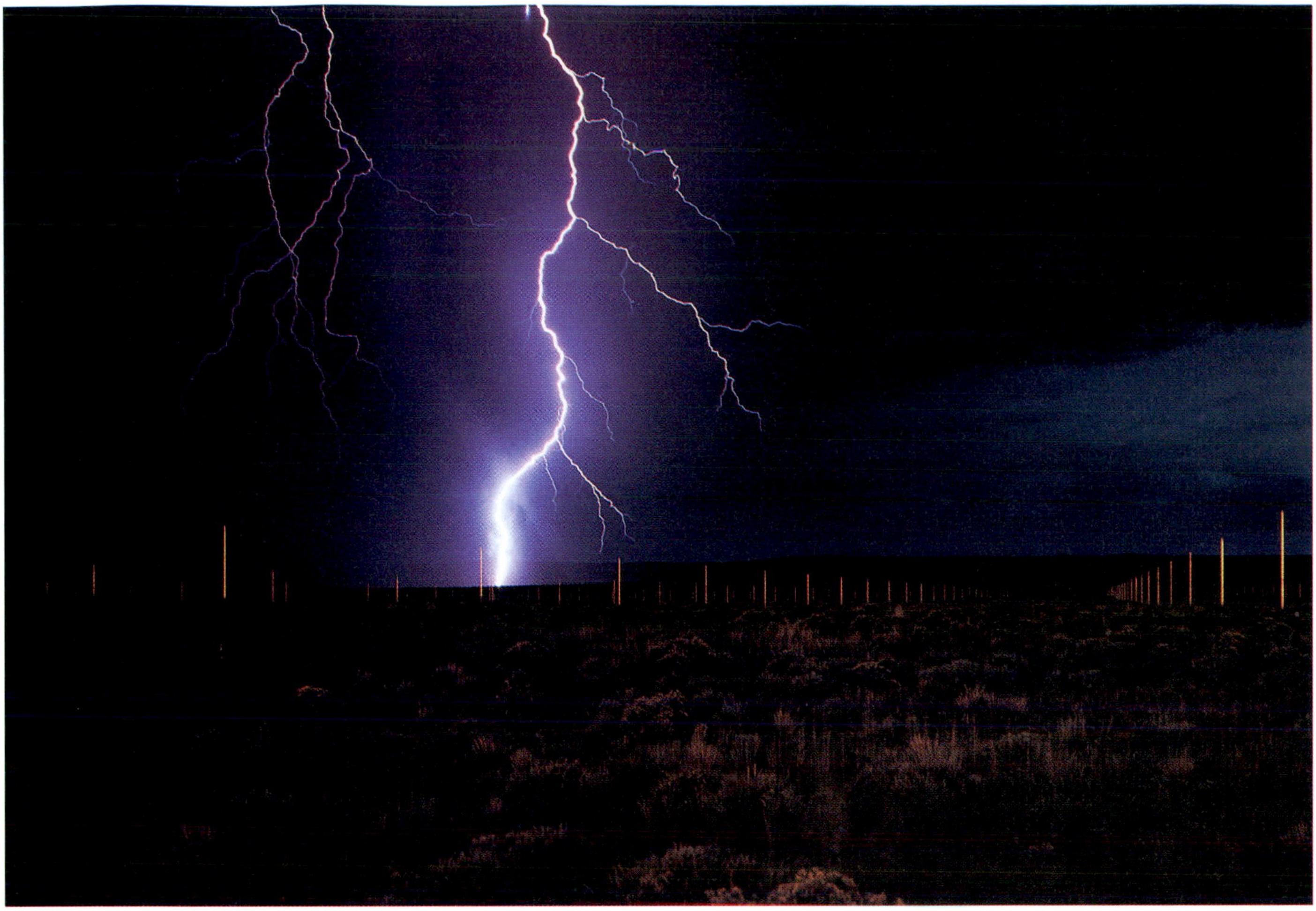

Fig. 361 Walter de Maria, *Lightning Field,* near Quemado, New Mexico, 1977.
Stainless-steel poles, average H. 20 ft. 7 ½ in.; overall dimensions 5,280 × 3,300 ft.
 Photograph by John Cliett.

holes cut into the walls of the tunnels duplicate the arrangement of the stars in four constellations—Draco, Perseus, Columba, and Capricorn—and the size of each hole is relative to the magnitude of each star. The work is designed to be experienced on site, imparting to viewers a sense of their own relation to the cosmos. "Only 10 miles south of *Sun Tunnels,*" Holt writes, "are the Bonneville Salt Flats, one of the few areas in the world where you can actually see the curvature of the earth. Being part of that kind of landscape . . . evokes a sense of being on this planet, rotating in space, in universal time."

In an isolated region near the remote town of Quemado, New Mexico, Walter de Maria has created an environment entitled *Lightning Field* (Fig. 361). Consisting of 400 steel poles laid out in a grid over nearly one square mile of desert, the work is activated between three and thirty times a year by thunderstorms that cross the region. At these times lightning jumps from pole to pole across the grid in a stunning display of pyrotechnics, but the site is equally compelling even in the clearest weather.

Visitors to the *Lightning Field* are met in Quemado and driven to the site, where they are left alone for one or two nights in a comfortable cabin at its edge. De Maria wants visitors to his environment to experience the space in relative isolation and silence, to view it over a number of hours, to see the stainless-steel poles change as the light and weather change, to move in and out of the grid at their leisure. He wants them to experience the infinite, to have some sense, posed in the vastness around them, of limitless freedom and time without end.

Mel Chin's Revival Field

One of the most prolific and diverse artists working today, Mel Chin creates art in any and every medium. In the spring of 1996, for instance, he was simultaneously working on a number of projects: He was creating a permanent sculptural redesign for a New York City subway station; he was working on a project creating a "condition of collaboration" between prime-time television, educational institutions, and the art world wherein art professionals and students create art to be exhibited in a famous television show; he was completing an icon-based software program for a Long Island school, which teaches ancient and modern cultural literacy; and he was shooting a series of "Public Service Questions"—as opposed to "Public Service Announcements"—which addressed the question of racisim in collaboration with the communities affected by the conditions that prompted the questions in the first place.

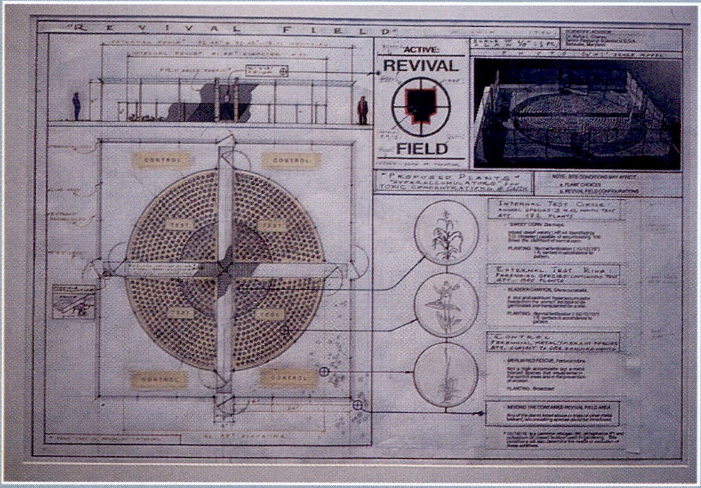

Fig. 362 Mel Chin, original plan and specifications for *Revival Field,* 1990.
Photograph by Mel Chin.

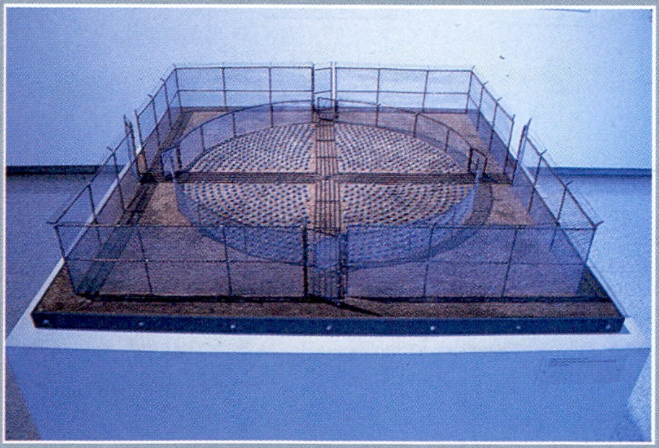
Fig. 363 Mel Chin, *Revival Field/Minnesota Maquette,* 1990.
Soil, steel, brass, metallic enamel, nylon, acrylic, mixed media.
Photograph by Mel Chin.

But one of Chin's more interesting, ongoing projects is a 1991 earthwork, first located outside St. Paul, Minnesota, entitled *Revival Field* (Fig. 364). The work is literally, and continually, "in progress." Chin had read about a group of plants known as hyper-accumulators, which are capable of absorbing heavy metals from the soil. His research led him to Rufus Chaney, an agronomist with the U. S. Department of Agriculture, who provided Chin with the scientific parameters for the project, as well as seeds for the plants.

At St. Paul's Pig's Eye landfill, Chin discovered a site full of heavy metals, including cadmium, the residue of leaking batteries. Sponsored by the National Endowment for the Arts and, later, by the Walker Art Center in Minneapolis, and with the cooperation of the Minnesota Waste Control Commission and the Minnesota Pollution Control Agency, Chin designed a landscape consisting of a circle within a square (Fig. 362). A traditional alchemical reference, it is also reminiscent of Leonardo's *Illustration of Proportions of the Human Figure* (Fig. 194). Leonardo wished to

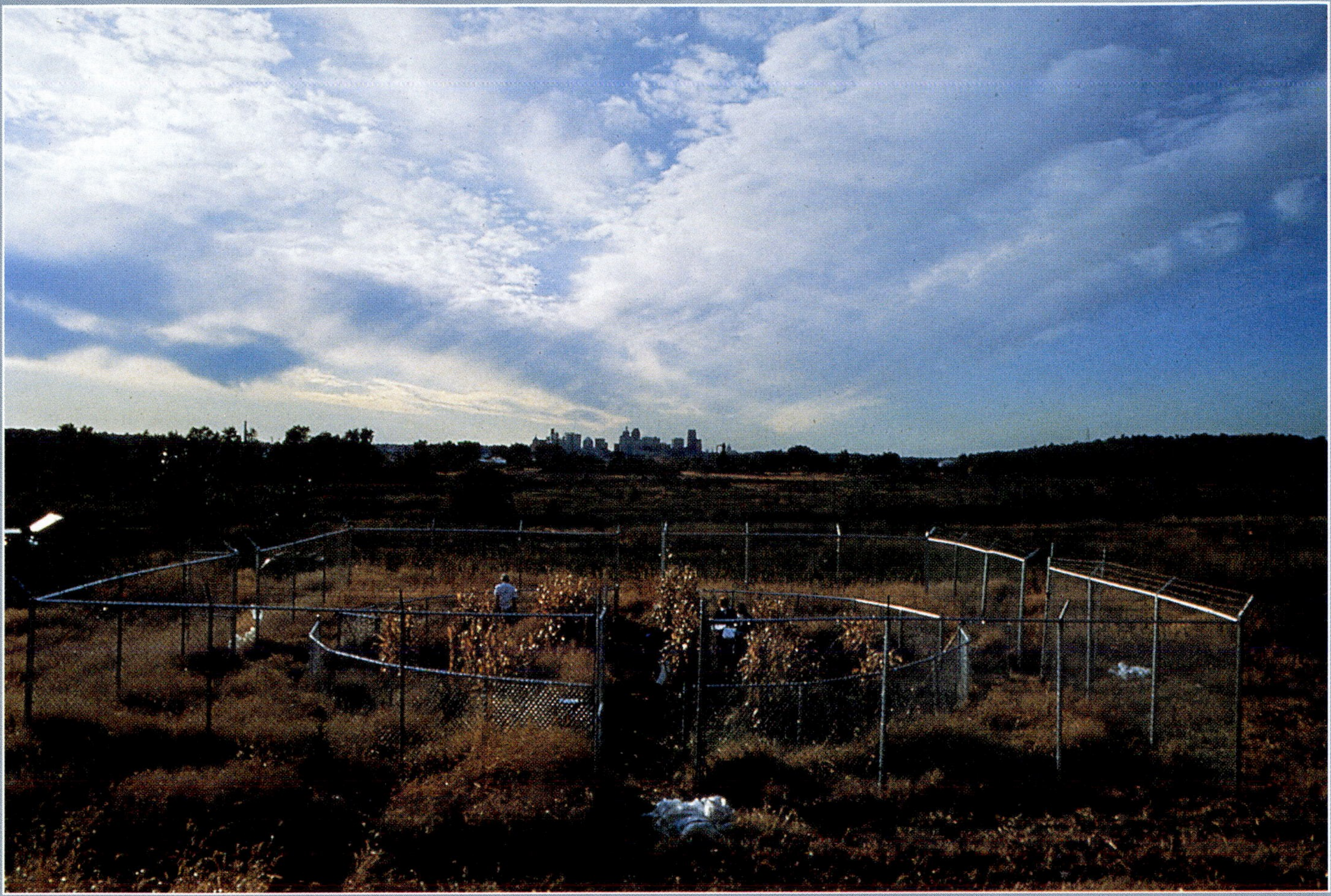

Fig. 364 Mel Chin, *Revival Field,* 1991–ongoing. Pictured: Harvest, 1993.
Plants, industrial fencing on a hazardous waste landfill, approx. 60 × 60 × 9 ft.
Pig's Eye Landfill, Saint Paul, Minnesota. Photo: Walker Art Center.

fit the square, symbolic of the finite, human world, into the circle, symbolic of the heavenly world, the cosmos, and to bring the two into balance. Chin's project is an attempt to reestablish an *ecological* balance that will allow the human figure to maintain its equilibrium in the environment. Chin's site is designed to restore us our harmony with the world.

A *maquette,* or model, of the site was designed first (Fig. 363). Two chainlink fences outline the circle and square, and the circle itself is crossed by two paths. The circular area, planted with the hyperaccumulators, serves as the actual test site, while the area outside the circle but inside the square serves as a control for the experiment. The site near St. Paul was planted with a variety of *Thlaspi,* a hyperaccumulator that *Revival Field* demonstrated absorbs significant amounts of cadmium through its vascular system, as well as with dwarf corn, romaine lettuce, and bladder campion—all tolerant of the site's conditions and capable of aiding in various aspects of the study.

Dismantled after three years, the Minnesota *Revival Field* has been replaced by a new *Revival Field* located in Palmerton, Pennsylvania, home of a National Priority Superfund Site notorious for a landscape devastated by heavy metal contamination. *Revival Field* is not only a model for successful art/science collaboration, it offers hope that hazardous contaminated sites might be transformed into living, productive environments.

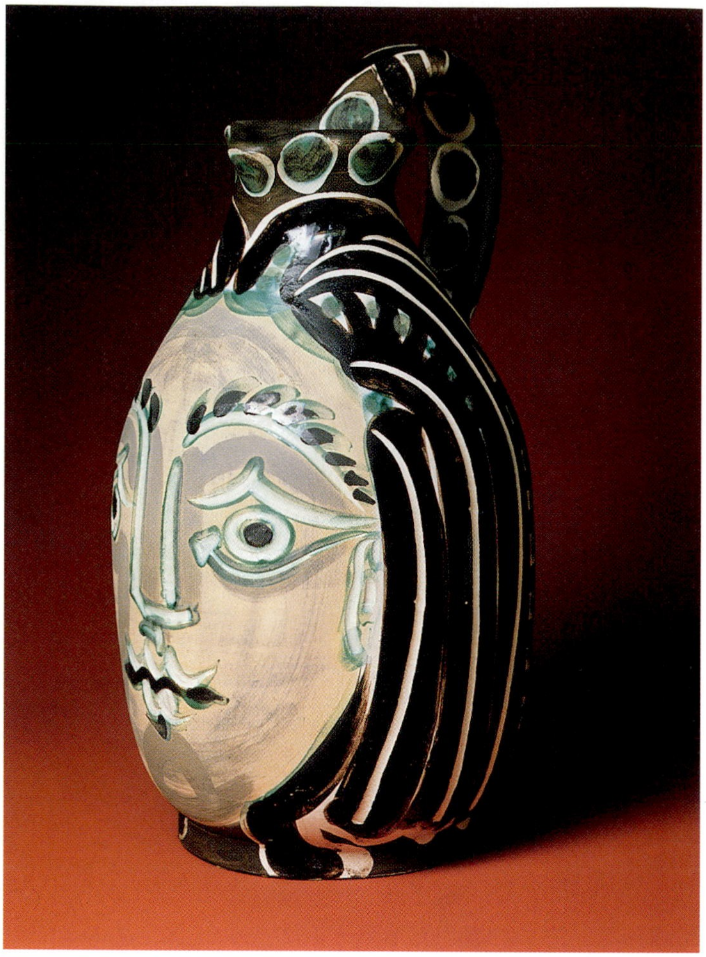

Fig. 365 Pablo Picasso (1881–1973), *Meed.*
Museum of Fine Arts, Moscow, Russia. Photo © SuperStock, Inc.

CRAFT MEDIA

Thus far in this chapter we have considered the traditional methods of making sculpture. But on more than one occasion we have discussed works that take advantage of media not associated so much with the fine arts as with the traditional crafts. Robert Arneson's ceramic *Case of Bottles* (Fig. 343) is a case in point, and so is Eva Hesse's fiber piece *Contingent* (Fig. 358). The line between the arts and the crafts is a fine one. **Craft** refers to expert handiwork, or work done by hand. And yet artists are expert with their hands. How is it that we don't call their work "craft" as well? Indeed, many artists would feel insulted if you complimented their work as being "craftful." These artists feel that a craft must be functional. That is, a craft object is something that can be used to satisfy our everyday needs. But the distinction between craft and artwork is not that clear-cut. For example, even if you poured wine out of Picasso's ceramic pitcher (Fig. 365), you would never call it craft. It is a work of art. Perhaps the only meaningful distinction we can draw between art and craft is this: if a work is primarily made to be used, it is craft, but if it is primarily made to be seen, it is art. However, the artist's intention may be irrelevant. If you buy an object because you enjoy looking at it, then whatever its usefulness, it is, for you at least, a work of art.

Ceramics

Ceramics are objects that are formed out of clay and then hardened by **firing,** or baking in a very hot oven, called a kiln. Ceramic objects are generally either flat and relief-like (think of a plate or a square of tile), or hollow, like cast sculpture (think of a pitcher). Unlike metal casts, the hollowness of ceramic objects is not a requirement of weight or cost so much as it is of utility (ceramic objects are made to hold things), as well as a requirement of the firing process itself. Solid clay pieces tend to hold moisture deep inside where it cannot easily evaporate, and during firing, as this moisture becomes superheated, it can cause the object to explode. In order to make hollow ceramic objects, a number of techniques have been developed.

Some types of ceramics are actually cast, like bronze or brass. Liquid clay is poured into a mold, fired, and hardened. As we will see in Chapter 15, "Design," mass-manufactured earthenware dishes, such as most of us eat on daily, are produced in this way. But most ceramic objects are created by one of three other means—*slab construction, coiling,* or *throwing* on a potter's wheel. Pieces made by any one of these techniques are then **glazed**—painted with a material that turns glassy when heated—and fired.

Koetsu's tea bowl named *Amaguno (Rain Clouds)* (Fig. 366) is an example of **slab construction.** Clay is rolled out flat, rather like a pie crust, and then shaped by hand. The tea bowl has a special place in the Japanese tea ceremony, the Way of the Tea. In small tea rooms specifically designed for the purpose and often decorated with calligraphy on hanging scrolls or screens, the guest was invited to leave the concerns of the daily world behind and enter a timeless world of ease, harmony, and mutual respect. Koetsu was an accomplished tea master. At each tea ceremony, the master would assemble a variety of different objects and utensils used to make tea, together with a collection of painting and calligraphy. Through this ensemble the master expresses his artistic sensibility, a sensibility shared with his guest, so that guest and host collaborate to make the ceremony itself a work of art.

This tea bowl, shaped perfectly to fit the hand, was made in the early seventeenth century at one of the "Six Ancient Kilns," the traditional centers of wood-fired ceramics in Japan. These early kilns, known as *anagama,* were narrow, underground tunnels dug out following the contour of a hillside. The pit was filled with pottery, and heat moved through the tunnel from the fire box at the lower end to the chimney at the upper end. The firing would take an average of seven days, during which temperatures would reach 2500°F. The coloration that distinguished these pieces results from wood ash in the kiln melting and fusing into glass on the pottery. The simplicity of these wood-fired pieces appealed to the devotee of the tea ceremony, and often tea masters such as Koetsu named their pieces after the accidental effects of coloration achieved in firing. The most prized effect is a scorch, or *koge,* when the firing has oxidized the natural glass glaze completely, leaving only a gray-black area. Such a *koge* forms the "rain clouds" on Koetsu's tea bowl.

María Martinez's black jar (Fig. 367) is an example of a second technique often used in ceramic construction, **coiling,** in which the clay is rolled out in long, ropelike strands that are coiled on top of each other and then smoothed. This pot is a specific example of a technique developed by María and her husband Julián in about 1919. Red clay is smothered in a dung-fueled bonfire during firing and painted with black-on-black designs.

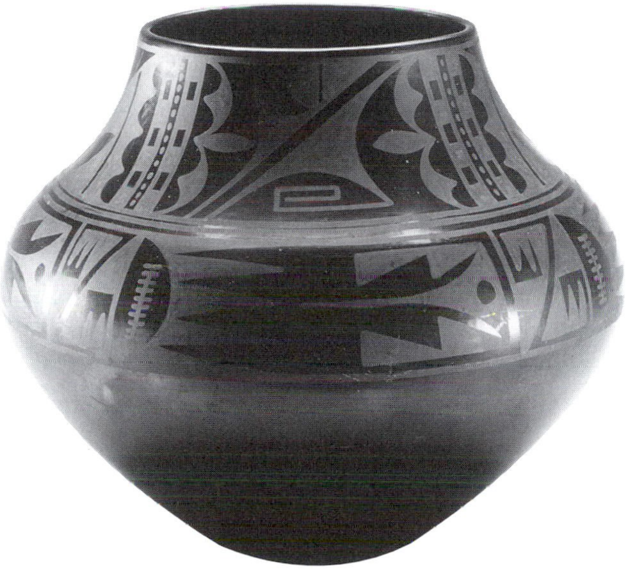

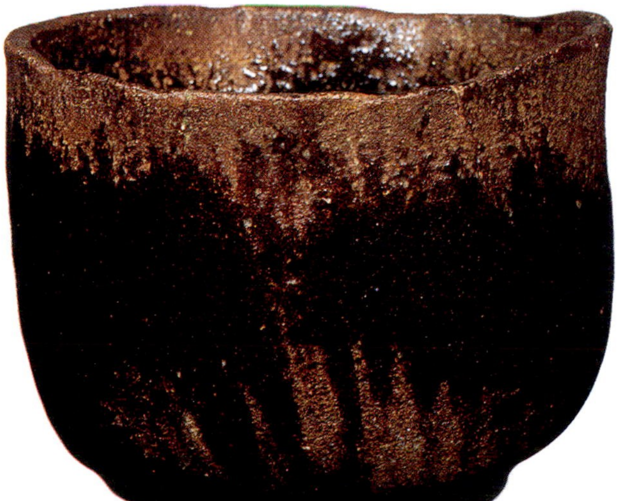

Fig. 366 (left) Hon'ami Koetsu (1558–1637), tea bowl named *Amagumo,* Momoyama or early Edo period.
3½ × 4 9/10 in.
Mitsuibunko, Section of Fine Arts, Tokyo.

Fig. 367 (above) María Montoya Martinez (1881–1980), *Jar,* San Ildefonso Pueblo, New Mexico, c. 1984.
Blackware, 11 1/8 × 13 in. (H. × D.).
The National Museum of Women in the Arts.
Gift of Wallace and Wilhelmina Holladay.

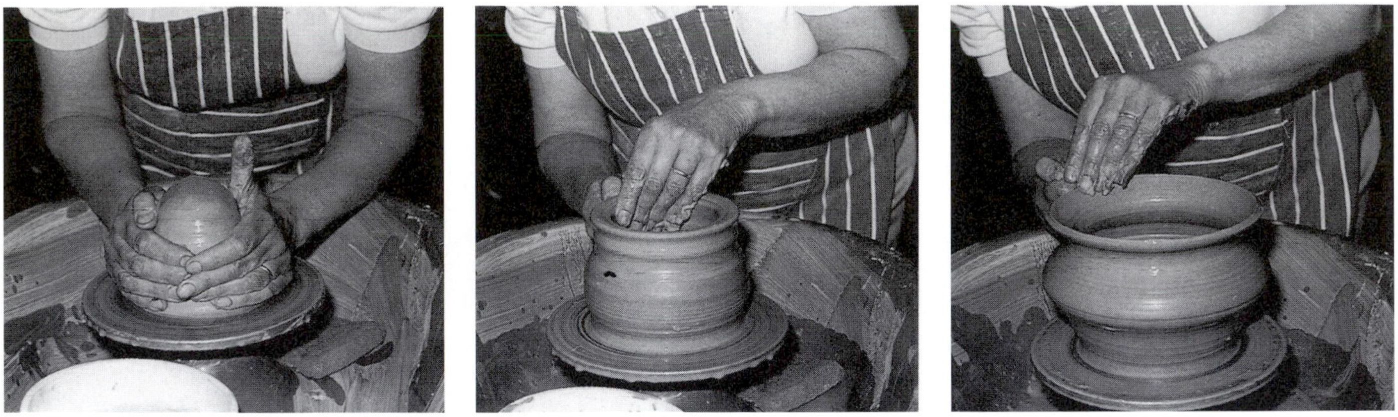

Fig. 368 Wheel-Throwing.

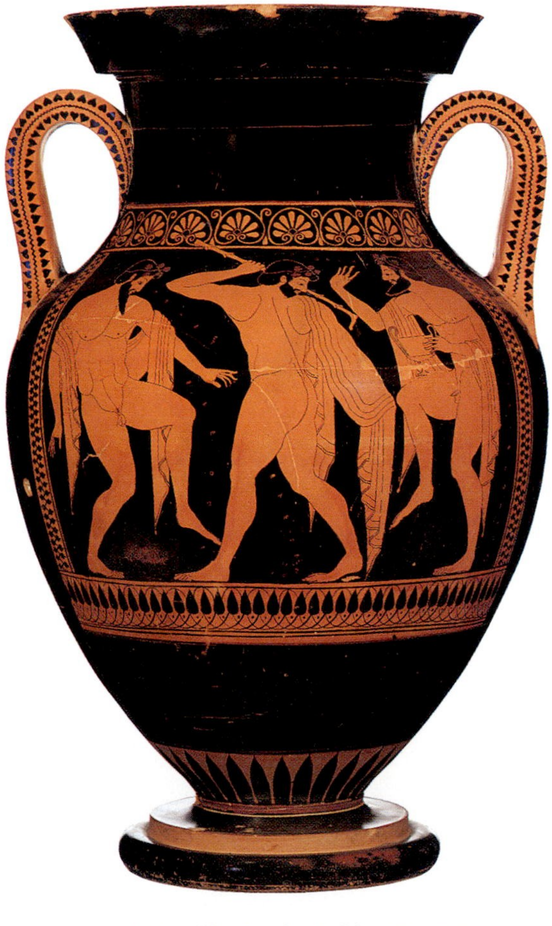

Fig. 369 Euthymides, *Revelers*, Vulci, c. 510–500 BCE.
H. approx. 24 in. Staatliche Antikensammulungen, Munich, Germany.

Native American cultures relied on coiling techniques, whereas peoples of most other parts of the world used the potter's wheel. Egyptian potters employed a wheel by about 4000 BCE, and their basic invention has remained in use ever since. The ancient Greeks became particularly skillful with the process. The **potter's wheel** is a flat disk attached to a flywheel below it, which is kicked by the potter (or driven by electricity in modern times), thus making the upper disk turn. A slab of clay, from which air pockets have been removed by slamming it against a hard surface, is centered on the wheel (see Fig. 368). As the slab turns, the potter pinches the clay between fingers and thumb, sometimes utilizing both hands at once, and pulls it upward in a round, symmetrical shape, making it wider or narrower as the form demands and shaping both the inside and outside simultaneously. The most skilled potters apply even pressure on all sides of the pot as it is thrown. The Greek amphora, or two-handled vase, known as *Revelers* (Fig. 369), is a thrown pot designed to store provisions such as wine, oil, or honey. An inscription on its bottom taunts the maker's chief competitor—"Euphronios never did anything like it," it reads—indicating the growing self-consciousness of the Greek artist, the sense that he was producing not just a useful object but a thing of beauty.

There are three basic types of ceramics. **Earthenware,** made of porous clay and fired at low temperatures, must be glazed if it is to hold liquid. **Stoneware** is impermeable to water because it is fired at high temperatures, and it is commonly used for dinnerware today. Finally, **porcelain,** fired at the highest temperatures of all, is a smooth-textured clay that becomes virtually transluscent and extremely glossy in finish during firing. The first true porcelain was made in China during the T'ang Dynasty (CE 618–906). By the time of the Ming Dynasty (1368–1644), the official kilns at Chingtehchen had become a huge industrial center producing ceramics for export. Just as the Greek artist painted his revelers on the red-orange amphora, Chinese artists painted elaborate designs onto the glazed surface of the the porcelain. Originally, Islam was the primary market for the distinctive blue-and-white patterns of Ming porcelain (Fig. 370), but as trade with Europe increased, so too did Europe's demand for Ming design.

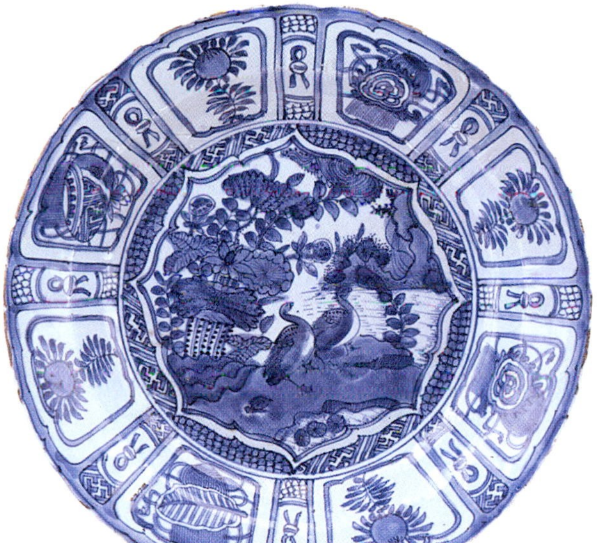

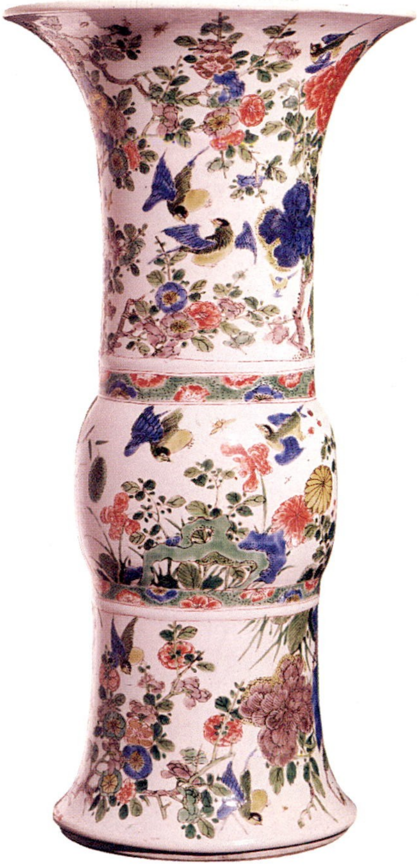

Fig. 370 (left) Plate, Ming Dynasty, late 16th–early 17th century.
Porcelain, D. 14 1/4 in.
The Metropolitan Museum of Art, New York. Rogers Fund, 1916. 16.13.

Fig. 371 (above) Vase, Ch'ing Dynasty, late 17th–early 18th century.
Porcelain painted in *famille verte* enamels and gilt, H. 18 in.
The Metropolitan Museum of Art, New York.
Bequest of John D. Rockefeller, Jr., 1961. 61.200.66.

The export trade flourished even after the Manchus overran China in 1644, establishing the Ch'ing Dynasty, which lasted into the twentieth century. This had a profound effect on Chinese design. The Chingtehchen potters quickly begin to make two grades of ware, one for export and a finer "Chinese taste" ware for internal, royal use. They also became dedicated to satisfying European taste. As a result, consistency and standardization of product were of chief concern.

One of the more beautiful Ch'ing Dynasty porcelains is this remarkable *famille verte* vase (Fig. 371), so-called because the palette of enamel paints used is marked by its several distinctive shades of green. Here birds, rocks, and flowers create a sense of the vibrancy of nature itself.

By the end of the eighteenth century, huge workshops dominated the Chinese porcelain industry, and by the middle of the nineteenth century the demands of mass production for trade led, throughout China, to the same lack of creative vitality so common in Western mass manufacturing.

Peter Voulkos's X-Neck

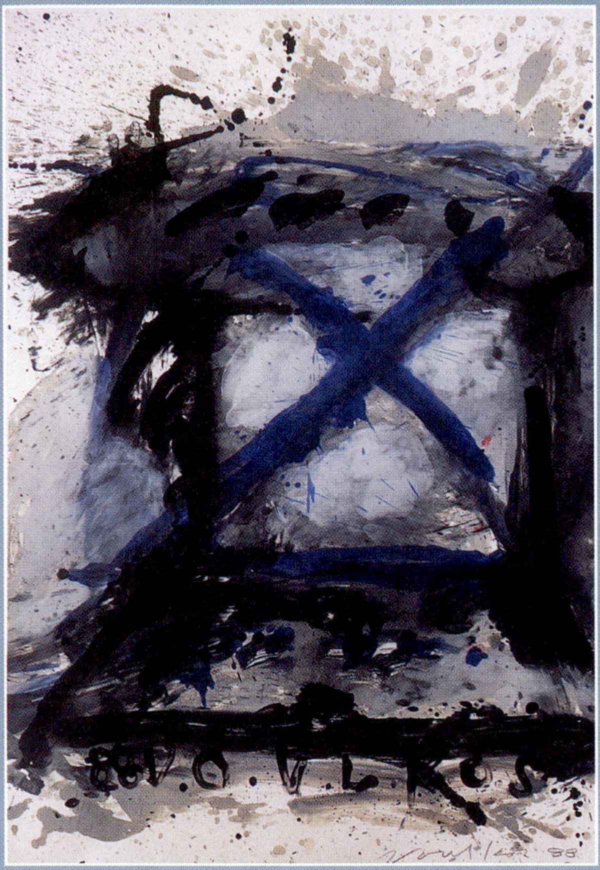

Fig. 372 Peter Voulkos, *"Untitled,"* 1988.
Monotype, 50 × 35 in.
Collection of Deborah Scripps, San Francisco.
Photo by Schopplein Studio. Copyright Peter Voulkos.

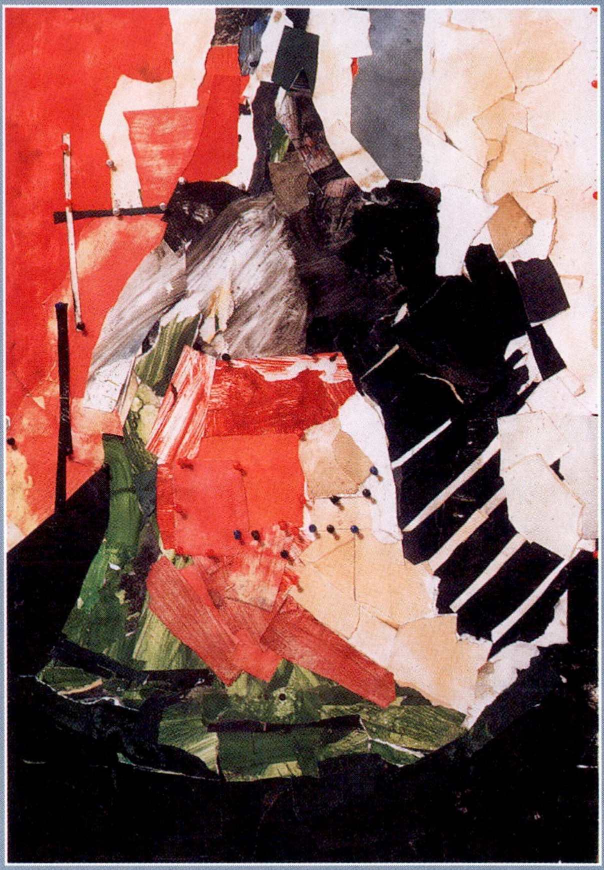

Fig. 373 Peter Voulkos, *"Pyramid of the Amphora,"* 1985.
Paper collage with pushpins, 52 × 37 in.
Collection Bruce C. and Monica Reeves, Alameda, California.
Photo by Schopplein Studio. Copyright Peter Voulkos.

In 1976, a young American ceramic artist by the name of Peter Callas built the first traditional Japanese *anagama,* or word-burning kiln, in the United States in Piermont, New York. Three years later, California artist Peter Voulkos was regularly firing his work in Callas's kiln. Voulkos's work is particularly suited to the wood-firing process, in which the artist must give up control of his work and resign himself to the accidental effects that result from submitting the work to a heat of 2500°F over the course of a seven-day firing. His "stacks," giant bottle-like pyramids of clay that average about 250 pounds, are so named because Voulkos literally stacks clay cylinders one on top of the other to create his form. Before they are quite dry, he gouges them, draws on them with various tools, and drags the clay in giant sweeps across the form's surface. Then he fires it in the *anagama.* Anything can happen in the firing. Depending on such factors as how the pieces in the kiln are stacked, the direction of the flame, where ash is deposited on the surface of the work, how a section near a flame might or might not melt, and undetectable irregularities in the clay itself, each stack will turn out differently. The Japanese call this "controlled accident." For Voulkos, it is the source of excitement in the work, "the expectancy of the unknown" that is fundamental to the process.

This interest in the possibilities of the accidental evidences itself in other ways in Voulkos's work. In many of his works, including both the untitled monotype reproduced here (Fig. 372) and the *X-Neck* stack (Fig. 374), a ragged "x" seems to be the focus of the piece. The "x" is, of course, a standard signature for those who cannot write, the signature of an absolute novice in the art of calligraphy. As was pointed out in the catalogue to Voulkos's 1995 retrospective exhibition, the "x" is also a reference to the Zen practice of *shoshin,* which means "beginner's mind." It is Voulkos's way of keeping in touch with what the Zen master Shunryu Suzuki describes as "the limitless potential of original mind, which is rich and sufficient within itself. For in the beginner's mind there are many possibilities; in the expert's mind there are few."

The form of the stacks of clay, however, is not accidental. It is a direct reference to the pyramid form, not only to the pyramids of ancient Egypt but also those of ancient Mexican Aztec and Mayan cultures. For Voulkos, the pyramid represents the mystery of the unknown. In utilizing this form, Voulkos makes contact between the ancient and the modern, between himself and the forces that have driven the human race for centuries. His collage, *Pyramid of the Amphora* (Fig. 373), has the stepped sides of a Mexican pyramid. On such structures, men and women were once sacrificed to the gods, their heads cut off, their hearts cut out. Red blood seems to flow across Voulkos's work. Even the tears in the paper and the pins pushed into the surface reflect this violence, and Voulkos's own manner of working with clay, the almost primitive violence of his approach to the material, is underscored by the collage.

His stacks make contact with the most elemental of emotions, our most intense, but human, feelings.

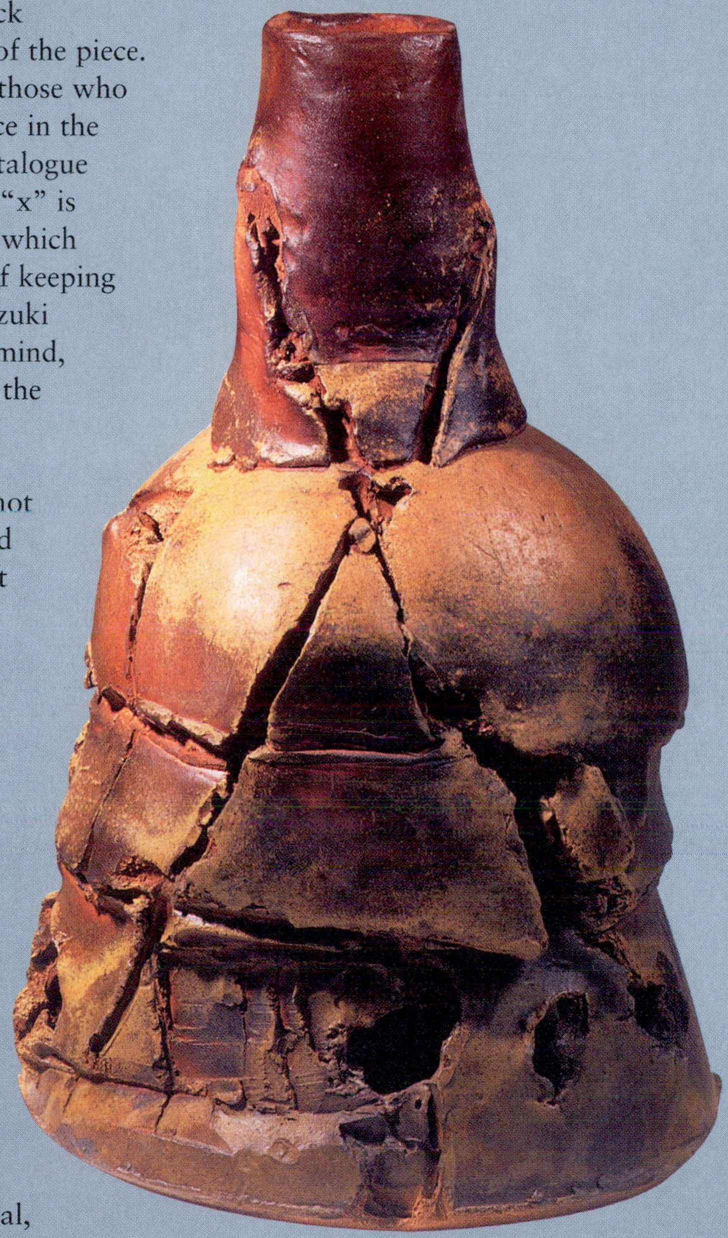

Fig. 374 Peter Voulkos, *X-Neck*, 1990.
Woodfired stoneware stack, H. 34 ½ in. × D. 21 in.
Private collection. Photograph by Schopplein Studio, Berkeley, California.
© 1997 Peter Voulkos.

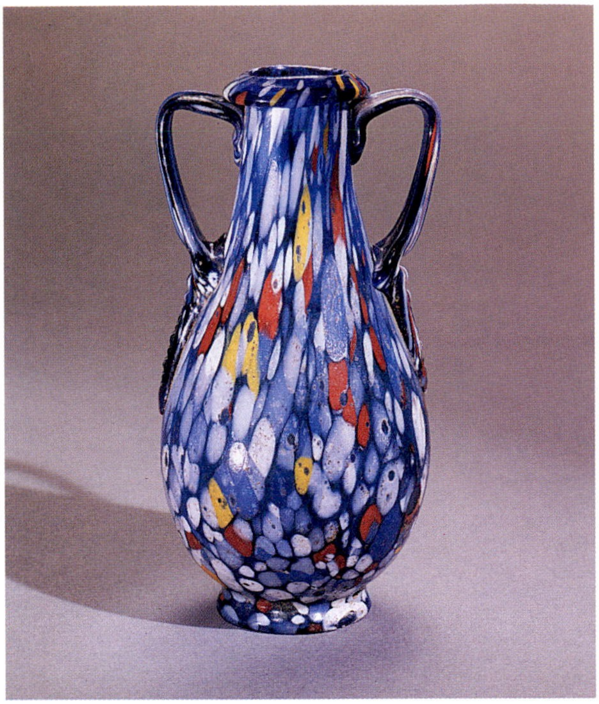

Fig. 375 Two-handled vase in dappled glass, Syrian, 1st century CE. H. 4 5/8 in. Corning Museum of Glass, Corning, New York.

Glass

Since ancient times glassware was made either by forming the hot liquid glass, made principally of silica, or sand, on a core or by casting it in a mold. The invention of glassblowing techniques late in the first century BCE so revolutionized the process that, in the Roman world, glassmaking quickly became a major industry. To blow glass, the artist dips the end of a pipe into molten glass and then blows through the pipe to produce a bubble. While it is still hot, the bubble is shaped and cut.

This two-handled vase (Fig. 375) was probably made in the second half of the first century CE in Syria, then part of the Roman Empire. It is made of transparent blue glass that was rolled on a surface strewn with chips of blue, white, red, and yellow opaque glass. These chips expanded and elongated in the blowing process, creating a decorative patchwork of dripping blobs and splotches. By the time this vase was made, demand for glass was so great that many craftsmen had moved from the Middle East to Italy to be near the expanding European markets.

Today, the Pilchuck Glass School in Washington State is one of the leading centers of glassblowing in the world, surpassed only by the traditional glassblowing industry of Venice, Italy. Dale Chihuly, one of Pilchuck's cofounders, has been instrumental in transforming the medium from its utilitarian purposes into more sculptural ends. As one of his drawings for his "basket" series makes clear (Fig. 376), he is interested in the interplay of line and space, in creating a web of interlaced line and transparent form. These works are not "baskets" per se, but rather sculpted containers that hold other sculpted forms within them. Inspired by having seen a group of Indian baskets in a museum storage room sagging under their own weight, works such as Chihuly's *Alabaster Basket Set* (Fig. 377) sag, bulge, push against, and flow into each other as if still in their liquid state. His work demonstrates another quality of glass—the way it is animated by light. At once reflective and transparent, the surface is dynamic, constantly transformed as both the light and the viewer's point of view changes.

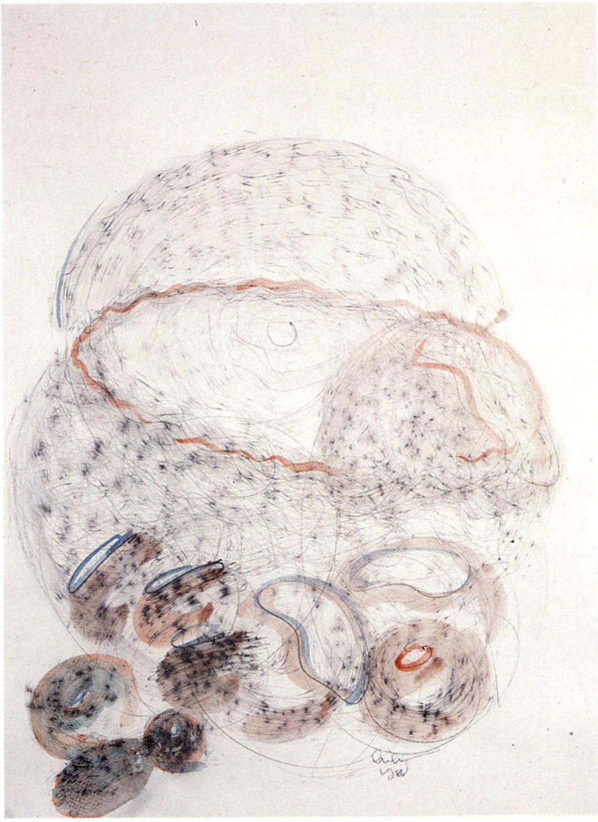

Fig. 376 Dale Chihuly, *Alabaster Basket* (Drawing), 1986. Graphite, colored pencil, and watercolor on paper, 30 × 22 in. Courtesy of Dale Chihuly.

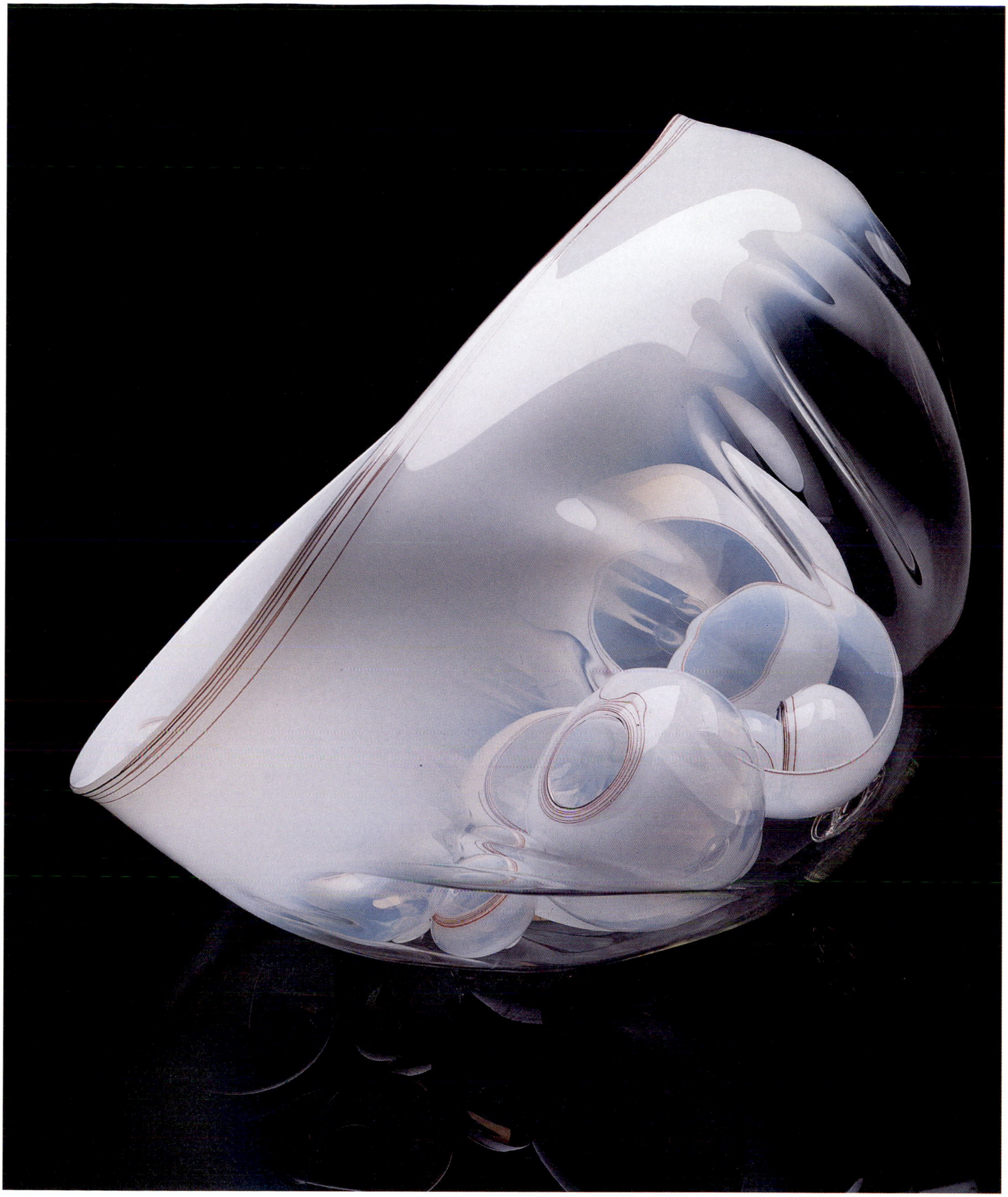

Fig. 377 Dale Chihuly,
***Alabaster Basket Set with Oxblood Wraps,* 1991.**
Glass, 18 × 27 × 21 in.
Courtesy of Dale Chihuly. Photograph by Claire Garoutte.

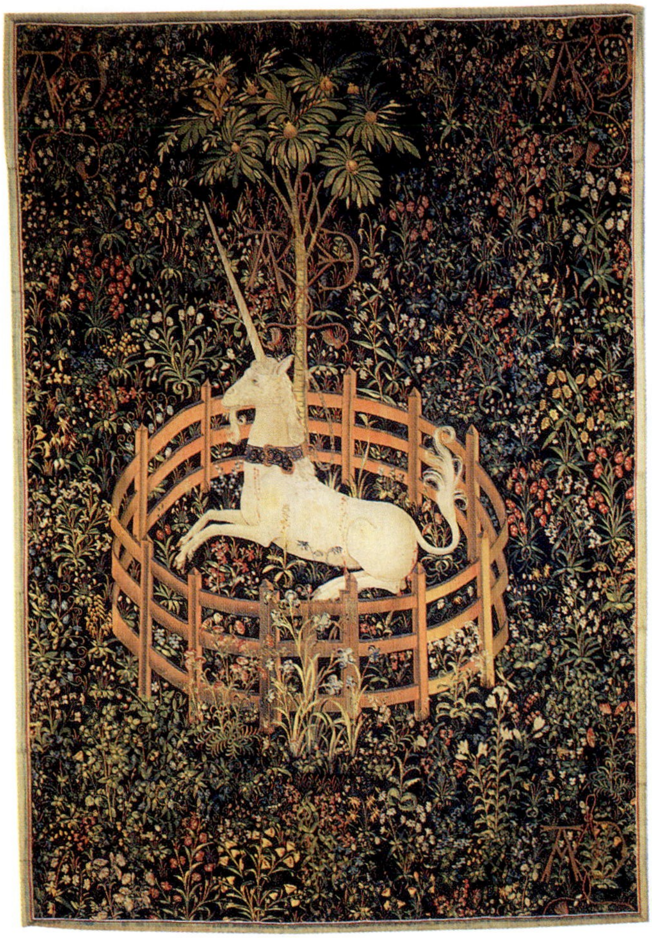

Fig. 378 ***The Unicorn in Captivity,* from the *Unicorn Tapestries,* c. 1500.**
Silk and wool, silver and silver-gilt threads, 12 ft. 1 in. × 8 ft. 3 in.
© The Metropolitan Museum of Art, New York, Gift of John D. Rockefeller, Jr.
The Cloisters Collection, 1937.

Fiber

We do not usually think of fiber as a three-dimensional medium. However, fiber arts are traditionally used to fill three-dimensional space, in the way that a carpet fills a room or that clothing drapes across a body. In the Middle Ages, tapestry hangings such as *The Unicorn in Captivity* on the left (Fig. 378) were hung on the stone walls of huge mansions and castles to soften and warm the stone. Fiber is an extraordinarily textural medium, and as a result it has recently become an increasingly favored medium for sculpture.

But all fiber arts, sculptural or not, trace their origin back to **weaving,** a technique for constructing fabrics by means of interlacing horizontal and vertical threads. The vertical threads—called the **warp**—are held taut on a loom or frame, and the horizontal threads—the **weft** or **woof**—are woven loosely over and under the warp. A **tapestry** is a special kind of weaving in which the weft yarns are of several colors and the weaver manipulates the colors to make a design as intricate as *The Unicorn in Captivity.*

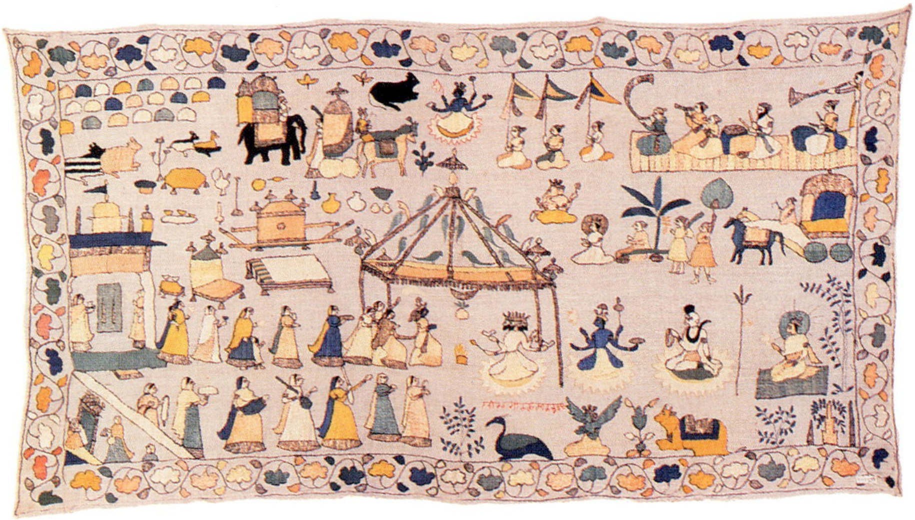

Fig. 379 Embroidered *rumal,* late 18th century.
Muslin and colored silks.
Victoria and Albert Museum, London.

In **embroidery,** a second traditional fiber art, the design is made by needlework. From the early eighteenth century onward, the town of Chamba was one of the centers of the art of embroidery in India. It was known, particularly, for its *rumals,* embroidered muslin textiles that were used as wrappings for gifts (Fig. 379). If an offering was to be made at a temple, or if gifts were to be exchanged between families of a bride and groom, an embroidered *rumal* was always used as a wrapping.

The composition of the Chamba *rumals* is consistent. A floral border encloses a dense series of images, first drawn in charcoal and then embroidered, on a plain white muslin background. For a wedding gift, as in the *rumal* illustrated here, the designs might depict the wedding itself. The designs were double-darned, so that an identical scene appeared on both sides of the cloth. Because of its location in the foothills and mountains of the Himalayas, offering relief from the heat of the Indian plains, the region around Chamba was a favorite summer retreat for British colonists, and its embroidery arts became very popular in nineteenth-century England.

One of the most important textile designers of this century was Anni Albers. The wall hanging at the right (Fig. 380) was done on a 12-harness loom, each capable of supporting a 4-inch band of weaving. Consequently, Albers designed a 48-inch wide grid composed of 12 of the 4-inch wide units. Each unit is a vertical rectangle variable only in its patterning, which is either solid or striped. The striped rectangles are themselves divided into units of 12 alternating stripes. Occasional cubes are formed when two rectangles of the same pattern appear side by side.

Anni Albers regarded such geometric play as rooted in nature. Inspired by reading *The Metamorphosis of Plants,* by Johann Wolfgang von Goethe, the eighteenth-century German poet and philosopher, she was fascinated by the way a simple basic pattern could generate, in nature, infinite variety. There is, in the design here, no apparent pattern to the occurrence of solid or striped rectangles or in the colors employed in them. This variability of particular detail within an overall geometric scheme is, from Albers's point of view, as natural and as inevitable as the repetition itself.

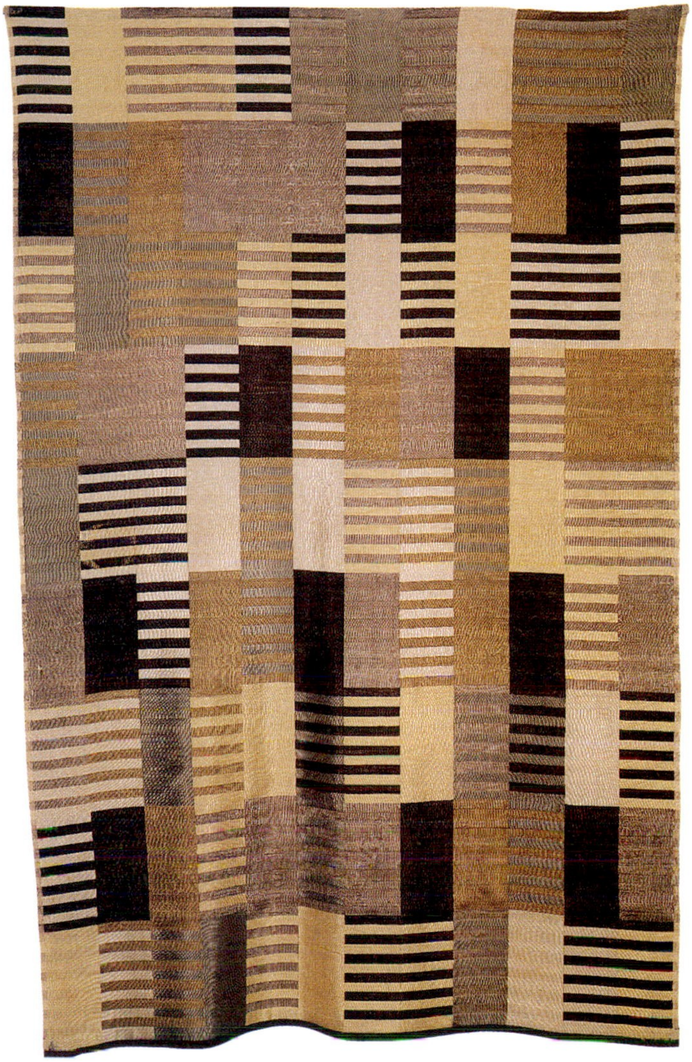

Fig. 380 Anni Albers, tapestry, 1926.
Three-ply weave, 72 × 48 in.
Courtesy of The Busch-Reisinger Museum, Harvard University; Association Fund.

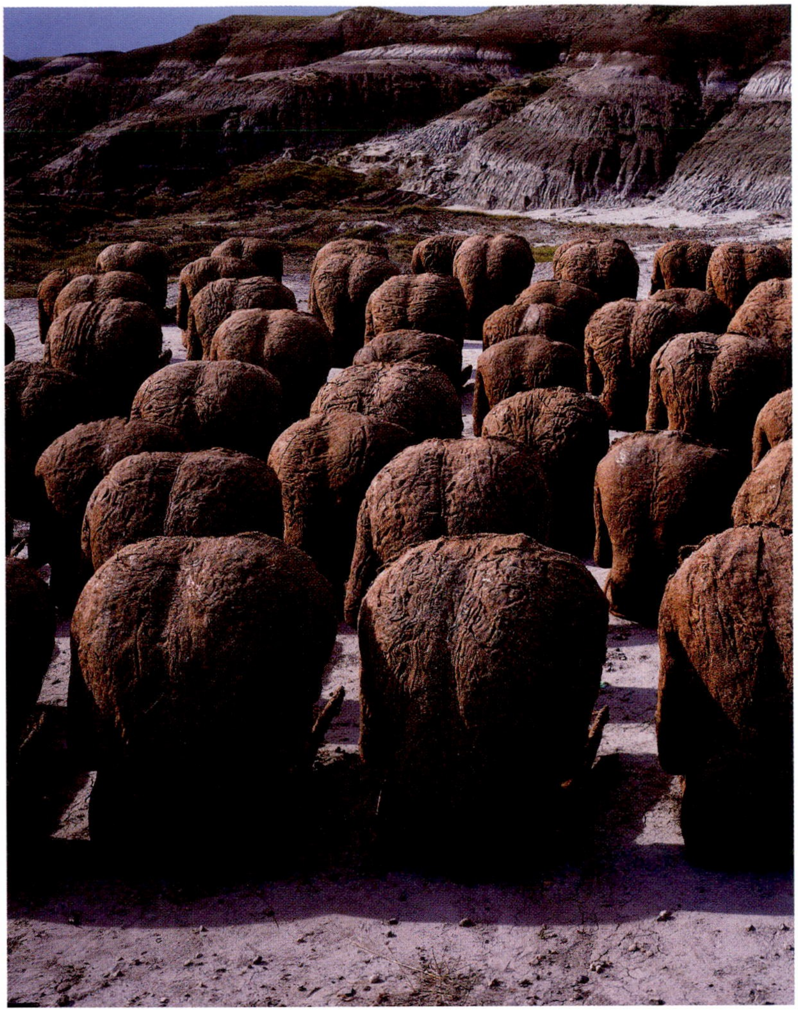

Fig. 381 Magdalena Abakanowicz, *Backs in Landscape,* 1978–1981.
Eighty sculptures of burlap and resin molded from plaster casts, over lifesize. Photo: © 1982 Dirk Bakker, Detroit, Michigan.

It was in the hands of Magdalena Abakanowicz, however, that fiber became, in this century, a tool of serious artistic expression, freed of any associations with utilitarian crafts. In the early 1970s, using traditional fiber materials such as burlap and string, Abakanowicz began to make forms based on the human anatomy (Fig. 381). She presses these fibers into a plaster mold, creating a series of multiples that, though generally uniform, are strikingly different piece to piece, the materials lending each figure an individual identity.

As we have already seen in the discussion of the Lotto rug in Chapter 7 (Fig. 177), and as Anni Albers's work also demonstrates, pattern and repetition have always played an important role in textile design. Abakanowicz brings new meaning to the traditional functions of repetitive pattern. These forms, all bent over in prayer, or perhaps pain, speak to our condition as humans, our spiritual emptiness—these are hollow forms—and our mass anxiety.

The textile wrappings also remind us of the traditional function of clothing—to protect us from the elements. Here, huddled against the sun and rain, each figure is shrouded in a wrap that seems at once clothing and bandage. It is as if the figures are wounded, cold, impoverished, homeless—the universal condition. As Abakanowicz reminds us, "It is from fiber that all living organisms are built—the tissues of plants, and ourselves. Our nerves, our genetic code, the canals of our veins, our muscles. We are fibrous structures. Our heart is surrounded by the coronary plexus, the plexus of most vital threads. Handling fiber, we handle mystery. . . . When the biology of our body breaks down, the skin has to be cut so as to give access to the inside, later it has to be sewn, like fabric. Fabric is our covering and our attire. Made with our hands, it is a record of our souls."

MIXED MEDIA

All of the media we have so far considered, from drawing to fiber, can be combined with one another to make a new work of art. In the twentieth century, in particular, artists have purposefully and increasingly combined various media. The result is **mixed media** work. In this section, we discuss three types of mixed media: collage, installation, and performance art. One of the most important results of mixed media has been to extend what might be called "the space of art." If this space was once defined by the picture frame—if art was once understood as something that was contained within that boundary and hung on a wall—that definition of space was extended in the hands of modern artists.

The two-dimensional space of the canvas was first challenged by Pablo Picasso and his close associate Georges Braque when they began to utilize collage in their work. **Collage** is the process of pasting or gluing fragments of printed matter, fabric, natural material—anything that is relatively flat—onto the two-dimensional surface of a canvas or panel. Collage creates, in essence, a low-relief assemblage. The logic of collage—the way in which collage rises off the flat surface—soon led artists to consider the room, or the gallery space as a whole, as the space of art. They thus began to create **installations,** or works created to fill an interior architectural space. Finally, the work of art came to integrate live human activity into its space. We call examples of these works **performance art.**

Collage

The motives for doing collage are many, but the primary one is that collage violates the the integrity of painting as a medium. It does this by introducing into the space of painting materials from the everyday world. Thus, in collage, the world of art collides with real life. Picasso's 1912 collage, *Bottle of Suze* (Fig. 382), is a perfect example. Here we have a table at a café, a bottle of aperitif sitting on it, the perfect image of a life of ease. But if we read the collaged fragments of newspaper that are incorporated into the work, a different story emerges. They describe a world in much greater turmoil than the Paris café scene would indicate. The newspaper describes current events in the Balkans:

> *I saw a hundred corpses. They were stretched out there where they had fallen during the march of the left convoy, in the ditches or across the road, and the files of cars loaded with the almost dead everywhere stretched themselves out on the devastated route. . . . I saw cadavers strewing the cursed route where a wind of death blows and I saw the dying march. . . . But I had seen nothing yet.*

Two worlds collide—the world of art, leisure, pleasure, and peace, and the world of death, misery, agony, and war. In the collage both stand in stark opposition.

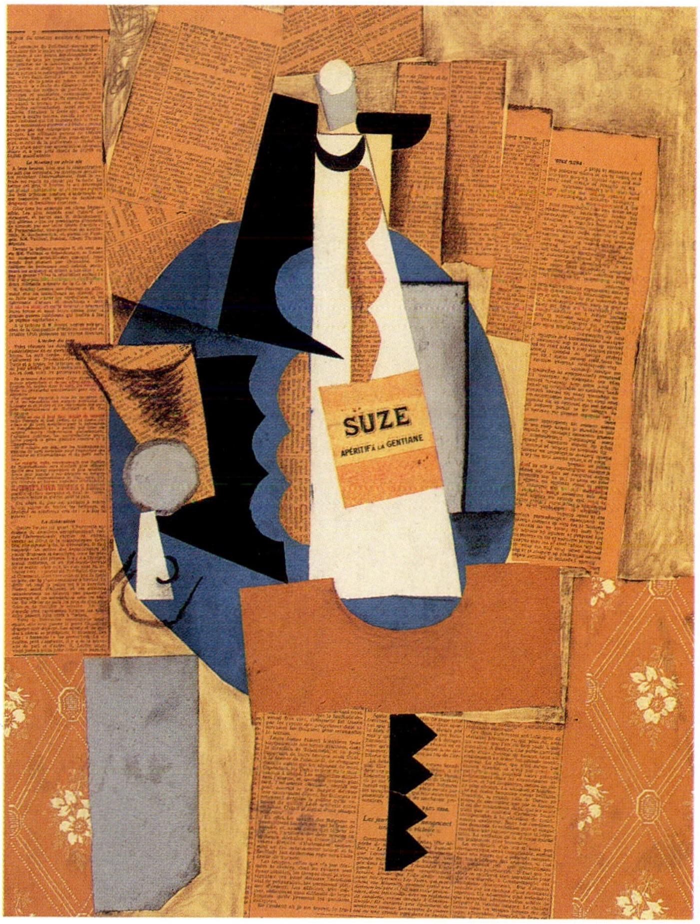

Fig. 382 Pablo Picasso, *Bottle of Suze,* 1912.
Pasted papers, gouache, and charcoal on paper, 25 3/8 × 19 3/4 in.
Washington University Gallery of Art, St. Louis, Missouri.
University purchase, Kende Sale Fund, 1946.

Robert Rauschenberg's Monogram

The movement of the two-dimensional into the three-dimensional that is suggested by collage is nowhere more forcefully stated than in the work of Robert Rauschenberg.

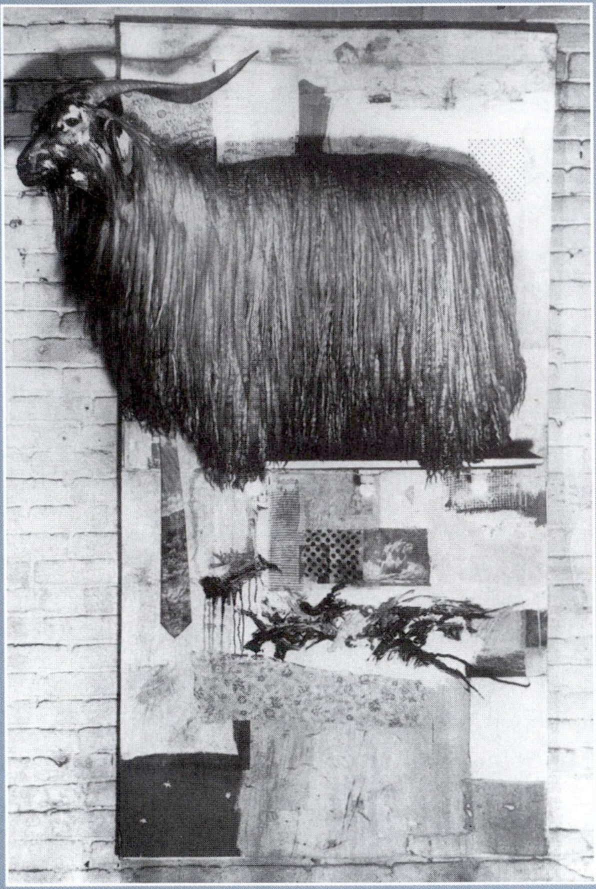

Fig. 383 Robert Rauschenberg, *Monogram, 1st State.*

Photograph by Harry Shunk.

Rauschenberg's work literally moves "off the wall"—the title of Calvin Tomkins's biography of the artist. There is probably no better example of this than *Monogram* (Fig. 385), a combine-painting, or high-relief collage, that Rauschenberg worked on over a five-year period from 1955 to 1959.

The composer John Cage once defined Rauschenberg's combine-paintings as "a situation involving multiplicity." They are a kind of collage, but more lenient than other collages about what they will admit into their space. They will, in fact, admit anything, because unity is not something they are particularly interested in. They bring together objects of diverse and various kinds and simply allow them to coexist beside each

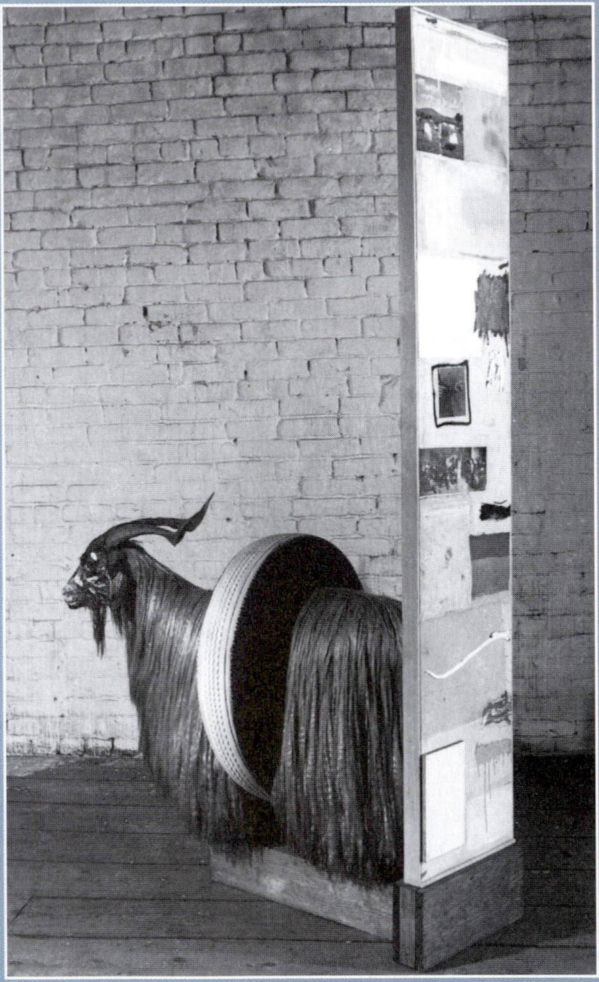

Fig. 384 Robert Rauschenberg, *Monogram, 2nd State.*

Photograph by Rudolph Burckhardt.

WORKS IN PROGRESS

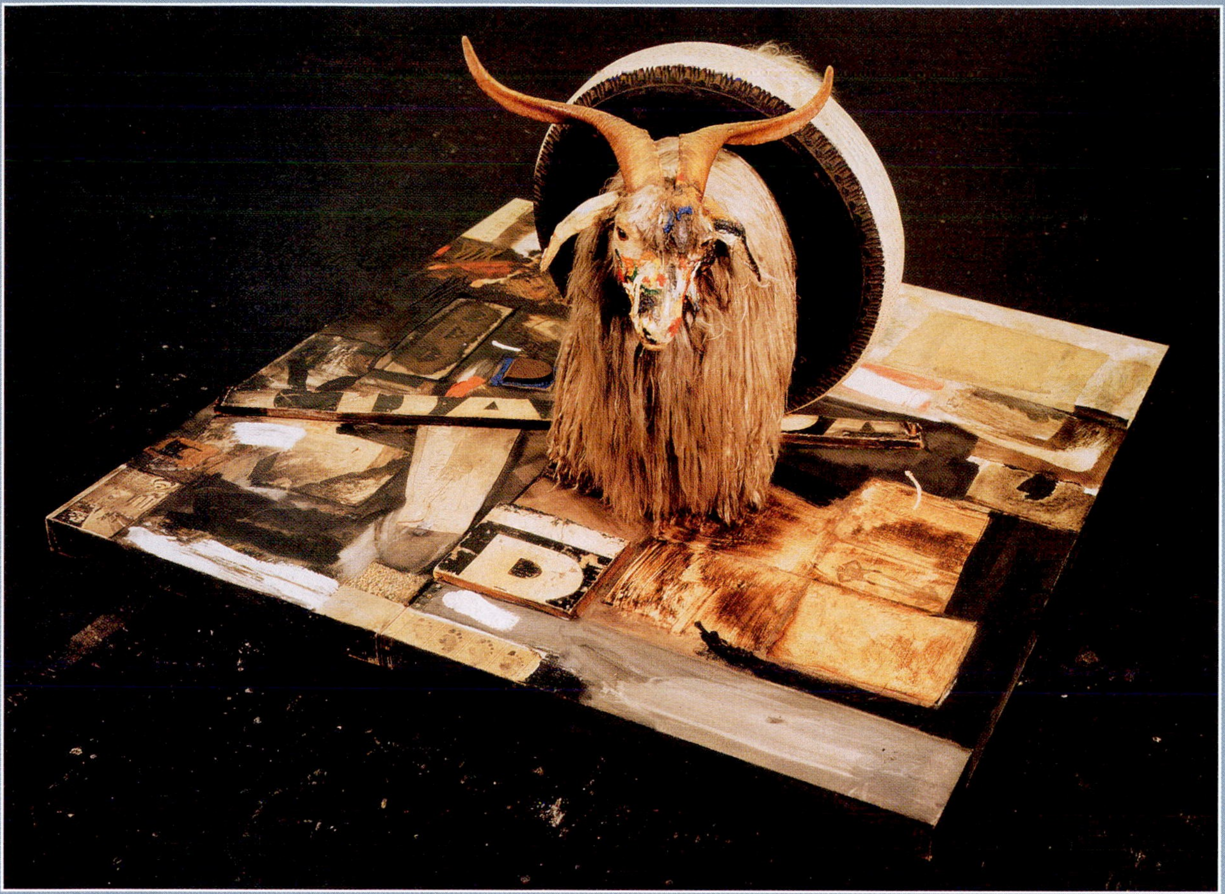

Fig. 385 Robert Rauschenberg, *Monogram,* 1955–1959.
Freestanding combine: oil, fabric, wood, on canvas and wood, rubber heel, tennis ball, metal plaque, hardware, stuffed Angora goat, rubber tire, mounted on four wheels, 42 × 63 ¼ × 64 ½ in.

other in the same space. In Rauschenberg's words, "A pair of socks is no less suitable to make a painting with than wood, nails, turpentine, oil and fabric." Nor, apparently, is a stuffed Angora goat.

Rauschenberg discovered the goat in a second-hand office furniture store in Manhattan. The problem it presented, as Tomkins has explained, was how "to make the animal look as if it belonged in a painting." In its earliest recorded state (Fig. 383) the goat is mounted on a ledge in profile in the top half of a six-foot painting. It peers over the edge of the painting and casts a shadow on the wall. Compared to later states of the work, the goat is integrated into the two-dimensional surface, or as integrated as an object of its size could be.

In the second state (Fig. 384), Rauschenberg brings the goat off its perch and sets it on a platform in front of another combine-painting, this one nearly ten feet high. Now it seems about to walk forward into our space, dragging the painting behind it. Rauschenberg has also placed an automobile tire around the goat's mid-section. This tire underscores its volume, its three-dimensionality.

But Rauschenberg was not happy with this design either. Finally, he put the combine painting flat on the floor, creating what he called a "pasture" for the goat. Here Rauschenberg manages to accomplish what seems logically impossible: the goat is at once fully contained within the boundaries of the picture frame and totally liberated from the wall. Painting has become sculpture.

The close connection between collage and sculpture is evident when we consider Louise Nevelson's *Sky Cathedral* (Fig. 386). The piece is a giant assemblage of wooden boxes, woodworking remnants and scraps, and found objects, such as a bowling pin. It is entirely frontal and functions like a giant high-relief altarpiece—hence its name—transforming and elevating its materials to an almost spiritual dimension. The real accomplishment here—and it is substantial—is that Nevelson has been able to make a piece of almost endless variety appear unified and coherent. Both its grid structure and the repetition of forms and shapes help accomplish this, but its overall black color does most. Black, Nevelson has explained, "means totality. It means: contains all. . . . Because black encompasses all colors. Black is the most aristocratic color of all. The only aristocratic color. . . . I have seen things that were transformed into black, that took on just greatness. I don't want to use a lesser word." It is this transformation of everyday things into greatness that defines not only Nevelson's *Sky Cathedral* but collage as a whole.

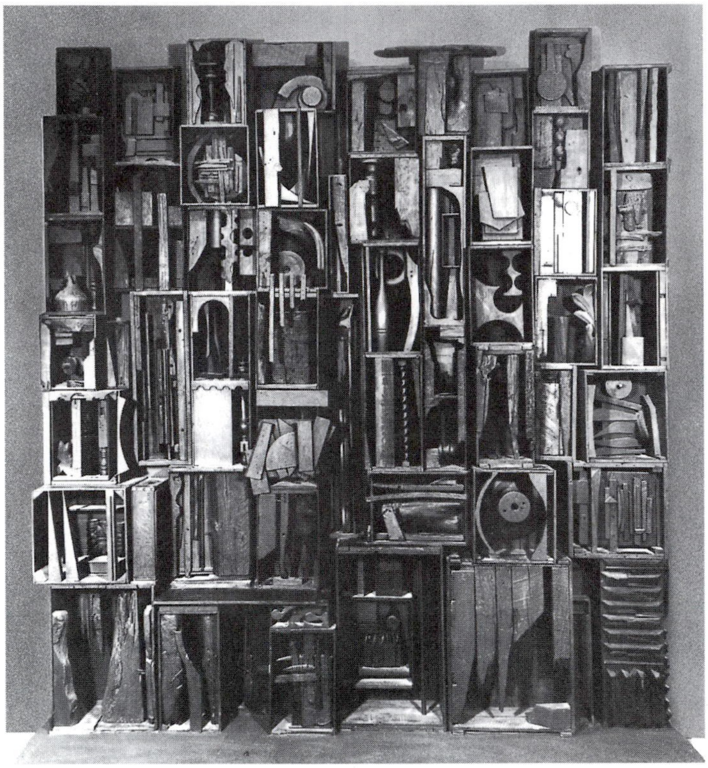

Installation

Collage is an inclusive medium. It admits anything and everything into its world. However, not everything that might be admitted into a collage can sit comfortably on a wall. We have already seen how collage begins to move into the space of the room. Judy Pfaff's *Rock/Paper/Scissor* (Fig. 387) completely escapes the wall, spilling out into the gallery as a whole. The piece insists on its lack of unity. It defiantly refuses to be classified. It even manages to ignore the unified architectural space of the gallery itself, turning it into a chaotic clutter of line, form, and color. The architecture of the room virtually disintegrates before our eyes.

This play with the predictable forms of interior architectural space is typical of installation art. Gaho Taniguchi's *Plant Body* (Fig.

Fig. 386 (above) Louise Nevelson, *Sky Cathedral,* 1958.
Assemblage: wood construction painted black, 11 ft. 3 ½ in. × 10 ft. ¼ in. × 18 in.
The Museum of Modern Art, New York.
Gift of Mr. and Mrs. Ben Mildwoff.

Fig. 387 (right) Judy Pfaff, *Rock/Paper/Scissor,* 1982.
Mixed media installation at the Albright-Knox Art Gallery, September 1982.
Albright-Knox Art Gallery, Buffalo, New York.

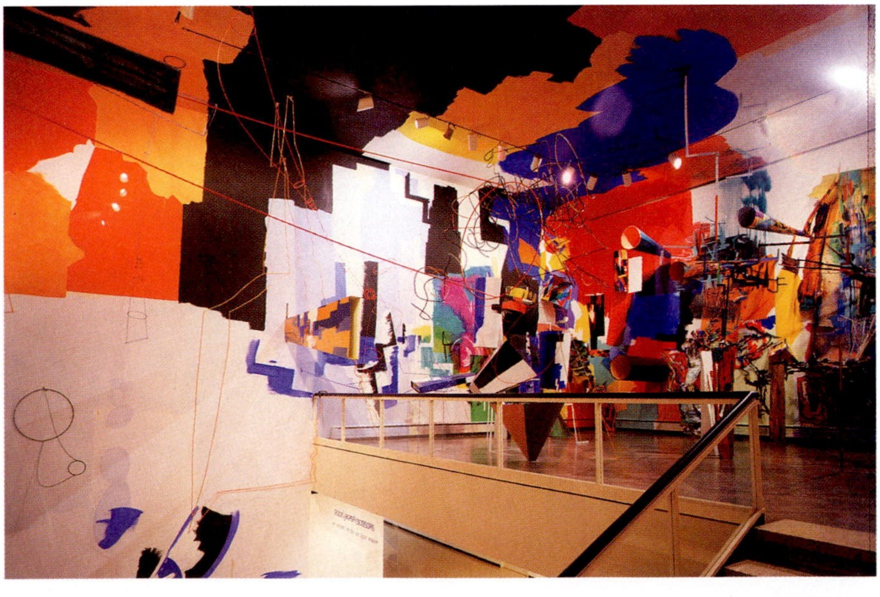

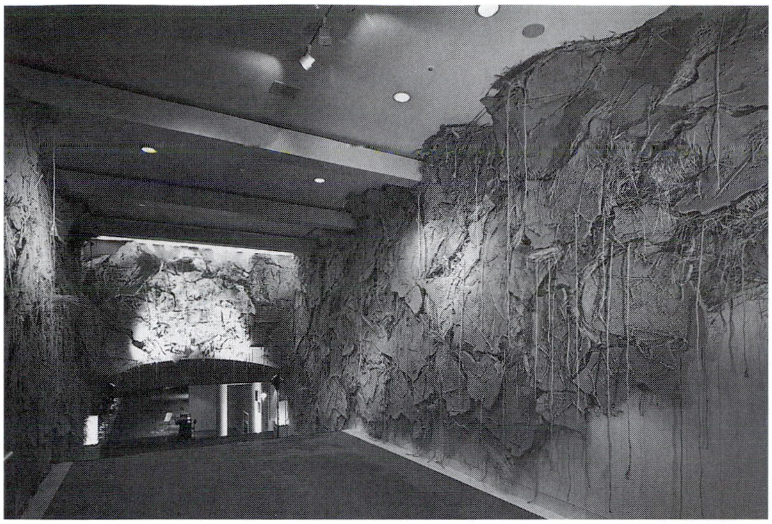

Fig. 388 (left) Gaho Taniguchi, *Plant Body,* 1987.
Installation at Spiral Garden, Wacoal Art Center, Tokyo. Soybeans, millet, rice, rope, straw mats, urethane, metal mesh, clay, 14 ft. 6 ¾ in. × 26 ft. 9 in. Spiral Garden, Tokyo/PPS.

Fig. 389 (below) George Segal, *The Aerial View,* 1970 (p.66).
Plaster, wood, plastic, incandescent and fluorescent light, 96 × 104 × 48 in. VAGA. Courtesy, Center for Creative Photography The University of Arizona, Tucson © 1991 Hans Namuth Estate. Sara Hilden Art Museum, Tampere, Finland.

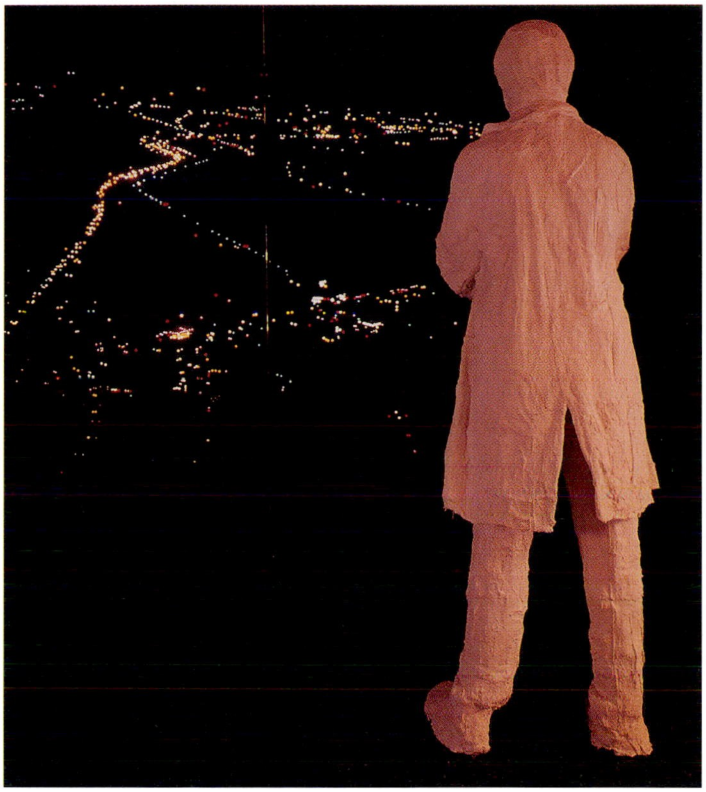

388) is designed to transform interior space entirely. It is inspired by the ancient Japanese art of flower arranging, *ikebana*. The philosophy behind *ikebana* stresses the notion of *mono no aware*, a sense of the poignancy of things, an attitude and feeling that can be traced back to early forms of Japanese Zen Buddhism. Both the ephemeral nature of the flower arrangement and the short life of the flower bear witness to the fact that all things beautiful must pass. *Ikebana,* then, seeks to capture the vanishing moment, and by doing this to celebrate the continual cycle of birth, death, and renewal.

Taniguchi was trained in the art of *ikebana,* and in *Plant Body,* she has implanted soybeans, rice, millet, straw, and rootlike rope into a surface of dried clay that seems barely to cling to the wall of the gallery. A sort of room-size live ceramic sculpture, the piece compresses the time of the seasons, from the wetness of the time when the seeds are planted to the hard dry soil of the harvest. The installation embodies, in interior space, the entire agricultural cycle.

George Segal's *The Aerial View* (Fig. 389) offers another model of installation art. Segal creates a life-size **tableau**—a three-dimensional, room-size environment into which we cannot enter. We view its space, as it were, through a window, and in this sense, it is like a three-dimensional painting. The power of Segal's installation derives from two separate effects. In the first place, his figure, a plaster cast of a real human form, stands in for us. Blank and anonymous, its view is our own. It looks out, from an extraordinary height—perhaps the top of a skyscraper—on an urban landscape. However, the depth of this space is an illusion. Segal has drilled hundreds of holes in a plywood board so that a pattern of colored lights, derived from slides Segal shot on a helicopter ride between Newark and Kennedy airports, shines through the black background. The irony of Segal's art is apparent—it is as if we contemplate the stars above, when in fact we only contemplate the ground beneath our feet.

Performance Art

One of the innovators of performance art was Allan Kaprow, who in the late 1950s "invented" what he called **Happenings,** which he defined as an "assemblages of events performed or perceived in more than one time and place. . . . A Happening . . . is art but seems closer to life." It was, in fact, the work of Jackson Pollock that inspired Kaprow to invent the form. The inclusiveness of paintings such as *Full Fathom Five* (Fig. 390)—it contains nails, tacks, buttons, a key, coins, cigarettes, matches, and other things buried in the paint that swirls across its surface—gave Kaprow the freedom to bring everything, including the activity of real people acting in real time, into the space of art. "Pollock," Kaprow wrote in 1958, "left us at the point where we must become preoccupied with and even dazzled by the space and objects of our everyday life, either our bodies, clothes, rooms, or, if need be, the vastness of Forty-Second Street. . . . Objects of every sort are materials for the new art: paint, chairs, food, electric and neon signs, smoke, water, old socks, a dog, movies, a thousand other things will be discovered by the present generation of artists. . . . The young artist of today need no longer say, 'I am a painter,' or 'a poet' or 'a dancer.' He is simply an 'artist.' All of life will be open to him."

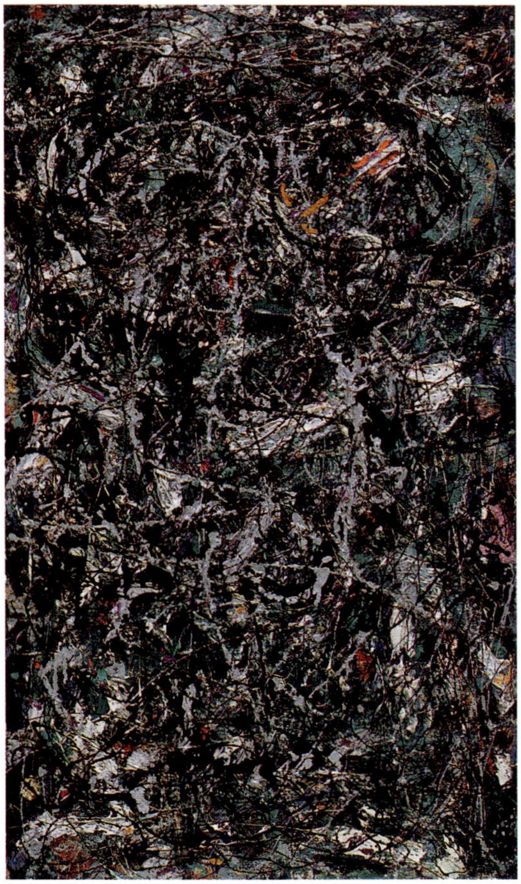

Fig. 390 Jackson Pollock, *Full Fathom Five,* 1947.
Oil on canvas with nails, tacks, buttons, key, coins, cigarettes, matches, etc., 50 7/8 × 30 1/8 in. Collection, The Museum of Modern Art, New York. Gift of Peggy Guggenheim.

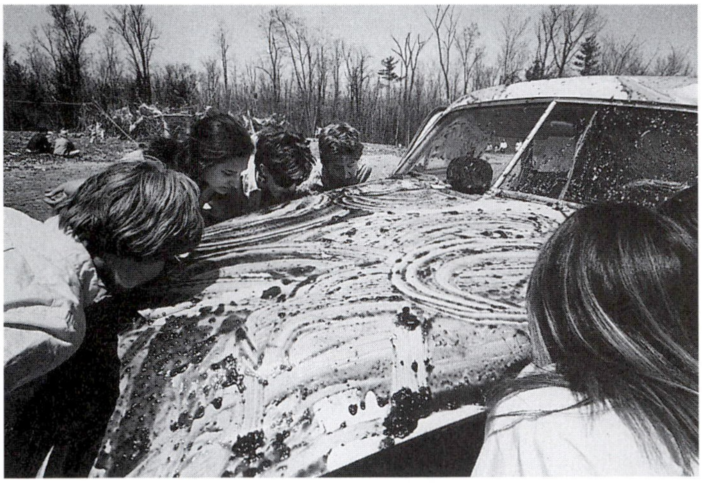

Fig. 391 Allan Kaprow, *Household,* 1964, near Ithaca, New York.

In the Happening *Household* (Fig. 391), there were no spectators, only participants, and the event was choreographed in advance by Kaprow. The site was a dump near Cornell University in Ithaca, New York. At 11 A.M. on the day of the Happening, the men who were participating built a wooden tower of trash, while the women built a nest of saplings and string. A smoking, wrecked car was towed onto the site, and the men covered it with strawberry jam. The women, who had been screeching inside the nest, came out to the car and licked the jam as the men destroyed their nest. Then the men returned to the wreck, and slapping white bread over it, began to eat the jam themselves. As the men ate, the women destroyed their tower. Eventually, as the men took sledge hammers to the wreck and set it on fire, the animosity between the two groups began to wane. Everyone gathered round and watched until the car was burned up, and then left quietly. What this Happening means, precisely, is not entirely clear, but it does draw attention to the violence of relations between men and women in our society and the frightening way in which violence can draw us together as well as drive us apart.

One of the most interesting and powerful performance artists was Joseph Beuys, who died in 1985. Beuys created what he preferred to call "actions." These were designed to reveal what he believed to be the real function of art—teaching people to be creative so that, through their creativity, they might change contemporary society. As he put it, "The key to changing things is to unlock the creativity in every man. When each man is creative, beyond right and left political parties, he can revolutionize time." Beuys's aims may have been didactic, but they were, nevertheless, almost always expressed in hauntingly poetic and moving images. In 1974, Beuys performed at the René Block Gallery in Manhattan a three-day piece, entitled *I Like America and America Likes Me* (Fig. 392). He had refused to visit the United States until it pulled out of Vietnam, and this performance not only celebrated his first visit to the country but addressed the still unhealed wounds of the Vietnam War, which had so divided the American people. When Beuys arrived at Kennedy International Airport, he was met by medical attendants, wrapped in gray felt, and driven by ambulance to the gallery, where, lying on a stretcher, he was placed behind a chain-link fence to live for three days and nights with a live coyote.

The coyote was comparable to the Native American in Beuys's eyes, a mammal subject to the same attack and persecution as they had been. For Beuys, the settling (or, rather, conquest) of the American West was a product of the same imperialist mentality that had led to the Vietnam War. The felt fabric in which Beuys wrapped himself is his most characteristic medium. It refers to his own rescue by Tartar tribesmen in the Crimea during World War II. After Beuys's plane crashed in a driving snowstorm, the Tartars restored him to health by covering his body with fat and wrapping him in felt. Thus wrapped in felt, Beuys introduced himself as an agent of healing into the symbolic world of the threatened coyote.

Man and coyote quickly developed a sort of mutual respect, mostly ignoring one another. About thirty times over the course of the three days, however, Beuys would imitate the coyote's every movement for a period of one or two hours, so that the two moved in a strangely harmonious "dance" through the gallery space. Often, when Beuys moved into a corner to smoke, the coyote would join him. For many viewers, Beuys's performance symbolized the possibilities for radically different "types" to coexist in the same space.

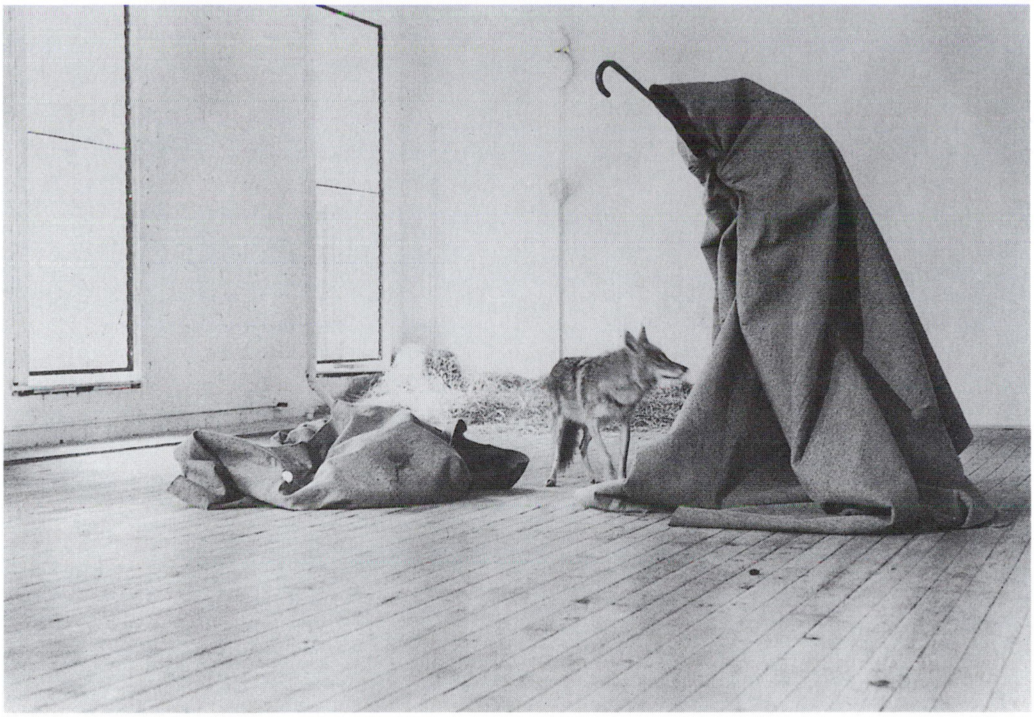

Fig. 392 Joseph Beuys, *I Like America and America Likes Me,* 1974.

Goat Island's How Dear to Me the Hour When Daylight Dies

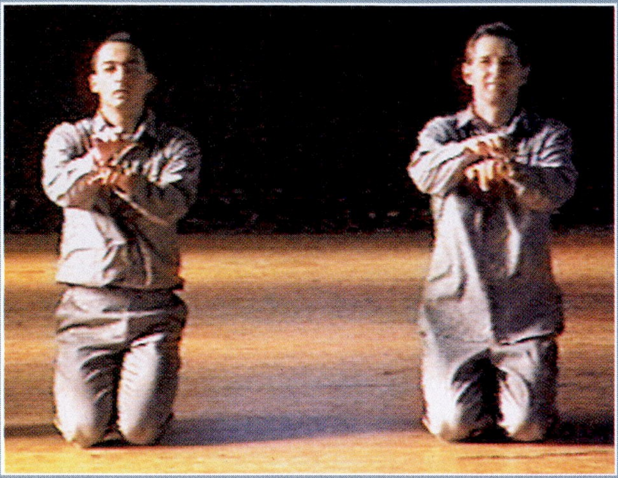

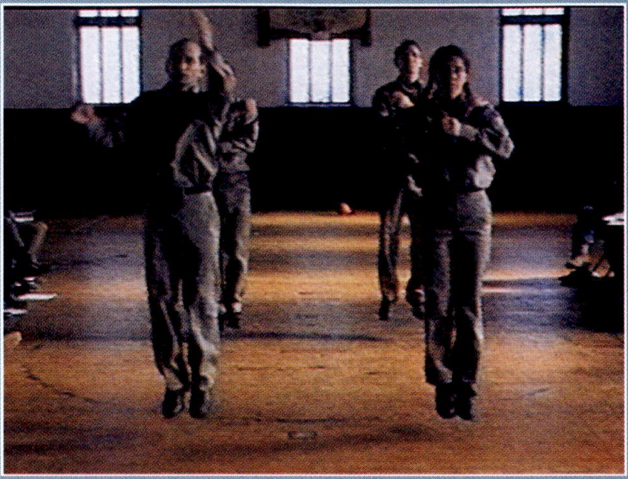

Figs. 393 and 394 Goat Island, *How Dear to Me the Hour When Daylight Dies,* 1995–1996.
Images from video documentation of work in progress, January 20, 1996. Courtesy Goat Island.

Goat Island's work is collaborative in nature. The group's four performers, and its director, Lin Hixson, all contribute to the writing, choreography, and conceptual aspects of each work.

Founded in 1987, the group has to date created five performance events, the last of which is *How Dear to Me the Hour When Daylight Dies,* which premiered in Glasgow, Scotland, in May 1996 and then subsequently toured across Scotland and England.

In each piece the troupe focuses on five major concerns: (1) they try to establish a conceptual and spatial relationship with the audience by treating the performance space, for instance, as a parade ground or a sporting arena; (2) they utilize movement in a way that is demanding to the point of exhaustion; (3) they incorporate personal, political, and social issues into the work directly through spoken text; (4) they stage their performances in non-theatrical spaces within the community, such as gyms or street sites; and (5) they seek to create striking visual images that encapsulate their thematic concerns.

The subject matter of their works is always eclectic, an assemblage of visual images, ideas, texts, physical movements, and music, that often have only the most poetic connection to each other. *How Dear to Me the Hour When Daylight Dies* began with their desire to share an intense group experience. To that end, in July 1994 the troupe traveled to Ireland to participate in the massive Croagh Patrick pilgrimage, a grueling four-hour climb up a mountain on the western seacoast near Westport, County Mayo, to a tiny church at the summit where St. Patrick spent forty days and forty nights exorcising the snakes from Ireland. Eleven days before the pilgrimage, on July 20, the father of Greg and Timothy McCain, two members of the troupe who have subsequently moved on to other endeavors, died in Indianapolis. The elder McCain had seen every Goat Island piece, some of them three times. The pilgrimage thus became not only an act of faith and penance, but one of mourning.

How Dear to Me begins with the troup performing a sequence of hand gestures, silently, thirty times, that evokes for them the memory of Mr. McCain (Fig. 393). The minimal exertion of these gestures contrasts dramatically with the intense physicality of the pilgrimage. But both actions, the hand movements and the pilgrimage, are acts of memory. And memory is in turn the focus of the next set of images in the performance.

Matthew Goulish plays the part of Mr. Memory, a sort of traveling sideshow character who claimed to commit to memory fifty new facts a day and who could answer virtually any question posed to him by an audience. After he answers a series of questions, the troupe breaks into a long dance number (Fig. 394). As all four perform this arduous and complex dance in absolute synchronous movement, it becomes clear that it is, at once, another version of the pilgrimage—the same physical exercise performed year after year, again and again—and an exercise in collaborative and communal memory, as each member of the troupe remembers just what movement comes next in the dance sequence.

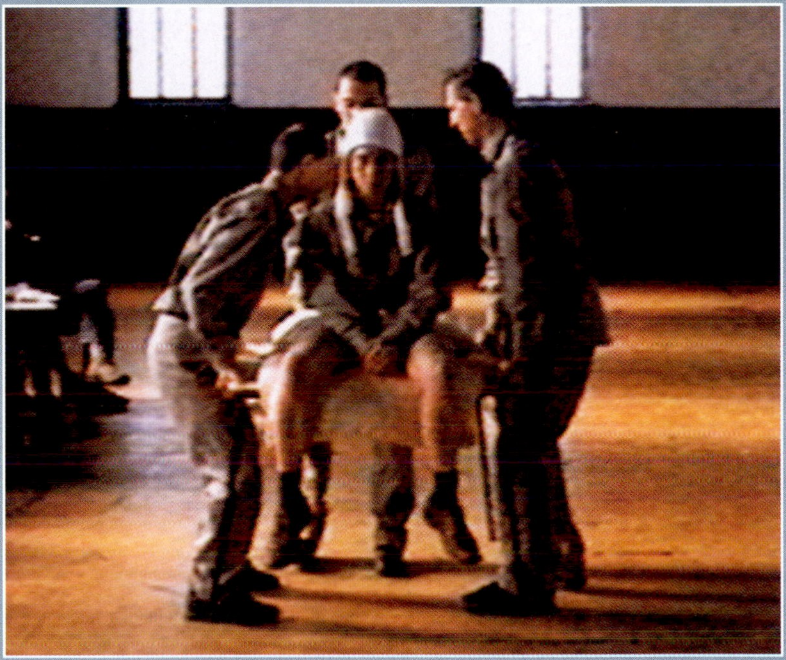

Fig. 395 Goat Island, *How Dear to Me the Hour When Daylight Dies,* 1995–1996. Image from video documentation of work in progress, January 20, 1996. Courtesy Goat Island.

After the dance, Mr. Memory is asked, "Who was the first woman to fly across the Atlantic Ocean?" The answer is Amelia Earhart, and, at that, Karen Christropher dons a flying cap and becomes Amelia Earhart herself. The mystery surrounding Earhart's death in the South Pacific in World War II is evoked, the mystery of her death is symbolic of the mystery of all death. In Figure 395, right, we witness the transformation of Christopher from her Earhart character into Mike Walker, "the world's fattest man," who in 1971 weighed 1,187 pounds. This transformation was necessitated by the discovery, during rehearsals, that Christopher was diabetic and would, as a result, need to eat during the course of each performance. The image of the three men carrying her emphasizes not only her weight but the gravity of her situation.

Many more images and ideas collide in the course of this one-and-one-half hour performance, too many to outline here; but this gives a sense of the remarkable energy, power, and inventiveness of Goat Island's collaborative and open-ended process.

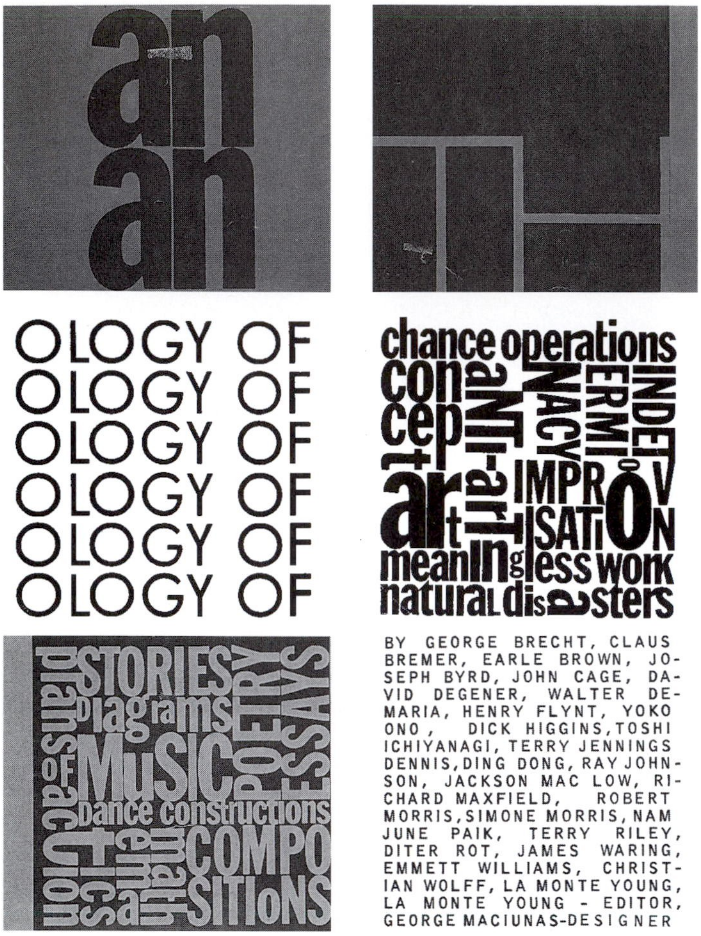

Fig. 396 George Maciunas, title pages of *An Anthology*, edited by La Monte Young, 1963.
Collection Gilbert B. and Lila Silverman. © 1963 by La Monte Young and Jackson Mac Low.

Performance art, it should be clear, exceeds limits of the visual sense to which we normally think of art as primarily appealing. As a result, it tends to be interdisciplinary, often combining elements not only of drama and poetry, but of music and dance as well. One of the major advocates of such an eclectic approach in the early 1960s was a loosely knit group of European, Japanese, Korean, Canadian, and American artists, many of whom trained first as musicians, which came to be identified by the name of Fluxus. Beuys often associated himself with the group, but more directly involved were people such as avant-garde musician La Monte Young, George Brecht, Dick Higgins, an accomplished assemblage artist, poet Jackson Mac Low, Yoko Ono, and, on occasion, John Lennon of the Beatles.

The composer John Cage's classes at the New School in New York were a catalyst for the group. Many of Cage's students began to investigate the implications of compositions such as his *4'33"* in their own work. The composition *4'33"* is literally four minutes and 33 seconds of silence, during which the audience becomes aware that all manner of noise in the room, incidental and otherwise, is, in the context of the piece, "music."

Thus Jackson Mac Low created poetry of chance-derived nouns and verbs improvised upon by the performer. La Monte Young's *X for Henry Flynt* required the performer to play an unspecified sound, or group of sounds, in a distinct and consistent rythmic pattern for as long as the performer wished, which, in Young's own performance, consisted of 600-odd beats on a frying pan. Dick Higgins's *Winter Carol* consisted of everyone going outdoors to listen to the snow fall for a specified amount of time. Events such as this were soon organized into Fluxus "concerts," events that admitted anything, including the audience's outrage. One of the first collections of Fluxus-like work, which served as something of a model for these concerts, was a publication called *An Anthology*, collected by La Monte Young and designed by George Maciunas. The innovative graphic design of its six title pages (Fig. 396), and its willingness to accept almost everything—even "anti-art"—as art are indicative of the inclusiveness of the movement as a whole.

Perhaps the most successful of the multimedia performance artists has been Laurie Anderson, who not only performs before large enthusiastic audiences in essentially commercial rock concert settings, but has successfully marketed both films and recordings of her work as well. Her performances—the most ambitious of which is the seven-hour, four-part, two-evening *United States* (Fig. 397)—involve a wide variety of technological effects. An electronic harmonizer lends her voice a deep male resonance that she describes as "the Voice of Authority . . . a corporate voice, a kind of 'Newsweekese.'" A "black box" delays, alters, and combines tapes of her voice so that she sounds like a chorus. Her "violin" is actually a tape playback head and her "bow" a strip of prerecorded audiotape that is transmitted as she draws it, at various speeds, in long or short sweeps, across the head.

These audio effects are matched by equally sophisticated choreography, lighting changes, and a wealth of complex visual imagery that inundates the audience in wave after wave of Americana. Anderson's performances wander through the psychological and emotional terrain of the United States, not so much in an effort to understand it as in submission to the impossibility of ever understanding it. "I mean my mouth is moving," she admits in *United States,* "but I don't really understand what I'm saying." It is as if she has no real voice of her own, only the voice of technology. She is not so much a person, a performer, as an assemblage, fabricated out of the American scene.

If it seems slightly odd that this chapter on three-dimensional media should conclude with discussion of a group of works that verge on becoming theater, you need only reflect back to where this chapter began. As a medium, sculpture is, by and large, more active than painting. We passively stand before a painting. But we walk around sculpture—or through it, in the case of earthworks—and it changes with our point of view. Even when we consider sculpture in relief, it is as if the scenes depicted in it are trying to emerge or escape from the confines of two-dimensionality.

One of the great myths that helps us to understand the power of sculpture is the story of Pygmalion. According to legend, Pygmalion fell in love with a statue of Venus that he himself had carved. When he prayed that he might have a wife as beautiful as the image he had created, to his amazement the statue came to life as his wife, Galatea. The story embodies the "liveliness" of all three-dimensional media, their tendency to move off the wall and actively engage us, not just imaginatively but physically as well. By modeling, carving, casting, and assembling, we create objects that enter our world, share our space, even confront us. When we work with clay or glass or fiber, we make things that we can physically use. Three-dimensional media engage our lives, just as collage engages the realities of the world around it by admitting such things as the news into the space of art. And as the space of art opens up, as room-size installations and then as performance, it literally comes to life like Galatea herself.

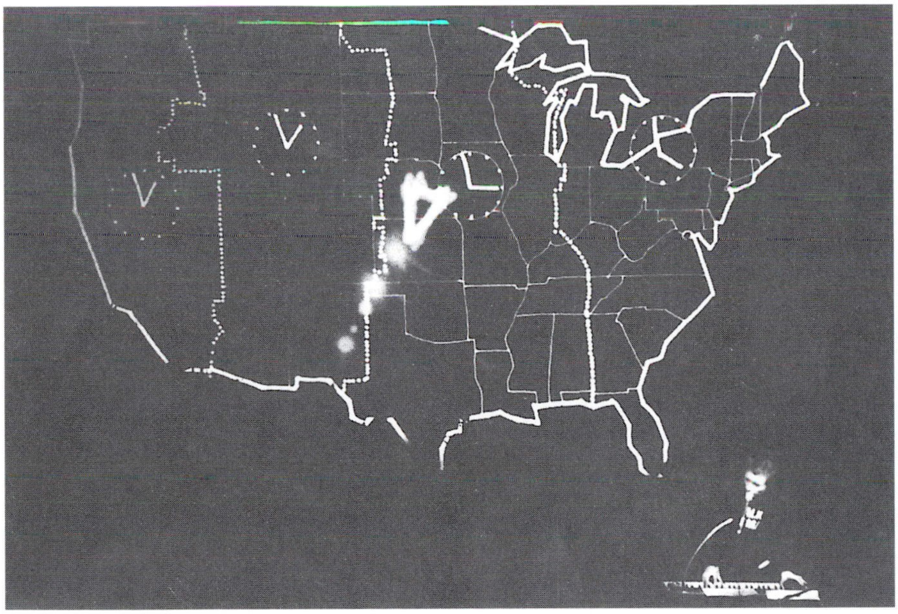

Fig. 397 Laurie Anderson, *United States Part II,* 1980.
Photograph by Paula Court.

CHAPTER 13

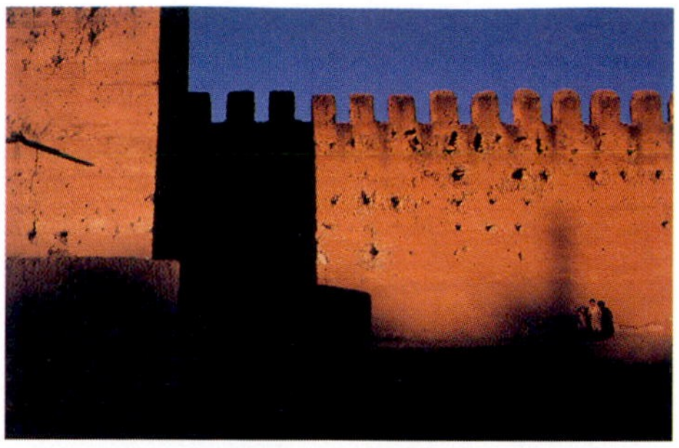

The Camera Arts

Photography
Early History
Form and Content

WORKS IN PROGRESS
Nicholas Nixon's *The Brown Sisters*

Film

Video

Thus far in Part III, we have discussed the two-dimensional media—drawing, printmaking, and painting—and the three-dimensional media—sculpture, the craft media, and new, mixed media forms. Now we turn to the camera arts, the media that allow the artist to explore the fourth dimension—time.

The images that come from still, motion picture, and video cameras are first and foremost informational. Cameras record the world around us, and the history of the camera is a history of technologies that record our world with ever increasing sophistication and expertise. Photography began with still images and added motion. To the silent moving image was next added sound. To the "talkie" was added color. And film developed in its audience a taste for "live" action, a taste satisfied by live television transmission, video images that allow us to view anything happening in the world as it happens. The history of the camera arts is thus a history of increasing immediacy. In this chapter we will survey that history, starting with still photography, moving to film, and, finally, to video. Our focus will be on works that stimulate the imagination, on these media as *art*.

PHOTOGRAPHY

Like collage, photography is, potentially at least, an inclusive rather than an exclusive medium. You can photograph anything you can see. According to artist Robert Rauschenberg, whose combine-paintings we studied in the last chapter (Fig. 385), "The world is essentially a storehouse of visual information. Creation is the process of assemblage. The photograph is a process of instant assemblage, instant collage." Walker Evans's photograph *Roadside Store between Tuscaloosa and Greensboro, Alabama* (Fig. 398) is an example of just such "instant collage." Evans's mission as a photographer was to capture every aspect of American visual reality, and his work has been called a "photographic equivalent to the Sears, Roebuck catalog of the day." But the urge to make such instant visual assemblages—to capture a moment in time—is as old as the desire to represent the world accurately. We begin our discussion of photography by considering the development of the technology itself, and then we will consider the fundamental aesthetic problem photography faces, the tension between form and content, the tension between the way a photograph is formally organized as a composition and what it expresses or means.

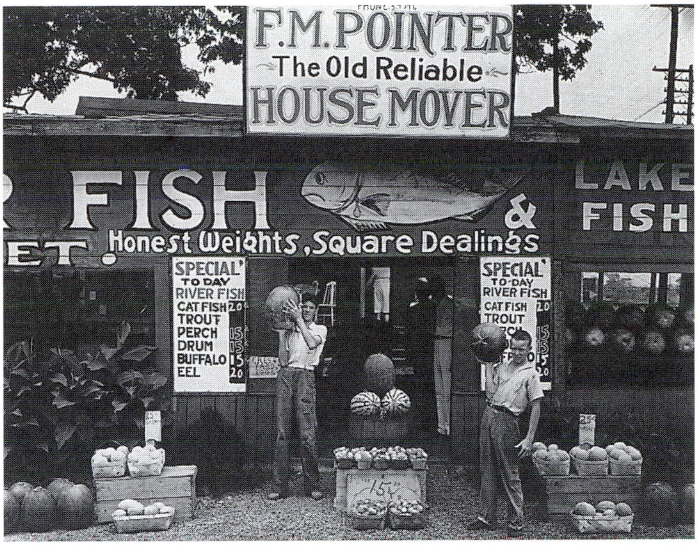

Fig. 398 Walker Evans,
***Roadside Store between Tuscaloosa and Greensboro, Alabama,* 1936.**
Library of Congress.

Early History

The word *camera* is the Latin word for "room." And, in fact, by the sixteenth century a darkened room, called a *camera obscura*, was routinely used by artists to copy nature accurately. The scientific principle employed is essentially the same as that used by the camera today. A small hole on the side of a light-tight room admits a ray of light that projects a scene, upside down, directly across from the hole onto a semitransparent white scrim. The *camera obscura* depicted here (Fig. 399) is a double one, with images entering the room from both sides. It is also portable, allowing the artist to set up in front of any subject matter.

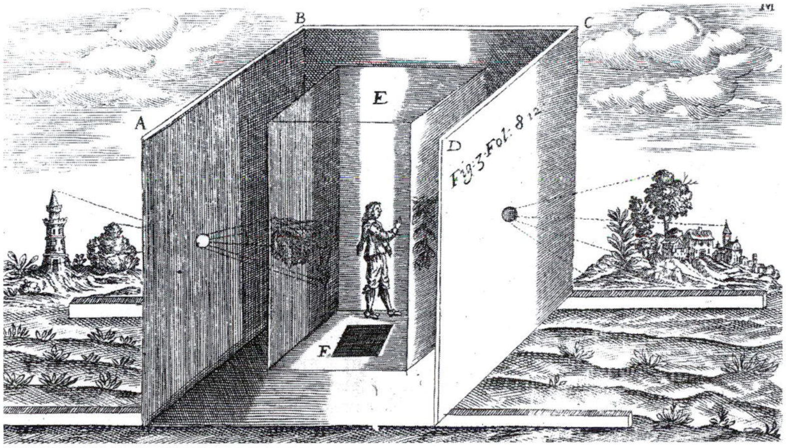

Fig. 399 *Camera Obscura.*
Engraving.
Courtesy of George Eastman House.
Unidentified photographer.

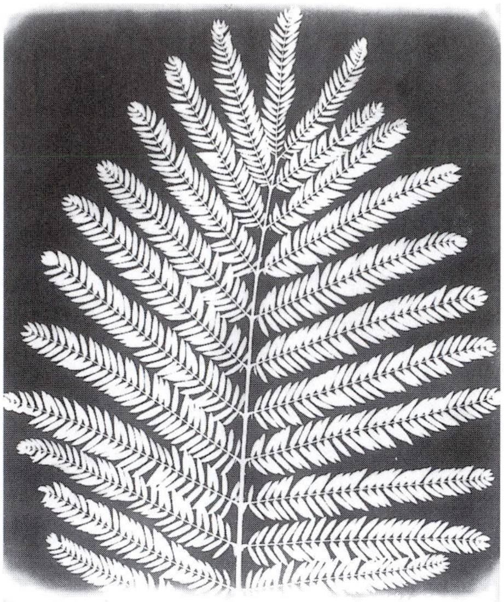

Fig. 400 William Henry Fox Talbot, *Mimosoidea Suchas, Acacia,* c. 1839.
Photogenic drawing.
Fox Talbot Collection, Science Museum, London.

But working with the *camera obscura* was a tedious proposition, even after small portable dark boxes came into use. The major drawback of the *camera obscura* was that while it could capture the image, it could not preserve it. In 1839, that problem was solved, simultaneously in England and France, and the public was introduced to a new way of representing the world.

In England, William Henry Fox Talbot presented a process for fixing negative images on paper coated with light-sensitive chemicals, which he called **photogenic drawing** (Fig. 400). In France, a different process, which yielded a positive image on a polished metal plate, was named the **daguerreotype** (Fig. 401), after one of its two inventors, Louis Jacques Mandé Daguerre (Joseph Nicéphore Niépce had died in 1833, leaving Daguerre to perfect the process and garner the laurels). Public reaction was wildly enthusiastic, and the French and English press faithfully reported every development in the greatest detail.

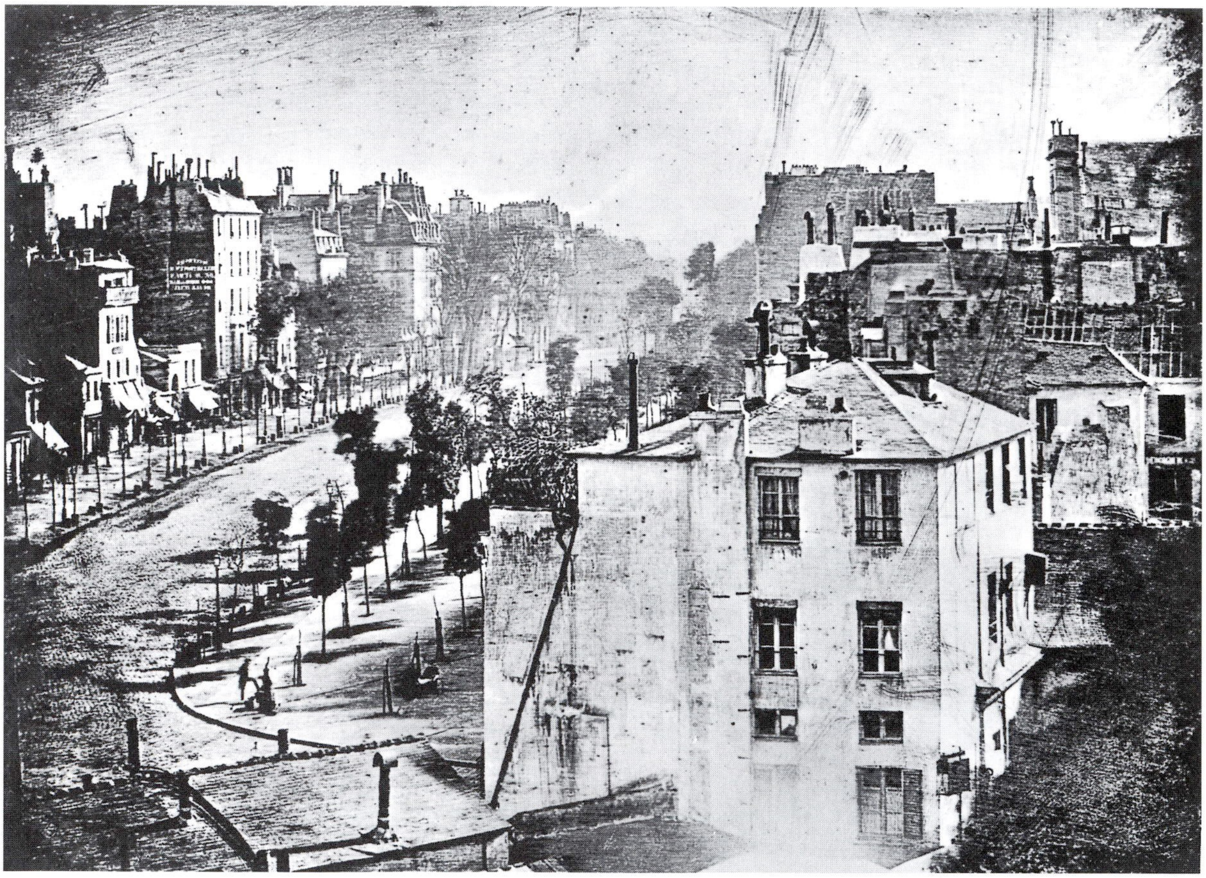

Fig. 401 Louis Jacques Mandé Daguerre, *Le Boulevard du Temple,* 1839.
Daguerreotype. Bayerisches National Museum, Munich.

When he saw his first daguerreotype, the French painter Paul Delaroche is reported to have exclaimed, "From now on, painting is dead!" Delaroche may have overreacted, but he nevertheless understood the potential of the new medium of photography to usurp painting's historical role of representing the world. In fact, photographic portraiture quickly became a successful industry. As early as 1841, a daguerreotype portrait could be had in Paris for 15 francs. That same year in London, Richard Beard opened the first British portrait studio, bringing a true sense of showmanship to the process. One of his first customers, the novelist Maria Edgeworth (Fig. 402), described having her portrait done at Beard's in a breathless letter dated May 25, 1841: "It is a wonderful mysterious operation. You are taken from one room into another upstairs and down and you see various people whispering and hear them in neighboring passages and rooms unseen and the whole apparatus and stool on a high platform under a glass dome casting a snapdragon blue light making all look like spectres and the men in black gliding about. . . ."

In the face of such a "miracle," the art of portrait painting underwent a rapid decline. Of the 1,278 paintings exhibited at the Royal Academy in London in 1830, over 300 were miniatures, the most popular form of the portrait; in 1870, only 33 miniatures were exhibited. In 1849 alone, 100,000 daguerreotype portraits were sold in Paris. Not only had photography replaced painting as the preferred medium for portraiture, it had democratized the genre as well, making portraits available not only to the wealthy but to the middle class, and even, with some sacrifice, to the working class.

The daguerreotype itself had some real disadvantages as a medium, however. In the first place, it required considerable time to prepare, expose, and develop the plate. Iodine was vaporized on a copper sheet to create light-sensitive silver iodide. The plate then had to be kept in total darkness until the camera lens was opened to expose it. At the time Daguerre first made the process public in 1839, imprinting an image on the plate took from eight to ten minutes in bright summer light. His own view of the Boulevard du Temple (Fig. 401) was exposed for so long that none of the people in the street, moving about their business, has left any impression on the plate, save for one solitary figure at the lower left who is having his shoes shined. By 1841, the discovery of so-called chemical "accelerators" had made it possible to expose the plate for only one minute, but a sitter could not move in that time for fear of blurring the image. The plate was finally developed by suspending it face down in heated mercury, which deposited a white film over the exposed areas. The unexposed silver iodide was dissolved with salt. The plate then had to be rinsed and dried with the utmost care.

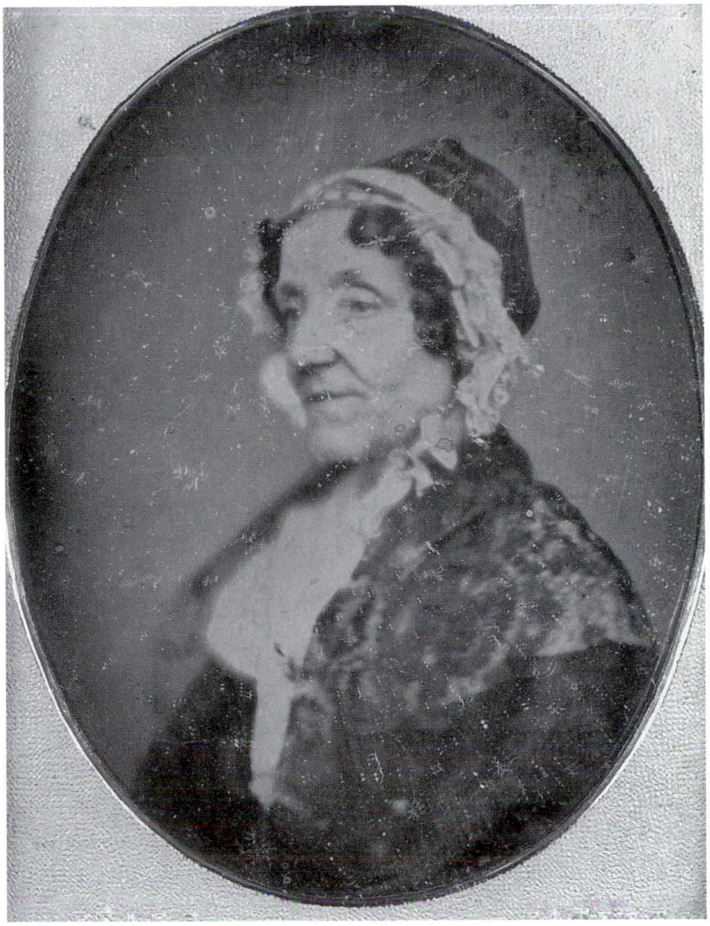

Fig. 402 Richard Beard, *Maria Edgeworth*, 1841.
Daguerreotype, 2 1/8 × 1 3/4 in.
National Portrait Gallery, London.

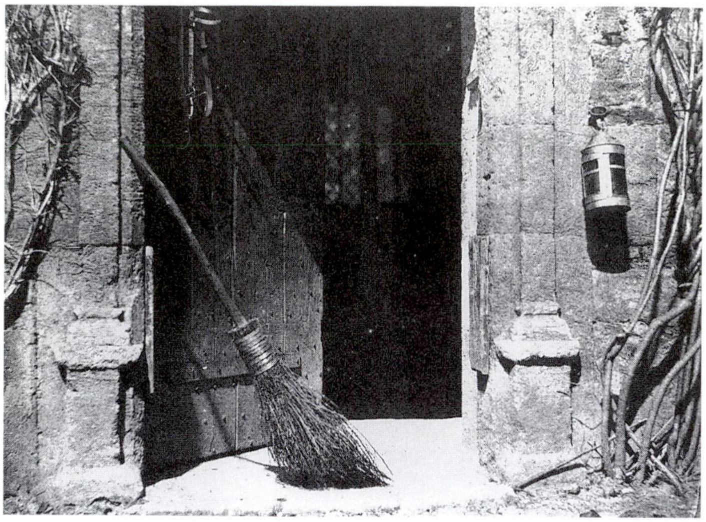

Fig. 403 William Henry Fox Talbot, *The Open Door,* 1843.
Calotype. Fox Talbot Collection, Science Museum, London.

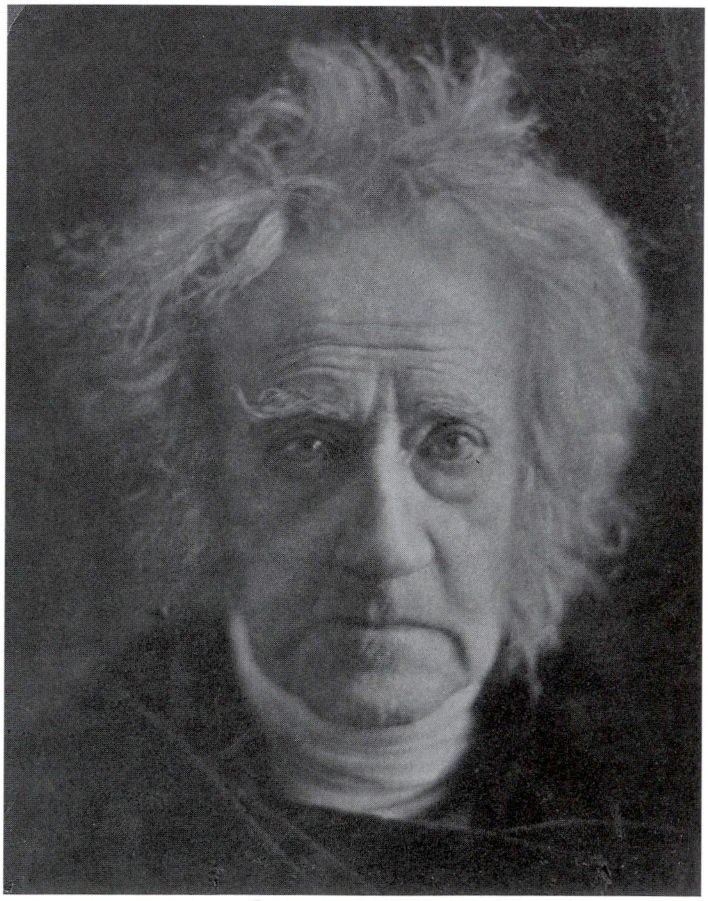

Fig. 404 Julia Margaret Cameron, *Sir John Herschel,* c. 1867.
Collodion/albumen print, 12 3/4 × 10 1/4 in.
Gift of Mrs. J. D. Cameron Bradley, Courtesy, Museum of Fine Arts, Boston.

An even greater drawback of the daguerreotype was that it could not be reproduced. Utilizing paper instead of a metal plate, Fox Talbot's photogenic process made multiple prints a possibility. Talbot quickly learned that he could reverse the negative image of the photogenic drawings by placing sheets of sensitized paper over them and exposing both again to sunlight. Talbot also discovered that sensitized paper, exposed for even a few seconds, held a *latent* image that could be brought out and developed by dipping the paper in gallic acid. This **calotype** process is the basis of modern photography.

In 1843, Talbot made a picture, which he called *The Open Door* (Fig. 403), that convinced him that the calotype could not only document the world as we know it, but become a work of art in its own right. When he published this calotype in his book *The Pencil of Nature*, the first book of photographs ever produced, he captioned it as follows: "A painter's eye will often be arrested where ordinary people see nothing remarkable. A casual gleam of sunshine, or a shadow thrown across his path, a time-withered oak, or a moss-covered stone may awaken a train of thoughts and feelings, and picturesque imaginings." For Talbot, at least, painter and photographer saw the world as one.

In 1850, the English sculptor Frederick Archer introduced a new **wet-plate collodion** photographic process that was almost universally adopted within five years. In a darkened room, he poured liquid collodion—made of pyroxyline dissolved in alcohol or ether—over a glass plate bathed in a solution of silver nitrate. The plate had to be prepared, exposed, and developed all within 15 minutes and while still wet. The process was cumbersome, but the exposure time short and the rewards quickly realized. On her forty-ninth birthday, in 1864, Julia Margaret Cameron, the wife of a high-placed British civil servant and friend to many of the most famous people of her day, was given a camera and collodion-processing equipment by her daughter and son-in-law. "It may amuse you, Mother, to photograph," the accompanying note said.

Cameron, who was friends with Sir John Herschel, the scientist with whom Fox Talbot had most often consulted, became one of the greatest of all portrait photographers. She set up a studio in a chicken coop at her home on the Isle of Wight, and over the course of the next ten years convinced almost everyone she knew to pose for her. Commenting on her photographs of famous men like Herschel (Fig. 404), she wrote in her *Annals of My Glass House,* "When I have had such men before my camera, my whole soul has endeavored to do its duty towards them in recording faithfully the greatness of the inner man as well as the features of the outer man. The photograph thus taken has been almost the embodiment of a prayer."

More than anything else, it was the ability of the portrait photographer to expose, as it were, the "soul" of the sitter that led the French government to give photography the legal status of art as early as 1862. But from the beginning, photography served a *documentary* function as well—it recorded and preserved important events. At the outbreak of the American Civil War, in 1861, Matthew Brady spent the entirety of his considerable fortune to outfit a band of photographers to document the war. When Brady insisted that he owned the copyright for every photograph made by anyone in his employ, whether or not made on the job, several of his best photographers quit, among them Timothy O'Sullivan (Fig. 405). One of the first great photojournalists, O'Sullivan is reported to have photographed calmly during the most horrendous bombardments, twice having his camera hit by shell fragments.

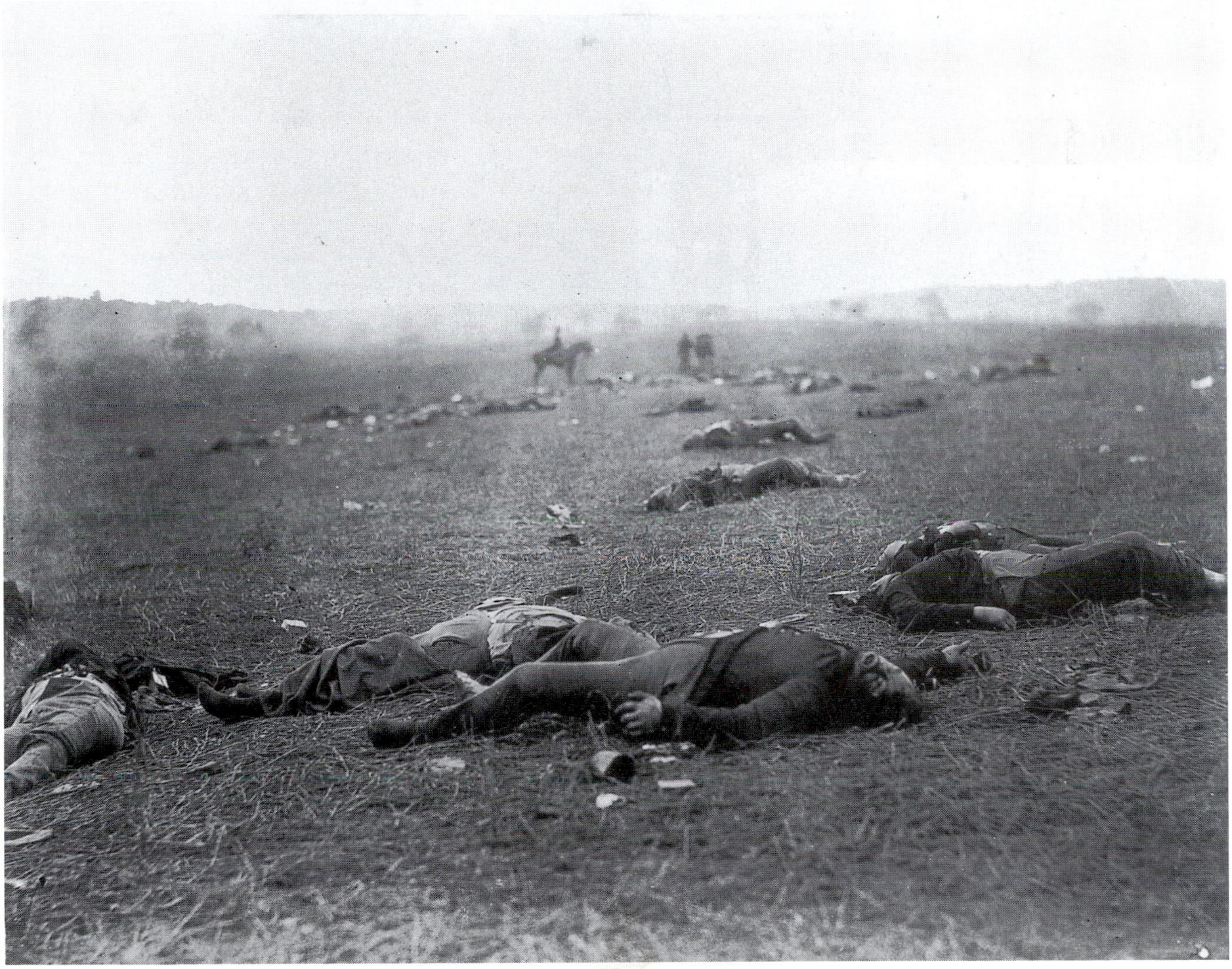

Fig. 405 Timothy O'Sullivan, *Harvest of Death, Gettysburg, Pa.,* 1863.
Collodion print. International Museum of Photography at George Eastman House, Rochester, New York.

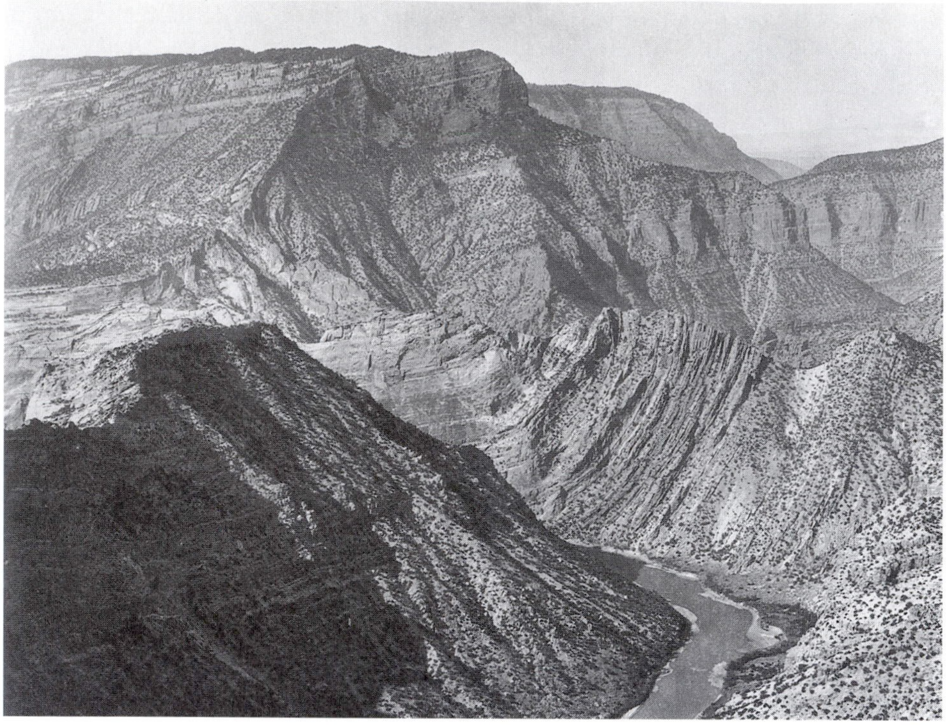

Fig. 406 Timothy O'Sullivan, *Green River (Colorado),* c. 1868.
Collodion print, 8 × 10 in. Library of Congress.

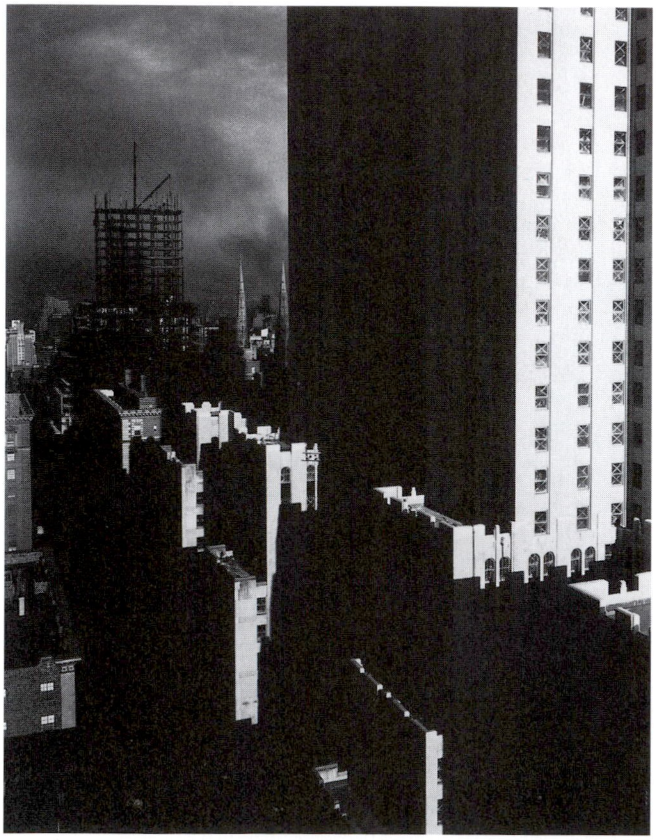

Fig. 407 Alfred Stieglitz, *From the Shelton, New York,* 1931.
Silver gelatin print.
©1993 National Gallery of Art, Washington, DC. Alfred Stieglitz Collection.

After the war, O'Sullivan packed his photography wagon, laden with glass plates, chemicals, and cameras, and joined Clarence King's Survey of the Fortieth Parallel in order to document a landscape few Americans had ever seen: the rugged, sometimes barren terrain stretching along the Fortieth Parallel between Denver, Colorado and Virginia City, Nevada. Hired to record the geological variety of the region, O'Sullivan quickly realized that on the two-dimensional surface of the photograph, the landscape yielded sometimes stunningly beautiful formal plays of line and texture. In his view of the Green River canyon (Fig. 406), brush dots the landscape in small, isolated flecks that create an almost dimensionless space, especially on the right. A geological upthrust, through which the river has apparently cut its way, sweeps up from the left, ending abruptly at the picture's center, almost reminding us of the broad brushwork of an abstract expressionist canvas.

Form and Content

It might be said that every photograph is an abstraction, a simplification of reality that substitutes two-dimensional for three-dimensional

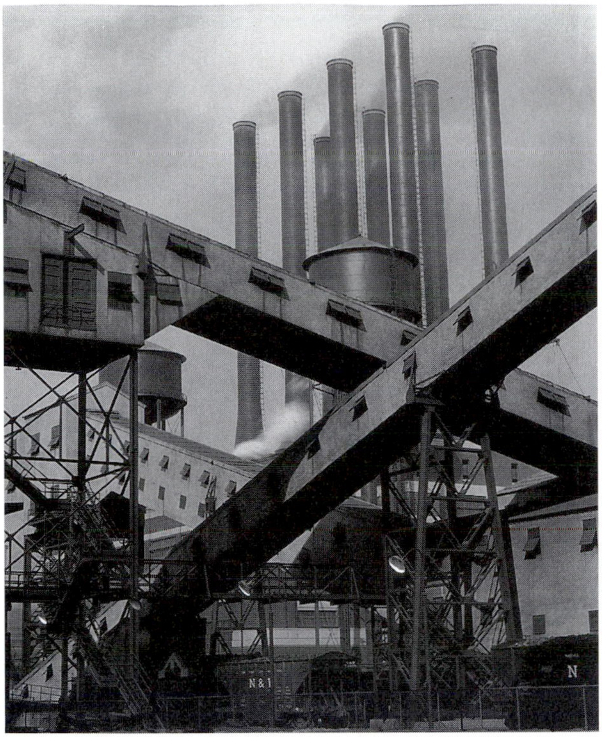

Fig. 408 Charles Sheeler, *Criss-Crossed Conveyors—Ford Plant,* 1927.
Gelatin-silver print, 10 × 8 in.
The Lane Collection, Courtesy, Museum of Fine Arts, Boston.

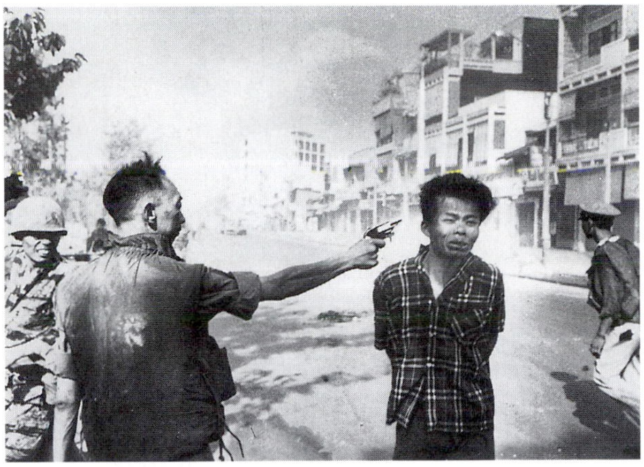

Fig. 409 Eddie Adams, Brigadier General Nguygen Ngoc Loan summarily executing the suspected leader of a Vietcong commando unit, Saigon, South Vietnam, February 1, 1968.
Wide World Photos.

space, an instant of perception for the seamless continuity of time, and, in black-and-white work at least, the gray scale for color. If the photographer additionally manipulates the space of the photograph in order to emphasize formal elements over representational concerns, as O'Sullivan seems to have done in his picture of the Green River canyon, then this abstract side of the medium is further emphasized. One of the greatest sources of photography's hold on the popular imagination lies in this ability to aestheticize the everyday—to reveal as beautiful that which we normally take for granted. In his photograph, *From the Shelton, New York* (Fig. 407), Alfred Stieglitz has transformed the three-dimensional space of the picture into a two-dimensional design of large, flat black-and-white shapes. By intentionally heightening the contrast between light and dark, and almost completely eliminating middle register grays, Stieglitz deemphasizes the literal content of his photograph and creates, instead, what he called "an affirmation of light. . . . Each thing that arouses me is perhaps but a variation on the theme of how black and white maintain a living equilibrium."

The geometric beauty of Stieglitz's work deeply influenced Charles Sheeler, who was hired by Henry Ford to photograph the new Ford factory at River Rouge in the late 1920s (Fig. 408). It was precisely Sheeler's task to aestheticize Ford's plant. His photographs, which were immediately recognized for their artistic merit and subsequently exhibited around the world, were designed to celebrate industry. They revealed, in the smokestacks, conveyors, and iron latticework of the factory, a grandeur and proportion not unlike that of the great Gothic cathedrals of Europe.

Even when the intention is not to aestheticize the subject, as is often true in photojournalism, the power of the photograph will come from its ability to focus our attention on that from which we would normally avert our eyes. The impact of Eddie Adams's famous photograph of Brigadier General Nguygen Ngoc Loan summarily executing the suspected leader of a Vietcong commando unit in Saigon, South Vietnam, February 1, 1968 (Fig. 409) lies in its sheer matter-of-factness. The photograph not only records the immediacy of death and the cold, ruthless detachment of its agent, it is unrelenting in its insistence on what might be called the "truth factor" of the photographic image. This *really* happened, and the photograph became, like Abraham Zapruder's film of John F. Kennedy's assassination or the television coverage of Jack Ruby shooting Lee Harvey Oswald, an icon of the political and moral ambiguity of the age.

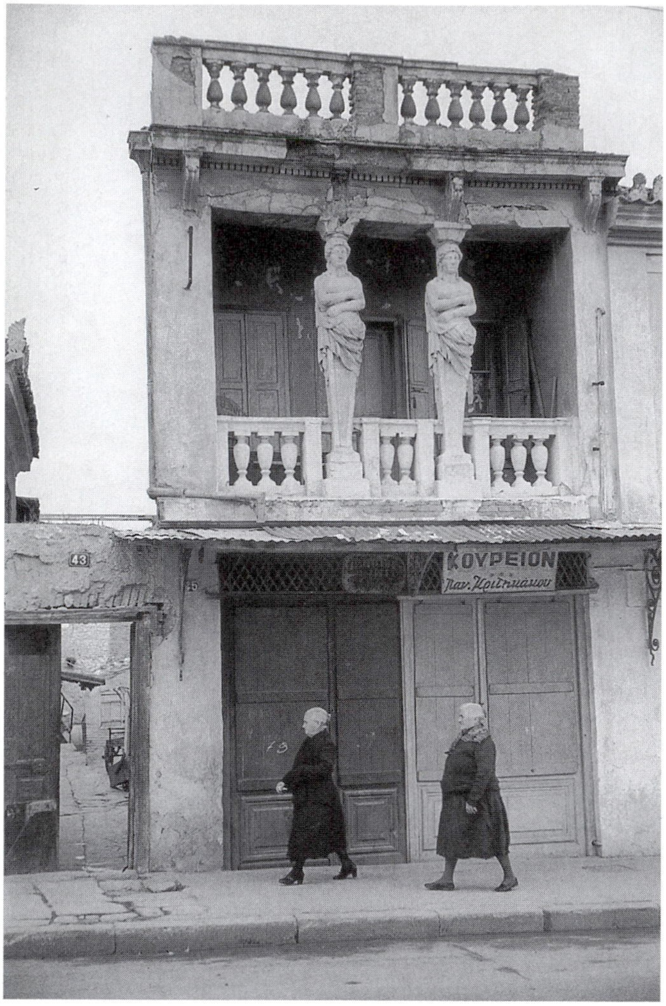

Fig. 410 Henri Cartier-Bresson, *Athens,* 1953.
Magnum Photos.

Both Sheeler's and Adams's photographs depend on much more sophisticated photographic equipment and film than was available to early practitioners like O'Sullivan. Since the day in 1888 when Kodak introduced the handheld camera, the technological advances have been staggering. But technological advances have not effaced the medium's primary concern with the tension and distance between form and content—between the photographic object, which exists out of time in aesthetic space, and the real event, the content, which takes place in both historical time and actual space.

Talking about the ways in which he arrives at the photographic image, Henri Cartier-Bresson has described the relation between form and content in the following terms:

> *We must place ourselves and our camera in the right relationship with the subject, and it is in fitting the latter into the frame of the viewfinder that the problems of composition begin. This recognition, in real life, of a rhythm of surfaces, lines, and values is for me the essence of photography. . . . We compose almost at the moment of pressing the shutter. . . . Sometimes one remains motionless, waiting for something to happen; sometimes the situation is resolved and there is nothing to photograph. If something should happen, you remain alert, wait a bit, then shoot and go off with the sensation of having got something. Later you can amuse yourself by tracing out on the photo the geometrical pattern, or spatial relationships, realizing that, by releasing the shutter at that precise instant, you had instinctively selected an exact geometrical harmony, and that without this the photograph would have been lifeless.*

Thus, in looking at this photograph (Fig. 410), we can imagine Cartier-Bresson walking down a street in Athens, Greece, one day in 1953, and coming across the second-story balcony with its references to the classical past. Despite the doorways behind the balcony, the second story appears to be a mere facade. Cartier-Bresson stops, studies the scene, waits, and then spies two women walking up the street in his direction. They pass beneath the two female forms on the balcony above, and, at precisely that instant, he releases the shutter. Cartier-Bresson called this "the decisive moment." Later, in the studio, the parallels and harmonies between street and balcony, antiquity and the present moment, youth and age, white marble and black dresses, stasis and change—all captured in this photograph—become apparent to him, and he prints the image.

These same conflicts between the ideal and the real animate Margaret Bourke-White's *At the Time of the Louisville Flood* (Fig. 411). Far less subtle than Cartier-Bresson's image, Bourke-White juxtaposes the dream of white America against the reality of black American lives. The dream is a flat, painted surface, the idealized space of the advertising billboard. In front of it, real people wait, indifferent in their hunger.

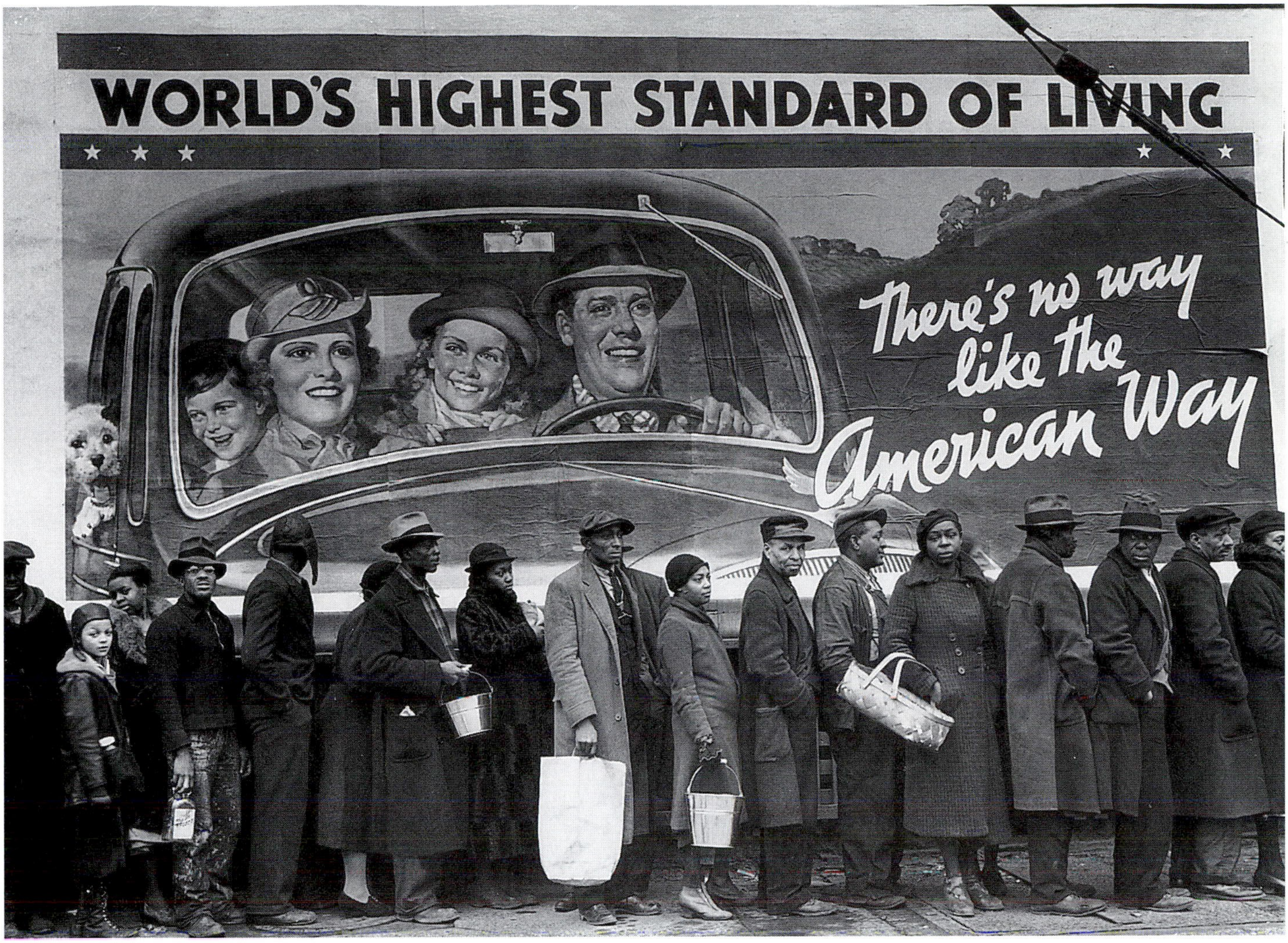

Fig. 411 Margaret Bourke-White, *At the Time of the Louisville Flood,* 1937.
Black-and-white photograph, *Life* Magazine © 1954, Time, Inc.

Bourke-White shot the scene in January 1937 on assignment for *Life* magazine. The Ohio River had flooded, inundating Louisville, Kentucky and killing or injuring over 900 people. Bourke-White flew into the city on the last flight before the airfield was flooded out. She hitchhiked on rowboats that were delivering food packages and searching for survivors. She shot photos of the churning river from a raft. *Life* ran *At the Time of the Louisville Flood* as its lead in a story featuring Bourke-White's photographs.

Life magazine, which started publication in November 1936, was conceived as a photojournalistic enterprise—heavy on pictures, light on words—and it became one of the primary outlets for American photography for the next 30 years. According to Bourke-White, it taught photographers an important lesson: "Pictures can be beautiful, but must tell facts too." Photographs have to balance form and content. But whatever *Life's* emphasis on content, the magazine still provided an enormous opportunity for creative work. "I could almost feel the horizon widening and the great rush of wind sweeping in," Bourke-White wrote of its arrival on the scene, "this was the kind of magazine that could be anything we chose to make it . . . everything we could bring to bear would be swallowed up in every piece of work we did."

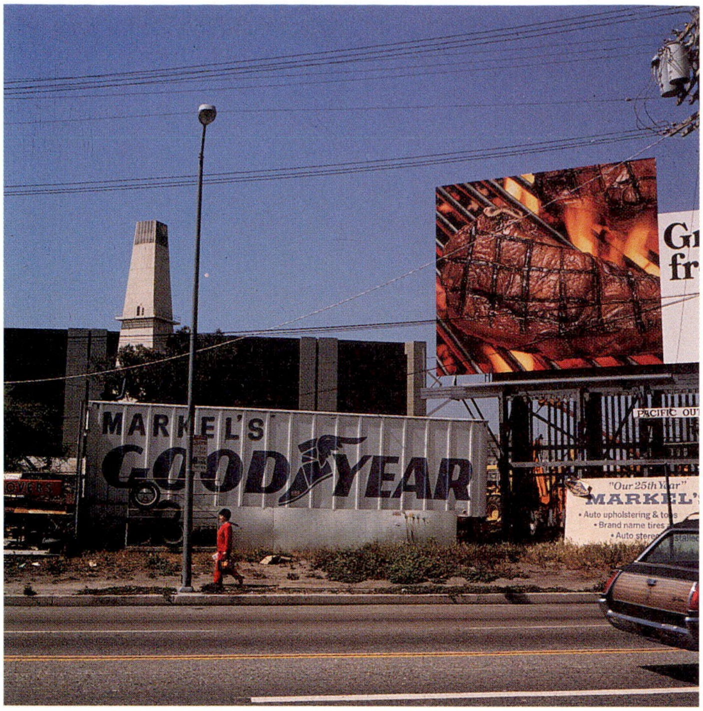

Fig. 412 **Kenneth McGowan, *Steak Billboard,* 1977.**
Courtesy of Brian Hagiwara, New York.

Black-and-white photography lends itself so well to investigating the relation between opposites in large part because, as a formal tool, it depends so much on the tension between black and white. In color photography, this formal tension is lost, but complementary color schemes often serve the same ends. Kenneth McGowan's *Steak Billboard* (Fig. 412), like Bourke-White's *At the Time of the Louisville Flood,* depends for its effects on a picture within a picture. There is, for instance, the enormous contrast in scale between the giant steak sizzling on the billboard and the real world passing by below. But it is the stunning contrast between the deep blue sky and the hot yellow, orange, and red fire on the grill that provides the greatest contrast. This color scheme is echoed in details throughout the photograph—by the red pantsuit of the woman walking down the street, by the yellow median strip, and by the car's taillights, all opposed to the

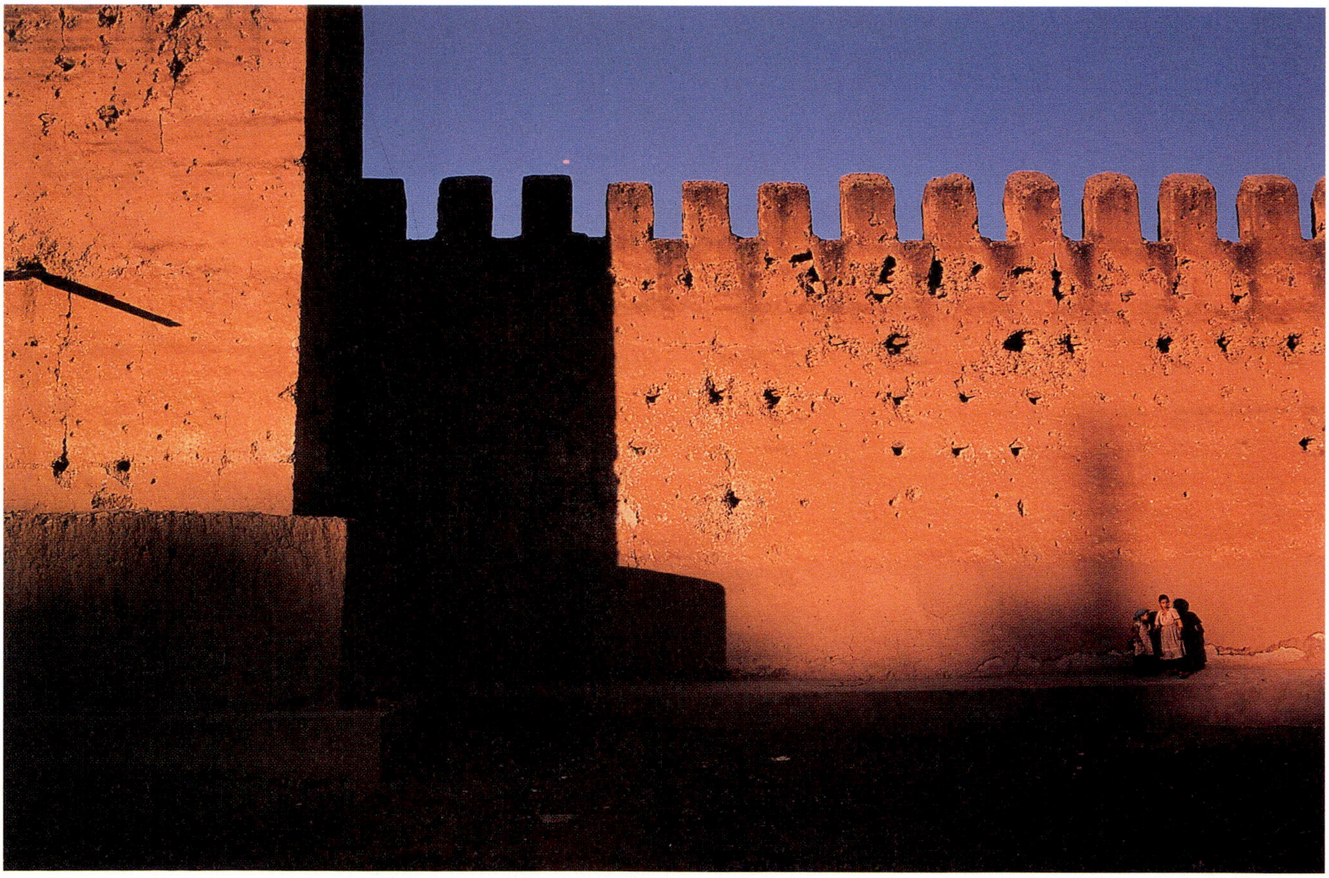

Fig. 413 **Harry Callahan, *Morocco,* 1981.**
Hallmark Photographic Collection, Kansas City, Missouri.

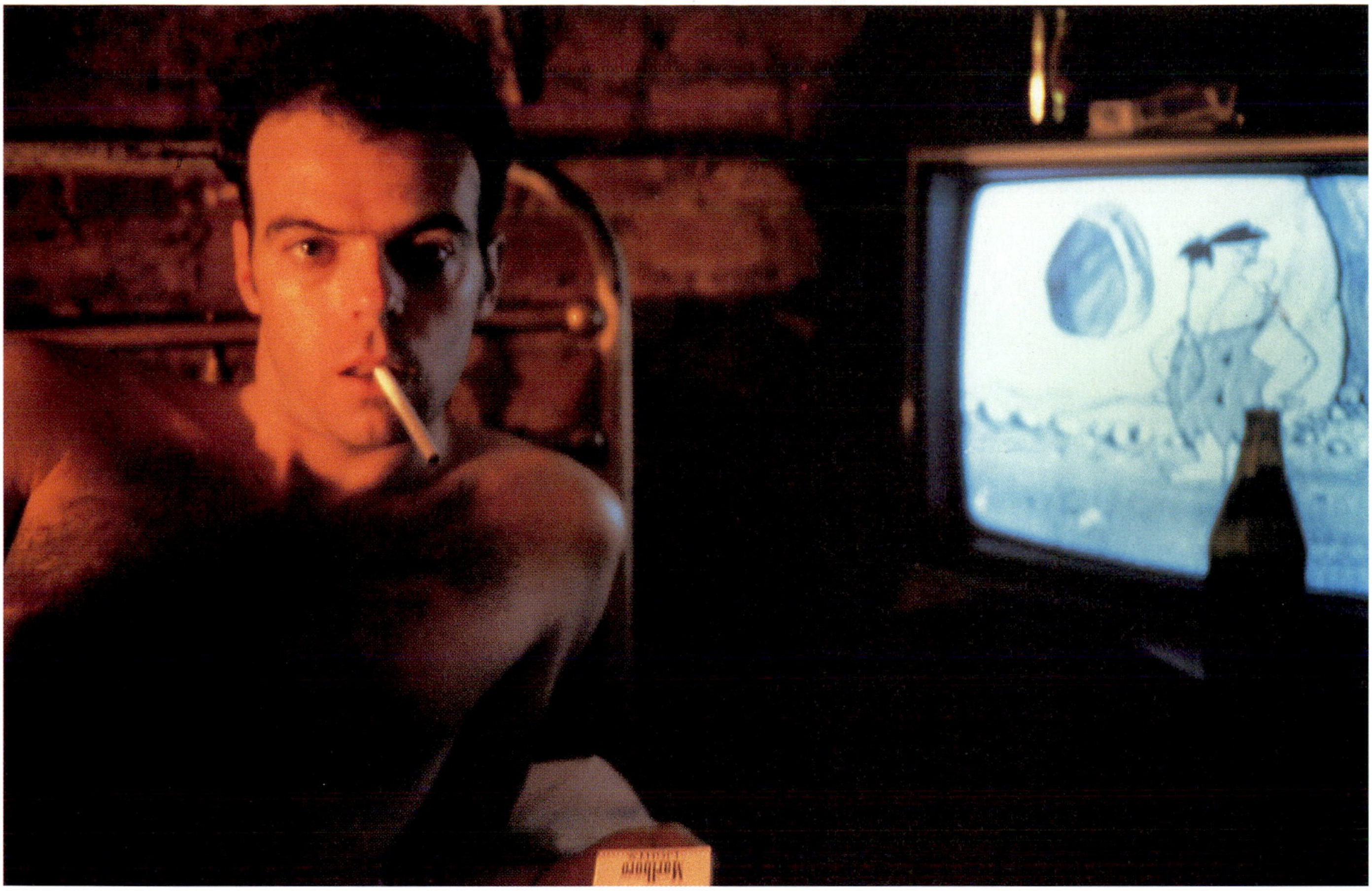

Fig. 414 Nan Goldin, *Brian with the Flintstones, New York City,* 1981.
From *The Ballad of Sexual Dependency* (Aperture Books, 1982). Pace/MacGill Gallery, New York.

blues of the Goodyear sign and even the pavement itself, which appears almost blue-violet.

Harry Callahan's *Morocco* (Fig. 413) is an exotic version of the same basic color scheme, now flattened in a simplified formal composition based on the highly dramatic conflict between light and dark. The photograph verges on geometric abstraction, a grid of horizontal and vertical lines that is classical in inspiration. But it is perhaps the two small figures huddled against the ancient fortress wall, children standing against the backdrop of historical time, that is most responsible for the photo's power.

Nan Goldin's *Brian with the Flintstones* (Fig. 414), a portrait of Goldin's boyfriend, uses color to different ends. Here the color is flat, the image unfocused, the scene depressingly familiar. In a series of photographs called *The Ballad of Sexual Dependency,* Goldin is self-consciously undermining what she calls "the mythology of romance." Her camera has bumped up against her boyfriend's almost numbing blank stare, in which we see an emptiness outdone only by the vapidity of Fred Flintstone. "A part of me," she says, "is challenged by the opacity of men's emotional makeup." Romance here is claustrophobic, and the romance is as dead as the color.

Nicholas Nixon's The Brown Sisters

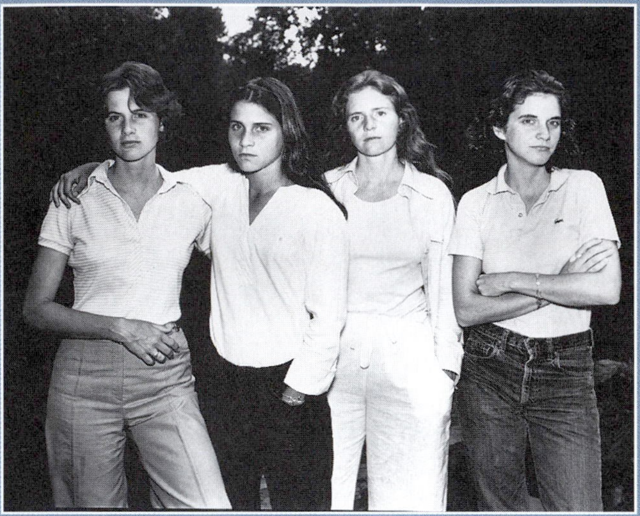

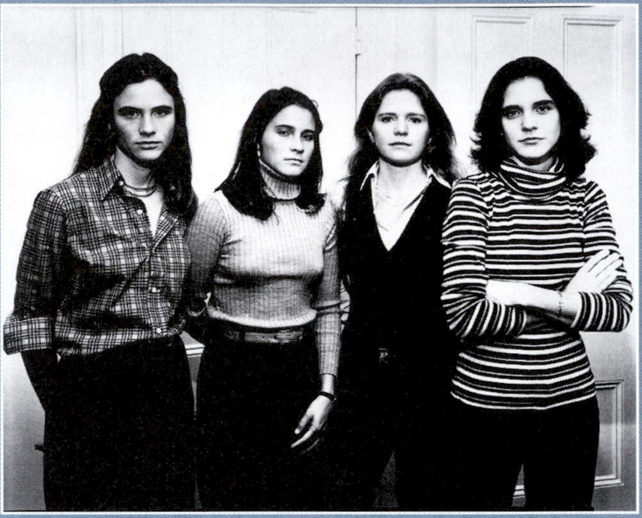

Figs. 415 and 416 Nicholas Nixon, *The Brown Sisters,* 1975 (left) and 1977 (right).
Gelatin-silver print. Photo by Roger Gass. Copyright © Nicholas Nixon. Courtesy Fraenkel Gallery, San Francisco.

Since 1975, the photographer Nicholas Nixon has taken a photograph of his wife and her three sisters once a year, every year (Figs. 415, 416, 417, and 418), an ongoing work in progress.

At first glance, the photographs seem familiar. Everything about them is recognizable. We may not know the women in them personally, but we know the photographs. There are thousands more or less like them everywhere, treasured in family albums, buried in dresser drawers, framed on desktops, and stationed prominently on mantelpieces. We recognize them so quickly, we take them in so casually, we think we understand them so completely, it is as if nothing need be said about them. They are simply family photographs—and we all know about family photographs. Off to the portrait studio the family goes. Everyone looks nice. Everyone smiles. Everyone *poses* for the photographer, whose presence Nixon makes absolutely clear in his portrait of 1984 (Fig. 417), where both he and his camera cast their shadow across the women. The family portrait is an artificial situation, an image that, in all likelihood, misrepresents the dynamics of the family itself. In the family portrait, we are recreated as if we were all television families in the 1950s, straight out of *Father Knows Best* or *Leave It to Beaver.* We "act out," in front of the camera, our idea of what a family should look like. Sitting for a family portrait is, in short, a kind of performance art.

But there is another way to think of Nixon's series. As the photographs have continued to accumulate, year after year, we have begun to see the sisters change. On these two pages we see them across a span of over a decade. Nixon's work becomes, then, not so much a series of family portraits, formal occasions that bring the family together, as a continuing essay on aging. Nixon is telling the story of the Brown women's lives, documenting their life's progress. And theirs is a journey, we come to recognize, that all of us must travel.

WORKS IN PROGRESS

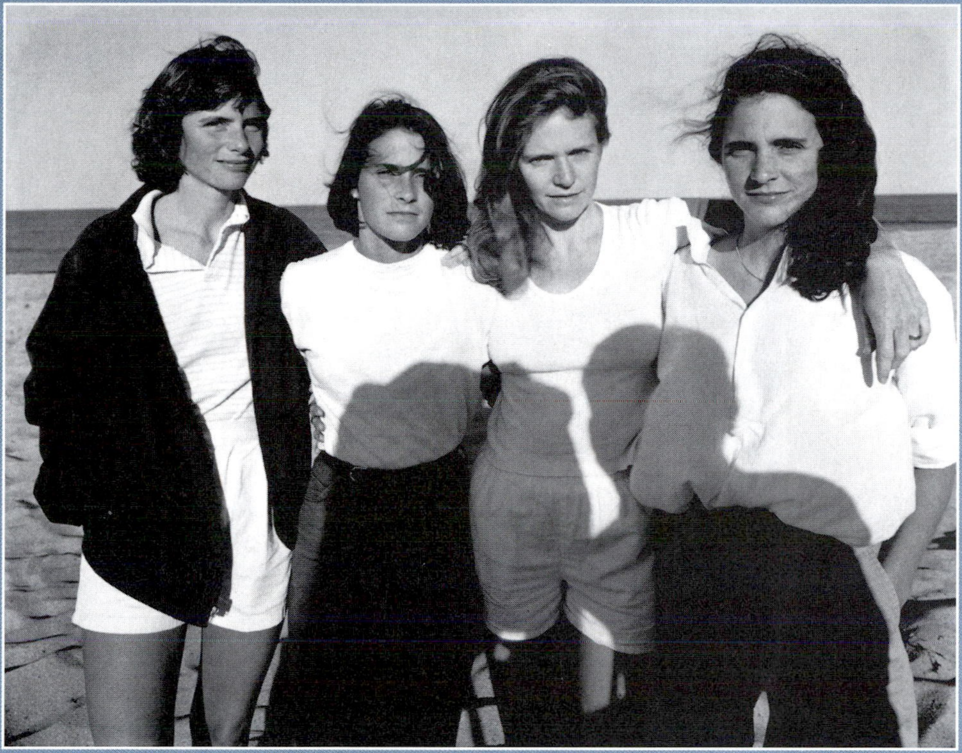

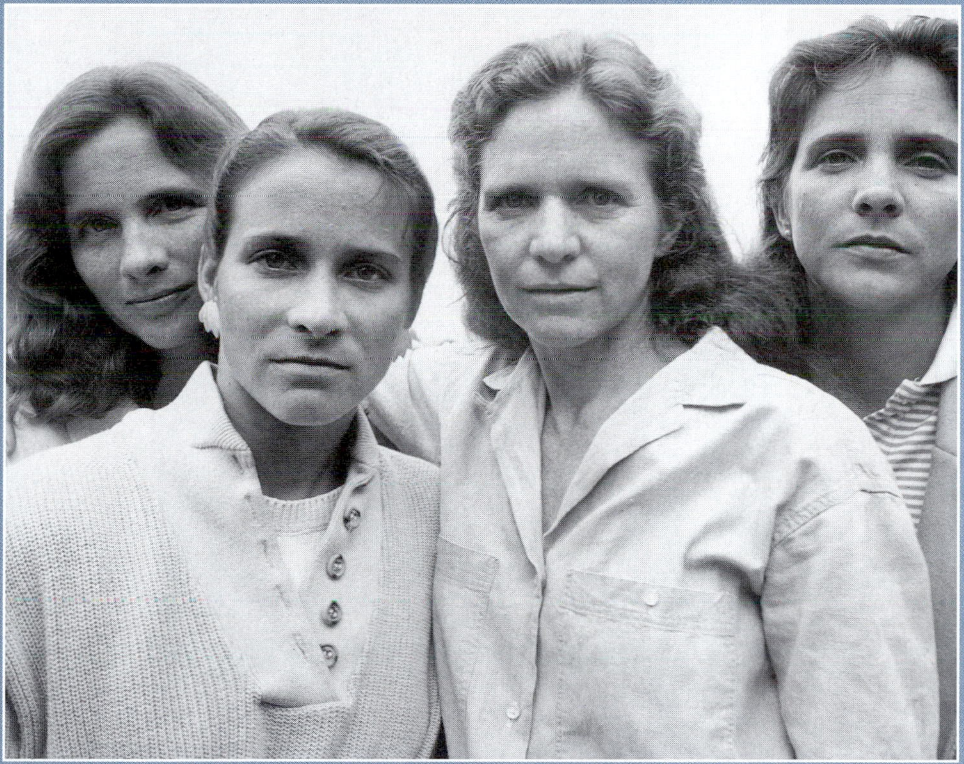

Figs. 417 and 418 Nicholas Nixon, *The Brown Sisters,* Heather Brown Sawitsky, Mimi Brown, Bebe Brown Nixon, Laurie Brown Tranchin, 1984 (top) and 1987 (bottom).

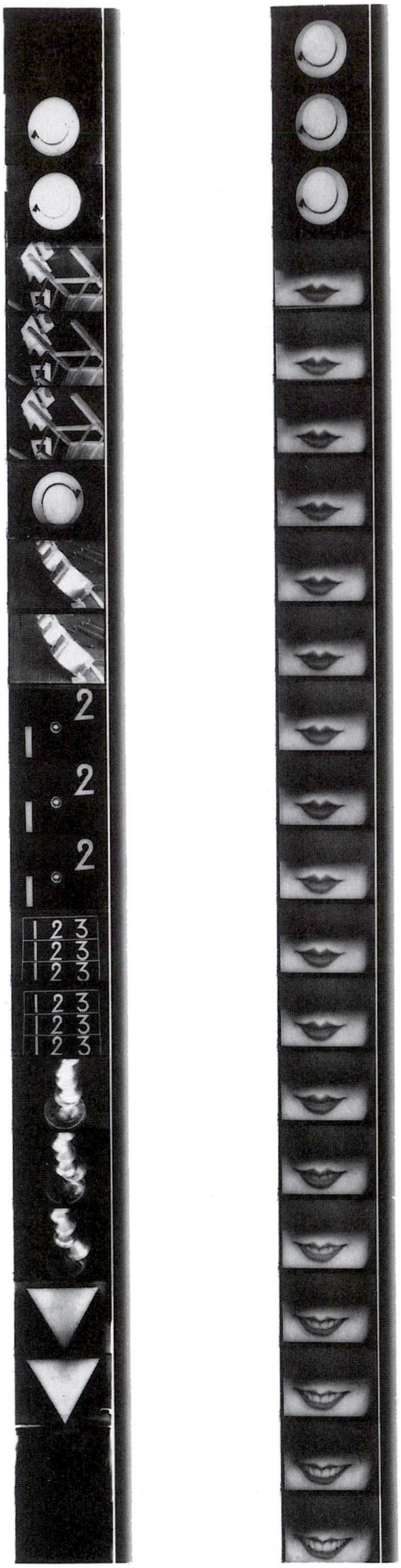

Fig. 419 **Fernand Léger, *Ballet Mécanique,* 1924.**
Courtesy the Humanities Film Collection,
Center for the Humanities, Oregon State University.

FILM

As we saw in Chapter 3, almost as soon as photography was invented, people sought to extend its capacities to capture motion. Eadweard Muybridge captured the locomotion of animals (Fig. 60) and Etienne-Jules Marey the locomotion of human beings (Fig. 61) in sequences of rapidly exposed photos. It was, in fact, the formal revelations of film that first attracted artists to it. As forms and shapes repeated themselves in time across the motion picture screen, the medium seemed to invite the exploration of rhythm and repetition as principles of design. In his 1924 film *Ballet Mécanique* (Fig. 419), the Cubist painter Fernand Léger chose to study a number of different images—smiling lips, wine bottles, metal discs, working mechanisms, and pure shapes, such as circles, squares, and triangles. By repeating the same image again and again at separate points in the film, Léger was able to create a visual rhythm that, to his mind, embodied the beauty—the ballet—of machines and machine manufacture in the modern world.

Assembling a film, the process of editing, is a sort of linear collage, as the Léger plainly shows. Although the movies may seem true to life, as if they were occurring in real time and space, this effect is only an illusion, accomplished by means of the editing. **Editing** is the process of arranging the sequences of a film after it has been shot in its entirety. It is perhaps not coincidental that as film began to come into its own in the second decade of the twentieth century, collage, constructed by cutting and pasting together a variety of fragments, was itself invented.

The first great master of editing was D. W. Griffith who, in *The Birth of a Nation* (Fig. 420) essentially invented the standard vocabulary of filmmaking. Griffith desired to create visual variety in the film by alternating between and among a repetoire of **shots,** each one a continuous sequence of film frames. A **full shot** shows the actor from head to toe, a **medium shot** from the waist up, a **close-up** the head and shoulders, and an **extreme close-up** a portion of the face. The image of the battle scene reproduced here is a **long shot,** a shot that takes in a wide expanse and many characters at once. Griffith makes uses of another of his techniques in this shot as well—the edge of the film is blurred and rounded in order to focus the attention of the viewer on the scene in the center. This is called an **iris shot.**

Related to the long shot is the **pan,** a name given to the panoramic vista, in which the camera moves across the scene from one side to the other. Griffith also invented the **traveling shot,** in which the camera moves back to front or front to back. In editing, Griffith combined these various shots in order to tell his story. Two of his more famous editing techniques are cross-cutting and flashbacks. The **flashback,** in which the editor cuts to narrative episodes that are supposed to have taken place before the start of the film, is now standard in film practice, but it was an entirely original idea when Griffith first utilized it. **Cross-cutting** is an editing technique meant to create high drama. The editor moves back and forth between two separate events—such as someone in jeopardy and the hero fighting his way to the rescue—in ever shorter sequences, the rhythm of shots eventually becoming furiously paced. Griffith borrowed these techniques of fiction writing to tell a visual story in film.

One of the other great innovators of film editing was the Russian filmmaker Sergei Eisenstein. Eisenstein did his greatest work in Bolshevik Russia after the 1917 revolution, in a newly formed state whose leader, Vladimir Lenin, had said, "Of all the arts, for us the cinema is the most important." In this atmosphere, Eisenstein created what he considered a revolutionary new use of the medium. Rather than concentrating

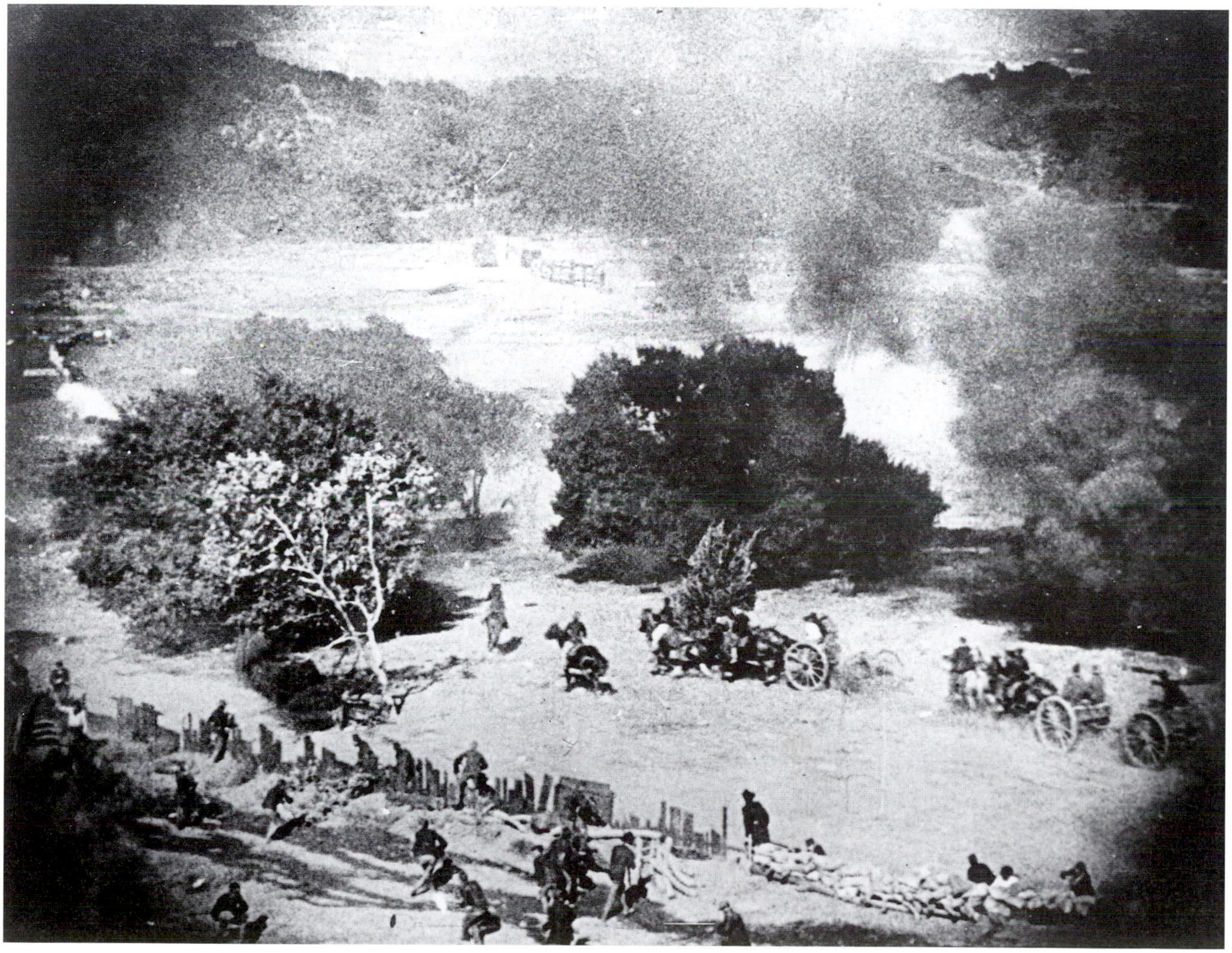

Fig. 420 D. W. Griffith, battle scene from *The Birth of a Nation,* 1915.
The Museum of Modern Art. Film Stills Archive.

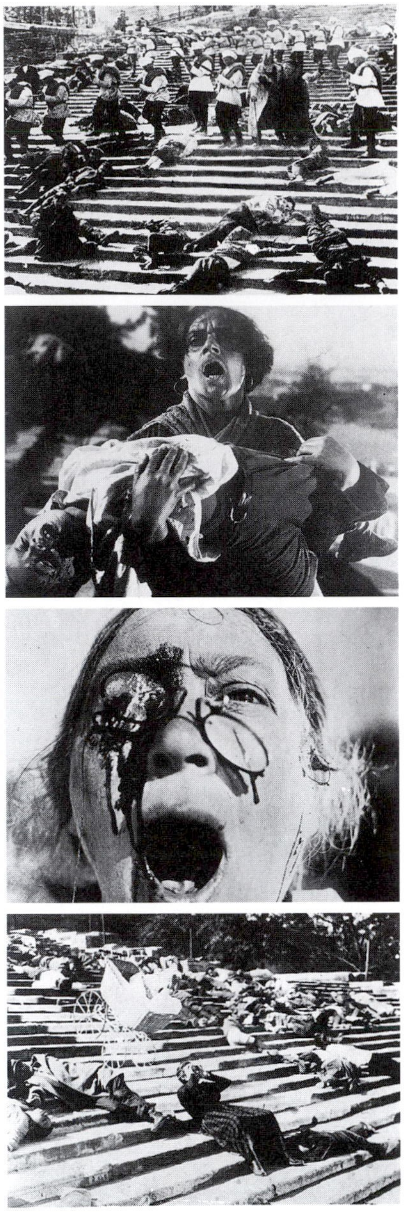

Fig. 421(a–d) Sergei Eisenstein, *Battleship Potemkin,* 1925.
Goskino. Courtesy of The Kobal Collection.

on narrative sequencing, he sought to create a shock in his film that would ideally lead the audience to perception and knowledge. He called his technique **montage**—the sequencing of widely disparate images to create a fast-paced, multifaceted image. In the famous "Odessa Steps Sequence" of his 1925 film *Battleship Potemkin,* four frames of which are reproduced here (Fig. 421), Eisenstein utilized 155 separate shots in four minutes and twenty seconds of film, an astonishing rate of 1.6 seconds per shot. The movie is based on the story of an unsuccessful uprising against the Russian monarchy in 1905, and the sequence depicts the moment when the crowd pours into the port city of Odessa's harbor to welcome the liberated ship *Potemkin.* Behind them, at the top of the steps leading down to the pier, soldiers appear, firing on the crowd. In the scene, the soldiers fire, a mother lifts her dead child to face the soldiers, women weep, a baby carriage careens down the steps. Eisenstein's "image" is all of these shots combined and more. "The strength of montage resides in this," he would write, "that it involves the creative process—the emotions and mind of the spectator . . . assemble the image."

The thrust of Eisenstein's work is to emphasize action and emotion through enhanced time sequencing. Just the opposite effect is created by Andy Warhol. Warhol equates, in the words of one critic, "reel" time with "real" time. Many of Warhol's films are the visual equivalent of John Cage's *4'33"*, discussed in the last chapter in connection with performance art, which consists of four minutes and thirty-three seconds of silence. In *Sleep* (1963), Warhol filmed the poet John Giorno sleeping. The only action in the six-hour-long film is that every 30 minutes the camera changes position when the film runs out and has to be reloaded. Each change is accompanied

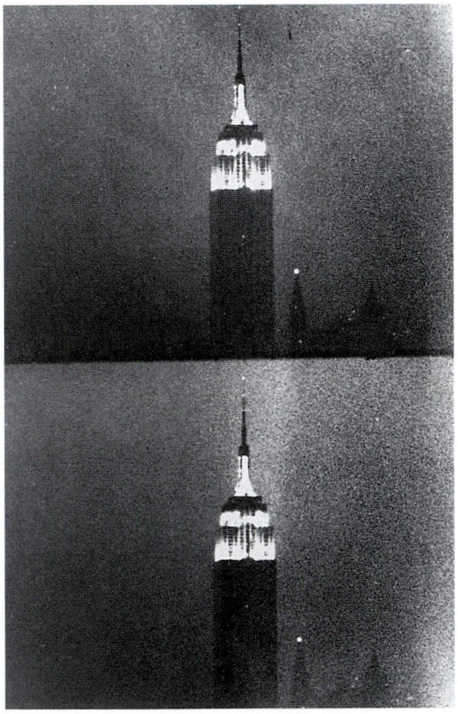

Fig. 422 Andy Warhol, film still from *Empire.*
© 1994 The Andy Warhol Foundation for the Visual Arts, Inc.

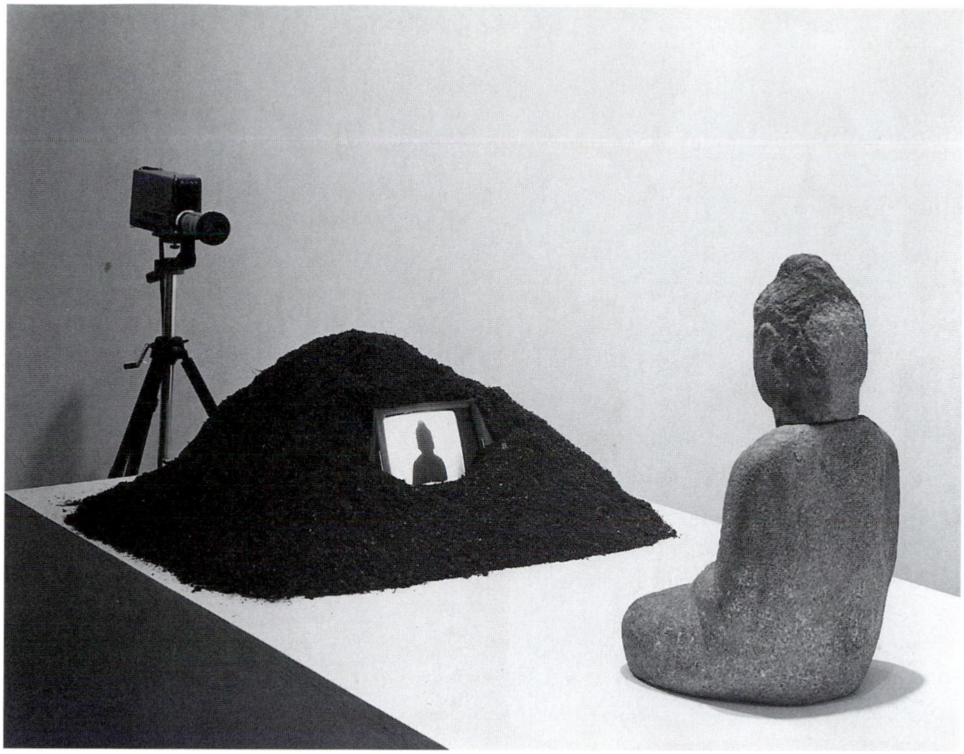

Fig. 423 Nam June Paik, *TV Buddha,* 1974–1982.
Mixed media, 55 × 115 × 36 in. Photo © Peter Moore, 1982.

by a white flash on the screen resulting from the film's exposure to light. For *Empire* (1964) (Fig. 422), Warhol filmed the Empire State Building for eight straight hours through the afternoon and evening, with a stationary camera set up on the 44th floor of the Time-Life building. To view either film is to understand the idea of *duration* in terms one might never before have experienced. In a darkened theater, where there is relatively little other visual stimulus, the viewer's attention is soon drawn beyond the screen to other elements in the surrounding environment. The slightest movement or sound in the theater becomes interesting in itself. The drama in these films, in fact, lies in the audience's reaction in real time to the monotony of the image.

VIDEO

One of the primary difficulties faced by artists who wish to explore film as a medium is the sheer expense of using it. The more sophisticated a film is in terms of its camera work, lighting, sound equipment, editing techniques, and special effects, the more expensive it is to produce. With the introduction in 1965 of the relatively inexpensive hand-held video camera, the Sony Portapak, artists were suddenly able to explore the implications of seeing in time. Video is not only cheaper than film but also more immediate—that is, what is seen on the recorder is simulataneously seen on the monitor. While **video art** tends to exploit this immediacy, commercial television tends to hide it by attempting to make videotaped images look like film.

Nam June Paik, originally a member of the Fluxus group, was one of the first people in New York to buy a Portapak. Since the late 1950s, he has been making video installations exploring the limits and defining characteristics of the medium. His *TV Buddha* (Fig. 423), for example, perpetually contemplating itself on the screen, is a self-contained version of Warhol's exercises in filmic duration. The work is deliberately and playfully ambiguous. It includes an inanimate stone sculpture shown "live" on TV. It is both peacefully meditative and mind-numbingly boring, simultaneously an image of complete wholeness and absolute emptiness. It represents, in short, the best and worst of TV.

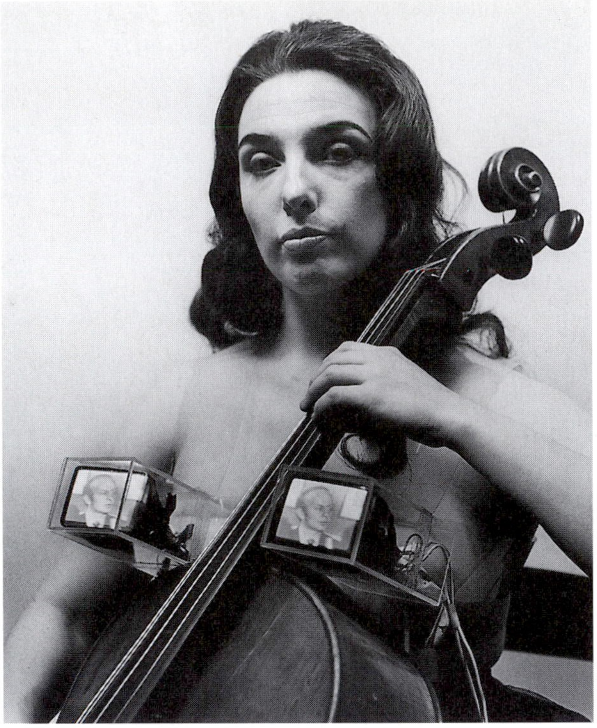

Fig. 424 Nam June Paik, *TV Bra for Living Sculpture*, 1969.
Performance by Charlotte Moorman with television sets and cello.
Photo ©Peter Moore, 1969.

The playfulness that Paik employs in *TV Buddha* is equally evident in the wordplay that underlies his *TV Bra for Living Sculpture* (Fig. 424), a literal realization of the "boob tube." The piece is a collaborative work, executed with the avant-garde musician Charlotte Moorman. Soon after Paik's arrival in New York in 1964, he was introduced to Moorman by the composer Karlheinz Stockhausen. Moorman wanted to perform a Stockhausen piece called *Originale,* but the composer would grant permission only if it was done with the assistance of Paik, who had performed the work many times. Paik's role was to cover his entire head with shaving cream, sprinkle it with rice, plunge his head into a bucket of cold water, and then accompany Moorman's cello on the piano as if nothing strange had occurred. So began a long collaboration. Like all of Paik's works, *TV Bra's* humor masks a serious intent. For Paik and Moorman, it was an attempt "to humanize the technology . . . and also stimulate viewers . . . to look for new, imaginative, and humanistic ways of using our technology." *TV Bra,* in other words, is an attempt to rescue the boob tube from mindlessness.

The clichéd mindlessness of commercial television has been hilariously investigated in a vast number of short videos by William Wegman. In one, called *Deodorant,* the artist simply sprays an entire can of deodorant under one armpit while he extols its virtues. The video, which is about the same length as a normal television commercial, is an exercise in consumerism run amok. In *Rage and Depression* (Fig. 425), Wegman sits smiling at the camera as he speaks the following monologue:

> *I had these terrible fits of rage and depression all the time. It just got worse and worse and worse. Finally my parents had me committed. They tried all kinds of therapy. Finally they settled on shock. The doctors brought me into this room in a straight jacket because I still had this terrible, terrible temper. I was just the meanest cuss you could imagine and when they put this cold, metal electrode, or whatever it was, to my chest, I started to giggle and then when they shocked me, it froze on my face into this smile and even though I'm still incredibly depressed—everyone thinks I'm happy. I don't know what I'm going to do.*

Wegman completely undermines the authority of visual experience here. What our eyes see is an illusion. He implies that we can never trust what we see, just as we should not trust television's objectivity as a medium.

In *Live/Taped Video Corridor and Performance Corridor* (Fig. 426), artist Bruce Nauman mounted a closed-circuit video camera on

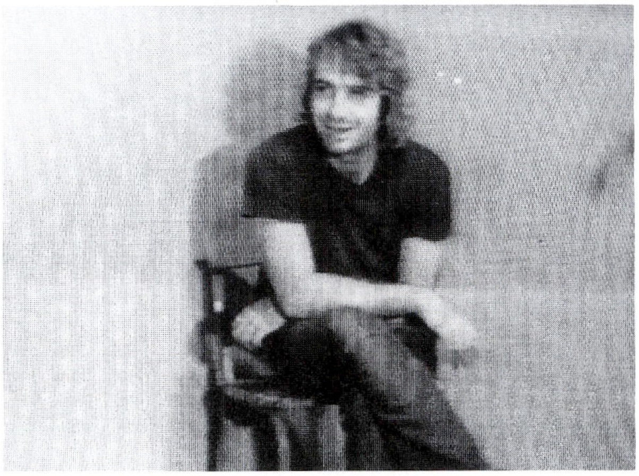

Fig. 425 William Wegman,
Still from *Rage and Depression,* Reel 3, 1972–1973.
Video, approx. 1 min. Courtesy of the artist.

the ceiling of a narrow corridor and placed two TV monitors at its end. In the top monitor, a video tape of the empty corridor continually plays; in the bottom one, viewers watch themselves enter the space. The act of entering disrupts the empty corridor and the black screen. It is as if the viewer becomes a performer in front of the camera, committing an act of aggression upon the space.

Video art has been used with particular effectiveness in installations such as Nauman's. At the end of Chapter 7, we discussed a video installation by Bill Viola to sum up the ways in which all the formal elements come into play (Figs. 192 & 193). Another of his installations, *Stations* (Fig. 427), consists of five video projections focusing on the human body submerged in water. Five cloth screens, three of which are visible in this reproduction, are suspended from the ceiling of a large, dark open space. Polished granite slabs lie flat on the floor underneath each screen. The projections of the floating bodies are upside down, causing their reflections on the polished granite below to appear rightside up. Underwater sounds can be heard near each screen. The images slowly drift out of the frame and then, suddenly, plunge into the water. Water, for Viola, is a kind of tangible space. In it, the body's relation to space becomes clear. The piece strips away the viewer's sense of gravity. Nothing is what it seems here. The reflecting pools are granite, up becomes down, to fall is to rise. The installation positions us somewhere between the dream state, our memory of birth, and the soul's flight from the body after death.

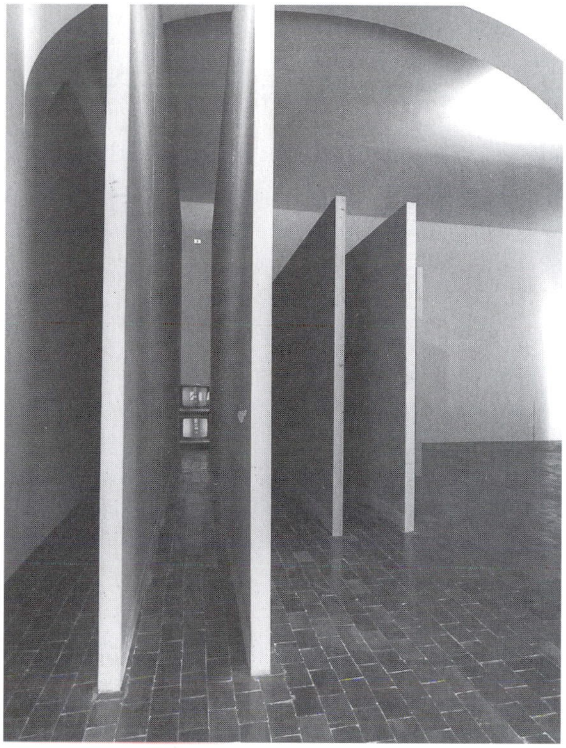

Fig. 426 Bruce Nauman, *Live/Taped Video Corridor and Performance Corridor,* 1968–1970.
Video installation. Collection of Giuseppe Panza di Biumo, Milan.
© 1993 Bruce Nauman/ARS New York.

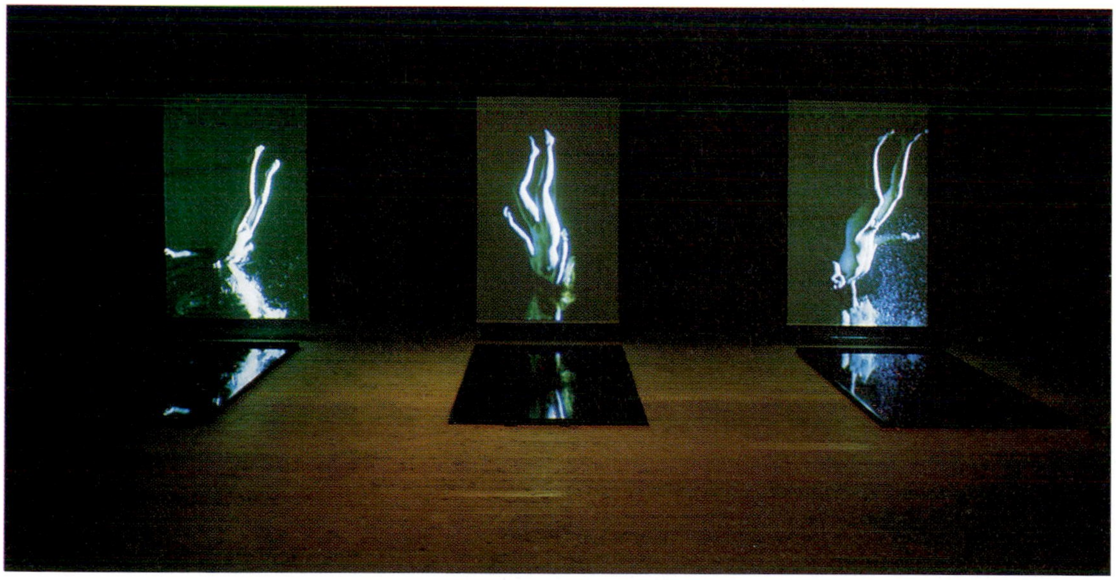

Fig. 427 Bill Viola, *Stations,* 1994.
Video/sound installation. Commissioned by the Bohen Foundation for the inaugural opening of the American Center, Paris.
© Bill Viola Studio. Photograph by Charles Duprat.

In his video installation *Crux* (Figs. 428 and 429), made in the mid-1980s, Gary Hill transforms the traditional imagery of the Crucifixion. The installation consists of five television monitors mounted on a wall in the shape of a cross. Hill shot the piece on a deserted island in the middle of the Hudson River in New York. Attached to his body were five video cameras, one on each shin facing his feet, one braced in front of his face and pointed directly back at him, and one on each arm aimed at his hands, which he extended out from his body. On his back he carried all the necessary recording equipment and power packs. The cameras recorded his barefooted trek across the island, through the woods and an abandoned armory to the river's edge. The 26-minute journey captures all the agony and pain of Christ's original ascent of Golgotha, as he carried his own cross to the top of the hill where he was crucified. But all we see of Hill's walk are his two bruised and stumbling feet, his two hands groping for balance, and his exhausted face. The body that connects them is absent, a giant blank spot on the gallery wall. This absence not only suggests the disappearance of Christ's body after the Resurrection, but it is also the "crux" of the title. A "crux" is a cross, but it is also a vital or decisive point ("the crux of the matter"), or something that torments by its puzzling nature. By eliminating his body, Hill has discovered a metaphor for the soul—that puzzling energy which is spiritually present but physically absent.

Women artists have been especially attracted to video art as a medium, in part because they have been denied ready acceptance as painters and sculptors, but also because they can use the medium to critique the ways in which women have been depicted and defined in our culture, and on television in particular. Dara Birnbaum's *Technology/Transformation: Wonder Woman* (Fig. 430) is a groundbreaking example of this direction in contemporary video art. It consists of a series of taped loops from the Linda Carter television series *Wonder Woman*, in which Wonder Woman transforms herself, like some spinning dervish, from her "normal" self into an all-powerful agent in the never-ending fight of good against evil. By

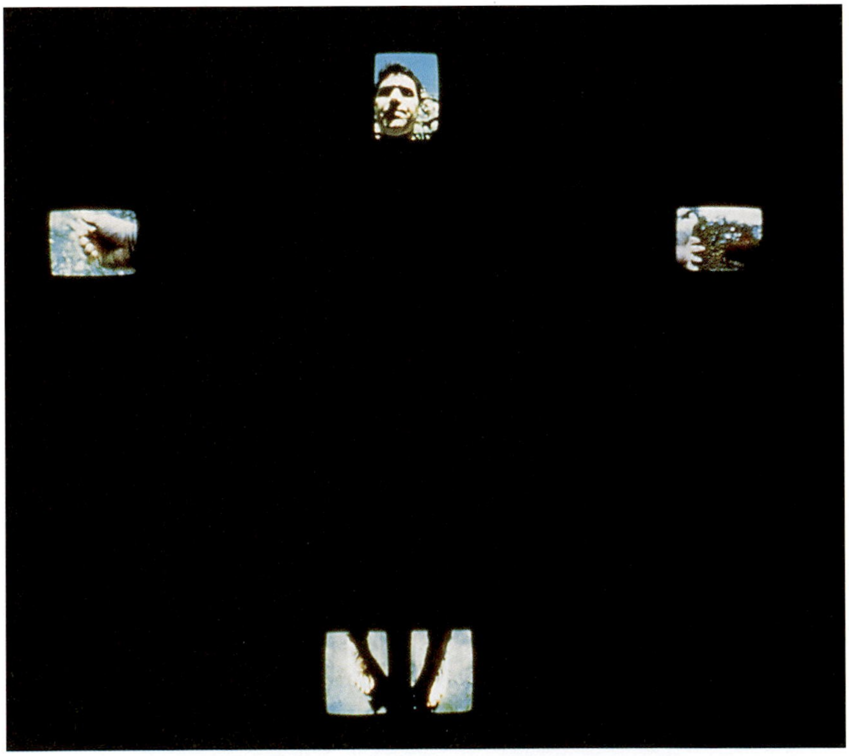

Fig. 428 Gary Hill, *Crux*, 1983–1987.
Five channel video/sound installation. Five color monitors and five speakers.
For full installation shot: Mark B. McLoughlin. Courtesy of Donald Young Gallery, Seattle.

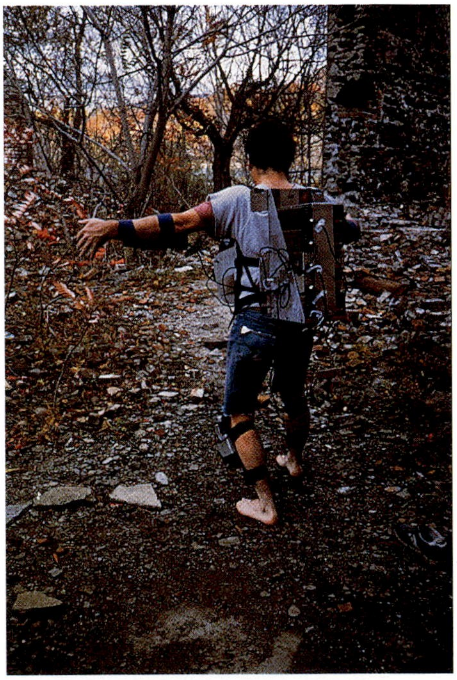

Fig. 429 Gary Hill, *Crux*, 1983–1987.
Five channel video/sound installation.
Five color monitors and five speakers.
For production shot at
Bannerman's Island: Ularn Curjel.
Courtesy of Donald Young Gallery, Seattle.

accompanying this transformation with a sound track of Wonder Woman and the Disco Land Band singing "Wonder Woman Disco," with its sexually suggestive lyrics ("This is your Wonder Woman talking to you / Said I want to take you down / Show you all the powers that I possess / Shake thy wonder maker"), Birnbaum exposes the underlying message of the series that being a normal woman somehow isn't enough. The show may seem to entertain the possibility that women can be powerful, but actually it does not.

Lynn Hershman's interactive art video disk, *Lorna* (Fig. 431) allows the viewer to participate in the story of Lorna, a middle-aged agoraphobic, fearful of leaving her tiny apartment. "The premise," according to Hershman, "[is] that the more she stayed home and watched television, the more fearful she became—primarily because she was absorbing the frightening messages of advertising and news broadcasts." In the disk, each object in her room is numbered and becomes a chapter in her life that viewers activate by means of their remote contol device. The plot has multiple variations, and three separate endings. The viewer is not helpless like Lorna. The mass media made a captive of her, but we are empowered to manipulate the media ourselves.

As forms of art, film and video are not the same as the movies and television. Film and video art seek to do more than merely entertain. They seek to discover new possibilities in their mediums, to transcend, in fact, the limitations inherent in producing work for the corporate film industry and the commercial networks. Photography, too, has its commercial and journalistic side. It is an inherently informational medium, but it transcends that limitation—its ability to record the facts—by presenting its content in a formally beautiful or interesting way. Obviously, there are great commercial and journalistic photographs just as there are great commercial films and even television shows. But what separates the *art* of photography, film, and video from mainstream production is the *aesthetic* sense. When a photograph or a film or a video triggers a higher level of thought and awareness in the viewer, when it stimulates the imagination, then it is a work of art.

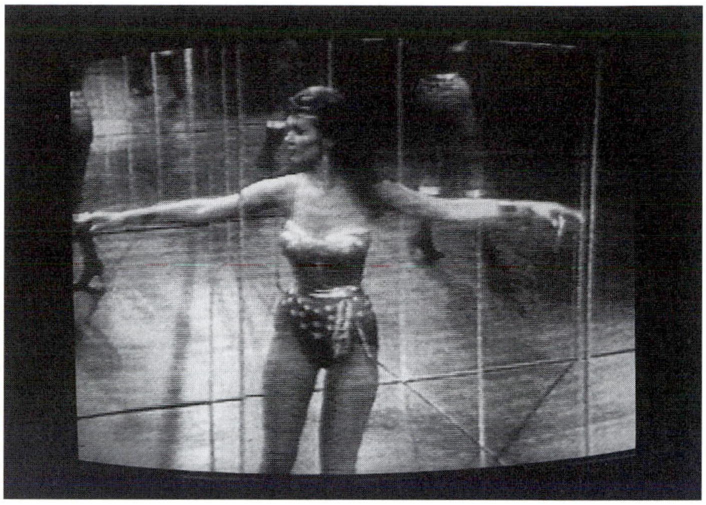

Fig. 430 Dara Birnbaum, *Technology/Transformation: Wonder Woman,* 1978–1979.
Color, stereo videotape, 7 min. Electronic Arts Intermix.

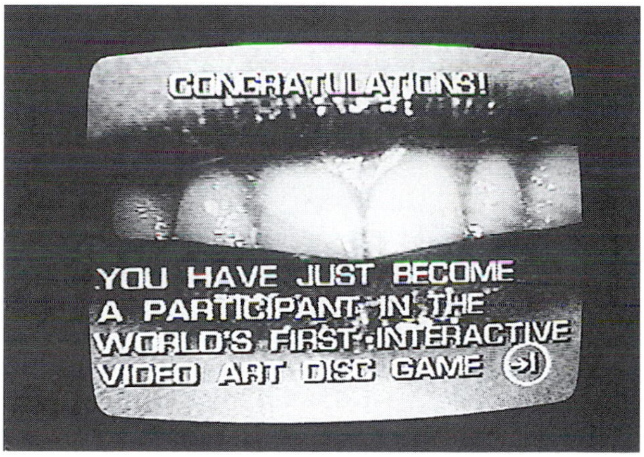

Fig. 431 Lynn Hershman, *Lorna,* 1983.
Interactive video disk. Courtesy of the artist.

PART IV

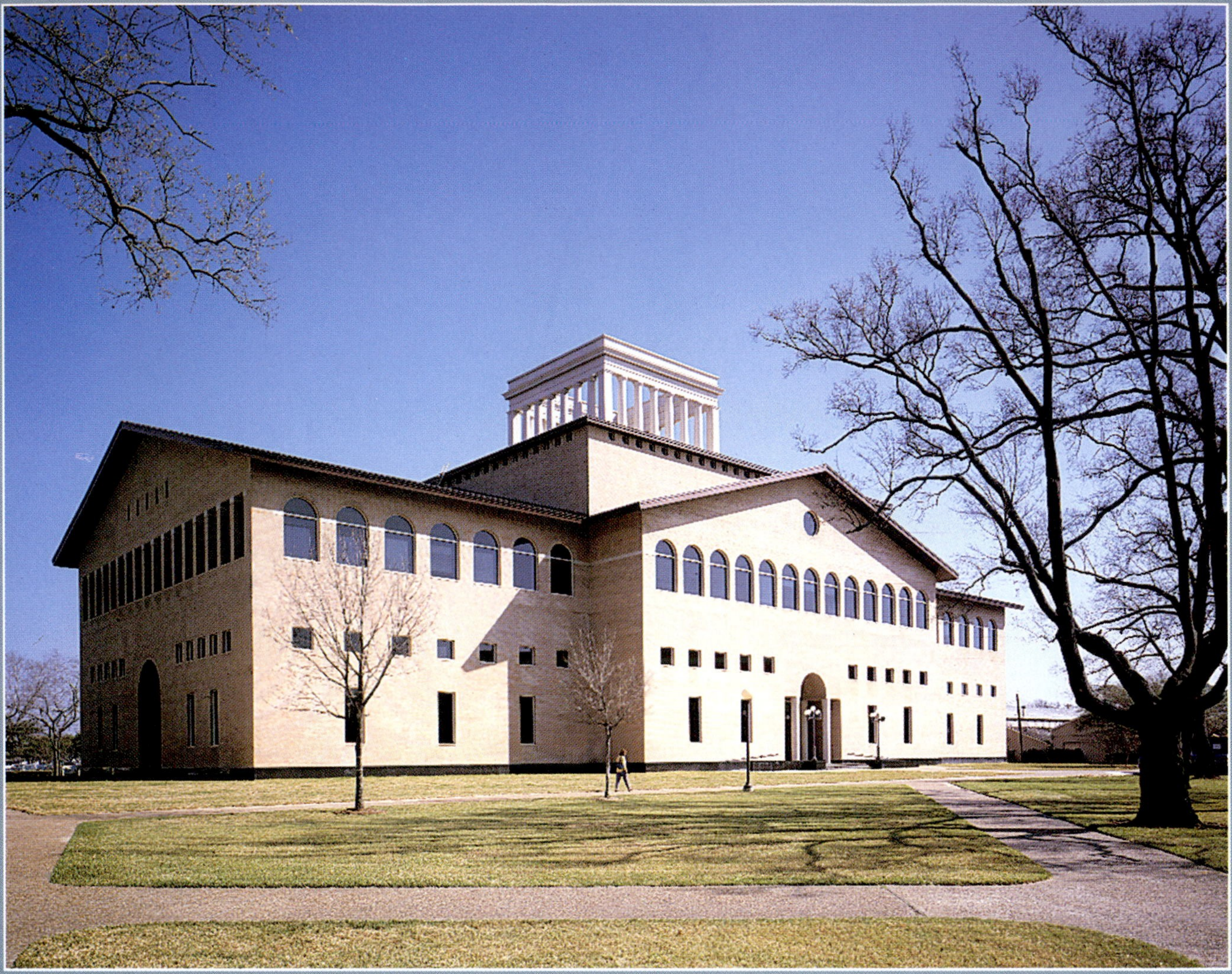

Fig. 432 Philip Johnson and John Burgee, College of Architecture, University of Houston, 1983–1985.
Photograph by Richard Payne.

THE VISUAL ARTS IN EVERYDAY LIFE

RECOGNIZING THE ART OF DESIGN

CHAPTER 14

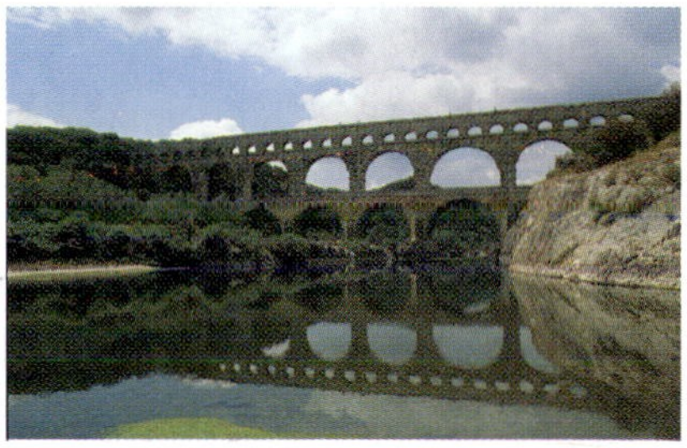

Architecture

The building that houses the College of Architecture at the University of Houston (Fig. 432), designed by architects Philip Johnson and John Burgee, is a sort of history of Western architecture from the Greeks to the present. Resting on its top is a Greek temple. The main building below is reminiscent of Italian country villas of the Renaissance. The entire building was inspired by

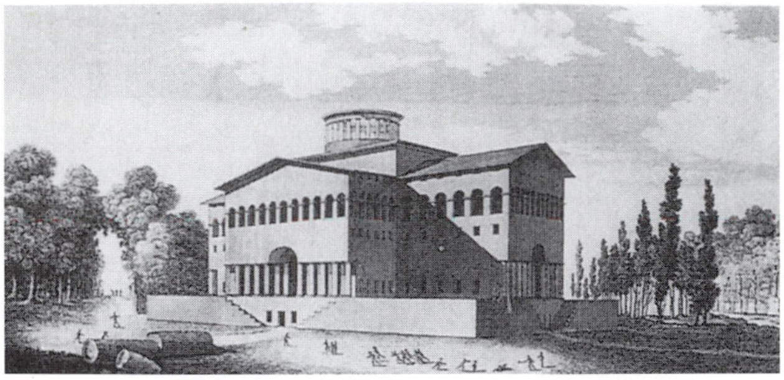

Fig. 433 Claude-Nicolas Ledoux, House of Education, Chaux project, 1773–1779. Engraved by Van Maelle and Mailla.

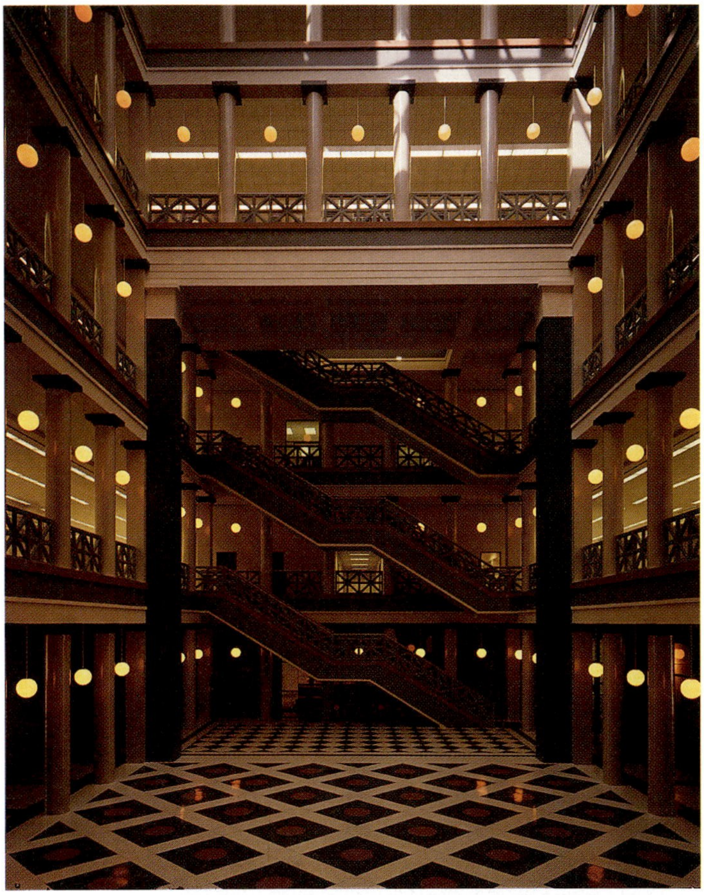

Fig. 434 Philip Johnson and John Burgee, College of Architecture, University of Houston, interior, 1983–1985. Photo by Richard Payne.

an eighteenth-century plan for a House of Education designed by Claude-Nicolas Ledoux (Fig. 433) for a proposed utopian community at Chaux, France, that never came into being. And the building itself is distinctly postmodern in spirit—it revels in a sense of discontinuity between its parts. One has the feeling that the Greek temple fits on the building's roof about as well as a marachino cherry would on a scoop of potato salad.

In this chapter we will consider how our built environment has developed—how we have traveled, in effect, from Greek temples and Anasazi cliff dwellings to skyscrapers and postmodernist designs We will see that the "look" of our buildings and our communities depends on two different factors and their interrelation—**topography,** or the distinct landscape characteristics of the local site, and **technology,** the materials and methods available to a given culture. Johnson's and Burgee's design for the College of Architecture at the University of Houston takes advantage of many of the technologies developed over the centuries, but at first glance it seems to ignore the local topography altogether. But when we consider its interior (Fig. 434), we can see that the cool atrium space that lies under the colonnade on the roof offers a respite from the hot Texas sun. The site has had a considerable influence on the design. Thus the key to understanding and appreciating architecture always involves both technology and topography. We will consider topography first.

TOPOGRAPHY

The built environment reflects the natural world and the conception of the people who inhabit it of their place within the natural scheme of things. A building's form might echo the world around it, or might contrast with it—but, in each case, the choices builders make reveal their attitudes toward the world around them.

The architecture of the vast majority of early civilizations was designed to imitate natural forms. The significance of the pyramids of Egypt (Fig. 435) is the subject of much debate, but their form may well derive from the image of the god Ra, who in ancient Egypt was symbolized by the rays of the sun descending to

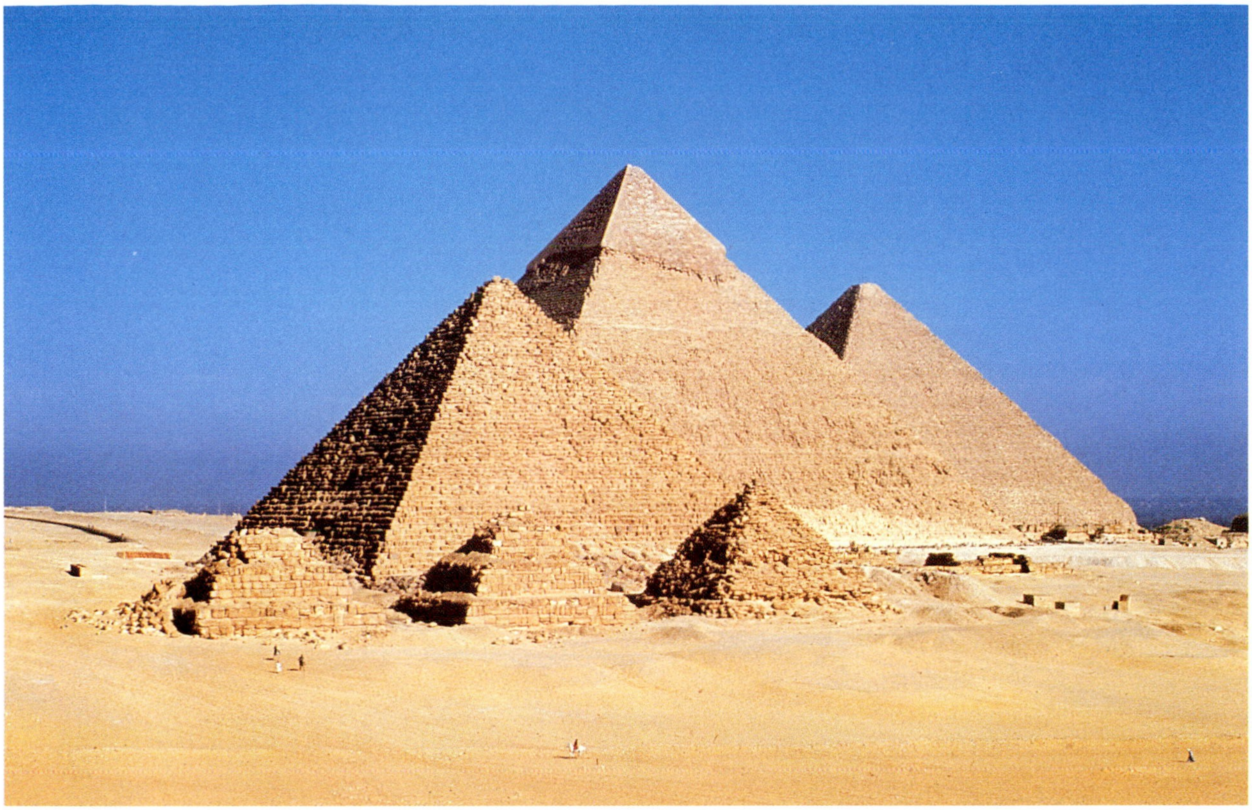

Fig. 435 Pyramids of Mycerinus (c. 2470 BCE), Chephren (c. 2500 BCE), and Cheops (c. 2530 BCE).
Original height of Pyramid of Cheops 480 ft., length of each side at base 755 ft. Photo by Superstock.

earth. A text in one pyramid reads: "I have trodden these rays as ramps under my feet." As one approached the mammoth pyramids, covered in limestone to reflect the light of the sun, the eye was carried skyward to Ra, the Sun itself, who was in the desert the central fact of life. In contrast, the pyramidlike structures of Mesopotamia, known as **ziggurats** (Fig. 436), are flatter and wider than their Egyptian counterparts, as if imitating the shape of the foothills that lead up to the mountains. The Sumerians believed that the mountaintops were not only the source of precious water, but the dwelling place of the gods. The ziggurat was constructed as an artificial mountain in which a god could reside.

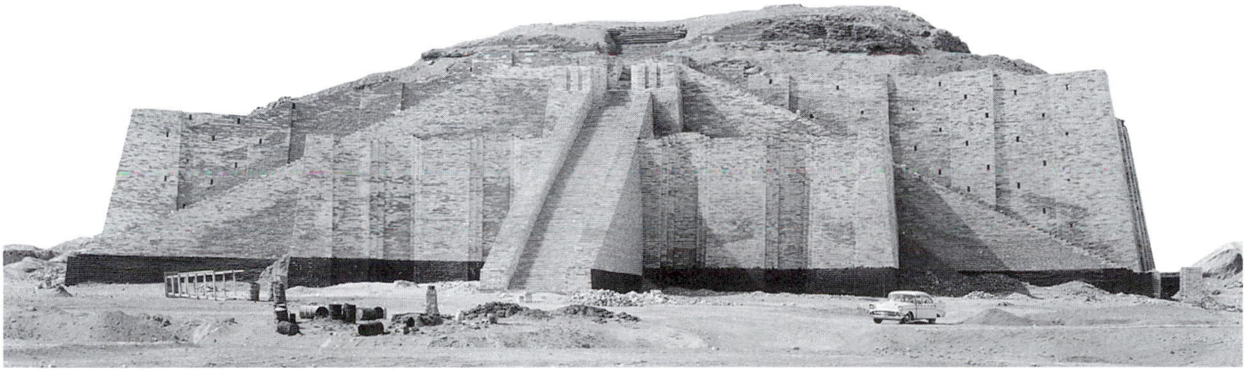

Fig. 436 Ziggurat, Ur, c. 2100 BCE.
Fired brick over mudbrick core, 210 × 150 ft. at base. Photo by Hirmer Fotoarchive.

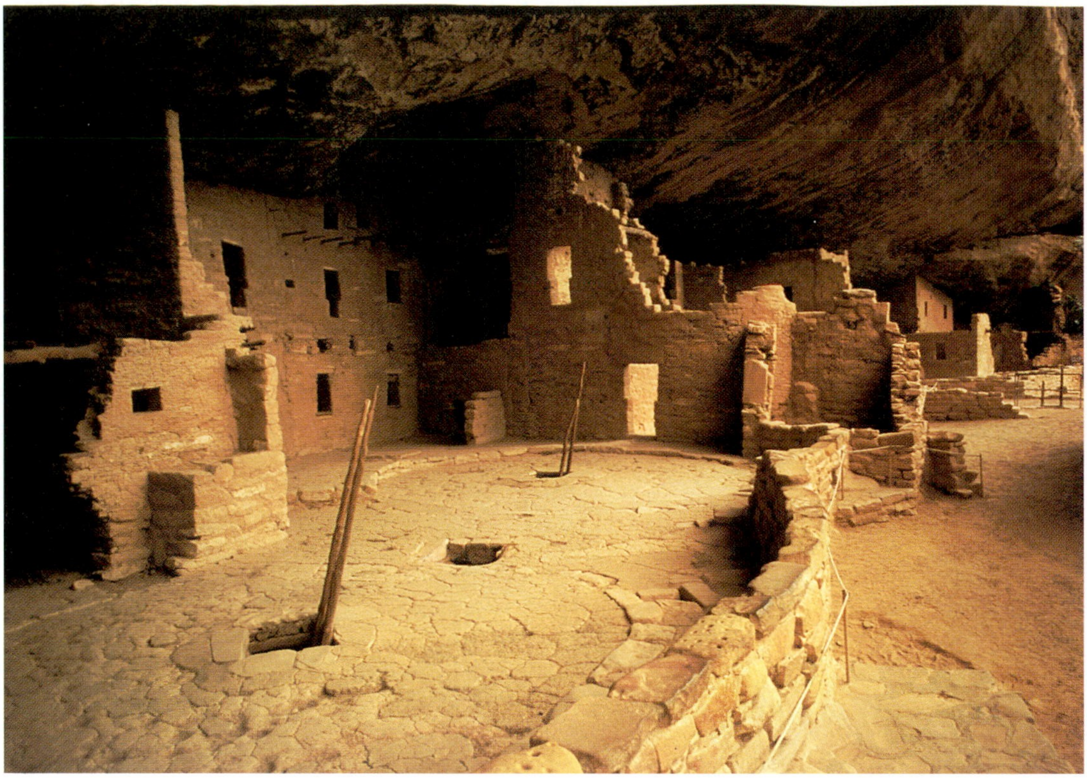

Fig. 437 Mesa Verde, Spruce Tree House, c. 1200–1300 CE.
Courtyard formed by restoration of the roofs over two underground kivas.
William M. Furguson and Arthur H. Rohn, *Anasazi Ruins in the Southwest in Color.* (Albuquerque: University of New Mexico Press.)

The Anasazi cliff dwelling known as Spruce Tree House (Fig. 437), at Mesa Verde National Park in southwestern Colorado, reflects a similar relation between humans and nature. The Anasazi lived in these cliffside caves for hundreds, perhaps thousands of years. The cave provided security, and in addition, to live there was to be closer to the people's origin and, therefore, to the source of their strength. For unknown reasons, the Anasazi abandoned their cliff dwellings in about 1300 CE. One possible cause was a severe drought that lasted from 1276 to 1299. It is also possible that disease, a shortened growing season, or warfare with Apache and Shoshone tribes caused the Anasazi to leave the highland mesas and to migrate south into Arizona and New Mexico.

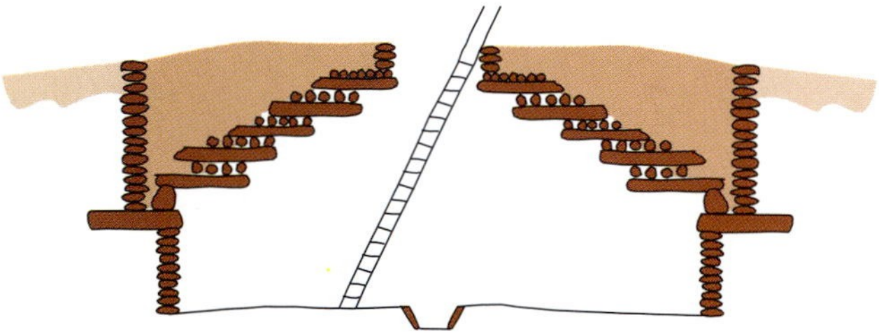

Fig. 438 Cribbed roof construction of a kiva.
After a National Park Service pamphlet.

At the heart of the Anasazi culture was the **kiva,** a round, covered hole in the center of the communal plaza in which all ceremonial life took place. The roofs of two underground kivas on the north end of the ruin have been restored. They are constructed of horizontally laid logs built up to form a dome with an access hole (Fig. 438). The people utilized these roofs as a common area. Down below, in the enclosed kiva floor, was a *sipapu,* a small, round hole symbolic of the Anasazi creation myth, which told of the emergence of the Anasazi's ancestors from the depths of the earth. In the parched Southwestern desert country it is equally true that water, like life itself, also seeps out of small fissures in the earth. Thus, it is as if the entire Anasazi community, and everything necessary to its survival, emerges from mother earth.

TECHNOLOGY

The structure of the kiva's roof represents a technological innovation of the Anasazi culture. Thus, while it responds directly to the topography of the place, it also reflects the *technology* available to the builder. The basic technological challenge faced by architecture is to construct upright walls and put a roof over the empty space they enclose. Walls may employ one of two basic structural systems: the **shell system,** in which one basic material provides both the structural support and the outside covering of the building, and the **skeleton-and-skin** system, which consists of a basic interior frame, the skeleton, that supports the more fragile outer covering, the skin.

In a building that is several stories tall, the walls or frame of the lower floors must also support the weight of the upper floors. The ability of a given building material to support weight is thus a determining factor in how high the building can be. The walls or frame also support the roof. The span between the elements of the supporting structure—between, for instance, stone walls, columns, or steel beams—is determined by the tensile strength of the roof material. **Tensile strength** is the ability of a building material to span horizontal distances without support and without buckling in the middle. The greater the tensile strength of a material, the wider its potential span. Almost all technological advances in the history of architecture depend on either the invention of new ways to distribute weight or the discovery of new materials with greater tensile strength. We begin our survey with the most basic technology and move forward to the most advanced.

Load-bearing Construction

The simplest method of making a building is to make the walls **load-bearing**—make the walls themselves bear the weight of the roof. One does this by piling and stacking any material—stones, bricks, mud and straw—right up to roof level. Many load-bearing structures, such as the pyramids or the ziggurat we have already seen, are solid almost all the way through, with only small open chambers inside them. Though the Anasazi cliff dwelling contains more livable space than a pyramid or a ziggurat, it too is a load-bearing construction. The kiva is built of adobe bricks—bricks made of dried clay—piled on top of one another, and the roof is built of wood. The complex roof of the kiva spans a greater circumference than would be possible with just wood, and it supports the weight of the community in the plaza above. This is achieved by the downward pressure exerted on the wooden beams by the stones and fill on top of them above the outside wall, which counters the tendency of the roof to buckle.

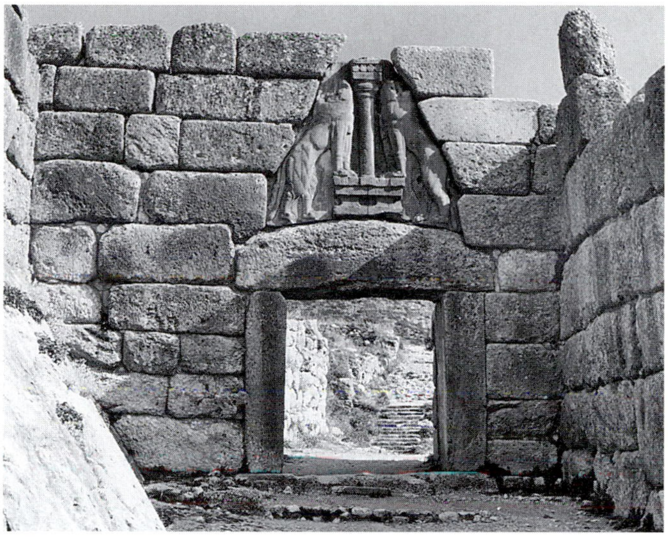

Fig. 439 The Lion Gate, Mycenae, Greece, 1250 BCE.
Hirmer/Fotoarchive.

Post-and-Lintel

The walls surrounding the Lion Gate at Mycenae in Greece (Fig. 439) are load-bearing construction. But the gate itself represents another form of construction, post-and-lintel. **Post-and-lintel construction** consists of a horizontal beam supported at each end by a vertical post or a wall. In essence, the downward force of the horizontal bridge holds the vertical posts in an upright position, and conversely, the posts support the stone above in a give-and-take of directional force and balance. So large are the stones used to build this gate—both the length of the **lintel** and the total height of the post-and-lintel structure are roughly 13 feet—that later Greeks believed it could only have been built by the mythological race of one-eyed giants, the Cyclops.

Post-and-lintel construction is fundamental to all Greek architecture. As can be seen in the Basilica at Paestum (Fig. 440), the columns, or posts, supporting the structure were placed relatively close together. This was done for practical reasons, since if stone lintels, especially of marble, were required to span too great a distance, they were likely to crack and eventually collapse. Each of the columns in the Basilica is made of several pieces of stone, called *barrels*. Grooves carved in the stone, called **fluting,** run the length of the column and unite the individual barrels into a single unit. Each column tapers dramatically toward the top and slightly toward the bottom, an architectural feature known as **entasis.** Entasis deceives the eye and makes the column look absolutely vertical. It also gives the column a sense of almost human musculature and strength. The columns suggest the bodies of human beings, holding up the roof like miniature versions of the giant Atlas, who carried the world on his shoulders.

The values of the Greek city-state were embodied in its temples. The temple was usually situated on an elevated site, above the city—an *acropolis,* from *akros,* meaning "top," of the *polis,* "city"—and was conceived as the center of civic life. Its **colonnade,** or row of columns set at regular intervals around the building and supporting the base of the roof, was constructed according to the rules of geometry and embodied cultural values of equality and proportion. So consistent were the Greeks in developing a generalized architectural type for their temples that it is possible to speak of them in terms of three distinct architectural types—the Doric, the Ionic, and the Corinthian, the last of which was rarely used by the Greeks themselves but later became the standard order in Roman architecture (Fig. 441). In ancient times, the heavier Doric order was considered masculine, and the more graceful Ionic order feminine. It is true that the Ionic order is slimmer and much lighter in feeling than the Doric.

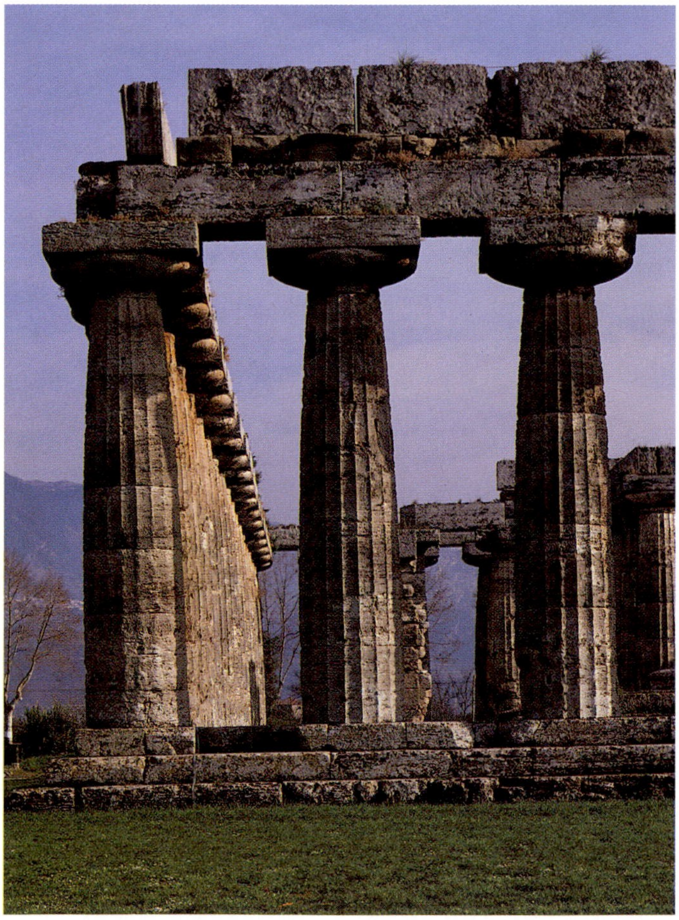

Fig. 440 Corner of the Basilica, Paestum, Italy, c. 550 BCE.
Canali Photobank.

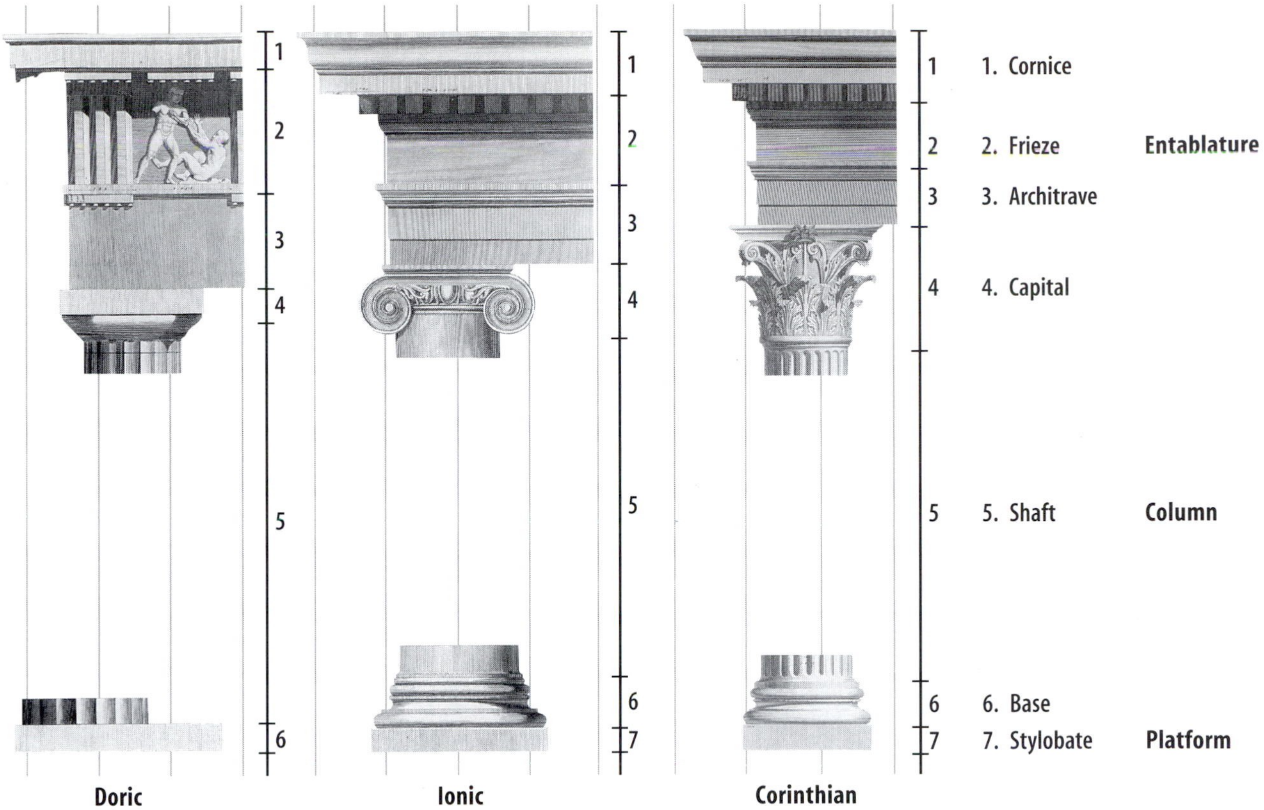

Fig. 441 **The Greek orders, from James Stuart, *The Antiquities of Athens,* London, 1794.**

The vertical design, or **elevation,** of the Greek temple is composed of three elements—the **platform,** the **column,** and the **entablature.** The relationship among these three units is referred to as its **order.** The Doric, the earliest and plainest of the three, is utilized in the Basilica at Paestum. The Ionic is later, more elaborate, and organic, while the Corinthian is more organic still. The elevation of each order begins with a platform, the **stylobate.** The column in the Doric order consists of two parts, the **shaft** and the **capital,** to which both the Ionic and Corinthian orders add a base. The orders are most quickly distinguished by their capitals. The Doric capital is plain, marked only by a subtle outward curve. The Ionic capital is much more elaborate and is distinguished by its scroll. The temple of Athena Nike (Fig. 442) is the oldest Ionic temple on the Acropolis in Athens. The Corinthian capital is decorated with stylized acanthus leaves. The entablature consists of three parts, the **architrave,** or weight-bearing and weight-distributing element, the decorated **frieze,** and the **cornice.**

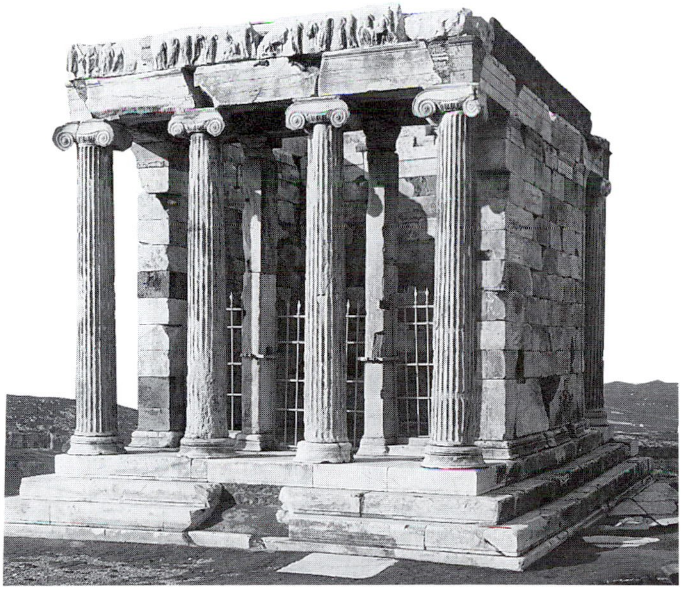

Fig. 442 **Temple of Athena Nike, Acropolis, Athens, 427–424 BCE.**
Vanni/Art Resource.

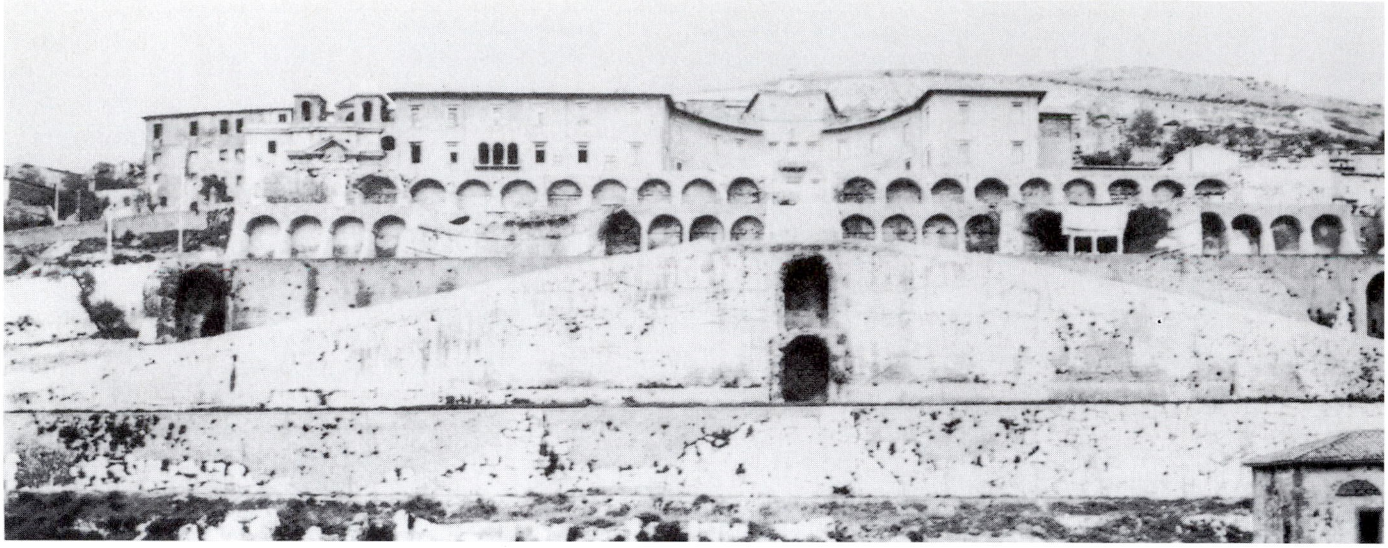

Fig. 443 **Sanctuary of Fortuna Primigenia, Praeneste (Palestrina), Italy. Early 1st century BCE.**

The geometrical order of the Greek temple suggests a conscious desire to control the natural world. So strong was this impulse that their architecture seems defiant in its belief that the intellect is superior to the irrational forces of nature. We can read this same impulse in Roman architecture—the will to dominate the site. The Sanctuary of Fortuna, or Fate, at Praeneste, in the foothills of the Apennines east of Rome (Figs. 443 and 444), seems to embrace the whole of the landscape below in one giant sweep of its mammoth ramps and terraces, as if it were literally the Roman Empire itself, engulfing the entire Mediterranean world. But despite its enormous size, the temple seems to fit into the hillside it occupies, as if in harmony with the landscape, not in opposition to it. As a temple to Fortune, or Fate, it seems to assert the inevitability of empire, the destiny of Rome to control and oversee the entire world. It is as if the Roman state is so large, so magnificent, it *is* nature.

Arches and Domes

The Sanctuary of Fortuna makes considerable use of colonnades—rows of columns—as do many Roman buildings, but it also employs arches as a major architectural feature. The

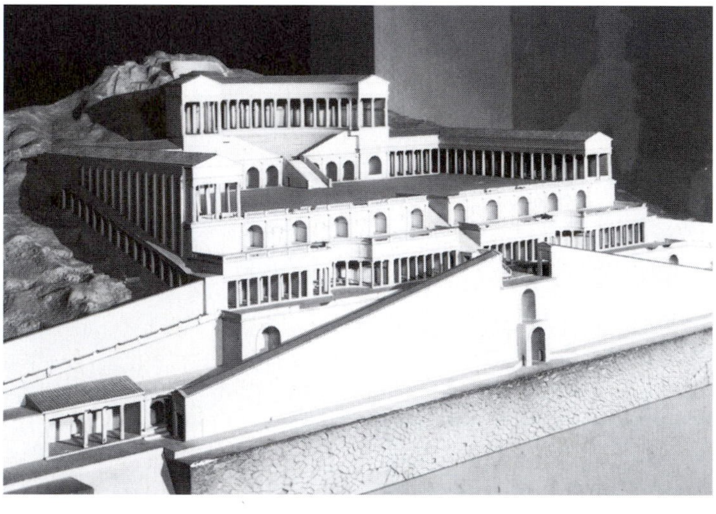

Fig. 444 **Reconstruction model of the Sanctuary of Fortuna Primigenia,** Praeneste (Palestrina), Italy. Museo Archeologico Nazionale, Palestrina, Italy.

development of the arch revolutionized the built environment. Although they did not invent the **arch** (Fig. 446), it was the Romans who, at the end of the first century CE, perfected its form. They recognized that the arch would allow them to make structures with a much larger span than was possible with post-and-lintel construction. Made of wedge-shaped stones, called ***voussoirs,*** each cut to fit into the semicircular form, an arch is not stable until the **keystone,** the stone at the very top, has been put into place. At this point, equal pressure is exerted by each stone on its neighbors, and the scaffolding that is necessary to support the arch while it is under construction can be removed. The arch supports itself, with the weight of the whole transferred downward to the posts. A series of arches could be made to span a wide canyon with relative ease. One of the most successful Roman structures is the Pont du Gard (Fig. 445), an aqueduct used to carry water from the distant hills to the Roman compound in Nîmes, France. Still intact today, it is an engineering feat remarkable not only for its durability, but, like most examples of Roman architecture, for its incredible size.

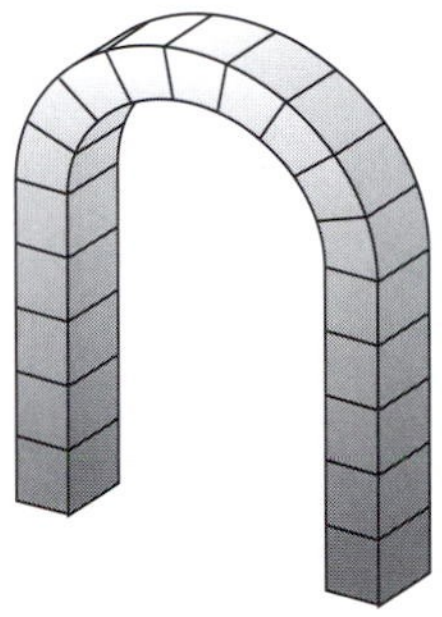

Fig. 446 Arch.

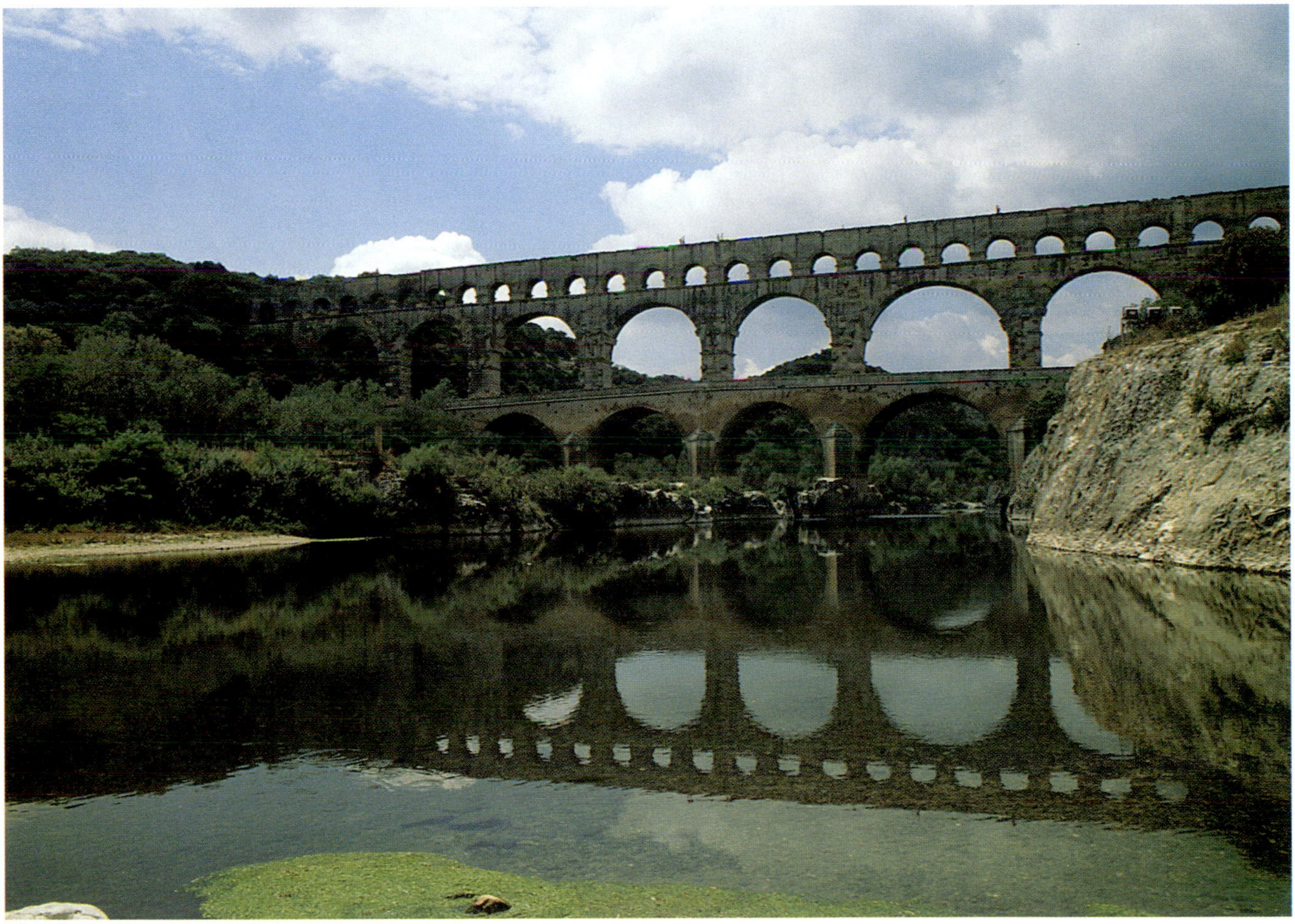

Fig. 445 Pont du Gard, near Nîmes, France. Late 1st century BCE.
Joelle Burrows.

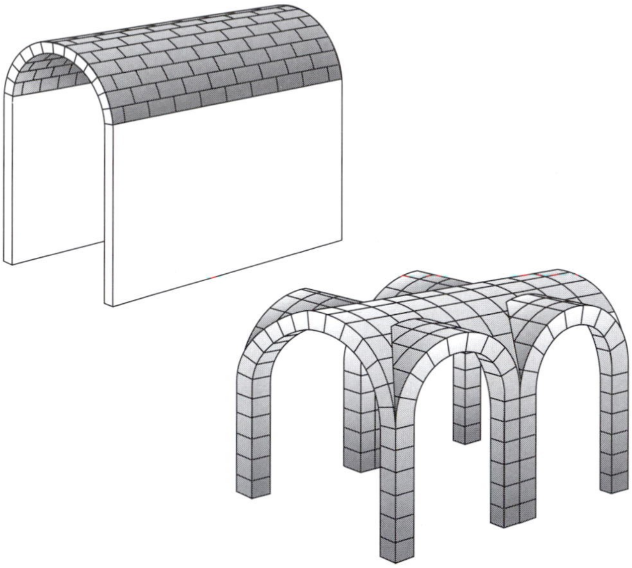

Fig. 447 Barrel vault (top) and groined vault (bottom) construction.

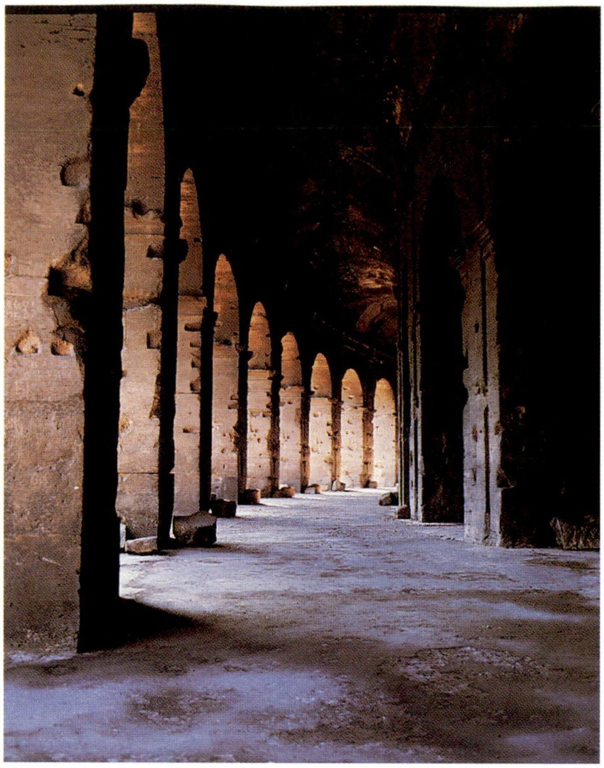

Fig. 449 Barrel vaulted gallery, ground floor of the Colosseum, Rome.
Scala/Art Resource.

With the development of the **barrel,** or *tunnel vault* (Fig. 447, top), which is essentially an extension in depth of the single arch by lining up one arch behind another, the Romans were able to create large, uninterrupted interior spaces. Such is the strength of the vaulting structure of the Roman Colosseum (Figs. 448

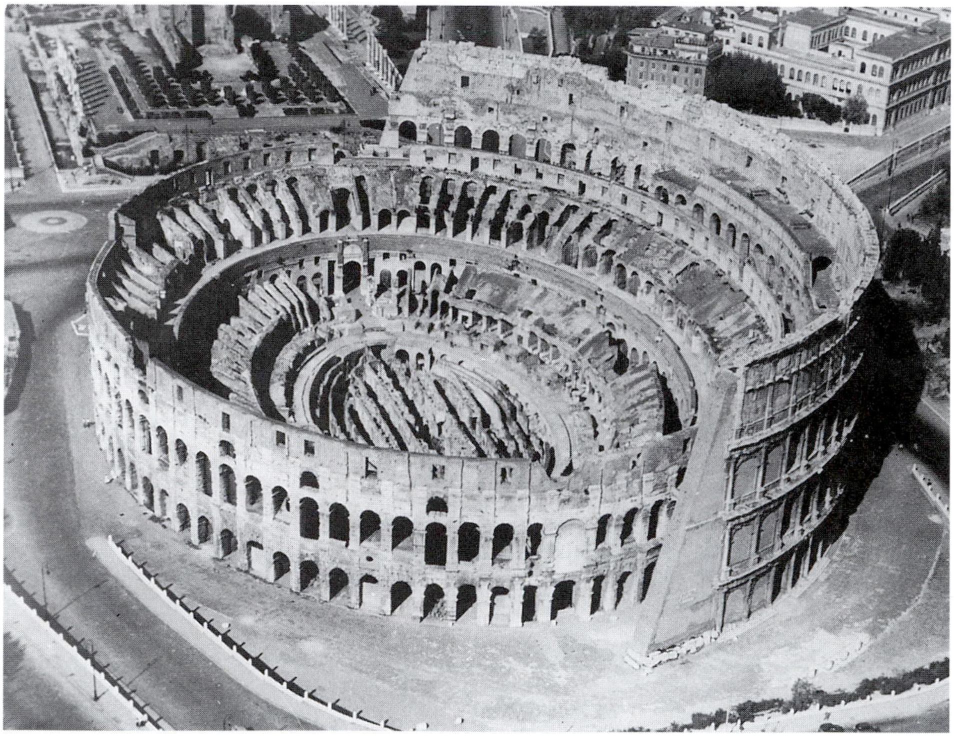

Fig. 448 The Colosseum (aerial view), Rome, 72–80 CE.
Italian Government Travel Office.

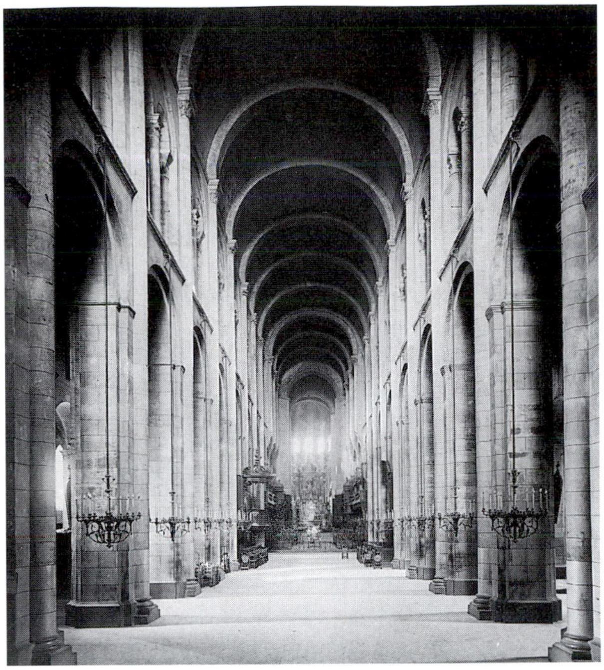

Fig. 450 Interior view of nave, St. Sernin, Toulouse, France, c. 1080–1120.
Marburg/Art Resource.

and 449), that more than 50,000 spectators could be seated in it. The Colosseum is an example of an *amphitheater* (literally meaning a "double theater"), in which two semicircular theaters are brought face to face, a building type invented by the Romans to accommodate large crowds. Built for gladiatorial games and other "sporting" events, including mock naval battles and fights to the death between humans and animals, the Colosseum is constructed both with barrel vaults and with **groined vaults** (Fig. 447, bottom), the latter created when two barrel vaults are made to meet at right angles. These vaults, originally covered with elaborate stucco decorations, provided so many exit and entry points that large crowds were able to flow rapidly in and out of the structure.

A thousand years after the Romans built the Colosseum, their system of vault construction was still in wide use throughout Europe. It was employed especially in Romanesque architecture—so called because it utilized so many Roman methods and architectural forms. The barrel vault at St. Sernin, in Toulouse, France (Figs. 450 and 451) is a magnificent example of Romanesque architecture. The plan of this church is one of great symmetry and geometric simplicity (Fig. 452). It reflects the Romanesque preference for rational order and logical development. Every measurement is based on the central square at the **crossing,** where the two **transepts,** or side wings, cross the length of the **nave,** the central aisle of the church used by the congregation, and the **apse,** the semicircular projection at the end of the church. Each square in the aisles, for instance, is one-quarter the size of the crossing square. Each transept extends two full squares from the center. The tower that rises over the crossing, incidentally, was completed in later times and is taller than it was originally intended to be.

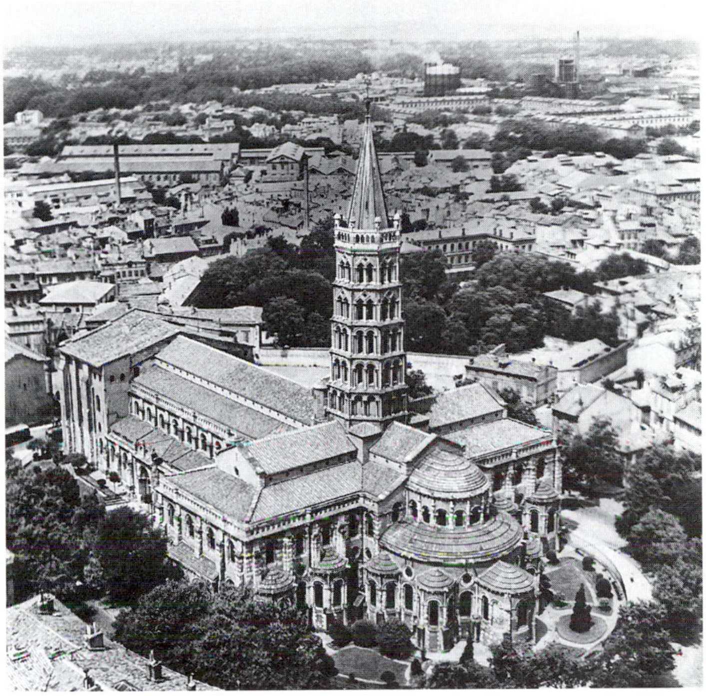

Fig. 451 St. Sernin, Toulouse, France, c. 1080–1120.
French Government Tourist Office.

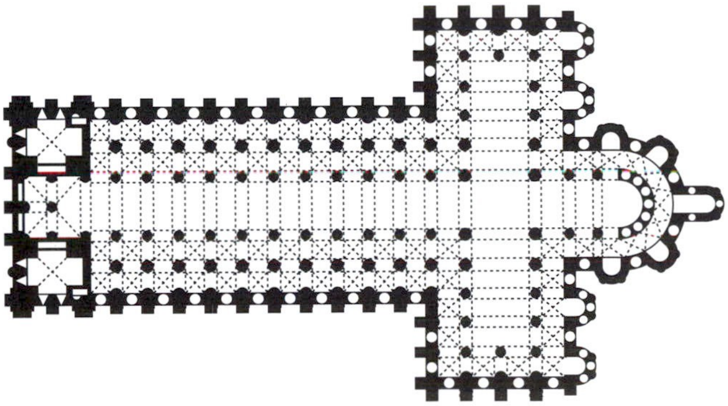

Fig. 452 Plan, St. Sernin.

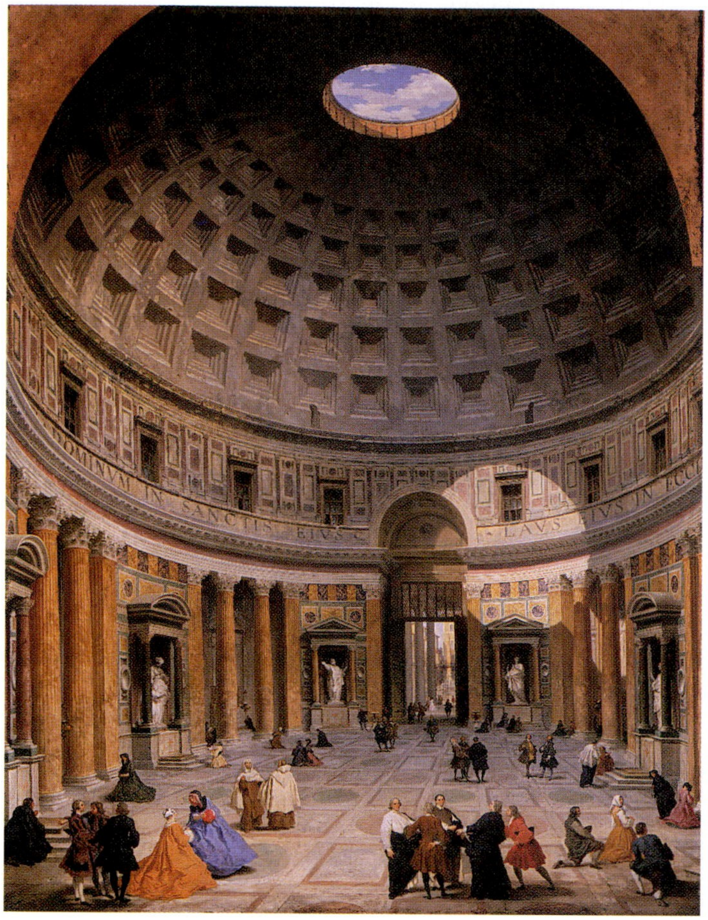

Fig. 453 Interior, Pantheon, 117–125 CE.
As seen in an 18th-century painting by Giovanni Paolo Panini.

The roof over the apse at St. Sernin is a half-dome. The Romans were also the first to perfect the **dome,** which takes the shape of a hemisphere, sometimes defined as a continuous arch rotated 360 degrees on its axis. Conceived as a temple to celebrate all their gods, the Roman Pantheon (Fig. 453)—from the Greek words *pan* ("every") and *theos* ("god")—consists of a 142-foot-high dome set on a cylindrical wall 140 feet in diameter. Every interior dimension appears equal and proportionate, even as its scale overwhelms the viewer. The dome is concrete, which was poured in sections over a huge mold supported by a complex scaffolding. Over 20 feet thick where it meets the walls—a point called the **springing**—the dome thins to only 6 feet at the circular opening, 30 feet in diameter, at the dome's top. Through this ***oculus*** (Latin for "eye"), the building's only source of illumination, worshipers could make contact with the heavens. As the sun shone through it, casting a round spotlight into the interior, it seemed as if the eye of Jupiter, king of the gods, shone upon the Pantheon walls.

The architectural inventions of the Romans provided the basis for building construction in the Western world for nearly 2,000 years. The idealism, even mysticism of the Pantheon's vast interior space, with its evocation of the symbolic presence of Jupiter, found its way into churches as the Christian religion came to dominate the West. Large congregations could gather beneath the high barrel vaults of churches, which were constructed on Roman architectural principles. The culmination of this spiritual direction is the immense interior space of the great Gothic cathedrals (Figs. 454 and 455), which arose throughout Europe beginning in about CE 1150. A building such as the Pantheon, with a 30-foot hole in its roof, was simply impractical in the severe climates of Northern Europe. As if in response to the dark and dreary climate outside, the interior of the Gothic cathedral rises to an incredible height, lit by stained-glass windows that transform a dull day with a warm and richly radiant light.

The great height of the Gothic cathedral's interior space is achieved by means of a system of pointed, rather than round, arches. The height of a rounded arch is determined by its width, but the height of a **pointed arch** (Fig. 456) can readily be extended by straightening the curve of the sides upward to a point, the weight descending much more directly down the wall. By utilizing the pointed arch in a scheme of groined vaults, the almost ethereal space of the Gothic cathedral, soaring upward as if toward God, is realized.

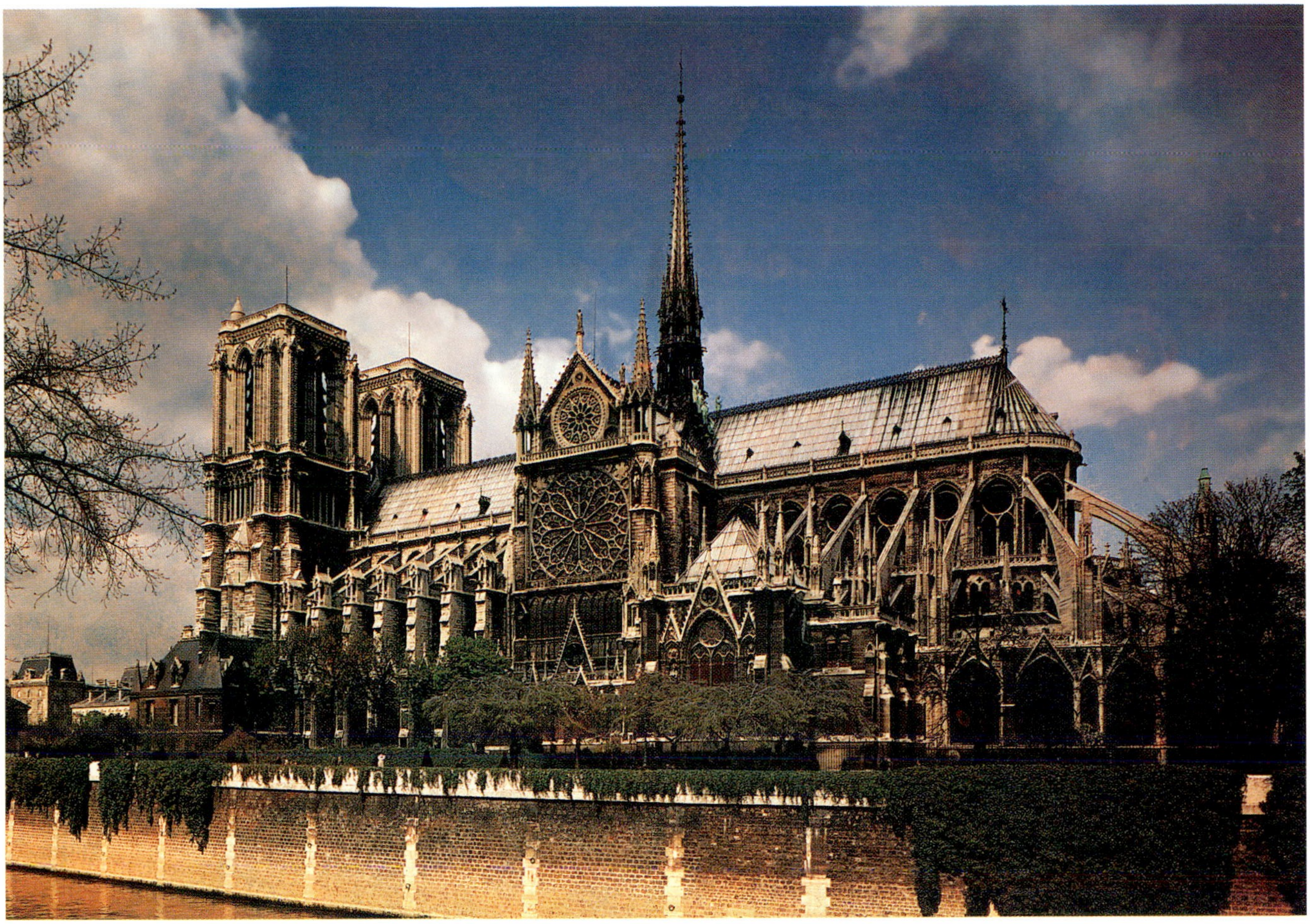

Fig. 454 **Cathedral of Notre-Dame, Paris, France, 1163–1250.**
Scala/Art Resource.

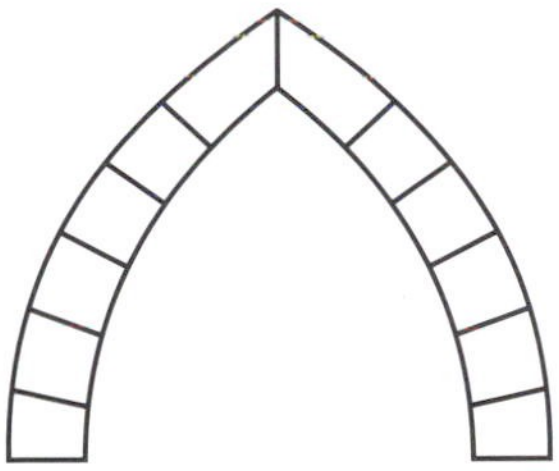

Fig. 456 (above) **Pointed arch.**

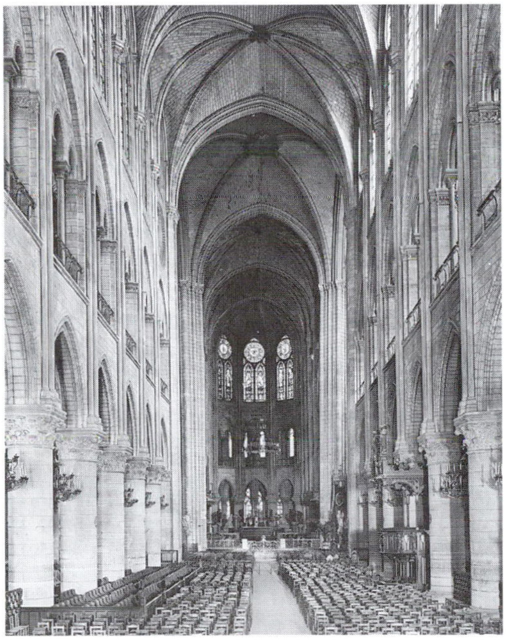

Fig. 455 **Interior, Notre-Dame, Paris.**
Alinari/Art Resource.

All arches tend to spread outward, creating a risk of collapse, and early on the Romans learned to support the sides of the arch to counteract this *lateral thrust*. In the great French cathedrals the support was provided by building a series of arches on the outside whose thrusts would counteract the outward force of the interior arches. Extending inward from a series of columns or *piers,* these **flying buttresses** (Figs. 457 and 458), so named because they lend to the massive stone architecture a sense of lightness and flight, are an aesthetic response to a practical problem. Together with the stunning height of the nave allowed by the pointed arch, the flying buttresses reveal the desire of the

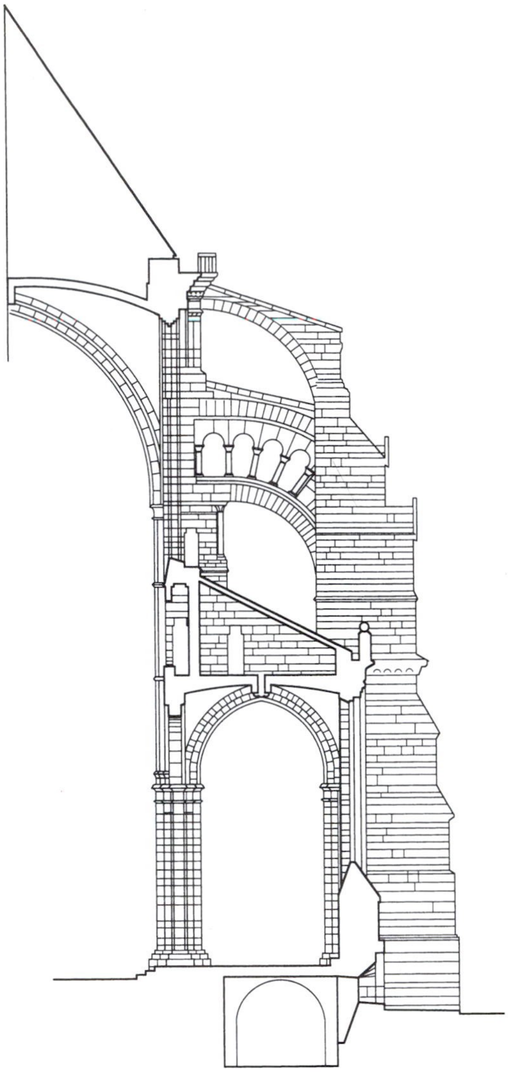

Fig. 458 Flying buttress.

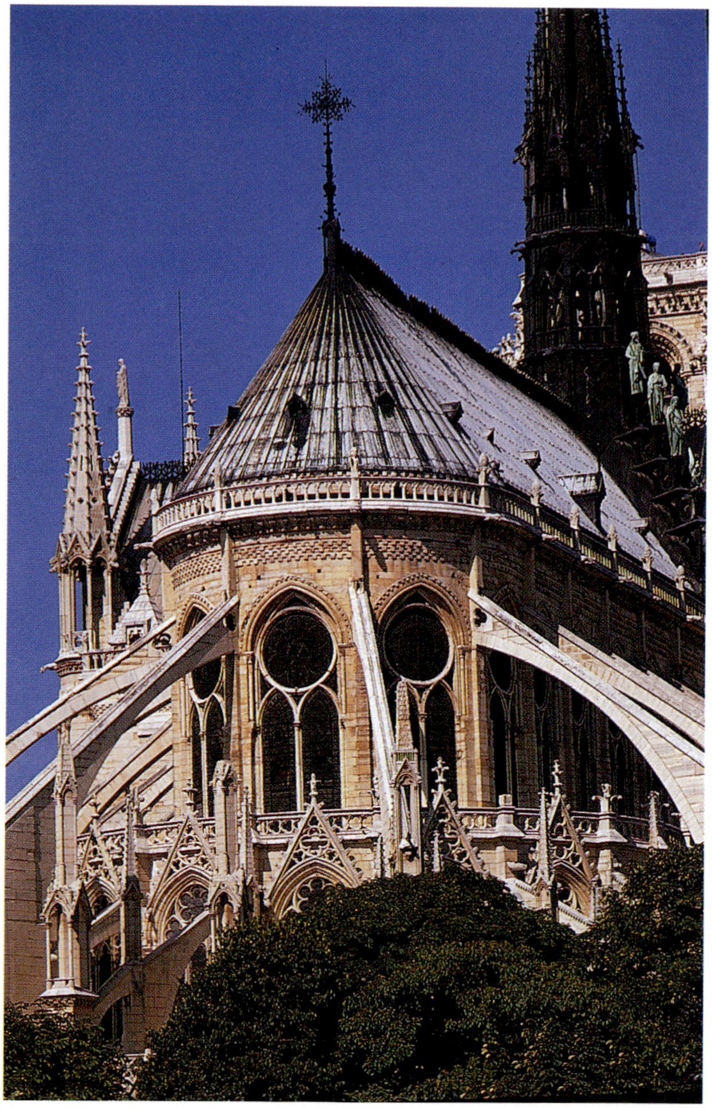

Fig. 457 Flying buttresses, Notre-Dame, Paris.
Jim Bryson.

builder to elevate the cathedral above the humdrum of daily life in the medieval world. The cathedral became a symbol not only of the divine, but of the human ability to exceed, in art and in imagination, our own limitations and circumstances.

Cast-iron Construction

Until the nineteenth century, the history of architecture was determined by innovations in the ways the same materials—mostly stone—could be employed. In the nineteenth century, a material that had been known for thousands of years but never employed in architecture absolutely transformed the built environment—iron. Wrought iron, which Hector Guimard used to construct his entrance for the Paris Métro (Fig. 459) in 1900, was soft and flexible, and, when heated, it could be easily

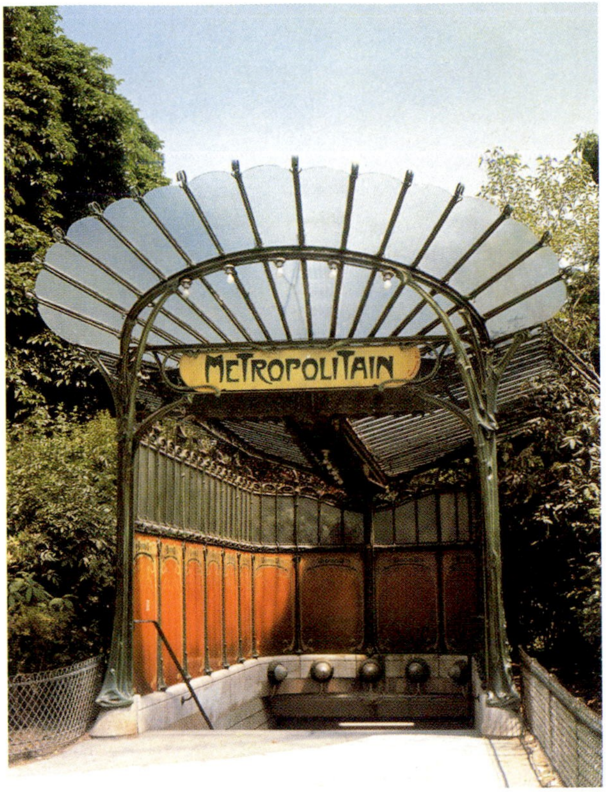

Fig. 459 Hector Guimard, Paris Métro entrance, 1900.
Roger-Viollet, Paris.

turned and twisted into the plantlike forms evident in Guimard's structure. But engineers discovered that by adding carbon to iron, a much more rigid and strong material, **cast-iron,** resulted. The French engineer Gustave Eiffel used cast iron in his new *lattice beam* construction technique, which produces structures of the maximum rigidity with the minimum weight by exploiting the way in which girders can be used to brace each other in three dimensions.

The most influential result was the Eiffel Tower (Fig. 460), designed as a monument to industry and the centerpiece of the international Paris Exposition of 1889. Nearly 1000 feet high, and at that time the tallest structure in the world by far, the Tower posed a particular problem—how to build a structure of such a height, yet one that could resist the wind. Eiffel's solution was simple but brilliant. Construct a skeleton, an open lattice beam framework that would allow the wind to pass through it. Though it served for many years as a radio tower—on July 1, 1913, the first signal transmitted around the world was broadcast from its top, inaugurating the global electronic network—the tower was essentially useless, nothing more than a monument. Many Parisians hated it at first, feeling that it was a blight on the skyline, but by the early years of the twentieth century it had become the symbol of Paris itself, probably the most famous structure in the world. Newspapers jokingly held contests to "clothe" it. But most importantly, it demonstrated the possibility of building to very great height without load-bearing walls. The tower inaugurated the skeleton-and-skin system of building. And the idea of designing "clothes" to cover such a structure soon became a reality.

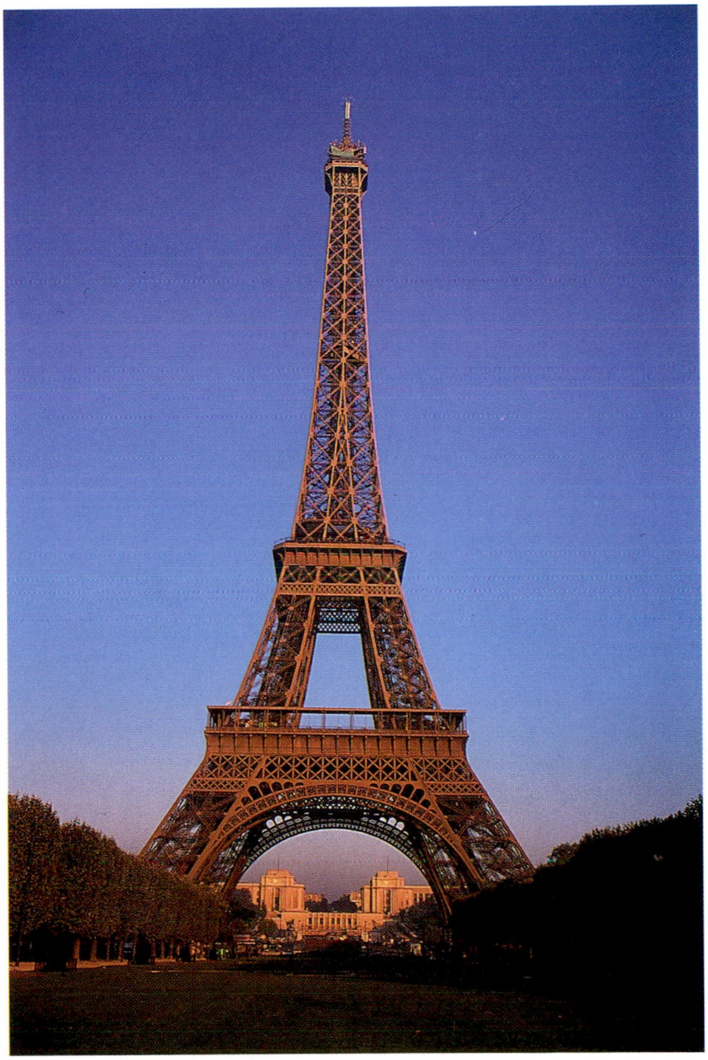

Fig. 460 Gustave Eiffel, Eiffel Tower, 1887.
Alain Evrard/Globe Press.

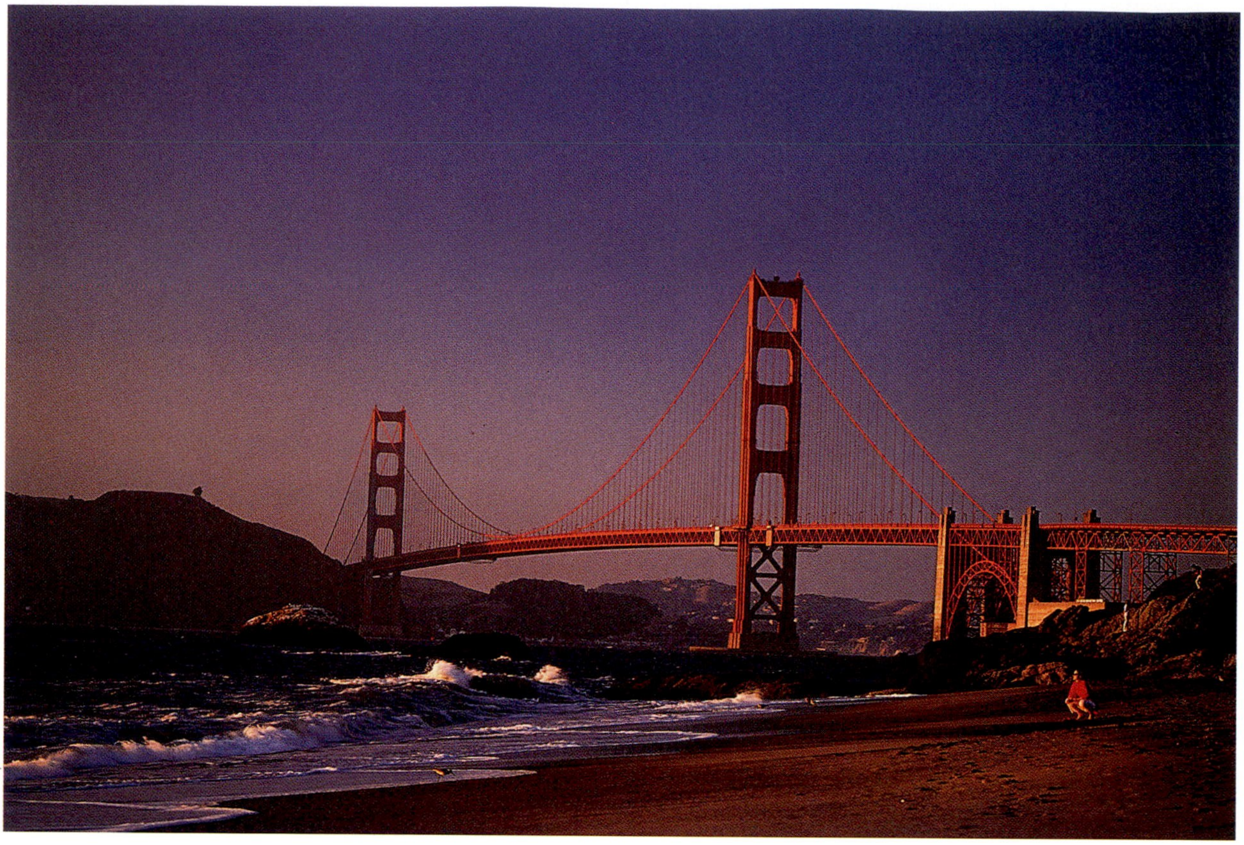

Fig. 461 Golden Gate Bridge, San Francisco, California.
David Weintraub.

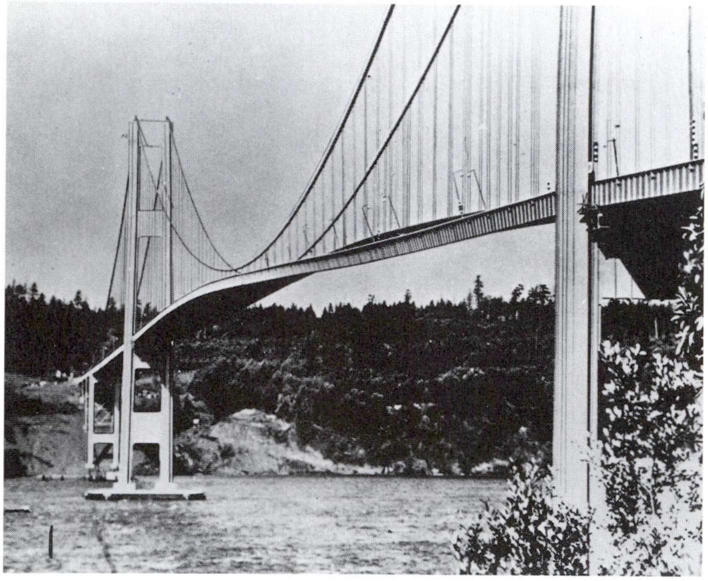

Fig. 462 Tacoma Narrows Bridge, morning of 7 November 1940, just before collapse.
Special Collections Division, University of Washington Libraries. Photograph by Professor F. B. Farquharson.

Suspension

While steel, made by mixing iron and carbon, was available in Eiffel's time, its superiority over iron as a building material was not well demonstrated until the turn of the century. Steel made possible one of the most beautiful forms in architectural engineering, the suspension bridge. The principle is simple: given the strength of steel cable, the weight of the entire span could be supported from cables hung between two vertical pylons.

Perhaps the most famous suspension bridge in the world is San Francisco's Golden Gate (Fig. 461), which for nearly 30 years after it opened in 1937 was the world's longest span—4200 feet. At 746 feet, its pylons remain the highest ever built. Three years after the Golden Gate opened, on November 7, 1940, the Tacoma Narrows suspension bridge in Washington State suddenly collapsed (Fig. 462). Its roadway had been rising and falling so constantly since opening ten months earlier that it had been nicknamed "Galloping Gertie." Engineers had miscalculated the effect of wind on the structure, and when 40 mile per hour winds blew into the area, the bridge began to oscillate. The roadway twisted violently from side to side, and the bridge finally collapsed into the water below. It was determined that the bridge's deck had been too flexible. We need only compare the lattice beam construction under the Golden Gate's roadway to the narrow sheath of steel under the Tacoma bridge to understand why the Golden Gate has never met the same fate.

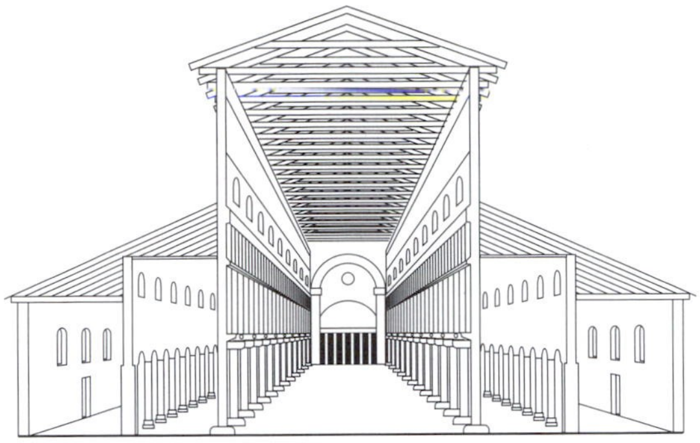

Fig. 464 Model of Old St. Peter's Basilica, Rome, c. 333–390.

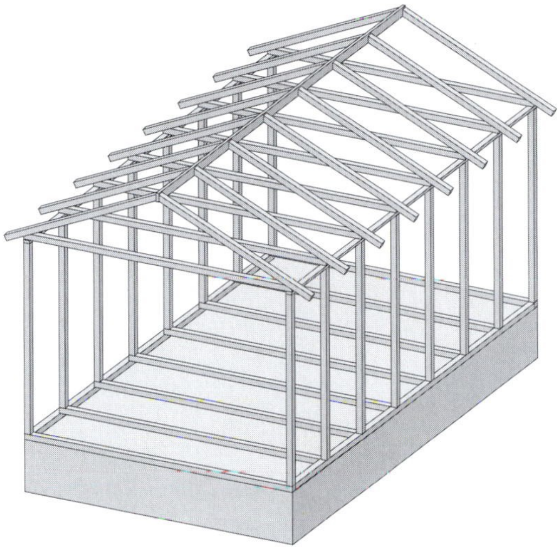

Fig. 463 Wood-frame construction.

Frame Construction

The role of iron and steel in changing the course of architecture in the nineteenth century cannot be underestimated—and we will consider steel in even more detail in a moment—but two more humble technological innovations had almost as significant an impact, determining the look of our built environment down to the present day. The mass production of the common nail, together with improved methods and standardization in the process of milling lumber, led to a revolution in home building techniques.

Lumber cannot easily support structures of great height, but it is perfect for domestic architecture. In 1933, in Chicago, the common **wood-frame** house (Fig. 463), a true skeleton-and-skin building method, was introduced. Sometimes called *balloon-frame* construction, because early skeptics believed houses built in this manner would explode like balloons, the method is both inexpensive and relatively easy. A framework skeleton of, generally, 2 × 4-inch beams is nailed together. Windows and doors are placed in the wall using basic post-and-lintel design principles, and the whole is sheathed with planks, clapboard, shingles, or any other suitable material. The roof is somewhat more complex, but as early as the construction of Old St. Peter's Basilica in Rome in the fourth century CE (Fig. 464), the basic principles were in use. The walls of St. Peter's were composed of columns and arches made of stone and brick, but the roof was wood. And notice the angled beams supporting the roof over the aisles. These are elementary forms of the **truss**, prefabricated versions of which most home builders today use for the roofs of their houses. One of the most rigid structural forms in architecture, the truss (Fig. 465) is a triangular framework that, because of its rigidity, can span much wider areas than a single wooden beam.

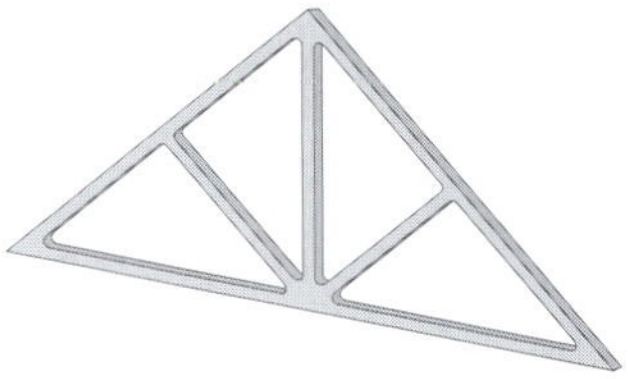

Fig. 465 Truss.

Fred Wilson at Project Row Houses

Fred Wilson, an artist/curator, in the Spring of 1996 was invited to Houston, Texas, to install a show of his own design at Project Row Houses. Project Row Houses (Fig 466) is an art and cultural community of 22 original "shotgun" houses founded in 1992 by local artist and community activist Rick Lowe. African-American artists in Houston wanted to establish a positive creative presence in their own community. The row houses, which were abandoned and in disrepair (Fig. 467), provided a unique opportunity for the realization of this dream.

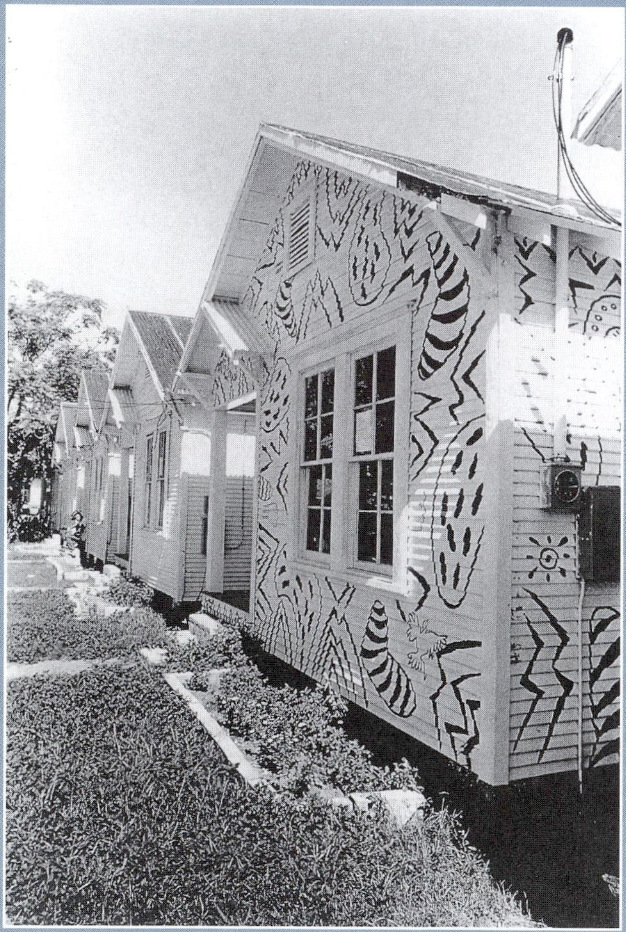

Fig. 466 Project Row Houses, Houston, Texas, 1992–continuing.
Fred Wilson, Artist/Curator.

Few examples of shotgun communities survive. The **shotgun house** is a single-story, wood-frame structure, one room wide and two or more rooms deep, capped by a gable-front roof (Fig. 468). It takes its name from the idea that if a shotgun were fired through the front door, the shot would travel straight through the house and out the back. After the Civil War, shotgun houses were the first homes of many newly freed African Americans, especially in the Florida panhandle, Mississippi, Louisiana, and Texas. In the hot climate of these areas, the open design, which has its roots in African housing, provided for ventilation.

As with all his projects, Wilson begins with research—in this case, into the history of the community and the people who lived there. "When I go into a project," he says, "I'm not looking to bring something to it. I'm responding more than anything else. You can still get a very personal emotional response from a situation or an individual who lived a hundred years ago. It's connecting over time that I'm responding to."

Not far from the row houses are the skyscrapers of downtown Houston, the Italian Romanesque buildings of Rice University, and the Johnson and Burgee postmodern College of Architecture at the University of Houston (Fig. 432). The basic question that Wilson asks in his installation (Fig. 469) developed from the contrast between the two types of building, between the simple and the elaborate, the *vernacular* or indigenous design of the row houses and the imported and fashionable styles of the others. What does architecture say about the community that built it? What stories can the row houses tell?

And what about the name "shotgun" house itself? Whose term is that? The Anglo community's or the African American's? The term's ironies are plain, but what can we learn from them? "Objects," Wilson says, "speak to me." As an artist, Wilson translates what they say to him for us all to hear.

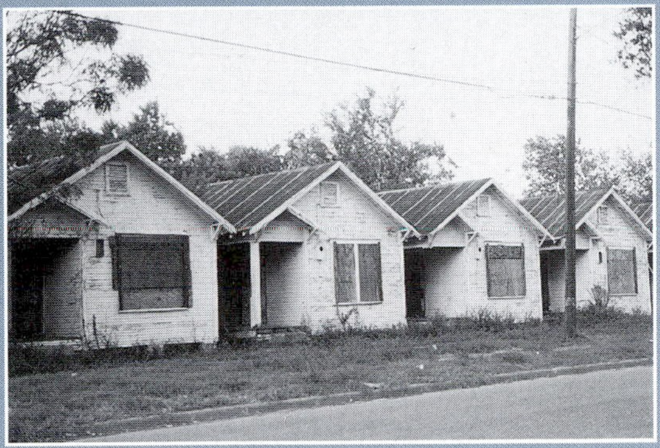

Fig. 467 Project Row Houses, September 1993, before work began. Fred Wilson, Artist/Curator.

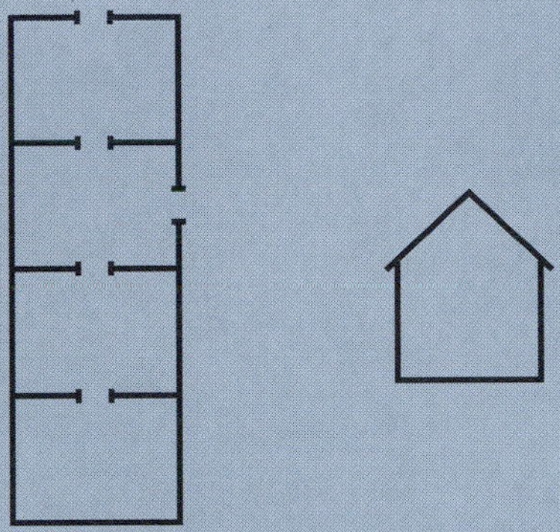

Fig. 468 Shotgun house plan.

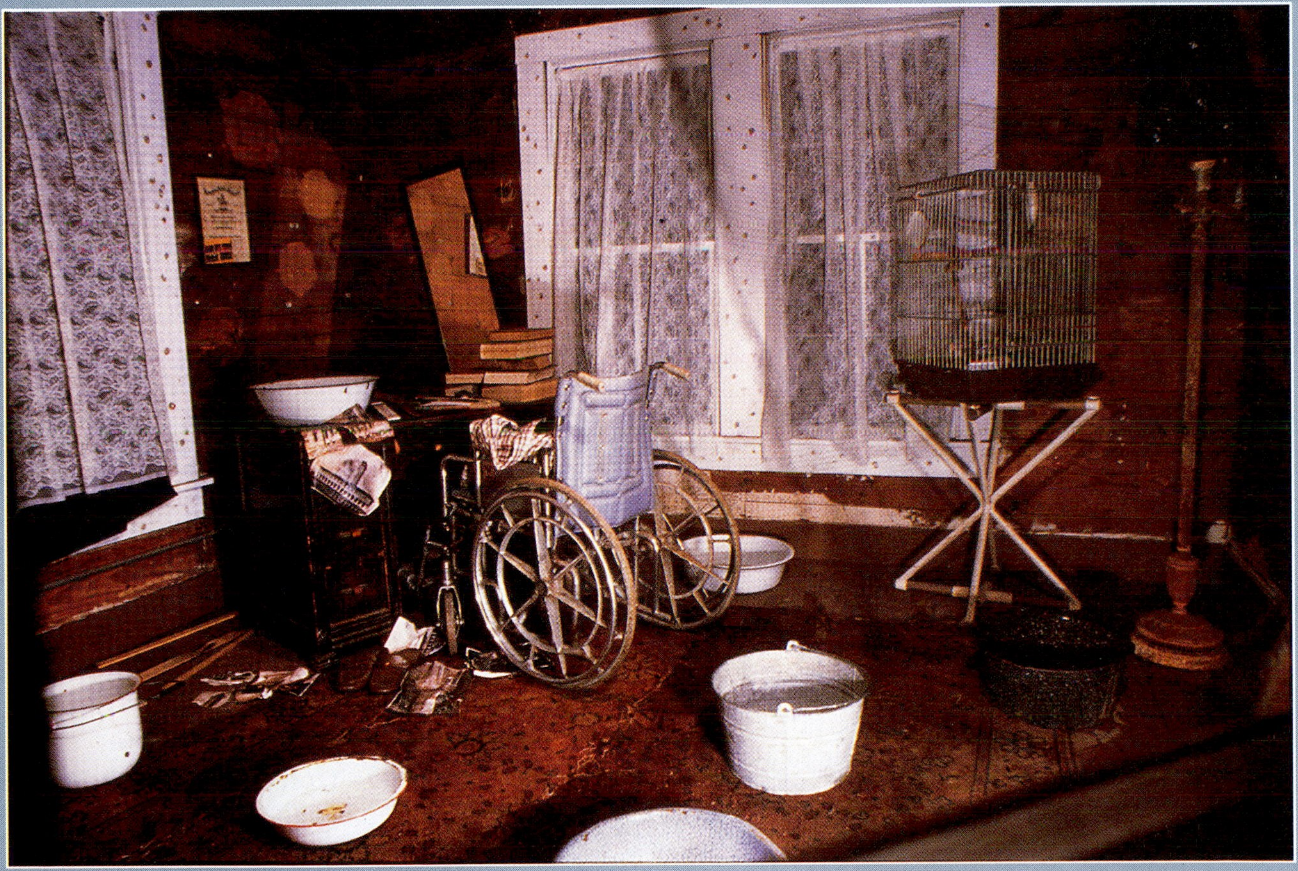

Fig. 469 Installation at Project Row Houses, 1996. Fred Wilson, Artist/Curator.

Steel and Reinforced Concrete Construction

It was in Chicago that frame construction was inaugurated, and it was Chicago that most impressed C. R. Ashbee, a representative of the British National Trust, when he visited America in 1900: "Chicago is the only American city I have seen where something absolutely distinctive in the aesthetic handling of material has been evolved out of the Industrial system." A young architect named Frank Lloyd Wright impressed him most, but it was Wright's mentor, Louis Sullivan, who was perhaps most responsible for the sense of vitality that Ashbee was responding to.

In 1870, fire had destroyed much of downtown Chicago, providing a unique opportunity for architects to rebuild virtually the entire core of the city. For Sullivan, the foremost problem that the modern architect had to address was how the building might transcend the "sinister" urban conditions out of which, of necessity, it had to rise. Most urban buildings were massive in appearance. Henry Hobson Richardson's Marshall Field Wholesale Store (Fig. 470), built after the fire, is a good example. Although Richardson employed a skeletal iron framework within the building to support its interior structure, its thick walls carried their own weight, just as stone walls had for centuries. Richardson's genius lay in his ability to lighten this facade by means of the three- and two-story window arcades running from the second through the sixth floors. But from Sullivan's point of view, the building still appeared to squat upon the city block rather than rise up out of the street to transcend its environment.

For Sullivan, the answer lay in the development of steel construction techniques, combined with what he called "a system of ornament." A fireproof steel skeletal frame, suggested by wood-frame construction, freed the wall of load-bearing necessity and opened it both to ornament and to large numbers of exterior windows. The horizontality of Richardson's building is replaced by a vertical emphasis as the building's exterior lines echo the upward sweep of the steel skeleton. As a result, the exterior of

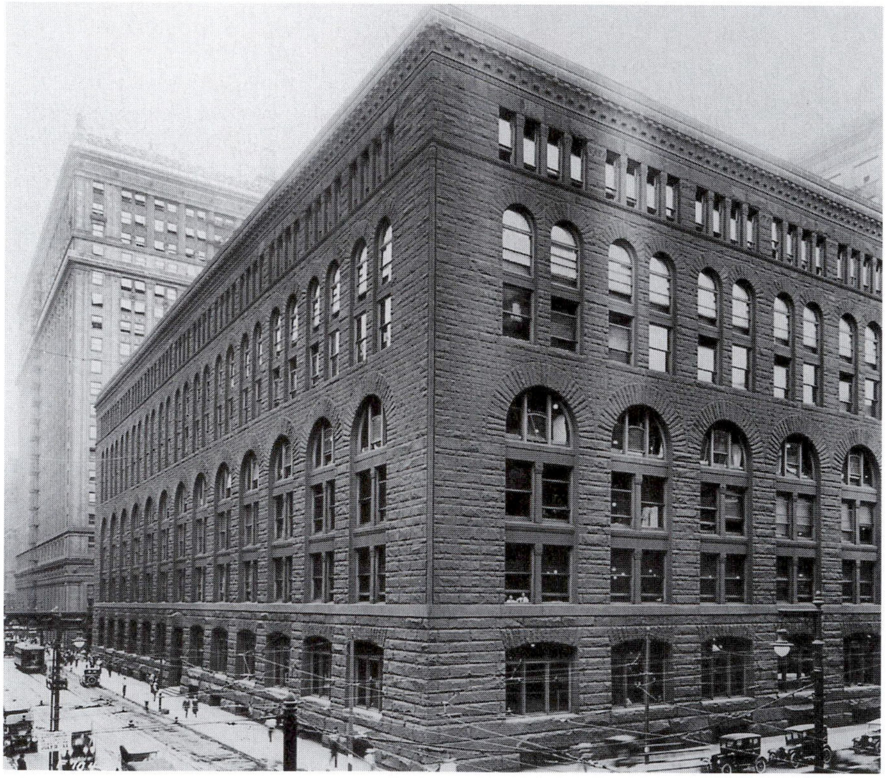

Fig. 470 H. H. Richardson, Marshall Field Wholesale Store, Chicago, 1885–1887.
Photograph courtesy of the Art Institute of Chicago.

the tall building no longer seemed massive; rather, it might rise with an almost organic lightness into the skies.

The building's real identity depended on the ornamentation that could now freely be distributed across its facade. Ornament was, according to Sullivan, "spirit." The inorganic, rigid, and geometric lines of the steel frame would flow, through the ornamental detail that covered it, into "graceful curves," and angularities would "disappear in a mystical blending of surface." Thus at the top of Sullivan's Bayard Building (Fig. 471)—a New York rather than a Chicago building—the vertical columns that rise between the windows blossom in an explosion of floral decoration.

Such ornamentation might seem to contradict completely the dictum that Sullivan is most famous for—"Form follows function." If the function of the urban building is to provide a well-lighted and ventilated place in which to work, then the steel frame structure and the abundance of windows on the building's facade make sense. But what about the ornamentation? How does it follow from the structure's function? Isn't it simply an example of purposeless excess?

Down through the twentieth century, Sullivan's original meaning has largely been forgotten. He was not promoting a notion of design akin to the sense of practical utility that can be discovered in, for instance, a Model T Ford. For Sullivan, "the function of all functions is the Infinite Creative Spirit," and this spirit could be revealed in the rhythm of growth and decay that we find in nature. Thus the elaborate, organic forms that cover his buildings were intended to evoke the Infinite. For Sullivan, the primary function of a building was to elevate the spirit of those who worked in it.

Almost all of Sullivan's ornamental exuberance seems to have disappeared in the architecture of Frank Lloyd Wright, whom many consider the first truly modern architect. But from 1888 to 1893, Wright worked as chief draftsman in Sullivan's Chicago firm, and Sullivan's belief in the unity of design and nature can still be understood as instrumental to Wright's work. In an article written for the *Architectural Record* in 1908, Wright emphasized that "a sense of the organic is indispensable to an architect," and as early as the 1890s, he was

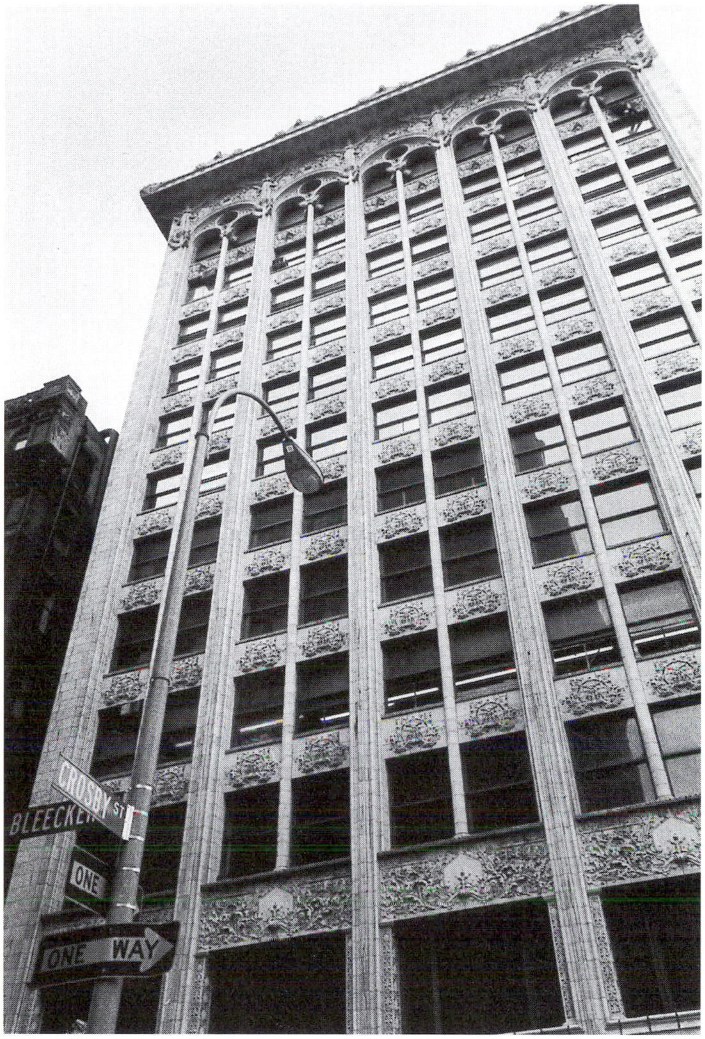

Fig. 471 Louis H. Sullivan, Bayard (Condict) Building, New York, 1897–1898.
Schles/Art Resource.

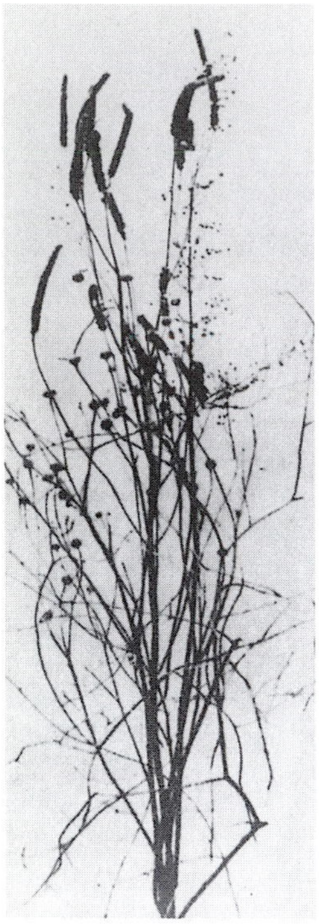

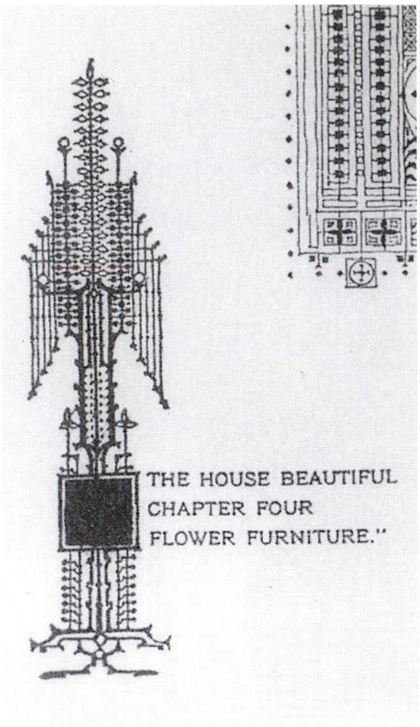

Figs. 472 and 473 Frank Lloyd Wright, left: photo of wild flowers; right: ornamental detail; both in William C. Gannett, *The House Beautiful,* 1896–1897.

routinely "translating" the natural and the organic into what he called "the terms of building stone." In the ornamental detail Wright designed for William C. Gannett's book *The House Beautiful,* Wright literally transformed the organic lines of his own photograph of some wildflowers into a geometric design dominated by straight lines and rectangular patterns (Figs. 472 and 473).

The ultimate expression of Wright's intentions is the so-called Prairie House, the most notable example of which is the Robie House in Chicago, designed in 1906 and built in 1909 (Fig. 474). Although the house is contemporary in feeling—with its wide overhanging roof extending out into space, its fluid, open interiors, and its rigidly geometric lines—it was, from Wright's point of view, purely "organic" in conception.

Wright spoke of the Prairie Houses as "of" the land, not "on" it, and the horizontal sweep of the roof and the open interior space reflect the flat expanses of the Midwestern prairie landscape. The **cantilever,** a horizontal form supported on one end and jutting out into space on the other, was made possible by newly

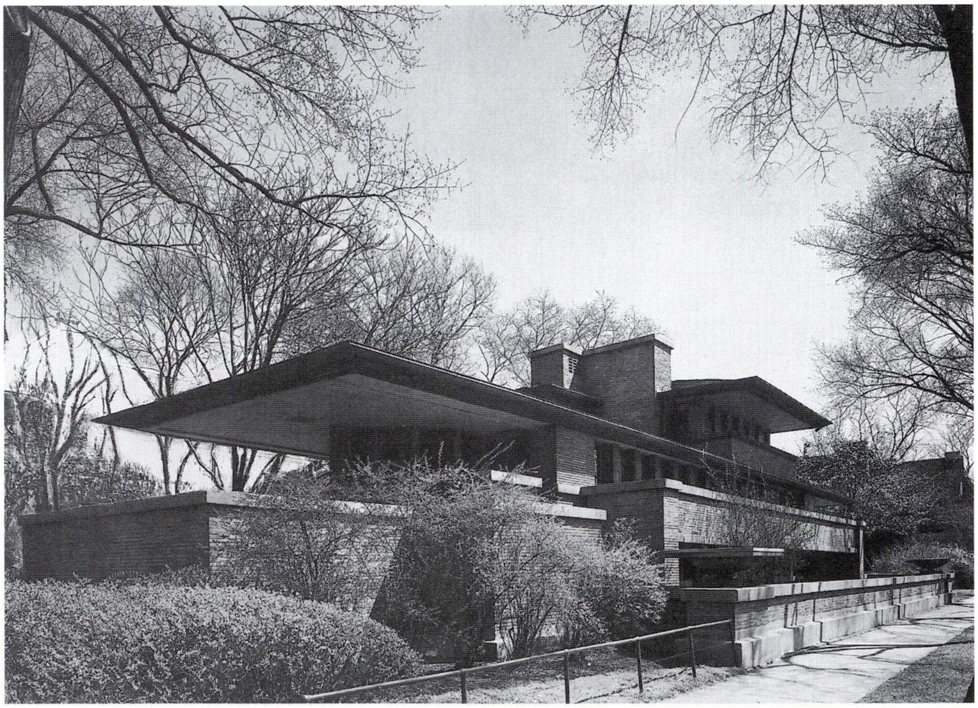

Fig. 474 Frank Lloyd Wright, Robie House, exterior, Chicago, 1909.
Chicago Convention and Tourism Bureau.

invented steel and reinforced concrete construction techniques. Under a cantilevered roof, one could be simultaneously both outside and protected. The roof thus ties together the interior space of the house and the natural world outside. Furthermore, the house itself was built of materials—brick, stone, and wood, especially oak—native to its surroundings.

The architectural innovations of Wright's teacher, Louis Sullivan, led directly to the skyscraper. It is the sheer strength of steel that makes the modern skyscraper a reality. Structures with stone walls require thicker walls on the ground floor the higher they rise. A 16-story building, for instance, would require ground-floor walls approximately six feet thick. But the steel cage, connected by concrete floors, themselves reinforced with steel bars, overcomes this necessity. The simplicity of the resulting structure can be seen clearly in French architect Le Corbusier's 1914 drawing for the Domino Housing Project (Fig. 475). The design is almost infinitely expandable, both sideways and upward. Any combination of windows and walls can be hung on the frame. Internal divisions can be freely designed in an endless variety of ways, or, indeed, the space can be left entirely open. Even the stairwell can be moved to any location within the structural frame.

In 1932, Alfred H. Barr, Jr., a young curator at the Museum of Modern Art in New York City, who would later become one of the most influential historians of modern art, identified Le Corbusier as one of the founders of a new "International Style." In an exhibition on "Modern Architecture," Barr wrote: "Slender steel posts and beams, and concrete reinforced by steel have made possible structures of skeletonlike strength and lightness. The modern architect working in the new style conceives of his building . . . as a skeleton enclosed by a thin light shell. He thinks in terms of volume—of space enclosed by planes and surfaces—as opposed to mass and solidity. This principle of volume leads him to make his walls seem thin flat surfaces by eliminating moldings and by making his windows and doors flush with the surface."

Taking advantage of the strength of concrete-and-steel construction, Le Corbusier lifted his houses on stilts (Fig. 476), thus creating, out of the heaviest of materials, a sense of lightness, even flight. The entire structure is composed of primary forms (that is, rectangles, circles, and so on). Writing in his first book, *Towards a New Architecture*, translated into English in 1925, Le Corbusier put it this way, "Primary forms are beautiful forms because they can be clearly appreciated."

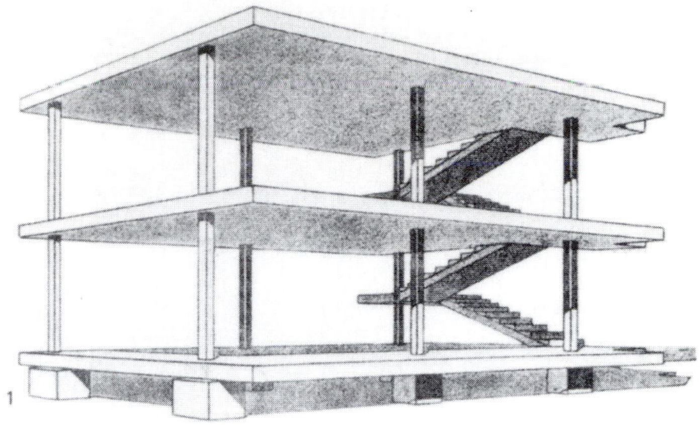

Fig. 475 Le Corbusier, Perspective drawing for Domino Housing Project, 1914.

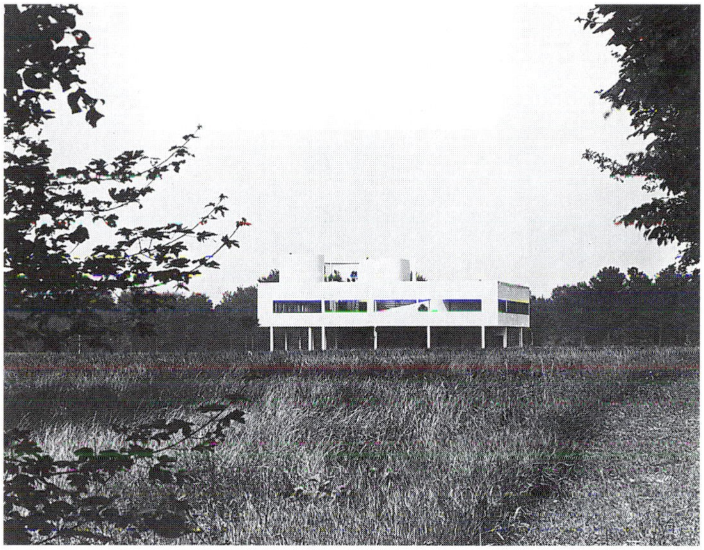

Fig. 476 Le Corbusier, Villa Savoye, Poissy-sur-Seine, France, 1928–1930.
Photograph courtesy The Museum of Modern Art, New York.

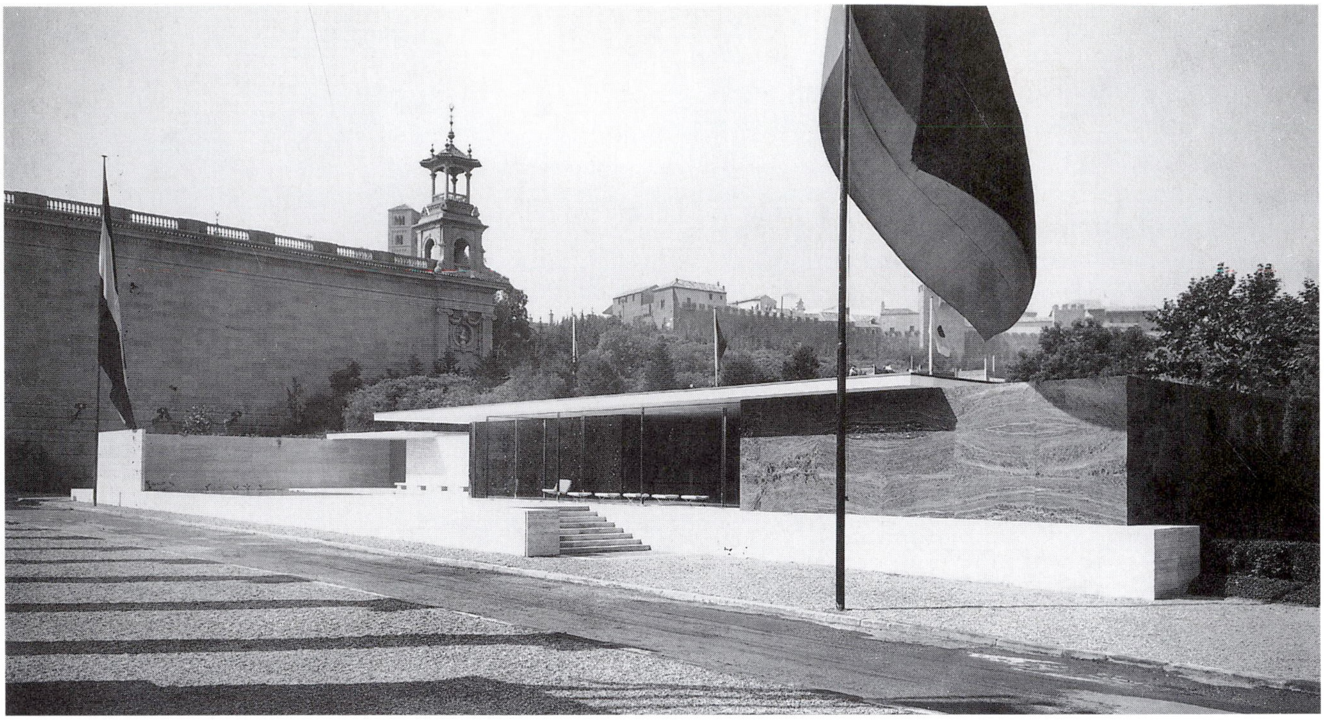

Fig. 477 Ludwig Miës van der Rohe, German Pavilion, International Exposition, Barcelona, Spain, 1929.
Photograph courtesy Miës van der Rohe Archive, The Museum of Modern Art, New York.

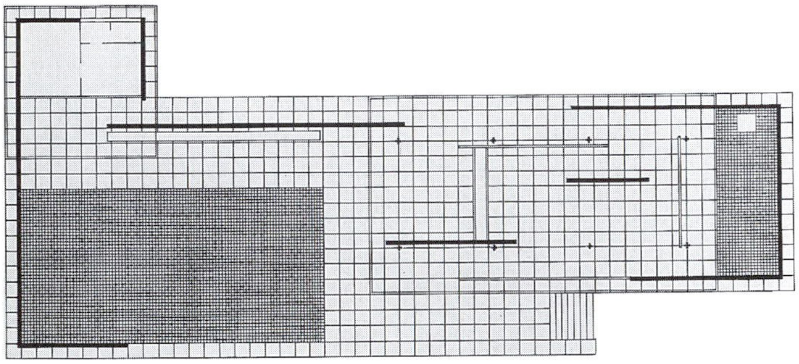

Fig. 478 Ludwig Miës van der Rohe, German Pavilion, International Exposition, Barcelona, Spain, 1929. Final scheme. Plan. Drawing made for publication, 1929.
Ink, pencil on paper, 22 ½ × 38 ½ in.
Collection, Miës van der Rohe Archive, The Museum of Modern Art, New York.
Gift of Ludwig Miës van der Rohe.

For Barr, Miës van der Rohe was the other great innovator of the International Style. His German Pavilion for the 1929 International Exposition in Barcelona (Fig. 477) was considered by Barr to be one of the most important buildings of the day. As the floor plan (Fig. 478) makes clear, Miës wanted most of all to open the space of architecture. The bands of marble walls and sheets of glass held between stainless steel poles extend back from the entry steps under a daringly cantilevered roof. The back wall encloses, but only barely, a large pool, visible in the lower left of the floor plan, that reflects both building and sky. As a result, as the visitor climbs the short set of stairs approaching the pavilion, the entire structure seems to shimmer in light. Built to showcase the German marble industry, the perfectly proportioned and immaculate building shines like a jewel.

Miës's Farnsworth House (Fig. 479), which was built in 1950, likewise opens itself to its surroundings. At once an homage to Le Corbusier's Villa Savoye and a reincarnation of the architect's own German Pavilion, the house is virtually transparent—both opening itself out into the environment and inviting it in.

But the culmination of Le Corbusier's steel and reinforced concrete domino plan is the so-called International Style skyscraper, the most notable of which is the Seagram Building in

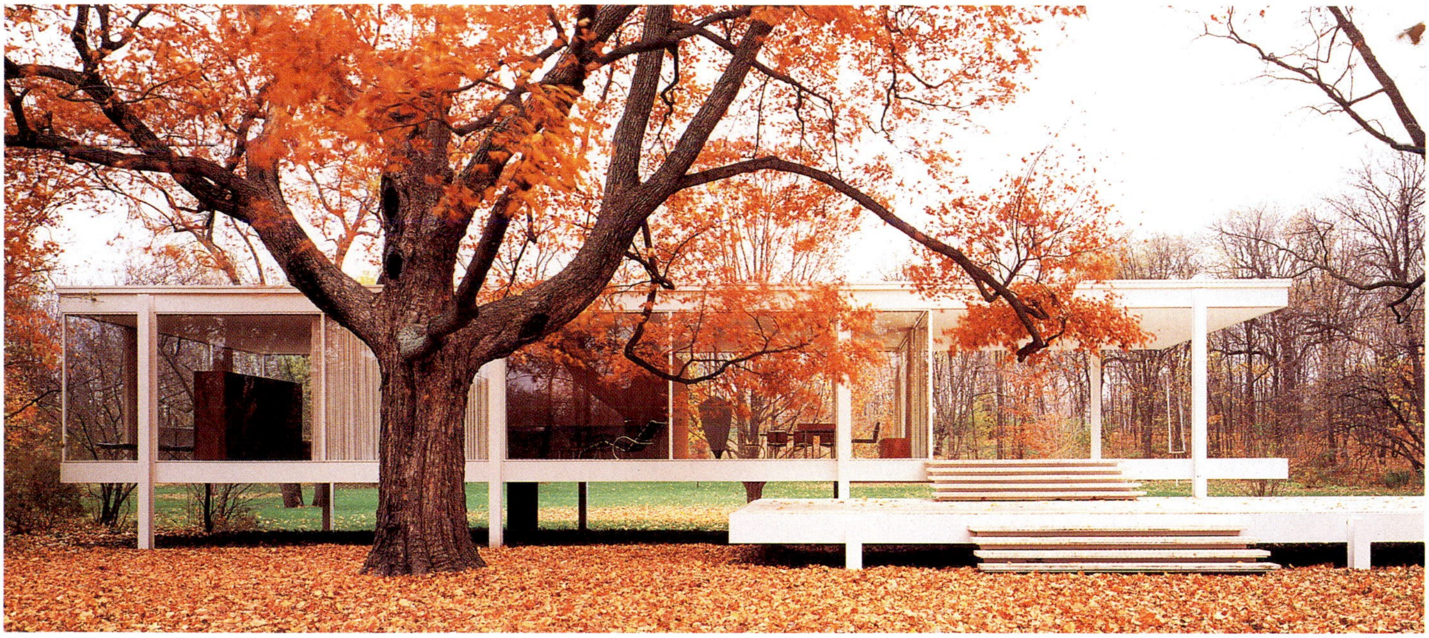

Fig. 479 Ludwig Miës van der Rohe, Farnsworth House, Fox River, Plano, Illinois, 1950.
Photograph by Bill Hedrich, Hedrich-Blessing.

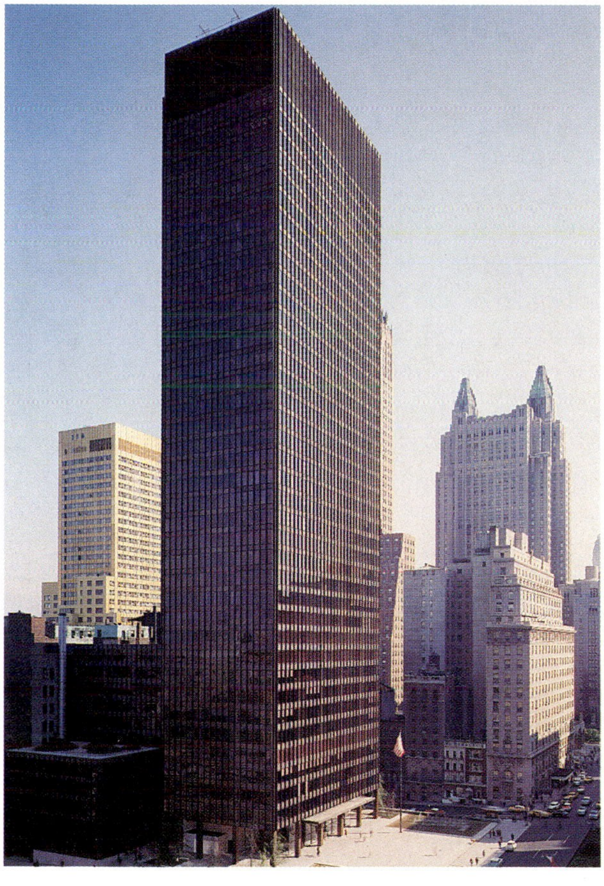

Fig. 480 Miës van der Rohe and Philip Johnson, Seagram Building, New York City, 1958.
Photograph by Ezra Stoller ©Esto. All rights reserved.

New York City (Fig. 480), a collaboration between Miës van der Rohe and Philip Johnson. Johnson is the architect whose design for the College of Architecture at the University of Houston opened this chapter and who, in 1932, had written the foreword to Barr's "Modern Architecture" catalogue. The **International Style** is marked by its austere geometric simplicity, and the design solution presented by the Seagram Building is extremely elegant. The exposed structural *I-beams* (that is, steel beams that seen in cross-section look like the capital letter "I") are finished in bronze to match the amber-tinted glass sheath. At the base, these exterior beams drop, unsheathed, to the courtyard, creating an open-air steel colonnade around a recessed glass lobby. New York law requires that buildings must conform to a "setback" restriction: buildings that at ground level occupy an entire site must stagger-step inward as they rise in order to avoid "walling-in" the city's inhabitants. But the Seagram Building occupies less than one-half its site, and as a result, it is free to rise vertically out of the plaza at its base. At night, the lighted windows activate the building's exterior, and by day, the surface of the opaque glass reflects the changing world around the building.

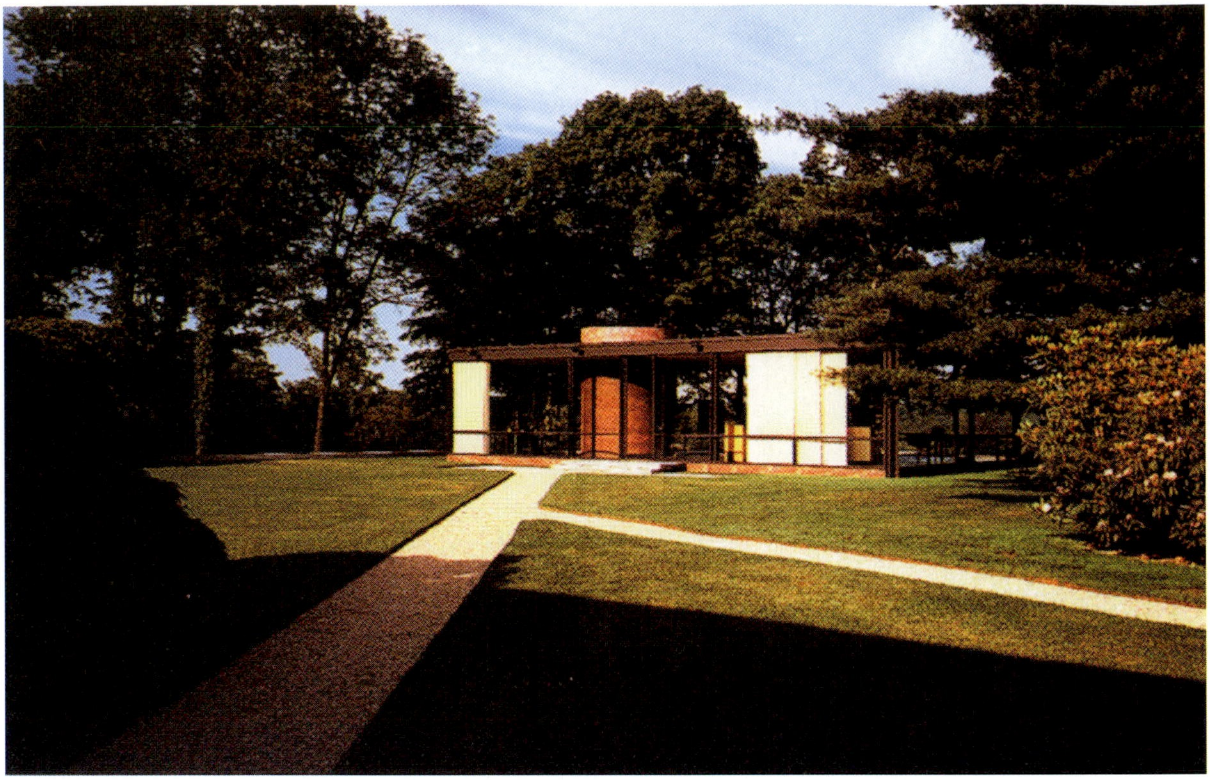

Fig. 481 Philip Johnson, Glass House, New Canaan, Connecticut, 1949.
Photograph by Ezra Stoller © Esto. All rights reserved.

Johnson's collaboration with Miës on the Seagram Buidling indicates his admiration for the older architect, but perhaps his greatest homage to Miës is his own home, built in 1949 in New Canaan, Connecticut (Fig. 481). Johnson's goal, and the goal of the International Style, was to speak a language of beauty so universal that it would, inevitably, appeal to all. The house defines this language as the language of simple primary forms in harmony with their surroundings. The glass block rises directly out of the surrounding space and opens, through its glass walls, into it. Except for the central round brick cylinder containing toilet and bath, the practical side of living in a transparent glass house has been almost entirely ignored. It is a pure aesthetic statement, meant to be considered only as a thing of beauty. In Johnson's own words, "If the business of getting the house to run well takes precedence over your artistic invention the result won't be architecture at all; merely an assemblage of useful parts."

Rejecting the International Style's emphasis on primary geometric forms, the architecture of Eero Saarinen demonstrates how steel and reinforced concrete construction can be utilized in other ways. Probably his two most successful buildings are airline terminals that were completed after his death in 1961. The TWA terminal at Kennedy International Airport in New York (Figs. 482 and 483), designed in 1956, is defined by a contrast between the openness provided by the broad expanses of window and the sculptural mass of the reinforced concrete walls and roof. What results is a constant play of light and shadow throughout the space. The exterior—two huge concrete wings that appear to hover above the runways—is a symbolic rendering of flight. Washington's Dulles International Airport (Fig. 484), designed in 1959, is much larger than the TWA terminal. Concrete piers hold a vast canopy in place so that the roof appears to be a giant wing, soaring in space. The air-traffic control tower, rising behind the terminal like a floating Chinese pagoda, underscores the international character of both the building and the cosmopolitan city it serves.

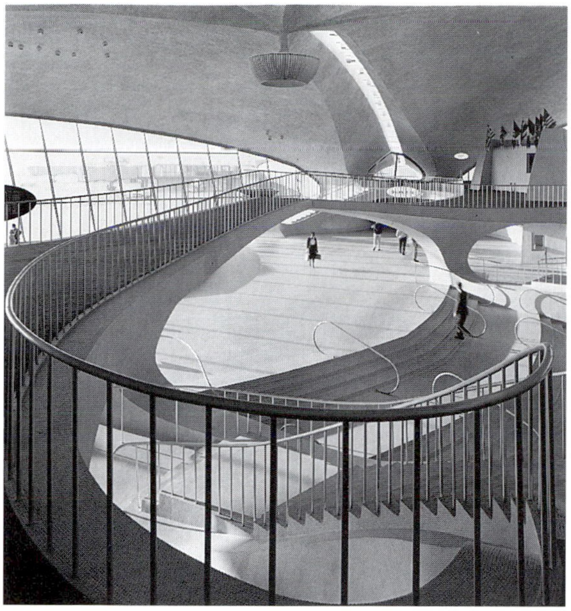

Figs. 482 (left) and 483 (middle) Eero Saarinen, TWA Terminal, Kennedy International Airport, New York, 1962.
Photographs by Ezra Stoller ©Esto.

Fig. 484 (bottom) Eero Saarinen, Dulles International Airport, Chantilly, Virginia, 1962.
Photograph by Ezra Stoller ©Esto.

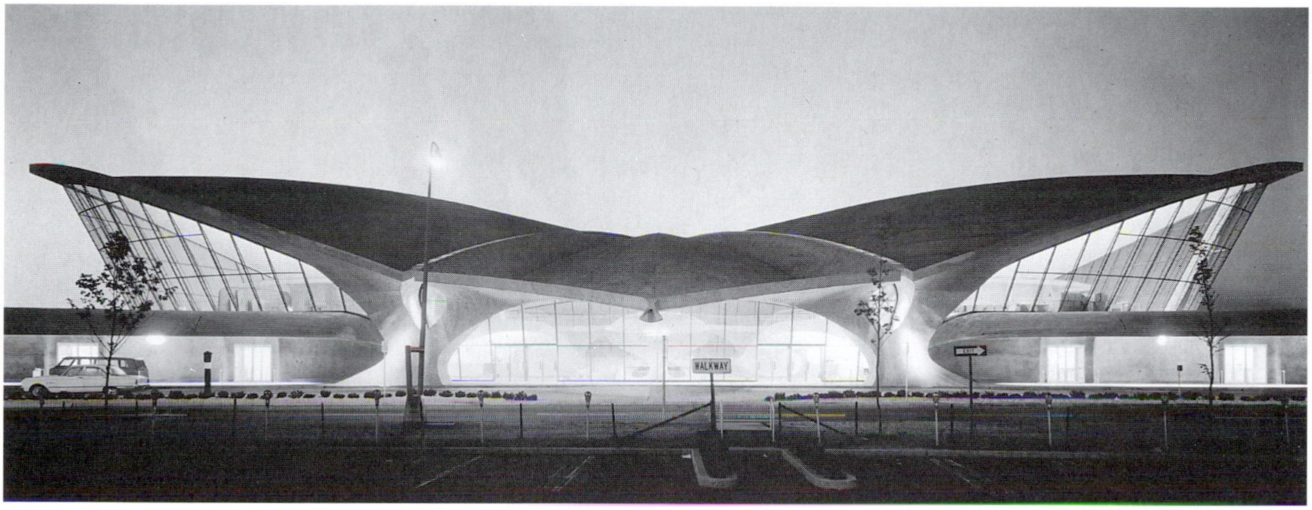

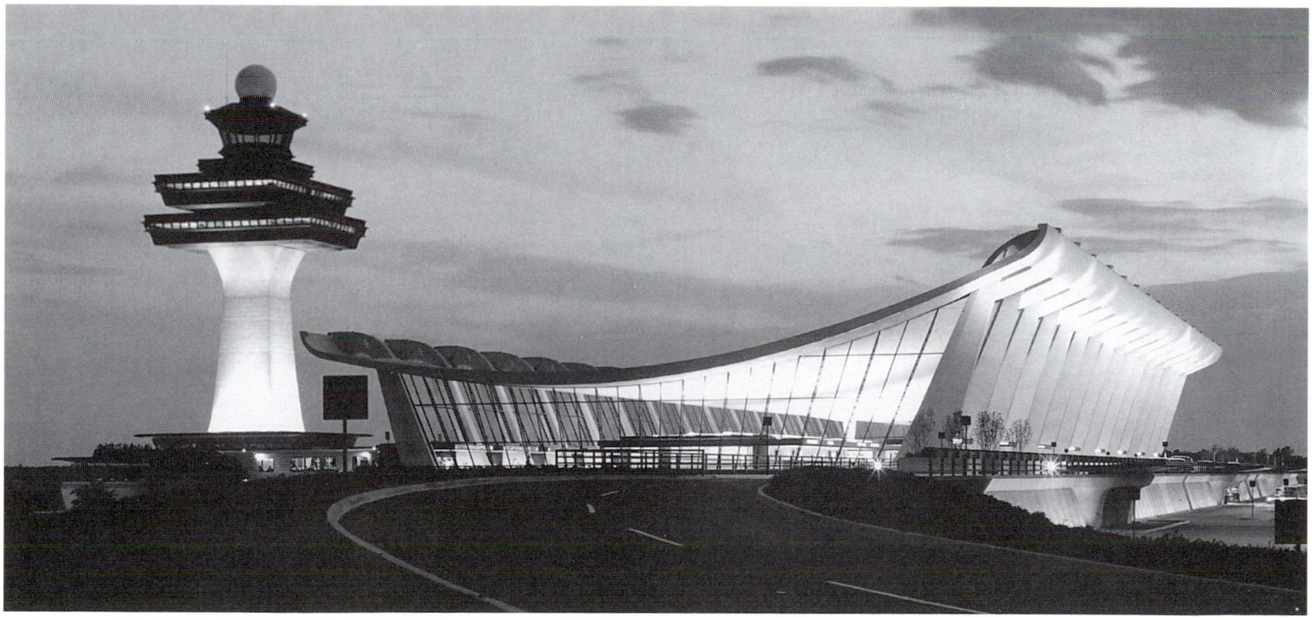

Frank Lloyd Wright's Fallingwater

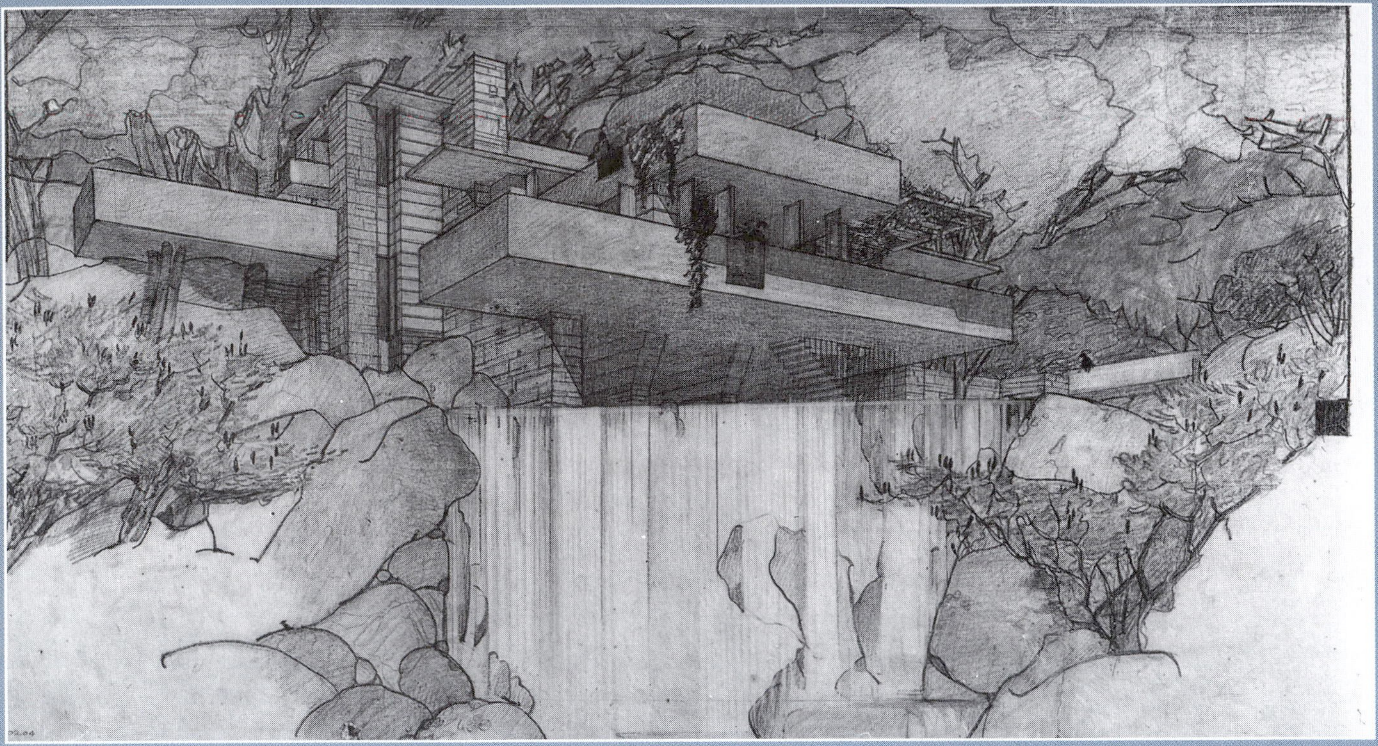

Fig. 485 Frank Lloyd Wright, drawing for "*Fallingwater*," Kaufmann House, Bear Run, Pennsylvania, 1936.
15 3/8 H × 27 1/4 W. The Frank Lloyd Wright Archives. Frank Lloyd Wright drawings are Copyright © 1997 The Frank Lloyd Wright Foundation.

Fallingwater (Fig. 486), Frank Lloyd Wright's name for the house he designed for Edgar and Lillian Kaufmann in 1935, is arguably the most famous modern house in the world. Edgar Kaufmann was owner of Kaufmann's Store in Pittsburgh, the largest ready-made men's clothing store in the country, and his son had begun to study with Wright in 1934. In November of that year, Wright first visited the site. There are no known design drawings until the following September. Writing a few years before about his own design process, Wright stated that the architect should "conceive the building in the imagination, not on paper but in the mind, thoroughly—before touching paper. Let it live there—gradually taking more definite form before committing it to the draughting board. When the thing lives for you, start to plan it with tools. Not before . . . . It is best to cultivate the imagination to construct and complete the building before working on it with T-square and triangle."

The first drawings were done in two hours when Kaufmann made a surprise call to Wright and told him he was in the neighborhood and would like to see something. Using a different colored pencil for each of the house's three floors on the site plan, Wright completed not only a floor plan, but a north-south cross section and a view of the exterior from across the stream (Fig. 485). The drawings were remarkably close to the final house.

Wright thought of the house as entirely consistent with his earlier Prairie houses. It was, like them, wedded to its site, only the site was markedly different. The reinforced concrete cantilevers mirrored the natural cliffs of the hillside down and over which the stream, Bear Run, cascades. By the end of 1935, Wright had opened a quarry on the site to extract local stone for the construction.

Meanwhile, the radical style of the house had made Kaufmann nervous. He hired engineers to review Wright's plan, and they were doubtful that reinforced concrete could sustain the 18-foot cantilevers that Wright proposed. When Kaufmann sent the engineers' reports to Wright, Wright told him to return the plans to him "since he did not deserve the house." Kaufmann apologized for his lack of faith, and work on the house proceeded.

Still, the contractor and engineer didn't trust Wright's plans for reinforcing the concrete for the cantilevers, and before the first slab was poured, they put in nearly twice as much steel as Wright had called for. As a result, the main cantilever droops to this day. Wright was incensed that no one trusted his calculations. After the first slab was set, but still heavily braced with wooden framing (Fig. 487), Wright walked under the house and kicked a number of the wooden braces out.

The house, finally, is in complete harmony with its site. "I came to see a building," Wright wrote in 1936, as the house was nearing completion, "primarily . . . as a broad shelter in the open, related to vista; vista without and vista within. You may see in these various feelings, all taking the same direction, that I was born an American, child of the ground and of space."

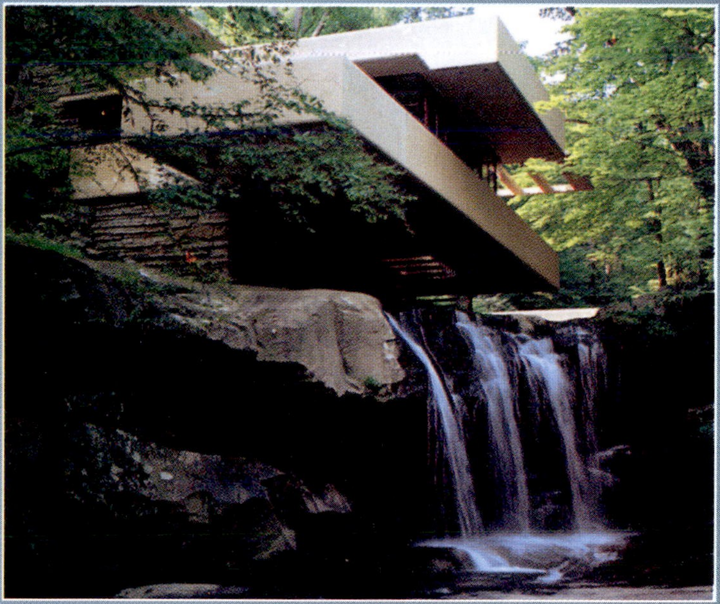

Figs. 486 Frank Lloyd Wright, *Fallingwater*, Kaufmann House, Bear Run, Pennsylvania, 1936.
M.E. Warren/Photo Researchers.

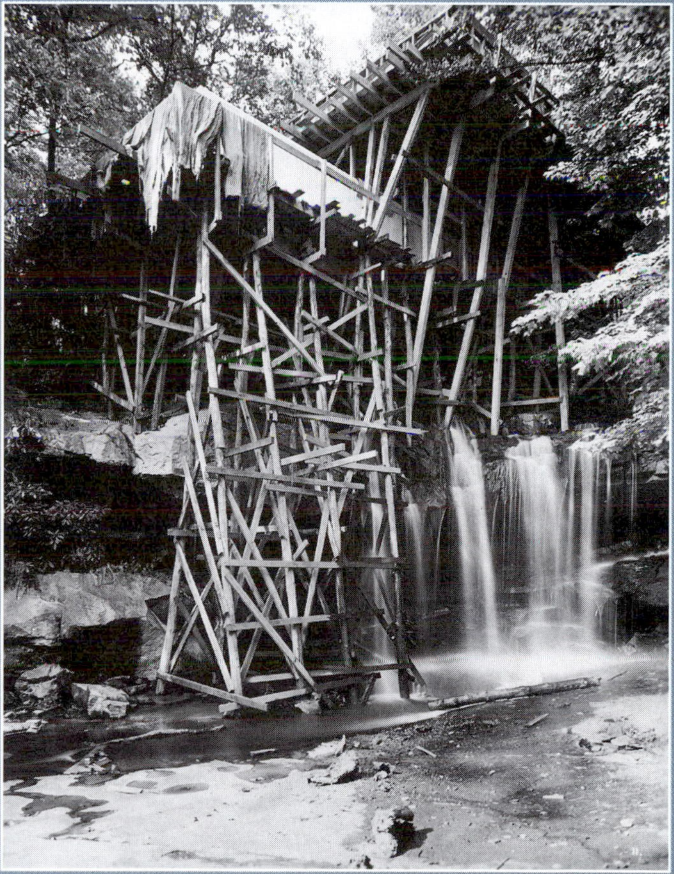

Figs. 487 *"Fallingwater Scaffolding"*, architect: Frank Lloyd Wright.
From the Fallingwater Collection at the Avery Archecturial and Fine Arts Library, Columbia University in the City of, New York.

COMMUNITY LIFE

However lovely we find the Seagram Building, the uniformity of its grid-like facade, in the hands of less skillful architects, came to represent, for many, the impersonality and anonymity of urban life. The skyscraper became, by the 1960s, a symbol of conformity and mediocrity. Moshe Safdie's Habitat (Fig. 488), created for the international trade fair EXPO 67 in Montreal, is an attempt to take the basic architectural unit as conceived by Le Corbusier and to enliven it by stacking the prefabricated units in unpredictable ways. This is architecture as assemblage, the roof of one unit providing a private deck for another. It recognizes the practicality of mass production, and yet its forms are rearranged to create a visually stimulating environment. The driving ambition for Safdie's design is to create a livable urban space, one in which collective life might be able to thrive.

Safdie's plan accepts the crowded conditions of urban life, even as it revises the city's visual vocabulary. So does Hiroyuki Wakabayashi's Children's Museum, in the Unagidani district of Osaka, Japan (Fig. 489). The Children's Museum is actually a tenant building with 22 stores, selling primarily children's clothing and toys. The building is a deliberate attempt on Wakabayashi's part to work against what he calls the "clean, square buildings in regular formation" that dominate urban life all over the world. "Despite some excellent design," he says, "it is becoming increasingly boring."

The Children's Museum was inspired by the architect's childhood in the same district of Osaka. "When I was a child," he explains, "I used to play in Unagidani, especially in the loft of an abandoned house near my home. For some reason that loft remains in my memory. The stairs twisted around, shacks occupied the narrow gaps between the buildings, and it was a complex mess of a place. For children there were many terrific hideouts. Now, as an adult, I need refined spaces, but some part of me still seeks the kind of spaces I played in as a child."

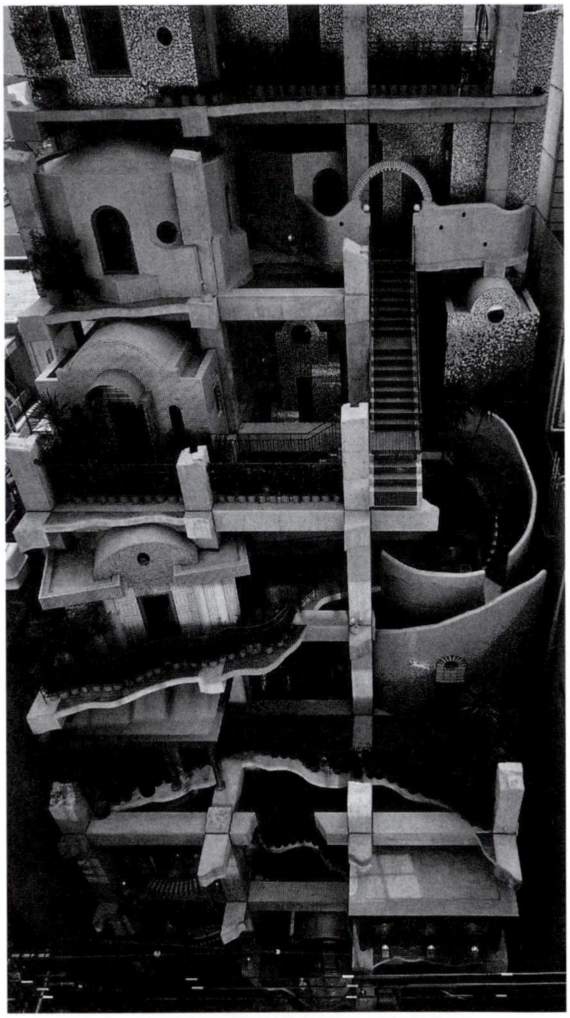

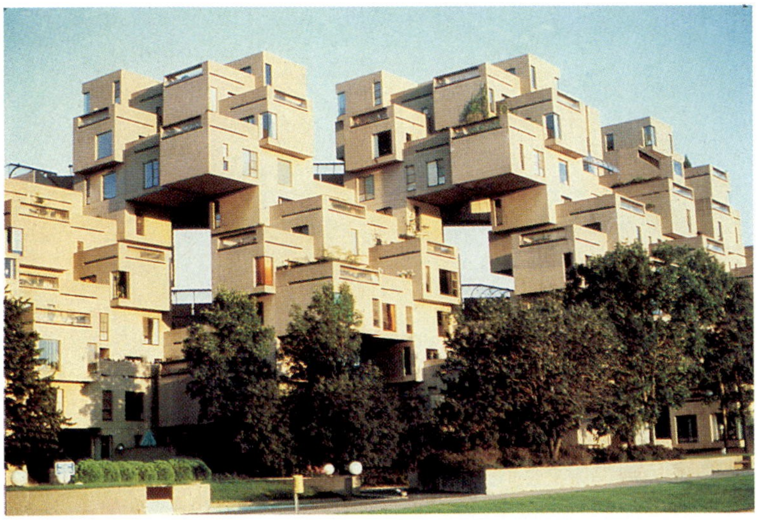

Fig. 488 (left) Moshe Safdie, Habitat, EXPO 67, Montreal, 1967.
Photograph by T. Safdie.

Fig. 489 (above) Hiroyuki Wakabayashi, Children's Museum, Osaka, Japan, 1989.
Emerging Japanese Architects of the 1990s, ed. Jackie Kestenbaum (New York: Columbia University Press.)

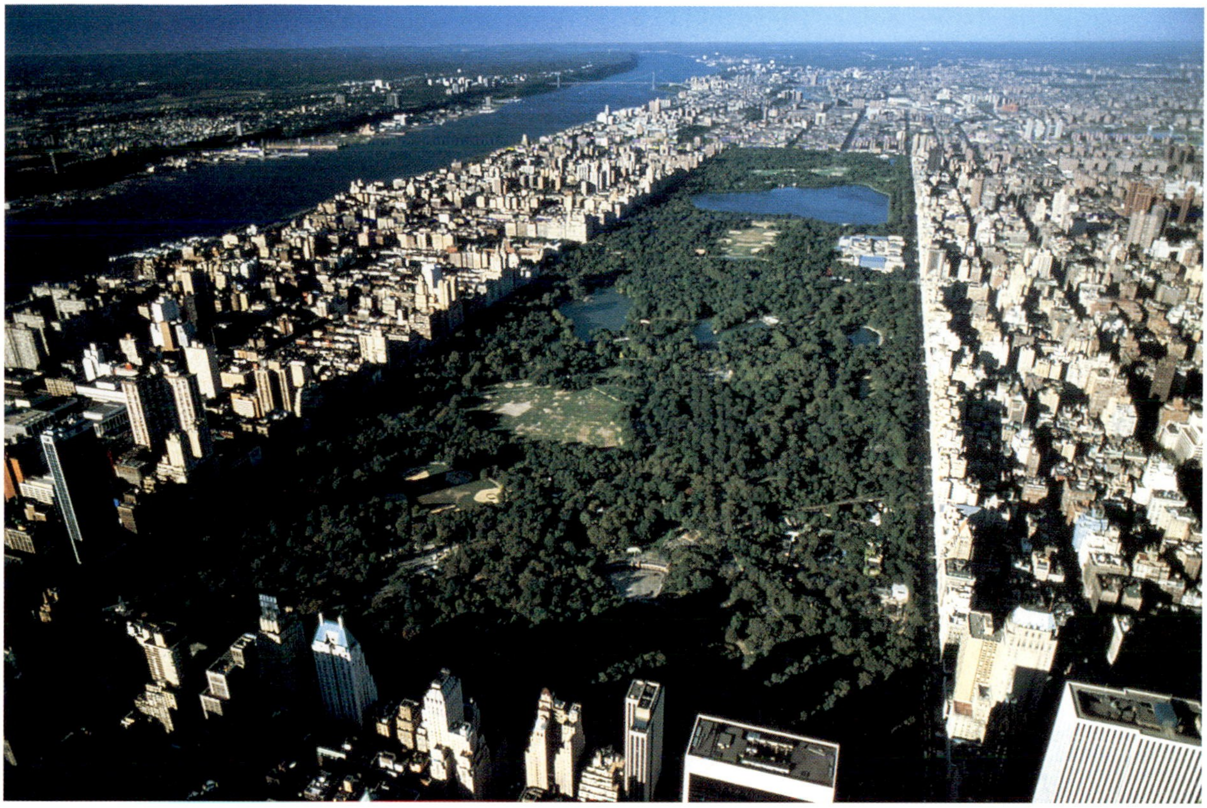

Fig. 490 Frederick Law Olmsted and Calvert Vaux, Central Park, aerial view, New York City, 1857–1887.
Photo by Steve Proehl/Image Bank.

The Children's Museum is actually composed in a rigid grid of posts and beams arranged in 60-square-meter sections. In each section is a scaled-down house, shrine, or temple, connected by a free-floating and unpredictable set of exterior balconies, stairways, and pathways. Almost surrealist in feeling, to Wakabayashi the whole is "like a dream freed from the cares of this world."

Wakabayashi's design reflects a strong sense of nostalgia, a wish to recapture a lost way of life. Since the middle of the nineteenth century, there have been numerous attempts to reestablish the values of lost rural life within the urban context. New York's Central Park (Fig. 490), designed by Frederick Law Olmsted and Calvert Vaux after the city of New York acquired the 840–acre tract of land in 1856, is an attempt to put city-dwelling humans back in touch with their roots in nature. Olmsted developed a system of paths, fields, and wooded areas modeled after the eighteenth-century gardens of English country estates. These estate gardens *appeared* wholly natural, but were in actuality extremely artificial, with man-made lakes, carefully planted forests, landscaped meadows, meandering paths, and fake Greek ruins.

Olmsted favored a park similarly conceived, with, in his words, "gracefully curved lines, generous spaces, and the absence of sharp corners, the idea being to suggest and imply leisure, contemplativeness and happy tranquility." In such places the rational eighteenth-century mind had sought refuge from the trials of daily life. Likewise, in Central Park, Olmsted imagined the city dweller escaping the rush of urban life. "At every center of commerce," he wrote, "more and more business tends to come under each roof, and, in the progress of building, walls are carried higher and higher, and deeper and deeper, so that now 'vertical railways' [that is, elevators] are coming in vogue." For Olmsted both the city itself and neoclassical Greek and Roman architectural features in the English garden offer geometries—emblems of reason and practicality—to which the "gracefully curved" lines of the park and garden stand in counterpoint.

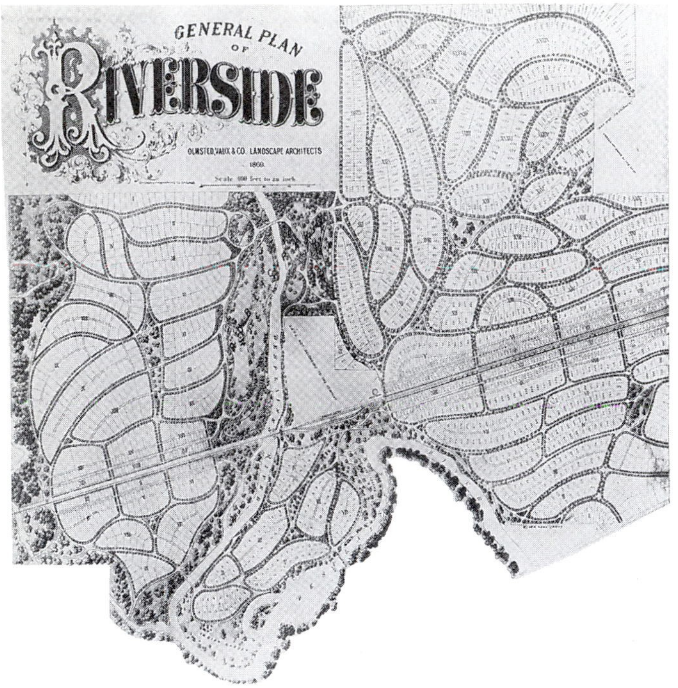

Fig. 491 Olmsted, Vaux & Co., landscape architects, General plan of Riverside, Illinois, 1869.
Frances Loeb Library, Graduate School of Design, Harvard University.

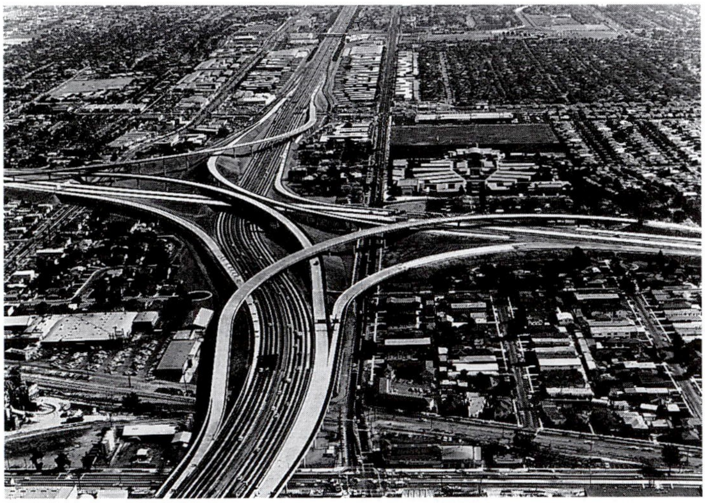

Fig. 492 Los Angeles Freeway Interchange.
Photograph courtesy California Division of Highways, Sacramento.

So successful was Olmsted's plan for Central Park that he was subsequently commissioned to design many other parks, including South Park in Chicago and the parkway system of the City of Boston, Mont Royal in Montreal, and the grounds at Stanford University and the University of California at Berkeley. But he perhaps showed the most foresight in his belief that the growing density of the city demanded the growth of what would later become known as the *suburb,* a residential community lying outside but within commuting distance of the city. "When not engaged in business," Olmsted wrote, "[the worker] has no occasion to be near his working place, but demands arrangements of a wholly different character. Families require to settle in certain localities which minister to their social and other wants, and yet are not willing to accept the conditions of town-life . . . but demand as much of the luxuries of free air, space and abundant vegetation as, without loss of town-privileges, they can be enabled to secure." As early as 1869, Olmsted laid out a general plan for the city of Riverside, Illinois, one of the first suburbs of Chicago (Fig. 491), which was situated along the Des Plaines River. The plan incorporated the railroad as the principle form of transportation into the city. Olmsted strived to create a communal spirit by subdividing the site into small "village" areas linked by drives and walks, all situated near common areas that were intended to have "the character of informal village greens, commons and playgrounds."

Together with Forest Hills in New York, Llewellyn Park in New Jersey, and Lake Forest, also outside Chicago, Olmsted's design for Riverside set the standard for suburban development in America. The pace of that development was steady but slow until the 1920s, when suburbia exploded. During that decade, the suburbs grew twice as fast as the central cities. Beverly Hills in Los Angeles grew by 2,500 percent, and Shaker Heights outside Cleveland by 1,000 percent. The Great Depression and World War II slowed growth temporarily, but by 1950, the suburbs were growing at a rate ten times that of the cities. Between 1950 and 1960, American cities grew by 6 million people or 11.6 percent. In that same decade, suburban population grew by 19 million, a rate of 45.6 percent. And, for the

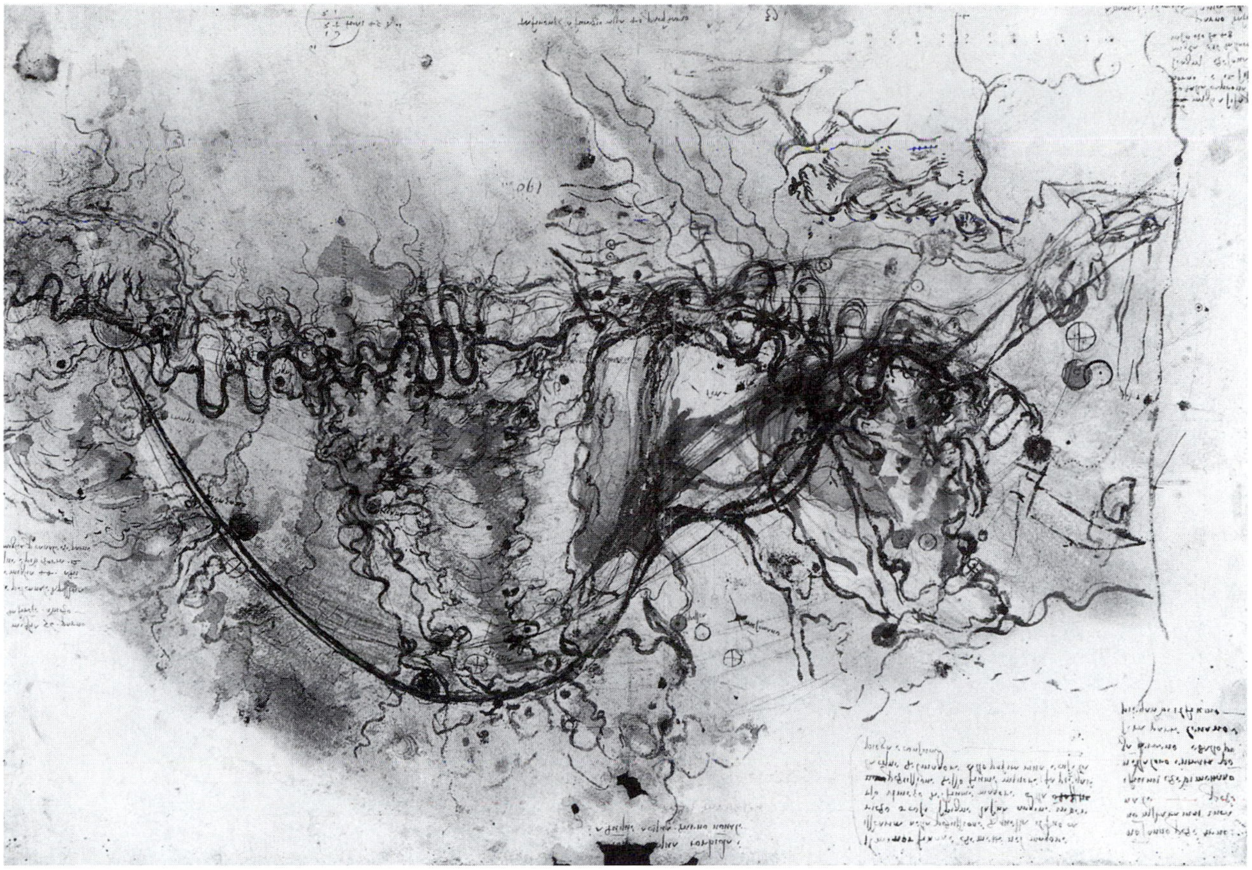

Fig. 493 Leonardo da Vinci, *Map of the River Arno and Proposed Canal,* c. 1503–1504.
Pen and ink over black chalk with washes, pricked for transfer, 13 3/16 × 19 in.

first time, some cities actually began to lose population: the populations of both Boston and St. Louis declined by 13 percent.

There were two great consequences of this suburban emigration: first, the development of the highway system, aided as well by the rise of the automobile as the primary means of transportation, and second, the collapse of the financial base of the urban center itself. As early as 1930, there were 800,000 automobiles in Los Angeles—two for every five people—and the city quite consciously decided not to spend public monies on mass transit but to support instead a giant freeway system (Fig. 492). The freeways essentially overlaid the rectilinear grid of the city's streets with continuous, streamlined ribbons of highway. Similarly, in 1940, the State of Pennsylvania opened a turnpike that ran the length of the state. Public enthusiasm was enormous, and traffic volume far exceeded expectations. That same year, the first stretches of the Pasadena Freeway opened. Today it is estimated that roads and parking spaces for cars occupy between 60 and 70 percent of the total land area of Los Angeles.

However, not only automobiles but also money—the wealth of the middle-class—drove down these highways, out of the core city and into the burgeoning suburbs. The cities were faced with discouraging and destructive urban decline. Most discouraging of all was the demise of the **infrastructure,** the systems that deliver services to people—water supply and waste removal, energy, transportation, and communications. The infrastructure is what determines the quality of city life. Artists such as Leonardo da Vinci have always been concerned with the quality of life, and, as a result, with the infrastructure. His plan for a canal on the Arno River (Fig. 493), which anticipates the route followed by the modern *autostrada,* or freeway, would have given the city of Florence access to the sea. If we think about many of the works of art we have studied in this

Mierle Ukeles's Fresh Kills Landfill Project

Maintenance is the subject of Mierle Ukeles's art. In 1969, responding to the discontinuity she felt between her work as an artist and the demands of family life, Ukeles wrote a "Manifesto for Maintenance Art," a work that has informed virtually all of her work since. "I am an artist. I am a woman," she wrote. "I am a wife. I am a mother. (Random order). I do a hell of a lot of washing, cleaning, cooking, renewing, supporting, preserving, etc. Also (up to now separately) I 'do' Art. Now I will simply do these maintenance things, and flush them up to consciousness, exhibit them, as Art."

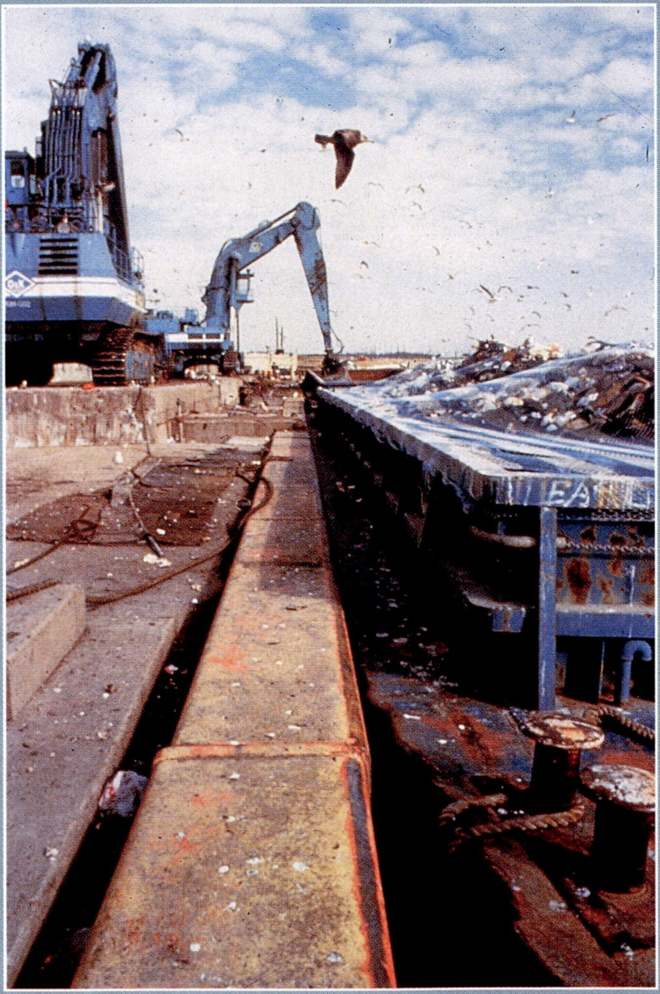

Fig. 494 "Fresh Kills Landfill, daily operation". Courtesy Ronald Feldman Fine Arts, Inc., New York. Photo Credit: Mierle Laderman Ukeles.

In the first place, Ukeles wanted to challege the notion of "women's work." In her 1973 piece *Wash,* she scrubbed the sidewalk, on her hands and knees, with a bucket of soap and water, in front of A. I. R. Gallery in New York. Very soon, she found herself verbally attacking people who walked on areas she had just cleaned, and her obsession with cleanliness revealed itself to be a form of tyranny. Furthermore, the possibility of ever adequately maintaining the city street was undercut by the very fact that it was public space. Community life and maintenance seemed to be at odds.

The city, she realized, was the ideal site for investigating the idea of maintenance. Maintenance of the city's infrastructure is an invisible process that is absolutely vital, and bringing the invisible to light is one of the artist's primary roles. For her *I Make Maintenance Art One Hour Every Day,* a 1976 project for a branch of the Whitney Museum of American Art located in New York's Chemical Bank Building, Ukeles asked the 300-person maintenance staff in the building, all of whom work invisibly at night, to designate one hour of their normal activities on the job as art and to document each night what they had done during that hour.

Soon after, Ukeles became the unsalaried artist-in-residence for the New York City Department of Sanitation. In New York, the collection and transportation of waste occurs 24 hours a day, every day of the year but

Christmas. One of her first pieces at the Department was a performance project in which, over a period of five years, she shook the hand of each of the Department's 8,500 employees.

Her most ambitious project for the Department is the redesign of the Fresh Kills Landfill on Staten Island (Figs. 494 and 495), an ongoing work with no end in sight. Landfills, she points out, are the city's largest remaining open spaces, and the Fresh Kills Landfill is the largest in the United States. She wants to transform it, to recapture it as public space, to reshape it. Just as Leonardo proposed to channel the Arno (Fig. 493), Ukeles proposes to reshape the land with Leonardo's same sort of fascination and reverence for the creative forces of nature.

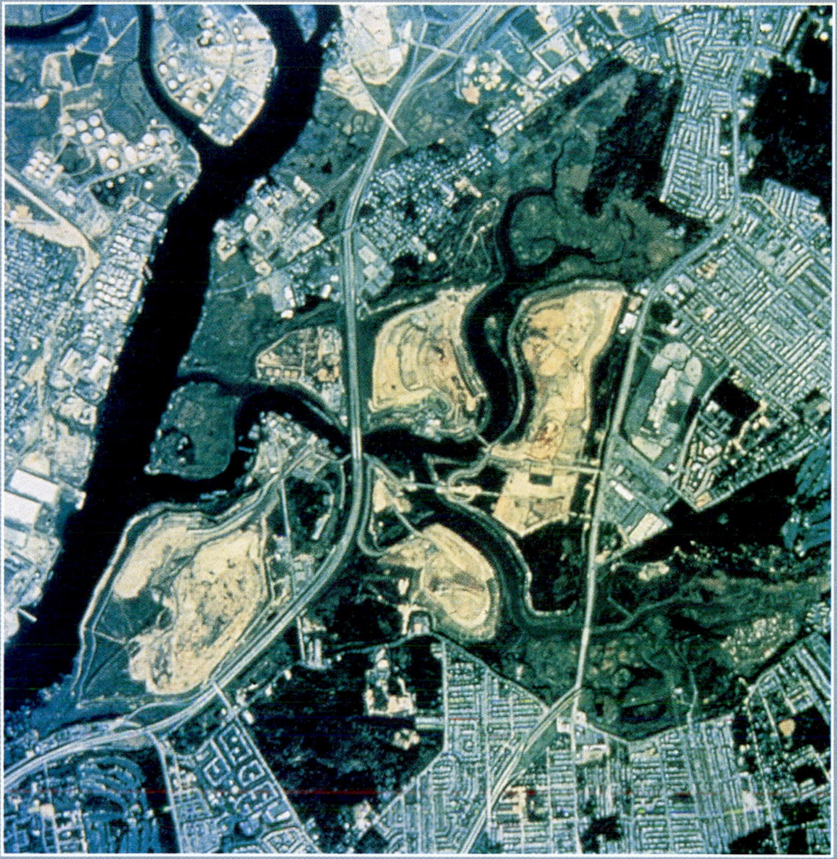

Fig. 495 "Fresh Kills Landfill, aerial view".
Courtesy Ronald Feldman Fine Arts, Inc., New York. Photo Credit: Mierle Laderman Ukeles.

Her project is based on the premise that there are four images of earth that have yielded four traditions of creation. In each, the earth is imaged as female. Earth as mother nourishes us and sustains us. Earth as virgin is, she says, "forever fresh, producing in us an attitude of reverence and devotion." Earth as wife is "enticingly wild and equally kempt . . . thoroughly domesticated because adequately Husbanded." For her, the perfect image of earth as wife is the artificial wilderness of Olmsted's Central Park. Finally there is the earth as whore, free and bountiful and endlessly available. This last image of earth is quickly becoming exhausted, as the planet's natural resources are increasingly diminished. To treat the earth as whore is to pretend that "one has no responsibility for one's actions." In Ukeles's plan, Fresh Kills Landfill will become public space, divided into three parts that mirror the first three images of earth. The fourth image will be banished.

Fresh Kills is a natural estuary, and Ukeles wishes to raise questions on the site, not only about waste disposal but about rivers and their role as fragile circulatory systems that continually cleanse our environment, nature's version of New York's sanitation workers. "Just think," Ukeles muses, "I could create a work that would make it possible for people to see what's really going on."

chapter, we can recognize that they were initially conceived as part of the infrastructure of their communities. For example, the Pont du Gard (Fig. 445) is a water supply aqueduct. The Paris Metro and the suspension bridges made possible by steel eased the difficulty of transportation in their communities. Public buildings such as temples, churches, and cathedrals provide places for people to congregate. Even skyscrapers are integral parts of the urban infrastructure, providing centralized places for people to work. As the infrastructure collapses, businesses close down, industries relocate, the built environment deteriorates rapidly, and even social upheaval can follow. To this day, downtown Detroit has never recovered from the 1967 riots and the subsequent loss of jobs in the auto industry in the mid-1970s. Block after block of buildings that once housed thriving businesses lie decayed and unused.

As early as the 1950s Boston and Baltimore began working to revitalize the core areas of their cities. At first, both tried to develop the downtowns by attracting office and corporate headquarters to the areas. Led by the Baltimore developer James Rouse, both cities turned their attention to redesigning their port areas (Fig. 496). Rouse restored old warehouse and market buildings to create multiple-use environments of boutiques, restaurants and bars, hotels, upscale residential areas, and major tourist attractions, such as aquariums and tall-masted schooners.

Baltimore's Inner Harbor and Boston's Quincy Market and Boston Waterfront projects were huge undertakings—the Baltimore project covers 250 acres and cost $260 million—but marked economic benefits were almost immediately realized. The idea was to create an essentially theatrical space in the heart of the city, a downtown area of spectacle

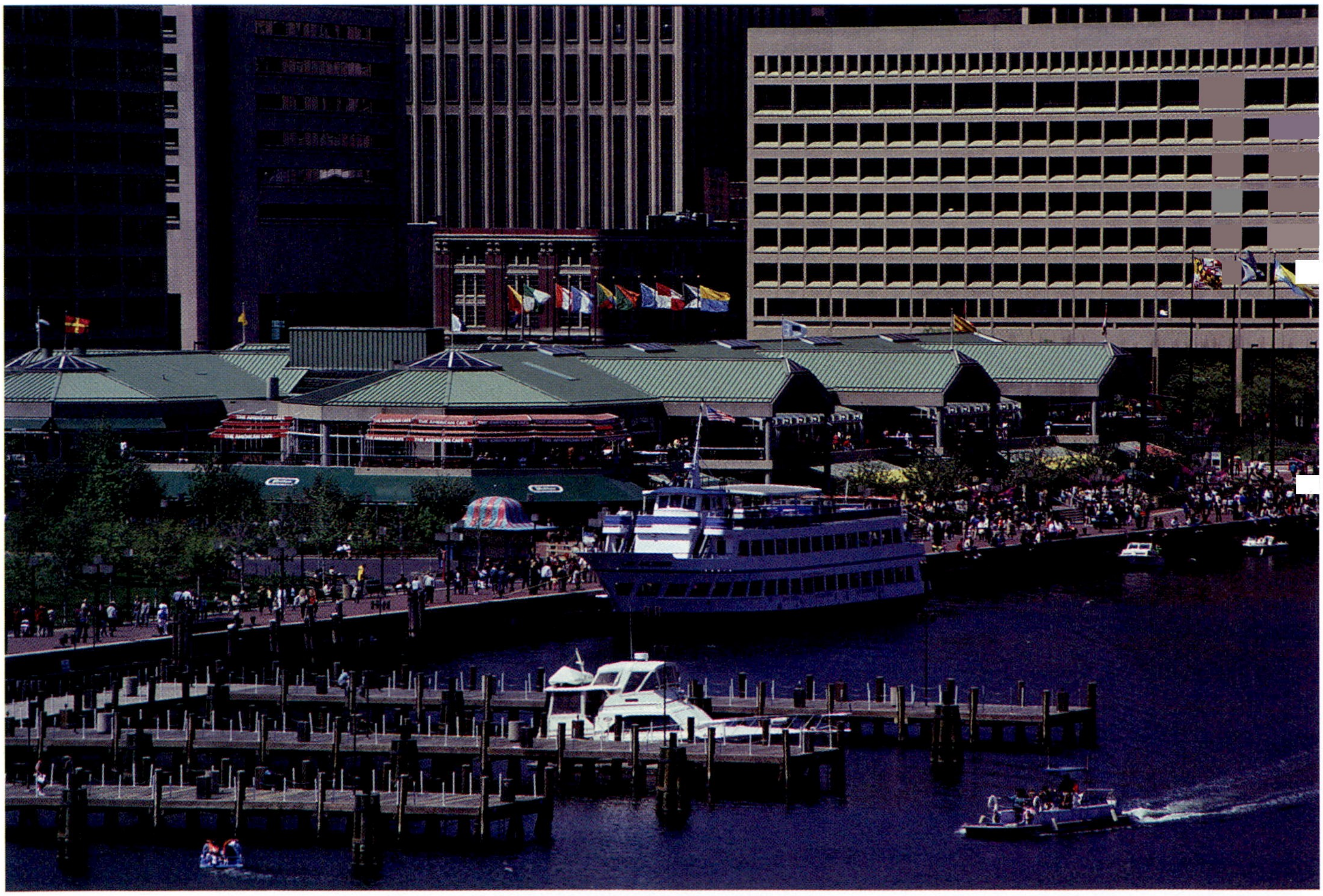

Fig. 496 Baltimore, Inner Harbor.
Gary Cralle/Image Bank.

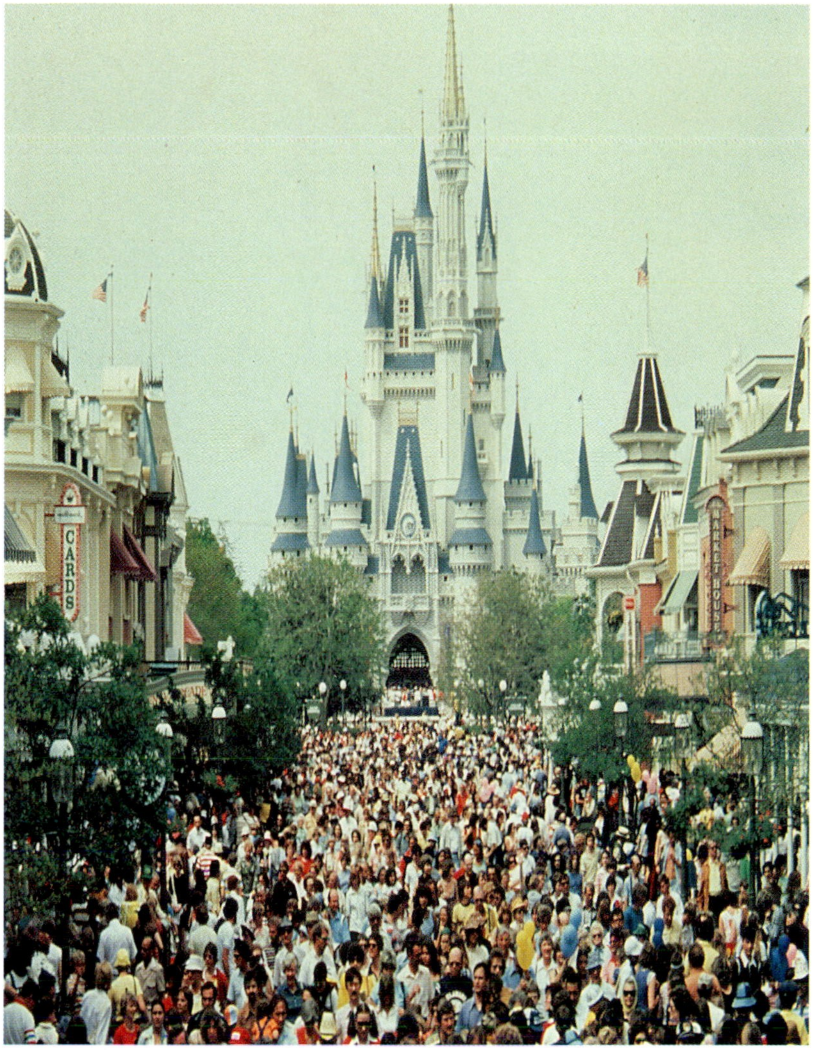

Fig. 497 Walt Disney World, Florida.
© The Walt Disney Company.

and glamour that would attract not only suburbanites (and their dollars) back into the city on a weekly or monthly basis but tourists as well. The downtown is thus reconceived not as a business center but as an entertainment complex. Today, Baltimore's Inner Harbor attracts over 22 million visitors a year, of whom 7 million are tourists, roughly comparable to the number who visit Walt Disney World in Florida. It is, in fact, Walt Disney World, with its Main Street, U.S.A. (Fig. 497), that provides the model for the new inner city—an arena of wholesome family entertainment, notably free of crime and drugs, thronging with happy people having a good time and spending money. Walt Disney World may be an imaginary kingdom, but it functions in the contemporary imagination like a continuous World's Fair, a Tomorrowland projection of how we would like the real world to appear.

Architecture is a design process, in many ways the ultimate design process, the process that determines what Main Street, U.S.A., looks like. The architect incoporates all other design—the products that surround us—into livable space. Architects are in charge of what could be called the art of everyday living. Their decisions determine how aesthetically pleasing our living space can be. But the architect depends on another group of designers, the men and women who design the products that fill our space. We turn our attention now to the work of these individuals, the people who mediate between art and industry, who make sure that the products we use both look good and function well.

CHAPTER 15

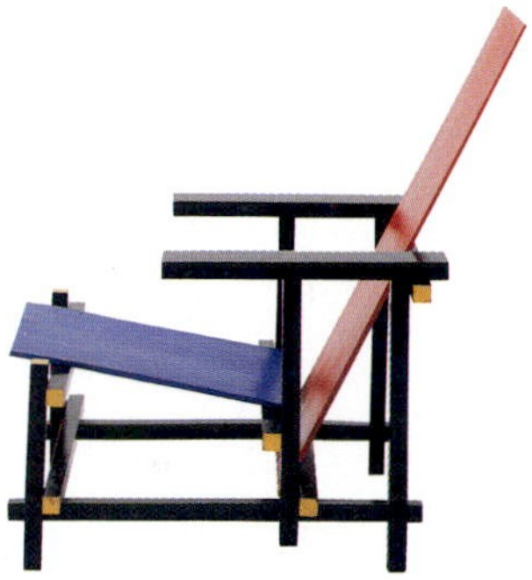

Design

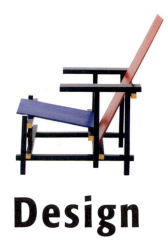

During the 1920s in the United States, many people who had once described themselves as involved in the graphic arts, the industrial arts, the craft arts, or the arts allied to architecture—even architects themselves—began to be referred to as *designers*. They were seen as serving industry. They could take any object or product—a shoe, a chair, a book, a poster, an automobile, or a building—and make it appealing, and thereby persuade the public to buy it or a client to build it. In fact, design is so intimately tied to industry that its origins as a profession can be traced back only to the beginnings of the industrial age.

DESIGN, CRAFT, AND FINE ART

On May 1, 1759, in Staffordshire, England, a 28-year-old man by the name of Josiah Wedgwood opened his own pottery manufacturing plant. With extraordinary foresight, Wedgwood chose to make two very different kinds of pottery; one he called "ornamental ware" (Fig. 498), the other "useful ware" (Fig. 499). The first were elegant handmade luxury items, the work of highly skilled craftsmen. The second were described in his catalogue as "a species of earthenware for the table, quite new in appearance . . . manufactured with ease and expedition, and consequently cheap." This new earthenware was made by machine. Until this moment, almost everything people used was handmade, and thus unique. With the advent of machine mass-manufacturing, the look of the world changed forever.

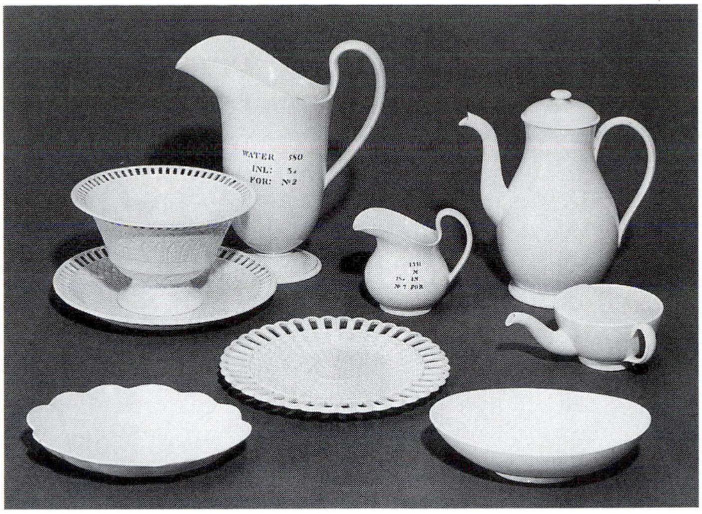

Fig. 499 Wedgwood Queen's Ware kitchen ware, c. 1850
The Wedgwood Museum, Barlaston, England.

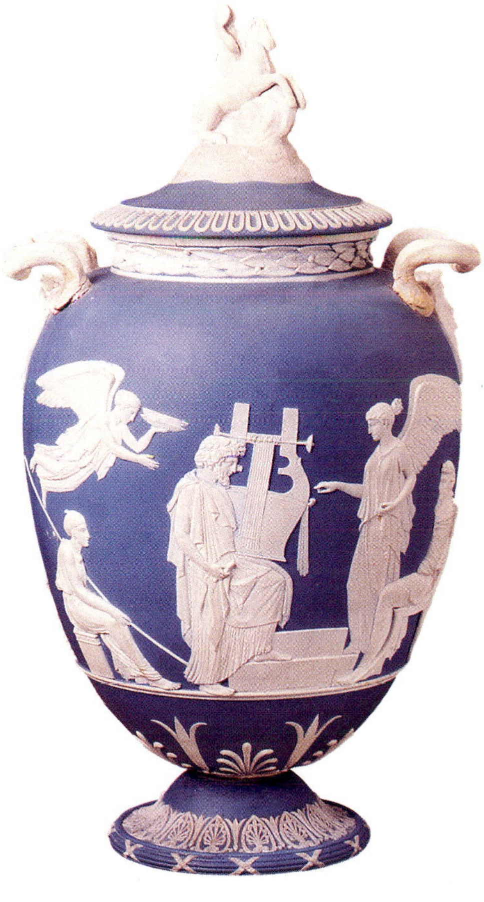

Fig. 498 Josiah Wedgwood, *Apotheosis of Homer Vase,* 1786.
Blue Jasper ware, H. 18 in. The Wedgwood Museum, Barlaston, England.

Wedgwood's business illustrates very clearly how the art of design has been differentiated from, on the one hand, the traditional **crafts** and, on the other, the so-called *fine arts,* like painting or sculpture. As we said in Chapter 12, when we speak of crafts, we are generally referring to *handmade* objects created by highly skilled artisans to serve useful functions. Designers are different from craftspeople in that they often have nothing to do with the actual making of the object, which is produced by mechanical means. A craft object is one-of-a-kind, and in order for it to sell only one person needs to like it. But designers create objects that are multiples. Their job is to make objects attractive to as large a public as possible. They must, as a result, appeal to the whims of fashion.

In these terms, craftspeople and fine artists have more in common with one another than either do with designers. They both equally share a hands-on relation to the objects they make. Wedgwood's ornamental ware, upon which he himself often worked, is more craft than is his useful ware, which was mechanically produced. In fact, Wedgwood's ornamental ware is aesthetic in its intention and was meant to be received as an object of fine art. But his useful ware was meant to be used daily, on the

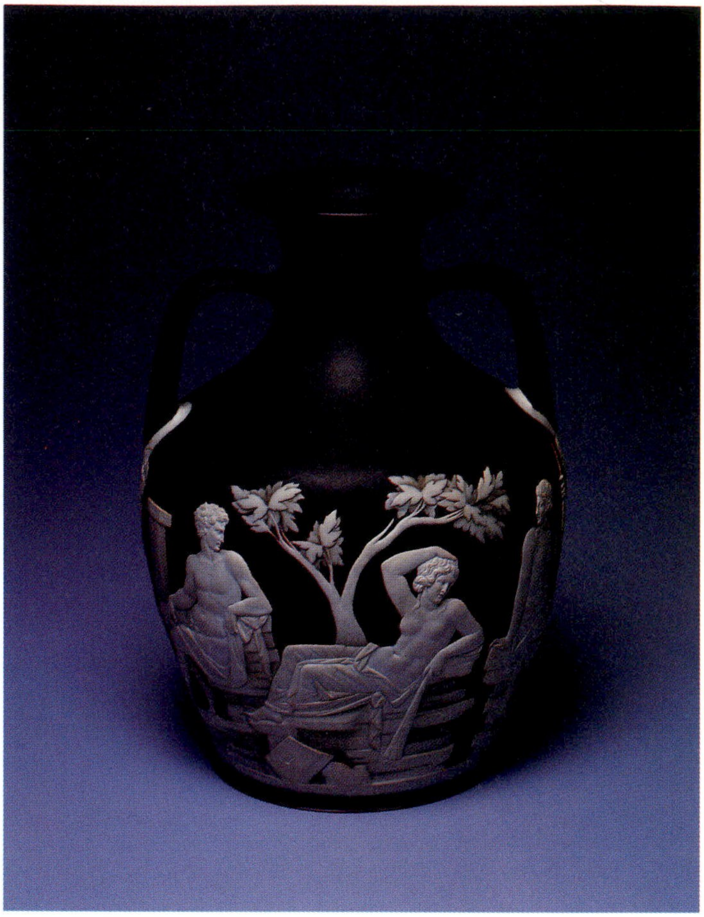

Fig. 500 Josiah Wedgwood, copy of *Portland Vase,* c. 1790.
Black Jasper ware, H. 10 in. The Wedgwood Museum, Barlaston, England.

table. Another way of putting this is to say that the word "ornamental" serves, in Wedgwood's usage, to remove the object from the ordinary, to separate it from the "useful," to lend it the status of art.

Though the Wedgwood factory has continued to produce various kinds of ornamental ware, Wedgwood's copy of the Portland Vase (Fig. 500) was his crowning achievement. The original, made around 25 BCE in Rome, is a cameo deep blue (virtually black) glass vase that the Dowager Duchess of Portland purchased in 1784 for her private museum. The duchess died within a year of her purchase, and her entire estate was auctioned off, but the vase stayed in the family when the third Duke of Portland bought it in June 1786. It was subsequently lent to Wedgwood so that he might copy it, and he contracted to sell a number of these copies to a group of "gentlemen" subscribers.

It took Wedgwood four years to reproduce the vase successfully. He was able to match the deep blue-black of the original, but the ornamental ware for which he is best known is generally of a much lighter blue, as pictured on the previous page. Some fifty numbered and unnumbered first edition copies of the Portland vase survive, and the factory has continued to produce editions over the years, most recently in 1980 for the 250th anniversary of Josiah's birth.

But Wedgwood's success as a manufacturer did not depend on such "ornamental" wares of refined taste and elegance. Rather it was his "useful" ware that supported his business. His cream-colored earthenware (dubbed Queen's Ware because the English royal family quickly became interested in it), was made by casting liquid clay in molds instead of by throwing individual pieces and shaping them by hand. Designs were chosen from a pattern book (Fig. 501) and printed by mechanical means directly on the pottery. Since Wedgwood could mass-produce his earthenware both quickly and efficiently, a reliable, quality tableware was made available to the middle-class markets of Europe and America.

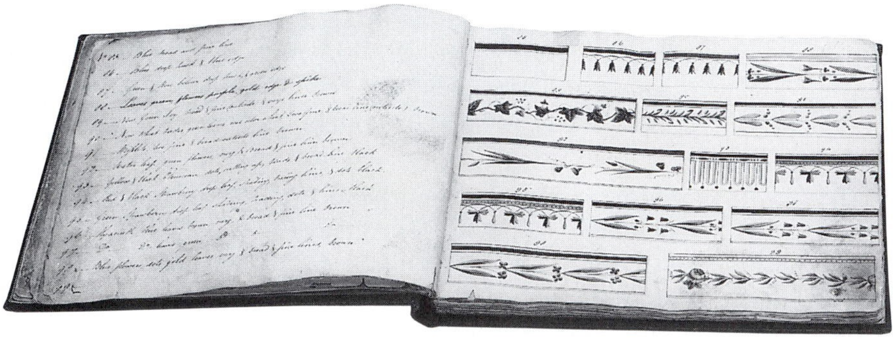

Fig. 501 First Wedgwood pattern book with border designs for Queen's Ware, 1774–1814.
The Wedgwood Museum, Barlaston, England.

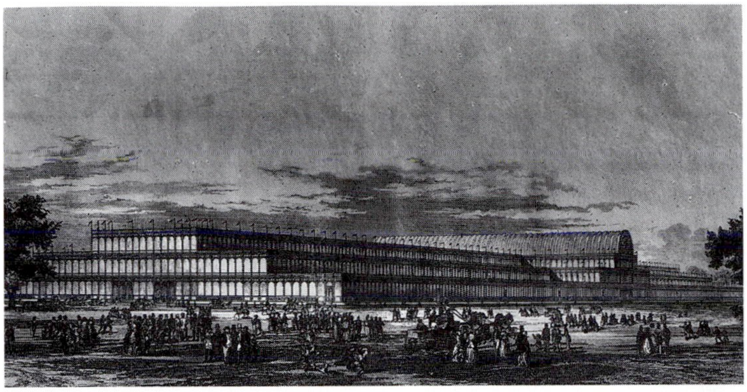

Fig. 502 (left) Joseph Paxton, Crystal Palace, Great Exposition, London, 1851. 1,848 ft. long, 408 ft. wide. Marburg/Art Resources.

Fig. 503 (below) Philip Webb, The Red House, Bexley Heath, 1859. Photograph courtesy of the National Monuments Record, Great Britain.

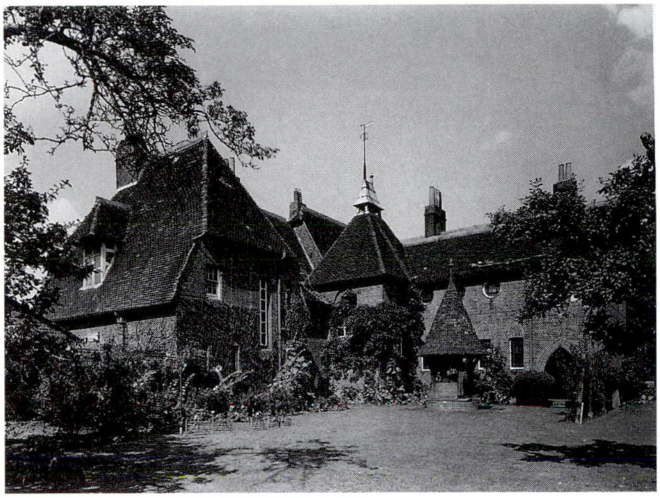

THE ARTS AND CRAFTS MOVEMENT

During the first half of the nineteenth century, as mass production became more and more the norm in England, the quality and aesthetic value of mass-produced goods declined. In order to expose England to the sorry state of modern design in the country, Henry Cole, a British civil servant who was himself a designer, organized the Great Exposition of 1851. The industrial production on exhibit demonstrated, once and for all, just how bad the situation was. Almost everyone agreed with the assessment of Owen Jones: "We have no principles, no unity; the architect, the upholsterer, the weaver, the calico-painter, and the potter, run each their independent course; each struggles fruitlessly, each produces in art novelty without beauty, or beauty without intelligence."

The building that housed the exhibition in Hyde Park was an altogether different proposition. A totally new type of building, which became known as the Crystal Palace (Fig. 502), it was designed by Joseph Paxton, who had once served as gardener to the Duke of Devonshire and had no formal training as an architect. Constructed of over 900,000 square feet of glass set in prefabricated wood and cast iron, it was three stories tall and measured 1,848 by 408 feet. It required only nine months to build, and it hailed in a new age in construction. As one architect wrote at the time, "From such beginnings what glories may be in reserve. . . . We may trust ourselves to dream, but we dare not predict."

Not everyone agreed. A. W. N. Pugin, who had collaborated on the new Gothic-style Houses of Parliament, called the Crystal Palace a "glass monster," and the essayist and reformer John Ruskin, who likewise had championed a return to a preindustrial Gothic style in his book *The Stones of Venice,* called it a "cucumber frame." Under their influence, William Morris, a poet, artist, and ardent socialist, dedicated himself to the renewal of English design through the renewal of medieval craft traditions. In his own words: "At this time, the revival of Gothic architecture was making great progress in England. . . . I threw myself into these movements with all my heart; got a friend [Philip Webb] to build me a house very medieval in spirit . . . and set myself to decorating it." Built of traditional red brick, the house was called the Red House (Fig. 503), and nothing could be further in style from the Crystal Palace. Where the latter reveals itself to be the product of manufacture—engineered out of prefabricated, factory-made parts and assembled, with minimal cost by unspecialized workers, in a matter of a few months—the former is a purposefully rural, even archaic building that rejects the industrial spirit of Paxton's Palace. It signaled, Morris hoped, a return to craft traditions in which workers were intimately tied to the design and manufacture of their products from start to finish.

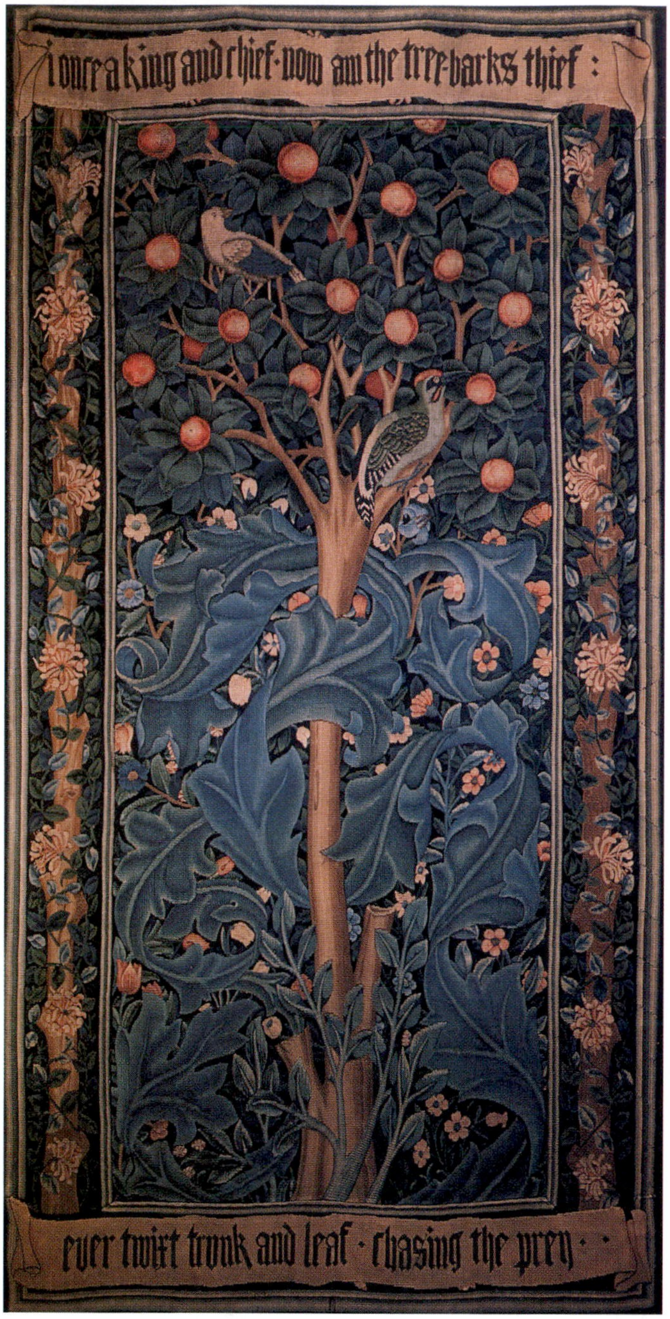

Fig. 504 Morris and Company, *The Woodpecker,* 1885.
Wool tapestry designed by Morris. William Morris Gallery, Walthamstow, England.

Morris longed to return to a handmade craft tradition for two related reasons. He felt that the mass manufacturing process alienated men from their labor, and he also missed the quality of handmade items. Industrial laborers had no stake in what they made, and thus no pride in their work. The result, he felt, was both shoddy workmanship and unhappy workers.

As a result of the experience of building the Red House and attempting to furnish it with objects of a medieval, handcrafted nature, a project that was frustrated at every turn, Morris decided to take matters into his own hands. In 1861 he founded the firm that would become Morris and Company. It was dedicated "to undertake any species of decoration, mural or otherwise, from pictures, properly so-called, down to the consideration of the smallest work susceptible of art beauty." To this end, the company was soon producing stained glass, painted tiles, furniture, embroidery, table glass, metalwork, chintzes, wallpaper, woven hangings, tapestries, and carpets.

In his designs, Morris constantly emphasized two principles, simplicity and utility. However, it is difficult, at first glance, to see "simplicity" in work such as *The Woodpecker* (Fig. 504). For Morris, however, the natural and organic were by definition simple. Thus the pattern possesses, in Morris's words, a "logical sequence of form, this *growth* looks as if it could not have been otherwise." Anything, according to Morris, "is beautiful if it is in accord with nature." "I must have," he said, "unmistakable suggestions of gardens and fields, and strange trees, boughs, and tendrils."

Morris's desire for simplicity—"simplicity of life," as he put it, "begetting simplicity of taste"—soon led him to create what he called "workaday furniture," the best examples of which are the company's line of Sussex rush-seated chairs (Fig. 505). Such furniture was meant to be "simple to the last degree" and to appeal to the common man. As Wedgwood had done 100 years earlier, Morris quickly came to distinguish this "workaday" furniture from his more costly "state furniture," for which, he wrote, "we need not spare ornament . . . but [may] make them as elaborate and elegant as we can with carving or inlaying or paintings; these are the blossoms of the art of furniture." A sofa designed by Morris's friend, the painter Dante Gabriel Rossetti, and displayed by Morris and Company at the International Exhibition of 1862 (Fig. 506), is the "state" version of the Sussex settee. Covered in rich, dark green velvet, each of the three panels in the back contains three personifications of Love, hand-painted by Rossetti. As Morris's colleague Walter Crane put it: "The great advantage . . . of the Morrisian method is that it leads itself to either simplicity or splendor. You might be almost plain enough to please Thoreau, with a rush bottomed chair, piece of matting, and oaken trestle-table; or you might have gold and luster gleaming from the sideboard, and jeweled light in your windows, and walls hung with rich arras tapestry."

By the 1870s, embroidered wall hangings were among the most popular items produced by Morris and Company. At first, Morris's wife, Jane, headed a large group of women, some of whom worked for the company full-time and others who worked more occasionally. In 1885, his daughter May, then 23 years old, took over management of the embroidery section.

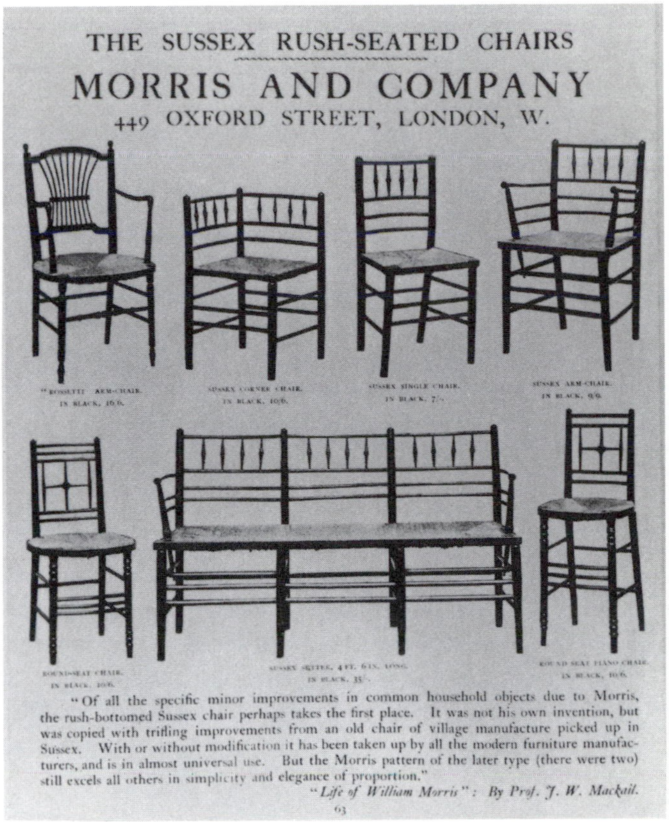
THE SUSSEX RUSH-SEATED CHAIRS

MORRIS AND COMPANY

449 OXFORD STREET, LONDON, W.

"Of all the specific minor improvements in common household objects due to Morris, the rush-bottomed Sussex chair perhaps takes the first place. It was not his own invention, but was copied with trifling improvements from an old chair of village manufacture picked up in Sussex. With or without modification it has been taken up by all the modern furniture manufacturers, and is in almost universal use. But the Morris pattern of the later type (there were two) still excels all others in simplicity and elegance of proportion."

"*Life of William Morris*": *By Prof. J. W. Mackail.*

63

Fig. 505 Morris and Company, Sussex rush-seated chairs.
Fitzwilliam Museum. University of Cambridge.

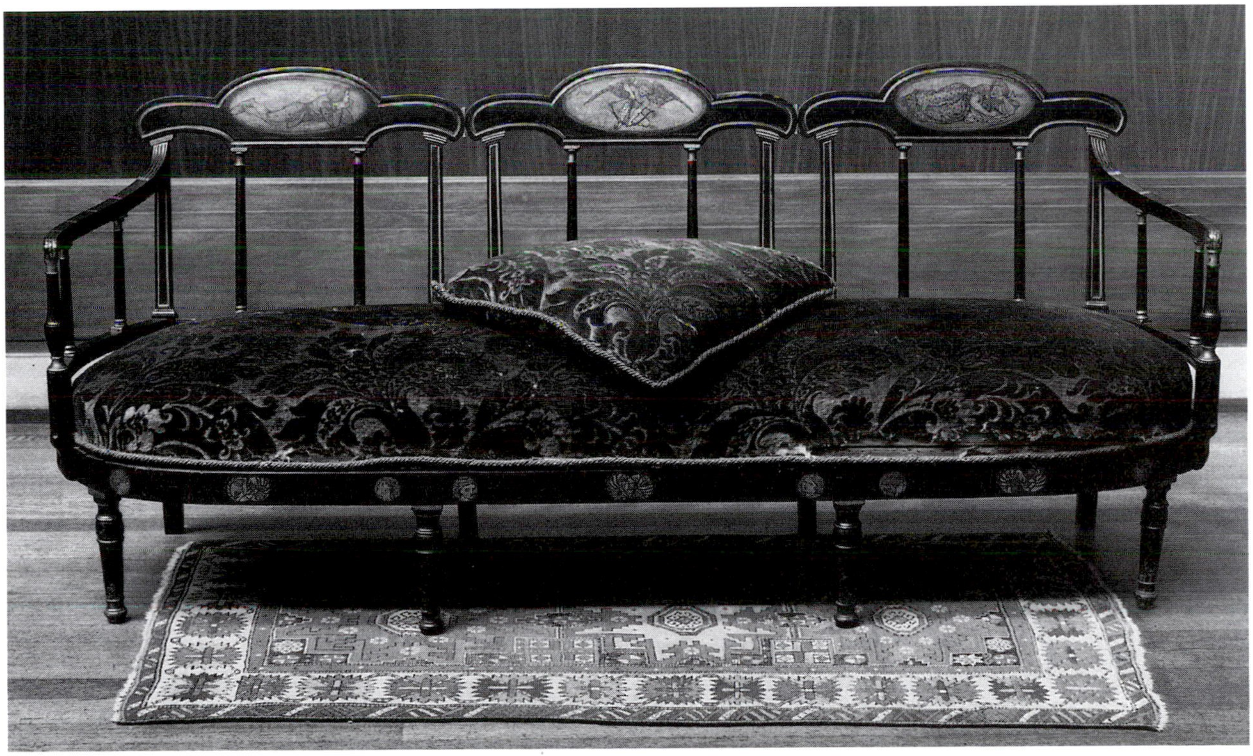

Fig. 506 Dante Gabriel Rossetti, sofa, 1862.
Wood, upholstered in velvet, W. 74 7/8 in. Fitzwilliam Museum, University of Cambridge.

For a quarter of a century, until about 1910, May Morris trained many women in the art of embroidery at her Hammersmith Terrace workshops, and many designs attributed to her father after 1885 are actually her own (apparently, she thought it important, at least from a commercial point of view, to give her father the credit).

The bed-hangings below were designed by her in 1916 for a lady's bedroom, "in which elaboration and luxury have been purposefully avoided" (Fig. 507). Shown at the Arts and Crafts Exhibition in London in the same year, the embroidery work was done by May Morris, the teacher Mary Newill, and Newill's students at the Birmingham School of Art. The fact that most of the women who worked for Morris and Company were relegated to the embroidery division demonstrates the rigidity of sex roles in English society at the turn of the century. Nevertheless, May Morris, a successful businesswoman, author, and lecturer, was an important role model for the women of her day. In 1907, she helped to found the Women's Guild of Art, the purpose of which was to provide a "centre and a bond for the women who were doing decorative work and all the various crafts."

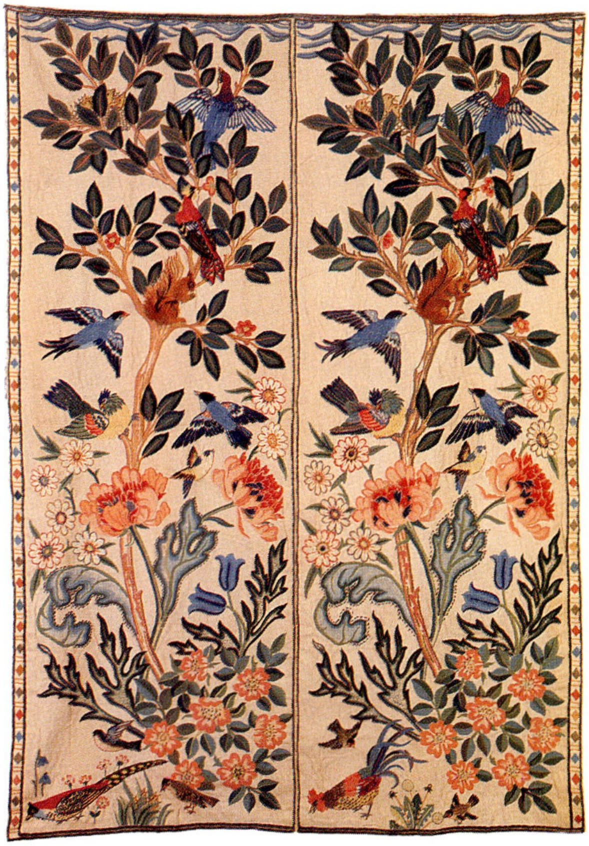

Fig. 507 May Morris, bed-hangings, 1916.
Wool crewel on linen, lined, 76 3/4 × 54 in.
Collection of Cranbrook Academy of Art Museum, Gift of George G. Booth.
Photograph by R. H. Hensleigh.

William Morris claimed that his chief purpose as a designer was to elevate the circumstances of the common man. "Every man's house will be fair and decent," he wrote, "all the works of man that we live amongst will be in harmony with nature . . . and every man will have his share of the *best.*" But common people were in no position to afford the elegant creations of Morris and Co. Unlike Wedgwood, whose common, "useful" ware made the most money for the firm, it was the more expensive productions—the state furniture, tapestries, and embroideries—that kept Morris and Co. financially afloat. Inevitably, Morris was forced to confront the inescapable conclusion that to handcraft an object made it prohibitively expensive. With resignation and probably no small regret, he came to accept the necessity of mass manufacture.

In the United States, Gustav Stickley's magazine *The Craftsman,* first published in 1901 in Syracuse, New York, was the most important supporter of the Arts and Crafts tradition. The magazine's self-proclaimed mission was "to promote and to extend the principles established by [William] Morris," and its first issue was dedicated exclusively to Morris. Likewise, the inaugural issue of *House Beautiful,* published in Chicago in 1896, included articles on Morris and the English Arts and Crafts movement. Stickley, recognizing the expense of Morris's handcrafted furniture and the philosophical dilemma that Morris faced in continuing to make it, accepted the necessity of machine manufacturing his own work. Massive in appearance, lacking ornamentation, its aesthetic appeal depended, instead, on the beauty of its wood, usually oak (Fig. 508).

By the turn of the century, architect Frank Lloyd Wright was also deeply involved in furniture design. Like Morris before him, Wright felt compelled to design furniture for the interiors of his Prairie Houses that matched the design of the building as a whole (Fig. 509). Though geometric, his designs were rooted in nature (see Figs. 472 and 473). "It is quite impossible," Wright wrote, "to consider the

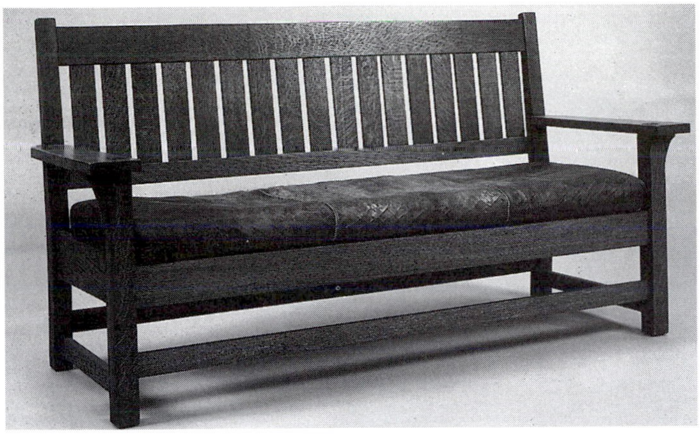

Fig. 508 Gustav Stickley, settee (for the Craftsman Workshops), 1909.
Oak and leather, back 38 × 71 7/16 × 22 in.; seat 19 × 62 in.
Gift of Mr. and Mrs. John J. Evans, Jr.,
© 1993 The Art Institute of Chicago, all rights reserved.

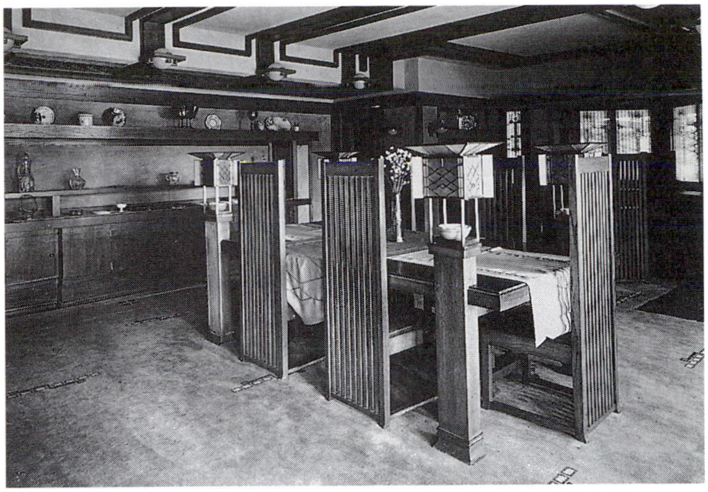

Fig. 509 Frank Lloyd Wright, Robie House, dining room with original furniture designed by Wright, 1909.
The Domino's Center for Architecture & Design.
Courtesy The Frank Lloyd Wright Archives, Scottsdale, AZ.

building as one thing, its furnishings another and its setting and environment still another. The Spirit in which these buildings are conceived sees these all together at work as one thing." The table lamp designed for the Lawrence Dana House in Springfield, Illinois (Fig. 510) is meant to reflect the dominant decorative feature of the house—a geometric rendering of the sumac plant that is found abundantly in the neighboring Illinois countryside, chosen because the site of the house itself was particularly lacking in vegetation. Given a very large budget, Wright designed 450 glass panels and 200 light fixtures for the house that are variations on the basic sumac theme. Each piece is unique and individually crafted.

Between them, the furniture designs of Morris, Stickley, and Wright point out the basic issues that design would face in the twentieth century. The first dilemma, to which we have been paying particular attention, was whether the product should be handcrafted or mass-manufactured. But formal issues have arisen as well. If we compare Wright's designs to Morris's, we can see that both use line completely differently. Even though both find the source of their forms in nature, Wright's forms are rectilinear and geometric, Morris's curvilinear and organic. Both believed in "simplicity," but the word meant two different things to the two men. Morris, as we have seen, equated simplicity with the natural. Wright, on the other hand, designed furniture for his houses because, he said, "simple things . . . were nowhere at hand. A piece of wood without a moulding was an anomaly, plain fabrics were nowhere to be found in stock." To Wright, simplicity meant plainness. The history of design continually confronts the choice between the geometric and the organic. The major design movement at the turn of the century, Art Nouveau, chose the latter.

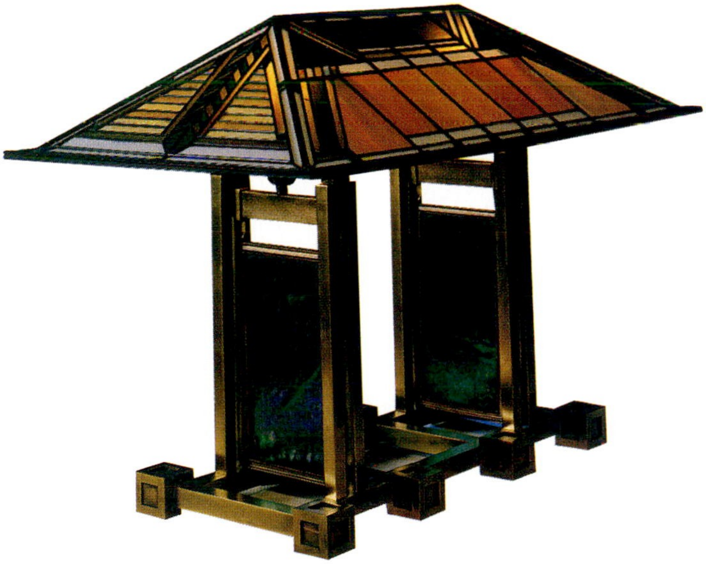

Fig. 510 Frank Lloyd Wright, table lamp, Susan Lawrence Dana House, Springfield, Illinois, 1903.
Bronze, leaded glass. Courtesy The Frank Lloyd Wright Archives, Scottsdale, AZ.

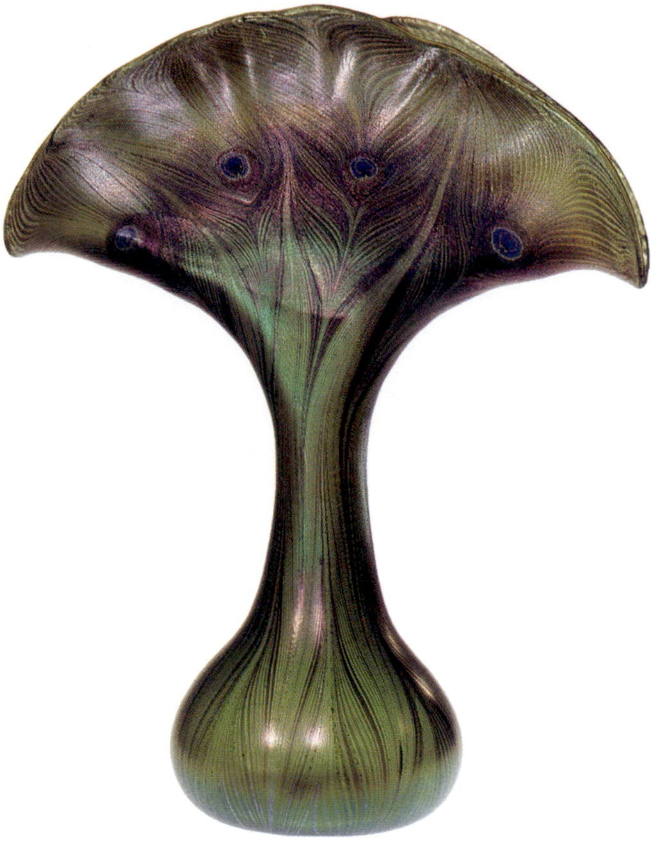

Fig. 512 **Louis Comfort Tiffany, *Peacock Vase*, c. 1910.**
Iridescent "favrile" glass, H. 14 1/8 in.; W. 11 1/2 in. The Metropolitan Museum of Art, New York. Gift of H. O. Havemeyer, 1896. 96.17.10.

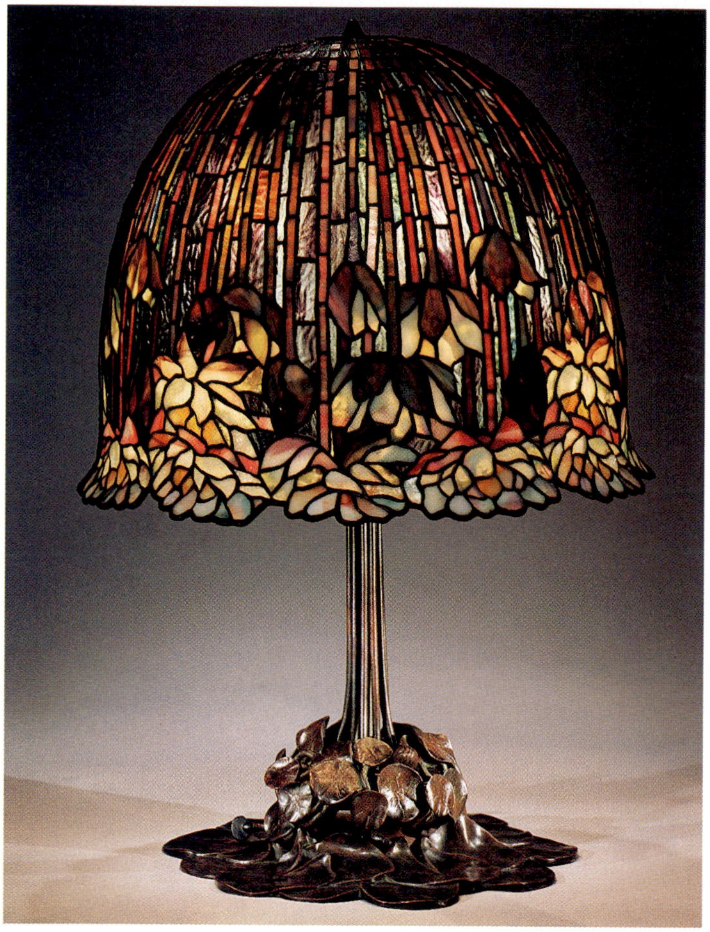

Fig. 511 **Louis Comfort Tiffany, lamp with leaded glass shade and bronze base, c. 1910.**
H. 26 1/2 in.; D. 18 1/2 in.
The Metropolitan Museum of Art, New York. Gift of Hugh J. Grant, 1974. 1974.214.15.

ART NOUVEAU

The day after Christmas in 1895, a shop opened in Paris named the Galeries de l'Art Nouveau. It was operated by one S. Bing, whose first name was Siegfried, though art history has almost universally referred to him as Samuel, perpetuating a mistake made in his obituary in 1905. Bing's new gallery was a success, and in 1900, at the Universal Exposition in Paris, he opened his own pavilion, Art Nouveau Bing. By the time the Exposition ended, the name **Art Nouveau** had come to designate not merely the work he displayed but a decorative arts movement of international dimension.

Bing had visited the United States in 1894. The result was a short book entitled *Artistic Culture in America*, in which he praised American architecture, painting, and sculpture, but most of all its arts and crafts. The American who fascinated him most was the glassmaker Louis Comfort Tiffany, son of the founder of the famous New York jewelry firm, Tiffany and Co. The younger Tiffany's work inspired Bing to create his new design movement, and Bing contracted with the American to produce a series of stained glass windows designed by such French artists as Henri de Toulouse-Lautrec and Pierre Bonnard. Since oil lamps were at that very moment being replaced by electric lights—Thomas Edison had startled the French public with his demonstration of electricity at the 1889 International Exhibition—Bing placed considerable emphasis on new, modern modes of lighting. From his point of view, a new light and a new art went hand in hand. And Tiffany's stained-glass lamps (Fig. 511), backlit by electric light, brought a completely new sense of vibrant color to interior space.

Even more than his stained glass, Bing admired Tiffany's iridescent Favrile glassware, which was named after the obsolete English word for handmade, "fabrile." The distinctive feature of this type of glassware is that nothing of the design is painted, etched, or burned into the surface. Instead, every detail is built up by the craftsperson out of what Tiffany liked to call "genuine glass." In the vase illustrated here (Fig. 512), we can see many of the design characteristics most often associated with Art Nouveau, from the wavelike line of the peacock feathers to the self-conscious asymmetry of the whole. In fact, the formal vocabulary of Art Nouveau could be said to consist of young saplings and shoots, willow trees, buds, vines—anything organic and undulating, including snakes and, especially, women's hair. The Dutch artist Jan Toorop's advertising poster for a peanut-based salad oil (Fig. 513) flattens the long, spiraling hair of the two women preparing salad into a pattern very like the elaborate wrought-iron grillwork also characteristic of Art Nouveau design. Writing about Bing's installation at the the 1900 Universal Exposition, one writer described Art Nouveau's use of line this way: "[In] the encounter of the two lines . . . the ornamenting art is born—an indescribable curving and whirling ornament, which laces and winds itself with almost convulsie energy across the surface of the [design]!"

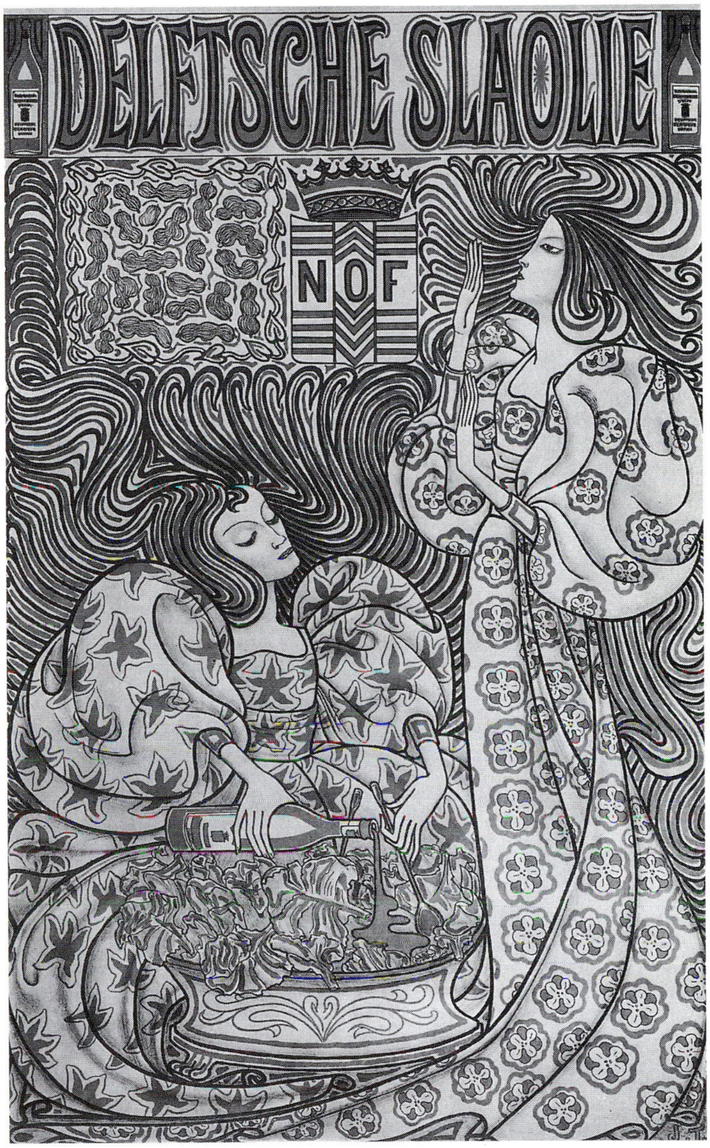

Fig. 513 Jan Toorop, poster for *Delftsche Slaolie* (Salad Oil), 1894.
Library of Congress.

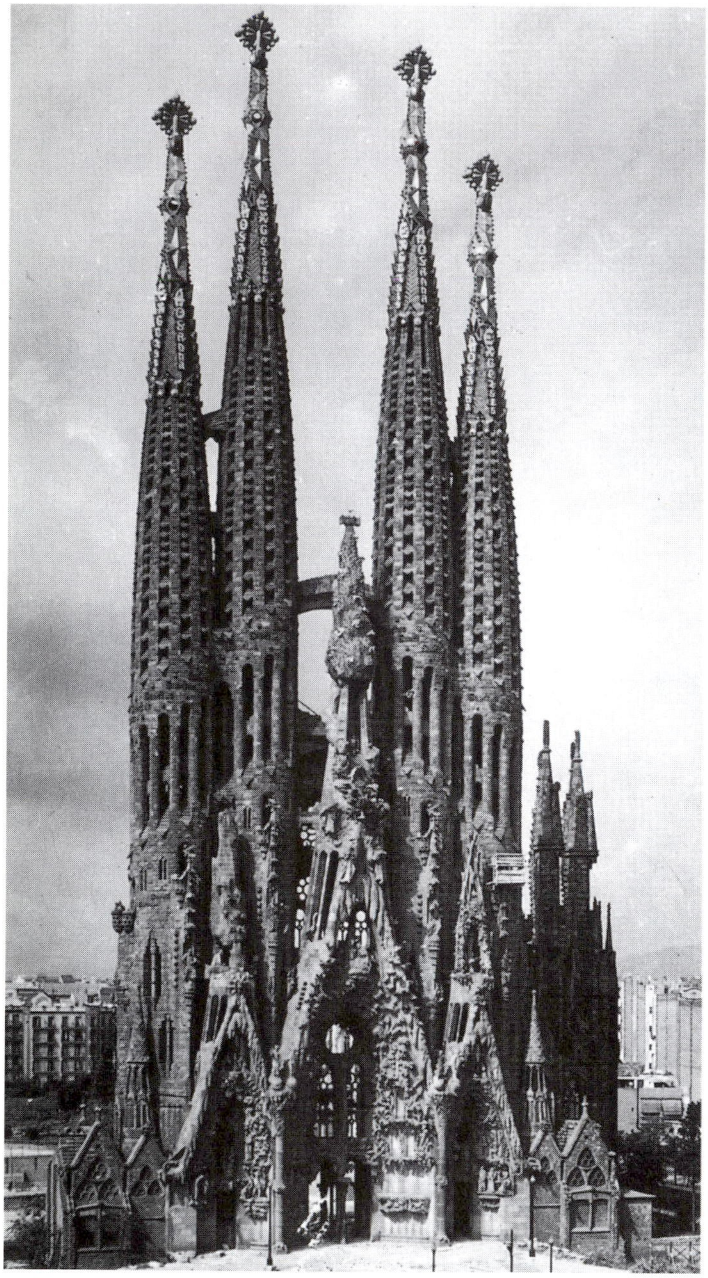

Fig. 514 Antoni Gaudí, Church of the Sagrada Familia, Barcelona, Spain, 1883–1926.

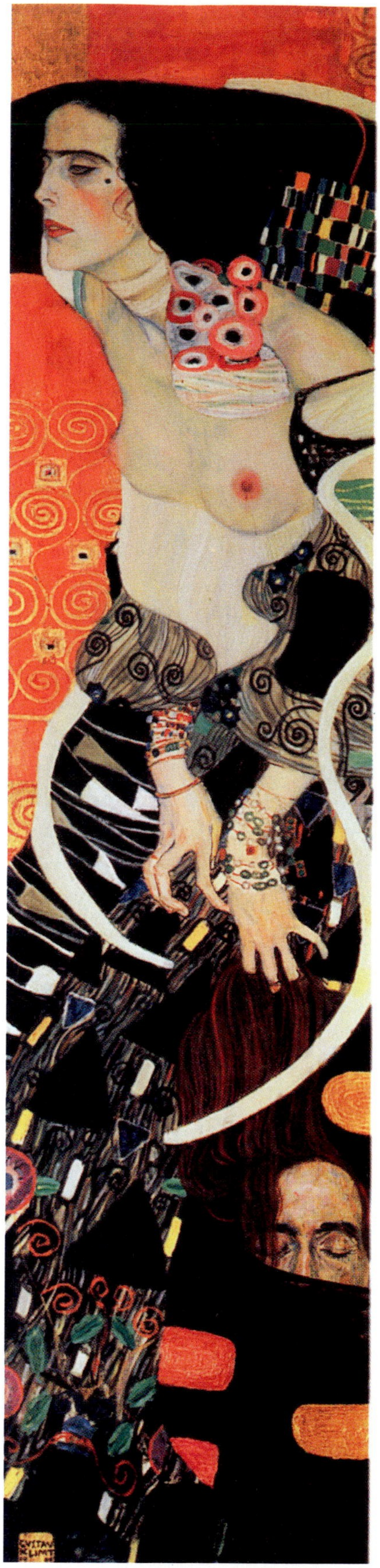

Fig. 515 Gustav Klimt, *Salomé,* 1909.
Oil on canvas, 70 1⁄8 × 18 1⁄8 in. Galleria d'Arte Moderna, Venice. Scala/Art Resource.

The organic, curvilinear qualities of Art Nouveau easily lent themselves to the development of an intensely personal and expressive style. In the hands of a master, such as the Spanish architect Antoni Gaudí, a level of formal invention was achieved that constitutes one of the most important artistic expressions of the period. Gaudí's Church of the Sagrada Familia (Fig. 514) is a twisting, spiraling, almost fluid mass of forms. In the architect's hands, masonry has been transformed into some pliable, natural material that seems as infinitely manipulable as his fantastic imagination is large.

Yet, for many, Art Nouveau seemed excessively subjective and personal, especially for public forms such as architecture. In Vienna, particularly, where Art Nouveau had flourished under the banner of the **Jugendstil**—literally, "the style of youth"—the curvilinear and organic qualities of Art Nouveau gave way to symmetry and simple geometry. Consider, for instance, the Palais Stoclet in Brussels (Fig. 516), designed by the Viennese architect Josef Hoffman. The exterior is starkly white and geometrical, and quite plain. But the interior was luxurious. Hoffman ringed the walls of the dining room, for instance, in marble inlaid with mosaics of glass and semiprecious stones including onyx and malachite designed by the Viennese painter Gustav Klimt. The theme of the mosaics was openly sexual. They were designed in the same spirit as paintings such as his *Salomé,* illustrated here (Fig. 515), which depicts a decadent society woman as if she were a temptress. For Hoffman, the interior of the house was private space, a place where fantasy and emotion could have free reign. Through the example of buildings like the Palais Stoclet, Art Nouveau became associated with an interior world of aristocratic wealth, refinement, and even emotional abandon, but it was also a style that realized the necessity of presenting, in its exteriors, a public face of order, simplicity, and control. In other words, the type of geometric and rectilinear design practiced by Frank Lloyd Wright began to find favor, and by the Exposition Internationale des Arts Décoratifs et Industriels Modernes—the International Exposition of Modern Decorative and Industrial Arts—in Paris in 1925, it held sway.

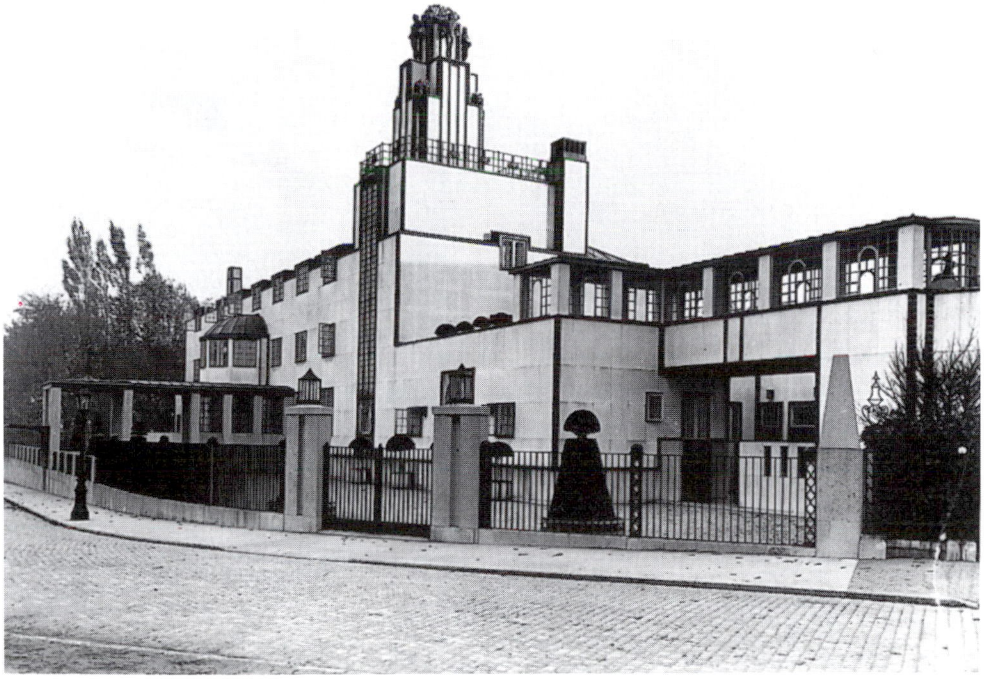

Fig. 516 Josef Hoffman, Palais Stoclet, Brussels, 1905–1911.
Marburg/Art Resource.

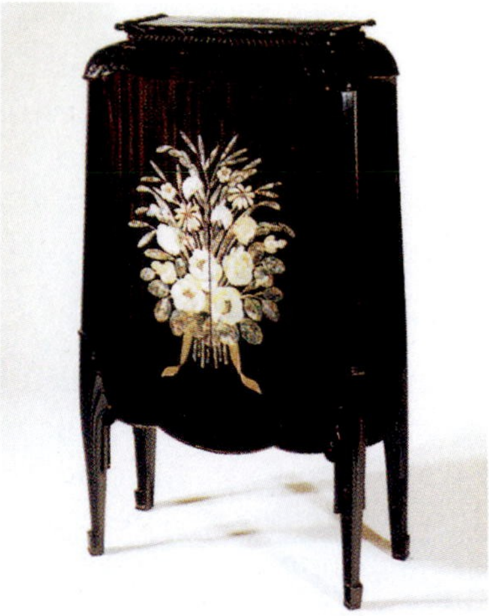

Fig. 517 Louis Süe and Andre Mare, *Cabinet*, 1927.
Ebony, mother-of-pearl, silver, 61 7/8 × 35 3/8 × 15 3/4 in.
Virginia Museum of Fine Arts, Richmond, VA.
Gift of Sydney and Frances Lewis Foundation. © Virginia Museum of Fine Arts.

ART DECO

The Exposition Internationale des Arts Décoratifs et Industriels Modernes was planned as early as 1907, during the height of Art Nouveau, but logistical problems—especially the outbreak of World War I—postponed it for almost 20 years. A very influential event, the exposition was the most extensive international showcase of the style of design then called *Art Moderne* and, since 1968, better known as **Art Deco.**

Not only did individual designers build their own exhibition spaces, but every great French department store, as well as the leading French manufacturers, built lavish pavilions as well. Throughout, the emphasis was on a particularly French sense of fashionable luxury. There was no evidence anywhere of the practical side of design—no concern with either utility or function. The cabinet designed by the French furniture company Süe et Mare (Fig. 517) is typical of the most elaborate form of the Art Deco style featured at the 1925 exposition. Made of ebony, the preferred wood of Art Deco designers because it was extremely rare and, therefore, expensive, and inlaid with mother-of-pearl, abalone, and silver, the cabinet is extraordinarily opulent. This richness of materials, together with the slightly asymmetrical and organic floral design of the cabinet door, link the piece to the earlier style of Art Nouveau.

But there was another type of Art Deco that, while equally interested in surface decoration, preferred more up-to-date materials—chrome, steel, and Bakelite plastic—and sought to give expression to everyday *"moderne"* life. The *Skyscraper Bookcase* by the American designer Paul T. Frankl (Fig. 518), made of maple wood and Bakelite, is all sharp angles that rise into the air, like the brand-new skyscrapers that were beginning to dominate America's urban landscape.

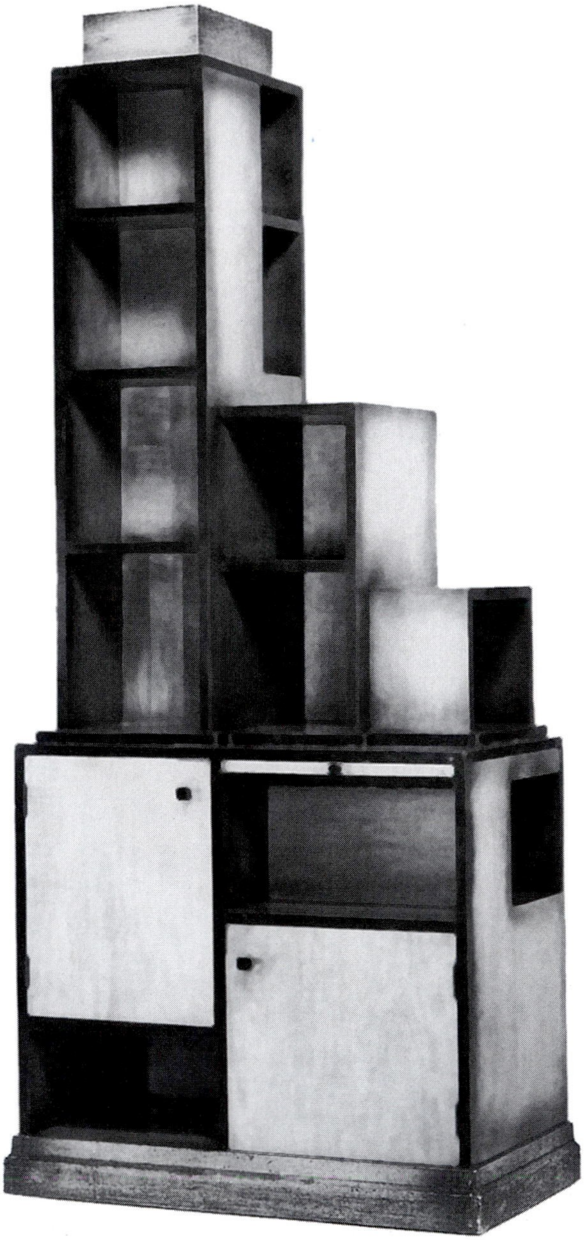

Fig. 518 Paul T. Frankl, *Skyscraper Bookcase*, 1925–1930.
Maple wood and bakelite, H. 79 7/8 in.; W. 34 3/8 in.; depth. 18 7/8 in.
The Metropolitan Museum of Art, New York. Theodore R. Gamble, Jr. Gift, in honor of his mother, 1982. 1982.30ab.

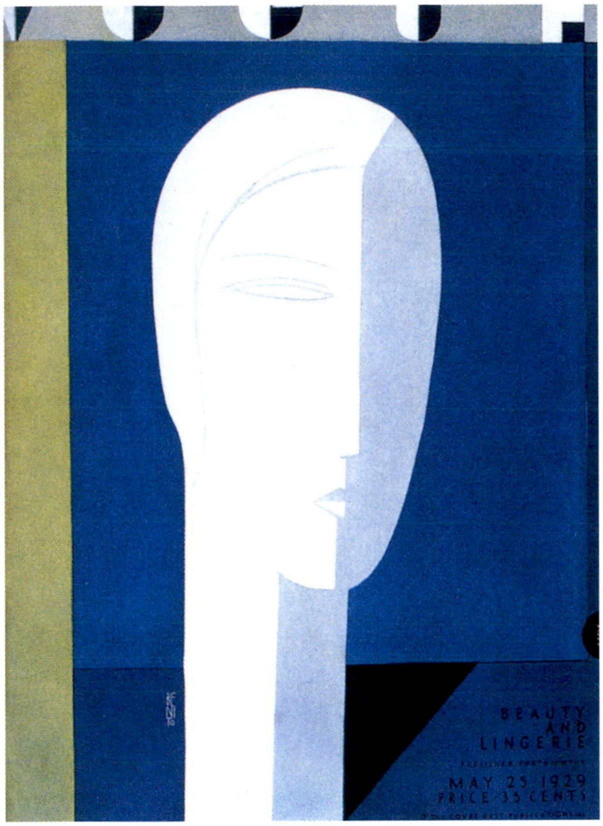

Fig. 519 Benito, cover illustration, *Vogue,* May 25, 1929.
Vogue Copyright ©1924, 1929 (renewed 1952, 1957) by The Conde Nast Publications Inc.

This movement toward the geometric is perhaps the defining characteristic of Art Deco. Even the leading fashion magazines of the day reflect this in their covers and layouts. In Edouardo Benito's *Vogue* magazine cover (Fig. 519), we can see an impulse toward simplicity and rectilinearity comparable to Frankl's bookcase. The world of fashion embraced the new geometric look. During the 1920s, the boyish silhouette became increasingly fashionable. The curves of the female body were suppressed (Fig. 520), and the waistline disappeared in tubular, "barrel"-line skirts. Even long, wavy hair, one of the defining features of Art Nouveau style, was abandoned, and the schoolboyish "Eton crop" became the hairstyle of the day.

THE AVANT-GARDES

At the 1925 Paris Exposition, one designer's pavilion stood apart from all the rest, not because it was better than the others, but because it was so different. As early as 1920, a French architect by the name of Le Corbusier had written in his new magazine *L'Esprit Nouveau* (The New Spirit) that "decorative art, as opposed to the machine phenomenon is the final twitch of the old manual modes; a dying thing." He proposed a *"Pavillon de l'Esprit Nouveau"* (Pavilion of the New Spirit) for the exposition that would contain "only standard things created by industry in factories and mass-produced; objects truly of the style of today."

To Le Corbusier, to make expensive, handcrafted objects, such as the cabinet by Süe et Mare (Fig. 517), amounted to making antiques in a contemporary world. From his point of view, the other designers at the 1925 exposition were out of step with the times. The modern world was dominated by the machine, and though designers had shown disgust for machine manufacture ever since the time of Morris and Company, they did so at the risk of living forever in the past. "The house," Le Corbusier declared, "is a machine for living."

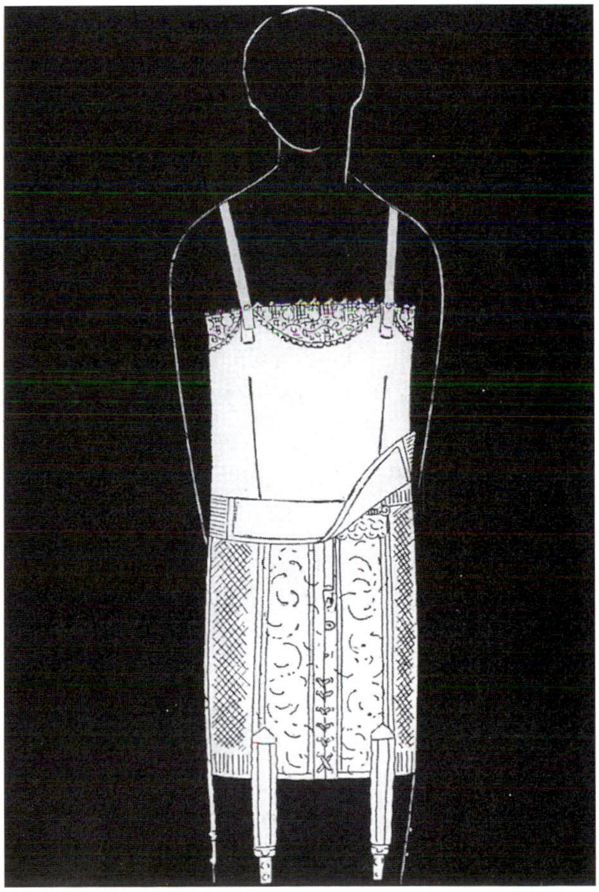

Fig. 520 Unidentified illustrator, corset, *Vogue,* October 25, 1924.
The Conde Nast Publications Inc.

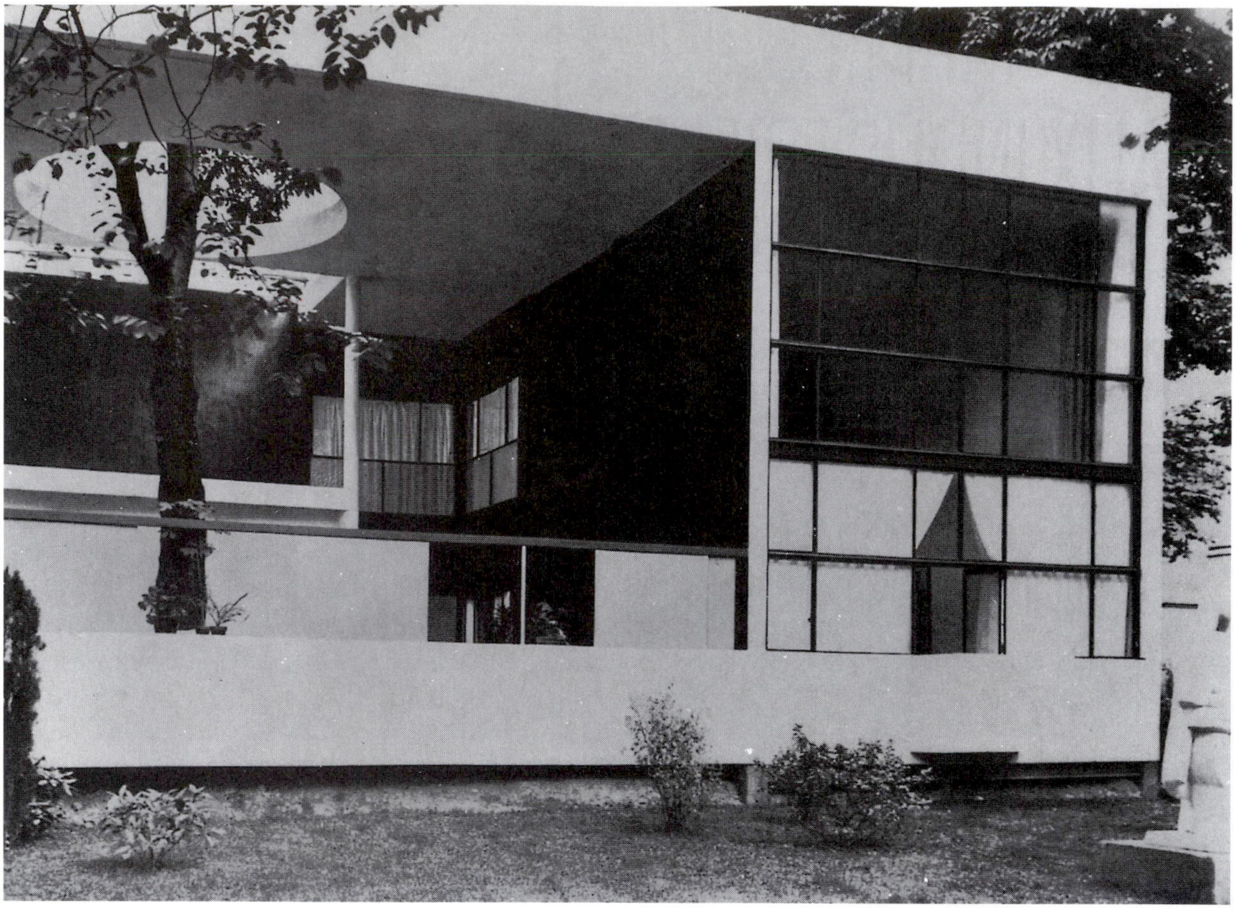

Fig. 521 Le Corbusier, Pavillon de l'Esprit Nouveau.
Exposition Internationale des Arts Décoratifs et Industriels Modernes, Paris, 1925.

Le Corbusier's "new spirit" horrified the exposition's organizers, and, accordingly, they gave him a parcel of ground for his pavilion between two wings of the Grand Palais, with a tree, which could not be removed, growing right in the middle of it. Undaunted, Le Corbusier built right around the tree, cutting a hole in the roof to accommodate it (Fig. 521). The pavilion was built of concrete, steel, and glass, and its walls were plain white. So distressed were Exposition officials that they ordered a high fence to be built completely around the site in order to hide it from public view. Le Corbusier appealed to the Ministry of Fine Arts, and finally the fence was removed. "Right now," Le Corbusier announced in triumph, "one thing is sure: 1925 marks the decisive turning point in the quarrel between the old and the new. After 1925, the antique lovers will have virtually ended their lives, and productive industrial effort will be based on the 'new.'"

The geometric starkness of Le Corbusier's design had been anticipated by developments in the arts that began to take place in Europe before World War I. A number of new **avant-garde** (from the French meaning "advance guard") groups had sprung up, often with radical political agendas, and dedicated to overturning the traditional and established means of art-making through experimental techniques and styles.

One of the most important was the **De Stijl** movement in Holland. De Stijl, which is Dutch for "The Style," took its lead, like all the avant-garde styles, from the painting of Picasso and Braque, in which the elements of the real world were simplified into a vocabulary of geometric forms. The De Stijl artists, chief among them Mondrian (see Figs. 223–227), simplified the vocabulary of art and design even further, employing only the primary colors—red, blue, and yellow—plus black and white. Their design relied on a vertical and horizontal grid, often dynamically broken by a curve or a circle or a diagonal line. Rather than enclosing forms, their compositions seemed to *open* out into the space surrounding them.

Gerrit Rietveld's famous chair (Fig. 522) is a summation of these De Stijl design principles. The chair is designed *against*, as it were, the traditional elements of the armchair. Both the arms and the base of the chair are insistently locked in a vertical and horizontal grid. But the two planes that function as the seat and the back seem almost to float free from the closed-in structure of the frame. Rietveld dramatized their separateness from the black grid of frame by painting the seat blue and the back red.

Rietveld's Schröder House, built in 1925, is an extension of the principles guiding his chair design. The interior of the box-shaped house is completely open in plan. The view represented here (Fig. 523) is from the living and dining area toward a bedroom. Sliding walls can shut off the space for privacy, but it is the sense of openness that is most important to Rietveld. Space implies movement. The more open the space, the more possibility for movement in it. Rietveld's design, in other words, is meant to immerse its occupants in a dynamic situation that might, idealistically, release their own creative energies.

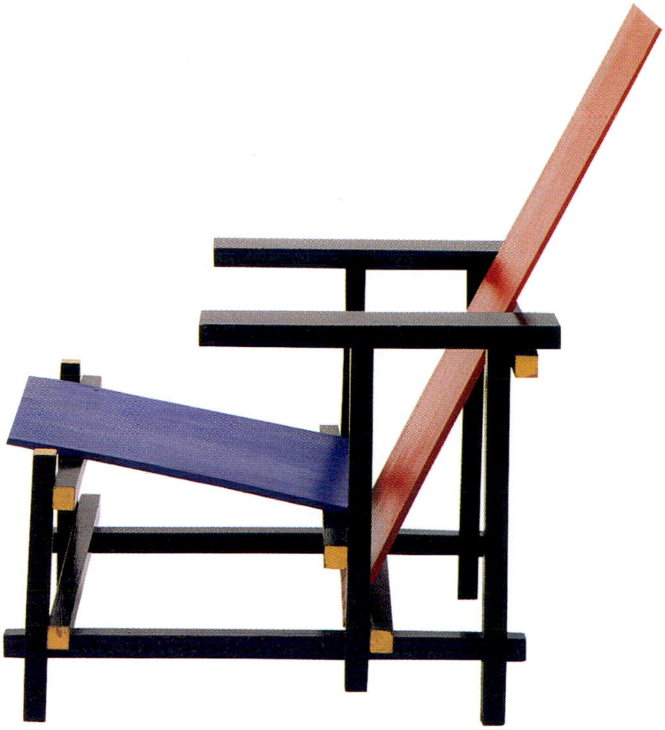

Fig. 522 Gerrit Rietveld, *Red and Blue Chair,* c. 1918.
Wood, painted, $34\,\frac{1}{8} \times 26 \times 33$ in.; seat height: 13 in.
Collection, The Museum of Modern Art, New York. Gift of Philip Johnson.

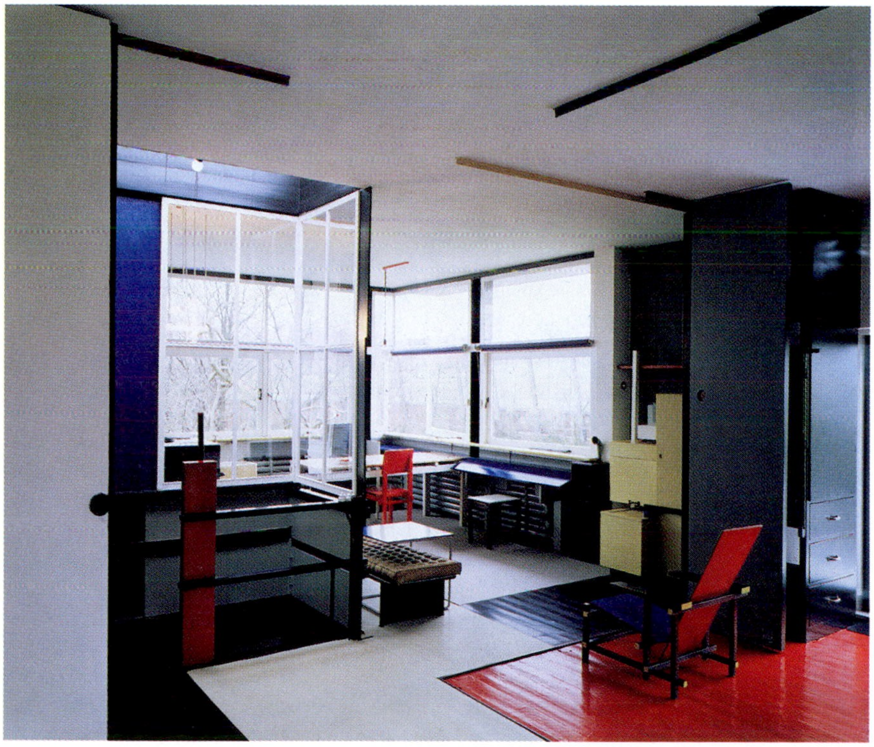

Fig. 523 Gerrit Rietveld (1888–1964), – First floor, 1987, view of the stairwell/landing and the living-dining area.
In the foreground the Red Blue chair. Rietveld Schroderhlis, 1924, Utrecht, The Netherlands. c/o Stichting Beeldrecht, Anstelveen.
Collection: Centraal Museum Utrecht/Rietveld-Schröder Archive. Photo: Ernst Moritz, The Hague.

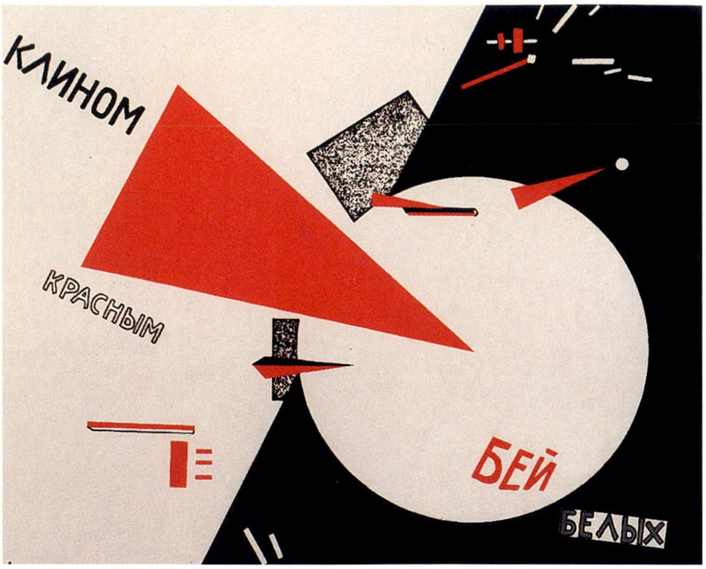

Fig. 524 El Lissitzky, *Beat the Whites with the Red Wedge,* 1919.
Lithograph. Collection Stedelijk Van Abbemuseum, Eindhoven, The Netherlands.

This notion of dynamic space can also be found in the work of the Russian **Constructivists,** who worked in the new postrevolutionary Soviet state and who dreamed of uniting art and everyday life through mass-production and industry. The artist, they believed, should "go into the factory, where the real body of life is made." They believed, especially, in employing nonobjective formal elements in functional ways. El Lissitzky's design for the poster *Beat the Whites with the Red Wedge* (Fig. 524), for instance, is a formal design with propagandistic aims. It presents the "Red" Bolshevik cause as an aggressive red triangle attacking a defensive and static "White" Russian circle. While the elements employed are starkly simple, the implications are disturbingly sexual—as if the Reds are male and active, while the Whites are female and passive—and the sense of aggressive action, originating both literally and figuratively from "the left," is unmistakable.

This same sense of geometrical simplification can be found in Liubov Popova's Constructivist costume design (Fig. 525). Prior to World War I and the revolutions in Russia that followed, the Russian textile industry had relied on French fabric designs. Popova's use of the large brown square, almost burying the figure in its plain geometry, suggests the new direction Soviet design would follow. She sought to break from former styles—to create a sense of "revolutionary" dress. The nonobjective forms of Constructivism were, in her view, free of all reference, and so they were the ideal place upon which to build a "classless" dress, a universal and egalitarian costume. But most important, this was not a "static" design, but a dynamic one. By definition, as the body moved beneath it, this block of geometric fabric would move as well.

Perhaps nowhere has the dynamism of Russian Constructivism been more powerfully expressed than in Vladimir Tatlin's visionary *Monument to the Third International* (Fig. 526). Though it was never constructed, Tatlin did make a large-scale model of the *Monument* for the U.S.S.R. pavilion at the 1925 Paris Exposition, and its affinities to Le Corbusier's Pavillon de l'Esprit Nouveau were noticed immediately. With its skeletal steel frame deliberately reminiscent of the Eiffel Tower, the *Monument* was intended to eclipse that Paris landmark and to become, at about 1,300 feet tall, the highest building in the world. The spiraling open-work construction was to have

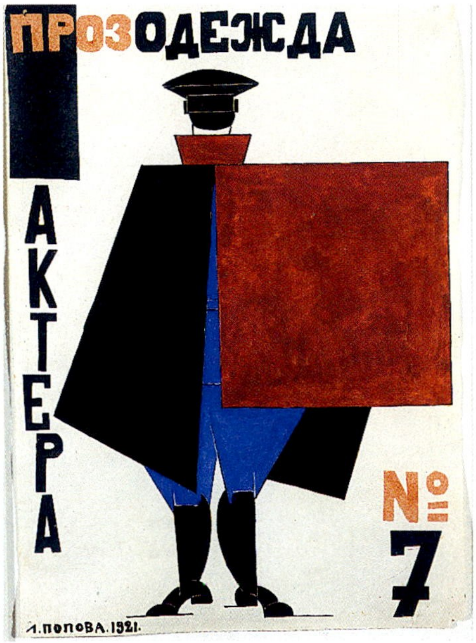

Fig. 525 Liubov Popova, *Production Clothing for Actor No. 7* for Fernand Crommelynch, *Le Cocu magnifique,* State Institute of Theatrical Arts, Moscow, 1922.
Ink, gouache, varnish, and collage on paper, 12 7/8 x 9 1/8 in. Collection Merrill C. Berman.

contained three monumental glass elements—a cube, a pyramid, and a cylinder, the essential forms of the Constructivist vocabulary—that would revolve on their axes at different speeds, one at a revolution of once per year, the second once a month, and the third once a day. The geometric forms were also intended to house the administrative, political, cultural, and scientific offices of the Communist International. For Tatlin, the spiral represented the inevitable advance of humanity under communism, the revolutionist's dream of never-ending progress toward a utopian workers' paradise.

Le Corbusier's l'Esprit Nouveau pavilion and Tatlin's *Monument* were not the only examples of the new rigorously geometric design sensibility at the 1925 Paris Exposition. The French abstract painter Sonia Delaunay also made a contribution in the form of daily fashion shows. Every evening during the run of the exposition, Delaunay dressed 20 models in her new geometric designs and paraded them through the grounds. Writing in the magazine *Surrealisme* in 1925, Claire Goll described the new dynamic Delaunay woman: "The black, white and red stripe runs down her almost like a new meander, giving her movements her own rhythm. And when she goes out, she slips into the delightful mole-coat, which is covered with wool embroidery, so it looks almost woven, and its lines filled in nuances of brown, rusty red and violet. When she has friends visiting, she wears an afternoon gown, in which a gaudy triangle cheerfully recurs. But in the evening she wears the coat that is worthy of the moon and that was born of a poem." For the exposition, Delaunay transposed the design of her motoring ensemble onto a Citroën B-12 roadster (Fig. 527). Here, Delaunay announces, is the design for a new machine age.

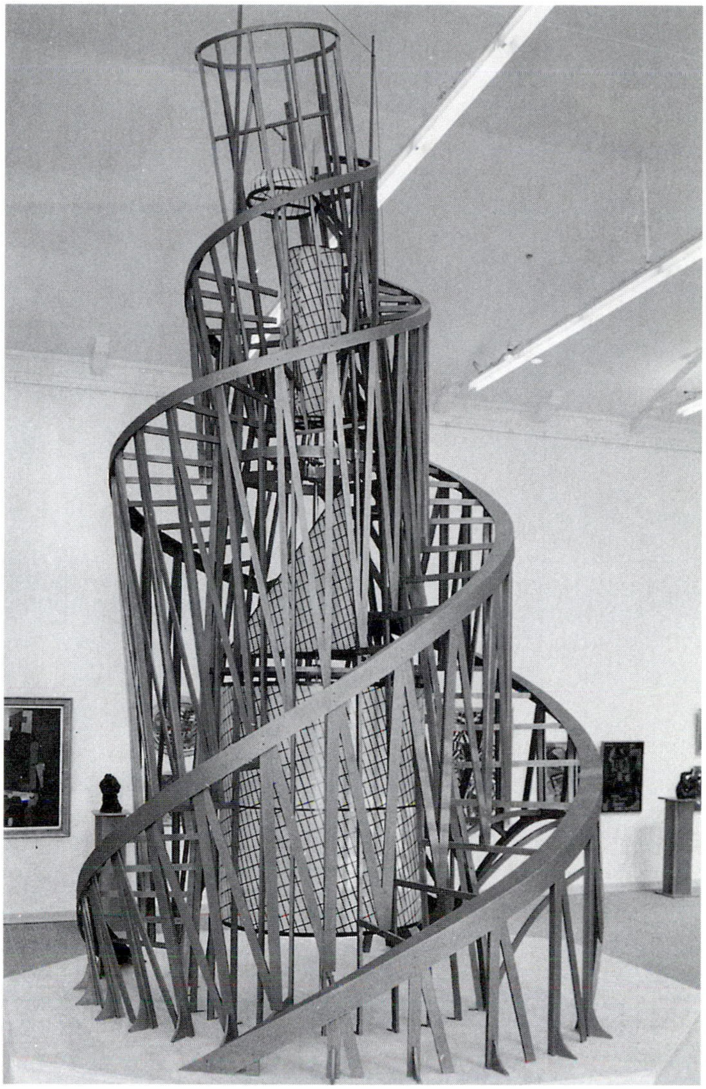

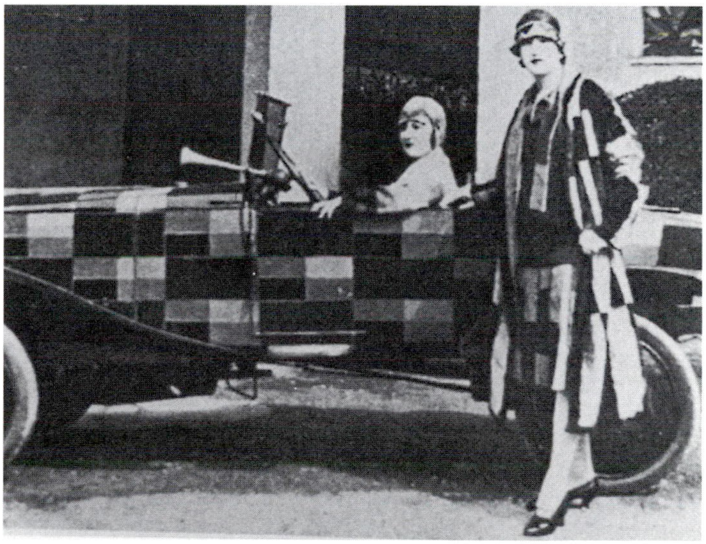

Fig. 526 (above right) Vladimir Tatlin, Model for *Monument to the Third International,* 1919–1920.
Original model destroyed; reconstruction 1968.
Wood, iron, and glass with motor, H. 15 ft. 5 in. Moderna Museet, Stockholm.

Fig. 527 (right) Models wearing Sonia Delaunay designs with a Delaunay–customized Citroën B-12. From *Maison de la Mode,* 1925.

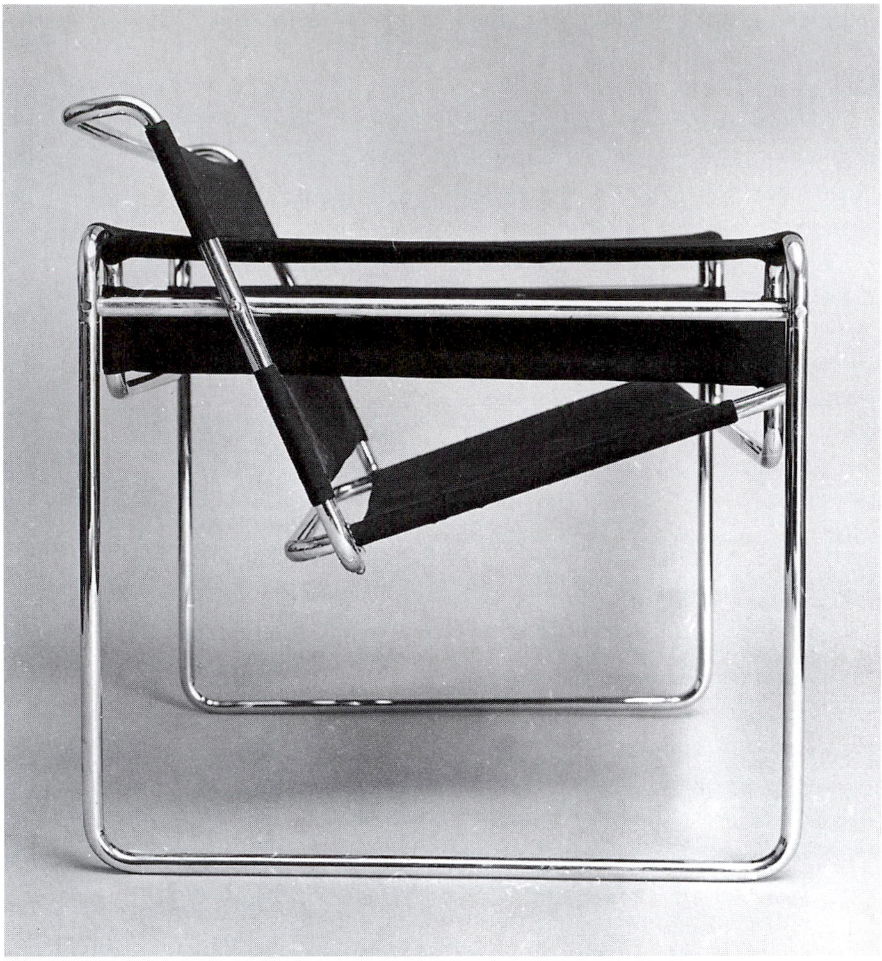

Fig. 528 Marcel Breuer, *Armchair,* model B3, late 1927 or early 1928.
Chrome-plated tubular steel, canvas, 28 1/8 × 30 1/4 × 27 3/4 in. Collection, The Museum of Modern Art, New York. Gift of Herbert Bayer.

THE BAUHAUS

At the German pavilion at the 1925 Paris Exposition one could see a variety of new machines designed to make the trials of everyday life easier—for instance, an electric washing machine and an electric armoire in which clothes could be tumble-dried. When asked who could afford such things, Walter Gropius, who in 1919 had founded a school of arts and crafts in Weimar, Germany, known as the **Bauhaus,** replied, "To begin with, royalty. Later on, everybody."

Like Le Corbusier, Gropius saw in the machine the salvation of humanity. And he thoroughly sympathized with Le Corbusier, whose major difficulty in putting together his Pavillon de l'Esprit Nouveau had been the unavailability of furniture that would satisfy his desire for "standard things created by industry in factories and mass-produced; objects truly of the style of today." Ironically, at almost exactly that moment, Marcel Breuer, a furniture designer working at Gropius's Bauhaus, was doing just that.

In the spring of 1925, Breuer purchased a new bicycle manufactured out of tubular steel by the Adler company. Impressed by the bicycle's strength—it could easily support the weight of two riders—its lightness, and its apparent indestructibility, Breuer envisioned furniture made of this most modern of materials. "In fact," Breuer later recalled, speaking of the armchair that he began to design soon after his purchase (Fig. 528), "I took the pipe dimensions from my bicycle. I didn't know where else to get it or how to figure it out."

The chair is clearly related to Rietveld's *Red and Blue Chair* (Fig. 522), consisting of two diagonals for seat and back set in a cubic frame. It is easily mass-produced—and, in fact, is still in production today. But its appeal was due, perhaps most of all, to the fact that it looked absolutely new, and it soon became an icon of the machine age. Gropius quickly saw how appropriate Breuer's design would be for the new Bauhaus building in Dessau. By early 1926, Breuer was at work designing modular tubular-steel seating for the school's auditorium, as well as stools and side chairs to be used throughout the educational complex. As a result, Breuer's furniture became identified with the Bauhaus.

But the Bauhaus was much more. In 1919, Gropius was determined to break down the barriers between the crafts and the fine arts and to rescue each from its isolation by training craftspeople, painters, and sculptors to work on cooperative ventures. There was, Gropius said, "no essential difference" between the crafts and the fine arts. There were no "teachers" either; there were only "masters, journeymen, and apprentices." All of this led to what Gropius believed was the one place where all of the media could interact and all of the arts work cooperatively together. "The ultimate aim of all creative activity," Gropius declared, "is the building," and the name itself is derived from the German words for building (*Bau*) and house (*Haus*).

We can understand Gropius's goals if we look at Herbert Bayer's design for the cover of the first issue of *Bauhaus* magazine, which was published in 1928 (Fig. 529). Each of the three-dimensional forms—cube, sphere, and cone—casts a two-dimensional shadow. The design is marked by the letter forms Bayer employs in the masthead. This is Bayer's Universal Alphabet, which he created to eliminate what he believed to be needless typographical flourishes, including capital letters. Bayer, furthermore, constructed the image in the studio and then photographed it, relying on mechanical reproduction instead of the handcrafted, highly individualistic medium of drawing. The pencil and triangle suggest that any drawing to be done is mechanical drawing, governed by geometry and mathematics. Finally, the story on the cover of the first issue of *Bauhaus* is concerned with architecture, to Gropius the ultimate creative activity.

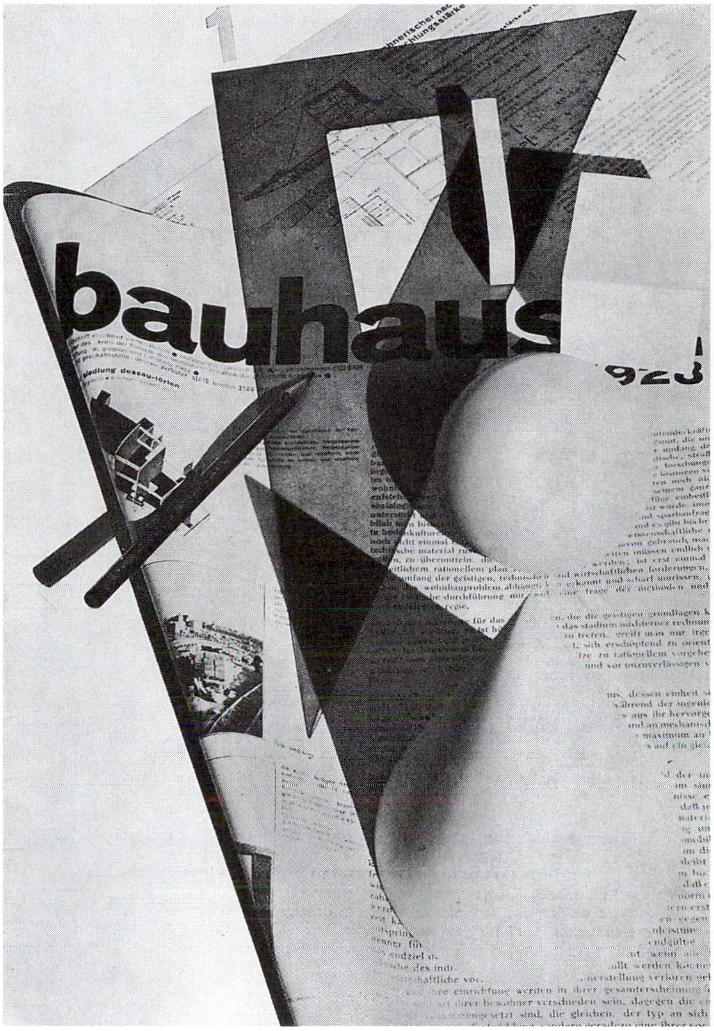

Fig. 529 Herbert Bayer, Cover for *Bauhaus 1*, 1928.
Photomontage. Bauhaus–Archiv, Berlin.
© VG Bild– Kunst, Bonn, Germany

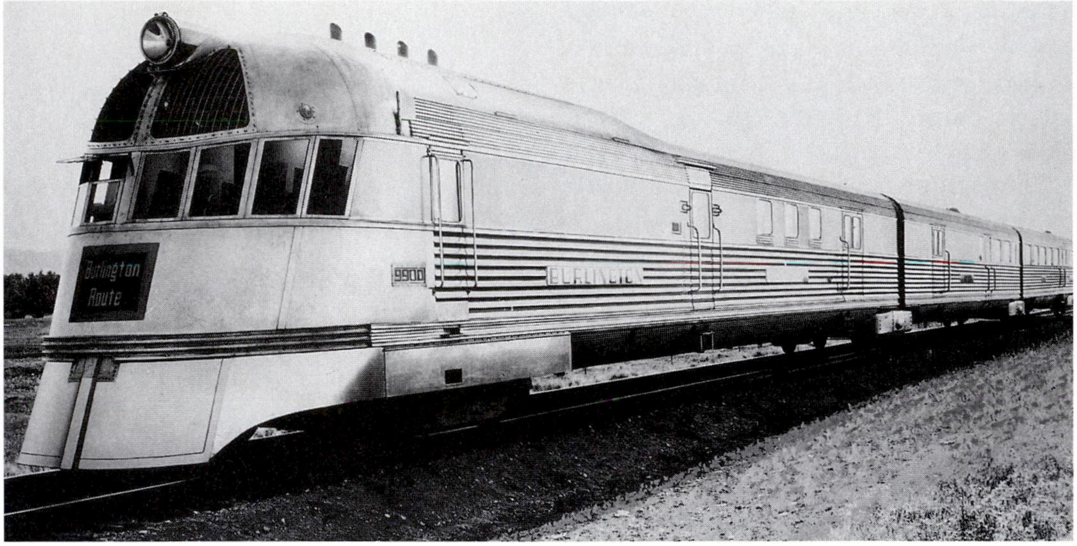

Fig. 530 Burlington *Zephyr #9900,* 1934.
Manufactured by the Edward G. Budd Company for the Chicago, Burlington and Quincy Railroad. Photograph courtesy Burlington Northern Co.

STREAMLINING

Even as the geometry of the machine began to dominate design, finding particular favor among the architects of the International Style (see Chapter 14), in the ebb and flow between the organic and the geometric that dominates design history, the organic began to flow back into the scene as a result of advances in scientific knowledge. In 1926, the Daniel Guggenheim Fund for the Promotion of Aeronautics granted $2.5 million to the Massachusetts Institute of Technology, the California Institute of Technology, the University of Michigan, and New York University to build wind tunnels. Designers quickly discovered that by eliminating extraneous detail on the surface of a plane, boat, automobile, or train, and by rounding its edges so that each subform merged into the next by means of smooth transitional curves, air would flow smoothly across the surface of the machine. Drag would thereby be dramatically reduced, and the machine could move faster with less expenditure of energy. "Streamlining" became the transportation cry of the day.

The nation's railroads were quickly redesigned to take advantage of this new technological information. Since a standard train engine would expend 350 horsepower more than a streamlined one operating at top speed, at 70 to 110 mph, streamlining would increase pulling capacity by 12 percent. It was clearly economical for the railroads to streamline.

At just after five o'clock on the morning of May 26, 1934, a brand new streamlined train called the Burlington *Zephyr* (Fig. 530) departed Union Station in Denver bound for Chicago. Normally, the 1,015-mile trip took 26 hours, but this day, averaging 77.61 mph and reaching a top speed of 112 mph, the *Zephyr* arrived in Chicago in a mere 13 hours and 5 minutes. The total fuel cost for the haul, at 5¢ per gallon, was only $14.64. When the train arrived later that same evening at the Century of Progress Exposition on the Chicago lakefront, it was mobbed by a wildly enthusiastic public. If the railroad was enthralled by the streamlined train's efficiency, the public was captivated by the its speed. It was, in fact, through the mystique of speed that the Burlington Railroad meant to recapture dwindling passenger revenues. Ralph Budd, president of the railroad, deliberately chose not to paint the *Zephyr's* stainless steel sheathe. To him it signified "the motif of speed" itself.

But the *Zephyr* was more than its sheathe. It weighed one-third less than a conventional train, and its center of gravity was so much lower that it could take curves at 60 mph that a normal train could only negotiate at 40. Because regular welding techniques severely damaged stainless steel, engineers had invented and patented an electric welding process to join its stainless steel parts. All in all, the train became the symbol of a new age. After its trips to Chicago, it traveled over 30,000 miles, visiting 222 cities. Well over 2 million people paid a dime each to tour it, and millions more viewed it from the outside. Late in the year, it became the feature attraction of a new film, *The Silver Streak,* a somewhat improbable drama about a high-speed train commandeered to deliver iron lungs to a disease-stricken Nevada town.

Wind-tunnel testing had revealed that the ideal streamlined form most closely resembled a teardrop. A long train could hardly achieve such a shape—at best it resembled a snake. But the automobile offered other possibilities. The first production model streamlined car was the Chrysler *Airflow* (Fig. 531), which abandoned the teardrop ideal and adopted the look of the new streamlined trains. (It is pictured here with the 1934 Union Pacific *Streamliner.*) The man who inspired Chrysler to develop the automobile was Norman Bel Geddes. Geddes was a poster and theatrical designer when he began experimenting, in the late 1920s, with the design of planes, boats, automobiles, and trains—things he thought of as "more vitally akin to life today than the theatre." After the stock market crash in 1929, his staff of 20 engineers, architects, and draftsmen found themselves with little or nothing to do, so Geddes turned them loose on a series of imaginative projects, including the challenge to dream up some way to transport "a thousand luxury lovers from New York to Paris fast. Forget the limitations." The specific result was his *Air Liner Number 4* (Fig. 532), designed with the assistance of Dr. Otto Koller, a veteran airplane designer. With a wingspan of 528 feet, Bel Geddes estimated that it could carry 451 passengers and 115 crew members from Chicago to London in 42 hours. It passenger decks included a dining room, game deck, solarium, barber shop and beauty salon, nursery, and private suites for all on board. Among the crew were a nursemaid, a physician, a masseuse and a masseur, wine stewards, waiters, and an orchestra.

Although Bel Geddes insisted that the plane could be built, it was the theatricality and daring of the proposal that really captured the imagination of the American public. Bel Geddes was something of a showman. In November 1932 he published a book entitled *Horizons* that included most of the experimental designs he and his staff had been working on since the stock market collapse. It was wildly popular. And its popularity prompted Chrysler to go forward with the *Airflow.* Walter P. Chrysler hired Bel Geddes to coordinate publicity for the new automobile. In one ad, Bel Geddes himself, tabbed "America's foremost industrial designer," was the spokesman, calling the *Airflow* "the first sincere and authentic streamlined car . . . the first *real* motor car." Despite this, the car was not a success. Though it drew record orders after its introduction in January 1934, the company failed to reach full production before April, by which time many orders had been withdrawn, and serious production defects were evident in those cars the company did manage to get off the line. The *Airflow* attracted over 11,000 buyers in 1934, but by 1937, only 4,600 were sold, and Chrysler dropped the model.

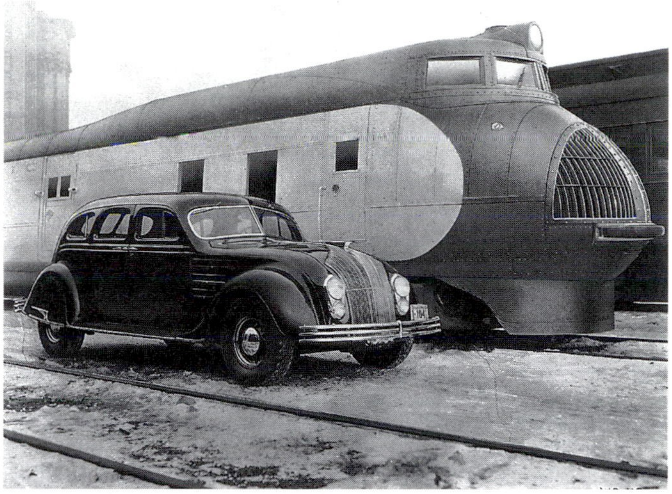

Fig. 531 Chrysler *Airflow* 4-door sedan, 1934.
Engine 8 cyl., L-head, 122 h.p. Steel body, broadcloth seats. Designer Chrysler Styling Section. Manufacturer Chrysler Corporation, Detroit. Chrysler Corporation Historical Archives, Detroit, Michigan.

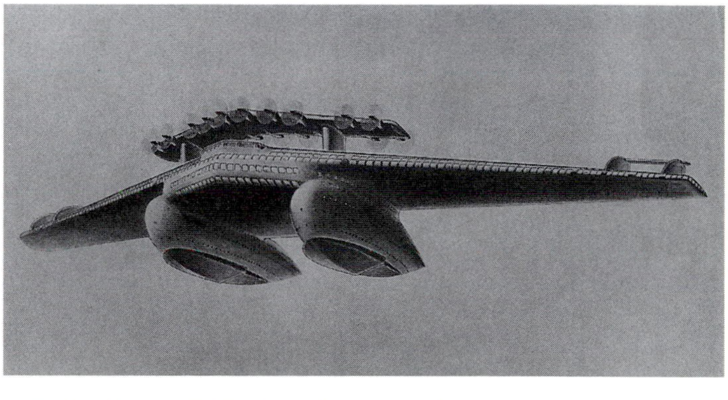

Fig. 532 Norman Bel Geddes, with Dr. Otto Koller, *Air Liner Number 4,* 1929.
Norman Bel Geddes Collection, Theatre Arts Collection,
Harry Ransom Humanities Research Center, The University of Texas at Austin.

R. Buckminster Fuller's Dymaxion Car

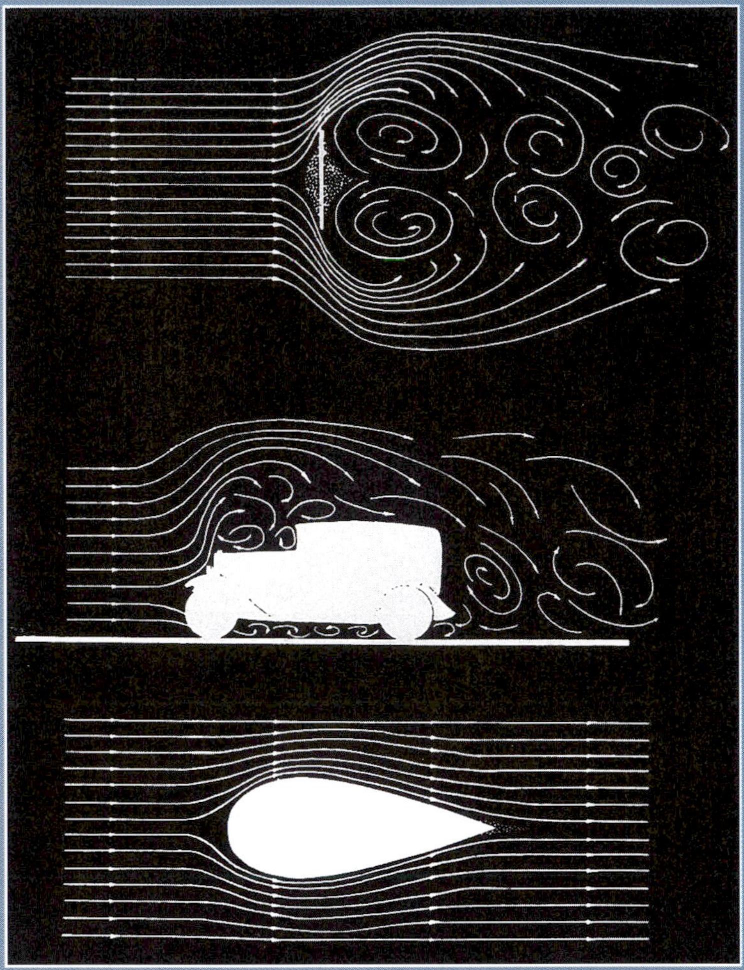

Fig. 533 R. Buckminster Fuller, airflow diagram, 1930.

In the mid-1920s, the visionary designer R. Buckminster Fuller had conceived of a future world in which everything would be mass-produced and energy efficient. He coined the word "dymaxion" to describe this world, fusing the ideas of "dynamism," "maximum" efficiency, and the "ion," or an electrically charged atom. To get around in this world people would need a *Dymaxion* car, first proposed in 1927 as a flying auto-airplane which Fuller described as "omni-directional transport." By 1930, he was studying the airflow effects around a conventional car contour and around the contour of the ideal teardrop streamlined form (Fig. 533), and three years later, in 1933, he rented a factory in Bridgeport, Connecticut, to develop a prototype. His friend, the sculptor Isamu Noguchi, built plaster scale models of the car, and then, on July 12, 1933, Fuller tested it on the factory's private speedway.

The car (Fig. 534) was unlike any other of its day, and boasted features such as front-wheel drive and a rear engine. It had three wheels, each capable of a ninety-degree turn, providing excellent maneuverability. A periscope not unlike those used on submarines rose through the roof above the driver's seat to provide rear vision. The car seated an incredible 11 passengers. Its efficiency on the highway was directly attributable to its streamlined, teardrop shape. Capable of reaching 120 mph with a 90 horsepower engine (a standard 1934 sedan required a 300 horsepower engine to attain the same speed), it consumed 30 percent less fuel at 30 mph and 50 percent less at 50 mph than comparable automobiles. It averaged over 30 miles to the gallon.

When the automobile first appeared on the roadways of New York City, it caused considerable excitement. But by the time it was presented to the nation at the Century of Progress Exposition in Chicago in 1934, the future of the *Dymaxion* automobile was in jeopardy. For one thing, few people believed it to be safe. Late in 1933, a representative of British car-racing interests who had gone to Chicago to test drive the *Dymaxion* was injured and his driver killed when the automobile collided with another near the Century of Progress Exposition. The public wanted the security of an engine out in front where they could see it. Engineers blamed the incident on "fishtailing": they noted that when a driver steered the front end of the *Dymaxion* car away from an oncoming vehicle, he also steered the rear end into it.

Fuller restored the car to its original condition and subsequently sold it, and it soon disappeared from view. But in 1942, Fuller found it again. It had been driven nearly 300,000 miles in the nine years. Once again, he restored the automobile to its original condition. It is housed today in Harrah's Automobile Collection in Reno, Nevada.

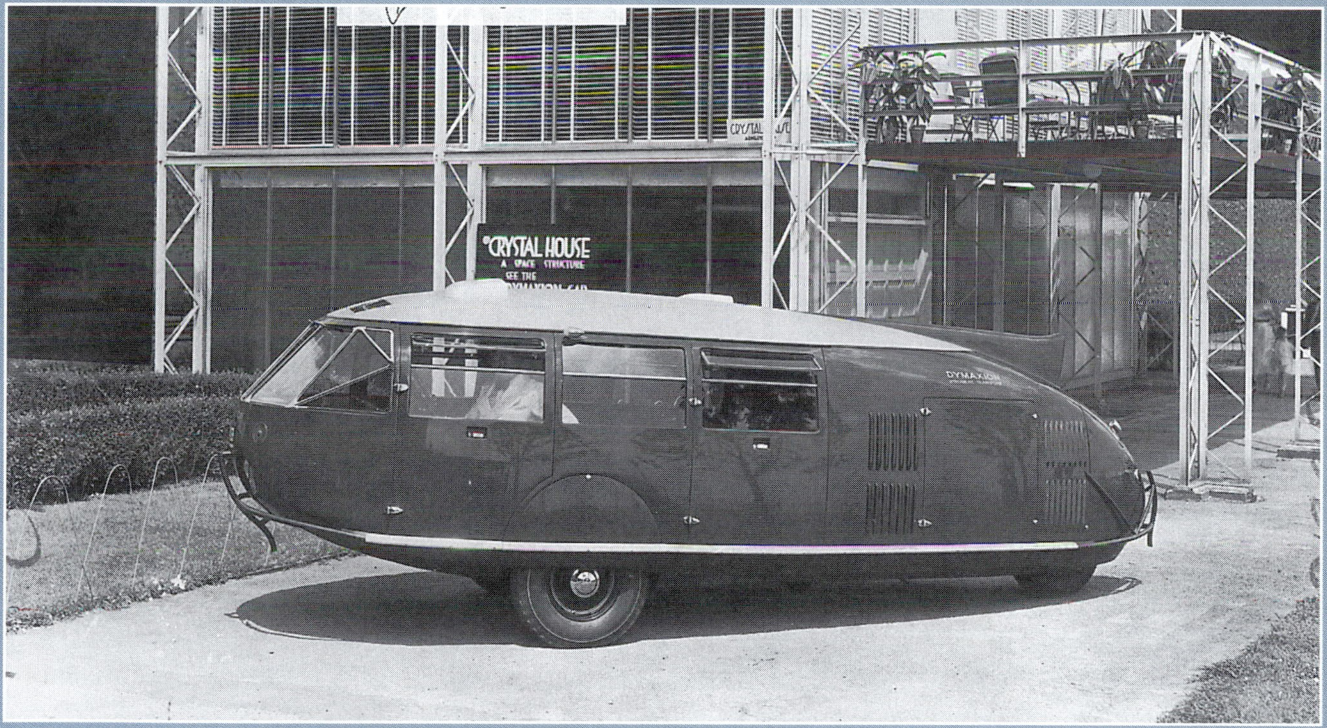

Fig. 534 R. Buckminster Fuller, *Dymaxion* car in front of the Crystal House, Chicago, 1934.
© 1960 The Estate of Buckminster Fuller; Courtesy Buckminster Fuller Institute, Los Angeles.

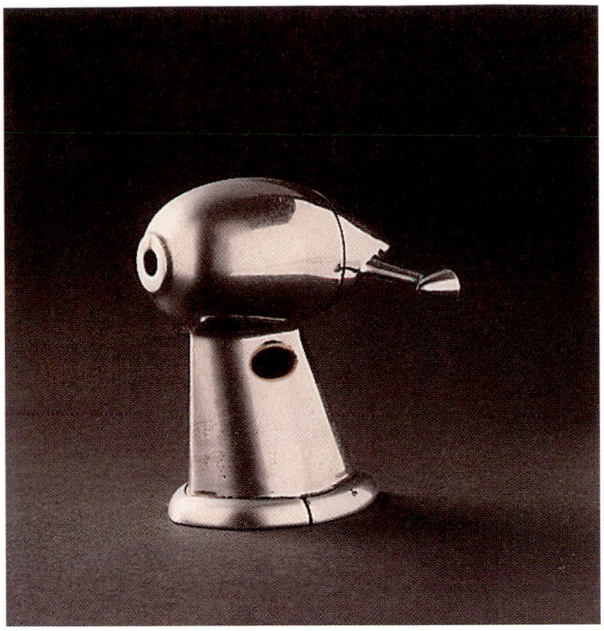

Fig. 535 Raymond Loewy, pencil sharpener, 1933.
Prototype. Collection Jack Solomon, Circle Fine Art Corporation.

However, streamlining had caught on, and other designers quickly joined the rush. For Raymond Loewy, one of the most successful American designers, streamlining was "a state of mind." For him, it was "the perfect interpretation of the modern beat." Streamlining, he wrote, "symbolizes simplicity—eliminates cluttering detail and answers a subconscious yearning for the polished, orderly essential." Thus it was no contradiction at all, from his point of view, to adopt a style created to satisfy the practical need for more efficient modes of transportation to an object as mundane as a pencil sharpener (Fig. 535). Writing in 1938, designer Russel Wright asserted that it was in objects such as Loewy's streamlined pencil sharpener and Wright's own streamlined tableware (Fig. 536) that the "American character" of a "distinct American design" could be felt.

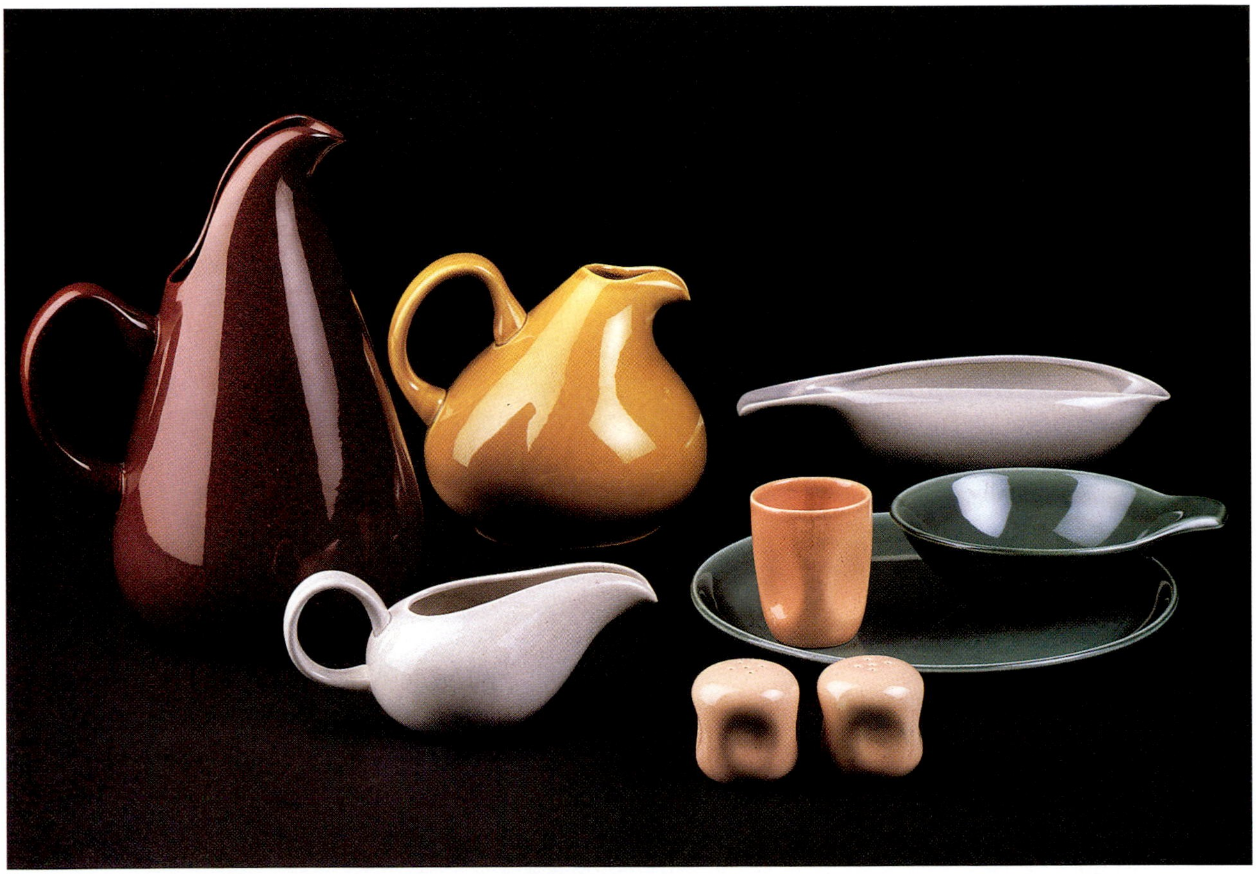

Fig. 536 Russel Wright, "American Modern" dinnerware, designed 1937, introduced 1939.
Made by Steubenville Pottery, East Liverpool, Ohio. Glazed earthenware.
Department of Special Collections, George Arents Research Library, Syracuse University.

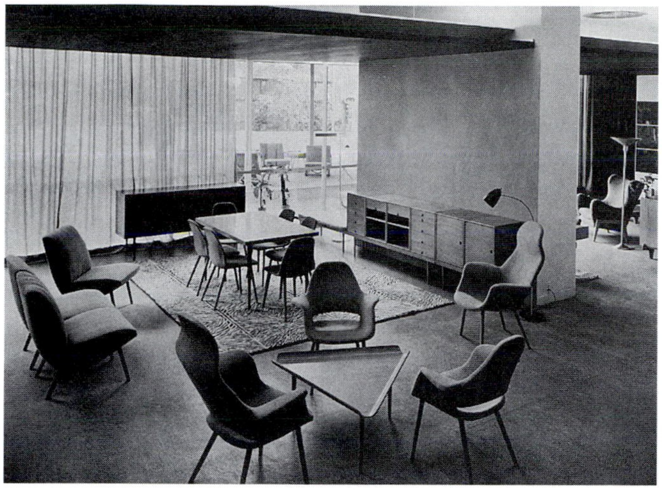

Fig. 537 Installation view of "Organic Design in Home Furnishings." September 24, 1941–November 9, 1941, The Museum of Modern Art, New York.
Photograph courtesy The Museum of Modern Art, New York.

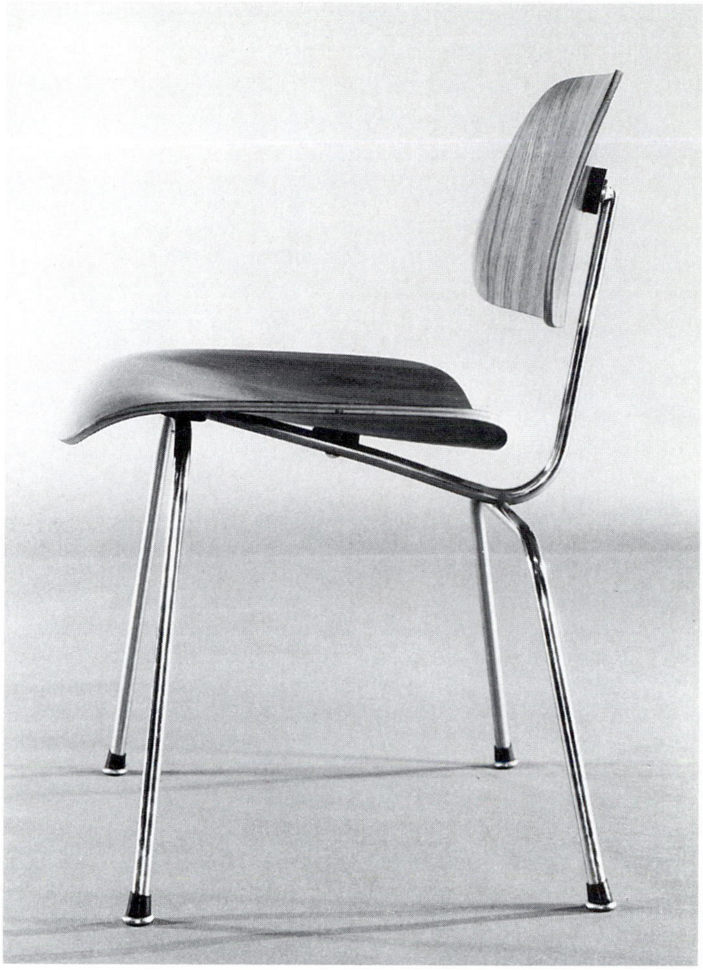

Fig. 538 Charles and Ray Eames, side chair, model DCM, 1946.
Molded walnut plywood, steel rods, and rubber shock mounts, H. 29 ½ × 20 ½ × 21 ½ in. Collection, The Museum of Modern Art, New York. Gift of Herman Miller Furniture Company.

THE FORTIES AND FIFTIES

The fully organic forms of Russel Wright's "American Modern" dinnerware announce a major shift in direction away from design dominated by the right angle and toward a looser, more curvilinear style. This direction was further highlighted when, in 1940, the Museum of Modern Art held a competition entitled "Organic Design in Home Furnishings." The first prize in that competition was awarded jointly to Charles Eames and Eero Saarinen, both young instructors at the Cranbrook Academy of Art in Michigan. Under the direction of the architect Eliel Saarinen, Eero's father, Cranbrook was similar in many respects to the Bauhaus, especially in terms of its emphasis on interdisciplinary work on architectural environments. It was, however, considerably more open to experiment and innovation than the Bauhaus, and the Eames-Saarinen entry in the Museum of Modern Art competition was the direct result of the elder Saarinen encouraging his young staff to rethink entirely just what furniture should be.

All of the furniture submitted by Eames and Saarinen to the show (Fig. 537) made use of molded plywood shells in which the wood veneers were laminated to layers of glue. The resulting forms almost demand to be seen from more than a single point of view. The problem, as Eames wrote, "becomes a sculptural one." The furniture was very strong, comfortable, and reasonably priced. Because of the war, production and distribution were necessarily limited, but, in 1946, the Herman Miller Company made 5,000 units of a chair Eames designed with his wife, Ray Eames, also a Cranbrook graduate (Fig. 538). Instantly popular and still in production today, the chair consists of two molded plywood forms that float on elegantly simple steel rods. The effect is amazingly dynamic: the back panel has been described as "a rectangle about to turn into an oval," and the seat almost seems to have molded itself to the sitter in advance.

Eero Saarinen took the innovations he and Eames had made in the "Organic Design in Home Furnishings" competition in a somewhat different direction. Unlike Eames, who in his

1946 chair had clearly abandoned the notion of the one-piece unit as impractical, Saarinen continued to seek a more unified design approach, feeling that it was more economical to stamp furniture from a single piece of material in a machine. His *Tulip Pedestal Furniture* (Fig. 539) is one of his most successful solutions. Saarinen had planned to make the pedestal chair entirely out of plastic, in keeping with his unified approach, but he discovered that a plastic stem would not take the necessary strain. Forced, as a result, to make the base out of cast aluminum, he nevertheless painted it the same color as the plastic in order to make the chair appear of a piece.

There was an explosion of new American design after the end of World War II, due, at least in part, to the rapid expansion of the economy as 12 million military men and women were demobilized. New home starts rose from about 200,000 in 1945 to 1,154,000 in 1950. These homes had to be furnished, and new products were needed to do the job. Passenger car production soared from 70,000 a year in 1945 to 6,665,000 in 1950, and in the following ten years Americans built and sold over 58 million automobiles. In tune with the organic look of the new furniture design, these cars soon sported fins, suggesting both that they moved as gracefully as fish and that their speed was so great that they needed stabilizers. The fins were inspired by the tail fins on the U.S. Air Force's P-38 "Lightning" fighter plane, which Harley Earl, chief stylist at General Motors, had seen during the war. He designed them into the 1948 Cadillac as an aerodynamic symbol. But by 1959, when the craze hit its peak, fins no longer had anything to do with aerodynamics. As the Cadillac (Fig. 540) made clear, it had simply become a matter of the bigger the better.

In many ways, the Cadillac's excess defines American style in the 1950s. This was the decade that brought the world fast food (both the McDonald's hamburger and the TV dinner), Las Vegas, *Playboy* magazine, and a TV in every home. But there were, in the 1950s, statements of real elegance. One of the most notable was the graphic design of the Swiss school, notably that of Armin Hofmann. Recognizing, in his words, that "the whole of sensory perception has been shifted by the photographic image," he freely incorporated photographs into his poster designs. Like Saarinen in his air terminal designs (Figs. 482–484), Hofmann placed his emphasis on finding a symbolic form or image appropriate to the content of his message. The poster for the ballet *Giselle* (Fig. 541) immediately conveys the idea of dance. It does this through the studied contrast between light and dark, between the blurred, speeding form of the dancer and the static clarity of the type, between, finally, the geometry of the design

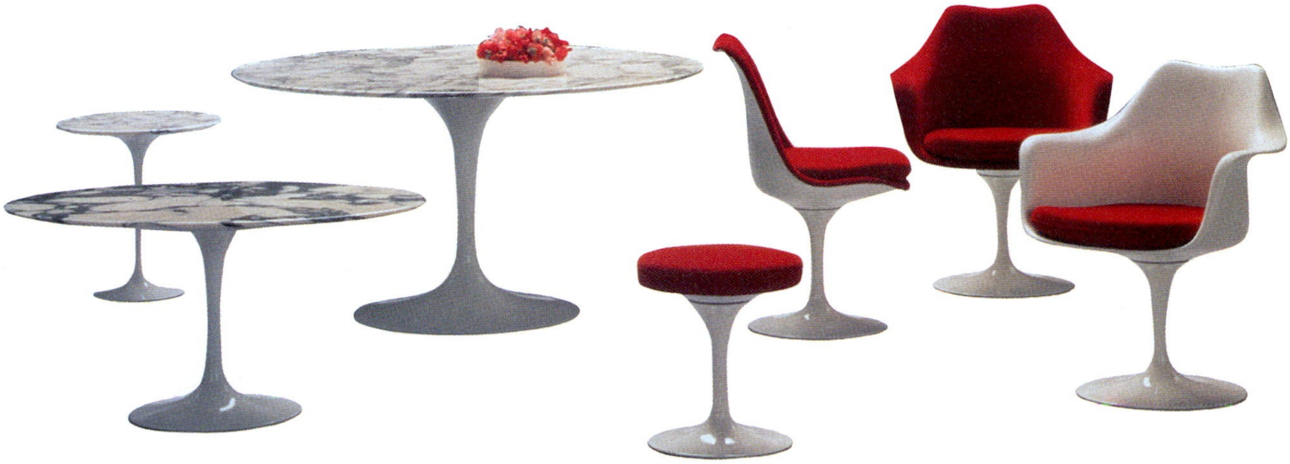

Fig. 539 Eero Saarinen, *Tulip Pedestal Furniture,* 1955–1957.
Chairs: plastic seat, painted metal base; tables: wood or marble top, plastic laminate base.
Saarinen Collection designed by Eero Saarinen in 1956 and 1957, courtesy of The Knoll Group.

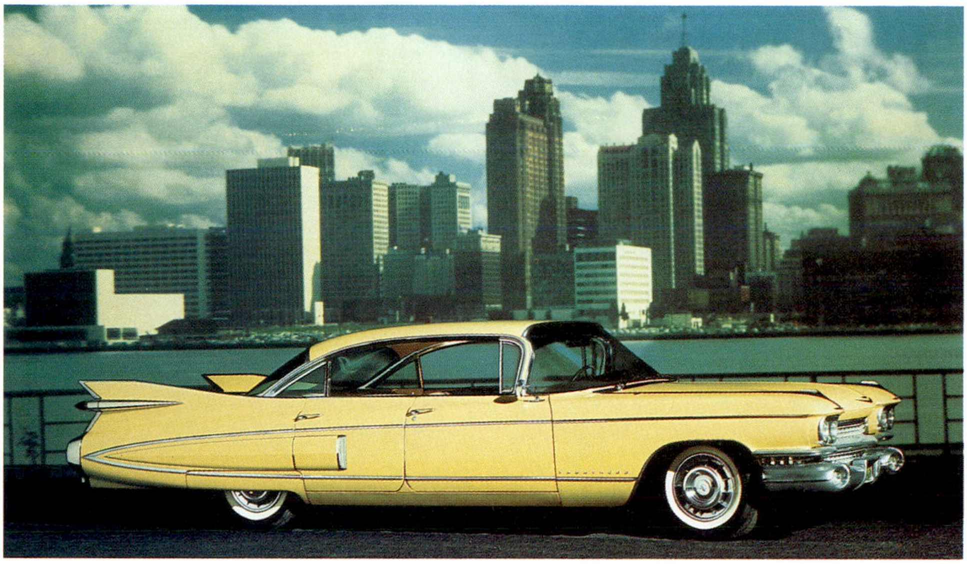

Fig. 540 Cadillac Fleetwood, 1959.
Courtesy General Motors Corp.

and the organic movement of the body. By these means, Hofmann arrives at a synthesis of the competing stylistic forces at work in the history of modern design.

CONTEMPORARY DESIGN

One way to view the evolution of design since 1960 is to recognize a growing tendency to accept the splits between the organic and the geometric and the natural and the mechanical that dominates its history as not so much an either/or situation as a question of both/and. In its unification of competing and contrasting elements, Hofmann's graphic design anticipates this synthesis. So, indeed, does the Eames chair, with its contrasting steel-support structure and molded plywood seat and back.

But, as we suggested in the earlier discussion of postmodernism, the contemporary has been marked by a willingness to incorporate anything and everything into a given design. This is not simply a question of the organic versus the geometric. It is, even more, a question of the collisions of competing cultures of an almost incomprehensible diversity and range. On our shrinking globe, united by television and the telephone, by the fax machine and the copier, e-mail and the World Wide Web, and especially by increasingly interdependent economies, we are learning to accept, perhaps faster than we realize, a plurality of styles.

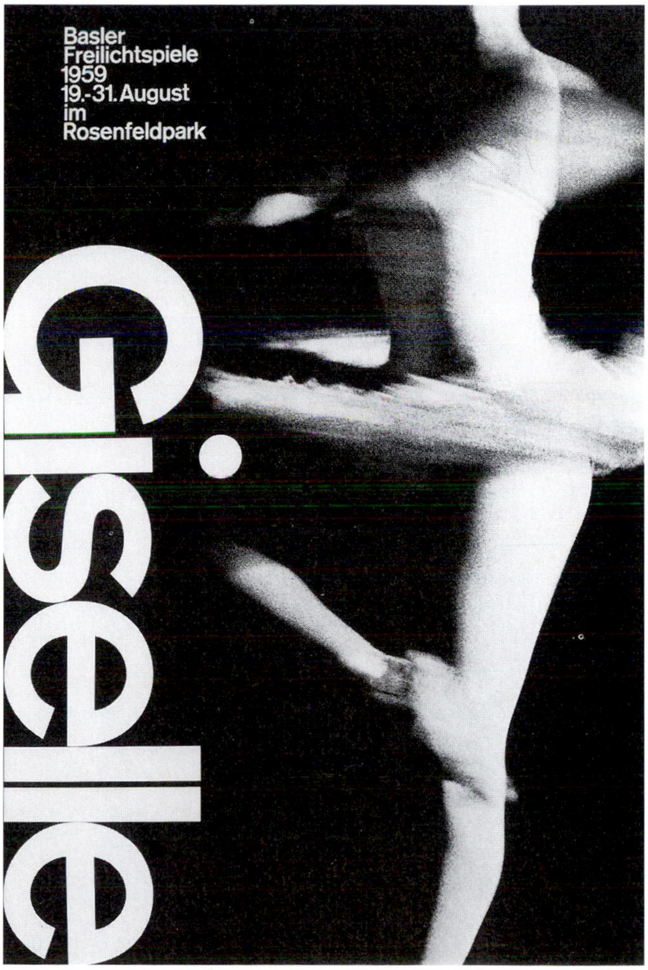

Fig. 541 Armin Hofmann, *Giselle,* 1959.
Offset lithograph, 50¾ × 35⅝ in.
Courtesy Reinhold-Brown Gallery, New York.

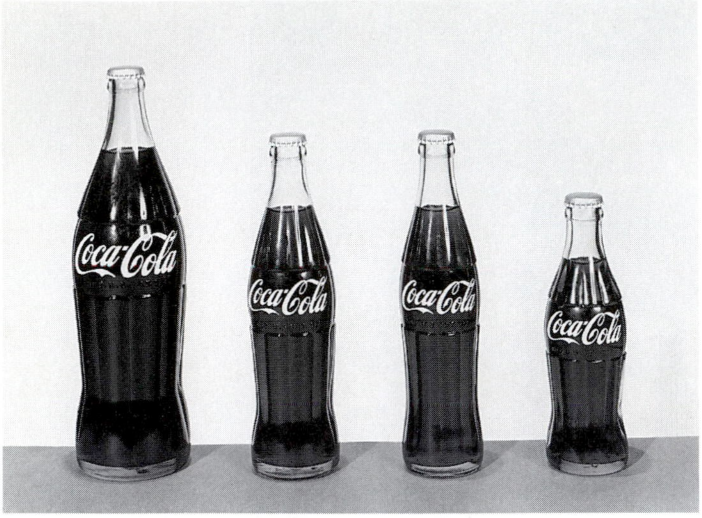

Fig. 542 Raymond Loewy, Coca-Cola bottle.
"Coke," "Coca-Cola," and the Dynamic Ribbon device are trademarks of The Coca-Cola Company and are used with permission.

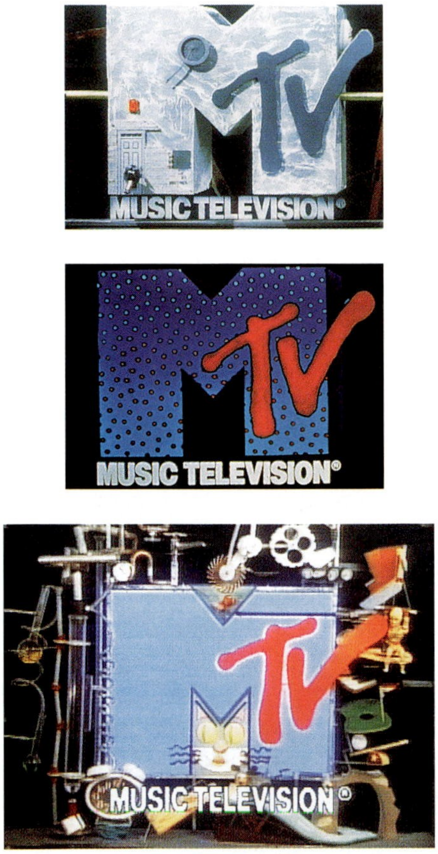

Fig. 543a, 543b, 543c MTV: MUSIC TELEVISION logo used by permission.
MTV Networks, a division of Viacom International Inc.
© 1996 MTV Networks. All Rights Reserved.

What we mean when we speak of the stylistic pluralism of contemporary design is clear if we compare a traditional corporate identity package with a conspicuously postmodern one. Although the Coca-Cola bottle has changed over the course of time, Raymond Loewy's 1957 redesign of the bottle (Fig. 542) makes it slightly more streamlined and sleeker than earlier versions and changes the embossed lettering to white paint. The script logo itself has remained constant almost since the day Dr. John Pemberton first served the concoction on May 8, 1886, at Jacob's Pharmacy in downtown Atlanta, Georgia. Coke claims that today more than 90 percent of the world's men, women, and children easily recognize the bottle.

By contrast, the Music Television Network, MTV, and the designers of Swatch watches, the Swiss husband and wife team Jean Robert and Käti Durrer, conceive of their design identities as kinetic, ever-changing variations on a basic theme (Figs. 543 and 545). In recent years, both the television and music industries have more and more turned from producing shows and recordings designed to appeal to the widest possible audience to a concentration on appealing to more narrowly defined, specialized audiences. Television learned this lesson with the series "St. Elsewhere," which had very low overall ratings, but which attracted large numbers of married, young, upper-middle-class professionals—yuppies—with enough disposable income to attract, in turn, major advertising accounts.

In the light of this situation, it is no longer necessary to standardize a corporate identity. It may not even be desirable. Illustrated here, in Figure 545, are eight of the approximately 300 watch designs produced by Robert and Durrer between 1983 and 1988, which were inspired by a variety of cultures, from Japanese to Native American, and styles. Each watch is designed to allow the wearer's unique individuality to assert itself. "In 1984," Robert and Durrer recall, "we saw a gentleman sitting in the back of his Rolls Royce. We couldn't help noticing a Swatch on his wrist. That showed us how great the breakthrough had been."

Nothing is perhaps more representative of the change from a uniform design sensibility to a pluralist vision than the poster at the right by

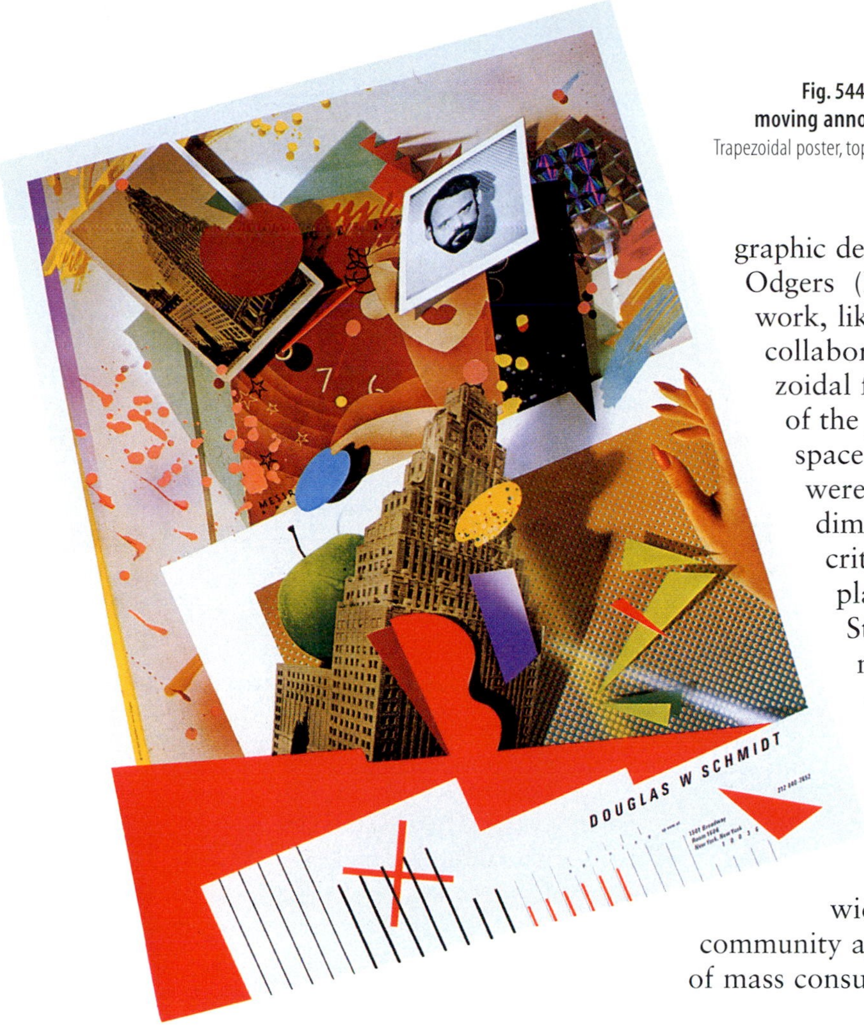

Fig. 544 April Greiman and Jayme Odgers, moving announcement for Douglas W. Schmidt, 1980.
Trapezoidal poster, top 17 in., bottom 21 in., H. 24 in. Courtesy April Greiman.

graphic designers April Greiman and Jayme Odgers (Fig. 544). Greiman, in all her work, likes to juxtapose opposites. In this collaboration with Odgers, the trapezoidal form of the design makes the top of the poster appear to move back into space away from the bottom, as if it were simultaneously two- and three-dimensional. In the words of one critic, "Her designs make opposites play on a common field: East/West, Stability/Change, Order/Randomness . . . Tension/Balance, Technical/Tribal . . . Classic/Eclectic, Cerebral/Sensual, New Wave/No Wave."

The development of this pluralist design vision has been aided and abetted by a widespread reaction in the design community against the "good taste" aesthetic of mass consumption. One of the chief figures

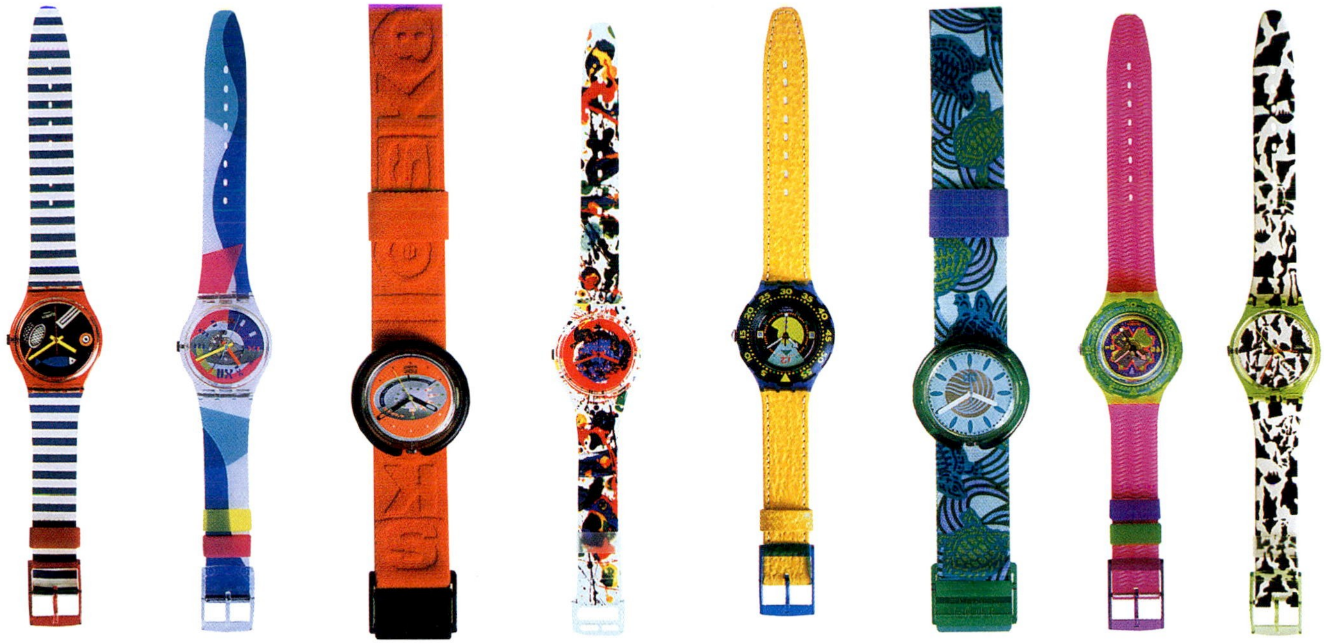

Fig. 545 Jean Robert and Käti Durrer, Swatch watches, 1983–1988.
Courtesy Swatch AG Biel.

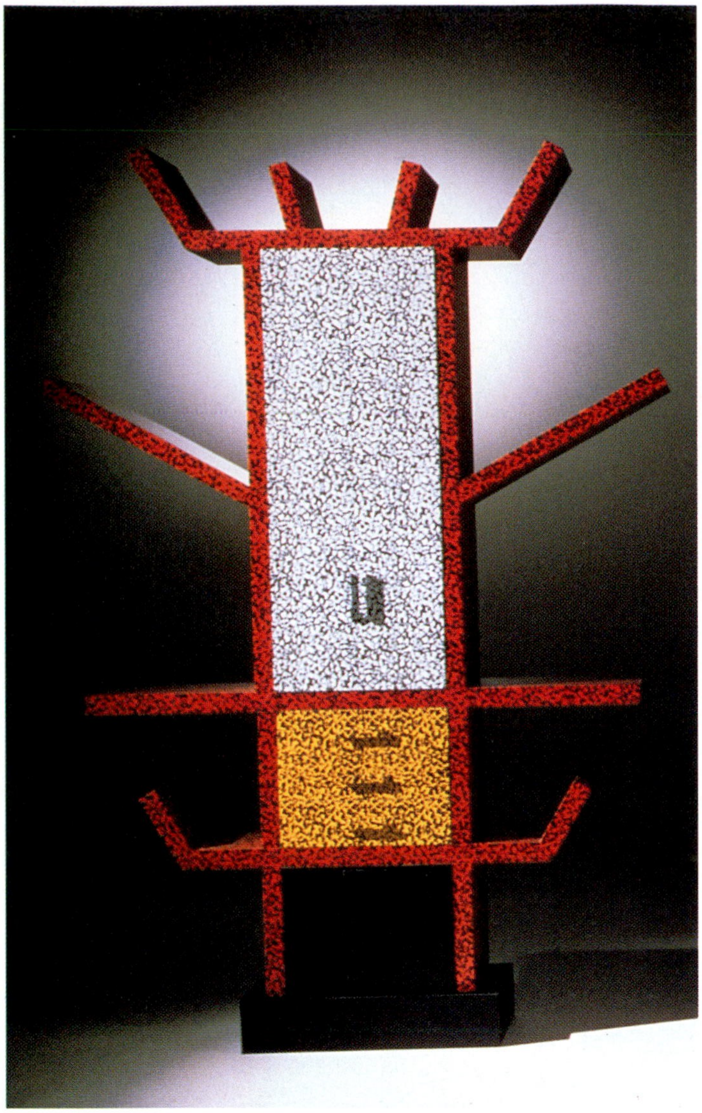

Fig. 546 Ettore Sottsass, *Casablanca* cabinet, 1981.
Laminate print. Production: Memphis srl, Milano.

in this movement has been the Italian Ettore Sottsass, who designed Olivetti's first electronic typewriter in 1958. In the mid-1970s, Sottsass spearheaded an Italian-based international design cooperative known as "Memphis." For Sottsass, personal expression takes precedence over mass appeal, and appearance is more important than function. His *Casablanca* cabinet (Fig. 546) does indeed function as a cabinet, but it is primarily a visual statement. As one Memphis designer has put it: "Industry must face up to a new strategy of production, no longer based on the great semantic reductions which classical design furnished, but rather based on a new and intensive process of imparting cultural significance to the product; a product able to choose its own user, able to create its own market, and most importantly able to exhibit qualities, no longer seemingly objective (and substantially anonymous), but personal and subjective. . . . From high-tech to high-touch."

The pluralist sensibility is also a function of the vast amount of information with which we are constantly bombarded in a technological society. The computer industry—especially in its personal computer and lap-top lines—has striven to create products designed to help us integrate and control this flow of information. An elegant example is Cranbrook graduate Lisa Krohn's 1986 *Phonebook*. (Fig. 547). At once a telephone and an answering machine, it stores telephone numbers and messages, as well as transcribing and thermally printing messages and conversations. Each of its functions is initiated with the flip of a page. The appeal of its design, however, depends on how it manages these operations at human scale, integrating high-tech and high-touch, the technology of the machine and the intimacy of the book. In many ways, Krohn's *Phonebook* brings us back, again, to the issues that have driven design since its beginning, the themes of this chapter. It is design made possible by technological innovation. Its high-tech look—its geometric simplicity—is countered by its high-touch feel—its organic relation to the human hand. And it seems, above all, useful, something we might want to own and use. Like all good design, it appeals to us as both a functional and aesthetic object.

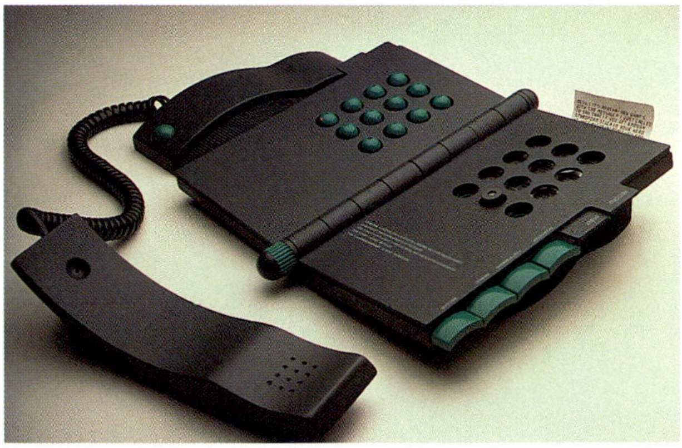

Fig. 547 Lisa Krohn, *Phonebook,* 1986.
Injection-molded plastic.

PART V

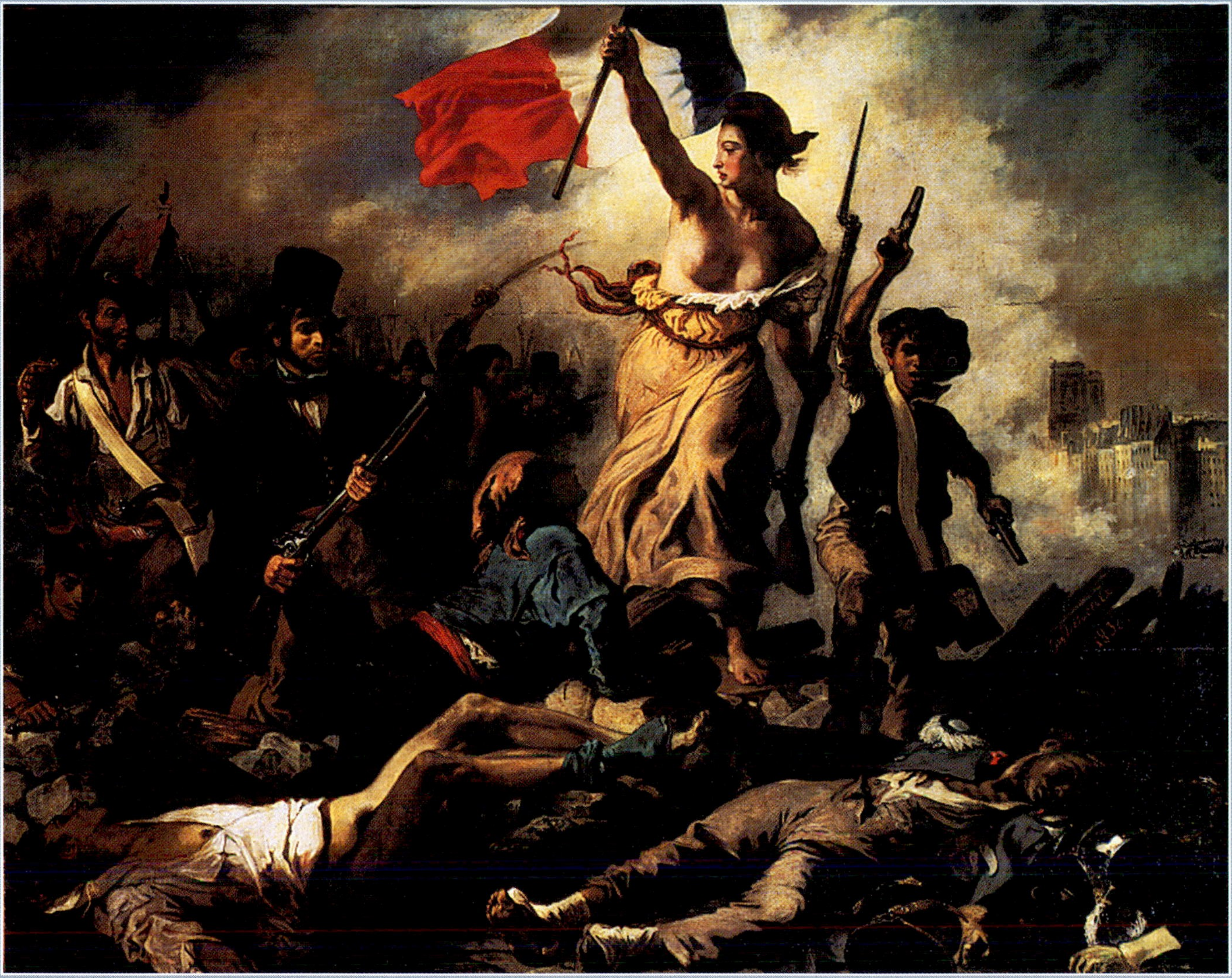

Fig. 548 Eugène Delacroix, *Liberty Leading the People*, 1830.
Oil on canvas, 8 ft. 6 3/8 in. × 10 ft. 8 in.
Musée du Louvre, Paris. Giraudon/Art Resource.

THE VISUAL RECORD

PLACING THE ARTS IN HISTORICAL CONTEXT

CHAPTER 16

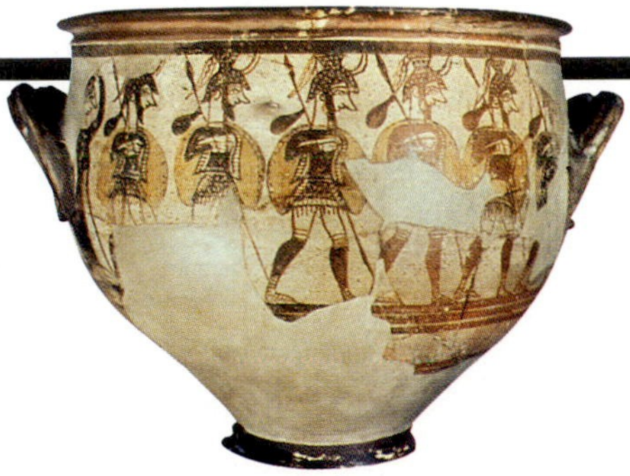

The Ancient World

The following chapters are designed to help place the works of art so far discussed in *A World of Art* into a broader historical context. The brief chronological survey and illustrations trace the major developments and movements in art from the earliest to the most recent times. To help you place the illustrations in these and earlier chapters in context, we have listed some important contemporaneous historical events across the tops of the pages. We will see how the history of art is inextricably tied to these broader cultural developments and in many ways reflects them.

Modern humans
arrive in Europe
40,000 BCE

22,000 BCE
Height of last
glacial advance in Europe

15,000 BCE

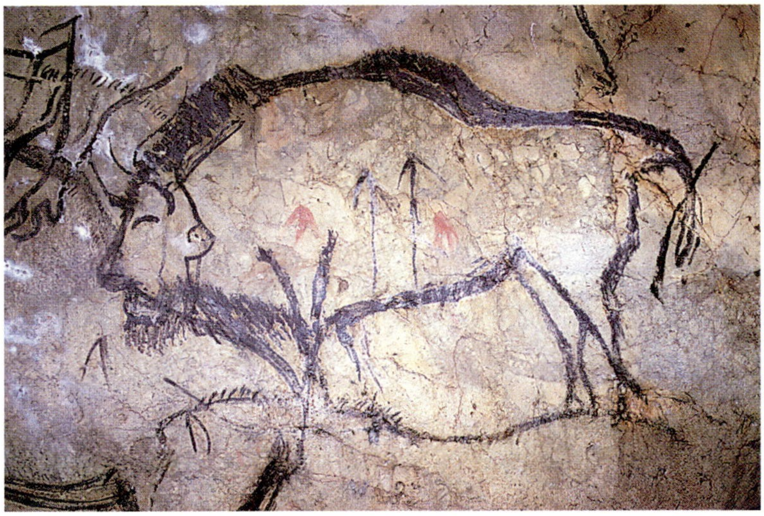

Fig. 550 *Bison with Arrows,*
Niaux, Ariège, France, c. 15,000–13,000 BCE.
L. 50 in.

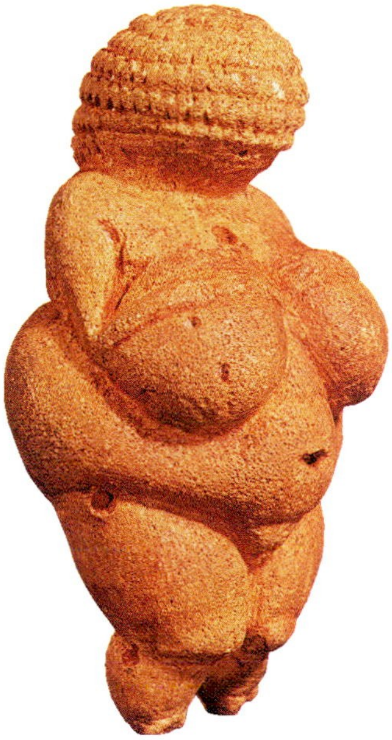

Fig. 549 *Venus of Willendorf,*
Lower Austria, c. 25,000–20,000 BCE.
Limestone, H. 4 1/2 in.
Naturhistorisches Museum, Vienna.

THE EARLIEST ART

It is not until the emergence of modern humans, *Homo sapiens,* in the Paleolithic Era, that we find artifacts that might be called works of art. The word "Paleolithic" derives from the Greek *palaios,* "old," and *lithos,* "stone," and refers to the use of stone tools, which represent a significant advance beyond the flint instruments used by Neanderthal people. With these tools, works of art could be fashioned. The earliest of these, representing animals and women, are small sculptural objects, which serve no evident practical function. Found near Willendorf, Austria, the so-called *Venus of Willendorf* (Fig. 549) is probably a fertility figure, judging from its exaggerated breasts, belly, and genitals, and lack of facial features. We know little about it, and we can only guess at its significance. Many sculptures of this kind are highly polished, a result of continuous handling.

The scale of these small objects is dwarfed by the paintings that have been discovered over the course of the last 125 years in caves concentrated in southern France and northern Spain. In 1879, near Santander in northern Spain, a local amateur archeologist, Marcelino de Sautuola, and his daughter were investigating the Altamira caves when the girl noticed the forms of some painted bulls on the low cave roof just above her father's head. These works were initially dismissed as forgeries, until cave after cave of similar paintings were discovered elsewhere in the region.

As with the carved objects, we can only guess at the significance of these paintings. The arrows in the bison from the cave at Niaux (Fig. 550) suggest that the paintings have something to do with hunting. In addition, sharp gouges in the side of the bison suggest that actual spears were hurled at this image, perhaps to invoke success in an upcoming hunt.

15,000 BCE

Beginnings of agriculture in Near East
8000 BCE

15,000 BCE
Cave paintings in France and Spain

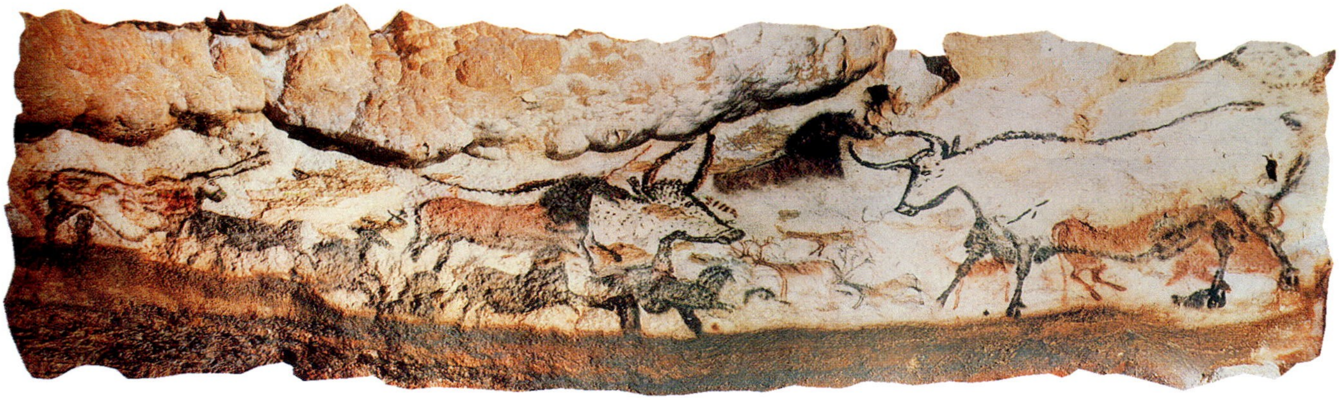

Fig. 551 Hall of Bulls, Lascaux, France, c. 15,000–13,000 BCE.
Approximately life size.

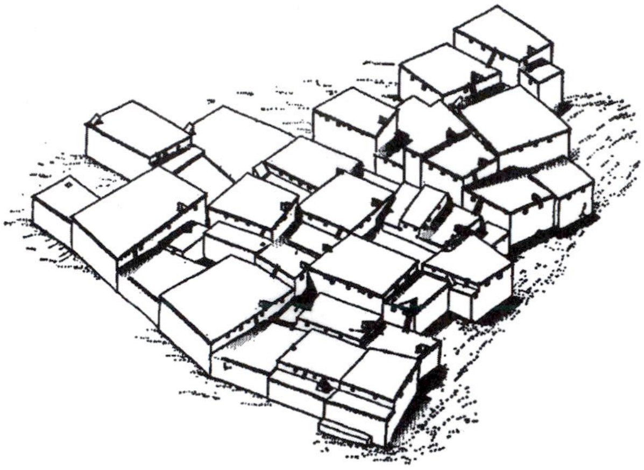

Fig. 552 Houses and shrines at Çatal Hüyük, Turkey, c. 6000 BCE.
Schematic reconstruction after J. Mellart.

The most magnificent of these caves was discovered at Lascaux, in the Dordogne region of France, near the city of Montignac, in 1940, when a dog belonging to some local boys fell into a hole. These drawings at Lascaux (Fig. 551) were done with chunks of red and yellow ocher that was mixed with something like animal fat as a medium. Many flat stones have been discovered that served as palettes for mixing colors. The caves were closed to the public in 1963, after it became evident that moisture and carbon dioxide from the breath of visitors were causing destructive fungi to grow over the paintings.

As the Ice Age waned, around 8000 BCE, humans began to domesticate animals and cultivate food grains, practices that started in the Middle East and spread slowly across Greece and Europe for the next 6,000 years, reaching Britain last. Gradually, Neolithic—or New Stone Age—peoples abandoned temporary shelters for permanent structures built of wood, brick, and stone. Crafts—pottery, and weaving in particular—began to flourish. Religious rituals were regularized in shrines dedicated to that purpose. Remains of highly developed Neolithic communities have been discovered at Jericho, which reached a height of development around 7500 BCE in modern-day Jordan, and at Çatal Hüyük, a community that developed in Turkey about 1,000 years later. Jericho was built around a freshwater spring, vital to life in the near-desert conditions of the region, and was surrounded by huge walls for protection. Çatal Hüyük (Fig. 552) was a trade center with a population of about 10,000 people. First excavated between 1961 and 1965, this village was built of mud bricks and timber. There were no streets, only courtyards, and people passed between houses via the rooftops.

Neolithic society developed most quickly in the world's fertile river valleys. By 4000 BCE, urban societies had developed on the Tigris and Euphrates rivers in Mesopotamia and on the

Invention of writing in Mesopotamia
3500 BCE

4000 BCE
Beginnings of agriculture in China

2000 BCE

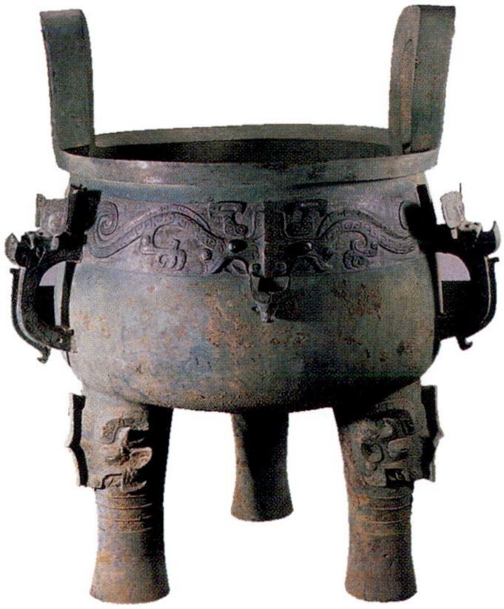

Fig. 553 Five-eared *ding* with dragon pattern, c. 1200 BCE.
Bronze: H. 48 in.; diameter at mouth, 32 3/4 in. Chunhua County Cultural Museum.

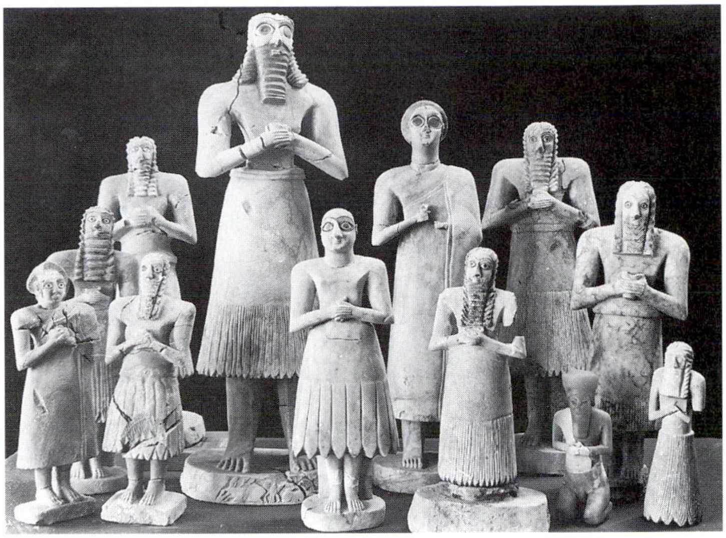

Fig. 554 Worshippers and deities from the Abu Temple, Tell Asmar, Iraq, c. 2700–2500 BCE.
Gypsum, H. of tallest figure, 30 in.
The Iraq Museum, Baghdad, and the Oriental Institute, University of Chicago.

Nile River in Egypt. Similarly complex urban communities were flourishing, by 2200 BCE, in the Indus and Ganges valleys of India and, by 2000 BCE, in the Huang Ho and Yangtze valleys of China (see map on p. 387). Excavations begun at Anyang in northern China, in 1928, have revealed the existence of what is known as the Shang dynasty, which ruled China from about 1766 to 1122 BCE. The great art form of the Shang dynasty was the richly decorated bronze vessel (Fig. 553), made by a casting technique as advanced as any ever used. This vessel was created to hold food during ceremonies dedicated to the worship and memory of ancestors. Many Shang vessels are decorated with symmetrical animal forms, often mythological, and the symmetrical animal mask that decorates it is typical of the bronze work of the period.

SUMERIAN CULTURE

Between 4000 and 3000 BCE, irrigation techniques were developed on the Tigris and Euphrates rivers in Mesopotamia. A complex society emerged, one credited, for instance, with both the invention of the wheel and the invention of writing. By the time they were finally overrun by other peoples in 2030 BCE, the Sumerians had developed schools, libraries, and written laws. Ancient Sumeria consisted of a dozen or more cities, each with a population of between 10,000 and 50,000, and each with its own reigning deity. Each of the local gods had the task of pleading the case of their particular communities with the other gods, who controlled the wind, the rain, and so on. The tallest figure in the collection of Sumerian figures above (Fig. 554) is Abu, the Sumerian god of vegetation. Next to him is a mother goddess. The smaller statues represent worshippers and are stand-ins for actual persons, enabling worshippers, at least symbolically, to engage in continuous prayer and devotion. Eyes were considered by the Sumerians to be the "windows to the soul," which explains why the staring eyes in these sculptures are so large. Communication with the god occurred in a *ziggurat*, a stepped temple, which rose high in the middle of the city (see Fig. 436). An early Mesopotamian text calls the ziggurat "the bond between heaven and earth."

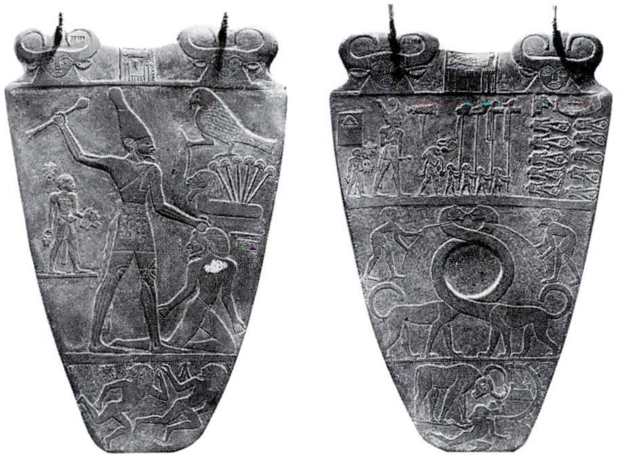

Fig. 555 ***Palette of King Narmer*** **(front and back), Hierakonpolis, Upper Egypt, c. 3000 BCE.**
Slate, H. 25 in. Egyptian Museum, Cairo.

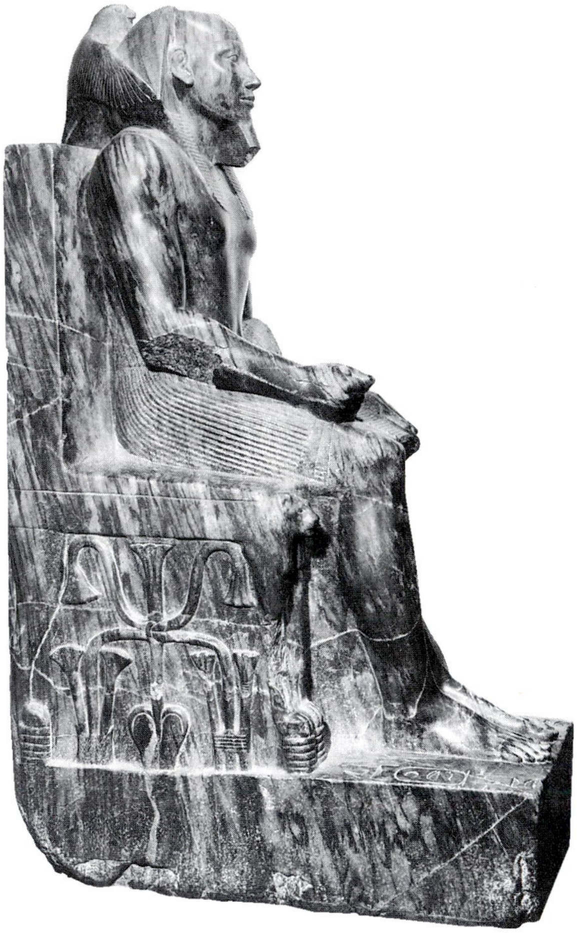

Fig. 556 ***King Chephren,*** **Giza, Egypt, c. 2530 BCE.**
Diorite, H. 66 1/8 in. Egyptian Museum, Cairo.

EGYPTIAN CIVILIZATION

At about the same time that Sumerian culture developed in Mesopotamia, Egyptian society began to flourish along the Nile River. As opposed to Sumeria, which was constantly threatened by invasion, Egypt, protected on all sides by sea and desert, cherished the ideals of order, stability, and endurance, and these ideals are reflected in its art.

Egyptian culture was dedicated to providing a home for the ***ka,*** that part of the human being that defines personality and that survives life on earth after death. The enduring nature of the *ka* required that artisans decorate tombs with paintings that the spirit could enjoy after death. Small servant figures might be carved from wood to serve the departed in the afterlife. The *ka* could find a home in a statue of the deceased. Mummification—the preservation of the body by treating it with chemical solutions and then wrapping it in linen—provided a similar home, as did the elaborate coffins in which the mummy would be placed. The pyramids (see Fig. 435) were, of course, the largest of the resting places designed to house the *ka*.

The enduring quality of the *ka* accounts for the unchanging way in which, over the centuries, Egyptian figures, especially the pharaohs, were represented. A canon of ideal proportions was developed that was almost universally applied. The figure is, in effect, fitted into a grid. The feet rest on the bottom line of the grid, the ankles are placed on the first horizontal line, the knee on the sixth, the navel on the thirteenth (higher on the female), elbows on the fourteenth, and the shoulders on the nineteenth. These proportions are utilized in the *Palette of King Narmer* (Fig. 555)—called a "palette" because eye make-up was prepared on it. The tablet celebrates the victory of Upper Egypt, led by King Narmer, over Lower Egypt, in a battle that united the country. Narmer is depicted

Great Sphinx and Pyramids of Giza
2500 BCE

2000 BCE

2000 BCE
Epic of Gilgamesh written in Mesopotamia

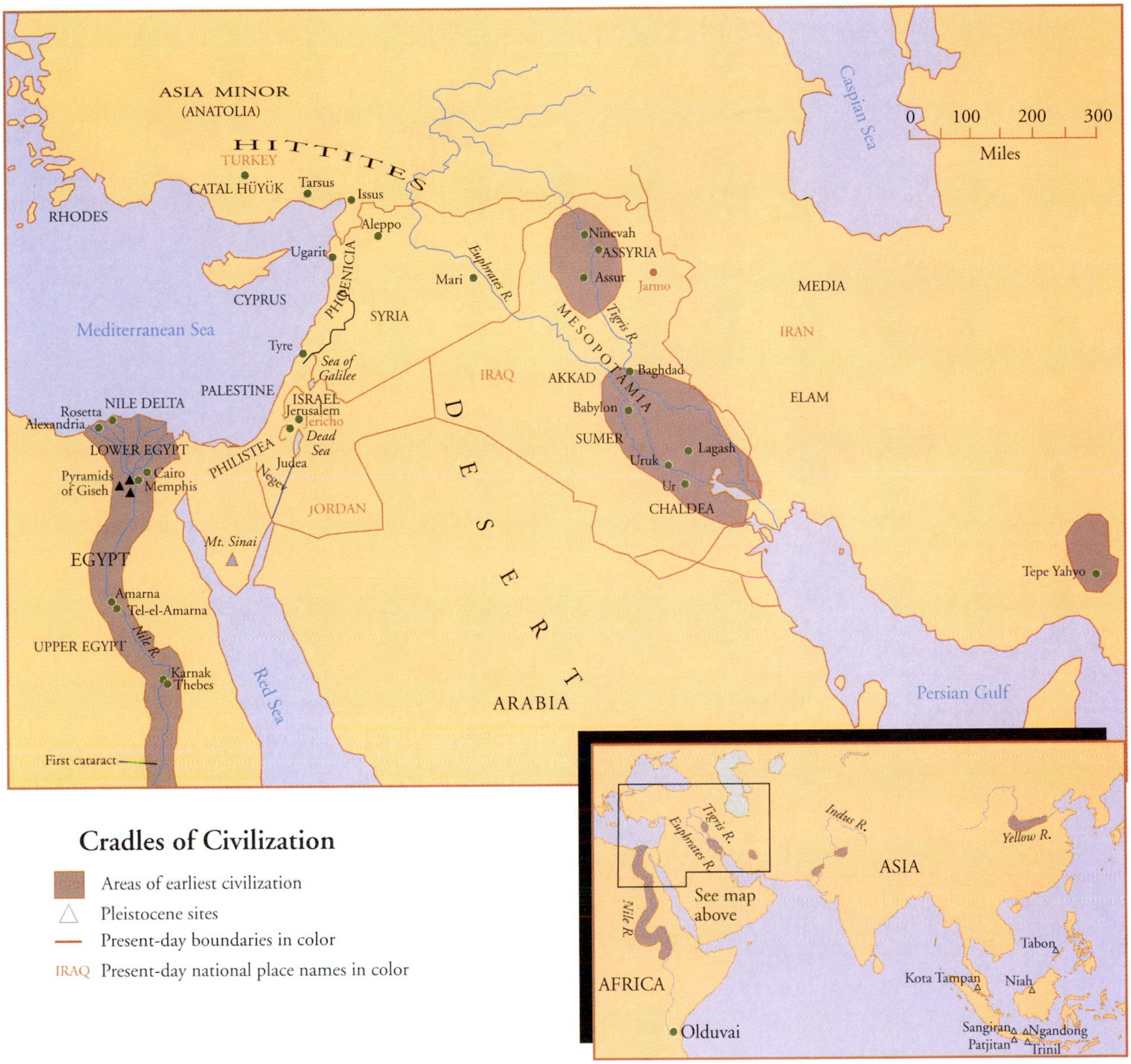

Cradles of Civilization

holding an enemy by the hair, ready to finish him off. On the other side he is seen reviewing the beheaded bodies of this foes. Narmer's pose is typical of Egyptian art. The lower body is in profile, his torso and shoulders full front, his head in profile again, though a single eye is portrayed frontally.

The rigorous geometry governing Egyptian representation is apparent in the statue of Chephren (Fig. 556). Chephren's frontal pose is almost as rigid as the throne upon which he sits. It is as if he had been composed as a block of right angles. The conventions of representation do not apply, however, to the face itself. Great care was taken in the realistic depiction of individual facial features, and, architecture aside, portraiture may be considered one of the greatest accomplishments of Egyptian art.

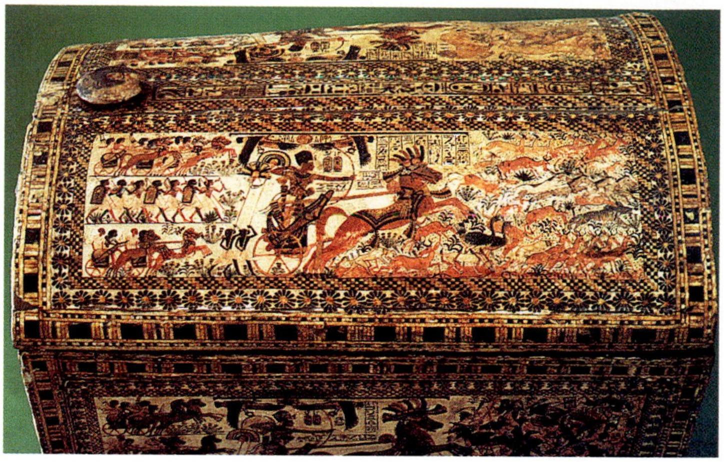

Fig. 558 Painted chest, tomb of Tutankhamen, Thebes, c. 1350 BCE.
L. approx. 20 in. Egyptian Museum, Cairo.

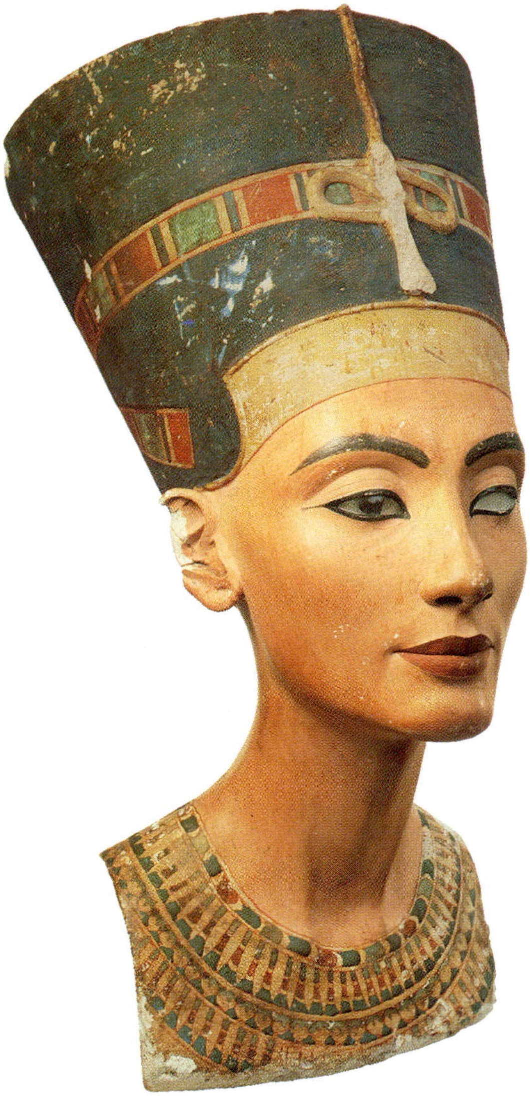

Fig. 557 *Queen Nefertiti,* Tell el Amarna, c. 1365 BCE.
Painted limestone, H. 19 5/8 in. Agyptisches Museum, Berlin.

For a brief period, in the fourteenth century BCE, under the rule of the Emperor Akhenaton, the realism of Egyptian portraiture was extended to the figure as a whole. Akhenaton declared an end to traditional Egyptian religious practices, relaxing especially the longstanding preoccupation with the *ka*. The Egyptians turned their attention to matters of life instead of death, and a sense of naturalistic form developed in their art that, until this time, could be seen only in representations of people of lower rank, such as entertainers. For the first time, Egyptian art showed a taste for the curved form and for a softness of contour, rather than the harshly rigid geometries of the Egyptian canon of proportion. Nowhere is the beauty of this new style more evident than in the famous bust of Akhenaton's queen, Nefertiti (Fig. 557). Both the graceful curve of her neck and her almost completely relaxed look make for a stunningly naturalistic piece of work.

The reason we know this style so well today is because it has survived in the only unplundered Egyptian tomb whose contents have come down to us. The tomb of Akhenaton's successor, Tutankhamen, the famous "King Tut," was discovered at Thebes in 1922. Among the thousands of artifacts recovered at that time was the tomb of King Tut himself, which consists of three coffins, one set within the other. The innermost coffin is made of 243 pounds of beaten gold inlaid in lapis lazuli, turquoise, and carnelian. The scene of the young king hunting, on a painted chest from the tomb (Fig. 558) shows Tutankhamen as larger than life in traditional heirarchical scale. Nevertheless, the sense of movement and action, and the abandonment of the traditional ground line in the wild chaos of the animals on the right, shows the influence of the freer Akhenaton style.

WORKS IN PROGRESS
Drawing in Ancient Egypt

For the ancient Egyptians, drawing was not only a preparatory medium—a design tool in the service of painting, sculpture, and architecture. It was also a self-sufficient medium that has survived in the form of papyrus illustrations (papyrus being a flat, paperlike material made from a water plant native to the Nile Valley), as well as in designs on pots, bowls, and other ceramic objects. Yet it is on what is known as *ostraka* that the majority of Egyptian drawings have come down to us.

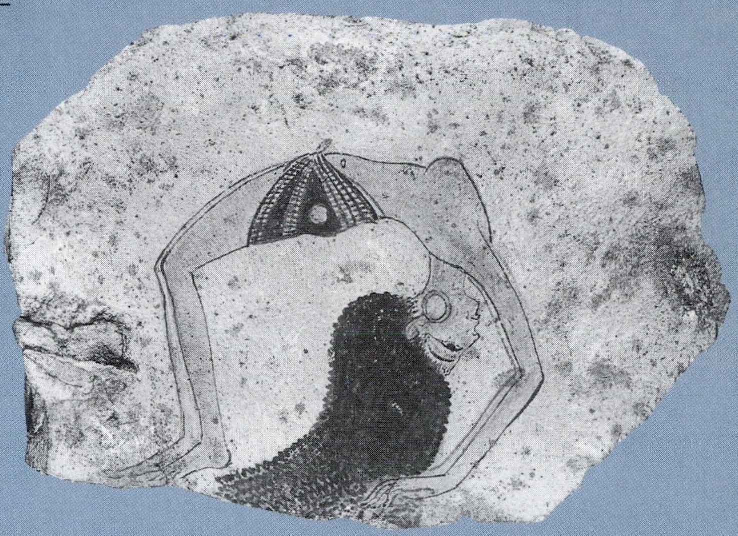

Fig. 560 Acrobatic dancer, Ramsside, c. 1305–1080 BCE. Ink on limestone, 4 ⅛ × 6 ⅝ in. Egyptian Museum, Turin, Italy.

Ostraka are limestone flakes upon which draftsmen made preparatory sketches (papyrus was too costly for such work). These sketches are often of the highest quality, and are similar in purpose to the cartoons for frescoes prepared by Renaissance painters in the West over 2,000 years later. Most of the *ostraka* known to us come from a village called Deir el Medina, which was built to house the artisans who decorated the royal tombs in nearby Thebes. They date from the period of the New Kingdom, during which Tutankhamun ruled, and they reflect the loose curvilinear style of his court.

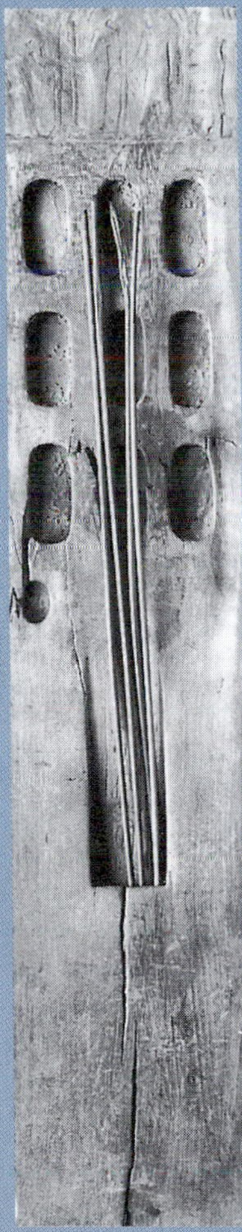

Fig. 559 Pen case of Amen-mes. Dynasty XVII, c. 1305–1196 B.C. Wood, 15 ⅞ × 3 in. Musée du Louvre, Paris; Cliche des Musées Nationaux – Paris. © R. M. N. – SPADEM.

The equipment used by the Egyptian artist consisted of a palette and pen case like the one depicted here, which is decorated with a head drawn in profile on its reverse side (Fig. 559). The depressions in the palette held cakes of pigment, the two most common being red ocher and black, which was obtained from soot. Rushes were used to create the pens. The rush was chiseled to a point, and then flattened to a greater or lesser degree depending on the width of line the artist wished to use. The pen was then dipped in water, the wet nib mixed with pigment, and the artist was ready to draw.

The *ostraka* above (Fig. 560) depicts one of the acrobatic dancers who were part of most religious ceremonies. Dancers such as this one even participated in funeral rituals. It is believed that their purpose was to create a mood of intense physical activity. Reporting on his Egyptian Expedition of 1925–1927, N. de Garis Davies wrote in the *Bulletin of the Metropolitan Museum of Art* that such acrobatic dancing was designed to help spectators and participants "reach a physical rhapsody, a throbbing emotion, which . . . must be induced by the sight of rapid physical action and the sound of strong monotonous rhythm." Notice that in this drawing, the dancer's large loop earring defies the laws of gravity, suggesting that the artist drew the body first, and then turned the *ostraka* upside down to draw the head.

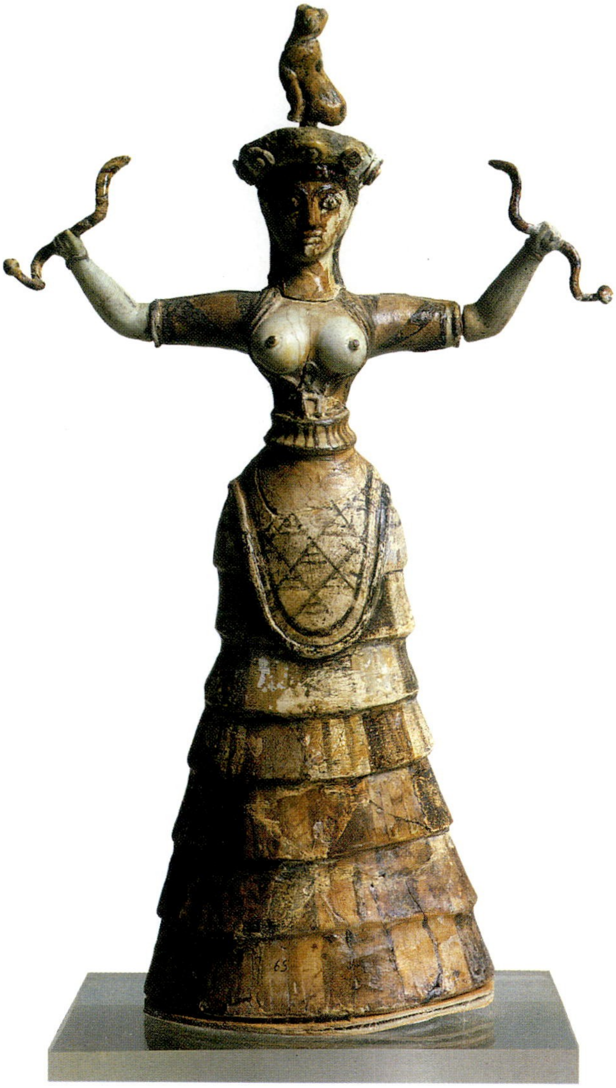

Fig. 561 ***Snake Goddess or Priestess*****, c. 1600 BCE.**
Faience, H. 11 5/8 in. Archeological Museum, Heraklion, Crete.

The Akhenaton style did not survive long in Egypt. Soon after King Tut's death, traditional religious practices were reestablished, and a revival of the old style of art, with its unrelentingly stiff formality, quickly followed. For the next 1,000 years, the Egyptians maintained the conventions and formulas that their forefathers had initiated in the first half of the third millennium BCE.

AEGEAN CIVILIZATIONS

The Egyptians had significant contact with other civilizations in the eastern Mediterranean, particularly with the Minoan civilization on the island of Crete and with Mycenae on the Greek Peloponnesus, the southern peninsula of Greece. The origin of the Minoans is unclear—they may have arrived on the island as early as 6000 BCE—but their culture reached its peak between 1600 and 1400 BCE. The chief deity of Minoan culture was a fertility goddess represented in several different forms. As she appears here (Fig. 561), her bare breasts indicate female fecundity, while the snakes she carries are associated with male fertility. Nothing like her has been discovered in any other culture.

The so-called *"Toreador" Fresco* (Fig. 562), from the Minoan palace at Knossos, does not actually depict a bullfight, as its title suggests. Instead, a youthful acrobat can be seen vaulting over the bull's back as one maiden holds the animal's horns and another waits to catch him. The similarity between this image and the Egyptian ostraka on the preceeding page demonstrates how much contact there was between the Minoans and the Egyptians. Both, at any rate, valued the activity, grace, and agility of athletes, something that the later Greeks, in founding the Olympic Games, would also value highly.

In Minoan culture, the bull was an animal of sacred significance. Legend has it that the wife of King Minos, after whom the culture takes its name, gave birth to a creature half-human and half-bull, that was the *Minotaur.* Minos had a giant labyrinth, or maze, constructed to house the creature, to whom Athenian youths and maidens were sacrificed until it was killed by the hero Theseus. The legend of the labyrinth probably arose in response to the intricate design of the palaces built for the Minoan kings.

It is unclear why Minoan culture abruptly ended in approximately 1450 BCE. Great earthquakes and volcanic eruptions may have

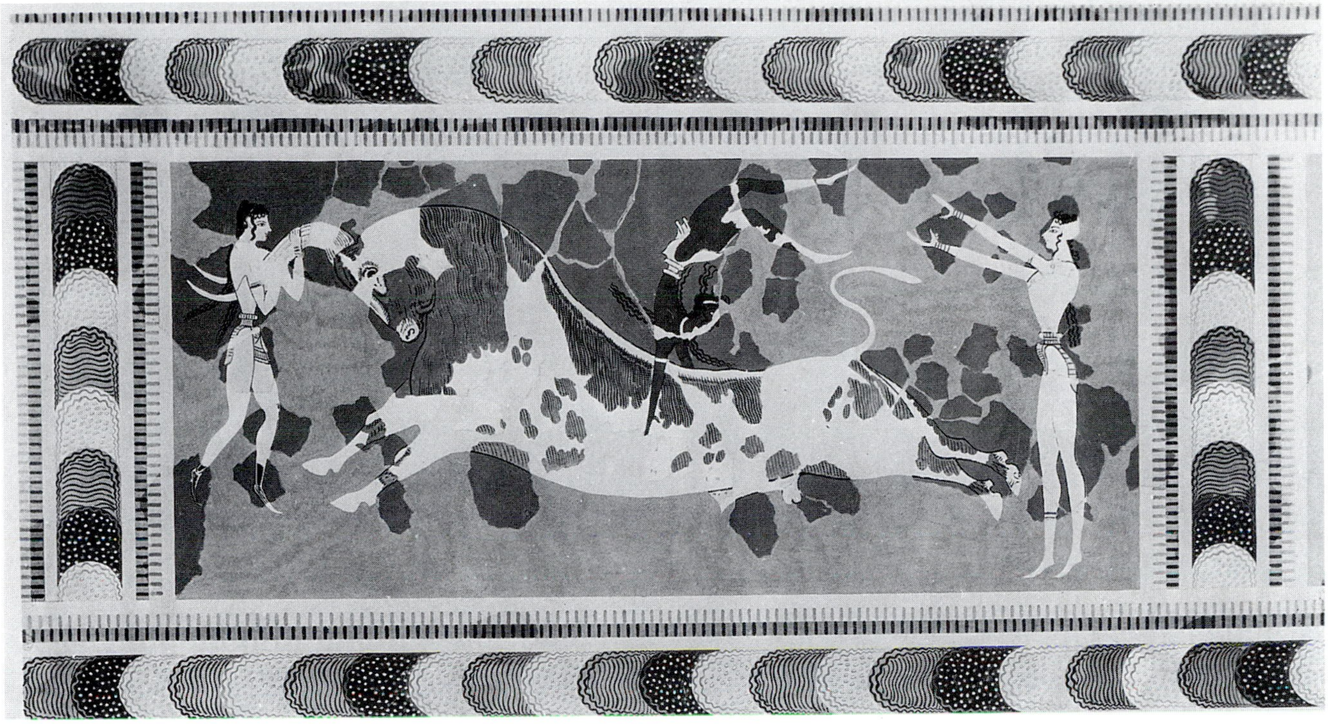

Fig. 562 ***The "Toreador" Fresco,*** **Knossos, Crete, c. 1500 BCE.**
H. including upper border approx. 24 ½ in. Archeological Museum, Heraklion, Crete.

destroyed the civilization, or, perhaps, it fell victim to the warlike Mycenaeans from the mainland, whose culture flourished between 1400 and 1200 BCE. Theirs was a culture dominated by military values. In the *The Warrior Vase* (Fig. 563) we see Mycenaean soldiers marching to war, perhaps to meet the Dorian invaders who destroyed their civilization soon after 1200 BCE. The Dorian weapons were made of iron and therefore were superior to the softer bronze Mycenaean spears. It is this culture, immortalized by Homer in the *Iliad* and the *Odyssey,* that sacked the great Trojan city of Troy. The Mycenaeans built stone fortresses on the hilltops of the Peloponnesus, a peninsula forming part of the Greek mainland. They buried their dead in so-called beehive tombs, which, dome-shaped, were full of gold and silver, including masks of the royal dead, a burial practice similar to that of the Egyptians.

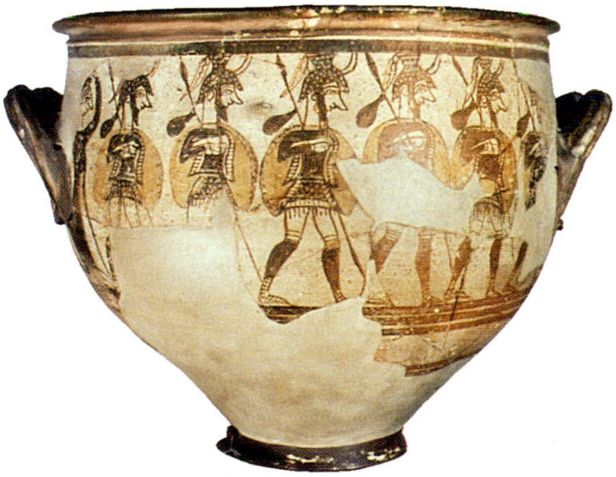

Fig. 563 ***The Warrior Vase,*** **Mycenae, c. 1200 BCE.**
H. approx. 14 in. National Museum, Athens.

Rule of the
Hebrew King, David
960–933 BCE

1200 BCE

c. 1000 BCE
Agriculture practices in village communities in American Southwest

c. 800 BCE
Homer writes *Iliad* and *Odyssey*

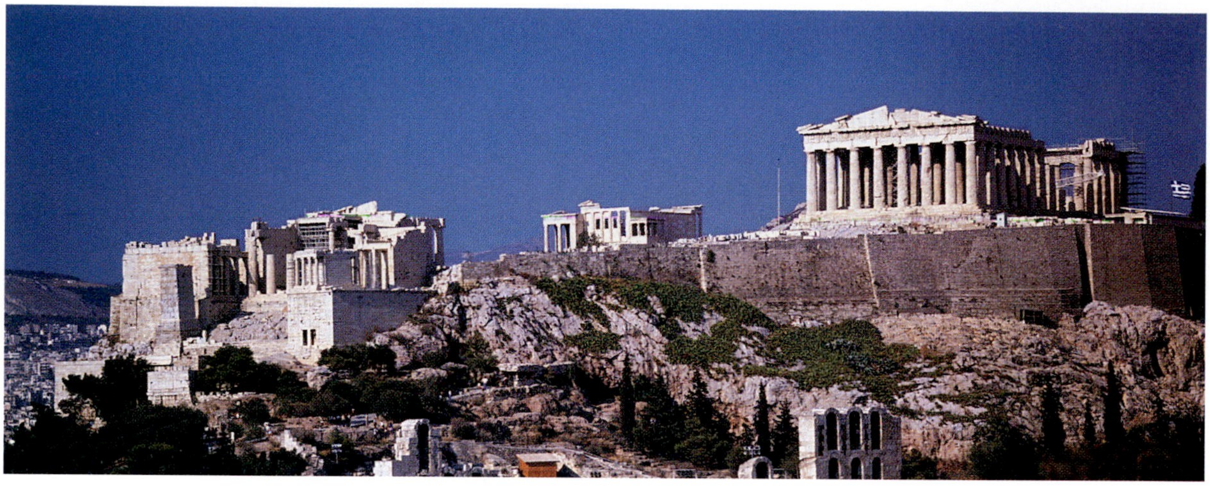

Fig. 564 The Acropolis today, viewed from the southwest, Athens, Greece. Parthenon at the right, constructed between 448 and 432 BCE.

GREEK ART

The rise of the Greek city-state, or *polis,* marks the moment when Western culture begins to celebrate its own human strengths and powers—the creative genius of the mind itself—over the power of nature. The Western world's gods now became personified, taking human form and assuming human weaknesses. Though immortal, they were otherwise versions of ourselves, no longer angry beasts or natural phenomena such as the earth, the sun, or the rain.

In about 1200 BCE, just after the fall of Mycenae, the Greek world consisted of various tribes separated by the geographical features of the peninsula, with its deep bays, narrow valleys, and jagged mountains. These tribes soon developed into independent and often warring city-states, with their own constitutions, coinage, and armies. We know that in 776 BCE these feuding states declared a truce in order to hold the first Olympic games, a moment so significant that the Greeks later took it as the starting point of their history.

The human figure celebrated in athletic contests is the most important subject of Greek art as well. Only during the short reign of Pharaoh Akhenaton, in Egypt (Fig. 557), had there been such concern to depict the human form in a realistic manner. By the fifth century BCE, this interest in humanity was reflected throughout Greek culture. The philosopher Plato developed theories not only about social and political relations but about education and aesthetic pleasure. The physician Hippocrates systematically studied human disease, and the historian Herodotus, in his account of the Persian Wars, began to chronicle human history. Around 500 BCE, in Athens, all free male citizens were included in the political system, and democracy—from *demos,* meaning "people," and *kratia,* meaning "power"—was born. It was not quite democracy as we think of it today: slavery was considered natural, and women were excluded from political life. Nevertheless, the concept of individual freedom was cherished.

The values of the Greek city-state were embodied in its temples. The temple was usually situated on an elevated site, above the city, and the **acropolis,** from *akros,* meaning "top," and *polis,* "city," was conceived as the center of civic life. The crowning achievement of Greek architecture is the complex of buildings on the Acropolis in Athens (Fig. 564), which was built to replace those destroyed by the Persians in 480 BCE. Construction began in about 450 BCE, under the leadership of the great Athenian statesman, Pericles. The central building of the new complex, designed by Ictinus and

Poet Sappho of Lesbos
c. 610–580 BCE

594 BCE
Solon's code of laws in Athens

Confucius in China
551–479 BCE

5th century BCE
Drama of Sophocles, Euripides, Aristophanes. Historical writings of Herodotus, Thucydides

400 BCE

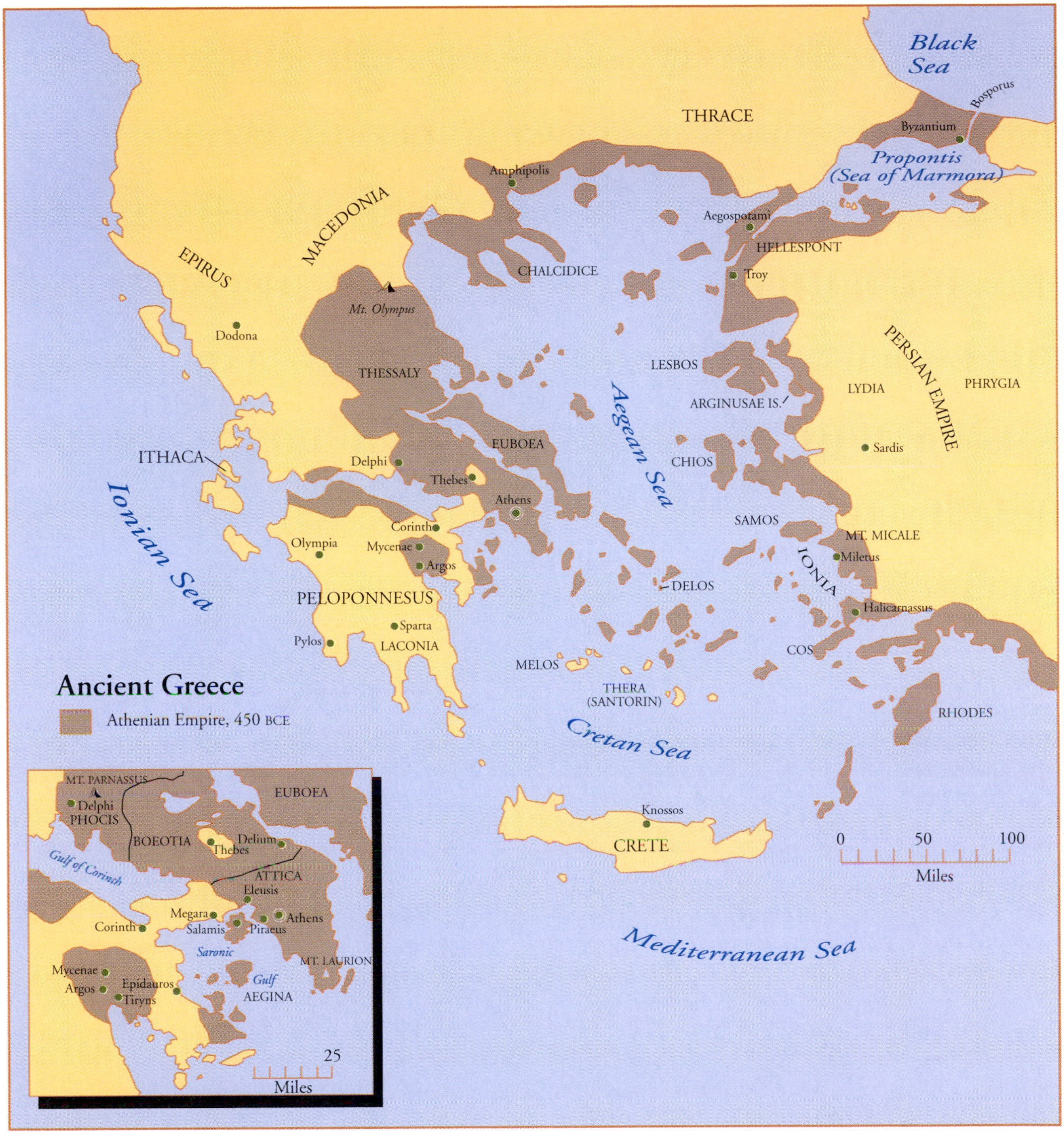

Callicrates, was the Parthenon, dedicated to the city's namesake, Athena Parthenos, the goddess of wisdom. A Doric temple of the grandest scale, it is composed entirely of marble. At its center was an enormous ivory and gold statue of Athena, sculpted by Phidias, who was in charge of all the ornamentation and sculpture for the project. The Athena is long since lost, and we can imagine his achievement only by considering the sculpture on the building's pediment (see Fig. 341) and its friezes, all of which reflect Phidias's style and may be his design.

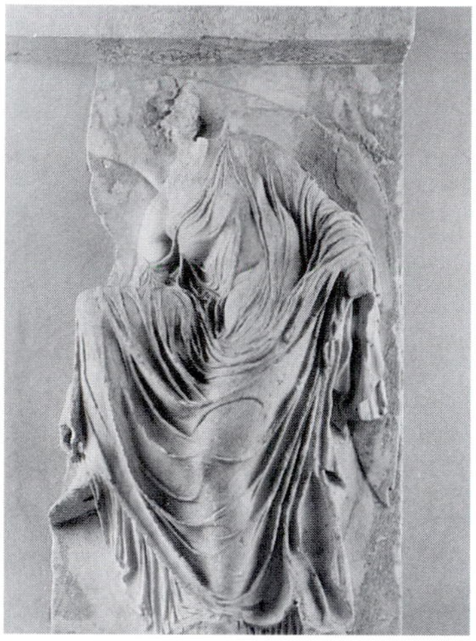

Fig. 565 ***Nike,* from the balustrade of the Temple of Athena Nike, c. 410–407 BCE.**
Marble, H. 42 in. Acropolis Museum, Athens.

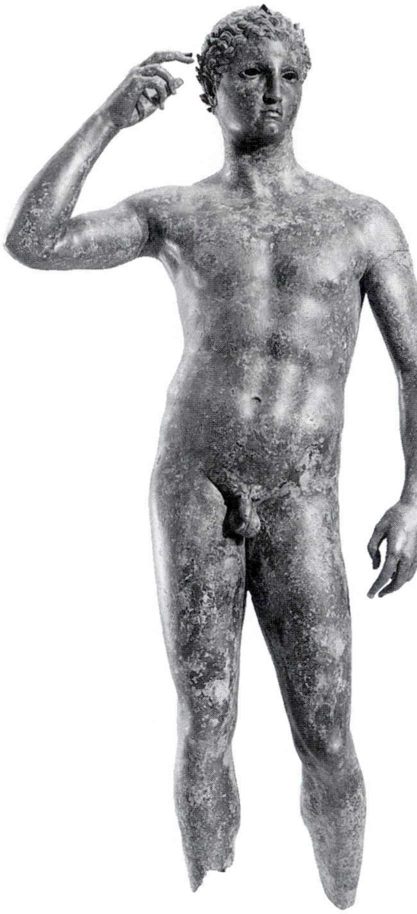

Fig. 566 Unknown, perhaps a pupil of Lysippos, *Statue of a Victorious Athlete,* Greek, last quarter of the 4th century BCE.
Bronze, 59 5/8 in. Collection of J. Paul Getty Museum, Malibu, California.

The Phidian style is marked by its naturalness. The human figure often assumes a relaxed, seemingly effortless pose, or it may be caught in the act of movement, athletic or casual. In either case, the precision with which the anatomy has been rendered is remarkable. The relief of *Nike* (Fig. 565), goddess of victory, from the balustrade of the Temple of Nike (see Fig. 442) is a perfect example of the Phidian style. As Nike bends to take off her sandal, the drapery both reveals and conceals the body beneath. Sometimes appearing to be transparent, sometimes dropping in deep folds and hollows, it contributes importantly to the sense of reality conveyed by the sculpture. It is as if we can see the body literally push forward out of the stone and press against the drapery.

The Greek passion for individualism, reason, and accurate observation of the world continued on even after the disastrous defeat of Athens in the Peloponnesian War in 404 BCE, which led to a great loss of Athenian power. In 338 BCE, the army of Philip, King of Macedon, conquered Greece, and after Philip's death two years later, his son, Alexander the Great, came to power. Because Philip greatly admired Athenian culture, Alexander was educated by the philosopher Aristotle, who persuaded the young king to impose Greek culture throughout his empire. **Hellenism,** or the culture of Greece, thus came to dominate the Western world. The court sculptor to Alexander the Great was Lysippos, known to us only through later Roman copies of his work. The *Statue of a Victorious Athlete* (Fig. 566), recently discovered in the Adriatic Sea, captures the body in its fleeting movements with such naturalness—the Lysippic ideal—that some scholars feel it may be the work of the master himself.

In the sculpture of the fourth century BCE, we discover a graceful, even sensuous, beauty marked by *contrapposto* and three-dimensional

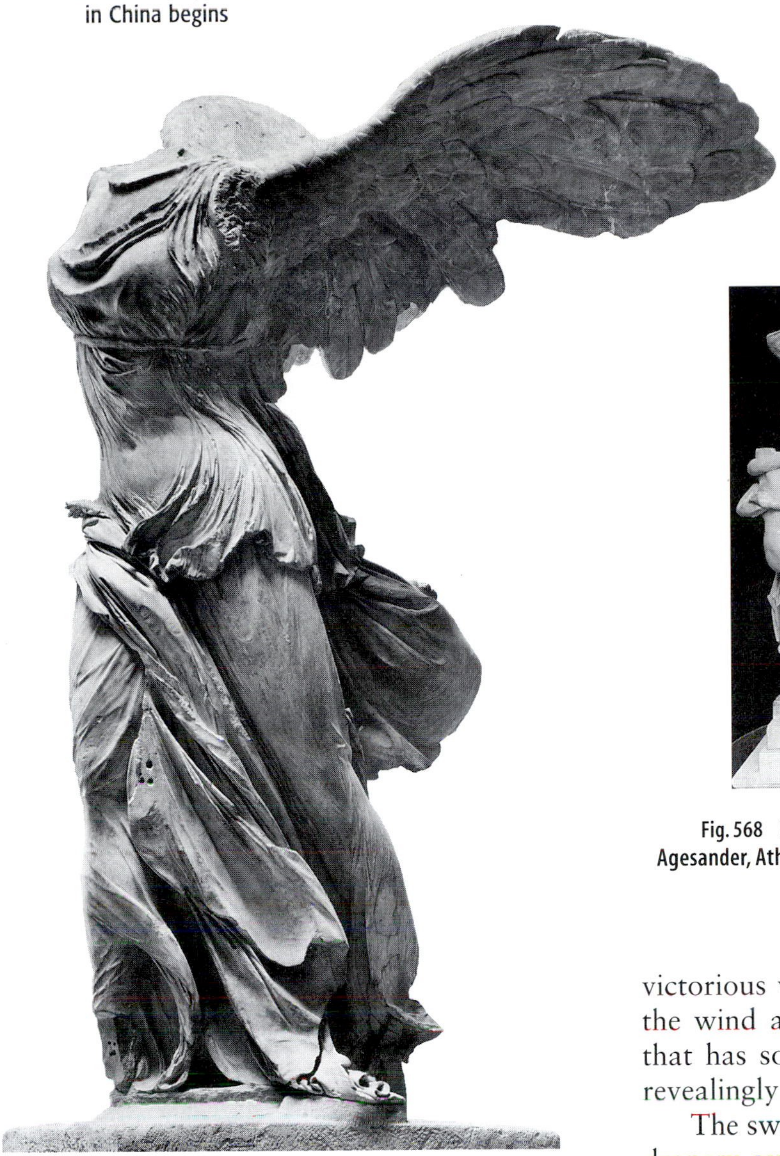

Fig. 567 ***Nike of Samothrace,*** **c. 190 BCE.**
Marble, H. approx. 8 ft. Musée du Louvre, Paris.

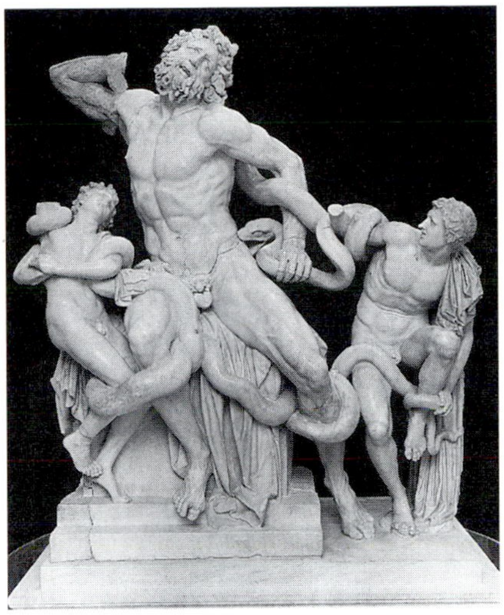

Fig. 568 ***The Laocoön Group,*** **Roman copy, perhaps after Agesander, Athenodorus, and Polydorus of Rhodes, 1st century CE.**
Marble, H. 7 ft. Vatican Museums, Rome.

realism (see Figs. 99 and 337). The depiction of physical beauty becomes an end in itself, and sculpture increasingly seems to be more about the pleasures of seeing than anything else. At the same time, artists strove for an ever greater degree of realism, and in the sculpture of the Hellenistic Age we find an increasingly animated and dramatic treatment of the figure. The *Nike of Samothrace* (Fig. 567) is a masterpiece of Hellenistic realism. The goddess has been depicted as she alights on the prow of a victorious war galley, and one can almost feel the wind as it buffets her and the surf spray that has soaked her garment so that it clings revealingly to her torso.

The swirl of line that was once restricted to drapery overwhelms the entire composition of *The Laocoön Group* (Fig. 568), in which Laocoön, a Trojan priest, and his two sons are overwhelmed by serpents sent by the sea-god Poseidon. We are caught in the midst of the the Trojan War. The Greeks have sent the Trojans a giant wooden horse as a "gift." Inside it are Greek soldiers, and Laocoön suspects as much. And so Poseidon, who favors the Greeks, has chosen to silence Laocoön forever. So theatrical is the group that to many eyes it verges on melodrama, but its expressive aims are undeniable. The sculptor is no longer content simply to represent the figure realistically; sculpture must convey emotion as well.

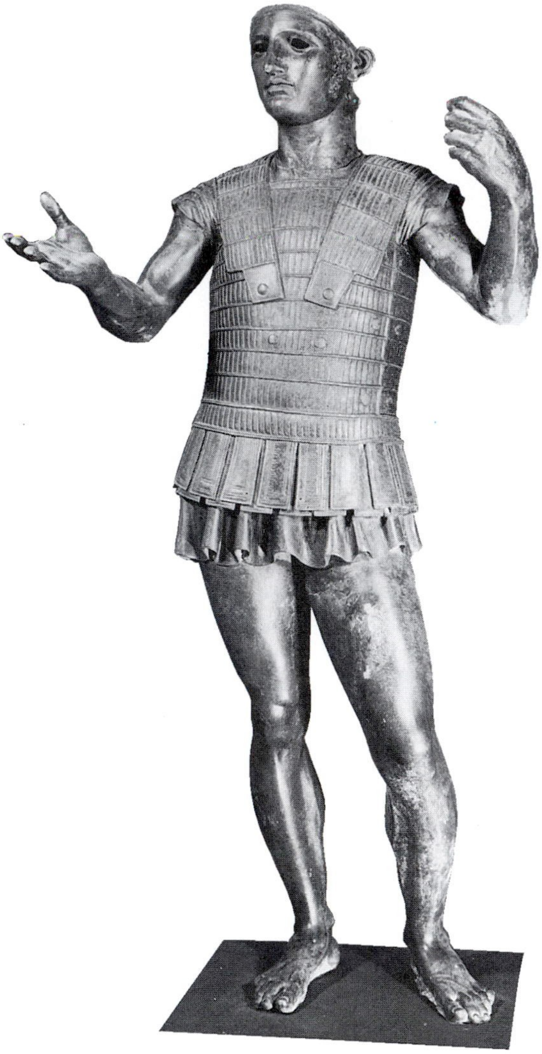

Fig. 569 ***Mars from Todi,*** **early 4th century BCE.**
Bronze, H. 56 in. Vatican Museums, Rome.

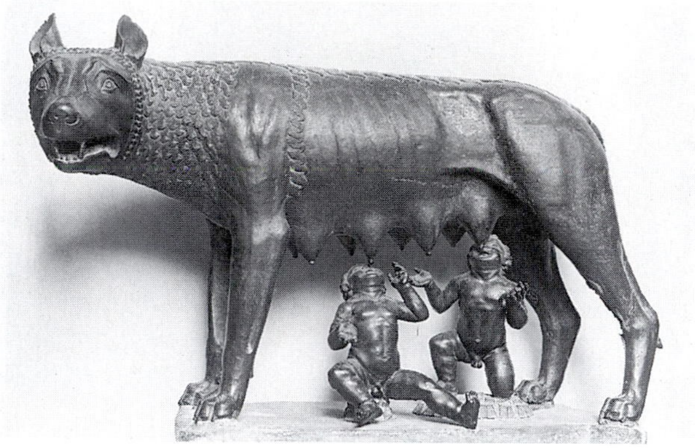

Fig. 570 ***She-Wolf,*** **c. 500 BCE.**
Bronze, H. 33 1/2 in. Museo Capitolino, Rome.

ROMAN ART

Although the Romans conquered Greece (in 146 BCE), like Philip of Macedon and Alexander, they regarded Greek culture and art as superior to any other. Thus, like the Hellenistic Empire before it, the Roman Empire possessed a distinctly Greek character. The Romans imported thousands of original Greek artworks and had them copied in even greater numbers. In fact, much of what we know today about Greek art, we know only through Roman copies. The Greek gods were adapted to the Roman religion, Jupiter bearing a strong resemblance to Zeus, Venus to Aphrodite, and so on. The Romans used the Greek architectural orders in their own buildings and temples, preferring especially the highly decorative Corinthian order. Many, if not most, of Rome's artists were of Greek extraction, though they were "Romanized" to the point of being indistinguishable from the Romans themselves.

Roman art derives, nevertheless, from at least one other source. Around 750 BCE, at about the same time the Greeks first colonized the southern end of the Italian peninsula, the Etruscans, whose language has no relation to any known tongue, and whose origin is somewhat mysterious, established a vital set of city-states in the area between present-day Florence and Rome. Little remains of the Etruscan cities, which were destroyed and rebuilt by Roman armies in the second and third centuries BCE, and we know the Etruscans' culture largely through their sometimes richly decorated tombs. At Veii, just north of Rome, the Etruscans established a sculptural center that gave them a reputation as the finest metalworkers of the age. They traded widely, and from the sixth century on, a vast array of bronze objects, from statues to hand mirrors, were made for export. Etruscan art was influenced by the Greeks, as

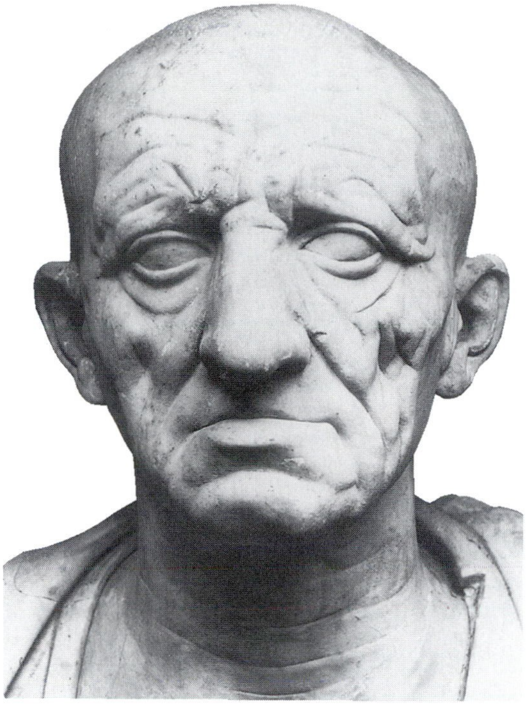

Fig. 571 ***Portrait of a Roman,* c. 80 BCE.**
Marble, lifesize. Palazzo Torlonia, Rome.
Metropolitan Museum of Art, New York. Rogers Fund, 1912.

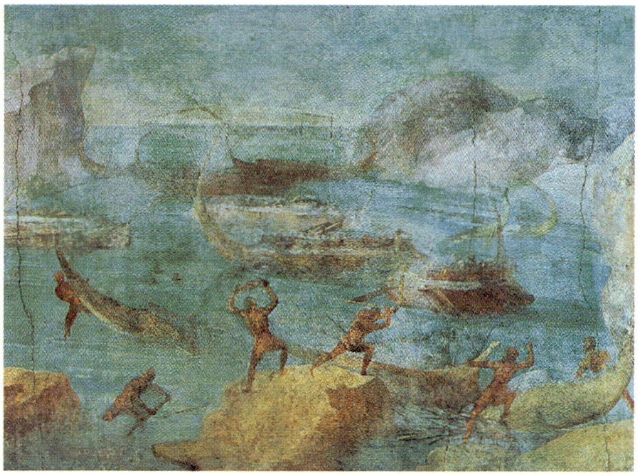

Fig. 572 ***Ulysses in the Land of the Lestrygonians,* from a Roman patrician house, 50–40 BCE.**
Fresco, H. 60 in. Vatican Library, Rome.

the lifesize portrait of a young man dressed as the god of war, *Mars from Todi* (Fig. 569), makes clear.

The Romans traced their ancestry to the Trojan prince Aeneas, who escaped after the sack of Troy and who appears in Homer's *Iliad*. The city of Rome itself was founded early in Etruscan times—in 753 BCE, the Romans believed—by Romulus and Remus, twins nurtured by a *She-Wolf* (Fig. 570). Though Romulus and Remus are Renaissance additions to the original Etruscan bronze, the image served as the totem of the city of Rome from the day on which a statue of a she-wolf, possibly this very one, was dedicated on the Capitoline Hill in Rome in 296 BCE. The she-wolf reminded the Romans of the fiercely protective loyalty and power of their motherland.

Beginning in the fifth century BCE, Rome dedicated itself to conquest and created an empire that included all areas surrounding the Mediterranean and that stretched as far north as present-day England. By the time the Romans conquered Greece, their interest in the accurate portrayal of human features was long established, and Hellenistic art only supported this tendency. But where the Greeks had sought to idealize their figures, to render them perfectly proportioned and beautiful to the eye, the Romans preferred absolute realism. As the bust of a Roman citizen makes clear (Fig. 571), no matter how unflattering the subject's features, they were portrayed as they were.

In painting, the Romans were dedicated to a similar *verism,* or truth to nature. They had still lifes and illusionistic "window views" painted in fresco on the walls of their villas (see Figs. 305 and 306). Atmospheric perspective was commonplace, and three-dimensional effects were achieved by means of *chiaroscuro*. The illusionistic landscape above (Fig. 572) portrays a moment from Homer's *Odyssey,* in which the Lestrygonians hurl rocks at Ulysses's fleet.

The perfection of the arch and dome and the development of structural concrete were, as we have seen in Part 4, the Romans' major architectural contributions. But they were

Romans destroy the Hebrew Temple in Jerusalem
CE 70

CE 1

CE 30
Crucifixion of Jesus

CE 180
Pax Romana begins to break down

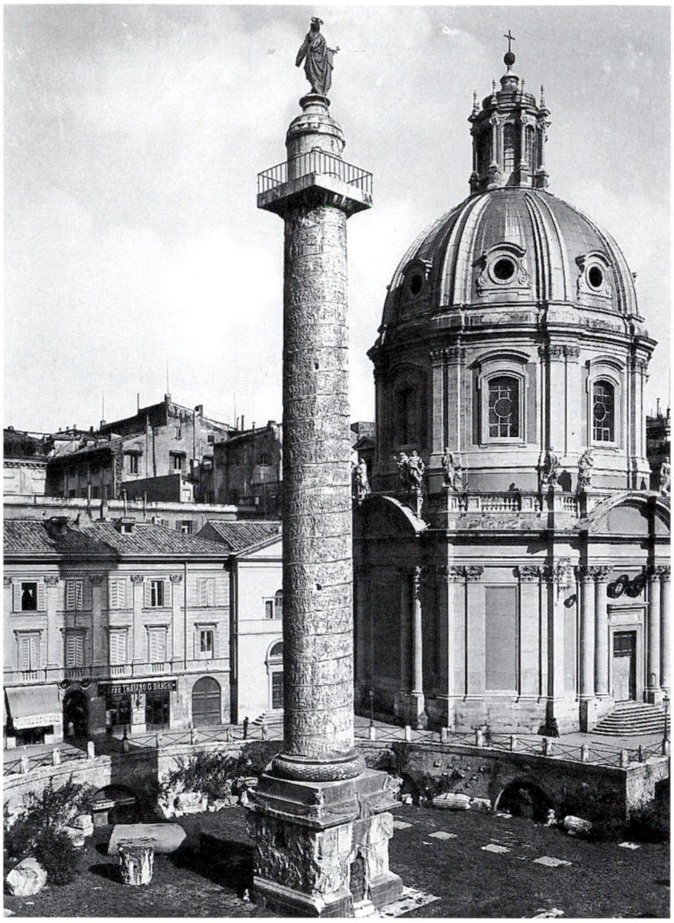

Fig. 573 Attributed to Apollodorus, *Column of Trajan*, CE 113.
Marble, H. originally 128 ft.; L. of frieze approx. 625 ft. Rome. Alinari/Art Resource.

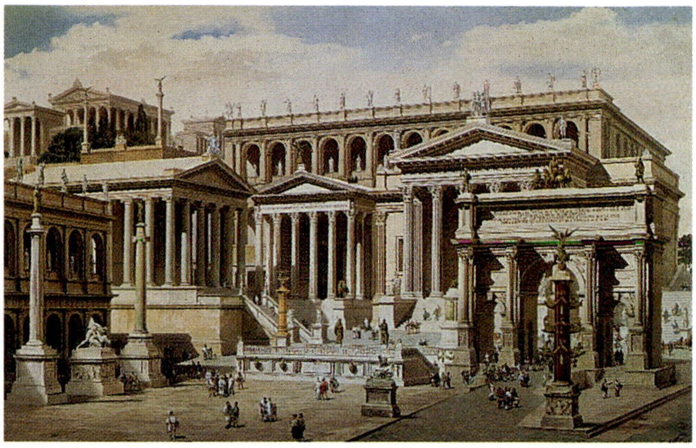

Fig. 574 Bechetti, *Reconstruction of the Roman Forum, Northern Part.*
Watercolor. Superintendent of Architecture, Rome. Scala/Art Resource.

extraordinary monument builders. Many of their triumphal arches still stand across Europe. One remarkable symbol of their power is the *Column of Trajan* (Fig. 573). Encircled by a spiraling band of relief sculpture 50 inches high and, if it were unwound and stretched out, 625 feet long, the column details the Emperor Trajan's two successful campaigns in present-day Hungary and Romania in the first century BCE. The 150 separate episodes celebrate not only military victories but Rome's civilizing mission as well.

As the empire solidified its strength under the Pax Romana—150 years of peace initiated by the Emperor Augustus in 27 BCE—a succession of emperors celebrated the glory of the empire in a variety of elaborate public works and monuments, including the Colosseum and the Pantheon (see Figs. 448 and 453). The most extravagant architectural expression of the Roman state was the Forum Romanum, the political center of Rome. At the time represented in this imaginary reconstruction (Fig. 574), around the first century CE, Rome's population approached 1 million. Most of its inhabitants lived in apartment buildings surrounding the Forum area. An archival record indicates that, at this time, there were only 1,797 private homes in the city. The Etruscans had developed the site as a marketplace, but in a plan developed by Julius Caesar and implemented by Augustus, the Forum became the symbol of Roman power and grandeur, paved in marble and dominated by colonnaded public spaces, temples, basilicas, and state buildings such as the courts, the archives, and the Curia, or senate house.

Though Rome became extraordinarily wealthy, the empire began to falter after the death of the emperor Marcus Aurelius in CE 180. Invasions of Germanic tribes from the north, Berbers from the south, and Persians from the east wreaked havoc upon the Empire's economic, administrative, and military structure. By the time the Emperor Constantine decided to move the capital to Byzantium in CE 323—renaming it Constantinople, today's

Barbarian invasions of China begin

c. 300

CE 400

313

Constantine gives Christianity favored status in Roman Empire

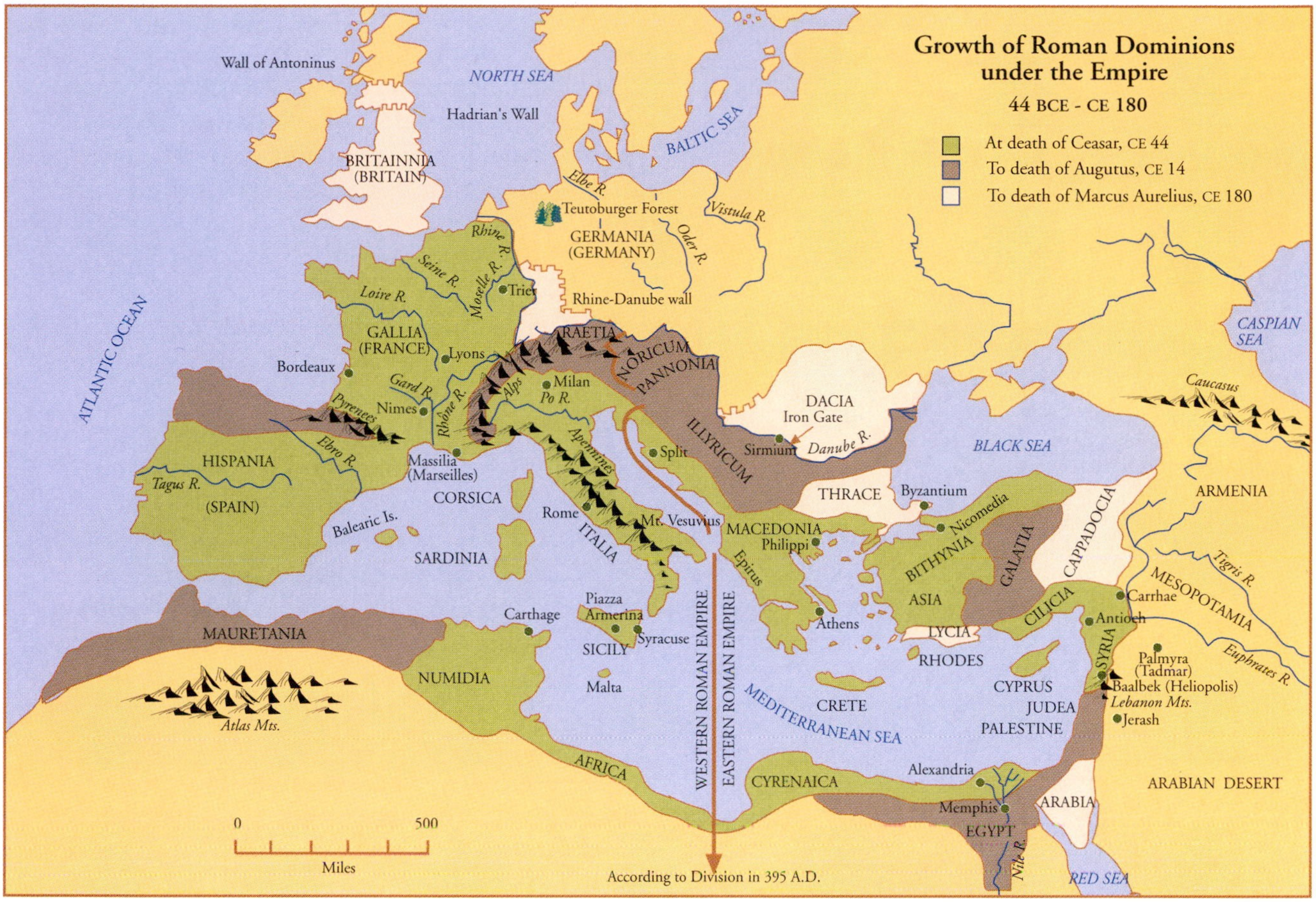

Istanbul—the empire was hopelessly divided, and the establishment of the new capital only underscored the division.

DEVELOPMENTS IN ASIA

Meanwhile, in Asia, the early artistic traditions developed during the Shang dynasty in China, particularly the casting of bronze (see Fig. 553), were continued. Even as the Roman Empire began to disintegrate, bronze casting in China reached new heights of subtlety and elegance. An example is *Flying Horse Poised on One Leg on a Swallow* (Fig. 575). It is perfectly balanced—almost impossibly so, defying gravity itself—so that it seems to have stolen the ability to fly from the bird beneath its hoof.

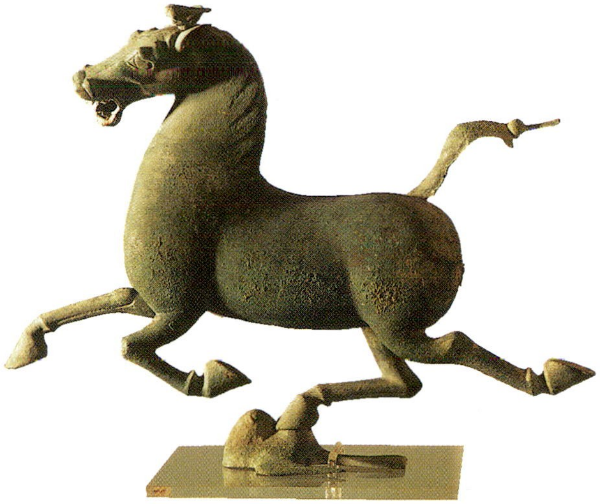

Fig. 575 ***Flying Horse Poised on One Leg on a Swallow,*** **from a tomb at Wuwei, Kansu, Late Han dynasty, 2nd century CE.**
Bronze, H. 13 1/2 in.; L. 17 3/4 in.
The Exhibition of the Archeological Finds of the People's Republic of China.

Cyrus the Great establishes the Iranian Empire in Persia
539 BCE

Life of Socrates
469–399 BCE

600 BCE

c. 500–200 BCE
Rise of Taoist and legalist schools of thought in China

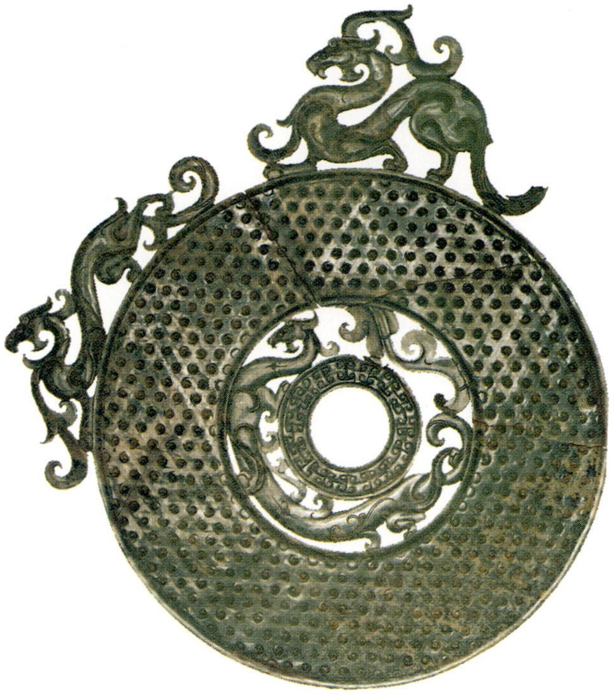

Fig. 576 Ritual Disc with Dragon Motif (*Pi*), Eastern Chou Dynasty, Warring States period 4th–3rd century B.C.;
Jade; diameter 6 ½" diameter (16.5 cm.) The Nelson-Atkins Museum of Art Kansas City, Missouri. (Purchase: Nelson Trust)

Though the traditions of bronze casting remained strong, that part of the world developed no less turbulently than the West. By the sixth century BCE, the Chinese empire had begun to dissolve into a number of warring feudal factions. The resulting political and social chaos brought with it a powerful upsurge of philosophical and intellectual thought that focused on how to remedy the declining social order. In the context of this debate, Confucius, who died in 479 BCE, ten years before the birth of Socrates, introduced the idea that high office should be obtained by merit, not birth, and that all social institutions, from the state to the family, should base their authority on loyalty and respect, not sheer might. At the same time, the Taoists developed a philosophy based on the universal principle, or Tao—the achievement by the individual of a pure harmony with nature (for an image embodying the Tao in a later Chinese painting, see Fig. 4).

The jade *Pi*, or disc (Fig. 576), illustrated here symbolizes the desire of the Chinese to unify their country. Made sometime between the 6th and 3rd centuries BCE, the disc is decorated with a dragon and a phoenix, which are today commonly found in the context of the Chinese wedding ceremony, hanging together as a pair over the table at the wedding feast. The tradition goes back to a time when the ancient peoples of China were united in an historic alliance between those from western China, who worshiped the dragon, and those from eastern China, who worshipped the phoenix. This particular disc was found in a tomb, probably placed there because the Chinese believed that jade preserved the body from decay.

Peace lasted in China from 221 BCE, when Shih Huang Ti, the first emperor of Ch'-in, whose tomb was discussed in Chapter 12 (Fig. 344), united the country under one rule. This lasted until the end of the Han dynasty in CE 220, when China once again endured a 400-year period of disorder and instability. The Han restored Confucianism to prominence. We know through surviving literary descriptions that the Han emperors built lavish palaces, richly decorated with wall paintings. In one of the few imperial Han tombs to have been discovered, that of the Emperor Wu Ti's brother and his wife, both bodies were dressed in suits made of over 2,000 jade tablets sewn together with gold wire. The prosperity of the Han dynasty was due largely to the expansion of trade, particularly the export of silk. The silk-trading routes reached all the way to Imperial Rome.

Elsewhere in Asia, the philosophy of Buddha, "The Enlightened One," was taking hold. Born as Siddhartha Gautama around 537 BCE, Buddha achieved *nirvana*—the release from worldly desires that ends the cycle of death and reincarnation and begins a state of permanent bliss. He preached a message of self-denial and meditation across northern India, attracting converts from all levels of Indian society. The religion gained strength for centuries after Buddha's death, and finally became institutionalized in

Kushite Empire of Africa reaches its pinnacle
c. 250 BCE

200 BCE

c. 256–206 BCE
Original Great Wall of China built

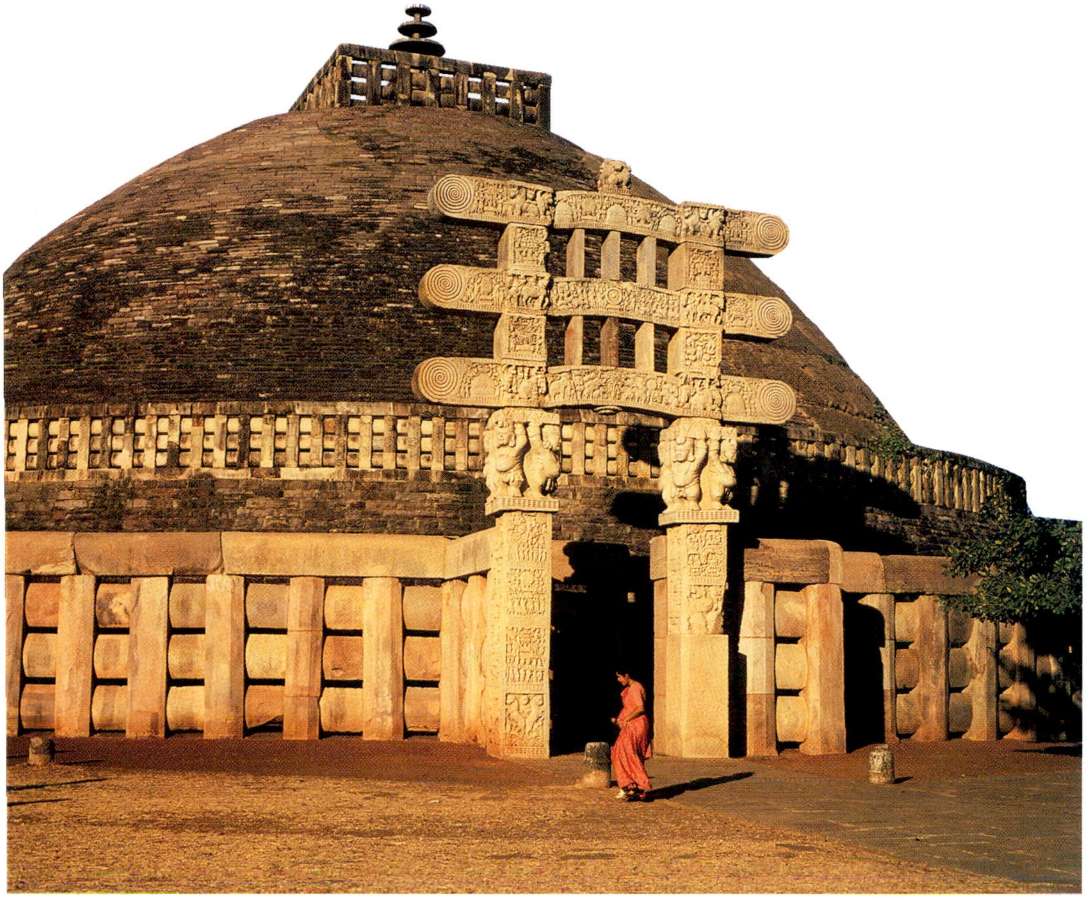

Fig. 577 The Great Stupa, Sanchi, India. Begun 3rd century BCE., with later additions.
Brick and rubble, originally faced with painted and gilded stucco, with rails of white stone. Four by Five/Superstock.

India under the rule of Asoka (273–232 BCE). Deeply saddened by the horrors of war, and believing that his power rested ultimately in religious virtue and not military force, Asoka became a great patron of the Buddhist monks, erecting some 84,000 shrines, called *stupas*, throughout India, all elaborately decorated with sculpture and painting. The ***stupa*** is literally a burial mound, dating from prehistoric times, but by the time the Great Stupa at Sanchi was made (Fig. 577)—it is the earliest surviving example of the form—it had come to house important relics of Buddha himself or the remains of later Buddhist holy persons. This *stupa* is made of rubble, piled on top of the original shrine, which has been faced with brick to form a hemispherical dome that symbolizes the earth itself. A railing—in this case, made of white stone and clearly visible in this photograph—encircles the sphere. Ceremonial processions moved along the narrow path behind this railing. Pilgrims would circle the *stupa* in a clockwise direction on another wider path, at ground level, retracing the path of the sun, thus putting themselves in harmony with the cosmos and symbolically walking the Buddhist Path of Life around the World Mountain.

All the ancient centers of civilization underwent wars, conquests, and dramatic cultural changes. And all produced great philosophers, great art, and great writing, much of which we still find current and useful today. All were organized around religion, and with the dawn of the Christian era, religion contined to play a central role in defining culture.

CHAPTER 17

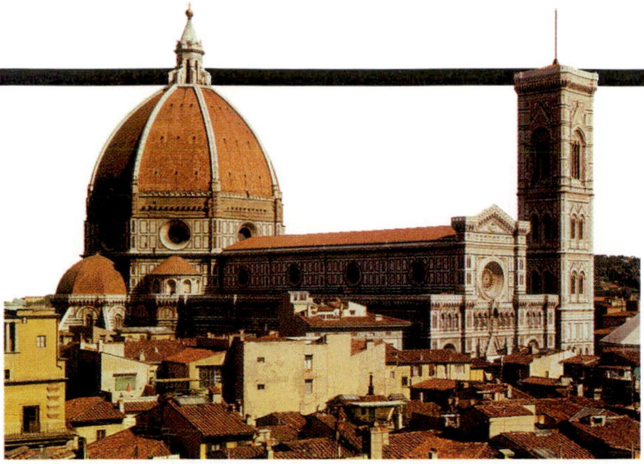

The Christian Era

Early Christian and Byzantine Art

Christian Art in Northern Europe

Romanesque Art

Gothic Art

Developments in Islam and Asia

Our study of the ancient world—from ancient fertility statues, to the Egyptian *ka,* to the rise of Buddhism—shows how powerful religion can be in setting the course of culture, and the advent of Christianity in the Western world makes this abundantly clear. So powerful was the Christian story that even the common calendar changed. From the 6th century on, time was recorded in terms of years "B.C." (before Christ) and years "A.D." (*anno Domini,* the year of Our Lord, meaning the year of His birth). Today usage has changed somewhat—the preferred terms, as we have used them in this text, are BCE (before the common era) and CE (the common era)—but the world's calendar remains Christian.

Camels first used for trans-Saharan transport
c. 200

c. 300
End of the Olmec civilization

Augustine writes *The City of God*
426

c. 400–500
Germanic tribes invade Rome

CE 550

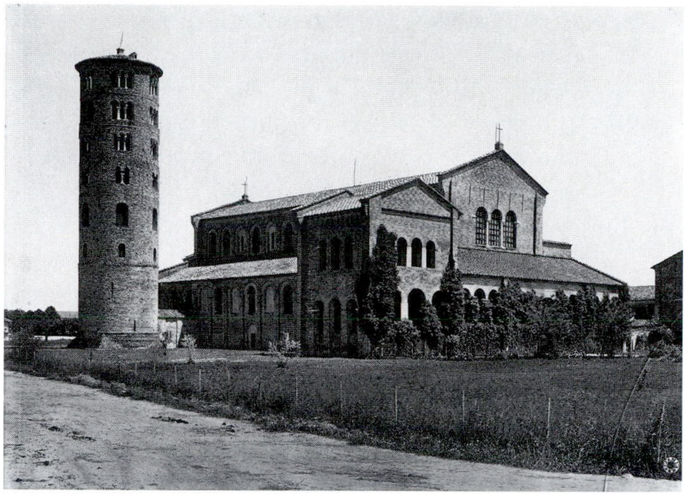

Fig. 578 Church of Sant' Apollinaire in Classe, the former port of Ravenna, Italy, 533–549.
Alinari/Art Resource.

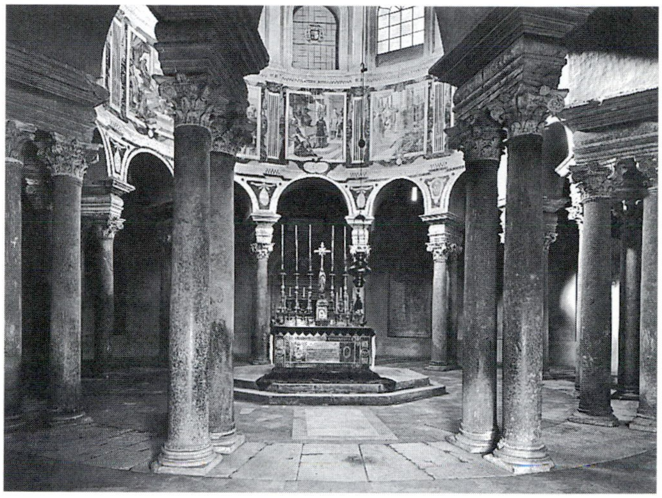

Fig. 579 Santa Costanza, Rome, CE 354.
Interior view. Alinari/Art Resource.

EARLY CHRISTIAN AND BYZANTINE ART

Christianity spread through the Roman world at a very rapid pace, in large part due to the missionary zeal of St. Paul. By CE 250, fully 60 percent of Asia Minor had converted to the religion, and when the Roman Emperor Constantine legalized it in the Edict of Milan in CE 313, Christian art became imperial art. The classical art of Greece and Rome emphasized the humanity of its figures, their corporeal reality. But the Christian God was not mortal, could not even be comfortably represented in human terms, and though His Son, Jesus, was human enough, it was the mystery of both his Immaculate Conception and His rising from the dead that most interested the early Christian believer. The world that the Romans had celebrated on their walls in fresco—a world of still lifes and landscapes—was of little interest to Christians, who were more concerned with the spiritual and the heavenly than with their material surroundings.

Constantine chose to make early Christian places of worship as unlike classical temples as possible. The building type that he preferred was the rectangular **basilica,** which the Romans had used for public buildings, especially courthouses. The original St. Peter's in Rome, constructed circa CE 333–390 but destroyed in the sixteenth century to make way for the present building, was a basilica (see Fig. 464). Sant' Apollinaire (Fig. 578), in Ravenna, Italy, is one of the earliest Christian basilicas to have survived intact. As at St. Peter's, wooden trusses support the gable roof of this essentially rectangular structure.

Equally important for the future of Christian religious architecture was Santa Costanza (Fig. 579), the small mausoleum built circa CE 354 for the tomb of Constantine's daughter, Constantia. Circular in shape and topped with a dome supported by a barrel vault, the building defines the points of the traditional Greek cross, which has four equal arms. Surrounding the circular space is a passageway known as an **ambulatory** that was used for ceremonial processions.

The circular form of Santa Costanza appears often in later Byzantine architecture. By the year 500, most of the western empire, tradi-

Founding of Benedictine Order
529

CE 500

529
Justinian's law code, the *Corpus Juris Civilis*

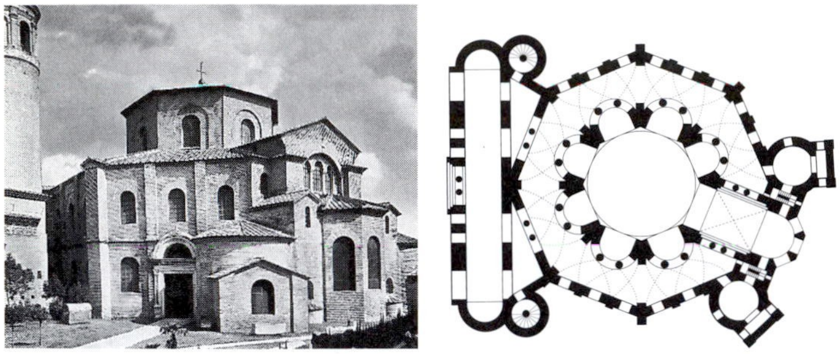

Fig. 580 San Vitale, Ravenna, CE 526–547.
Exterior view and floor plan. Alinari/Art Resource.

tionally Catholic, had been overrun by barbarian forces from the north. When the Emperor Justinian assumed the throne in Constantinople in 527, he dreamed of restoring the lost empire. His armies quickly recaptured the Mediterranean world, and he began a massive program of public works. At Ravenna, Italy, at one time the imperial capital, Justinian built San Vitale (Fig. 580), a new church modeled on the churches of Constantinople. Although the exterior is octagonal, the interior space is essentially circular, like Santa Costanza before it. Only in the altar and the apse, which lie to the right of the central domed area in the floor plan, is there any reference to the basilica structure that dominates western church architecture. Considering that Sant' Apollinaire was built at virtually the same time and in virtually the same place, there is some reason to believe that San Vitale was conceived as a political and religious statement, an attempt to persuade the people of the Italian peninsula to give up their Catholic ways and to adopt the Orthodox point of view—that is, to reject the leadership of the Church by the pope.

Sant' Apollinaire and San Vitale share one important feature. The facades of both are very plain, more or less unadorned local brick. Inside, however, both churches are elaborately decorated with marble and glittering mosaics. At St. Vitale two elaborate **mosaics**—small stones or pieces of tile arranged in a pattern—face each other on the side walls of the apse, one depicting Theodora, the wife of Justinian (Fig. 581), and the other Justinian himself (Fig. 582). Theodora had at one time been a circus performer, but she became one of the emperor's most trusted advisers, sharing with him a vision of a Christian Roman Empire. In the mosaic, she carries a golden cup of wine, and Justinian, on the opposite wall, carries a bowl containing bread. Together they are bringing to the Church an offering of bread and wine for the celebration of the Eucharist. The haloed Justinian is to be identified with Christ, surrounded as he is by twelve advisors, like the Twelve Apostles. And the haloed Theodora, with the three Magi bearing gifts to the Virgin and newborn Christ embroidered on the hem of her skirt, is to be understood as a figure for Mary. In this image, Church and state become one and the same.

These mosaics bear no relation to the naturalism that dominated Greek and Roman culture. Here, the human figures are depicted wearing long robes that hide the musculature and cause a loss of individual identity. Although each face has unique features—some of Justinian's attendants, for example, are bearded, while others are not, and the hairstyles vary—all have identical wide open eyes, curved brows, and long noses. The feet of the figures turn outward, as if to flatten the space in which they stand. They are disproportionately long and thin, a fact that lends them a heavenly lightness. And they are motionless, standing before us without gesture, as if eternally still. The Greek ideal of sculpture in the round, with its sense of the body caught in an intensely personal, even private moment—Nike taking off her sandal, for instance, or Laocoön caught in the intensity of his torment—is gone. All sense of drama has been removed from the idea of representation.

Mosaics are made of small pieces of stone called ***tesserae,*** from the Greek word *tesseres*, meaning "square." In Hellenistic Rome, they were a favorite decorative element, used because of their durability, especially to embellish villa floors. But the Romans rarely used

Birth of Mohammed
c. 570

First book printed in China
600

597
Pope Gregory sends Augustine to Christianize Britain

607
Japan begins sending embassies to China

CE 600

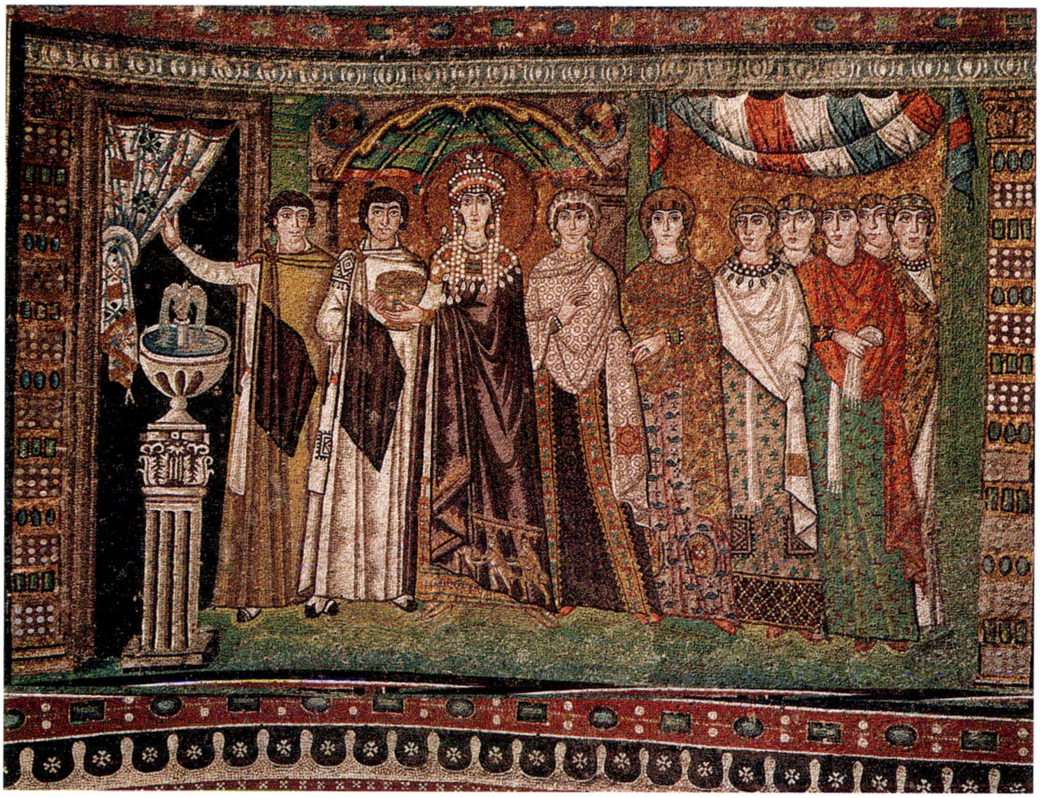

Fig. 581 (above) ***Theodora and Her Attendants*****, c. 547.**
Mosaic, sidewall of the apse, San Vitale. Scala/Art Resource.

Fig. 582 (right) San Vitale, interior view, looking into the apse at *Justinian and His Attendants*, c. 547.
Canali/Photobank.

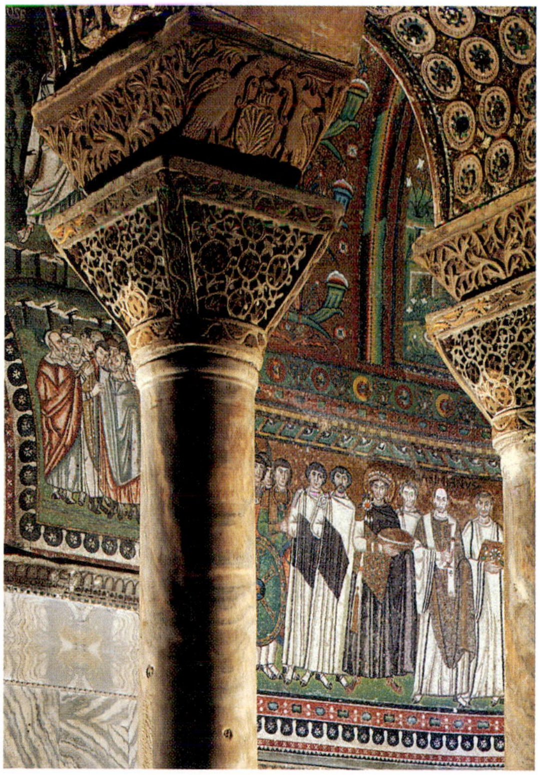

mosaic on their walls, where they preferred the more refined and naturalistic effects that were possible with fresco. For no matter how skilled the mosaic artist, the naturalism of the original drawing would inevitably be lost when the small stones were set in cement.

The Byzantine mosaic artists, however, had little interest in naturalism. Their intention was to create a symbolic, mystical art, something for which the mosaic medium was perfectly suited. Gold tesserae were made by sandwiching gold leaf between two small squares of glass, and polished glass was also used. By setting the tesserae unevenly, at slight angles, a shimmering and transcendent effect was realized, which was heightened by the light from the church's clerestory windows.

Sung Dynasty in China
600

Charlemagne comes
to the throne
768

CE 600

607
Flowering of court literature
in Heian Japan

800
City of Machu Picchu
built in Peru

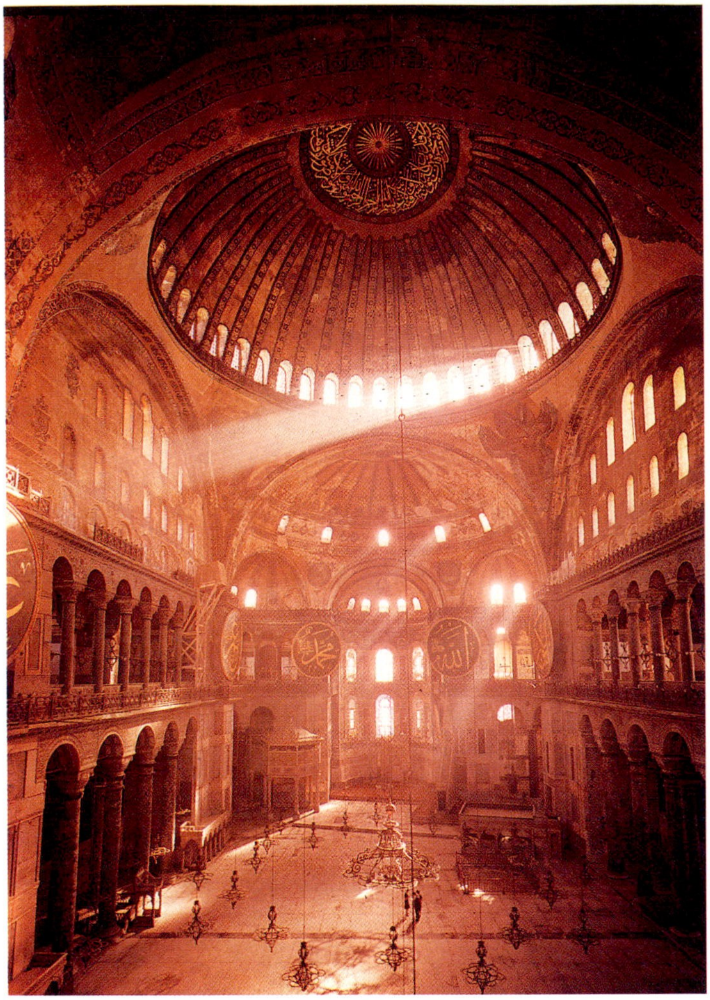

Fig. 583 Anthemius of Tralles and Isidorus of Miletus, Hagia Sophia, Istanbul, 532–537.
Interior view. Erich Lessing/Art Resource.

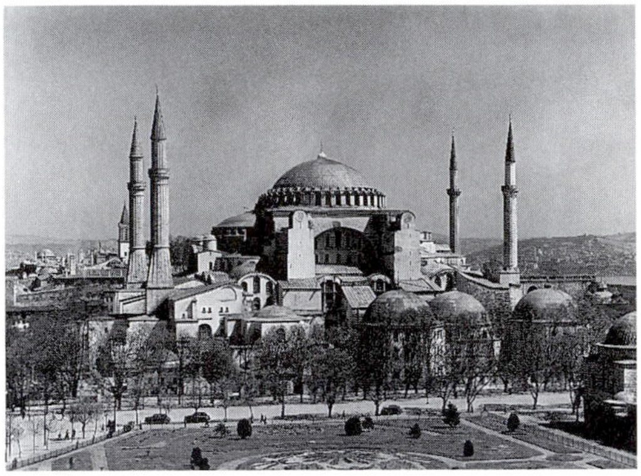

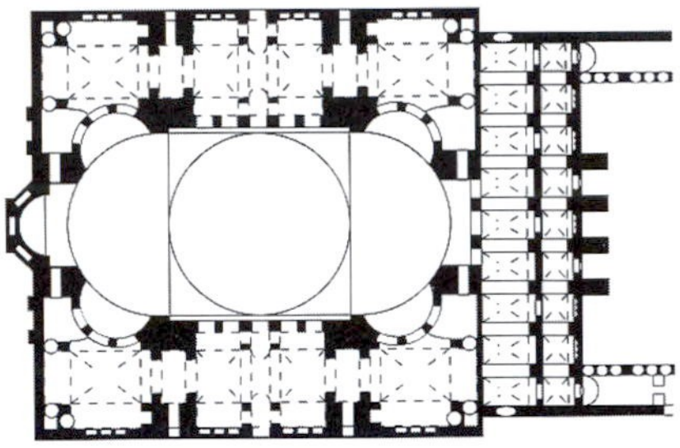

Fig. 584 Anthemius of Tralles and Isidorus of Miletus, Hagia Sophia, Istanbul, 532–537.
Exterior view and plan. G.E. Kidder Smith.

Justinian attached enormous importance to architecture, believing that nothing better served to underscore the power of the emperor. The church of Hagia Sophia, meaning "Holy Wisdom," was his imperial place of worship in Constantinople (Figs 583 and 584). The huge interior, crowned by a dome, is reminiscent of the circular, central plan of Ravenna's San Vitale, but this dome is abutted at either end by half-domes that extend the central core of the church along a longitudinal axis reminiscent of the basilica, with the apse extending in another smaller half-dome out one end of the axis. These half-domes culminate in arches that are repeated on the two sides of the dome as well. The architectural scheme is, in fact, relatively simple—a dome supported by four **pendentives,** the curved, inverted triangular shapes that rise up to the rim of the dome between the four arches themselves. This dome-on-pendentive design was so enthusiastically received that it became the standard for Byzantine church design.

Many of the original mosaics that decorated Hagia Sofia, Justinian's magnificent church in Constantinople, were later destroyed or covered over. During the eighth and ninth centuries, Iconoclasts, meaning "image-breakers," who believed literally in the Bible's commandment against the worship of "graven" images, destroyed much Byzantine art. Forced to migrate westward, Byzantine artists discovered Hellenistic naturalism and incorporated it into later Byzantine design. The mosaic of Christ from Hagia Sophia (Fig. 585) is representative of that later synthesis.

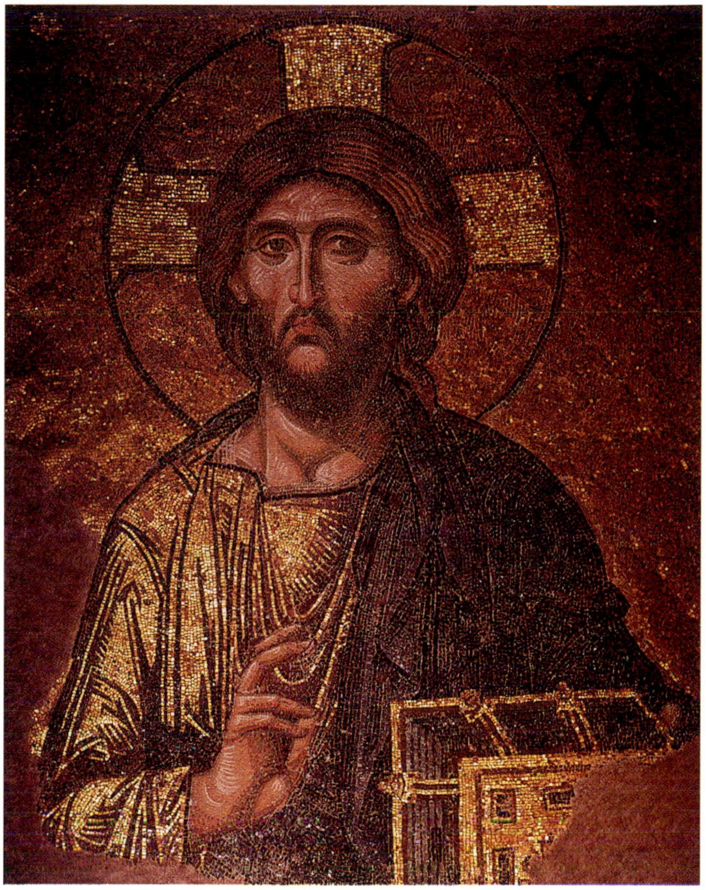

Fig. 585 ***Christ,*** **from** ***Deësis*** **mosaic, 13th century.**
Hagia Sophia, Istanbul. Erich Lessing/Art Resource.

Though only a few of the original mosaics have been restored, and later mosaics were few in number, the light in the interior is still almost transcendental in feeling, and one can only imagine the heavenly aura when gold and glass reflected the light that entered the nave through the many windows that surround it. In Justinian's own words: "The sun's light and its shining rays fill the temple. One would say that the space is not lit by the sun without, but that the source of light is to be found within, such is the abundance of light. . . . The scintillations of the light forbid the spectator's gaze to linger on the details; each one attracts the eye and leads it on to the next. The circular motion of one's gaze reproduces itself to infinity. . . . The spirit rises toward God and floats in the air."

Justinian's reign marked the apex of the early Christian and Byzantine era. By the seventh century, barbarian invaders had taken control of the western empire, and the new Muslim empire had begun to expand to the east. Reduced in area to the Balkans and Greece, the Byzantine empire nevertheless held on until 1453 when the Turks finally captured Constantinople and renamed it Istanbul, converting Hagia Sophia into a mosque.

CE 400

461 Death of St. Patrick in Ireland

c. 450 Angles, Saxons, and Jutes invade England

476 Last Roman emperor dethroned

527 Justinian comes to the throne of Byzantium

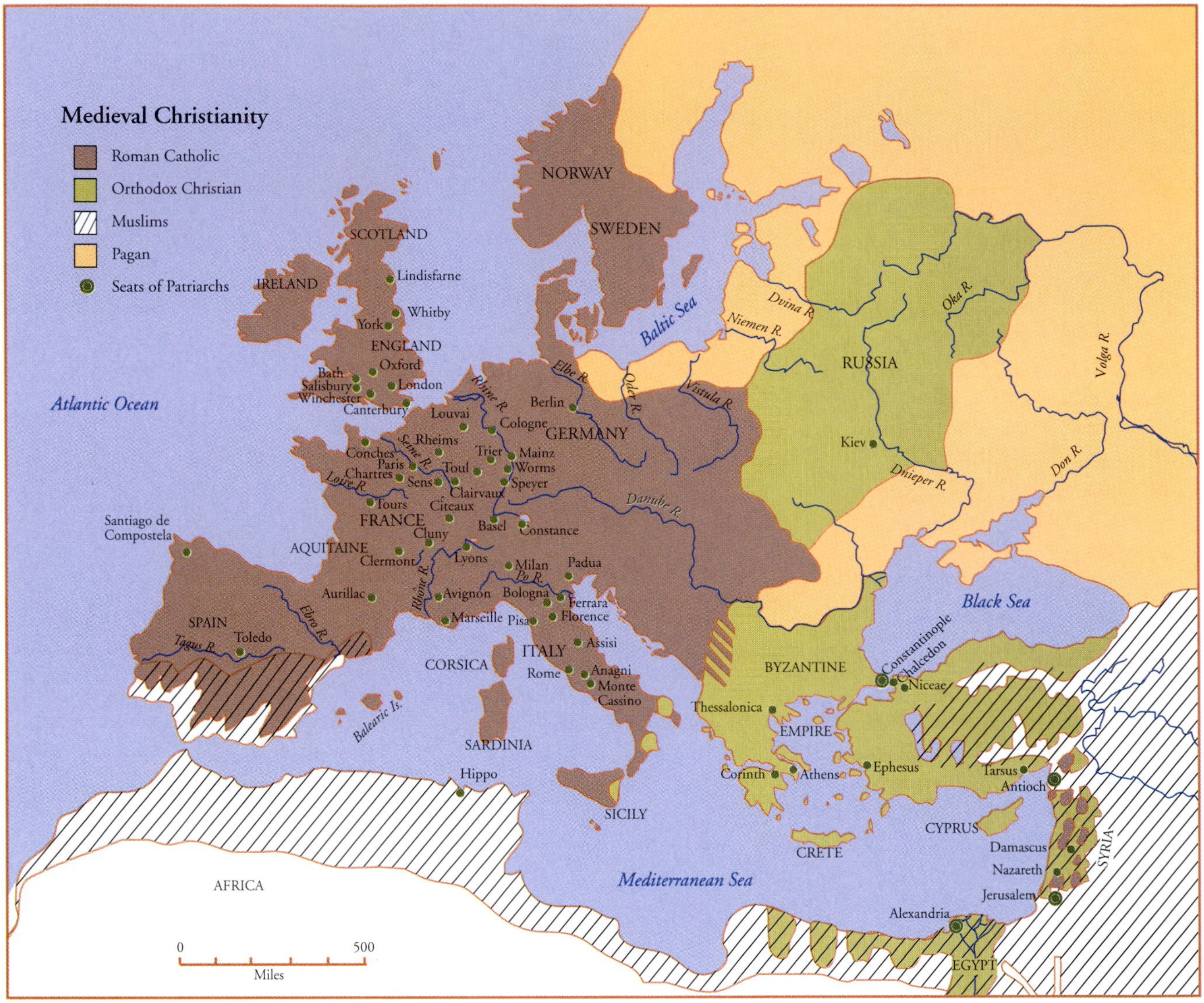

CHRISTIAN ART IN NORTHERN EUROPE

Until the year 1000, the center of Western civilization was located in the Middle East, at Constantinople. In Europe, tribal groups with localized power held sway: the Lombards in what is now Italy, the Franks and the Burgundians in regions of France, and the Angles and Saxons in England. Though it possessed no real political power, the Papacy in Rome had begun to work hard to convert the pagan tribes and to reassert the authority of the Church. As early as 496, the leader of the Franks, Clovis, was baptized into the Church. Even earlier (c. 430), St. Patrick had undertaken an evangelical mission to Ireland, establishing monasteries and quickly converting the native Celts. These new monasteries were designed to serve missionary as well as educational functions. At a time when only priests and monks could read and write, the sacred texts they produced came to reflect native Celtic designs. These designs

Expansion of Islam
633–725

CE 700

c. 600
Slave trade between sub-Saharan Africa and Mediterranean begins

7th century
Anglo-Saxon epic *Beowulf* is composed

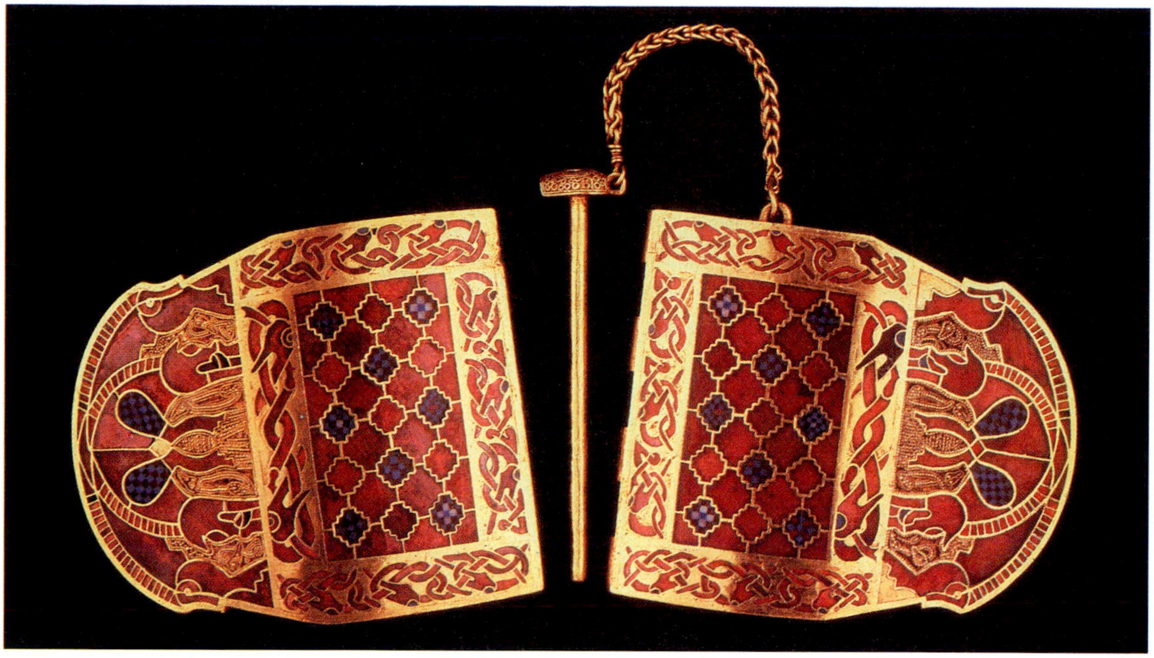

Fig. 586 Hinged clasp from the Sutton Hoo burial ship, 7th century.
Gold with garnets, mosaic, glass, and filigree. British Museum, London. Bridgeman/Art Resource.

are elaborately decorative, highly abstract, and contain no naturalistic representation. Thus, Christian art fused with the native traditions, which employed the so-called *animal style*. Some of the best examples of this animal style, such as the hinged clasp above (Fig. 586), have been found at Sutton Hoo, north of present-day London, in the grave of an unknown 7th-century East Anglian king. At the round end of the each side of the hinge are animal forms, and the entire clasp is covered with intricate traceries of lines and bands.

In 597, Gregory the Great, the first monk to become pope, sent an emissary, later known as Saint Augustine of Canterbury, on a mission to convert the Anglo-Saxons. This mission brought Roman religious and artistic traditions into direct contact with Celtic art, and slowly but surely Roman culture began to dominate the Celtic-Germanic world. The difficulties that the artist trained in the linear Celtic tradition faced in coping with the naturalistic traditions of Roman art are evident in the painting of Saint Matthew above (Fig. 587), copied from an earlier Italian original. Here, the image is flat, the figure has not been modeled, and the perspective is completely askew. It is pattern—and the animal style—that really interests the artist, not accurate representation.

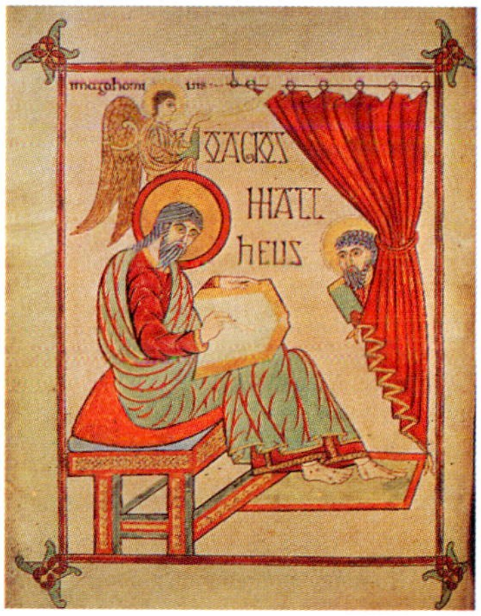

Fig. 587 *St. Matthew* from the *Lindisfarne Gospels*, c. 700.
Approx. 11 × 9 in. British Library, London. Bridgeman/Art Resource.

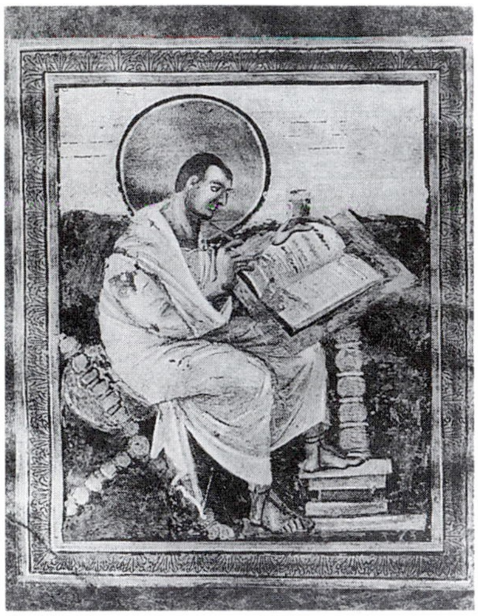

Fig. 588 ***St. Matthew*** **from the** ***Gospel Book of Charlemagne,*** **c. 800–810.**
13 × 10 in. Kunsthistorisches Museum, Vienna.
Marburg/Art Resource.

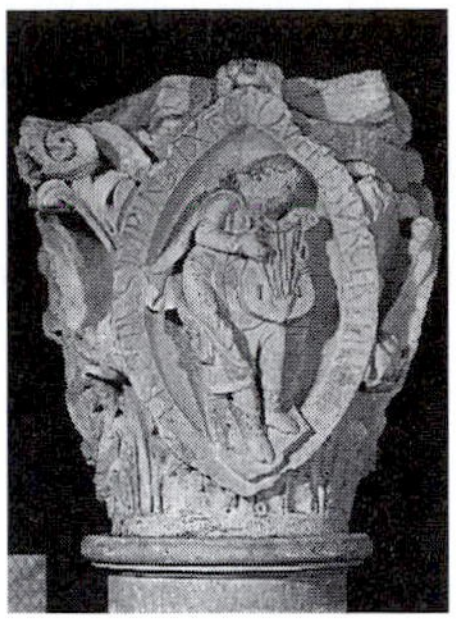

Fig. 589 Capital with relief representing the Third Tone of Plainsong, from the choir, Abbey Church of St. Pierre, Cluny.
Musée Lapidaire du Farinier, Cluny, France.
Giraudon/Art Resource.

When Charlemagne (Charles, or Carolus, the Great) assumed leadership of the Franks in 771, this process of Romanization was assured. At request of the Pope, Charlemagne conquered the Lombards, becoming their King, and on Christmas Day, 800, he was crowned Holy Roman Emperor by Pope Leo III at St. Peter's Basilica in Rome. The fusion of Germanic and Mediterranean styles that reflected this new alliance between Church and state is known as **Carolingian art,** a term referring to the art produced during the reign of Charlemagne and his immediate successors.

Charlemagne was intent on restoring the glories of Roman civilization. He actively collected and had copied the oldest surviving texts of the classical Latin authors. He created schools in monasteries and cathedrals across Europe in which classical Latin was the accepted language. A new script, with Roman capitals and new lowercase letters, the basis of modern type, was introduced. A second depiction of St. Matthew (Fig. 588), executed 100 years after the one on the previous page, demonstrates the impact of Roman realism on northern art. Found in Charlemagne's tomb, this illustration looks as if it could have been painted in classical Rome.

ROMANESQUE ART

After the dissolution of the Carolingian state in the ninth and tenth centuries, Europe disintegrated into a large number of small feudal territories. The emperors were replaced by an array of rulers of varying power and prestige who controlled smaller or larger *fiefdoms*, areas of land worked by persons under obligation to the ruler, and whose authority was generally embodied in a chateau or castle surrounded by walls and moats. Despite this atomization of political life, a recognizable style that we have come to call **Romanesque** developed throughout Europe beginning about 1050. Although details varied from place to place, certain features remained constant for nearly 200 years.

Romanesque architecture is characterized by its easily recognizable geometric masses—rectangles, cubes, cylinders, and half-cylinders. The wooden roof that St. Peter's Basilica had utilized was abandoned in favor of fireproof stone and masonry construction, apparently out of bitter experience with the invading nomadic tribes, who burned many of the churches of Europe in the ninth and tenth centuries. Flat roofs were replaced by vaulted ceilings. By structural necessity, these were supported by massive walls that often lacked windows sufficient to provide adequate lighting. The churches were often built along the roads leading to pilgrimage centers, usually monasteries that housed Christian relics, and they had to be large enough to accommodate large crowds of the faithful. For instance, St. Sernin, in Toulouse, France (Figs. 450–452) was on the pilgrimage route to Santiago de Compostela, in Spain, where the body of St. James was believed to rest.

Conquest of England by the Norman French
1066

Beginning of First Crusade
1096

1135

1054
Schism between Latin and Greek Christian churches

1071
The fork is introduced to Europe by a Byzantine princess

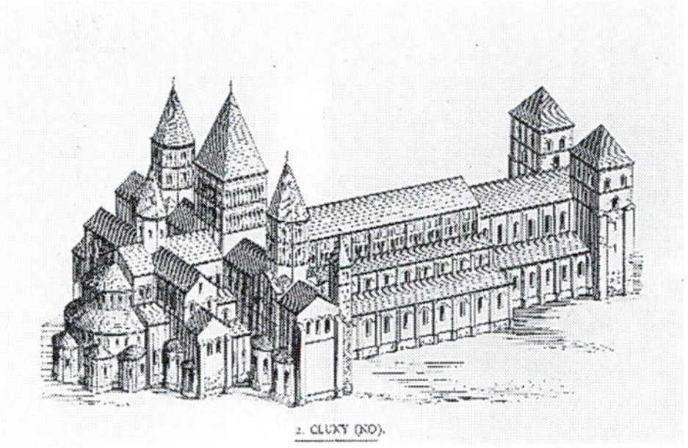

Fig. 590 Reconstruction of the third Abbey Church of St. Pierre, Cluny, France, c. 1085–1130.
Marburg/Art Resource.

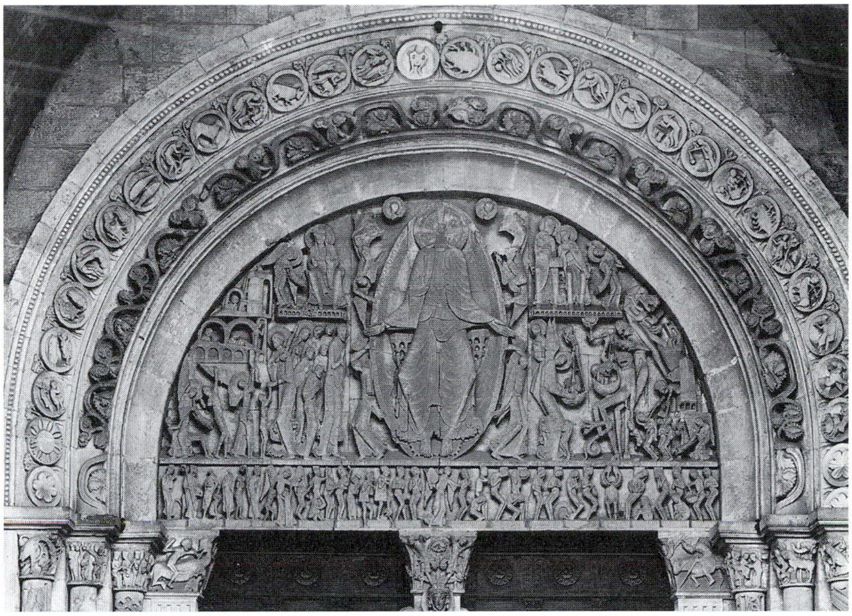

Fig. 591 Gislebertus, *Last Judgment,* tympanum and lintel, west portal, Cathedral, Autun, France, c. 1125–1135.
Marburg/Art Resource.

Thanks in large part to Charlemagne's emphasis on monastic learning, monasteries had flourished ever since the Carolingian period, many of them acting as feudal landlords as well. The largest and most powerful was Cluny, near Maçon, France (Fig. 590). Until the building of the new St. Peter's in Rome, the church at Cluny was the largest in the Christian world. It was 521 feet in length, and its nave vaults rose to a height of 100 feet. The height of the nave was made possible by the use of pointed arches. The church was destroyed in the French Revolution, and only part of one transept survives.

The Benedictine order at Cluny stressed the intellectual life, the study of music, and the pursuit of the arts. A Corinthian capital (Fig. 589), one of ten that survives from the original Abbey Church at Cluny, shows the continued importance of Roman art even in a Christian context. The almond-shaped inset hollowed into the acanthus leaves contains a figure playing a lyre, underscoring the importance of the arts in the Clunaic order. Surviving examples such as this demonstrate how richly decorated Cluny was.

With the decline of Hellenistic Rome, the art of sculpture had largely declined in the West, but in the Romanesque period it began to reemerge. Certainly the idea of educating the masses in the Christian message through architectural sculpture on the facades of the pilgrimage churches contributed to the art's rebirth. The most important sculptural work was usually located on the **tympanum** of the church, the semicircular arch above the lintel on the main door. It often showed Christ with His Twelve Apostles. Another favorite theme was the Last Judgment, full of depictions of sinners suffering the horrors of hellfire and damnation. To the left of Gislebertus's *Last Judgment* at Autun, France (Fig. 591), the blessed arrive in heaven, while on the right, the damned are seized by devils. Combining all manner of animal forms, the monstrosity of these creatures recalls the animal style of the Germanic tribes.

Rise of Chivalric poetry
written in the vernacular
12th century

1137

1100
Third Pueblo period
in American Southwest

12th and 13th centuries
Growth of trade and towns
as trading centers

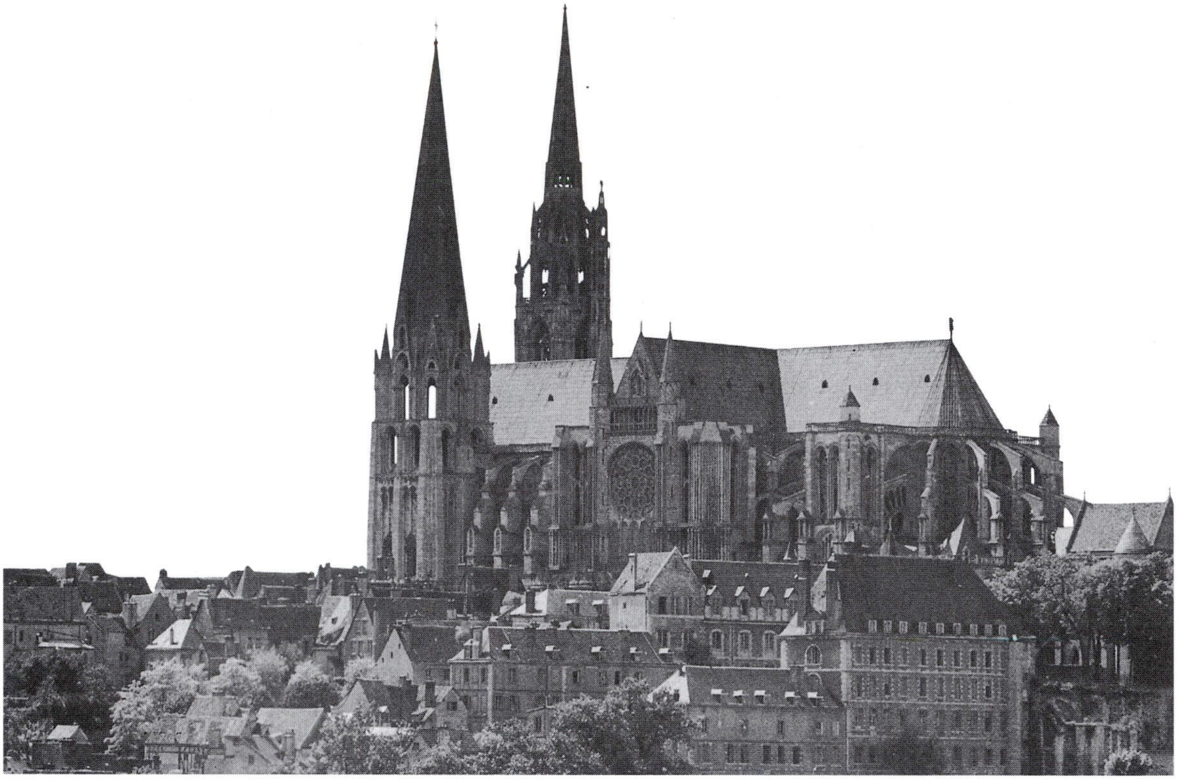

Fig. 592 Chartres Cathedral, 1145–1220.
Photograph Courtesy of Standard Oil Co. (NJ)

GOTHIC ART

The great era of **Gothic** art begins in 1137 with the rebuilding of the choir of the abbey church of St. Denis, located just outside Paris. Abbot Suger of St. Denis, saw his new church as both the political and the spiritual center of a new France, united under King Louis VI. Although he was familiar with Romanesque architecture, which was then at its height, Suger chose to abandon it in principle. The Romanesque church was difficult to light because the structural need to support the nave walls from without meant that windows had to be eliminated. Suger envisioned something different. He wanted his church flooded with light as if by the light of Heaven itself. The new St. Denis, he wrote, "will shine with the wonderful and uninterrupted light of the most luminous windows, pervading the interior beauty [of the church]." For Suger, this light was deeply theological in meaning. "Marvel not at the gold and the expense but at the craftsmanship of the work," he wrote. "Bright is the noble work; but, being nobly bright, the work should brighten the minds, so that they may travel, through the true light, to the True Light where Christ is the true door."

St. Denis contains many Romanesque features, notably a choir and an apse surrounded by an arcaded ambulatory. But instead of creating separate chapels behind the ambulatory, as was customary, the ambulatory and chapel areas were merged into a continuous open space. This space consists of seven wedge-shaped areas, articulated by columns and arches, that fan out from the center of the apse (Fig. 593). The stained-glass windows at the back of each wedge fill the entire wall area, admitting a relatively

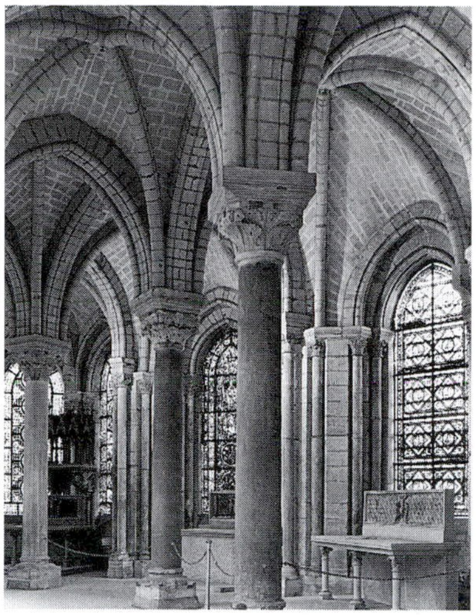

Fig. 593 St. Denis, near Paris, 1140–1144.
Interior view. C.N.M.H.S./S.P.A.D.E.M.

large amount of light into the church. Thus filled with light, the walls seem to disappear. Supported by the buttress system, the interior stonework was made to appear almost fragile, even weightless, especially where it framed the stained glass.

What made this all possible was the flying buttress, which we have already discussed in Chapter 14 (Figs. 457 and 458). With this unique combination of pointed arches, groined vaults, and flying buttresses, the architect of the Gothic church was able to vault the central nave to an extraordinary height. Chartres Cathedral is a good example (Fig. 592). To this day, its spires dominate the countryside and can be seen for miles around.

The Gothic style spread rapidly throughout Europe, though each particular region modified it to suit local tastes and conditions. In Germany's Cologne Cathedral (Fig. 594), the width of the nave has been narrowed to such a degree that the vaults seem to rise higher than they actually do. The cathedral was not finished until the nineteenth century, though built strictly in accordance with thirteenth-century plans. The stonework is so slender, incorporating so much glass into its walls, that the effect is one of almost total weightlessness.

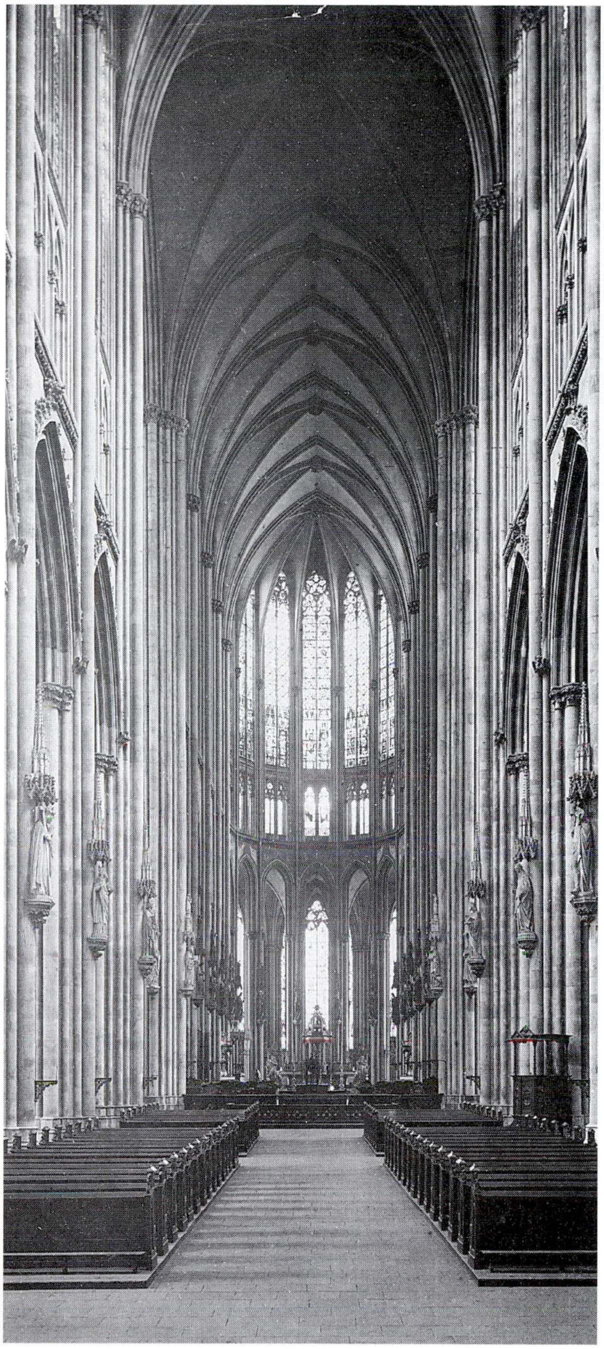

Fig. 594 Choir of Cologne Cathedral, Germany, 13th–14th century.
A.C. Champagne.

1250

Dante Alighieri
1265–1320

c. 1300
Dante writes
The Divine Comedy

Aztecs arrive
in the Valley of Mexico
c. 1325

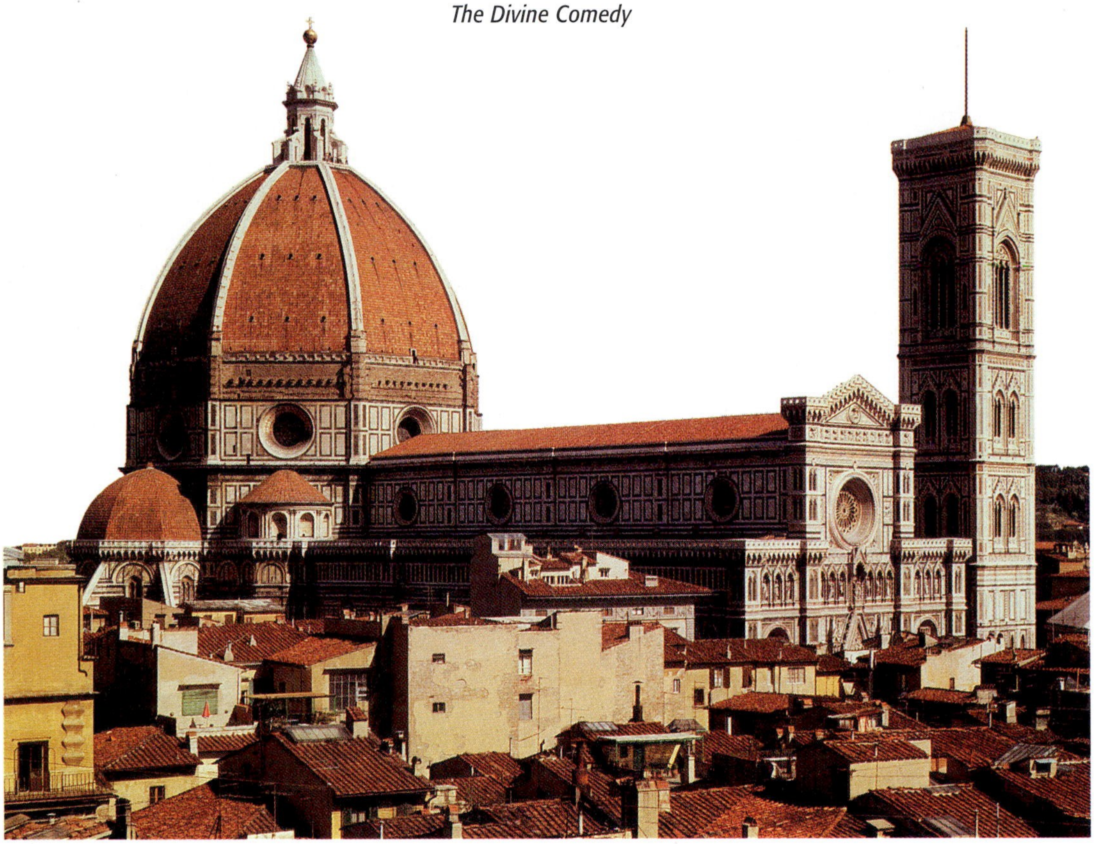

Fig. 595 Florence Cathedral (Santa Maria del Fiore), begun by Arnolfo de Cambio, 1296; dome by Filippo Brunelleschi, 1420–1436. Scala/Art Resource.

The Gothic style in Italy is unique. For instance, the exterior of Florence Cathedral (Fig. 595) is hardly Gothic at all. It was, in fact, designed to match the dogmatically Romanesque octagonal Baptistry that stands in front of it. But the interior space is completely Gothic in character. Each side of the nave is flanked by an arcade that opens almost completely into the nave by virtue of four wide pointed arches. Thus nave and arcade become one, and the interior of the cathedral feels more spacious than any other. Nevertheless, rather than the mysterious and transcendental feelings evoked by most Gothic churches, Florence Cathedral produces a sense of tranquility and of measured, controlled calm.

The Gothic style in architecture inspired an outpouring of sculptural decoration. There was, for one thing, much more room for sculpture on the facade of the Gothic church than had been available on the facade of the Romanesque church. There were now three doors where there had been only one before, and doors were added to the transepts as well. The portal at Reims (Fig. 596), which notably substitutes a stained-glass rose window for the Romanesque tympanum and a pointed for a rounded arch, is sculpturally much lighter than, for instance, the tympanum at Autun, France (see Fig. 591). The elongated bodies of the Romanesque figures are distributed in a very shallow space. In contrast, the sculpture of the Gothic cathedral is more naturalistic. The proportions of the figures are more natural, and the figures assume more natural poses as well. The space they occupy is deeper—so much so that they appear to be fully realized sculpture in-the-round, freed of the wall behind them. Most important

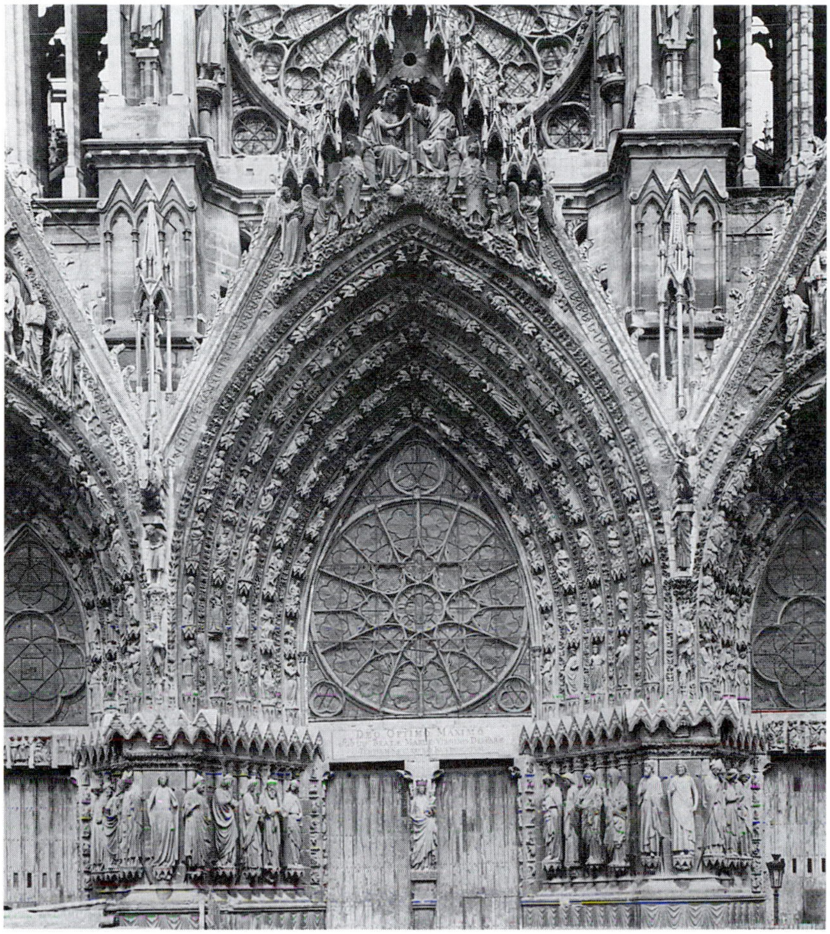

Fig. 596 Central portal of the west facade of Reims Cathedral, c. 1225–1290.
Giraudon/Art Resource.

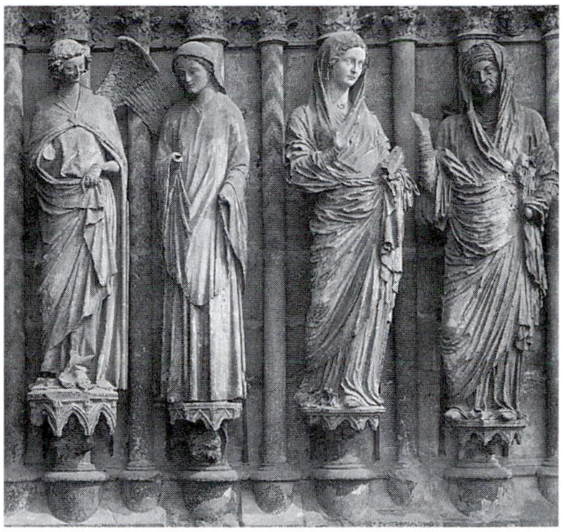

Fig. 597 Detail, west portal, Reims Cathedral, c. 1225–1245.
Giraudon/Art Resource.

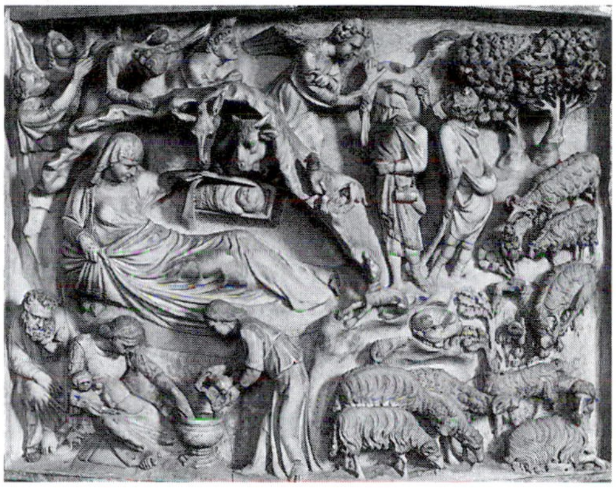

Fig. 598 Giovanni Pisano, *The Nativity*, detail of pulpit, Pisa Cathedral, 1302–1310.
Marble. Alinari/Art Resource.

of all, many of the figures seem to assert their own individuality, as if they were actual persons. The generalized "types" of Romanesque sculpture are beginning to disappear. The detail of figures at the bottom of the Reims portal (Fig. 597) suggest that each is engaged in a narrative scene. The angel on the left smiles at the more somber Virgin. The two at the right seem about to step off their pedestals. What is most remarkable is that the space between the figures is bridged by shared emotion, as if feeling can unite them in a common space. The Renaissance is about to dawn, as we can witness in Giovanni Pisano's Nativity for the Pisa Cathedral (Fig. 598). Pisano sets the figures in this relief loose of their architectural mooring by situating them in a landscape. Notice, particularly, how the sheep below the tree on the right seem to come toward us as they graze down the hillside. The Virgin is, realistically speaking, too large, showing the continued influence of medieval hierarchies, but Pisano has nevertheless given expression to his naturalistic impulses.

First Muslim invasion of India
c. 710

600

644-656
Koran text established

732
Furthest point of Muslim advances in Western Europe

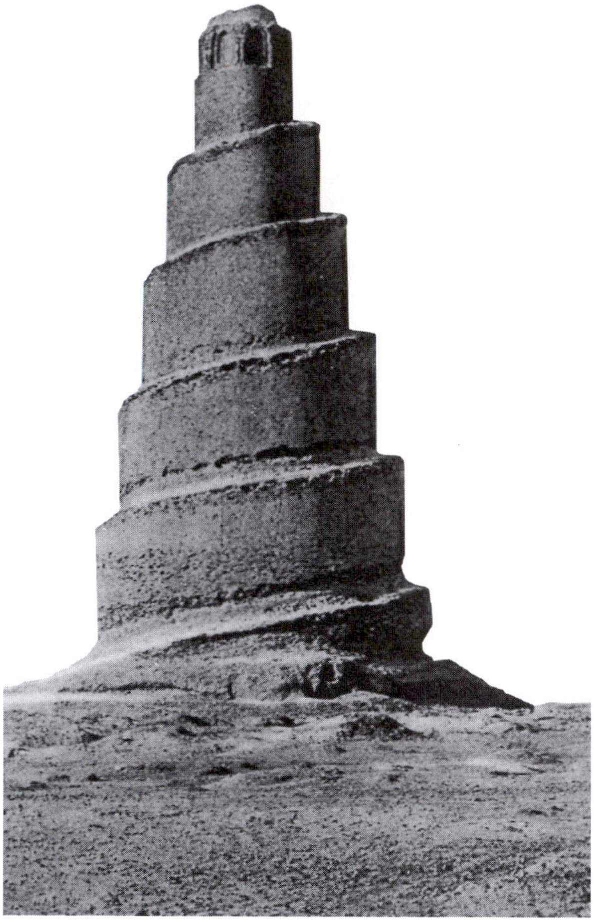

Fig. 599 **Great Mosque at Samarra, Iraq, 648–852.**
Marburg/Art Resource.

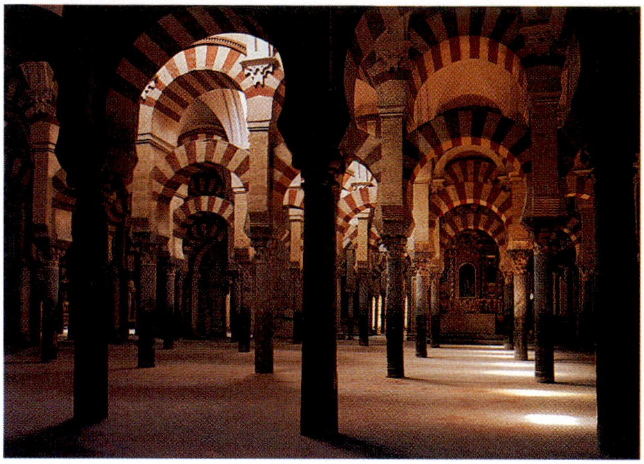

Fig. 600 **Interior of the sanctuary of the mosque at Córoba, Spain, 786–987.**
Werner Forman/Art Resource.

DEVELOPMENTS IN ISLAM AND ASIA

In 1096 Pope Urban II declared the First Crusade to liberate Jerusalem from control by the Muslims. Ever since the Prophet Mohammed had fled Mecca for Medina in 622, the Muslim empire had expanded rapidly. By 640, Mohammed's successors, the Caliphs, had conquered Syria, Palestine, and Iraq. Two years later, they defeated the army of Byzantium at Alexandria, and, by 710, they had captured all of northern Africa and moved into Spain. They advanced north until 732, when Charles Martel, grandfather of Charlemagne, defeated them at Poitiers, France. But the Caliphs' foothold in Europe remained strong, and they did not leave Spain until 1492. Even the Crusades failed to reduce their power. During the First Crusade, 50,000 men were sent to the Middle East, where they managed to hold Jerusalem and much of Palestine for a short while. The Second Crusade, in 1146, failed to regain control, and in 1187, the Muslim warrior Saladin reconquered Jerusalem. Finally, in 1192, Saladin defeated King Richard the Lion-Hearted of England in the Third Crusade.

The major architectural form of Islam was the mosque. Now ruined, the mosque at Samarra was once the largest in the Islamic world. Its single **minaret** (Fig. 599), modeled on the ziggurats of ancient Mesopotamia, stood before the entrance, opposite the ***mihrab*** on the ***qibla wall.*** The *mihrab* is symbolic of the spot in Mohammed's house at Medina where he stood to lead communal prayers. The *qibla* wall faces in the direction of Mecca, the holy site toward which all Muslims turn in prayer. The minaret overlooked a ten-acre wooden roof supported by 464 columns arranged in aisles around an open center court. With its 36 piers and 514 columns, the mosque at Córdoba (Fig. 600) gives us some sense of what Samarra might once have looked like. Between 786 and 987, it

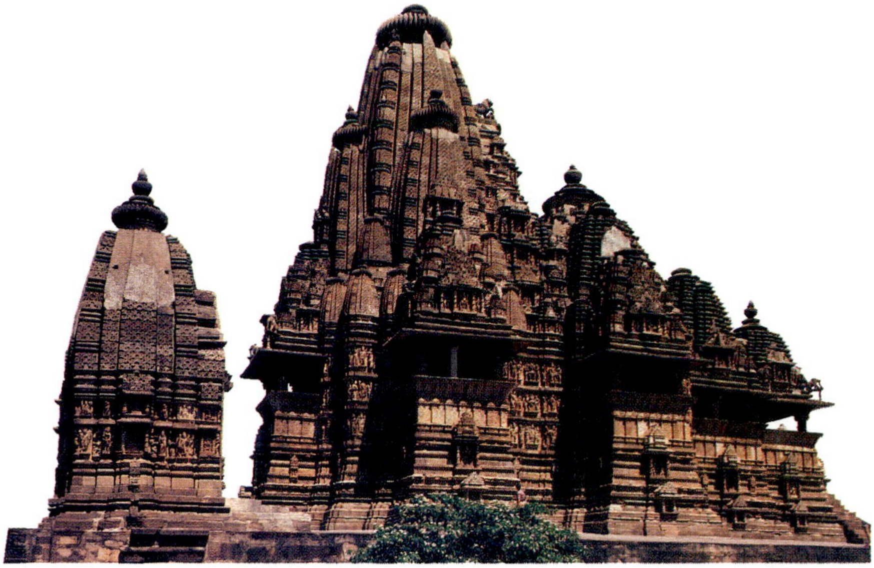

Fig. 601 Kandariya Mahadeva Temple, Khajuraho, India, 10th–11th century.
George Holton/Photo Researchers.

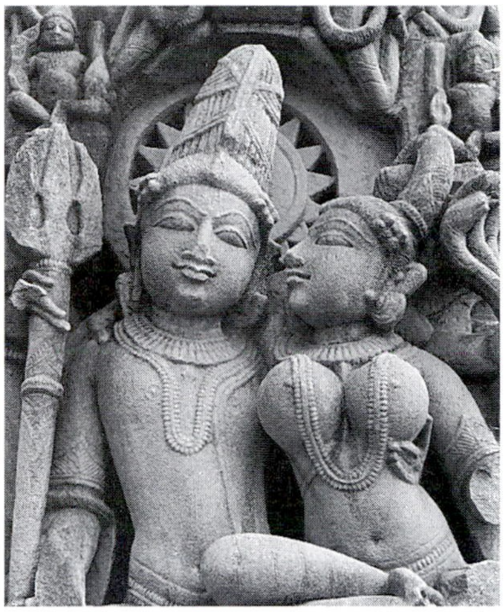

Fig. 602 Wall relief, Kandariya Mahadeva Temple, Khajuraho, India, 10th–11th century.
George Holton/Photo Researchers.

was enlarged seven times, showing the versatility of its construction method. All Muslim design is characterized by a visual rhythm realized through symmetry and repetition of certain patterns and motifs, a rhythm clearly evident in the interior of the Córdoba mosque.

As early as 1500 BCE Aryan tribesmen from northern Europe invaded India, bringing a religion that would have as great an impact on the art of India as Islam had on the art of the Middle East. The Vedic traditions of the light-skinned Aryans, written in religious texts called the *Vedas*, allowed for the development of a class system based on racial distinctions. Status in one of the four classes—the priests (Brahmans), the warriors and rulers (kshatriyas), the farmers and merchants (vaishayas), and the serfs (shudras)—was determined by birth, and one could escape one's caste only through reincarnation. Buddhism, which began about 563 BCE, was in many ways a reaction against the Vedic caste system, allowing for salvation by means of individual self-denial and meditation, and it gained many followers.

The Hindu religion, which evolved from the Vedic tradition, has myriad gods, headed by the trinity of Brahma, Vishnu, and Shiva. Brahma is the creator of the cosmos, who contains all things. Hindu temples were designed to capture the rhythms of the cosmos, of Brahma. Completed only a few years before the great Romanesque cathedrals of Europe, the main tower at Kandariya (Fig. 601) is like a mountain peak, showing the summit of the paths one must follow to attain salvation. The entirety is covered by intricate reliefs representing the gods, stories from Hindu tradition, and erotic encounters (Fig. 602). The pleasures of erotic love were understood as reflecting the pleasures of the eventual union with the god, and carnal love was seen as an aspect of spiritual love. The achievement of sexual bliss was thus considered to be one of the many paths of virtue leading to redemption. Indeed, the Hindu gods usually incorporate all aspects of the human personality.

Meanwhile, in Europe, the naturalistic impulses evident in the facade of Reims Cathedral (Fig. 597) and in Pisano's *Nativity* (Fig. 598) were asserting themselves ever more forcefully. A new era, marked by a rebirth of classical values, was about to unfold.

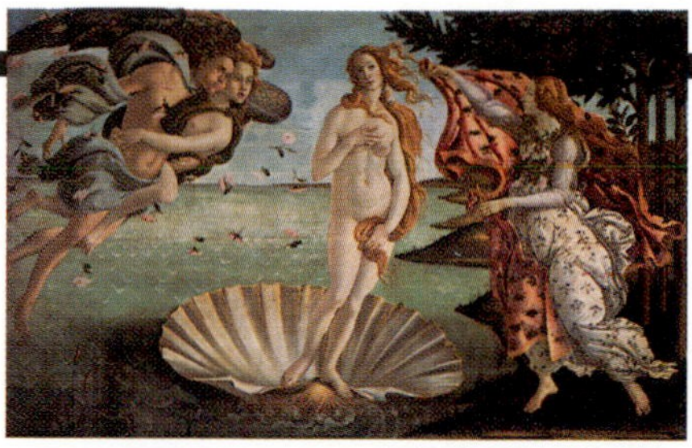

CHAPTER 18

The Renaissance through The Baroque

The Early Renaissance

The High Renaissance

Art in China

Pre-Columbian Art in Mexico

Mannerism

The Baroque

Just when the Gothic era ended and the Renaissance began is by no means certain. In Europe, toward the end of the thirteenth century, a new kind of art began to appear, at first in the South, and somewhat later in the North. By the beginning of the fifteenth century, this new era, marked by a revival of interest in arts and sciences that had been lost since antiquity, was firmly established. We have come to call this revival the **Renaissance,** meaning "rebirth."

The Gothic era has been called a long overture to the Renaissance, and we can see, perhaps, in the sculptures at Reims Cathedral (Fig. 597), which date from the first half of the thirteenth century, the beginnings of the spirit that would develop into the Renaissance sensibility. These figures are no longer archetypical and formulaic representations; they are almost real people, displaying real emotions. This tendency toward more and more naturalistic representation in many ways defines Gothic art, but it is even more pronounced in Renaissance art. If the figures in the Reims portal seem about to step off their columns, Renaissance figures actually do so. By the time of the Limbourg Brothers' early fifteenth-century manuscript illumination for *Les Très Riches Heures du Duc de Berry* (Fig. 603), human beings are represented, for the first time since classical antiquity, as casting actual shadows upon the ground. The architecture is also rendered with some measure of perspectival accuracy. The scene is full of realistic detail, and the potential of landscape to render a sense of actual space, evident in the earlier Pisano Nativity, is fully realized.

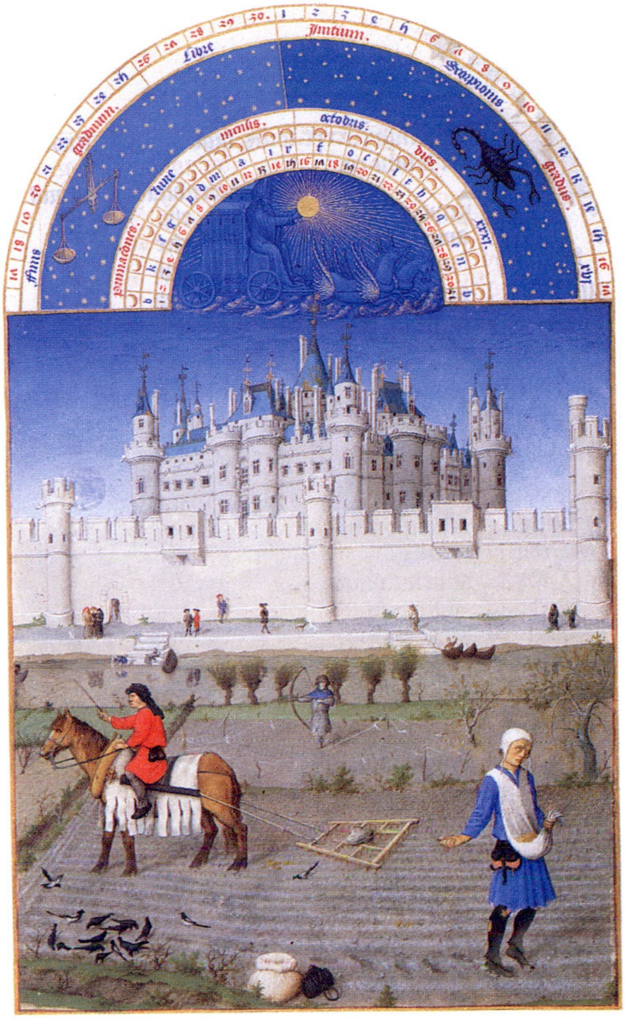

Fig. 603 The Limbourg Brothers, *October*, from *Les Très Riches Heures du Duc de Berry*, 1413–1416.
Musée Condé, Chantilly. Giraudon/Art Resource.

THE EARLY RENAISSANCE

The Renaissance is, perhaps most of all, the era of the individual. As early as the 1330s, the poet and scholar Petrarch had conceived of a new Humanism, a philosophy that emphasized the unique value of each person. Petrarch believed that the birth of Christ had ushered in an "age of faith," which had blinded the world to learning and thus condemned it to darkness. The study of classical languages, literature, history, and philosophy—what we call the "humanities"—could lead to a new enlightened stage of history. People should be judged, Petrarch felt, by their actions. It was not God's will that determined who they were and what they were capable of; rather, glory and fame were available to anyone who dared to seize them.

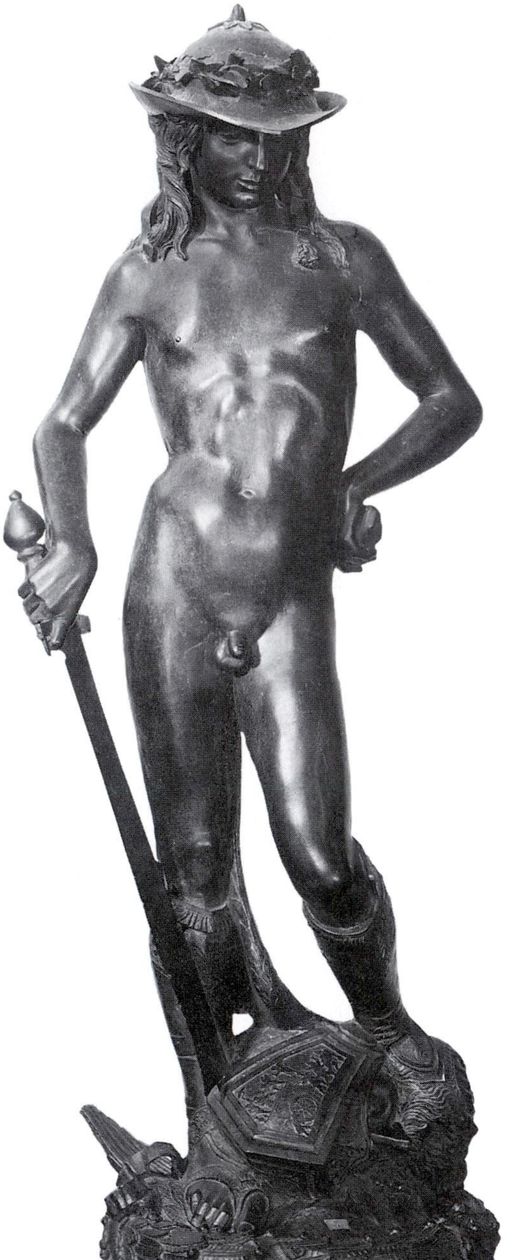

Fig. 604 Donatello, *David*, c. 1425–1430.
Bronze, H. 62¼ in.
Museo Nazionale del Bargello, Florence. Alinari/Art Resource.

Writing in 1485, the philosopher Giovanni Pico della Mirandola—Pico, as he is known—addressed himself to every ordinary (male) person: "Thou, constrained by no limits, in accordance with thine own free will . . . shalt ordain for thyself the limits of thy nature. We have set thee at the world's center . . . [and] thou mayst fashion thyself in whatever shape thou shalt prefer." Out of such sentiments were born not only the archetypical Renaissance geniuses—men like Michelangelo and Leonardo—but also Niccolò Machiavelli's wily and pragmatic Prince, for whom the ends justify any means, and the legendary Faust, who sold his soul to the devil in return for youth, knowledge, and magical power.

Under the leadership of the extraordinarily wealthy and beneficent Medici family—with first Cosimo de' Medici and, subsequently, his grandson, Lorenzo the Magnificent, assuming the largest roles—the city of Florence became the cultural center of the early Renaissance. The three leading innovators of the arts in fifteenth-century Florence—the painter Masaccio, who died in 1428 at the age of 27, having worked only six short years; the sculptor Donatello, and the architect Filippo Brunelleschi—were already firmly established by the time Cosimo assumed power in 1434. Brunelleschi was the inventor of geometric, linear perspective, a system he probably developed in order to study the ruins of ancient Rome. In 1420, he accepted a commission to design and build a dome over the crossing of the Florence Cathedral (see Fig. 595). The result, which spans a space 140 feet wide, was a major technological feat. But it was, above all, his sense of measure, order, and proportion that defined his sensibility—and that of the Italian Renaissance as a whole. Brunelleschi's God is a reasonable one, not the mysterious force that manifests itself in the ethereal light of the Gothic cathedral.

Donatello had traveled to Rome in 1402 with his friend Brunelleschi. The Greek and Roman statuary he studied there had a great influence on his own work, which reflects the

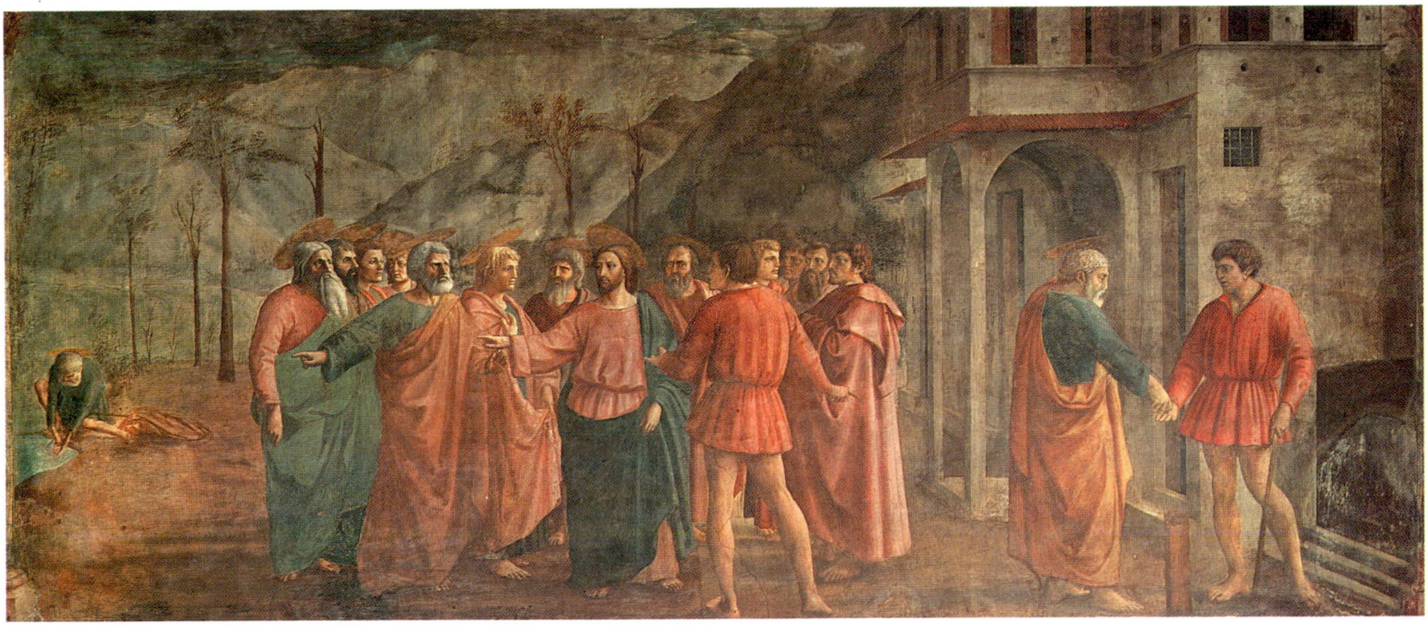

Fig. 605 Masaccio, *The Tribute Money*, c. 1427.
Fresco. Brancacci Chapel, Santa Maria del Carmine, Florence. Scala/Art Resource.

classical interest in the human body in motion and in articulating that body through the use of drapery. The first lifesize nude sculpture since antiquity, Donatello's *David* (Fig. 604) is posed in perfectly classical ***contrapposto***. But the young hero—almost antiheroic in the youthful fragility of his physique—is also fully self-conscious, his attention turned, in what appears to be full-blown self-adoration, upon himself as an object of physical beauty.

Masaccio, 15 years younger than Donatello and 24 years younger than Brunelleschi, learned from them both, translating Donatello's naturalism and Brunelleschi's sense of proportion into the art of painting. In his *The Tribute Money* (Fig. 605), painted around 1427, Christ's disciples, especially St. Peter, wonder whether it is proper to pay taxes to the Roman government when, from their point of view, they owe allegiance to Christ, not Rome. But Christ counsels them to separate their earthly affairs from the spiritual obligations—"Render therefore unto Caesar the things which are Caesar's; and unto God the things that are God's"(Matthew 22:21). To that end, Christ tells St. Peter and the other disciples that they will find the coin necessary to pay the imperial tax collector, whose back is to us, in the mouth of a fish. At the left, St. Peter extracts the coin from the fish's mouth, and, at the right, he pays the required tribute money to the tax collector. The figures here are modeled by means of chiaroscuro in a light that falls upon the scene from the right (notice their cast shadows). We sense the physicality of the figures beneath their robes; the landscape is rendered through atmospheric perspective; the building on the right is rendered in a one-point perspective scheme, with a vanishing point behind the head of Christ. All of these artistic devices are in themselves innovations; together, they constitute one of the most remarkable achievements in the history of art, an extraordinary change in direction from the flat, motionless figures of the Middle Ages toward a fully realistic representation.

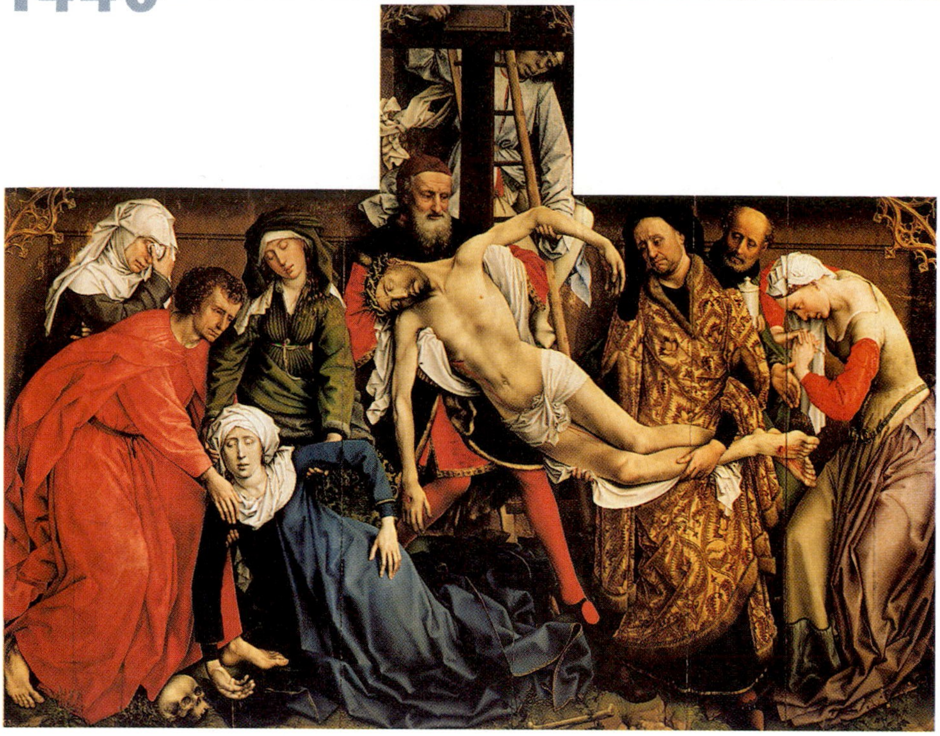

Fig. 606 Rogier van der Weyden, *Deposition,* c. 1435–1438.
Oil on wood, 7 ft. 1 5/8 in. × 8 ft. 7 1/8 in. Museo del Prado, Madrid. Scala/Art Resource.

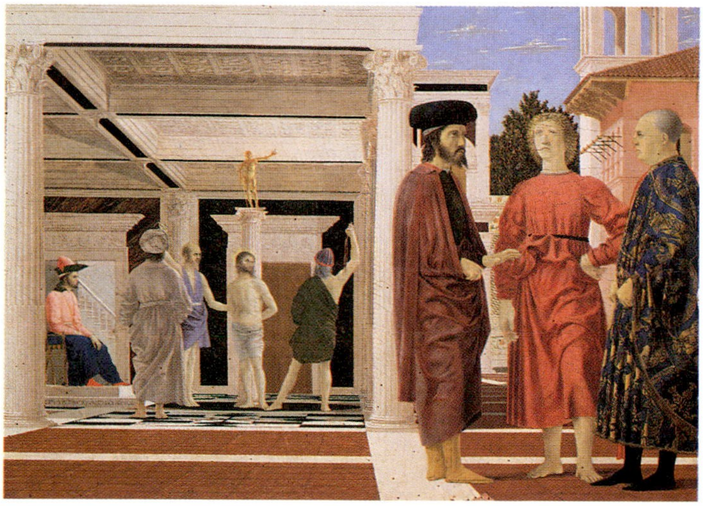

Fig. 607 Piero della Francesca, *The Flagellation of Christ,* c. 1451.
Tempera on wood, 32 3/4 × 23 1/3 in.
Palazzo Ducale, Galleria Nazionale delle Marche, Urbino. Scala/Art Resource.

In the North of Europe, in Flanders particularly, a flourishing merchant society promoted artistic developments that in many ways rivaled those of Florence. The Italian revival of classical notions of order and measure was, for the most part, ignored in the North. Rather, the Northern artists were deeply committed to rendering believable space in the greatest and most realistic detail. The *Mérode Altarpiece,* executed by the Master of Flémalle (see Fig. 312), is almost exactly contemporary with Masaccio's *Tribute Money,* but in the precision and clarity of its detail—in fact, an explosion of detail—it is radically different in feel. The chief reason for the greater clarity is, as we discussed in Part III, a question of medium. Northern painters developed oil paint in the first half of the fourteenth century. With oil paint, painters could achieve dazzling effects of light on the surface of the painting—as opposed to the matte, or nonreflective, surface of both fresco and tempera. These effects recall, on the one hand, the Gothic style's emphasis on the almost magical light of the stained-glass window. In that sense, the effect achieved seems transcendent. But it also lends the depicted objects a sense of material reality, and thus caters to the material desires of the North's rising mercantile class.

If we compare Rogier van der Weyden's *Deposition* (Fig. 606) to Piero della Francesca's *The Flagellation of Christ* (Fig. 607), the differences between the northern, Flemish and the southern, Italian sensibilities become evident. Virtually a demonstration of the rules of linear perspective, Piero's scene depicts Pontius Pilate watching as executioners whip Christ. Although

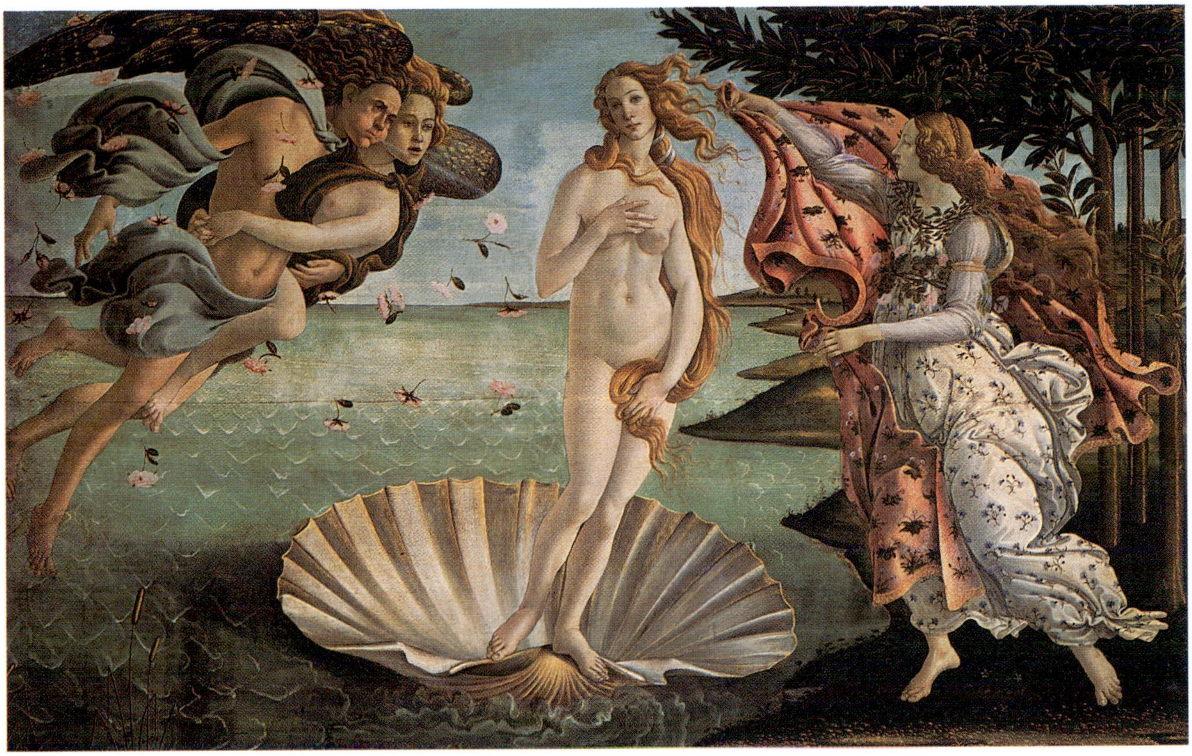

Fig. 608 Sandro Botticelli, *The Birth of Venus*, c. 1482.
Tempera on canvas, 5 ft. 8 7/8 in. x 9 ft. 1 7/8 in. Galleria degli Uffizi, Florence. Scala/Art Resource.

it is much more architecturally unified, the painting pays homage to Masaccio's *Tribute Money*. Emotionally speaking, Rogier's *Deposition* has almost nothing in common with Piero's *Flagellation*. It is as if Piero has controlled the violence of his emotionally charged scene by means of mathematics, while Rogier has emphasized instead the pathos and human feeling that pervades his scene of Christ being lowered from the cross. While Piero's composition is essentially defined by a square and a rectangle, with figures arranged in each in an essentially triangular fashion, Rogier's composition is controlled by two parallel, deeply expressive, and sweeping curves, one defined by the body of Christ and the other by the swooning figure below him. Next to the high drama of Rogier's painting, Piero's seems almost static, but the understated brutality of Christ's flagellation in the background of Piero's painting is equally compelling.

THE HIGH RENAISSANCE

When Lorenzo de' Medici assumed control of his family in 1469, Florence was still the cultural center of the Western world. Lorenzo's predecessor had founded the Platonic Academy of Philosophy, where the artist Sandro Botticelli studied a brand of Neoplatonic thought that transformed the philosophic writings of Plato almost into a religion. According to the Neoplatonists, in the contemplation of beauty, the inherently corrupt soul could transform its love for the physical and material into a purely spiritual love of God. Thus, Botticelli uses mythological themes to transform his pagan imagery into a source of Christian inspiration and love. His *Birth of Venus* (Fig. 608), the first monumental representation of the nude goddess since ancient times, represents innocence itself, a divine beauty free of any hint of the physical and the sensual. It was this form of beauty that the

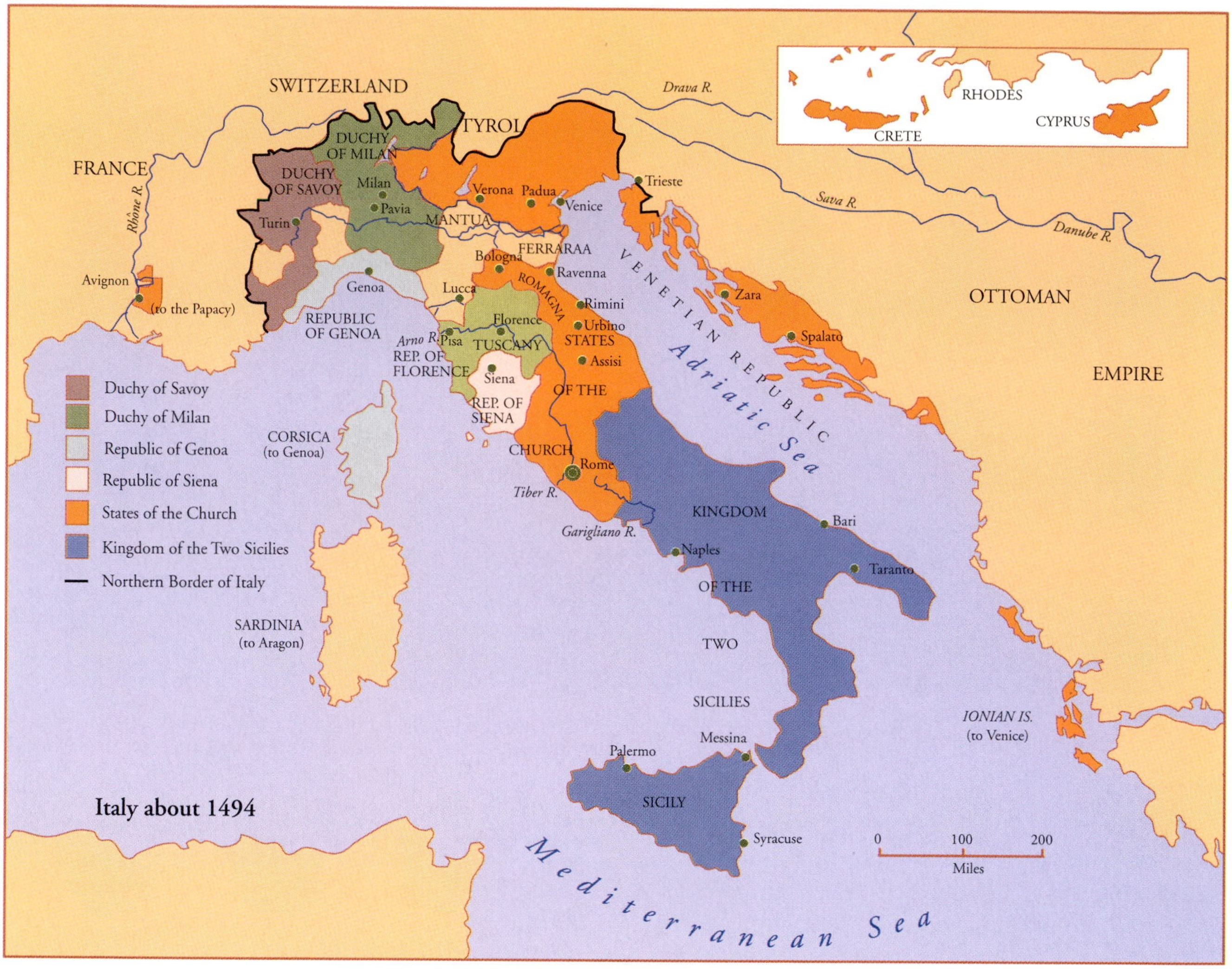

soul, aspiring to salvation, was expected to contemplate. But such meanings were by no means clear to the uninitiated, and when the Dominican monk Girolamo Savonarola denounced the Medicis as pagan, the majority of Florentines agreed. In 1494, the family was banished.

Still, for a short period at the outset of the sixteenth century, Florence was again the focal point of artistic activity. The three great artists of the High Renaissance—Leonardo, Michelangelo, and Raphael—all lived and worked in the city. As a young man, Michelangelo had been a member of Lorenzo de' Medici's circle, but with the Medicis' demise in 1494, he fled to Bologna. He returned to Florence seven years later to work on a giant piece of marble left over from an abandoned commission. Out of this, while still in his twenties, he carved his monolithic *David* (Fig. 69).

Leonardo, some 23 years older than Michelangelo, had left Florence as early as 1481 for Milan. There he offered his services to the great Duke of Milan, Ludovico Sforza, first as a military engineer and, only secondarily, as an architect, sculptor, and painter. His drawing of *A Scythed Chariot, Armored Car, and Pike* (Fig. 609), is indicative of his work for Sforza. "I will make covered vehicles," he wrote to the

Vasco da Gama reaches India by sea
1497

c. 1500
Rise of modern European nation-states

Portuguese dominate the East Coast of Africa
1506

1510

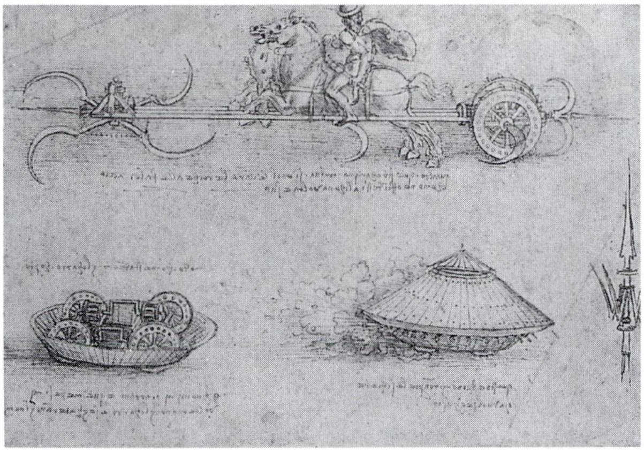

Fig. 609 Leonardo da Vinci, *A Scythed Chariot, Armored Car, and Pike,* c. 1487.
Pen and ink and wash, $6\frac{3}{4} \times 9\frac{3}{4}$ in. The British Museum, London.

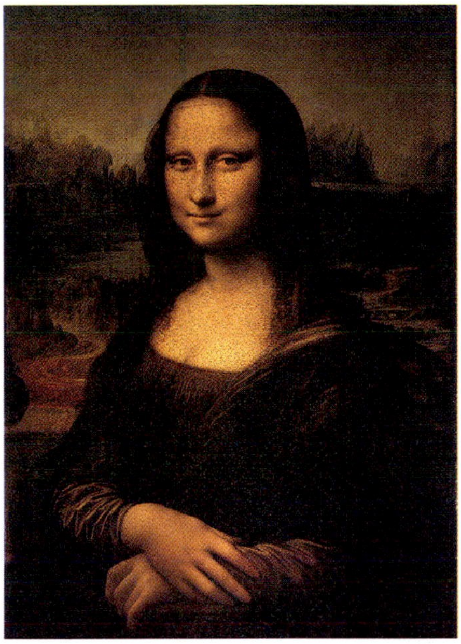

Fig. 610 Leonardo da Vinci, *Mona Lisa,* c. 1503–1505.
Oil on wood, $30\frac{1}{4} \times 21$ in.
Musée du Louvre, Paris. Erich Lessing/Art Resource.

Duke, "which will penetrate the enemy and their artillery, and there is no host of armed men so great that they will not be broken down by them." The chariot in the drawing is equipped with scyths to cut down the enemy, and the armored car, presented in an upside down view as well as scooting along in a cloud of dust, was to be operated by eight men. But Leonardo's work for Sforza was not limited to military operations. From 1495 to 1498, he painted his world famous fresco *The Last Supper* (Fig. 112), which many consider to be the first painting of the High Renaissance, in Santa Maria delle Grazie, a monastic church under the protection of the Sforza family. Leonardo left Milan soon after the French invaded in October 1499, and by April he had returned to Florence, where he concentrated his energies on a lifesize cartoon for *Virgin and Child with St. Anne and Infant St. John* (see Fig. 237). This became so famous that throngs of Florentines flocked to see it. At about this time he also painted the *Mona Lisa* (Fig. 610). Perhaps a portrait of the wife of the Florentine banker Zanobi del Giocondo, the painting conveys a psychological depth that has continued to fascinate viewers up to the present day. Its power derives, at least in part, from a manipulation of light and shadow that imparts a blurred imprecision to the sitter's features, lending her an aura of ambiguity and mystery. This interest in the pyschology, not just the physical looks, of the sitter is typical of the Renaissance imagination.

When Raphael, 21 years old, arrived in Florence in 1504, he discovered Leonardo and Michelangelo locked in a competition over who would get the commission to decorate the city council chamber in the Palazzo Vecchio with pictures celebrating the Florentine past. Leonardo painted a Battle of Anghiari and Michelangelo a Battle of Cascina, neither of which survives. We know the first today only by reputation and early drawings. A cartoon survived well into the seventeenth century and was widely copied, most faithfully by Peter Paul Rubens. Of the Michelangelo we know very little. What is clear, however, is that the young Raphael was immediately confronted by the cult of genius that in many ways has come to define the High Renaissance. Artists of genius and inspiration were considered to be different from everyone else, and to be guided

The Prince written by Niccoló Machiavelli
1513

Martin Luther posts his ninety-five theses
1517

1510

1517
Spain authorizes slave trade between West Africa and New World colonies

1519–22
First circumnavigation of the world

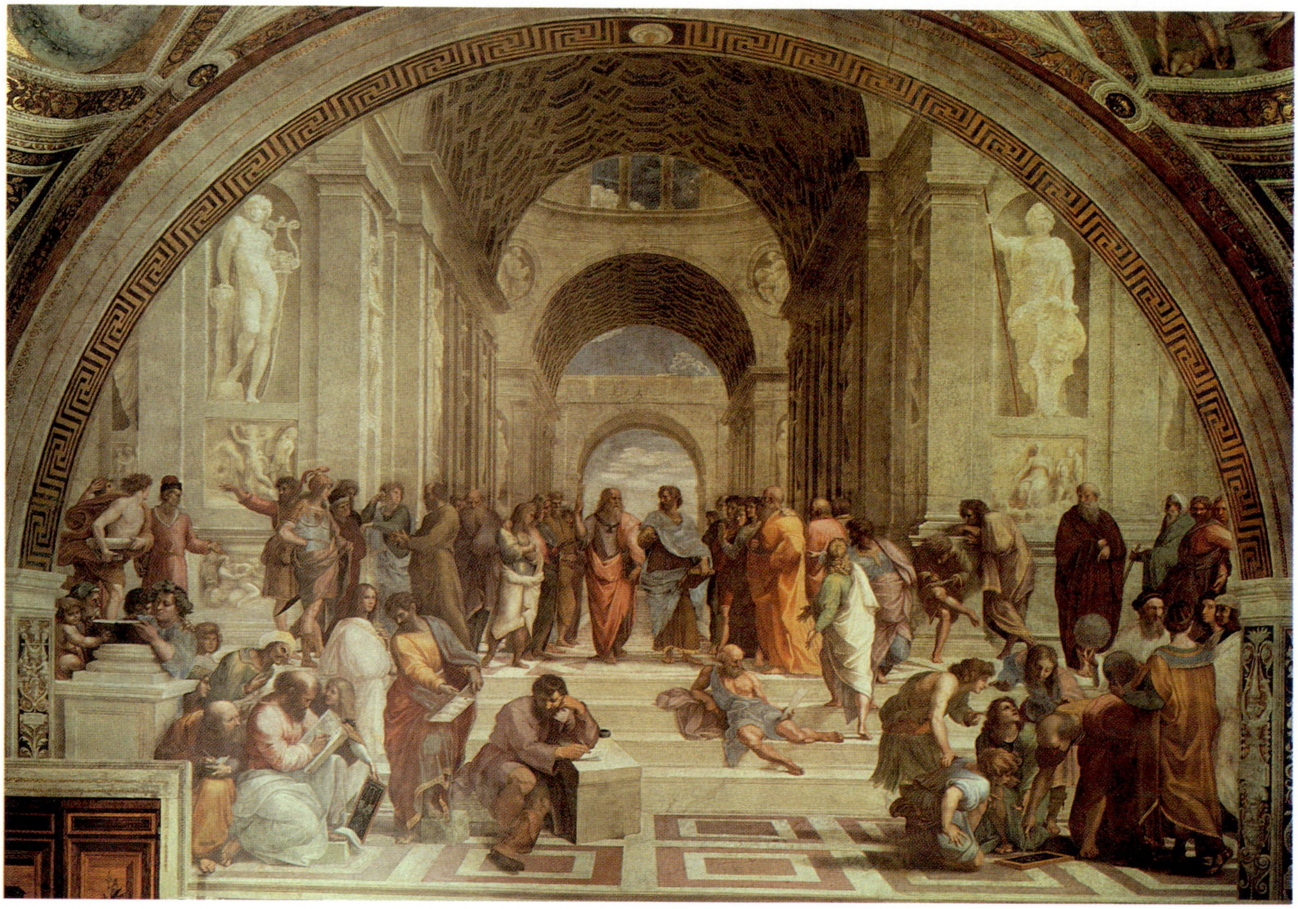

Fig. 611 Raphael, *The School of Athens,* 1510–1511.
Fresco. Stanza della Segnatura, Vatican Palace, Rome. Scala/Art Resource.

in their work by an insight that, according to the Neoplatonists was divine in origin. The Neoplatonists believed that the goals of truth and beauty were not reached by following the universal rules and laws of classical antiquity—notions of proportion and mathematics. Nor would fidelity to visual reality guarantee beautiful results; in fact, given the fallen condition of the world, quite the opposite was more likely, as Leonardo's studies of the faces of his fellow citizens had demonstrated (see Fig. 27). Instead, the artist of genius had to rely on subjective and personal intuition—what the Neoplatonists called the "divine frenzy" of the creative act—to transcend the conditions of everyday life. Plato had argued that painting was mere slavish imitation of an already existing thing—it was a diminished reality. The Neoplatonists turned this argument on its head. Art now exceeded reality. It was a window, not upon nature, but upon divine inspiration itself.

Raphael learned much from both Leonardo and Michelangelo, and, in 1508, he was awarded the largest commission of the day, the decoration of the papal apartments at the Vatican in Rome. On the four walls of the first room, the Stanza della Segnatura, he painted frescos representing the four domains of knowledge—Theology, Law, Poetry, and Philosophy. The

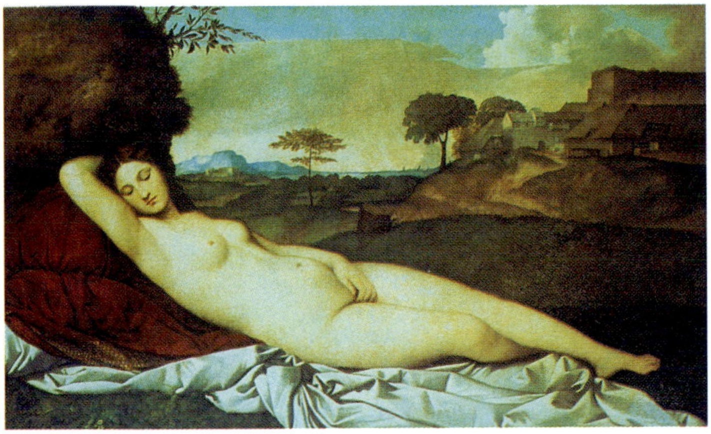

Fig. 612 Giorgione (completed by Titian), *Sleeping Venus*, c. 1510.
Oil on canvas, 42 3/4 × 69 in.
Staatliche Gemäldegalerie, Dresden. Scala/Art Resource.

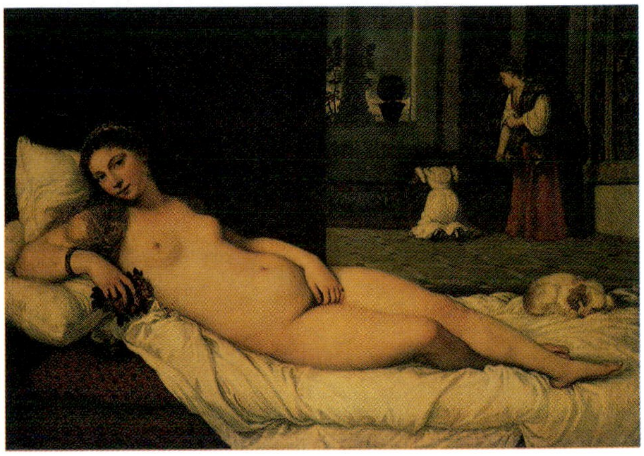

Fig. 613 Titian, *Venus of Urbino*, 1538.
Oil on canvas, 47 × 65 in.
Galleria degli Uffizi, Florence. Scala/Art Resource.

most famous of these is the last, *The School of Athens* (Fig. 611). Raphael's painting depicts a gathering of the greatest philosophers and scientists of the ancient world. The centering of the composition is reminiscent of Leonardo's *Last Supper,* but the perspectival rendering of space is much deeper. Where, in Leonardo's masterpiece, Christ is situated at the vanishing point, in Raphael's work, Plato and Aristotle occupy that position. These two figures represent the two great, opposing schools of philosophy, the Platonists, who were concerned with the spiritual world of ideas (thus Plato points upwards), and the Aristotelians, who were concerned with the matter-of-factness of material reality (thus Aristotle points over the ground upon which he walks). The expressive power of the figures owes much to Michelangelo, who, it is generally believed, Raphael portrayed as the philosopher Heraclitus, the brooding, self-absorbed figure in the foreground.

Raphael's commission in Rome is typical of the rapid spread of the ideals of the Italian Renaissance culture to the rest of Italy and Europe. In Venice, however, painting developed somewhat independently of the Florentine manner. The emphasis in Venetian art is on the sensuousness of light and color and the pleasures of the senses. The closest we have come to it so far is in the mysterious glow that infuses Leonardo's *Mona Lisa,* but what is only hinted at in Leonardo's work explodes in Venetian painting as full-blown theatrical effect. Partly under the influence of Leonardo, who had visited Venice after leaving Milan in 1499, Giorgione developed a painting style of blurred edges and softened forms. After his teacher's death in the great plague of 1510, Giorgione's student, Titian, took this style even further, developing a technique that employed a painterly brushstroke to new, sensuously expressive ends. Two paintings of Venus, the first by Giorgione, probably completed by Titian after his teacher's death (Fig. 612), and the second executed 28 years later by Titian himself (Fig. 613), demonstrate the sensuality of the Venetian style. Giorgione's life-size figure, bathed in luminous light, is frankly erotic, but Titian's is even more so. Positioned on the crumpled sheets of a bed, rather than in a pastoral landscape, she is not innocently sleeping but gazes directly at us, engaging us in her sexuality.

Death of Song poet
Su Tung-p'o
1101

1000

1105
Genghis Khan begins
Mongol invasions

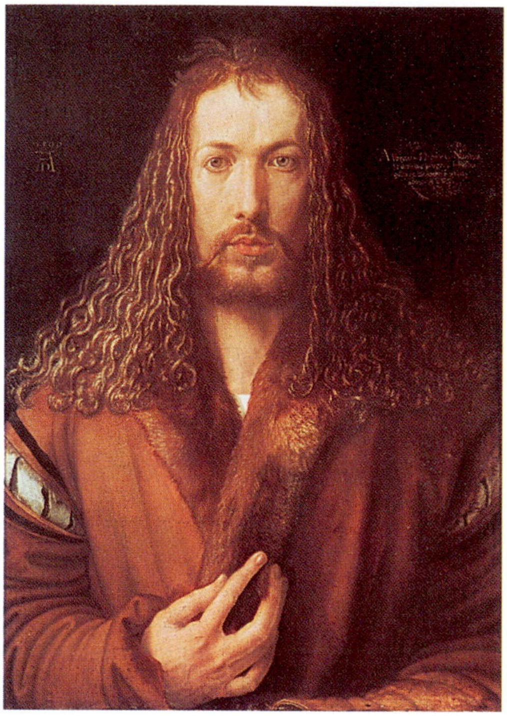

Fig. 614 Albrecht Dürer, *Self-Portrait,* 1500.
Oil on panel, 26 1/4 × 19 1/4 in. Pinakothek, Munich.

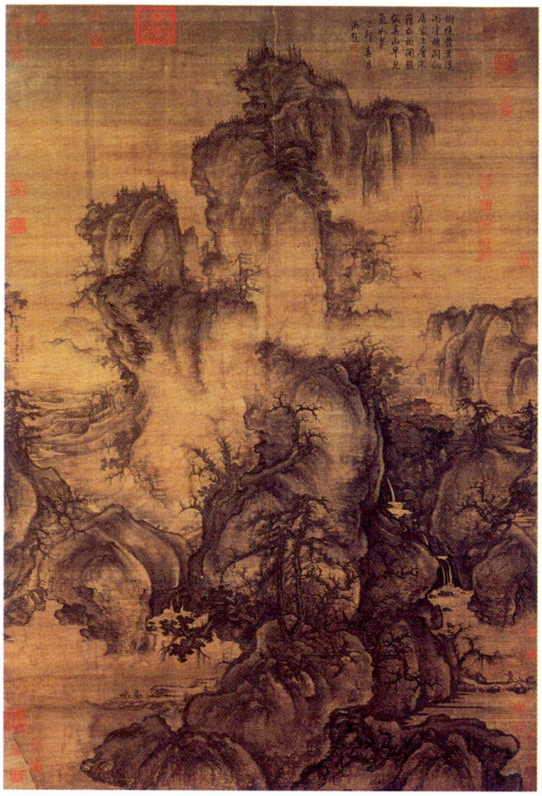

Fig. 615 Guo Xi, *Early Spring,* 1072 (Northern Song dynasty).
Hanging scroll, ink and slight color on silk, L. 60 in.
Collection of the National Palace Museum, Taipei, Taiwan, R. O. C.

In the North of Europe, the impact of the Italian Renaissance is perhaps best understood in the work of the German artist Albrecht Dürer. As a young man he had copied Italian prints, and, in 1495, he traveled to Italy to study the Italian masters. From this point on, he strived to establish the ideals of the Renaissance in his native country. The first artist to be fascinated by his own image, Dürer painted self-portraits (Fig. 614) throughout his career. In this act, he asserts his sense of the importance of the individual, especially the individual of genius and talent, such as himself. Meaning to evoke his own spirituality, he presents himself almost as if he were Christ. Yet, as his printmaking demonstrates (see Fig. 283), not even Dürer could quite synthesize the northern love for precise and accurate naturalism—the desire to render the world of real things—with the southern idealist desire to transcend the world of real things.

ART IN CHINA

In 1275, a young Venetian by the name of Marco Polo arrived in Peking, China, and quickly established himself as a favorite of the Mongol ruler Kublai Khan, first emperor of the Yuan dynasty. Polo served in an administrative capacitiy in Kublai Khan's court and for three years ruled the city of Yangchow. Shortly after his return to Venice, in 1295, he was imprisoned after being captured by the army of Genoa in a battle with his native Venice, and while there he dictated an account of his travels. His description of the luxury and magnificence of the Far East, by all accounts reasonably accurate, was virtually the sole source of information about China available in Europe until the nineteenth century.

First Mongul invasion of Japan
1274

1368
Founding of Ming Dynasty

Chinese voyages to India and Africa begin
1405

1400

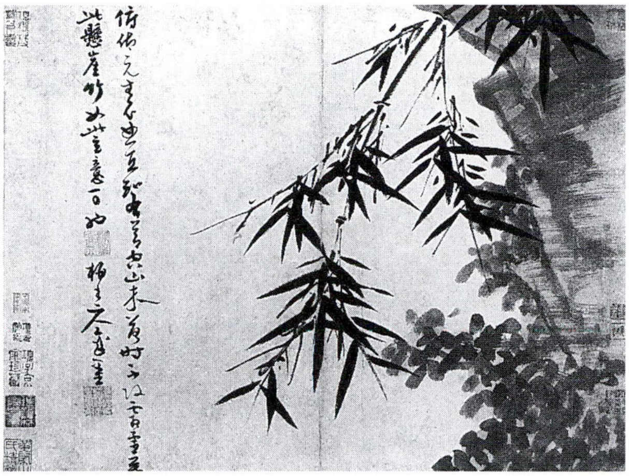

Fig. 616 Wu Chen, *Bamboo,* 1350.
Album leaf, ink on paper, 16 × 21 in.
Collection of the National Palace Museum, Taipei, Taiwan, Republic of China.

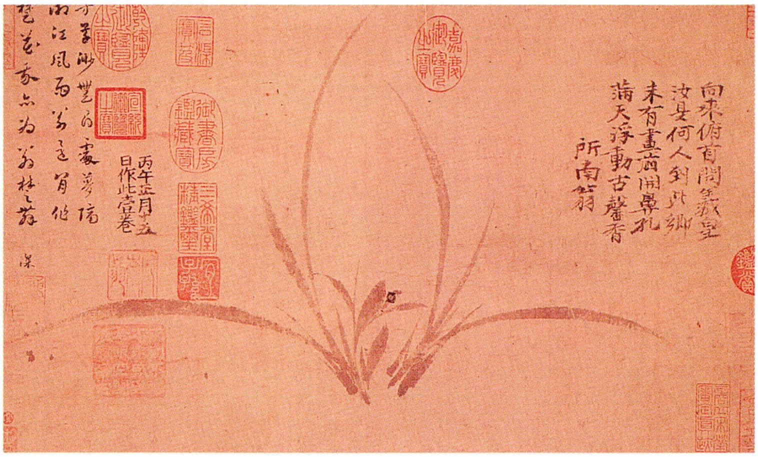

Fig. 617 Cheng Sixiao, *Ink Orchids,* Yuan dynasty, 1306.
Handscroll, ink on paper, 10 1/8 × 16 3/4 in.
Municipal Museum of Fine Art, Osaka/PPS.

Since the time of the Song dynasty, which ruled the empire from 960 until it was overrun by Kublai Khan in 1279, the Taoists in China had emphasized the importance of self-expression, especially through the arts. Poets, calligraphers, and painters were appointed to the most important positions of state. After calligraphy, the Chinese valued landscape painting as the highest form of artistic endeavor. For them, the activity of painting was a search for the absolute truth embodied in nature, a search that was not so much intellectual as intuitive. They sought to understand the *li,* or "principle," upon which the universe is founded, and thus to understand the symbolic meaning and feeling that underlies every natural form. The symbolic meanings of Guo Xi's *Early Spring* (Fig. 615), for instance, have been recorded in a book authored by his son, Guo Si, entitled *The Lofty Message of the Forests and Streams.* According to this book, the central peak here symbolizes the Emperor, and its tall pines the gentlemanly ideals of the court. Around the Emperor, the masses assume their natural place, just as around the mountain, the trees and hills fall, like the water itself, in the order and rhythms of nature.

At the time of Marco Polo's arrival, many of the scholar-painters of the Chinese court, unwilling to serve under the foreign domination of Kublai Khan, were retreating into exile from public life. In exile they conscientiously sought to keep traditional values and arts alive by cultivating earlier styles in both painting and calligraphy. The bamboo in Wu Chen's painting (Fig. 616) was a political symbol aimed at the hated non-Chinese rulers—the plant might bend, but it would not break. Wu Chen's efforts to keep the traditions of China alive are also evident in his inscription to this painting, written in the wild "cursive" of the Tang dynasty. According to the inscription on Cheng Sixiao's *Ink Orchids* (Fig. 617) this painting was done to protest the "theft of Chinese soil by invaders," referring to the Mongol conquest of China. The orchids, therefore, have been painted without soil around their roots, showing an art flourishing even though what sustains it has been taken away.

In 1368, the Mongols were overthrown when Zhu Yuanzhang drove the last Yuan emperor north into the desert and declared himself first emperor of the new Ming dynasty. China was once again ruled by the Chinese.

Olmec civilization
c. 1500–300 BCE

4000 BCE

before 3000 BCE
Maize domesticated
in Mexico

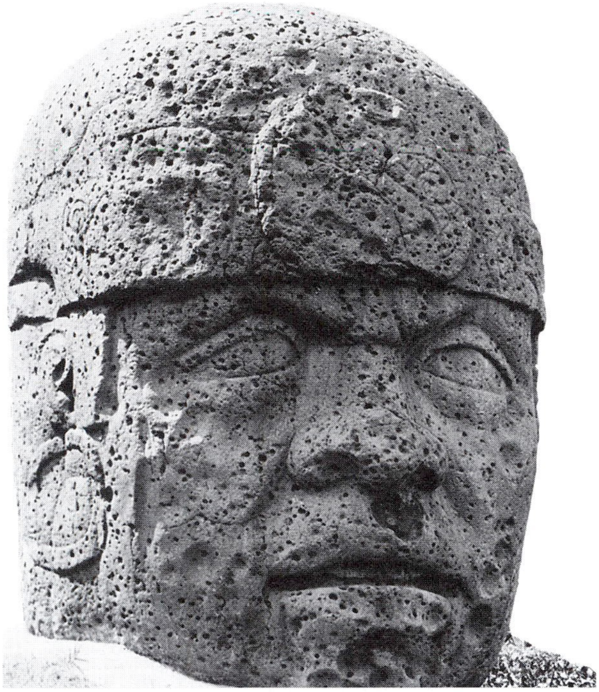

Fig. 618 Colossal head, Villahermosa, Mexico, Olmec culture, c. 800–200 BCE.
Basalt, H. 7 ft. Museo Nacional de Antropologia, Mexico City.

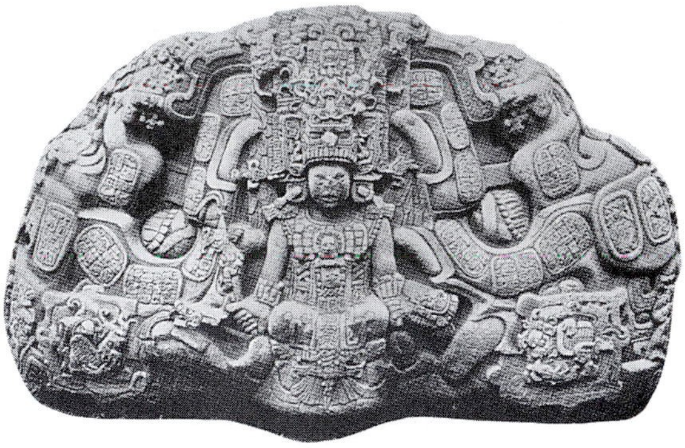

Fig. 619 *Great Dragon,* Maya, Quiriguá, Mexico, 6th century CE.
H. 7 ft. 3 in.

PRE-COLUMBIAN ART IN MEXICO

The term **Pre-Columbian** refers to the cultures of all the peoples who lived in Mexico, Central America, and South America prior to the arrival of the Europeans at the end of the fifteenth century. The cultures of the Pre-Columbian peoples are distinguished by their monumental architecture and their preference for working in stone, both of which lend their art a quality of permanence that differentiates it from the more fragile art forms of the Native American peoples who lived in what is now the United States and Canada. The permanence of Pre-Columbian art was the result of a cultural stability gained around 4000 BCE, when they developed agricultural, as opposed to nomadic civilizations based especially on the production of maize, or yellow corn.

The major cultures of Mexico were the Olmec; the Maya, the civilization that developed with the great city of Teotihuacán as its center; and the Aztec, who called themselves Mexica, and whose culture was not even 200 years old at the time of the Spanish conquest of Mexico in 1519. Led by Hernándo Cortés, the Spanish discovered, at the Aztec capital of Tenochtitlan (now Mexico City), a city that was, in the words of one of Cortés's men, "like the enchantments in the book of [the late medieval romancer] Amadís, because of the high towers . . . and other buildings, all of masonry, which rose from the water. Some of our soldiers asked if what we saw was not a dream." Albrecht Dürer recounts seeing the treasures Cortés sent home to King Charles V: "a sun entirely of gold, a whole fathom broad; likewise a moon entirely of silver, just as big . . . all so precious that they were valued at a hundred thousand guilders. I have never seen in all my days that which so rejoiced my heart, as these things." Within 75 years of the Spanish conquest, disease had ravaged the native peoples of the region, reducing their population from about 20 million to about 1 million, and the Pre-Columbian culture that Dürer praised had vanished from the face of the earth. Indeed, the treasures themselves were melted down for currency.

Classic period of Teotihuacán civilization
300–900

Aztecs arrive in the Valley of Mexico
c. 1325

Cortés invades Mexico
1519

1519

c. 164 BCE
Oldest Mayan monuments

c. 1000–1500
Inca civilization in South America

1369
City of Tenochtitlan founded

The first Pre-Columbian culture was that of the Olmecs, who lived in present-day Tabasco and Vera Cruz, states on the southern coast of the Gulf of Mexico. As early as 1500–800 BCE, the Olmecs created a huge ceremonial center at La Venta. La Venta's design, the basis of planning in Mexico and Central America for many centuries to come, centered on a pyramid, perhaps echoing the shape of a volcano. This pyramid faced a ceremonial courtyard, laid out on an axis that was determined astronomically. The courtyard was decorated with four giant stone heads, three to the south and one to the north (Fig. 618). More than a dozen such heads have been discovered, some of them 12 feet high. The closest source for the stone used to make this head from La Venta, in present-day Villahermosa, is 60 miles away, across swampland.

Mayan civilization began to reach its peak in southern Mexico and Guatemala around CE 250, shortly after the rise of Teotihuacán in the north, and it flourished until about the year 900. Narrative relief carving was one of the predominant means of artistic expression in Mayan culture. The so-called *Great Dragon* relief (Fig. 619), carved on the face of a huge river boulder, shows one of the last rulers of the Mayan city of Quiriguá, in present-day Guatemala. The king is shown sitting in the gaping mouth of a giant monster and wearing an elaborate headdress. The monster does not so much threaten the ruler as evoke his power.

By about the sixth century BCE, widespread use of both a 260-day and a 365-day calendar system began to appear throughout Mexico. The latter corresponds to the true solar year, while the former is based on the length of human gestation, from the first missed menstrual flow to birth. Both calendars were often used simultaneously. A given day in one calendar will occur on the same day in the other every 52 years, and each new 52-year cycle was widely celebrated, particularly by the Aztecs. Such calendar systems, which were inscribed in stone, provide a sense of continuity between the Pre-Columbian cultures. Particularly among the Aztecs, who traced their ancestry to the merging of Mayan and Toltec cultures at Chichen Itzá, on the Yucatan peninsula, the calendar's tie to the menstrual cycle required blood sacrifice. *Coatlicue* (Fig. 620) was the Aztec goddess of life and death. Her head is composed of two fanged serpents, which are symbolic of flowing blood. She wears a necklace of human hearts, severed hands, and a skull. The connection of blood to fertility is clear in the snake that descends between her legs, which suggests both menstruation and the phallus.

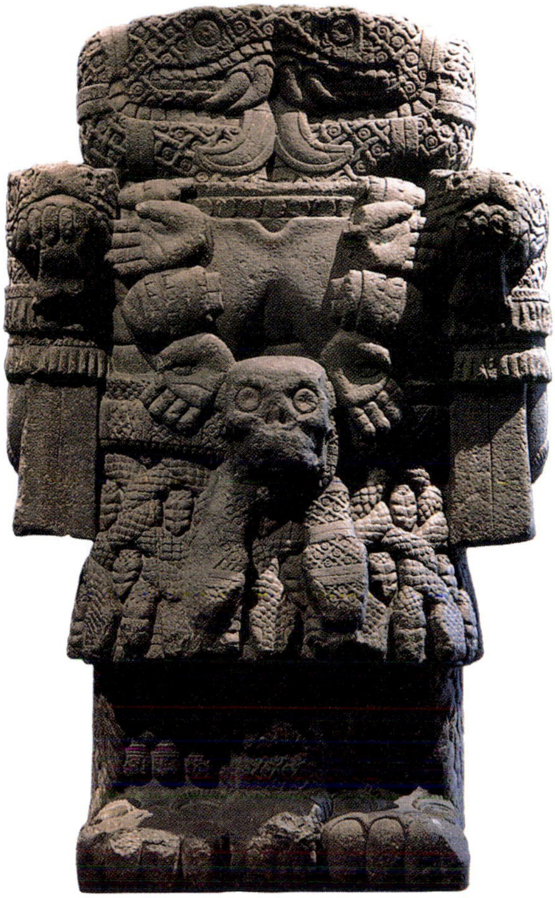

Fig. 620 ***Coatlicue,*** **Aztec, 15th century.**
H. 8 ft. 3 in. Werner Forman/Art Resource.

Copernicus publishes
On the Revolution of the Heavenly Spheres
1543

1520

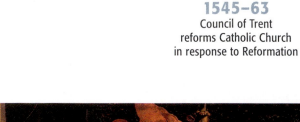

1521–22
Luther translates
New Testament into German

1545–63
Council of Trent
reforms Catholic Church
in response to Reformation

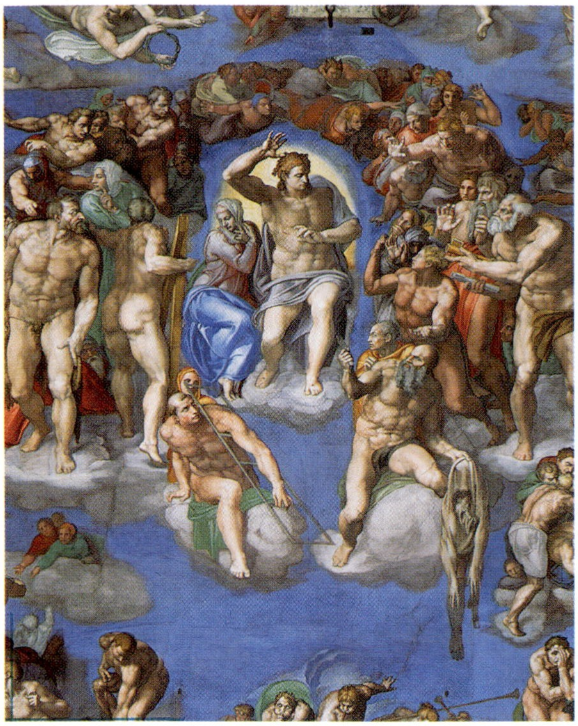

Fig. 621 Michelangelo, *The Last Judgment, "Guidizio Universale"* (detail), Sistine Chapel, 1531–1541.
Fresco, on altar wall of Sistine Chapel.
Photo: Zigrossi Bracchetti, October 1996. The Vatican Museums, Rome.
©Nippon Television Network Corporation Tokyo; 1

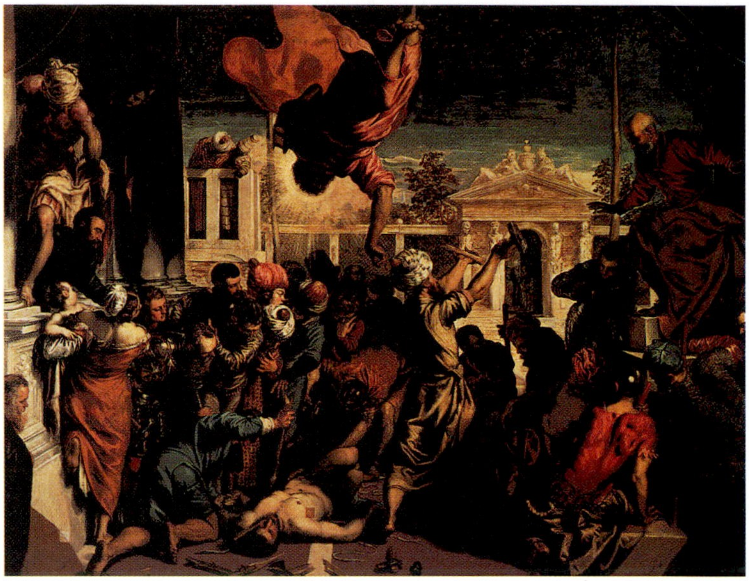

Fig. 622 Tintoretto, *The Miracle of the Slave,* 1548.
Oil on canvas, approx. 14 × 18 ft. Galleria dell' Academia, Venice. Scala/Art Resource.

MANNERISM

Shortly after the Spanish conquest of separatist States within Spain in 1519 and the death of Raphael in 1520, many Italian painters embarked on a stylistic course that was highly individualistic and *mannered,* or consciously artificial. The call word of this **Mannerist** style was "invention," and the technical and imaginative virtuousity of the artist became of paramount importance. Each Mannerist artist may, therefore, be identified by his own "signature" style. Where the art of the High Renaissance sought to create a feeling of balance and proportion, quite the opposite is the goal of Mannerist art. In the late work of Michelangelo, for example, particularly the great fresco of *The Last Judgment* on the altar wall of the Sistine Chapel (Fig. 621), executed in the years 1534–1541, we find figures of grotesque proportion arranged in an almost chaotic, certainly athletic swirl of line. Mannerist painters represented space in unpredictable and ambiguous ways, so that bodies sometimes seem to fall out of nowhere into the frame of the painting, as in Tintoretto's *The Miracle of the Slave* (Fig. 622). The drama of Tintoretto's painting is heightened by the descent of the vastly foreshortened St. Mark, who hurtles in from above to save the slave from his executioner. The rising spiral line created by the three central figures—the slave, the executioner, holding up his shattered instruments of torture, and St. Mark—is characteristic of Mannerism, but the theatricality of the scene, heightened by its dramatic contrast of light and dark, anticipates the Baroque style, which soon followed.

Often the space of a Mannerist painting seems too shallow for what is depicted, a feeling emphasized by the frequent use of radical foreshortening, as in the Tintoretto. Or the figure

Birth of
William Shakespeare
1564

Defeat of Spanish Armada
by English fleet
1588

1600

1584
First English attempt to
colonize North America (Roanoke)

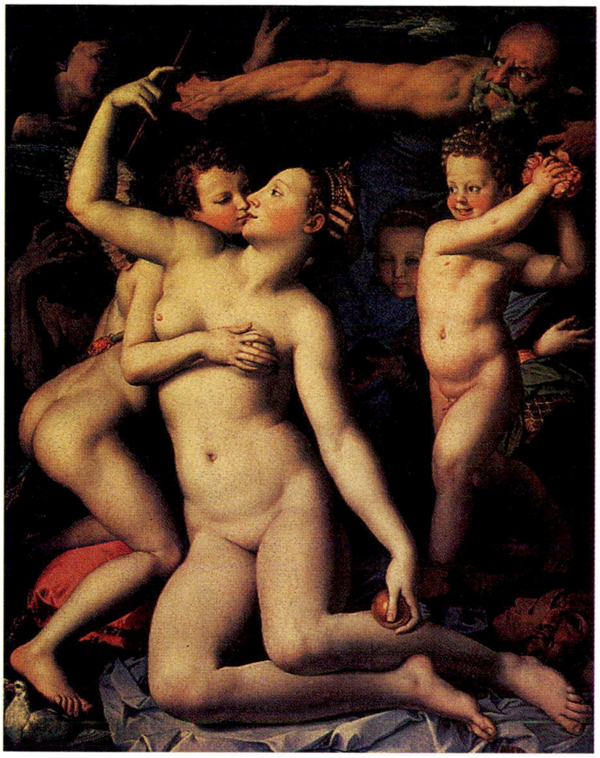

Fig. 623 Bronzino, "*Venus, Cupid, Folly, and Time (The Exposure of Luxury)*", c. 1546.
Oil on wood, approx. 61 × 56 3/4 in.
National Gallery, London.

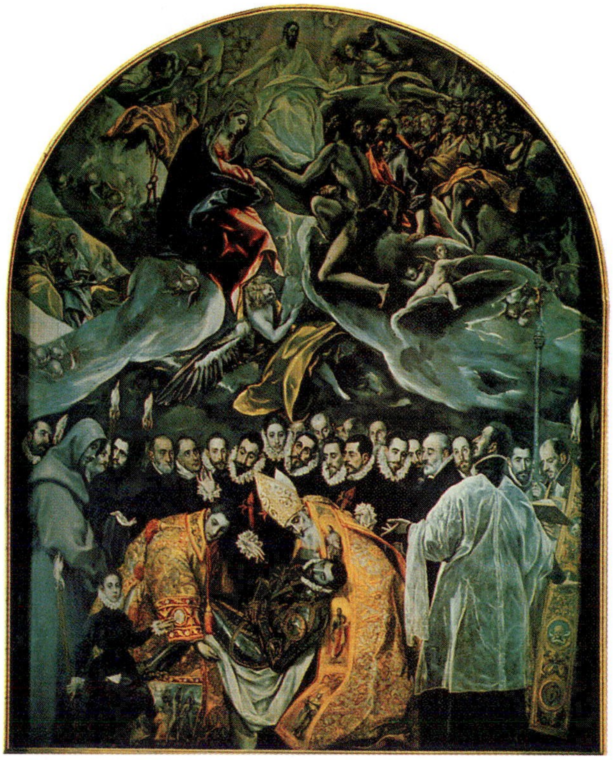

Fig. 624 El Greco, *The Burial of Count Orgaz*, 1586.
Oil on canvas, 16 ft. × 11 ft. 10 in. S. Tomé, Toledo, Spain. Superstock.

itself may be distorted or elongated, as in Bronzino's *Venus, Cupid, Folly, and Time (The Exposure of Luxury)* (Fig. 623). The colors are often bright and clashing. At the upper right of Bronzino's painting, Time, and, at the upper left, Truth, part a curtain to reveal the shallow space in which Venus is fondled by her son Cupid. Folly is about to shower the pair in rose petals. Envy tears her hair out at center left. The Mannerist distortion of space is especially evident in the distance separating Cupid's shoulders and head.

As in El Greco's *The Burial of Count Orgaz* (Fig. 624), Mannerist painting often utilizes more than one focal point, and these often seem contradictory. Born in Crete and trained in Venice and Rome, where he studied the works of Titian, Tintoretto, and the Italian Mannerists, El Greco moved to Toledo, Spain, in 1576, and lived there for the rest of his life. In the painting we see here, the realism of the lower ensemble, which includes local Toledo nobility and clergy of El Greco's day, (even though the painting represents a burial that took place over 200 years earlier, in 1323), gives way in the upper half to a much more abstract and personal brand of representation. El Greco's elongated figures—consider the hand of St. Peter, in the saffron robe behind Mary on the upper left, with his long piercing fingers on a longer, almost drooping hand, to say nothing of the bizarrely extended arm of Christ himself—combine with oddly rolling clouds that rise toward an astonishingly small representation of Christ. So highly eclectic and individual is this painter's style that it is difficult to label it even as Mannerist.

1600

Death of Elizabeth I of England
1603

Jamestown founded in Virginia
1609

1603
Cervantes begins *Don Quixote*

1608
Quebec founded by the French

1611
King James translation of the Bible completed

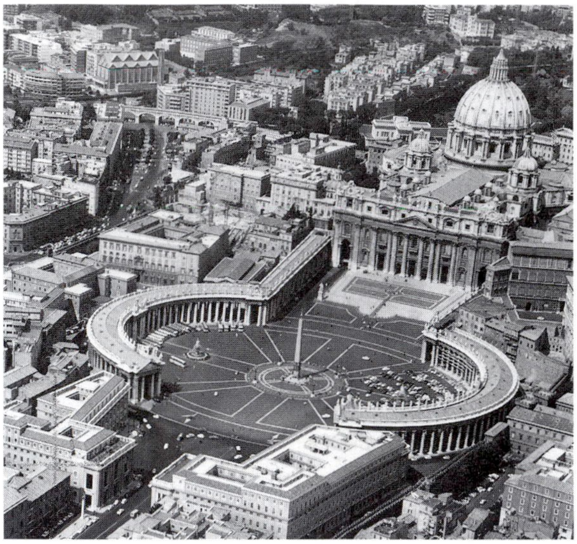

Fig. 625 Aerial view of St. Peter's, Rome. Nave and facade by Carlo Moderno, 1607–1615, colonnade by Gianlorenzo Bernini, 1657.
Photo by Ratkin, P.F.I.

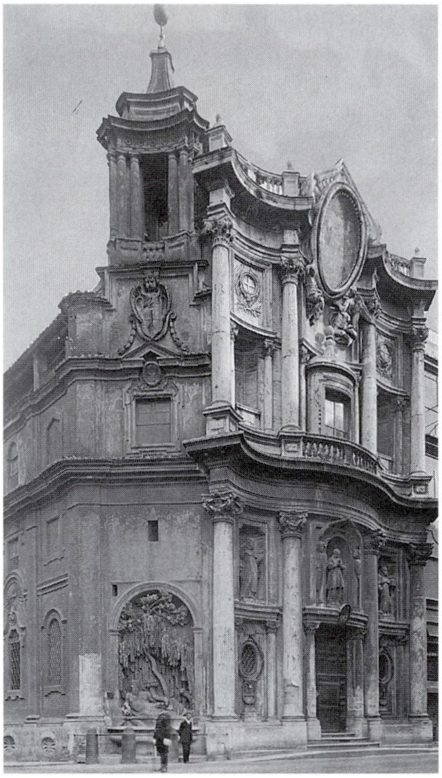

Fig. 626 Francesco Borromini, facade, San Carlo alle Quattro Fontane, Rome, 1665–1667.
Marburg/Art Resource.

THE BAROQUE

The **Baroque** style, which is noted particularly for its theatricality and drama, was, in many respects, a creation of the Papacy in Rome. Around 1600, faced in the North with the challenge of Protestantism, which had grown steadily more powerful ever since Martin Luther's first protests in 1517, the Vatican took action. It called together as many talents as it could muster with the clear intention of turning Rome into the most magnificent city in the world, "for the greater glory of God and the Church." At the heart of this effort was an ambitious building program. In 1603, Carlo Maderno was assigned the task of adding an enormous nave to Michelangelo's central plan for St. Peter's, converting it back into a giant basilica (Fig. 625). Completed in 1615, the scale of the new basilica was even more dramatically emphasized when Gianlorenzo Bernini added a monumental oval piazza surrounded by colonnades to the front of the church. Bernini conceived of his colonnade as an architectural embrace, as if the church were reaching out its arms to gather in its flock. The wings that connect the facade to the semicircular colonnade tend to diminish the horizontality of the facade and emphasize the vertical thrust of Michelangelo's dome.

As vast as Bernini's artistic ambitions were, he was comparatively classical in his tastes. If we compare Bernini's colonnade at St. Peter's to Francesco Borromini's facade for San Carlo alle Quattro Fontane in Rome (Fig. 626), we notice immediately how symmetrical Bernini's design appears. Beside Borromini's facade, Bernini's colonnade seems positively conservative, despite its magnificent scale. But Borromini's extravagant design was immediately popular. The head of the religious order for whom San Carlo alle Quattro Fontane was built wrote with great pride, "Nothing similar can be found anywhere in the world. This is attested by the foreigners who . . . try to procure copies of the plan. We

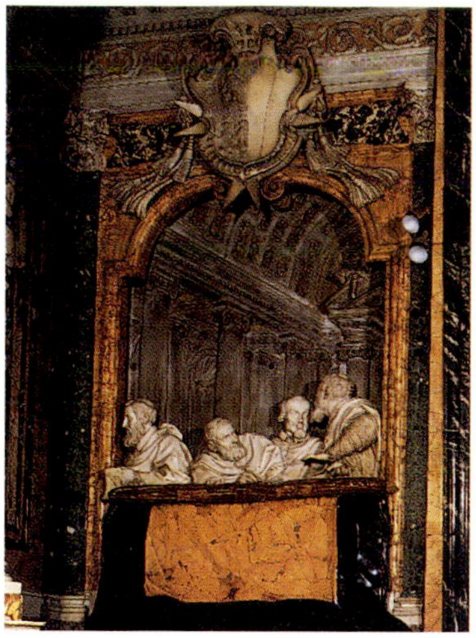

Figs. 627 and 628 Gianlorenzo Bernini, the Cornaro family in a theater box (marble, lifesize); and *The Ecstasy of St. Theresa* (marble, lifesize); both 1645–1652, Cornaro Chapel, Santa Maria della Vittoria, Rome.
Scala/Art Recource.

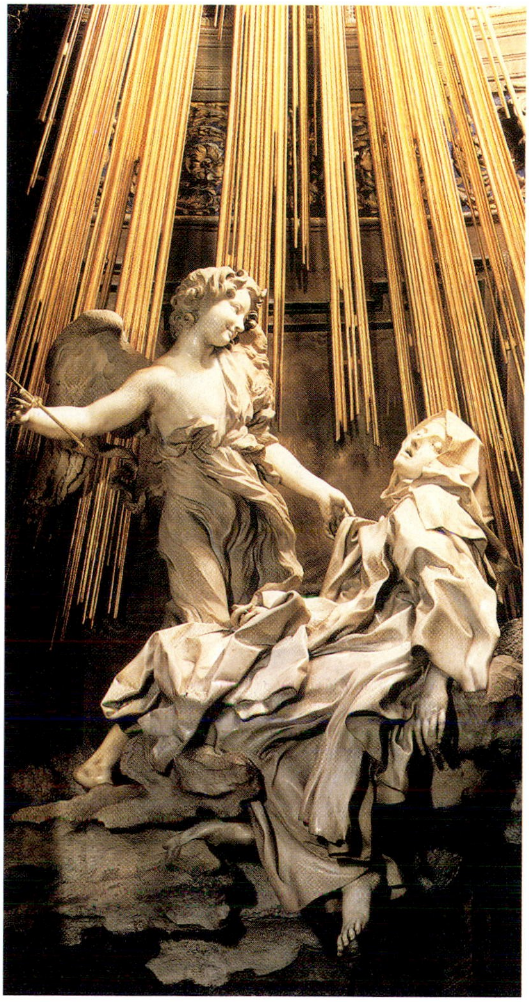

have been asked for them by Germans, Flemings, Frenchmen, Italians, Spaniards, and even Indians." We can detect, in these remarks, the Baroque tendency to define artistic genius more and more in terms of originality, the creation of things never before seen. Bernini's colonnade makes clear that the virtues of the classical were continually upheld, but emerging for the first time, often in the work of the same artist, is a countertendency, a sensibility opposed to tradition and dedicated to invention.

One of the defining characteristics of the Baroque is its insistence on bringing together various media to achieve the most theatrical effects. Bernini's Cornaro Chapel in Santa Maria della Vittoria (Figs. 627 and 628) is perhaps the most highly developed of these dynamic and theatrical spaces. The altarpiece depicts the ecstasy of St. Theresa. St. Theresa, a nun whose conversion took place after the death of her father, experienced visions, heard voices, and felt a persistent and piercing pain in her side. This was caused, she believed, by the flaming arrow of Divine Love, shot into her by an angel: "The pain was so great I screamed aloud," she wrote, "but at the same time I felt such infinite sweetness that I wished the pain to last forever. . . . It was the sweetest caressing of the soul by God." The paradoxical nature of St. Theresa's feelings is typical of the complexity of Baroque sentiment. Bernini fuses the angel's joy and St. Theresa's agony into an image that depicts what might be called St. Theresa's "anguished joy." Even more typical of the Baroque sensibility is Bernini's use of every device available to him to dramatize the scene. The sculpture of St. Theresa is illuminated by a hidden window above, so that the figures seem to glow in a magical white light. Gilded bronze rays of heavenly light descend upon the scene as if from the burst of light painted high on the frescoed ceiling of the vault. To the left and right of the chapel are theater boxes containing marble spectators, like ourselves witnesses to this highly charged, operatic moment.

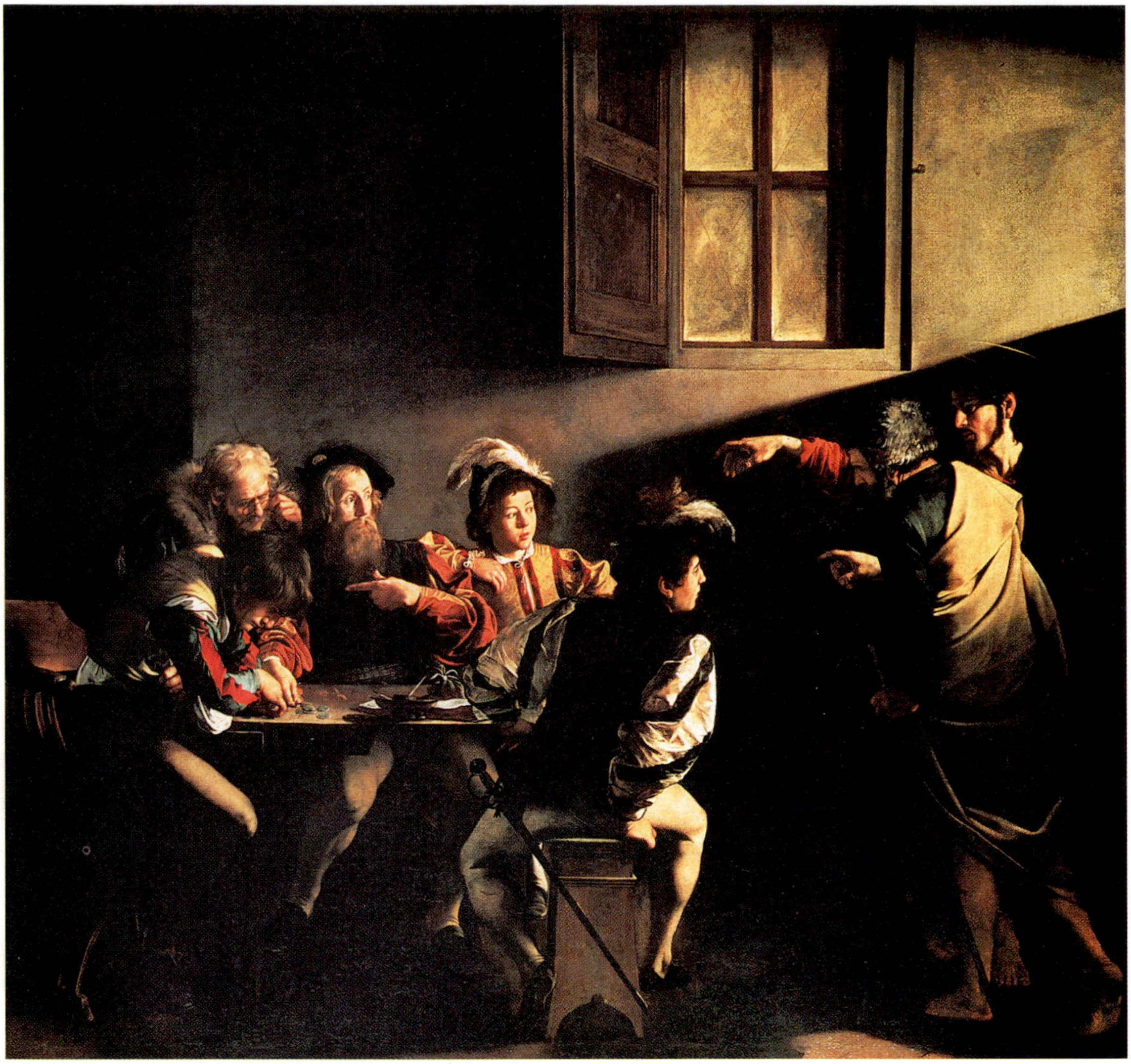

Fig. 629 Caravaggio, *The Calling of St. Matthew*, c. 1599–1602.
Oil on canvas, 11 ft. 1 in. × 11 ft. 5 in. Contarelli Chapel, San Luigi dei Francesci, Rome.
Scala/Art Resource.

The Baroque style quickly spread beyond Rome and throughout Europe. Elaborate Baroque churches were constructed, especially in Germany and Austria. In the early years of the seventeenth century, furthermore, a number of artists from France, Holland, and Flanders were strongly influenced by the work of the Italian painter Caravaggio. Caravaggio openly disdained the great masters of the Renaissance, creating instead a highly individualistic brand of painting that sought its inspiration not in the proven styles of a former era but literally in the streets of contemporary Rome. Upon viewing his work it is often difficult to tell that his subject is a religious one, so ordinary are his people and so dingy and commonplace his settings. Yet despite Caravaggio's desire to secularize his religious subjects, their light imbues them with a spiritual reality. It was, in fact, the contrast in his paintings between light and dark, mirroring the contrast between the spiritual content of the painting and its representation in the trappings of the everyday, that so powerfully influenced painters across Europe.

Caravaggio's naturalism is nowhere so evident as in *The Calling of St. Matthew* (Fig. 629) painted, somewhat surprisingly, for a church. The scene is a tavern. St. Matthew, originally a tax collector, sits counting the day's take with a band of his agents, all of them apparently prosperous, if we are to judge from their attire. From the right, two barefoot and lowly figures, one of whom is Christ, enter the scene, calling St. Matthew to join them. He points at himself in some astonishment. Except for the undeniably spiritual quality of the light, which floods the room as if it were revelation itself, the only thing telling us that this is a religious painting is the faint indication of a halo above Christ's head.

Though not directly influenced by Caravaggio, Rembrandt, the greatest master of light and dark of the age, knew Caravaggio's art through Dutch artists who had studied it. Rembrandt extends the sense of dramatic opposition Caravaggio achieved by manipulating light across a full range of tones, changing its intensity and modulating its brilliance, so that one feels in every beam and shadow a different emotional content. In his *Resurrection of Christ* (Fig. 630), Rembrandt uses the emotional contrast between light and dark to underscore emotional difference. He contrasts the chaotic world of the Roman soldiers, sent reeling into a darkness symbolic of their own ignorance by the angel pulling open the lid of Christ's sepulchre, with the quiet calm of Christ himself as He rises in a light symbolic of true knowledge. Light becomes, in Rembrandt's hands, an index to the psychological meaning of his subjects, often hiding as much as it reveals, endowing them with a sense of mystery even as it reveals their souls.

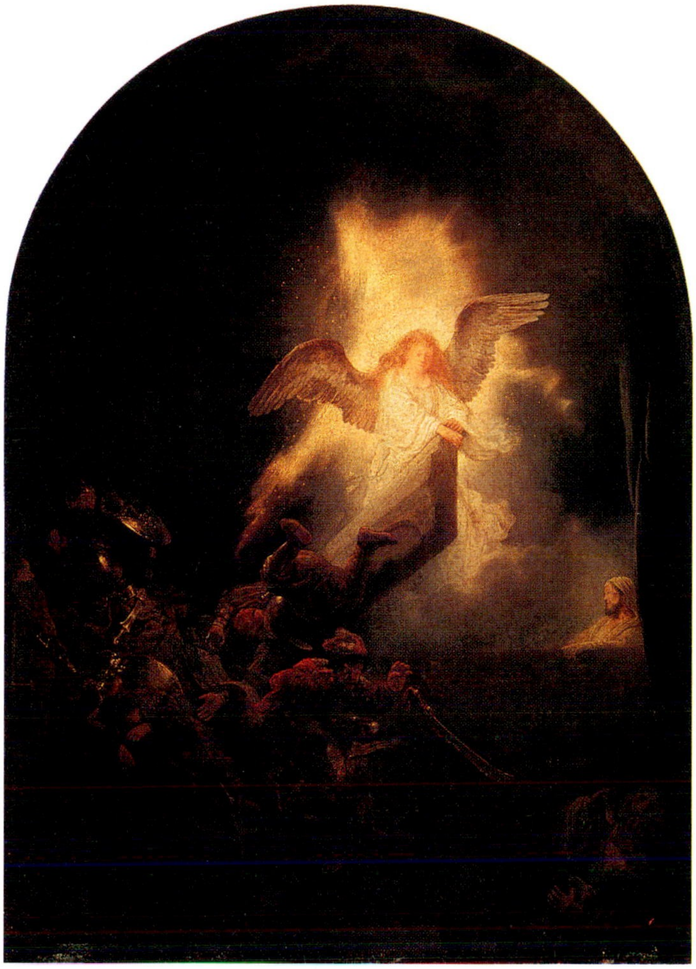

Fig. 630 Rembrandt van Rijn, *Resurrection of Christ*, c. 1635–1639. Oil on canvas, 36 1/4 × 26 3/8 in. Alte Pinakothek, Munich. Artothek.

1652
First Cape Colony settlement by Dutch East India Company

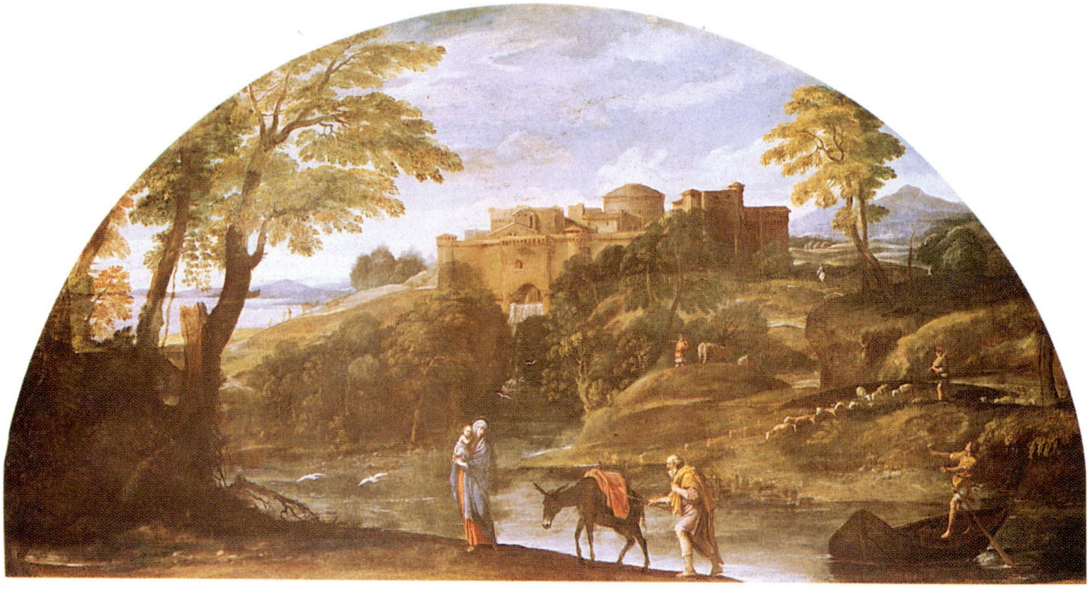

Fig. 631 Annibale Carracci, *Landscape with Flight into Egypt,* c. 1603.
Oil on canvas, 48 1/4 × 98 1/2 in. Galleria Doria Pamphili, Rome. Scala/Art Resource.

In Northern Europe, where strict Protestant theology had purged the churches of religious art (see Fig. 34), and, furthermore, classical subjects were frowned upon as pagan, realism thrived. Works with secular, or nonreligious, subject matter became extremely popular: still life painting was popular (see Jan de Heem's *Still Life with Lobster,* Fig. 314), as were representations of everyday people living out their daily lives (genre painting), and landscapes. In Spain, where the royal family had deep historical ties to the North, the visual realism of Velázquez came to dominate painting (see Fig. 206). Spurred on by the great wealth it had acquired in its conquest of the New World, Spain helped to create a thriving market structure in Europe. Dutch artists quickly introduced their own goods—that is, paintings—into this economy, with the Spanish court as one of its most prestigious buyers. No longer working for the Church, but for this new international market, artists painted the everyday things that they thought would appeal to the bourgeois tastes of the new consumer.

Of all of the new secular subject matter that arose during the Baroque Age, the genre of landscape perhaps most decisively marks a shift in Western thinking. In Annibile Carraci's *Landscape with Flight into Egypt* (Fig. 631) the figure and the story have become incidental to the landscape. Joseph has dreamed that Herod is searching for the infant Jesus to kill him, and he flees into Egypt with Mary and the child, to remain there until after Herod's death. But this landscape is hardly Egypt. Rather, Caracci has transferred the story to a highly civilized Italian setting. This is the pastoral world, a middle ground between civilization and wilderness where people can live free of both the corruption and decadence of city and court life and the uncontrollable forces of nature. One of the most idyllic of all landscape painters goes even further. Claude Lorrain—Claude, as he is usually known—casts the world in an eternally

London Plague kills 100,000 people
1665

1667
Publication of Milton's *Paradise Lost*

Construction of Versailles Palace begins outside Paris
1668

1669
Ottoman Turks seize the island of Crete

Native American population reduced to around 70,000
1675

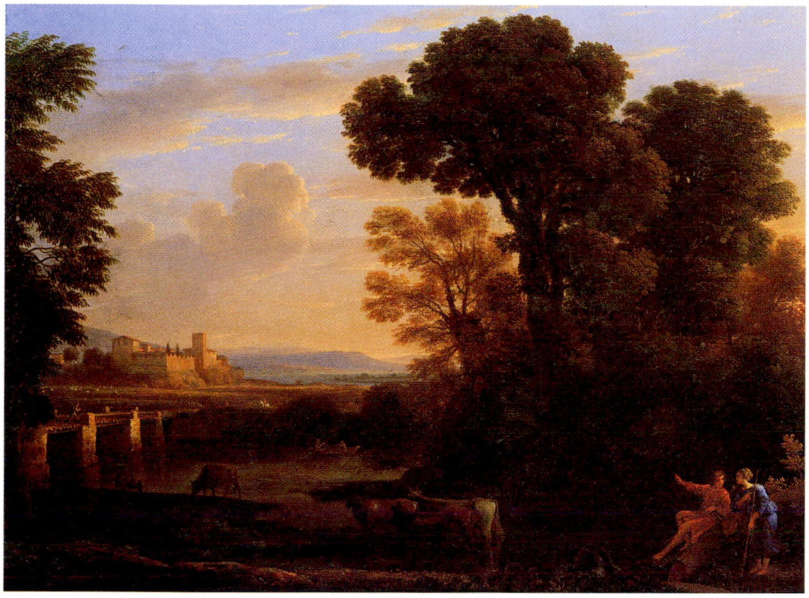

Fig. 632 Claude Lorrain, *A Pastoral Landscape*, c. 1650.
Oil on copper, 15 ½ × 21 in.
Yale University Art Gallery, New Haven, Connecticut. Leo C. Hanna, Jr., Fund.

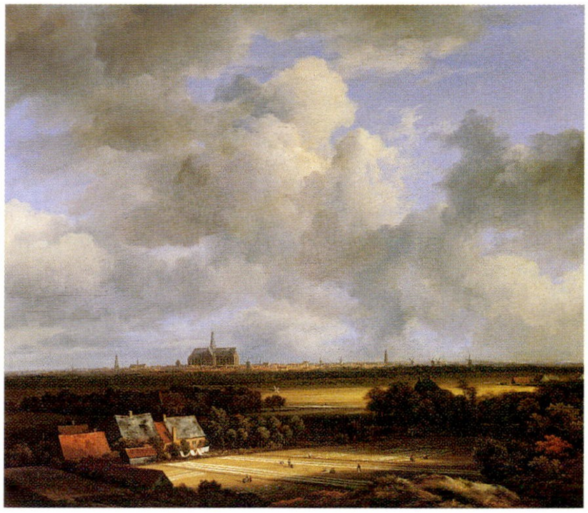

Fig. 633 Jacob van Ruisdael, *View of Haarlem from the Dunes at Overveen*, c. 1670.
Oil on canvas, 22 × 24 ⅜ in.
Mauritshuis, The Hague, The Netherlands.

poetic light. In his *A Pastoral Landscape* (Fig. 632), he employs atmospheric perspective to soften all sense of tension and opposition and to bring us to a world of harmony and peace. In this painting, and many others like it, the best civilization has to offer has been melded with the best of a wholly benign and gentle nature.

Landscape painters felt that since God made the earth, one could sense the majesty of His soul in His handiwork, much as one could sense emotion in a painter's gesture upon canvas. The grandeur of God's vision was symbolically suggested in the panoramic sweep of the extended view. Giving up two-thirds of the picture to the infinite dimensions of the heavens, Jacob Ruisdael's *View of Haarlem from the Dunes at Overveen* (Fig. 633) is not so much about the land as it is about the sky—and the light that emanates from it, alternately casting the earth in light and shadow, knowledge and ignorance. Rising to meet the light, importantly, is the largest building in the landscape, the church. The beam of light that in Caravaggio's painting suggests the spiritual presence of Christ becomes, in landscape, a beam of light from the "Sun/Son," a pun popular among English poets of the period, including John Donne. By the last half of the seventeenth century, it is as if the real space of the Dutch landscape had become so idealized that it is almost Edenic.

The example of landscape offers us an important lesson in the direction art will take from the late seventeenth century down to our own day. The spiritual is no longer found exclusively in the church. It can be found in nature, in light, in form, even, as we progress toward the modern era, in the artist's very self. And by the end of the seventeenth century, the church is no longer the major patron of art as it had been for centuries. From Spanish kings, to wealthy Dutch merchants, to an increasingly large group of middle class bourgeoisie with disposable incomes and the desire to refine their tastes, the patrons of art will change until, by the middle of the twentieth century, art comes to be bought and sold in an international "art market."

CHAPTER 19

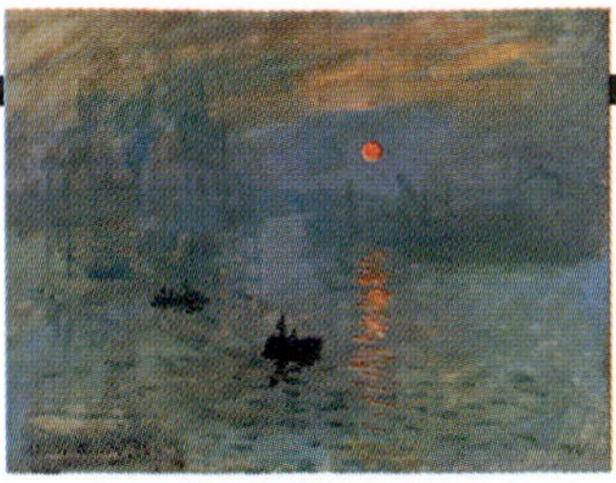

The Eighteenth and Nineteenth Centuries

The Rococo

Neoclassicism

Romanticism

WORK IN PROGRESS
Théodore Géricault's *Raft of the Medusa*

Realism

Impressionism

Post-Impressionism

The conflict of sensibility that became evident when, in the last chapter, we compared the architecture of Bernini to that of his contemporary Borromini—the one enormous in scale but classical in principle, the other extravagant in form and so inventive that it seems intentionally anticlassical—dominates the history of European art in the eighteenth century. In France, especially, anticlassical developments in Italian art were rejected. As early as 1665, Jean-Baptiste Colbert had invited Bernini to Paris to complete construction of the Louvre, the palace of King Louis XIV. But Louis considered

La Salle takes possession of Mississippi River for France
1682

Glorious Revolution establishes constitutional monarchy in Britain
1688–89

1700

1687
Newton publishes his law of motion

1690
John Locke publishes Second *Treatise of Government*

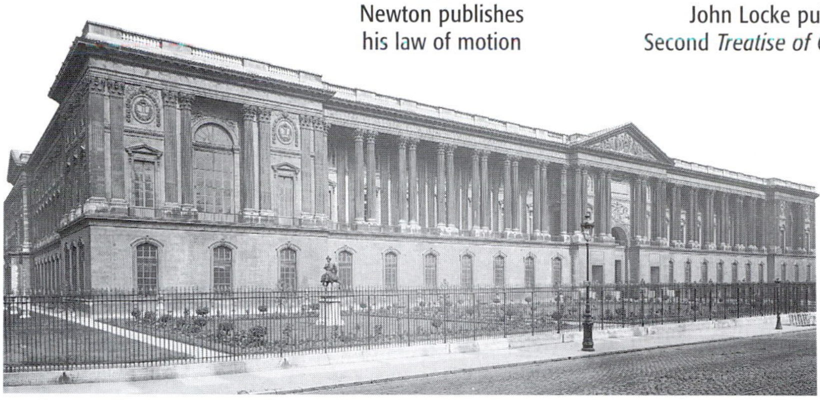

Fig. 634 Claude Perrault, with Louis Le Vau and Charles Lebrun, east front of the Louvre, Paris, 1667–1670.
Giraudon/Art Resource.

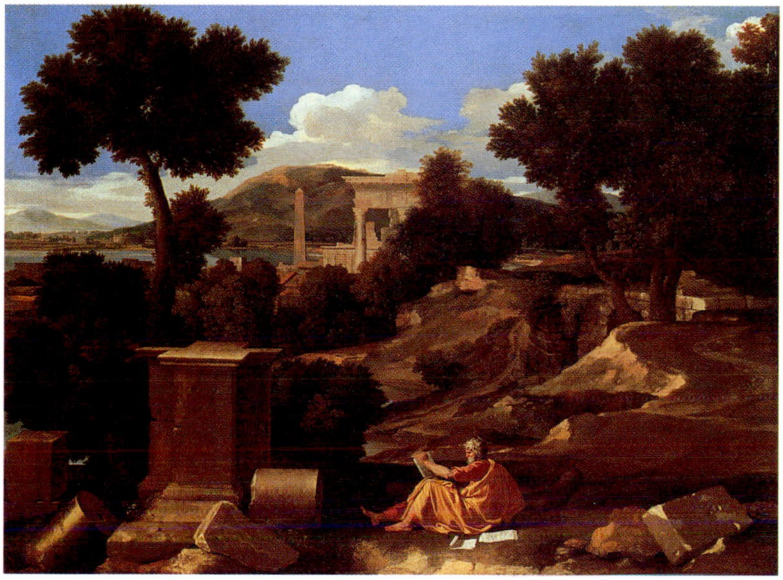

Fig. 635 Nicolas Poussin, *Landscape with St. John on Patmos,* 1640.
Oil on canvas, 40 × 53 ½ in.
A. A. Munger Collection, © 1993

Bernini's plans too elaborate—he envisioned demolishing all the extant palace—and the Louvre finally was built in a highly classical style, based on the plan of a Roman temple (Fig. 634).

The classicism of Bernini's colonnade for St. Peter's in Rome has been fully developed here. All vestiges of Baroque sensuality have been banished in favor of a strict and linear classical line. At the center of the facade is a Roman temple from which wings of paired columns extend outward, each culminating in a form reminiscent of the Roman triumphal arch.

One of the architects of this new Louvre was Charles Lebrun, a court painter who had studied in Rome with the classical painter Nicolas Poussin. Poussin believed that the aim of painting was to represent the noblest actions of men with absolute clarity as far as possible. To this end, distracting elements—particularly color, but anything that appeals primarily to the senses—had to be suppressed. In Poussin's *Landscape with St. John on Patmos* (Fig. 635), the small figure of St. John is depicted writing the *Revelations.* Not only do the architecture and the architectural ruins lend a sense of classical geometry to the scene, but even nature has been submitted to Poussin's classicizing order. Notice, for instance, how the tree on the left bends just enough as it crosses the horizon to form a right angle with the slope of the distant mountain.

As head of the Royal Academy of Painting and Sculpture, Lebrun installed Poussin's views as an official, royal style. By Lebrun's standards, the greatest artists were the ancient Greeks and Romans, followed closely by

Louis XV assumes the French throne
1715

Christianity banned in China
1742

1700

18th century
Literacy becomes widespread

1726
Gulliver's Travels published

mid-18th century
Beginning of Industrial Revolution

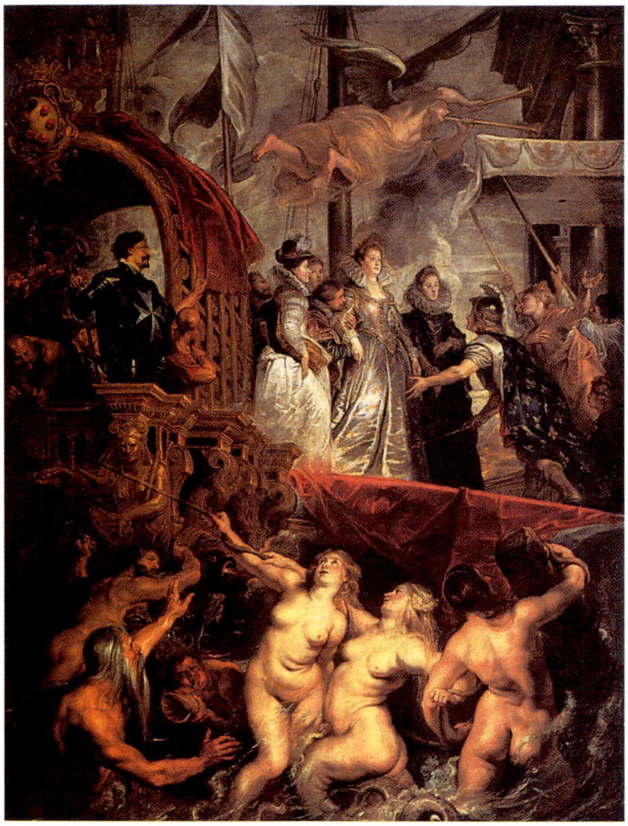

Fig. 636 Peter Paul Rubens and his workshop, *The Arrival and Reception of Marie de' Medici at Marseilles,* 1621–1625.
Oil on canvas, 13 × 10 ft. Musée du Louvre, Paris. Giraudon/Art Resource.

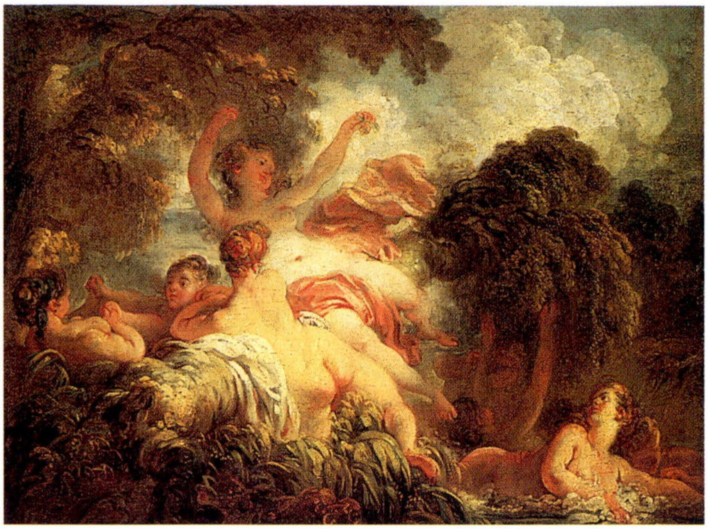

Fig. 637 Jean-Honoré Fragonard, *Bathers,* c. 1765.
Oil on canvas, 25 1/4 × 31 1/2 in. Musée du Louvre, Paris. Scala/Art Resource.

Raphael and Poussin; the worst painters were the Flemish and Dutch, who not only "overemphasized" color and appealed to the senses, but also favored "lesser" genres, such as landscape and still life.

By the beginning of the eighteenth century, Lebrun's hold on the French Academy was questioned by a large number of painters who championed the work of the great Flemish Baroque painter Peter Paul Rubens over that of Poussin. Rubens, who had painted a cycle of 21 paintings celebrating the life of Marie de' Medici, Louis XIV's grandmother, was a painter of extravagant Baroque tastes. Where the design of Poussin's *Landscape with St. John on Patmos* (Fig. 635) is based on horizontal and vertical elements arranged parallel to the picture plane, Rubens's forms in *The Arrival and Reception of Marie de' Medici at Marseilles* (Fig. 636) are dispersed across a pair of receding diagonals. In this painting, which depicts Marie's arrival in France as the new wife of the French king, Henry IV, our point of view is not frontal and secure, as it is in the Poussin, but curiously low, perhaps even in the water. Poussin in his design focuses on his subject, St. John, who occupies the center of the painting, while Rubens creates a multiplicity of competing areas of interest. Most of all, Poussin's style is defined by its linear clarity. Rubens's work is painterly, dominated by a play of color, dramatic contrasts of light and dark, and sensuous, rising forms. Poussin is restrained, Rubens exuberant.

THE ROCOCO

With the death of Louis XIV in 1715, French life itself became exuberant. This was an age whose taste was formed by society women with real, if covert, political power, especially Louis XV's mistress, Madame de Pompadour. The *salons,* gatherings held by particular hostesses on particular days of the week, were the

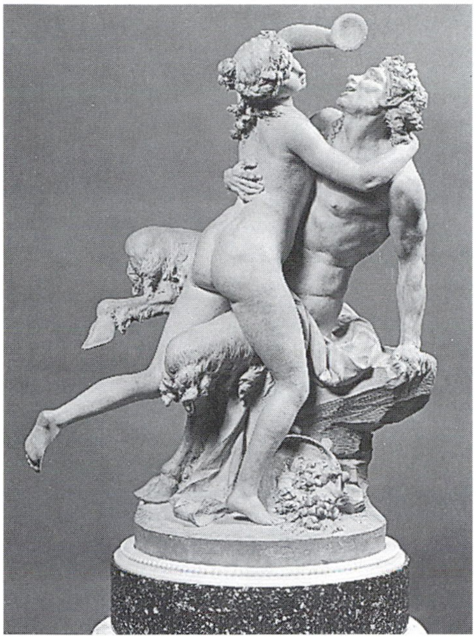

Fig. 638 Claude-Michel Clodion, *Bacchante and Faun*, c. 1775.
Terracotta, H. 23 1/4 in. The Metropolitan Museum of Art, New York. Bequest of Benjamin Altman, 1913. 14.40687.

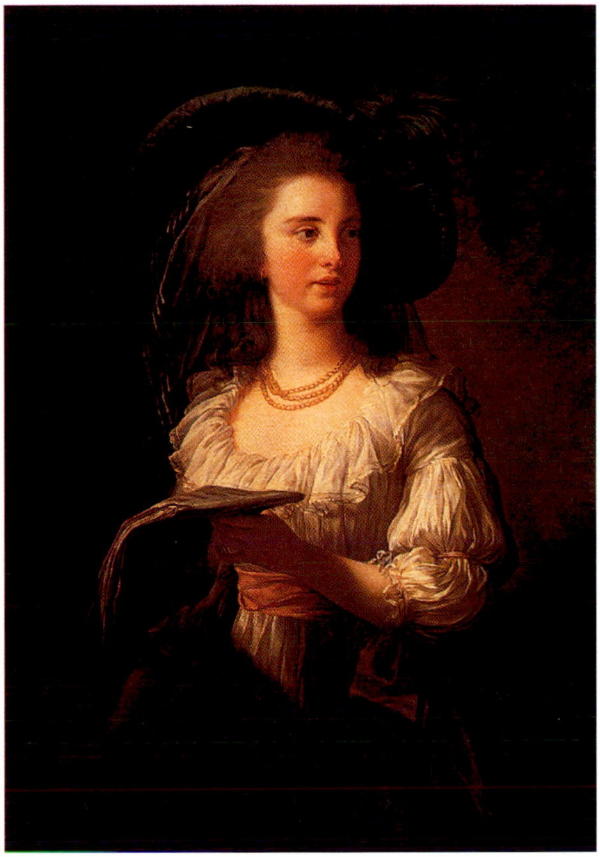

Fig. 639 Marie-Louise-Elisabeth Vigée-Lebrun, *The Duchess of Polignac*, 1783.
Oil on canvas, 38 3/4 × 28 in.
© The National Trust Waddesdon Manor, England/Art Resource.

social events of the day. A famous musician might appear at one salon, while at Mme. Geoffrin's on Mondays, artists and art lovers would always gather. A highly developed sense of wit, irony, and gossip was necessary to succeed in this society. So skilled was the repartee in the salons that the most biting insult could be made to sound like the highest compliment. Sexual intrigue was not merely commonplace but expected. The age was obsessed with sensuality, and one can easily trace the origins of Fragonard's *Bathers* (Fig. 637) back to the mermaids at the bottom of Rubens's painting (Fig. 636). Fragonard was Madame de Pompadour's favorite painter, and the *Bathers* was designed to appeal to the tastes of the eighteenth-century French court.

It is the age of the **Rococo,** a word derived from the French *rocaille,* referring to the small stones and shells that decorate the interiors of grottoes, the artificial caves popular in landscape design at the time. Architecturally, Rococo was an extension of Borromini's curvilinear Baroque style. In sculpture, the Rococo was the Baroque eroticized. Clodion's *Bacchante and Faun* (Fig. 638), a small sculpture designed for a table top, is cloaked in the respectability of its Greek theme, but its purpose was to lend an erotic tone to its environment. In painting, the Rococo was deeply indebted to the Baroque sensibility of Rubens, as Fragonard's *Bathers* demonstrates. Vigée-Lebrun's portrait of *The Dutchess of Polignac* (Fig. 639) combines in exquisite fashion all of the tools of the Baroque sensibility, from Rembrandt's dramatic lighting to Rubens's sensual curves and, given the musical score in the Duchess's hand, even Bernini's sense of theatrical moment.

1789	U. S. Bill of Rights **1791**	Eli Whitney invents the cotton gin **1793**		
	1789 Beginning of French Revolution	**1793** Louis XVI of France is beheaded	**1798** Wordsworth and Coleridge publish the *Lyrical Ballads*	

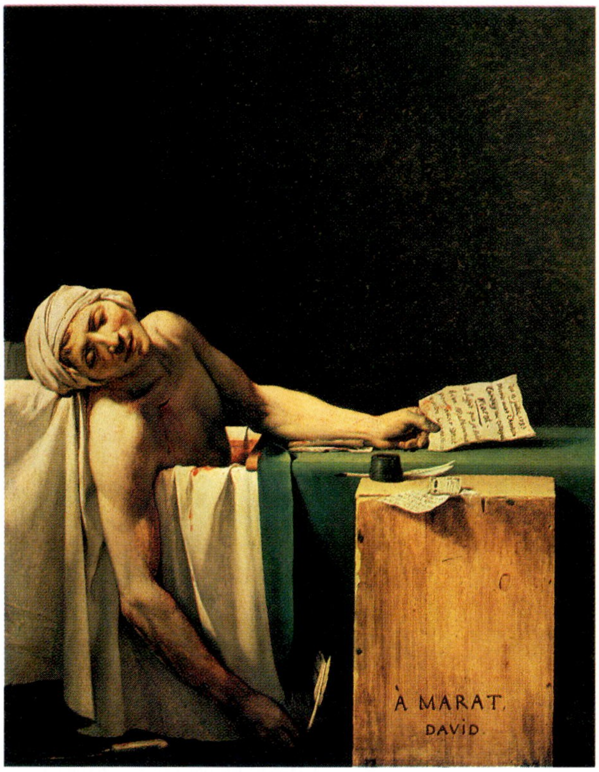

Fig. 640 Jacques Louis David, *The Death of Marat,* 1793.
Oil on canvas, 65 × 50 ½ in.
Musées Royaux des Beaux-Arts de Belgique, Brussels. Giraudon/Art Resource.

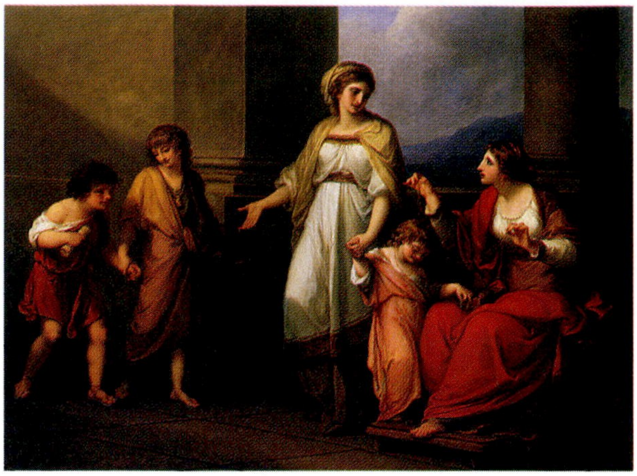

Fig. 641 Angelica Kauffmann, *Cornelia, Pointing to Her Children as Her Treasures,* ca. 1785.
Oil on canvas, 40" × 50" (101.6 × 127.0 cm.).
Virginia Museum of Fine Arts, Richmond, VA.
The Adolph D. and Wilkins C. Williams Fund. © Virginia Museum of Fine Arts.

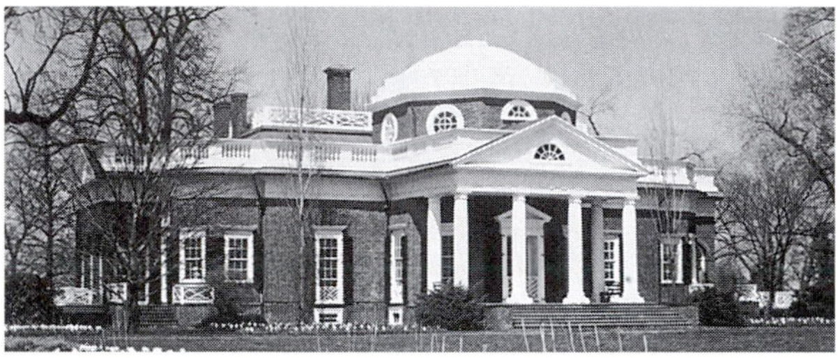

Fig. 642 Thomas Jefferson, Monticello, Charlottesville, Virginia, 1770–1784; 1796–1806.

NEOCLASSICISM

Despite the Rococo sensibility of the age, the seventeenth-century French taste for the classical style that Lebrun had championed did not disappear. When Herculaneum and Pompeii were rediscovered, in 1738 and 1748 respectively, interest in Greek and Roman antiquity revived as well. The discovery fueled an increasing tendency among the French to view the Rococo style as symptomatic of a widespread cultural decadence, epitomized by the luxurious lifestyle of the aristocracy. The discovery also caused people to identify instead with the public-minded values of Greek and Roman heroes, who placed moral virtue, patriotic self-sacrifice, and "right action" above all else. A *new* classicism—a *neo*classicism—supplanted the Rococo almost overnight.

The most accomplished of the Neoclassical painters was Jacques Louis David, whose work has been discussed at length in this text (see Figs. 94, 95, and 210). David took an active part in the French Revolution in 1789, recognizing as an expression of true civic duty and virtue the desire to overthrow the irresponsible monarchy that had, for two centuries at least, squandered France's wealth. His *Death of Marat* (Fig. 640) celebrates a fallen hero of the Revolution. Slain in his bath by a Monarchist—a sympathizer with the overthrown king—Marat is posed by David as Christ is traditionally posed in the Deposition (compare, for instance, Rogier 's *Deposition,* Fig. 606), his arm draping over the edge of the tub. A

Napoleon becomes First Consul and absolute ruler of France
1799

1803
Louisiana Purchase

Napoleon crowns himself Emperor of France
1804

1807
Serfdom abolished in Prussia

Wars of independence in Latin America begin
1808

1810

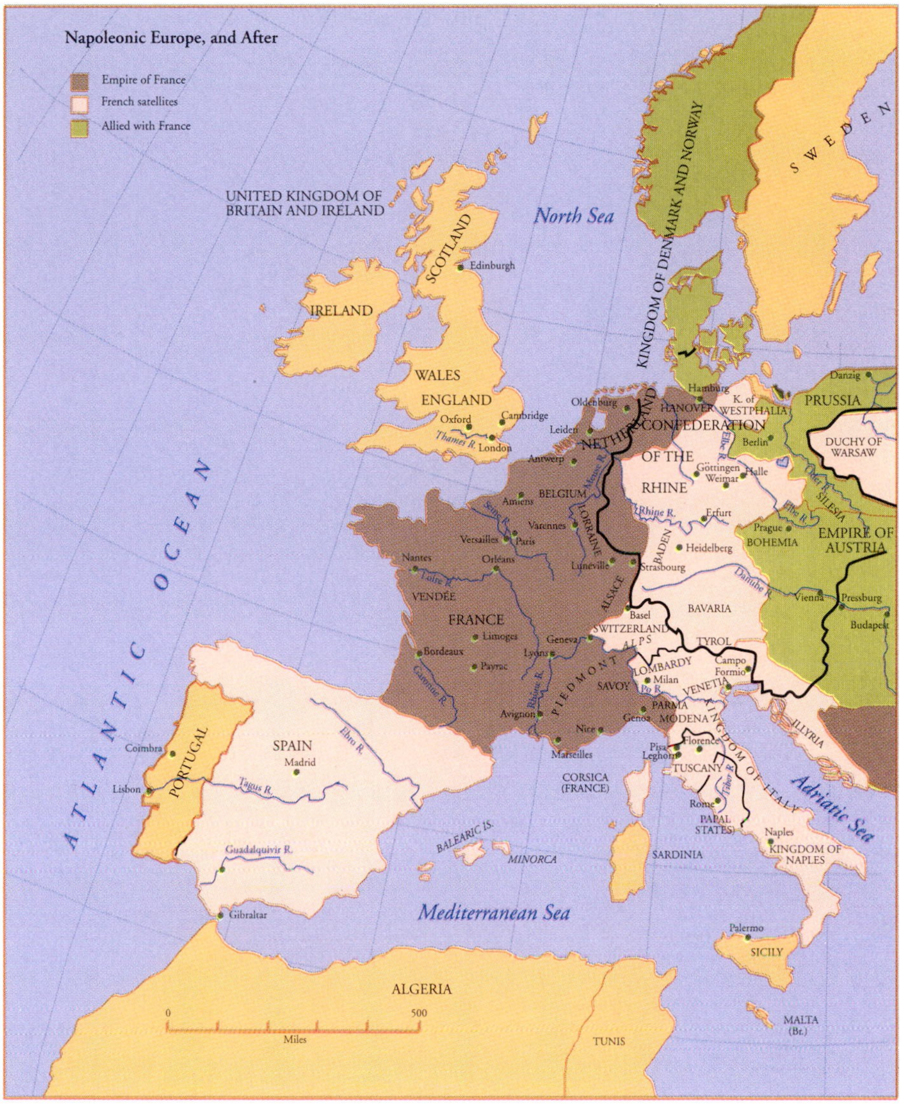

dramatic Caravaggesque light falls over the revolutionary hero, his virtue embodied in the Neoclassical simplicity of David's design.

Virtue is, in fact, the subject of much Neoclassical art—a subject matter distinctly at odds with the early Rococo sensibility. Women are no longer seen cavorting like mermaids, or even luxuriously dressed like the Duchess of Polignac. In Angelica Kauffmann's *Cornelia, Pointing to Her Children as Her Treasures* (Fig. 641), Cornelia demonstrates her Neoclassical virtue by declaring her absolute devotion to her family, and, by extension, to the state. Her virtue is reinforced by her clothing, particularly the simple lines of her bodice.

The same sensibility informs the Neoclassical architecture of Thomas Jefferson. For Jefferson, the Greek orders embodied democratic ideals, possessing not only a sense of order and harmony but a moral perfection deriving from measure and proportion, and thus he utilized them on the facade of his own home at Monticello (Fig. 642). The colonnade thus came to be associated with the ideal state, and, in the United States, Jefferson's Neoclassical architecture became an almost official Federal style.

Neoclassicism found official favor in France with the rise of Napoleon Bonaparte. In 1799, Napoleon brought the uncertain years that followed the French Revolution to an end when he was declared First Consul of the French Republic. As this title suggests, Napoleon's government was modeled on Roman precedents. He established a centralized government and instituted a uniform legal system. He invaded Italy and brought home with him many examples of classical sculpture, including the *Laocoön* (Fig. 568) and the *Apollo Belvedere* (Fig. 25). In Paris itself, he built triumphal Roman arches, including the famous Arc de Triomphe, a column modeled on Trajan's in Rome, and a church, La Madeleine, modeled after the temples of the first Roman emperors. In 1804, Napoleon was himself crowned Emperor of the largest empire since Charlemagne's in the ninth century.

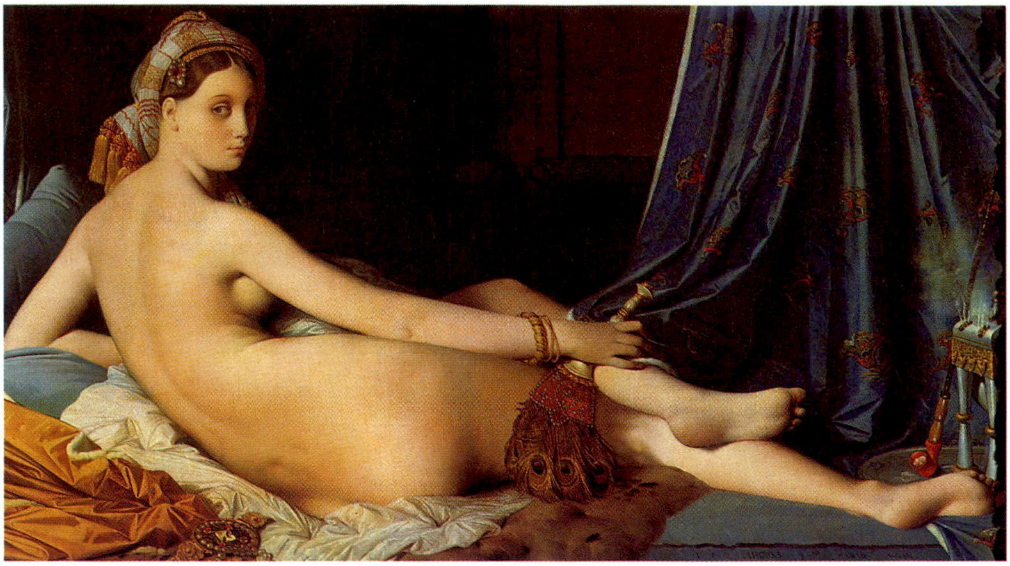

Fig. 643 Jean-Auguste-Dominique Ingres, *Grande Odalisque,* 1814.
Oil on canvas, 35 1/4 × 63 3/4 in.
Musée du Louvre, Paris. Giraudon/Art Resource.

Neoclassical art was used to legitimate this empire. David saw Napoleon as the salvation of France (so chaotic had Revolutionary France been that David himself had been imprisoned, a sure sign, he thought, of the confusion of the day), and he received important commissions from the new emperor. But it was David's finest pupil, Jean-Auguste-Dominque Ingres who became the champion of Neoclassical ideals in the nineteenth century. In 1806, he painted *Napoleon on his Imperial Throne* (see Fig. 37), and in the same year was awarded the Prix de Rome. Ingres departed for Italy, where he remained for 18 years, studying Raphael in particular and periodically sending new work back to France, including the astonishing *Jupiter and Thetis* (see Fig. 100).

Ingres's Neoclassicism was "looser" than his master's. While Jupiter, for instance, is dogmatically classical in spirit, the sensuous Thetis is almost Rococo in treatment. Looking at a painting such as the *Grande Odalisque* (Fig. 643), with its long, gently curving limbs, we are more clearly in the world of Mannerist painting than that of the Greek nude. Ingres's color is as rich as Bronzino's in *The Exposure of Luxury* (see Fig. 623), and, in fact, his theme is much the same. An "odalisque" is a Turkish harem girl, and Ingres's subject seems more decadent than not, deeply involved in a world of satins, peacock feathers, and, at the right, hashish. Certainly, it is not easy to detect much of the high moral tone of earlier Neoclassical art.

But beside Eugène Delacroix's own *Odalisque* (Fig. 644), Ingres's classicism becomes more readily apparent. To Ingres, Delacroix, who was a generation younger than himself, represented a dangerous and barbaric Neo-Baroque sensibility in contrast to his own Neoclassicism.

Ingres and Delacroix became rivals. Each had his critical champions, each his students and followers. For Ingres, drawing was everything. Therefore, his painting was, above all, linear in style. Delacroix, however, was fascinated by the texture of paint itself, and in his painterly attack upon the canvas we begin to sense the artist's own passionate temperament. Viewed beside the Delacroix, the pose of the odalisque in Ingres's painting is positively conservative. In fact, Ingres

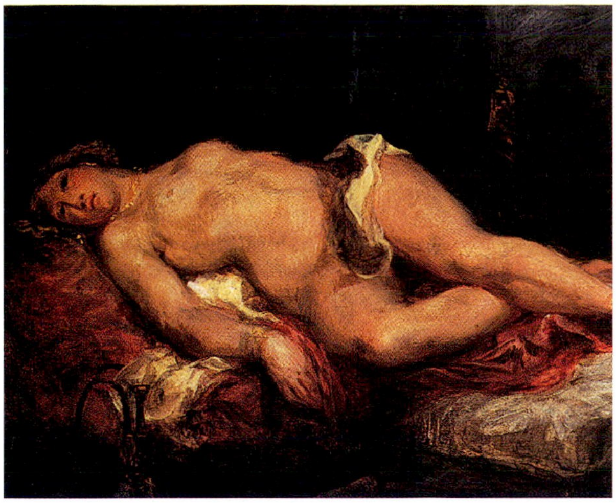

Fig. 644 Eugène Delacroix, *Odalisque,* 1845–1850.
Oil on canvas, 14 7/8 × 18 1/4 in.
Fitzwilliam Museum, University of Cambridge, England.

felt he was upholding traditional values in the face of the onslaught represented by the uncontrolled individualism of his rival.

ROMANTICISM

We have come to call the kind of art exemplified by Delacroix **Romanticism.** At the heart of this style is the belief that reality is a function of each individual's singular point of view, and that the artist's task is to reveal that point of view. Individualism reigned supreme in Romantic art, and, as a result, it sometimes seems to have as many styles as it has artists. What unifies the movement is more a philosophical affirmation of the power of the individual mind than a set of formal principles.

One of the most individual of the Romantics was the Spanish painter Francisco de Goya y Lucientes. After a serious illness in 1792, Goya turned away from a late Rococo style and began to produce a series of paintings depicting inmates of a lunatic asylum and a hospital for wounded soldiers. When Napoleon invaded Spain in 1808, Goya recorded the atrocities in both painting and a series of etchings, *The Disasters of War,* which remained unpublished until long after his death. His last, so-called "Black Paintings," were brutal interpretations of mythological scenes that revealed a universe operating outside the bounds of reason, a world of imagination unchecked by a moral force of any kind. In one of these, *Saturn Devouring One of His Sons* (Fig. 645), which was painted originally on the wall of the dining room in Goya's home, Saturn is allegorically a figure for Time, which consumes us all. But it is the incestuous cannibalism of the scene, the terrible monstrosity of the vision itself, that tells us of Goya's own despair. The inevitable conclusion is that, for Goya, the world was a place full of terror, violence, and horror. What we recognize in his work is his own despair.

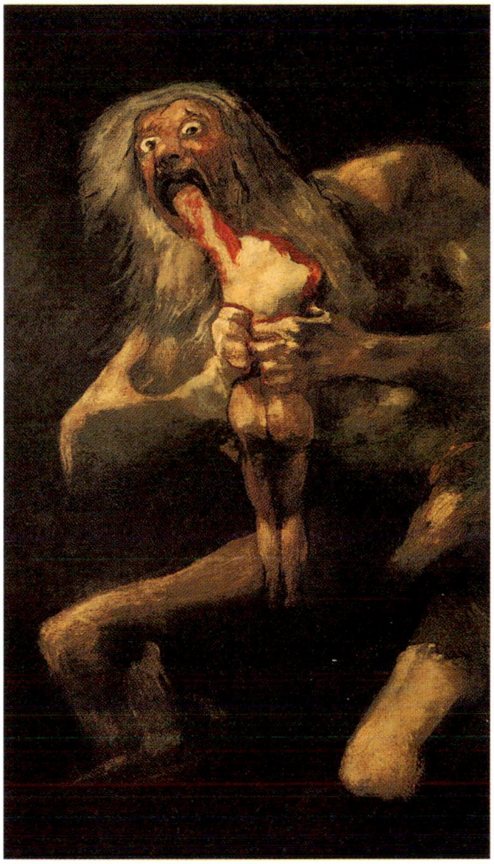

Fig. 645 Francisco Goya, *Saturn Devouring One of His Sons,* 1820–1822.
Fresco, transferred to canvas, 57 7/8 × 32 5/8 in.
Museo del Prado, Madrid. Scala/Art Resource.

WORKS IN PROGRESS

Théodore Géricault's Raft of the Medusa

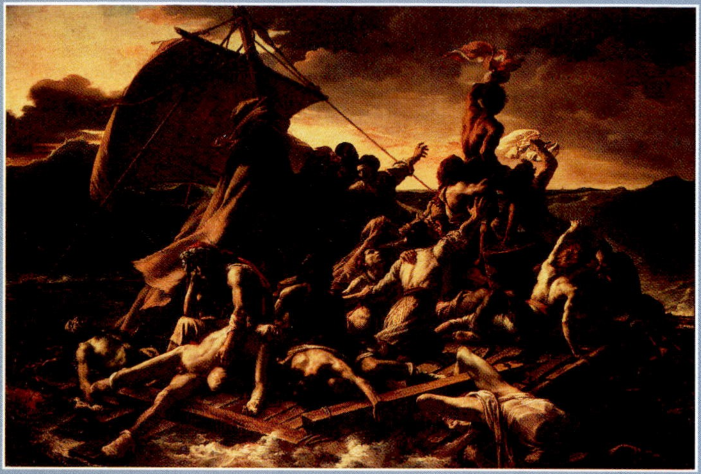

Fig. 646 Théodore Géricault, *The Raft of the Medusa*, 1819.
Oil on canvas, 16 ft. 1 ¼ in. × 23 ft. 6 in.
Musée du Louvre, Paris.
Giraudon/Art Resource, New York.

On July 2, 1816, the French frigate *Medusa* was wrecked on a reef off the African coast. The overloaded ship had been carrying soldiers and settlers to Senegal. The captain and other senior officers escaped in lifeboats, leaving 150 behind to fend for themselves on a makeshift wooden raft. After 12 harrowing days on the raft, only 15 survived. The naval officer who rescued them reported: "These unhappy people had been obliged to fight a great number of their comrades who staged a revolt in the hope of taking over the remaining provisions. The others had been swept out to sea, had died of hunger, or gone mad. The ones I saved had been feeding on human flesh for several days, and when I found them, the ropes serving as maststays were loaded with pieces of such meat, hung there for drying."

The incident infuriated the young painter Théodore Géricault. The captain's appointment had depended on his connections with the French monarchy, which had been restored after Napoleon's defeat at Waterloo. Here, therefore, was clear evidence of the nobility's decadence. To illustrate his beliefs and feelings, Géricault planned a giant canvas, showing the raft just at the moment that the rescue ship, the *Argus,* was spotted on the horizon (Fig. 646). He went to the Normandy coast to study the movement of water. He visited hospitals and morgues to study the effects of illness and death on the human body. He had a model of the raft constructed in his studio and arranged wax figures upon it. His student, Delacroix, posed face down for the central nude.

And all the while he was sketching. An early sketch (Fig. 647) is horizontal in composition, a crowded scene from early on in the ordeal, a claustrophobic and amorphous mass of humanity, with no real focal point or sense of order. The final painting (above, left) turns the raft on its axis, creating two contradictory pyramidal points of tension. On the left, the mast not only suggests the crucifix but also reveals that the raft is sailing away from its rescuers, while on the right, the pyramid of survivors climb desperately in their attempt to be seen. Géricault's horrifying picture, exhibited only a few months after it was conceived, would fuel the Romantic movement with the passion of its feelings.

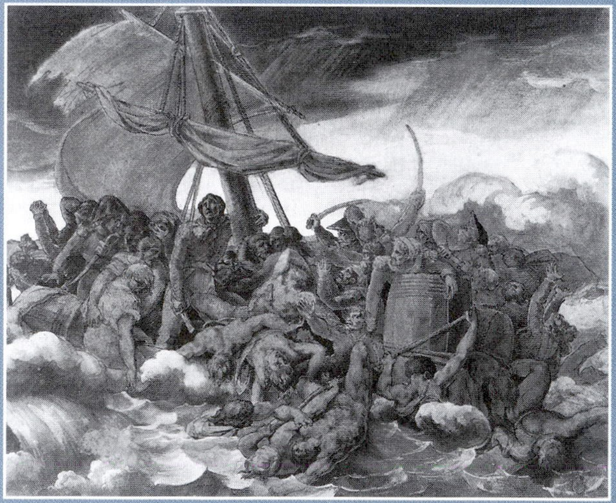

Fig. 647 Théodore Géricault, *Sketch for The Raft of the Medusa*, 1818.
Gouache on paper, 15 ¾ × 20 in.
Fogg Art Museum (bequest of Grenville L. Winthrop),
Harvard University, Cambridge.

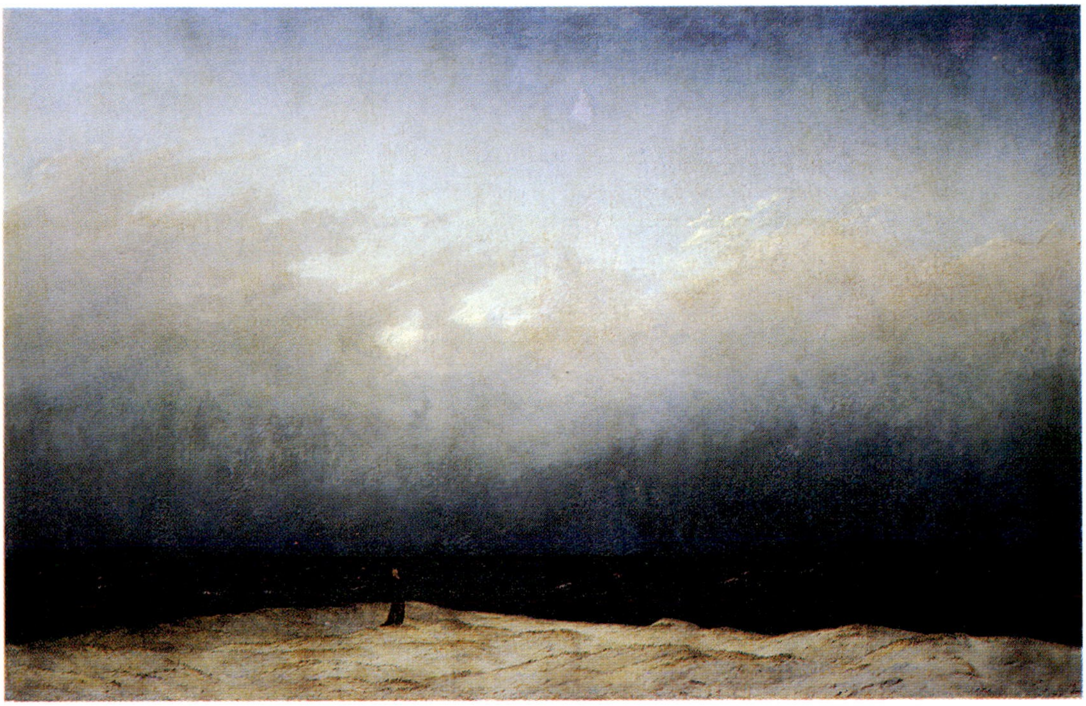

Fig. 648 Caspar David Friedrich, *Monk by the Sea,* 1809–1810.
Oil on canvas, 42 ½ × 67 in. Schloss Charlottenburg, Berlin. Bildarchiv Preussischer Kulturbesitz.

This sense of the terrible is by no means unique to Goya. In his own *Journal,* Delacroix would write, "[The poet] Baudelaire . . . says that I bring back to painting . . . the feeling which delights in the terrible. He is right." It was in the face of the Sublime that this enjoyment of the terrible was most often experienced. Theories of the **Sublime** had first appeared in the seventeenth century, most notably in Edmund Burke's *Inquiry into the Origin of Our Ideas of the Sublime and the Beautiful* (1756). For Burke, the Sublime was a feeling of awe experienced before things that escaped the ability of the human mind to comprehend them—mountains, chasms, storms, and catastrophes. The Sublime exceeded reason; it presented viewers with something vaster than themselves, thereby making them realize their smallness, even their insignificance, in the face of the infinite. The Sublime evokes the awe-inspiring forces of Nature, as opposed to the Beautiful, which is associated with Nature at her most harmonious and tranquil. A pastoral landscape may be beautiful; a vast mountain range, Sublime.

No painting of the period more fully captures the terrifying prospect of the Sublime than Caspar David Friedrich's *Monk by the Sea* (Fig. 648). It indicates just how thoroughly the experience of the infinite—that is, the experience of God—can be found in Nature. But the God faced by this solitary monk is by no means benign. The infinite becomes, in this painting, a vast, dark, and lonely space—so ominous that it must surely test the monk's faith. The real terror of this painting lies in its sense that the eternal space stretching before this man of faith may not be salvation but a meaningless void.

American landscape painters such as Albert Bierstadt (see Fig. 3), Thomas Moran (see Fig. 275), and Frederic Church continually sought to capture the Sublime in their paintings of the

Age of the realistic novel begins
1840s

1845

1847
Charlotte Brontë, *Jane Eyre*

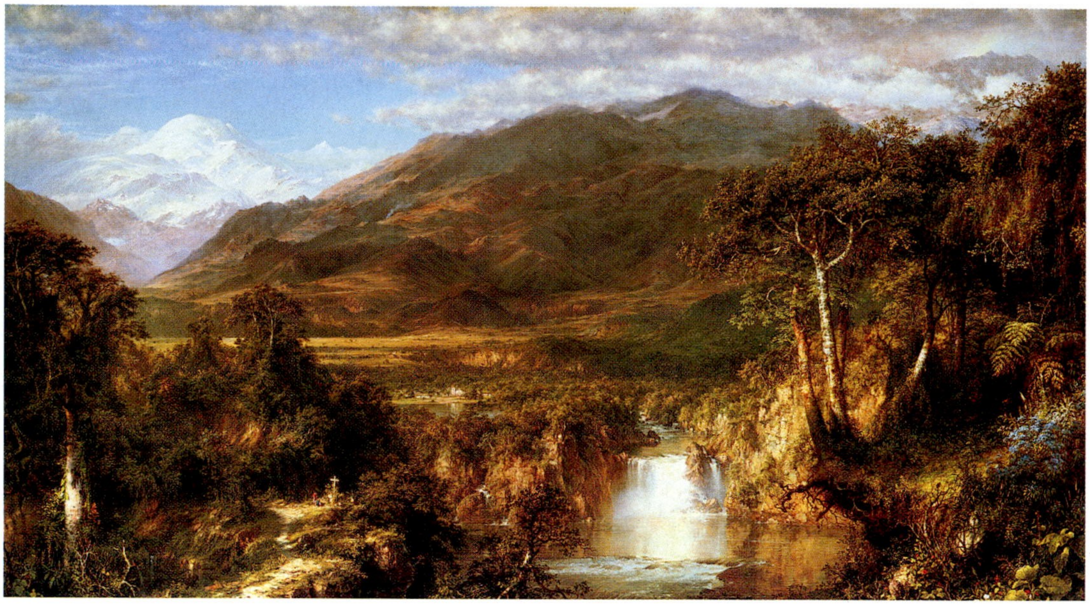

Fig. 649 Frederic Edwin Church, *The Heart of the Andes,* 1859.
Oil on canvas, 66 1/8 × 119 1/4 in. The Metropolitan Museum of Art, New York. Bequest of Margaret E. Dows, 1909.09.95.

vast spaces of the American West. Church even traveled to South America in order to bring evidence of its exotic and remarkable landscapes to viewers in America and Europe. His painting *The Heart of the Andes* (Fig. 649) was first exhibited in 1859 in New York in a one-picture, paid-admission showing. The dramatic appeal of the piece was heightened by brightly lighting the picture and leaving the remainder of the room dark, and by framing it so that it seemed to be a window in a grand house looking out upon this very scene. Deemed by critics "a truly religious work of art," it was a stunning success. The insignificance of man can be felt in the minuteness of the two figures praying at the cross in the lower left, but the scene is by no means merely Sublime. It is also beautiful and pastoral in feeling, and, in the careful rendering of plant life, almost scientific in its fidelity to nature.

The Romantic painter was, in fact, interested in much more than the Sublime. A Romantic artist might render a beautiful scene as well as a Sublime one, or one so pastoral in feeling that it recalls, often deliberately, Claude's soft Italian landscapes (see Fig. 632). It was the love of Nature itself that the artist sought to convey. In Nature, the American poet and essayist Ralph Waldo Emerson believed, one could read eternity. It was a literal "sign" for the Divine Spirit.

The painter, then, had to decide whether to depict the world with absolute fidelity or to reconstruct imaginatively a more perfect reality out of a series of accurate observations. As one writer put it at the time, "A distinction must be made . . . between the elements generated by . . . direct observation, and those which spring from the boundless depth and feeling and from the force of idealizing mental power." As we have seen in our discussion of painting in Chapter 11, it was the idealizing force of the imagination in painting that distinguished it from mere copywork. Nevertheless, and though Church's *Heart of the Andes* is an idealist compilation of diverse scenes, in many of its details—in, for instance, the accuracy with which the foliage has been rendered—it depends on direct observation.

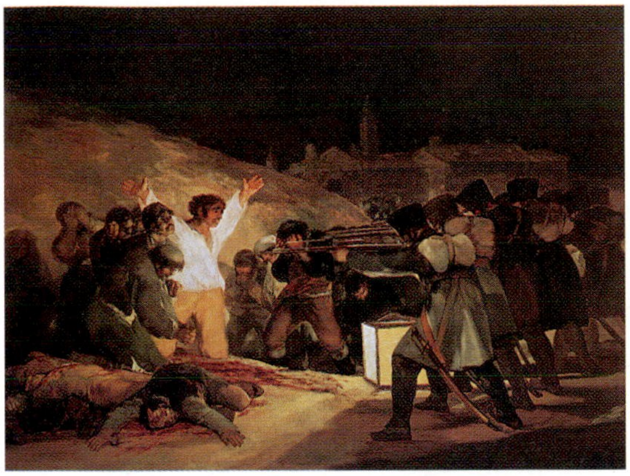

Fig. 650 Francisco Goya, *The Third of May, 1808,* 1814–1815.
Oil on canvas, 8 ft. 9 in. × 13 ft. 4 in.
Museo del Prado, Madrid. Scala/Art Resource.

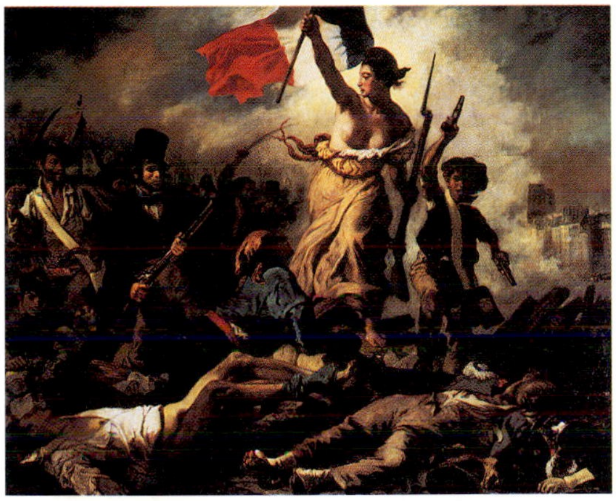

Fig. 651 Eugène Delacroix, *Liberty Leading the People,* 1830.
Oil on canvas, 8 ft. 6 3/8 in. × 10 ft. 8 in.
Musée du Louvre, Paris. Giraudon/Art Resource.

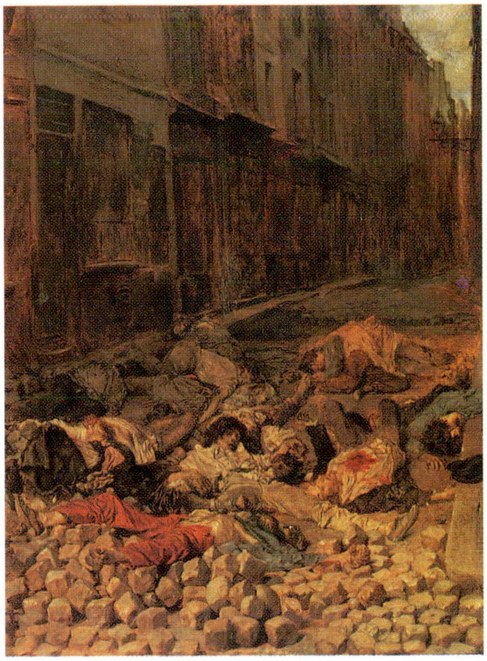

Fig. 652 Ernest Meissonier, *Memory of Civil War (The Barricades),* 1849.
Oil on canvas, 11 1/2 × 8 3/4 in.
Musée du Louvre, Paris. Scala/Art Resource.

REALISM

Church's accurate rendering of foliage reflects the importance of scientific, empirical observation to the nineteenth century as a whole, an urge for **realism** that runs counter to, and exists alongside, the imaginative and idealist tendencies of the Romantic sensibility. If we compare three history paintings from the first half of the nineteenth century, we can see how the idealizing tendency of the Romantic sensibility gradually faded away. Faced with the reality of war, idealism seemed absurd. Francisco Goya's *The Third of May, 1808* (Fig. 650) depicts an actual event, the execution of the citizens of Madrid by Napoleon's invading army. Its dramatic lighting and the Christ-like outstretched arms of the man about to be shot reflect the conventions of Baroque religious art, but the promise of salvation seems remote. The church in the background is shrouded in darkness, and the man will fall forward, like the others before him, a bloody corpse. Eugène Delacroix's *Liberty Leading the People* (Fig. 651) represents Liberty as an idealized allegorical figure, but the battle itself, which took place during the July Revolution of 1830, is depicted in a highly realistic manner, with figures lying dead on the barricades beneath Liberty's feet and Notre Dame Cathedral at the distant right shrouded in smoke. In Ernest Meissonier's *Memory of Civil War (The Barricades)* (Fig. 652) all the nobility of war has been drained from the picture. The blue, white, and red of the French flag has been reduced to piles of tattered clothing and blood, what one contemporary gruesomely described as an "omelette of men."

World population reaches about 1.1 billion
1850

Admiral Perry's visit ends Japanese isolation
1854

1850

1851
Herman Melville, *Moby Dick*

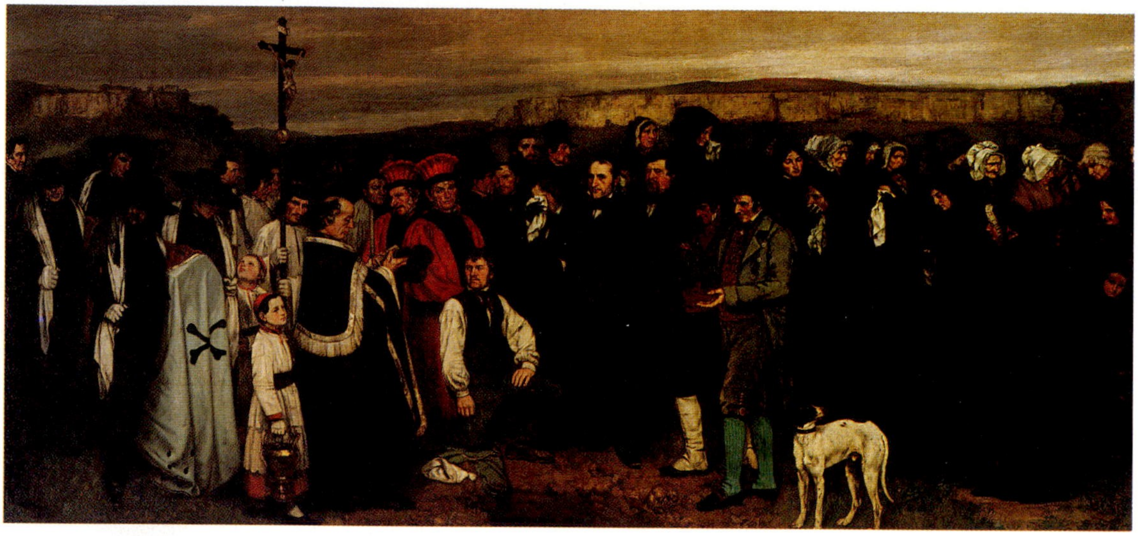

Fig. 653 Gustave Courbet, *Burial at Ornans,* 1849.
Oil on canvas, 10 ft. 3 ½ in. × 21 ft. 9 in. Musée d'Orsay, Paris. Giraudon/Art Resource.

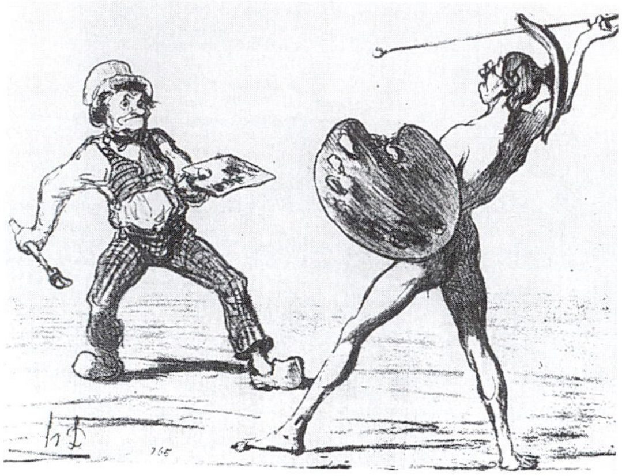

Fig. 654 Honoré Daumier, *Fight between Schools, Idealism and Realism,* 1855.

So thoroughly did the painter Gustave Courbet come to believe in recording the actual facts of the world around him that he would declare, in 1861: "Painting is an essentially concrete art and can only consist of the presentation of real and existing things. It is a completely physical language, the words of which consist of all visible objects." Artists should confine their representation to accurate observation and notation of the phenomena of daily life. No longer was there necessarily any "greater" reality beyond or behind the facts that lay before their eyes. Courbet's gigantic painting, *Burial at Ornans* (Fig. 653) seems, at first glance, to hold enormous potential for symbolic and allegorical meaning, but just the opposite is the case. In the foreground is a hole in the ground, the only "eternal reward" Courbet's scene appears to promise. No one, not even the dog, seems to be focused on the event itself. Courbet offers us a panorama of distraction, of common people performing their everyday duties, in a landscape whose horizontality reads like an unwavering line of monotony. If the cruxifix rises into the sky over the scene, it does so without deep spiritual significance. In fact, its curious position, as if it were set on the horizon line, lends it a certain comic dimension, a comedy that the bulbous faces of the red-cloaked beadles also underscore. The painting was rejected by the jury of the Universal Exposition of 1855, and to emphasize his distain for the values of the establishment, Courbet opened a one-person exhibition outside the Exposition grounds, calling it the Pavilion of Realism. The cartoonist Honoré Daumier immediately responded with a cartoon depicting the *Fight between*

1859
Charles Darwin,
On the Origin of Species

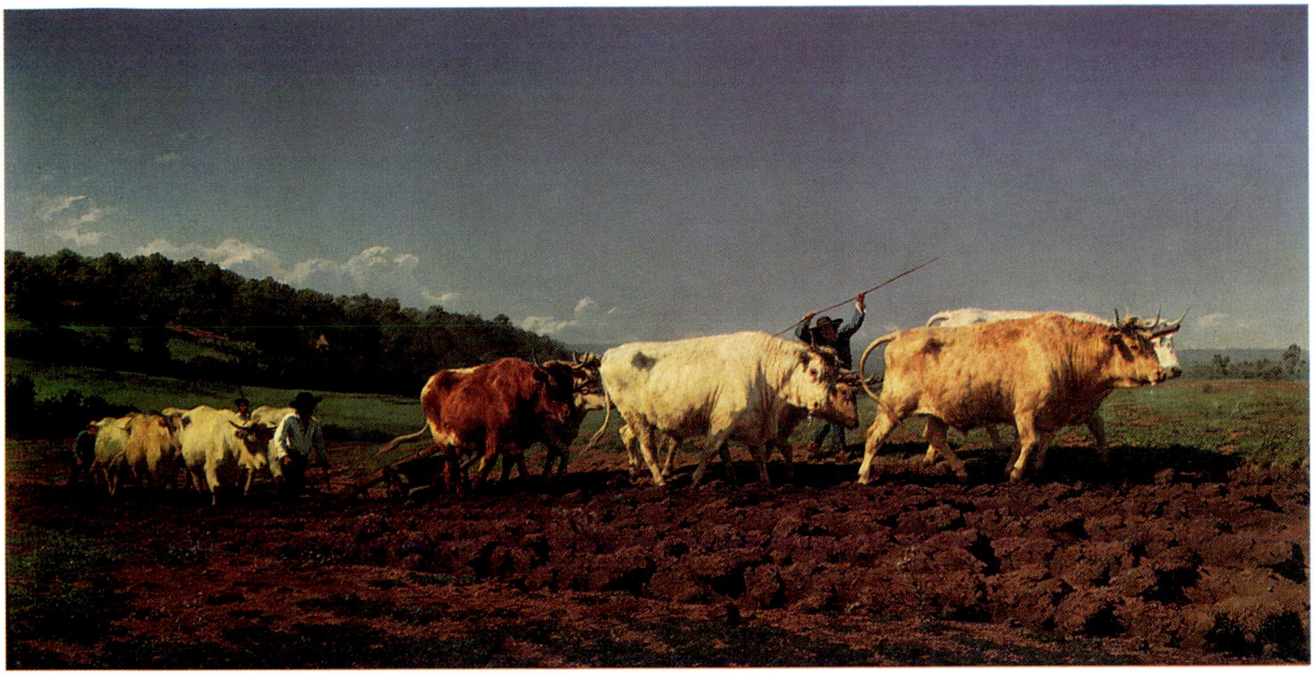

Fig. 655 Rosa Bonheur, *Plowing in the Nivernais,* 1849.
Oil on canvas, 5 ft. 9 in. × 8 ft. 8 in. Musée d'Orsay, Paris.

Schools, Idealism and Realism (Fig. 654). The Courbet-like realist, with his square palette, house painter's brush, and wooden shoes, battles the aged, classically nude idealist, who wears, atop his head, the helmet of a Greek warrior.

It was, at least in part, the realist impulse that led to the invention of photography in the 1830s (see Figs. 400–406). And it was also in this spirit that Karl Marx, in *The Communist Manifesto,* would say: "All that was solid and established crumbles away, all that was holy is profaned, and man is at last compelled to look with open eyes upon his conditions of life and true social relations." Marx's sentiments, written in response to the wave of revolutions that swept Europe in 1848, are part and parcel of the realist enterprise. Rosa Bonheur's *Plowing in the Nivernais* (Fig. 655) was commissioned in response to the French Revolution of 1848. It reveals her belief in the virtue of toil and the common life of the French peasant. But it is her realism, her extraordinary ability to depict animals, that made her the most famous woman artist of her day. It was, suddenly, socially and aesthetically important, even imperative, to paint neither the Sublime nor the beautiful nor the picturesque, but the everyday, the commonplace, the low, and the ugly. Painters, it was felt, must represent the reality of their time and place, whatever it might look like.

As Daumier's cartoon makes clear, the art of the past, exemplified by the Classical model, was felt to be worn-out, incapable of expressing the realities of contemporary life. As the poet Charles Baudelaire put it, *"Il faut être de son temps"*—"it is necessary to be of one's own time." He looked everywhere for a "painter of modern life." The modern world was marked by change, by the uniqueness of every moment, each instant like a photograph different from the last. Painting had to accommodate itself to this change. There were no longer any permanent, eternal truths.

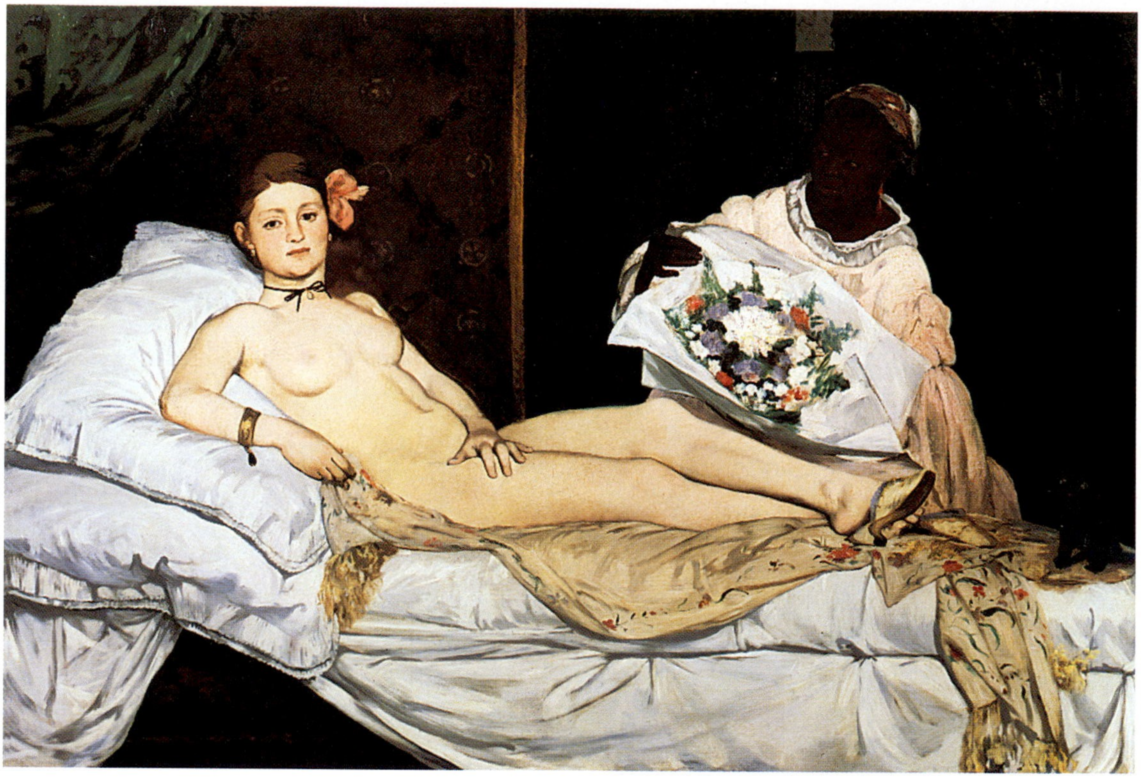

Fig. 656 Edouard Manet, *Olympia,* 1863.
Oil on canvas, 51 × 74¾ in. Musée d'Orsay, Paris. Giraudon/Art Resource.

Baudelaire's painter of modern life was Edouard Manet. As we have already seen in Chapter 3, Manet's *Luncheon on the Grass* (Fig. 57), more commonly known by its French name *Déjeuner sur l'herbe,* caused an outcry when it was first exhibited in 1863. Two years later, at the Salon of 1865, Manet exhibited another picture that caused perhaps an even greater scandal. *Olympia* (Fig. 656) was a depiction of a common prostitute posed in the manner of the traditional odalisque. Though it was not widely recognized at the time, Manet had, in this painting, by no means abandoned tradition completely in favor of the depiction of everyday life in all its sordid detail. *Olympia* was directly indebted to Titian's *Venus of Urbino* (compare Fig. 613), just as the *Déjeuner sur l'herbe* had been based on a composition by Raphael (Fig. 58). Manet's sources were classical. His treatment, however, was anything but. What most irritated both critics and public was the apparently "slipshod" nature of his painting technique. Olympia's body is virtually flat. Manet painted with large strokes of thick paint, and if he distorted perspective in *Le Déjeuner*—the bather in the background seems about to spill forward into the picnic—then he eliminated perspective altogether in the shallow space of the *Olympia,* where the bed appears to be no wider than a foot or two.

Manet's rejection of traditional painting techniques was intentional. He was drawing attention to his very modernity, to the fact that he was breaking with the past. His manipulation of his traditional sources supported the same intentions. In Marx's words, Manet is looking "with open eyes upon his conditions of life and true social relations." Olympia's eyes directly confront us. The visitor, who is implicitly male, becomes a voyeur, as the female body is subjected to the male gaze. It is as if the visitor, who occupies our own position in front of the scene, has brought the flowers, and the cat, barely discernible at Olympia's feet, has arched its back to hiss at his approach. The Venus that once strode the heights of Mt. Olympus, home of the gods, is now the common courtesan. "Love" is now a commodity, something to be bought and sold.

In his brushwork, particularly, Manet pointed painting in a new direction. His friend, the novelist Emile Zola, who was the first to defend *Olympia,* described it this way: "He catches his figures vividly, is not afraid of the brusqueness of nature and renders in all their vigor the different objects which stand out against each other. His whole being causes him to see things in splotches, in simple and forceful pieces." Manet was something of a professional observer—a famous *flâneur,* a Parisian of impeccable dress and perfect manners who strolled the city, observing its habits and commenting on it with the greatest subtlety, wit, and savoir-faire. The type can be seen strolling toward the viewer in Gustave Caillebotte's *Place de l'Europe on a Rainy Day* (Fig. 114). Wrote Manet's friend Antonin Proust, "With Manet, the eye played such a big role that Paris has never known a *flâneur* like him nor a *flâneur* strolling more usefully."

Edgar Degas's *The Glass of Absinthe* (Fig. 657) was painted a decade after Manet's *Olympia* but was directly influenced by Manet's example. Degas's wandering eye has caught the underside of Parisian café society. Absinthe was an alcoholic drink that attacked the nerve centers, eventually causing severe cerebral damage. Especially popular among the working classes, it was finally banned in France in 1915. In the dazed, absent look of this young woman, Degas reveals the consequences of absinthe consumption with a shockingly direct realism worthy of Courbet.

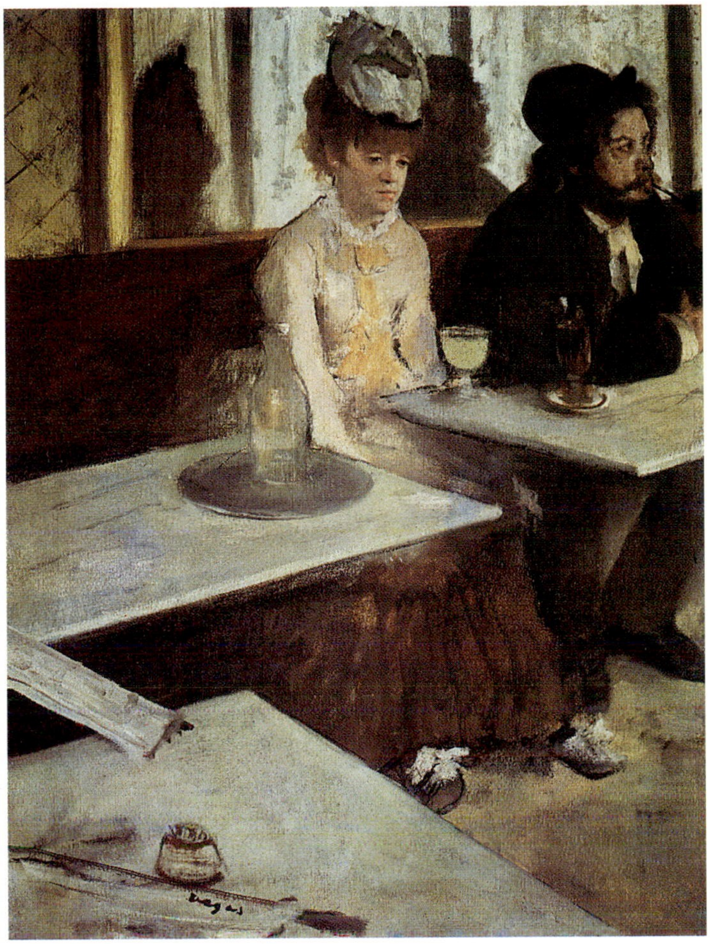

Fig. 657 Edgar Degas, *The Glass of Absinthe,* 1876.
Oil on canvas, 36 × 27 in. Musée d'Orsay, Paris. Scala/Art Resource.

1870

1870s
European birth and death rates begin to decline

European powers carve up Africa
1870s and 1880s

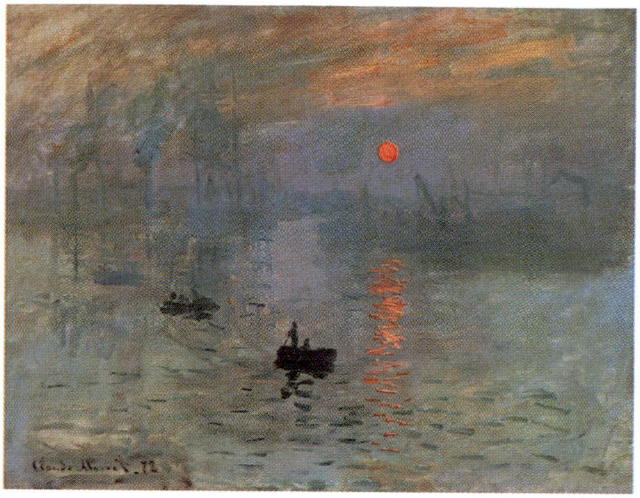

Fig. 658 Claude Monet, ***Impression-Sunrise,*** **1872.**
Oil on canvas, 19 1/2 × 25 1/2 in. Musée Marmottan, Paris.

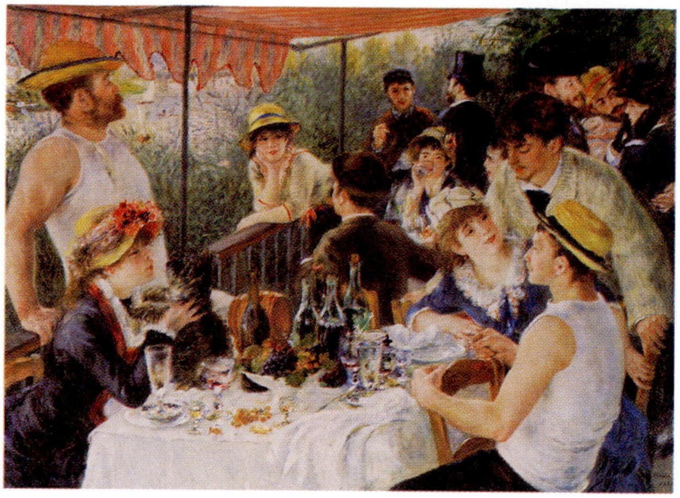

Fig. 659 Auguste Renoir, ***A Luncheon at Bougival*** **(or** ***The Luncheon of the Boating Party),*** **1881.**
Oil on canvas, 51 × 68 in. ©The Phillips Collection, Washington, DC.

IMPRESSIONISM

In the late 1860s, the young painter Claude Monet began to employ the same rich, thick brushstrokes Manet was already using, but with an even looser hand. Combining two or more pigments on a single wide brush, he allowed them to blend as they were brushed onto the canvas. He would paint "wet on wet"—with wet pigment over and through an already painted surface that had not yet dried. Most of all, he painted with the intense hues made possible by the development of synthetic pigments.

Others followed his lead, and together, in April 1874, they held a group exhibition. They called themselves "Painters, Sculptors, Engravers, etc. Inc.," but before long they would be known as the **Impressionists.** The painting that gave them their name was Monet's *Impression-Sunrise* (Fig. 658). Monet, the critic Théodore Duret wrote in 1878, "is the Impressionist painter par excellence. . . . [He] has succeeded in setting down the fleeting impression which his predecessors had neglected or considered impossible to render with the brush . . . the fleeting appearances which the accidents of atmosphere present to him . . . a singularly lively and striking sensation of the observed scene. His canvases really do communicate impressions." The paintings, in fact, have the feel of the sketches, as if they were executed spontaneously, even instantaneously, in the manner of photographic snapshots.

The Impressionists' subject matter sets them apart from their predecessors at least as much as their technique does. Unlike the Realist painters of a generation earlier, the Impressionists were less interested in social criticism than in depicting in their work the pleasures of life, including the pleasures of simply seeing. If Impressionism is characterized by a way of seeing—by the attempt to capture the fleeting effects of light by applying paint in small, quick strokes of color—it is also defined by an intense interest in images of leisure. The Realists would have rejected these images as unworthy of their high moral purposes. The Impressionists painted life in the Parisian theaters and cafés, the grand boulevards teeming with shoppers, country gardens bursting with flowers, the racetrack and seaside, the suburban pleasures of boating and swimming on the Seine. Auguste Renoir's

Invention of phonograph
1877

1880

1877
First public telephone system installed in New Haven, Connecticut

1880
Invention of electric lights

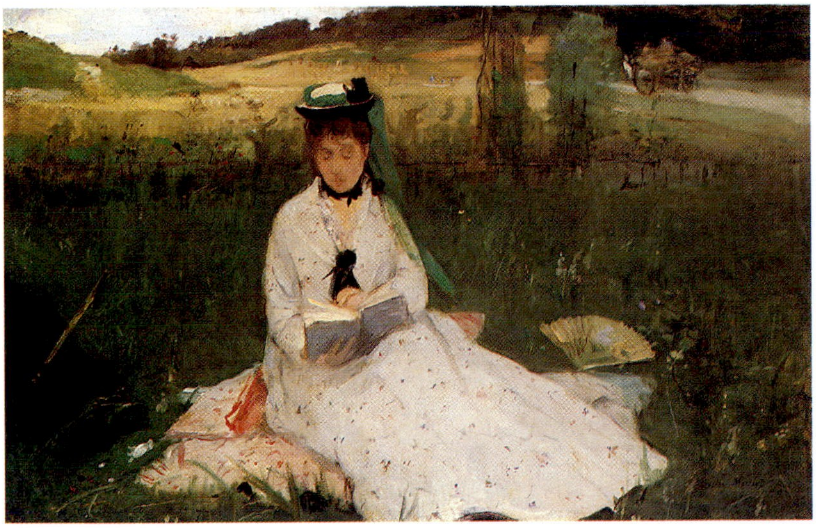

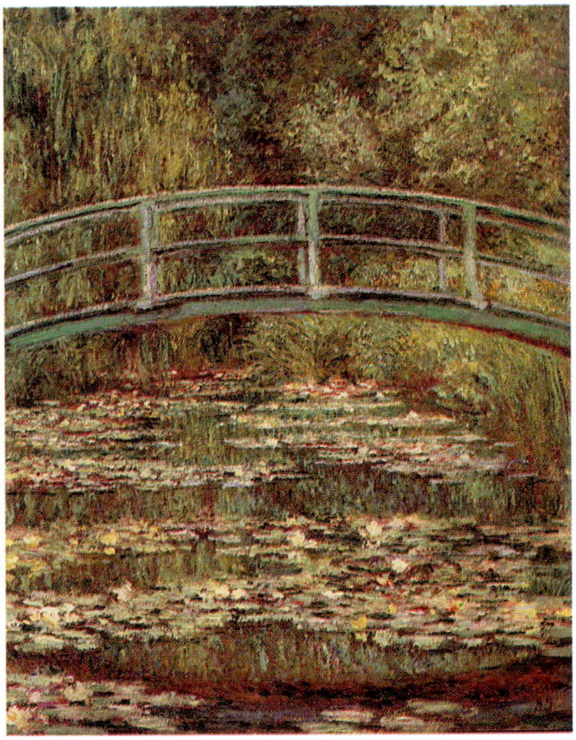

Fig 660 (above) Berthe Morisot, *The Artist's Sister, Mme. Pontillon, Seated on the Grass*, 1873.
Oil on canvas, 17 3/4 × 28 1/2 in. Cleveland Museum of Art. Gift of the Hanna Fund, 50.89.

Fig. 661 (right) Claude Monet, *Bridge over a Pool of Water Lilies*, 1899.
Oil on canvas, 36 1/2 × 29 in. The Metropolitan Museum of Art, New York. Bequest of Mrs. H. O. Havemeyer, 1929. The H. O. Havemeyer Collection. 29.100.113.

A Luncheon at Bougival (or *The Luncheon of the Boating Party*) (Fig. 659) is typical. All of the figures in the painting are Renoir's friends, including his future wife, Aline Charigot, pursing her lips at the little dog. When he saw the painting in 1882, one critic accurately summarized the spirit of both it and the party it depicts: "For them eternity is in their glass, in their boat, and in their songs."

The distance of Impressionist painting from its Realist predecessors is summed up in Berthe Morisot's *The Artist's Sister, Mme. Pontillon, Seated on the Grass* (Fig. 660), probably one of four paintings Morisot exhibited at the first Independents Exhibition in 1874. In the background, a farmer's cart heads down the road, the proper subject matter of the Realist. But Morisot's sister has no interest in what passes behind her, and neither really does the painter herself. The cart is rendered in few loose, rapid brushstrokes, as is the entire landscape. Leisure is Morisot's subject.

Increasingly, this urge to observe the world in its most minute particulars led to the investigation of optical reality in and for itself. As early as the 1870s, in his paintings of boats on the river at Argenteuil (see Fig. 234), Monet began to paint the same subject over and over again, studying the ways in which the changing light transformed his impressions. This working method led to his later serial studies of the grainstacks (Figs. 24 and 162), Rouen Cathedral, and his garden at Giverny (Fig. 661), where he moved in 1883. By the turn of the century, he had given up painting "modern life" altogether, concentrating instead on capturing the "presentness" of his garden, the panoramic views that would be installed in the Orangerie in Paris in 1927 (see Figs. 182 and 183).

For many, painting began to be an end in itself, a medium whose relation to the actual world was at best only incidental. In England, the American expatriate painter James McNeill Whistler equated his paintings to musical com-

Germany introduces the first social security laws
1883

1880

1883
First skyscraper built in Chicago

1884–5
International Conference in Berlin to decide the future of Africa

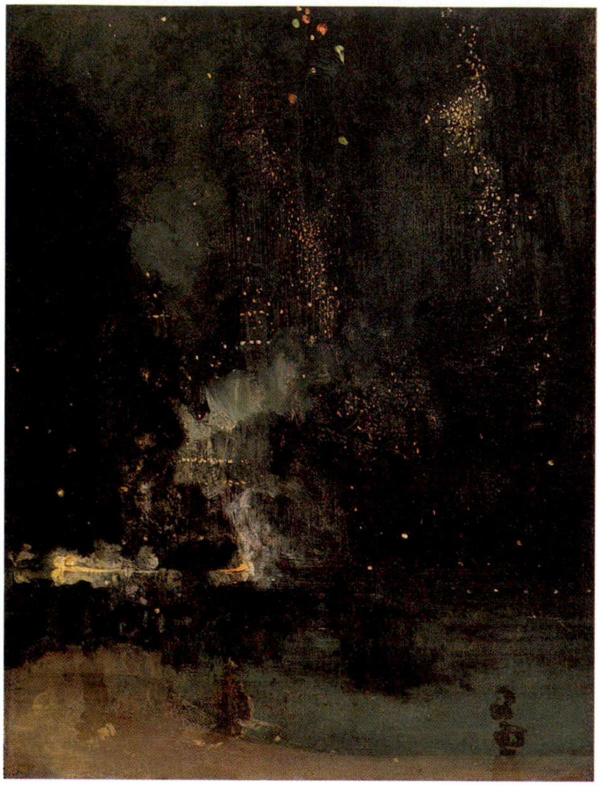

Fig. 662 James McNeill Whistler, *Nocturne in Black and Gold, the Falling Rocket*, c. 1875.
Oil on oak panel, 23 3/4 × 18 3/8 in.
© The Detroit Institute of Arts. Gift of Dexter M. Ferry, Jr.

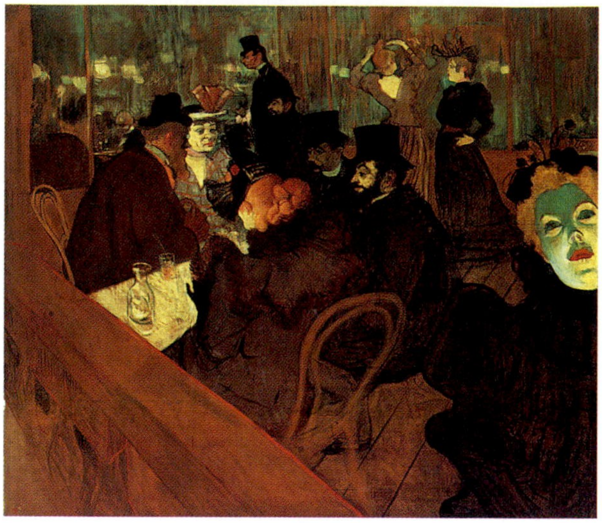

Fig. 663 Henri de Toulouse-Lautrec, *At the Moulin Rouge*, 1892–1895.
Oil on canvas, 48 3/8 x 55 1/4 in. Helen Birch Bartlett Memorial Collection.

positions by titling them "nocturnes" and "symphonies." He painted, he said, "as the musician gathers his notes, and forms his chords, until he brings forth from chaos glorious harmony." Painting was, for Whistler, primarily an abstract arrangement of shapes and colors; only incidentally did it refer to the world. Believing that art should possess strong moral content, the English essayist John Ruskin was blind to Whistler's abstraction. After viewing *Nocturne in Black and Gold, the Falling Rocket* (Fig. 662), an image of fireworks falling over the Thames, Ruskin wrote that Whistler was "flinging a pot of paint in the public's face." Whistler, in turn, sued Ruskin for libel. A lengthy trial followed, and in 1878 Whistler finally won his case, but was awarded damages of only a farthing, approximately half a U. S. cent. If artists were free to paint anything they wanted, they also had to accept whatever criticism came their way.

POST-IMPRESSIONISM

Although, by the 1880s, Impressionism's subject matter had come to seem trivial to many artists, they were still interested in investigating and extending its formal innovations and in reexamining the symbolic possibilities of painting. Monet's work at Giverny can be seen as an example of just such an ongoing formal exploration. A number of other painters—among them Henri de Toulouse-Lautrec, Vincent van Gogh, Paul Gauguin, Georges Seurat, and Paul Cézanne—embarked on a similar brand of **Post-Impressionism,** each dedicated to redirecting the Impressionist enterprise. Toulouse-Lautrec returned to the kind of direct criticism of modern life that had marked the work of Manet and Degas. His painting *At the Moulin Rouge* (Fig. 663), for instance, celebrates Parisian night life like the work of the

Kodak camera invented
1888

1889
Eiffel Tower built in Paris

1890

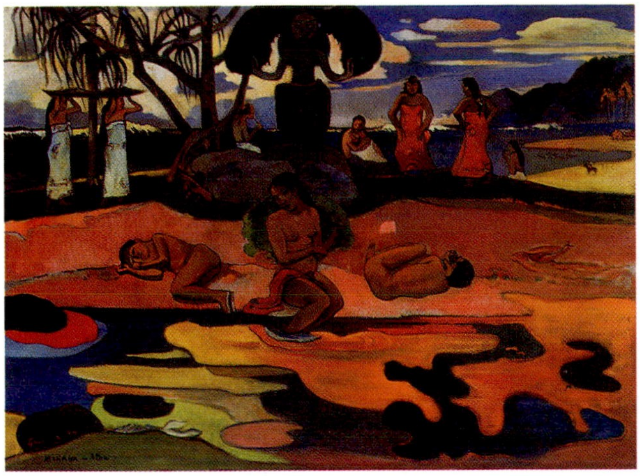

Fig. 664 Paul Gauguin, *The Day of the Gods (Mehana no Atua)*, 1894. Oil on canvas, 26 7/8 × 36 1/8 in. Helen Birch Bartlett Memorial Collection.

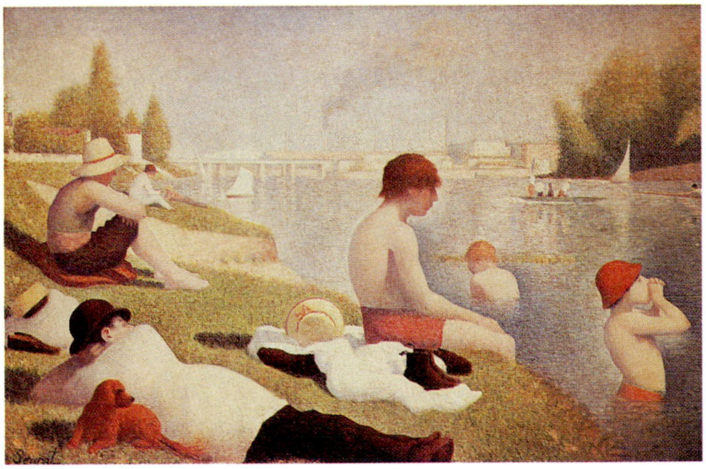

Fig. 665 Georges Seurat, *The Bathers*, 1883–1884. Oil on canvas, 79 1/2 × 118 1/2 in. The National Gallery, London. Reproduced by courtesy of the Trustees. Erich Lessing/Art Resource.

Impressionists before him, but the grotesquely gas-lit features of the woman on the right capture a decadence that, by century's end, pervaded Parisian life. Van Gogh and Gauguin, it was felt even at the time, released artists from the need to copy nature. Color could now be used arbitrarily to express emotions (see van Gogh's *The Night Café*, Fig. 169).

Like Toulouse-Lautrec, Gauguin criticized the conditions of modern life, but he did so by leaving Europe and seeking out a new life in the South Seas. There, in paintings such as *The Day of the God (Mahana no Atua)* (Fig. 664), he tried to capture the mystery and magic of the "primitive" culture, a world of unity, peace, and naked innocence far removed from the turmoil of civilized life. The perfect balance of the painting's composition and the brilliant color of the scene are structural realizations of paradise on earth.

In paintings such as *A Sunday Afternoon on the Island of the Grande Jatte* (Fig. 155), Georges Seurat sought to impose a formal order upon the world, and in the process revealed its rigidity, its lack of vitality. Though Seurat's subject matter in *The Bathers* (Fig. 665) is Impressionist, his composition is not. It is architectural, intentionally returning to the seventeenth-century compositional principles of Poussin (see Fig. 635). And it subtly critiques the image of Impressionist leisure. These are not well-to-do middle class Parisians, but workers (their costume gives them away), swimming in the Seine just down river from the factory town of Asnières. Smokestacks belch soot in the distance. The spot, as observant Parisians knew, was directly across from the outlet of the great collective sewer from Paris. In the summer of 1884, according to the local press, "more than 120,000 cubic feet of solids had accumulated at the sewer's mouth; several hundred square meters of which are covered with a bizarre vegetation, which gives off a disgusting smell." Suddenly, the green material floating in the water is transformed.

Of all the Post-Impressionist painters, Cézanne, working alone in the south of France, most thoroughly emphasizes the formal aspects of painting at the expense of subject matter, and in this he looks forward most to the direction of art in the twentieth century. He pushed toward an idea of painting that established for

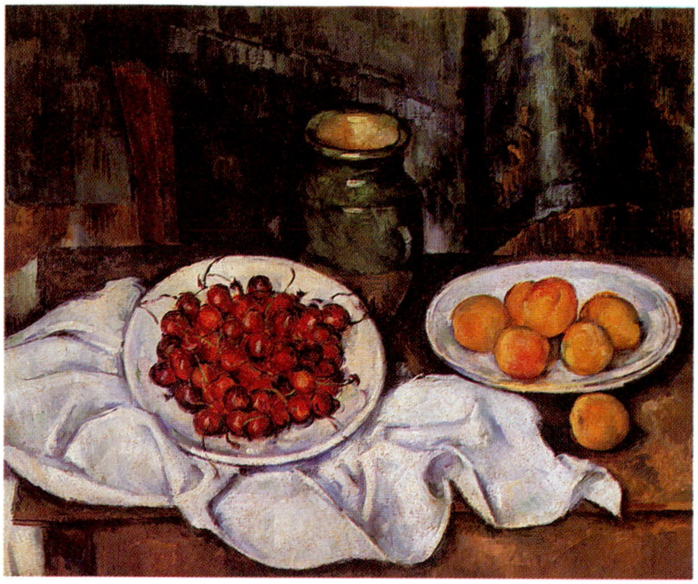

Fig. 666 Paul Cézanne, *Still Life with Cherries and Peaches,* 1883–1887.
Oil on canvas. $19\frac{3}{4} \times 24$ in.
Los Angeles County Museum of Art, Mrs. Armand S. Deutsch.

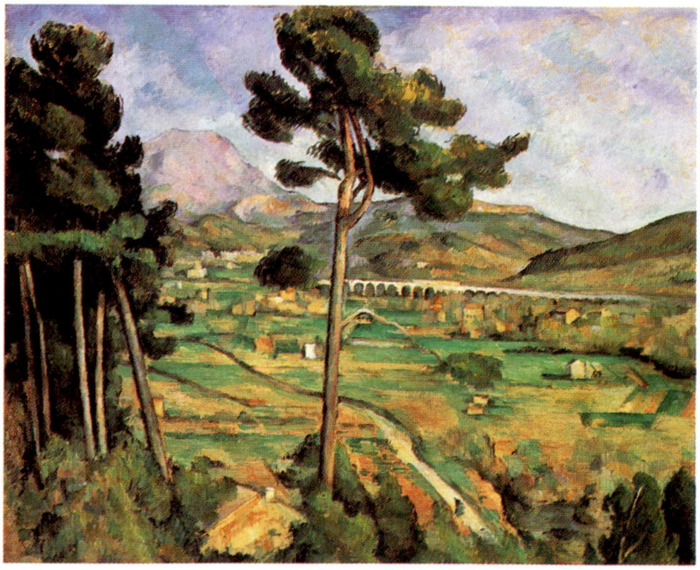

Fig. 667 Paul Cézanne, *Mont Sainte-Victoire, Seen from Bellevue,* also known as *The Viaduct,* 1882–1885.
Oil on canvas, $25\frac{3}{4} \times 32\frac{1}{8}$ in. The Metropolitan Museum of Art, New York.
Bequest of Mrs. H. O. Havemeyer, 1929. The H. O. Havemeyer Collection. 29.100.64.

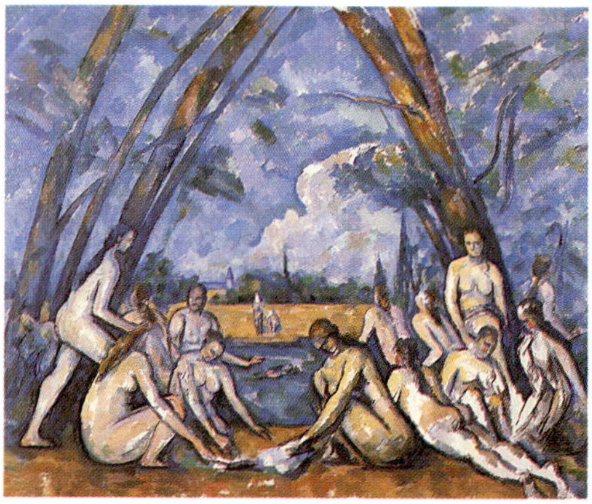

Fig. 668 Paul Cézanne, *The Large Bathers,* 1906.
Oil on canvas, 82×99 in.
Philadelphia Museum of Art. Purchased: The W. P. Wilstach Collection.

the picture an independent existence, to be judged in terms of the purely formal interrelationships of line, color, and plane. In his *Still Life with Cherries and Peaches* (Fig. 666), he emphasizes the *act* of composition itself, the process of seeing. It is as if he has rendered two entirely different views of the same still life simultaneously. The peaches on the right are seen from a point several feet in front of the table, while the cherries on the left have been painted from directly above. As a consequence, the table itself seems to broaden out behind the cherries.

Similarly, his *Mont Sainte-Victoire, Seen from Bellevue* (Fig. 667) collapses the space between foreground and background by making a series of formal correspondences between them, by the repetition of the shape of the lower righthand branch of the tree, for instance, the road below it, and the shape of the mountain itself. Finally, in the *Large Bathers* (Fig. 668), the pyramidal structure of the composition draws attention to the geometry that dominates even the individual faceting of the wide brushstrokes, which he laid down as horizontals, verticals, and diagonals. The simplification of the human body evident here, as well as Cézanne's overall emphasis on form, would have a profound effect on painting in the twentieth century. It is in Cézanne that the art of the twentieth century dawns.

CHAPTER 20

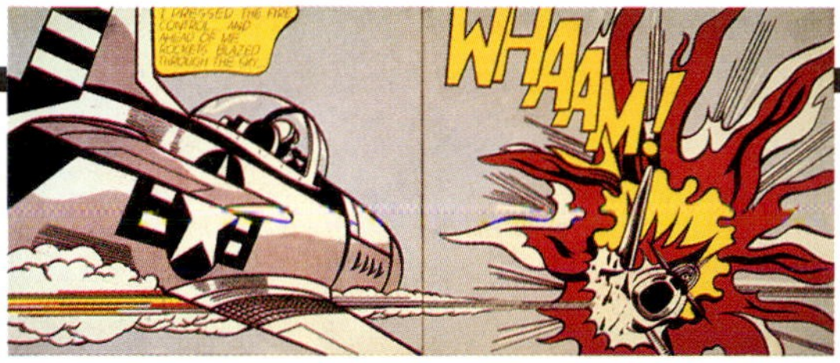

The Twentieth Century

Cubism

The Fauves

German Expressionism

Futurism

Dada and Surrealism

WORK IN PROGRESS
Pablo Picasso's *Guernica*

American Modernism and Abstract Expressionism

Pop Art and Minimalism

Postmodern Directions

In the autumn of 1906 and throughout 1907, Pablo Picasso painted his portrait of *Gertrude Stein* (see Fig. 41) and then embarked on his monumental and groundbreaking painting *Les Demoiselles d'Avignon* (Fig. 49). At the time, Paris was inundated by exhibitions of the work of Cézanne, which were to have a profound effect on the development of modern art. Soon after he died, in October 1906, a retrospective of 79 of Cézanne's last watercolors was exhibited at the Bernheime-Jeune Gallery. At the Salon in the autumn of 1907, another retrospective of Cézanne's late paintings, mostly oils, appeared.

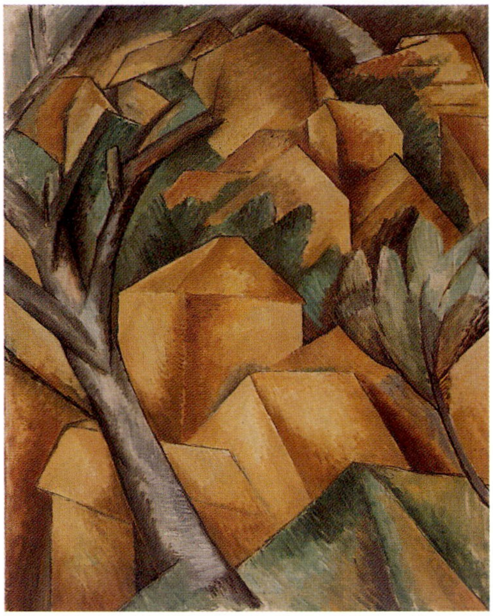

Fig. 669 Georges Braque, *Houses at l'Estaque,* 1908.
Oil on canvas, 28 3/4 × 23 3/4 in.
Kunstmuseum, Berne, Hermannn and Margit Rupf Foundation.

In his letters to the painter Emile Bernard, which were published posthumously in the Paris press, Cézanne advised painters to study nature in terms of "the cylinder, the sphere, the cone."

CUBISM

Picasso was already under the influence of Cézanne when he painted *Les Demoiselles*, and when Georges Braque saw first Picasso's painting and then Cézanne's, he began to paint a series of landscapes based on their formal innovations. His *Houses at l'Estaque* (Fig. 669) takes Cézanne's manipulation of space even further than the master did. The tree that rises from the foreground seems to meld into the roofs of the distant houses near the top of the painting. At the right, a large, leafy branch projects out across the houses, but its leaves appear identical to the greenery that is growing between the houses behind it. It becomes impossible to tell what is foreground, what is not. The houses that descend down the hill before us are themselves spatially confusing. Walls bleed almost seamlessly into other walls, walls bleed into roofs, roofs bleed into walls. Braque presents us with a design of triangles and cubes as much as he does a landscape.

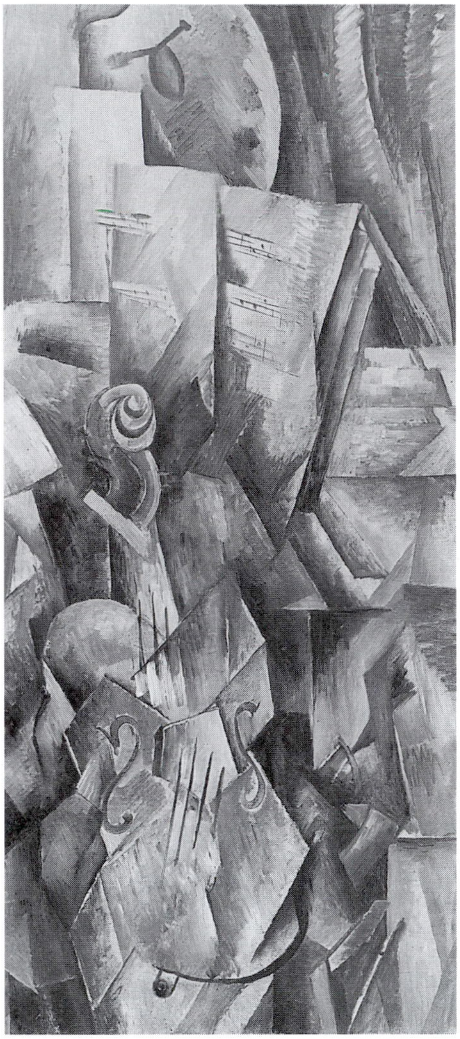

Fig. 670 Georges Braque, *Violin and Palette,* 1909.
Oil on canvas, 36 1/8 × 16 7/8 in.
Solomon R. Guggenheim Museum, New York. Photograph by Robert E. Mates.

Together, over the course of the next decade, Picasso and Braque would create the movement known as **Cubism,** of which Braque's *Houses at l'Estaque* is an early example. The name derived from a comment made by the critic Louis Vauxcelles in a small review that appeared directly above a headline announcing the "conquest of the air" by the Wright brothers: "Braque . . . reduces everything, places and figures and houses, to geometric schemes, little cubes." It was, as the accidental juxtaposition of Cubism and the Wright brothers suggested, a new world.

Other artists soon followed the lead of Picasso and Braque, and the impact of their art can be felt everywhere—from the work of Stuart Davis (see Fig. 161) and Jacob Lawrence (see Figs. 221 and 324) to the photography of Charles Sheeler (see Fig. 408), to the graphic design Benito (see Fig. 519). For the Cubist, art was primarily about form. Analyzing the object from all sides and acknowledging the flatness of the picture plane, the Cubist painting represented the three-dimensional world in increasingly two-dimensional terms. The curves of the violin in Braque's *Violin and Palette* (Fig. 670) are flattened and cubed, so much so that in places the instrument seems as flat as the sheets of music above it. The highly realistic, almost *trompe-l'oeil* nail at the painting's top introduces another characteristic of Cubist work. Casting its own shadow, it can be seen either as part of the painting, holding up the palette, or as real, holding the painting to the wall. Such play between the reality of painting and the reality of the world soon led both Picasso and Braque to experiment with collage, which we discussed in Chapter 12. Perhaps most important, Cubism freed painting of the necessity to represent the world. From henceforward, painting could be primarily about painting.

THE FAUVES

Though the Cubists tended to deemphasize color in order to emphasize form, Henri Matisse favored the expressive possibilities of color. Matisse, in a sense, synthesized the art of Cézanne and Seurat, taking the former's broad, flat zones of color and the latter's interest in setting complementary hues beside one another. Under the influence of van Gogh, whose work had not been seen as a whole until an exhibition at the Bernheim-Jeune Gallery in 1901, Matisse felt free to use color arbitrarily. A number of other young painters joined him, and in the fall of 1905 they exhibited together at the Salon, where they were promptly labeled **Fauves** ("Wild Beasts"). Not long after the exhibition, Matisse painted a portrait of his wife known as *The Green Stripe* (Fig. 671) for the bright green stripe that runs down the middle of her face. The painting is a play between zones of complementary colors, and in its emphasis on blue-violet, red-orange, and green, it anticipates Matisse's attempt to generate light in *Dance II* (Fig. 167). Although some critics ridiculed them, the Fauves were seen by others as promising a fully abstract art. The painter Maurice Denis wrote of them: "One feels completely in the realm of abstraction. Of course, as in the most extreme departures of van Gogh, something still remains of the original feeling of nature. But here one finds, above all in the work of Matisse, the sense of . . . painting in itself, the act of pure painting."

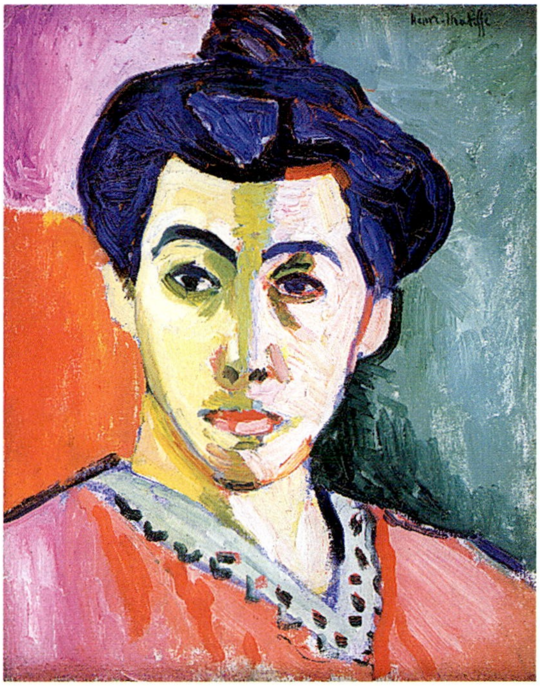

Fig. 671 Henri Matisse, *The Green Stripe (Madame Matisse)*, 1905.
Oil and tempera on canvas, 15 7/8 × 12 7/8 in.
Statens Museum for Kunst, Copenhagen. J. Rump Collection.

1912
Titanic sinks on its maiden voyage

1914
Panama Canal opens

1910
Stravinsky, *The Firebird*

1914
10.5 million immigrants enter the U. S.

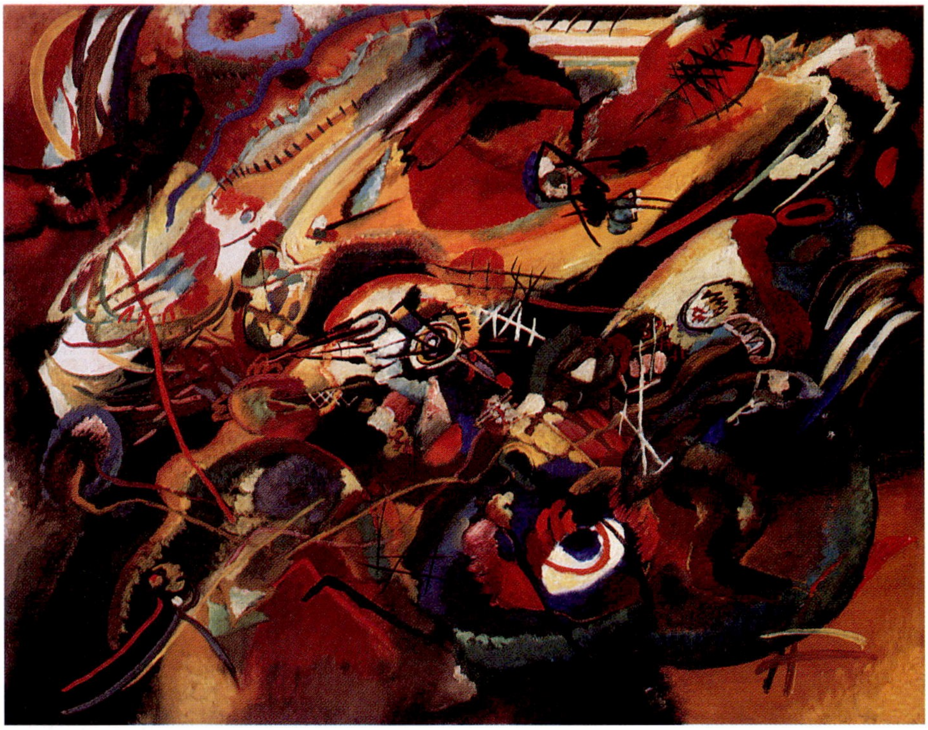

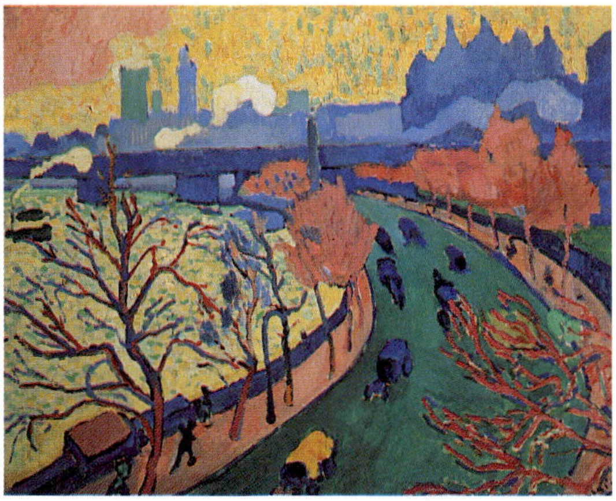

Fig. 672 (above) Wassily Kandinsky, *Sketch I* for *"Composition VII,"* 1913.
India ink, 30 3/4 × 39 3/8 in. Kunstmuseum, Bern, Switzerland. Collection Felix Klee.

Fig. 673 (left) André Derain, *Westminster Bridge,* 1906.
Oil on canvas, 31 7/8 × 39 1/8 in. Musée d'Orsay, Paris. Giraudon/Art Resource.

GERMAN EXPRESSIONISM

It was in Germany that Denis's idea of "pure painting" would fully take hold. In Dresden, a group of artists known as *Die Brücke* ("The Bridge"), among them Ernst Kirchner and Emil Nolde (see Fig. 270), advocated a raw and direct style, epitomized by the slashing gouges of the woodblock print. A group of artists known as *Der Blaue Reiter* ("The Blue Rider") formed in Munich around the Russian Wassily Kandinsky. They believed that through color and line alone works of art could *express* the feelings and emotions of the artist directly to the viewer—hence the name **Expressionism.**

In the 1890s, Kandinsky had seen an exhibition of Monet "Haystacks." Noting how the haystacks themselves seemed to disintegrate in the diffuse light, Kandinsky was convinced that "the importance of an 'object' as the necessary element in painting" was suspect. Nothing of the geometry of Cubism can be detected in Kandinsky's early paintings such as *Sketch I* for *"Composition VII"* (Fig. 672). Like Whistler before him, Kandinsky considered his painting to be equivalent to music, and his

D. W. Griffith, *Birth of a Nation* 1915

Worldwide influenza epidemic 1918–19

1920

1914–18 World War I

1917 Bolsheviks seize power in Russia

1920 Carl Jung publishes *Psychological Types*

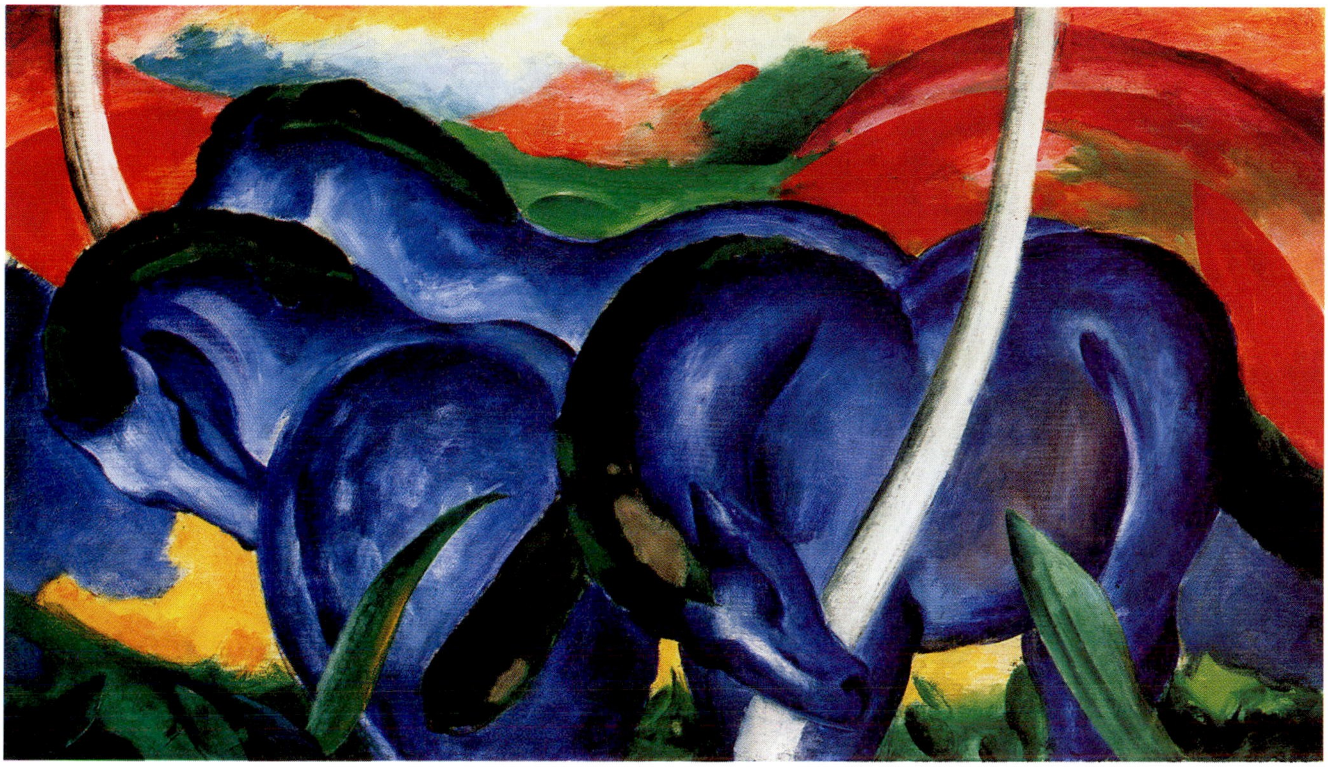

Fig. 674 Franz Marc, *The Large Blue Horses*, 1911.
Oil on canvas, 41 5/16 × 71 1/4 in. Collection, Walker Art Center, Minneapolis.
Gift of T.B. Walker Foundation, Gilbert M. Walker Fund, 1942.

works are alive in nonfigurative movement and color. Each color and each line carried, for Kandinsky, explicit expressive meaning (see Fig. 170). He believed that paintings like his had "the power to create [a] spiritual atmosphere" that would "lead us away from the outer to the inner basis."

The paintings of the Fauves, such as André Derain's *Westminster Bridge* (Fig. 673), convinced Kandinsky that through color he could eliminate the object altogether. "Color," Kandinsky wrote in his 1911 essay *Concerning the Spiritual in Art,* "is able to attain what is most universal yet at the same time most elusive in nature: its inner force."

Kandinsky's ideas find remarkable expression in the work of another member of the Blue Rider group, Franz Marc, who adopted Kandinsky's color symbolism to the depiction of animals. "I try to heighten my feeling for the organic rhythm of all things," Marc wrote, "to feel myself pantheistically into the trembling and flow of the blood of nature." More than any other German painter, Marc understood the sensuality of Matisse's line and employed it in his work. His use of color, which echoes, of course, the name of the movement to which he belonged, is liberated from the world of appearance, but it is highly emotional. He painted horses over and over again (Fig. 674). Sometimes they were blue—Marc associated blue with masculinity, strength, and purity—sometimes red, sometimes yellow, depending on his emotions as he was painting. Marc never fulfilled his promise as a painter. He was killed fighting on the Western front in 1916.

Arnold Schoenberg develops 12-tone music
1921

Adolf Hitler, *Mein Kampf*
1925

1920

1922
Mussolini assumes power in Italy

1925
Formulation of quantum mechanics

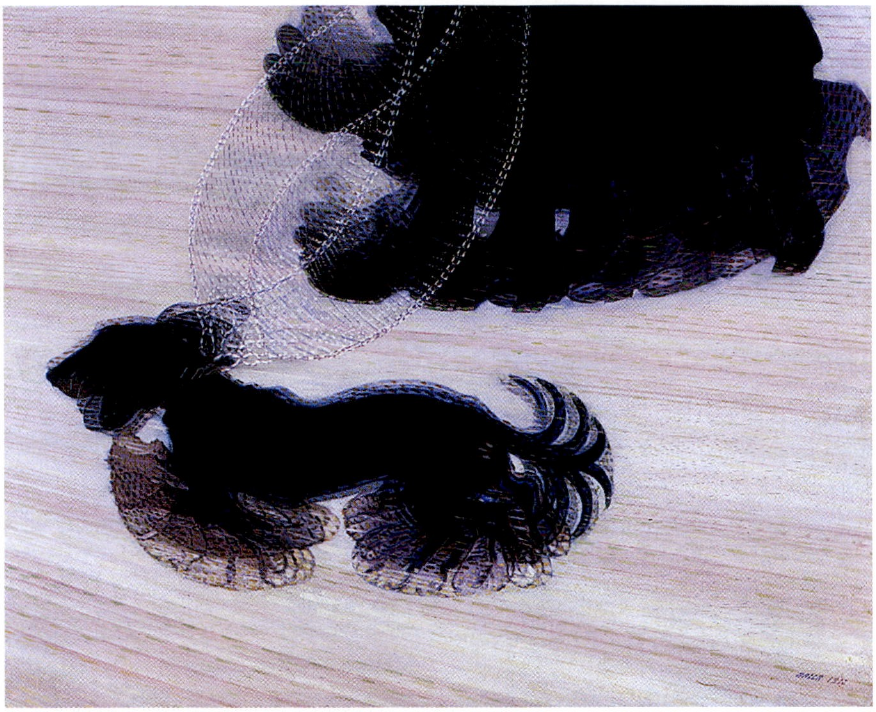

Fig. 675 Giacomo Balla, *Dynamism of a Dog on a Leash,* 1912.
Oil on canvas, 35 3/8 × 43 1/2 in.
Albright-Knox Art Gallery, Buffalo, NY. Bequest of A. Conger Goodyear and Gift of George F. Goodyear, 1964.

FUTURISM

If abstraction was the hallmark of the new century, certain thematic concerns defined it as well. The world had become, quite literally, a new place. In the summer of 1900, with the opening of the World's Fair, Paris found itself electrified, its nights almost transformed to day. The automobile, a rarity before the new century, dominated the city's streets by 1906. People were flying airplanes. Albert Einstein proposed a new theory of relativity and Neils Bohr a new model for the atom. It seemed to many that there could be no tradition, at least not one worth imitating, in the face of so much change.

In February 1909, an Italian poet named Filippo Marinetti published in the French newspaper *Le Figaro* a manifesto announcing a new movement in modern art, **Futurism.** Marinetti called for an art that would champion "aggressive action, a feverish insomnia, the racer's stride . . . the punch and the slap." He had discovered, he wrote "a new beauty; the beauty of speed. A racing car whose hood is adorned with great pipes, like serpents of explosive breath . . . is more beautiful than the Victory of Samothrace." He promised to "destroy the museums, libraries, academies," and "sing of the multicolored, polyphonic tides of revolution in the modern capitals." There were, at the time, no Futurist painters. Marinetti had to leave Paris, go back to Italy, and recruit them. But as they exhibited their show of Futurist painting around Europe from 1912 until the outbreak of World War I in 1914, outraging as many as they pleased, these painters—Umberto Boccioni, Carlo Carrà, Luigi Russolo, Giacomo Balla, and Gino Severini—embodied the spirit of the machine and of rapid change that seemed to define the

Discovery of penicillin
1928

First Soviet 5-year plan
1928

1927
Charles Lindbergh flies nonstop from New York to Paris

1928
First television broadcast

1929
U. S. stock market crash; Great Depression begins

1930

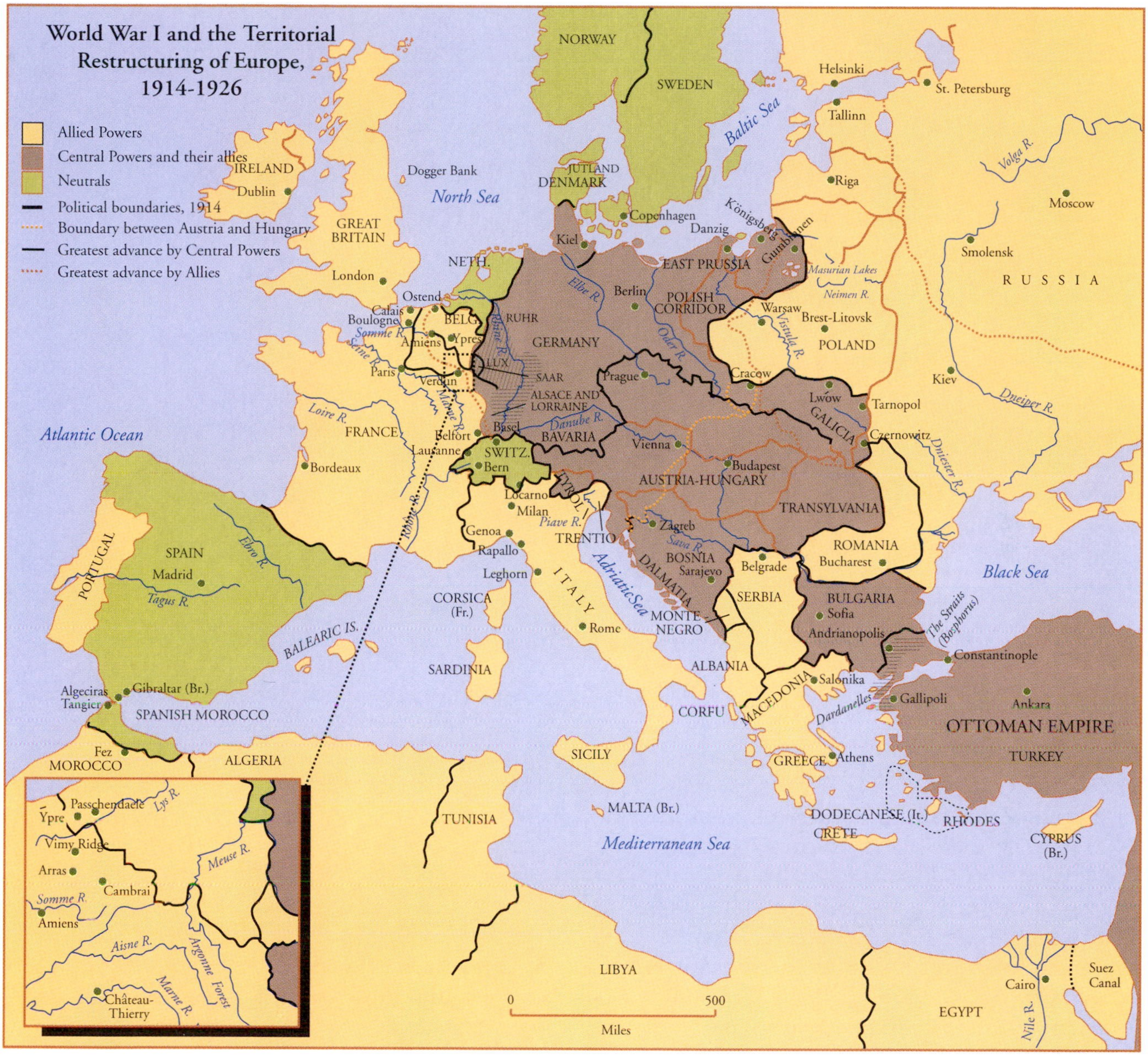

century itself. Balla's *Dynamism of a Dog on a Leash* (Fig. 675) captures the Futurist fascination with movement. It demonstrates, as well, its debt to new technological media—in particular, photography, as in Muybridge's and Marey's work (see Figs. 60 and 61), and the new art of film.

But World War I more than dampened this exuberance. The war was catastrophic. As many as 10 million men were killed and 20 million wounded, most in grueling trench warfare on the Western front, a battleline which remained virtually stationary for three years and ran from Oostend on the Dutch coast, past Rheims and Verdun, to Lunéville in France. World War I represented to many the bankruptcy of Western thought, and it served notice that all that had come before needed to be swept away.

Amelia Earhart first woman to fly across the Atlantic alone
1932

Hitler comes to power in Germany
1933

1930

1932
30 million unemployed in U. S. and Europe

1932–33
Mass famine in the U. S. S. R.

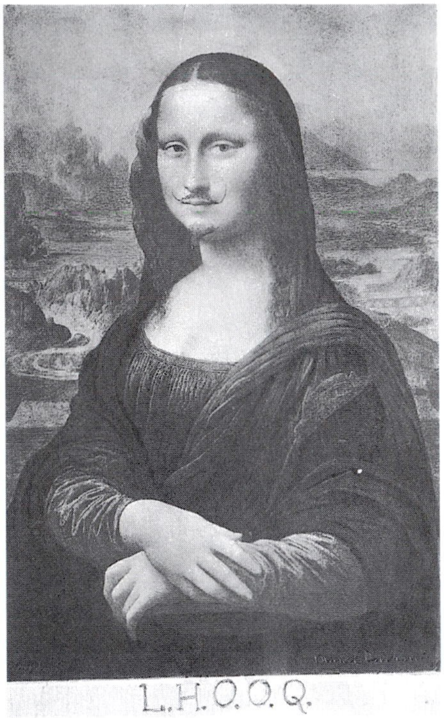

Fig. 676 Marcel Duchamp, *L.H.O.O.Q.*, 1919.
Rectified Readymade (reproduction of Leonardo da Vinci's Mona Lisa altered with pencil), 7 3/4 × 4 1/8 in. Private collection, Paris.

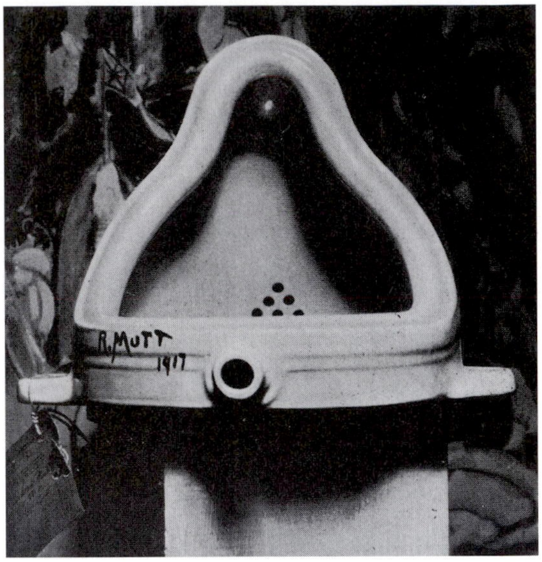

Fig. 677 Marcel Duchamp, *The Fountain*, 1917.
Photograph by Alfred Stieglitz in *The Blind Man*, no. 2 (May 1917); original lost.

DADA AND SURREALISM

Founded simultaneously in Zurich, Berlin, Paris, and New York during the war, **Dada** took up Futurism's call for the annihilation of tradition but, as a result of the war, without its sense of hope for the future. It was thus a *nihilist* art form. Its name referred, some said, to a child's first words; others claimed it was a reference to a child's hobbyhorse; and still others celebrated it as a simple guttural nonsense sound. As a movement, it championed senselessness, noise, and illogic. Dada was, above all, against art, at least art in the traditional sense of the word. Its chief strategy was insult and outrage. Perhaps Dada's chief exponent, Marcel Duchamp, always challenged tradition in a spirit of fun. His *L. H. O. O. Q.* (Fig. 676) is an image of Leonardo's *Mona Lisa* with a moustache drawn on her upper lip. Saying the letters of the title with French pronunciation reveals it to be a pun, *elle a chaud au cul,* roughly translated as "she's hot in the pants." Such is the irreverence of Dada.

In New York, Duchamp submitted a common urinal to the Independents Exhibition in 1917, titled it *Fountain,* signed it R. Mutt, and claimed for it the status of sculpture (Fig. 677). At first it was rejected, but when Duchamp let it be known that he and R. Mutt were one and the same, it was accepted. Thus, whether something was art depended on who made it—or found it, in this case. It also depended on where it was seen—in the museum it was one thing, in the plumbing store, quite another. Furthermore, on its pedestal, in the context of the museum, Duchamp's "fountain" looked to some as if it were indeed sculpture. Duchamp did not so much invalidate art as authorize the art world to consider all manner of things in aesthetic terms. His logic was not without precedent. Cubist collage had brought "real things" like newspaper clippings into the space of painting, and photography, especially, often revealed aesthetic beauty in common experience. But Duchamp's move, like Dada generally, was particularly

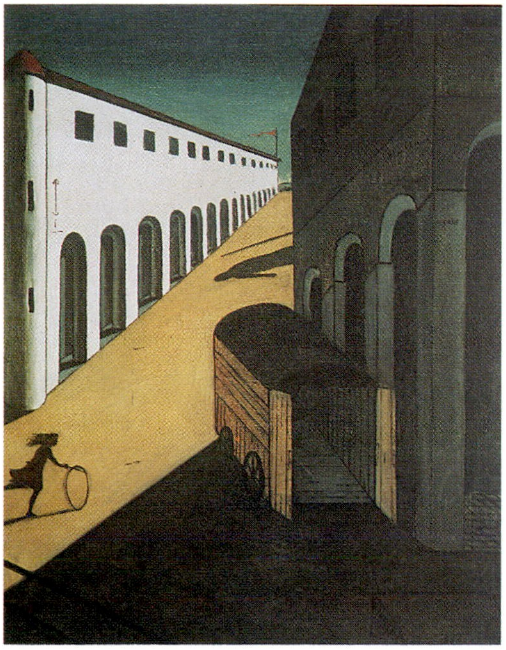

Fig. 678 Giorgio de Chirico, *Melancholy and Mystery of a Street,* 1914.
Oil on canvas, 24 1/4 × 28 1/2 in. Private collection.

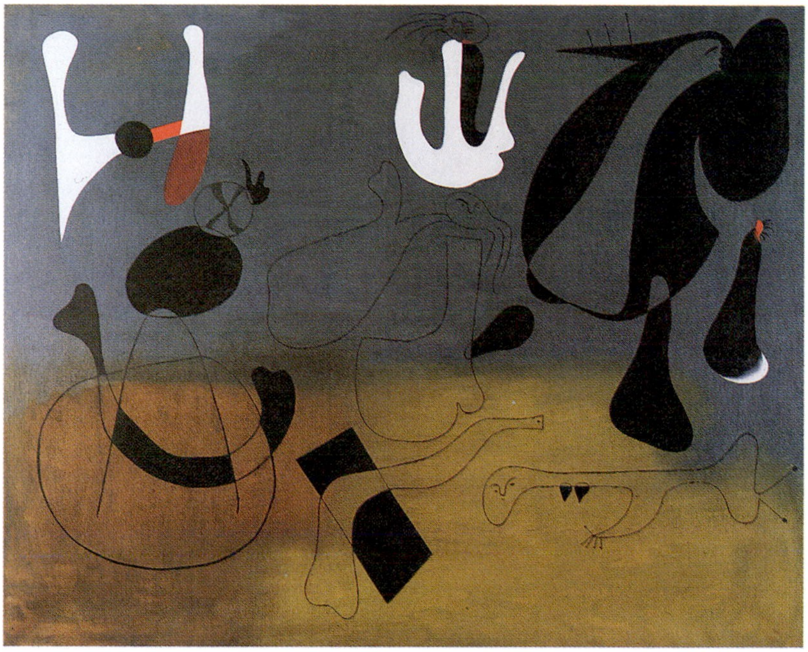

Fig. 679 Joan Miró, *Painting,* 1933.
Oil on canvas, 51 3/8 × 64 1/8 in.
Wadsworth Atheneum, Hartford. The Ella Gallup Sumner and Mary Catlin Sumner Collection.

challenging and provocative. "I was interested," he explained, "in ideas—not merely in visual products."

The art of **Surrealism** was born of Dada's preoccupation with the irrational and the illogical, as well as its interest in ideas. When the French writer André Breton issued the First Surrealist Manifesto in 1924, it was clear that the nihilist spirit of Dada was about to be replaced by something more positive. Breton explained the direction his movement would take: "I believe in the future resolution of these two states, dream and reality, which are seemingly so contradictory, into a kind of absolute reality, a surreality." To these ends, the new art would rely on chance operations, automatism (or random, thoughtless, and unmotivated notation of any kind), and dream images—the expressions of the unconscious mind. Two different sorts of imagery result. The first contained recognizable if fantastic subject matter. It was typified by the work of Salvador Dali and René Magritte (see Figs. 42 and 315), and Giorgio de Chirico, who was acknowledged as an important precursor to the Surrealist movement by the Surrealists themselves. De Chirico claimed not to understand his own paintings. They were simply images that obsessed him, and they conveyed, Breton felt, the "irremediable anxiety" of the day. Thus, in *Melancholy and Mystery of a Street* (Fig. 678), the little girl rolls her hoop toward the ominous black shadow of a figure lurking behind the wall.

The other type of surrealist painting was virtually abstract, presenting us with a world of undecipherable visual riddles. The painting of the Spanish artist Joan Miró and many of the early mobiles of Alexander Calder (see Fig. 81) fall into this category. In Miró's *Painting* (Fig. 679), biomorphic, amoebalike forms float in a space that suggests a darkened landscape. If we look closely, however, faces, hair, and hands begin to appear. Everything in this composition appears fluid, susceptible to continuing and ongoing mutation, back and forth between representation and abstraction.

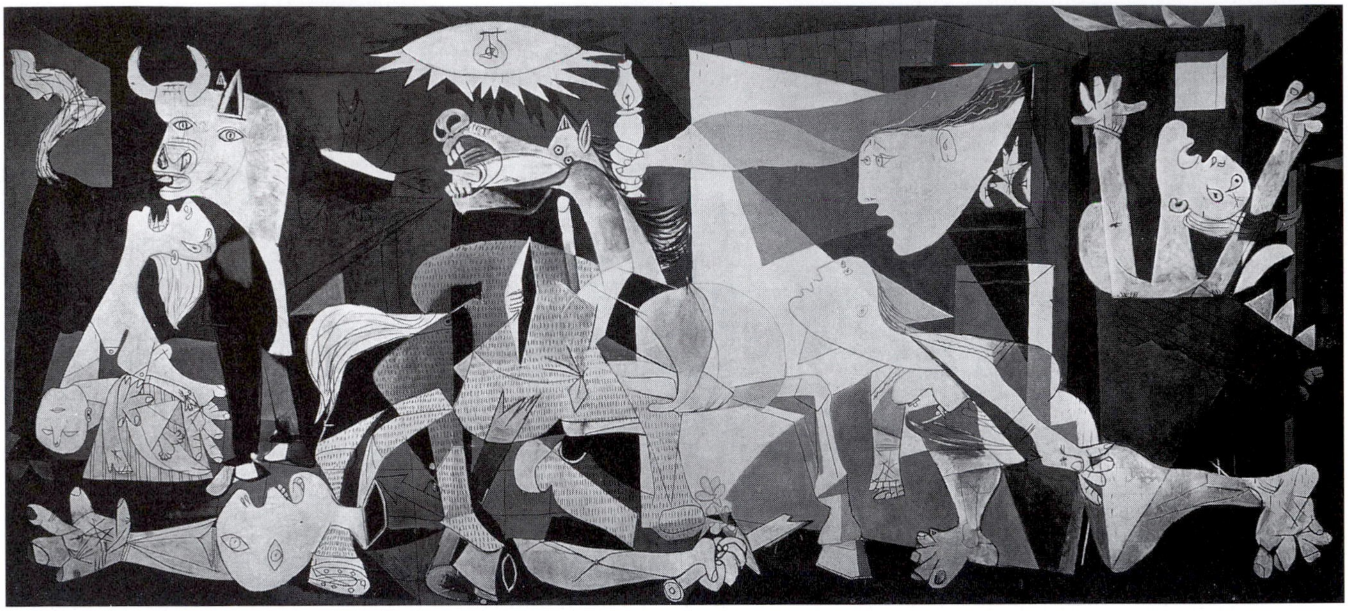

Fig. 680 Pablo Picasso, *Guernica*, 1937.
Oil on canvas, 11 ft. 5 1/2 in. × 25 ft. 5 1/4 in. Centro de Arte Reina Sofia, Madrid. ©ARS, N.Y. Giraudon/Art Resource, New York.

One of the greatest paintings of the Surrealist era is Pablo Picasso's *Guernica* (Fig. 680). It represents an event in the Spanish Civil War that occurred on April 26, 1937. That day, Republican Basque troops, who were fighting the Fascist forces of General Francisco Franco, were retreating toward Bilbao on the nothern Spanish coast. A bridge over the Mandaca River, at the edge of a town of seven thousand people called Guernica, was the last escape route for vehicles in the area, and the German air force, which had come to the aid of Franco, was determined to destroy it. The attack was planned by Wolfram von Richthofen, the cousin of the almost mythical German ace of World War I, Manfred von Richthofen, the Red Baron, and a man eager to create his own legend. The strike force consisted of three squadrons—a total of 33 planes. Each was loaded with 3,000 pounds of bombs, as well as several hundred small incendiary cylinders. The attack, a type of sudden coordinated strike that would soon come to be known as a *blitzkrieg,* commenced at 4:30 in the afternoon and lasted continously for three and a quarter hours. The first bombs were dropped near the railroad station—the bridge was ignored—and from that point on, the planes released their bombs indiscrimanently into the smoke and dust raised by the first explosions. By the time the fires subsided three days later, the entire central part of the town—fifteen square blocks—was totally destroyed. Nearly one thousand people had been killed.

Picasso, who was sympathetic with the Republican side and who considered himself exiled in Paris, was outraged at the events. Many elements of the painting refer to surrealist dream symbolism. The horse, at the center left, speared and dying in anguish, represents the fate of the dreamer's creativity. The entire scene is surveyed by a bull, which represents at once Spain itself, the simultaneous heroism and tragedy of the bullfight, and the Minotaur (see Fig. 562), the bull-man who for the Surrealists stood for the irrational forces of the human psyche. The significance of the electric lightbulb, at the top center of the painting, and the oil lamp, held by the woman reaching out the window, has been much debated, but they represent, at least, old and new ways of seeing.

WORKS IN PROGRESS
Pablo Picasso's Guernica

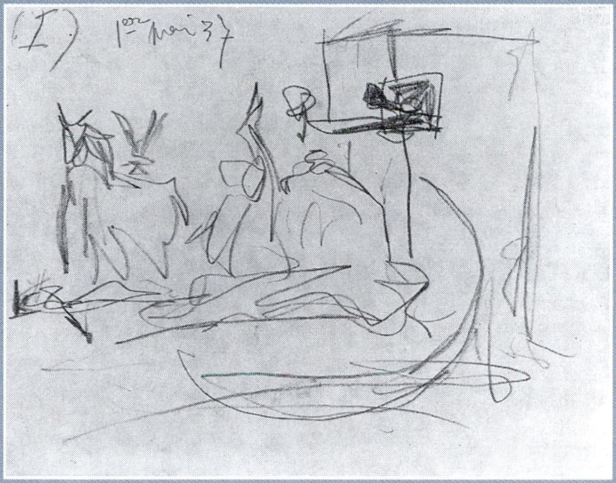

Fig. 681 Pablo Picasso, Sketch I, *Composition Study,* 1 May 1937.
Pencil, 8 ¼ × 10 ⅝ in. Casón del Buen Retiro, Museo del Prado, Madrid.

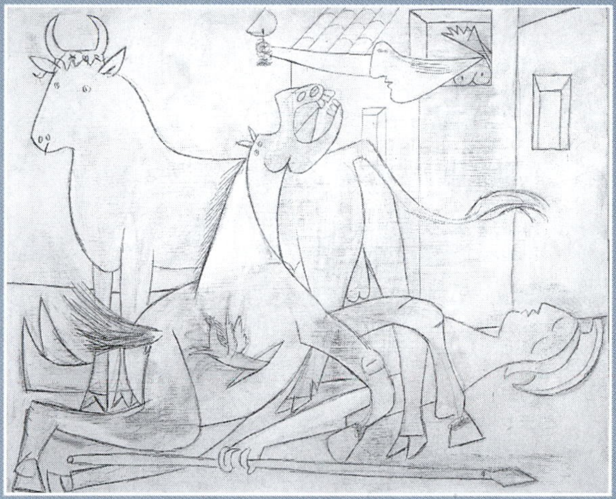

Fig. 682 Pablo Picasso, Sketch 6, *Composition Study,* 1 May 1937.
Pencil, 21 ⅛ × 25 ½ in. Casón del Buen Retiro, Museo del Prado, Madrid.

In January 1937, nearly four months before the bombing of Guernica, Picasso had been approached by representatives of the freely elected Republican government of Spain, who hoped that he might contribute a large mural for the entrance hall of a Spanish pavilion at the 1937 World's Fair in Paris. On May 1, as Paris papers headlined the tragedy that had occurred four days before, Picasso took pencil to paper, executing six sketches for the 25½-foot painting. Time was short. The pavilion was scheduled to open on May 28. Picasso would finish the painting on June 4.

The first sketch (Fig. 681) outlines the idea in the most cursory fashion. The bull is present, and so is the woman reaching out of the house, oil lamp in hand. Rising in the middle is the shape that will become the twisted neck and head of the horse. By the end of the day, the composition's themes have begun to be worked out (Fig. 682). Out of the wound in the horse's side, the animal's spirit seems to take wing. A slain soldier lies beneath it, and the bull watches over the scene. Here, the theme of the bullfight is introduced—the victorious bull, the slain picador (the chief antagonist of the bull who, on horseback, torments him with a lance), and the fallen horse are equated to the war in Spain. But the bull's victory is temporary. In the bullfight, the bull's death is inevitable, just as death is inevitable for us all.

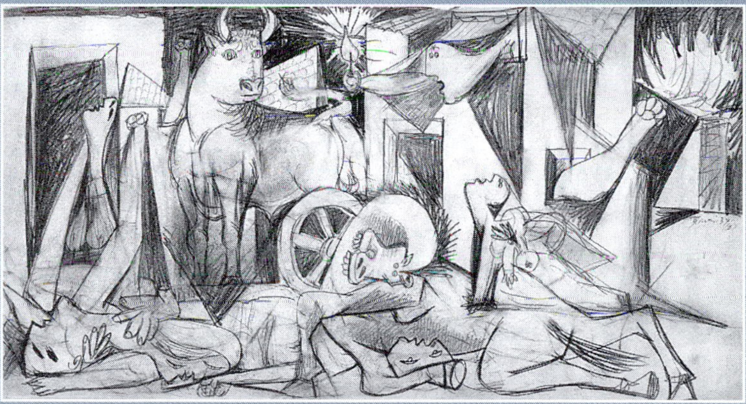

Fig. 683 Pablo Picasso, Sketch 15, *Composition Study,* 9 May 1937.
Pencil, 9 ½ × 17 ⅞ in. Casón del Buen Retiro, Museo del Prado, Madrid.

Within a week, Picasso had essentially arrived at the final composition. In a sketch of May 9 (Fig. 683), the idea of mass human suffering is finally introduced. The dead lying across the ground, the woman lifting her dead child in a scream of terror, the dramatic contrast between light and dark, all point to the final composition, which Picasso would arrive at four days later, on May 13.

1940

U. S. enters World War II
1941

Enrico Fermi splits the atom
1942

1940
Germans invade France

1941–45
The Holocaust

1944
Allied invasion of Europe, led by U. S. forces

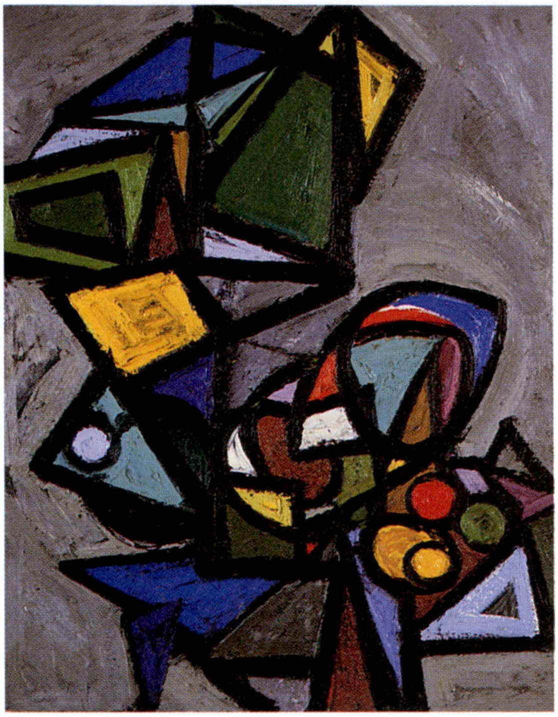

Fig. 684 Lee Krasner, *Untitled*, c. 1940.
Oil on canvas, 30 × 25 in.

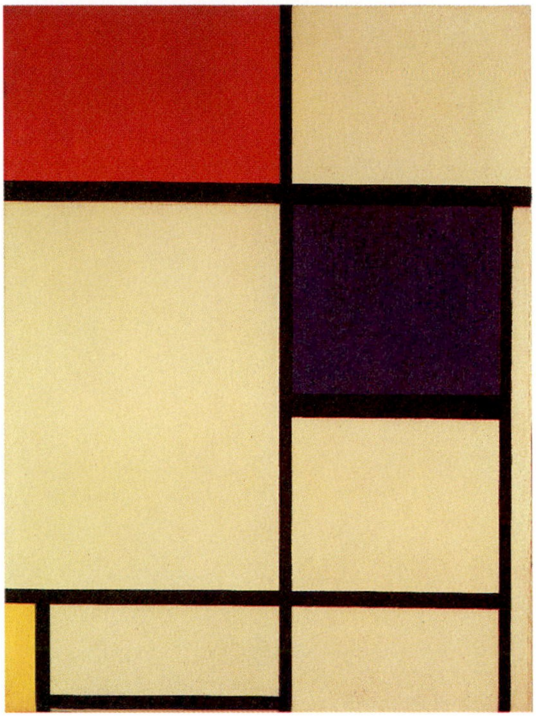

Fig. 685 Piet Mondrian, *Composition (Blue, Red, and Yellow)*, 1930.
Oil on canvas, 28 ½ × 21 ¼ in.
Courtesy Sidney Janis Gallery, New York.

AMERICAN MODERNISM AND ABSTRACT EXPRESSIONISM

With the outbreak of World War II, Picasso decided that *Guernica* should stay in the United States. He arranged for it to be kept at the Museum of Modern Art in New York, where it was to be held until the death of Franco and the reestablishment of public liberty in Spain. Franco, however, did not die until 1975, two years after Picasso himself. The painting was returned to Spain, finally, in 1981. It hangs today in a special annex of the Prado Museum in Madrid.

The painting profoundly affected American artists. "Picasso's *Guernica* floored me," Lee Krasner reported. "When I saw it first . . . I rushed out, walked about the block three times before coming back to look at it. And then I used to go to the Modern every day to see it." Krasner's own *Untitled* painting (Fig. 684) done soon after *Guernica's* arrival in New York in 1939, reflects its angular forms and turbulent energy. But it differs in important ways from *Guernica*. It is totally abstract, and where *Guernica* is a monochrome gray-brown, like burnt newsprint, Krasner's painting is vibrant with color. Probably more than any other artist of her day, Krasner understood how to integrate the competing aesthetic directions of European abstraction, fusing the geometric and expressionist tendencies of modern art in a single composition.

Like Krasner, and somewhat earlier, the Dutch painter Piet Mondrian, who had himself emigrated to New York in 1940, purged from his work all reference to the world (see Figs. 223–227). In paintings such as *Composition (Blue, Red, and Yellow)* (Fig. 685), he relied only upon horizontal and vertical lines, the three primary colors, and black and white,

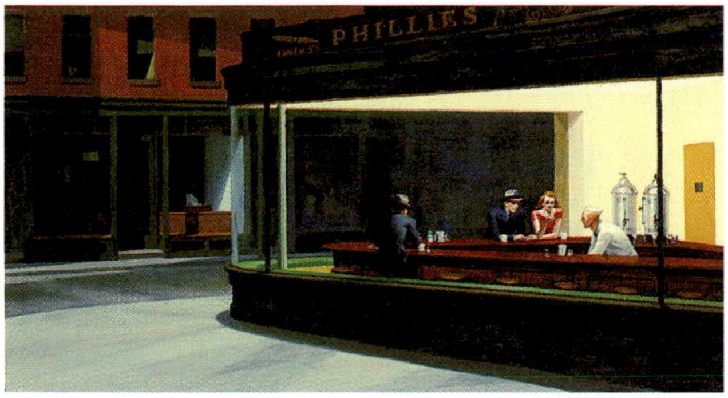

Fig. 686 Edward Hopper, *Nighthawks,* 1942.
Oil on canvas, 30 × 60 in. Friends of American Art Collection,

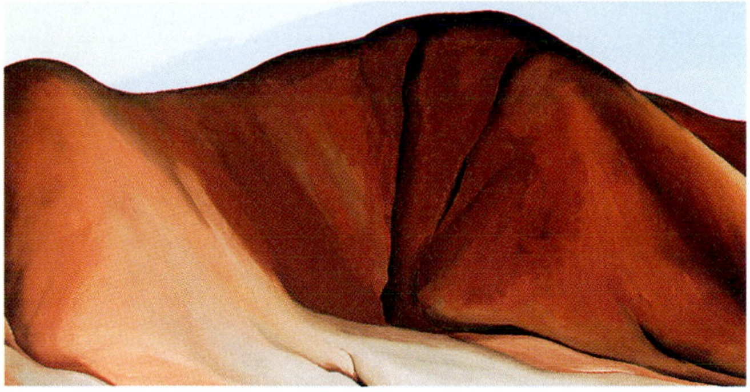

Fig. 687 Georgia O'Keeffe, *Purple Hills Near Abiquiu,* 1935.
Oil on canvas, 16 1/8 × 30 1/8 in.
San Diego Museum of Art. Gift of Mr. and Mrs. Norton S. Walbridge.

which were, he felt, "the expression of pure reality." Like the Russian Suprematists before him (see Fig. 23), who had sought to create a new art to match the spirit of the Russian Revolution, Mondrian's aims were, essentially, ethical—he wanted to purify art in order to purify the spirit. Krasner complicates, as it were, Mondrian's art, opening it to the color of the German Expressionists, and to the sometimes terrifying whirl of modern life that Picasso had captured in his art.

Until 1940, abstraction such as Krasner's was not very well accepted in the United States. To be sure, American **Modernism** had been responsive to trends in European painting since the early years of the century, but instead of pushing toward abstraction, as had happened in Europe, American modernists tended to utilize European painting's formal innovations in more realist painting. Many artists preferred a realist approach, which was supported, on the one hand, by the growing popularity of photography, and, on the other, by an increasing conviction that art, in the face of the harsh realities of the Great Depression of the 1930s, should deal with the problems of daily life. Still, they were willing to learn from the formal discoveries of their more abstraction-oriented contemporaries, and we are often as attracted to the form of their work as to their subject matter. In a painting like *Nighthawks* (Fig. 686), Edward Hopper depicts the emotional isolation of the average American. But the composition is powerfully supported by the visual simplicity of his design, a geometry inspired by the example of Mondrian. It is as if his figures are isolated from one another in the vast horizontal expanse of the canvas. In her *Purple Hills near Abiquiu* (Fig. 687), Georgia O'Keeffe utilizes the sensuous line of the German Expressionist painter Franz Marc (see Fig. 674) to create a landscape that almost seems to be alive, a body capable of moving and breathing like one of Marc's animals.

The Great Depression and the outbreak of World War II, nevertheless, provided the impetus for the development of abstract painting in the United States. President Roosevelt's WPA (Works Progress Administration) had initiated, in 1935, a Federal Art Project that supported artists financially and thus allowed them to work as they pleased. Furthermore, many leading European artists emigrated to the United States to escape ever-worsening conditions in Europe. Suddenly, in New York, American painters could not only see Picasso's *Guernica* but found themselves in the company of Fernand Léger, Piet Mondrian, Yves Tanguy, Marcel Duchamp, and André Breton. A style of painting referred to as **Abstract Expressionism** soon developed. It harked back to Kandinsky's nonobjective work of 1910–1920, but it was

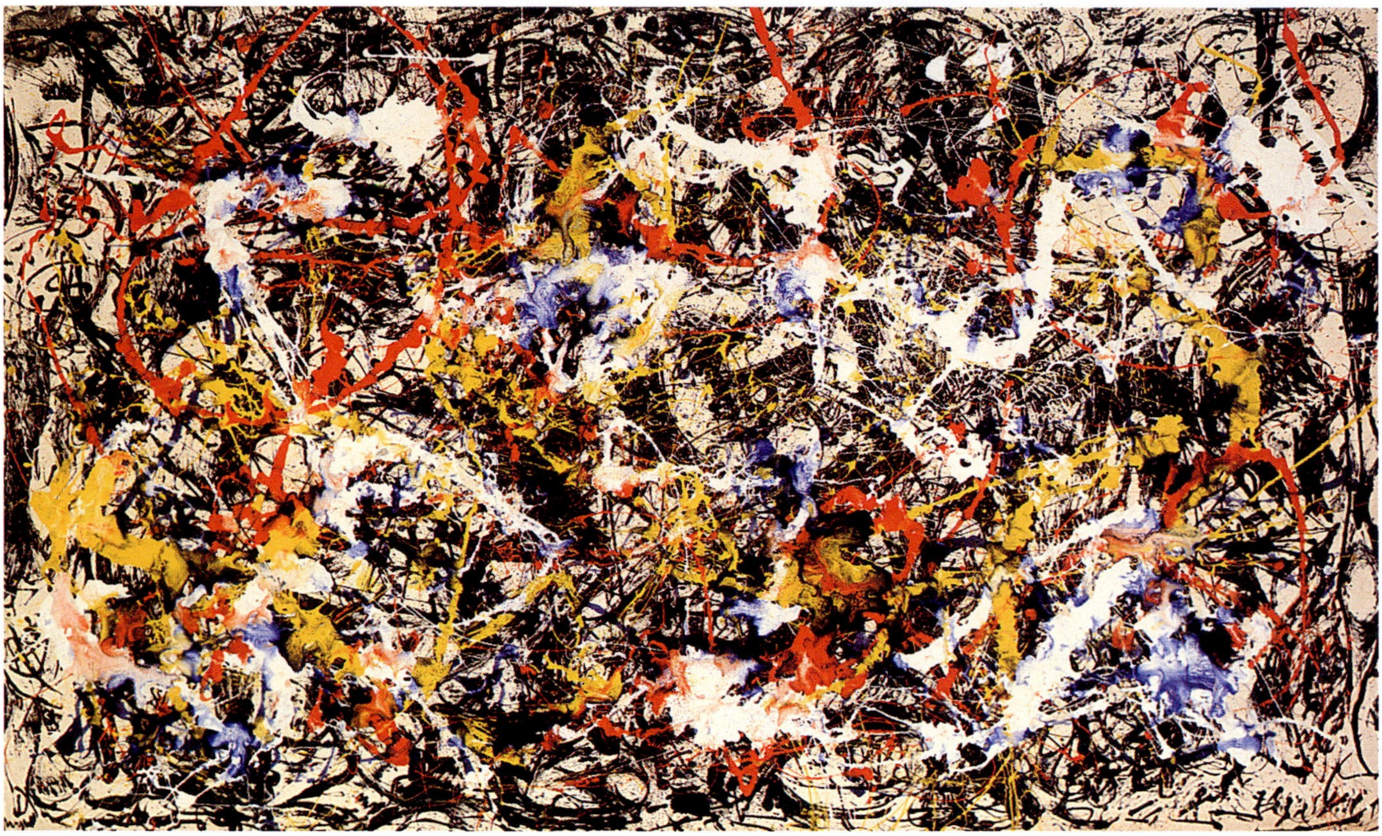

Fig. 688 Jackson Pollock, *Convergence*, 1952.
Oil on canvas, 93 ½ × 155 in.
Albright-Knox Art Gallery, Buffalo, New York. Gift of Seymour H. Knox, 1956.

not unified in its stylistic approach. Rather, the term grouped together a number of painters dedicated to the expressive capacities of their own individual gestures and styles.

Jackson Pollock was deeply influenced by the Surrealist notion of *automatism*, the direct and unmediated expression of the self. Pouring and flinging paint onto canvas, usually on the floor, he created large "all-over"—completely covered, large-scale—surfaces with no place for the eye to rest (see Figs. 184 and 186). In reproduction it is difficult to feel the way in which a painting like *Convergence* (Fig. 688) absorbs the viewer, drawing the eye into its web of line and color. The space, created by swirling lines of paint that pass over each other again and again, has aptly been labeled "galactic," and almost seems to mimic the energy released by an exploding nebula.

Because of the energy and movement of such paintings, the Abstract Expressionism of Pollock has been labeled "Action Painting." Willem de Kooning's work, with its visible application of paint to the surface, is the definitive example of this approach. Though his paintings of women, including *Woman and Bicycle* (Fig. 689), are often seen as an attack upon women, de Kooning's hashed-out, scribbled-over, loosely gestural painting is equally a celebration of his own freedom from the conventions of figural representation. "I do not think . . . of art," he explained, "as a situation

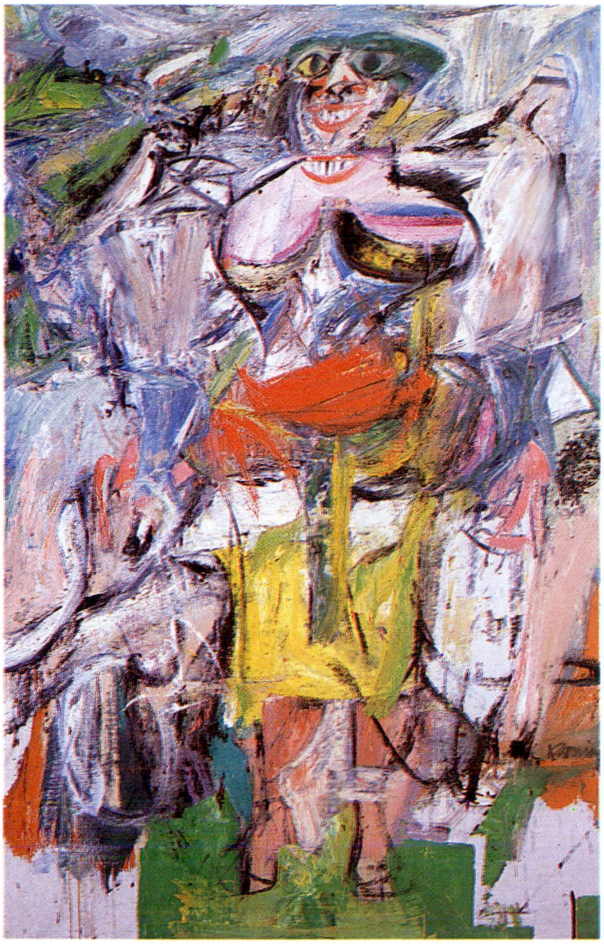

Fig. 689 Willem de Kooning, *Woman and Bicycle,* 1952–1953.
Oil on canvas, 76 1/2 × 49 in.
Collection of Whitney Museum of American Art, New York. Purchase, 55.35.

Fig. 690 Mark Rothko, *Four Darks in Red,* 1958.
Oil on canvas, 102 × 116 in.
Collection of Whitney Museum of American Art, New York.
Purchase, with funds from the Friends of the Whitney Museum of American Art, Mr. and Mrs. Eugene M. Schwartz, Mrs. Samuel A. Seaver, and Charles Simon, 68.9.

of comfort." What de Kooning liked most in Mondrian's work, for instance, was the instability, the vibration that occurs where black lines cross (see Fig. 227). This shimmer, he said, made him feel like he was about to fall out of the painting.

The monumental quietness of Mark Rothko's canvases (Fig. 690) conveys almost the opposite feeling. To call this "action painting" would be a misnomer. The painting produces a meditative, not active, space. In place of action, we find a carefully modulated field of color that suggests the luminous space and light of Monet's *Haystacks,* only without the realistic image. However, because Rothko emphasizes the horizontal band and the horizon line, his paintings often suggest the point where land meets sky. The bands of color bleed mysteriously into one another or into the background, at once insisting on the space they occupy by the richness of their color and dissolving at the edges like mist. "I am interested only in expressing the basic human emotions—tragedy, ecstasy, doom, and so on," Rothko would explain, "and the fact that lots of people break down and cry when confronted with my pictures shows that I communicate with those basic human emotions. The people who weep before my pictures are having the same religious experience I had when I painted them."

First manned space flight
1961

Cuban missile crisis
1962

The Beatles, *I Want to Hold Your Hand*
1963

Major increase in U. S. commitment to Vietnam War
1965

1960

1961
Berlin Wall erected

1963
President John F. Kennedy assassinated

1964
Passage of U. S. Civil Rights Act

POP ART AND MINIMALISM

By the middle of the 1950s, as Abstract Expressionism established itself as the most important style of the day, a number of young painters began to react against it. Robert Rauschenberg parodied the high seriousness of the Action Painters by using its gestures—supposed markers of the artist's sincerity—to paint over literal junk. Like the Cubists before him, he cut out materials from newspapers and magazines and silkscreened media images into his prints (see Fig. 293). Rauschenberg went further, however, incorporating stuffed animals, tires (see Fig. 385), even his own bedding when he was short of canvas, into the space of art. In *Bed* (Fig. 691), Rauschenberg literally splashes paint over the "dream fabric." The formal vocabulary of both Abstract Expressionism and Surrealism is present here, but without the high seriousness of either.

In the 1960s, inspired by Rauschenberg's example, a group of even younger artists, led by Andy Warhol, Claes Oldenburg, and Roy Lichtenstein, invented a new American realism, **Pop Art.** Pop represented life as America lived it, a world of Campbell's soup cans, Coca-Cola bottles, and comic strips. Based on an actual Sunday cartoon strip, Lichtenstein's giant painting *Whaam!* (Fig. 692) indicates, by its very size, the powerful role of popular culture in our emotional lives. This is an image of power, one that most American boys of the 1950s were raised to believe in wholly. One of the chief tactics of the Pop artists, in fact, was to transform the everyday into the monumental, as Oldenburg turned a clothespin or a garden trowel into giant sculptural objects (see Figs. 212 and 298). Most important perhaps, Pop Art left behind traditional artistic media like painting. Artists turned instead to slick renderings made by mechanical reproduction techniques, such as photolithography, that evoked commercial illustration more than fine art.

Another reaction against Action Painting led, in the same period, to a style of art known as **Minimalism.** In contrast to Pop works,

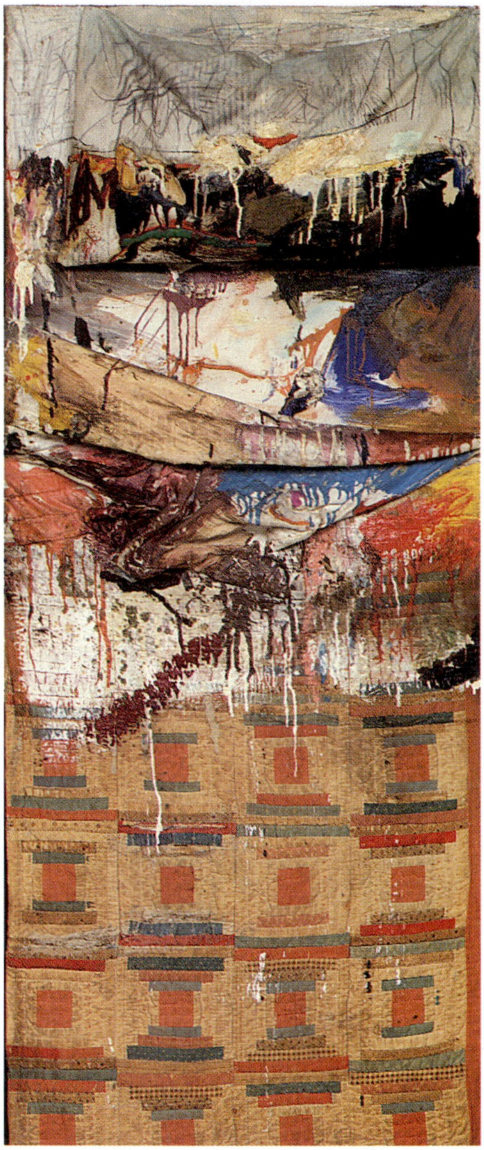

Fig. 691 Robert Rauschenberg, *Bed,* 1955.
Combine-painting: oil and pencil on pillow, quilt, and sheet on wood supports, 6 ft 3 1/4 × 31 1/2 × 8 in. Fractional gift of Leo Castelli in honor of Alfred H. Barr, Jr., to The Museum of Modern Art, New York.

Minimalist pieces were, in their way, elegant. They addressed notions of space—how objects take up space and how the viewer relates to them spatially—as well as questions of their dogmatic material presence. For Frank Stella, the shape of the painting determined its content,

First manned moon landing
1969

1970

1965–69
Cultural Revolution in China

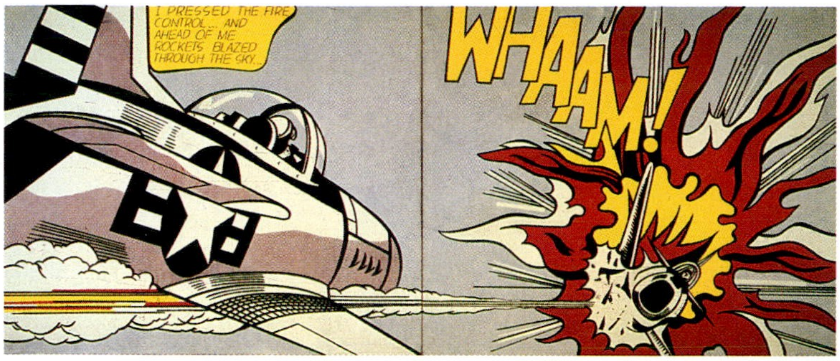

Fig. 692 Roy Lichtenstein, ***Whaam!*** **1963.**
Magna on two canvas panels, 5 ft. 8 in. × 13 ft 4 in.
Tate Gallery, London.

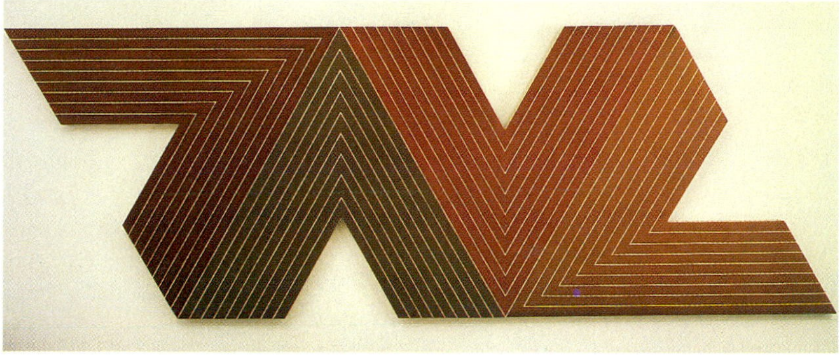

Fig. 693 Frank Stella, ***Empress of India,*** **1965.**
Metallic powder in polymer emulsion on shaped canvas, 6 ft. 5 in. × 18 ft. 8 in.
Collection, The Museum of Modern Art, New York.
Gift of S. I. Newhouse.

which might consist of a series of parallel lines that could have been drawn with a compass or protractor. "I always get into arguments with people who want to retain the old values in painting," Stella muses. "My painting is based on the fact that only what can be seen is there. It is really an object. . . . All I want anyone to get out of my paintings, and all I ever get out of them is the fact that you can see the whole idea without confusion. What you see is what you see." Thus, despite its title, *Empress of India* (Fig. 693) is contentless painting. It has no spiritual aspirations. It does not contain the emotions of the painter. It is simply there, four interlocked V's, before the viewer, a fact in and of itself. Stella has deliberately set out to make a work of art that has no narrative to it, that cannot, at least not very easily, be written about.

POSTMODERN DIRECTIONS

From the time of Gauguin's retreat to the South Pacific and Picasso's fascination with African masks, Western artists have turned to non-Western cultures for inspiration, seeking "authentic" new ways to express their emotions in art. The African features of the two figures on the right of Picasso's *Les Demoiselles d'Avignon* (Fig. 49) are a prime example of this. At the same time, other cultures have been dramatically affected by Western traditions. Although we normally think of the Western world's impact on these other cultures in negative terms—in the process of Westernization, ancient customs are lost, at the same time that cultural artifacts are looted and carried off for display in Western museums—many non-Western artists have incorporated the art of the West into their own in positive ways. As Native American artist Jimmie Durham has put it: "We took glass beads, horses, wool blankets, wheat flour for fry-bread, etc., very early, and immediately made them identifiably 'Indian' things. We are able to do that because of our cultural integrity and because our societies are dynamic and able to take in new ideas." Similarly, the aboriginal painters of Australia have adopted the use of acrylic paint, integrating the

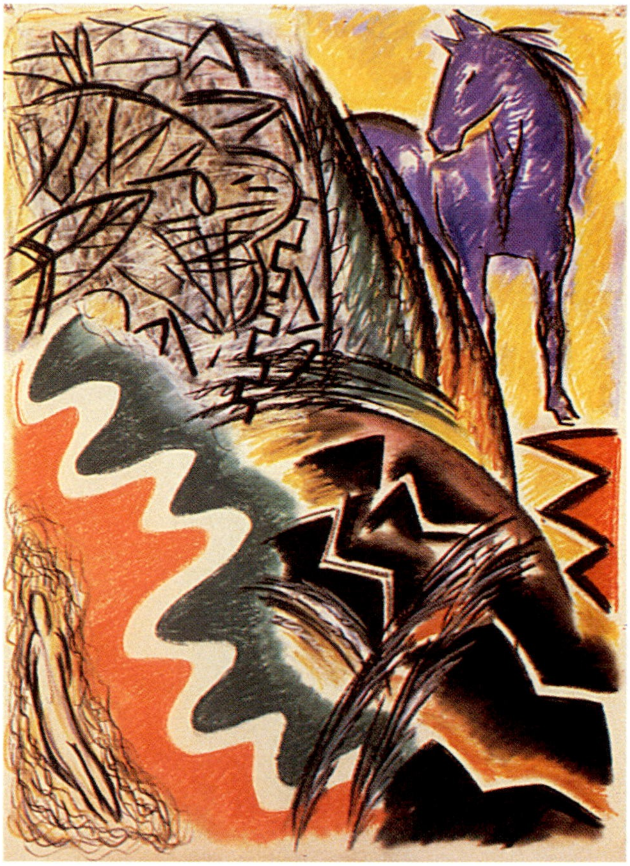

Fig. 694 Jaune Quick-to-See Smith, *Petroglyph Park,* 1986.
Pastel on paper, 30 × 22 in.
Courtesy Steinbaum Krauss Gallery, New York.

medium into their own cultural traditions (see Fig. 5). Native American painter Jaune Quick-to-See Smith, who studied at the University of New Mexico, puts it this way, "With a university training, you're exposed to classic art and traditions from around the world. You wouldn't be true to yourself if you didn't incorporate what you were familiar with." In her *Petroglyph Park* (Fig. 694), Quick-to-See Smith makes direct allusion to the Blue Rider of Kandinsky and Marc, drawing an analogy between the fate of the wild horse and the fate of the Native American. Everything in this painting refers to lost peoples—from the makers of the petroglyphs to Marc's early death in World War I—and the presence of those peoples in our memory. The simultaneous presence of diverse traditions in a single work is indicative of what we have come to call **Postmodernism.**

Since the mid-1970s, the world of art has become increasingly diverse and plural in character, and new voices have continually entered into the arena. One of the most important of these has been feminism. Since the early 1970s, when the feminist movement began to take hold in this country, women have played an increasingly important role in defining the issues and directions of contemporary art. One important consequence is that women have retrieved for art history figures previously relegated to the sidelines or ignored altogether. These include artists such as Artemisia Gentileschi (Fig. 138 and 301), Anna Valayer-Coster (Fig. 203), Elisabeth-Louise Vigée-Lebrun (Fig. 204 and 639), Angelica Kauffmann (Fig. 641), Elaine de Kooning (Fig. 292), Lee Krasner (Fig. 684), and, illustrated here, Frida Kahlo. Kahlo's *Las Dos Fridas (The Two Fridas)* (Fig. 695) has become almost an icon for the woman artist. Like Elaine de Kooning, married to Willem, and Lee Krasner, married to Jackson Pollock, Kahlo was married to a successful painter, the Mexican muralist Diego Rivera (see Fig. 309), and like both of these women, she sacrificed her own work and her reputation to further her husband's. Painted soon after their divorce in 1939, *The Two Fridas* represents Rivera's rejection of her. According to Kahlo, the Frida on the right, in native Tehuana costume, is the Frida whom Rivera had loved. The Frida on the left is the rejected Frida. A vein runs between them both, originating in a small photo of Rivera as a child on the once-loved Frida's lap, through both hearts, and terminating in the unloved Frida's lap, cut off by a pair of surgical scissors. But the flow of blood cannot be stopped and continues to drip, joining the embroidered flowers on her dress.

A work that contributed significantly to the resuscitation of women's place in the art world was Judy Chicago's *The Dinner Party* (Fig. 696). Chicago was trained as a painter, but she aban-

Death of Mao Tse-Tung
1976

Islamic fundamentalist revolution in Iran; U. S. hostages held
1979

1980

1975
South Vietnam falls to Vietcong

1979
Egypt–Israeli peace treaty

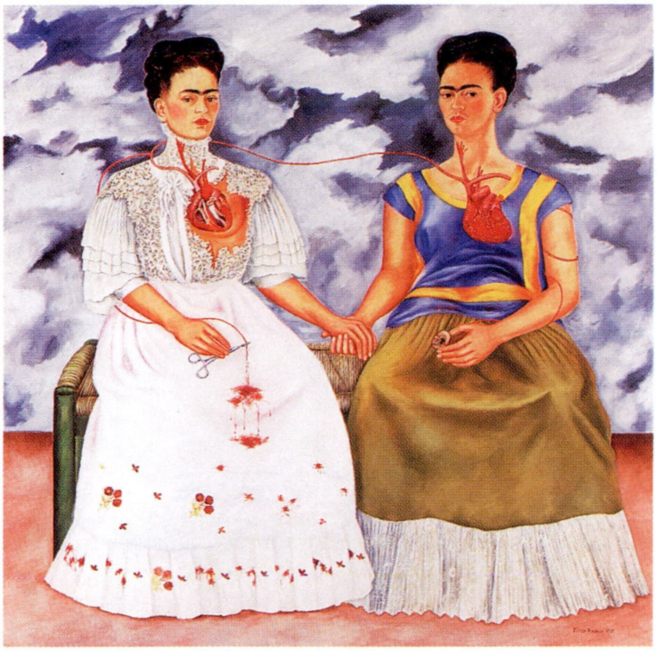

Fig. 695 Frida Kahlo, *Las Dos Fridas,* 1939.
Oil on canvas, 69 1/5 × 69 1/5 in.
Museo de Arte Moderno, Mexico, D.F. Photograph by Bob Schalkwijk/Art Resource.

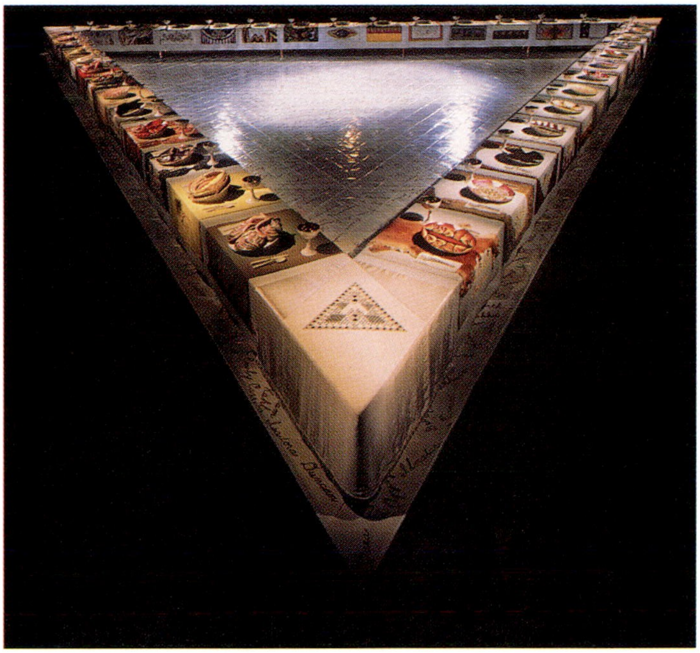

Fig. 696 Judy Chicago, *The Dinner Party,* 1979 (installed).
Mixed media. Triangle, 48 ft. each side.
Photograph © Donald Woodman/Through the Flower.

doned painting because, in the 1960s and '70s, it was a field dominated by men and by men's way of thinking. The art world at the time emphasized formal issues and devalued personal narrative of the kind evident in, for instance, Frida Kahlo's work. This led Chicago, and colleagues like Suzanne Lacy (see Fig. 74) and Miriam Schapiro (see Fig. 179) to explore new means of expression. Performance art was an immediate outgrowth of this attitude. So too was an interest in traditional craft media and collaborative art processes.

The Dinner Party was a collaborative project that involved over 300 woman artisans working together over a period of five years to create a visual celebration of women's history. The dinner table is 48 feet on each side and shaped as a triangle, the earliest symbol of female power—the sign of the goddess, and a reference to the female genitalia. It is set with 39 places, thirteen on a side, each celebrating a woman who has made an important contribution to world history. The names of 999 additional women, all of whom have made significant contributions to history in their own right, are inscribed in ceramic tiles along the table's base. Each place setting consists of a needleworked fabric runner and a ceramic plate in honor of the woman whom it celebrates. The first plate is dedictated to the Great Goddess, and the third to the Cretan Snake Goddess (see Fig. 561). Around the table, the likes of Eleanor of Aquitaine, English author Virginia Woolf, and painters Artemisia Gentileschi and Georgia O'Keeffe are celebrated.

An important aspect of feminist art has been its critique of traditional ways of seeing, ways of seeing prescribed and institutionalized by men. As we saw in Chapter 4, conventional representations of the male and female nude carry with them recognizably sexist implications—man as strong and rational, woman as

1980

1980s Beginnings of AIDS epidemic

1983 First CDs marketed

1984 Apple Macintosh computer first sold

1984 Mikhail Gorbachev introduces *glasnost* in U.S.S.R.

1984 Ozone hole above Antarctica discoverd

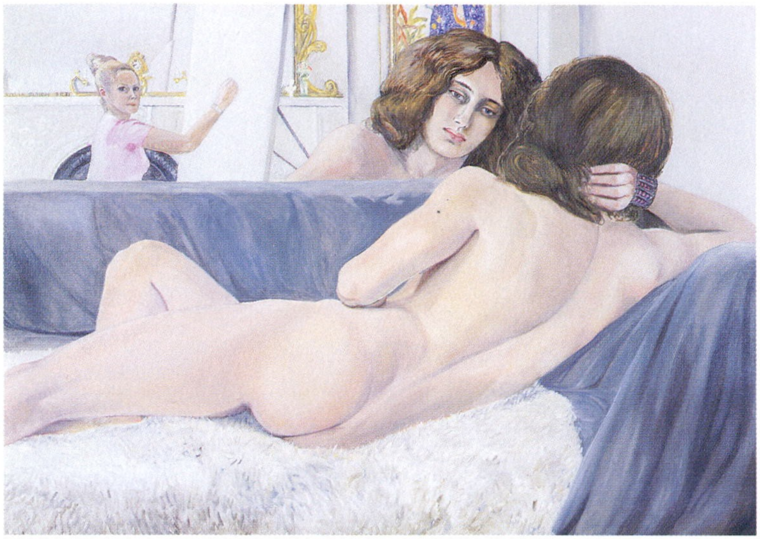

Fig. 697 Sylvia Sleigh, *Philip Golub Reclining,* 1971.
Oil on canvas, 42 × 60 in. Courtesy of the artist.

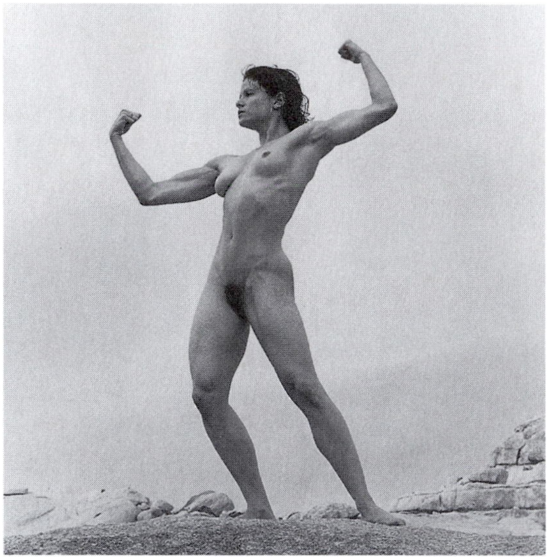

Fig. 699 Robert Mapplethorpe, *Lisa Lyon,* 1980.
© 1980 The Estate of Robert Mapplethorpe.

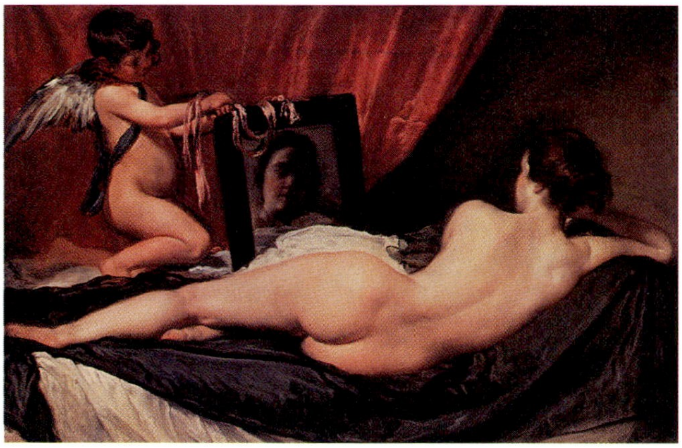

Fig. 698 Diego Velázquez, *Venus and Cupid* (known as the *Rokeby Venus*), c. 1651.
Oil on canvas, 48 1/4 × 69 3/4 in.
National Gallery, London.

weak and given to emotional outbursts. But in the hands of women artists these conventions have been reversed. Sylvia Sleigh's *Philip Golub Reclining* (Fig. 697) depicts a male model in a distinctly feminine pose, reminiscent of Velázquez's *Rokeby Venus* (Fig. 698). Sleigh's portrait is composed of sensual, curvilinear lines, in stark contrast to the forceful and upright representation of the painter herself, reflected in the mirror behind the sofa. Conversely, Robert Mapplethorpe's photograph of *Lisa Lyon* (Fig. 699) is a collaboration with his model, the First World Women's Bodybuilding champion. Lyon has self-consciously composed herself, especially her upper torso and arms, in an arrangement of right angles, as hard as the rocks on which she stands. Both artists reverse stereotypes in these works. Mapplethorpe subverts conventional representations of the female, and Lyon reveals the male position as a sort of posturing in its own right. Sleigh's reclining nude disconcertingly submits the male figure to a female gaze that has culturally always been the right of the male. The point of both works is a simple one: we recognize both

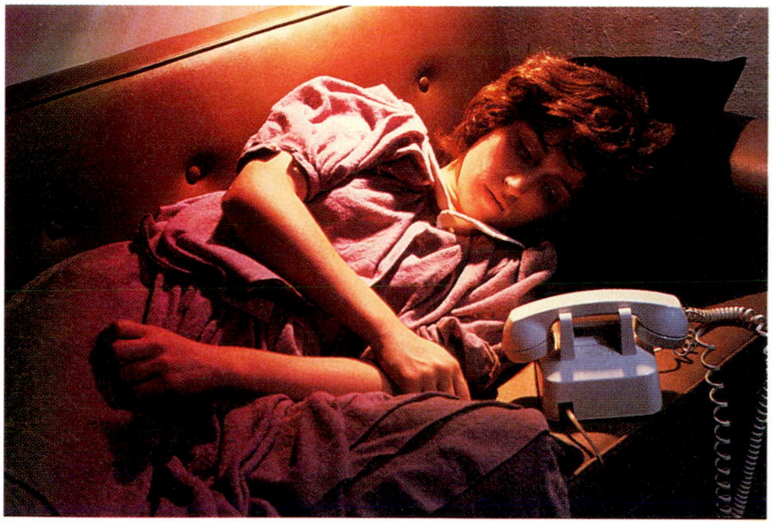

Fig. 700 Cindy Sherman, *Untitled #96,* 1981.
Color photograph, 24 × 48 in.
Courtesy Metro Pictures, New York.

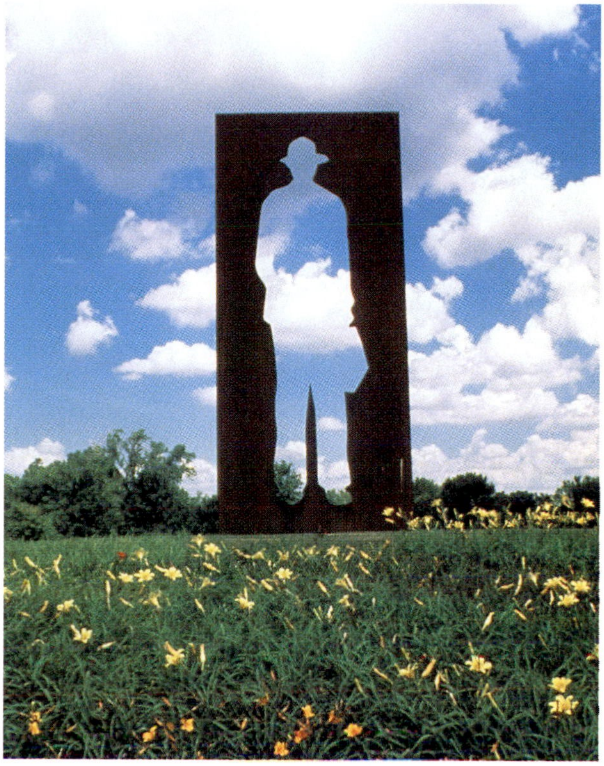

Fig. 701 Jonathan Borofsky, *Man with a Briefcase,* 1987.
Cor-Ten steel, 30′ × 13′6″ × 2″.
General Mills, Minneapolis, Minnesota.
Courtesy Paula Cooper Gallery, New York.

of these works as reversals of the norm because we approach representations of the male and female nude with culturally encoded expectations. These expectations encompass the kinds of line and form that can and should be used to depict the male and female bodies. The works challenge these expectations.

As our assumptions and expectations have become increasingly challenged, the art world has become increasingly unbound by any rules or by any ruling "isms." Artists can draw on personal experiences or stylistic trends and address their work to a wide audience or a relatively narrow one. But one overriding characteristic of contemporary art is its struggle with the question of identity. Cindy Sherman's untitled photographs, for instance, are self-portraits (Fig. 700), sometimes presented at the scale of the film still and other times at the scale of a large poster. They are actually performances that address issues such as voyeurism, vulnerability, and loneliness. In this case, we are witness to an unnamed adolescent reverie, at once ordinary and touching.

The implication is that Sherman's life, and by extension our own, is a series of performances, that, chameleonlike, we change identities as readily as we change our clothes, picking and choosing who we are from media images. Thus, Jonathan Borofsky's *Man with a Briefcase* (Fig. 701) is, on the one hand, a monument to the faceless mass of American workers. At the same time, however, it addresses questions of personal identity in a manner quite comparable to Sherman's self-portraits. Borofsky explains: "This figure is me too—the traveling salesman who goes around the world with his briefcase full of images and thoughts. The briefcase has always been a metaphor for my brain."

1990

Nelson Mandela released from prison in South Africa
1990

End of Communist rule in Russia; breakup of Soviet Union
1991

Nelson Mandela becomes President of South Africa
1994

1990
Reunification of East and West Germany; Berlin Wall torn down

1993
Israel and Palestinians sign peace accord

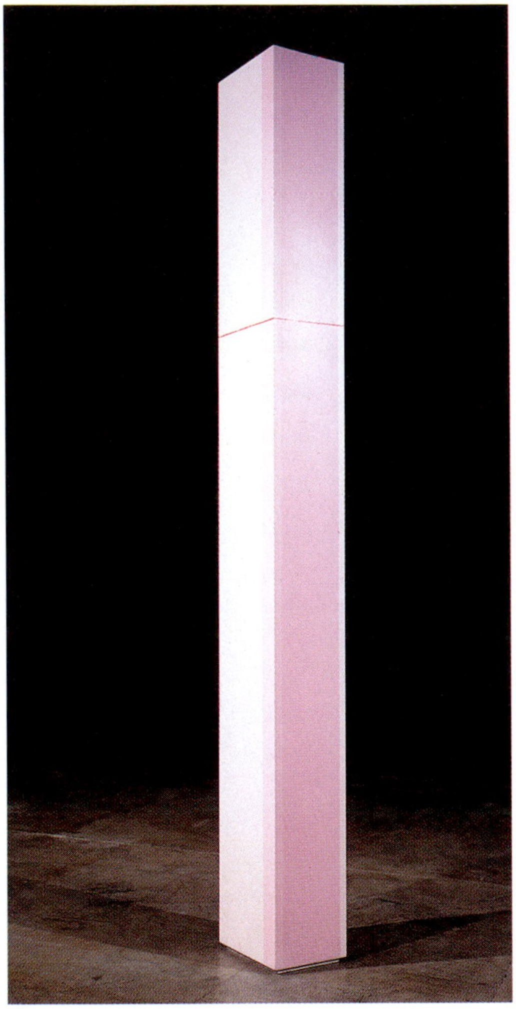

Fig. 702 Anne Truitt, *Nicea*, 1977.
Painted wood, 84 ½ × 10 × 8 in.
Courtesy André Emmerich Gallery, New York.

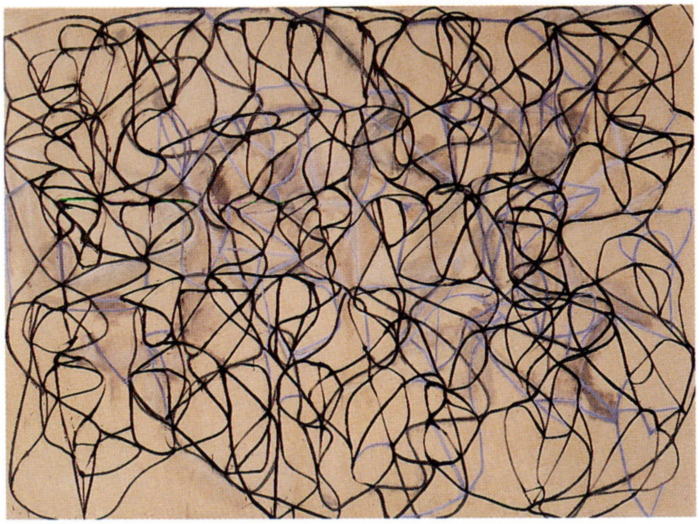

Fig. 703 Brice Marden, *Cold Mountain 3*, 1989–1991.
Oil on linen, 9 × 12 ft.
Courtesy Mary Boone Gallery, New York.

Anne Truitt's sculptures, such as *Nicea* (Fig. 702), seem minimalist and nonobjective, but like Sherman's and Borofsky's work, they are autobiographical. The formal innovation of this subtly colored piece lies in the way its colors "turn" the corner, at once emphasizing the verticality of the column and drawing us around it. But it is also deeply autobiographical, relating directly to the architectural forms of Truitt's youth in Delaware, and can best be approached through her published journals, *Daybook* (1982) and *Turn* (1986). In *Turn* she describes her love for geometric simplicity, tracing its source back to her childhood:

> *The people around me, except for my baby nurse . . . and my father when he was well, were not only inexpressive but preoccupied. I turned to my physical environment, the garden's trees, grass, flowers, bushes. The garden was bisected by a brick path. I noticed the pattern of its rectangles, and then saw that they were repeated in the brick walls of the houses of Easton [Delaware]; their verticals and horizontals were also to be found in clapboard walls, in fences, and in lattices. In my passion (no other word will do for the ardor I felt) for something to love, I came to love these proportions—and years later, in 1961, when I was forty years old, this love welled up in me and united with my training in sculpture to initiate and propel the work that has occupied me ever since.*

Truitt's work seems superficially to fulfill the desire of modernism to create art that explores the formal dimensions of its own medium. But it is her autobiographical anecdote that lends the work its special richness.

Almost 19,000 McDonald's restaurants in business worldwide
1996

1995
Oklahoma City bombing

2000

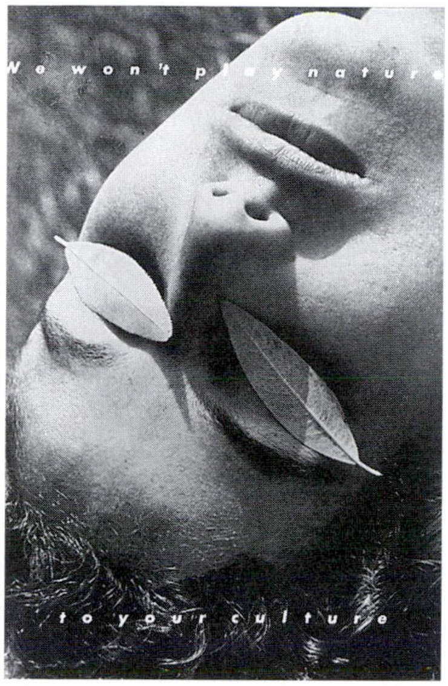

Fig. 704 Barbara Kruger, ***Untitled (We won't play nature to your culture),*** **1983.**
Photograph, 72 × 48 in. Courtesy Ydessa Hendeles Art Foundation, Toronto.

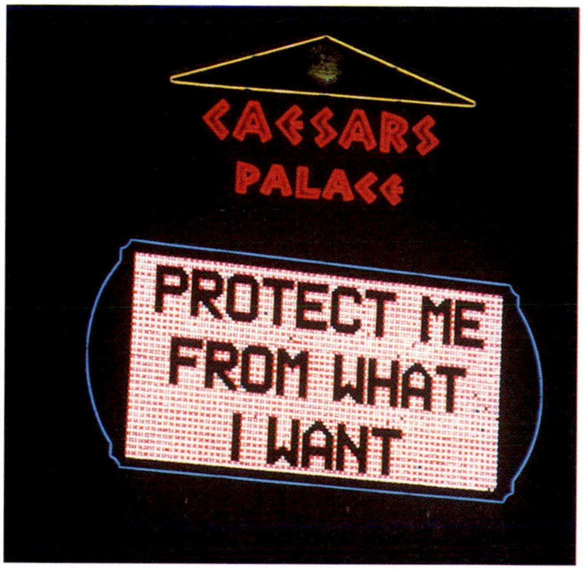

Fig. 705 Jenny Holzer, selection from "The Survival Series," 1986.
Dectronic Starburst double-sided electronic display signboard, 10 × 40 ft. Installation, Caesar's Palace, Las Vegas. Courtesy Barbara Gladstone Gallery, New York.

In painting, the styles of the past—from Mannerism to the Rococo, from Cubism to Abstract Expressionism—have been raided and appropriated to the context of the present. An example is Brice Marden's *Cold Mountain 3* (Fig. 703), one of a series of recent works that takes its name from the Chinese poet called Cold Mountain. This painting is like a minimalist version of Jackson Pollock. It is as if the high energy of Pollock had turned meditative, and the quick, almost violent motion of Pollock's line had been reinvented as a sort of slow dance suspended in a quiet space.

One of the distinguishing characteristics of Postmodernism in art has, in fact, been its antiformalist mood, its willingness to let all manner of things having little or nothing to do with its formal qualities invade and inform the work. Pop Art's introduction of mass culture into the arena of "high art" was an invitation for the arts as a whole to critique the cultural institutions of the day, and the purely visual aspirations of modernism have been supplanted by work that self-consciously reflects social, political, and economic reality.

The mass media—from television and video to electronic signboards and commercial photography—are increasingly not only the subject of contemporary art but its means. Barbara Kruger's word-and-photograph pieces relate to billboard imagery, but they continue the feminist imperative of contemporary art, addressing issues of gender. In *Untitled (We won't play nature to your culture)* (Fig. 704) Kruger exposes the traditional nature/culture dichotomy for what it is—a strategy that authorizes the cultural and intellectual domination of the male over a passive and yielding female nature. Jenny Holzer's medium is language displayed on the electronic signboard (Fig. 705). From New York's Times Square to the Las Vegas strip, Holzer's sayings eerily invade the space of advertising like messages from our own cultural subconscious. It is, perhaps above all, the new electronic technologies that are most affecting art at century's end. Today, CD-ROMs, laser discs, the fax machine, and cable television all promise to expand the world of art into an electronic "global village," a brave new world of art, in which our ways of seeing are almost limitless.

GLOSSARY

Words appearing in italics in the definitions are also defined in the glossary. Page numbers following the entries refer to the page or pages in the text where a detailed discussion of the term begins and where appropriate illustrations can also be found.

absolute symmetry Term used when each half of a composition is exactly the same (140).

abstract In art, the rendering of images and objects in a stylized or simplified way, so that though they remain recognizable, their formal or *expressive* aspects are emphasized (22). Compare both *representational* and *nonobjective art.*

Abstract Expressionism A painting style of the late 1940s and early 1950s, predominantly American, characterized by its rendering of *expressive* content by *abstract* or *nonobjective* means (473–74).

acropolis The elevated site above an ancient Greek city conceived as the center of civic life (392).

acrylic A plastic resin that, when mixed with water and pigment, forms an inorganic and quick-drying paint *medium* (243).

actual texture As opposed to *visual texture,* the literal tactile quality or feel of a thing (124).

actual weight As opposed to *visual weight,* the physical weight of material in pounds (140).

additive 1) In color, the adjective used to describe the fact that when different *hues* of colored light are combined, the resulting mixture is higher in *key* than the original hues and brighter as well, and as more and more hues are added, the resulting mixture is closer and closer to white (106). 2) In sculpture, an adjective used to describe the process in which form is built up, shaped, and enlarged by the addition of materials, as distinguished from *subtractive* sculptural processes, such as carving (245).

aerial perspective See *atmospheric perspective.*

aesthetic Pertaining to the appreciation of the beautiful, as opposed to the functional or utilitarian, and, by extension, to the appreciation of any form of art, whether overtly "beautiful" or not (4, 38, 42).

afocal art Work in which no single point of the composition demands our attention any more or less than any other and in which the eye can find no place to rest (149).

afterimage In color, the tendency of the eye to see the *complementary* color of an image after the image has been removed (111).

ambulatory A covered walkway, especially around the *apse* of a church (403).

analogous colors Pairs of colors, such as yellow and orange, that are adjacent to each other on the *color wheel* (109).

analytic line Closely related to *classical line,* a kind of line that is mathematical, precise, and rationally organized, epitomized by the vertical and horizontal grid, as opposed to *expressive line* (72).

apse A semi-circular recess placed, in a Christian church, at the end of the *nave* (323).

aquatint An *intaglio* printmaking process, in which the acid bites around powdered particles of resin resulting in a *print* with a granular appearance. The resulting *print* is also called an aquatint (209).

arbitrary color Color that has no *realistic* or natural relation to the object that is depicted, as in a blue horse, or a purple cow, but which may have emotional or *expressive* significance (117).

arch A curved, often semicircular architectural form that spans an opening or space built of wedge-shaped blocks, called *voussoirs,* with a *keystone* centered at its top (321).

architrave In architecture, the *lintel,* or horizontal beam, that forms the base of the *entablature* (319).

Art Deco A popular art and design style of the 1920s and 1930s associated with the 1925 Exposition Internationale des Arts Décoratifs et Industriels Modernes in Paris and characterized by its integration of organic and geometric forms (362).

Art Nouveau The art and design style characterized by undulating, curvilinear, and organic forms that dominated popular culture at the turn of the century, and that achieved particular success at the 1900 International Exposition in Paris (358).

assemblage An *additive* sculptural process in which various and diverse elements and objects are combined (259).

asymmetrical balance Balance achieved in a composition when neither side reflects or mirrors the other (142).

atmospheric perspective A technique, often employed in landscape painting, designed to suggest *three-dimensional space* in the *two-dimensional space* of the *picture plane,* and in which forms and objects distant from the viewer become less distinct, often bluer or cooler in color, and contrast among the various distant elements is greatly reduced (97).

autographic line Any use of line that is distinct to the artist who employs it and is therefore recognizable as a kind of "signature" style (69).

avant-garde Those whose works can be characterized as unorthodox and experimental (364).

axonometric projection A technique for depicting space, often employed by architects, in which all lines remain parallel rather than receding to a common *vanishing point* as in *linear perspective* (88).

Baroque A dominant style of art in Europe in the seventeenth century characterized by its theatrical, or dramatic, use of light and color, by its ornate forms, and by its disregard for *classical* principles of composition (434).

barrel vault A masonry roof constructed on the principle of the *arch,* that is, in essence, a continuous series of arches, one behind the other (322).

basilica In Roman architecture, a rectangular public building, entered on one of the long sides. In Christian architecture, a church loosely based on the Roman design, but entered on one of the short ends, with an *apse* at the other end (403).

bas-relief See *low-relief.*

Bauhaus A German school of design, founded by Walter Gropius in 1919 and closed by Hitler in 1933 (368).

bilateral symmetry Term used when the overall effect of a composition is one of *absolute symmetry,* even though there are clear discrepancies side to side (140).

binder In a *medium,* the substance that holds *pigments* together (173, 221).

buon fresco See *fresco.*

burin A metal tool with a V-shaped point used in *engraving* (203).

burr In *drypoint* printing, the ridge of metal that is pushed up by the *engraving* tool as it is pulled across the surface of the plate and that results, when inked, in the rich, velvety *texture* of the drypoint *print* (208).

calligraphy The art of handwriting in a fine and aesthetic way (16).

calotype The first photographic process to utilize a negative image. Discovered by William Henry Fox Talbot in 1841 (294).

Canon (of *proportion*) The "rule" of perfect proportions for the human body as determined by the Greek sculptor Polykleitos in a now lost work, known as the *Canon,* and based on the idea that each part of the body should be a common fraction of the figure's total height (157).

cantilever An architectural form that projects horizontally from its support, employed especially after the development of reinforced concrete construction techniques (334).

capital The crown, or top, of a *column,* upon which the *entablature* rests (319).

Carolingian art European art from the mid-8th to the early 10th century, given impetus and encouragement by Charlemagne's desire to restore the civilization of Rome (410).

cartoon As distinct from common usage, where it refers to a drawing with humorous content, any full size drawing, subsequently transferred to the working surface, from which a painting or *tapestry* is made (171).

cast shadow In *chiaroscuro,* the shadow cast by a figure, darker than the shadowed surface itself (100).

casting The process of making sculpture by pouring molten material—often bronze—into a mold bearing the sculpture's impression (254). See also *lost-wax casting.*

ceramics Objects formed out of clay and then hardened by *firing* in a very hot oven, or kiln (253, 268).

chiaroscuro In drawing and painting, the use of light and dark to create the effect of *three-dimensional, modeled* surfaces (100).

cire-perdue See *lost-wax casting.*

classical line Closely related to *analytic line,* a kind of line that is mathematical, precise, and rationally organized, epitomized by the vertical and horizontal grid, as opposed to *expressive line* (74).

Classical style In Greek art, the style of the 5th century BCE, characterized by its emphasis on balance, proportion, and harmony; by extension, any style that is based on logical, rational principles (74).

closed palette See *palette.*

close-up See *shot.*

coiling A method of *ceramic* construction in which long ropelike strands of clay are coiled on top of one another and then smoothed (269).

collage A work made by pasting various scraps or pieces of material—cloth, paper, photographs—onto the surface of the *composition* (279).

colonnade A row of *columns* set at regular intervals around the building and supporting the base of the roof (318).

color wheel A circular arrangement of *hues* based on one of a number of various color theories (105, 111).

column A vertical architectural support, consisting of a *shaft* topped by a *capital,* and sometimes including a base (319).

complementary colors Pairs of colors, such as red and green, that are directly opposite each other on the *color wheel* (110).

composition The organization of the formal elements in a work of art (24).

connotation The meaning associated with or implied by an image, as distinguished from its *denotation* (220).

Constructivism A Russian art movement, fully established by 1921, that was dedicated to *nonobjective* means of communication (366).

Conté crayon A soft drawing tool made by adding clay to graphite (180).

content The meaning of an image, beyond its overt *subject matter* (18); as opposed to *form,* (24).

contour line The visible border of an object in space (65).

contrapposto The disposition of the human figure in which the hips and legs are turned in opposition to the shoulders and chest, creating a counter-positioning of the body (421).

convention A traditional, habitual, or widely accepted method of representation (26).

cornice The upper part of the *entablature*, frequently decorated (319).

craft Expert handiwork, or work done by hand (268).

creativity The ability to bring to fruition, or produce, whatever is imagined or envisioned (10).

cross-cutting In film, technique when the editor moves back and forth between two separate events in increasingly shorter sequences in order to heighten drama (305).

cross-hatching Two or more sets of roughly parallel and overlapping lines, set at an angle to one another, in order to create a sense of three-dimensional, *modeled* space (101). See also *hatching*.

crossing In a church, where the *transepts* cross the *nave* (323).

Cubism A style of art pioneered by Pablo Picasso and Georges Braque in the first decade of the 20th century, noted for the geometry of its forms, its fragmentation of the object, and its increasing abstraction (462).

cyberspace See *virtual reality*.

Dada An art movement that originated during World War I in a number of world capitals, including New York, Paris, Berlin, and Zurich, which was so antagonistic to traditional styles and materials of art that it was considered by many to be "anti-art" (468).

daguerreotype One of the earliest forms of photography, invented by Louis Jacques Mandé Daguerre in 1839, made on a copper plate polished with silver (292).

delineation The descriptive representation of an object by means of *outline* or *contour* drawing (178).

denotation The direct or literal meaning of an image, as distinguished from its *connotations* (220).

De Stijl A Dutch art movement of the early 20th century that emphasized abstraction and simplicity, reducing form to the rectangle and color to the *primary colors*—red, blue, and yellow (364).

diagonal recession In *perspective*, when the lines recede to a *vanishing point* to the right or left of the *vantage point* (83).

dimetric projection A kind of *axonometric projection* in which two of the three measurements—height, width, and depth—employ the same *scale* while the third is different (88).

dome A roof generally in the shape of a hemisphere or half-globe (324).

drypoint An *intaglio* printmaking process in which the copper or zinc plate is incised by a needle pulled back across the surface leaving a *burr* . The resulting *print* is also called a drypoint (208).

earthenware A type of *ceramics* made of porous clay and fired at low temperatures that must be *glazed* if it is to hold liquid (271).

earthwork An *environment* that is out-of-doors (248, 264).

editing In filmmaking, the process of arranging the sequences of the film after it has been shot in its entirety (304).

edition In printmaking, the number of *impressions* authorized by the artist made from a single master image (195).

elevation The side of a building, or a drawing of the side of a building (319).

embroidery A traditional fiber art in which the design is made by needlework (277).

encaustic A method of painting with molten beeswax fused to the support after application by means of heat (222).

engraving An *intaglio* printmaking process in which a sharp tool called a *burin* is used to incise the plate. The resulting *print* is also called an engraving (203).

entablature The part of a building above the *capitals* of the *columns* and below the roof (319).

entasis The slight swelling in a *column* design to make the column appear straight to the eye (318).

environment A form of art that is large enough for the viewer to move around in (248).

etching An *intaglio* printmaking process in which a metal plate coated with wax is drawn upon with a sharp tool down to the plate and then placed in an acid bath. The acid eats into the plate where the lines have been drawn, the wax is removed, and then the plate is inked and printed. The resulting *print* is also called an etching (206).

ethnocentric Pertaining to the imposition of the point of view of one culture upon the works and attitudes of another (27).

Expressionism An art that stresses the psychological and emotional content of the work, associated particularly with German art in the early 20th century (464). See also *Abstract Expressionism*.

expressive Anything that springs directly from the artist's emotions or feelings (69).

expressive line A kind of line that seems to spring directly from the artist's emotions or feelings—loose, gestural, and energetic—epitomized by curvilinear forms (69); as opposed to *analytic* or *classical line*, (72).

extreme close-up See *shot*.

Fauvism An art movement of the early 20th century characterized by its use of bold *arbitrary color*. Its name derives from the French word "fauve," meaning "wild beast" (463).

figure-ground reversal Term used in a two-dimensional work, in which the relationship between a form or figure and its background is reversed so that what was figure becomes background and what was background becomes figure (80).

firing The process of baking a *ceramic* object in a very hot oven, or *kiln* (268).

fixative A thin liquid film sprayed over *pastel* and charcoal drawings to protect them from smudging (179).

flashback A narrative technique in film in which the editor cuts to episodes that are supposed to have taken place before the start of the film (305).

fluting The shallow vertical grooves or channels on a *column* (318).

flying buttress On a Gothic church, an exterior *arch* that opposes the lateral thrust of an arch or vault, as in a *barrel vault,* arching inward toward the exterior wall from the top of an exterior *column* or pier (326).

focal point In a work of art, the center of visual attention, often different from the physical center of the work (146).

foreshortening The modification of *perspective* to decrease distortion resulting from the apparent visual contraction of an object or figure as it extends backwards from the *picture plane* at an angle approaching the perpendicular (91).

form 1) The literal *shape* and *mass* of an object or figure. 2) More generally, the materials used to make a work of art, the ways in which these materials are utilized in terms of the formal elements (line, light, color, etc.), and the *composition* that results (24).

fresco Painting on plaster, either dry *(fresco secco)* or wet *(buon* or *true fresco)*. In the former, the paint is an independent layer, separate from the plaster proper; in the latter, the paint is chemically bound to the plaster, and is integral to the wall or support (223).

fresco secco See *fresco.*

frieze The part of the *architrave* between the *entablature* and the *cornice,* often decorated (246, 319).

frontal recession In *perspective,* when the lines recede to a *vanishing point* directly across from the *vantage point* (83).

frottage The technique of putting a sheet of paper over textured surfaces and then rubbing a soft pencil across the paper (126).

full shot See *shot.*

Futurism An early 20th century art movement, characterized by its desire to celebrate the movement and speed of modern industrial life (466).

gesso A plaster mixture used as a *ground* for painting (226).

glaze 1) In oil painting, a thin, transparent, or semitransparent layer put over a color, usually in order to give it a more luminous quality (230). 2) In *ceramics,* a material that is painted on a ceramic object that turns glassy when *fired* (268).

Golden Section A system of *proportion* developed by the ancient Greeks obtained by dividing a line so that the shorter part is to the longer part as the longer part is to the whole, resulting in a ration that is approximately 5 to 8 (157).

Gothic A style of architecture and art dominant in Europe from the 12th to the 15th century, characterized, in its architecture, by features such as *pointed arches, flying buttresses,* and a verticality symbolic of the ethereal and heavenly (412).

gouache A painting medium similar to *watercolor,* but opaque instead of transparent (238).

grid A pattern of horizontal and vertical lines that cross each other to make uniform squares or rectangles (73).

groined vault A masonry roof constructed on the *arch* principle and consisting of two *barrel vaults* intersecting at right angles to one another (322).

ground A coating applied to a canvas or printmaking plate to prepare it for painting or *etching* (206, 221).

Happening A spontaneous, often multimedia, event conceived by artists and performed not only by the artists themselves but often by the public present at the event as well (284).

hatching An area of closely spaced parallel lines, employed in drawing and *engraving,* to create the effect of shading or *modeling* (101). See also *cross-hatching.*

heightening The addition of *highlights* to a drawing by the application of white or some other pale color (177).

Hellenistic art The art of the 3rd and 2nd centuries BCE in Greece characterized by its physical realism and emotional drama (394).

highlight The spot or one of the spots of highest *key* or *value* in a picture (100).

high- (haut-) relief A sculpture in which the figures and objects remain attached to a background plane and project off of it by at least half their normal depth (246).

hue A color, usually one of the six basic colors of the *spectrum*—the three *primary colors* of red, yellow, and blue, and the three *secondary colors* of green, orange, and violet (102, 106).

hyperspace See *virtual reality.*

iconography The images and symbols *conventionally* associated with a given subject (29).

illusionistic art Generally synonymous with *representational art,* but more specifically referring to an image so natural that it creates the illusion of being real (19).

impasto Paint applied very thickly to canvas or support (124–25, 228).

implied line A line created by movement or direction, such as the line established by a pointing finger, the direction of a glance, or a body moving through space (65).

impression In printmaking, a single example of an *edition* (195).

Impressionism A late 19th-century art movement, centered in France, and characterized by its use of discontinuous strokes of color meant to reproduce the effects of light (456).

infrastructure The systems that deliver services to people—water supply and waste removal, energy, transportation, and communications (345).

installation An *environment* that is indoors (248, 282).

intaglio Any form of printmaking in which the line is incised into the surface of the printing plate, including *aquatint, drypoint, etching, engraving,* and *mezzotint* (202).

intensity The relative purity of a color's *hue,* and a function of its relative brightness or dullness; also known as *saturation* (106).

intermediate colors The range of colors on the *color wheel* between each *primary color* and its neighboring *secondary colors;* yellow-green, for example (105).

International Style A 20th-century style of architecture and design marked by its almost austere geometric simplicity (337).

in-the-round As opposed to *relief,* sculpture that requires no wall support and that can be experienced from all sides (247).

investment In *lost-wax casting,* a mixture of water, plaster, and powder made from ground-up pottery used to fill the space inside the wax lining of the mold (256).

iris shot In film, a *shot* which is blurred and rounded at the edges in order to focus the attention of the viewer on the scene in the center (305).

isometric projection A kind of *axonometric projection* in which all three measurements—height, width, and depth—employ the same *scale* (88).

Jugendstil The "style of youth" in turn-of-the-century German art and design, closely related to *Art Nouveau* (361).

ka In ancient Egypt, the immortal substance of the human, in some ways equivalent to the Western soul (250, 386).

key The relative lightness or darkness of a picture or the colors employed in it (102); used in preference to *value,* (103–4).

keystone The central and uppermost *voussoir* in an *arch* (321).

kiln An oven used to bake *ceramics* (253).

kinetic art Art that moves (66, 134).

kiva In Anasazi culture, the round, covered hole in the center of the communal plaza in which all ceremonial life took place (316).

linear perspective A system for depicting *three-dimensional space* on a *two-dimensional* surface that depends on two related principles: that things perceived as far away are smaller than things nearer the viewer, and that parallel lines receding into the distance converge at a *vanishing point* on the horizon line (83).

linocut A form of *relief* printmaking, similar to a *woodcut,* in which a block of linoleum is carved so as to leave the image to be printed raised above the surface of the block. The resulting *print* is also known as a linocut (201).

lintel In architecture, the horizontal beam stretching between two posts. See also *post-and-lintel construction* (317).

lithograph Any print resulting from the process of *lithography* (210).

lithography A printmaking process in which a polished stone, often limestone, is drawn upon with a greasy material; the surface is moistened and then inked; the ink adheres only to the greasy lines of the drawing; and the design is transferred to dampened paper, usually in a printing press (210).

load-bearing construction In architecture, construction where the walls bear the weight of the roof (317).

local color As opposed to *optical color* and *perceptual color,* the actual *hue* of a thing, independent of the ways in which colors might be mixed or how different conditions of light and atmosphere might affect the color (115).

long shot In film, a *shot* that takes in a wide expanse and many characters at once (304–5).

lost-wax casting method A bronze-casting method in which a figure is molded in wax and covered with clay; the whole is fired, melting away the wax and hardening the clay; the resulting hardened mold is then filled with molten metal (256–57).

low- (bas-) relief A sculpture in which the figures and objects remain attached to a background plane and project off of it by less than one-half their normal depth (246).

Mannerism The style of art prevalent especially in Italy from about 1525 until the early years of the 17th century, characterized by its dramatic use of light, exaggerated *perspective,* distorted forms, and vivid colors (432).

mass Any solid that occupies a *three-dimensional* volume (79).

matrix In printmaking, the master image (195).

medium 1) Any material used to create a work of art (170). Plural form, **media.** 2) In painting, a liquid added to the paint that makes it easier to manipulate (106).

medium shot See *shot.*

metalpoint A drawing technique, especially *silverpoint,* popular in the 15th and 16th centuries, in which a stylus with a point of gold, silver, or some other metal was applied to a sheet of paper treated with a mixture of powdered bones (or lead white) and gumwater (177).

mezzotint An *intaglio* printmaking process in which the plate is ground all over with a *rocker,* leaving a burr raised on the surface that if inked would be rich black. The surface is subsequently lightened to a greater or lesser degree by scraping away the burr. The resulting *print* is also known as a mezzotint (209).

mihrab A niche set in the wall of a mosque indicating the direction of Mecca (416).

mimesis The concept of imitation, involving the creation of *representations* that transcend or exceed mere appearance by implying the sacred or spiritual essence of things (220).

minaret A tall, slender tower attached to a mosque from which the people are called to prayer (416).

Minimalism A style of art, predominantly American, that dates from the mid-20th century, characterized by its rejection of expressive content and its use of "minimal" formal means (476).

mixed media The combination of two or more *media* in a single work (279).

modeling In sculpture, the shaping of a form in some plastic material, such as clay or plaster (252); in drawing, painting, and printmaking, the rendering of a form, usually by means of *hatching* or *chiaroscuro,* to create the illusion of a *three-dimensional form* (100).

Modernism Generally speaking, the various strategies and directions employed in 20th-century art—*Cubism, Futurism, Expressionism,* etc.—to explore the particular formal properties of any given *medium* (473).

monotype A printmaking process in which only one *impression* results (217).

montage In film, the sequencing of widely disparate images to create a fast-paced, multifaceted visual impression (306).

mosaic An art form in which small pieces of tile, glass, or stone are fitted together and embedded in cement on surfaces such as walls and floors (404).

mudra The various hand positions of the Buddha (29).

narrative art A *temporal* form of art that tells a story (129).

naturalistic art Generally synonymous with *representational art;* but more specifically meaning "like nature"; descriptive of any work that resembles the natural world (19).

nave The central part of a church, running from the entrance through the *crossing* (323).

negative shape or space Empty space, surrounded and shaped so that it acquires a sense of form or volume (80).

Neoclassicism A style of the late 18th and early 19th centuries that was influenced by the Greek *Classical style* and that often employed Classical themes for its subject matter (444).

nonobjective art Art that makes no reference to the natural world and that explores the inherent expressive or aesthetic potential of the formal elements—line, shape, color—and the formal *compositional* principles of a given *medium* (23).

nonrepresentational art See *nonobjective art.*

objective As opposed to *subjective,* free of personal feelings or emotion; hence, without bias (35).

oblique projection A system for projecting space, commonly found in Japanese art, in which the front of the object or building is parallel to the picture plane and the sides, receding at an angle, remain parallel to each other, rather than converging as in *linear perspective* (88).

oculus A round, central opening at the top of a *dome* (324).

one-point linear perspective A version of *linear perspective* in which there is only one *vanishing point* in the *composition* (83).

open palette See *palette.*

optical color Spots or dots of pure *hues* set beside each other and mixed by the viewer's eye (116).

Optical Painting (Op Art) An art style particularly popular in the 1960s in which line and color are manipulated in ways that stimulate the eye into believing it perceives movement (134).

order In Classical architecture, a style characterized by the design of the *platform,* the *column* and its *entablature* (319).

original print A *print* created by the artist alone and which has been printed by the artist or under the artist's direct supervision (195).

outline The edge of a shape or figure depicted by an actual line drawn or painted on the surface (65).

overlapping A way to create the illusion of space by placing one figure behind another (82).

palette Literally a thin board, with a thumb-hole at one end, upon which the artist lays out and mixes colors, but by extension, the range of colors used by the artist. In this last sense, a *closed* or *restricted palette* is one employing only a few colors and an *open palette* is one utilizing the full range of *hues* (107).

pan In film, a *shot* in which the camera moves across the scene from one side to the other (305).

pastel 1) A soft crayon made of chalk and pigment. Also any work done in this *medium* (182). 2) A pale, light color (182).

pattern A repetitive motif or design (123, 127).

pencil A drawing tool made of graphite encased in a soft wood cylinder (180).

pendentive A triangular section of a masonry hemisphere, four of which provide the transition from the vertical sides of a building to a covering *dome* (407).

penumbra The lightest of the three basic parts of a shadowed surface, providing the transition from the lighted area to the *umbra,* or core of the shadow (100).

perceptual color The color as perceived by the eye, changed by the effects of light and atmosphere, in the way, for instance, that distant mountains appear to be blue (116). See also *atmospheric perspective.*

performance art A form of art, popular especially since the late 1960s, that includes not only physical space but the human activity that goes on within it (279).

perspective A formula for projecting the illusion of *three-dimensional space* onto a *two-dimensional* surface (83). See also *linear perspective, one-point linear perspective, two-point linear perspective,* and *atmospheric perspective.*

photogenic drawing With the *daguerreotype,* one of the first two photographic processes, invented by William Henry Fox Talbot in 1839, in which a negative image is fixed to paper (292).

photorealistic art Generally used to describe *two-dimensional* images, a kind of *super realistic art* rendered with such a high degree of *representational* accuracy that it appears to be photographed rather than drawn or painted (22, 31).

picture plane The surface of a picture (82).

pigments The coloring agents of a *medium* (173, 221).

planographic printmaking process Any printmaking process in which the *print* is pulled from a flat, planar surface, chief among them *lithography* (210).

platform The *base* upon which a *column* rests (319).

plein air painting Painting done on site, in the open air (116).

pointed arch An *arch* that is not semicircular but rather rises more steeply to a point at its top (324–25).

polychromatic color scheme A color composition consisting of a variety of *hues* (115).

ponderation The principle of the weight shift, in which the relaxation of one leg serves to create a greater sense of naturalism in the figure (250).

Pop Art A style arising in the early 1960s characterized by its emphasis on the forms and imagery of mass culture (476).

porcelain The type of *ceramics* fired at the highest temperature that becomes virtually translucent and extremely glossy in finish (271).

position In the art process, a method of establishing space in a *two-dimensional* work by placing objects closer to the viewer lower and objects further away higher in the picture (88).

post-and-lintel construction A system of building in which two posts support a crosspiece, or *lintel,* that spans the distance between them (317).

Post-Impressionism A name that describes the painting of a number of artists, working in widely different styles, in the last decades of the 19th century in France (458).

Postmodernism A term used to describe the willfully plural and eclectic art forms of contemporary art (163, 478).

potter's wheel A flat disk attached to a flywheel below that is kicked by the potter or driven by electricity, allowing the potter to pull clay upward in a round, symmetrical shape (270).

Pre-Columbian The cultures of all the peoples of Mexico, Central America, and South America prior to the arrival of the Europeans at the end of the 15th-century (430).

primary colors The *hues* that in theory cannot be created from a mixture of other hues and from which all other hues are created—namely, in pigment, red, yellow, and blue, and in light, red-orange, green, and blue-violet (105).

print Any one of multiple *impressions* made from a master image (195).

proof A trial *impression* of a *print,* made before the final *edition* is run, so that it may be examined and, if necessary, corrected (195).

proportion In any composition, the relationship between the parts to each other and to the whole (152).

qibla wall The wall of a mosque that, from the interior, is oriented in the direction of Mecca, and that contains the *mihrab* (416).

radial balance A circular composition in which the elements project outward from a central core at regular intervals like the spokes of a wheel (145).

realism Generally, the tendency to render the facts of existence, but specifically, in the 19th century, the desire to describe the world in a way unadulterated by the imaginative and idealist tendencies of the Romantic sensibility (451).

realistic art See *representational art.*

registration In printmaking, the precise alignment of *impressions* made by two or more blocks or plates on the same sheet of paper, utilized particularly when printing two or more colors (201).

relief 1) Any sculpture in which images and forms are attached to a background and project off it. See *low-relief* and *high-relief* (246). 2) In printmaking, any process in which any area of the plate not to be printed is carved away, leaving only the original surface to be printed (196).

Renaissance The period in Europe from the 14th to the 16th century characterized by a revival of interest in the arts and sciences that had been lost since antiquity (418).

repetition See *pattern* and *rhythm.*

replacement A term for casting, by for instance the *lost-wax* process, in which wax is replaced by bronze (257).

representation Any image that refers to something other than itself (16, 18).

representational art Any work of art that seeks to resemble the world of natural appearance (19).

reserve An area of a work of art that retains the original color and texture of the untouched surface or *ground* (82).

rhythm An effect achieved when shapes, colors, or a regular *pattern* of any kind is repeated over and over again (158).

rocker A sharp, curved tool utilized in the *mezzotint* printmaking process (209).

Rococo A style of art popular in the first three-quarters of the 18th century, particularly in France, characterized by curvilinear forms, *pastel* colors, and light, often frivolous subject matter (443).

Romanesque art The dominant style of art and architecture in Europe from the 8th to the 12th centuries, characterized, in architecture, by Roman precedents, particularly the round *arch* and the *barrel vault* (410).

romantic Pertaining to works of art possessing the characterisitics of *Romanticism* (74).

Romanticism A dramatic, emotional, and *subjective* art arising in the early 19th century in opposition to the austere discipline of *Neoclassicism* (447).

saturation See *intensity.*

scale The comparative size of a thing in relation to another like thing or its "normal" or "expected" size (82, 152).

scumbling In painting, the working of an opaque layer of paint over another layer of a different tone or color so that the lower layer is not entirely obliterated (235).

secondary colors *Hues* created by combining two *primary colors;* in pigment, the secondary colors are traditionally considered to be orange, green, and violet; in light, yellow, magenta, and cyan (105).

serigraphy Also known as screenprinting, a stencil printmaking process in which the image is transferred to paper by forcing ink through a mesh; areas not meant to be printed are blocked out (216).

shade A color or *hue* modified by the addition of another color, resulting in a *hue* of lower *key* or *value,* in the way, for instance, that the addition of black to red results in maroon (102).

shaft A part of a *column* (319).

shape In *two-dimensional* media, an area, the boundaries of which are measured in terms of height and width (79). More broadly, the *form* of any object or figure.

shell system In architecture, one of the two basic structural systems in which one basic material both provides the structural support and the outside covering of a building (317).

shot In film, a continuous sequence of film frames (304), including a *full shot,* which shows the actor from head to toe, a *medium shot,* which shows the actor from the waist up, a *close-up,* showing the head and shoulders, and an *extreme close-up,* showing a portion of the face. Other shots include the *long shot,* the *iris shot,* the *pan,* and the *traveling shot* (304–5).

shotgun house A single-story, wood-frame structure, one room wide and two or more rooms deep. After the Civil War, such houses were the first homes of many newly freed African Americans (330–31).

silkscreen Also known as a serigraph, a print made by the process of *serigraphy* (216).

silverpoint See *metalpoint.*

simultaneous contrast A property of *complementary colors* when placed side by side, resulting in the fact that both appear brighter and more intense than when seen in isolation (111).

sinopie The *cartoon* or underpainting for a *fresco* (178).

sizing An astringent crystalline substance called alum brushed onto the surface of paper so that ink will not run along its fibers (199).

skeleton-and-skin system In architecture, one of the two basic structural systems, which consists of an interior frame, the skeleton, that supports the more fragile outer covering of the building, the skin (317).

slab construction A method of *ceramic* construction in which clay is rolled out flat, like a pie crust, and then shaped by hand (268).

solvent A thinner that enables paint to flow more readily and that also cleans brushes; also called *vehicle* (221).

spectrum The colored bands of visible light created when sunlight passes through a prism (105).

springing The lowest stone of an *arch,* resting on the supporting post (324).

state In printmaking, an *impression* pulled part way through the process so that the artist can study how the image is progressing (204).

still life A work of art that consists of an arrangement of inanimate objects, such as flowers, fruit, and household objects (43).

stippling In drawing and printmaking, a pattern of closely placed dots or small marks employed to create the effect of shading or *modeling* (202).

stoneware A type of *ceramics* fired at high temperature and thus impermeable to water (271).

stopping out In *etching*, the application of varnish or *ground* over the etched surface in order to prevent further etching as the remainder of the surface is submerged in the acid bath (207).

stupa A large mound-shaped Buddhist shrine (401).

stylobate The base, or *platform*, upon which a *column* rests (319).

subject matter The literal, visible image in a work of art, as distinguished from its *content*, which includes the *connotative*, symbolic, and suggestive aspects of the image (18).

subjective As opposed to *objective*, full of personal emotions and feelings (35).

sublime That which impresses the mind with a sense of grandeur and power, inspiring a sense of awe (5, 449–50).

subtractive 1) In color, the adjective used to describe the fact that, when different *hues* of colored pigment are combined, the resulting mixture is lower in *key* than the original hues and duller as well, and as more and more hues are added, the resulting mixture is closer and closer to black (106). 2) In sculpture, an adjective used to describe the process in which form is discovered by the removal of materials, by such means as carving, as distinguished from *additive* sculptural processes, such as *assemblage* (245).

super realistic art A work of art so *illusionistic* or true to life that it appears to be real (22, 31).

support The surface on which the artist works—a wall, a panel of wood, a canvas, or a sheet of paper (221).

Surrealism A style of art of the early 20th century that emphasized dream imagery, chance operations, and rapid, thoughtless forms of notation that expressed, it was felt, the unconscious mind (36, 469).

symmetry Term used when two halves of a *composition* correspond to one another in terms of size, shape, and placement of forms (140).

tableau A *three-dimensional*, room-size *environment* into which we cannot enter (283).

tapestry A special kind of *weaving*, in which the *weft* yarns are of several colors that the weaver manipulates to make a design or image (276).

technology The materials and methods available to a given culture (170, 314).

tempera A painting *medium* made by combining water, pigment, and, usually, egg yolk (226).

temperature The relative warmth or coolness of a given *hue*, those in the yellow-orange-red range considered to be warm, and those in the green-blue-violet range considered cool (109).

temporal art Any form of art that possesses a clear beginning, middle, and end, or that takes place over time (129).

tenebrism From the Italian *tenebroso*, meaning murky, a heightened form of *chiaroscuro* (100).

tensile strength In architecture, the ability of a building material to span horizontal distances without support and without buckling in the middle (317).

tesserae Small pieces of glass or stone used in making *mosaic* (404).

texture The surface quality of a work (124).

three-dimensional space Any space that possesses height, width, and depth (80).

tint A color or *hue* modified by the addition of another color resulting in a hue of higher *key* or *value*, in the way, for instance, that the addition of white to red results in pink (102).

topography The distinct landscape characteristics of a local site (314).

transept The crossarm of a church which intersects, at right angles, with the *nave*, creating the shape of a cross (323).

traveling shot In film, a *shot* in which the camera moves back to front or front to back (305).

trimetric projection A kind of *axonometric projection* in which all three measurements—height, width, and depth—employ a different *scale* (88).

trompe l'oeil A form of *representation* that attempts to depict the object as if it were actually present before the eye in *three-dimensional space;* literally "eye-fooling" (230–31).

truss In architecture, a triangular framework that, because of its rigidity, can span much wider areas than a single wooden beam (329).

tusche A greasy material used for drawing on a *lithography* stone (213).

two-dimensional space Any space that is flat, possessing height and width, but no depth, such as a piece of drawing paper or a canvas (82).

two-point linear perspective A version of *linear perspective* in which there are two (or more) *vanishing points* in the *composition* (84).

tympanum The space between the *arch* and *lintel* over a door, often decorated with sculpture (411).

Ukiyo-e A style of Japanese art, meaning "pictures of the transient or floating world," that depicted, especially, the pleasures of everyday life (198).

umbra The heart, or core, of a shadow (100).

value See *key*. Also the worth, monetarily and culturally, of a work (45).

vanishing point In *linear perspective*, the point on the horizon line where parallel lines appear to converge (83).

vanitas A kind of still life painting designed to remind us of the vanity, or frivolous quality, of human existence (42).

vantage point In linear perspective, the point where the viewer is positioned (83).

vehicle See *solvent*.

verisimilitude In *representation*, the apparent "truth" or accuracy of the depiction (92).

video art An art form that employs television as its *medium* (307).

virtual reality An artificial three-dimensional *environment*, sometimes called *hyperspace* or *cyberspace*, generated through the use of computers, that the viewer experiences as real space (94).

visual literacy The ability to recognize, understand, and communicate the meaning of visual images (16).

visual texture A *texture* on the surface of a work that appears to be actual but is an illusion (126).

visual weight As opposed to *actual weight*, the apparent "heaviness" or "lightness" of a shape or form (140).

voussoir A wedge-shaped block used in the construction of an *arch* (321).

warp In *weaving*, the vertical threads, held taut on a loom or frame (276).

wash Large flat areas of ink or *watercolor* diluted with water and applied by brush (189).

watercolor A painting *medium* consisting of *pigments* suspended in a solution of water and gum arabic (236).

weaving A technique for constructing fabrics by means of interlacing horizontal and vertical threads (276).

weft In *weaving*, the loosely woven horizontal threads, also called the *woof* (276.)

weight An important element in creating balance in a *composition*. As opposed to *actual weight*, which is the physical weight of material in pounds, *visual weight* is the apparent "heaviness" or "lightness" of a shape or form (140).

wet-plate collodion process A photographic process, developed around 1850, that allowed for short exposure times and quick development of the print (294).

wood engraving Actually a *relief* printmaking technique, in which fine lines are carved into the block resulting in a *print* consisting of white lines on a black ground. The resultant print is also called a *wood engraving* (200).

woodcut A *relief* printmaking process, in which a wooden block is carved so that those parts not intended to print are cut away, leaving the design raised. The resultant *print* is also called a *woodcut* (196).

wood-frame construction A true skeleton-and-skin building method, commonly used in domestic architecture to the present (329).

woof See *weft*.

ziggurat A pyramidal structure, built in ancient Mesopotamia, consisting of three stages or levels, each stage stepped back from the one below (315, 385).

PRONUNCIATION GUIDE

an—*man, tan*
ay—*day, play*
aw—*draw, saw*
ah—*that, cat*
eh—*pet, get*
er—*her, fur*
ih—*fit, spit*
oh—*toe, go*
ohn—*phone, tone*
ow—*cow, now*
uh—*bud, fuss*
ye—*sky, try*

No pronunciation guide is perfect, and this one is like all others. It is meant solely to assist North American readers in pronouncing, with some assurance that they will not be embarrassed, unfamiliar names and phrases. Foreign names and phrases, particularly, are not rendered here with perfect linguistic accuracy. Many of the subtleties of French pronunciation are ignored (in part because many North Americans cannot hear them), as are the gutteral consonants of German and its related languages. The Guide suggests, for instance, that Vincent van Gogh be pronounced "van GOH"—a perfectly acceptable North American pronunciation that wholly ignores the throaty glottal click of the the Dutch "g." Often, there is, even among scholars, disagreement about how a name is pronounced. We have tried to offer alternatives in such instances.

A simplified phonetic system has been employed. Some of the less obvious conventions are listed at the left.

Abakanowicz, Magdalena mahg-daw-LAY-nuh aw-baw-kaw-NOH-vich
Akenaten aw-keh-NAH-ten
Anthemius of Tralles ahn-THAY-mee-us of TRAW-layss
Aphrodite ahph-roh-DYE-tee
architrave ARK-ih-trayv
Balla, Giacomo JAH-coh-moh BAW-law
Barela, Patrocinio pah-troh-CHEE-nee-oh baw-RELL-uh
Bartolommeo, Fra fraw bar-toh-loh-MAY-oh
Baselitz, Georg GAY-ohrg BAZ-eh-litz
Basquiat, Jean-Michel jawn mee-SHELL boss-kee-AW
Bel Geddes, Norman bel geh-DEES
Bellini, Giovanni jyoh-VAHN-ee bell-EE-nee
Benin beh-NEEN
Bernini, Gianlorenzo jawn-loh-REN-soh behr-NEE-nee
Beuys, Joseph YO-sef BOYS
Bonheur, Rosa buhn-ER
Bonnard, Pierre pee-AIR boh-NAWR
Borromini, Francesco frahn-CHAY-skoh bore-oh-MEE-nee
Botticelli, Sandro SAN-droh boh-tee-CHEL-lee
Boucher, François frahn-SWAH boo-SHAY
Braque, Georges jorjh BRAHK
Breuer, Marcel mar-SELL BROO-er
Bronzino brawn-ZEEN-oh
burin BYOOR-in
Caillebotte, Gustave goos-TAWV kye-BAWT
camera obscura KAM-er-aw ob-SKOOR-uh
Caravaggio caw-raw-VAW-jyoh
Carracci, Annibale on-NEE-ball-ay car-RAW-chee
Cartier-Bresson, Henri on-REE car-TEE-ay Bress-OH(n)
Cassatt, Mary kaw-SAWT
Cézanne, Paul say-ZAN
Chardin, Jean Baptiste Siméon jawn ba-TEEST see-may-ohn shar-DAN
Chartres SHAR-tr'
Cheng Sixiao jong see-SHO
chiaroscuro kee-ar-oh-SKOOR-oh
Chihuly, Dale Chih-HOO-lee
Chirico, Giorgio de JOR-gee-oh day KEE-ree-coh
Christo KRIS-toh
Cimabue chee-maw-BOO-ay
cire perdue seer payr-DOO
Clodion, Claude-Michel klodh-mee-SHELL kloh-dee-OH(n)
contrapposto kohn-traw-POH-stoh
Corbusier, Le luh kor-boo-SEE-ay
Courbet, Gustave goos-TAWV koor-BAY
cruciform KROO-suh-form
Daguerre, Louis Jacques Mandé loo-ee JAWK man-DAY daw-GAYR
Dali, Salvador sal–vaw-DOHR DAW-lee or daw-LEE
Daumier, Honoré ohn-ohr-AY dohm-YAY
David, Jacques Louis jawk loo-EE daw-VEED
Degas, Edgar ed-GAWR deh-GAW
Déjeuner sur l'herbe, Le luh day-joon-AY ser LAIRB
de Kooning, Willem VILL-um duh KOON-ing
Delacroix, Eugène you-JEHN duh-law-KRWAW
Demoiselles d'Avignon, Les lay duh-mwoi-ZELL dah-veen-YON
Derain, André awn-DRAY deh-RAN
Diebenkorn, Richard DEE-ben-korn
Donatello dohn-aw-TAY-loh
Dubuffet, Jean jawn doo-boo-FAY
Duchamp, Marcel mar-SELL doo-SHAW(n)
Dürer, Albrecht AWL-breckt DYUR-er
El Greco ell GRAY-koh
El Lissitzky ell lih-ZITZ-kee
entasis EN-taw-sis
Fauve fohv
Fragonard, Jean-Honoré jawn oh-noh-RAY fraw-goh-NAWR
Frankenthaler, Helen FRANK-en-thawl-er
Friedrich, Caspar David FREED-rik
frieze freez
Gaudí, Antoni ahn-TOH-nee gow-DEE
Gauguin, Paul goh-GAN
Gentileschi, Artemisia ar-tay-MEES-jyuh jen-till-ESS-kee
Géricault, Théodore tay-oh-DOHR jeh-ree-COH
gesso JESS-oh
Giorgione gee-or-gee-OH-nay
Giotto gee-YAW-toh
Giovanni da Bologna joh-VAWN-ee daw bo-LOHN-yaw

Gislebertus geez-lay-BARE-tuss
Goethe, Wolfgang von GUH-tuh
Gohlke, Frank GOHL-kee
Gómez-Peña, Guillermo Ghee-AIR-moh GOH-mes PAIN-yuh
gouache gwawsh
Goya, Francisco de frawn-SEES-coh day GOY-yaw
Grünewald, Matthias maw-TEE-ess GROON-eh-vawlt
Guernica GARE-nee-caw
Guimard, Hector heck-TOR GWEE-mar
Guo Xi gow zee
haut-relief OH ree-leef
Hesse, Eva hess
Hiroshige, Ando AWN-doh heer-oh-SHEE-gay
Hokusai, Katsushika kat-s'-SHEE-kaw HOH-k'-sye
Hung Liu hung loo
impasto im-PAW-stoh
Ingres, Jean Auguste Dominique jawn oh-GOOST dohm-een-EEK AING-r'
intaglio in-TAWL-yoh
ka kaw
Kahlo, Frieda FREE-duh KAW-loh
Kandinsky, Wassily vaw-SEE-lee kan-DIN-skee
Kaprow, Allan KAP-roh
Kirchner, Ernst Airnst KEERCH-nair
Klimt, Gustav goos-TAHV KLEEMT
Knossos KNAW-sohs
Koetsu, Hon'ami HOHN-aw-mee ko-ET-zoo
Kollwitz, Käthe KAYT-eh KOHL-vitz
Laocoön lay-AW-coh-un
Lascaux las-COH
Lautrec, Henri de Toulouse- awn-REE deh too-LOOS loh-TREK
Ledoux, Claude-Nicolas klawd-NEE-coh-law Leh-DOO
Léger, Fernand fair-NAN LAY-zhay
Leonardo da Vinci lay-oh-NAHR-doh daw VEEN-chee (in the U.S., often lee-oh-NAHR-doh)
Liang Kai lee-ong kye
Limbourg lam-BOOR(g)
Loewy, Raymond LOH-ee
Lorrain, Claude Klodh lor-REHN
Maciunas, George mass-ee-YOU-nehs
Magritte, René reh-NAY ma-GREET
Malevich, Kasimir kaw-zee-MEER MAW-lay-veech
Manet, Edouard ayd-WAHR ma-NAY
Mantegna, Andrea awn-DRAY-uh mawn-TAYN-yaw
Mapplethorpe, Robert MAYP-'l-thorp
Marey, Etienne-Jules ay-TEE-an jool ma-RAY
Marisol Maw-ree-SOHL
Masaccio maw-SAW-chee-oh
Matisse, Henri on-REE ma-TEESE
Maya MYE-yaw
Mesa Verde MAY-suh VAYR-day
mezzotint MET-soh-tint
Michelangelo mye-kel-AN-jel-oh; also mee-kel-AN-jel-oh
Mies van der Rohe, Ludvig LOOD-vig meese van dur ROH(uh)
mihrab MEE-rawb
Miró Joan HWAHN meer-OH
Mondrian, Piet PAYT MOHN-dree-awn
Monet, Claude klodh moh-NAY
Morisot, Berthe BAYR-t' mohr-ee-SOH
mudra muh-DRAW
Muybridge, Eadweard ED-ward MY-bridj
Mycenae my-SEEN-ay or my-SEEN-ee
Nauman, Bruce NOW-man
Neri, Manuel man-WHALE NAY-ree
Nolde, Emile ay-MEEL KNOWL-d'
Olmec OHL-mek
Paik, Nam June NAWM joon PIKE
Pfaff, Judy paff
Philippe de Champaigne fee-LEEP duh sham-PAYN
Piero della Francesca pee-AYR-oh DAY-law frawn-CHEE-skaw
Piéta pee-ay-TAW
plein air PLEHN-air
Pollock, Jackson PAWL-uck
Polykleitos pawl-ee-KLY-tohs
Pollaiuolo poh-LYE-you-oh-loh
Pont du Gard pohn doo GAHR
Poussin, Nicolas nee-coh-LAW poo-SAN
Pozzo, Fra Andrea fraw an-DRAY-uh POHTS-zoh
Quarton, Enguerrand in-gher-AWN kwar-TON
quiblah KEEB-law
Raphael RAF-fye-ell, or RAFF-yell
Rauschenberg, Robert ROW-shen-burg
Rembrandt van Rijn rem-BRANT fahn RINE
Renoir, Pierre-August pee-ayr oh-GOOST rehn-WAHR
Rietveld, Gerrit GARE-it REET-felld
Rococo roh-coh-COH
Rodin, Auguste oh-GOOST roh-DAN
Rogier van der Weyden roh-JEER van dur VYE-den
Ruisdael, Jacob van YAW-kohb fahn ROYS-dawl
Saarinen, Eero EER-roh SAWR-uh-nen
Saenredam, Peter SANE-reh-dawm
Safdie, Moshe MOSH-uh SAWF-dee
St. Denis san deh-NEE
St. Sernin san sayr-NAN
St. Vitale san vee-TAHL-ay
santos SAWN-tohs
Seurat, Georges jorjh suh-RAW
Siqueiros, David Alfaro see-KAYR-ohs
Sirani, Elisabetta ay-leez-eh-BAY-tuh seer-AW-nee
Sottsass, Ettore ay-TOR-ay SAWT-sahs
Steir, Pat steer
Stieglitz, Alfred STEEG-litz
stupa STOO-paw
Taniguchi, Gaho GAW-hoh tan-ih-GOOCH-ee
Teotihuacán tay-OH-tee-hwaw-CAWN
tesserae TESS-er-ee
Tiepolo, Giovanni Battista gee-oh-VAWN-ee baw-TEES-taw tee-EH-poh-loh
Tinguely, Jean jawn TANG-lee
Tintoretto teen-toh-RAY-toh
Titian TEE-shan, or TISH-an
Toorop, Jan YAWN tour-AWP
trompe l'oeil trump LOY
Tutankhamum toot-an-KAW-mun

Ukeles, Mierle merl YOU-kell-ees
Ukiyo-e OO-kee-oh-ee
Utamaro, Kitagawa kee-taw-GAW-waw oo-taw-MAR-oh
Vallayer-Coster, Anna AWN-naw val-law-YAH cohs-TAY
Van Doesburg, Théo TAY-oh van DOHS-burg
Van Eyck, Jan YAWN van IKE
Van Gogh, Vincent van GOH
vanitas VAWN-ee-taws
Van Ruisdael, Jacob YAW-cub van ROYS-dawl
Vasari, Giorgio gee-OR-gee-oh va-SAHR-ee
Velázquez, Diego dee-YAY-goh vay-LAWSS-kess
Vermeer, Jan YAWN Vare-MEER
Vigée-Lebrun, Elisabeth ay-leez-eh-BETT vee-SJAY leh-BROH(n)
Viola, Bill vee-OH-luh
Voulkos, Peter VOOL-kohs
voussoir voo-SWAWR
Wakabayashi, Hiroyuki hir-oh-YOU-kee waw-kaw-baw-YAW-shee
Willendorf VILL-en-dohrf
Wu Chen woo jehn

INDEX

All references are to page numbers. **Boldface** numbers indicate an illustration.

d

e

f

k

l

m

n

t

u

V

W